THE TRAVELS OF
MENDES PINTO

DATE DUE	
UPI 261-2505	PRINTED IN U.S.A.

PEREGRINAÇAM
DE FERNAM MENDEZ
PINTO.

EM QVE DA CONTA DE MVYTAS E MVY-
to eſtranhas couſas que vio & ouuio no reyno da China, no da Tartaria, no do Sornau, que vulgarmente ſe chama Siaõ, no do Calaminhan, no de Pegù, no de Martauaõ, & em outros muytos reynos
& ſenhorios das partes Orientais, de que neſtas noſſas
do Occidente ha muyto pouca ou
nenhũa noticia.

E TAMBEM DA CONTA DE MVYTOS CASOS PARTI-
culares que acontecerão aſi a elle como a outras muytas peſſoas. E no fim della trata bre-
uemente de algũas couſas, & da morte do ſanto Padre meſtre Franciſco Xauier,
vnica luz & reſplandor daquellas partes do Oriente, & Reytor
nellas vniuerſal da Companhia de Ieſus.

Eſcrita pelo meſmo Fernão Mendez Pinto.

Dirigido à Catholica Real Mageſtade del Rey dom Felippe o III.
deſte nome noſſo Senhor.

Com licença do ſanto Officio, Ordinario, & Paço.

EM LISBOA. Por Pedro Crasbeeck. Anno 1614.

A cuſta de Belchior ſde Faria Caualeyro da caſa del Rey noſſo
Senhor, & ſeu Liureyro.　　*Com priuilegio Real.*

Eſtà taixado eſte liuro a 600 reis em papel.

Title page of the first edition (Lisbon, 1614).
Courtesy of the James Ford Bell Library,
University of Minnesota

THE TRAVELS OF
MENDES PINTO

Fernão Mendes Pinto

Edited and Translated by
REBECCA D. CATZ

 The University of Chicago Press
CHICAGO AND LONDON

REBECCA D. CATZ is a research associate in Renaissance and medieval studies at the University of California, Los Angeles.

The map of Asia printed on the endsheets is from Abraham Ortelius, *Theatrum orbis terrarum* (Antwerp, 1570). Courtesy of the Edward E. Ayer Collection, The Newberry Library, Chicago

This publication has been supported by grants from the Calouste Gulbenkian Foundation of Lisbon and the National Endowment for the Humanities, an independent federal agency.

The University of Chicago Press, Chicago 60637
The University of Chicago Press, Ltd., London
© 1989 by The University of Chicago
All rights reserved. Published 1989
Printed in the United States of America

98 97 96 95 94 93 92 91 90   5432

LIBRARY OF CONGRESS CATALOGING-IN-PUBLICATION DATA

Pinto, Fernão Mendes, d. 1583.
    [Peregrinaçam. English]
    The travels of Mendes Pinto / Fernão Mendes Pinto ; edited and
translated by Rebecca D. Catz.
        p.   cm.
    Translation of: Peregrinaçam.
    Bibliography: p.
    1. Asia—Description and travel.   2. Pinto, Fernão Mendes, d.
1583—Journeys—Asia.   I. Catz, Rebecca.   II. Title.
DS7.P5513 1989
910.4—dc19   88-39778
    ISBN 0-226-66951-3   CIP

∞ The paper used in this publication meets the minimum requirements of the American National Standard for Information Sciences—Permanence of Paper for Printed Library Materials, ANSI Z39.48-1984.

Contents

vii   *CONTENTS*

Illustrations

Acknowledgments

I was turned down by several colleagues whom I had asked to read the manuscript. Who can blame them? Time is short and Pinto's book is long.

But there was one man, to whom I am extremely grateful—Marion A. Zeitlin of the University of California at Los Angeles—who, appropriately enough, was my first professor of Portuguese. He alone found the time to read, correct, suggest, and encourage me in what was to be a long and arduous labor of love. We did not always see eye to eye, but the exchange was always stimulating and fruitful. How can I thank him?

I am also indebted to Professor Francis M. Rogers of Harvard University, who read a good part of the manuscript, to which he gave his blessings, though not without some critical comments intended to eradicate a few errors in form and content.

At the same time I would like to express my most cordial thanks to the following institutions that supplied illustrations for this edition: the National Maritime Museum of Greenwich, the Academia das Ciencias of Lisbon, the Kunsthistorische Museum of Vienna, and the City Museum of Kobe. Especially warm thanks are due to John Parker of the University of Minnesota's John Ford Bell Library and Robert Karrow of the Newberry Library, who were extraordinarily helpful.

And last but not least, I am profoundly indebted to the National Endowment for the Humanities and the Calouste Gulbenkian Foundation of Lisbon for much appreciated financial support.

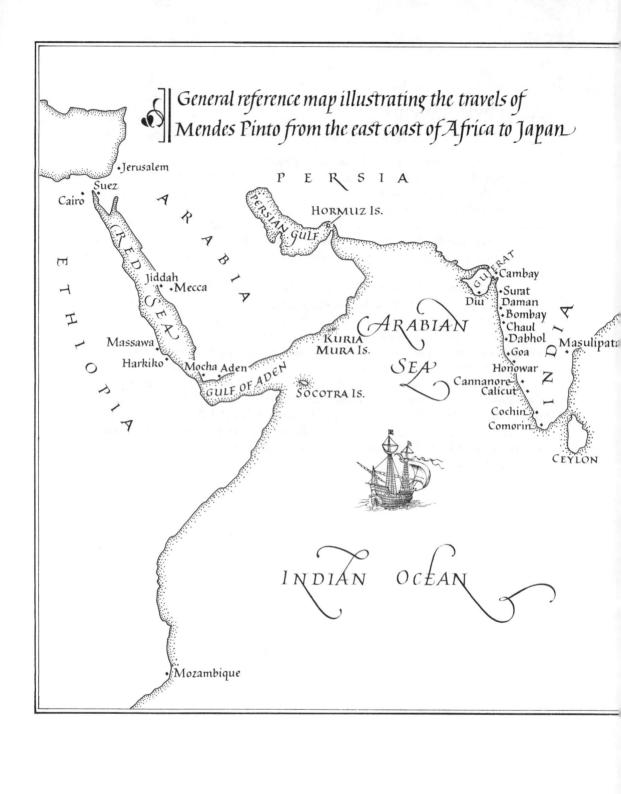

General reference map illustrating the travels of Mendes Pinto from the east coast of Africa to Japan

PERSIA

ARABIA

ETHIOPIA

RED SEA

PERSIAN GULF

HORMUZ Is.

GUJERAT

ARABIAN SEA

INDIA

CEYLON

GULF OF ADEN

KURIA MURA Is.

SOCOTRA Is.

INDIAN OCEAN

•Jerusalem
•Suez
Cairo•
Jiddah•
•Mecca
Massawa•
Harkiko•
•Mocha Aden
Diu•
•Cambay
•Surat
•Daman
•Bombay
•Chaul
•Dabhol
•Goa
•Masulipata
Honowar•
Cannanore•
Calicut•
Cochin•
Comorin•
•Mozambique

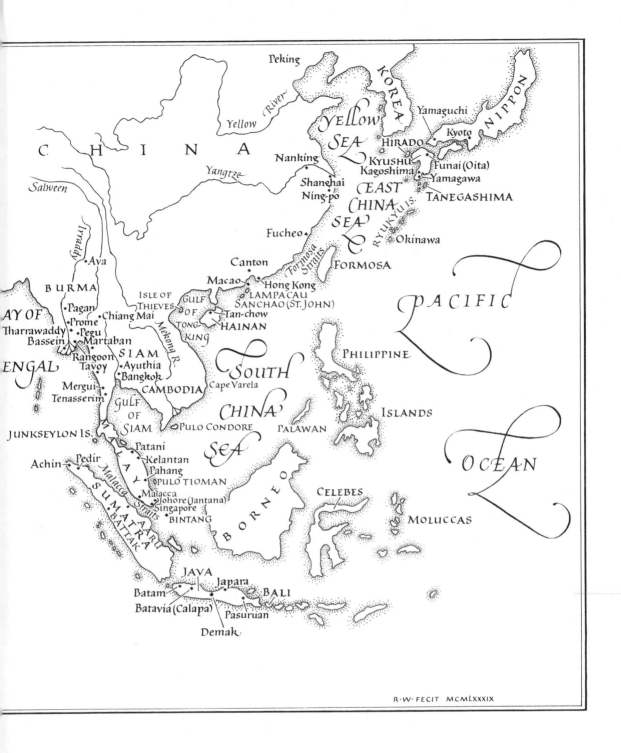

Peking

Yellow *River*

KOREA

NIPPON

C H I N A

Yangtze

YELLOW
SEA

Yamaguchi

Kyoto

HIRADO

Salween

Nanking

KYUSHU
Kagoshima

Funai (Oita)
Yamagawa

Shanghai
Ning-po

EAST
CHINA
SEA

TANEGASHIMA

Irrady

Fucheo

RYUKYU IS.

Okinawa

•Ava

Canton

FORMOSA

Formosa Straits

BURMA

Macao

Hong Kong

PACIFIC

ISLE OF
THIEVES

GULF
OF
TONG-
KING

LAMPACAU
SANCHAO (ST. JOHN)

•Pagan

•Chiang Mai

Tan-chow

HAINAN

AY OF

Tharrawaddy
Bassein

•Prome
•Pegu
•Martaban

Mekong R.

PHILIPPINE

SIAM

Rangoon
Tavoy

•Ayuthia
Bangkok

SOUTH

ENGAL

CAMBODIA

Cape Varela

Mergui
Tenasserim

GULF
OF
SIAM

CHINA

ISLANDS

JUNKSEYLON IS.

•Pulo Condore

PALAWAN

SEA

OCEAN

Patani

Achin

•Pedir

•Kelantan
Pahang

PULO TIOMAN

BORNEO

CELEBES

Malacca
Johore (Jantana)
Singapore

MOLUCCAS

S
U
M
A
T
R
A

Malacca Straits

A
R
U

BINTANG

BATTAK

JAVA

Japara

Batam

BALI

Batavia (Calapa)

Pasuruan

Demak

R·W· FECIT MCMLXXXIX

Introduction

Little is known about Fernão Mendes Pinto except that he was born (1510?) and died (1583) in Portugal, that he spent the best years of his life in Asia, and that he wrote a book which he never lived to see published. His total literary production is represented by his *Peregrinaçao* [*Travels*], which appeared in 1614, some thirty years after the author's death, plus three extant letters, the first of which was written from Malacca on 5 December 1554 and published immediately after it was received in Portugal; the second, written from Macao on 20 November 1555, was not published until the beginning of this century. The third letter, written from Almada on 15 March 1571, was purchased by Harvard University in 1966 and published in 1983.

Pinto was still a young man in his late twenties when, in the year 1537, he sailed for India. There he amassed a considerable fortune as a merchant adventurer, only part of which he brought home. On one of his voyages to Japan he met and befriended Francis Xavier, to whom he lent money to build the first Christian church in Japan. In 1554 he joined the Society of Jesus and took part in and paid for a diplomatic and evangelical mission to Japan. Two years later he was separated from the order, at his own request, and not long afterwards, in the year 1558, he returned to Portugal, after an absence of twenty-one years.

Disappointed in his hopes of obtaining a royal sinecure, he left the court of Lisbon after four and a half years of fruitless petitioning, married, and retired to a modest estate in Almada, a town opposite Lisbon, on the other side of the Tagus River. There he devoted the remainder of his life to raising a family and writing a book that was to become a classic in Portuguese literature, a book that in the seventeenth century rivalled in popularity that of Cervantes's famous classic.

But the book's popularity abroad declined, due in great part to a proliferation of faulty and bigoted translations which to this day have not been corrected. From the beginning, Pinto's work was misunderstood but thoroughly enjoyed as an amusing traveler's tale or an imaginative adventure book, the first in European literature to tell of pirate battles on the high seas in the distant lands of the little-known Orient. This was far from the author's intention.

A close reading of Pinto's *Travels* reveals that it is a work of corrosive satire in which the author attacks all the religious and political institutions of sixteenth-century Portugal. More than that, it represents a sweeping condemnation of the ideology of the crusade, which was the mythic lifeline of the overseas empire of the Portuguese. This was a dangerous subject in an age when a person's innermost thoughts were the particular object of episcopal censorship. Yet this is what makes the *Travels* a unique document in the history of Western thought. It is a rare book indeed, in a period of religious strife, that makes a plea for religious tolerance as a moral injunction from God. It is an early example, if not the first in a period that witnessed the beginnings of the age of European imperialism, of a book that questions the morality of the overseas conquests of the Portuguese, which the author views as barbaric acts of piracy, and much of which he claims to have seen in his lifetime, a lifetime that spans almost all of the sixteenth century.

At about the time that Pinto was born, the Portuguese had acquired a line of scattered maritime possessions that stretched from the coasts of Brazil to West Africa, East Africa, Persia, the Malabar coast of India, Ceylon, the Malay Archipelago, and the Moluccas. When Pinto died in 1583, Portugal had ceased to exist as an independent nation. In 1580 he witnessed the shameful absorption of his country into the empire of Philip II, who supported his claim to the Portuguese throne with well-placed money and military might. This tumultuous period of history is reflected in the book and needs to be known by anyone who would read it with understanding and appreciation.

Europe under Charles V (1500–55)

By the end of the fifteenth century Europe had emerged from a period of economic, demographic, and political depression. The hundred years from 1450 to 1550 witnessed the consolidation of royalism in Europe, notably in Spain under the Hapsburgs, in England under the Tudors, and in France, where the house of Valois achieved an unprecedented degree of centralized power. The emergence of the national state led to an exhaustive military and diplomatic struggle between three strong and willful men: Francis I of France; his rival Charles V, king of Spain, Holy Roman Emperor, and brother-in-law of the Portuguese king, John III; and Henry VIII of England, who shifted his alliance from one opponent to the other as suited his interests. The rise of royal power was accompanied by the resurgent temporal ambition of the Holy See in Rome, which not only played an active part in diplomatic and political affairs but deployed armies on the field of battle. The sack of Rome in 1527 by the troops of Charles V had tremendous ideological repercussions in Europe, and the news was received with extreme sensitivity by the court of Lisbon, where John III was instrumental in patching up the quarrel between his brother-in-law and Pope Clement VII. Such a quarrel between the two greatest political powers of Europe ran counter to the national interests of Portugal. Her very existence as a maritime nation rested in great part on the shadowy legitimacy accorded her overseas expansion by the Holy See in the bull *Inter Caetera* of 1493. Moreover, Portugal's mission to spread the faith depended on freedom from embroilment in the continental wars and freedom of the seas, which could only be assured by deflecting the military energies of the Christian powers against the Grand Turk. The conduct of war itself was radically changing, partly because of new weapons, especially the improvement of artillery, partly because of feudalism's decline, and partly because kings could now afford to raise larger and better-equipped armies.

The growth of national conflicts intensified economic rivalry, which was stimulated by the exploitation of the newly opened East and the newly discovered West. The importation of gold from the New World, as well as the more skillful working of mines in Europe, introduced enormous and disastrous inflationary pressures at a time when national economies were coming to be based more firmly on money. For the distribution of the large quantities of produce and merchandise brought from India, a powerful syndicate was formed in Lisbon by the great New Christian mercantile and banking house of Francisco and Diogo Mendes, who established for the purpose warehouses and *comptoirs* in Antwerp. The firm and their partners, chiefly the Italian Affaitati, enjoyed a monopoly of the distributing trade in the north of Europe, competing with the Fuggers and the Hanseatic League, who had previously enjoyed a similar monopoly in regard to the overland trade. The age produced for the first time in modern Europe the phenomenon of vast private wealth. Charles V was able to out-bid Francis I in bribing the German electors who made him emperor only by recourse to the funds of the private merchant house of the Fuggers. The wealth of the Mendes spice trust in Antwerp filled the coffers of Rome, persuading the Holy See for seventeen years to resist the pressure put on it by John III for the establishment of a free and untrammelled Inquisition in Portugal. The social and moral results of this trend were complex and incalculable.

Flowering of the Renaissance

The age was a time of intense intellectual excitement for a widening elite in western Europe. The excitement derived chiefly from a cultural event of the first magnitude: the sensation of recovering the civilization of classical antiquity. By the end of the fifteenth century the invention of the printing press had permitted the publication in Italy of a large corpus of Greek texts, and Latin translations existed to help the curious beginner. The Hellenist movement in France was spurred by the contact with Italy resulting from the periodic invasions of that country beginning in 1494. The new classical scholars won an important victory in 1530 when Francis I permitted the creation of the Lecteurs Royaux, which was to become the Collège de France, a bastion of philosophical study. The individual took on transcendant importance and became the point of departure for all knowledge of the universe.

This new trend was too rich in revolutionary implications to escape violent opposition. The recovery of ancient culture revealed a mode of human life in sharp contrast to the medieval Christian tradition; it suggested unfamiliar potentialities to the artistic imagination, a wider liberty, and an alternative dignity. From Italy the contagion drifted northward, to alter radically the self-consciousness of Western man. In 1440 the Italian humanist Lorenzo Valla published his *Constitutum Constantini*. It undermined papal authority and introduced the potential questioning of all sacrosanct authority. Thus the science of philology, devised to establish the most reliable texts of ancient writers, was destined to clash with the discipline of theology.

The confrontation reached a crisis in 1516, when the great humanist Desiderius Erasmus published his New Testament containing the Greek text, with notes, and his own new Latin translation. It revealed the fact that the Vulgate, the Bible of the Church, was not only a secondhand document but, in places, an erroneous document. The influence of Erasmus's translation was profound and durable. When he followed this edition with further challenges—notably a commentary on the Greek text of Saint Luke—all study of Greek was prohibited by the theological faculty of the University of Paris, a stronghold of reaction. Erasmus's *Adagia*, a collection of proverbs gathered from classical writers with essayistic commentary, his *Colloquia*, and his *Praise of Folly* were so popular that they underwent numerous editions and made their author's ideas familiar throughout Europe. Even in the Iberian peninsula, where new ideas were slow to penetrate, we find the Council of Valladolid concerned about the number of Erasmus's books circulating.

No doubt the strongest force of Erasmus's influence was negative. His attacks on the papacy and church hierarchy, on monasticism, on pilgrimages, on the cult of saints, on many other alleged social and ecclesiastical abuses, and above all on the formalism of Christian worship, prepared and hastened the religious upheavals he lived to witness. Much weaker in the long run was the positive force of Erasmus's teaching, based in part on the *Devotio Moderna*, the spirit of the imitation of Christ. Erasmus's Christian message was a call literally to imitate the life of Christ he discerned in the Gospels, a life of charity, humility, tolerance, and reasonable self-restraint. In reality, the Erasmian philosophy represented a middle course between the existing Catholic doctrine and the hardening Protestant movement.

In 1517 Martin Luther challenged the Church by protesting the sale of indulgences and later went on to intensify Erasmus's attacks on alleged abuses, denounce the Church's claims of the necessity of mediation, deny the validity of several sacraments, insist on the prime authority of scripture, and assert Saint Paul's doctrine of justification by faith alone. Erasmus died in 1536, the year of the publication of Jean Calvin's *Institution de la religion chrétienne*. Calvinist theology lays stress, even more firmly than the Lutheran, on the absolute corruption of fallen man, his inability unaided to will anything but evil, his total dependence on divine grace, and the importance of his works to win him salvation.

When Pinto left Europe in 1537 the polarization of belief was accelerating rapidly. In 1534, the so-called "affaire des placards" turned Francis I vigorously and finally against the reformist party when he awoke to find the walls of Paris, and his own bedroom door at Amboise, covered with posters condemning the Mass. As the movement toward Protestantism continued in large parts of Germany, Scandinavia, the Low Countries, and England, the religious coherence of France deteriorated, culminating in devastating civil wars and frightful persecutions of the Huguenots. Thus the flowering of humanism in the north accompanied a second movement that overlapped it but that remained in essence profoundly different: the drive to reform the doctrine and institutions of the Church of Rome. This drive came from all quarters of western Europe, with Charles V himself taking the lead in calling for a general assembly of the Church.

After many long delays and passive resistance on the part of the papacy, the Council of Trent began its historic sessions in 1545. This great ecumenical council of the Roman Catholic Church, which convened intermittently during the years 1545−47, 1551−52, and 1562−63, was in the process of rendering final the rift with Protestantism, of reinterpreting and stiffening orthodox doctrine, and of fostering those developments within the Church which were to be known collectively as the Counter-Reformation. The council's work struggled forward despite formidable conflicts of interest and powerful opposition, but the crucial importance of its achievements in determining the future of modern Europe can scarcely be exaggerated.

Pinto returned to Portugal in 1558. He was there when the final session of the Council of Trent met. He was there that summer of 1572 when the Saint Bartholomew's Day massacre was celebrated in Lisbon with joyous processions and prayers of thanksgiving. The result of the council's work was the resumption of the civil wars that were to tear France apart until the accession of Henri IV in 1589, who abjured his Protestantism and reunited the war-torn country with his pragmatic "Paris vaut bien une messe."

Henry VIII and Francis I both died in 1547 within a few months of each other. In 1554 Charles V began a series of abdications, which divided the Hapsburg dominions between Austria and Spain. He gave Naples and Milan to his son Philip, whose second marriage to Queen Mary I of England took place the same year. In 1555 he turned over the Netherlands to Philip, and in 1556 he made him king of Spain and Sicily. In 1556 also, he practically surrendered the empire to his brother Ferdinand, and in 1558 he formally abdicated as emperor. Though he retired to the monastery of Yuste in 1556, he took an active interest in politics until his death in 1558. During Charles's rule the Spanish empire had been tremendously expanded by the conquest of Mexico and Peru, and Magellan circumnavigated the globe under his auspices. In Italy, Spanish power had become paramount. Even England seemed about to fall to Spain through Philip's marriage, and it was Charles's marriage with Isabel of Portugal that was to bring the Portuguese crown to Philip in 1580. Charles had indeed ruled over an empire on which "the sun never set."

Yet Charles failed in his purpose to return the Protestants to the Church of Rome, and the human and financial cost of constant warfare drained the resources of his empire, warfare that was motivated less by religious conviction than by political considerations.

Spain under Philip II (1556–98)

Philip II, king of Spain, Naples, and Sicily, ascended the throne on the abdication of his father, Emperor Charles V, who had previously made over to him the Low Countries, Franche-Comté, and the duchy of Milan. Following Philip's marriage to Queen Mary I of England in 1554, and his arrival in London, England officially returned to the Roman Church. Extremely unpopular with the English, Philip left London soon afterwards, frustrated by Parliament in his attempt to win coronation. Continuing his father's war on Henri II of France, he drew England into the conflict in 1557. After Mary's death in 1558, Philip offered his hand in marriage to Queen Elizabeth I, but was put off in the capricious manner that characterized the political courtships of her reign. After the treaty of Cateau-Cambrésis in 1559, general peace made Spain the strongest power in Europe and left it the greatest colonial power in the world.

At the beginning of his reign Philip also made war (1556–57) on Pope Paul IV because the papacy, fearing that Spanish supremacy in Italy would destroy its temporal power and result in Spanish dominance, supported France. The suppression of the Moriscos, especially after the revolt of 1568–71, assured Spanish religious unity; its main purpose, however, was to prevent the Moriscos from helping the Turks to invade Spain. In 1571, Philip's half-brother, Don Juan of Austria, led the combined forces of Venice, Spain, and Rome in a decisive naval victory against the Turkish fleet in the Gulf of Lepanto. The victory at Lepanto caused great rejoicing among the Catholic powers (although not in France, then allied with the sultan), but the triple alliance soon fell apart. The victory at Lepanto was of little lasting importance because Philip failed to follow up his advantage. In 1573, Venice signed a separate peace treaty with Turkey. The sultan quickly rebuilt his fleet, and in 1574 the Turks took Tunis from Spain. Philip later found it more expedient to bribe the Turkish vizirs, who then turned their military thrust eastward, leaving Philip free to pursue his wars in the west. Despite Elizabeth's machinations with the Grand Turk, whom she urged in frequent and flowery correspondence to attack the Spaniards, in the end Philip's money prevailed; and while the Turks were busy campaigning in Persia, Philip prepared his "invincible armada" for the invasion of England in 1588.

The revolt of the Netherlands was the greatest setback of Philip's reign. He appointed the duque de Alba to replace his half-sister, Margaret of Parma, as governor of the Netherlands, but when Alba's cruel methods failed to quell the revolt, Philip supported the conciliatory tactics of Alba's successors—Requesens, Don Juan of Austria, and Duke Alessandro Farnese—who managed to reconquer the southern provinces, or approximately what is now modern Belgium. But Antwerp, the most flourishing city in all of Europe, was destroyed and never fully recovered from the devastation wrought by the armies of Spain. Lord Burghley, Elizabeth's principal advisor, recoiling in horror from the dreadful waste, was said to have told de Gueras, the Spanish agent then in London, "You people are of a sort that wherever you set foot no grass grows and you are hated everywhere."

Philip undertook his fateful expedition against England for supporting the rebels in the Netherlands and challenging Spanish sea power. A further pretext for Philip's expedition against England was the last will of Mary Stuart, queen of Scots, who before her execution in 1587 was alleged to have disinherited her son James in favor of Philip as claimant to the English throne. Philip was fitting out the armada when, in 1587, Sir Francis Drake sacked the port of Cadiz and intercepted a Spanish squadron at Cape Saint Vincent. But Philip went ahead with his plans for the "invincible armada," which eventually was battered and scattered along the coasts of the British Isles.

Philip's third wife, Elizabeth of Valois, died in 1568, the same year as Philip's son from his first marriage, the mad Don Carlos, around whose mysterious death many legends arose. Philip's daughter by Elizabeth of Valois was his favorite and constant companion during his later years. After the assassination of Henri III, Philip tried in vain to place her on the throne of France, but was thwarted by the French Salic laws and the general opposition to a daughter of Spain. Philip's fourth wife, Anne of Austria and the mother of his successor, Philip III, died in 1580, the same year that Portugal became part of Spain. The only major military success of Philip's later reign was the conquest of Portugal, to which he had claim as the son of Isabel of Portugal, daughter of Manuel I; and this was accomplished with relatively little resistance and with the aid of princely bribes.

Philip saw himself as God's chosen instrument to stamp out heresy and drained Spain's energies in constant, unceasing warfare. In Flanders he was intensely disliked, even by the Catholic aristocracy, for while he had sworn to respect their ancient freedoms, his authoritarian rule would brook no institutions guaranteed by laws. The latter half of his reign was marked by constant conflict with two capricious women, Elizabeth of England and Catherine de Medici, who controlled the fortunes of France. The debilitating effects of persecution, of depopulation, of colonial overexpansion, and of the influx of gold began to make itself strongly felt. American gold and the proceeds of an increasingly burdensome taxation were wasted on Philip's foreign wars and interventions and had to be supplemented with loans. The embodiment of the hard-working civil servant and bureaucrat, he sought to direct the destinies of a world empire from the seclusion of his cabinet, devoting infinite time and pains to the minutest administrative details, which he was unwilling to delegate. However, the decline of Spain and, ultimately, Portugal, had begun long before Philip's time. After seven centuries of crusading against the Moors, the Spaniards had become unable to distinguish between political and religious aims. Nation and faith became one, and the only useful citizens the soldier and the priest. The Inquisition became a national institution and agriculture an object of disdain. While the rest of Europe was transformed by the Renaissance, Spain alone resisted and, in large measure, remained unchanged.

Portugal under Manuel I (1495–1521) and John III (1521–57)

Pinto died under the rule of a Spanish king who honored him for his services, although his lifetime spanned the reigns of four Portuguese monarchs who failed to recognize those services. Pinto was born during the first decade of the sixteenth century, which opened with the glittering reign of Manuel I, who reaped the harvest sown by his predecessors. The annual voyages of discovery begun by Henry the Navigator (1394–1460) nearly a hundred years before culminated in the voyage of Vasco da Gama (1497–99) and the discovery of the maritime route to India. The following year, in 1500, Brazil was discovered. Thereafter, every year of Manuel's reign witnessed some new discovery to bring Portugal pride and glory. The Portuguese empire was flung far across the world—Asia, Africa, America—and the conquering genius of Afonso de Albuquerque, governor of Portuguese India until 1515, gave Manuel the monopoly of the eastern trade and made him the richest king in Christendom.

Manuel was especially anxious to add Spain to his worldwide possessions and made three marriages with that end in view. There is no question but that the long series of royal marriages between the two countries brought Portugal under the moral and political influence of Spain and—eventually—under her heel. As a condition of his first marriage to Isabel (widow of John II's only son and heir, and eldest daughter of Isabel and Ferdinand of Spain) Manuel undertook to expel from Portugal all refugees who had been condemned by the Spanish Inquisition. Acting under this impulsion and the urgings of his confessor, he issued in 1497 a general edict of expulsion of all Jews, excepting children under the age of fourteen, who were taken from their parents and placed in Catholic foster homes.

But Manuel was too wise a statesman to permit the dislocation that would result from the expulsion of some of the richest and most industrious people in his kingdom, and when the Jews had gathered in the ports assigned for their departure, it soon became apparent that Manuel had no intention of letting them go. By various means they were prevented from departing and eventually forced to accept baptism en masse. Manuel soon tempered these coercive measures by exempting the Jews from persecution for twenty years, extending this protection again in 1512 until 1534. Despite the king's protection, popular aversion to the New Christians ran high and culminated in the bloody Lisbon massacre of 1506. Manuel meted out swift and severe punishment to the priests responsible for the bloodbath, which lasted for three days. In 1507 he lifted the restrictive laws of 1499 and permitted the New Christians to come and go as they pleased. Although in 1515 he made a fainthearted attempt to establish the Inquisition in Portugal, throughout the rest of his reign the New Christians enjoyed a measure of toleration and prosperity.

John III was only a youth of twenty when he ascended the throne in 1521. Henry Lea, the distinguished historian of the Inquisition, describes him as a fanatic of narrow mind and limited intelligence, but in the early years of his reign the influence of his father's counsellors prevailed and procured the confirmation of the privileges granted to the New Christians by the late king.[1]

Continuing the tradition of royal marriages with Spain followed by his thrice-married father, two marriages were arranged in 1525: that of John III himself with Catherine, the sister of Charles V, and that of Isabel, the sister of John III, with Charles V, marriages that were to draw the destinies of Spain and Portugal still closer.

Though the golden age apparently continued, Portugal began to decline in the reign of John III. Emigration drained the best blood of the country; the East corrupted while it enriched its conquerors; the cultivation of the soil was either abandoned or left to slaves; and the government could not make both ends meet. Taking advantage of the predispositions of his mind, the advocates of persecution continually urged the monarch to establish a tribunal of faith identical with that of Spain. In 1524 the king took the first step that was to lead to the establishment of the Inquisition in Portugal by directing that secret investigations be made concerning the mode of life of the New Christians in Lisbon. Catherine, the new queen of Portugal, had been accustomed since her childhood to regard the Inquisition as a tribunal indispensable for the maintenance of the faith. The only queen with a seat in council, she brought with her in 1525 the ideas and prejudices of the court of Spain against the New Christians. The support of the queen and her influence over her husband, already inclined to intolerance, redoubled the efforts of the adversaries of the New Christians.

In 1531, Gil Vicente, whom Herculano refers to as "our Shakespeare," was in Santarém when an earthquake occurred. His courage and prompt action averted a repetition of the massacre of 1506, for the town's friars had begun to preach that the earthquake was a punishment of God for the sins of the Jews. Gil Vicente's letter to the king, describing the events in Santarém, proves that toleration was still possible in 1531.[2] Yet in the same year the decision to establish an Inquisition had already been taken by the king. Instructions were given to the ambassador at Rome that he was to obtain from Clement VII, with the utmost secrecy, a bull that should serve as a basis for the intended establishment of the Inquisition. On 17 December 1531, the pope granted such a bull, but with limitations which dissatisfied John, who continued to negotiate with the Holy See in an effort to obtain more acceptable terms. These negotiations were to drag on for seventeen years—marked on both sides by the most flagrant mercantilism—with the successive popes extending to the New Christians a tenuous protection that fluctuated with the amount of gold that reached them from Flanders, where Diogo Mendes, the wealthiest and most influential of the Portuguese converts, and Gracia Mendes, widow of his brother Francisco, provided the greater part of the money.

The following year, on 14 June 1532, a law was enacted forbidding the New Christians to leave the kingdom. Finally, on 23 May 1536, Pope Paul III, Clement VII having died in the meantime, granted a new bull, acceding to the pressure applied on him by Charles V, who happened to be in Rome after his victory in Tunis. This is the generally accepted date for the establishment of the Inquisition in Portugal. However, this Inquisition was still not satisfactory to John III. On 16 August 1536, a list of crimes punishable by the Inquisition was published, and the people were urged to come forward and confess, and to denounce others. This was the state of affairs in Portugal when Fernão Mendes Pinto sailed for India on 11 March 1537.

Finally, under a date of 16 July 1547, came the long-sought-for bull, instituting a vigorous and vengeful Inquisition in Portugal. Its methods divided the nation into spies and victims and encouraged blackmail and false denunciations, yet the Inquisition was popular nonetheless. It is therefore all the more remarkable that John failed to extend the Inquisition to his colonial possessions. As early as 1545 Francis Xavier had written to the king, urging on him the necessity of a tribunal in Goa where the New Christians, living in comparative freedom in the multiracial society of Portuguese India, observed far less caution than their brethren at home. This state of affairs was soon to end. Early in 1558, while Pinto was waiting in Goa for a ship to take him home, the first group of New Christians were arrested and sent back to Lisbon in chains, to be tried by the Inquisition.[3]

When Pinto reached Lisbon on 22 September 1558, Portugal was about to experience the worst oppressions of the Inquisition. John III had died the year before, and the queen was acting as regent for her three-year-old grandson Sebastian. By 1560 the Inquisition in Portugal was functioning on the terms originally sought by John, free of the restrictions the popes had attempted to impose on him; and in the same year the regency founded an Inquisition in Goa, which in time earned a sinister renown as the most pitiless in Christendom. In 1562, John's brother, Cardinal Henrique, assumed the regency while at the same time acting as inquisitor-general, a post he had held for twenty-three years.

In 1568 Sebastian ascended the throne, at the tender age of fourteen. A fanatic headstrong youth, raised in the by then outmoded traditions of the Middle Ages, he dreamed of reconquering the North African empire, an enterprise that had been gradually and prudently abandoned by his grandfather. This quixotic campaign, brashly conceived and badly executed, stripped the country of its last remaining resources and ended in complete disaster. The young king himself died unnoticed on the battlefield of Alcacer-Quibir in 1578, where his body was discovered, completely naked, by a page, and later was returned to Portugal for burial. The mysterious circumstances surrounding his death gave rise to the legend that he would return, a legend that blossomed into a peculiar messianic belief known as "Sebastianism" that lasted well into the nineteenth century and which—ironically enough—was born of the messianic fervor that had gripped the New Christians, whose messianism in turn was the strongest pretext advanced for the establishment of the Inquisition in Portugal.

In 1578, the inquisitor-general, Cardinal Henrique, was crowned king at the age of sixty-six, with hardly any prospect of issue—though he tried in vain to receive a dispensation from the pope to marry. His brief and desolate reign was marked by national mourning, famine, pestilence, and agitation over the rivalries among the pretenders to the throne. He convoked the Cortes for the purpose of choosing a successor, urging on them as his choice his nephew—Philip II of Spain.

Publication History of the Book

The circumstantial history of Pinto's *Travels,* its fortunes, and its impact on Europe have received much critical attention on the part of investigators, most of whom have looked to it—perhaps inordinately—to explain the work of art itself. Many questions concerning its posthumous fate are still hotly disputed by the critics, some even going so far as to accuse the Jesuits of having persecuted the author and emasculated the manuscript—out of spite—for Pinto's having left the order. Even the royal chronicler, Francisco de Andrade, who was assigned the task of editing and preparing the manuscript for publication, has come in for a share of blame and abuse.

It is a maverick book, an enigma to readers and critics alike. For centuries it has puzzled the literary experts, who have never fully explained the author's purpose or the manifest errors and inconsistencies of its design. But did the original manuscript really suffer alteration, as some claim? Was it withheld from publication, and if so, by whom? Was its author the liar seventeenth-century Europe reputed him to be?

Though modern investigation has vindicated Pinto in great part, many questions still hang fire.

Written sometime between the years 1569 and 1578, the *Travels* was not published until 1614, some thirty-odd years after the author's death. Although the book is known to have circulated in manuscript form long before the date of publication, the original manuscript copies are lost. The earliest reference to Pinto's book appears in a letter written from Coimbra on 22 February 1569 by the Jesuit Father Cipriano Soares to Father Diogo Mirón, also a Jesuit, in Rome. In answer to the latter's query about the progress being made by the royal chronicler, João de Barros, on his *Décadas*—three volumes of which had already been published—Soares writes that the historian had relied principally on Pinto for his information about Japan until the letters of the Jesuit missionaries began to arrive from Asia; after which, Barros turned to the letters for his source material instead. Thus it was generally known in 1569, at home and abroad, that Pinto was writing a book; moreover, the foremost Portuguese historian of his day had consulted him for firsthand information on the Orient.[4]

In 1582, when Pinto was nearing the end of his life, he was interviewed by the Jesuit historian Maffei, who had been commissioned by the crown to write a history of the Portuguese in India that would enhance their evangelical role. The questions directed at Pinto by Maffei and his collaborators seem to have been limited to China and Japan. The answers given by Pinto—with only slight variations—were taken directly from the *Travels,* as it has come down to us.[5]

Pinto died the following year. His daughters delivered the precious manuscript, in obedience to their father's last will and testament, to the Casa Pia das Penitentes, a charitable house for wayward women in Lisbon. The bequest, in itself, would seem to suggest a desire to have the book published. In the ensuing years, the Casa Pia was visited by many luminaries who came to consult Pinto's book—Father Maffei among them.

In 1588, Maffei published his *Historiarum Indicarum Libri XVI,* and though he disdained the information obtained from Pinto during the interview, it is apparent that he adopted Pinto's version of the events relating to Saint Francis Xavier in the Far East. He was not alone in this. In 1594, H. Tursellini, S.J., published his *De Vita Francisci Xaverii Libri Sex,* in which he drew upon Pinto's book for his life of the saint; as did João de Lucena, S.J., in his *História da vida do Padre Francisco de Xavier* (1600), and Fernão Guerreiro, S.J., in his *Relaçam Anual* (1602–12). None of these writers acknowledged their indebtedness to Pinto, a not uncommon practice in those days.

An early printed reference to Pinto appears in Giovanni Botero's *Relationi Universali,* first published in Rome in 1591–92. Botero is unique in that he acknowledges Pinto as the source for his chapter on Pegu (Burma), though with only a simple parenthetical observation: "(come scrive Fernando Mendes)." However, Botero's source may have been Pinto's letter of 5 December 1554, which was published in a Jesuit letter-book in 1555 and widely circulated in several languages. Also, it is doubtful if anything about Burma had been printed in Europe prior to that time. A printed reference to Pinto's as yet unpublished *Travels* appears in a bibliography appended to Melchior Estácio do Amaral's shipwreck narratives, published in 1604. But by that date the first steps to publication had already been taken.

With the *Travels* receiving so much attention, it was only natural that the Casa Pia should want to publish it; and in 1603, the same year that application was made, permission was granted by the authorities to do so, accompanied by the warmest praise from the censor, who signed the "Nihil Obstat" of the Inquisition on 25 May 1603. But eleven years were to elapse before the book was finally published in 1614. Several reasons for the delay have been suggested, particularly by Maurice Collis, who points out that Pinto had not left the manuscript ready for publication. It was an immense work and required careful revision. The dates and names were confused in places, there were no chapter divisions, the curious place-names were hard to read, some passages might require cutting or modification. Collis also suggests that no publisher could be found who was willing to bring out a book of such length, dealing with events that had occurred sixty to eighty years before. Furthermore, the subject matter may no longer have seemed fresh: in the thirty-one years since Pinto's death, historians like Barros, Castanheda, and Couto, to say nothing of Camões and the biographers of Francis Xavier, had already published their works. Most of these rival accounts of the East had been backed by official funds, whereas Pinto's *Travels* was strictly a commercial proposition.

Collis's suggestions seem plausible, for who could foresee that none of these obstacles would make any difference to its later success? It seems even more plausible to suppose that Pinto could have had the book published himself—had he so desired. But no evidence exists to show that he took any steps in that direction. Pinto's apparently modest protestations that he was writing the book solely for the benefit of his children, as a sort of ABC chart and as a legacy for them, are borne out neither by the terms of his last will and testament nor by the work itself. Pinto's ABC primer certainly was not intended for his children alone, for he had written what he believed to be an ABC of human conduct, a code of ethics, a guideline, for all to follow. His life— or rather, what he chose to depict as one man's journey through life—is presented with the conviction that those who do what "must be done" will unfailingly be protected by a divine Providence. All of Pinto's hair-raising adventures and narrow escapes, through which he alone miraculously survives, are so fashioned as to make of him the symbol of the righteous man, tried by hardships and misfortunes, overcoming travail, watched over by the divine Father. Pinto further states (chap. 1) that he is writing his book in obedience to the divine will, a detail often overlooked by the critics who have never fully explained the author's purpose or his moral philosophy:

> when I consider that God always watched over me and brought me safely through all those hazards and hardships, then I find that there is not as much reason to complain about my past misfortune as there is reason to give thanks to the Lord for my present blessings, for He saw fit to preserve my life so that I could write this awkward, unpolished tale.

There can be little question but that Pinto was afraid to publish his book. The times were dangerous, and he had written a dangerous book criticizing—albeit indirectly—every institution, sacred and profane, of his country. He must have been afraid not only for himself, for he would not have wished his children to live under the opprobrium that might accrue to them from an unwelcome reception of the work. Far better to leave the manuscript to a pious institution under whose orthodox aegis the book would have a sponsor both unsuspecting and above suspicion and could safely be transmitted to posterity. Good sense and good reason dictated this course. Pinto had written a satire, woven of the subtlest threads of irony—a subversive book—that deceived his countrymen and threatened the very foundation of his society. Moreover—and this cannot be stressed enough—he was well aware of the profusion of error and contradiction in the book. The inconsistencies and improbabilities of the *Travels* are an integral part of its design, a deliberate puzzle that has teased admirers and detractors alike for four hundred years. Thus, Pinto very wisely avoided the need to explain those "errors" to his contemporaries—a need that certainly would have arisen, for many of them were still alive and had been in Asia with him.

Pinto understood the peculiar mentality of his countrymen all too well, and though he was fairly certain that his ironies would pass over the heads of the authorities, he could not risk it. Pinto's irony was directed at that small but elite audience with which satire is content—the "pauci lectores" of which the Roman satirist Horace speaks. The year 1578, when Pinto finished his book, was a significant date in the history of Portugal. It was the year that Pinto saw his countrymen go down, under the fanatic King Sebastian, in the catastrophic defeat at Alcacer-Quibir, which marked the end of Portugal's independence as a nation—a divine punishment visited on a people who, in Pinto's philosophy, had failed to do what "must be done." Pinto set out to castigate the Portuguese for their sins, but with methods (as will be discussed below) of the most subtle indirection and duplicity. His book pays lip service to the orthodoxy of his day and is superficially overlaid with the same hypocrisy he ultimately sought to expose. Pinto understood the spirit of an age which laid great stress on the formal observance and outward trappings of piety; his careful protestations of faith more than satisfied the censor.

Ten years after the necessary licenses to publish had been granted, the Royal Privilege was obtained, under date of 6 November 1613. The book finally appeared in print in 1614, at the expense of Belchior de Faria, for the benefit of the Casa Pia das Penitentes of Lisbon, to whom the profits would accrue for a period of ten years.

The task of editing and preparing the voluminous manuscript for press was assigned to the royal chronicler, Francisco de Andrade, who has been blamed for bungling the job entrusted to him. Andrade's death one year following the publication of the *Travels* left unanswered the criticism directed at him by the Spanish translator, Francisco de Herrera Maldonado, who appeared on the scene shortly afterwards. In a long prefatory "Apologia" in the Spanish edition (1620), well larded with Latin quotations and overburdened with stuffy erudition, Herrera criticizes Andrade for his editorial deficiencies. Herrera's main objection seems to be that Andrade did nothing to "improve the primitive style" of the author and that he confined himself to dividing the work into chapters and composing relevant chapter headings or titles.

If Herrera's "Apologia" has any value for us today, it does not lie in the validity of his opinions, but rather in the relative assurance it affords us that the manuscript suffered very little alteration, if any, at the hands of the royal chronicler. Nevertheless, with the original manuscript lost, it is impossible to assess the changes—if any, we repeat—made by Andrade, or anyone else for that matter. More important for literary history is the charge, put forward by some nineteenth-century critics, that the Jesuits either censored, mutilated, or altered the original manuscript of the *Travels*. There is, however, no evidence for this assertion. I believe that the royal chronicler who edited the manuscript was just as hard put to explain the manifest errors and contradictions of the work as have been four centuries of critics and investigators, and that Andrade very sensibly thought it best to leave matters as they were—for which the world of literature owes him a debt of gratitude. Moreover, it is my contention that very little of Pinto's *Travels* as it has come down to us is out of place; the work shows a remarkable integrity of purpose and design.

The success of the *Travels* was enormous. It was followed six years later by the Spanish translation, which was published in 1620 in two variant editions. Herrera's translation was reprinted in 1627, 1628, 1645, 1664, and 1666, so that it received considerable circulation long before the second Portuguese edition was published in 1678. In the seventeenth century alone the *Travels* ran into a total of nineteen editions in six languages: two Portuguese, seven Spanish, three French, two Dutch, two German, and three English editions, not including the extracted version that appeared in *Purchas His Pilgrimes,* published in London in 1625.

"How enormous was the success is not fully conveyed by the number of editions," writes Collis. "In the seventeenth century, the reading public was small and confined to the top. The figures, in fact, indicate that most educated people in Europe had read it before 1700. By that date Pinto had as many readers as Cervantes, whose *Don Quixote* was published in 1604 (first part) and 1615 (second part)."[6]

With publication of the *Travels* Pinto quickly gained a wide reputation as a liar. Herrera's "Apologia" was already defensive about Pinto's veracity. A seventeenth-century reader's reaction to Pinto's book has come down to us in the form of a charming letter written by Dorothy Osborne to Sir William Temple, two representative figures of the intellectual elite of the period.

> Have you read the Story of China written by a Portuguese, Fernando Mendez Pinto I think his name is? if you have not, take it with you, tis as diverting a book of the kinde as ever I read, and is as handsomly written, you must allow him the Priviledge of a Travellour and he dos not abuse it, his lyes are as pleasant harmlesse on's as lyes can bee, and in noe great number considering the scope hee has for them; there is one in Dublin now that ne're saw much further, tolde mee twice as many (I dare swear) of Ireland.[7]

Dorothy Osborne's opinion was widely shared. And when in 1695 the Restoration dramatist, William Congreve, had one of his characters say, in the comedy *Love for Love* (act 1, sc. 1), "Ferdinand Mendez Pinto was but a type of thee, thou liar of the first magnitude," his audiences understood the allusion all too well, for by the end of the century, Pinto's name had become synonymous with the word "liar."

The line just quoted from Congreve, mistakenly attributed to Shakespeare by the historian Hugh Murray in an 1820 edition of his *Travels in Asia,* was picked up by several of the nineteenth-century Portuguese critics who unjustly included the illustrious name of Shakespeare among Pinto's detractors. Cervantes too was said to have called Pinto a liar, but no one yet has shown where or when. And if, on the one hand, an eighteenth-century Latin poem, "Hippodromus Pedroucianus," by Jorge Garcês, perpetuates Pinto's fame as a liar, on the other hand, an early twentieth-century poem, written by J. M. Symns, reflects the poet's respect for Pinto's veracity, for he has apprehended the criticism of the Portuguese implicit in the *Travels* as his theme for the poem, "When Pinto Came to Martaban." And according to the historian W. A. R. Wood, "Sir Richard Burton, in one of his footnotes to the third voyage of *Sindbad the Sailor,* when discussing the huge serpent which ate his companions, mentions Mendes Pinto and calls him 'The Sindbad of Portugal, though not so respectable.'"[8]

In short, Pinto shared the same fate as that renowned Venetian traveler before him who was dubbed "Marco Milione" by an incredulous Europe. It was an incredulity born of ignorance.

Today, modern investigation has disclosed that Pinto's *Travels* is indeed based, in large part, on historical fact, though some disagreement still exists as to the exact proportion of fact to fancy. All the apparatus of modern scholarship is still at work, both among the supporters and detractors of Pinto, in an effort either to undermine or buttress the historical framework of the book. Whatever the results, they can never diminish thereby the stature of the artist, for it is as a literary work that the *Travels* must finally be judged.

Translations

In addition to its lengthy "Apologia," the Spanish translation is notable for its inaccuracy and its preoccupation with what the translator calls "style." Furthermore, Herrera's translation was influenced by his religious zeal, and his conception of style was conditioned by the baroque then in vogue. As a result, he took many unwarranted liberties with the text, rewriting and adding entire paragraphs at will, all of which detracts and distorts rather than—as he boasts in his "Apologia"—improves on the beauty and simplicity of Pinto's style. He shows little respect for the original text and no understanding of the author's subtle criticism. In favor of the Spanish translation is the fact that it contains all 226 chapters of the original, though they are much longer than the original, inflated by the baroque style and pious sermons inserted here and there. Herrera's translation was made from 1614 Portuguese *princeps*, though he claims to have seen the manuscript and even cites some differences between them that are of minor importance. Strangely enough, despite the high demand for the Spanish editions in the seventeenth century—there were seven altogether—no others appeared in later centuries.

The French edition was translated by a Bernard Figuier (probably Bernardo Figueiro), about whom nothing is known—though he is described on the title page as a "gentilhomme portugais"—and published in Paris in 1628, 1645, 1663, and, perhaps, 1678, making a total of three or four printings in the seventeenth century. Figuier appears to have made use of both the Portuguese and Spanish editions for his translation. He had sense enough to omit the extra verbiage inserted by Herrera, but unfortunately was influenced by some of his other mistakes. However, the liberties he took are not as audacious as those of the Spanish translator, so that of all the European translations, the French is the best. But that does not make it praiseworthy. In many respects it falls far short of the original because of the translator's overreliance on the Spanish version and his ignorance of the subject matter, which was little known to a European of his day. It contains all 226 chapters of the original and was reprinted in 1830.

The Dutch translation is really an abridged version of the original by an unknown translator, and was published in Amsterdam in 1652 and 1653. By the end of the seventeenth century the Dutch had driven the Portuguese out of their fortress-factories and were writing their own accounts of events in Asia. This may explain the lack of further editions.

The German translation was published in Amsterdam in 1671 in two variant editions. This too is an abridged version of the original that compresses the events of 226 chapters into 63. The unknown translator states in his preface that he relied on the Dutch and French editions for his translation. There were no further German editions.

The English translation was published in London in 1653, 1663, and 1692. A facsimile edition of the English *princeps* appeared in London in 1969. The translator, a Henry Cogan, who published five other translations in a three-year period, apparently relied on the French translation. Where the Spanish translator is guilty of sins of commission, Cogan is guilty of sins of omission, for he shortened the work considerably by condensing the 226 chapters of the original into eighty-one and by omitting all the chapters relating to Saint Francis Xavier—the same chapters that made the book so popular in the Catholic countries—as well as chapter 225, which deals with the missionary aspects of Pinto's last voyage to Japan. However, in all fairness to Cogan, it should be pointed out that his truncated version of Pinto's *Travels* was dictated by historical circumstances, for it was published during Oliver Cromwell's administration, and all references to the hated "popists" had to be omitted. Similar historical circumstances may have affected the work of the other Protestant translators.

The English historian G. E. Harvey, who consulted Cogan's *Voyages and Adventures of Fernand Mendes Pinto, a Portugal,* for his *History of Burma* (1925), complains that "Cogan's translation of Pinto is thoroughly bad; not only does it mangle the sense and take serious liberties with proper names but also it miscopies dates so badly that it is useless for purposes of chronological comparison." Besides omitting the chapters on Saint Francis and other pious Catholic phrases or references, Cogan shortens the work by omitting entire passages that he found repetitive or boring. Also, when he comes to a difficult passage or an ambiguous word or phrase, he simply omits it. When Pinto gives both the Asian name of a temple and its meaning in Portuguese, such as a temple by the name of "*Hifaticau,* meaning 'love of God,'" Cogan omits the Asian name and renders the name of the temple merely as "Love of God," thereby destroying the historical reference, as well as the literary effects the author sought to achieve. Other mistranslations were picked up from the French edition, which in turn were picked up from the Spanish edition, such as "Fortune saw fit to take me from the caresses and cockering of my mother"—a tender touch added by the Spanish translator, despite the fact that Pinto never mentions his mother in the book. In short, Cogan's translation is a truncated version of the original, teeming with errors and written in Jacobean English which is difficult for the modern nonspecialist reader to comprehend.

It should be added that the first Japanese translation of the *Travels* was published recently in Tokyo (1979–80) in three volumes. The translator, Takiko Okamura, is a professor at the Sophia University of Tokyo. This edition is sparsely annotated, but it has the distinction of being the first new, complete translation published in this century. Interestingly enough, in 1973 the Japanese also published a facsimile edition of the Portuguese *princeps* of 1614. Both of these editions would seem to indicate that the Japanese have come to appreciate the importance of Pinto's contribution to their history.

Over the years, numerous abridged or partial editions of Pinto's *Travels* have been published, all of them based on the poor seventeenth-century translations, including a Czech (1966) and an Italian (1970) edition.

I have heard of, but not seen, an abridged Cantonese translation of the *Travels,* supposedly published in Macao in 1982. A Chinese professor from the Beijing Institute of Foreign Languages, who recently received a grant to translate the Chinese episodes of the *Travels* into Mandarin, has defected in Lisbon, and I have lost all contact with him.

Until now, no good critical, annotated edition has been published in any language.

Summary of the Text

Pinto begins the story of his wanderings with a brief account of his early life in Portugal beset by hardship and poverty, a pirate encounter at sea, and his years of service in the households of the rich and powerful. Dissatisfied with his lot and the paltry pay he received—that is the reason he gives—he decided, like many of the young men of his day with poor prospects at home, to seek his fortune in India.

On 11 March 1537, Pinto sailed for India. After an uneventful journey around the Cape of Good Hope and a brief stop in Mozambique, he arrived on 5 September 1537 at Diu, a fortified island and town northwest of Bombay, which had come into the possession of the Portuguese two years before. At the time of his arrival, the fortress was under threat of siege from the combined Moslem forces, headed by Suleiman the Great, who were determined to throw the Portuguese out of India and maintain their monopoly of the eastern trade.

Enticed by tales of money to be made by attacking Moslem shipping, Pinto joins a reconnaissance mission to the Red Sea, with a brief stop in Ethiopia to deliver a message to the Portuguese soldiers then guarding the mother of Prester John in her mountain fortress. After departing from the Ethiopian port of Massawa, they engage three Turkish galleys, are beaten, taken to Mocha—a port on the Red Sea in southwest Arabia—and put on the auction block. Pinto is sold to a Greek Moslem, a cruel master, he says, who in turn, frightened by Pinto's threats of suicide, sells him to a Jewish merchant. His new master takes him along the caravan route to Hormuz, the leading mart in the Persian Gulf, where Pinto signs on with a Portuguese cargo ship.

After several naval engagements in the Arabian Sea, Pinto reaches Goa, then the capital of Portuguese India. Broken, bruised, and destitute, he decides that the life of a soldier is not the way to make one's fortune. He enters the service of Pero de Faria, the newly appointed captain of Malacca. From 1539 on he seems to have been based in Malacca. There he served the captain as a sort of ambassador-at-large and was sent out on ostensibly diplomatic missions to the petty kingdoms of Sumatra, then allied with the Portuguese against the Moslems of Achin in northern Sumatra. These missions permitted him to engage in private trade, while at the same time looking after the commercial interests of the officials he served, many of whom, as he maliciously points out, enriched themselves by engaging in private trade to the detriment of their allies, who are allowed to go down in defeat.

His next mission takes him to Patani, on the eastern shore of the Malay Peninsula, where he meets up with a group of his countrymen. In a joint business venture, they send a shipload of merchandise up the coast to Siam, where huge profits are to be made. However, a sudden attack by a Moslem pirate leaves the Portuguese of Patani penniless. Thirsting for vengeance, the Portuguese set out in search of the pirate who victimized them and in the process become pirates themselves, in a swashbuckling episode that functions within the work as a parody of the overseas action of the Portuguese. After many months of operating profitably in the Gulf of Tongking, in and around Indochina and the waters of the South China Sea, and on up to the northern coasts of China to raid the emperor's tombs, the expedition ends in shipwreck, and a small band of survivors is tossed up on the shores of China, where they are arrested for vagrancy, tried, and sentenced to one year of hard labor on the Great Wall of China.

Before Pinto and his companions have completed their sentence, the Tartars invade China and capture them. They win the favor of the cruel Tartar invaders by showing them how to storm a fortress and from them, in return, win their freedom. In the company of a Tartar ambassador they travel overland to Cochinchina, whence they are conducted to the coast of China, where they hope to take a ship for India. On the way, they meet up with a popelike figure, strongly reminiscent of the Dalai Lama, who had never been heard of in Europe. Arriving too late in the season and faced with the prospect of cold and starvation on the barren, deserted islands off the coast of Canton, Pinto and two of his companions board a Chinese pirate junk, which is driven by a storm to the Japanese island of Tanegashima, just south of Kyushu. Landing in 1542 or 1543, Pinto makes the plausible claim that his was the first group of Europeans to set foot in Japan. The pirate captain, posing as a peaceful merchant, sells his goods at enormous profit. The Portuguese endear themselves to the local feudal lord, who is enchanted by their tales of their country at "the other end of the world" and especially by their gift of an arquebus—the first firearm the Japanese have seen—which they copy and rapidly reproduce, thereby turning the tide of the civil wars then raging in Japan.

Pinto returns to the coast of China, to Ning-po—a Portuguese enclave near Canton—with tales of the riches to be gained by trading with the newly discovered land of Japan. In their rush to be the first to get there, the Portuguese merchants of Ning-po set out against the monsoon and are shipwrecked off the Ryukyu [Lu-chu] Islands, where they are arrested and charged with piracy. Thanks to the compassionate women of Ryukyu, who plead for their lives, they are released, though not absolved, and Pinto returns once more to Malacca.

There he reports to Pero de Faria, who is still serving as captain of Malacca, and is sent on a mission to Martaban, a small, wealthy state—today part of Lower Burma, but then tributary to Pegu, which had recently been conquered by the Burmese. He arrives in the midst of a siege and takes refuge in the camp of the Portuguese mercenaries who had abandoned the "king"—actually the viceroy—of Martaban and passed over to the Burmese, attracted by the higher pay. The chapters devoted to the fall of Martaban, the betrayal of the king, the cruel executions that follow, and the frenzied sack of the city, form one of the most dramatic episodes in the book. They are an impassioned condemnation of war, tyranny, and man's capacity for brutality.

At the end of the siege, Pinto, betrayed by a Portuguese mercenary, is made a captive of the Burmese and placed in the charge of the king's treasurer, who takes him on a journey to the kingdom of Calaminhan—identified by modern scholars as Luang Prabang. On that journey he learns of strange religious customs among the heathens and witnesses bloody scenes of self-sacrifice strongly resembling the Juggernaut festival, which in the sixteenth century was reputed to be the most dreadful scene of religious frenzy in all of Asia. On his return, while the Burmese are besieging Sandoway, Pinto escapes and makes his way back to Goa.

There Pinto meets up with Pero de Faria, now ex-captain of Malacca, who sends him to Java to buy pepper destined for China. While waiting for the monsoon, forty of the Portuguese merchants in the port of Bantam are invited to join forces with the Moslem emperor of Demak, supreme ruler of Java, in a holy war against the Hindu

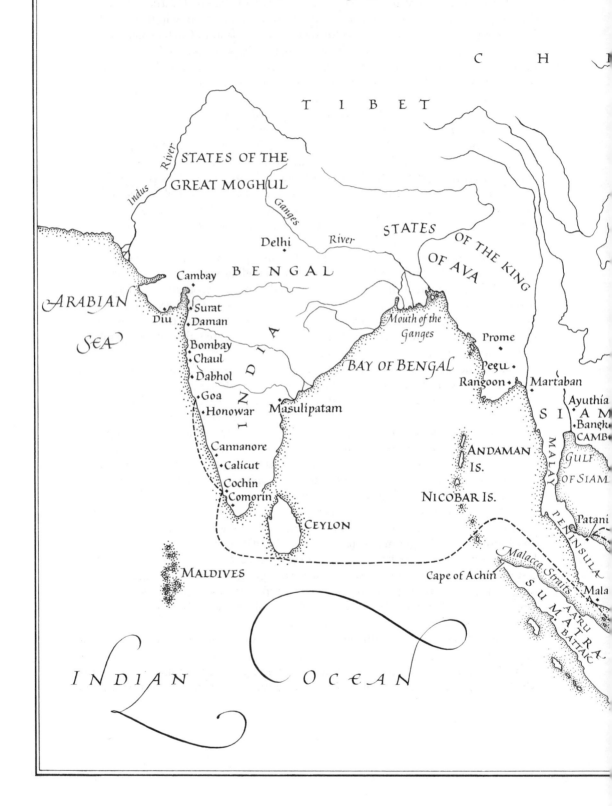

✒] Mendes Pinto's route to Japan

C   H   CHI

T I B E T

STATES OF THE

GREAT MOGHUL

Indus River

Ganges

Delhi

River

STATES

OF THE KING

OF AVA

B E N G A L

Cambay

ARABIAN

Surat

Diu

Daman

Mouth of the Ganges

Prome

SEA

Bombay

Chaul

Pegu

BAY OF BENGAL

Rangoon

Martaban

Dabhol

Goa

Honowar

Masulipatam

Ayuthia

S I A M

Bangk

CAMB

Cannanore

ANDAMAN

IS.

GULF

OF SIAM

Calicut

Cochin

Comorin

NICOBAR IS.

Patani

CEYLON

M A L A Y

P E N I N S U L A

MALDIVES

Cape of Achin

Malacca Straits

Mala

A A R U

S U M A T R A

B A T T A K

I N D I A N

O C E A N

I N D I A

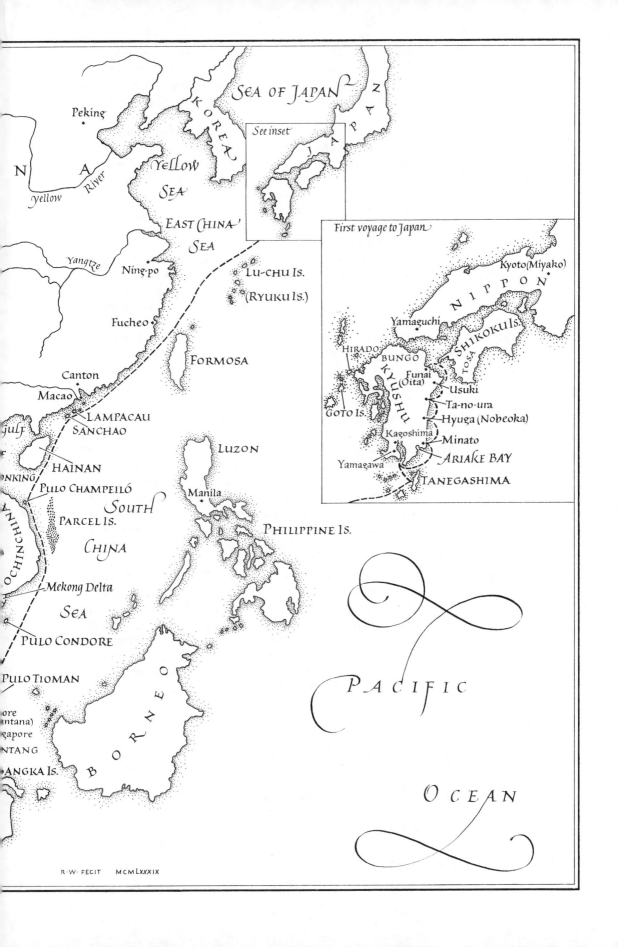

SEA OF JAPAN

KOREA

JAPAN

Peking

Yellow River

yellow

N
A

YELLOW SEA

EAST CHINA SEA

Yangtze

Ning-po

Lu-chu Is.
(Ryuku Is.)

Fucheo

FORMOSA

Canton

Macao

LAMPACAU
SANCHAO

gulf

HAINAN

NKING

Pulo Champeiló

PARCEL Is.

SOUTH
CHINA

OCHINCHINA

Mekong Delta

SEA

Pulo Condore

Pulo Tioman

ore
(ntana)
gapore

NTANG

ANGKA Is.

B O R N E O

Luzon

Manila

PHILIPPINE Is.

See inset

First voyage to Japan

Kyoto(Miyako)

N I P P O N

Yamaguchi

HIRADO

BUNGO

SHIKOKU Is.

TOSA

Funai
(Oita)

Usuki

KYUSHU

Ta-no-ura

Hyuga (Nobeoka)

GOTO Is.

Kagoshima

Minato

Yamagawa

ARIAKE BAY

TANEGASHIMA

P A C I F I C

O C E A N

king of Pasaruan, a small independent royalty at the eastern end of the island. The crusade comes to a sudden halt when the emperor is slain by his page boy over a ridiculous point of honor. The Portuguese, alarmed by the chaos and anarchy that mark the election of a successor, return to their ship, already loaded with pepper, and set sail for China.

The voyage is disastrous for them. They are driven off by the Japanese Wako (pirates) then ravaging the coasts of China, are shipwrecked in the Gulf of Siam, their raft tossed up on the coast of Java, where they stoop to cannibalism and sell themselves as slaves in order to be taken out of the swamps by a passing riverboat. They are then sold to a Celebes merchant and resold to the king of Calapa (Batavia), who generously sends them back to Sunda whence they had departed.

From Sunda, Pinto sails for Siam to start anew on borrowed money. Shortly after his arrival, the king of Siam sets out to quell a revolt on his northern borders and invites the Portuguese residents of Siam to join him. On his return from the wars, the good king of Siam is poisoned by his adulterous queen, who murders the nine-year-old heir and succeeds in placing her lover on the throne. The usurper in turn is murdered, and during the interregnum and the unrest that follow, the king of Burma lays siege to Ayuthia, the capital of Siam. The siege is suddenly lifted when the Burmese receive word of rebellion at home. Though he does not claim to have been present throughout, Pinto dwells at great length on the palace intrigues and the Burmese wars of unification. As for his description of these events, scholars are generally agreed that Pinto had a genius for grasping the essentials of Burmese politics at a time when nothing had been written on the subject in Europe.

Pinto makes a second voyage to Japan. As he is preparing to leave from the port of Kagoshima, he takes on board a Japanese fugitive by the name of Anjiro, snatching him from the arms of his pursuers. On his arrival in Malacca he hands Anjiro over to Francis Xavier, the "Apostle of the Indies," as the saint later came to be known. Xavier converts Anjiro, baptizes him Paul of the Holy Faith, and sails with him to Japan in 1549, to begin missionary work that was to bear fruit for the next hundred years, until the Japanese closed their doors to all foreigners. On his third voyage to Japan, in 1551, Pinto encounters Francis again and is present at the saint's disputations with the Japanese Buddhist priests at the court of Bungo. Later that year, Pinto departs from Japan with Francis Xavier as his shipmate.

Fifteen chapters are devoted to the saint, his miracles, his disputations with the Japanese Buddhist priests, and his lonely death, in 1552, on the doorstep of China, where he is forbidden to enter. Pinto makes a fourth and final voyage to Japan (1554–56) in the company of Xavier's successor, as the ambassador of the viceroy of Portuguese India to the daimyo of Bungo, on the island of Kyushu. In the last chapter he rapidly covers his return to Portugal in 1558, the four and a half years he spent cooling his heels at the court of Lisbon, and his disappointment at not obtaining a royal sinecure for his twenty-one years of service to God and king.

Influences

There is no question but that Pinto's *Travels* draws upon everything he ever saw, heard, and read about Asia. Occasionally the germ of an idea or an episode can be traced to its source.

Albert Kammerer, an expert on the Near East, doubts that Pinto ever set foot in

Ethiopia, and this despite the fact that Pinto's account is fairly accurate. He even concedes that the few mistakes made by Pinto were made as well by other more respected writers on the early history of Ethiopia. Nevertheless, Kammerer regards Pinto's relation as "d'authenticité douteuse."[9] It is highly probable that Pinto based his description of Ethiopia on Father Francisco Alvares's *Verdadera informaçam das terras do Preste Joam* (A True Relation of the Lands of the Prester John), written in 1520 but not published until 1540 at Lisbon. It is even more probable that Pinto had purchased the second edition of this work, which was translated into Spanish by Thomas de Padilla and published in Saragossa (1561) under the title of *Historia de las cosas de Ethiopia*. In support of this claim I offer the fact that appended to this second edition was a Jesuit letterbook containing Pinto's letter of 5 December 1554, written from Malacca. Pinto may well have had this book in his library.

That Pinto read the Jesuit letterbooks is apparent from a comparison between the episode following his departure from Ethiopia (chap. 5) and a letter written by Brother Fulgencio Freire to the patriarch of Ethiopia. In both instances the Portuguese engage a Turkish man o' war, are beaten, and are taken captive to a Red Sea port. And in both instances the circumstances are too similar to be accidental. Brother Fulgencio's letter of August 1560 was published in Barcelona in 1562, which was just about the time that Pinto was preparing to write his book.[10]

For his description of China, especially for the interior of China, Pinto borrowed freely from Gaspar da Cruz's *Treatise on China* (1569), as well as from the reports, written and oral, of the Portuguese prisoners in China who later escaped or were ransomed by their countrymen. While it is true that Pinto himself visited the islands off Canton several times on trading voyages, it is not known for certain that he visited any other part of China. He may possibly have accompanied Father Belchior Nunes Barreto to Canton to ransom the Portuguese prisoners, but still, at the time that Pinto was there (1555), none of the Portuguese had ever travelled freely in the interior of China. Pinto keeps true to this fact by presenting the protagonist (himself) in the China episode as a prisoner being taken in chains as far north as Peking, where he is in turn taken prisoner by the Tartars who invade China in the year 1550.

Of the medieval travelers who preceded him, Pinto is most indebted to Odoric of Pordenone, who traveled in Asia from 1316 to 1330 and from whose relation he borrowed his description of suttee, or the rite of widow burning. To Odoric's *Travels* he also owes his description of the figure he calls the *talapicor* of Lechune, who is strongly reminiscent of the Dalai Lama. Of less importance but of striking similarity is the image of the dancing girls who waited on table at the banquet for Antonio de Faria, borrowed no doubt from the "musical damsels" who fed the rich man of Manzi in chapter 46 of Odoric's relation. But most important of all is his description of the Juggernaut festival, the germ of which was undoubtedly taken from Odoric's chapter on "customs of the idolaters." Much enlarged in Pinto's work, the episode of the Juggernaut festival is of crucial importance as a commentary on the role of religion in the lives of the Asians.

On 5 December 1554, during his brief career as a member of the Society of Jesus, Pinto wrote a letter from Malacca to his brethren in Portugal in which he says,

> Two hundred and fifty leagues from here [from China] and a hundred leagues before arriving in Japan, are the Ryukyu Islands, where some Portuguese were shipwrecked. The King of the Ryukyus gave them a ship and *everything else they needed, but he refused to*

see them, saying that it would not please God for him to see with his own eyes, people who were in
the habit of stealing from others. He said that because of the lands conquered by the Portuguese
in India. I mention this, dear brothers, to show you the kindness of these people who have no
knowledge of their Creator.

The portion in italics was deleted from the copies of this letter in the codexes of the three Jesuit colleges in Portugal, as well as from the many printed copies of the Jesuit letterbooks published in the sixteenth and seventeenth centuries, with the exception of the Italian version, *Diversi avisi particolari dall'Indie di Portogallo* (Venice, 1565).

The letter proves that the episode of the shipwreck off the Ryukyu Islands (chaps. 138–43) is based on information Pinto obtained from an unknown source. Though the Portuguese are put on trial for piracy in this episode, they are later pardoned by the king with words similar to those in Pinto's letter. Pinto characterizes the Luchuans, whom he probably never met, as a gentle and compassionate people, which accords well with the description given of them by Basil Hall two centuries later, in his *Voyage to Loo-Choo* (1826).

An example of an interesting "borrowing" appears in chapter 136, where Pinto describes a shooting accident in which the young prince of Bungo is wounded. In chapter 137 Pinto describes how he cures the prince. Such an accident actually did occur, but not exactly at the time or under the circumstances described by Pinto. It was proven by Schurhammer, who cites a letter written by Yoshishige, the "king" of Bungo and brother of the wounded prince, describing the arquebus accident and attributing the cure to a Portuguese named Jorge de Faria,[11] and not Fernão Mendes Pinto. Interestingly enough, Charles Boxer refers to the same accident but attributes the cure to a Diogo Vaz de Aragão.[12]

The Historical Author

In dealing with a work that is purportedly autobiographical, one would naturally expect that the task of constructing the author's life would be made easier. That is not the case with Pinto's *Travels*. It must be borne in mind that for Pinto, autobiography is but a pretext—a framework on which to build his fiction—so that the problem faced by his biographers is one of separating the facts from fancy; and given Pinto's penchant for ambiguity and indirection, the results are often open to question. Fortunately, other sources do exist which can be drawn on to support the basic structure of fact on which Pinto's *Travels* is so imaginatively fashioned.

For the little we know with any certainty of Pinto's life, we are indebted to the Jesuits who were his contemporaries, who either knew him or heard about him, wrote about him, and—best of all—preserved their records. The Jesuit writings, including the two letters written by Pinto himself, cover the events of the years 1551–57 and make up an important contribution to Pinto's biography, for they contain information about which Pinto himself chose to remain silent. As such, they add an important chapter to his life which is missing from the book, namely the events leading up to Pinto's return to Portugal in 1558. For the rest, we must rely in great part on what he tells us in the book.

Most biographers place the date of Pinto's birth somewhere between the years 1509 and 1511. This is based solely on the book's assertion that he was ten or twelve years old when King Manuel died, which was Saint Lucy's Day, 13 December 1521.

Pinto remembers that date quite clearly, he says, because his uncle brought him to Lisbon on the day they were breaking the escutcheons for the death of the king. Pinto begins the *Travels* with the information that he "lived in abject misery and poverty until about the age of ten or twelve, in my father's humble house in the village of Montemor-o-Velho." Montemor-o-Velho, a town halfway between the port of Figueira da Foz and the university city of Coimbra, has been accepted unquestioningly by his biographers and critics alike as Pinto's birthplace. However, no proof has ever been adduced, and until birth or baptismal documents are produced, Pinto's birthplace remains uncertain.

Pinto probably came of a poor family that may have been distantly related to the wealthy Mendes family of Lisbon and Antwerp, the powerful New Christians who early in the century had been awarded the monopoly of the spice trade by the Portuguese crown. This would explain the uncle who brought him to Lisbon and placed him in the service of a noblewoman of distinguished lineage. Unfortunately, his uncle's ambitious plans for him did not turn out as he had hoped. For after he had served about a year and a half in the household of this unnamed noblewoman, something dreadful occurred—or, as he puts it, "something happened that placed me in such great jeopardy that I was forced to leave the house at a moment's notice and flee for my life." No reason for the sudden flight is given. The reader is left to conjecture about what could possibly have happened that placed the youthful Pinto in such great danger. He did not stop running, he tells us, until he reached the Alfama port district, where he signed on board a caravel in the Tagus River estuary that was sailing for Setúbal, a nearby port about twenty miles southeast of Lisbon. The following morning, when they were within fifteen miles of their destination, the caravel was attacked by the French pirates who constantly infested the waters in those days, preying on Spanish and Portuguese shipping. Pinto was taken captive by the pirates who, he says, intended to sell him to the slave traders of the Barbary coast. However, en route to Africa the pirates captured an even richer prize and decided to return home with their booty. Pinto was then put ashore at Melides, along with a few companions, who, half naked and wounded from the lash, made their way to Santiago de Cacém, where they were cared for by the townspeople. As soon as he was well enough to travel, Pinto made his way to Setúbal, where, inexplicably enough, this penniless castaway and refugee was accepted into the household and employ of a nobleman, Francisco de Faria. As a reward for his faithful service of four years, the latter recommended him to Dom Jorge, the bastard son of John II, and grand master of the Order of Santiago.

He remained in Dom Jorge's employ only a year and a half when, dissatisfied with the paltry remuneration, he decided to seek his fortune in India. Dom Jorge may have been instrumental in obtaining passage for him as a soldier aboard one of the three ships belonging to King John III that sailed from Portugal on 11 March 1537. If, as Pinto says, he was ten or twelve years old in 1521, then he must have been twenty-six or twenty-eight years old when he departed for India. Of these sixteen years—that is, the period from 1521 to 1537—he accounts for only seven years: one and a half years in the service of the unnamed noblewoman whose house he fled; four years with the nobleman Francisco de Faria; and one and a half years with the bastard prince Dom Jorge. Thus, nine years of his life during this period are passed over in silence.

During Pinto's twenty-one years in Asia, from 1537 until 1558, he was a slave, soldier, merchant, pirate, ambassador, missionary, doctor—the list is not complete. He claims to have been shipwrecked, taken captive, and sold sixteen or seventeen times.

He seems to have been based in Malacca, where he arrived in 1539, in the employ of the captain of the fortress, Pero de Faria. If he is to be believed, he served the latter for as long as his term of office lasted, as a troubleshooter or ambassador-at-large to the neighboring friendly kingdoms of Sumatra, Malaysia, and Martaban. Also, it is fairly certain, from his letters and from Jesuit sources, that he lived for some years in Pegu (Burma) and Siam. He next shifted his activities to trading voyages in the China seas. That he did in fact make four voyages to Japan is accepted, although his claim to have been among the first group of Europeans to set foot in Japan cannot be proven.

We come now to the best documented period of Pinto's life. Though in the book he complains constantly of his penury, we know that sometime during his twenty-one years in Asia Pinto amassed a considerable fortune. It was as a wealthy merchant, on his third voyage to Japan, that he befriended Francis Xavier in the year 1551. There it was that he lent the saint money to build the first Christian church in Japan. In 1554 Pinto decided to return home with his fortune, settle down, and raise a family. While in Goa, waiting for the homeward-bound ships, Pinto underwent a mystic conversion and divested himself of a large part of his fortune on behalf of the Society of Jesus, which accepted him into its ranks as a lay brother. Concurrently with these events a letter arrived in Goa from Otomo Yoshishige, the daimyo, or feudal lord, of Bungo, asking the viceroy to send Francis Xavier back to Japan and holding out a promise for Otomo's conversion. The daimyo's letter arrived at about the same time that the saint's corpse was being viewed in Goa by thousands of fervent worshippers.

It was decided that Father Belchior Nunes Barreto, vice-provincial and rector of the Society of Jesus in Asia, should head a religious mission to Japan. Pinto was to accompany the mission, but in the capacity of ambassador, sent by the viceroy, to establish diplomatic relations between Japan and Portuguese India. Though Pinto had already been sworn in as a member of the Jesuit Society, it was agreed that he would not don his religious robes until after the completion of the mission, the cost of which was borne almost entirely by Pinto.

As it turned out, the evangelical side of the mission was a failure, though Pinto seems to have carried out his embassy with some degree of success. It had taken almost two years for them to reach Japan, and by the time they arrived, Otomo Yoshishige was embroiled in a civil war and could hardly risk alienating his people by converting to a foreign faith. Twenty-two years were to pass before Otomo converted in 1578. Pinto may or may not have been aware of it, for in the same year in Almada he was just putting the finishing touches to the *Travels*, which makes no mention of this important conversion.

Sometime between this last voyage to Japan and his return to Goa in 1557, something must have happened to Pinto—about which we can only speculate—that caused him to undergo a change of heart. He was separated from the Society of Jesus, apparently at his own request and on good terms with the order. Lending credence to this supposition is the fact that years later, in 1582, Pinto was interviewed in his retirement by the official Jesuit historians of India, and shortly thereafter Philip II, then reigning monarch of Portugal, granted him a stipend in the form of wheat, which was the equivalent of about three loaves of bread a day.

When Pinto returned to Portugal on 22 September 1558, he was already well known as the author of an edifying letter that had been published by the Society of

Jesus in 1555. In 1558 the dowager Queen Catherine was in her second year as regent. Pinto complains bitterly of the four and a half years he wasted as a hanger-on at court, hoping to receive some award or compensation for his services to the crown. On 23 December 1562, Catherine handed over the reins of government to her brother-in-law, Cardinal Henrique. It must have been in the early months of the latter's regency when Pinto came to realize that his cause was hopeless, for under the cardinal's rule the strictest economy was practiced at court. With his claims unrecognized, Pinto retired a disappointed man to a small estate near Almada, opposite Lisbon, where he married a Maria Correia de Brito and settled down to raise a family. He had acquired somewhat of a reputation as an old China hand, for there he was consulted by João de Barros, the most famous historian of his day, for information about China and Japan. Between 1569 and 1571 he was visited by an ambassador of the grand duke Cosimo de' Medici, who had come to Lisbon in search of information on China. In 1573 and again in 1578, he was elected president of the Board of Guardians of the Hospital of Saint Lazarus in Almada, a post usually reserved for the rich and powerful. Sometime between the years 1569 and 1578 he wrote the *Travels*. Pinto died on 8 July 1583, only three months after he had received the small but long-awaited stipend from the crown, in recognition of his long years of service to God and king.

Of Pinto's family little is known for certain except the information derived from Jesuit sources. Even the two extant letters written by him when he was a member of the society contain no information about his family and very little about himself, despite the fact that he writes that the father master had instructed him to compose a long letter about his life. From a letter written by Francis Xavier to King John III in 1551 we learn that he had two brothers, António and Álvaro, and that the latter was present at the siege of Malacca in 1551. Other letters reveal that one of his brothers suffered martyrdom in Bintang, that he had "sisters and a brother" in Lisbon in 1554 and a wealthy cousin named Francisco Garcia de Vargas, who was present in Cochin in 1557. We also know that the children he refers to in his book were daughters, for it was they who, after his death, donated the manuscript of his *Travels*—as was his wish—to the Casa Pia das Penitentes.

Pinto must have been a kind and generous man, to judge from the picture painted of him by another letter writer of the period who tells us that he freed many slaves, though three of them threw themselves at his feet, protesting that they wanted to die with him in Japan. But if we know from the work a little about Pinto's mind, and a great deal about his imagination, the man himself remains unknowable, hidden as much as revealed by the *Travels,* which alone has given substance to his name.

Satire and the Fictive Author

The narrator or fictive author of the *Travels* is not to be confused with the historical author. He is a persona, a character or identity assumed by the satirist in order to realize his critical purposes. As a rhetorical instrument, the persona is highly flexible, because it allows Pinto to speak alternately in three or more distinguishable voices:

1. the voice of the stoic *vir bonus,* or the "good man," who wins our confidence in his personal morality by projecting an image of himself as a fundamentally kind and virtuous man;

2. the voice of the *ingénu,* the naif who wins our sympathy by presenting an

image of himself as an innocent man, the simple heart, slightly dim-witted, who lays no claim to talent or literary pretensions; the speaker of this voice is usually the vehicle of ironies about matters he professes not to understand;

3. the voice of the hero, the patriot, the defender of the faith (*fidei defensor*), who opens before our eyes a world in which the discernment of evil is always accompanied by the courage to attack;

4. the voice of the *picaro*, who reveals the foolishness and knavery of others by dissimulating approbation of, and by his participation in, the very evil he wishes to condemn.

This "poor inoffensive me," this false *ingénu*, travels throughout the world as a wolf in sheep's clothing. He takes us on a voyage in which he reveals, in the most realistic terms, the overseas actions of the Portuguese. The opposite of the "matchless chiefs" of the *Lusiads*, the Portuguese of Pinto's *Travels* are the very incarnation of evil. He shows us the ugliest and most cruel aspects of their overseas adventures but at the same time pretends not to see anything ignoble in them. On the contrary, he appears to be proud of the colonial enterprise and of his part in it. But beware of this *faux ingénu*, for every episode is artfully contrived to make a criticism.

Again and again, episodes are presented first from the Portuguese point of view, but then the perspective gradually shifts to that of the Asians, who express their criticism of the Portuguese in the strongest terms. The protagonist frequently is only an observer who merely repeats the words spoken by Asians. It's not his fault if the Chinese boy found on board a ship captured by the Portuguese pirate, Antonio de Faria, accuses the Portuguese of being robbers and hypocrites. He only repeats what he hears, without giving much thought to it. Nor is it his fault if the Asians accuse the Portuguese of coming to Asia disguised as merchants, to spy out the land, only to return later to conquer it, an accusation that agrees with the actions described by the innocent narrator.

This pose permits Pinto to express, albeit indirectly, the most crushing condemnation of the ideology of the crusade—through, for instance, the Tartar king who says (chap. 122), "The fact that these people journey so far from home to conquer territory indicates clearly that there must be very little justice and a great deal of greed among them," to which an old man replies:

> It would certainly seem so, for when men, by dint of industry and ingenuity, fly over all the waters in order to acquire possessions that God did not give them, it means either that there is such great poverty among them that it makes them completely forget their homeland, or that the vanity and blindness engendered in them by their greed are so great as to cause them to deny God and their fathers.

The same accusations are made to the shipwrecked Portuguese on the Ryukyu Islands, who then protest that "the God in whom we believed forbade us in his holy Law either to kill or to steal" (chap. 140). But the innocent narrator pretends not to see the irony when, once the Portuguese are pardoned by the king of the Ryukyus, the narrator, speaking now in the voice of the patriot, invites the Portuguese to come and conquer the islands.

The last voyage to Japan of the historical Fernão Mendes Pinto, just as it is described in his letter of 20 November 1555 from Macao, also appears in the *Travels*, but with this difference—the protagonist does not mention his role as missionary and puts in the mouth of the friendly king of Patani the following words (chap. 220): "Wouldn't it be better for these people, as long as they are exposing themselves to such great hardship, to go to China to get rich rather than to foreign kingdoms to preach nonsense?" Evidently Pinto's point of view on the evangelical mission he undertook in 1554–56 changed considerably years later when he was writing his *Travels*.

At times the narrator speaks to us in the voice of the *picaro*, but only in certain episodes in which he establishes what can be called a reciprocal relationship between "master" and "servant." The most significant of those mutual relationships is the contract that the protagonist makes with Antonio de Faria, the leader of the Portuguese pirates. The motive that he gives for joining the band of pirates is one of the basic devices of picaresque satire—hunger. The Antonio de Faria episode constitutes by itself a parody of the overseas conquests of the Portuguese, but at the same time it contains all the elements of the picaresque. Throughout the entire episode, our *picaro*, always ready to be corrupted, directs all of his power of praise on his "master," who is praised for being "a brave and good Christian" (chap. 56), who is "by nature a very generous person" (chap. 58), and who ennobles his ugly cause by making "a speech, like a good Christian—which indeed he was" (chap. 60). And while the "servant" recounts all this in his characteristic tone of ironic neutrality, our attention is directed to the villainy of his "master."

This relationship of the *picaro* to Antonio de Faria can be compared with that of Lazarillo de Tormes to his fifth master, the seller of papal indulgences. In this particular episode in the *Life of Lazarillo de Tormes* (c. 1554)—the most famous work in the literature of roguery—there is no friction between master and servant. While the servant reports, our attention is centered on the master's chicanery. He is a bad master, not because he beats his servant or starves him, but because he is a bad example, a corrupting instructor. Since the *picaro* is never quite so corrupt as the society he enters, he has to be taught the tricks of the trade, and in the process much that is underhanded is exposed and analyzed for the reader. The degeneration portrayed is not so much in the master-servant relationship itself as in the occupation of the master, into which the servant is drawn and initiated.

A natural corollary of the flexibility of Pinto's persona is its inconsistency. As a result, we find the satirist constantly changing his mood, manner, and mores, whenever it suits his purpose. But his purpose, it should be noted, is unswervingly consistent, for the satirist never loses sight of his goal. His primary intention—and in this he is inflexible—is to portray a consistent moral philosophy.

Once the *persona* has established an image of himself as a somewhat foolish and artless creature, the reader is better prepared to accept the many careless—or what appear to be careless—errors and inconsistencies that are artfully woven into the narrative. Supporting the shadowy fiction that the satirist creates in pursuit of his goal are the frequent references to genuine historical particulars and realistic detail, which provide the necessary touches of verisimilitude. Nothing is out of place and nothing is done without a purpose. But the resulting scene is one of premeditated paradox and ambiguity.

For example, the chronology of the *Travels* is glaringly and daringly inaccurate. More than that, it is absurd, a fact that no one will dispute, from the casual reader who has but lightly skimmed over its pages to the most careful critic who still persists in defending its absurdity, as many of the defenders of the veracity of Pinto have done. As we have seen, the Spanish translator of the *Travels* even went so far as to accuse the royal chronicler, Francisco de Andrade, of having emasculated the manuscript, while he himself presumed to correct the manifest errors of the original by changing the chronology or omitting dates. The truth is that the arguments advanced by the defenders, as well as those advanced by Pinto's detractors, are equally plausible, given the *Travels'* deliberate ambiguity, which permits wide latitude on both sides. The dual nature of satire invites the reader to doubt the extrinsic meaning of the work and to probe beneath the surface for the intrinsic meaning of the satire.

The episode of the protagonist's wanderings in China is presented in the form of a utopian satire. It depends for its effects on the strategem of the innocent observer who travels the world over and discovers civilizations superior to his own. It falls to the reader to work out an endless series of implied contrasts and comparisons. With notable frequency the narrator calls attention to manifest absurdities among the heathens, but just as frequently these absurdities turn out to be a distorted version of the same or similar evils existing at home. For example, the "letters of exchange" and the plenary indulgences that he ridicules among the heathens bear a striking resemblance to the papal indulgences and the jubilee pardons of Rome.

Very often the simpleminded *ingénu* fails to understand the strange workings of Chinese justice and asks—with exaggerated naivete—why his charitable benefactors refuse to accept bribes or to use their influence with the judge in order to obtain a more rapid or more favorable resolution of their case. In Pinto's utopian China such practices are looked upon with loathing and are represented as a sin against the Almighty, so that it must be carefully explained to this barbarian—for such is the Chinese perspective—that the ultimate dispensation of justice has its source in heaven and that, therefore, punishment is also a manifestation of the divine will. The exaggerated wealth of China, on which the author lavishes many pages, forms a striking contrast with the poverty at home in Portugal. Within the fiction of the work, poverty is a divine punishment, whereas abundance is represented as heavenly compensation.

The pagans of the utopias of the *Travels*—and there are several, not only China—never heard of Jesus Christ, but they obey the Commandments of the Lord. Among them tolerance exists: the freedom to worship God in different ways, and even the freedom not to believe in God. Pinto clearly appears to suggest that there is a morality possible outside the bounds of the established church. His utopian China also functions within the work as a symbol of a celestial kingdom where the Portuguese are not permitted to enter, not even the saintliest among them, Francis Xavier, whose death on the doorstep of China stands as a symbol of the failure of the ideology of the crusade.

Pinto also makes careful use of analogy in his satire. He presents a portrait of the cruelty and destructiveness of the Tartar conqueror—in sharp contrast, I might add, to the utopian Chinese—and pointedly shows the Portuguese helping, and even surpassing, the Tartars in military spirit and ingenuity. The satirist focuses on the strong affinity between these two warlike peoples and exaggerates the respect and admiration on the part of the Tartars for Portuguese military prowess.

The episode of the discovery of Japan functions, by satiric analogy, in somewhat the same manner as that of the Tartar episode. Naotoki, feudal lord of the island of Tanegashima, where the first Portuguese discoverers landed, is delighted at the prospect of friendship with the "southern barbarians" whose glorious conquests are known to him, and believes that "no king on earth can consider himself fortunate unless he is a vassal of a monarch as great as the emperor of these people" (chap. 133). The

Japanese craze for firearms, which Naotoki esteems much "more . . . than all the wealth of China" (chap. 134), is deliberately exaggerated, as is the huge quantity of firearms manufactured by the Japanese in the space of a few months, the point of which is to portray the Japanese as a warrior nation. The Japanese are also analogous to the Portuguese in their love of fine raiment, in their love of honor, and in their disdain for the merchant and their respect for the warrior and priestly castes. The sickly "king" of Bungo is cheered by the sight of the protagonist, whom he insists on meeting because he has heard that the Portuguese are "men whose ways are very compatible" to the Japanese, and who "dress in silken garments and gird on swords, not like merchants engaged in trade, but like men who love honor, in the name of which they seek to cover themselves with glory" (chap. 135).

The episode of the discovery of Japan also functions, within the fiction, as a symbol of Portuguese greed. For when the news of the discovery of a new land where profits are high reaches Ning-po—a Portuguese enclave in China and a microcosm of Lisbon—Japan becomes the special target of the onslaught of merchant and missionary alike. That is when the rush to Japan begins "against the wind, against the monsoon, against the tide, and against all reason, without a moment's thought for the perils of the sea" (chap. 137). The *persona* protects himself by an assumption of guilt, for he too is one of this mad company. Inevitably, the consequences of this mad scramble for gold is punishment, which strikes in the form of a shipwreck off the coast of the Lu-chu Islands—and, years later, the total destruction of the Portuguese enclave of Ning-po.

The Asia of Mendes Pinto is full of violent wars, motivated by greed covered by hypocrisy and instigated almost always by Moslem warrior-priests, trying to force men to abandon the faith of their fathers. The greatest Catholic saint of his time, Francis Xavier, is obliquely presented in the work as a warrior-priest who instigates men to combat. The portrait of Francis Xavier contrasts with that of the heathen priests of Pinto's utopias, who are forbidden to carry arms. On those terms, how can the Portuguese, whom Pinto paints in the darkest colors, hope to convert the Asians who live in accordance with God's laws and who are prepared to go to greater lengths, to make greater sacrifices—as in the case of the heathens of Calaminhan—than the greatest Catholic saint of his time, in an effort to apprehend the eternal? This question is implicitly posed again and again in the *Travels,* together with warnings of divine punishment that falls on the sinners at every step of their peregrination through life.

In their efforts to determine the historicity of the *Travels* scholars have frequently failed to see that Pinto's masterpiece belongs not to history, but to literature, specifically to the genre of satire. Satire is seldom "honest," but at the same time it does not stray far from the truth. Not all critics would agree on a definition of satire, but Edward W. Rosenheim, Jr., is one who insists that satire be identified in terms of its concern with historic facts: "All satire is not only an attack; it is an attack upon *discernible, historically authentic particulars.*"[13] Pinto was indeed concerned with historically authentic particulars, which he rearranged to suit his purposes.

Nevertheless, the debate on Pinto's veracity and reliability continues. Veracity and reliability, it must be stressed, should be seen as two distinct problems. This delicate distinction becomes important when we stop to consider that if Pinto—to take the question of the discovery of Japan as an example—was not actually present on that historic occasion, he was certainly among the earliest group of travelers to arrive on the scene. As such he was close enough to events to have been in a position to pass on a fairly accurate description of the discovery, which cannot easily be dismissed by the historian as unreliable, or as any less reliable than hearsay European accounts, written long after the facts.

The Dutch historian, P. A. Tiele, writing in 1880, did not believe that Pinto was actually present in person during the Javanese campaign against the Pasaruans, but that he wrote his account from information received. "For all that," Tiele states, "Pinto provides us with a document which cannot be disregarded, for little is known of Javanese history at this period."[14] Indeed, an Asian expert like Maurice Collis, who like Pinto lived in those parts for twenty years, insists that even in the most fantastic episodes of his *Travels* there is a note that rings true. As Collis notes, Pinto had an instinct for picking out the essentials of the Asian scene, and he had the genius to throw it all together in the most dramatic and artistic form. Although Collis cautions that "no episode can be wholly taken as a direct source for history,"[15] he believes that Pinto has given us in the *Travels* "the most authentic and complete picture of sixteenth-century Asia that had been written, or that would ever be written."[16] For in a certain sense, Pinto surpassed the historians of his day. He took the essence of history and extracted from it a moral lesson urgent in his own time and still valid today.

A Note on the Translation

To the reader of Portuguese, Pinto's style appears to be simple enough; indeed, it is so deceptively simple that the seventeenth-century Spanish translator, who was himself attuned to the baroque of the period, characterized it as "primitive." Essentially, it is an oral style, skillfully contrived to appear as though it were written, or rather spoken, in one long breathless sentence. At the same time, and this cannot be stressed enough, it is a style devised to fit the image of the simple-minded persona Pinto created. Of that he leaves no room for doubt. In case his readers are not perceptive enough to notice, he tells them, in the opening chapter of the book, that he has written an "awkward, unpolished tale," solely for the benefit of his children. He elaborates on this bit of fiction even further (in chapter 105) by reminding us that his "intention in writing this book . . . was none other than to leave it to my children as a primer of sorts. . . . I thought it mattered little if I wrote it in my own crude style, which is . . . the way that Nature taught me, without looking for circumlocutions or words borrowed from others with which to enhance my weak, unpolished wit."

In keeping with his rhetorical aims, Pinto often changes his style to suit his purpose. He prefers the style of the weak-witted first-person narrator who wins the readers over by taking them into his confidence. Occasionally he shifts to indirect discourse, especially when relating or paraphrasing what he chooses to have his Asian characters say on his behalf, or what he fears to say on his own behalf. At times he allows those characters, who are never fully rounded, to speak for themselves, quoting them in direct dialogue, in order to have them voice the criticism he fears to utter. In addition, he makes use of ostensibly genuine letters and documents—to which he could not possibly have had access—all of them composed in a rather rich, ornate style, supposedly reminiscent of the Orient. A Chinese bride-to-be writes to her groom, who is late in arriving: "If it were proper for me, a mere woman, to come and gaze upon thy countenance without sullying my reputation . . . I would fly, swift as the hungry falcon newly released from its bonds, to kiss thy lingering feet" (chapter 47). Somehow the metaphor of the falcon bears a closer resemblance to the courtly language of love than to the Orient, where kissing is despised. A letter from the Ryukyu women to their dowager queen begins with a long series of dazzling metaphors: "To our sainted pearl, set in the largest oyster in the profoundest depths of the sea, heavenly star, shining as bright as fire, skein of golden hair intertwined in a garland of roses . . ." (chapter 141). Other letters and documents, presumably composed in a similar vein by Asian potentates, end with the year of the ruler's reign. This is a genuine dating system of the Orient, designed to lend a touch of verisimilitude to the spurious documents.

As for the translation, it is more literary than literal. Indeed, it could not be otherwise in view of Pinto's painfully long and convoluted sentences, almost totally devoid of punctuation. Among the difficulties encountered in unraveling his sentences were those involved in reducing them to manageable proportions and adjusting the word order and tenses to the nearest English equivalents. Especially troublesome were the many gerunds and conjunctions, for which the author has an annoying predilection. In addition, there are errors of syntax in the original Portuguese, as well as an over reliance on relative pronouns, which are quite often used in such a way that it is difficult to determine to whom or to what they relate. Moreover, the translator is overwhelmed by a plethora of technical terms relating to ships and the sea. As if that were not enough, the text is liberally strewn with Asian words, phrases, and titles, some genuine, some gibberish and some borrowed from the Malay language, which Pinto probably knew best, and attributed, either deliberately or erroneously, to speakers of other tongues. Also, there are catalogs of Asian coins, currencies, weights, and measures, some long since fallen into disuse. Here and there some old Portuguese words of forgotten meaning are to be found along with hundreds of place names, a few of which have been difficult to recognize or identify, but all of which have been listed in the respective glossaries and gazetteer prepared for ease of consultation.

Finally, it should be noted that the edition used for the translation is a facsimile of the 1614 *editio princeps,* published by the Tenri Central Library of Tokyo in 1973.

THE TRAVELS OF
MENDES PINTO

I
The Early Years

Whenever I look back at all the hardship and misfortune I suffered throughout most of my life, I can't help thinking I have good reason to complain of my bad luck, which started about the time I was born and continued through the best years of my life. It seems that misfortune had singled me out above all others for no purpose but to hound me and abuse me, as though it were something to be proud of. As I grew up in my native land, my life was a constant struggle against poverty and misery, and not without its moments of terror when we barely escaped with our lives. If that were not enough, Fortune saw fit to carry me off to the Indies, where, instead of my lot improving as I had hoped, the hardship and hazards only increased with the passing years.

But on the other hand, when I consider that God always watched over me and brought me safely through all those hazards and hardships, then I find that there is not as much reason to complain about my past misfortune as there is reason to give thanks to the Lord for my present blessings, for he saw fit to preserve my life, so that I could write this awkward, unpolished tale, which I leave as a legacy for my children— because it is intended only for them. I want them to know all about the twenty-one years of difficulty and danger I lived through, in the course of which I was captured thirteen times and sold into slavery seventeen times,[1] in various parts of India, Ethiopia, Arabia Felix, China, Tartary, Macassar, Sumatra, and many other provinces of the archipelago located in the easternmost corner of Asia, which is referred to as "the outer edge of the world"[2] in the geographical works of the Chinese, Siamese, *Gueos,*[3] and Ryukyu, about which I expect to have a lot more to say later on, and in much greater detail. And this may serve, on the one hand, as an example for all men, not to let the misfortunes of life discourage them from doing what has to be done, for there are no misfortunes so great that human nature, with God's help, cannot overcome. On the other hand, it may inspire them to join with me in giving thanks to the almighty Lord for the infinite mercy he has shown me, in spite of all my sins, which I confess— and I believe it sincerely—were the source of all my troubles, for his mercy gave me the strength and courage to endure them, and to survive.

I'll begin this tale of my wanderings with what happened to me during my early years in Portugal, where I lived in abject misery and poverty until the age of ten or twelve, in my father's humble house in the village of Montemor-o-Velho.[4] An uncle of mine, apparently anxious to see me get a good start in life, brought me to the city of Lisbon and placed me in the service of a lady of very high birth, who was related to some of the noblest families in the kingdom, hoping that her influence as well as the connections of her powerful relatives would help me reach the goals he had set for me. This was at the time when they were breaking the escutcheons in the city of Lisbon at the funeral of King Manuel[5] of glorious memory, which took place on Saint Lucy's Day, 13 December 1521, an event I remember quite vividly, though I have no recollection of anything else that happened to me in Portugal prior to that time.

My uncle's plans for me did not turn out as well as he expected. On the contrary, for after more or less a year and a half in the employ of this noblewoman, something happened that placed me in such great jeopardy that I was forced to leave the house at a moment's notice and run for my life. And I kept on running, so crazed with fear that I didn't know where I was going, for I thought I saw death staring me in the eyes, keeping pace with me every step of the way. I finally reached the Stone Wharf, where I found an Alfama[6] caravel loading the horses and household goods of some nobleman bound for Setúbal,[7] where King John III,[8] may he rest in peace, had moved with his entire court to escape from an epidemic then raging in many parts of the kingdom.

I embarked on this caravel, which departed shortly afterwards, and the following morning, when we had sailed about as far as Sesimbra,[9] we were attacked by a French pirate. After he had gotten the grappling hooks into us, he rushed fifteen or twenty of his men on board, and without the slightest opposition or resistance on our part, they soon took command of the ship. Once they had stripped her of everything they could find—a plunder that netted them over six thousand *cruzados*[10]—they sent her to the bottom. Seventeen of us who escaped with our lives were transferred to their ship, bound hand and foot, to be sold as slaves in Larache,[11] where they were said to be heading with a cargo of arms for trading with the Moors.

They proceeded on this course for thirteen more days, treating us to liberal doses of the lash at every opportunity, when at sundown of the thirteenth day, it was their good fortune to sight a sailing vessel. After a whole night spent following in her wake, like old hands at the game, they finally caught up with her before the end of the midwatch. After firing three broadsides they got their grappling hooks into her with a fine show of bravery, and even though they encountered some resistance on the part of our men, it was not enough to prevent them from boarding her and killing six Portuguese, along with ten or twelve slaves. This ship was a beautiful *nao*[12] that belonged to a merchant from Vila do Conde[13] by the name of Sylvester Godinho, and she had been chartered by some Lisbon traders at São Tomé[14] for a heavy cargo of sugar and slaves, which the poor merchants, bewailing their misfortune, valued at 40,000 *cruzados*. As soon as the corsairs found themselves with such a rich prize on their hands, they changed their minds and decided to head back to France, taking some of our people with them to man the captured vessel. The rest were put ashore one night on the beach at Melides,[15] naked, barefoot, and some with their flesh still raw from the floggings they had received. And in this condition, we reached Santiago de Cacem[16] the next day, where we were generously supplied with everything we needed by the local inhabitants, especially a lady there by the name of Dona Brites, who was the daughter of the count of Vilanova and wife of Alonso Perez Pantoja, commander and mayor of the town.

As the sick and wounded began to recover, they all went their separate ways in search of a living. As for poor me, I joined up with a group of six or seven others equally forlorn, and we made our way to Setúbal, where it was my luck to be hired by a nobleman by the name of Francisco de Faria, who was attached to the household of the grand master of the Order of Saint James.[17] I served him for four years, and at the end of that time, in recognition of my years of good service, he recommended me to the grand master himself, whom I served in turn as a valet for a year and a half.

But since the salary paid by princes in those days was not enough for me to live on, I decided to leave for India, meager as my resources were, and I was perfectly willing to accept, for better or worse, whatever fate had in store for me.

2
The Passage to India

On 11 March 1537, I left Portugal with a squadron of five *naos*. There was no flagship[1] in this fleet, which was commanded respectively by the following captains:[2] the *Rainha*, by Dom Pedro da Silva,[3] or the "Rooster," as he was nicknamed, son of the admiral, Count Dom Vasco da Gama, who was commanding the same ship on which he had brought his father's remains back to Lisbon, where King John, then in residence, arranged for him to be given the most elaborate funeral that has ever been seen to this day for a lesser man than a king; the *São Roque*, by Dom Fernando de Lima,[4] son of Diogo Lopez de Lima, lord mayor of Guimarães, who died in Hormuz[5] a year later, in 1538, while serving as captain of the fortress there; the *Santa Barbara*, by his cousin, Jorge de Lima,[6] who had just been appointed captain of the fortress of Chaul[7] and was on his way to take up his duties there; the *Flor de la Mar*, by Lopo Vaz Vogado,[8] who was a master seaman in his own right; and the *Galega*—on which Pero Lopez de Sousa[9] was shipwrecked afterwards—by Martim de Freitas,[10] a native of the island of Madeira, who died later that year in Daman,[11] along with thirty-five of his men.

Proceeding on its course, the entire fleet, with God's help, made port safely at Mozambique, where we found the *nao São Miguel* laid up for the winter. She was owned and operated by a merchant named Duarte Tristão,[12] and on the way back to Portugal this richly laden vessel disappeared at sea and has never been heard from since. But then, that was the same fate that befell a number of other ships on the East India run—a price we paid for our sins.

As soon as the fleet was provisioned and made ready to sail from Mozambique, Vicente Pegado,[13] who was in command of the fortress there, presented the five captains with an order from Governor Nuno da Cunha[14] to the effect that all ships arriving from Portugal that year were to proceed directly to Diu[15] and to leave the men there to garrison the fortress, for there was good reason to fear that the Turks would send an armada against them in reprisal for the death of Sultan Bahadur[16] of Cambay[17] the previous summer, for which the governor had been responsible. A meeting was then called to discuss the matter, and it was unanimously agreed that the three *naos* belonging to the crown should proceed directly to Diu, in compliance with the governor's order, but that the two merchantmen in our fleet should go on to Goa[18] to discharge their cargo, mainly because of a number of complaints and protests that had already been lodged by their agents over the expropriation of private property that had taken place recently.

And they departed on their separate ways, the three crown ships setting a course for Diu and the two merchantmen for Goa, and with God's help, they all made port safely. The arrival of those three *naos* in the harbor of Diu, on the fifth of September in that same year of 1538,[19] was a joyful occasion for Antonio da Silveira,[20] brother of the Count of Sortelha, Luis de Silveira.[21] He greeted them with a great deal of fuss and fanfare and saw to it that everyone was well taken care of at his expense, for he not only provided food for over seven hundred men, he also showered them continuously with gifts of money and other kind favors. Impressed by this show of generosity and the abundance of things they saw all around them, on top of which they were offered salary and sustenance, practically all of the soldiers in the fleet voluntarily agreed to remain, so there was no need to apply any pressure or coercion, as was always the practice when a fortress was under threat of siege.

After disposing of their cargo at a good profit, the three *naos* proceeded on their way to Goa with just the crew and the ship's officers aboard, where they remained for a few days, until they received permission from the governor to depart for Cochin.[22] And from there, after loading new cargo, all five of the original ships in the fleet returned safely to Portugal, in consort with another *nao* that had been built in India, called the *São Pedro,* which joined them for the homeward voyage. Her captain's name was Manuel de Macedo,[23] and it was this ship that carried the famous basilisk, that huge piece of ordnance which is known in Portugal as the "cannon of Diu,"[24] for the name of the place where it was captured with two other matching pieces, at the time that Sultan Bahadur, king of Cambay, was slain. These guns were part of the original fifteen pieces of artillery that Rumi-Khan,[25] admiral of the Turkish fleet, had brought with him from Suez in 1534, when Dom Pedro de Castelbranco came to our aid with the twelve caravels that sailed from Portugal in November.[26]

3
A Renegade in the Red Sea

Only seventeen days after my arrival at the fortress of Diu, I embarked on one of the two foists[1] that were being made ready in the harbor for a reconnaissance mission to the Straits of Mecca,[2] for the purpose of gathering accurate information about the Turkish armada, which was a matter of growing concern in India.[3] The captain was a friend of mine, who led me to believe, by promising to look out for my interests on the voyage, that I would soon be rich, which was all that I cared about at the time. Taken in by his promises and letting my imagination run away with me, I embarked with this friend of mine on a foist called the *Silveira,* without ever stopping to consider that most get-rich schemes end up costing dearly, or that I was risking my life by venturing out to sea at the wrong time of year, or that we might run into the things that actually happened to us later—because of my sins and those of my companions.

After their departure from the fortress of Diu, the two foists were navigating in consort—under a hard gale, at the end of winter, in a heavy downpour, against the monsoon[4]—when they sighted the islands of Kuria-Muria[5] and Abd al-Kuri,[6] where we came close to total disaster and nearly lost our lives. We turned about, proceeding on a southwesterly course, and with God's help, we anchored off the tip of the island of Socotra,[7] a league below the site where the first viceroy of India, Dom Francisco de Almeida, built a fortress on his outward voyage from Portugal in the year 1507.[8] We took on water and traded for provisions with the natives, who are descendants of the early Christians converted in ancient times by the apostle Saint Thomas[9] in that part of India and along the coast of Coromandel.[10]

We departed from this island, setting a course for the mouth of the straits,[11] and in nine days under a fair wind we reached the latitude of Massawa[12] where, shortly before sunset, we sighted a sailing ship. We gave chase and made such good time that we caught up with her before the end of the first watch.[13] And when we tried to engage the captain in a friendly conversation, for the purpose of finding out what we wanted to know about the armada of the Grand Turk[14]—whether or not it had already left Suez, or what news there was of it—the answer we got from the company on board the *nao* was far from what we expected; for without a word in reply they surprised us by firing a dozen cannonballs at us—five of which came from falcons[15] and stone throwers,[16] and seven from culverins[17]—to say nothing of the many arquebuses they also fired, treating us as if we were child's play for them. And every now and then they let out wild jeers and catcalls, waving their banners and turbans contemptuously, while from the top of the poop deck they were jabbing the air with naked swords as though challenging us to approach.

At first, all their bluster and bravado caught us off guard, but after a hurried conference between the two captains and the men, it was decided by majority voice not to let the enemy get away with it, but to try as hard as we could to wear them down with our artillery until daylight, when it would be easier and less risky for us to grapple them. And that is exactly what we did, chasing them for the rest of the night until, as God willed, just before dawn, they gave up, after sixty-four of the eighty men on board lay dead. As for those still alive, practically all of them jumped overboard, no doubt preferring a watery grave to a fiery death from the powder pans[18] we tossed at them. Thus, out of the original company of eighty, only five survived, and they were badly wounded. One of them was the captain of the *nao*, who confessed under torture that he was coming from Jidda,[19] his native town, and that the armada of the Grand Turk had already departed from Suez and was on its way to take Aden[20] and build a fortress there before launching its attack on India, in compliance with the orders the pasha of Cairo[21] had received from the Grand Turk in Constantinople, who had appointed him admiral of the fleet.

And we also got a lot of other important information out of him that was extremely useful for our purposes; and among other things, he confessed that he was a Christian renegade, a Mallorcan national, born in Cerdagne,[22] the son of a merchant named Paulo Andrés, and that he had converted to Islam only four years earlier, for love of a Greek Moslem girl whom he married. Then both captains asked him if he wanted to return to the faith and become a Christian again, to which he replied in so harsh and senseless a manner, one would have thought he had been born and raised in that cursed religion. When they heard this poor soul carrying on like a madman and blindly resisting any attempt on their part to make him see the holy Catholic truth—when by his own admission he had been a Christian just a short time before—both captains lost their tempers, and in a fit of holy zeal for the honor of God, they had him bound hand and foot with a huge stone at the neck and thrown alive into the sea, where the devil carried him off to join in the torments of Mohammed, in whom he believed so fervently. And the *nao*, along with the rest of them, was sent to the bottom since the cargo consisted mainly of bales of dyed cloth of a tint similar to our pastel,[23] which were of no use to us at the time, with the exception of some bolts of camel's-hair cloth that the soldiers saved to make clothes for themselves.

4
The Land of Prester John

From here we departed for Arkeeko,[1] in the land of Prester John,[2] to deliver a letter that Antonio da Silveira had written to his factor, a man by the name of Henrique Barbosa, who had been sent there three years before by Governor Nuno da Cunha.

This Barbosa and forty of his men had escaped from the uprising at Shihr,[3] where they captured Dom Manuel de Menezes,[4] along with 160 Portuguese, and made off with 400,000 *cruzados* and six Portuguese *naos*. These were the same *naos* that were used later as military supply ships by the viceroy of Cairo, Suleiman Pasha,[5] when he laid siege to the fortress of Diu in the year 1538, for he had received the ships and sixty of the Portuguese captives as a gift from the king of Shihr, who presented the rest of them to his Mohammed,[6] but I believe all this information can be found in much greater detail in the chronicles dealing with the Nuno da Cunha administration of India.

When we arrived at *Gotor,* about a league below the port of Massawa, we were greeted by the natives and a Portuguese soldier we found there by the name of Vasco Martins de Seixas, originally from the village of Óbidos,[7] who had been posted there by Henrique Barbosa with instructions to wait for any Portuguese ship entering the harbor, and at the time we arrived, he had already been waiting there for a month with a letter from Henrique Barbosa that he delivered to our captains. The letter contained information about the Turks as well as an urgent request from Barbosa to send a party of our men into the interior to confer with him on a matter of vital importance to God and king, since he himself was unable to leave the fortress of *Gileytor,*[8] where he and his forty Portuguese soldiers were guarding the princess of Tigremahom,[9] mother of Prester John.[10] The two captains called a meeting, and everyone present agreed that a party of four should be sent, in the company of Vasco Martins, to deliver Antonio da Silveira's letter to him, and that is precisely what was done.

Early the following day, the four of us—for I was one of them—accompanied by six Abyssinians, set out on the journey, traveling overland on some pretty good mules that the *tiquaxy,* the local military commander, provided for us, in compliance with a written order that Vasco Martins had brought with him from the princess, the prester's mother. That night we slept at a monastery in a compound of stately, elegant buildings called *Satilgão;* and early the next morning we continued on our way, following the banks of a river for five more leagues until we came to a town by the name of *Bitonto.*[11] There we stopped for the night at a fine monastery called Saint Michael's, where we were welcomed in quite a festive manner by the prior and all the priests who lived there. While we were there we received a visit from a son of the *barnagais,*[12] governor of this empire of Ethiopia. He was seventeen years old, a fine-looking lad, who was accompanied by thirty bodyguards mounted on mules, though he himself rode a horse saddled in Portuguese style, with purple velvet trappings fringed in gold, that Governor Nuno da Cunha had sent him from India two years before with a man named Lopo Chanoca,[13] who was later captured in Cairo. The young prince sent a Jewish merchant from Azebibe[14] to ransom him, but by the time he got there, Lopo Chanoca was dead, and they say the prince was deeply grieved. And Vasco Martins told us that he had arranged for him to have, right there in that very same monastery of Saint Michael, the most impressive funeral services he had ever seen, attended by some four thousand priests and an even greater number of novices they call *santileus*. Nor did the prince neglect the widow and three small daughters that were left behind in Goa in dire poverty, for he sent them a charitable gift of three hundred gold *oqueas*,[15] which are worth about twelve *cruzados* in our money.

The following day we departed from this monastery on some excellent horses provided by the prince, who also sent four of his own men to look after us, and they certainly did a splendid job, taking care of our every need for the rest of the way. We spent that night in some large buildings they call *betenigus*,[16] meaning "the king's houses," which were surrounded for more than three leagues by dense forests of very tall cedar and cypress, and groves of coconut and date palms, like the ones that grow in India.

We continued on our way, keeping to our regular schedule of five leagues per day, traveling across very large, beautiful fields of grain, until we arrived at a mountain range called *Vangaleu,* that was populated by Jews,[17] white people, of good physique, but very poor, as far as we could tell. And from there, in two and a half days, we reached a good-sized town called *Fumbau,* two leagues from the fortress of *Gileytor,* where we found Henrique Barbosa and the forty Portuguese soldiers, who were overjoyed to see us, though they broke down and cried. For even though, as they assured us, they were well treated in Ethiopia and were living there like absolute lords of the land, they were terribly homesick and very unhappy about being exiled in a foreign country so far from home. But since it was quite late at night when we got there, Henrique Barbosa did not think it was the proper time to inform the princess of our arrival.

The following morning, which fell on a Sunday, October 4,[18] we accompanied him and the forty Portuguese to the princess's apartments, and when she heard we were there, she immediately had us ushered into the chapel where she was preparing to hear mass. We kneeled down before her and kissed the fan she was holding, and went through some other ceremonies in keeping with the court etiquette that the Portuguese there had taught us.

"Ah, true Christians," she greeted us joyfully, "I am so happy to have you here before me, now, always, and every hour of the day, for the eyes in my head delight in gazing upon you as much as the flowers in the garden desire to drink of the evening dew. Welcome! Welcome! And may your visit to my house prove to be as auspicious an occasion as was that of Queen Helena's[19] to the holy land of Jerusalem!"

And after commanding us to be seated on some floor mats about four or five paces from her, with her face wreathed in smiles, she began to ply us with questions, which they said she was quite fond of doing, in order to elicit some new or interesting items of information she might not have heard before. For example, she asked about the pope, what was his name, how many kings were there in Christendom, if any of us had ever been to the Holy land, why the Christian princes did not make a greater effort to destroy the Grand Turk, how great would we say was the power of the Portuguese king in India, how many fortresses did he have there, where were they located, and so on; and as far as we could tell, she was perfectly satisfied with all our answers. And when this was over, she dismissed us and we returned to our quarters.

Nine days later we went to take our leave of her, and as we kissed her hand, she said, "It truly grieves me to see you depart so soon, but since it cannot be helped, I wish you Godspeed; and may your return voyage to India be favored with such good fortune that your people will welcome you upon your arrival as the ancient Solomon welcomed our queen of Sheba into his great, admirable house!"[20]

At her command, all four of us received twenty gold *oqueas,* which is the equivalent of 240 *cruzados* in our money; and she also arranged for a *naique*[21] and twenty Abyssinians to guard us against thieves and to provide us with food and horses back to the port of Arkeeko, where our foists were waiting. And Vasco Martins de Seixas was entrusted with an expensive gold service as a present[22] for the governor of India, which was lost on the way, as we shall soon see.

5
Captive in Mocha

Back in the port of Arkeeko, where we rejoined our companions, we waited nine more days until they finished careening the foists and loading all the necessary provisions, and we departed on a Wednesday, the sixth of November, in the year 1537,[1] taking with us Vasco Martins de Seixas, who was to deliver the gift and a letter from the mother of Prester John to the governor; and we also took along an Abyssinian bishop[2] who was planning to come to Portugal, and from here to Santiago de Galicia,[3] Rome, then Venice, and from there to Jerusalem.

We weighed anchor an hour before dawn and went gliding along the coast with a following wind until close to vespers, and when we had gone about as far as the tip of *Gocão,*[4] just this side of the Isle of the Reef,[5] we sighted three sails riding at anchor. Believing them to be *gelvas*[6] or *terradas*[7] from the opposite coast,[8] we headed towards them under sail and oars, for by then the wind was beginning to fail. Nevertheless, by dint of hard pulling, in barely two hours we got close enough to them to be able to distinguish their oarbanks; but that was close enough to convince us that they were Turkish galliots, and we turned back towards the coast as fast as we could, trying desperately to escape from the danger we had blundered into.

Knowing full well, or perhaps suspecting, what we were up to, the Turks let out a yell, and in less time than it takes to recite the Credo, they were under way, tacking in our wake with their colorful checkered sails full of wind and their silk flags flying. And since they were favored by a wider breeze athwart, they rapidly gained ground to windward and were soon bearing down on us with hardly any effort; and as they came within cannon-shot range, they fired all their guns at us, killing nine men instantly and wounding twenty-six others; and with our foists disabled by then, for most of the rigging was thrown into the sea, the Turks lay so close aboard that from their poop deck they were cutting us up with their lances.

At this point only forty-two of our men were still able to fight, and since they knew all too well that their only chance for salvation lay in hand-to-hand combat, they attacked the flagship, which was carrying the admiral, Suleiman Dragut, bravely throwing themselves on board with such a sudden rush that they mopped it up from stem to stern, killing twenty-seven Janissaries.[9] But the other two ships in the squadron that had been lagging a short distance behind now moved in, and forty Turks bounded aboard. These reinforcements proved to be the undoing of our men, who were so badly mauled that, out of the original number of fifty-four, only eleven survived, and two of them died the following day. Their bodies were drawn and quartered by the Turks, who hung them from the top of the spars as a battle trophy, and they were taken that way to the city of Mocha,[10] which was under military command of the father-in-law of our captor, Suleiman Dragut.

As we were entering the port, he was already there on the beach waiting with all the townspeople to welcome his son-in-law and congratulate him on his victory. Also with him was a *qasis*[11] of theirs, a *moulana*,[12] whom they regarded as a holy man because he had recently returned from a pilgrimage to Mecca. Sitting in a carriage, protected from the sun's glare by a silk awning, he was bestowing blessings and salaams on all sides and urging the crowd to give thanks to Mohammed for having granted the victory to the Turk.

The nine survivors were led ashore in chains, including the Abyssinian bishop, who was so badly wounded that he died the following day, like a model Christian, setting an inspiring example, which proved to be a great consolation to us in our misery. The crowd that had seen us arrive in chains knew that we were Christian captives, and they set upon us with such fury that I swear I never thought we would escape from their clutches, for they were incited by the *qasis*, who made them believe that they would earn plenary indulgence if they abused us and cursed us.

And in this manner we were herded triumphantly through the whole city, to the accompaniment of mingled shouts and sounds of music, and even the purdah women from the seclusion of their balconies, and children of all ages, poured the contents of their bedpans over us as a measure of their hatred and disdain for the Christian name. It was close to sundown when they finally threw us into an underground dungeon, where we remained for seventeen days, suffering under the worst imaginable conditions, with no more than a pinch of barley meal for our daily ration in all that time, though on some days they gave us the raw grain moistened in water, and not a single scrap of anything else to go with it.

6
On the Slave Block

Considering the condition we poor wretches were in, what with most of us critically wounded, and then subjected to such inhuman treatment in that miserable prison, it was no wonder that two of the nine men were found dead the following morning. One was called Nuno Delgado and the other André Borges, both wellborn, courageous men, but it was because they had received deep head gashes in the fighting and gone without benefit of medical care, or any other kind of attention for that matter, that they succumbed so fast.

When the *mocadão*,[1] or caretaker of that prison, discovered the bodies, he immediately ran to inform the *guazil*,[2] an official whose function is similar to that of our local magistrates. He came in person, ceremoniously accompanied by a lot of ominous-looking police guards, and issued orders to have the dead men's handcuffs and shackles removed; then, by means of ropes tied to their feet, he had them dragged out and taken that way through the entire city, where they were followed by a mob of howling youngsters who kept on pelting them with stones until their bodies were tossed into the sea.

The next afternoon, the seven surviving captives were taken out to be sold at auction in a public square where the whole town had gathered. The first one the auctioneer laid hold of to open the proceedings was poor me; and just as he was calling for the opening bid, the *caciz moulana,* who was already out there with a group of about ten or twelve of his followers, also *cazizes* of that cursed sect, interrupted him by demanding that Heredim Sofo, military commander of the city, present us as a gift to the House of Mecca, where he was shortly planning to make a pilgrimage, in the name of the townspeople. He pointed out that it would be most unbecoming and dishonorable for a man in the commander's position to send a representative to pay his respects to the body of the Prophet *Noby*[3] with empty hands, for after all, without a suitable gift, the Rajah *Dato*[4] *Moulana,* headman of the city of Medina,[5] would not even deign to receive him, let alone grant the pardons he was seeking on behalf of the people of Mocha, who were so sorely in need of God's favor for their sins. To this the commander replied that he did not have the right to dispose of the captives so freely and suggested that he speak to his son-in-law, Suleiman Dragut, who he thought would be quite willing to grant his request.

The *caciz* retorted that matters pertaining to God, such as offerings in His name, were too sacred to be bandied about from one person to another as he had suggested, and that he saw no reason to discuss it any further with anyone else, since he alone was commander of the city and the people gathered there, and as such, it was incumbent on him alone to grant permission for something so righteous, so holy, and so gratifying to the Prophet *Noby Mafamede;* and what's more, he added, it was entirely due to the intercession of the Prophet that the victory over those captives had been won by his son-in-law, and not to the courage of the soldiers, as he seemed to think.

When he heard the remarks of the *caciz,* which cast aspersions on him and all the others responsible for our capture, one of the captains of the three galleys, a Janissary by the name of *Khoja*[6] Geinal, who was highly esteemed and respected among them, broke in.

"It would be far better for the salvation of your soul," he said, in a voice tinged with sadness, "if you distributed some of your excess income to these poor soldiers instead of constantly trying to rob them of what is rightfully theirs with your hypocritical speeches. And if, as you say, you can't go empty handed, then use the money your father left you for bribing the *cazizes* of Mecca in your own personal interest, instead of taking the captives we paid for so dearly with the many lives now buried at sea and with the blood spilled so profusely by the ones who are still alive. But then I don't see any bloodstains on your *cabaya*,[7] which is something no one can say about mine, or the ones that these poor soldiers are wearing."

The captain's protest, so freely voiced on behalf of the soldiers, was deeply resented by the *moulana caciz,* who replied in an extremely arrogant and irritating manner, which only succeeded in antagonizing Captain Geinal and the other Turkish and Moorish soldiers even more. As a result, a fight broke out between them and the townspeople, all of whom sided with the *moulana,* who knew full well that he could count on their support, which is why he spoke so brashly in the first place. The disorder lasted for the rest of the day, and even Heredim Sofo, as commander-in-chief of the city, was powerless to control it.

At any rate, to make a long story short, the rioting escalated into such a harsh, furious battle that, when it finally ended, more than six hundred lives were lost on both sides, and more than half the city was sacked. The *moulana*'s house was also looted, and his body drawn and quartered and thrown into the sea, along with his seven wives and nine children and all the other relatives the soldiers could lay their hands on, for they were determined not to spare a single member of his clan.

And in the meantime, there we were, as I was saying, all seven Portuguese left standing in the middle of the square waiting to be sold at auction; but when the fighting started, we decided, for our own protection, to beat a hasty retreat back to the dungeon, without benefit of police guards or any other kind of escort, and we were grateful to the *mocadão* when he shut the prison door behind us, for we thought he was doing us a tremendous favor.

This violent and dangerous uprising was finally quelled, thanks to the leadership of Suleiman Dragut, captain of the galleys, who decided to take matters into his own hands after Heredim Sofo, his father-in-law and commanding officer of the city, took to his bed with an arm wound he sustained in the course of the fighting.

And thirteen days later, when quiet had once more been restored to the city, they put us up for auction again, together with all the booty in ordnance and supplies they had taken from our two foists, on all of which they realized a sizable profit. As for poor me, perhaps the unluckiest of all, I had the misfortune to be purchased by a Greek renegade, whom I shall curse as long as I live. He used me so badly that during the three months I was his slave there were at least six or seven times when I nearly took my life with poison—but the good Lord mercifully stayed my hand each time—in order to make him lose the money he had spent on me, for as far as I was concerned, he was the most cruel and inhuman foe that anyone in the world ever had.

At the end of three months, thanks be to God, some of his neighbors warned him that he was running the risk of losing all the money he had invested in me, a possibility that frightened him into trading me for about twelve thousand *réis*'[8] worth of dates to a Jew by the name of Abraham Mussa, a native of the city of Tor,[9] located about two and a half leagues from Mount Sinai.[10] He took me as far as Hormuz in a merchant caravan traveling from Babylonia[11] to Qishm,[12] and he offered me to both Dom Fernando de Lima, who was then captain of the fortress of Hormuz, and Doctor Pero Fernandez,[13] the king's special magistrate for Indian affairs, who had been sent there just a few days before by Governor Nuno da Cunha on a mission for the crown. And with the funds they collected throughout the city, plus the money they both contributed personally, they were able to ransom me from the Jew for two hundred *pardaus*,[14] and with that he considered himself well paid.

7
The Siege of Diu

Sixteen days after I reached Hormuz and, by the mercy of God, free of the suffering I described, I shipped out on a *nao* belonging to a Jorge Fernandez Taborda that was bound for India with a cargo of horses. Proceeding on our course with a following wind, after seventeen days of an uneventful voyage, we came in sight of the fortress of Diu. Having decided to stop for news of what was going on there, we began our approach to land, and by nightfall we were able to distinguish a lot of fires all along the coast as well as the occasional burst of artillery. Not knowing what to make of it, we shortened sail and hove to for the rest of the night until daybreak, when we got a clear view of the fortress surrounded by an enormous number of lateen-rigged vessels.

Startled by the sight, which was most unusual, the men began arguing excitedly among themselves, offering all sorts of explanations for it, though most of them thought it was the governor recently arrived from Goa to make peace for the slaying of Sultan Bahadur, king of Cambay, whom he had killed not long before; and some were of the opinion, which they wagered heavily on, that it was the Infante Dom Luis,[1] brother of King John III, who had just arrived from Portugal, and that the large number of lateen sails we were looking at were the caravels of his outbound fleet, for it was widely believed at the time that he was in India. Others claimed that it was the *Patemarcá*,[2] with the hundred foists of the *samorim*,[3] king of Calicut; and still others said it was the Turks, and their reasons for saying so made good sense.

While we were arguing back and forth and becoming gradually more alarmed by the possibilities confronting us, five ships moved out from the middle of the fleet. They were huge galleys, with their fore-and-aft sails in a checkerboard pattern of green and purple, the deck awnings literally covered with flags, and long banners streaming so far down from the mastheads that the ends brushed the surface of the water. And as we watched, they pointed all five bows in our direction and came heading toward us, luffing and gaining ground to windward, which was enough to convince us that they were Turks.

The moment we realized who they were, we unfurled the mainsail, which had been hoisted in readiness, and quickly steered for the open sea in a frenzy of fear that, because of our sins, we would shortly be overtaken by a disaster very much like the one I described before. The enemy followed in our wake until almost nightfall when—God be praised—they suddenly turned shoreward and headed back in the direction they had come from.

Our *nao*, happily out of danger, arrived in Chaul two days later, where the skipper and the merchant passengers immediately went ashore to see Simão Guedez,[4] captain of the fortress, to tell him about what had happened on our voyage.

"There's no doubt," he replied, "that you all have good reason to give thanks to God for delivering you from such great danger."

Then he went on to explain that, twenty days earlier, Antonio da Silveira had been besieged by a huge Turkish armada commanded by Suleiman Pasha, viceroy of Cairo, and that the large number of sails we had seen were fifty-eight galleys of both the royal and bastard type,[5] each capable of firing five pieces of artillery over the bow—some of them quite heavy guns too, such as wall-breakers,[6] lions,[7] and spheres[8]—and eight huge *naos* carrying many Turkish reinforcements to replace their dead, as well as large stores of food and munitions said to include three hundred battering guns, twelve of them basilisks.

We were all thoroughly shaken by this news and offered up many prayers of thanks to the Lord for having delivered us from such grave danger.

8
Impressment at Sea

Early the next day we left Chaul bound for Goa, and when we had sailed about as far as the *Carapatão* River,[1] we met up with Fernão de Morais.[2] He was commanding a squadron of three foists bound for Dabul,[3] with orders from the viceroy Dom Garcia de Noronha,[4] who had just arrived from Portugal, to try to capture or destroy a Turkish *nao* anchored in the harbor of Dabul, where it had been sent by the pasha to load provisions. After hailing our *nao*, this Fernão de Morais spoke to our captain and demanded that he transfer fifteen of our twenty soldiers to his fleet because he was short of men, due to the urgency with which the viceroy had ordered him to depart, in the name of service to God and king. Following a heated argument between them, which I shall pass over for the sake of brevity, they finally agreed that the captain of our *nao* should hand over twelve men instead of the fifteen originally demanded by Fernão de Morais, and that satisfied him. I was also one of them, since I was always the first to be cast aside, and they both parted on friendly terms.

The *nao* continued on its way to Goa, and Fernão de Morais proceeded to the port of Dabul with his three foists, arriving at nine o'clock on the following day. And there he seized a Malabari *paguel*,[5] laden with cotton and pepper, that was riding at anchor in the middle of the bay. He immediately applied the torture to her skipper and pilot, who confessed that, a few days before, one of the pasha's *naos* had entered the harbor to pick up some provisions and that there was an ambassador on board who had come to deliver a gift of an elaborate *cabaya* to the *Adil-Khan*,[6] which he refused, knowing full well that its acceptance would make him a vassal of the Grand Turk, for among the Moors it was the custom for a lord to present these *cabayas* only to a vassal; and that, as a result of this disagreement, the *nao* departed without taking on provisions or anything else; and that the *Adil-Khan* had replied to the proposals made by the pasha in the name of the Grand Turk that he preferred the friendship of the king of Portugal, who had taken Goa away from him, to the friendship of the Grand Turk, who had promised to restore it to him; and that the *nao* had departed only two days before; and that her captain, a man by the name of Sidi Ali, had publicly declared war on the *Adil-Khan,* vowing that as soon as they captured the fortress of Diu—which would take no more than a week, considering the state it was in now—the *Adil-Khan* would lose his kingdom and his life and then he would find out how little the Portuguese could avail him.

Since there was nothing more for him to do there, Fernão de Morais headed back to Goa to report to the viceroy, arriving there two days later. And there we found Gonzalo Vaz Coutinho[7] anchored in the harbor, readying a fleet of five foists for an expedition to Honowar,[8] the purpose of which was to ask the reigning queen to hand over a galley that had sought shelter there after becoming separated in bad weather from the rest of Suleiman's fleet.

One of the five captains in this fleet was a very good friend of mine who felt sorry for me when he saw how shabby I looked. Since he wanted to help me in some way, he suggested that I enlist with him, and he would see to it that I was immediately paid five *cruzados*. I accepted gladly, for I thought that, with God's help, I would now have the means to buy myself a better suit of clothes than the one I was wearing at the time, for all I had to my name was what I hoped to acquire with my own two hands. And then the soldiers on the foist came to my aid with a few essential items I was badly in need of, so that before I knew it, I was outfitted from head to toe in patches like the rest of my companions in the fleet who were no better off than I was.

The following morning, which was a Saturday, we sailed from the bar harbor of Bardez,[9] and on Monday we anchored in the port of Honowar with a thunder of artillery and with the spars lashed together in the form of a sword, as a sign of war, playing the fife and drum as loud as we could for the benefit of the local people, trying to make it appear with this outward show of bravery that we were not afraid of the Turks.

9
The Queen of Honowar

After the fleet was anchored and the salvos fired in port, as I said, Captain Gonzalo Vaz Coutinho immediately sent the queen a letter he was carrying for her from the viceroy. It was delivered by a Bento Castanho, a discreet, well-bred man, who was instructed to tell her why he had come there, and to ask her, since Her Highness was a friend of the king of Portugal, to whom she had long been bound by peace and friendship treaties, why she was sheltering the Turks in her port when they were our worst enemies.

To which she replied that his lordship and his entire company were most welcome there, and that what he had said about her long-standing friendship with the king of Portugal and his governors was quite true and would continue to hold true as long as she lived; but as for his complaint about the Turks, as God was her witness, they had come there against her will; and since his lordship had brought with him enough troops to expel them, by all means, let him do so, and she would favor him in that respect as much as possible, but more than that she could not do, for as his lord-ship well knew, she was not powerful enough, nor did she dare, to engage such a superior force; and she swore by the golden sandals of her idol, that if God should grant him the victory over them, it would make her as happy as being invited to dine with the king of Narsinga,[1] whose slave she was, and seated at table with his wife.

Gonzalo Vaz Coutinho was disappointed when he heard the queen's message, polite as it was, but he thought it best to disguise his true feelings, and he quietly went about gathering information from the local people, trying to find out what sort of opposition he could expect from the Turks, where they were hiding, and what they were up to. After the matter had been discussed in council and carefully weighed, it was finally decided by all who took part in the deliberations that for the honor of the flag of the king, our lord, the Turkish galley should be attacked and captured, if pos-sible; if not, then we would do our utmost to try and destroy it by fire, for there was no doubt that the Lord our God, in whose name we were fighting, would come to our aid against these enemies of his holy faith. This was agreed and sworn to by all, and a document was drawn up to that effect which everyone signed. Once this business was disposed of, the admiral proceeded further up the river for a distance of twice the range of a falcon shot.

But before he could drop anchor, a native *almadia*[2] came rowing up to his foist with a Brahman on board who spoke Portuguese quite well. He gave the admiral a message from the queen to the effect that she strongly urged him, for the sake of the lord viceroy, not to launch an attack against the Turk under any circumstances, for she had learned through her spies whom she had sent out for that purpose, that they were extremely well entrenched in a stockade they had built near the ditch to which they had moved their galley and that, in her opinion, he would need a much larger force for such an undertaking than the one he had and that God alone knew the deep pain and anguish she was suffering for fear that he would meet with some disaster.

To this the admiral replied, measuring his words carefully and courteously, that he kissed the hands of Her Highness for favoring him with her sound advice, but that under no circumstances would he desist from attacking the Turks because it was not the custom of the Portuguese to run from a fight for fear of being outnumbered by the enemy; and that the more there were, the better, for then their losses would be higher.

And with this reply the Brahman was dismissed, quite contented with the gifts he received from the admiral, of a bolt of green camel's-hair cloth and a hat with a red satin lining.

10
Defeat at Honowar

After he had dismissed the Brahman, Admiral Gonzalo Vaz Coutinho was more determined than ever to press his attack against the Turks, but first he ob-tained reports from his spies about the strategy the Turks were planning to use against us, and about how that night, with the approval of the queen, as it was rumored, they had moved their galley into a drainage ditch and built a stockade nearby with very high parapets on which they had installed twenty-six pieces of artillery.

Nevertheless, the admiral headed straight for the enemy position, and when he came within a culverin-shot's distance, he disembarked with eighty soldiers, leaving a hundred of the men he had brought with him from Goa to guard the foists in the river; and after lining his men up in proper military formation, he began to march towards the enemy.

When the foe saw our troops advancing resolutely upon them, they decided on their stand with equally brave determination and came forward to meet our men about twenty-five or thirty paces outside their stockade, engaging them in a swift and violent assault that left forty-five men lying dead in the field in less time than it takes to recite two Credos, though only eight of the dead were ours and the rest theirs. The admiral closed in on them again, and as God willed, they suddenly turned and fled, retreating in a disorderly fashion, to all appearances, like men who had been completely routed. Seeing them run, our men followed them into the stockade, where they turned about and faced us once more. At this point, the confusion and the press of bodies was so great that some of the men received blows in the face from the pommels of their own swords.

In the meantime, our foists came rowing in along the beach, and with a rallying battle cry they fired all the artillery into the enemy ranks, cutting down ten or twelve of the Janissaries wearing those green velvet caps that are a sign of the Turkish nobility. Disheartened by these casualties, the enemy fled the field. At this point our admiral decided to set fire to the galley, and he tossed five firepots into her. When the flames started licking away at the deck awnings, the enemy rushed in fearlessly and extinguished the fire in no time at all; nevertheless, our men still persisted stubbornly in trying to enter the ditch, but the enemy countered by firing a heavy artillery piece that, judging from the size of the cannonball, must have been a camel[1] of very large caliber. It sprayed us with stone shot and killed six of our men outright, one of whom was Diogo Vaz Coutinho, the admiral's son, wounded fifteen or sixteen others, and left us totally defeated.

Aware of the damage they had inflicted on us, the enemy began to shout victory, calling aloud to Mohammed, a name that had an immediate effect on the admiral.

"Christian soldiers!" he cried, rallying his men. "If these dogs can call on the devil to help them, then let us call on the Lord Jesus Christ to help us!"

At the sound of this rallying battle cry our men made another dash for the stockade, but the crafty enemy turned and fled to the galley, preparing to take up a stronger position there; nevertheless, those of our men who had entered with them in the first rush managed to gain the better part of the stockade. It was then that they touched off a mine near the entrance, killing outright six Portuguese and eight of their slaves—to say nothing of others who were badly burned—and enveloped us all in such a huge cloud of smoke that we couldn't even see each other.

For fear of additional losses as severe as the ones we had just suffered, the admiral withdrew to the beach, closing ranks in good order, with the dead and wounded being carried in the arms of others who were placed in the middle. And when he reached the waiting foists, he climbed aboard and rowed back to the inlet he had set out from, and there, with deep sorrow and tears, he buried the dead and attended to the large number of men who had been wounded or burned.

II
The Queen's Treachery

That same day, which was indeed a tragic one for us, muster was taken in order to determine what the attack on the galley had cost us, and it showed that fifteen out of the eighty soldiers were dead and fifty-four wounded—nine of whom turned out to be permanently disabled—and the remainder of that day and the night that followed went by with great hardship and heightened vigilance on our part.

Early in the morning a messenger arrived from the queen with a huge *sauguate*[1] consisting of a generous supply of fresh poultry and eggs, which the admiral refused to accept; but instead, letting his anger get the better of him, he lashed out against her and said a few things that were perhaps unduly harsh; and he added that the lord viceroy would soon find out how faithfully she served the king of Portugal and how beholden he was to her, so that in due time he could repay her for what she had done. And as a pledge of his word, to prove that he meant what he said, he was leaving the body of his son behind along with the others for whose death she was to blame by her treachery in aiding and abetting the Turks, and only then would he thank her for the gift she was sending him in order to cover up what she had done.

The messenger was dismissed with this reply, half frightened out of his wits by the oaths and threats with which the admiral had punctuated his words now and then, so that when he delivered his message to the queen he made her believe that without any doubt, because of the galley, she would soon lose her kingdom; and that the extreme urgency of the situation called for her to do everything in her power to effect a reconciliation with the admiral. And after consulting with her advisers, she sent another message to the admiral, this time with a very close relative of hers, an elderly, dignified Brahman, who carried himself with an air of authority. The admiral received him courteously, and after they had dispensed with the formalities of mutual honor and respect, the Brahman spoke up.

"Sir," he began, "if you will give me leave to speak, I will impart to you the purpose of my mission on behalf of the queen, my mistress."

The admiral answered that all ambassadors were granted personal immunity and license to speak freely on any matter relating to their missions, and that he should proceed without being afraid of saying whatever he had a mind to. The Brahman thanked him and continued.

"It would be impossible for me to convey to you in so many words, Sir Admiral, the sadness and distress of the queen over the death of your son and the other Portuguese soldiers who lost their lives in yesterday's fighting, for I solemnly swear to you, by her life, and by this *linha*,[2] with which I was invested as a child, that when she heard of the disaster that befell you and its unfortunate outcome, she could not have been more aggrieved if she had been forced to eat cow's meat this very day in front of the main entrance of the temple where her father lies buried. That should give you some idea of how deeply she shares your grief. But since, much as she desires, the sad events of the past cannot be undone, she begs and implores you to renew the peace treaty that the former governors of India had granted her, since the viceroy has empowered you to do so; and she in turn gives you her word of honor that she will immediately have the galley burned and the Turks driven from her shores, which is the best she can do, for as you well know, she is not powerful enough to go beyond that. However, she requests that you grant her at least four days in which to do so."

The admiral, fully aware of the gravity of the situation, accepted her promise and renewed the peace treaty, which was sworn to then and there and confirmed by both parties in accordance with Hindu traditions.

And the queen tried in every way possible to keep her word, but the condition of the wounded men in the fleet was such that the admiral could not risk waiting the entire four-day period she had asked for, and he departed in the afternoon of that same day. However, at the suggestion of the queen, he left behind in his place a certain Jorge Nogueira, who was to report to the viceroy on the events that transpired.

12
Departure for Malacca

The following day Admiral Gonzalo Vaz Coutinho and his fleet arrived in Goa, where he was welcomed by the viceroy, whom he informed about everything that had happened to him on the voyage and about the agreement he had made with the queen of Honowar, not only to burn the galley, but to expel the Turks from her kingdom as well, and the viceroy was satisfied with that.

Twenty-three days after we arrived in Goa, when I had recovered fully from the two wounds I received during the fighting in the stockade, finding myself destitute, with no means of support, I took the advice of a priest who was a good friend of mine and went to offer my services to a respected nobleman by the name of Pero de Faria.[1] He had just been appointed captain of Malacca, and at that time he was providing free board to any and all comers willing to take advantage of it. He accepted me into his service and promised to look after my personal interests insofar as possible during his forthcoming term of office, since I was willing to accompany him on his expedition with the viceroy Dom Garcia de Noronha, who was preparing to go to the aid of the fortress of Diu in response to their appeal for help, for they could no longer hold out against the besieging Turks.

For that purpose he had gathered a huge, beautiful armada of 225 sails that was said to be carrying a total expeditionary force of ten thousand elite troops, along with thirty thousand deckhands, able-bodied seamen, and Christian slaves, though only eighty-three of the ships, counting the *naos,* galleons, and caravels, were multiple-decked vessels, and the rest, galleys, brigantines, and foists.

The pasha was being kept informed of the progress of this powerful armada by daily messages he received from the *Adil-Khan,* the *samuri,* king of Calicut, the *nizam-ul-mulk,*[2] the *Asad-Khan,*[3] and many other native rulers, both Hindu and Mohammedan, all of whom had their own spies operating secretly in Goa. And when it was time to depart and the armada was ready and fully equipped with everything necessary, the viceroy embarked on a Saturday, November 14, in the year 1538.[4] Five days later, while he was still on board and waiting for the rest of the people—and they were many—to finish boarding, a cutter arrived from Diu with letters from Antonio da Silveira, the captain of the fortress, informing him that the Turks had withdrawn and that the siege had been lifted. The news spread deep gloom among the soldiers in the fleet, for they had all been so eager to meet up with these enemies of our holy faith.[5]

The viceroy delayed here for another five days to attend to some official business for the State of India, and from where he was anchored, he dispatched two *naos* to Portugal under the respective commands of Martim Afonso de Sousa[6] and Vicente Pegado.[7] And he sent with them the comptroller-general, Doctor Fernão Rodriguez de Castelbranco,[8] to oversee the loading of the pepper cargo in Cochin and to make arrangements for the homeward voyage of the outgoing governor of India, Nuno da Cunha, who had been waiting there for days on board the *nao Santa Cruz,* in poor health and none too happy about the lack of respect that had been shown him, which he felt was undeserved in view of the services he had rendered the state.[9]

Once these matters had been taken care of, the viceroy departed from the bar of Goa on a Thursday morning, the sixth of December.[10] On the fourth day of his voyage he dropped anchor in Chaul, where he stayed for three days, attending to some business with the *nizam-ul-mulk* that was of vital importance to the security and welfare of the fortress; and while he was there, he also finished outfitting several ships in the armada that were still short of a few things, especially deckhands and provisions.

From there he departed for Diu, and when he was halfway across the gulf, as far north as the peaks of Dahanu,[11] he was struck by a storm of such great violence that it scattered the fleet in all directions and sank some of the ships. One of the vessels lost was the galley *Bastarda,* commanded by the viceroy's son and admiral of the sea, Dom Alvaro de Noronha,[12] which was wrecked on the bar of Dabul. Another was the galley *Espinheiro,* which went down in the gulf. Her captain was João de Sousa, who went by the nickname "Rates,"[13] because he was the son of the prior of a village by that name. However, most of the men on the galley were rescued by Dom Cristóvão da Gama, son of the count admiral, who happened to be nearby when she sank—the same Cristóvão da Gama who was later slain by the Turks in the land of Prester John.[14] Seven other ships also went down, but I don't remember their names. At any rate, more than a month went by before the viceroy was able to recover from these losses and gather together what the storm had tossed in different directions.

When he finally reached Diu on the sixteenth of January, in the year 1539, he immediately set about rebuilding the fortress, since most of it had been leveled by the Turks, and the fact that it had been able to hold out seemed more like the working of a miracle than anything wrought by man. Dividing the reconstruction work among the various captains in the fleet, he assigned Pero de Faria—since he had a large number of men in his company—to the job of repairing the bastion facing the sea, with the armor plate on the land side; and within twenty-six days, working with only three hundred soldiers, he restored it to better condition than it had been in before.

And by that time, since March fourteenth was upon us and the monsoon for Malacca had already begun, Pero de Faria departed for Goa, where, in keeping with the viceroy's orders, he finished outfitting the ships with enough and to spare of all the necessities; and on April thirteenth, he sailed from Goa with a total complement of six hundred men in a fleet of eight *naos,* four foists, and one galley; and with a favorable monsoon, he arrived in Malacca on June fifth, in the same year of 1539.

13
The Battak Envoy

At the time that Pero de Faria arrived in Malacca, Dom Estêvão da Gama[1] was still serving as captain of the fortress, in which capacity he continued for a few more days until his term of office expired.[2] Nevertheless, since Pero de Faria was the newly appointed captain who would presently assume command, shortly after he arrived at the fortress, the neighboring kingdoms began to send their ambassadors to call on him and congratulate him on his appointment, with offers to renew the peace and friendship treaties they had maintained with the king of Portugal. Among those who came was an envoy from the king of the Battak,[3] who resides on the ocean side of the island of Sumatra in the presumed vicinity of the Isle of Gold, the exact location of which King John III, acting on information received from some of his captains in this area, had made several attempts to discover.[4]

This ambassador, whose name was *Aquareng Dabolay* and who was a brother-in-law of the king of the Battak, brought Pero de Faria a valuable gift of eaglewood,[5] calambac,[6] and five quintals[7] of aromatic benzoin crystals,[8] as well as a letter, inscribed on palm leaf,[9] which read as follows:

"I, *Angeesiry Timorraja*,[10] king of the Battak, desirous above all others to be of service to the Crowned Lion, whose throne of awesome splendor spans the ocean waves, over which he reigns with incredible power wherever the four winds blow, that magnificent prince of great Portugal, thy lord and mine, to whom once again I pay homage by rendering obedience to thee, Pero de Faria, thou tower of strength, in a spirit of true and sacred friendship; and from this day forward, I promise to be a faithful subject to him, with all the purity of love and devotion befitting a loyal vassal.

"Being most eager to renew our friendship pact, I propose to enrich thy subjects with all the products of my soil, by entering into a new trade agreement with thee that will fill the storehouses of thy sovereign and mine, with gold, pepper, camphor, eaglewood, and benzoin, on condition that I be given a safe-conduct pass,[11] written in thy hand and guaranteed by the force of thy word, permitting my *lancharas*[12] and *jurupangos*[13] to navigate in freedom and safety wherever the four winds blow. And to seal this new friendship treaty, I also ask the favor of thy assistance in the form of some military supplies that may be lying in some forgotten corner of thy arsenal, for I find that at the moment I am sorely in need of cannonballs and gunpowder; and with the aid of this *sauguate* as the first sign of thy friendship, I shall be able to punish the perfidious Achinese,[14] who have long been bitter foes of thy ancient Malacca. And I swear that as long as I live, I shall never keep either peace or friendship with them until after I have been avenged for the blood of my three sons, a vengeance called for by the tears that flow incessantly from the eyes of the noble mother who conceived them and nourished them at her breast; for they met their death in the village of *Jacur* and *Lingau,* at the hands of that cruel Achinese tyrant, concerning which *Aquareng Dabolay,* brother of the grieving mother who bore these three sons, will have more to say to thee, in my name, for it is he whom I am sending to renew the bonds of friendship and to discuss with thee my lord, whatever else he may deem necessary for the service of God and the welfare of thy people. Dated at *Panaju,* on the fifth *mamoco*[15] of the eighth moon."

This ambassador was given a fine reception by Pero de Faria, complete with all the honors and ceremonies performed in their fashion. And after delivering the letter—which was immediately translated from the Malay language into Portuguese—he explained to Pero de Faria, through an interpreter, the reason for the strained relations existing between the Achinese tyrant and the king of the Battak, which arose out of the following:

Not long before, this bitter enemy of theirs had proposed to the king of the Battak, who was a Hindu, that he convert to Islam, and that if he would put aside his wife of twenty-six years, who, like him, was also a Hindu, he would give him one of his sisters in marriage. When the Battak refused, the Achinese tyrant, at the instigation of his *caciz,* declared war on him. Mobilizing their armies, they threw them into the field in a battle that raged without pause for three hours until the Achinese, faced with mounting losses in his ranks, was forced to concede the military superiority of his foe and retreated to a mountain range called *Cagerrendão,* where the Battak kept him encircled for twenty-three days. But by then the Achinese, with his camp ravaged by disease, and his opponent, with his army running short of supplies too, agreed to terminate the hostilities and signed a peace treaty that called for the Achinese to make reparations of five *bahars*[16] of gold, or the equivalent of 200,000 *cruzados* in our money, which the Battak needed to pay his mercenaries; also, the Battak agreed to give his oldest son in marriage to the sister of the Achinese, over whom the dispute had arisen in the first place. Once the terms of the agreement had been carried out, the Battak returned to his country, dismantled his camp, and demobilized his army.

The blessings of this peace treaty lasted for only two and a half months, which was all the time the Achinese needed for the three hundred Turks he had been expecting to reach him. They arrived from the Straits of Mecca in the four *naos* he had originally sent there with a cargo of pepper, and on their return the holds were filled with many crates of muskets and other arms, including some heavy artillery made of bronze and cast iron. Spreading rumors to the effect that he was on his way to Pasay[17] to punish one of his own captains who had rebelled against him, the Achinese set out with these arms and reinforcements; but instead, he fell upon two Battak villages called *Jacur* and *Lingau.* Finding them off guard, lulled by the false security of the peace treaty only recently signed, he captured them without any difficulty, killing three sons of the Battak, along with seven hundred *ourobalões,*[18] who are their best soldiers and the noblest men in the kingdom.

Outraged by the enormity of this treachery, the Battak king swore by the head of the holiest idol in his Hindu faith, *Quiay Hocombinor,*[19] "god of justice," to abstain from eating fruit, or salt,[20] or anything else that tasted good to him, until he had avenged the death of his sons and regained the territory taken from him, or die in the attempt.

Fully determined on this course of action, the Battak king mobilized an army of fifteen thousand men, both native and foreign, which he assembled with the help of some friendly princes. And not content with this, he also wanted to avail himself of our good will. That is why he sent his ambassador with an offer to renew the friendship treaty discussed above, which Pero de Faria gladly accepted, knowing full well how important it was to the service of the king and the security of the fortress, and how much it would add to the revenues of the customs house—to say nothing of his own personal interests and those of the other Portuguese who were trading in those parts to the south.

14
Through the Jungles of Sumatra

After he had read the letter from the king of the Battak and grasped the full import of the ambassador's mission, Pero de Faria arranged for him to be given the most honorable accommodations that were available at the time. And within seventeen days of his arrival in Malacca, the entire matter was expedited to the satisfaction of the ambassador, who departed quite pleased with the results of his mission, because he was given a few extra items he had not asked for, such as a hundred powder pans, grapeshot, and firebombs. He was so happy with the treatment he received in the fortress that one day, bursting into tears of joy, he turned around, facing the main door of the church and raised his arms, as though speaking to God, and in front of all the people in the church plaza, he cried aloud for all to hear, "Almighty Lord, reigning in peace and deep joy amidst the rich spiritual treasure shaped by thy will, if thou shouldst see fit to grant us the victory over the Achinese tyrant and restore all that he took from us in the two villages of *Jacur* and *Lingau,* in a sneak attack of such outrageous perfidy and treachery, I promise thee, in the name of my king, that out of deep loyalty and gratitude we shall always acknowledge the holy truth of the Portuguese faith, wherein lies the good of all mankind; and we will build thee new and sweet-smelling temples in our country, where all living men may worship thee with upraised arms as they have always done and still do to this day in the land of mighty Portugal; and I further promise thee, and I swear to it with all the good faith of a loyal, devoted vassal, that my king shall never bow to any king other than the great Portuguese monarch who is now lord of Malacca."

Then he climbed aboard the same *lanchara* that had brought him to Malacca and departed, escorted by a fleet of ten or twelve *balões*[1] that accompanied him for a little more than half a league as far as the island of Upi,[2] where the *bendara*[3] of Malacca, who is the highest-ranking official among the Moors in power, honor, and the administration of justice, tendered him a lavish, Moorish-style banquet, by order of Pero de Faria. Entertainment was provided by a band that played on shawms, trumpets, and timbals, as well as a choir of fine voices singing Portuguese songs to the accompaniment of an orchestra of harps, flageolets, and rebecs. He was so thoroughly impressed by it all that he kept putting his finger in his mouth, in a gesture of amazement that is very characteristic of these people.[4]

Since Pero de Faria was most anxious to get his hands on the huge profits that some Moors told him were to be made on shipments of Indian goods to the Battak—

to say nothing of the even higher profits to be earned on the return cargo—twenty days after the departure of this ambassador, he outfitted a ship about the size of a small caravel that they call *jurupangos* in those parts, on which, at the time, he was only willing to risk ten thousand *cruzados,* and he entrusted the business end of the voyage to a local Moor who was to act as his agent. And he asked me if I would be willing to go along, while at the same time letting me know how happy it would make him if I were to pay a visit to the Battak king on his behalf, in the guise of an ambassador, and accompany him as a military observer to Achin, where he was then preparing to march with his army. He pointed out that there would be an opportunity for me to make a bit of profit on the side, and that I would be in a position to obtain an accurate description of the area from firsthand observation; and also, that there too I might hear some talk about the Isle of Gold, regarding which he was planning to send His Highness a full report.

I couldn't very well refuse to accept his proposal, though at first I had some qualms about making the voyage, not only because it meant traveling into unknown territory inhabited by treacherous people, but also because I only had a hundred *cruzados* of my own at the time, on which I couldn't expect to make much profit. At any rate, I finally embarked in the company of the Moor who was responsible for the merchandise.

After making the crossing from Malacca to the port of *Surotilau,*[5] off the coast of the kingdom of Aaru,[6] the pilot sailed along the island of Sumatra, in the inland sea, as far as a river called *Hicanduré.*[7] Proceeding on this course for five more days, he reached a beautiful bay called *Minhatoley,*[8] nine leagues from the kingdom of Pedir[9] at eleven degrees latitude. And from here he sailed around the tip of the island, which at this point is only twenty-three leagues wide, until we came in full view of the ocean on the opposite coast; and after navigating along it for four more days under fair winds, he entered a small river seven fathoms deep, which was called *Guateamgim.*[10] Sailing along this river for six or seven leagues, we could see between the thick jungle growth a large number of snakes and other creatures of such extraordinary sizes and shapes that one would very much fear to mention it, at any rate, to people who have not seen much of the world, for inasmuch as they have seen little, they are also apt to give little credence to what others have seen a great deal of.

All along the river, which was not very wide, there were a great many lizards,[11] though serpents would be a more appropriate name for them because some of them were as big as a good-sized *almadia,* with scales on their backs and mouths more than two spans wide; and from what the natives told us, they were extremely bold and quick to attack, and very often they would lunge at an *almadia* that had only three or four blacks on board, upsetting it with a swish of the tail and devouring the occupants one by one as they floundered in the water, without tearing them to pieces, just swallowing them whole.

We also saw here what was for us a very unusual and strange-looking animal that the natives call *caquessitão,*[12] about the size of a big duck, deep black in color, covered with scales, a row of spines running down the back for about the length of a quill pen, wings like a bat, the neck of a cobra, a horn on the head like a cockspur, and a very long, greenish-black tail, of the same color as the large lizards that abound here. These creatures, which fly as though leaping through the air, live by hunting monkeys and other animals from the treetops.

Also, we saw a great many hooded cobras[13] here that were as thick as a man's thigh and so venomous, the blacks said, that if the saliva dripping from its mouth touched any living creature, it would drop dead on the spot, and that there was no known cure or antidote for it. We saw some other cobras [14] that were neither hooded nor as poisonous as these, but much longer and thicker, with a head the size of a calf. These animals, we were told, also hunted their prey on the ground in the following manner. They slither up one of the trees that grow wild and abundantly all over the country, and wrap their tails around one of the upper branches with the head hanging down on the underbrush below, keeping an ear close to the jungle floor and listening for the sound of anything that stirs in the dead of night; and if an ox, or boar, or deer, or any other animal wanders by, they seize it by mouth as they swing from the bough; and any prey that comes within their grasp is swallowed alive, so that it is impossible for any living thing to escape.

We also saw a lot of brown apes [15] here, about the size of a huge mastiff, which the blacks fear more than any other beast in the jungle because they attack with such ferocity that no one can offer any resistance.

15
At the Court of the Battak

We proceeded up the river for about seven or eight leagues until we came to a small town called *Batorrendão* [1]—meaning "fried stone" in our language—located roughly about a quarter of a league from the city of *Panaju*, where the king of the Battak was busy with preparations for his war against the Achinese.

As soon as he heard that I was arriving with a gift and a letter from the captain of Malacca, he sent out a welcome party headed by the *shahbandar*, [2] the highest-ranking naval officer and the one who has the final say in all matters relating to the movement of ships. He came to meet me at the port where I was anchored, arriving with five *lancharas* and twelve *balões* that escorted me noisily with timbals and bells and crewmen shouting all the way up to *Campalator*, [3] as they call one of the city piers; and there the *bendara,* governor of the kingdom, was waiting for me with a large group of *ourobalões* and *amborrajas,* [4] who are the noblest members of the royal court. However, most of them, or nearly all, were an extremely seedy-looking lot, who were dressed quite shabbily, leaving me with the impression that this country was not as rich as they seemed to think in Malacca.

After reaching the king's palace compound, I passed through the outer court-yard, and there at the entrance to the inner patio stood an elderly woman, in the company of some other people who were much more distinguished looking and better dressed than the party escorting me. She motioned to me, inviting me to enter, and welcomed me in a solemn, dignified manner.

"Man from Malacca," she said to me, "your coming here into this land of the king, my lord, is as gratifying to him as the raindrops falling on our rice fields in a time of drought. Enter, and have no fear, since, by the grace of God, we are all people like you; and we trust in Him that it will always be so, forever and ever, until the end of time."

I passed into the interior of the building where the king was waiting and greeted him with due respect, touching my knee to the floor three times as I handed over the letter and the gift, with which he was obviously delighted, and he asked me what had brought me there.

I replied, in accordance with the instructions I had received, that I had been sent to serve His Highness on his forthcoming military campaign, and to see the city of Achin and its fortifications with my own eyes and take soundings of the river to determine if it was deep enough for our large *naos* and galleons to enter, because the captain of Malacca had decided to come to the aid of His Highness and hand the Achinese over to him as soon as more men arrived from India. And since this was so much in accord with what he desired, the poor king believed it was true. Rising from the *bailéu*,[5] a sort of platform he had been sitting on, he went to kneel down before some kind of shelf or mantelpiece on which was displayed the skull of a cow,[6] its horns all gilded and decorated with the branches of many fragrant trees; and raising his arms to it, he prayed out loud, choking back the tears.

"Oh thou boundless source of nourishment! Thou who givest freely of thy milk to all who desire it, with the instinct of a mother for her child, though nature constrains thee not, for unlike those of whom we are born, thou has not known the pangs and suffering of the flesh that bind them to us—I implore thee, from the depths of my heart and call upon thee there in the sunny meadows where thou dost dwell, reaping a harvest of contentment for the good thou hast done here on earth—to preserve for me the new friendship of this good captain, so that the words I have just heard may come true!"[7]

To this prayer his people all responded with a loud cry, raising their arms and repeating three times the words *Pachy parau tinacor!*—meaning, "Oh but to live to see it come true and gladly die!"

Then they lapsed into a silence tinged with sadness as the king turned back to me, wiping the tears that the intensity of the prayer had brought to his eyes, and resumed the conversation by asking me a few questions about India and Malacca that didn't take long. He terminated the audience graciously and promised to arrange for the profitable sale of the captain's merchandise which the Moor was handling, and it was that, more than anything else, that I was interested in at the time.

But since my arrival had coincided with the king's scheduled departure for Achin, he had no time for other matters, and nine days after I had reached the city of *Panaju,* capital of the Battak kingdom, he departed with his men for a town five leagues away called *Turbão,*[8] where most of his army was already waiting for him. He arrived within an hour of sunset without fanfare or any other sign of joy, because of their grief over the death of his three sons, which was quite obvious, for there was always an air of deep sadness about them.

16
Observing the Battak at War

Early the following day the king departed for Achin, which was located eighteen leagues from the town of *Turbão*, from where he started out with an army of fifteen thousand men, only eight thousand of whom were Battak nationals; the rest consisted of troops from Menangkabow,[1] Luzon,[2] Indragiri,[3] Jambi,[4] and Borneo that the princes of those nations had sent to his aid. He also had forty elephants and twelve wagons of light ordnance consisting mainly of falcons and culverins, but included among them were two camels and one half-sphere[5] of bronze stamped with the coat of arms of France that had been taken from a French *nao* that appeared there in the year 1526 when Lopo Vaz de Sampaio[6] was governing the State of India, though the captain and pilot of that *nao* was a Portuguese by the name of Rosado[7] who came from the town of Vila do Conde.

Advancing in regular marches of five leagues a day, the Battak king came to a river called *Quilém*, where he learned from some Achinese spies picked up in the area that the king was in *Tondacur*, two leagues outside the city, waiting and ready to meet him on the battlefield, and that he had many foreign troops with him, including some Turks, Gujeratis,[8] and Malabaris from the coast of India. After consulting with his captains, the Battak was advised to strike before the enemy had a chance to build up his strength. And having decided to do so, he set out immediately from the riverbank, quickening his pace a little, and shortly before ten o'clock at night, he reached the foot of a mountain, half a league from the site where the opposing army was encamped; and after resting there for a little over three hours, he resumed the march in very good order, with his troops divided into four battalions. As he was rounding a bend in the mountain, just before reaching the end he saw a broad stretch of rice fields where the enemy was waiting in tightly closed formation divided into two large battalions.

The moment they sighted each other they sounded the trumpets, drums, and bells, filling the air with incredibly wild screams and shouts as they threw themselves bravely into battle. After loosening a barrage of bombs and arrows and other fire projectiles in their arsenal they closed in on each other with a sudden rush, displaying such tremendous spirit and courage that the sight alone was enough to make me quake with fear. The battle continued at this furious pace for a little over an hour without any noticeable gain on either side; but when he saw that his men, suffering from fatigue and badly wounded, were beginning to lose ground, the Achinese started to withdraw in the direction of a knoll a little farther back to the south, about the distance of a sphere shot, with the intention of digging in at the top of a hill where there were some ditches that looked like they had been prepared for rice or vegetable crops. However, a brother of the king of Indragiri cut him off by placing two thousand men in his line of retreat, and the battle flared up all over again as furiously as before. Judging from the way they fought, wounding each other so unmercifully, no other nation can surpass them, for even before the Achinese could reach the line of trenches, he had lost more than fifteen hundred men, including the 160 Turks who had arrived a few days before from the Straits of Mecca, plus two hundred Malabari Moors and some Abyssinians, who comprised the elite of his army.

Since it was almost noon by then and the heat was intense, the Battak withdrew to the mountain, where he remained for the rest of the day until close to nightfall, when he had enough to occupy him tending to the wounded and burying the dead. Not daring to make the next move until he could see what the enemy was up to, he stayed there all night, keeping a careful lookout. At daybreak there was not a soul to be seen in the trenches the Achinese had retreated to the day before, from which the Battak concluded that the enemy had been completely routed. He decided to follow up on his victory, and from there, after discharging the wounded who were in no condition to fight, he took off in pursuit of the Achinese, marching right up to the city, which he reached at two hours before sundown.

Anxious to do something to show the enemy that he still had the upper hand, before making camp he set fire to two good-sized towns on the outskirts of the city as well as four *naos* and two galleons that were careened on shore, in which the Turks had arrived from the Straits of Mecca. And as the fire raged with tremendous force through these six ships, without the enemy so much as daring to venture forth from the city, the Battak king in person, convinced that fortune was on his side, tried to make the most of it by attacking a stockade that was sweeping the entrance of the river—which was called *Penacão*—with twelve pieces of heavy artillery. He went into the assault with about seventy or eighty ladders and managed to scale the walls with the loss of only thirty-seven of his men, penetrating the fort, where he put them all to the sword, unwilling to give quarter to anyone found inside, and there must have been as many as seven hundred people there. So that the first day he arrived he accomplished three very outstanding feats which lifted the morale of his men and inspired them to so much daring that they would have attacked the city itself that same night had he let them; but since it was a very dark night and the men were exhausted, he contented himself with what he had done thus far and offered up a fervent prayer of thanks to God.

17
The Battak Army in Retreat

The Battak king held this city under siege for twenty-three days, during which time the enemy made two sorties, though one of them is hardly worth mentioning since the death toll on both sides came to only ten or twelve. But just as a victory, or any successful engagement on the battlefield, tends to increase the daring and self-confidence of the victor, so too there are times when the weaker opponent reacts to a military setback by overcoming his fear completely and throwing himself boldly into the most difficult and arduous exploits, winning some and at times losing others. This was especially true from what I observed when I was with the Battak, for when they saw that the Achinese had kept on retreating, apparently in defeat, their courage and pride increased to the point where they thought they were invincible, and twice they were nearly wiped out because of this vain and blind opinion of themselves which led them to take foolish risks; for when the enemy sallied forth from the city the second time, the Battak attacked them courageously on two sides, but as soon as the fighting became a little heavy, the Achinese, feigning weakness, began to withdraw towards the stockade where a few days before the Battak king had captured the twelve pieces of artillery. Elated by what he thought was a sure victory, one of the Battak captains pursued them, his ranks in total disorder, and succeeded in driving them into the trenches. However, the enemies turned about to face him and defended themselves courageously. At this point in the fighting, with some men determined to enter and others determined to prevent them from entering, the Achinese touched off a huge mine, which exploded near the edge of a counterscarp made of dry masonry, sending the Battak captain and more than three hundred of his men flying through the air in pieces, in the midst of the most horrendous noise and smoke, in what seemed like a portrait of hell.

When this happened the enemy began cheering wildly and the Achinese king in person came dashing out of the city, throwing himself full force against the Battak with more than five thousand *amucks;*[1] and since the powder smoke was still so thick they could hardly see each other, what followed was a confused yet extremely cruel battle; and since I do not dare to describe in detail what actually happened at this point, I'll sum it up by saying that the fighting lasted for little more than a quarter of an hour and when it ended, over four thousand lay dead on both sides, though most of these casualties were sustained by the Battak king, who retreated soon afterwards with the rest of his army to a hill called *Minacaleu,* where he tended to the wounded, whose numbers, it was said, came to over two thousand, not counting the dead who were thrown into the river since they were unable to bury them.

Following this it was quiet on both sides for a period of four days when one morning, in the middle of the river, towards the *Penacão* side, there appeared a gaily bedecked armada of eighty-six sail, covered with silken banners and bunting, joyfully announcing its arrival with a lot of fanfare and merrymaking, all of which spread confusion in the ranks of the Battak, who were totally at a loss to explain it. However, that same night, their spies captured five fishermen who confessed under torture that this was the same armada that the Achinese king had sent two months before to Tenasserim[2] in his war with the *Sornau,*[3] king of Siam, in which five thousand Luzons and Borneans, all hand-picked men, were said to be returning, under the command of a Turk by the name of Hamed Khan, nephew of the pasha of Cairo.

In a meeting with his war council, which he had called to discuss the information obtained from the fishermen, the king was advised to withdraw and not to waste any time going about it, in view of the gravity of the situation which would not brook even an hour's delay, not only because the Achinese power was now much greater than his, but also because he was said to be expecting additional reinforcements of foreign mercenaries who were due to arrive from Pedir[4] and Pasay[5] in a fleet of ten *naos.* Bowing to their advice, the king departed that same night, extremely dejected by the failure of his campaign and by the fact that he was returning with an army considerably reduced by the death of well over thirty-five hundred men, to say nothing of an equal number that had been wounded in battle and burned by the mine.

Five days later he was back in *Panaju,* where he demobilized his troops, both native and foreign, and departed up the river in a small *lanchara,* refusing to allow any more than two or three men to accompany him. His destination was a town called *Pachissaru,* where he remained in seclusion for fourteen days at a pagoda dedicated to an idol called *Guinasseró,* "god of sadness," as though he were observing novena devotions.

When he returned to *Panaju* he sent for me and the Moor who was handling Pero de Faria's merchandise, and he questioned him in great detail about the sale of the goods, wanting to know if there was any money still due him and if so, he would see to it that he was paid at once. The Moor and I assured him that we had done quite well, mainly because of the interest His Highness had shown in the matter, and that the merchants had already paid us in full and that no one owed us anything, and that this favor would soon be repaid by the captain of Malacca, who would avenge him on the Achinese enemy and restore to him all the land that had been taken from him.

"Ah, Portuguese, Portuguese!" the king exclaimed, after reflecting a moment on what I said. "How do you expect me to answer you? Please, don't think me foolish enough to believe that someone who has not been able to avenge himself in thirty years can possibly help me. When I consider that your king and his governors failed to punish this same enemy after he captured your fortress in Pasay,[6] and the galley bound for the Moluccas,[7] and the three *naos* off Kedah,[8] and the galleon from Malacca in the days of Garcia de Sá,[9] and later on, the four foists at Selangor,[10] and the two *naos* from Bengal, and the junk, and Lopo Chanoca's ship,[11] and many other vessels I can't think of at the moment, on which I was told he had killed more than a thousand Portuguese, to say nothing of all the valuable prizes he made off with, long before he set out to destroy me—how can I place any hope in what you say? No, there's nothing left for me to do but remain where I am, the way I am now, with three sons dead and most of my kingdom gone, and for you Portuguese to hang on in Malacca, in a none-too-secure position."[12]

I must confess that I felt quite embarrassed and ill at ease when I heard his reply, delivered as it was with such deep feeling, for I knew all too well that what he had said was true, and I never said another word to him about our coming to his aid, nor did I dare to repeat the promises I had made him before, for the sake of our honor.

18
The Battak's Warning

The Moor and I returned to our lodgings, where we remained for four more days until we finished loading some hundred *bahars* of tin and thirty of benzoin that were still on shore. And since everything owed to us had been paid in full and there was nothing to keep us there, I went down to the *passeivão*[1] of the king's residence and informed him that everything was now on board and that I was ready to leave if His Highness would grant me permission.

"I was extremely pleased yesterday," he began, after a gracious reception, "when my *shahbandar* told me that the captain's cargo was sold at a handsome profit. However, since it is possible that he was not so much concerned with telling me the truth as he was with telling me what I wanted to hear, for he was well aware of the personal interest I have taken in this matter all along, I beg you to tell me if it is true, and if the Moor who brought the merchandise is leaving in a happy frame of mind, for I would not want them cursing the merchants of *Panaju* in Malacca, at the expense of my honor, or saying that they are not to be trusted, or that there is no king there to force them to pay their debts, for I swear to you, by my faith as a good Hindu, that that would be as great an indignity to me, in my position, as signing a peace treaty now with the Achinese enemy, without having avenged myself on that lying tyrant."

To which I replied that everything had been taken care of to our entire satisfaction, that all the merchandise had been paid for, and that no one owed us anything.

"I am delighted to hear it," he said. "And as long as there is nothing more for you to do here, it would be advisable for you to leave at once, without any further delay, for apart from the fact that the monsoon is almost over, there is also the danger of your running into the gulf doldrums, which have often forced ships into the harbor of Pasay. God forbid that it should happen to you, for I can assure you, if you were unlucky enough to get caught there, the Achinese would eat you up alive, especially the king, who would relish each mouthful more than anyone else; for of all the titles he boasts, the one he is most proud of is 'Drinker of the impure blood of the cursed foreign kaffirs[2] who have come from the end of the world to usurp other men's kingdoms in the lands of India and the islands of the sea, by brute force and tyranny.' His people are all extremely impressed with that title because it was conferred on him this year by the House of Mecca out of gratitude for the gift of the golden lamps he sent as an offering to the *Al-Koran*[3] of his Mohammed, as is his custom every year. And be sure and tell the captain of Malacca on my behalf, even though I have already written him, that he must be on constant guard against the Achinese enemy, who thinks of nothing, night and day, but how to drive you out of India and supplant your power with that of the Turk from whom, they say, he expects to receive a great deal of help for that purpose. But I trust that God in His wisdom will see to it that all his sly, malicious schemes turn out to be the complete opposite of what he expects."

And so saying, he handed me a letter in reply to my official embassy as well as a gift consisting of six gold-shafted assegais,[4] twelve catties[5] of calambac, and a gold-trimmed tortoise-shell box filled to the brim with baroque seed pearls and sixteen extra large ones. He was also kind enough to make me a gift of two catties of gold and a small dagger, trimmed in gold too.

After taking leave of him, overwhelmed with honors, which he had always shown me—as if to prove that the friendship pact he had just signed with us was quite firm on his part—I boarded the ship, accompanied by his brother-in-law, the same *Aquareng Dabolay* he had sent as his ambassador to Malacca, as I mentioned earlier.

We departed from the port of *Panaju,* and about two hours after dark we reached a small island called *Apefingau,*[6] located approximately a league and a half from the bar, that was inhabited by extremely poor people who live by fishing for shad, of which, owing to a scarcity of salt in those parts, they keep only the roe of the female, which is cured by the same method the river folk of Aaru and Siak[7] use on the eastern seaboard of Sumatra.

19
A Malay Tyrant

The next morning we departed from this island of *Fingau*[1] and ran along the ocean coast for a distance of twenty-six leagues until we reached the mouth of the *Minhagaru Strait*[2] through which we had come before. Passing through them to the other side of the island in the inland sea, we proceeded on our course along the coast as far as *Pulo Bugay,* from where we crossed over to the mainland. Steering a course for the port of Junkseylon,[3] we ran under fair winds for two and a half days and came to anchor in the Perlis River[4] in the kingdom of Kedah, where we stayed for five days, owing to contrary winds. While we were there, on the advice of some of the local merchants, the Moor and I went to pay our respects to the king, bringing him an *odiá,*[5] or gift (as we would say), of a few articles of sufficient value to serve our purpose, and he gave us a good reception.

At the time we arrived in Kedah, the king was in the midst of conducting elaborate funeral services for his father, whom he had stabbed to death in order to marry his mother, who was pregnant with his child. As part of the ceremonies, which were performed with a great deal of pomp and splendor, there was music making, dancing, shouting, screaming, and free meals for the poor who flocked there in great numbers. In order to stamp out public indignation that was aroused by this horrendous and utterly abominable crime, the king had issued a proclamation to the effect that anyone heard gossiping about what had happened would be ruthlessly put to death, and from what we were told, he had already carried out this threat by executing, in an exceptionally brutal manner, some of the most important people in the kingdom, as well as a considerable number of merchants, whose property he had confiscated, thus enriching his treasury by two *contos*[6] of gold.

Due to this state of affairs, at the time I arrived all the people were already so frightened that no one dared breathe a word. And since *Khoja* Ali, the Moor who was traveling with me, was by nature a very loose-tongued fellow who was in the habit of speaking his mind whenever he felt like, he thought that, as a foreigner, especially one who was known to be acting as agent of the captain of Malacca, he would be freer to do so than the natives, and that the king would have to be more lenient with him than with his own subjects. One day he was invited to dinner by another Moor, a foreign merchant from Patani,[7] who was supposed to be a relative of his. It seems, from what they told me later, that at the height of the banquet, when they had already had too much to eat and drink, the guests began talking about the affair quite openly, and that it was immediately reported to the king by the many spies he had posted around for that purpose. Upon being informed, the king had the guest house surrounded, and all seventeen members of the party were taken into custody and brought before him bound hand and foot. And without any semblance of justice, without making the slightest attempt to determine their guilt or innocence, he had them all executed by an extraordinarily cruel method they call *gregoge,*[8] which consists of sawing a live man to death, starting with the feet, then the hands, the neck, and the chest, all the way down the back to the bottom of the spine, which is the way I saw them all afterwards. That same night, out of fear that the captain might take offense at his having executed an agent of his along with the other condemned men and use that as a pretext to seize some merchandise he had shipped to Malacca, the king sent his men to fetch me from the *jurupango,* when I was fast asleep and had not the faintest idea of what was going on.

By the time I reached the outer courtyard of the palace it was already past midnight, and the first thing I noticed were the many guards posted about, armed to the teeth with lances, swords, and shields, which struck me as rather unusual, and I began to get nervous. I suspected that there was some kind of treachery afoot, of the sort that had formerly taken place in that country, and I wanted to leave immediately. But the men who had brought me there would not let me go, telling me not to be afraid of whatever I had seen, and that the armed men present there were merely a police patrol that the king was sending out to arrest a thief; but I must confess, their explanation did not satisfy me in the least. By this time I was stammering so badly that nothing I said made any sense. Somehow, I managed to ask them if they would let me return to the *jurupango* to look for some keys I had forgotten, and I offered to pay them forty *cruzados* in gold immediately if they would let me go.

"Not for all the gold in Malacca!" all seven of them protested. "It's not worth the risk of having our heads cut off!"

About this time another fifteen or twenty of the other guards joined them, and together they formed a ring around me and kept me locked in that way until dawn, for only then did they inform the king of my presence. He had them bring me in immediately, and God only knows what a state I was in by that time—poor me—I was more dead than alive!

When I reached the inner courtyard, I found the king mounted on an elephant, with more than a hundred men around him, not counting the guards, who were there in even greater number. Observing the deplorable condition I was in, he tried to reassure me.

"Jangão tacor!" he said, repeating it twice. "Don't be afraid! Come over here and I will tell you why I have sent for you."

At a sign from him, ten or twelve people moved back, and he motioned to me to look at something. I turned to look in the direction he was pointing to, and I saw a heap of bodies lying face down on the floor in a pool of blood, and there among them I recognized the remains of the Moor, *Khoja* Ali, the captain's business agent who had accompanied me on the voyage. At the sight of him lying there I became so panic-stricken that without knowing what I was doing I threw myself at the feet of the elephant.

"I beg you, sir," I cried, unable to control the tears, "please take me for your slave instead of having me killed like them, for I swear by my faith as a Christian that I have done nothing to deserve it. And don't forget that I am the nephew of the captain of Malacca, who will gladly pay any amount of money to ransom me. And then there's the *jurupango* in the harbor with all its valuable cargo which is yours for the taking whenever you please."

"Good God, man!" he exclaimed. "What are you saying? Do you think I'm as bad as all that? Now, now, calm yourself, you have nothing to fear. Just sit down and rest a while, for I can see that you are upset. Then after you have regained your composure, I will explain why I ordered the execution of that Moor you brought with you. And I swear by my faith, I would never have done such a thing if he had been a Portuguese, or a Christian, even if he were guilty of murdering one of my sons."

Then he had them bring me a pan of water, from which I drank long and thirstily, and he also made me feel more comfortable by having them fan me, in the process of which more than an hour went by. Finally, when he saw that I had recovered enough from my fright to be able to make some sense, he resumed where he had left off.

"Portuguese," he began, "I am well aware of the fact that they have already told you that I murdered my father a few days ago. I did so because I found out that he was planning to kill me, all because of a plot hatched against me by some evil men who told him that I had made my mother pregnant—something I never even dreamed of doing. But since my father believed this baseless accusation and had already decided to kill me, I had no other choice but to kill him first. God only knows how I hated to do it, because I had always been a good son to him. And since I did not want to see my mother remain poor and defenseless—which is the fate of many widows—I married her; and as a result I had to refuse many other good offers of marriage I had been considering, to women in Patani, *Berdio,* Tenasserim, Siak, Jambi, and Indragiri, all of them sisters and daughters of kings who would have brought me fabulous dowries. Now, in order to stop the slander being spread by evil people who have no fear of saying the first thing that comes into their heads, I had proclamations posted throughout the kingdom forbidding anyone to speak about it any more. That Moor of yours is lying there because last night, in the company of other dogs like him, who had had too much to drink, he said so many disrespectful things about me that I am ashamed to repeat them to you; and since he was heard saying publicly, in a loud voice, that I was a pig, and worse than a pig, and that my mother was a bitch in heat, I was forced, for the sake of my honor, to punish him, along with those other dogs, who were no better than he. Therefore, I beg you, as a good friend, do not think unkindly of me for what I have done, because it would upset me very much. And if by chance you think I was looking for a pretext to confiscate the cargo belonging to the captain of Malacca, believe me, such a thought never crossed my mind—and you can assure him of that in all truth because I swear to it by my faith—for I have always been a good friend of the Portuguese, and I always will be, as long as I live."

By this time I was beginning to overcome my fear somewhat, though I was still far from calm, and I told him that His Highness had performed a great act of friendship for his brother, the captain of Malacca, by killing the Moor, because he had been robbing him shamelessly, and that I too was obliged to him because the Moor had tried to poison me twice to make sure that I would not tell the captain about his tricks, and that he was such an evil dog that he was always getting drunk and saying whatever he had a mind to, like a dog barking at every passerby.

This crude answer of mine, which I blurted out without even realizing what I was saying, satisfied the king completely, and it made him so happy that he bade me come closer.

"I can tell from the way you answered me," he said, "that you are indeed a very fine fellow and a good friend of mine. That's why the things I did do not seem as bad to you as they did to those dirty dogs lying there."

Then he took a gold-embossed kris from his belt and handed it to me, along with a letter for Pero de Faria containing all sorts of lame excuses for what he had done.

I took my leave of him as best as I could, telling him that I would have to remain there for another ten or twelve days, and I embarked immediately; and as soon as I set foot aboard the *jurupango,* without a moment's delay, I cut the cables and clapped on full sail, though I was still unable to shake off the sensation that the entire country was coming after me, an illusion created by the harrowing experience I had been through just a few hours before.

20
The Elusive Isle of Gold

After my hasty departure from the Perlis River on a Saturday close to sundown, I proceeded on my course until Tuesday at noon, when, as God willed, I reached the island of Pulo Sambilang,[1] the first landfall on the coast of Malaya, where I found three Portuguese *naos,* two of them inbound from Bengal and the other from Pegu.[2] The captain and owner of the ship from Pegu was a certain Tristão de Gá,[3] a former tutor to Viceroy Dom Francisco de Almeida's son, Dom Lourenço,[4] who was killed in the harbor of Chaul by Emir Hussein,[5] in a battle that has been described at great length in the chronicles dealing with the discovery of India.[6] This Tristão de Gá readily supplied me with many things I was short of, such as cables, sailors, two soldiers, and a pilot, and he and the other two *naos* escorted me safely all the way to the port of Malacca.

The moment I landed I went straight to the fortress to see the captain and informed him about everything that had happened on the voyage. I gave him a detailed report on the exploration of the hitherto uncharted rivers, ports, and bays I had entered along both the ocean and inland sea coasts of the island of Sumatra, including a description of the trading practices among the inhabitants, who up until that time had never had any commercial relations with us. I had mapped and taken soundings of all the ports and rivers along the entire coast, carefully recording this information with the respective place-name and degree of latitude, in keeping with his instructions.

I also brought back information about the bay in which Rosado,[7] the captain of the French *nao,* was shipwrecked. He was a fellow officer of Brigas, captain of the other *nao* that in the year 1529 was driven by bad weather into the harbor of Diu, where Sultan Bahadur, king of Cambay, who was still alive at the time, took all eighty-two Frenchmen into custody and forced them to convert to Islam, making use of these renegades later on as artillerymen in his war against the Moghul king, in 1533,[8] where every single one of them lost their lives. And I also informed him about the anchorage in the Bay of Pulo Butum,[9] where the *nao Biscay,*[10] said to have belonged to Magellan, once entered, but which was shipwrecked later on in the mouth of the Sunda Straits[11] while crossing over to the island of Java.

I also gave him a description of the many different nations that live along the ocean coast and the Lampong River,[12] from where the gold of Menangkabow[13] is shipped to the kingdom of Kampar[14] via the Jambi[15] and *Broteo*[16] rivers. The inhabitants of this region tell of reading in their chronicles that the queen of Sheba[17] once had a trading post there which supplied her, presumably, as some claim, through the intermediary of an agent of hers by the name of Naussim, with a large quantity of gold, which she contributed to the temple of Jerusalem when she visited King Solomon, by whom she is said to have begotten a son who later became emperor of Ethiopia—commonly known here in Europe as Prester John[18]—a lineage of which the Abyssinian nation is extremely proud. I informed him also about the seed-pearl fishery located between Pulo Ticos[19] and *Pulo Quenim,* from where the Battak used to ship these pearls in former days to Pasay and Pedir, trading them with the Turks of the Mecca Straits and the *naos* of Jidda for other merchandise they brought from Cairo and the ports of Arabia Felix.

And in addition, I told him many other things I had learned from the Battak king and from my contacts with the merchants of *Panaju.* And I also gave him, in writing, the information he had particularly requested in his instructions to me, about the Isle of Gold, which they all say lies on the ocean side of the *Calandor* River at five degrees south, surrounded by numerous reefs and swift currents, at a distance of about 160 leagues from the northern tip of the island of Sumatra.

Convinced of the accuracy of this information, not only from what I told him, but also from what the Battak wrote in the letter I delivered to him, Pero de Faria forwarded all of it that year to King John III, of glorious memory. As a result, the following year, the king granted the captaincy of an expedition to discover this island to a knight of the royal household, Francisco de Almeida,[20] a man of many parts and one quite equal to the task, who had been asking for it for a long time in compensation for the many services he had performed in the islands of Banda,[21] the Moluccas, Ternate, and Jailolo.[22] However, on his way there from India, this Francisco de Almeida died of a fever on the Nicobar Islands.[23] Once the news of his death was confirmed, His Highness granted the captaincy the second time to a Diogo Cabral, a native of the island of Madeira who later was punished by being removed from his command by Martim Afonso de Sousa,[24] because he was said to have insulted him, during his term as governor; and he gave it instead to a Jerónimo de Figueiredo,[25] a nobleman in the service of the duke of Braganza, who departed from Goa in 1542 with a company of eighty soldiers and sailors in two foists and a caravel. But this voyage came to naught because it seems, from what they learned later, that he wanted to get rich quicker than was to be expected from keeping to his course; and instead, he crossed over to the coast of Tenasserim, where he seized some vessels arriving from the Straits of Mecca, from Aden, El Quseir,[26] Jidda, and other ports of the Persian Gulf; and because he did not get along well with the soldiers there and did not share the booty with them, as they had every right to expect, they mutinied against him; and after many other things that happened which are better left unsaid, they tied him hand and foot and put him ashore in the port of Galle[27] on the island of Ceylon. Then they delivered the two foists and the caravel to Governor Dom João de Castro,[28] who pardoned them when they agreed to join the armada he was preparing to take to the defense of Dom João de Mascarenhas[29] in the fortress of Diu, then under siege by the captains of the king of Cambay. And from that time on, no effort has been made to discover this island which it seems will be very beneficial for the general welfare of this empire, if our Lord should some day see fit to let this island be discovered.

21
The Ambassador from Aaru

Only twenty-six days had gone by since I returned to Malacca with the letter from the king of the Battak I was discussing, and Dom Estêvão da Gama[1] was still serving as captain of the fortress when an ambassador arrived from the king of Aaru,[2] which is on the island of Sumatra. He had come to request military aid for his king, who was asking for men and a quantity of munitions, such as cannonballs and powder, which he needed to defend himself against imminent invasion by a huge armada that the king of Achin was preparing to send against him as part of an overall plan to seize control of his kingdom and obtain a nearby base[3] from which to carry out operations against Malacca, a plan set in motion by the arrival of three hundred Turks from the Straits of Mecca.

Aware of its importance to the service of the king and the security of the fortress, Pero de Faria immediately brought the matter to the attention of Dom Estêvão, who remained in office for another month and a half.[4] But he refused to deal with this request for military aid, excusing himself on the grounds that his term was ending and that it was a matter of greater concern to Pero de Faria since he was staying in Malacca and would have to contend with what they feared lay ahead. To this Pero de Faria replied that he should authorize him to give orders in the arsenal, and he would provide whatever military assistance he deemed necessary.[5] To make a long story short, I'll skip the details of what went on between the two of them and sum it all up by saying that the ambassador's request was refused by both of them, on the pretext by one that his term of office was ending, and by the other that his term had not yet begun. And thus he departed without receiving any of the things he had come for.

Dismayed by what he regarded as utterly unjustifiable conduct towards his king, one morning, as he was preparing to embark, when both captains were standing at the gates of the fortress, he turned to them, and almost in tears, he cried aloud for all to hear, "I call upon the almighty God who reigns on high in majesty supreme, with sighs of anguish welling up from the very depths of my soul, to pass judgement in this matter on how proper and just is the petition that I address to both your lordships in the name of my king, loyal vassal of the powerful ruler of all the nations and peoples of India and the land of great Portugal, who has always honored the oath of fealty his ancestors swore to him long ago at the hands of Albuquerque, roaring lion of the ocean waves, who promised us then that as long as the kings of Aaru upheld their oath of loyalty, his king and his successors would assume the obligation to defend us against all our enemies, in keeping with the duty of a powerful liege lord, such as he was. And in view of the fact that we have never violated our oath, I ask your lordships, what reason can you possibly have for refusing to honor your obligation and the word of your king, when you know full well that it is on account of our loyalty to him that the Achinese enemy has set out to destroy us, giving as his reason that my king is as much a Portuguese and a Christian as though he had been born in Portugal? And now when my king turns to you as to true friends, to defend him against this outrage, you refuse him with flimsy excuses, when all it would take to satisfy us and protect our kingdom against these enemies is only about forty or fifty Portuguese soldiers with their muskets and arms to train us and lift our spirits in battle, and four kegs of powder, with a supply of two hundred cannonballs for the culverins. And we will consider this bit of help—which is insignificant in comparison to the large reserves you still have—as a quite satisfactory token of your friendship; and our king will thereby be deeply obliged to you and will always remain a loyal and devoted slave of the prince of great Portugal, who is your lord and king as well as ours, on whose behalf, and in the name of my king, I appeal to both you gentlemen, once, twice—nay, a hundred times—do not fail to honor your obligations, for the manner in which you respond to the emergency I publicly proclaim here will determine whether or not you can have the kingdom of Aaru for your own and the fortress of Malacca safe from the Achinese enemy who is determined to conquer it. He already has the means to do so, for he is continuously receiving help from many nations and is even now, at this very moment, mobilizing foreign troops on his soil for that purpose. And because our country is of greater strategic importance to him than any other for his sinister purpose, he is making preparations to conquer it in order to gain naval supremacy of the Malacca Straits and cut you off, as his people openly boast they will, from all your spice commerce with the Banda and Molucca islands, and block all your trade routes to China, Sunda, Borneo, Timor, and Japan.[6] Those are the conditions of the pact, as we have learned, that he has just signed with the Grand Turk, through the intermediary of his new protector, the pasha of Cairo, who has filled him with hopes of receiving all kinds of assistance, as you already know from the letters I brought you. Need I remind you that the petition I bring you today in the name of my king is of utmost importance to the service of your king, on whose behalf I once more appeal to you to restrain this monster who is about to put into effect the evil he has conceived—while it is still in your power to do so. And do not refuse with excuses from one of you that your term of office is ending and from the other that it has not yet begun, when both of you know that one is equally as obligated as the other to do so."

And when he had finished pleading his case—which availed him little at the time—he picked up two stones from the ground and rapped them ceremoniously against a bombard as he exclaimed, almost in tears, "The Lord who created us will defend us!"

And with that he boarded his ship and departed immediately, quite unhappy about the prospect of returning with such bad news.[7]

Five days after he left, as was to be expected, someone told Pero de Faria that people were talking quite openly about the lack of respect that both he and Dom Estêvão had shown this king who was such a good friend of ours and who was about to lose his kingdom precisely because he had so often demonstrated his friendship to the fortress of Malacca. Only then, when he was made to see that he had been remiss—or perhaps he was even ashamed of it—though he still tried to make excuses for it, he decided to help the king. He arranged to send him three quintals of bombard powder, two arrobas[8] of musket powder, a hundred grenades, a hundred cannonballs for culverins and fifty for falcons, twelve muskets, forty clusters of stone grapeshot, sixty fuses, a laminated breastplate[9] with gilt rivets, lined with red satin, for the personal use of the king, as well as other articles of clothing such as a score of saris and sarongs for his wife and daughters, which is what they usually wear in that country.

And when it had all been loaded on board an oar-equipped *lanchara*, he asked me to be good enough to deliver it to this king, since it was a mission of great importance in the service of His Highness, promising to reward me on my return, not only with additional pay, but with the choice of a trading voyage. And I—sinner that I was—accepted gladly, and I say this because of what happened afterwards.

I weighed anchor on a Tuesday morning, 5 October 1539,[10] proceeding on my course until the following Sunday when I reached the *Puneticão*[11] River, on which the capital of Aaru is located.

22
The Aaru on the Eve of War

When I reached the *Puneticão* River I disembarked and went straight to the fortifications at the mouth of the river which the king was then constructing in an effort to forestall an enemy landing. He gave me a fine welcome, plainly showing that he was delighted to see me; and I delivered a letter to him from Pero de Faria written in such a way as to make him believe that sometime in the future he would personally come to his aid, if it so pleased him; and it was also full of many other expressions of courtesy and respect which cost little but which were deeply appreciated by the king, who was taken in by the whole thing. And after he had seen the gifts, the gunpowder, and the other munitions I had brought, he embraced me joyfully.

"Believe me, my good friend," he exclaimed happily, "all last night I dreamed that the wonderful things I now see before my eyes were being sent to me from the fortress of my lord, the king of Portugal; and with my hope in God, I will use them to defend my country, so as to be in a position to render many services to him, as I have done all along, with a loyalty that the former captains of Malacca can vouch for."

And after asking me a few things he wanted to know about India and Portugal too, he turned over to his men the job of fortifying the barrier on which they were all working feverishly; then he took me by the arm, and together with six or seven of the young noblemen who were there with him, and which was all the retinue he had, he led me that way on foot to the city, which must have been almost a quarter of a league away; and he gave a banquet in my honor at his residence, where I was treated with a great display of hospitality, and he showed me his wife, which is something that is rarely done in that part of the world; and he spoke to me this way, shedding many tears.

"Portuguese, you can see for yourself," he said, "why I am so distressed about the enemy invasion, for I am a victim of necessity and honor bound to do my duty. If I were not forced by poverty to stay and defend myself here, I swear to you, by my faith as a good Moslem,[1] I would have done to him first what he is doing to me now, and I would have done it without having to rely on anyone but myself and my own people, for I have known about the Achinese king's treachery for a long time and have taken the full measure of his power. Actually, his only strength lies in the huge sums of money[2] at his command, which he uses to mask the cowardice of his people by hiring hordes of foreign mercenaries to fight for him. To give you a better idea of how vile and degrading this miserable and hateful thing called poverty is, and of how detrimental it can be to kings who are as poor as I am,[3] come with me and I will show you how little I have to my name and how shabbily Fortune has treated me."

He led me to some thatched huts that housed his entire arsenal and began to show me what he had stored there, which was so little that one could say—and with good reason—that it was nothing compared to the huge quantities needed to defend oneself against an armada of 130 ships full of people as bellicose as the Achinese, with a mixture of Turks and Malabaris to boot. And then, in a rather sad voice, as though he were unburdening his heart to me, he described the difficult situation he was in and the enormous outrage he was faced with; and he told me that he already had an army of five thousand men, exclusively Aaru, with no foreign mercenaries, and forty pieces of light ordnance, such as falcons and culverins, including a half-sphere that had been sold to him some time before by a Portuguese named Antonio Garcia,[4] former quartermaster of the Pasay fortress, whom Jorge de Albuquerque[5] later had drawn and quartered in Malacca for corresponding secretly with the king of Bintang[6] about some act of treason he was committing.

He also told me he had forty muskets, twenty-six elephants, and fifty horsemen to guard the shore, ten or twelve thousand charred wooden stakes dipped in poison, which they call *saligues*,[7] about fifty lances, and a good quantity of shields coated with red clay for the use of the men defending the trenches, a thousand pots of powdered quicklime to be used instead of grenades when grappling a ship, about three or four *batéis*[8] laden with stones, plus some other miserable, worthless weapons that failed by a long shot to meet the requirements of a man in his difficult position; so that just by looking at what he had there, I could see how easy it would be for the enemy to conquer his kingdom.

And when he asked me what I thought about the abundant store of munitions he had in his arsenal, and if it was enough with which to welcome the guests he was expecting, I told him that he had more than enough to entertain them with; to which, after a thoughtful pause, he replied, shaking his head, "If the Portuguese king knew at this moment how much he would gain by my not losing, or how much he would lose if the Achinese took Aaru from me, I am sure he would punish the longtime negligence of his captains who, in blind pursuit of their own selfish interests, have permitted this enemy to build up his strength and power to the point where I fear he will no longer be able to restrain him once he decides to do so; and if he should succeed in doing so, he will have to pay a heavy price for it, in his own resources."

And when I tried to respond to what he was saying with such deep sadness in his voice, he destroyed all my arguments with a few remarks that were so obviously true, that I no longer dared utter a single word in reply. I knew all too well that his charges could not be denied because he pointed to a few rather ugly, criminal deeds committed by certain individuals which I don't care to dwell on since it is not my purpose here to expose the wrongdoings of others. And he culminated the conversation by taunting me about the light punishment meted out to the ones who were guilty of these crimes and the high honors he had seen conferred on people who did not deserve them, and concluded by saying that any king who wanted to carry out the responsibilities of his office with complete integrity and who was bent on conquering and maintaining control of nations so far from his shores by means of armed force, would find that it was just as necessary for him to punish the bad as it was to reward the good. However, if he should happen to be the sort of king who, in the name of clemency, showed too much laxity and negligence in meting out punishment where it was due, then his people, once they came to recognize this as characteristic of him, would have no fear of treading wherever they pleased, and in the course of time, this would or could have the effect of reducing the strength of his conquests to the condition that Malacca was in at the present time.

With that he withdrew into a house and arranged for me to be lodged in another belonging to a Hindu merchant from Indragiri who banqueted me splendidly throughout the five days I was there, though at the time I would rather have eaten any kind of unsavory food any place but there, where I could feel more secure, far from the many alarms and warning bells that sounded every hour; for the day after I arrived the king was reliably informed that the Achinese fleet had already left its home port and was due to arrive within a week.

The moment he received this news he redoubled his efforts and rushed about attending to what was still undone as well as giving orders for the evacuation of all the women and other noncombatants who were being sent into the forest about four or five leagues from the city, whose misery and helplessness, owing to the disorderly and undisciplined manner in which it was carried out, was such a pitiful sight to see that I was utterly dismayed, and God knows how much I regretted ever having come there. The queen went off on a female elephant, accompanied by only forty or fifty old men, all of whom were so thoroughly frightened that I was convinced, without any doubt, that the enemy would have no trouble conquering that country.

Five days after my arrival the king sent for me and asked me when I wanted to leave, and I replied, whenever His Highness saw fit, but that I would prefer to leave right away because I was due to take a shipment of the captain's goods to China.

"You are quite right," he replied.

Then he removed from his arm two gold *loyas,*[9] which are solid gold bracelets twisted around in one piece, that both weighed eighty *cruzados,* and he gave them to me, saying as he did so, "Please do not think I am a miser for giving you so little, for I assure you that my thoughts at present are such, and always have been, that I wish I had more in order to be able to give more. And this letter with this diamond you will give to the captain. Tell him that I know I owe him much more in return for the love he has shown me by coming to my aid with the munitions you brought; but I must leave it for a time when I shall be rid of my enemies and can bring it to him personally, with greater peace of mind than I have now."

23
Shipwrecked off the Island of Sumatra

After bidding the king farewell I embarked immediately and by the time I got under way it was close to sundown. I proceeded down the river by oar until I reached a village near the bar where there were about fifteen or twenty thatched huts, inhabited by extremely poor people who support themselves solely in that area by killing lizards and making poison from their livers in which to dip the arrows they fight with. And according to them, the poison produced in the kingdom of Aaru—which is called *pocausilim*—and especially the one that comes from this village, is the best in those parts because there is no known cure or antidote for it.

The following morning we departed from this village and went sailing along the coast under a land breeze until after vespers when we rounded the *Anchepisão* Islets;[1] and from there, still taking advantage of the southeast wind, though it was a bit foul, we headed out to sea, keeping to our course for the remainder of the day and part of the night. Shortly after the middle of the first watch we were struck by a thunderstorm coming out of the northwest—the kind that usually prevails over the island of Sumatra throughout most of the year—which was completely disastrous for us because the wind whipped us to pieces, sails and poles and all, leaving the *lanchara* dismasted, with three gaping holes near the keel. We sank so fast that nothing could be saved and only a few survived, for out of the twenty-eight people on board, twenty-three drowned in less time than it takes to recite the Credo; and the five of us that managed to escape with our lives—solely by the mercy of our Lord, and badly wounded at that—spent the rest of the night clinging to the reefs and weeping bitterly over the terrible disaster that had befallen us. And since we couldn't make up our minds at the time about what to do next or where to go from there—for the entire shore was a swampland covered by jungle growth so thick that not even the smallest bird could have flown between the thorns on the tightly laced branches of the mangrove trees—we remained there that way for three days, squatting on the rocks, with nothing to eat in all that time but some seaweed we scooped up from the ocean spray.

At the end of that time, confused and dazed with pain, unable to decide what to do with ourselves, we walked along the island of Sumatra all that day, sinking waist deep in the slime, until just before sunset when we reached the mouth of a small river, slightly wider than a crossbow shot;[2] but since it was quite deep and we were completely exhausted, we did not dare to cross it. And up to our necks in water, we settled down for the night, which we spent in agony, tortured by the sand flies and mosquitoes that came swarming out of the jungle, stinging us so viciously that before long we were all covered with blood.

When morning came I asked the four sailors who were with me if they were familiar with the country and if they knew of a town nearby. One of them, a man advanced in years, with a wife and family in Malacca, answered me in tears.

"Sir, the closest place to you and me," he replied, "if God by some miracle does not save us, is the one where a painful death awaits us, and where very soon we will be called to account for our sins, and that will be much more agonizing than what we are going through now, so the sooner we prepare for it, the better, by resigning ourselves once and for all to whatever fate God has in store for us. So don't be disheartened by anything you may see, which is inspired by fear, for all things considered, it makes little difference whether we die today or tomorrow."

Then, clutching me in a tight embrace with the tears coursing down his cheeks, he asked me to make him a Christian right then and there because he realized, as he freely confessed, that therein lay the only path to salvation, and not in the wretched faith of Mohammed he had followed all his life, for which he asked God to forgive him. And no sooner had he spoken these words than he expired, probably because of the weak condition he was in, for his head had been split wide open and the gray matter was all crushed and exposed and oozing pus, owing to lack of medical treatment; and on top of that, his wounds were full of saltwater and badly bitten by the sand flies and mosquitoes, so that must have been the reason why he succumbed so quickly. But I—for my sins—was never able to help him, not only because the time was too short, but also because I myself was so weak that I kept falling into the water with every step I took, from sheer dizziness and loss of blood that kept draining from the wounds and lacerations all over my back.

Nevertheless, we buried him in the slime as best as we could under the circumstances, and then we—the three sailors and I—decided to cross the river and spend the night in some tall trees that were visible on the other side, as a precaution against the tigers and *reimões*[3] roaming all over the area, to say nothing of all the many other different kinds of poisonous animals lurking around, plus an infinite number of hooded cobras and some other kind of green and black speckled snakes which were venomous enough to kill with a whiff of the breath.[4]

Once all four of us had made this decision, I urged two of them to go ahead and the other to stay with me and help me because by then I was extremely weak. One of the two sailors promptly threw himself into the water and the other jumped in right after him, with both of them calling out to me as they went to follow them and not be afraid. But just when they had gone a little past the middle of the river, two huge lizards[5] lunged at them, cutting each of them into four pieces in no time at all, reddening the river with their blood and dragging them down to the bottom. I was so frightened out of my wits by the sight of it that I couldn't even scream, nor do I have any recollection of how I ever got out of the water, nor how I escaped with my life, because at the time it happened I had already waded chest deep into the river with the other black, who was holding me by the hand and who was so frightened himself that he hardly knew where he was or what he was doing.

24
Captive in Siak

There I was, as I was saying, so completely frightened out of my wits that I was in a state of shock for over three hours without so much as being able to utter a sound or shed a tear. Finally, the other sailor and I returned to the sea and remained there in the surf until morning, when we caught sight of a coastal barge that was heading for the mouth of the river. As soon as it came alongside we emerged from the water in all our nakedness, threw ourselves down on our knees, and with arms upraised, pleaded with them to take us on board.

The occupants of the boat stopped rowing when they saw us, and after taking in our situation for a moment, for they could easily tell from the pitiful state we were in that we had been cast up by the sea, they moved in closer and asked us what we wanted. We told them we were Christians from Malacca and that we had been shipwrecked nine days before on our return voyage from Aaru, and we begged them, for the love of God, to take us with them wherever they were going.

"From the looks of you, you're not even worth feeding," said one of them, who appeared to be the leader of the group. "But if you have any money hidden on you, hand it over first, and then maybe we will be moved to pity by your tears—otherwise, you're out of luck."

And so saying, they made as if to move off, but once again we pleaded with them, in tears, to take us along as captives and sell us for ransom wherever they felt like, making a point of the fact that they could get any price they wanted for me, no matter where, since I was a Portuguese and a close relative of the captain of Malacca.

"That's different," they replied. "We'll gladly take you along on those terms, but we must warn you, if it doesn't turn out the way you say, we'll thrash you within an inch of your lives and throw you overboard alive, tied hand and foot."

We readily agreed. And then four of them jumped ashore and helped us into the boat because by that time we were in such bad shape we could hardly move. Once they had us on board they seemed to think that by threatening and beating us they could make us confess where we had some money hidden away, which they thought all along they could get out of us; so they tied us to the foot of the mast, and with two rattan canes folded in half they flogged us till the blood flowed, showing no mercy. And since I was already half dead by that time, they did not make me drink the foul stuff they forced down the throat of my unfortunate companion, which was some kind of lime mixed with urine that made him throw up his guts, as a result of which, he died an hour later. And because they did not find any gold in his vomit, as they thought they would, that was why—as it pleased God—they spared me the same treatment and instead, they applied the same concoction to my lash wounds to make sure I wouldn't die of them, but the pain was so excruciating, it nearly killed me.

After our departure from this river—which was called the *Arissumhé*—we anchored the following day at vespers in front of a large village of thatched huts called Siak, in the kingdom of Jambi, where they kept me for twenty-seven days, during which time—God be praised—I recovered from the flogging.

But when the seven partners who owned me came to realize that they could find no use for me in their occupation, which always kept them out on the water fishing, they put me up for auction three times, each time without success, for no one was willing to bid for me. As a result, having given up hope of ever finding a buyer for me, they threw me out, so as not to have to feed me, for I was of absolutely no use to them.

For thirty-six days I was left to shift for myself, like a sorry old nag put out to pasture, begging from door to door for a bite to eat, which I very seldom received because the people in that country are all extremely poor, until one day, as God willed, when I was lying on the beach in the sun lamenting my misfortune, a Moor from the island of Palembang[1] chanced to pass by. He had been to Malacca several times, where he had come to know the Portuguese, and when he saw me lying half-naked on the sand that way he asked me to tell him if I was a Portuguese and to be truthful about it. I told him I was and that I belonged to a very wealthy family, and that if he would take me to Malacca, they would ransom me for any price he asked because I was the nephew of the captain of Malacca, the son of one of his sisters.

"If you are who you say you are," he replied, "what sin did you commit to bring you to the sad state I see you in now?"

Then I gave him a detailed account of my shipwreck at sea and how the seven fishermen had brought me there and how they had thrown me out later because they couldn't find anyone to buy me.

He listened in open-mouthed amazement and then finally, after a thoughtful pause, spoke up.

"As you can see," he said, "I am only a poor merchant—so poor as a matter of fact that I could never manage to scrape together any more than a hundred *pardaus*[2] at one time. That is why I went into this business of selling shad roe, in hopes of bettering myself. Unfortunately, things did not turn out as well as I had expected. Now, it so happens, I have just heard of a good business opportunity in Malacca, and I would like to go there if only I could be sure of not being cheated by the captain and his customs officers, which is what I have heard they have been doing, for many of the merchants who have been there have complained about the way their goods have been handled at that fortress. But if you are willing to use your influence to protect me so that I can trade there without having to worry about being cheated or mistreated, then I will arrange to buy you from the fishermen who own you."

I answered with the tears running down my cheeks that I was well aware of the fact that my appearance was not one to inspire much confidence in anything I might say, not only because of the lowly condition I had been reduced to, but also because he might think that in order to persuade him to ransom me from such a miserable captivity, I was pretending to have more influence in Malacca than he might find was actually the case when he got there; but if he would take my word for it, which was all I had to pledge, then I would swear to him, and I would even put it in writing, that if he brought me to Malacca, the captain would treat him with all due honor and respect, and that no part of his merchandise would be touched, and that he would be paid ten times more than it cost him to ransom me.

"All right, I will be glad to buy you and take you to Malacca," the Moor replied, "as long as you don't say a word about this to anybody, for otherwise they will raise the price so high that it will be impossible for me to help you, much as I'd like to."

And I swore to him that I would do exactly as he said, with enough and to spare of whatever I thought necessary at the time to suit my purpose, and he was easily convinced.

25
Back in Malacca

Four days after I made this agreement with the Moor, he entered into secret negotiations with the seven fishermen, using one of the natives as an intermediary to discuss the price with them. By this time they were disgusted with me, not only because of my poor state of health but also because I was of absolutely no use to them; then too, nearly a month had gone by since they had thrown me out, and there were seven people who had a share in me, and they were no longer getting along as well as they had before, plus a number of other factors that God permitted to enter into it, all of which combined to make them set very little store by me. As a result, through the third party acting as agent for the Moor, they all agreed to sell me to the merchant for a price of seven *maces*[1] of gold, which is equal to fourteen hundred *réis* in our money, at the rate of half a *cruzado* per *mace,* which he immediately paid and took me straight home with him.

Five days after I was out of their hands, with my health somewhat improved owing to the decent treatment I was then receiving from my new master, he departed for another town five leagues from there by the name of Surabaya,[2] where he finished loading the merchandise he dealt in, which, as I said before, was the roe of the shad fish that thrive so abundantly in these rivers that they only make use of the eggs of the female, averaging above two thousand shiploads annually, with capacity loads of 150 to 200 jars[3] containing a thousand each, which is the maximum they can hold.

Once he had finished loading the *lanchara,* which was the vessel he was using for his cargo, the merchant departed for Malacca, arriving three days later. He took me straight to the fortress to see the captain and told him what had happened to me. When he saw the way I looked, Pero de Faria recoiled, as though in horror, and with tears in his eyes he told me to say something out loud so he could be sure of my identity, for my features and my whole frame had become so altered and emaciated that he could hardly recognize me; and since they had not heard from me in over three months and had presumed me dead, the fortress could not hold all the people who came crowding in to see me, wanting to know, with tears in their eyes, what misfortune had befallen me that could account for the way I looked. And after I had told them the whole story of my ill-starred voyage, in all its details, they were all so astounded, that without a word, they filed silently out of the fortress, crossing themselves as they went. And, as was the custom in those days, most of them contributed their alms to me, so that in the end I was richer than I had been before.

As for the merchant who had brought me there, Pero de Faria saw to it that he received sixty *cruzados* and two bolts of Chinese damask; and he also issued orders in the name of the king, exempting his merchandise from the required customs duties, which amounted to almost as much; and he was not wronged in any way, so that all in all he was quite satisfied and content and considered himself well paid for the bargain he had struck with me.

As for me, the captain made arrangements for me to be lodged at the home of one of the clerks of the trading post who was married to a native woman,[4] because he thought I would be better cared for there than elsewhere, which indeed proved to be true. And I kept to my bed for over a month, during which time, as God willed, I completely recovered my health.

26
The Achinese Threat to Portuguese Power

When I had fully recovered my health, Pero de Faria summoned me to the fortress and asked me what had happened with the king of Aaru and how and where I was shipwrecked; and I gave him an account, at great length, of all the events surrounding my voyage and shipwreck, which left him utterly astounded.

However, before I go any further, I thought it necessary to relate the outcome of the Achinese war and what they eventually accomplished with their huge armada, the point being to provide a basis for understanding the reason for my gloomy predictions and why I have been so worried all along about our fortress in Malacca, whose importance to the State of India has apparently been forgotten by those who, by right, should remember it most; for the way I see it, and it stands to reason, we have no alternative but to destroy the Achinese or face up to the fact that, because of them, we will eventually lose the entire area to the south, which includes Malacca, Banda, the Moluccas, Sunda, Borneo, and Timor, to say nothing of the area to the north, China, Japan, the Ryukyus, and many other countries and ports where the Portuguese, thanks to the intercourse and commerce they engage in, are assured of far better prospects for earning a living than in any or all of the other nations discovered beyond the Cape of Good Hope, an area so vast that its coastline extends for more than three thousand leagues, as anyone can see by looking at the respective maps and charts, provided, of course, that they are accurately drawn. Moreover, if we should lose all that—which I pray that God in his infinite mercy will forbid, no matter how great our sins and the errors of our ways—we also run the risk of losing the Mandovi[1] Customs House in the city of Goa, which is our most prized possession in India, since the main part of its revenue is derived from the ports and islands mentioned above, to say nothing of the spice shipments of clove, nutmeg, and mace that are sent to Portugal from those islands. As for the rest that I could say on the subject from firsthand observation, I don't care to go into it any further, because from this alone I believe one can grasp the tremendous importance of all that is involved here, and once it is understood, I have no doubt that the proper steps will be taken to remedy the situation. And now back to my story.

The Achinese tyrant had been told by his advisors that if he wanted to capture Malacca, he would never succeed in doing so by investing her from the sea as he had tried to do six times before in the days of Dom Estêtão da Gama[2] and other captains before him. Instead, they advised him to begin by conquering the kingdom of Aaru and fortifying himself in the *Paneticão*[3] River, from where his armada would be in a better position to continue the war that he was planning to wage against Malacca, by operating from a closer base; for then, at very little cost to him, he would be able to blockade the Strait of Singapore and Sabang[4] and prevent our *naos* from passing into the China Sea, to Sunda, Banda, and the Moluccas. That way too, he could easily have access to all of the spice trade in that archipelago and thus comply with the terms of the new treaty he had signed with the Grand Turk, through the intermediary of the pasha of Cairo.

Convinced that this was the best course of action to follow, the king immediately gave his approval and set about preparing a fleet of 160 sails, comprised mainly of oar-propelled *lancharas* and galliots, as well as some Javanese *calaluzes*[5] and fifteen multiple-decked vessels loaded with provisions and munitions; and he put seventeen thousand men aboard these ships, counting twelve thousand soldiers and the rest sappers and sailors; and among those twelve thousand fighting men he had a regiment of four thousand foreign mercenaries—Turks, Abyssinians, Malabaris, Gujeratis, and Luzons from Borneo. As field marshal he appointed Heredim Mohammed, governor of the kingdom of Barros,[6] and brother-in-law of the king himself, who was married to one of his sisters. This fleet reached the *Paneticão* River safely, where the king of Aaru was then fortifying the stockade I mentioned earlier, in which he stationed six thousand Aaru soldiers,[7] with no foreign contingents among them, not only because he was too poor to hire them, but also because the land was not productive enough to feed them.

As soon as the Achinese arrived they opened fire on the city and kept up a steady barrage for six days in a row with many pieces of artillery. However, those inside defended themselves bravely, though not without some bloodshed on both sides, forcing Heredim Mohammed to send all his men ashore, where they set up an artillery emplacement of twelve heavy cannon, consisting of camels and spheres; and after three intense rounds of fire one of the two bulwarks defending the mouth of the river was breached, and at dawn they broke through it, carrying bales of cotton as shields. Their captain was an Abyssinian by the name of Mahmud Khan who had arrived from Jidda less than a month before to ratify and swear allegiance to the new league and treaty arranged by the pasha of Cairo with the king of Achin in the name of the Grand Turk, in exchange for which he was granted the exclusive rights to a trading factory in the port of Pasay. Leading a company of sixty Turks, forty Janissaries, and some other Moors from the Malabar coast, this Abyssinian captain gained control of the river fortifications, hoisting five flags aloft as well as many other banners and pennons.

Then the king of Aaru spurred his men on with words and promises required by the circumstances, to which they responded with forceful determination by throwing themselves against the enemy, regaining control of the bulwark and killing the Abyssinian captain and the rest of the men who had followed him inside. Apparently anxious for a victory, the king decided to take advantage of his good fortune and quickly ordered the gates of the stockade thrown open, sallying forth into the field with part of his troops, and engaging the enemy in such fierce combat that he routed them all and succeeded in capturing eight of their twelve pieces of artillery; after which he withdrew safely and strengthened his position as best as he could at the time, in preparation for what lay ahead.

27
The Death of the King of Aaru

When he saw how disastrous that day had been for him, what with the death of the Abyssinian captain and the loss of the eight pieces of artillery—which he regretted far more than the deaths of all the others combined—the Achinese king consulted his people about what to do next, and a decision was reached, with the approval of all the captains, that the siege should be continued and the stockade invested on all sides, and steps were immediately taken to implement it, with no effort spared.

And in the seventeen days that they were still there, they launched nine assaults, with the aid of so many ingenious military devices invented for them by a Turkish engineer in their ranks that they succeeded in demolishing most of the stockade, including the two main bastions on the southern bank and a section of the earthworks protecting the entrance to the river. But throughout it all, the men inside resisted with such great courage, that the enemy losses, by fire and sword, came to twenty-five hundred—not counting a much higher toll among the wounded and burned, who eventually died for lack of attention.

As for the Aarus, their losses amounted to only four hundred; but since they were so few and far outnumbered by the better-armed enemy, in the final assault, which took place on the thirteenth day of the moon, they were completely wiped out owing to the fact that the king, acting on the advice of his most trusted *caciz*—who had sold out to the enemy for a *bahar* of gold worth forty thousand *cruzados*—sallied forth from the city, engaging the enemy in bitter combat. At the height of the battle, with the king of Aaru clearly getting the best of it, that dog of a *caciz,* who had been left in command of the stockade, came dashing out with about five hundred of his men, on the pretext of helping the king press his advantage. Seeing his chance, an enemy captain, a Malabar Moor by the name of *Cutiale Marcá,*[1] commanding a unit of six hundred Gujerati and Malabar Moors, made a rush for the gates which had been left unguarded by the *caciz* because of the bribe they had given him. Encountering no resistance, he easily gained control of the stockade, slaughtering all the sick and wounded he found inside, sparing none, and from what was said, they numbered well over fifteen hundred.

Seeing the stockade in the hands of the enemy, the hapless king was forced to abandon the field in order to come to the aid of his highest-ranking *caciz,* whose treachery he never suspected. And just as he began his retreat and was withdrawing to the nearest line of trenches, as luck would have it, he was struck down, shot through the heart by a Turkish arquebus; and it was all over for the Aarus, owing to the enormous disorder and confusion following in the wake of his death.

Seizing the poor king as he lay dead on the field, the enemy disembowelled and salted his body, placed it in a chest and delivered it to the Achinese king who, in an elaborate public display of justice, commanded that the corpse be sawed to pieces and boiled in a cauldron of tar and oil, accompanying the proceedings with a frightful proclamation that went like this:

"Hear ye! Hear ye! Hear the punishment decreed by Sultan Alaradim, king of the land from sea to sea,[2] incense of the golden lamps of the chapel of the Prophet *Nobi,*[3] at whose wish and command the body of this Moor has been dismembered and boiled, so that, in like manner, his soul may suffer the torments of hell for transgressing against the Law of the Koran and the flawless creed of the Mussulmen of the House of Mecca—a righteous punishment, in accordance with the holy precepts written in the Book of Flowers, executed upon one who defied God by continuously sending secret messages about this kingdom to those cursed dogs from the other end of the world who, by the most tyrannous means, aided by our sinful negligence, have become masters of Malacca!"

And the people responded with a tumultuous roar, "Small punishment for so great a crime!"

And that is exactly how, in all truth, the kingdom of Aaru was lost, with the death of this poor king, who was such a good friend of ours and who, I believe, could have been saved with very little cost and effort on our part if, at the beginning of this war, we had given him the help he sought through his ambassador. But who was to blame for it—if blame there was—is not for me to judge. Let Him—who has the right to do so—be the judge.

28
The Queen of Aaru Seeks Revenge

With the king of Aaru slain the way I described and his army routed, the city soon fell and the entire kingdom was very easily captured; and Heredim Mohammed, admiral of the fleet, repaired and fortified the stockade, providing it with everything required for the security of the rest that he had won. Leaving eight hundred of the best soldiers in the fleet behind, under the command of a Moor from Luzon by the name of Sapetu de Rajah, he departed with the remainder of his force for Achin, where it was said the tyrant king overwhelmed him with very high honors for the successful outcome of the campaign, conferring on him the title of king of Barros whereas previously he had only been governor and *bendara* of Barros (as mentioned earlier); and from that time on he was called sultan of Barros, which is the word for king among the Moors.

A few days later, the queen of Aaru (who all this time had been hiding seven leagues away in the forest, where she had fled for safety, as was said before), upon being reliably informed of the death of the king, her husband, and everything else that had occurred in this tragic case, immediately wanted to set herself afire,[1] in fulfillment of a solemn vow she had made to him before his death. However, her people would not consent to it, offering her many reasons to dissuade her from doing so. Giving in to them, she replied, "I can assure you, in all truth, that neither the reasons you have given me, nor the things you have pointed out along with them, nor the kind words inspired by the devotion of loyal vassals, could have been enough to sway me from so holy a purpose as the one I had promised my king and lord, if God had not given me to feel in my soul that I had to dedicate my life to avenging his death; and I swear to you all, by the blood he shed, that as long as I live, I shall always seek out every possible means of doing so; and to that end I would even go so far as to become a Christian, a thousand times over if necessary, in order to achieve, within my lifetime, what I so much desire."

And without any further delay, carried away by the fervor of the moment, she mounted an elephant and rode off, accompanied by three hundred of her personal guards and many others who joined her later, swelling the ranks of her followers to seven hundred strong; and with them she headed straight for the city, determined to set it afire so as to prevent the enemy from gathering the spoils; and she found about four hundred Achinese there engaged in plundering what was still left; and urging her men to turn themselves into *amucks*, reminding them, with the tears streaming down her cheeks, of their obligation to do so, she fell upon the enemy so courageously that, according to what was said later in Malacca, not a single one of the four hundred escaped alive.

And when she realized that she was not powerful enough to do as much as she would have liked to, she withdrew once more to the forest from where, in just the twenty days she still remained there, she harassed her enemies so effectively and ambushed them so many times when they came in search of water and firewood and other things they needed, that they no longer dared to venture out of the city or even to try to obtain what they needed; and had it been possible for her to continue this guerrilla war for another twenty days, they would have been forced by hunger to surrender, in spite of themselves. But since the rain was falling continuously, owing to the season, and the ground was ordinarily swampy and wet, and the fruit of the forest on which they depended for their nourishment lay rotting on the ground, and most of the people were falling sick, and there was no way to care for them, the queen was forced to cross a river five leagues from there called *Minhasumbá*,[2] where she embarked on sixteen rowing vessels, including a number of fishing prows[3] that she managed to procure, and with them she arrived in Malacca, fully believing that, by coming there in person, she would not be denied a single thing, no matter what she asked for.

29
The Queen of Aaru in Malacca

Having been reliably informed that the queen of Aaru was arriving, Pero de Faria sent a reception party to meet her, headed by Alvaro de Faria,[1] his son and admiral of the sea, who set out in a fleet comprised of one galley, five foists, two cutters, and twenty *balões*. Accompanied by three hundred men as well as a huge crowd of natives, he escorted her to the fortress, where she was honored with a formal gun salute that lasted for well over an hour.

When she came ashore she was taken on a tour of the city and shown a few things that Pero de Faria wanted her to see that were intended to impress her, such as the arsenal, the waterfront, the fleet, the trading station, the customs house, the powder factory, and a few other things that had been prepared in advance for that purpose. Afterwards, she was provided with excellent accommodations, while her followers, who numbered perhaps six hundred, were put up in cabins and tents in the field of Hilir,[2] which were the best arrangements that could be made for them at the time.

And throughout the entire length of her stay, which must have been about four or five months, she never lost sight of her purpose in coming there, which was to ask for our help in avenging the death of her husband, persisting in her request for aid with enough well-founded arguments that could not be denied. And at the end of that time, when she realized that we could be of little help to her, and that all we were doing was wasting her time with words that were leading her nowhere, she decided to confront Pero de Faria and find out once and for all exactly what he proposed to do about keeping his promise. And she waited for him on a Sunday, at the main entrance to the fortress, at a time of day when the outer courtyard was crowded with people and he was just leaving to attend mass. There she waylaid him, and after the usual exchange of courtesies, she spoke up.

"My dear brave, noble Captain," she began, "I beseech you, for the sake of your illustrious lineage, spare me but a few minutes of your time and hear me out, for even though I am a Moslem and, for my sins, blind to the pure light of your holy faith, still, you owe me the courtesy, not only as a woman, but as one who was once a queen, of looking upon me, helpless as I am, with a little Christian charity."

At her words Pero de Faria stopped, removed his cap, and bowed graciously to her. For a moment they were both silent and then the queen, after bowing reverently in the direction of the church door opposite them, said to Pero de Faria, "From the beginning, I was filled with such an overwhelming desire to avenge the death of the king, my husband, that I determined to seek out all possible means of doing so, since it is my fate to have been born a woman, too weak to bear arms. Believing as I did that the best means of achieving this goal lay here, I turned to you first, placing far more hope in you than in any of the other possibilities open to me. And filled with trust, growing out of our ancient friendship treaty, and knowing how deeply obligated this fortress is to me, for many reasons that you, sir, are well aware of, I came here with tears in my eyes, to ask you, in the name of His Most Serene Highness, the king of Portugal, my lord, whom my husband always served as a loyal subject and vassal, to please help me and support me in my hour of need. To this plea you responded publicly, with words from your own mouth, in the presence of many noblemen who were there at the time, that you would do so without fail. And now, after making that promise, which was made the more precious by the treasure of your faith, instead of keeping it, you tell me, or rather you excuse yourself by telling me, that you have written about the matter to the viceroy, when I have no need of all the assistance you say I can get from him; for with less than a hundred men, together with my people who are hiding all over the countryside, waiting for my return, I dare, woman that I am, to reconquer my entire kingdom in less than a month and avenge the death of my husband—which is what I desire above all else—with the help of almighty God, in whose name I beseech you and urge you, for the service and the honor of His Most Serene Highness, the king of Portugal, my lord, my shield, my sole support, to keep your promise, since you are able to do so; but make haste, because time is of the essence in deciding the outcome of this matter; and by acting promptly you will thwart the enemy's long-range ambitions which depend for their success on the destruction of this fortress, which, from the way he is going about it, should be perfectly obvious to you; and if you decide to give me the help I am asking for, then I will wait; if not, tell me the truth, for either way you do me as much harm by making me wait without helping me and wasting my time, as you do by denying me outright the help I have so urgently sought from you—the help which, by your Christian faith, you owe me, as the almighty Lord, God of heaven and earth, on whom I call as my judge in this instance, well knows!"

30
The Queen of Aaru Departs in Anger

As he stood there listening to what the queen in her despair was saying, reminding him, in public too, of his obligation to comply with her request, Pero de Faria felt embarrassed by his negligence and almost ashamed of his failure to comply; and he replied that, by his Christian faith and on his word of honor, he could assure her that he had already written to the viceroy twice about the matter and that, without fail, he was expecting troops and an armada to arrive with the monsoon, provided no emergency arose in India to prevent it; and that therefore, he was advising her and urging her to do him the favor of remaining in Malacca until then, when that brief span of time would prove to her that he was telling the truth.

But when she protested that there was no way of knowing for certain whether or not such help would arrive, Pero de Faria nearly reached the end of his patience, for he thought she was doubting his word, and in his anger he let slip a few words that were unduly sharp, bringing tears to the eyes of the unhappy queen; and with her arms upraised to heaven and her eyes fixed on the door of the church not far from her, she replied, sobbing so uncontrollably that she could hardly speak, "The God that is worshipped in that house is like a fountain of pure water from whose mouth nothing but the truth issues forth; but the men who reside here in this land are like pools of stagnant water, whose foul depths provide a natural breeding ground for vice and folly, and he who places his trust in the words that issue from their mouths is as good as damned. For I assure you, my dear Captain, ever since I can remember, everything I have ever seen or heard points to but one thing—that the more unfortunate people like my husband and me do for you Portuguese, the less you do for them, and the more you owe, the less you repay; from which, I dare say, it is perfectly obvious that rewards are distributed by the Portuguese mainly on the basis of influence, rather than on the merit of the person. And oh, how I wish to God that the king, my husband, had known twenty-nine years ago what I, for my sins, now know about you, for then he would not have spent his life so foolishly trusting in you, nor would he have lost it in the end as he did, because of you. But since that is the way matters stand, all I have left to console me for my pains is the knowledge that there are many others as deeply outraged by your friendship as this poor unfortunate woman standing here before you. And if you did not dare, or did not care, to help me, then why did you give your word so lightly to this unhappy woman, leaving her now equally bereft of what she sought and thought she could get from you, as she is deceived by the generosity of your promises?"

No sooner had she spoken these words than she turned her back on the captain, refusing to hear what he had to say for himself, and went straight back to her house. And she immediately ordered her ships to prepare for departure; and on the following day she sailed for Bintang where the king of Jantana[1] was then in residence, and where, according to what was said later in Malacca, he paid her the highest honors. She told him what had happened between her and Pero de Faria and how disappointed she was in our friendship, relating to him the entire course and outcome of the events that had taken place.

To which, they say, the king replied that, as for what she said about our being untrustworthy, he was not in the least surprised, nor did he see why she should be, for we had demonstrated it often enough to the world at large; and to prove his point he cited a few examples of some things in particular he said we had done, which at first sight appeared to serve his purpose; still, since he was a Moor, he tried to undermine us by making them appear even uglier and far more serious than they actually were.

And after telling her about many very bad things we had done, which he called lies, robberies, tyrannies, and by many other very ugly names, without trying to explain the reasons for them or any of the extenuating circumstances that might have existed at the time, even if they had really been as abominable as he made them out to be, he concluded by saying that he promised her, on his word as a good king and a good Moslem, that with his help she would soon have her entire kingdom restored to her, without losing a single handspan of territory. And to prove to her that she could trust in his promise, he would be happy to receive her as his wife, if she would have him, for in that way he would have just and legal grounds for taking up her cause and declaring war against the king of Achin, which he would be forced to do if he refused to hand over the captured territory peacefully.

To this she replied that, even though his proposal was a very great honor for her, she would not accept it unless he promised her as part of the dowry and marriage contract that he would avenge the death of the king, her husband, since, as she assured him, that was all that she desired; otherwise, she would not consent to be the wife of any man, even if he were to make her queen of the world.

On the advice of his counsellors the king agreed to her terms and took a solemn oath, which he swore to by placing his head upon a book of his faith, to sanctify the promise he had made to her.

31
Jantana Lays Claim to Aaru

After the *Raja Moulana,* his chief *caciz,* had finished administering this oath to him, on one of their holy days in the month of Ramadan,[1] the king departed for the island of Kampar;[2] and there, once the wedding celebration was over, he met with his counsellors to decide what to do about the situation he had gotten himself into, for he was well aware of the fact that it would be quite difficult, inasmuch as he would be forced to risk a large share of his own resources on it. The meeting ended with a unanimous resolution to the effect that before making any move he should notify the king of Achin about his newly acquired right to the kingdom of Aaru as a result of his recent marriage to the queen, and then, depending on the response he got, he would decide what to do next. The king approved of this advice and immediately dispatched an ambassador with instructions to deliver an expensive gift of gold objects and silk cloth to the king of Achin, along with a letter that went like this:

"I, *Siribi Iaia Quendou Pracamá de Raja,* legitimate king, by right of succession, of my captive Malacca, forcefully and unlawfully usurped by the tyrant infidels, king of Jantana, Bintang, and the vassal states of Indragiri and Lingga[3]—

"To thee, *Siri* Sultan Aaradim, king of Achin and all the land bounded by both seas, my true brother, a kinship accorded us by the ancient friendship of our forefathers; fortunate recipient of the golden seal of the holy House of Mecca, proclaiming to all that thou art a good and faithful dervish,[4] as revered as the *Datos Moulanas* of old, who, for the greater glory of the Prophet *Nobi,* followed the path of self-renunciation throughout the weary days of this wretched life;—

"I, thy flesh and blood kinsman, hereby make known to thee, through my ambassador, that in days past, during the seventh moon of the present year, the noble widow *Anchesini,* queen of Aaru, appeared before me, complaining of outrage and injury. With woeful countenance and tear-filled eyes she prostrated herself before me, and digging her fingernails into her cheeks, she tore at her flesh as she told me that thy captains had overrun her kingdom from the *Laué*[5] to the *Paneticão* rivers, killing her husband *Alibomcar* along with five thousand of his *amborrajas* and *ourobalões,* the flower of his nobility, and enslaving three thousand innocent children who were bound hand and foot and beaten as mercilessly and relentlessly as though they had been born of infidel mothers.

"Wherefore, I, thy brother, acting in compassion, as the holy Koran teaches and commands us to do, took her under my protection, the better to be able to ascertain the reason or good cause thou mightst have on thy side. However, when I found, after carefully weighing her sworn statements, that thou hadst none, I took her for my wife, so that I might freely and lawfully plead her cause before God.

"Wherefore, I pray thee, as thy true brother, give up what thou hast taken, like a good Moslem, by making free and proper restitution of all that belongs to her, in compliance with the tenets of our faith. As for the manner in which this should be done, I beg thee to follow the procedure set forth in the instructions that my ambassador, *Siribi Khan,* will present to thee.

"In the event that thou shouldst refuse to do so, in conformity with what I, in all justice, beg of thee, then thou mayest well regard me as one who has declared himself against thee, and in favor of the woman to whom I solemnly swore, as part of the marriage contract, that I would take up her cause which she, a poor helpless woman, is too weak to defend."

On his arrival, the ambassador was given an honorable reception by the Achinese king, who accepted the letter he was carrying; but after it had been read and shown to him, he wanted to have him killed on the spot, and this might well have happened, had not cooler heads among his advisors prevailed, cautioning against such an outrageous act. Instead, he dismissed him summarily, refusing to accept the gifts as a sign of disdain, and replied with words to this effect:

"I, Sultan Alaradim, king of Achin, Barros, Pedir, Pasay, and the vassal states of Dayá[6] and Battak, prince of all the land bounded by the ocean and the inland sea, the mines of Menangkabau, and the kingdom of Aaru, recently conquered with just cause;—

"To thee, thou merry old king, playfully trying to snatch a dubious legacy: I have seen thy letter, obviously written at the nuptial feast, and judging by its frivolous contents, I dare say that thy counsellors were still drunk, and I would not even have deigned to reply, had it not been for mine, who urged me to do so.

"Therefore, I say to thee, do not seek to exculpate me in thy eyes, for I can assure thee that I have no need of thy praise. As for the kingdom of Aaru, never mention it again if thou dost value thy life! Suffice to say that it was conquered on my orders and that it is mine, as thine will be too, very shortly. And if thou didst wed thy wife *Anchesini,* in order to acquire thereby the right to a kingdom that is no longer hers, then thou wilt have to do with her as other wedded men do with their wives, supporting themselves by cultivating the soil by the sweat of their brows. First take back Malacca, since it once was thine, and then thou wilt look to a kingdom that never was thine, at which time I will be happy to favor thee as a vassal, but never as a brother, as thou didst call thyself.

"Written at my grandiose palace in prosperous Achin, on the same day of the arrival of thy ambassador, whom I promptly dismissed, refusing to see or hear any more of him, as he will inform you."

32
Jantana and Achin at War

Having been dismissed with this reply on the same day he was received in audience, which among them is usually a sign of the utmost contempt, the ambassador of the king of Jantana arrived in Kampar where the king was then residing, returning with the gift, which had also been refused to further humiliate and offend the same ambassador who was delivering it.

When he learned about all this, they say that the king was so angry, that some of his intimates claimed that they had seen him crying in secret a few times, showing how deeply he resented being treated with such little regard by the Achinese tyrant. He called his council together again to decide what to do about the situation, and it was agreed that they should embark on an all-out war against the Achinese, as though he were a mortal enemy; and that first and foremost they should concentrate all their efforts on capturing the kingdom of Aaru and the fortress of *Paneticão* before the Achinese had a chance to strengthen his position any further. And to that end the king soon gathered, with the greatest possible speed, a huge armada of two hundred oared sailing vessels, consisting mainly of *lancharas, joangás,*[1] and *calaluzes,* as well as fifteen multiple-deck sailing junks, which he loaded with provisions and munitions and the rest of the supplies he needed for this undertaking, placing it under the command of his admiral, the great *Laque Xemena,*[2] whose name is frequently mentioned in the chronicles of India, providing him with ten thousand soldiers and four thousand seamen, all of them handpicked men, experienced in warfare.

The admiral departed immediately with the entire fleet, and when he reached the *Paneticão* River where the enemy fortress was located, he assaulted it five times, employing three scaling ladders in the attempt to take it, as well as many ingenious incendiary weapons; and when this proved to be ineffective, he began to batter it with forty pieces of heavy artillery, firing night and day without pause; and after seven days of this continuous pounding, most of the fortress was leveled. Displaying great courage, they rushed into the attack, penetrating the fortress and killing fourteen hundred Achinese, most of whom had come there a day before the fleet arrived, under the command of a Turkish captain named *Morado Arraiz,* nephew of the pasha of Cairo who was also slain there, along with two hundred Turks in his company, for *Laque Xemena* refused to spare the lives of a single one of them. And he immediately set about repairing the damaged walls with stakes and rubble, assigning most of his men to the task, who worked at such a feverish pace that within twelve days the fortress was restored to its original condition, with the added advantage of two more bastions.

News of the fleet that the king of Jantana was preparing in the ports of Bintang and Kampar soon reached the Achinese tyrant, who, in fear of losing what he had won, immediately gathered another fleet of 180 sail, comprised of foists, *lancharas,* galliots, and fifteen galleys of twenty-five oarbanks, on which he embarked fifteen thousand men, of whom twelve thousand were scaffold fighters, or *bailéu*[3] fighters, as they call them, and the rest oarsmen. And as commander of this fleet he chose the same Heredim Mohammed who had previously captured the kingdom for him, as mentioned earlier, because he regarded him as one who was extremely courageous and lucky in war.

Departing with the entire fleet, Heredim Mohammed reached a town called *Apessumhé,* four leagues from the *Paneticão* River, where he found out from some fishermen captured in the area everything that had happened in the meantime, and that *Laque Xemena,* now in complete control of the fortress and the kingdom, both by land and by sea, was lying in wait for him; and they say that Heredim Mohammed was completely disconcerted by this news, for in all truth, he never dreamed that the enemy was capable of accomplishing so much in so short a time.

He then met with his war council to decide what to do, and it was said that the majority favored immediate withdrawal in view of the fact that the fortress and the kingdom had already been captured, that their men had all been slain, that the enemy was in so powerful a position, both by land and by sea, and that in any event they should turn back at once because the situation was not what they had expected it to be. However, Heredim Mohammed declared himself to be strongly opposed to their view and said that he would rather die fighting like a man than live out his life in dishonor, like a woman, and that as long as his king had chosen him for this undertaking, God forbid that he should lose one whit of the esteem in which he was held by all; and so he threatened and swore by the bones of Mohammed and by all the lamps that perpetually burned in his shrine, that anyone who disagreed with him would be executed as a traitor by being boiled alive in a cauldron of tar, which was precisely the fate he had in mind for *Laque Xemena* himself.

And in a frenzy of excitement, he departed from his anchoring place, heading under full sail and oar for the mouth of the river, amidst a deafening clamor of shouts and screams and all the racket they generally make under similar circumstances with their drums and bells and martial music. And when they came in sight of *Laque Xemena*'s fleet, they found him ready and waiting with large numbers of fresh reinforcements of fine soldiers who had recently come to his aid from Perak,[4] Bintang, Siak, and other nearby places. *Laque Xemena* came out to meet him in the middle of the river, and after the usual opening rounds of artillery, they went after each other at full speed; and since they were all spoiling for a fight, the battle that ensued was so fierce that for nearly an hour and a half no advantage could be discerned on either side until the moment when Heredim Mohammed, the Achinese commander, was killed by a fire bomb that hit him in the chest, severing him in two. And with his death, his men lost heart to such a degree that when they tried to withdraw to a point in the river called *Batoquirim,* intending to close ranks and take up a firm stand there until nightfall brought them respite, they were thwarted in their efforts by the swift river currents which scattered them in all directions.

And that was the way the Achinese tyrant's armada fell into the hands of *Laque Xemena,* with only fourteen ships managing to escape, while the other 166 were captured, and 13,500 men killed, not counting the 1,400 who had died in the trenches.

On their return to Achin, the fourteen ships reported to the king; and they say that he was so stricken by the news they brought him that he went into complete seclusion for twenty days. At the end of that time he issued orders to have the fourteen ship captains beheaded, while the rest of the men who had served under them were ordered to shave their beards, and on pain of being sawn to pieces alive, they were ordered henceforth to dress like women at all times, drawing attention to themselves in public, no matter where they went, by striking a tambourine; and in addition, when swearing by something, they were to use expressions like "May God bring my husband back to me," or "May the children I bore bring me joy." And when these men found themselves condemned to such shameful punishment, most of them fled into exile and many took their own lives, some by poison, others by hanging, and still others by the sword.

And that is the true story, exactly the way I told it, in all its details, of how the kingdom of Aaru was freed from the yoke of the Achinese tyrant. And it remained in the possession of the king of Jantana until the year 1564, when this same Achinese set sail with an armada of two hundred ships, spreading the word abroad that he was going against Patani; but instead, in a sneak attack one night, he fell upon Jantana where the king was then in residence. Caught off guard, the king, his wives and children, and many other people were all captured and taken to Achin, where he had them all, without exception, cruelly executed, and where he had the king's brains dashed out with a heavy club.

And once again the Achinese came into possession of the kingdom of Aaru, which he handed over to his oldest son, on whom he conferred the title of king, the same one that was killed later on when he went to lay siege to Malacca, during the captaincy of Dom Leonis Pereira,[5] son of the count of Feira, whose staunch defense of the fortress seemed more like the working of a miracle than anything wrought by natural means, for by that time the enemy had grown so powerful, and our men were so few in comparison to theirs, that one could say in all truth that there were two hundred Moors for every Christian there.

33
Rescue at Sea

And now to return to where I left off before. As I was saying, having fully recovered from the illness I contracted during my captivity in Siak, I was sent by Pero de Faria, who wanted to give me an opportunity to acquire something of my own, on a voyage to the kingdom of Pahang,[1] in an oared *lanchara,* laden with a cargo of his merchandise worth ten thousand *cruzados,* which I was to deliver to an agent of his residing there by the name of Tomé Lobo,[2] and from there, go on to Patani, another hundred leagues further, with a letter and a gift for the king, to negotiate for the release of some five Portuguese imprisoned by his brother-in-law, the *monteu* of Banchá,[3] in the kingdom of Siam.

With this in view, I departed from Malacca, and one night, on the seventh day of my voyage, not quite halfway through the morning watch,[4] when I had sailed as far as Pulo Tioman,[5] about ninety leagues from Malacca and ten or twelve from the bar of Pahang, we were startled by loud cries, which we heard twice, coming from somewhere at sea. Unable to see anything, for it was still quite dark, we were groping about in suspense, wondering what it could be. We reefed the sails and went yawing back in the direction the sound had come from, with all of us peering over the sides, straining to make out what it could be. We continued in this state of excitement for about an hour, when we noticed a shapeless mass of something dark and flat way off in the distance. Filled with uncertainty, for we still could not tell what it was, we conferred with each other again to decide what to do. And even though there were only four of us Portuguese on board the *lanchara,* a wide variety of suggestions were made, including one to the effect that I mind my own business and go on my way to where Pero de Faria had sent me instead of wasting time that way when I knew full well that the loss of even so much as an hour in that latitude could affect the entire outcome of the voyage, placing the cargo at risk, and leaving me to give a poor account of myself in the event of a disaster.

My answer to this was that under no circumstances would I abandon the search, and if it turned out, as they said, that I was wrong, then I would have to answer to Pero de Faria, to whom the *lanchara* and all its cargo belonged, and not to them, who had no more at stake than their lives, which were worth no more than mine.

And while we were arguing this way, it pleased God that the dawn came up, and in the early morning light we distinctly saw a group of shipwreck victims floating on some planks. Without any further ado, we sped off resolutely in their direction under sail and oar, and when we were close enough for them to see us they raised their voices, crying out loud, repeating the same words over and over, about six or seven times, "Lord God, have mercy on us!"

It was a pathetic sight, and we were all so badly shaken by it that we were almost beside ourselves, but we lost no time sending the *lanchara* rowers over the side and getting them all aboard. There were twenty-three of them altogether, counting fourteen Portuguese and nine slaves, and their features were so horribly distorted that we could not bear to look at them, and they were so exhausted they could hardly speak. But after we had gotten them all settled on board and done as much as we could for them, we asked them how their misfortune came to pass.

"Gentlemen," one of them spoke up, the tears streaming down his cheeks, "my name is Fernão Gil Porcalho. As you can see, one of my eyes is missing. I lost it in the trenches when the Achinese attacked Dom Estêvão da Gama the second time.[6] And because he wanted to compensate me for my services, especially when he saw how destitute I was at the time, he gave me permission to make a voyage to the Moluccas, where I wish to God I had never gone, since this was the outcome. After departing from the port of Talangame,[7] which is the roadstead serving our fortress at Ternate, in a junk loaded with a thousand *bahars* of clove, worth more than 100,000 *cruzados,* we navigated for twenty-three days under a fair wind, with all hands quite pleased by the way things were going, when suddenly, just as we were sailing on a course bearing northwest from the tip of Surabaya, off the island of Java, it was my misfortune, for the many times I have sinned against God, to be struck by a heavy gale out of the north, that tossed us about in a crossed sea of mountainous waves, splitting the junk open along the stempost and forcing us to jettison everything on the deck. All that night we ran under bare poles without daring to expose a single span of sail to the fierce gusts of wind that lashed at us repeatedly. We struggled on painfully until midway through the morning watch, when the junk suddenly sank to the bottom; and the 23 of us who are here now are the only ones who survived out of 147 people on board. And we have been drifting on those planks for fourteen days, with nothing to eat in all that time but the body of one of my black slaves who had died in the meantime, which sustained us for a week; but even though two of the Portuguese died last night, we refused to eat them, though our need was great, for we thought that death would surely come by morning and put an end to our suffering."

34
Tomé Lobo in Danger

We all listened with rapt attention to this man's story, thoroughly amazed by what we heard and by the deplorable state to which he and his companions had been reduced; and we could not help but marvel at the miraculous way in which our Lord in his mercy had seen fit to save them, and for that we all offered up many prayers of thanks; and we consoled our new guests, comforting them with words of Christian solace, such as we were capable of at the time, considering our limited powers of understanding. And we also shared our clothes with them, making up somewhat for what they lacked in that respect; and we made them lie down in our beds and plied them with remedies we thought most likely to induce rest, for it seems that, having gone so long without sleep, they were subject to dizzy spells and would suddenly collapse in a fit of trembling, from which it would take them a good hour to recover.

From here we headed for the bar of Pahang, arriving close to midnight, where we anchored at the mouth of the bar, opposite a small town called *Campalarau;* and at daylight we rowed up the river to the city, for what must have been a little more than a league, where we found Tomé Lobo who, as I said before, was residing there as agent for the captain of Malacca, and I delivered the cargo to him.

That same day, three of the fourteen shipwrecked Portuguese died, among them Fernão Gil Porcalho, the captain of the junk, as well as five of the Christian slaves. We buried them all at sea that night, weighing their bodies down with stones at the feet and neck to make them sink, because we had been refused permission to bury them ashore even though Tomé Lobo had offered them forty *cruzados* to let us do so. And the reason they gave for refusing was that the ground would be cursed and that nothing would ever grow again because the bodies had not been cleansed of the great quantities of pork consumed, and this, to their way of thinking, was the worst sin imaginable. As for the other survivors of the shipwreck, Tomé Lobo gave them shelter and provided them with everything they needed until they were well enough to depart for Malacca.

A few days later, when I was getting ready to leave for Patani, my next port of call, Tomé Lobo tried to stop me, insisting that I remain, because, as he claimed, he did not feel safe in that town. He explained that someone had told him that a certain *Tuão*[1] *Xerrafão,* a prominent local resident, had sworn to set his house afire and burn him alive with all the goods stored there because, as he was heard to say, an agent of the captain in Malacca had cheated him by sending him, in return for a five-thousand-*cruzado* shipment of benzoin, silk, and eaglewood, a lot of rotten dry goods, arbitrarily evaluated at far more than they were worth; and that as a result, out of the five thousand *cruzados* he had invested in his cargo—which was worth more than ten thousand in Malacca, to say nothing of the profit he could have made if he had received some decent merchandise, which in turn would have earned him almost as much—he had a profit of only seven hundred *cruzados* to show for it; and that twice already, they had tried to provoke him with feigned disturbances, just to make him come out and get himself killed; and that was why he thought it would be a good idea for me to stay, for in case something happened, as he feared, then I would be around to save the merchandise he had there, which would otherwise be lost if no one were there to look after it.

After giving him various excuses for not being able to stay, all of which he brushed aside, I finally ended up by asking him that if it was true, as he said, that they were trying to kill him, in order to steal the merchandise, how could I be sure that they would not kill me too? And if, as he assured me, he was firmly convinced that the information they had given him was true, then why did he allow the eleven Portuguese to leave, or why did he not go with them to Malacca?

"God only knows how much I regret it!" he exclaimed. "But since I failed to do so, then you must do as I say. And I insist upon it, in the name of the captain, to whom I shall write at once, giving him a full report of what I have gone through with you. And I do not think he will take very kindly to your leaving me here alone, with no one to help me look after his merchandise in which he has a thirty-thousand-*cruzado* investment—to say nothing of mine, which is worth almost as much!"

I found myself in a difficult situation, and I hesitated about which of the two extremes to choose, for I knew that if I stayed, as he insisted, I would be exposing myself to great danger. Finally, after thinking it over, I was forced, for my own good, to come to some sort of an understanding with him, and we agreed upon the following solution: I would give him two weeks in which to trade all the merchandise for gold and precious stones, both of which were in plentiful supply locally, and if at the end of that time he was not ready to board the *lanchara* with me for Patani, then I would be free to go on my way without him. He accepted this compromise, and from then on we remained on the best of terms.

35
Murder of the King of Pahang

Apparently frightened by the reports he had received, Tomé Lobo was in such a hurry to dispose of the merchandise that he offered it for sale at bargain prices, and in less than a week the dry goods that had been stored in the warehouses were cleared out; and since he was unwilling to accept either pepper or clove or any of the other spices that were too bulky, he traded them exclusively for gold from Menangkabou and for diamonds brought in by the *jurupangos* from *Laué* and *Tanjampura*,[1] as well as for pearls from Borneo and Solor.[2]

And when almost everything had been taken care of and we were getting ready to depart the next day, the devil contrived to set in motion a series of frightful events that began the night before we were supposed to leave. What happened was that a very wealthy man by the name of *Khoja* Geinal,[3] who had been residing at the court of Pahang for about three or four years as ambassador of the king of Borneo, murdered the king because he discovered him with his wife. This led to disorders among the people throughout the city, which bore no resemblance to anything human but seemed more like all of hell put together.

Then some vagrants and idlers, who are always on the lookout for a chance like this, seeing that the time and the occasion was most favorable for doing what they would not have dared to do before for fear of the king, banded together in a huge company of nearly five or six hundred, divided into three gangs, and descended upon the warehouse where Tomé Lobo lived. And despite all our efforts, there was little we could do to stop them from breaking into the buildings in about six or seven different places and killing eleven of our men, including the three Portuguese who had set out from Malacca with me. And Tomé Lobo escaped with six sword cuts, though one of them laid open the right side of his face clear down to the neck and nearly cost him his life. As a result, we were both forced to abandon the warehouse to them with all its merchandise and seek refuge on board the *lanchara,* on which, thanks be to God, we managed to escape, along with five of the slaves and eight sailors. However, there was no escape for the merchandise, which in gold and precious stones alone was worth over fifty thousand *cruzados.*

We spent some rather anxious moments aboard the *lanchara* that night, closely watching the general unrest that was spreading among the people and waiting to see what would develop. In the morning, when we saw that the situation was steadily growing worse, we decided that it would be better for us to proceed to Patani instead of running the risk of getting killed there, which is what happened to four thousand other people.

We departed immediately, and six days later we arrived in Patani, where we were welcomed by the Portuguese residents there, who were quite upset when they heard about what had happened to us in that miserable city. Determined to do something about it, and motivated solely by deep loyalty to their fellow Portuguese, they went down in a body to the king's palace and complained bitterly about the outrage perpetrated against the captain of Malacca, and asked for permission to indemnify themselves for the stolen goods, which the king readily granted.

"By all means!" he replied. "It is only fair that you should do unto others as they do unto you, and steal from others who steal from you—and especially from the captain of Malacca, to whom you are all so beholden."

The Portuguese all thanked him kindly for the favor granted and returned to their lodgings, where it was decided that they would help themselves to anything they found that was from the kingdom of Pahang, until the losses had been fully compensated.

Nine days later they heard about three richly laden China junks belonging to some Moorish merchants, natives of the kingdom of Pahang, that had been forced by bad weather to seek shelter in the Kelantan River[4] about eighteen leagues away. Plans were quickly made for the attack, and eighty out of the three hundred Portuguese residing there made ready to sail on two foists and a square-rigger that were fully equipped with everything they needed for the planned undertaking. And within three days they departed at top speed, out of fear that the local Moors might discover what they were up to and warn the other Moors they were going after to be on their guard.

In command of these three ships was a certain João Fernandes de Abreu, a native of the island of Madeira, and son of the lord high steward of King John's household, who was on board the square-rigger with forty soldiers; and the captains of the two foists were Lourenço de Gois and his cousin, Vasco Sarmento, both natives of the city of Braganza, all of them fearless men, experienced in naval warfare.

The following day our ships reached the Kelantan River and there they sighted the three junks they had heard about, riding at anchor. They fell upon them with great courage, and even though the men on board did all they could to defend themselves, in the end it was to no avail, for in less than an hour they were completely overcome, with a death toll of seventy-four on their side and only three on ours, though we had many wounded.

And since I think it is not necessary to mention in particular what one side or the other did, I will limit myself to the important details. With the defeated and captured junks in tow, our ships sailed out of the river, for by this time the alarm had spread through the entire countryside. Navigating under a fair wind, they arrived in Patani at vesper time on the following day and anchored in the port with a great deal of merry-making and a noisy salvo of artillery, much to the annoyance of the local Moors. And even though they were on good terms with us and passed for our friends, they still tried in every way possible, by bribing the local officials and the king's favorites, to make him punish us and expel us from the country for what we had done. But the king refused, insisting that under no circumstances would he do anything to mar the peaceful relations that his ancestors had always maintained with Malacca. Instead, he offered to act as mediator between us and the injured parties, and he solved the problem by asking us not to take any more from the three *necodás*[5]—the owners of the junks—than was taken in Pahang from the captain of Malacca, and to return the vessels to them freely, which João Fernandes de Abreu and the other Portuguese consented to, only to please the king, for it was obviously his wish. The king beamed happily and thanked them profusely for the good will they had shown.

And that is how Pero de Faria and Tomé Lobo recovered the fifty thousand *cruzados* they had lost; and from then on the Portuguese continued to reside in that country, honored and respected by all and deeply feared by the Moors. As for the three junks that were captured, there was a report, attributed to those on board at the time, that they had been carrying 200,000 *taels*[6] in silver alone—which comes to 300,000 *cruzados* in our money—to say nothing of all the other cargo that filled the holds to bursting.

36
Disaster in the Harbor of *Lugor*

I had been here in Patani for twenty-six days and had just finished expediting a small cargo of goods from China in preparation for my return, when a foist arrived from Malacca. Her captain was a certain Antonio de Faria e Sousa[1] who had been sent there by Pero de Faria to discuss some business with the king as well as to renew the peace treaty he had long maintained with Malacca, and to thank him for the good treatment the Portuguese were getting from him in his kingdom, plus a few other things of that sort designed to build up friendly relations that were of vital importance to our trade, which, frankly speaking, was our chief concern at the time. However, our real intentions were masked by a letter, delivered under the guise of an embassy, along with a costly gift, presented in the name of His Majesty the king and purchased at the expense of his treasury, as is the custom with all the captains in those parts of Asia.

This Antonio de Faria arrived with a cargo of Indian calicoes that were worth about ten or twelve thousand *cruzados,* which he had borrowed in Malacca; but since there was so little demand for them locally, not a single offer came his way. In desperate straits, with hardly any prospects in view, he decided to lay up for the winter and try his best, some way or other, to dispose of them. Some longtime residents in the area advised him to send the goods to *Lugor,*[2] a rich, heavily trafficked seaport in Siam, a hundred leagues to the north, that was always crowded with junks from the island of Java and from the ports of *Laué, Tanjampura,* Japara,[3] Demak,[4] Panaruca,[5] Sidayo,[6] Pasuruan,[7] Solor, and Borneo, because they usually paid well there, in gold and precious stones, for that kind of merchandise.

Acting promptly on this advice, which he found to his liking, Antonio de Faria made arrangements to send a local vessel up there because the foist he had come on was not suitable for that purpose, and as his agent he chose a Cristóvão Borralho, who was a good businessman. He was joined by a group of sixteen other men, both merchants and soldiers, who had goods to sell, all of whom went along expecting to turn over a profit of at least six or seven hundred percent, not only on what they were taking with them, but on what they would be returning with as well. And poor me, I happened to be one of them.

Departing from here on a Saturday morning, we navigated all the way along the coast under fair winds, and on the following Thursday morning, we arrived at the bar of *Lugor.* We dropped anchor at the mouth of the river and remained there for the rest of the day, making detailed inquiries that were important, not only for the sale of the merchandise, but for our own personal safety as well. And the news we heard was good, for we found out that the market was so favorable that we could easily expect to make a profit of almost 600 percent. As for the rest, ample security was provided for all, along with free port privileges and customs exemptions that were to remain in effect for the entire month of September, as decreed by the king of Siam for the period of the royal *zumbaias.*[8] But in order to appreciate what this is all about, some explanation is called for.

There is a great king who rules over the entire coastal region and interior of Malaysia. Of all his titles, the one by which he is best known is *Prechau Saleu,*[9] emperor of all the *Sornau,*[10] which is a province comprising thirteen separate kingdoms, otherwise known as Siam. Subject to him are fourteen lesser kings who are required to pay him tribute every year. According to ancient custom, they were forced to make an annual journey to the city of Ayuthia,[11] capital of the *Sornau* empire and kingdom of Siam, in order to deliver the required tribute personally and perform the *zumbaia,* a ceremony that consists of kissing the sword at his side. Since this city is fifty leagues inland and is accessible only by a rapidly flowing river, it was not unusual for these petty kings to be left stranded for the entire winter, entailing vast expenditures for them. As a result, the fourteen kings got together and petitioned the *prechau,* king of

Siam, to relieve them of such an onerous burden and to find a less costly method of paying the tribute. He responded with a decree to the effect that a viceroy, called *poyho*[12] in their language, should represent him in the city of *Lugor*, and that every three years the fourteen kings should pay homage to him in person, as they had done formerly to the emperor himself, and deliver to him in one lump sum the total tribute assessed for the three-year period. Moreover, during the month in which they came to pay homage, they were to be granted customs exemptions on all their goods, the same privilege being extended to all other merchants entering or leaving the harbor, whether native or foreign.

And since the duty-free regulations were in effect at the time we arrived, as I said before, the city was so crowded with merchants from everywhere that it was said that well over fifteen hundred richly laden vessels had entered the harbor with an enormous variety of cargo from many different places. That was the news we heard when we anchored in the mouth of the river, and we were all so happy and excited about it that we decided to enter the river as soon as the sea breeze shifted.

But it was our misfortune, sinners that we were, that what we had been looking forward to with such great anticipation, never came to pass, for shortly before ten o'clock, just as we were sitting down to dinner, with the hawser at short stay and everything made ready for us to sail when we had finished eating, we saw a huge junk coming out of the river with only her foresail and mizzen set. As she came alongside, she dropped anchor a little to windward of us, but once they had anchored, it did not take them long to notice that we were Portuguese, that there were very few of us, and that our ship was very small. They slackened their lines, letting the junk drift till it lay on our starboard, and as soon as it was even with our bow, they threw out a pair of grappling hooks attached to two very long iron chains, dragging us alongside; and since their ship was much larger than ours, we lay aboard, held fast beneath the curve of their prow, right below the hawse.

Then, about seventy or eighty Moors, including some Turks, came bursting out of the deckhouse where they had been hiding, screaming wildly and hurling stones, javelins, lances, and spears in such profusion that it looked like rain from heaven; and in less time than it takes to recite the Credo, twelve out of the sixteen Portuguese on board were dead, as well as thirty-six of the slaves and sailors. Four of us escaped by plunging into the sea, where one drowned immediately, but the three remaining survivors managed to reach the shore and take cover in the jungle, all battered and bruised, and sinking in mud up to our waists.

The Moors on the junk quickly boarded our ship and finished off six or seven of the boys they found lying wounded on deck, sparing none. Working rapidly, they transferred all the cargo they could find to their junk, then smashed a huge hole in the side of our ship, sending it to the bottom; next, they cut the grappling irons they had secured us with, clapped on all sail and quickly sped away out of fear of being discovered.

37
Lady of the Swamp

Finding ourselves wounded and destitute, the three of us who survived the disaster suddenly broke down and cried; and we began hitting ourselves like madmen, for we nearly went out of our minds at the thought of what we had witnessed less than half an hour before. We carried on that way for the rest of the day, and having noticed that the terrain all around us was swampy and teeming with lizards and snakes, we decided that we had better stay there for the night also, which we spent almost shoulder deep in the slime.

At daybreak the next morning we followed the river until we came to a small tributary which we were afraid to cross, not only because it was too deep but also because it was swarming with lizards. And so another night went by in agony, which continued unabated for five more days without our being able to make any progress either backwards or forwards, for no matter which way we turned we encountered nothing but swamp and tall grass. It was about this time that one of our companions died, a rich, honorable man by the name of Bastião Henriques, who had lost eight thousand *cruzados* on the *lanchara*. And the two remaining companions, Cristóvão Borralho and I, broke down and cried over his half-buried body, too exhausted to speak, yet fully determined to spend what we thought were our last few hours of life right there, without moving from the edge of the river.

The following day, the seventh since our misfortune, just before sundown we saw a barge laden with salt, coming up the river by oar. As it came alongside, we asked the rowers on bended knee to please take us on board. They stopped and stared for a moment, amazed by the sight of us there on our knees with upraised arms, as though we were praying. Without a word they made as if to move off, throwing us into a panic. We both started shouting, and with the tears streaming down our cheeks we pleaded with them again not to leave us there to die. Upon hearing our cries, a woman came out from under the awning. She was somewhat advanced in years and appeared to be as kindly and noble a person as indeed she later turned out to be. She was moved to pity by our plight the moment she saw us there displaying our wounds. Acting in compassion, she reached for a pole and brought the barge nearer to shore, cracking it three or four times over the backs of the sailors for refusing to help; after which, six of them jumped ashore and carried us aboard on their shoulders. Appalled by our condition and the extent of our wounds, with our shirts and trousers all muddied and bloodied, this noble woman saw to it that we were promptly washed with many buckets of water, and that each of us received one of her sarongs to cover ourselves with in the meantime; and then she made us sit down beside her while she sent for food, which she herself placed in front of us.

"Come now, eat, eat up, you poor strangers," she urged us, "and do not despair at finding yourselves in such a sad state. Look at me. Here I am, a woman, barely fifty years of age, and less than six years ago I found myself suddenly taken captive, robbed of a personal fortune worth over 100,000 *cruzados*, and stricken by the death of three sons; and I saw my husband, who was dearer to me than life itself, and my whole family—father and sons, two brothers, and son-in-law—all torn to pieces in front of my eyes by the trunks of the elephants of the king of Siam. Though sick at heart and weary of life, I endured all these misfortunes and many others almost as bad when, in the same manner, I saw three virgin daughters, my mother and father, and thirty-two members of my family—nephews, nieces, and cousins—thrown alive into flaming ovens, uttering screams to pierce the very gates of heaven, calling on God to avail them in that hour of unbearable pain and torment. But I had committed too many sins for their cries to be heard in the court of His infinite mercy, and the Lord of Lords turned a deaf ear to what I thought were their just pleas; but the truth is that whatsoever God ordains is the best for us and we must accept it."

We responded to this by telling her that it was because we too had sinned that God had permitted this calamity to befall us.

"In the face of adversity," she said, mingling her tears with ours, "when we feel the hand of the Lord, it is always best to acknowledge the reason for it and to confess to the truth of it with our own mouths; but you must believe it sincerely, deep down in your heart, with a pure and steadfast faith; for therein often lies the reward for our suffering."

And after speaking in this manner for a while, she asked us how our misfortune had come about and what had occurred to bring us to such a sorry pass. We told her everything that had happened but that we did not know who had done it to us or why. Hearing this, some of the men in her crew volunteered the information that the huge junk we were talking about belonged to a Gujerati Moor by the name of *Khoja* Hassim, who had sailed out of the river that morning, bound for Hainan[1] with a cargo of brazilwood.[2]

"Well, strike me dead, if that isn't so!" this dignified woman exclaimed, beating her breast in amazement, "because that same Moor has been heard boasting in public to all who would listen that he had slain quite a number of those men from Malacca on several different occasions, and that he hated them with such a passion that he had vowed to his Mohammed that he would yet kill as many more."

Astounded by such unheard-of news we asked her to tell us more about this man and why he went around telling everyone that he hated us so. As for the reason why, she said that all she knew was that she had once heard him say that a great captain of ours by the name of Heitor da Silveira[3] had killed his father and two of his brothers on a *nao* he had captured in the Straits of Mecca, that was bound from Jidda to Dabul. And for the rest of the journey she continued talking about that Moor, going into great detail about the deep hatred he had for us and the terrible things he said about us.

38
Antonio de Faria Swears Vengeance

Departing from where she had found us, this honorable woman proceeded up the river under sail and oar for about two leagues, stopping overnight at a little village; and early the next morning she departed for the city of *Lugor,* five leagues further, arriving close to midday. After landing, she went straight to her house where she took us and kept us for twenty-three days, nursing us back to health and providing for all our needs with the utmost generosity.

This woman was a member of a distinguished family, as we learned later, and the widow of the *shahbandar* of *Prevedim* who, in 1538, in the city of *Banchá,*[1] had been slain by the *pate*[2] of *Lasapará,* king of *Quaijuão,* on the island of Java; and at the time she rescued us in the manner described, she was returning from a junk she owned that was anchored outside the bar, laden with salt; and since it was too heavy a vessel to cross the sandbank, she had been unloading it little by little onto the river barge.

And at the end of the twenty-three days I referred to, when, with God's help, we had recovered completely and were well enough to travel, she recommended us to a kinsman of hers, a merchant bound for Patani, about eighty-five leagues from there, who took us aboard the oar-propelled *calaluz* that he himself was traveling on, and seven days later we reached Patani, after navigating along a wide, freshwater river called *Sumèhitão.* And since Antonio de Faria was searching the horizon, watching and waiting for us or for some word of his merchandise, as soon as he saw us and heard what had happened he was so upset that it was more than half an hour before he could speak.

By this time our lodgings could not hold all the Portuguese who came crowding in, most of whom had invested their money on the ill-fated *lanchara* that had been carrying a cargo worth more than sixty thousand *cruzados* in her hold, the bulk of it in the form of minted silver to be traded for gold. And when some well-meaning people there tried to console him for the loss of the twelve thousand *cruzados* he had borrowed in Malacca, Antonio de Faria, who had been left destitute, replied quite candidly that he did not dare to face his creditors in Malacca for fear that they would force him to honor the notes he had signed, which he was in no position to do at the time, and that it made more sense to him to go after the ones who had stolen his money than be in default with the ones who had lent it to him. And right then and there, in front of everyone, he swore on the holy Gospels, and said that, apart from the oath he was taking, he was also promising God that he would immediately go in search of the thief who had stolen his property and make him pay dearly one way or another, by fair means or foul, though he felt that fair play alone was too good for someone like that who had murdered sixteen of his Portuguese soldiers as well as thirty-six of the Christian slaves and sailors, and that it would not be right to let him off so easily without some kind of punishment, for otherwise, with each passing day we would see another atrocity of the same sort, and then another, and so on, until a hundred had been committed.

All the bystanders praised him highly for the stand he had taken, and a lot of young men, and good soldiers too, offered him their services, and still others offered to lend him money to buy arms and whatever else he needed. He immediately accepted all the offers made by his friends and went about making preparations as fast as he could; and within eighteen days he had enlisted a company of fifty-five soldiers.

As for poor me, I was forced to join him too, because I had not a farthing to my name, nor anyone who would so much as give me or lend me one; besides, I owed more than five hundred *cruzados* to some friends in Malacca, which together with five hundred of my own had been carried off—for my sins—by that dog, in one fell swoop, with the rest of the stolen booty mentioned above; and out of it all, the only thing I was able to save was my skin, and even that was in not too good a shape after having received three spear wounds and the blow of a stone to the head, which had left me hovering between life and death three or four times; and even here in Patani I still had to have a bone removed before I recovered completely. As for my companion Cristóvão Borralho, he was in far worse condition than I from an equal number of wounds he had received in return for the twenty-five hundred *cruzados* that were stolen from him along with the rest.

39
In Search of *Khoja* Hassim

As soon as he had completed his preparations, Antonio de Faria departed from Patani on a Saturday, May 9, in the year 1540, setting his course north-northwest for the kingdom of Champa,[1] with the intention of exploring the ports and inlets along the coast and, while he was at it, looking around for some decent plunder to make up for a few of the shortages that still existed on board; for he had been in such a hurry to leave Patani that he was not well outfitted enough to get by without replenishing a lot of stores, mainly in the way of provisions, munitions, and gunpowder.

Keeping to our course for seven days, we came in sight of an island called Pulo Condore[2] at eight and one-third degrees north latitude that lay almost northwest by southeast with the bar of Cambodia; and after rounding it completely we discovered a good anchorage called *Bralapisão* on the eastern side, a little over six leagues from the mainland. And there we found a Ryukyu Island junk that was bound for Siam with an ambassador on board from the *nautaquim*[3] of *Lindau,* prince of the island of Tosa,[4] which lies at latitude thirty-six degrees, who immediately got under way when he saw us. Antonio de Faria sent his Chinese pilot to deliver a very courteous message to him, with an offer of friendship, to which they replied that the time would come when they would communicate with us in the friendship and spirit of the true faith of the God of infinite mercy who died so that all men might live forever in the dwelling place of the good people, as they believed it was meant to be past the middle of the middle of time. And with this reply came a gift of a rich, ornamental sword, its scabbard and hilt all made of gold, in addition to twenty-six pearls in a jewel box, also made of gold, fashioned in the shape of a little saltcellar. Antonio de Faria sorely regretted his inability to reciprocate properly, for by the time the Chinese pilot returned with this message, they had been swallowed up in the distance more than a league away.

We went ashore on this island and stayed there for three days, taking on fresh water and fishing for endless quantities of sea bream and croakers that swam abundantly in the area, and afterwards, we headed for the coast of the mainland in search of a river called *Pulo Cambim*[5] which divides the domain of Cambodia from the kingdom of Champa at latitude nine degrees, arriving on a Sunday, the last day of May.[6] The pilot moved on to anchor three leagues up the river, opposite a large town called

Catimparu,[7] where, after some friendly arrangements had been made, we stayed for twelve days, peacefully going about the business of outfitting ourselves with abundant supplies of everything necessary.

And since Antonio de Faria was by nature a very curious fellow, he made every effort to find out from the local residents what sort of people lived in the interior of that country and where the headwaters of that large river were located. He was told that the river had its source in a lake called *Pinator,*[8] 260 leagues east of the sea in the kingdom of *Quitirvão;*[9] and that the lake was ringed by huge mountains at the foot of which, all around the shore, were nestled thirty-eight towns, only thirteen of them large and the others quite small, but that there was a gold mine in only one of the larger towns called *Xincaléu,*[10] which was so big that, according to the people who lived there, it produced one and a half *bahars* of gold daily, which in our money comes to twenty-two million in gold per year. This mine was owned by four men who were so greedy that they were constantly fighting among themselves, with each one trying to gain exclusive control of the mine; and one of these men by the name of *Raja Hitau* had jars buried neck deep in the courtyard of his house, containing six hundred *bahars* of gold dust, of the same quality as that which comes from Menangkabow on the island of Sumatra; and that if three hundred men of our nation with a hundred muskets were to attack, there was no doubt whatsoever that they would easily gain control of it; and that also, in another one of those towns called *Buaquirim,* there was a quarry from which they extracted huge quantities of rough diamonds, from old rock, that were worth much more than the ones found in *Laué* and *Tanjampura,* on the island of Java.[11]

And in reply to a lot of other questions about certain things he was particularly interested in, Antonio de Faria was told many other things about the wealth and fertility of the country further inland up the river that were extremely tempting and, from the way it sounded, just as easy and inexpensive to conquer.

40
Pirates off the Coast of Champa

After we departed from the *Pulo Cambim* River we navigated along the coast of the kingdom of Champa until we came to a bay called *Saleyjacau,* seventeen leagues to the north, which we entered, but since we did not see anything there we could lay our hands on, we just sailed around it until shortly before sunset and left, without having done any more than observe and count the number of settlements located along the shore. There were six altogether, five of them hardly more than villages, though the sixth one looked like a good-sized town of over a thousand hearths, surrounded by a huge forest with many freshwater streams that descended from the mountains towering above it on the south like a protective wall; but we made no attempt to climb them for fear of alarming the countryside.

The following morning we reached a river called *Tobasoy,* where Antonio de Faria dropped anchor outside the mouth because the pilot was afraid to enter since, as he pointed out, he had never been there before and did not know how deep it was. And while we were there, still arguing about whether or not to enter the river, we sighted a large sailing vessel coming in from the high seas and heading straight for the port. Excited at the prospect of welcoming her with everything necessary, in a manner befitting our calling and lofty intentions, we waited for her, without moving from the spot.

As she came alongside, we hoisted our merchant flag in what they call the *charachina* [1] salute, making all the appropriate signs and signals of friendship, in keeping with local custom. However, instead of acknowledging our salute in like manner, as was only proper, the people on board the *nao*—who had apparently recognized us as Portuguese for whom they had no great love—answered by showing us, from the top of the deckhouse, the naked behind of a kaffir, which was hardly a courteous reply. On top of that, they set up a terrible racket, banging drums, tooting horns, clanging bells, shouting, and jeering in what was a general demonstration of scorn and contempt, obviously intended for us.

Deeply offended by such a response, Antonio de Faria ordered a broadside fired from a culverin, to teach them better manners. They answered with five cannonballs, three of them discharged from a falcon, and two from a heavy camel, placing him and everyone else in quite an embarrassing position. A meeting was called to decide what to do, and it was agreed that we should remain anchored where we were for the time being instead of rushing headlong into something we were not sure of, and that in the morning we would try to learn more about those people and how well armed they were; and depending on what we found out about them, we would decide what to do next—which sounded like excellent advice to Antonio de Faria as well as all the others. After taking all the necessary precautions and posting a careful lookout, we stayed right where we were, to wait until morning.

At two hours past midnight we noticed three black objects floating on the water close to the horizon. We immediately called the captain, who happened to be on the quarterdeck at the time, sleeping on top of a hen coop, and we pointed it out to him. He looked, made up his mind in a flash, and began shouting three or four times—"To arms! To arms!" And he did not have to wait long to see his order obeyed. At the time, we were still in doubt about what those objects could be, but gradually, as we watched, we were able to distinguish three rowboats coming towards us. The men all armed themselves quickly, and the captain posted them at the most critical stations. Since it was obvious from the stealthiness of the oars that these were our enemies of the previous day—for there was certainly nothing to fear from the local people—he addressed the soldiers this way:

"Men! My brothers!" he began. "What we are up against is nothing but a thief who is out to attack us because he thinks that there cannot be more than six or seven of us here, which is how we usually sail on these *lorchas.* [2] Now, in the name of Christ, if we are to accomplish something worthwhile, at no risk to ourselves, I want you all to lie low and keep out of sight, so that they can't see anyone on board from out there, and then we will find out what they are up to or what they want with us. Also, see to it that the powder pots are kept on the ready, because I think that with them and a few well-placed sword thrusts we can resolve the whole matter. But keep your wicks covered and don't let them see any fire on board, and that way they will think that everyone is asleep."

His instructions were carried out to the letter with extreme caution and perfect teamwork all around.

When they were within slightly more than a crossbow-shot distance from our *lorcha,* the three boats rowed all around us, examining the ship from stem to stern; and after they had looked us over carefully, they met again, apparently to consult with each other, and parted after more or less a quarter of an hour, heading in opposite directions, with the two smaller boats moving to our stern while the sampan, the larger one, which was carrying the main body of their forces, made straight for our starboard. Then altogether, from different directions, the enemy quickly climbed aboard, and in less time than it takes to recite the Credo, there were more than forty of them swarming all over the *lorcha.*

With a cry of "*Santiago*[3]—and at 'em!" Antonio de Faria dashed out of the deckhouse where he had been hiding with about forty of his men, rushing at them so forcefully and fearlessly that in no time at all nearly all of them lay dead. They followed up with many powder pans, which were quickly tossed at the occupants of the three boats below, finishing them off and spilling them into the sea. Carried away with enthusiasm, some of our soldiers jumped down into the boats, capturing all three of them; and as a result, thanks be to God, everything fell safely into our hands.

We managed to pull out of the water five of the enemy who had jumped overboard but were still alive and kicking, one of them the kaffir who had showed us his behind. We also came up with a Turk, two Achinese, and the captain of the junk himself, a man by the name of Similau, who was a notorious pirate and a declared enemy of the Portuguese. Antonio de Faria immediately had them put to the torture to make them tell who they were, where they came from, or what they wanted of us. We could not get any reasonable answers out of the Achinese or the Turk, so he turned to the kaffir, who was already tied up by that time, but just as we were about to hoist him on the rack,[4] he began crying and bellowing that we should not hurt him, that he was as Christian as anyone of us, and that he would tell us anything we wanted to know without benefit of torture.

Antonio de Faria then ordered him released and sat him down beside him. He offered him a piece of biscuit and even a swig of wine; and in a gentle tone of voice he asked him, since he claimed to be a Christian, to tell him the whole truth.

"If I'm not telling your lordship the truth," he exclaimed, "then don't take me for what I said I was! My name, sir, is Bastião. I used to be Gaspar de Melo's slave until two years ago when that dog you have tied up over there killed him, in Ning-po,[5] along with the twenty-six other Portuguese he had on board his *nao.*"

"Enough! Stop right there!" Antonio de Faria cried out in amazement. "I don't want to hear any more! You mean to say that that one over there is the dog of a Similau who killed your master?"

"Yes, sir!" he replied. "And he was trying to do the same to your lordship. He couldn't wait to embark because he did not think he would find more than six or seven of you here. And he said he intended to take you all alive and have your brains squeezed out with a crossbar,[6] like he did to my master. But it is God's will that he should pay for his sins."

Antonio de Faria listened closely to everything the kaffir boy had to say, and when he repeatedly assured him that that dog had brought all his soldiers with him, leaving only forty Chinese sailors behind on the junk, he decided that it was too good an opportunity to miss.

After disposing of Similau and his cohorts, by having their brains squeezed out with a crossbar—which is what he had done to Gaspar de Melo and the other Portuguese in Ning-po—Antonio de Faria set out immediately in the longboat and the *manchuas,*[7] the boats the enemies had arrived in, taking thirty soldiers along; and in less than an hour, with the wind and the tide in his favor, he reached the spot where the junk was anchored, just a league up the river from us.

In a sneak attack, without making the slightest sound, he promptly took command of the afterdeck. From there, with the aid of only four powder pots tossed on to the main deck where the crew was asleep, he sent them all jumping into the water, where ten or twelve of them drowned; and since the rest were yelling for help, Antonio de Faria had them fished out because he needed them to man the junk, which happened to be an extremely large and majestic vessel.

And that is how it happened, exactly the way I described it, that the good Lord, in the supreme wisdom of his divine justice, ordained that this dog's arrogance should be the instrument of the punishment he deserved for his evil deeds, by leading him directly into the hands of the Portuguese, who made him pay for what he had done to them.

By the time it was over it was almost morning. When an inventory of the plunder was made, thirty-six thousand *taels* in Japanese silver were found; and in our money, calculated at the rate of six testons[8] per *tael,* that comes to fifty-four thousand *cruzados,* to say nothing of a large assortment of other fine-quality merchandise which we did not have time to appraise, for by then the alarm had spread and fire rafts[9] were being prepared, making it necessary for Antonio de Faria to clap on all sail and get under way as fast as he could.

41
Exploring Champa

It was a Wednesday morning, on the eve of Corpus Christi,[1] in the year 1540, when Antonio de Faria sailed out of the *Tobasoy* River. And he made his way along the coast of the kingdom of Champa to avoid the risk of being blown off course by the violent easterly winds that prevail in that latitude most of the year, especially during the conjunctions of the new and full moon. And the following Friday he reached the river that the natives call *Tinacoreu,* though the Portuguese know it as the Varela.[2] And he thought it would be a good idea to enter the river, as some of the men advised him to do, to pick up some information about a few things he wanted to know and, at the same time, see if there was any news about the *Khoja* Hassim he was looking for, since that river was the usual stopping place on the China run for all the junks from Siam and the entire coast of Malaya; and sometimes, they would even trade their merchandise very profitably there for gold, calambac wood, and ivory, which are in plentiful supply throughout the whole kingdom.

As we anchored inside the bar opposite a little village by the name of *Taiquileu,* a fleet of refreshment prows came rowing out to meet us, but when they realized that we were a new race of people that had never been seen there before, they became quite frightened and began talking excitedly among themselves in this vein: "How strange that they should come here! This must be a visitation from God. Let us hope that the good Lord did not send us that notorious race of bearded men who enrich themselves by spying out the land, acting like merchants, but returning later to attack and plunder like thieves. Let us head for the jungle before they set fire to our houses and fields with the sparks from those firebrands dangling from their mouths, turning into white ash as they puff on them. That is what usually happens when those people set foot on foreign soil."

"God forbid!" still others exclaimed. "But since, for our sins, they are already on our doorstep, don't let them know that we fear them as enemies, otherwise they will show their true colors sooner. Let us speak softly and ask them in a friendly manner what they are doing here, and once we have learned the truth from them we will write to the *Hoyá*[3] *Paquir* who is now in *Congrau.*"

Pretending not to understand a word of what they were saying, though there were many interpreters on board, Antonio de Faria welcomed them pleasantly and put them in a receptive mood by paying what they asked for their refreshments without permitting any haggling over prices. And when they asked him where he was from, or what he was doing there, he told them that he had come from the kingdom of Siam where he lived, in the foreign quarter of Tenasserim, and that he was a merchant on his way to the Ryukyu Islands, where he intended to sell his cargo, and that the only reason he had entered their river was to look for a friend of his, a merchant by the name of *Khoja* Hassim who was headed in the same direction, and that he just wanted to find out if his friend had passed this way before him, and if not, then he would be on his way because he was afraid of losing the monsoon, apart from the fact that he could see that this was no place for him to sell his merchandise.

"You are quite right in that respect," they replied, "because there is nothing to be had in this town but fishnets and fishing prows, which barely provide us with a living. But if you continue on your way up the river you will reach the city of *Pilaucacém,* which is where the king resides; and there, we can assure you, in less than five days you will be able to sell ten times as much as your junk can hold, no matter how expensive the merchandise is, because you will come across some very important merchants who come there to trade in elephant, ox, and camel caravans, from all over the land of the Laotians, *Pafuás,* and *Gueos,*[4] where the people are very wealthy."

Seeing his chance, now that he had set them at ease, Antonio de Faria began interrogating them in great detail, and a few of them, who seemed to be better informed than the rest, answered his questions in a way that suited him perfectly.

"The river you are anchored in now," they said, "is called the *Tinacoreu,* though there were some in ancient days who called it the *Taraulachim,* meaning 'land of plenty,' which was a very appropriate name for it, from what the old folks still have to say about it. This river, the way you see it here, in the same depth and width, extends as far as *Moncalor,* which is a mountain range about eighty leagues from here; but from there on the river widens and becomes more shallow, and in some parts, it spreads out into low-lying marshes where there are an enormous number of birds covering the entire area; and owing to the presence of so many birds, the whole kingdom of the *Chintaleuhos,* which took eight days to cross, was abandoned by the population forty-two years ago. Once you pass the bird swamps, you enter an entirely different region that is much more forbidding, with large mountain ranges, inhabited by many other animals far worse than the birds, such as elephants, yak,[5] lions, boar, buffalo, and other wild herds of cattle roaming around in such huge numbers, that it is impossible for a man to grow anything there to feed himself, and there is nothing that can be done about it. And in the middle of this country or kingdom, which is what it was formerly, there is a big lake the natives call *Cunebeté,* though others call it the Chiang Mai.[6] That lake empties into this river and three other rivers besides, that provide water for a great part of the land. The writers who have described it state that the lake measures sixty *jaus*[7] in circumference, with three leagues to a *jau,* and that all around it there are many mines of silver, copper, tin, and lead, which are in constant production and yield huge quantities of these metals which are then carried by merchants in elephant and yak caravans to the kingdoms of the *Sornau,* or Siam, *Passiloco,*[8] *Savady,*[9] Toungoo,[10] Prome,[11] *Calaminhan,*[12] and other provinces in the interior beyond this coast, that take two to three months to cross and are divided into seigniories and kingdoms, some inhabited by white people, some by light-brown people, and still others by men of a darker complexion; and they return laden with a lot of gold, diamonds, and rubies, which they receive in exchange for their goods."

When asked if these people possess any sort of arms, they said no, just charred wooden spears and krisses with blades two handspans long. They also said that it would take from two to two and a half months to get there by voyaging along that river, and that the reason it took so long was because the waters descended with tremendous force during the greater part of the year, but that the return voyage took only eight to ten days.

And apart from these questions, Antonio de Faria plied them with many more, and from their answers he learned many other interesting things about that country that are worthy of the attention of some high-minded individual capable of acting on them, for then perhaps we would derive far greater benefits from them, at less cost in blood and all that goes with it, than we do from all of India on which to this day we have expended so much of our energy and resources.

42
Night Raid off Hainan Island

The following Wednesday we left the Varela River, otherwise known as the *Tinaçoreu,*[1] and from there the pilot thought it best to head for Pulo Champeiló,[2] which is an uninhabited island at the entrance to the Gulf of Cochinchina[3] at latitude fourteen degrees and a third to the north. On our arrival, we anchored in a sheltered cove, and after three days there, which we spent getting things ready and putting the ordnance in condition for what we had in mind, we departed for the island of Hainan, where Antonio de Faria thought he might find the *Khoja* Hassim he was looking for.

After sighting the *Pulo Capás* hill, which is the first landmark at the tip of the island, he came in close enough to shore to be able to survey the rivers and harbors and see what their entrances were like, which is all he wanted to do that day. And at nightfall, with the approval of all the soldiers, before making any other move, he ordered them to transfer to the better of the two ships, since the *lorcha* in which he had set out from Patani was taking on too much water; and this was done without any further ado.

And after reaching a river we had seen towards the east at sundown, he issued orders to drop anchor about a league out to sea, because the big junk he was on drew a lot of water and he was afraid of the many shoals we had seen all day long. And he ordered Cristóvão Borralho and his fourteen soldiers to take the *lorcha* up the river to find out what those fires were that we saw up ahead; and he departed without a moment's delay.

When he had gone more than a league upstream, he came upon a fleet of forty huge, imposing junks, each of which had two to three crow's nests aloft; and fearing that they might be part of the mandarin's armada, about which we had heard some vague reports, he anchored a little to shoreward of them; and towards midnight, when the tide was beginning to come in, he weighed anchor very quietly and moved on further up the river to where he had seen the fires, most of which had been extinguished by this time, though two or three still appeared at intervals, guiding him along the way. As he continued up the river this way, he ran into an enormous number of ships both large and small, which some of the men estimated roughly at over two thousand sails. He made his way among them, cutting the water silently with the oars, until he came to the city, which turned out to be a good-sized town of over thirty thousand inhabitants, surrounded by a brick wall with towers and ramparts built into them, just like ours, with a barbican, and two moats running all around. Here, a party of five out of the fourteen soldiers on the *lorcha* went ashore, taking with them two Chinese sailors whose women had been left behind on the junk as hostages. They looked the whole town over from the outside and spent almost three hours there without their presence being detected, then they reembarked and departed under sail and oar without making the slightest sound or commotion, out of fear that, if they were to cause any disturbance there, none of them would escape alive. As they were coming out of the river, they saw what appeared to them to be a junk from the opposite coast that had anchored at the bar a short time before.

When they got back to Antonio de Faria they informed him about everything they had seen, from the huge fleet up the river to the junk they had found at the bar, which, as they repeated several times, probably belonged to that dog of a *Khoja* Hassim they were looking for. This news filled him with such excitement that he could not wait to get started, and without a moment's delay he weighed anchor and set sail, telling us all the while that he had a premonition about it, and that he was so sure that he had found him that he was willing to stake his life on it, and that if he turned out to be right, he could say without any hesitation that it would be well worth it to lay down his life for a chance to avenge himself on someone who had done him so much harm; and he swore, by the word of a decent man, that he was not saying so because of his twelve thousand *cruzados,* which he had forgotten all about, but because of the fourteen Portuguese who had been killed by that dog.

As he came within sight of the junk, he ordered the *lorcha* around to the other side so that both of them could attack her simultaneously, while at the same time cautioning them not to fire a single shot, so that the junks anchored up the river would not be attracted by the sound of the artillery and come running to see what was going on. No sooner did our ships reach the spot where the junk was anchored than she was firmly grappled and boarded by twenty soldiers who promptly took command of the vessel without encountering any resistance from her company, most of whom had jumped overboard. Once they had recovered from their surprise, some of the braver souls among the enemy tried to fight back; however, Antonio de Faria threw himself into the fray with twenty more soldiers, and rushing at them with a battle cry of *Santiago,* he cut down more than thirty of them. As for those who were still alive after jumping overboard, he had them picked up because he needed them to man the vessel.

And since he was interested in knowing who they were and where they were from, he ordered about four of them put to the torture; but two of them obstinately preferred to die rather than tell us anything. Then they laid hold of a young boy, and just as they were about to do the same thing to him, an old man lying there, who was his father, protested loudly, crying out that they should listen to him first before they did the boy any harm. Antonio de Faria commanded the torturers to stop what they were doing and told him to go ahead and say whatever he wanted to, but that he had better speak the truth, for if he caught him in a lie, he could rest assured that both he and his son would be thrown alive into the sea, and that if he told the truth, he would release both of them and put them ashore along with all their goods, provided they swore under oath that it was theirs.

"Sir, I accept that promise," the Moor replied, "and I will take your word for it, even though the occupation you are presently engaged in is not much in keeping with the Christian faith you professed at your baptism."

Antonio de Faria was so taken back by these words that he did not know what to say. Instead, he had the man brought closer to him and interrogated him in a kind, gentle manner, without threatening him any further.

43
The Armenian's Story

When the man reached his side Antonio de Faria could see that he was as white as the rest of us, and he asked him if he was a Turk or a Parsee.[1] He answered no, but that he was a Christian and a native of Mount Sinai, where the body of the blessed Saint Catherine was buried.[2] To this Antonio de Faria responded, since he was a Christian, as he said, why was he not traveling with Christians? To which he replied that he was a merchant, of good family, by the name of Thomas Mostangue, and that one day, in the year 1538, while he was on board one of his *naos* anchored in the port of Jidda, the viceroy of Cairo, Suleiman Pasha, had commandeered his *nao* and seven others as supply ships for the sixty-galley fleet he arrived in, with orders from the Grand Turk to restore Sultan Bahadur to his throne in the kingdom of Cambay from which he had then been ousted by the Moghul, and at the same time, throw the Portuguese out of India. And when he got there, traveling on the same *nao* in order to make some repairs and collect the freight payments promised him, the Turks, on top of having lied to him about everything, as they usually do, laid hold of his wife and a small daughter traveling with him and dishonored them publicly before his eyes; and because one of his sons protested in tears against this outrage, they bound him hand and foot and threw him alive into the sea. He himself was put in chains and subjected to daily floggings; and they confiscated his cargo, which was worth more than six thousand *cruzados,* with the explanation that it was unlawful for anyone but just and saintly Mussulmen like them to enjoy the blessings of God. His wife and daughter having died in the meantime, one night, in desperation, he and that young son of his threw themselves into the sea, off the bar of Diu, from where they made their way overland to Surat.[3] From there, he sailed to Malacca on a *nao* belonging to Garcia de Sá,[4] the captain of Bassein;[5] and from Malacca, he was sent by Dom Estêvão da Gama[6] on a voyage to China with Cristóvão Sardinha,[7] a former crown steward in the Moluccas, who was killed one night, while they were anchored off Singapore, by *Quiay Taijão,* the owner of that junk, along with twenty-six other Portuguese; and due to the fact that he was an expert artilleryman, they had spared his life and taken him along as their chief gunner.

At this point, Antonio de Faria let out a yell, hitting his head in amazement.

"Good God!" he exclaimed. "Good God! I can't believe my ears!"

And turning to the soldiers who were standing there, he told them the whole life story of *Quiay Taijão,* affirming that he had on several occasions killed over a hundred Portuguese on ships that he had found lost at sea and undermanned, robbing them altogether of well over 100,000 *cruzados;* and that even though his real name was *Quiay Taijão,* as the Armenian had said, ever since he had killed Cristóvão Sardinha in Singapore he had been going under the alias of "Captain Sardinha," as a way of boasting about what he had done. Anxious to know where he was or where he could find him, he asked the Armenian, who said that he was hiding, badly wounded, in the rope locker of the forward section of the junk, along with six or seven others.

Antonio de Faria immediately jumped up and hurried over to that dog's hiding place with the rest of the soldiers behind him. As he lifted the scuttle to see if what the Armenian had said was true, the dog and his six henchmen made their way out through another hatchway a little further down; and running amuck, they threw themselves against our soldiers, despite the fact that there were more than thirty of us, to say nothing of our forty slaves. And once again the fighting broke out with such fury, that before our men had a chance to finish them off—which took them a little longer than it would normally take to recite the Credo three times—they had killed two Portuguese and seven slaves, and wounded more than twenty, including Captain Antonio de Faria himself, who emerged in very bad condition with two sword cuts to the head and one on the arm.

Once they had done with this havoc, they attended to all the wounded; and since it must have been close to ten o'clock by then, the order was given to set sail for fear of being discovered by the forty-junk armada up the river. After putting plenty of distance between us and the shore, we dropped anchor shortly before nightfall on the opposite coast of Cochinchina, where we began to take inventory of what this thief had been carrying on his junk. We found five hundred *bahars* of pepper, weighing fifty quintals per *bahar,* as well as sixty of sandalwood, forty of nutmeg and mace, eighty of tin, thirty of ivory, twelve of beeswax, and five *bahars* of fine-quality eaglewood, all of which, estimated at the local market value, was probably worth as much as sixty thousand *cruzados,* to say nothing of the artillery we found—a camel, four falcons, and thirteen bronze culverins—mostly of Portuguese make, which had been stolen by that Moor from Cristóvão Sardinha's *nao,* João de Oliveira's junk, and Bartolomeu de Mato's ship. Three leather-bound chests were also found, containing a large assortment of Portuguese bedding and clothes, a gilded silver washbasin with matching jug and saltcellar, twenty-two spoons, three candlesticks, five gilded goblets, fifty-eight muskets, and sixty-two scores of Bengalese garments, all of which had belonged to the Portuguese, as well as eighteen quintals of gunpowder, and nine little children between the ages of six and eight, who were all shackled at the arms and legs, lying there in such dreadful condition that it was pitiful to see, for there was nothing left of them but skin and bones.

44
The Pearl Fishers of Quemoy

The following day Antonio de Faria departed from where he had been anchored and headed back to Hainan. He tacked along the coast all day and night in twenty-five to thirty fathoms until dawn, when he came out in the middle of a large bay where there were a number of barges engaged in fishing for seed pearls.[1]

Unable to make up his mind about where to proceed from there, he spent the whole morning seeking advice and listening to many different opinions on the matter. Some thought it would be a good idea to seize the barges that were fishing there for seed pearl while others said no, that it would be better to trade with them, for that way we would be able to get rid of most of the cargo in exchange for the many pearls they had there. Finally, after the various points of view had been presented, the meeting ended with the decision to follow the safest and wisest course of action, and he ordered the flag of commerce hoisted aloft, in keeping with Chinese custom.

At the sign of the flag two *lanteias*[2]—which are similar to the foist—came out from shore, laden with all sorts of refreshments. After the usual greetings, their occupants climbed aboard the junk that Antonio de Faria was on, but when they noticed that we were a different kind of people that had never been seen there before, they became quite frightened and asked us who we were and what we were doing there. The answer they got was that we were merchants, natives of the kingdom of Siam, and that we had come there to trade with them, if they were willing. An elderly man, who appeared to have more of an air of authority about him than the others answered yes, but that we were in the wrong place, and that we would have to proceed to another port further up called *Guamboy* where the official trading station for foreigners was located; and that we would have to transact our business there in the same way as it was done in Canton, *Chincheo,*[3] *Lamau,*[4] *Comhay,*[5] *Sumbor,*[6] Ning-po, and the other coastal cities where foreign navigators were allowed to disembark; and that, speaking as chief administrative officer for the others, they advised Antonio de Faria to depart at once, because he was in a restricted area that had been set aside as a pearl fishery for the benefit of the treasury of the House of the Son of Heaven; and that by order of the *tutão*[7] of *Comhay*, who was the military governor over all of Cochinchina,[8] the area had been placed off limits to all except the fishing barges assigned to work there; and that, in compliance with the law, any unauthorized vessel found there would immediately be set afire with the entire ship's company aboard; but since he was a foreigner who was unfamiliar with the local laws and customs, they were letting him know that he had better leave right away before the mandarin of the fleet returned; and that he was expected back in three or four days from a place called *Buhaquirim*, about seven leagues from there, where he had gone to load provisions.

And when Antonio de Faria asked him what kind of ships the mandarin had in his fleet and what sort of complement they carried, he told him that he had forty big junks and twenty-five oar-propelled *vancões*[9] with a total of seven thousand men on board, or five thousand fighting marines and two thousand sailors. And when he was asked how long the mandarin remained in the area, he said that he stayed for the entire fishing season which lasted for six months, from early March to the end of August. And continuing with his questions, Antonio de Faria asked how much they paid in royalties for their fishing rights, and how much was the annual revenue collected in those six months. He answered that they paid by handing over two-thirds of the pearls weighing five carats or more, one-half of the lesser-quality pearls, and one-third of the seed pearls. As for the annual revenue, he could not say for certain because the catch varied from year to year, but he thought that on the average it yielded about 400,000 *taels*.

Hoping to get more detailed information out of them, Antonio de Faria went out of his way to be hospitable, and he gave the old man a few gifts—two cakes of wax, a sack of pepper, and an ivory tusk—which pleased him immensely and left them all in an expansive mood. Resuming his questions, he asked how big was this island of Hainan about which he had heard so many wonderful things.

"First tell us who you are," they replied, "and why you have come here, and then we will answer your questions. To tell the truth, we have never in all our lives seen as many well-mannered and elegantly dressed young men on board a merchant ship as those that you have here. One would think that Chinese silks are so cheap in your country that they are worth practically nothing; either that, or they have been obtained at prices far below their value, for judging by what we see going on here, as a simple pastime, your men stake a bolt of damask on a throw of three dice with the sort of indifference one shows toward something that was acquired at little cost."

Antonio de Faria smiled a bit wryly at the inference that his men were gambling with stolen goods, but he explained it away by saying that such behavior was only to be expected from the sons of rich merchants who were too young to appreciate the value of things.

"Certainly," they replied, trying not to show that they had already surmised the truth, "it may well be as you say."

Antonio de Faria then made a sign to his men to put away the dice and hide the silks they were wagering with, so that those men would not realize that we were thieves, and they immediately obeyed. And since he was anxious to dispel the doubts of the Chinese, who still suspected that we were a bad lot, he ordered the hatches opened on the junk we had captured the night before from "Captain Sardinha," so that they could see that the hold was crammed full of pepper, which cleared the air a bit and made them somewhat less suspicious.

"Now that we know that they are genuine merchants," they said to each other, "we can feel free to answer their questions. After all, we do not want them to think that we refused out of ignorance, or that all we can talk about is fishing and diving for oysters."

45
Gathering Information in Hainan

The merchant tried to satisfy Antonio de Faria's curiosity to some extent by answering his questions in the following manner:

"Now that I know who you are, sir," he began, "and that your questions come from a pure heart, I will tell you what I have learned from listening to former governors of this *anchacilado*[1] at various times. They say that this island was once a sovereign, independent nation, ruled by a very rich king who styled himself the *Prechau*[2] *Gamu*—a title higher and nobler than any used by the reigning kings of his day. When he died without leaving an heir, fighting broke out over a successor to the throne, which soon escalated into a full-scale civil war and led to so much bloodshed that, according to the chronicles dealing with the events of the period, a total of sixteen *lacasás*[3] of men—a *lacasá* being equal to 100,000—perished by the sword in only four and a half years. The decline in the population left the island in such a vulnerable position that it was easy for the Cochinese king to conquer it with only the seven thousand troops sent to him by the Tartar king from the city of *Tuymicão,* then the capital of his empire. Once Hainan was completely subdued, the Cochinese monarch returned to his kingdom, leaving one of his captains behind as governor of this island, a man by the name of *Hoyha*[4] *Paguarol* who, for some very valid reasons of his own, rebelled against him and sought the protection of the king of China for an annual tribute of 400,000 *taels*—or 600,000 *cruzados* in foreign currency—which in turn obligated the Chinese king to defend him against his enemies whenever necessary. During the thirteen years that this pact was in effect, the Cochinese king was defeated on the battlefield five times. And when *Hoyha Paguarol* died without a son to succeed him, in gratitude for the protection he had received in his lifetime from the king of China, he named him in his last will and testament as his legitimate heir and successor to the throne; and ever since then, for two hundred and thirty-five years, this island of Hainan has been under the scepter of the great Chinese king. As for the rest of your questions regarding the treasures, revenues, and people of this island, I only know what I have heard from some of the ancients who once ruled this *anchacilado* of Hainan in their official capacity as *tutões* and *chaens,*[5] and who claimed that the gross national income, including the silver mines and the duties collected at all the seaports, came to two and a half million *taels*."

Antonio de Faria and the other Portuguese there gasped in amazement at the enormity of the figure mentioned by the merchant.

"If you are all so impressed by that meager sum," he went on, "what would you do if you ever saw the city of Peking, where the Son of Heaven resides permanently with his court, whose treasury receives the combined revenue of the thirty-two king-doms of the monarchy which they say, in gold and silver alone that he gets from its eighty-six mines, amounts to more than fifteen thousand piculs?"[6]

After thanking him for having answered his questions so much to the point, Antonio de Faria asked him to recommend a place for him to sell his cargo where he would feel safe and find the best people to deal with, since he no longer had the mon-soon to take him to Ning-po.

"Let me give you a word of friendly advice," he replied. "Do not enter any of the ports on this island of Hainan, and do not trust any of the Chinese you find here, for I can assure you that none of them, regardless of what they say, will tell you the truth. You can trust me because I happen to be a wealthy man who has nothing to gain by lying to you. I would advise you to sail into this bay until you come to a large river called *Tanauquir*, but make sure you sound the depths as you go because of the many dangerous shoals in the area. The anchorage is good in that river and you will be per-fectly at ease and safe there; and in two days you will be able to sell all your cargo and even twice as much, if you had it to sell. However, I would not advise you to unload your goods ashore because the mere sight of wealth is capable of arousing greed in the breast of even a decent, law-abiding citizen, let alone an unruly person with no con-science who is inclined by nature to take what does not belong to him, rather than share what he has with the poor and needy, for the love of God."

And so saying, he and his party took their leave of the captain and the Por-tuguese with an effusive stream of polite and flowery words, with which, as a general rule, they are by no means frugal. And in return for the gift he had received, he gave Antonio de Faria a tortoise-shell jewel box, about the size of a little saltcellar, filled to the brim with grains of seed pearl as well as twelve good-sized pearls, while at the same time asking him to excuse him for not trading with him there, for they were afraid they would be killed if they did, in conformity with the strict law of the land; and he urged him to leave right away, because if the mandarin of the fleet were to find him there on his return he would surely burn his ships.

Antonio de Faria had no desire to ignore this man's advice since he feared that what he had told him might well be true, and he immediately set sail, passing over to the southern side of the opposite coast where, within two days, under westerly winds, he reached the *Tanauquir* River and anchored in front of a little village called *Neytor*.

46
Encounter with a Chinese Pirate

We anchored for the night outside the mouth of the *Tanauquir* River intending, first thing in the morning, to go up to the city five leagues from there to see if somehow or other we could sell the cargo, for we were so heavily laden that hardly a day went by without our scraping the reefs two or three times, and in some areas, where the ridges extended for four or five leagues, the sand was so close to the surface that we did not dare sail except in broad daylight, and even then, we were constantly heaving the lead. As a result, it was agreed not to undertake anything until we had gotten rid of the merchandise we were carrying, and naturally, Antonio de Faria had only one thing in mind—to get to a port where he could sell it.

The good Lord having shown us the way to a port where this could be done, we spent practically the entire night tugging and straining to enter the mouth of the river; but the currents were so strong that even with all sail unfurled we were driven back to leeward of the port. And while we were concentrating all our efforts on this, with the main deck so cluttered up with hawsers and cables that there was hardly enough room to turn around, two huge junks came out of the river. They were armed with movable fighting platforms from stem to stern, with silk awnings fluttering over the maintops, and the hulls protected all around with wooden shields painted in red and black, all of which combined gave them a very warlike appearance. And as they came, they chained themselves together to double the impact and bore down upon us so fast that we never even had a chance to prepare for them and were forced to scoop up the halyards and cables and throw them overboard in order to get at the guns, which was all that mattered at the time.

As the junks neared us, letting out screams and making a tremendous racket with drums and bells, we noticed that the first of the three broadsides they greeted us with came from a battery of twenty-six guns that included nine falcons and camels. This was a sure sign that we were dealing with people from the opposite coast of Malaya, and it came as a bit of a surprise to us. However, the moment he saw the two of them linked together, Antonio de Faria, like the shrewd man that he was, knew immediately what they were up to and headed out to sea, pretending to be fleeing from them, not only to gain time, but also to make them think they were dealing with people other than our sort. But they too were old hands at the game, and since they had no intention of letting their prey escape, they disconnected the chains that bound them, the better to chase us. Catching up, they grappled us immediately and sent so many lances flying through the air that it looked as if nothing could withstand them.

Taking up a position under the quarterdeck castle with the twenty-five soldiers he had on his junk as well as ten or twelve slaves and sailors, Antonio de Faria played along with them, responding with arquebus fire for nearly half an hour until he had made them use up all their ammunition, which they had plenty of, judging by what lay strewn all over the deck.

Determined to see it through to the end, forty of their apparently bravest men boarded our junk, bent on gaining control of the bow, which forced our captain to come out to receive them. They rushed at each other enthusiastically, engaging in such heated combat that in little more time than it takes to recite the Credo three times, the good Lord saw fit to leave twenty-six out of the forty stretched out on the deck and to send the rest diving over the side.

Taking advantage of this favorable turn of events presented by the hand of God, twenty of our men jumped into the enemy ship where they met with hardly any resistance, since their best men had already been slain. And after they had cut down everyone they could find, killing them right and left, the crew finally surrendered, but their lives had to be spared because we did not have enough seamen to handle so many ships.

Once this was out of the way, Antonio de Faria sped as fast as he could to Cristóvão Borralho's ship, which had been grappled by the other junk and was in a very precarious position because most of our men had been wounded; but with his aid—thanks be to God—the enemy jumped into the water, where most of them drowned, leaving both their junks in our hands.

Counting up our casualties, we found that this victory had cost us the lives of one Portuguese, five slaves, and nine sailors, to say nothing of the wounded; as for the toll in enemy ranks, there were eighty dead and almost as many taken captive.

After tending to our wounded and making them as comfortable as we could, Antonio de Faria issued orders to pick up the sailors who had jumped overboard, most of whom were floundering about shouting for help and yelling that they were drowning; and once they had been brought on board the big junk that Antonio de Faria was on he had them all put in chains. Interrogating them in an effort to find out who owned the junks, what their captain's name was, and whether he was still alive, not a single one of them would respond properly, and while they were stubbornly allowing themselves to die, unmindful of the torture we applied, we heard Cristóvão Borralho shouting from the other junk.

"My lord! My lord! Come quick!" he cried. "There's more work to be done here than we thought!"

Antonio de Faria leapt aboard the junk with fifteen or sixteen soldiers and asked him what was wrong.

"I hear a lot of voices coming from the bow," he replied. "There must be some more people hiding there."

Hurrying forward with all his men at his heels, he ordered the hatches thrown open and heard coming from below a loud cry of "Lord God, have mercy!" It was accompanied by such frightful moaning and wailing that it seemed unreal, as though a spell of enchantment had been cast over all. Thoroughly amazed by it, he and some of our men peered into the opening and saw a large number of people in chains, lying in the hold. And still unable to grasp the meaning of what he was seeing with his own eyes, the captain ordered someone down to take a closer look. At his bidding, two of the slaves jumped down and brought up a group of seventeen Christians—two Portuguese men, five children, and ten slaves, two of them female—whose condition was such that it was a most pitiful sight to see. They were promptly relieved of their shackles—collars, handcuffs, and very heavy iron chains—and provided with all the necessities, for most of them were stark naked, with not a stitch of clothing to cover their bodies.

After this had been taken care of, one of the two Portuguese—since the other was half-dead—was questioned about the children, whom they belonged to, and how they happened to fall into the hands of that thief, and what was his name. He replied that the thief had two names, one Christian and the other pagan, and that his pagan name, by which he was known at the time, was *Necodá Xicaulém,* and that his Christian name was Francisco de Sá; and that five years before he had converted to Christianity in Malacca, during the captaincy of Garcia de Sá, who acted as godfather at his baptism and gave him that name and married him off to a young half-breed orphan, an extremely genteel woman and the daughter of a very honorable Portuguese, in order to make him feel more like a member of the community; and that in the year 1534, while on a voyage to China on a huge junk he owned, with his wife and twenty of the wealthiest and most honorable Portuguese of Malacca on board, he stopped at the island of Pulo Catão[1] to take on fresh water, intending to proceed from there to the port of *Chincheo;* but on the second day of his stopover, the entire crew, which had been hired by him and, like him, were all Chinese, rose up one night while the Portuguese were asleep, killing them and their slaves with those little hatchets they carry, refusing to show mercy to anyone who called himself a Christian; and he tried to persuade his wife to become a pagan and to worship an idol that his *tucão*,[2] the ship's master, kept in a chest, and that once she had renounced the Christian faith he would marry her off to the *tucão*, who in turn was willing to give him one of his sisters, also a pagan Chinese, who was traveling with him; and because the wife refused to worship the idol or to consent to the rest of his plans, that dog dashed her brains out with a hatchet; and that after embarking from there he had proceeded to the port of Ning-po, where he traded that year; and since he was afraid to show himself in Patani on account of the Portuguese who lived there, he laid over for the winter in Siam; and the following year he returned to the port of *Chincheo*, where he seized a small junk inbound from Sunda with ten Portuguese on board, killing them all; and since by that time the news of the evils he had perpetrated against us had spread all over the country and he was afraid that he might run into some of our forces, he had gone to this Gulf of Cochinchina, where he had been living as both a merchant and a pirate, trading when he could and freebooting when he dared; and that it was now three years since he had turned this river into his private hunting grounds, mainly because he thought he would be safe from us here, knowing that we did not ordinarily trade in the gulf ports or the island of Hainan.

And when Antonio de Faria asked him if the children belonged to the Portuguese he had referred to, he said no, that they belonged to Nuno Preto, Gião Dias, and Pero Borges,[3] who also owned the slaves, and that he had killed them too, in *Mompollacota*, off the bar of the river of Siam, on a junk belonging to João de Oliveira,[4] along with sixteen other Portuguese who were on board; and that he had spared both their lives only because he was a carpenter and the other a caulker; and that he had been taking them with him for nearly four years now, killing them slowly by starving and flogging them; and that at the time he attacked us he had no idea that we were Portuguese, mistaking us for Chinese merchants like the ones he usually robbed whenever he could catch them unawares as he had expected to catch us.

And when he was asked if he would be able identify the thief among the dead, he said yes. Antonio de Faria immediately stood up, took him by the arm, helping him over to the other junk which had rammed him, but after he had looked at all the corpses strewn about the deck, he said he was not there. Ordering the *manchuas* made ready, Antonio de Faria went personally to look for him among the bodies floating in the water, where he found him, with a deep gash in the head and a sword wound right through his heart. After he had carried him on to the deck of the junk he asked the man again to identify him, and this time he did, without any hesitation. And Antonio de Faria believed it because he was wearing a thick gold chain around his neck, with a two-headed idol fashioned in the shape of a lizard, also made of gold, with an enamel coating on the tail and paws of green and black. And he had his body dragged over to the bow, where it was beheaded and cut to pieces.

47
The Unlucky Bride

Once the victory had been achieved as described, the wounded attended to, and the prisoners placed under guard, an inventory was taken of the cargo found on both junks; and it showed that the prize captured was worth perhaps a little over forty thousand *taels,* which was then placed in the custody of Antonio Borges,[1] who was the factor in charge of the booty; and this inventory did not include the value of the bare hulls of the two junks, for even though they were brand new we were forced to scuttle one of them because there were only enough hands for one. Also, seventeen bronze artillery pieces were found—four falcons, one camel, and twelve culverins—most of them, or practically all, stamped with the royal coat of arms, which that dog had stolen from the three ships on which he had killed the forty-six Portuguese.

The following morning Antonio de Faria wanted to go back to the river mouth but was advised against it by some fishermen captured during the night, who told him that under no circumstances should he venture into the city, where they had already heard the news of what he had done to that thief with whom the *chileu,*[2] commanding officer and governor of the province, had formed a partnership and was getting a third of all the prizes he took; and that as a result, things were in such a state of turmoil there that even if he tried to give the merchandise away for nothing, much less sell it for money, they would not take it; and that two huge rafts, piled high with firewood and barrels of tar and pitch, had already been placed at the entrance to the harbor, ready to be launched against him the moment he appeared, to say nothing of the more than two hundred oar-propelled prows with large companies of archers and fighting men stationed on board that were lying in wait for him. After hearing that report, António de Faria bowed to the counsel of those who knew better and agreed to sail to another port called *Mutipinão,* about forty leagues further east, where many wealthy merchants, both native and foreign, came by caravan, heavily laden with silver, from the land of the Laotians, the *Pafuás,* and the *Gueos.*

Departing with the three junks and the *lorcha* on which we had started out from Patani, we sailed along the coast under a head wind, going from one board to the other until we came in sight of a hill called *Tilaumera,* where we dropped anchor, owing to contrary currents.

We had been riding here at anchor for thirteen days, growing frustrated with the gale winds blowing dead on end, and beginning to run low on provisions, when sometime in the afternoon we were lucky enough to meet up with four oar-propelled *lanteias,* which are similar to the foist. They were escorting a bride to a village called *Panduré,* nine leagues from there, and since they were all in a festive mood, they were belaboring the drums, gongs, and bells and making such a racket that it was impossible to be heard above the noise of their merriment. Since our men had no idea of what it was all about, the first thing that occurred to them was that they were spies sent by the armada of the captain of *Tanauquir* to look for us, and Antonio de Faria quickly slackened the lines and prepared himself for whatever might happen. And with the ships gaily bedecked and other signs of festivity on board, he stood by and waited for the *lanteias* to come alongside. As soon as they saw us standing there all together, responding to their gaiety in the same way, they headed straight towards us as merry as could be, mistaking us for the bridegroom's party which was supposed to meet them there; and after we had exchanged salutes in the *charachina* way, as is the custom among these people, they bore off and dropped anchor near the shore.

Since we, for our part, had no way of knowing the reason for their unusual behavior, we all agreed with the captain that they were spies from the armada we had left behind, which would catch up with us before long; and we spent what little remained of the day and nearly two hours past nightfall, watching and waiting in suspense until finally the bride, who was on board one of the *lanteias,* distressed by the groom's failure to send someone to pay his respects, as was only fitting, decided to make the first move and show him, apparently, how much she loved him, by sending an uncle of hers on one of the four *lanteias* to deliver a letter to him that went like this:

"If it were proper for me, a mere woman, to come and gaze upon thy countenance without sullying my reputation, believe me, I would fly, swift as the hungry falcon newly freed from its bonds, to kiss thy lingering feet. But now, my lord, since I have journeyed all the way from my father's house to meet thee here, it is up to thee to leave thy vessel and come to mine, where I await thee, but a shadowy substance that cannot come into being without seeing thee; for if thou shouldst fail to come now, in the dark of night, who can say if, in the light of day, thou willst still find me amongst the living. My uncle, *Licorpinau,* will reveal to thee the secrets locked deep in my heart, for not only am I beyond the power of speech, but I can no longer bear to be so mercilessly deprived of the pleasure of seeing thee. Therefore, I implore thee to come unto me or else give me leave to come unto thee. For the sake of the love I have always borne thee, do not deny me this favor, so that God in his justice may not chastise thee for such ingratitude and cut thee off from the estate that thou hast inherited from thy forebears at the very moment when I am on the threshold of womanhood and about to take the marriage vows that will make thee my lord and master until death alone do us part—from which I pray God will spare thee for as many thousands of years to come as the number of times the sun and the moon have spun around the earth since the world began."

When the *lanteia* that was carrying the bride's uncle with this letter came alongside, Antonio de Faria ordered all the Portuguese to keep out of sight, allowing no one but the Chinese sailors to remain on deck, so as not to arouse their suspicions. Having reached the junk, just as sure of themselves as could be, three of the occupants of the *lanteia* climbed aboard and asked for the bridegroom, and in reply our men grabbed them and threw them down the hatch as they came, one by one. And since they were all, or nearly all of them, quite drunk, even the ones who were still on board the *lanteia* were not aware of what was happening despite the noise we were making; nor were they in any condition to react fast enough to get clear of the rope that was dropped on their masthead from the top of the poop castle, dragging them alongside in such a way as to make it impossible for them to ever disentangle themselves. And after we had tossed a few fire pots at them from above—which sent them all flying overboard—six or seven soldiers and an equal number of sailors jumped down and took possession of the *lanteia,* which they had to use later to pick up the poor hapless creatures who were flailing about in the water, yelling that they were drowning.

Once they had been rescued and placed under guard, Antonio de Faria went after the other three *lanteias* that were anchored about a little more than a quarter of a league away. The first one he reached was the one the bride was on, and he grappled it without encountering the slightest resistance since there were no soldiers on board, just the sailors at the oars, and about six or seven respectable-looking men, judging from the way they were dressed, relatives of the poor bride who had been escorting her, as well as two young boys, her brothers, who were both very fair and handsome; and the rest were elderly women musicians whose services are usually hired for such occasions, in keeping with Chinese custom.

Realizing that there was trouble afoot, the other two *lanteias* cut their lines and sped off under full sail and oar as though the devil himself were after them; but even so, that did not prevent us from capturing one of them, and thus we obtained possession of three out of the four. This done, we returned to our ships.

Since it was almost midnight by then, all we did was transfer the booty to the junk and put the captives below deck, where they stayed until morning. And when he saw what a sad lot they were, mainly old women who were of no use to us, Antonio de Faria had them all put ashore, except for the bride and her two brothers, since they were fair and handsome young lads, as well as twenty seamen who were very useful for manning the junks which were still somewhat shorthanded.

Sometime later we learned that the bride was the daughter of the *anchaci*[3] of *Colem*—an official somewhat like our magistrate—and that she was betrothed to a young man who was a son of the *chi-fu*,[4] or captain, of *Panduré*, who, they say, had written her that he would meet her there in that place with three or four junks belonging to his father, who was a very wealthy man, and that is why they were deceived by us.

The following afternoon, when we had already departed from the place we called the "bride's rendezvous," the groom came looking for her in a fleet of five gaily bedecked ships, saluting us happily as he passed with a burst of music and other signs of rejoicing, without having the vaguest idea of his misfortune or the fact that we were carrying his bride off. And in that manner, covered with bunting and many silk awnings, he turned the bend of the *Tilaumera* River where we had been the day before, and anchored there to wait for his bride, as he had written he would.

From here we proceeded on our course, and three days later, with God's help, we reached the port of *Mutipinão*, which was where we were heading because Antonio de Faria had heard that he would be able to sell the cargo there.

48
No Word of the Lord

Having reached this port we dropped anchor in the middle of a bay formed by a stretch of land jutting out towards a little island just south of the entrance to the bar, where we remained quietly, without saluting the port or making any noise, having decided, as soon as it was dark, to sound the river and gather the information we were looking for. At moonrise, which must have been shortly before eleven, Antonio de Faria sent out one of his *lanteias* with a well-armed party of twelve soldiers under the command of Valentim Martins de Alpoim, a clever, capable fellow, who had already given a good account of himself on previous missions of this sort. As soon as he started out he began taking river soundings, and he kept on heaving the lead until he reached the city anchorage, where he captured two men he found sleeping on a barge laden with earthenware. Returning aboard without incident, he gave Antonio de Faria a complete report of his findings, from the large size of the town to the small number of ships in port. Based on this information, he thought it would be perfectly safe for him to enter the harbor, for even if something unforeseen occurred that would prevent him from trading there as he wished, no one would be able to stop him from leaving whenever he felt like, since the river was wide and clear all the way and free of the danger of reefs and shoals.

At a meeting called to decide what to do next, the majority agreed that the two Moors taken captive should not be interrogated under torture as originally planned, not only to avoid scandalizing them, but because there was no need for it. And at daybreak, when everyone had recited the Litany with deep devotion, accompanied by vows of fine, rich offerings for the adornment of the Church of Our Lady of the Mount in Malacca,[1] Antonio de Faria took it upon himself to interrogate the two Moors. He began gently, calming their fears as he questioned them carefully about what he was especially interested in finding out. Both of them replied in one voice that, as far as entering the river was concerned, there was nothing to fear, because it was the safest in the entire gulf, and that much larger ships than his frequently entered and departed, for even in the shallowest areas it measured fifteen to twenty fathoms deep; and as for conditions on shore, there was nothing to worry about because the local inhabitants were fainthearted by nature and did not possess arms; and as for the foreigners there, most of them were merchants who had arrived nine days before from the kingdom of *Benão* in two caravans of five hundred oxen each, laden with large quantities of silver, eaglewood, silk, linen dry goods, ivory, wax, lac, benzoin, camphor, and gold dust of the same quality found on the island of Sumatra; and that they had all come to trade their goods for pepper, spices, and pearls from the island of Hainan. And when they were asked if there were any armadas along the coast they said no, because most of the military campaigns carried out by or against the *prechau*, emperor of the Cochinese, were fought on land, and that when they did fight on the rivers, they used small oared craft, not ships as large as his, because there was not enough draft for them. And when asked if their *prechau* was in the area, they said that he was only a twelve-days' journey from there, in the city of *Quangepaarù*,[2] where he resided most of the time with his household and court, governing his kingdom from there in peace and justice. And when asked how much treasure and revenue he had, they replied that the metal mines reserved for the crown yielded a good fifteen thousand piculs of silver, half of which, by divine law of the Lord of all Creation, belonged to the poor who cultivated the soil for the sustenance of their families; but that those rights had been voluntarily surrendered by the consent of all, in exchange for an agreement exempting them thereafter from the payment of tribute or any other form of oppressive taxation, an agreement which the former *prechaus,* in national assemblies that were convoked, had sworn to uphold for as long as the sun sheds light on earth.

When he felt that they were in the proper frame of mind, Antonio de Faria asked them about some other things of interest to him, such as their knowledge of what they saw with their own eyes by night in the heavens, and by day in the clarity of the sun, about which he had heard so much. To this they replied that the highest truth of all, which they adhered to and believed in above all others, was that there was an all-powerful, universal God who created and preserved all things; and that, if at times, our human understanding becomes clouded and confused by our selfish desires, it was not the fault of the Creator, in whom there could be no imperfection, but rather the fault of the sinner, who, for lack of forbearance, judged all things according to his own inclinations. And when asked if there was anything in their law that taught that God had once come down to earth in human shape and form, they said no, because they could not conceive of anything that could force him to such an extreme, for by the very perfection of his divine nature, he was free of our human miseries and very far indeed from coveting the treasures of this earth, since all things were reduced to naught in the presence of his divine splendor.

And in this way, by means of the above questions and a few others put to them by Antonio de Faria, we realized that, to this day, these people had never heard about our true faith, and that all they did was acknowledge with words what they saw with their eyes in the canopy of the sky and the beauty of the day, by continually raising their arms heavenward as they make their *zumbaias,* repeating these words: "By thy deeds, O Lord, we acknowledge thy grandeur!"

Following this, António de Faria had them put ashore, sending them freely on their way with a few gifts which made them very happy.

About this time the sea breeze was beginning to blow and he set sail in a festive mood, the maintops covered with silk awnings, and the flag of commerce hoisted in *charachina* style so that anyone seeing him that way would take him for a merchant and not for anything else. And an hour later he anchored in front of the city quays, saluting the port with very little noise of artillery. In response, ten or twelve canoes laden with refreshments came out from shore, and even though they were surprised by the sight of us and could tell from our features and clothes that we were neither Siamese, nor Javanese, nor Malaysians, nor people of any other nation that they had seen before, they greeted us with these words: "May tomorrow dawn upon us all as bright and promising as the afternoon which has been graced by your presence here!"

Yet out of all the canoes there, only one ventured to come alongside and request permission to board. In reply they were told to feel free to do so, that there was nothing to fear since we were all brothers; but even so, only three of the dugout's nine occupants boarded the junk. Antonio de Faria welcomed them graciously, and after seating them comfortably on a carpet, he told them that he was a merchant from the kingdom of Siam, and that on his way to the island of Hainan where he had been planning to trade, someone had told him that prices and conditions here in this city were better than elsewhere, because the merchants and people in this area were more trustworthy than the Chinese living along the coasts of the gulf and the island of Hainan.

"You are absolutely right," they replied, "and if you are a merchant, as you appear to be, then you may rest assured that you will be treated honorably here in every respect, and you can sleep soundly, for there is nothing to fear."

49
Problems Unloading the Cargo

Out of fear that some message or word of what he had done to the thief in the *Tanauquir* River might arrive overland and that it might harm him in some way, Antonio de Faria refused to unload the cargo ashore as the customs officials requested of him, and twice the whole business was completely undone as a result of the problems and difficulties that arose. And when he realized that soft words were not enough to bring them around to his way of thinking, he sent a merchant who was usually available as a go-between to deliver a message to them explaining that he appreciated the fact that they were within their rights in asking him to put the cargo ashore, as was customary, but he pointed out that he was not in a position to do so since they were now at the tail end of the monsoon and it was urgent that he leave right away in order to repair his big junk, which was taking on so much water that seventy seamen had to be kept busy at the three pumps night and day and he was in imminent danger of sinking to the bottom right there, cargo and all; and that as far as the king's duties were concerned, he would be very happy to pay them; however, not at thirty percent as they demanded, but at ten, which was what they paid in other countries and which he would be willing to pay immediately; but instead of replying they arrested the man who brought them the message.

When the messenger failed to return, Antonio de Faria set sail with the ships gaily bedecked, acting as if it mattered little to him whether or not he sold the cargo. Seeing him leave the port—for which they blamed the obstinacy of the *nautarel*[1]— and along with him the merchandise with which they had hoped to conclude their business, the foreigners who had come there by caravan got together and demanded of the *nautarel* that he recall him, threatening otherwise to denounce him to the king for the injustice he was doing them by driving out of the port the merchandise that they had hoped to buy. Afraid of being punished and turned out of office, the *nautarel* and the other *capisondos*[2] of the customs house gave in to their demands, but on the condition that they pay five percent more—since we were only willing to pay ten—in order to cover the king's half of the duties, which was perfectly agreeable to them.

Releasing the merchant who had been detained, they sent him to deliver a very courteous letter explaining the terms of the agreement that had been reached. Antonio de Faria replied that under no circumstances would he return to the port, for at the end of the monsoon he could not afford so many comings and goings, but that if they were willing to come and buy the entire cargo, all at the same time, bringing enough silver with them to pay for it on the spot, he would sell it to them; otherwise, he did not want anything more to do with them because he was deeply offended by the *nautarel*'s lack of respect in ignoring his messages; and that if this arrangement was satisfactory to them, they should let him know within the hour, for that was all the time he would give them, and if not, he would proceed on his way to Hainan, where he could sell his goods on far better terms than here.

Faced with this ultimatum, which they believed to be final, they accepted it, for they were afraid of losing this opportunity to wind up their affairs and go home; and they set out immediately, in five big barges laden with chests full of silver and a large supply of gunny sacks for loading the pepper. When they reached the junk that was flying the admiral's flag, they received a warm welcome from Antonio de Faria, who listened as they repeated the story of what had happened in the city with the *nautarel,* complaining bitterly about his evil nature and some of the things he had done to them which they considered unfair; however, as long as they had managed to appease him with fifteen percent, of which they were willing to pay five, they asked him to pay the ten percent he had promised, otherwise, they would not be able to buy his merchandise. Antonio de Faria replied that he would gladly do so, but mainly out of consideration for them and not because it was to his liking, for which they thanked him, thus concluding the agreement in a peaceful manner, without much ado.

Rushing about frantically to unload the cargo, it took us only three days to weigh it and bag it and deliver it to the owners, whose accounts were duly verified and paid for in silver. The total transaction came to 130,000 *taels,* calculated, as I have said several times before, at the rate of six testons per *tael.* But even though it was done in the shortest possible time, it was still not quick enough, for we had not quite finished when the news of what we had done to the thief in the *Tanauquir* River arrived and caused such an uproar ashore that no one would venture aboard any more, and as a result, Antonio de Faria was forced to set sail, and rather hastily at that.

50
Victory in the *Madel* River

As we were sailing away from this river port of *Mutipinão,* with the bow facing north, Antonio de Faria thought it would be better to turn back to the coast of Hainan in search of a river called *Madel,* with the intention, since the big junk was leaking badly, of running it aground on the tide, or exchanging it somehow or other, for a better and more watertight ship. And after twelve days of navigating against foul winds, he reached the hill of *Pulo Hinhor,* on *Coconut* Island; but since he could not find any news there of the *Khoja* Hassim he was looking for, he changed course and headed back to the southern coast, where he captured a few good prizes, which, from our way of looking at it, were fairly come by; for it was never his intention to steal from anyone but the pirates who had murdered and robbed the many Christians frequenting the gulf and coast of Hainan, where these pirates operated freely under the protection of the port mandarins, who received handsome bribes for allowing them to sell on shore what they stole at sea. But since the Lord our God has a way of bringing forth great good from great evil, he saw fit, in the wisdom of his divine justice, that as a result of the robbery perpetrated against us by *Khoja* Hassim off the bar of *Lugor,* as described above, Antonio de Faria should decide, as he did that day in Patani, to track him down and make him serve as an example to other thieves, who richly deserved the punishment they got from the Portuguese.

After a few days of navigating in the Gulf of Cochinchina under the most difficult conditions, we put into a port called *Madel;* and while we were there, on the feast of the Nativity of Our Lady, the eighth of September,[1] feeling quite apprehensive about the new moon—which in that latitude often brings with it a terrible storm the Chinese call "typhoon," accompanied by rain and high winds too furious for any ship to withstand—when for the past three or four days the skies had been lowering and showing signs of what we had been dreading, and the junks had been hurrying into the nearest haven, it was the will of the Lord that, among the many ships entering this harbor, one of them should belong to a well-known pirate by the name of *Hinimilau,* a Chinese heathen who had converted to Islam a short time before. And it seems that under the influence of the *cacizes* of the Moslem faith to which he had recently converted, as was presumed, he had become such a fierce enemy of the Christians, that he would go about saying in public that God owed him the kingdom of heaven for the invaluable service he was performing for Him by ridding the earth little by little of that evil race of Portuguese who, owing to some substance absorbed with their mother's milk, got as much pleasure out of offending God as do the demons inhabiting the House of Smoke; and with such words and others like them he would go around saying the most obscene, abominable things about us, such as had never before been imagined.

This pirate came sailing into the river on a huge, majestic junk, with the entire ship's company busily engaged in reefing the sails, for by then the weather had closed in with gusts of wind and rain; and as he went past, he saluted us in the *charachina* way, to which we responded in like manner, as is the custom in those ports, without their having as yet recognized us as Portuguese, nor we them, for that matter, having taken them for just another one of the Chinese ships that had been coming into port every hour, seeking shelter from the storm. However, they had some prisoners on board, five Christian slaves, who did recognize us and who cried out the minute they saw us, shouting in unison three times over, "Lord God, have mercy!"

At the sound of this cry we all jumped up and ran to the side to see what it was all about, though at the time we were far from imagining what was to follow. Recognizing the boys as Christians, we shouted to the seamen to douse the sails, but they refused; and instead, they answered us contemptuously by letting out three loud jeers to the beat of a drum, while they pranced around, jabbing the air with their naked swords in a threatening manner, trying to frighten us.

After they had anchored about a quarter of a league beyond us, Antonio de Faria decided to investigate and sent a well-armed *balão* after them which met with such a heavy shower of stones as it came alongside that its occupants were all in danger of being killed; and so they turned around and came back, with the sailors all cut and bruised and the lone Portuguese on board badly injured from the two enormous stones that were dropped on him.

At the sight of him all covered with blood Antonio de Faria asked him what it was all about.

"I have no idea, sir," he replied, "but look at us, and the manner in which we are returning."

And he showed him the wounds on his head while giving him a full description of the welcome they had received; and when he had finished, Antonio de Faria remained silent, brooding over it for quite a while.

"Come on, men!" he exclaimed finally, taking in everyone around him. "Get ready! And let there not be a single comrade on board who is unprepared to fight, for in the name of Christ, we are going to find out what this is all about! Something tells me it is the work of that dog of a *Khoja* Hassim, and maybe today we will have a chance to make him pay, and pay well, for our merchandise!"

And filled with the fervor of the moment, he immediately gave orders to cast off the lines and got under way as quickly as possible with all three of the junks and the *lanteias*. Arriving within musket-shot range of them, he sent over a salvo of thirty-six pieces of artillery, including twelve falcons and camels, in addition to a bronze sphere that fired cast-iron balls. This caught the enemy so completely by surprise that the only thing they could think of at the time was to cut their lines and let the junk drift shoreward. But it did not turn out the way they thought it would, or the way they would have liked it to, because Antonio de Faria understood what they were trying to do and he intercepted them before they could carry it out by ramming them with the combined force of the junks and *lanteias* under his command.

And then a beautiful battle broke out at this point, with swords being thrust at the ones who were near and spears and fire pots thrown at the ones who were far, while upwards of a hundred arquebuses were firing continuously as the fighting raged on for nearly half an hour without either side gaining the upper hand, until at last, as God willed, the enemy, badly wounded and burned, threw themselves into the water, while our men, fully avenged, filled the air with shouts as they freely followed up on that great victory.

When he saw his enemies drowning in the swift and turbulent waters, Antonio de Faria had two *balões* made ready and armed; and embarking with a party of soldiers as fast as he could, he managed to rescue some sixteen of them, unwilling to let them die along with the others because he was sorely in need of crewmen for the *lanteias*, since most of them had died in the previous fighting.

51
The Corsair's Confession

After achieving this victory in the manner described, the first thing we turned our attention to was the care of some of the men who had been wounded, since that was the most important order of business; and after that, having been reliably informed that one of the sixteen men he had rescued was the pirate, Antonio de Faria had him brought before him; and after seeing to it that the two wounds he had were attended to, he asked him where the Christian boys were, to which he obstinately replied that he did not know. And when the question was put to him again, with threats, he said that first they should give him a little water because his throat was so dry that he could not speak. And when the water was brought to him he drank it so fast that he spilled most of it. Still not satisfied he asked for more, promising by his Moslem faith and the whole Koran to tell them anything they wanted to know as long as they would give him enough water to quench his thirst. Antonio de Faria had it brought immediately along with a jar of preserves, which he refused, but he drank an enormous amount of water. And this time when he was asked where the Christian boys were, he said that they would find them in the forward hold.

Antonio de Faria immediately sent three soldiers to look for them, and when they opened the hatch to call them up, they saw them all lying there below with their heads cut off. Horrified by the sight they let out a frightful scream and started shouting, "Jesus! Jesus! Jesus! Come here, your lordship, and you will see something most pitiful!"

Antonio de Faria and all the others who were with him jumped up at once and ran forward; and when he saw those boys lying there all dead, one on top of the other, he was so overcome by the sight that he was unable to hold back the tears, and with arms upraised and his gaze turned heavenward he cried out loud in a voice filled with grief, "O my Lord Jesus Christ! Blessed art thou for the pity and mercy thou showest in suffering such a grave offense!"

And when he had them brought up on deck not a single man present was able to control the tears or keep from going to other extremes upon seeing a woman and two children about six or seven years of age, both so beautiful and innocent, mercilessly beheaded, and the five boys who had called out to us, with their bodies slashed and their guts hanging out.

Taking his seat again, Antonio de Faria asked the pirate why he had done such a cruel thing to those innocent victims lying there; and he said that he did it because they had betrayed him by revealing themselves to the Portuguese who were his worst enemies, and because they had called on their God to avail them; and as for the two little ones, the fact that they were children of the Portuguese, whom he had never liked, was reason enough for him. And he answered some other questions that were put to him in the same indifferent manner and with as much obstinacy as though he were the devil himself in the flesh.

And when asked if he was a Christian he said no, but that he had formerly been one in the days when Dom Paulo da Gama[1] was captain of Malacca. And when Antonio de Faria asked him, since he had once been a Christian, what made him leave the faith of Christ, in which his salvation was certain, for that of Mohammed, in which his soul would most certainly be damned, he said that it was because after he had become a Christian he was always treated with deep contempt by the Portuguese, whereas previously, when he had been a heathen, they would all remove their hats when they spoke to him and address him politely as *quiay necodá*,[2] which was like calling him "Sir Captain;" but once he had become a Christian they showed him very little respect; and that he went to Bintang to become a Moslem, and that there, after he was converted, the king of Jantana, who was there at the time, always treated him in the most honorable manner, and the mandarins all addressed him as "brother." As a result, he had taken a vow and sworn to it on the Book of Flowers, that as long as he lived he would always be the greatest enemy of the Portuguese and all other people who professed the Christian faith, an oath for which he was highly praised by both the king and the *caciz moulana*, who assured him that if he kept his word his soul would be eternally blessed.

When asked how long it had been since he rebelled against the Portuguese, what ships of theirs he had captured, how many of them he had slain, and how much merchandise he had stolen from them, he replied that seven years before, the first ship he had captured, in the river of Ning-po, was a junk belonging to Luis de Paiva,[3] laden with four hundred *bahars* of pepper only, no other spices, on which he had killed eighteen Portuguese, apart from their slaves, who did not count because they did not really satisfy the oath he had taken; but that later on, by a fortunate combination of circumstances at sea, he had captured four more ships on which he had killed nearly three hundred people, though probably not more than seventy of them were Portuguese; and that he reckoned that altogether he must have captured about fifteen or sixteen hundred *bahars* of pepper and other assorted goods, more than half of which he had to give to the king of Pahang in exchange for allowing him to seek refuge in his country and for protecting him against the Portuguese by providing him with an armed force of a hundred men who sailed with him and obeyed him as though he were a king.

And when asked if those were the only Portuguese he had slain or had encouraged others to slay, he said no, but that two years before, while anchored in the *Choaboquec* River off the coast of China, a big junk with many Portuguese on board arrived, and her captain happened to be a very good friend of his by the name of Rui Lobo,[4] who had been sent there on a trading voyage by Dom Estévão da Gama, then captain of Malacca; and that after he had finished trading, Rui Lobo had departed with his ship gaily bedecked because he was returning rich; however, five days after he had departed he ran into a heavy sea that split the junk open, and since he was unable to ride it out he was forced to return to the port from which he had departed; and as he was coming in under a high wind and full sails so as to gain time, the junk suddenly sank to the bottom, though Rui Lobo and seventeen Portuguese as well as some slaves survived and managed to make their way to the island of *Lamau* on board their sampan without sail, water, or food; and trusting in their old friendship, Rui Lobo had begged him on bended knee, with tears in his eyes, to take him on board his junk which was then preparing to leave for Patani, promising in return, and swearing by his faith as a Christian, to pay him two thousand *cruzados,* an offer which he had agreed to; but after he had taken him aboard, the Moors advised him not to trust in the friendship of a Christian if he wanted to stay alive, warning him that as soon as they had regained their strength they would take over his junk and all its cargo, for that was the way they usually behaved, no matter where they were, and that since he was afraid that there might be some truth to what the Moors had said, he killed them all one night while they were asleep, though later on he had regretted it many times.

Antonio de Faria and the others around him were as deeply shocked by the enormity of that ugly deed as one would expect them to be; and since he no longer had any desire to interrogate him, he gave orders to have him killed and thrown overboard, along with the four others who were still alive.

52
King of the Sea

After this pirate and the others had received their punishment, an inventory was taken of what the junk was carrying, and the value of the prize was estimated at nearly forty thousand *taels* in silk, bolts of satin and damask, silk yarn, and musk, apart from a large quantity of fine porcelain and some other goods that had to be burned along with the junk for lack of a crew to sail her.

This honorable exploit had such an amazing impact on the Chinese that whenever they heard any mention of the Portuguese they trembled. Realizing that the same thing could happen to each one of them, the *necodás* or owners of the junks in that port organized a meeting they call a *bichara*,[1] at which they chose two of their most respected associates who were best qualified to represent them for what they had in mind, and they sent them as ambassadors to Antonio de Faria, as king of the sea, to ask him, on his word of honor, to protect them, so that they might leave port safely and proceed on their way before the end of the monsoon, in consideration of which they would immediately acknowledge themselves as his slaves and subjects and pay him, as their lord, a tribute of twenty thousand *taels* in silver, without any further ado.

Antonio de Faria received them graciously and granted their request, and swore to do just as they wished by giving them the security of his word of honor and assuring them that henceforth no thief would steal a single piece of their merchandise. And while one of the two remained behind as hostage, the other left to get the twenty thousand *taels*. He returned in less than an hour with the silver as well as a number of expensive items as a personal gift from all the *necodás*.

And since Antonio de Faria wanted to favor one of his slaves, a boy by the name of Costa, he appointed him as the official scribe and put him in charge of the safe-conduct passes that were to be issued to the *necodás* at a fixed rate of five *taels* for the junks, and two for the *vancões, lanteias,* and barges. He did so well for himself that in just the thirteen days that it took to issue the passes, this boy earned—according to what was said by those who envied him—more than four thousand *taels* in silver alone, to say nothing of the many fine gifts they all gave him to get him to take care of them faster. And the safe-conduct passes read as follows:

"This is to certify that *Necodá* So-and-So has been granted the right to navigate freely along the entire coast of China, with the assurance, backed by my word of honor, that he will not be molested by any of my men, on condition that he treat all Portuguese as brothers wherever they chance to meet." And at the bottom it was signed, "Antonio de Faria."

All of these passes were scrupulously honored, with the utmost integrity. And from that time forward, he was so deeply feared along that entire coast that even the *chaem* of Hainan, the viceroy of the island himself, owing to what he had heard about him, sent a representative to call on him with an expensive gift of pearls and a gold service; and he wrote him a letter informing him that he would be very pleased to have him enlist in the service of the Son of Heaven as admiral of the coastal area extending from *Lamau* to Ning-po, at an annual salary of ten thousand *taels;* and that if he lived up to their expectations, as they had every reason to believe he would, judging by his reputation, he could assure him that, at the end of three years, he would be promoted to the rank of one of the forty *chaens* in the government, whose word was supreme in the administration of justice; and at the same time he pointed out to him that from there, a man like him, if he proved to be loyal, could eventually rise to become one of the twleve *tutões* in the government, whom the Son of Heaven, Crowned Lion on the Throne of the World, admitted to his chamber and board as intimate members of his household by reason of the high honors and positions of command conferred on them, at a salary of 100,000 *taels*.

Antonio de Faria thanked him very much for the offer and turned it down in the flowery stylized language they use, with the excuse that he did not consider himself worthy of the high honors being offered to him, but that he would always be ready to serve him, without remuneration, whenever the *tutões* of Peking chose to call on him.

After that, departing from the port of *Madel* where he had spent fourteen days, once again he ran along the coast inside the gulf, trying to see if he could find some trace of *Khoja* Hassim; for inasmuch as that had been his main purpose from the start, for the reasons I explained before, he never once lost sight of that goal, which was to keep on searching all over for him, and that was the only thing he could think of, night and day. And because it seemed to him that he would find him in that gulf, he remained there for more than six months, exposing himself to considerable hardship and personal risk. At the end of that time he reached a very noble city called *Quangiparù*,[2] where there were many sumptuous buildings and temples. He anchored in the harbor and remained there for a whole day and night, behaving to all outward appearances like a merchant, peacefully going about the business of purchasing what was brought on board. But since it was a city of over fifteen thousand hearths, as some of the men estimated, he slipped away early the next morning, without the local people taking any notice of us.

Once again he headed out to the open sea in spite of the fact that the wind was a bit foul, and in twelve days, under difficult sailing conditions, he ran up and down the whole coast, covering both shores from south to north, without being able to find anything in the entire area that he could lay his hands on. Both coasts were dotted with small settlements of some two hundred to five hundred inhabitants, and though some of them were surrounded by brick walls, they were hardly strong enough to defend themselves against an attack by a company of some thirty decent soldiers, because the people there are all fainthearted; moreover, they possess no weapons to speak of, only charred wooden stakes and some short-bladed swords, along with shields fashioned of pine boards and painted in red and black.

But as for the location of the area itself, it is the best and the most fertile and bounteous in all things of any that I have ever seen; and there is so much cattle that it would be impossible to even hazard a guess at the number; and there are huge expanses of wide, flat, open fields of wheat, rice, barley, millet, and many different kinds of vegetables, the sight of which left us all gaping in amazement; and in some parts there were huge forests of chestnut, pine, and angely[3] trees like the ones that grow in India, which could be used for building an infinite number of ships; and according to the information Antonio de Faria obtained from some merchants, the area is also rich in mines—copper, silver, tin, saltpeter, and sulphur—to say nothing of the many fields of good fertile land lying fallow, and all of it wasted on those fainthearted people, for if it were in our possession, perhaps we would be far better off than we are these days in India, sinners that we are.

53
Shipwreck off the Isle of *Thieves*

For seven and a half months Antonio de Faria remained in that gulf, sailing back and forth, from river to river, up and down both coasts from north to south and around the island of Hainan, without being able to find any trace of *Khoja Hassim* in all that time. Sick and tired of all the hardship they had endured for so long, the soldiers all got together and demanded of him that everything that had been acquired in the meantime be divided up according to a signed statement he had given them, so that they could each take their share and return to India or wherever else they wanted to go.

There was quite a bit of ill feeling over this, and though tempers flared during the discussions, in the end they agreed to lay up for the winter in Siam, where all the cargo on the junks would be sold, converted to gold, and distributed accordingly. Once this agreement had been signed and sworn to by everyone, they went on to the Isle of *Thieves,* as it was called, and dropped anchor there because of its location at the outermost point of the gulf, intending to begin the return leg of the voyage from there with the first breezes of the monsoon.

After we had been waiting there for twelve days, with everyone anxious to put the agreement into effect, as Fortune would have it, with the conjunction of the new moon in the month of October, which was something we always dreaded, we were struck by a raging storm, accompanied by rain and winds of such tremendous force that it could not be attributed to natural causes. And since we were short of cables at the time, and the ones that we had were nearly all badly frayed and half rotten to begin with, as soon as the sea began to swell and the southeast wind swept over the coast, catching us in an exposed position, such a huge surge of mountainous waves arose, that much as we tried in every possible way to save ourselves—by cutting away the masts, razing the deckhouses and upper works from stem to stern, jettisoning everything on deck, taking turns at the pumps, throwing cargo overboard, splicing hawsers and cables and clinching them onto anchors improvised out of the heavy artillery that had been removed from the gun carriages—all of our efforts were of no avail; and with the night so dark, the temperature so low, the seas so heavy, the winds so fierce, the waters so crossed, the waves so high, and the force of the storm so terrifying, there was nothing left for us to do but throw ourselves on the mercy of the Lord, upon whom we kept calling continuously, shouting at the top of our voices and shedding bitter tears.

But since, sinners that we were, we were unworthy of being shown this mercy, the good Lord, in the wisdom of his divine justice, ordained that at two hours past midnight we were struck by a wind of such tremendous force that all four of the ships were blown against the coast and dashed to pieces, killing 586 people, including twenty-eight Portuguese. Those of us who survived by the grace of God—twenty-two Portuguese and the rest seamen and slaves, making fifty-three altogether—sought shelter, bleeding and naked, in some shallow pools where we managed to get through the night. In the morning we made our way to the beach and discovered that it was completely strewn with corpses. It was such an unbearably painful sight that not a man among us could stand up under the shock of it and everyone collapsed, reeling in horror from it, filling the air with the most plaintive sounds of weeping and beating their breasts in anguish.

They carried on this way until close to vespers, when Antonio de Faria, who, thank God, was among the survivors, which made us feel somewhat better—repressing the grief that the rest of us could not hide, appeared before us dressed in a scarlet *cabaya* he had stripped off one of the corpses lying there, and with dry eyes and a cheerful countenance, made a brief speech in which he touched every now and then on the false and fleeting nature of the material things of this world; and that was why he was asking them, in a brotherly fashion, to try as hard as they could to forget about such things, since dwelling on them would only cause them further grief; and that if we stopped to think about the circumstances and the wretched condition to which Fortune had reduced us, because of our sins, then we would appreciate what he was saying and would realize how important it was for us to heed his advice; for he trusted that the Lord our God, right there in that dense and uninhabited jungle, would send them the means to save themselves; and that one had to firmly believe that He would never permit any evil unless it were meant for some greater good; and that was why he, for one, believed with all his heart that, even though we had lost 500,000 *cruzados* there, we would soon get back 600,000 or more.

They heard him out as he delivered this brief talk, but there were many tears shed all around, and with heavy hearts they turned to the task of burying the dead that were strewn all over the beach. Two and a half days were devoted to it, and during that time we also salvaged some of the wet provisions we needed to keep alive, but though the supply was plentiful, it only lasted for five out of the fifteen days we spent there because it was soaked in salt water, and as a result was so spoiled that we got little good out of eating it.

At the end of these fifteen days, during which we endured unspeakable hardship, our Lord, who never abandons those who truly trust in Him, miraculously sent us the means, naked and bare as we were, to save ourselves, as I will explain.

54
Marooned

Those of us who survived the disastrous shipwreck I have described above wandered about the beach and through the woods, naked and barefooted, suffering from the extremes of cold and hunger to such a degree that many of our comrades, while talking to each other, suddenly dropped dead of exhaustion; and it was not so much from the lack of food as it was from the harm done us by the food we had eaten which was moldy and spoiled, to say nothing of the fact that it smelled so bad and tasted so bitter that you could not bear to put it in your mouth. But since the Lord our God by his very nature is infinitely good, there is no place on earth, however remote or forsaken, where the suffering of sinners can escape him and where he cannot succor them with certain effects so far beyond our imagination that if we stop to think about the way they come to pass, it becomes perfectly clear that they are miracles wrought by his divine hands rather than the natural course of events, as we so often delude ourselves into thinking.

The reason I say this is because, one day, the very day on which the feast of the archangel Saint Michael[1] is celebrated, when we had abandoned all hope of human aid and were weeping in despair—a weakness we attributed to our misery and lack of faith—a sea hawk chanced to fly by, appearing from behind a knoll that rose toward the southern part of the island; and as it flew overhead, wheeling and dipping its outspread wings in the air, a fresh mullet, about a handspan in length, fell from its claws and landed at the feet of Antonio de Faria. He stood there a little puzzled, not knowing what to make of it, until he realized what it was and then, after staring briefly at the fish, he got down on his knees, and with the tears streaming down his cheeks, he heaved a deep sigh and uttered this prayer:

"Lord Jesus Christ, eternal son of God, I humbly beseech thee, by the wounds of thy sacred Passion, do not condemn us for the lack of faith we have shown in a moment of weakness induced by our misery, for I truly believe that thou wilt be as merciful to us, here and now, as thou wast to Daniel in the lion's den, in days of old, when thou hadst him delivered by the prophet Habakkuk,[2] and so shalt thou be any time, any place, where any sinner invokes thy aid with unswerving faith and hope in his heart. Therefore, I pray thee, my Lord and my God, not for my sake but for thine own, and through the intercession of thy holy angel whose feast day is observed this day by thy holy church, look not upon how little we merit of thee, but rather how much merit thou didst earn for us by thy suffering on the Cross. I ask this so that thou mayest be pleased to grant us the remedy for our suffering which can only come from thee; and lead us in thy mercy to a Christian land where, persevering in thy holy service, we can live out our lives as true believers!"

He picked up the mullet and roasted it on some embers and gave it to the sick who needed it most. And then, looking in the direction of the hill from which the hawk had come, we saw many of them soaring and descending in the air, which gave us to understand that those birds were feeding on some kind of game or fresh quarry. Since we were all anxious to do something for our sick comrades, and there were many among us who were ailing, we formed a procession and headed in that direction, hobbling as best as we could and reciting a litany through our tears. When we reached the top of the hill we discovered a completely level valley with a wide variety of fruit trees growing there and a freshwater stream flowing right through the middle; but before we even reached it, the Lord placed a freshly killed deer in our path, its throat slashed, on which a tiger was just beginning to feed. He dropped his prey when he heard our shouts and went fleeing into the thickest part of the woods, leaving it behind for us just where it lay.

We took this for a good omen and descended to the riverbank, where we settled down for the night after feasting on a marvelous banquet we prepared not only with the deer, but also with the many mullet we picked up, thanks to the great number of hawks that came down to the river in droves, for quite often our screams would frighten them into dropping some of the many fish they caught.

We continued fishing this way at the riverbank from the Monday on which we arrived until the following Saturday when, early in the morning, we saw a sail heading for the island. Since we were not sure whether or not it would anchor there, we went down to the beach where we had been shipwrecked, and after watching it for nearly half an hour we saw that it was a small thing, and as a result we were forced to hide in the woods so they would not see us.

Once in port, this boat—which was a beautiful oared *lanteia*—was secured by the crew with two mooring lines fore and aft, to a high bank formed by the point of the cove, to enable them to let a gangplank down on shore. There were more or less about thirty people on board, and when they had all disembarked they immediately set to work on their chores, taking on water, collecting firewood, washing clothes, and cooking dinner, while some even amused themselves with wrestling and other sport, never dreaming that there might be anyone there who could interfere with them.

When he saw them all going about their business in such a carefree and disorderly manner, and that there was no one on board to stand in our way, Antonio de Faria gathered us all about him.

"Men, brothers," he said, "I do not have to tell you that we are in such a sad situation because we have sinned. You all know that well enough, though I am firmly convinced, and I confess it freely, that my sins alone are to blame for it. But since our Lord is infinitely merciful, I trust in him that he will not allow us to end our days here in such a miserable way. And even though I know that there is no need to tell you how important it is for us to try to capture this boat which the Lord has miraculously sent us, still, I just want to mention it so that all of us together, just as we are—with his holy name on our lips and in our hearts—may make a dash for it and get on board before they discover us. And once we have reached it, please keep in mind that the most important thing is to gain possession of the weapons we find there, since we will need them to defend ourselves and take control of this one thing which—after God—is our sole salvation. And as soon as I say the words, 'Jesus, in the name of Jesus!' three times, do exactly what you see me do!"

Everyone promised that they would without fail. And once we were all ready and set to go after the worthy goal we had set ourselves, Antonio de Faria gave us the signal he had chosen, and dashed off with the rest of us at his heels. Reaching the *lanteia*, we promptly gained control of it without encountering any opposition, and casting off the mooring lines, we moved out to sea for about the distance of a crossbow shot.

Hearing the noise, the unsuspecting Chinese quickly ran down to the beach, but when they saw their ship had been captured, they were so astounded that not one of them could determine what to do about it; and after an iron demi-culverin that we found on board had been fired at them, they all ran off to the woods where they remained, crying over their misfortune, just as we, up until then, had cried over ours.

55
A Precocious Child

Once we were all safe aboard the *lanteia* and secure in the knowledge that there was nothing the Chinese could do about it, we sat down to a leisurely dinner that an old man had prepared for them, consisting of two large skillets full of duck and rice mixed with bits of salt pork, a meal that tasted quite good to us at the time, considering the appetites we all brought to it.

After we had finished eating and given thanks to God for His mercy, we inspected the *lanteia's* cargo and found that she was carrying silks—floss, satin, damask—and three large demijohns of musk, all of which we estimated roughly at about four thousand *cruzados,* not counting a good store of provisions, rice, sugar, ham, and two coops of hens, which were prized above all as a remedy for the sick, many of whom had not fully recovered; and then one by one, since there was nothing to fear, we set about picking through the bolts of silk and helping ourselves to make up for all the things we had gone without.

Noticing a rather fair and handsome young lad of about twelve or thirteen who was also on board, Antonio de Faria asked him where the *lanteia* had come from, why it had stopped there, to whom it belonged, and where it was bound.

"It belonged to my poor unlucky father," the boy replied, "who was unfortunate enough to have you steal from him in less than an hour what it took him more than thirty years to earn. He was coming from a town called *Quoamão,* where he had bought and paid for in silver all the cargo you have there, and he was on his way to sell it to the Siamese junks in the port of *Comhay;* but since he was running low on water, his sad fate led him to stop here for it so that you could rob him of his cargo without the slightest fear of punishment from heaven above."

Antonio de Faria told him not to cry and caressed him as much as he could and promised to treat him like a son, assuring him that that was the way he felt about him and that he would always feel that way.

"Don't think because I am still a child," the boy replied, looking at him with a scornful smile, "that I am stupid enough to believe that the man who robbed me of my father could treat me like a son. And if you really mean it, then I beg you, for the love of your God, please, please, please, let me swim back to that lonely island where the man who gave me life remains behind, for he is my real father, and I would rather die there in the woods where I can just see him crying his heart out over me, than live here with such evil people as you!"

Some of the men standing there scolded the boy and told him not to talk that way, that it was not right.

"Do you know why I said that?" he replied. "Because I saw you, after you had filled your bellies, praising God with upraised arms and greasy lips, acting as if you think it is enough to mumble a few words to heaven instead of paying for what you have stolen. Well you ought to know that the almighty Lord does not command us to move our lips in prayer so much as he forbids us to take another man's property, and worst of all—to rob and kill—which are the two most dreadful sins, as you will find out after you die from the terrible punishment that his divine justice has in store for you!"

Impressed by the boy's words, Antonio de Faria asked him if he wanted to become a Christian.

"I have no idea what that is," the boy replied, turning to look at him, "so I cannot understand what you are asking of me. First tell me what it means, then I will know how to answer."

After Antonio de Faria had explained it to him, with well-chosen words, as only he could, the boy, instead of replying directly, looked up to heaven, raised his arms, and cried out, "Blessed art thou, O Lord, for thy patience, which suffers the presence of people on earth who speak so well of thee and observe so little of thy divine Law as these blind, wretched creatures who think that robbing and preaching can satisfy thee, as they do the tyrant princes that reign on earth!"

And refusing to answer any more questions, he went off to cry by himself in a corner, where he remained for three whole days without touching any of the food they brought him.

At a meeting that was called at the time to decide where to go from there or what course to follow, whether north or south, some radically different opinions were expressed; but it was finally agreed that we should go to Ning-po, a port about 260 leagues to the north, because there along the coast it would probably be easier for us to get hold of a bigger ship, one that was better suited for our purpose, since the one we had was too small for such a long voyage, and we were afraid of the many storms that strike the coast of China during the period of the new moon, when so many ships are continually lost at sea.

With this in view, we set sail from the island just as the sun was beginning to set, leaving the dazed Chinese behind us on the beach. All that night we ran with the bow facing east-northeast, and at daybreak we sighted a little island called *Guintó*, where we captured a fishing vessel loaded with a heavy catch of fresh fish from which we took what we needed along with eight of the twelve men we found on board, for handling the *lanteia*, because our own men were still too weak and exhausted from our recent hardship to do it themselves.

And when we asked these eight fishermen what ports were located along that coast as far as *Chincheo*, where we would be likely to find some *nao* inbound from Malacca, they said there was a very good river port called *Xinguau*, with excellent anchorage, about eighteen leagues away, where a lot of junks were always to be found loading salt, alum, olive oil, mustard, and sesame, and that there we would be able to fit out the vessel and obtain abundant supplies of all that we needed; and that at the mouth of the river there was a small town called *Xamoy*, inhabited by fishermen and other poor people, but that three leagues further upstream was the city, where there were large quantities of silk, musk, porcelain, and other assorted merchandise which were carried for trading to many different places.

Armed with this information, we headed for that river, arriving the following afternoon and taking the precaution of anchoring about a league out to sea for fear that our sins might bring us here some misfortune similar to the ones we had experienced in the past.

That same night we captured a fishing prow and interrogated the crew about the junks that were anchored up the river, how many of them there were, what kind of crew they were carrying, and other questions of the sort that suited our purpose. They answered that there probably were only about two hundred junks still in the city because most of them had already departed for Hainan, *Sumbor, Lailó,*[1] and other ports of Cochinchina, but that we would be perfectly safe in the town of *Xamoy*, where they would sell us all the provisions we needed. After that we entered the river and anchored near the town.

It must have been sometime around midnight, which means that we had been there only half an hour when Antonio de Faria got to thinking that the *lanteia* we were on was not a fit vessel on which to make the voyage to Ning-po, which is where we were planning to lay up for the winter, and he decided, with the approval of the rest of the soldiers and comrades, to acquire a better ship for himself. And even though we were in no condition at the time to undertake anything of the sort, still, we were forced by necessity to go beyond the limits of our strength.

At the time there happened to be a small junk in port, anchored in a spot all by itself with no other ships nearby, with very few men on board, and all of them deep in slumber. Seeing it as a perfect opportunity to carry out his plans, Antonio de Faria immediately ordered the cables slackened, letting our vessel drift to an even keel with theirs; and choosing a party of fifteen out of the twenty-seven soldiers he had there, as well as eight slaves, he climbed aboard the main deck of the junk, without anyone so much as suspecting his presence. He found six or seven Chinese sailors sleeping there and had them bound hand and foot, sealing their lips by threatening to slit their throats if they made any noise. Cutting both her anchor cables, he sailed out of the river as fast as he could and ran all the rest of the night with the bow pointing out to sea. At dawn he found himself near an island called *Pulo Quirim,* nine leagues from where he had departed.

Three days later, with God's help and a fair wind filling the sails, we dropped anchor at an island called *Luxitay,* where we had to spend two weeks in order to give the sick a chance to recover completely. It was a perfect spot, not only because of the wholesome climate and good water, but also because we were able to obtain fresh food from fishermen in exchange for rice.

There the entire junk was searched and nothing was found in the hold but rice, which they had been selling in the port of *Xamoy,* but the bulk of it was jettisoned in order to lighten the junk and make her better able to withstand the dangerous voyage ahead. After transferring the *lanteia*'s cargo to the junk, we careened her ashore to scrape her bottom because she would be needed for taking on water in the various ports we would be stopping at.

It took us two weeks, as I said before, to finish up at this island, and during that time the sick recovered completely, and we departed on our way to the kingdom of Ning-po, where we had heard that there were many Portuguese, inbound from Malacca, Sunda, Siam, and Patani, all of whom, in those days, used to go there for the winter.

56
Partners in Piracy

After two days of navigating along the coast of *Lamau* with a fair wind and moderate sea, it was God's will that we should happen to meet up with a Patani junk returning from the Ryukyus. It belonged to a Chinese pirate by the name of *Quiay Panjão* who was very friendly to the Portuguese and extremely fond of our manner of dress. In his company were thirty Portuguese, all of them handpicked soldiers who, besides the regular wages they got from this pirate, received many other benefits which he bestowed on them every hour of the day, thereby making them all rich men.

Mistaking us for people of another sort, the moment he caught sight of us he set his junk on a collision course, and like an old hand at the pirate's game, with all sails full he swung her around to windward of us, covering nearly three-quarters of our wake. Aiming at a point directly between both clews, he came bearing down on our stern, and when he got within a little more than a culverin-shot's distance, he sent over a salvo of fifteen artillery pieces, which left us in a difficult position, since they were mainly falcons and rock throwers.

But Antonio de Faria spurred his men on like a brave and good Christian, stationing them at the most crucial points—such as the main deck, stem, and stern—and posting reserves wherever they might be needed most. And while he was going about all this, his mind made up to see it all the way through, taking his chances on whatever Fortune decreed, it was the will of the Lord that we should distinguish a large banner of the Cross flying on her poop, as well as a large number of people on top of the deckhouse who were wearing the red caps that were the usual headgear of our men in those days when fighting at sea. That was enough to convince us that they were Portuguese who most likely were coming from Ning-po and bound for Malacca, a common run during the season of the monsoon. Thereupon we also exhibited some signs that would enable them to recognize us, and as soon as they realized that we were Portuguese they let out a shout, and in deference to our signals, they lowered both foresails simultaneously and followed this up by sending out a well-armed *balão* with two Portuguese on board to find out who we were and whence we had come. The moment they recognized us and were convinced of the truth about us, they increased their speed, and after making their salvos, to which we also responded, they climbed aboard.

Antonio de Faria welcomed them effusively, and since some of the men in our company were acquainted with them, they spent quite a bit of time with us, talking about many things that were of particular interest to us, in view of our plans. Antonio de Faria sent Cristóvão Borralho along with the two of them to pay a visit to *Quiay Panjão* and wrote him an extremely courteous letter with an offer of deep friendship, which made the pirate *Panjão* feel so pleased and flattered that he was bursting with pride. Bringing his junk in closer to ours, he gave orders to strike sail and embarked in the sampan that served as the ship's boat, and accompanied by a party of twenty Portuguese he came to pay a call on Antonio de Faria, bringing him an expensive gift of amber, pearls, gold, and silver plate that was worth well over two thousand *cruzados;* and Antonio de Faria gave him and the Portuguese in his company a joyous welcome and treated them all with the greatest courtesy and respect.

After everyone had been sitting around for a while conversing pleasantly as befitted the occasion, Antonio de Faria began to tell them the whole story of his shipwreck and all the other misfortunes he had encountered on his voyage, and about his decision to set a course for Ning-po to fit himself out with more men and rowing ships so that he could go back and run along the coast of Hainan again and through the Gulf of Cochinchina to the mines of *Quoanjaparù,* where he had been told there were six large buildings full of silver, to say nothing of a much greater quantity being smeltered at the water's edge and where, at no risk to themselves, they could all become very rich.

"As for me, Sir Captain," *Panjão* replied, "I am not as rich as some people think I am, though at one time I was, and I have also suffered disasters of Fortune similar to the one you have just described, which deprived me of the greater part of my wealth. That is why I am afraid to go back to Patani, where my wife and children reside, because I know for certain that the king will confiscate all my possessions on the pretext that I left without his permission, and he is bound to make much ado about it so he can have an excuse to rob me as he had done to others several times for even less cause than he has against me. That is why I say to you, if it would please you, or if you would be willing to have me join up with you on the voyage you are planning to make, along with the hundred men I have on my junk, my fifteen artillery pieces and thirty muskets—to say nothing of another forty carried by the Portuguese who sail with me—I would be very happy to do so, provided I get a one-third share of the prizes. And to seal the bargain, if you please, sir, you would have to give me a signed statement and swear by your faith that you will strictly adhere to it."

Antonio de Faria gladly accepted his offer, and after he had thanked him profusely and embraced him repeatedly for it, he swore by some of the holy Gospels to do exactly as he had asked him to, without fail, and then he handed him a signed statement to that effect, which was witnessed by ten or twelve of the most respected men.

After this pact had been made, both of them departed for a river called *Anay* five leagues from there, where they outfitted themselves with everything they needed in exchange for a one-hundred-*cruzado* bribe which they gave to the mandarin in command of the city.

57
News of *Khoja* Hassim

Having left the *Anay* River fully equipped with everything necessary for the projected voyage, Antonio de Faria, acting on the advice of *Quiay Panjão*—whom he always treated with the greatest respect so as to keep his friendship—decided to drop anchor in the port of *Chincheo* in order to obtain information from the Portuguese who came there from Sunda, Malacca, Timor, and Patani, about a few things that were necessary to know for what he had in mind, and to see if they had any news from Ning-po, where it was rumored that an armada of four hundred junks and 100,000 men had been sent by the king of China with orders to seize the Portuguese living there and burn their *naos* and settlements, for he no longer wanted them in his country owing to the fact that he had recently been informed that our people were not as trustworthy and peace loving as he had been led to believe.

When we got to *Chincheo* we found five *naos* belonging to some Portuguese who had arrived there the month before from the places I have mentioned, and they gave us a hearty welcome, accompanied by a great deal of joy and merrymaking all around. After giving us a report of the local news, the cargo being traded, and the peaceful conditions existing in the port, they told us that as for what was happening in Ning-po, all they knew was what the Chinese had told them—that there were many Portuguese laid up there for the winter, and others recently arrived from Malacca, Sunda, Siam, and Patani, who were quietly going about their business; and that the huge armada we were so concerned about had not gone there at all but was believed to have gone instead to the Goto Islands,[1] in aid of the *sucão*[2] of *Pontir*, whose throne, it was said, had been tyrannically usurped by a brother-in-law of his; and since this *sucão* had recently become a subject of the king of China, at an annual tribute of 100,000 *taels,* the king had sent him that armada of four hundred junks, said to be carrying 100,000 men, to restore him to the kingdom or domain that had been taken from him. This information set our minds at rest, and in return we offered up many prayers of thanks to the Lord. Nine days later we departed from this port of *Chincheo* with thirty-five more soldiers who had transferred to our ship's company from the other five *naos,* attracted by a good offer Antonio de Faria had made them, and we proceeded on our way to the kingdom of Ning-po.

And after five days of navigating against foul winds, tacking from port to starboard without being able to make any headway, one night, during the first watch, we met up with a small fishing prow with eight badly wounded Portuguese on board. One of the men there was called Mem Taborda and another Antonio Henriques—and I make a point of mentioning the names of these two because they were rich, highly respected men who were well known in those parts—and both of them, as well as all the others with them, were in such a disastrous state that it was pitiful to see.

As soon as the prow came alongside his junk, Antonio de Faria had these eight Portuguese picked up immediately, and as they came on board, one by one, they threw themselves at his feet the moment they saw him; and he welcomed them with the utmost kindness and consideration and shed many tears over them, deeply touched by the way they looked, their bodies mangled, naked, barefooted, and bathed in their own blood.

Seeing them that way he asked them how they happened to meet with their misfortune, and they began by telling him, their voices choked with emotion, that seventeen days before, they had left Ning-po, bound for Malacca, intending to go on to India from there if the monsoon prevailed; but when they had sailed as far as the island of *Sumbor,* they were attacked by a Gujerati thief named *Khoja* Hassim, in a fleet of three junks and four *lanteias,* with an armed force on these seven ships of five hundred men, including 150 Moors from Luzon, Borneo, Java, and Champa, all of them from parts east of Malaya; and that he finally overcame them after a battle that lasted from one to four o'clock in the afternoon and left eighty-two people dead, including eighteen Portuguese, to say nothing of an equal number taken captive and the cargo on the junk that they made off with, which belonged to them as well as some other investors and was worth well over 100,000 *taels;* and in addition, they related some other particulars that were so distressing, you could see pain and anguish welling up in the eyes of some of the men who were listening there.

Antonio de Faria remained silent for a long time, but his mind was working rapidly as he thought over the possibilities of what these men had just told him.

"Tell me, gentlemen," he said after a while, turning back to them, "if the fighting was as bad as you said it was, how did you, out of all the others there, manage to escape?"

"After holding them off for about an hour to an hour and a half with the bombards," they replied, "the three big junks managed to ram us five times with such shattering impact that they opened a big hole in our junk near the sternpost that sent the water rushing in so fast we nearly sank. That was the beginning of the end for us because, in order to get at the leak, we were forced to shift much of the cargo around; and while we were concentrating on that, the enemy pressed in all the harder, and we were also forced to stop what we were doing and rush back up on deck to defend ourselves. In the meantime, while we were desperately trying to beat them off, with most of our men wounded and some already slain too, one of their junks caught fire, and since the flames were beginning to spread to the one right next to it, they were forced to release the grappling irons in order to get clear of each other; but much as they tried, they could not work fast enough to prevent one of them from burning clear down to the waterline, forcing everyone on board to jump into the sea, where most of them drowned. By this time our junk had drifted onto the stakes of the fishing traps located in the shoals this side of the river mouth, where the Siamese pagoda now stands; and the moment that dog of a *Khoja* Hassim—who was the one who had grappled us—saw us stuck on the piles that way, he made a sudden rush for us with a large company of Moors all armed with cuirasses and skirts of mail, and as they came aboard, swarming all over us, they promptly cut down over fifty of our men, including eighteen Portuguese. As for those of us who are here, wounded and burned as your lordship sees us, we jumped into a *manchua* we kept tied to the stern of our junk— since there was no other way out—and with God's help, just fifteen of us managed to escape on it, though two died only yesterday, and the thirteen who miraculously survived—eight Portuguese and five of our slaves—arrived here in the state your lordship now sees us in. Yet all the time we were fleeing in the *manchua,* we had to keep close to the reefs, picking our way carefully between the stakes and the shore in order to stay out of their reach. And after the *lanteias* had finished picking up their men who were still floundering about in the water, they headed for our junk, shouting and making a racket with their martial music, but once there, they got so carried away by their greed for plunder—the Lord be praised—that they lost interest in us; and by that time, since it was close to sundown, they went on up the river in a festive mood, banging away at their instruments, jeering at us all the while as they loudly celebrated their triumph over us in all our misery."

"From what you say," Antonio de Faria observed, "they must still be there in that river, since they suffered as much damage as you described. And it seems to me that neither your junk nor the one that was entangled with the burning junk can be of much use to them; and you must have killed and wounded some of the men that were on the big one that grappled yours."

Both of them assured him that they had killed and wounded quite a few.

At which Antonio de Faria, removing his cap, kneeled down and raised his arms and eyes heavenward.

"Lord Jesus Christ," he prayed, the tears flowing freely, "since thou, my God, art the true hope of all who believe in thee, I, the greatest sinner among all men, humbly entreat thee, in the name of these servants of thine, whose souls thou didst redeem with thy precious blood, give us strength and courage, and grant us the victory over this enemy, this cold-blooded killer of countless Portuguese, whom I am determined to seek out with thy help and favor, for the glory of thy holy name, as I have been trying to do all this time, and to see to it that he pays, at the hands of these thy servants and faithful soldiers, a debt long overdue!"

"After them!" everyone shouted in unison. "After them, in the name of Christ! Let's make that dog pay nine times over what he owes us and our poor friends here!"

Whipped to a frenzy, shouting and screaming all the while, they trimmed the sails astern for the port of Lailó, eight leagues further back where, once the council that was called approved of it, Antonio de Faria headed to make his preparations for the forthcoming battle with this pirate for whom he had been searching so long, as mentioned previously, without having been able to find any trace of him until that moment, in any of the many ports through which he had passed.

58
Preparations for the Attack

The following morning we dropped anchor in the port of Lailó, where *Quiay Panjão,* who had joined forces with Antonio de Faria—and who, as I said before, was Chinese and had many relatives there and was well known and liked by everyone in town—asked the local mandarin in command of the port to let us buy what we needed, to which he agreed, not only because he was afraid some harm might befall him, but also because of a thousand-*cruzado* bribe that Antonio de Faria gave him, which helped to persuade him.

Disembarking, some of our men rushed about buying all the necessary supplies, items such as saltpeter and sulphur for making gunpowder, lead, cannonballs, provisions, cordage, oil, tar, wadding, wooden beams, planks, weapons, javelins, charred stakes, spars, shields, yards, rock fragments, tackle, halyards, and anchors. And they took on fresh water and signed on more seamen, for even though it was a small town of only about three to four hundred inhabitants, so many of these things were available there and in the neighboring villages that I say in all truth that I cannot find enough words that would do credit to it, for this land of China excels above all others in that it has a greater abundance of everything one could desire, more so than all other countries in the world. And since Antonio de Faria was by nature a very generous person and was spending money from the general fund, he paid for these things entirely at the whim of the seller, so it was little wonder that mountainous loads of everything were delivered to him. As a result, he departed from this port thirteen days later with two new huge, majestic junks purchased in exchange for the small ones he had, and two brand-new oar-propelled *lanteias,* fresh from the drydock, and 160 sailors, counting deckhands as well as able seamen.

Once all these necessities had been taken care of, the sails set, the anchors at short stay, and everything in readiness for departure, a general roll call of the fleet was made, and the final tally showed a full complement of five hundred, counting both soldiers and sailors. This count included ninety-five Portuguese, all young lads, ready and willing to fight for any good cause, while the rest consisted of our slave boys, sailors, and soldiers from the east coast of Malaya whom *Quiay Panjão* kept on his payroll, who were also highly experienced in warfare at which, as corsairs, they had been engaged for the last five years. Also, an inventory showed that the fleet was equipped with 160 muskets; forty bronze pieces of artillery, counting twelve falcons, two camels, one sphere, five rock throwers firing stone shot, and the rest culverins; as well as two dogs[1] similar to the half-sphere; sixty quintals of powder—fifty-four for the bombards and six for the muskets, not counting the powder that had already been issued to the arquebusiers—nine hundred fire pots, four hundred of them filled with powder and the rest with unslaked lime such as the Chinese use; a large quantity of stone missiles, arrows, lances, and firebombs that a Levantine was paid to make for us; four thousand iron-tipped *zargunchos,* which are the first missiles used when a ship is grappled; and six boatloads of rock fragments, which are something the whole crew can fight with; twelve grappling hooks, attached to very long iron chains; and many other types of firearms that the Chinese devised for us out of greed for the huge sums of money they got for them.

This done, we departed from the town of Lailó gaily bedecked, the maintops dressed with silk awnings, and the junks and *lorchas* protected broadsides with a double row of wooden shields, with fighting platforms fore and aft, topped by other movable platforms that could be raised or lowered as the need arose. And as God willed, within three days we reached the fishing traps where *Khoja* Hassim had captured the Portuguese junk; and at nightfall, Antonio de Faria sent a reconnaissance party up the river where he had been told that he could find him.

His spies returned with a fishing prow they had captured, with six natives on board who said that the pirate was anchored two leagues from there, in a river called *Tinlau,* repairing the junk taken from the Portuguese, preparing to depart with her and two other junks for Siam, which is where he came from, and that he was expecting to sail within ten days. Armed with this information, Antonio de Faria decided, with the approval of some of the men who were summoned for that purpose, that it would still be better to see for ourselves because there was too much at stake to risk venturing into it blindly without first making some careful observations of our own, and that, depending on what was learned for certain from firsthand observation, we would do whatever everyone thought best.

Removing the six fishermen from their prow, they replaced them with a crew of sailors from *Quiay Panjão*'s junk, since they were more reliable and trustworthy, choosing only two of the captives to go with them while the rest stayed behind as hostages, and with them they sent a soldier by the name of Vicente Morosa, a brave fellow, and very clever too, dressed in Chinese clothes to avoid being recognized. After reaching the spot where the enemy was anchored, he pretended to be fishing as others were doing, while he watched and spied for as long as necessary; and once he was back on board he reported on what he had seen and declared that the enemy was practically in our hands, so much so, that there would be very little for us to do when we got there.

Thus informed, everyone gathered on board *Quiay Panjão*'s junk because Antonio de Faria wanted to give him the honor of holding the meeting there so as to spur him on and show him favor; and there the decision was made that at nightfall we would drop anchor at the mouth of the river, from where we would proceed in the predawn hours, with the name of Christ on our lips, to attack the enemy. When the meeting was over, having ended with complete agreement on all sides, Antonio de Faria issued orders for the formation and strategy that was to be followed when entering the river and attacking the enemy.

Dividing up the men, he placed thirty Portuguese on *Quiay Panjão*'s junk, allowing him to select the ones he wanted, since it was necessary to let him have his way all the time; and he assigned six men to each of the two *lanteias,* twenty to Cristóvão Borralho's junk, and the rest, thirty-three all told, remained with him, to say nothing of the slaves and many other Christians, all of them very brave and loyal.

Thus, with everything arranged in the necessary order for what we hoped to accomplish with the help of our Lord, he set sail for the river of *Tinlau,* arriving shortly before the Ave Maria hour; and after a night spent in careful vigil, at three hours past midnight he got under sail and headed straight for the enemy's position, about a little over half a league up the river.

59
A Glorious Victory

With the wind and tide in our favor—thanks be to the Lord—we sailed up the river, and in less than an hour we came within sight of our enemies, who up until that time had never even suspected our presence in the area. But after all, they were thieves, and since they were fearful of reprisals from the local inhabitants whom they victimized day after day, they kept a sharp lookout for trouble and were so well prepared to meet it that the moment they spied us they sprang into action, beginning with the sound of a bell that created such an uproar among them from ship to shore that it was impossible to be heard above the tumult going on.

Observing the situation, Antonio de Faria acted quickly.

"Let's go, men!" he shouted. "At them, at them, in the name of Christ! And be quick about it, before their *lorchas* come to their aid! *Santiago!*—and at 'em!"

He opened up at them with all our artillery which—the Lord be praised— hit the mark so well that their bravest men, who by this time were already on top of the poop deck, were promptly mowed down, most of them blown to bits, and with this we were off to a great start. After that, at a given signal, our arquebusiers—about 160 of them—began firing all at the same time, and they were so effective at clearing the decks of the crowds that had been seen on both junks before, that none of the foe dared show himself again.

Next, our two junks sank the grappling hooks into the two enemy junks right where they lay, and the fighting broke out on all sides with such fury that, to tell the truth, I could not possibly describe in detail what went on at the time even though I was there, because it was still not daylight, and the battle raging between the enemy forces and ours was so fierce, and it was accompanied by the noise of drums, gongs, and bells, mixed on both sides with shouts and screams, to say nothing of the frequent bursts of fire from the artillery and the arquebuses, and the echoes rumbling through the hills and valleys, that it was enough to make the flesh quiver with fear.

The fighting continued this way for about a quarter of an hour until their *lorchas* and *lanteias* began arriving from shore with large numbers of reinforcements. As they were coming, a fellow by the name of Diogo Meireles on *Quiay Panjão's* junk noticed that the latter's artillery officer kept missing the mark, mainly because he was so scared he did not know what he was doing; and just as he was about to fire a camel, his hand all atremble, this Meireles grabbed hold of him and threw him aside so forcefully that he went flying down the hatch.

"Out of my way, you yokel!" he shouted after him as he went, "this isn't a job for the likes of you! Let a real man take over here!"

Adjusting the sights of the camel carefully, in accordance with all the rules of gunnery of which he had a fairly good command, he fired the piece which had been loaded with cannonball and stone shot, scoring a direct hit on the nearest *lorcha,* apparently the flagship in command of four, ripping it apart on the starboard side from stem to stern and from the gunwale down to the waterline, causing it to sink so fast that there was no time for anybody on board to save himself. The rock munition carried over it, hitting the main deck of another *lorcha* a short distance astern, killing her captain and six or seven others near him. This put such a scare into the other two *lorchas* that in their haste to return to shore they became so entangled in each other's vangs that neither one of them could get free, and they remained there like sitting ducks without being able to move either backward or forward.

Seeing the chance they had been waiting for, the captains of our own two *lorchas,* Gaspar de Oliveira and Vicente Morosa, proudly vying with each other, moved in to attack simultaneously with huge quantities of fire pots, setting them ablaze; and trapped as they were, they burned together right down to the waterline, forcing most of their men to throw themselves into the sea where our men finished them off with the javelins, unwilling to let a single one of them escape alive.

On these three *lorchas* alone, upwards of two hundred people died; and the fourth one carrying the dead captain did not escape either, because *Quiay Panjão* went after her in his sampan, which served as his ship's boat, and captured her when she had almost touched shore, though by then there was no one left on board, for the entire company had jumped into the water, where most of them perished also, against the rocks on the beach. Seeing all this, the enemies who were still on board the junks— and there must have been as many as 150 of them, all Moors from Luzon and Borneo, with a few Javanese to boot—began to show signs of weakening, as many of them were already jumping over the sides.

Meanwhile, seeing his ranks fall apart, that dog of a *Khoja* Hassim, who up until that time still had not shown himself, suddenly appeared on the scene, dressed in a laminated breastplate lined with crimson satin fringed in gold, that had formerly belonged to the Portuguese.

"Lah hilah hilah lah Muhamed roçol halah!"[1] he shouted aloud three times for all to hear. "Oh, Mussulmen! Oh, righteous men who believe in the holy Law of Mohammed! How can you let yourselves be conquered by these cowardly Christian dogs who have no more spirit than a bunch of white hens and bearded women? Go after them, men! After them! For we have the sacred promise of the Book of Flowers wherein the Prophet *Noby* gratified the dervishes of the House of Mecca with wondrous delights. He will do the same for you and me today if we bathe ourselves in the blood of these savage infidels!"

Spurred on by the devil himself, as soon as they heard these cursed words, they turned back and grouped themselves into a single body of *amucks,* and it was indeed amazing to see how courageously they threw themselves in the path of our swords.

Then, in like fashion, Antonio de Faria also exhorted his soldiers.

"Oh Christians! Brothers all!" he shouted. "If these people can take strength in the cursed faith of the devil to fight like that, then let us take strength in Christ our Lord who died on the Cross for us, and who will never forsake us, no matter how great our sins, for after all, unlike those dirty dogs, we are his people, and they are not!"

Filled with ardor and zeal for the faith, he rushed at *Khoja* Hassim, eager to get at him, and brought his double-grip sword down on his head with such force that he cut right through a mail helmet he was wearing and knocked him off his feet; then, doubling back with a reverse stroke, he severed both his legs, making it impossible for him to get up again. At the sight of this his men let out a blood-curdling scream and five or six of them made a wild dash for Antonio de Faria, pitting themselves against him with such great courage and daring that they managed to inflict two sword cuts on him that nearly laid him out despite the thirty Portuguese soldiers surrounding him. Seeing this, our men rushed in quickly, and our Lord instilled them with so much strength that in little more time than it takes to recite two Credos, forty-eight of the enemy were lying dead on top of *Khoja* Hassim, and just fourteen of ours, of whom only five were Portuguese and the rest slave boys, who were all very loyal and devoted Christians.

By this time the ones still fighting had begun to weaken, and they started a disorderly retreat in the direction of the forecastles, intending to fortify themselves there. But twenty of the thirty soldiers on *Quiay Panjão*'s junk quickly dashed in and cut them off before they could achieve their objective, pressing them so hard in hand-to-hand combat that before long they had them all jumping overboard so frantically that they were falling on top of each other.

Their spirits high, inspired by the name of Christ our Lord, upon whom they kept calling, secure in the knowledge that the victory was theirs and conscious of the great honor they had achieved, our men finished off the rest of them, with the exception of only five, who were taken alive. After being tied hand and foot, these five were thrown down the hatch to be interrogated later under torture; but they cut each other's throats with their teeth, out of fear of the death that awaited them.

Their bodies were drawn and quartered by our slave boys and also tossed into the sea to join the company of that dog of a *Khoja* Hassim, their captain and high *caciz* of the king of Bintang, also known as the "shedder and drinker of Portuguese blood," as he styled himself at the beginning of all his correspondence, and as he publicly proclaimed to all the Moors, because of which, and because of the superstitions of their cursed faith, he was deeply revered by them.

60
After the Battle

Regarding the events of this cruel, ruthless battle, which ended with the glorious victory I have just described, I must say that I have deliberately chosen to present them in a brief and concise manner, for if I were to dwell at length on every little detail, not only about our men and how well they carried themselves but also about our enemies and the courage they displayed in defending themselves, apart from the fact that I do not possess the ability required for such a task, it would entail far too much and my story would be even longer than it is. However, since my intention here is only to touch upon these events, on the run, so to speak, I always try to limit myself to as few words as possible in my approach to many things that perhaps other people with more imagination than I have would have dwelt on at greater length had they been there to witness them or write about them. And now to return to my story. But first I felt I had to explain that I am only going to touch briefly on those things that could not possibly have been omitted.

Once the victory was ours, the first thing Antonio de Faria turned his attention to was the care of the wounded, who numbered altogether about ninety-two—mainly Portuguese and our slave boys. Next, since he wanted to know how many had died, a casualty count was taken which showed forty-two on our side, eight of them Portuguese—a loss that Antonio de Faria regretted above all else—and 380 on the enemy side, only 150 of whom had died by fire and sword, and the rest by drowning. And even though everyone was elated by the victory, many tears were shed openly and privately for the death of our companions, their bodies still unburied, most of them lying where they had fallen, their heads split open by the hatchets with which the enemy fought.

And though he was suffering from three wounds himself, Antonio de Faria went ashore, taking with him all the men who were in condition to accompany him; and there the first thing they did was bury the dead, which took them the better part of the day. Next, Antonio de Faria set out on an expedition around the island to see if there were still any people about, and he came upon a very pleasant valley dotted with many vegetable gardens and orchards producing a wide variety of fruits. Nestled in the valley was a tiny hamlet of forty or fifty one-story houses that had been sacked and its occupants slain by *Khoja* Hassim—at least those of them who were unable to escape.

In the valley below, about a bow-shot's distance, at the edge of a cool, freshwater stream teeming with mullet, trout, and robalo, there was a large single-story structure or building that looked like the village temple, which *Khoja* Hassim had been using as a hospital. It was filled to capacity with all his sick and wounded, among them some Moors who were close relatives of his, and some others too, high-ranking officers whom he kept on his payroll, who altogether numbered ninety-six. The moment they saw Antonio de Faria they let out a loud scream, as though begging for mercy, which he would not hear of, because, as he explained, one could not spare the life of anyone who had killed so many Christians. He ordered the building put to the torch in six or seven places, and since it was constructed of tarred wood and covered with dry palm leaves, the flames shot up so rapidly that it was frightful to see, and in a way, it was pitiful too, because the poor wretches trapped inside let out the most horrible screams as the fire spread all around. Some of them tried to escape by throwing themselves out of the openings in the roof, but our men, who seemed quite put out by this, received them with many a lance and spear in such a way that they were impaled on them as they fell through the air.

Having done with this cruel deed, Antonio de Faria returned to the beach, where the junk that *Khoja* Hassim had captured twenty-six days before from the Portuguese of Ning-po was being repaired. He immediately set to work getting it launched, for by this time it had been made seaworthy; and when it was afloat he delivered it to Mem Taborda and Antonio Henriques, who were the original owners, as I mentioned before. After making both of them place their hands on a prayerbook he was holding, he said to them, "In the name of my brothers and comrades, both living and dead, who, as you saw today, paid a very high price for your junk with their lives and blood, I, as a good Christian, hereby return it to you with all that was on it; and may the Lord God who reigns on high count it as an act of charity and see fit to pardon us for our sins in this life, and grant us his glory in the next, as I trust he will do for our brothers who laid down their lives today like good and faithful Christians, for their holy Catholic faith. However, I insist upon one condition, which I admonish you to keep in accordance with the oath I am administering to you, and it is that you take only what belongs to you and to the others who invested in your junk, and by that I mean the cargo you were carrying when you left Ning-po, for that is all that I am giving you and that is all that is due you; otherwise, we would both be guilty of wrongdoing—I by giving, and you by taking, what is not yours."

Mem Taborda and Antonio Henriques, who perhaps had not expected that much of him, threw themselves at his feet, their eyes wet with tears, and as they tried to find words to express their gratitude for the favor he had shown them, they were so overwhelmed by emotion that they broke down and cried; and then everyone joined in and once again there arose the sad, mournful sounds of weeping for the dead who had just been buried, the earth covering them still stained with their blood.

Both of them set about making arrangements for the recovery of their merchandise, and with the assistance of fifty to sixty slaves lent them by their owners for that purpose, they went around the entire island, picking up the still-wet silk they found hanging on the trees which were all covered with it; and in addition they found, stored away in two buildings, the dry and least-damaged silk which they said represented a joint investment of 100,000 *taels* by a group of more than a hundred men, counting the people who had remained behind in Ning-po, together with those in Malacca to whom the goods were being shipped. And the merchandise that these two men still were able to gather was probably worth more than 100,000 *cruzados,* though the rest, which was about a third of the original shipment, was lost due to rot, moisture, breakage, and thievery, about which nothing more was ever heard.

After this, Antonio de Faria returned to his ship and devoted the rest of the day to nothing but visiting and attending to the wounded, and to feeding and bedding the soldiers, for by then it was almost nightfall. And early the next morning he boarded the big junk he had captured, which was still strewn with the bodies of the men killed the day before, and he had them thrown overboard, just as they were, with the exception of that dog of a *Khoja* Hassim, since he was more prestigious and deserving of more pomp and ceremony in his funeral rites. He ordered him taken up just as they found him, fully dressed and armed, and had his body drawn and quartered before it was also thrown into the sea, to a tomb that was fitting and proper for a man of his stature and deeds, which was waiting for him in the bellies of the huge lizards swarming by the junk, feeding on the corpses that were being thrown overboard. And in his honor, instead of the prayer that was recited for the soul, Antonio de Faria intoned the following: "Off to the devil with you, where your darksome soul is probably reveling in the wondrous delights of Mohammed, as yesterday you so loudly proclaimed to those other evil dogs like you!"

Next, he had all the captive slaves on his ship, both the sound and the wounded, brought out before him, and he also sent for their owners, and when they were all gathered he made them a speech, like a good Christian—which indeed he was—urging them, for the love of God, to see fit to free their slaves, in keeping with the promise he had made them before the battle, and telling them that they could name their price, for he himself would reimburse them out of his own pocket. In reply, they all said that they would be glad to do so since his lordship thought it right, and that from that day on they held them to be free and independent men. And a document was drawn up at once for them to sign, which had to serve the purpose until they got to Ning-po where, later on, they all received their letters of manumission.

After this, an inventory was taken of the merchandise that was clearly visible—not counting what had been given to the Portuguese—and it was appraised at 130,000 *taels* in Japanese silver and clean, saleable goods such as satin, damask, silk, yarn, taffeta, musk, and very fine porcelain wrapped in straw, for at the time no inventory was made of the rest of the merchandise that this pirate had stolen up and down that coast from *Sumbor* to Foochow,[1] where he had been operating for more than a year.

61
Grounded on the Coast of China

After spending twenty-four days in the *Tinlau,* which gave the wounded men time to recover, Antonio de Faria departed for Ning-po, where he had decided to lay up for the winter, and from there, at the beginning of summer, undertake the voyage to the mines of *Quãogeparu,* as agreed upon with *Quiay Panjão,* who was accompanying him. When he had sailed about as far as the tip of *Micuy,* situated at latitude twenty-six degrees, he was struck by a fierce contrary wind coming out of the northwest, and on the advice of the pilots, he hove to, so as not to lose the distance already covered. As the afternoon wore on, the weather grew worse, bringing rain and heavy seas which the two oar-driven *lanteias* were unable to withstand, and at the approach of nightfall they headed for shore, intending to seek shelter in the *Xilendau* River, which was located about a league and a half from there. Also, in fear of impending disaster, Antonio de Faria moved off as fast as he could, following in their wake with only about five or six spans of sail exposed, not only to keep from swamping them, but also because the wind was too strong to carry any more. But since darkness had now closed in, and he was blinded by the spray of the breaking waves, he did not notice the ridge between the little island and the tip of the reef, and he passed over it, hitting the shoals with a shuddering impact that split the keelson apart in four different places, as well as a section of the keel below. But when his master gunner wanted to fire a falcon to bring the other junks to his aid, he would not allow it, insisting that if it was the will of the Lord for them to die there, he did not want the others—nor was there any reason why they should—to lose their lives because of him; instead, he urged everyone to help by showing openly what they could do with their hands, and by praying secretly with their hearts, asking God for forgiveness for their sins and grace to mend their ways, for if they did so with all sincerity, he assured them that they would very soon find themselves safe and sound, with nothing to worry about.

And so saying, he hurried over to the mainmast and had them cut it away close to the carlings on the deck below, and as it came crashing down, the junk settled down to a slightly more even keel, though its fall cost the lives of three sailors and one of our slaves, who were caught underneath and crushed to pieces. Next, he also had all the other masts cut away, both fore and aft, and the cabins razed, until there was nothing left clear down to the lower deck; and even though we worked as quickly as possible to get this done, it was hardly of any avail, because the storm was so violent, the seas so rough, the night so dark, the waves so high, the rain so heavy, and the force of the wind, beating against us with furious gusts, so insufferable, that no man could hold his head up against it. Also, about this time, the other four junks sent out distress signals to let us know they were in trouble, and when he heard them, Antonio de Faria looked up to heaven, clasped his hands and prayed out loud for all to hear.

"Lord Jesus Christ," he cried, "just as thou, my God, didst mercifully take it upon thyself to expiate the sins of mankind on the Cross, so I beseech thee, for thy name's sake, let me alone receive thy divine punishment so that I may atone for the sins these men have committed against thee; and spare them the suffering my sins have brought upon me this sad night, for if it had not been for me, they would never have offended thy divine goodness. Therefore, in the name of all, I entreat thee, O Lord, with aching heart, unworthy sinner that I am, heed my prayer, not for my sake, but for thy name's sake, and for the sake of the price thou didst pay for us all in thy infinite mercy!"

At his words they all cried out, "Lord God, have mercy on us!" It was a cry of such deep anguish that everyone there, without exception, was beside himself with pain and sorrow.

And since it is only natural for a man at a time like this to think of nothing but saving himself, here too, that was all that mattered to them; and so intense was each man's desire for salvation, that they gave not a thought to anything else but the means of attaining it, and completely forgetful of their greed, they decided to get rid of the cargo as quickly as possible. And about a hundred men jumped down into the hold—Portuguese, as well as slaves and sailors—and in less than an hour they had cleared out everything. There was nothing you could name that had not been tossed into the sea. And in their desperation, these men even went so far as to jettison every single one of twelve crates of silver bullion that had been taken from *Khoja* Hassim in the recent battle, right down to the last one, oblivious of their contents—to say nothing of other very valuable things that, along with the rest, went along that sad course.

62
The Storm's Ravages

After that harrowing night which left us battered, bedraggled, bare-footed, and exhausted from the great hardships we had undergone, with the coming of dawn God willed that the winds should die down a bit, allowing the junk to settle a little, though she was sitting on top of the reef and had taken on thirteen spans of water; and all the men were hanging over the side clinging to ropes, to keep from being swept overboard and drowned by the huge waves breaking over the ship or from being dashed against the rocks, which had already happened to ten or twelve of them who had neglected to take similar precautions.

And at daybreak, as God willed, we were sighted by the junk belonging to Mem Taborda and Antonio Henriques, which had hove to all night under bare poles, with large wooden rafts lashed astern in the *charachina* fashion, an emergency measure devised by their ship's officers to help them ride out the storm. It headed towards us the minute they spied us, and as they came near they threw out many planks tied to ropes for us to cling to, which we lost no time doing. It took almost an hour to complete this rescue operation, which turned out to be a very arduous task because of the disorder and frenzy accompanying it, with each man wanting to be the first to be saved. As a result, twenty-two drowned, including five Portuguese, which Antonio de Faria regretted far more than the loss of the junk and all its cargo, though it was by no means an insignificant loss, bearing in mind that the silver alone was worth well over 100,000 *taels* and that most of the captured prizes, as well as the loot taken from *Khoja* Hassim, had been placed aboard Antonio de Faria's junk, it being a bigger and better vessel, where it seemed that it would be in less danger than on the other ships which were not as well constructed nor half as safe.

After tremendous hardship, and at great risk to our lives, we finally found ourselves aboard Mem Taborda's junk, where the rest of the day was spent crying and lamenting over our sad plight, without any notion of what had happened to the rest of the company. However, late in the afternoon, as God willed, we caught sight of two sailing ships that were going about from one board to another with unusually short tacks, looking as if they were deliberately trying not to make any headway, and from this we gathered that they were part of our fleet; but since night was coming on, it was thought best, for various reasons, not to approach them, and instead we sent up a signal, to which they responded accordingly. Halfway through the morning watch they reached us, and as they came alongside they saluted us rather sadly and inquired about the admiral and the rest of the company, but they were told that their questions would be answered in the morning and that for the time being they should haul off until daylight because the seas were still heavy and they would be courting disaster.

As soon as the morning star appeared and the day dawned clear, two of the Portuguese on *Quiay Panjão*'s junk came aboard. After they saw how Antonio de Faria had taken refuge on Mem Taborda's junk because his own had been lost, they too, upon hearing the story of his misfortune, had a tale to tell which was almost as bad as ours. It included a description of how three of their men had been swept up by a fierce gust of wind and carried out to sea as far as you could shoot a stone, a thing which, indeed, had never been seen or heard of before. And they also described how the small junk went down with fifty people on board, most of them, or practically all, Christians, seven of them Portuguese, including her captain, Nuno Preto, an honorable and extremely courageous man, as he had amply demonstrated throughout our past adversities, whose loss was deeply felt by Antonio de Faria.

About this time, along came one of the two *lanteias*, whose fate until then had been uncertain; and they too had a tale to tell about all the hardship they had endured. They informed us that the other *lanteia* had snapped its cables in the storm and had been swept ashore and dashed to pieces right before their eyes; and that out of the entire ship's company only thirteen had managed to save themselves, and that these survivors—five Portuguese and eight Christian slaves—had been captured by the local inhabitants and carried off to a village called *Nouday*.

So that all in all, this unfortunate storm was responsible for the loss of two junks and a *lorcha*, or *lanteia*, as well as the lives of more than a hundred people—eleven of them Portuguese—not counting the captives. As for the total loss, both in merchandise and in silver, luxury items, boats, artillery, arms, munitions, and provisions—it was estimated at over 200,000 *cruzados*, leaving the captain and all the soldiers with nothing to call their own but the clothes on their backs.

And sudden storms like this come up on this coast of China more often than any place else in the world, so that no one can be sure of navigating there in any given year without running into some disaster, especially if at the conjunction of the full moon they neglect to seek shelter in one of the many excellent roadsteads outside their ports, which can be entered safely because they are all shoal free, with the only exception of *Lamau* and *Sumbor,* where there are some sandbanks located to the south, about half a league from the bar harbors.

63
The Prisoners of *Nouday*

Once the storm in all its fury had passed completely, Antonio de Faria transferred to the other big junk he had captured from *Khoja* Hassim, which he had left under the command of Pero da Silva de Sousa. Clapping on full sail he departed with the rest of the company, now consisting of three junks and a *lorcha,* or *lanteia* as the Chinese call them, and dropped anchor in the bay of *Nouday,* in an effort to see what he could learn about the fate of the thirteen men captured there. As soon as it was dark he sent out two fully armed *balões* with instructions to spy out the port, sound the river, check the roadstead, get the lay of the land, note the kind of ships in the harbor, and gather other information he needed for putting his plans into effect. And he ordered them to make a special effort to capture a few natives of the city, from whom he could obtain specific information to go by and find out what had become of the Portuguese, for by this time he was afraid that they had been taken further inland.

The *balões* departed immediately, and at two hours past midnight they reached a small town called *Nipafau,* located near the entrance to the bar at the edge of a cove where, with God's help, they managed things so well that before dawn they returned with a barge they had found anchored in the middle of the river, laden with earthenware and sugarcane, carrying eight men, two women, and a little boy about six or seven years old, who were so scared when they were put aboard Antonio de Faria's junk that he had a hard time calming their fears because they all thought they were going to be killed.

And when he tried to interrogate them, all he could get out of them was "Suqui hamidau nivanquao lapapoa dagatur," which means, "Don't kill us like this without any reason, for we are poor and humble folk, and you will have to answer to God for spilling our blood."

And they carried on that way, crying and trembling so uncontrollably that they could hardly speak.

When he saw that he was not getting anywhere with these simple people in the abject state they were in, Antonio de Faria decided to postpone the interrogation for the time being, and instead, hiding his true intentions for quite a while, he handed them over to a Christian Chinese woman who was traveling with the pilot and asked her to take care of them and try to calm them down enough to be able to get some intelligent answers out of them. They responded so well to the warmth and affection she lavished on them that in less than an hour she got them to tell her that, if the captain would allow them to leave freely in their own boat just as it was when it had been taken from them, then they would confess the truth of everything they had seen and heard. Antonio de Faria promised he would and gave them elaborate assurances to that effect.

Then one of them, who was the oldest and apparently the most authoritative member of the group, spoke up.

"I still do not trust very much in the generosity of your words," he said, "because you went too far, so much so, that I fear you will fail me in carrying out what they promise. I would rather hear you swear by the waters of the sea that keep you afloat, for then, if you tell a lie under oath, you can be sure that the Lord will be so angry, that his mighty arm will strike out against you and cause the winds above you and the waters beneath you to run forever contrary to your desires, no matter where you chance to sail; for I swear to you by the beauty of the stars of his heaven above, that a lie is as vile and hateful in the eyes of the Lord as the overweening pride shown by those who administer justice here on earth when they speak, in a contemptuous and discourteous manner, to the parties who appear before them, to demand the righteousness of his justice."

And only after Antonio de Faria had sworn to keep his promise, with all the solemnity he thought necessary for his purposes, did the Chinese appear to be satisfied.

"As for the men you are inquiring about," he said finally, "two days ago I saw them being thrown into the *chifanga*[1] of *Nouday,* where they were put in leg irons and formally charged with the crime of piracy on the high seas."

Antonio de Faria said nothing, though it infuriated him to think that it was probably true. However, realizing that the situation was too dangerous to brook any further delay, he hastened to put his plans for freeing the men into operation and wrote them a letter, to be delivered by one of the Chinese, who departed early in the morning, leaving the others behind as hostages. And since these Chinese were anxious to obtain their freedom, the man chosen to deliver the letter—who was married to one of the two women captured on the earthenware barge and now being held hostage on the junk—was in such a hurry to have done with it, that he returned by noon with a reply, written on the back of the letter and signed by all five Portuguese, in which they briefly described the horrible prison conditions and the grim prospect of the death sentence hanging over them; and they begged him, by the sacred passion of our Lord Jesus Christ, not to let them die there alone and friendless, but to remember his faith and the trust they had placed in him, for, as he well knew, it was because of him that they now found themselves in this sad plight, plus a lot of other pious words to that effect, as was only to be expected from men who were prisoners in the power of such cruel, cowardly people like the Chinese.

Antonio de Faria read this letter aloud and asked for advice on what was to be done in the matter, but since quite a number of people had something to say on the subject, there were many different opinions offered, which was not at all to his liking. As a result, after a lengthy and heated argument, when he saw that he was getting nowhere because of the wide diversity of opinions, he reached the end of his patience.

"Gentlemen! Brothers!" he exclaimed, "as far as I am concerned, I have sworn a solemn oath to God not to leave this place until I have freed those poor soldiers and comrades of mine by hook or crook, even though it means risking my life a thousand times, to say nothing of the personal expense involved for me, about which I care little. Therefore, I beg you, gentlemen, and I am addressing myself to each and every one of you, please, please, please, as a favor to me, do not put any obstacles in the way of a decision on which my honor depends, because I swear to the shrine of our Lady of Nazareth[2] that anyone who is opposed will have me for an enemy to the same degree as he shall be, to my way of thinking, an enemy of my soul!"

To this they all replied that what his lordship had decided was the best and wisest course of action to follow and that by all means, for the good of his conscience, he should not let anything prevent him from doing what he thought was right, because they would support him all the way and were ready to lay down their lives for him. He thanked them and embraced them all, with his hat in his hand, and expressed his appreciation in the most courteous manner, with tears in his eyes; and once again he assured them that from then on he would repay them with deeds and not just words, which were all he had to offer them at the moment; and it ended with complete agreement on all sides, to the entire satisfaction of everyone.

64
The Mandarin's Reply

Once this matter had been resolved, it was placed before the council to decide how to go about putting it into effect. It was agreed that first they should try to make some sort of a friendly arrangement with the mandarin whereby they could obtain the release of the captives in exchange for a reasonable sum of money; and then, depending on his response, they would decide what to do next. After that a formal petition was drawn up, phrased in the elegant language of the court, and Antonio de Faria sent it off to the mandarin with two of the most respectable-looking Chinese selected from among the captives, who also took with them an *odiá*[1] that was worth two hundred *cruzados,* which he thought would be more than enough to satisfy a gentleman of quality. However, it did not turn out that way, as we shall soon see.

The Chinese messengers departed with the petition and the gift and returned early the next morning with a brief reply, written on the back of the petition, that went like this: "Come read thy petition at my feet and after thou hast been heard, I shall consider the merits of thy case."

When he was shown the mandarin's unfavorable reply, phrased in such a haughty and disagreeable manner, Antonio de Faria felt a little sad and disheartened, for it meant that he was off to a bad start and that he was going to have a difficult time freeing the captives. He discussed the matter privately with some of the men who were chosen for that purpose, and again, there were some differences of opinion. Finally, it was agreed that he should try again, by sending him another message with an offer of two thousand *taels* in silver and merchandise in exchange for the release of his men, while at the same time letting him know in no uncertain terms that, one way or another, he had no intention of leaving without them; for then maybe, once he had convinced him that he was determined to have his way, fear might prove to be more effective in persuading him than an appeal to his self-interest.

The same two Chinese departed again carrying this message, which was folded and sealed like an ordinary letter from one person to another, written in plain language, without the ceremoniousness of a formal petition or any of the vain flattery demanded by their heathen customs, so that the mandarin would see from the straightforward style of the letter that he meant business.

However, before going any further, I want to mention just two of the main points in the letter that were responsible for the complete breakdown of negotiations. One of them was that Antonio de Faria told him that he was a foreign merchant, of Portuguese nationality, who was on his way to trade in the port of Ning-po, where many merchants lived, going about the business of trading their goods on which they paid the regular taxes and duties as established by law, without ever having committed a single act of piracy or any other crime such as he had accused them of. The other thing the mandarin objected to was his saying that if they had come there it was because the king of Portugal, their lord, was a brother and a true friend of the king of China, just as the Chinese merchants, for the same reason, were in the habit of going to Malacca, where they were treated with the greatest consideration, in all honesty and fairness, and never given any cause for complaint. And though the mandarin took exception to both of these points, it was the second one, where the king of Portugal was referred to as the brother of the king of China, that offended him most. He became so enraged by this particular point[2] that, without stopping to think of the consequences, he had the two messengers whipped, their ears cut off, and sent back that way with a reply for Antonio de Faria written on a scrap of paper, that went like this:

"Thou miserable maggot, born of a filthy fly and bred in the foulest dung heap ever to be found in a dirty dungeon inhabited by unwashed prisoners! How dost thou dare, lowly creature that thou art, to meddle with the divine? As I was listening to thy petition, in which thou didst ask me, as thy lord, to take pity on thee, for thou wert poor and wretched, I, who am by nature noble and generous, was beginning to feel well inclined towards thee and was willing to accept the paltry ransom offered. But then thy arrogant blasphemy fell on my ears, and I heard thee say that thy king is the brother of the Son of Heaven, the Crowned Lion who sits on the throne of the world over which he rules with incredible power, beneath whose feet humbly lie the crowns of all others who govern on earth with royal scepter and command, always ready at his beck and call, to be used as buckles on his sandals, downtrodden in the path of his heels, as testified to, in their true faith, by the writers of the golden *bralas*,[3] all the world over, wherever people inhabit the earth. Because of this outrageous heresy, I had thy letter burned, as a ritual representation of the cruel sentence handed down against thee, which I would like to see executed upon thy person as well, for the heinous sin that hast committed. Therefore, I command thee, immediately, without any further delay, to sail away, if thou wouldst not be cursed by the waters that sustain thee."

As soon as the interpreter—who is called a *tansu*[4] there—finished reading and translating the letter, everyone who heard it felt quite humiliated, and especially Antonio de Faria, who was more humiliated and offended by it than all of them put together. And for a long time they felt somewhat helpless, because they had given up all hope of ever being able to ransom the captives.

And after discussing the offensive language of the letter and the mandarin's bad manners, they finally decided to send a landing party ashore to attack the city, for they could count on our Lord's protection to be equal to the good intentions that inspired them. And to implement their decision, they lost no time arranging for landing craft, which consisted of four fishing barges that were captured that same night.

A roll call of the men available for this mission showed a total of three hundred—seventy of them Portuguese and the rest, slaves and sailors—counting *Quiay Panjão*'s people, among whom there were 160 arquebusiers, while all the others were armed with lances, javelins, firebombs, and many other different kinds of weapons needed to bring this affair to a successful conclusion.

65
The Sack of *Nouday*

The following morning, shortly before daybreak, Antonio de Faria sailed up the river with the three junks, the *lorcha,* and the four fishing barges he had seized, and dropped anchor in six and a half fathoms of water right up against the walls of the city. Dispensing with the noisy salvo of artillery, he lowered the sails and hoisted the flag of commerce in keeping with Chinese custom, intent upon observing all the outward signs of peace and leaving nothing undone by way of complying with the formalities, though he knew full well, from the way matters stood with the mandarin, that it would do him no good.

From here he sent him another letter which was extremely polite and friendly in tone, offering to raise the ransom for the captives; but it made that dog of a mandarin so angry, that he had the poor Chinese messenger crucified on an X-shaped cross and exhibited from the top of the wall in full view of the fleet. The sight was enough to make Antonio de Faria abandon the last shred of hope to which some of the men still made him cling, and at the same time, it made the soldiers so furious that they told him that, as long as he had decided to go ashore, there was no point in his waiting any longer because he would just be giving the enemies time to increase their strength.

Since this seemed like good advice to him, he embarked immediately with all the men who were determined to go ashore, leaving orders behind for the junks to direct a steady barrage of fire against the enemies and the city, wherever major gatherings were to be seen, provided he was not engaged in battle with them. And after disembarking at a spot about a culverin-shot's distance below the roadstead, without encountering the slightest opposition, he marched along the shore in the direction of the city where, by this time, many people were stationed on top of the walls, waving an enormous number of silk banners, trying to put on a brave show by shouting and playing their martial music and generally carrying on like people who put more stock in words and outward appearances than in actual deeds.

As our men came within a musket-shot's distance of the moat surrounding the wall, about 1,000 to 1,200 soldiers—a guess hazarded by some—sallied forth from two gates; and of this number, about 100 to 120 were mounted on horseback, or to put it in a better way, they were mounted on some rather sorry-looking nags. They began by putting on a fine show of skirmishing, running back and forth just as free and easy as you please, getting in each other's way most of the time, and often colliding and falling down in heaps of three and four, from which it was obvious that they were country bumpkins who were there not so much out of a desire to fight, but because they had been forced to come.

Antonio de Faria gaily spurred his men on, and after signalling to the junks, he waited for the enemy out in the field, for he thought that they would want to engage him there, judging by the brave show they were putting on. But instead, they went right on with their skirmishing, running around in circles for a while, as though they were threshing wheat, thinking that this alone would be enough to scare us off. However, when they saw that we would not turn tail and run as they thought or probably hoped we would, they got together in a huddle and remained that way for a while, in a single body, in great disorder, without coming any closer.

Seeing them that way, our captain ordered all the muskets, which had been silent until then, to fire at once; and, as God willed, they hit the mark so well that more than half of the cavalrymen, who were in the vanguard, were knocked to the ground. Off to a good start, we rushed at them all together, calling on the name of Jesus as we went; and he, in his mercy, caused the enemy to abandon the field to us and sent them fleeing so wildly that they were falling on top of each other; and when they reached the bridge spanning the moat, they got themselves jammed in there so tightly that they were unable to move either backward or forward.

At this juncture, the main body of our men caught up to them and handled them so efficiently that, before long, more than three hundred of them were lying on top of each other—a pitiful sight indeed—for not a single one of them ever drew a sword.

Exhilarated by this victory, we made a dash for the gate, and there in the entrance we found the mandarin, surrounded by nearly six hundred men, mounted astride a fine horse, wearing an old-fashioned gilt studded breastplate of purple velvet, which we found out later had belonged to a certain Tomé Pires,[1] whom King Manuel, of glorious memory, had sent as an ambassador to China on board Fernão Peres de Andrade's[2] *nao* in the days when Lopo Soares de Albergaria[3] was governing the State of India.

The mandarin and his men tried to stop us at the entrance, where a cruel battle ensued, during which, little by little, in the time it would take to recite four or five Credos, they began to drive us back with a lot less fear than the ones on the bridge had shown, and they would have given us a difficult time had it not been for one of our slave boys who knocked the mandarin off his horse with a musket ball that struck him right in the chest. At that, the Chinese became so frightened that they all spun around immediately and began retreating through the gates in complete disorder, and we along with them, knocking them down with our lances, while not a single one of them had enough presence of mind to shut the gates. And off we went, chasing them before us like cattle, down a very long road, until at last they swept through another gate that led to the forest where every last one of them disappeared from sight.

Next, to prevent disorder, Antonio de Faria gathered his soldiers together and, in a single corps, marched with them straight to the *chifanga,* which was the prison where they were holding our men, who at the sight of us let out such a loud and terrifying cry of "Lord God, have mercy on us!" that it was enough to send the shivers down one's spine. He immediately had the prison doors and bars broken with axes, a task that our men threw themselves into with such great enthusiasm that it took but a moment to smash everything to bits and to remove the prisoners' shackles, so that in a very short time, all our companions were unfettered and free.

The order was given to our soldiers and the others in our company that each man was to lay hold of as much as he could for himself, because there would be no sharing of the spoils, and everyone was to keep whatever he could carry; but he asked them to be quick about it, for he would allow them no more than the brief space of half an hour in which to do it. And they all answered that they would be perfectly satisfied with that.

And then they all disappeared into the houses, while Antonio de Faria headed straight for the mandarin's, which he had staked out for himself, and there he found eight thousand *taels* in silver alone, as well as five huge jars of musk, all of which he had gathered up. The rest, which he left for the slaves accompanying him, consisted of large quantities of silk, yarn, satin, damask, and fine-quality porcelain packed in straw, which they carried until they were ready to collapse.

As a result, the four barges and three sampans that had been used as landing craft had to make four trips to transfer the loot to the junks, and there was not a slave or sailor among them who did not speak of his booty in terms of whole cases and bales of piece goods, to say nothing of the secrets each one kept locked in his heart.

When he saw that more than an hour and a half had gone by, Antonio de Faria quickly ordered the men to return to the ships, but there was absolutely no way of getting them to stop their looting, and this was especially true of the men of most account. But with night coming on, he was afraid some disaster might befall them, and he had the torch put to the city in ten or twelve different places; and since most of the buildings were constructed of pine and other woods, the fire spread so fiercely that in less than a quarter of an hour it looked like a blazing inferno.

Withdrawing to the beach with all the men, he embarked, with not a murmur of protest from any of them, for they were all leaving very rich and happy; and they had many pretty girls in tow, which was really pathetic to see, for they were tied up with musket wicks by fours and fives, and they were all crying while our men were laughing and singing.

66
Pirates at the Gates of Ning-po

Since it was already late when Antonio de Faria and all his men got back to the ship, there was no time left for anything but to attend to the wounded, who numbered fifty—eight of them Portuguese and the rest slaves and sailors—and to bury the dead, who numbered nine, counting one Portuguese.

And after spending the night with a careful lookout on account of the junks up the river, at daybreak he departed for a small town located at the water's edge on the opposite bank, and discovered that it was completely deserted, all the inhabitants having fled. But he found the houses filled to overflowing with their goods and enormous quantities of food which Antonio de Faria had loaded on board the junks out of fear that in the ports along the way people would refuse to sell him anything because of what he had done.

After that it was decided, since everyone thought it best and advised him to do so, that the three winter months he still had to wait before he could set out on his voyage should be spent on a deserted island called *Pulo Hinhor*,[1] located out to sea fifteen leagues from Ning-po, where there was fresh water and good anchorage, because he thought that his presence in Ning-po would be detrimental to the commerce of the Portuguese merchants who spent their winters there peacefully carrying on their trade. And everyone praised him highly for this decision and his good intentions.

We departed from the port of *Nouday*, and after five days of sailing between the mainland and the islands of *Comolém*, at midday on a Saturday we were attacked by a robber named *Prematá Gundel*, a bitter enemy of the Portuguese people, who had already done them a great deal of harm several times before, not only in Patani but in Sunda and Siam and other places as well, wherever he chanced to meet them in a way that suited his purposes. Mistaking us for Chinese, he attacked us with two huge junks carrying two hundred fighting men, not counting the crew that worked the sails. One of them, after sinking its grappling hooks into Mem Taborda's junk, nearly finished him off. However, when *Quiay Panjão*, who was a little way out to sea, saw what was happening, he turned back and rammed the enemy junk, going after it under full sail and smashing into its starboard quarter with such force that both of them promptly sank to the bottom, leaving Mem Taborda free of the danger threatening him. Then three of our *lorchas*, which Antonio de Faria had brought from the port of *Nouday*, came running to the rescue at top speed and—thanks be to God—they saved most of our people while those on the enemy side all drowned.

About this time, *Prematá Gundel* had reached the big junk that Antonio de Faria was on and tackled it with a pair of grappling hooks attached to very long iron chains, immobilizing him fore and aft, and engaging him in a battle that was truly remarkable to see. For more than half an hour the enemy fought so bravely that most of Antonio de Faria's men were wounded, leaving him, on two occasions, in danger of being taken. However, at that point the three *lorchas* and a small junk commanded by Pero da Silva came to his aid, and—as God willed—with their help our men soon regained the ground they had lost. They pressed the enemy so hard that in no time at all the whole business was over, ending with the death of the eighty-six Moors who had boarded Antonio de Faria's junk and given him such a bad time that the only part of the ship still held by our men was the poop deck. And from here, they boarded the pirate's junk and put everyone they found on it to the sword, sparing none, though the crew had already dived into the sea.

However, the price of this victory was not cheap by any means, for it cost us the lives of seventeen men, five of them Portuguese—the best and bravest soldiers in the whole company—and left forty-three badly wounded, one of them Antonio de Faria, who came out of it with a spear injury and two sword cuts.

The battle over, an inventory was taken of what was found on the enemy junk and the booty was appraised at eighty thousand *taels*, the bulk of it in Japanese silver that the pirate had stolen from three merchant junks bound from Hirado[2] to *Chincheo*. That meant that, on this one ship alone, the pirate was carrying 120,000 *cruzados;* and they said that he had been carrying almost as much on the junk that went down, which aggrieved many of our men.

With this prize, Antonio de Faria withdrew to a little island called *Buncalou,* located three or four leagues to the west where there was fresh water and good anchorage. He went ashore and remained there for eighteen days, sleeping in huts that were improvised for the large numbers of wounded men where—as it pleased the Lord—all of them regained their health.

And from there, we proceeded on our determined course with Antonio de Faria on his big junk, Mem Taborda and Antonio Henriques on theirs, Pero da Silva on the small one that had been captured in *Nouday,* and *Quiay Panjão* and all his people on the one just taken from the robber, which was given to him to compensate him for the one he had lost, in addition to twenty thousand *taels* from the common funds, with which he felt completely satisfied and well paid for his trouble; and all our men were also pleased with this arrangement because Antonio de Faria had been most adamant about it and had promised to make up for it handsomely in the future.

We went sailing along in this manner, and within six days we reached the Gates of Ning-po, which are actually two islands located three leagues from where the Portuguese traded in those days. It was a town they had built ashore with over a thousand houses that was governed by a city council, a high court magistrate, constables, six or seven judges, and administrative officers of state, where the notaries would sign the legal documents they drew up in the following manner: "I, So-and-So, Notary Public of the Archives and Judiciary of the city of Ning-po, in the name of His Majesty, the King . . . ," as though it were situated between Santarém[3] and Lisbon. And they felt so sure of themselves and were so complacent about it that they had gone so far as to build homes costing between three and four thousand *cruzados,* all of which, from large to small, were later destroyed and completely leveled by the Chinese—for our sins—with not a trace of them left to show for it, as I will explain more fully at the proper time when I come to it.[4] And then it will be plain to see how uncertain things are in China, about which there is such great interest in Portugal and for which some people mistakenly have such high regard, for at every hour of the day they are exposed to all kinds of disasters and misfortunes.

67
A Message from Ning-po

Between these two islands—which are called the Gates of Ning-po[1] by the natives and navigators who frequent that coast—there runs a channel a little wider than twice the distance of a musket shot and about twenty to twenty-five fathoms deep; and in some parts it has small inlets with good anchorage and freshwater streams that descend from the mountaintop among forests thickly wooded with cedar, oak, and different varieties of pine, where many ships stop to gather the lumber they need for making spars, masts, planking and other kinds of timber, at no cost to themselves.

On a Wednesday morning, shortly after Antonio de Faria had dropped anchor at these islands, Mem Taborda and Antonio Henriques requested permission to proceed to Ning-po to inform the town of his arrival and to find out what was going on in the country and whether or not there was talk or any rumors about what he had done in *Nouday;* for if it should turn out that his presence would in any way be harmful to the peace and security of the Portuguese living there, then he would go on to spend the winter on the island of *Pulo Hinhor* as he had originally planned to do; but that in any event, they would let him know one way or the other in very short order.

To this he replied that he approved of the idea and granted permission for them to proceed as requested. He also wrote a few letters for them to deliver to the most honorable members of the local government, relating all the events of his voyage and asking them to advise him and to command him to do as they wished inasmuch as he was ready to obey them at a moment's notice, and other gracious words to that effect which cost nothing and turn out to be quite advantageous at times. Antonio Henriques and Mem Taborda departed that same afternoon, and Antonio de Faria remained there at anchor, waiting for a reply.

It was two hours after dark by the time these two reached the city, where the townspeople reacted with deep amazement, as was only to be expected, when they had seen them and heard the full story of the voyage. Appearing in response to the bells of the Church of Our Lady of the Immaculate Conception—which was the mother church of six or seven others throughout the land—they assembled to discuss among themselves the news that these two men had brought; and in view of Antonio de Faria's generosity towards them and all the others who had a share in the junk's cargo, they decided, since their means were limited and they could not repay him in full for all that he had done, that they would repay him in part, with a demonstration of love and gratitude.

In reply to his letter they composed one in common that was signed by all, as though it had come out of a special session of the council; and they had it delivered to him along with two *lanteias* laden with a good supply of fresh food by a gray-haired nobleman named Jerónimo do Rego, who was a very learned man and a leading member of the community. And in the letter, which contained many expressions of deep gratitude, they told him how highly obligated they all felt towards him, not only for the favor he had done them by recovering their merchandise from the hands of the enemy, but also for the great love he had shown them by his generous treatment of them, for which they hoped that the Lord our God would repay him with a great abundance of blessings in His glory; and that, as for his fear of spending the winter there because of what he had done in *Nouday,* there was no reason to worry about it since there was too much unrest in the country at the moment for anyone to take notice of it, not only on account of the death of the king of China,[2] but also because of the dissensions that had broken out all over the kingdom among the thirteen pretenders to the throne, all of whom were already encamped in the field with their armies, fully determined to effect a decision through force that could not be reached through justice; and that the *Tutão Nay,* who, after the king, held the highest position in the government, with all the supreme and divine powers of royal majesty, was surrounded in the city of Quoansy, by the *Prechau Muão,*[3] emperor of the Cochinese, to whose side the king of the Tartars was expected to rally with an army of 900,000 men; and that as a result, there was so much confusion and division among them that, even if his lordship had destroyed the city of Canton, they would hardly have paid any attention to it, let alone the city of *Nouday,* which in China, compared to many other cities, was of far less importance than in Portugal, Oeiras[4] is, compared to Lisbon; and that as a favor, in return for such reassuring good news, they requested his lordship to remain anchored where he was for six more days, in order to give them time to prepare suitable accommodations for him, since they could be of no other use to him for the time being, nor were they able to show him at the moment, much as they all desired, how deeply indebted they were to him; and other courteous words to that effect which were used profusely throughout the letter; and since he wanted to let them have their way, he replied in a manner he thought was proper, by agreeing to do what they asked of him.

And on the two *lanteias* that they had used to bring him the fresh food, he sent back the sick and wounded of the fleet, whom the people of Ning-po received most charitably, dividing them up among the wealthiest households where they nursed them back to health and provided them with everything necessary, in the most solicitous manner, seeing to it that nothing was overlooked.

And throughout the six days that Antonio de Faria waited here at anchor, not a single person of any importance in the town, or city, as they called it, failed to come and pay his respects to him, bringing him many gifts of ingeniously prepared delicacies, fresh food, and fruit, in such abundance that we were amazed by what we saw, and particularly by the lavish display and pageantry that accompanied all these things.

68
Antonio de Faria's Reception in Ning-po

Antonio de Faria remained anchored off these islands for all six of the days he waited here, as the people of Ning-po had asked him to do. At the end of that time, in the predawn hours of a Sunday, which was the day they had appointed for him to enter the port, they came to serenade him with a beautiful sunrise song, performed by an excellent chorus, to the accompaniment of soft musical instruments, that was a pleasure to hear. And they gave it a typical Portuguese ending when they struck up a frolic in double time, performed to the beat of drums, tambourines, and sistra, which we thoroughly enjoyed because it made us feel at home.

Slightly more than two hours before dawn, in the still of night, under a bright moon, he got under way with the entire fleet, the ships gaily bedecked with many silken flags and awnings, the topsails and topgallant sails decorated with fine silver mesh and very long streamers of the same stuff, escorted by numerous rowing barges from which could be heard the sounds of many trumpets, shawms, flutes, fifes, drums, and many other musical instruments both Portuguese and Chinese; and every one of the musical groups on board these boats had a different style of playing, each one better than the other. Then, at daybreak, when he still had a little more than half a league to go to reach port, the wind died down, and immediately, twenty well-equipped rowing *lanteias* appeared on the scene and took the entire fleet under tow, bringing it to its berth in less than an hour.

However, before it got there, more than sixty boats, *balões* and *manchuas,* moved in alongside Antonio de Faria's junk. They were bedecked with silk awnings and flags and plush carpets and were carrying over three hundred men on board who were dressed in all their finery with many gold collars and chains around their necks, and with their swords, also decorated in gold, worn bandolier style, as they do in Africa. And all these things were done to perfection, with such good taste, that everyone looking on was extremely pleased and no less astonished.

In this manner Antonio de Faria arrived in port, where he found anchored and lined up in order, twenty-six *naos* and eighty junks, and a much greater number of *vancões* and barges, tied one behind the other and lined up in two rows to form a long passageway; and all of them were decorated with branches of pine, laurel, and green cane, shaped into many arches covered with cherries, pears, lemons, oranges, and many other kinds of green foliage and fragrant herbs, which were also entwined in the masts and rigging.

After he had dropped anchor in the spot especially prepared for him near shore, Antonio de Faria fired his salvos with many a piece of fine artillery, to which all the *naos,* the junks, and the other craft mentioned responded in order, one by one, in what was indeed a remarkable sight that left the Chinese merchants gaping in amazement. And they asked who was that man that was getting such a splendid reception, was he a brother or relative of our king, or did he have some other connection with the royal family. Some of the courtesans replied by saying no, that he was not related, but that his father was in fact the blacksmith who shoed the horses that the king of Portugal rode and that that was why he was so honorable a personage that all the others there might well be his servants, fit to wait on him hand and foot like slaves.

The Chinese, believing every word of it, looked at each other in amazement.

"There are undoubtedly very great monarchs in the world," they exclaimed, "who are not mentioned in our ancient chronicles because our authors never heard about them. And it seems that one of them, who should be shown great respect, must be the king of these men, for according to what we have heard about him, he is richer, more powerful, and the lord of much more territory than either the Tartar or Cochinese kings; and one might even go so far as to say—if it were not a sin—that he is the equal of the Son of Heaven, the Crowned Lion on the Throne of the World."

All those listening agreed.

"Of course," they replied. "That's perfectly obvious, judging from the enormous wealth these bearded men have acquired throughout the world by sheer force of arms, in defiance of all other nations."

Once all the ships had completed their salvos, an expertly rowed *lanteia* moved in alongside Antonio de Faria's junk. It was completely covered with a fresh forest of chestnut trees with their prickly burrs just as nature created them, the branches all decorated with great quantities of roses and carnations intertwined with some other greenery a lot fresher and sweeter smelling than those which the natives call "lichees." And all this foliage was so thick, you could not see the oarsmen, who were also decorated in the same manner. On top of the quarterdeck of this vessel there was a richly adorned platform mounted on six legs and draped with brocade that had a silver chair on it surrounded by six very pretty young girls ranging in age from twelve to fifteen who were professional musicians and singers with beautiful voices that had been hired for the occasion and brought there from the city of Ning-po, seven leagues away, for this type of entertainment and many others like it are available for a price whenever necessary, and many merchants grow rich just from providing these things which are in great demand there for parties and other pastimes.

Antonio de Faria embarked on this *lanteia* and when he arrived at the pier there was a deafening racket of trumpets, shawms, timbals, fifes and drums, and many other instruments used by the Chinese, Malays, Chams, Siamese, Borneans, Ryukyu Islanders, and other nations who came to that port seeking the protection of the Portuguese against the pirates infesting those waters. And there they took him ashore in a luxurious sedan chair used for state occasions, as though he were one of the twenty-four *chaens* who comprise the governing body of this empire. It was carried by eight bearers dressed in fine mesh cloth, accompanied by twelve footmen holding silver maces, and by sixty halberdiers, their *panouras*[1] and poleaxes inlaid with gold, who had also been hired out from the city, and by eight men on horseback holding white damask banners, and as many more, with crimson and green satin parasols, who every now and then shouted in the *charachina* style to make the crowds fall back.

After he had landed and been officially welcomed, the noblest and richest people in town came to call on him, and one by one, as a gesture of courtesy, they prostrated themselves on the ground before him, which took up some time.

This done, two elderly noble gentlemen who resided there, one called Tristão de Gá[2] and the other Jerónimo do Rego, approached him, and in the name of all delivered a speech to him in which they praised him highly in rather eloquent and elegant terms, giving him a place, for his generosity, far above Alexander's, using very forceful and factual arguments to prove it, and comparing him advantageously, for his courage, with Scipio, Hannibal, Pompey, Julius Caesar, plus a lot of other things to that effect.

From here they took him to the church, passing through a very long street lined with laurel and pine trees, the walks completely strewn with flowers and shaded above with awnings made of many bolts of satin and damask. And in many places along the way there were tables set up with silver incense burners giving off all sorts of fragrances and perfumes, and some very clever theatrical interludes going on, that had been produced at great expense.

Fairly close to the end of the street there was a wooden tower constructed of pine and painted to look like stone, with three spires, each one topped by a gilded weather vane and a white damask banner displaying the royal coat of arms in gold. Framed in a window of this tower, two children and a middle-aged woman were weeping, and down below at the foot of the tower there was a man, his body drawn and quartered, in what was a very realistic depiction of his slaying by ten or twelve Castilians who were fully armed, with their lances and halberds painted blood red; and altogether it was a very enjoyable spectacle because of the great pomp and pageantry with which it was presented. And they say the inspiration for it came from the life of a certain John Doe from whom the true Farias[3] are descended, for they say that that was the way he earned his patent of nobility during the wars that were fought in ancient times between Portugal and Castile.

About this time, a bell at the very top of the tower, like a lookout point, was struck three times, signalling the crowds to be silent; and when the hubbub, which was considerable, had subsided, an old man wearing a purple damask surplice stepped out, accompanied by four attendants carrying silver maces; and after bowing deeply to Antonio de Faria, he told him, in carefully chosen words, how much they were all obliged to him for the great generosity he had shown them by restoring their goods; and that as a result, they would henceforth regard themselves as his subjects and vassals, and pay him due homage as his tributaries for as long as he lived. And he told him to gaze upon the figure of the hero close by, wherein he would see, as clearly as in a mirror, the manner in which his ancestors' great devotion to duty had earned so honorable a name for his descendants, as was well known to all the peoples of Spain;[4] and therein, he would also see how perfectly natural it was for him to do what he had done, and this applied to the courage he had shown as well as to all his other actions with respect to them; and that therefore, speaking in the name of all, he was asking him to accept this small token he was offering him in the meantime, to defray the cost of fuses for the soldiers, and to consider it as the initial payment of the tribute that they, as his vassals, were obliged to give him; and as for the rest of what they owed him, they promised to pay it in due time; and with that they presented him with five cases of silver bullion containing a total of ten thousand *taels*.

Antonio de Faria thanked them at great length for the honors they had already shown him and for the gift they were offering him, but under no circumstances would he accept it, no matter how hard they all insisted upon it.

69
The Vicar of Ning-po

Setting out from here, they wanted to lead Antonio de Faria beneath a richly adorned canopy being held in readiness for him by six of the most prominent men in the community. But he flatly refused, protesting that he had never been born for so high an honor as they wished to confer on him, and he continued on his way in the same manner, with no more ostentation than before, still accompanied by a large crowd of people, Portuguese, natives of the area and of many other nations who came there to trade, for in those days it was known as the best and richest port in all that part of the world. Moving ahead of him there were many dancers, *pélas*,[1] frolics, games, and different kinds of dramatic interludes which the local people who traded with us—some upon request and others forced by the penalties imposed on them— also performed like the Portuguese. And all this was accompanied by the music of many instruments, trumpets, shawms, flutes, horns, flageolets, harps, rebecs, together with fifes and drums, and a heavy babble of voices in the singsong *charachina* style, producing such an incredible racket that made it all seem unreal.

When he reached the church door, eight priests, ceremoniously arrayed in cloaks of brocade and richly wrought fabrics, came out to meet him, accompanied by a procession singing the *Te Deum Laudamus,* while another excellent choir sang the response with organ music that was as fine as any ever heard in the private chapel of a great prince.

And in the midst of this splendid procession he marched with measured steps up to the main altar of the church, where a white damask dossel had been hung, right next to a crimson velvet chair with matching footrest. And seated in this chair he heard a beautifully arranged vocal and instrumental mass, at which the vicar Estêvão Nogueira, a very honorable old man, officiated. But since, for lack of practice, he was not well versed in pulpit usage—to say nothing of the fact that he was a weak preacher and had little or no learning to begin with and, on top of this, was vain and conceited about being almost noble—in his anxiety to show how much he knew and what an expert orator he was, since this was an auspicious occasion, he devoted the entire sermon exclusively to a eulogy of Antonio de Faria, speaking in such an incoherent and generally disorganized manner that, when it became apparent to his listeners that Antonio de Faria was showing signs of discomfort bordering on annoyance, some of the vicar's friends tugged at his surplice three or four times to make him shut up. And when he finally caught on, he reacted like someone waking up to a fight.

"By God!" he exclaimed in a voice loud enough to be heard by all, though he pretended that he was responding to his friends. "I'm speaking the Gospel truth, so leave me alone! I swear to God that I would be willing to butt my head against the walls for the man who saved me seven thousand *cruzados* that I invested on the junk, which that dog of a *Khoja* Hassim had already made off with, like some ball player, using the fender timber for his stick. May God grant his soul the torments of hell where he now lies, and let us say amen!"

And this conclusion to the sermon was followed by such a loud roar of laughter that it was impossible for anyone in the church to be heard above the noise they were making.

When the laughter had died down and everyone was quiet, six little boys came out of the sacristy, dressed like angels and carrying gilded harps. Then the vicar himself knelt down before the altar of Our Lady of the Immaculate Conception, and gazing upon the image with upraised arms, his eyes brimming with tears, he intoned a prayer in a voice choked with emotion, as though he were speaking directly to the image: "Our Lady, thou art the rose"; to which the six little boys responded in unison, "Our Lady, thou art the rose," harmonizing so sweetly as they accompanied themselves on their harps that everyone there without exception burst into tears, overwhelmed by the deep devotion it inspired in them.

After this, accompanying himself on a large old-fashioned viol he was holding, the vicar intoned a few stanzas of this hymn in the same chanting voice, which were extremely devout and most appropriate to the occasion. And at the end of each stanza the children responded with the refrain, "Our Lady, thou art the rose."

It was generally so well liked by everyone, not only because of the excellent musical arrangement with which it was presented, but also because of the deep devotion it inspired in all, and as a result, there were many tears shed throughout the church.

70
A Banquet in Honor of Antonio de Faria

Once mass was over, the four leading members of the governing body of the town, or city, of Ning-po, as our people called it—namely, Mateus de Brito,[1] Lançarote Pereira,[2] Jerónimo do Rego, and Tristão de Gá—came over to Antonio de Faria. Placing themselves on either side of him, they led him off, accompanied by the whole Portuguese colony of probably over a thousand men, to a large garden terrace fronting their homes which was completely enclosed by a dense hedge of chestnut trees, heavily laden with burrs, fresh from the forest, their boughs decorated above with many silk banners and flags, and the ground below covered with arrowhead, mint, and roses, both red and white, which grew abundantly in China.

Within this hedged area, three very long tables had been set up along some myrtle bowers running all around the terrace where many sprinklers had been installed with water flowing through pipes, from one to the other by means of some mechanical devices invented by the Chinese, which were so highly sophisticated and ingenious that no one was ever able to figure out how they operated, for with the force of the blast of air from something like an organ bellows, to which they were all connected, they squirted the water so high that when it fell to earth it came down in tiny droplets as gentle as dew, requiring only a single jug of water to spray the entire terrace, which was as large as a big city square.

In front of these three tables there were three matching buffets laden with a large quantity of extremely fine porcelain and six oversized gold pitchers which the Chinese merchants had brought from the city of Ning-po, where they had borrowed them from the mandarins, whose table service consists exclusively of gold vessels because silver is used by people of lesser quality and lower station in life. They had also brought many other serving pieces, such as large platters, saltcellars, and goblets, also made of gold, which were indeed delightful to behold, if the sight did not bring on an occasional twinge of envy.

After the people who had not been invited to the banquet bade their farewells, only the guests remained, and there were perhaps seventy or eighty of them, not counting Antonio de Faria's soldiers, who numbered above fifty. And once they were seated at table, they were waited on by very pretty girls, richly clad in mandarin style, who sang a song, accompanied by background music played by others, every time they served a dish. And Antonio de Faria was waited on personally by eight extremely fair gentlewomen, the daughters of honorable merchants, whose fathers had brought them there from the city, out of consideration for Mateus de Brito and Tristão de Gá. These girls were all dressed like sirens, and they waited on table with mincing steps, as though they were dancing, to the sound of instrumental music which simply delighted everyone listening and left all the Portuguese gaping with amazement but full of praise for the perfection with which everything they were seeing and hearing had been arranged and presented. And when it was time to serve the drinks, they struck up the band with shawms, trumpets, and timbals. The banquet went on like this for nearly two hours, and during that time they also presented some theatrical interludes, one in Chinese and the other in Portuguese.

As for the excellence and abundance of the food, I will not even touch upon the subject, for if I were to try to describe in detail all the things that were served that day it would take me forever; but one thing I will say, and it is that I doubt very much that in very few places in the world, could a banquet be given that would surpass this one in any respect.

When the tables were cleared, and it must have been close to two in the afternoon by then, they moved on to another terrace enclosed all around with many reviewing stands that were crowded with people who watched the running of ten bulls and five wild horses, which was the most enjoyable spectacle ever seen, accompanied by the playing of many trumpets, timbals, fifes and drums, and many different kinds of theatrical interludes.

By the time this was over it was almost evening, and Antonio de Faria wanted to return to his ship, but they would not hear of it, and instead, Tristão de Gá and Mateus de Brito offered him their homes, which had already been prepared for him with connecting passageways from one to the other, where he remained very comfortably installed for the entire five months of his stay in Ning-po. And during that time there were always many diversions such as fishing trips, falconry and hawking, hunting for deer, boar, bulls, and wild horses which abound on this island, in addition to many other sports and pastimes in the form of plays and all sorts of variety performances, along with splendid banquets that were given on Sundays, feast days, and a great number of weekdays; so that the five months we spent here seemed like barely five days to us.

At the end of that time, Antonio de Faria made ready with men and ships for the voyage to the mines of *Quoangeparù*. However, owing to the death in the meantime of *Quiay Panjão,* which he sorely regretted, he was advised not to attack them because there were rumors, which were believed to be true, that there was a great deal of unrest in that country due to the wars being carried on by the *Prechau Muhão*[3] against the kings of Chiang Mai,[4] the *Pafuás,* and Champa. But they suggested that he get together with a very famous pirate there called Similau,[5] whom he then contacted. He had a long talk with him, and this fellow told him many wonderful things about an island named *Calempluy,*[6] where there were seventeen tombs of the kings of China, who had been buried in some golden chapels with a huge number of idols, also of gold, where he said that the only trouble or difficulty they would encounter was no more than that of loading the ships. And he also told him many other things of such great majesty and splendor that I will pass over for fear they may raise doubts in the mind of the reader.

And since Antonio de Faria was by nature a very curious person, and not wholly devoid of greed either, he immediately became so taken with the ideas of this Chinese that, on his word alone, without any other proof, he decided to throw all caution to the winds and undertake this voyage; and he was unwilling to seek anyone else's advice on the matter, which scandalized a few of his friends somewhat, and not without reason.

71
The Voyage to *Calempluy*

The season arrived, and since all the necessary preparations for the new voyage he had decided to make were completed by then, Antonio de Faria departed from here on a Monday, the fourteenth of May, in the year 1542, laying his course for the island of *Calempluy*. He embarked on two *panouras,*[1] which are like galliots, only a bit taller, having been advised against making the voyage on ocean-going junks, not only to avoid being detected, but also because the big ships he was using at the time would never be able to make any headway, not even under full sail, against the strong currents and heavy volume of water flowing into the Gulf of Nanking during the months of May, June, and July, when the winter snows of Tartary and *Nixiumflão* begin to melt, descending in that direction with tremendous force.

Sailing on board these two ships were fifty-six Portuguese and a priest to say mass, as well as forty-eight seamen to handle the oars and sails, all natives of Patani who had been offered good terms because they were a loyal and trustworthy crew. In addition to these men we were taking forty-two of our slaves, so that altogether we had a company of 146 and no more, because the corsair Similau, who was our pilot, wanted it that way; nor would he allow any more ships for fear of arousing suspicion, since we would have to cross the Gulf of Nanking and pass through heavily trafficked rivers, and he was very much afraid of running into one or another of the many disasters to which we were exposing ourselves.

The first day and night we made our way past all the islands of *Angitur* and proceeded on our voyage, steering a course on out to seas that had never before been seen or navigated by the Portuguese. Deeply preoccupied by thoughts of the perils that lay ahead, on we went, under a fair wind, keeping within sight of land for the first five days, until we reached the mouth of the gulf where the fishing waters of Nanking begin. Here we crossed a gulf forty leagues wide and sighted a very high mountain range called *Nangafau*, along which we sailed for another five days, heading due north, until the wind began to fail us. And since the seas here were already quite rough, Similau sought the shelter of a small river with good anchorage that was populated by a very fair people, of good stature, with narrow eyes like the Chinese, but otherwise quite different from them in both speech and dress.

And in the three days we were here, the men we encountered steadfastly refused to engage in any form of conversation with us; on the contrary, many of them would band together and run down to the beach near where we were anchored, shouting and gesticulating wildly, with menacing expressions on their faces, and they would shoot their slings and arrows at us, running back and forth, and generally carrying on as if they had something to fear from us.

At the end of these three days, when the weather and the seas had improved enough for us to continue our journey, Similau, who was then in complete command and whose orders everyone obeyed, set sail with the bow pointing east-northeast, a course he maintained steadily for the next seven days, keeping constantly within sight of land; and from here, after heading due east across another gulf, he reached the entrance to a strait ten leagues wide at the mouth called *Sileupaquim,* through which he ran for five more days, passing many noble towns and cities along the way. This river or strait was heavily congested with an enormous number of ships; and since he was afraid of being discovered here, and having been assured that if he were, there would be no salvation for him, Antonio de Faria decided to turn back. But Similau balked at this decision, though everyone else was in favor of it.

"It's too late," he protested, "for your lordship or anyone else in our company to talk about sins, because I warned you publicly in Ning-po, during the general meeting at the church, in the presence of over a hundred Portuguese, that we would all be taking enormous risks, and I more so than any of you, because I am Chinese, and on top of that, the pilot. All they would do to your lordships would be to kill you once;

but me, they would kill two thousand times, if that were possible. So you see, I am in no position to betray you; on the contrary, I am forced to be loyal, extremely loyal, as I am now and always will be, not only insofar as this voyage is concerned, but in all other matters as well, regardless of what the troublemakers have been telling your lordship about me. But if you are so afraid of this danger you are talking about and prefer to go a different way, one that is traveled by fewer people and ships, it will take us longer, but we will be able to sail with nothing to fear. And so it is up to you, sir, to make that decision with your soldiers, but do so right away or let us turn back, for I am ready to do whatever you say."

Antonio de Faria was very grateful to him for this and showed it by embracing him many times. And when he asked him what course he would take since the one they were on was not to his liking for the many dangers to which they were exposed, Similau told him that 170 leagues further north there was a river slightly wider than half a league, called *Sumèpadão,* where they would meet with no obstacles, for unlike the Gulf of Nanking they happened to be in at that time, the area was uninhabited; however, the voyage would take them a month longer because of the wide detour they would be making if they went by way of that river.

And since Antonio de Faria thought that risking a delay was far better than risking their lives, he agreed to Similau's suggestion and turned about and left the Gulf of Nanking the way he had entered. He coasted along the shore for five more days, and at the end of that time, as it pleased the Lord, we sighted a very high mountain range with a round hill to the east, which Similau said was called *Fanjus.* We headed for it and soon found ourselves entering an extremely beautiful bay, forty fathoms deep, that was completely sheltered from the wind because of its half-moon shape, in which two thousand *naos,* no matter how big, could easily ride at anchor.

Here Antonio de Faria went ashore with a party of ten or twelve soldiers and scoured the entire area without finding anyone who could give him information about the course he was following. He was quite shaken by this and was beginning to repent of what he had so arbitrarily undertaken, without consulting anyone or considering anyone else's feelings or inclination but his own, and though he was suffering for this mistake, he tried hard not to show it so his men would not interpret it as a sign of weakness on his part.

Here in this bay, in front of everyone, Antonio de Faria spoke to Similau again about the way they were navigating, so blindly.

"Believe me, Sir Captain," he replied, "if I could pledge to you a jewel of greater value than my own head, I would gladly do so, because I am so sure that I am on the right course that I would have no qualms about giving you a thousand of my sons as hostages for the promise I made to you in Ning-po. And even now, I am telling you again, if you have any regrets, or if you are afraid to continue the journey because of the things your men keep whispering in your ear about me, as I have seen and heard them do all along, then command me as you wish, for I am ready to obey you in all things. As for what they keep telling you, that I am now making the voyage longer than I promised you in Ning-po, you know perfectly well the reason why I did so, and you saw nothing wrong with it at the time I explained it to you; and since you approved of it then, set your mind at rest now and do not go back on your decision, and you will see how much profit you will derive from the hardship you are suffering now."

This made Antonio de Faria feel somewhat better and he told him to go whichever way he thought best, and that, as for the soldiers' grumbling, to pay it no heed, for what else could one expect from idle people but criticizing other people's lives instead of looking after their own; but that henceforth they would hold their tongues or he would punish them severely; and with that Similau felt satisfied.

72
A Doubtful Course

Departing from this inlet, we sailed along the coast for thirteen more days, keeping constantly within sight of land, until we came to a bay called *Buxipalem* at latitude forty-nine degrees, where we found the climate already somewhat colder. It was teeming with fish and serpents of so many different varieties that I must say, it really fills me with dread to relate the highly incredible things that Similau told Antonio de Faria about them, not only about what had been found there before, but also about what could be heard in the night, especially during the interlunar periods of November, December, and January, when the rainstorms begin and darkness sets in; and he pointed some of them out to him right in front of his eyes, which led us to believe that the rest of what he said might well be true.

We saw some fish here like our rays which our men called "blanket fish," which measured more than four fathoms around, with flat snouts like an ox's. We saw some others like huge lizards that had green and black spots all over, with three rows of sharply pointed spines down the back the thickness of an arrow and nearly three handspans long, and the rest of the body completely covered with them, though these spines were not as thick and long as the others. These fish, which Similau said the Chinese called *puchissucões,* would occasionally bristle like porcupines, acquiring a fearsome aspect, and they had a very sharp black snout with teeth nearly two handspans long protruding from the jaw like a boar's. We also saw some other dark black fish resembling the sea devil, but so monstrously large that the head alone was more than six handspans across, and when swimming with their fins spread out, they measured more than a fathom around, according to those who saw them.

And I am not mentioning many other different kinds of fish we saw here because I do not think it is necessary to spend too much time on something that has no bearing on my story. I will only add that on the two nights we were anchored here, we felt far from safe with all those huge lizards, whales, fish, and sea serpents we had seen around there in the daytime, because there was such a weird chorus of howls, grunts, and snorts rising from the water, along with the barking noises of the sea horses [1] coming from the beach, that I would not even attempt to put it into words.

After departing from this Bay of *Buxipalem,* which our men named the "River of Serpents," Similau kept on his course for a distance of fifteen more leagues and dropped anchor in another much more beautiful and deeper bay called *Calindão* that swept around in a semicircle measuring perhaps more than six leagues, somewhat like a cove, which was completely surrounded by very high mountains and dense forests, with many streams running down to the beach from the highest peaks. There was a confluence in this cove of four very large rivers which all emptied into the bay through openings that had been formed in different parts of the land. And here Similau told us that, because of the huge amount of animal remains carried by these rivers when swollen by the melting winter snows, all the beasts we had seen both here and in the other bay came to feed, which did not happen in any other part of the coast we had left behind.

And when Antonio de Faria asked him where the headwaters of those rivers were located, he said he did not know, but that if what was written about them was true, two of them descended from a huge lake called *Moscumbiá,* and the other two from a province called *Alimania,*[2] where there were large mountain ranges covered with snow all the year round; and that that was the reason why, in the summertime, when most of the snow was melting, those rivers descended as forcefully and with as great a volume of water as we had seen, to a far greater extent than at any other time of the year; and that we were anchored at the mouth of one of those rivers called *Patèbenão,* along which, with the name of the Lord of heaven on our lips, we would have to sail, heading east and east-southeast, in order to again reach the Gulf of Nanking which we had left 260 leagues behind, having traveled that distance several times over at a greater latitude than where the island we were looking for was located; and even though, by doing this, we might undergo some hardship, he urged Antonio de Faria not to think of it as wasted effort, because he had done it all for the best, with the safety of all in view.

And when Antonio de Faria asked him how many days he might spend navigating that river along which he was taking them, he said only about fourteen to fifteen days, and he promised him that once we had sailed out of it, within five days he would put him ashore on the island of *Calempluy,* where they would indulge themselves to their heart's content and look back at all the hardship they were now complaining about as having been well worth it. Then Antonio de Faria embraced him and made him great promises of friendship; and he reconciled him with the soldiers about whom he had been complaining all along, so that everyone was quite happy.

Completely reassured by this good news and by what Similau had told him about the new route that would lead him into such a great and powerful domain, Antonio de Faria spurred his men on as he prepared himself in a manner suited to his purposes, not only with regard to the artillery which had been kept under cover till then, but also inspecting the arms, appointing captains of the lookout teams, and doing everything else necessary to provide for any contingency that might arise. And it was then that Father Diogo Lobato, who was part of the company as I said before, and who was our patron and second in command on board, delivered a brief sermon to all of us there, in order to instill us with spirit and courage for what lay ahead; and in it he touched on some matters of vital importance to our worthy goal, with such fine words, and in a manner so discreet and so appropriate to the occasion, that everyone who had hitherto been quite despondent and frightened, suddenly, as was plain to see, became imbued with a new spirit of derring-do, shaking off their doubts and committing themselves wholeheartedly to the undertaking they had begun.

Burning anew with ardor, they fired a devout salvo before an image of our Lady, at the foot of which everyone promised fearlessly to carry out this expedition on which they had embarked. And in a pitch of excitement we reefed the sails; and with the bow facing due east, we entered the mouth of the river that Similau had indicated, calling out frequently as we went, with many tears and with all our hearts, for the help and protection of the Lord on high who sits at the right of the Eternal Father, praying to him to keep us in his all-powerful hand.

73
Of Men and Beasts

We proceeded on our course with the bow pointed in different directions as we followed the bends in the river, and the next day we reached a very high mountain range called *Botinafau*, flowing with many streams of water and abounding in tigers, *badas*,[1] lions, *caleus*,[2] wildcats, zebras, and many other different kinds of wild beasts that were darting about chasing their prey, obeying only their strong, primitive instincts as they engaged in a cruel and never-ending war against other kinds of wild beasts and animals of a weaker nature, such as the deer, boar, ape, jackal, monkey, fox, and wolf—a sight we enjoyed for quite a while, and though we shouted and hooted at them, it did not frighten them much since they were not accustomed to hunters.

It took us six days to pass this mountain range, covering a distance of forty-five to fifty leagues, after which we found ourselves entering another mountain range no less wild, called *Gangitanou;* and from here on the rest of the country is very mountainous, rugged, almost inaccessible, and so densely forested that neither the sun's rays nor its warmth could possibly penetrate it. Similau said that this mountain range was unpopulated for ninety leagues around because the soil was not suitable for cultivation, with the exception of the foothills, which were inhabited by a monstrous race of people called *Gigauhós*. They were a primitive tribe that lived exclusively on the wild game they hunted and a little rice that some merchants from certain parts of China brought them in exchange for raw hides. And it was said, judging by the duties paid for these hides to the customs at *Pocasser*[3] and Nan-t'ou,[4] that twenty thousand catties[5] of these skins had been traded; and with sixty skins to the catty or bale, it is obvious, that is, if Similau was telling the truth, that the total number of skins traded amounted to 1,200,000. They were used by people in the wintertime for lining their clothes, for hangings, and for bed covers, and since it gets very cold there, they were commonly used by everyone.

Amazed by all of the many things Similau told him regarding this as well as other matters, and especially by what he had said about these *Gigauhós* and the deformity of their bodies and limbs, Antonio de Faria begged him to try as hard as possible to let him catch a glimpse of one of them because, as he assured him, it meant more to him than all the wealth of China.

"Sir," he replied, "I know how important it is for me to do so, not only to gain credibility in your eyes, but also to silence the grumblers who keep nudging each other with their elbows every time they hear me speak. But, to make them believe one thing because of another, before sundown, you will be talking to more than a pair of them—only on condition that you do not go ashore as you have been doing all along, lest some disaster befall you like the many that happen here everyday to merchants who like to hunt birds in strange forests. For I can assure you that these *Gigauhós* never deal with anyone in good faith, not only because it is something they never learned at their mother's breast, but also because of their fierce, primitive instincts, which makes them inclined to nourish themselves on flesh and blood, like any of the beasts in the jungle."

We proceeded along the shore in the same manner, under sail and oar, observing the dense growth of the vegetation, the ruggedness of the mountains and forests, the multitude of monkeys, apes, jackals, wolves, deer, boar, and large numbers of many other wild animals, running, leaping, weaving in and out amongst each other, and screeching so loud that in many places we could not hear ourselves speak—though it kept us amused for quite a while—when all at once we saw a beardless youth approaching from behind a point of the land, prodding six or seven cows before him as though leading them to pasture. The boy stopped when he saw Similau waving a towel at him and waited for us to get in closer to the water's edge where he was standing. And after displaying a bolt of green taffeta, which he said they were very fond of, Similau asked him in sign language if he wanted to buy it. Moving as close as he could to us, he replied in a very discordant kind of speech: "Quiteu paraó fau fau," which meant nothing to us because none of the men on board the ships could speak or understand that language, and it was only by making signs that Similau could handle the exchange of the merchandise he was displaying.

Antonio de Faria told him to give him a length of about three or four ells from the bolt of taffeta they had shown him, as well as six pieces of porcelain. He took it all with a great deal of excitement and exclaimed, "Pur pacam pochy pilaca hunangue doreu,"—words which, again, nobody understood. The boy was apparently very pleased with the things they had given him, and pointing in the direction from which he had come, he went dashing off into the woods, leaving the cows behind him.

This boy was dressed in tiger skins with the fur side out, his arms and legs were bare, he had absolutely nothing on his head, and he carried a crude stick in his hand. His limbs were well proportioned, and he had rather frizzly reddish hair that reached down to his shoulders and must have been more than ten spans long, according to what some people said.

He returned a little more than a quarter of an hour later with a live deer slung over his back, accompanied by thirteen people, eight men and five women, leading three cows tied with ropes, all of them dancing to the sound of a drum which, at intervals, they beat five times, then clapped their hands five times, saying in loud and discordant voices, "Cur cur hinau falem." To make them think we were merchants, Antonio de Faria gave orders to show them five or six bolts of cloth and many pieces of porcelain, all of which they thoroughly enjoyed looking at.

This whole group of people, both men and women, were dressed alike, with nothing in the way of clothing to tell them apart, except that the women were wearing thick tin bracelets on their upper arms, and their hair, which was much longer than the men's, was decorated with some flowers, like arrowhead blossoms, called lilies in this country, and around their necks they wore a large string of red shells about the size of oysters. The men carried heavy sticks in their hands that were bound halfway down with the same skins they were wearing, and they all had heavy, coarse features, with thick lips, short flat noses, and wide nostrils. Their bodies are somewhat disproportionate in size, though not as much as people in Portugal think, because Antonio de

Faria had them measured and he did not find a single one over ten and a half spans tall—except for only one elderly man there who was almost eleven—and the women are a little under ten. But still, I believe that they are a very crude, primitive race, of far less intelligence than all the other people discovered up till now in our conquests or anyone else's.

Antonio de Faria gave them three scores of porcelain, a bolt of green taffeta, and a basket of pepper; after which they all threw themselves down on the ground, raised both hands with closed fists, and said, "Vumguahileu opomguapau lapão lapão lapão," which words we took for expressions of gratitude, judging by the motions that went with them, since they prostrated themselves three times. And after presenting us with three cows, the deer, and a huge amount of leaf chard, they once again uttered in their loud, discordant voices, a jumble of words after their fashion which I cannot recall, but which, like the others before them, nobody understood. And after more than three hours of conversing with them in sign language, with us as amazed by the looks of them as they were with ours, they disappeared into the jungle from whence they had come, howling to the accompaniment of the five drum beats, leaping up and down from time to time as if to show how delighted they were with what they were carrying.

From here we proceeded up the river on our course for another five days, and during that time we always saw them along the edge of the water, sometimes bathing in the nude, but we never had any further communication with them.

Once we had passed this stretch of land which must have been a distance of about forty leagues, give or take a little, we continued on our way under sail and oar for another sixteen days without seeing any people in all that time, as though the country were uninhabited, except for two nights when we observed some fires far inland. At the end of these sixteen days—as it pleased the Lord—we reached the Gulf of Nanking, just as Similau had said we would, hoping that within five or six days we would see the outcome of our desires.

74
Similau Disappears

When we reached the Gulf of Nanking Similau advised Antonio de Faria to keep the Portuguese out of sight, no matter what, for he feared that if the Chinese saw them it would cause a commotion, since no foreigners had ever been seen in those parts before; and that they alone were sufficient for handling any questions that might be asked of them. He was also of the opinion that they should sail in the middle of the gulf rather than along the shore because of the constant coming and going of the *lorchas* and *lanteias* that were passing them on all sides; and this was done, since everyone was of the same opinion.

After we had been sailing on for six days on a course east by north, we came in sight of a big city called *Sileupamor* and headed straight for it, and by the time we entered the port it was two hours past nightfall. It was a beautiful bay nearly two leagues around, where we saw a huge number of sails at anchor, perhaps more than three thousand, according to those who ventured a guess, and the sight of them put such a scare into us that, without daring to cause the slightest disturbance, we turned around and slipped very quietly away. Crossing the river, which must have been six or seven leagues wide, we ran on our course for the rest of the day along a large open plain, with the intention of taking on some provisions wherever we might find it most suitable to our purpose; and since we were already running quite low on victuals and had been put on short rations, we went through thirteen days of extreme hunger and thirst during which each man was allotted only three scant mouthfuls of boiled rice and nothing more.

And it was while we were going through all this misery that we reached a group of very ancient buildings called *Tanamadel*, where we went ashore one morning at dawn and descended upon one of the buildings that was a little further removed from the others; and there—as the Lord willed—we found a huge store of rice and beans, many pots full of honey, smoked ducks, onions, garlic, and sugarcane, to which we helped ourselves freely. Some Chinese we captured there told us that that building served as the storehouse for a charity hospital located two leagues from there, where pilgrims could obtain provisions when passing through on their way to visit the tombs of the kings.

We reembarked, and with the ships now well victualled, proceeded on our voyage for seven more days, which by then made a total of two and a half months since we had departed from Ning-po. By this time Antonio de Faria had lost all confidence in what Similau had told him. He truly regretted ever having set out on that voyage, and he let everyone know how he felt about it. However, since there was nothing to be done at that point but commend oneself to God and take precautions for what lay ahead, that is precisely what he did at all times, with great courage.

And one morning, when he asked him what heading he was taking, Similau answered him in a way that did not make any sense, as though he had lost his bearings and could not tell where he was. As a result, Antonio de Faria became so enraged that he reached for a dagger at his waist and would have killed him on the spot if many men had not come between them and cautioned him not to, for then all would be lost. Getting control of himself, he yielded to the advice of his friends, but he was still so angry that he swore, as he pulled on his beard, that if within three days Similau did not somehow prove or disprove his lies, he would stab him to death. This put such a fright into Similau that the following night, when we were anchored close to shore, he very quietly jumped into the river, without the men on duty suspecting anything until the end of the watch, when they informed Antonio de Faria. He was caught completely off guard by the news and was so beside himself that he came close to losing his patience entirely, but out of fear of a mutiny, which was already beginning to take shape, he spared the lives of the two watchmen who had been negligent in their duty.

He immediately went ashore with all his men and went around looking for Similau almost until dawn without being able to find him or a living soul who could give him any information as to his whereabouts. After returning to the ships he discovered that of the forty-six Chinese sailors in the company, thirty-two had fled, for they too, in fear of the danger facing them, had decided to save themselves that way. Antonio de Faria and all those with him were so overcome that they clasped their hands together, and gazing heavenwards, remained silent, so that only their tears spoke for them, giving mute testimony to what they felt in their hearts; but considering all the events leading up to that moment, and the turmoil and grave danger in which they found themselves, losing one's courage, judgment, and understanding— let alone one's power of speech—was the least.

A meeting was called to decide upon what to do next, but for a long time the matter remained in abeyance without any conclusion being reached because of the many and wide variety of opinions that were offered on the subject. Finally it was agreed that we should still go forward with our original plans, and that we should try, as stealthily as possible, so as not to alarm the countryside, to capture someone who could give us some idea of how far we were from there to the island of *Calempluy;* and that if, from the information obtained, we could determine that it was as easy to attack as Similau had said it was, then we should go ahead; and that if it was not, we would turn back, navigating downstream on the current in the middle of the river because it would bring us on its natural course to the sea. Having reached this decision by majority vote, we proceeded on our way forward with distraught minds and terror in our hearts, for we knew full well, alone and friendless as we were, that we were exposing ourselves to the danger of death.

The next night, towards the end of the midwatch, we saw right off our bow a barge anchored in the middle of the river which, owing to dire need and the crisis confronting us, we were forced to board without causing an uproar or tumult of any kind; and there we captured five men we found asleep, who were each interrogated separately by Antonio de Faria to see if he would get the same answers from all of them. In reply to his questions they all said that we were in an area of the country called *Tanquilem,* from where it was only a distance of ten leagues to the island of *Calempluy.* And when he questioned them in detail about many other things that were necessary for our safety and salvation, all of them, one by one, answered very much to the point, which made Antonio de Faria and all the others feel quite satisfied and, most of all, extremely sorry about their past blunders, for they knew all too well that without Similau, who was the guiding star of our voyage, we could not do anything right.

Antonio de Faria took these five Chinese along, chained to the benches, and proceeded on his course for two and a half more days; and at the end of that time it was the Lord's will that just when we were rounding a point of the land called *Guinaytarão,* we discovered this island of *Calempluy* that we had been searching for for eighty-three days, in the midst of all the turmoil caused by the hardships and fears described above.

75
The Fabulous Isle of *Calempluy*

Having rounded, as I said, this point *Guinaytarão,* we saw, about two leagues ahead of us, right in the middle of the river, a flat stretch of land, like a floodplain, which appeared to be a little over a league in circumference. As Antonio de Faria came in close to it, he felt a deep surge of excitement, mixed with no small amount of fear, for up until that moment he had not yet realized that he had gotten, not only himself, but all the others into a very dangerous situation.

It was more than three hours past nightfall when he dropped anchor about a culverin-shot's distance from the island. And at daybreak, all those who were called into conference for the purpose agreed that, since it did not seem likely that anything as magnificent as that, of such obvious splendor and majesty, would be left unguarded, it would probably be wise to sail completely around it first, as silently as possible, in order to see what landing places it had and what obstacles there might be to our disembarking, and that, depending on what was discovered, we would decide what to do.

Antonio de Faria ordered this resolution to be carried out; and without making the slightest sound, he moved in close to shore and sailed all the way around it, looking it over at will and taking special note of everything for as far as the eye could see.

This island was encircled by a raised embankment twenty-six handspans tall, of jasper stonemasonry, the slabs so beautifully cut and set that the entire wall appeared to be made of one piece, a feat of construction that left everyone gasping with amazement, because they had never seen anything like it before anywhere in the world, either in or outside of India. The base of this wall was set in the very bottom of the river, and from there to the surface of the water, it measured another twenty-six handspans, so that altogether it was fifty-two spans high. At the top of the embankment where the wall ended, there was a border running all the way around, also made of jasper, carved in the shape of a twisted rope, like the waist cord of a monk's robe, about as thick as a four-almud[1] barrel; and on top of this, a brass railing, fashioned by lathe, with balusters spaced six arm's lengths apart, also made of brass, each of which supported a female idol holding a sphere in her hands, which at that time had no special significance for us.

Running along the inside of this railing, there was a row made up of an infinite number of cast-iron monsters, holding hands like dancers, encircling the entire island, which, as I said before, measured nearly a league in circumference. Behind these monstrous idols, forming a concentric circle around the floodplain, there was a row of arches so exquisitely wrought that the eyes could never have their fill of admiring them. And all the rest within the enclosure consisted of a very dense grove of dwarf orange trees, in the middle of which had been built 360 chapels dedicated to the gods of the year, about whom these pagans have written a great deal of nonsense in their histories, to compensate for their inability to see the light.

Further up, about a quarter of a league, on a land elevation rising to the east, there appeared some buildings with seven façades, like those of a church, all covered in gold from top to bottom for as far as the eye could see, with very tall spires, which appeared to be belfry towers; and on the exterior, running all around these buildings, were two streets covered with arches which matched the seven façades and were all, from the top of the towers all the way down to the ground, covered with gold, which was why everyone thought this was probably a very sumptuous temple of exceedingly great wealth.

After a careful examination of this island or floodplain, which was possible because, as I have said, it was situated in the middle of the river, Antonio de Faria decided, in spite of the late hour, to go ashore and see if he could find somebody in one of the chapels who could give him the information he needed to help him decide whether he should proceed or withdraw.

And after posting the necessary guards on both ships, he went ashore with a landing party of forty soldiers and twenty slaves, made up of both lancers and arquebusiers, along with four Chinese—who had visited the place several times before and were familiar with the area—to act as guides and interpreters, leaving Father Diogo Lobato behind in command of the two *panouras,* since he was an intelligent and extremely courageous man.

And after touching shore without encountering a single person or detecting any kind of sound or movement up to that moment, he passed quickly through one of the eight entrances to this compound, made his way through the middle of the orange grove, and headed for a chapel coming in view that was located about twice a musket-shot's distance from our point of disembarkation, where he found—what we shall see in a moment.

76
Desecration of the Tombs

Antonio de Faria made straight for the chapel ahead of him, treading as softly as he could and not without some trepidation, for he still had no idea of what he had gotten himself into; and with each man keeping the name of Jesus on his lips and in his heart, we reached a small courtyard in front of the door, without encountering a single person along the way.

Antonio de Faria, who had been in the lead all the while, with a broadsword in his hands, tried the door and felt that it was locked from the inside. He ordered one of the Chinese near him to knock, which he did, rapping twice.

"Blessed be the Creator who painted the beauty of the heavens above!" a voice from within replied. "Come around to the other side and I will hear what you desire."

The Chinese went around the chapel and entered through a side door. Then he opened the other one for Antonio de Faria, who rushed in with all his people and found an old man there who looked like he was more than a hundred years old. He was dressed in a very long robe of purple damask and appeared to be a noble personage, which, as we found out later, he was indeed. But the sight of the soldiers crowding in was too much for him to bear, and he collapsed. He fell face down on the floor and lay there, with his feet and hands atremble, and incapable, for the moment, of uttering a word. However, once he had gotten over the initial shock, which took quite some time, he regained complete control of himself. Then he looked around at everybody, and though his smile was sweet, his words were blunt as he asked us who we were or what we were doing there.

Speaking through the interpreter, Antonio de Faria told him that he was the captain of that group of foreigners, and a native of the kingdom of Siam, and that while on his way to the port of Ning-po, where he was bound on a trading voyage in a heavily laden junk of his, he had been lost at sea, and that it was only by a miracle that he and all those men there with him had been saved; and that because he had vowed to make a pilgrimage to this holy land, to give thanks to God for saving him from the grave peril he had been faced with, he had come there now to fulfill his promise and, at the same time, to ask him for a bit of charity, to help him get a new start in life; and that he could assure him, that within three years, he would repay him double the value of whatever he took from him now.

The Hiticou, as the hermit was called, thought about what he had heard for a while before he spoke.

"I have listened very closely to what thou hast said," he replied, looking straight at Antonio de Faria. "Also, I have understood what thy purpose is, and that it is an evil one, clouded by thy blindness, which, like a pilot of hell, is leading thee and the others straight to the Lower Depths of the Lake of the Night; for instead of giving thanks to God for the great mercy thou sayest he has shown thee, thou comest to rob him. Now I ask thee—if thou dost such a thing, what canst thou expect of divine justice when the time comes for thee to draw thy last breath? Put aside thy evil purpose! Do not allow the thought of such a dreadful sin to cross thy mind, and God will put aside the punishment awaiting thee. Trust in me, for I am speaking the truth—so help me God as long as I live!"

Pretending that he approved of his advice, Antonio de Faria begged him not to get upset, for he assured him that, at the moment, he had no more certain way to gain a living than what he had come there to do. At this, the hermit raised his arms and turned his gaze heavenward.

"Blessed art thou, O Lord!" he exclaimed, with tears in his eyes, "for suffering the presence here on earth of men who will commit offenses against thee to gain a living, rather than serve thee a single day to gain the certainty of eternal glory!"

He remained somewhat preoccupied by these thoughts and a little distraught over what he was witnessing, but after a moment, he looked up at all the noise and commotion we were making by pulling down the coffins and breaking them open; then he looked at Antonio de Faria who was standing there at the time, leaning on his broadsword, and asked him to come and sit next to him for a moment, which Antonio de Faria did with the utmost courtesy and signs of respect. However, that did not prevent him from motioning to the soldiers to continue with what they were doing— that is, ransacking the coffins and picking out the silver objects that were to be found among the bones of the dead. The hermit was so deeply affected by what was going on that twice he lost consciousness and slid off the bench he was sitting on, as though overcome by the dreadful sin being committed before his eyes, and with a heavy heart he resumed his conversation with Antonio de Faria.

"I wish to declare unto thee," he said, "as one would to a man of sound judgement, which thou seemst to be, how one can obtain pardon for the sin thou hast so many times pointed out to me, in order that thou mayest not perish for ever and ever with thy last breath. Since, as thou hast said, it was sheer necessity that drove thee to commit such a dreadful crime, and that thou hast every intention of restoring what thou hast stolen before death comes to thee—if the opportunity should present itself—then thou must do these three things: First, thou must return everything that thou hast stolen before thou diest, so as to remove from thy path all obstacles to the clemency of the Lord on high. Second, thou must implore him, with tears in thy eyes, to forgive thee, for what thou hast done is extremely offensive to him, and for that reason thou must mortify thy flesh continuously, night and day. And third, thou must share whatever thou hast with God's poor, distributing thy charity with thine own hands judiciously and discreetly, with the same generosity thou wouldst show thyself, so that the Servant of Darkness will not have a case to argue against thee on the Day of

Judgement. And in keeping with this advice, I urge thee to instruct thy men to pick up the bones of the saints and not to profane them by leaving them on the ground."

Antonio de Faria promised he would and treated him with every mark of courtesy, which mollified the hermit somewhat, but did not satisfy him completely. Moving still closer to him, he tried to make him feel better by speaking to him soothingly and gently, in loving and courteous terms, protesting that after hearing what the hermit had just told him he already repented of having undertaken the voyage, but that his men were saying that they would kill him if he were to turn back now, and that he was telling him this in great secrecy.

To which the hermit replied, "Please God, let it be so, for then thou, at least, wilt receive a lighter punishment than these other Ministers of the Night who behave like a pack of hungry dogs and whom, it seems to me, all the silver in the world could never satisfy."

77
The Old Hermit of *Calempluy*

After all the booty had been collected and sent off to the ships, everyone thought it would be better not to make any more commotion for the time being—not only because it was too close to nightfall, but also because we were unfamiliar with the territory—and that instead we should leave it for the next day, when we hoped to be able to do as we pleased with greater facility.

Before embarking, Antonio de Faria decided first to take leave of the hermit. He consoled him with kind words, telling him, please, for the love of God, not to take it so hard, because, as he assured him, it was only the extreme poverty he was suffering from that had made him do something that was not really in his nature to do; and that after their conversation, he had repented of it and had wanted to turn back immediately, but that those men had all opposed him and sworn to kill him if he tried to do so; and that it was only out of fear for his life that he had kept quiet and consented to what he knew perfectly well was a great sin, as he had said; and that as a result, he had made up his mind that as soon as he could get rid of them, he would travel around the world doing as much penance as he thought necessary to atone for such a great crime.

"May it please the Lord who reigns above in the beauty of his stars," the hermit replied, "that the great knowledge that thou hast of God, as is apparent from thy words, will not in the end be held against thee, for I assure thee that he who understands the ways of the Lord, and knowingly breaks his Commandments, runs a greater risk than the ignorant man with no knowledge of God, whose lack of understanding is enough to excuse him in the eyes of the Lord and of the world."

At this point one of our men, a fellow by the name of Nuno Coelho decided to break into the conversation by telling the old man not to get so excited about such a trifling matter.

"Much more trifling is the fear thou hast of death since thou spendest thy life committing deeds as foul as I believe thy soul to be, from the outside of that dunghill of thy body to the inside, through and through. And if thou art hungry for more silver—as is apparent from thy greedy look—to cram into the insatiable pouch of thy infernal appetite, thou shalt find enough in the other buildings around here on which to gorge thyself to the bursting point. And perhaps that will be a good idea after all, for as long as thou art condemned to hell for what thou hast already stolen, thou mayest as well go to hell for stealing the rest—for the heavier the burden on thy head, the quicker shalt thou sink to the bottom, as anyone can tell from the evil deeds that bear witness against thee."

And when Nuno Coelho replied by telling him to accept everything with patience, because that was what God in his holy Law commanded, the hermit clapped his hand to his forehead in a gesture of amazement, shaking his head five or six times and smiling over what he had heard.

"There is no doubt," he exclaimed, "that I now have before me something I never dreamed I would ever see or hear—inborn wickedness and feigned virtue all in one, that is—to steal and to preach! How profoundly blind thou must be to rely with such confidence on thy fine words and spend thy life committing such foul deeds! I wonder if God will jest with thee on the Day of Judgement.

Refusing to hear any more of what he had to say, he turned to Antonio de Faria, who by this time had risen to his feet, and with his arms upraised, he appealed to him urgently to stop our men from spitting on the altar, because that to him was more painful than a thousand deaths; to which Antonio de Faria replied that he certainly would and that everything else that the Hiticou were to command would be promptly done, which made the latter feel a little better.

And since it was quite late by then, Antonio de Faria decided not to lose any more time there. However, just as he was leaving, he realized that he needed to get some more information to allay his fears about a few things that were troubling him, and he asked the hermit how many people there were altogether in those chapels. He replied that there were only 360 *talagrepos*,[1] or one for each chapel, in addition to forty *menigropos*,[2] who took care of them from the outside, bringing them food, and attending to a few who were sick.

When he asked him if the kings of China ever visited that place during any special year or time of year, he answered no, because the king was the Son of Heaven and, as such, was able to absolve everyone and could not be condemned by anyone. And when asked if those hermits had any kind of weapons in their possession, he answered no, for he who desired to walk in the path of heaven had no need of arms to attack, but of patience, to forbear. And when asked why the silver was among the bones in the coffins, he said that it had been placed there as an offering to the dead who carried it with them up there to the Moon Heaven, where they used it to take care of their needs.

After many other questions, he finally asked him if they had any women. He replied that it was very necessary for those who were supposed to sustain the life of the soul, not to waste any time on the pleasures of the flesh, for it was obvious that in the sweet honeycomb was bred the bee that with her sting attacked and wounded those who ate the honey.

Then, after embracing him and begging his pardon many times over, in keeping with their customs—which they call the *charachina* way—Antonio de Faria embarked, just before nightfall, having made up his mind that on the following day he would raid the other chapels, where he had heard they had a very large quantity of silver as well as some gold idols. But our sins prevented us from ever seeing the outcome of what we had risked our lives for, and striven for so painfully, for more than two and a half months—as I will explain shortly.

78
The Hermit Spreads the Alarm

After Antonio de Faria and all of us got back on board—which must have been close to the Ave Maria hour by then—we rowed over to the other side of the island and dropped anchor about a falcon-shot's distance from the shore. We remained there until nearly midnight, having decided, as I said before, that at first light the next day we would go ashore again to raid the chapels of the tombs of the kings, less than a quarter of a league from where we were, and finish loading both ships from there. And perhaps that might well have been the case if matters had been handled properly, or if Antonio de Faria had been willing to heed the advice they gave him, which was, that since no one had as yet discovered our presence in the area, he should take the hermit along with him to make sure that he would not send word of what we had done to the House of the Bonzes.[1] But Antonio de Faria refused, and said he was sure that it was all right, for the hermit was much too old and his legs so swollen with the gout that he could hardly stand up on them, let alone walk. However, it did not turn out the way he thought it would, for, as we learned later, the moment the hermit saw us embark, crippled as he was, he crawled on his hands and knees to the other hermitage, which was about a crossbow-shot's distance from his own, informed the hermit in charge about what we had done, and asked him to go immediately to the House of the Bonzes and spread the alarm, since he was in no condition to go himself because of his dropsy; and the other hermit lost no time going about it.

Also, from where we were, we soon became aware of what was happening, because at one hour past midnight we saw a very long string of fires that looked like signals, burning on top of the wall of the large pagoda where the tombs of the kings were located. We asked our Chinese what they thought it meant, and they all replied that there was no doubt whatsoever that we had been discovered, and therefore they advised us to get under sail without any further delay.

This was immediately reported to Antonio de Faria who was sleeping at the time. He roused himself quickly, cut the cable, set the oars in motion, and nearly out of his mind, he rowed right up to the island to see if there was any kind of excitement going on. Arriving at the wharf, we heard all the chapel bells ringing out loudly and every now and then, the sound of voices.

"Sir," the Chinese protested, "you have already seen and heard enough! Let's get out of here, for the love of God, or you'll get us all killed!"

However, Antonio de Faria paid no attention to them and jumped ashore with six men armed with swords and shields, and scrambled up the steps of the wharf. His pride wounded, he was nearly beside himself as he climbed crazily over the fence which, as I said before, surrounded the entire island, and he went running back and forth like a madman without observing anything out of the ordinary.

Returning to the ships, his mood one of deep outrage, he called everyone together to discuss what should be done about it. After many opinions had been expressed, all of which he dismissed, the majority of the soldiers demanded that, no matter what, they should depart without delay. Afraid of mutiny, he agreed, but said that for the sake of his honor it was incumbent on him to find out first what it was they were running away from; and that therefore, he asked them, as a favor, to wait there for him because he wanted to see if he could capture someone who could talk, for he was still not sure of how well founded their suspicions were, and that he was only asking for half an hour to do this since there was still time enough for everything before dawn.

And when some of the men tried to remonstrate with him, he refused to listen, and instead, leaving them all there that way—after first making them swear allegiance to him on the holy Gospels—he and his party of six disappeared into the wooded area ashore. Once inside, he walked for a distance of more than four musket shots when he heard a bell ringing up ahead of him. By following the sound, he came out upon a chapel, far more stately and richly decorated than the one we had entered the day before, in which there were two men, both about the same age, dressed in religious robes with beads around their necks, which told him that, obviously, they were hermits. And quick as a flash he fell upon them, capturing them both and leaving one of them so shaken that it was a long time before he could utter a sound that made any sense. Four of our six men entered the chapel and grabbed off the altar a good-sized silver idol that had a gold mitre on its head and a wheel in its hand, the significance of which we were unable to determine at the time; and they also took three silver chandeliers attached to some very long chains.

Retracing his steps, Antonio de Faria hurried back to the ships, practically dragging the two gagged hermits behind him, and once aboard, set sail immediately, following the river downstream. And when he interrogated the one captive who seemed to be in greater possession of his wits than the other, threatening him with dire punishment if he lied, he replied that it was true, that in the dead of night, a holy man from one of the chapels, by the name of Pilau Angirou, had appeared at the House of the Tombs of the Kings, rapping excitedly at the door and shouting at the top of his voice, "'O ye unhappy men, sunk in the drunken stupor of carnal slumber, ye who have solemnly sworn to uphold the honor of the goddess Amida,[2] the rich reward of our toil—wake up, wake up, and hear this most miserable of creatures who wishes he had never been born! I have come to let you know that some foreigners from the end of the world, with long beards and bodies as strong as steel, have broken into the House of the Twenty-seven Pillars, and, as I was told by the holy man who is caretaker there, they have stolen the treasure of the saints and have contemptuously thrown their bones on the ground, spitting on them and contaminating them with their putrid and evil-smelling spittle, laughing over and over as they went about it, like obstinate demons proudly bent on committing the greatest of the cardinal sins. Therefore, I advise you to have a care for your personal safety, for it is said that they have sworn to return in the morning and kill us all. Now, either run for your lives or call upon someone to come to your aid, since, as men of God, ye are forbidden to take anything in your hand that draws blood!'

"His shouts woke everybody up, and when they ran quickly to the door they found him lying on the ground half dead from grief and exhaustion, for he was a very old man; after that, all the *grepos*[3] and *menigrepos* lit up the fires you saw burning and hastened to send a message to the cities of *Corpilem* and *Fumbana,* asking them to come to their aid as quickly as possible with as many men as they could muster, and to alert the entire countryside to join forces with them too. Therefore, I can assure you, without any doubt, that in just the time it takes them to gather together, they will come, for they would fly through the air if they could, as swift as hungry falcons when unleashed. And now that you know the truth about everything that is happening, I demand that you set us free, and I warn you not to kill us, for then you would be guilty of a greater sin than you committed yesterday. And remember that God has taken us under his protection because of the penitence we practice, and that he watches over us almost every hour of the day. And you must try to seek salvation for yourselves, because I can assure you that the earth, the air, the winds, the waters, the people, the beasts of the field, the fish, the birds, the grass, the plants, and everything in creation under the sun will surely rise up against you and attack you so mercilessly that only He who lives in the heavens above will be able to avail you."

Convinced that this man's information was an accurate account of the situation, Antonio de Faria promptly set off, sailing downstream as fast as he could, tearing at his beard and beating his breast for having lost, through his own carelessness and ignorance, such a great thing as he had undertaken, if only he had carried it through to the end.

79
Antonio de Faria Meets His End

For seven days we sailed down the Gulf of Nanking, keeping to the middle where the current was strong so as to gather speed, as if our salvation depended on that alone, but with all of us so downhearted and discontent that not one of us, like men beside ourselves, could utter a word that made any sense. On the seventh day of our voyage we reached a village called *Susoquerim,* and since no news of us or where we had come from had reached them as yet, we dropped anchor in the port. After loading some provisions and inquiring indirectly about the course we should take, we departed within two hours and turned, as fast as we could, into a river estuary called *Xalingau,* that was less trafficked than the gulf waters we had just passed through. And there we ran for nine more days, covering a distance of 140 leagues.

Then, turning back into the same Gulf of Nanking, which at this point was already over ten or twelve leagues wide, we sailed along our course for thirteen more days, tacking from one board to the other under westerly winds, growing sick and tired of all the fear and hardship we were going through and, by this time, running out of food. And just as we came within sight of the mines of *Conxinacau,* at latitude forty-one and two-thirds, we were struck by a storm coming out of the south—which the Chinese call a typhoon—that closed in on us darkly with winds and rain so fierce, that it seemed like something beyond the bounds of nature. And since our ships were oar propelled, not very large, low-built, weak, and shorthanded, our situation was so precarious that we saw very little hope of being able to save ourselves, so we let ourselves roll coastwards on the waves, taking it for the lesser of two evils to be dashed against the rocks than to drown at sea.

And as we were proceeding on our way, trying without much success to keep to this pitiful course, which we had chosen as a lesser evil and a less burdensome way to go, sometime in the afternoon the wind suddenly shifted and veered to the north-northwest, causing the waves to surge to enormous heights in a sea so crossed that the sight was terrifying. Filled with fear we began to jettison everything we had on board, and so great was the madness with which we went about this arduous task that even the provisions and crates of silver went over the side. And after that, we cut away both masts, for by then the wind was on the quarter, and we ran that way under bare poles for the rest of the day.

Shortly before midnight we heard a loud cry of "Lord God, have mercy!" coming from Antonio de Faria's *panoura,* from which we gathered that he was sinking; and when we responded to their cry in like manner, there was no reply, as if they had already been swamped. It had such a terrifying effect on us that for a good long hour we were all so frightened out of our wits that no one was capable of uttering a word that made any sense.

That sad night went by in agony and affliction, and then, at an hour before dawn, our ship cracked open above the keelson and the water rushed in immediately, flooding us eight spans deep, which meant that nothing could prevent us from sinking to the bottom. From this we assumed that it was the Lord's will that our lives and labors come to an end then and there.

When the day dawned clear and we were able to get a good view of the entire expanse, there was no sign of Antonio de Faria. That left us all so frozen with fear that none of us were capable of doing anything. We remained in this agonizing state, gripped by indescribable fear, until nearly ten o'clock, when we reached the coast; and half waterlogged as we were, the waves sent us rolling towards a rocky point jutting out ahead of us, against which, with one last heave of the sea, we were promptly dashed to bits. We all clung to each other, raising our voices in a loud cry of "Lord God, have mercy on us!"; and of the twenty-five of us Portuguese, only fourteen were saved, while the other eleven drowned, along with eighteen Christian slaves and seven Chinese sailors. And this disaster occurred on a Monday, the fifth day of August, in the year 1542. May the Lord be praised forevermore.

80
Castaways in China

The fourteen of us that escaped by the mercy of our Lord Jesus Christ spent all that day and night bemoaning our misfortune and the terrible distress we were in, without being able to make up our minds about what to do, not only because of the terrain, which was extremely mountainous and rugged, but also because we had not seen a single person in all that time who could guide us. After consulting with each other, trying to decide what would be the best thing for us to do under the circumstances, it was agreed that we should head inland, where sooner or later we were bound to meet up with someone who would take us captive and feed us until the day it should please the Lord to put an end either to our lives or our suffering.

With this in mind we began to walk along a mountain range, and after trekking six or seven leagues, we discovered an immense swamp on the other side that stretched on endlessly for as far as the eye could see, without any other sign of land beyond it. As a result, we were forced to turn back and retrace our footsteps to the scene of our shipwreck, which we reached just before sundown on the following day. And there on the beach we found the bodies of all our men washed up by the sea, and again we broke down and wept mournfully over them. The following morning we buried them in the sand to make sure that their bodies would not be devoured by the many tigers roaming about in the area. It was a painful and arduous task that took us the better part of the day, for what with there being thirty-six of them in all, and their stench by that time being unbearable, since they were already in an advanced stage of decomposition, and what with our not having any other tools but just our hands to work with, it took us nearly half an hour to scratch out a grave for each one of them.

After burying them we settled down for the night in a pool of water, where we remained until nearly dawn, as a precaution against the tigers. From here we set out in a northerly direction, making our way through brush and bramble so thick that in some places we had difficulty getting through. We went on this way for three more days until we came to an estuary, without having caught sight of a single person in all that time. The first four to attempt to swim across—three Portuguese and a slave—drowned immediately, because by that time they were too weak and exhausted to negotiate a river as wide and swift as that was, and the strength of their arms gave out when they had gone only a third of the way across. These three Portuguese were all highly respected men, two of them brothers, the one named Belchior Barbosa and the other Gaspar Barbosa, and the third was a cousin of theirs named Francisco Borges Caeiro. All three of them came from the town of Ponte de Lima,[1] and they were all splendid fellows, much admired for their courage and other fine personal qualities.

After seeing the wretched end to which our companions had come and realizing that little by little, with each passing hour, our ranks were growing smaller, those of us who were left—eleven Portuguese and three more slaves—broke down and cried, sobbing and sighing uncontrollably at the thought, not only of what had happened to them, but of what might eventually happen to us.

We spent the night that way—a dark, cold night, filled with rain, wind, tears, and sighs—and in the early dawn it was the will of God that we should see, off to the east, a huge fire burning; and as the sun rose, guided by the feeble reckonings of a few of the men still capable of making any, we began to walk in the direction of the fire, trusting in the almighty Lord to whom alone we looked for relief from all our pain and suffering.

We continued on our way along the river, and after a forlorn journey that took us the better part of the day, just before sundown we reached a clearing in the woods where five men were busy making charcoal. When we got close to them we threw ourselves at their feet and begged them, for the love of God, to tell us where we could turn for the help they could see we needed.

"I wish the only thing you needed was food to help still your hunger," one of them replied, "but I see that your needs are far greater and that all the sacks we have here would not be enough to cover your badly torn bodies. However, may our good will be acceptable to God, for whose sake we will give you a bit of rice we had prepared for our dinner, and with some hot water to wash it down, instead of wine, that should hold you for the night, if you are willing. But better still, what you should do, even though it may be added hardship for you, is to go on ahead to that village you see up there in the distance, where you will find a shelter reserved for the wayfarers who constantly pass this way."

We thanked them wholeheartedly for the kindly interest they had taken in us and for their charitable offer, which we accepted, though we took only two mouthfuls apiece of the rice, for there was so little that it did not go any farther.

And without any further delay, we bid them farewell, and in accordance with their directions, we set out for the town where the shelter was located, walking as fast as our wobbly legs could carry us.

81
The Wayside Shelter

It must have been dark for about an hour when we reached the town where the shelter was located, in what turned out to be a little village. We headed straightway for it, and when we came inside we received a warm welcome from the four men in charge, who very charitably put us up for the night.

Early the next morning they asked us who we were or what had happened to bring us to such a plight. We told them that we were foreigners, natives of the kingdom of Siam, and that two weeks before, while bound from the port of Ning-po to the fishing waters of Nanking, we had been shipwrecked in a bad storm at sea out of which nothing had been saved but those wretched carcasses of ours, as bare and battered as we stood before them. Then they asked us what we intended to do or where we wanted to go. To the city of Nanking, we replied, where we would be able to ship out as oarsmen aboard the *lanteias* bound for Canton or *Comhay,* where our fellow countrymen carried on their trade, with the permission of the *aytao*[1] of Peking and the protection afforded them by the word of the Son of Heaven, Crowned Lion on the Throne of the World; and that that was why we were asking them, for the love of God, to please let us stay there until we recovered our strength and were well enough to make the journey on foot, and to give us some sort of clothing with which to cover ourselves.

"It is no more than right that we should grant your tearful request for garments to cover your nakedness," all four of them replied, "but at the moment the house is so short of funds that, if we were to comply with your request, we would be unable to take care of all our other obligations. However, we will be very glad to do whatever we can for you."

Then, naked as we were, they led us through the entire village, which might have had some forty to fifty inhabitants, more or less, all of them, from what we could see, very poor, who earned a living by the sweat of their brows; and they collected alms for us that came to two *taels* in cash, half a sack of rice, a small amount of flour, some beans and onions, as well as some old clothes, which improved our situation a little bit. And they themselves added two silver *taels* to it, which they withdrew from the shelter's funds. But they would not allow us to stay, explaining that the rules of the house did not permit the poor to remain longer than three to five days, with the exception of the sick, and pregnant women, who received special consideration because they were unable to walk without danger; and that under no circumstances could they break this rule which had been established in ancient times by learned and religious men; but that three leagues from there, in a large town called *Sileyjacau,* there was a very wealthy hospice open to the poor of every kind, where we would be better cared for than in their shelter, which was as small and impoverished as the town itself; and that to help us, they would give us a letter of recommendation, signed by all those of their brotherhood, that would ensure us of an immediate reception.

We expressed our deep thanks for this, telling them to let it be done in the name of God.

At this, one of the four, an old man, exclaimed, "You may be sure that it is being done for that reason alone, and not for any worldly reason, because there is an enormous difference between the ways of God and the ways of the world, in both deeds and the conditions under which they come to pass. Since the world is a poor and miserable place, no good can be expected of it, whereas God is infinitely rich and a friend to the poor who, from the depths of their poverty, humbly and patiently sing his praises. The world is vindictive, and God is forbearing; the world is wicked, and God is all goodness; the world is voracious, and God is abstinent; the world is rebellious and resentful, and God is peace loving and forbearing; the world is lying and deceitful with its own, and God is all truth and light, and sweet and gentle with those who turn to him in prayer; the world is sensual and avaricious, and God is generous and purer than the light of the sun and all the stars that we can see as well as those far more excellent stars which are not given to us to see, but which are always there in full view of his radiant countenance. The world is torn by conflicting opinions, puffed up with false vainglorious airs, and God is pure and constant in his truth, by means of which the humble and pure of heart shall find eternal glory; the world is full of folly and ignorance, and God is pure knowledge of all truth. And therefore, my friends, though you may find yourselves in wretched straits today, do not despair of the promises he holds forth, for I can assure you that if you, for your part, are not unworthy of him, he, for His part, will not fail you, because he has never failed his own, though there are some blind people in the world who hold to the contrary because they are constantly oppressed by wretched poverty and despised by the world."

Then he handed us the letter of recommendation for the hospice, and we took it and departed. By then it was close to midday, and when we got to the town it was about an hour or two before sunset. We went directly to the "resthouse of the poor," as the Chinese call it, though I use the word "hospice" here in order to be understood, because that is what we usually call it. And the moment we handed the letter we were carrying to the *tanigores* of the brotherhood, who were all sitting at a table, attending to the affairs of the poor, they accepted it with an unusual ceremony of respect and passed it to the clerk to be read out loud. He rose to his feet, and turning to all those seated at the table, in a singsong voice, he read the letter, which was phrased as follows:

"We, the poorest among the poor, unworthy servants of the Lord whose glorious deeds the stars in heaven bear silent witness to in the dark of night, duly elected to succeed to our posts here in the Lord's House of *Buatendó,* situated in this village of *Catihorau,* do hereby reverently and respectfully beseech your humble persons, as dedicated servants of the Lord, to extend the hand of charity to these fourteen foreigners, by sheltering them and assisting them in any way possible, three of whom are dark-skinned men and the other eleven of a lighter color, whose bare flesh and dire poverty will convince you at a glance that we have done the right thing by requesting this favor for them, since they and all their possessions were cast away by the impetuous waters of the sea which, with their customary fury, executed a sentence imposed by His mighty hand, for He frequently allows disasters to occur, as punishments of His righteous justice, that show clearly how much His judgement is to be feared, from which, may He deliver us all on the day we die, so that we may not see the awesome indignation of His countenance."

Once this letter had been read, they arranged for us to be lodged in a spotlessly clean building where fourteen cots had been properly set up, along with a table and plenty of chairs, where they served us a delicious meal.

And early the next morning, the clerk, acting on orders from his superiors, asked us who we were, what country we came from, where we had been shipwrecked, and other questions of that sort, which we answered exactly the same way as we had in the other town so that they would not catch us in a lie. Then he asked us what we intended to do, and we told him that we would like to stay there long enough to regain our health, if they would allow us to, because we were quite ill and unable to walk. He answered, by all means, for that was their main function, which they carried out constantly in the service of God; for which we all thanked him, weeping and putting on such a good show to suit our purposes that the tears rose to his eyes. And he immediately sent for a doctor, instructing him to take good care of us because we were so poor that all we possessed in the world was what the house could give us. Then he recorded our names in a book, which we all signed, a formality he said was necessary in order for them to keep track of what they spent on us.

82
Thrown to the Leeches

After eighteen days in this hospice, where we were more than generously provided with all the necessities, thanks be to God, we recovered completely; and as long as we were well enough to walk by then, we departed for a town five leagues from there called *Suzoangané,* which we reached by sundown.

And since we were extremely weary when we arrived, we sat down at the edge of a water fountain located just outside the entrance to the town, where we rested a while, trying to orientate ourselves and to decide which way to go from there. In the meantime, people coming to draw water stopped dead in their tracks when they saw us there like that, without daring to approach the fountain, and many of them turned back with their pitchers empty, to spread the alarm.

Most of the villagers rushed out to see for themselves, and amazed by the unusual sight we presented, for people like us had never been seen there before, they got together to consult with each other. After a lengthy argument, for there seemed to be some disagreement among them, they sent a very elderly woman over to ask us who we were, or what we were doing there at the edge of the town's fountain.

We told her that we were poor foreigners, natives of the kingdom of Siam, and that we had been shipwrecked in a bad storm at sea, from which God had saved us, leaving us in the condition they could see we were in. "Well, what would you like us to do for you?" she asked, "or what were you planning to do? Because this town does not have a resthouse for the poor where you can stay."

At this, one of our men, with just the right touch of tears and gestures to achieve the desired effect, replied that he was confident that God, for his name's sake, would not fail to give us the support of his powerful hand by touching their hearts and moving them to have pity on us and our poverty; and that we were determined to make the journey on foot, in that poor manner, all the way to the city of Nanking, where we would sign on as oarsmen aboard the merchant *lanteias* bound for Canton, and from there, to the port of *Comhay,* where there were many junks from our country on which we could embark.

"Well, if that is your situation," she replied, "wait here, and I will let you know what these people decide to do about you."

She went back to her people, of whom by this time a crowd of over a hundred had gathered, and she stood there arguing intensely with them. Finally, she returned with a priest of theirs who was dressed in a long flowing houppelande of purple damask—which is the ornamental attire of the highest dignitaries among them—and who was carrying a sheaf of wheat in his hand.

When he reached the fountain he called us to come closer to him, and we immediately did so, being careful to observe all the courtesies due him, which he barely acknowledged, because he saw that we were poor. Then he threw the sheaves of grain into the water and instructed us to place our hands on them, which we all hastened to do, regarding it as necessary for the peace and conformity we desired to have with them. The moment we touched the wheat, he exclaimed, "By this solemn oath that you take before me on these two substances, water and bread, which the almighty Creator of all things of his own will formed to sustain those born into the world in their pilgrimage through this life, confess and swear if what you told this woman is the truth; for if it is, we will take you in with us in conformity with the charity that by the law of reason one should show God's poor; but if it is not, I admonish and order you in his name to depart at once under pain of being bitten and chewed up in the jaws of the Ravenous Serpent of the Lower Depths of the House of Smoke!"

To this we answered that everything we had told the woman was absolutely true, and he was satisfied with that.

"Now that I know that everything you have told us about yourselves is true," he said, "come with me, and do not be afraid, for you have my word."

Then he led us over to where his people were waiting and told them that it was all right for them to offer us alms for he was giving them permission to do so. They then took us all into town with them, where they settled us in some sheds attached to the local pagoda and lost no time providing us with two sleeping mats and what was necessary in the way of food.

At daybreak we went through the town begging from door to door, collecting four *taels* in silver which we used later to buy some of the things we needed badly.

From here we set out for another town two leagues from there called *Xiangulé*, with the intention of journeying like that from one town to another until we reached the city of Nanking, 140 leagues away, because we thought that we would be able to get from there to Canton, where our *naos* traded in those days, provided that Fortune did not prevent it.

It was almost vesper time when we got there, and we sat down to rest in the shade of a tree just outside of town, where we found three young men tending to some cattle, who started to run the minute they saw us, shouting "Thieves! Thieves!"

The townspeople immediately responded to their cries, running up with many crossbows and lances, and shouting at the top of their voices "Navacarangué! Navacarangué!" meaning, "Nab those thieves! Nab those thieves!"

And they came chasing after us, for by this time we were on our feet and making a run for it; and in the pursuit they landed so many well-placed stones and blows that every one of us was hit, and one of the three slaves who were with us received wounds from which he subsequently died; and once they had caught us all, they tied us around the biceps with our hands behind our backs and led us back to town as prisoners.

After a warm reception at which we were treated generously with slaps and blows, they stuck us waist deep in a cistern of stagnant water, literally swarming with leeches, where we remained for two days that seemed like a hundred years of hell to us, with not a moment of respite in all that time, and not a single bite to eat.

At the end of those two days, a man arrived from *Suzoangané*, the village from which we had come. When he happened to hear about what they had done to us, he swore to the local people, by all that he held sacred, that we were not the sort they thought we were, but that we were foreigners who had been shipwrecked at sea, and that they had committed a great sin by arresting us and treating us that way. And on this man's word, thanks be to God, they hauled us out of the cistern, dripping with as much blood as water, owing to the swarm of leeches, which had bled us so much that, had we been left there for one more day, there is no doubt that it would have been the end for all of us.

It was already close to sundown when, deeply outraged, we departed from this village and went on our way, with all of us weeping bitter tears over our misfortunes.

83
An Upper-Class Chinese Family

After leaving the village of *Xiangulé*, we reached a tiny settlement inhabited by poor people, where we found three men beating flax. The minute they spied us they dropped what they were doing and fled into a clump of pine trees at the top of the hill, from where they shouted to everyone passing to keep away from us because we were thieves.

Afraid of getting into the same sort of situation we had been in before, which, from the way it appeared, was already in the making, we departed immediately, even though it was almost dark by then, and we took to the road again without the slightest idea of where we were going. On we went, completely frustrated by the fact that we did not know which road to take until, in the midst of the deep gloom, darkness, and rain, we stumbled upon some cow pens, where we settled down for the night on top of a little dunghill, rising at daybreak to find our way back to the road.

Just as the sun came up we discovered a meadow dotted by many trees, in the middle of which, close by a stream, was a group of stately buildings with many towers tapering into spires with their gilded weather vanes at the top. Approaching them, with the name of Jesus constantly on our lips, we sat down at the edge of a fountain outside the entrance to a courtyard that led to the buildings, having gone that far without seeing a soul.

We spent part of the day that way, puzzled by the mystery surrounding the place, when we saw a young man coming along who was probably about seventeen or eighteen years of age, mounted on a fine horse, accompanied by four footmen, one of them carrying two hares and the others carrying five *nivatores*[1]—which are wild fowl similar to the pheasant—and he with a falcon resting on his wrist, and around him a pack of six or seven hounds.

The young man reined in his horse when he saw us and asked us who we were or what we were doing there, which we answered at great length by telling him the entire story of our shipwreck, and from his expression we could see that he was moved by what we had told him.

"Wait here," he said, as he turned into the courtyard. "I will send someone to take care of you at once, and it will be for the sake of the One who reigns above in the glory of his great riches, in the highest of all the heavens."

And shortly afterwards he sent an old woman to fetch us who was wearing some long flowing garments with some beads around her neck, a style of dress affected by those women whom the people look upon as being overly pious.

"The son of the lord who provides us with our daily rice has sent for you," she said. "Follow me with humility so that anyone seeing you will not take you for the sort of people who would rather beg than work for a living."

From here we followed her into another courtyard, far more beautiful than the first, which was completely surrounded by a double row of arcades, like a monastery cloister, decorated with hunting scenes depicting women on horseback with falcons on their wrists. At the front of this courtyard, over the staircase leading up to it, there was a huge archway of elaborately wrought woodwork, in the middle of which, hanging from a silver chain, was a coat of arms, like a shield; and on it, enclosed in a circle, was a painting of a man, that looked almost like a tortoise, in an upside down position, as well as some lettering that read, "Ingualec finguau, potim aquarau," meaning, "Everything about me is like this."

They said that this monstrous figure represented the world, which the Chinese paint upside down, since everything in it is deceptive. It is a way of telling all those who value the things of this world too highly not to be deceived, for "Everything about me is like this"—upside down, so to speak.

From here we climbed a broad staircase made of well-laid stone and entered a large house where a woman, who looked to be about fifty years of age, was sitting on a dais. Next to her were two very lovely young girls, richly attired, with strings of pearls around their necks; and between them was an old man lying on a couch, who was being fanned by one of the girls; and near him was the young man who had sent for us. Beyond the dais were nine young girls, dressed in crimson and white damask, working on an embroidery frame.

As soon as we reached the dais, we threw ourselves on our knees and begged for alms. And just when we had launched into our speech with a few tears and well-chosen words inspired by the occasion and our necessity, the old woman motioned to us to stop.

"Please don't!" she exclaimed. "That's enough! Enough! I cannot bear to see you cry, and I already know that you are forced to beg for alms."

Then the old man who was lying on the couch called us over and asked if anyone of us knew how to cure fevers. At this, his daughter, the one who was fanning him, looked at her mother and smiled.

"Oh come now, sir!" she said to her father. "They are in greater need of having their hunger cured than of being asked if they can do something they probably know nothing about! You would do better to first tend to what they need most, and then later we can talk to them about what matters less."

"You chatterbox!" her mother scolded. "When are you going to learn to speak when you are spoken to? One of these days I will break you of that nasty habit."

"My lord, first see to it that their fast is broken," she laughingly replied. "As for my bad habit, she can break me of that anytime she feels like it."

Nevertheless, the old man, with the peevishness of the sick, refused to let us go and asked us who we were, where we came from, where we were going, and other questions of that sort. We told him what we thought was necessary under the circumstances, explaining how and where we had been shipwrecked, how many had drowned, and how we had been wandering around there lost, without the slightest idea of where to turn next.

After a moment of thoughtful silence, he turned to his son and said, "What do you think about what you have just heard these foreigners say? I want you to remember it well, so that you will come to know God and be grateful to him, and to acknowledge it by offering up many prayers of thanks to him for giving you a father who, in order to spare you from that kind of suffering as well as many other kinds to be found in the world, has provided for you with his life and learning the three best properties in this *anchacilado,* the least of which is worth over 100,000 *taels.* But you are the kind of boy who thinks that bagging a hare is of greater consequence than all of this!"

His only response to this was the smile he directed towards his sisters.

Then he ordered food brought to us there in front of him, and he urged us to eat, which we did most heartily, while he, out of his sickness and boredom, showed great pleasure in watching us. But the ones who appeared to enjoy it most were the sisters, his daughters, for while we ate they were having a good time joking with their brother about the way we were eating with our hands; for throughout the entire Chinese empire, people are not in the habit of eating with their hands, as we do, but with two little sticks that look like spindles.

After we had offered a prayer of thanks to God, which he took good note of in us, he raised his arms to heaven and shed many tears as he prayed aloud, "O Lord, thou who reignest on high, in the serenity of thy great wisdom, I praise thee with humble heart for permitting that these foreigners, born at the farthest ends of the earth, without any knowledge of thy doctrine, should sing thy praises and give thanks to thee, in accordance with their limited capacity, which thou, for thy name's sake, wilt accept as though it were a magnificent offering of gentle music to thy ears!"

Then he saw to it that we received three bolts of linen cloth and four silver *taels*, and insisted upon our spending the night there since by then it was too dark outside for us to set out. We accepted his hospitality, and all of us thanked him for it with many expressions of courtesy in keeping with their etiquette; and he was apparently pleased with this, and his wife and daughters very happy.

84
Arrested in *Taypor*

At daybreak the following morning we bade our host farewell and departed; and from there we went on to a hamlet four leagues away called *Finginilau,* where we stopped for three days. And we continued our daily marches from hamlet to hamlet, from village to village, always avoiding the big cities and towns out of fear of being noticed by the police. We wandered like this for nearly two months without anyone ever bothering us in any way, and during that time we might very well have reached the city of Nanking if we had had someone to guide us; but not knowing how to get there, we frequently mistook the way, needlessly wasting all that time and exposing ourselves to terrible hardship and danger.

At the end of that two-month period, we reached a small town called *Chautir,* where elaborate funeral ceremonies were being conducted according to their rites, with no expense spared, for the soul of a very wealthy woman who had disinherited all her relatives, leaving her entire estate to the local pagoda where she was buried. Since we were poor, we were invited to attend the funeral and to partake of the food that was served at the graveside, as is their custom. When the three days we spent there were over, for that was how long the funeral ceremonies lasted, they gave us six *taels* in alms and urged us to always remember the soul of the departed woman in our prayers.

From this village we went on to another called *Guinapalir,* from where we resumed our daily marches from place to place for nearly two months, until we reached a town called *Taypor* where, as punishment for our sins, and unbeknownst to us, there happened to be present at the time a *chumbim,*[1] a fellow who is something like the head of a circuit court district, who tours all the provinces of the kingdom every three years, overlooking the affairs of the local magistrates and justices of the peace. When he saw us begging from door to door, he called out to us from the window where he stood watching us and, in the presence of three law clerks and a crowd of people that had quickly gathered in the meantime, he asked us who we were, what country we came from, and why we were going around begging that way.

We told him that we were foreigners, natives of the kingdom of Siam, who, after being shipwrecked in a bad storm at sea, were wandering about, begging from door to door to support ourselves with the alms we received from good people until we could reach our destination, which was the city of Nanking, hoping there to board one of the merchant *lanteias* bound for Canton, where our ships lay in port.

He would have let us go with this explanation if one of the law clerks had not stepped in and advised him not to, since we were nothing but idlers and vagrants who spent our lives loafing about in people's doorways, living on charity handouts we did not deserve; wherefore, according to the statute relevant to the case, recorded in volume 7 of the twelve books of the ordinances of the realm, it was expressly forbidden for him to release us for any reason, at the risk of being severely punished for it when his record was examined at the end of his term in office; therefore, as a loyal servant of his, he would advise him to put us under lock and key immediately, to make sure that we would not get away. This the *chumbim* hastened to do, with such an excess of cruelty as was to be expected of a godless heathen like him.

And after an indictment had been hastily drawn up, based, as usual, on false evidence, alleging the most appalling crimes, he had us thrown into a bare prison cell where he kept us handcuffed and shackled in iron collars and leg chains, starved and brutally whipped, for twenty-six unspeakable days, after which he ordered us transferred to the jurisdiction of the *chaem*[2] of Nanking, because it was not within his power to sentence any prisoner to death.

85
Transferred to Nanking

As I was saying, we spent twenty-six days in this horribly wretched prison, though to us it seemed like twenty-six thousand years, for we could clearly see that our end was near and that there was no hope for us. It was so appalling that one of our companions, a fellow by the name of João Rodrigues Bravo, died right in front of us, eaten up by the lice, without our being able to help him in any way, for we too were suffering from that plague, which we escaped as if by a miracle.

They took us out of here one morning, heavily shackled as we were and by that time so sick and feeble that we could hardly speak, and they bound us all together in a single chain and shipped us off along with thirty or forty other prisoners convicted of high crimes, who were also being sent to Nanking on appeal.

This city, as I have said before, is the second largest in the kingdom of China and is the permanent seat of a *chaem* of the supreme court, whose title is as high as that of a viceroy. Assisting him in his jurisdiction is a huge staff of 120 *gerozemos*[1] and *ferucuas*,[2] who are the appeal judges, chancellors, and examiners, to whom all civil and criminal cases are referred, and whose decisions are not subject to further review, appeal, or resort, except to a special court they have which has power even over the king himself, so that to all intents and purposes, when one appeals to that court, it is like appealing to heaven.

In order to have a better understanding of all this, it is necessary to know that, inasmuch as this court and others like it around the empire in its important cities were given the supreme authority by the king to make the final decision in all matters pertaining to civil and criminal law, without any recourse to further appeal or review, they constituted another body higher than that of the crown's, to which, in some extraordinary instances, one can appeal. It is called the Bench of the Creator of All Things, and it is made up of twenty-four *menigrepos* who are known as the "Men of Austere Life," which is some sort of religious order, like that of the Capuchins, from whom a great deal could be expected if they were Christians, because of the austere lives they lead and the penitence they do. Ordinarily, they are not eligible to sit on this bench until the age of seventy or more, and even then their appointments depend on the permission and apportionment of their prelates. And in every case that comes to them on appeal, they are so upright and so thoroughly incorruptible in their judging that, once they have handed down a decision, there is nothing more on earth to be said; for even if it involved a suit against the king himself, or against as many powerful interests in the world as one can imagine, no amount of pressure could be brought to bear that would make them deviate in the slightest degree from what they view as justice.

After we had been shipped out in the manner I described, we stopped in the late afternoon of that day to spend the night at a large town called *Potimleu,* where we remained in the local jail for nine days, owing to the heavy rains that fell at the conjunction of the new moon. And it was the will of the Lord that we should find in custody there a German,[3] who welcomed us most cordially. And when we asked him in Chinese—which was the language we used to communicate with him—where he was from, and how he came to be there, he told us that he was originally from a city that was called *Hiquegens,* in Muscovy, and that he had been convicted five years before on a murder charge and sentenced to life imprisonment. However, as a foreigner, he had the right to appeal his sentence to the tribunal of the *aytau* of *Batampina*[4] in the city of Peking—the maritime court presided over by the highest-ranking admiral of the fleet, who was the supreme commander of the thirty-two admirals assigned to the thirty-two subject kingdoms of the empire—since this particular admiral had sole jurisdiction over all foreigners and mariners from abroad; and he was appealing to this bench for revocation of his sentence so that he would be set free to die a Christian among Christians.

Nine days later they shipped us out again; and after navigating up a very great river, within seven days we reached the city of Nanking, which, in addition to being the second most important city in this whole monarchy, is the capital of the three kingdoms of Ning-po, *Fanjus,* and *Sumbor.* Here they kept us in jail for a month and a half, suffering from great hardship and privation and reaching such extreme depths of misery that we were visibly dying in utter abandonment, with no help for it but to weep and turn our gaze heavenward; for on the very first night we arrived we were immediately robbed of everything we had, leaving us with not even a shirt to our backs; for since the prison building was very large and overcrowded, containing, according to what they said, over four thousand inmates, there was no place a person could sit down without being immediately robbed and covered with lice.

At the end of this month and a half, the *anchaci* assigned to our case, one of the two judges who ordinarily heard these pleas, handed down a sentence, upon the recommendation of the prosecutor, who argued to the effect that the indictment drawn up by the *chumbim* of *Taypor* proved that there was something evil about us; and whereas we had presented not a shred of evidence in our own defense to disprove the charges, and that, as for what we had said, our credibility did not measure up to what the law required in such cases, therefore he recommended, for the time being, that we be publicly flogged on the buttocks, a punishment that would·teach us to mend our ways; and in addition, he recommended the cutting-off of our thumbs which, as one could safely assume from the circumstantial evidence, had been used to commit robbery and other crimes, for which the Sovereign Judge who reigns on high would eventually punish us, with all the power of his righteous justice, on the very last day of our days; and as for the rest of the punishment we deserved, he was appealing for justice to the tribunal of the *aytau* of *Batampina,* within whose higher jurisdiction the case belonged.

This sentence was read to us in prison, where we were more fit to die than to withstand the terribly cruel flogging we promptly received, from which we all bled so profusely that the whole ground was covered with our blood; and to such a degree that, out of the eleven who were there, only nine of us survived by a miracle, for two of us, as well as a slave boy, died three days later.

86
Legal Aid for the Poor

After having been flogged in the manner I described, we were taken to a building within the prison compound used for an infirmary, where there were many sick and wounded lying around, some on beds, others on the floor; and there our wounds were treated with all kinds of concoctions and washes, squeezed out, pressed tight, and covered with powder, which helped somewhat to ease the pain of the lashing. These treatments were administered by honest men, something like our Brothers of Mercy, who serve here for months at a time, giving of themselves very charitably, out of love of God, and seeing to it that the patients receive everything they need with a great deal of abundance and cleanliness.

On the eleventh day of our treatment here, when we were beginning to feel somewhat better, though still bemoaning the harshness of the thumb-cutting sentence handed down against us, it pleased God that one morning there should happen to come by two men dressed in long, flowing robes of purple satin who were holding some white wands in their hands that looked like scepters. The moment they set foot in the hospital all the patients greeted them with a loud cry of "Pitau hinacur chendoo," meaning, "Blessed be the ministers of God's works!"

To this they responded, raising their wands, "May the Lord give to all of you the patience to endure your hardship and adversity!"

They began to distribute money and clothing, starting first with the ones nearest them, until they reached us too. After a kindly greeting, which showed how affected they were by our tears, they asked us who we were, what land or nation we were from, and why we had been imprisoned.

We replied, with the tears rolling down our cheeks, that we were foreigners, natives of the kingdom of Siam, from a land called Malacca, where we lived as merchants possessing an abundance of worldly goods; and that one day, while bound for the port of Ning-po with our merchandise, we had been shipwrecked in a bad storm off the islets of *Lamau,* where we lost everything we were carrying without being able to salvage anything but our wretched skins, which were in the shape they could see; and that after making our way, in that condition, to a town called *Taypor,* we were arrested by the *chumbim* of the justice department, for no apparent reason, and charged with being a band of thieves and vagabonds who loitered around one doorway after another, eating off the charity of others, which we did not deserve, in order to avoid having to work for a living; and that after drawing up an arbitrary indictment, he had put us in irons and sent us off to that prison, where for the past forty-two days we had been suffering unbearably from sickness and starvation, without anyone caring to hear what we had to say in our own defense, not only because we did not have anything with which to bribe them, but also because we did not know how to communicate with them; and that for no reason at all we had been condemned to the lash and to having our thumbs cut off like thieves; and that the cruel penalty of the lash had been carried out immediately, with such severity, and in such an excessively brutal manner as they could see with their own eyes from looking at our pitiful flesh; and that therefore, we were appealing to them, as men who had dedicated their lives to the service of God, not to abandon us, for we were despised by everyone and subjected to the most shameful treatment because of our extreme poverty.

They had both listened very closely to us, and after a moment of thoughtful silence, they knelt down, and with tears in their eyes, they looked up to heaven and prayed, "Almighty Lord who reigns on high with infinite forbearance, O thou who dost allow the anguished cries of the poor and helpless to thunder in thy ears so that the grave offenses constantly committed against thee by our officers of the law may not go unpunished, offenses for which, sooner or later, we trust in thy holy law, thou wilt punish them!"

After questioning some of the people standing around about what we had told them, they immediately summoned the court registrar, commanding him, under pain of dire punishment, to bring them the entire record of the proceedings in our case. He came at once and informed them about everything that had transpired and about how far these irregularities had gone.

Since there was nothing that could be done about the flogging we had already received, they petitioned for a review of the thumb-cutting sentence, directing it to the *chaem,* who replied through the normal appellate channels as follows:

"Mercy has no place where justice loses face. Petition denied."

This dispatch was signed by the *chaem* himself as well as eight *conchacis*[1] who are like associate justices of the criminal bench.

When these two "defenders of the poor for the honor of God"—which is the name they go by because of the work they do—saw how summarily our petition had been rejected, they immediately drew up another one, since they were anxious to have us spared the indignity of the thumb cutting, addressing it to a court known as *Xinfau Nicor Pitau,* meaning "the sweet smile of the Lord of Creation," in which we confessed, like sinners, that we were guilty of the crime as charged and threw ourselves on the mercy of the court. It was quickly delivered to this bench on which sat twenty-four *talagrepos,* who are holy men, similar to our Capuchin friars, of the greatest integrity and authority in the eyes of both the people and the king, who review all the judgements handed down against the poor and other people who are not powerful enough to defend their rights in court.

As soon as they received this petition they all came together, summoned in session by the ringing of a bell. After an examination of the legal proceedings from beginning to end, including all the petitions, dispatches, and everything else that had happened, from which they realized that our case could be lost for a total lack of support, they immediately sent two of their members to deliver a letter with seals attached, enjoining the *chaem* to transfer the case from his jurisdiction to theirs. The injunction was acknowledged immediately by means of a dispatch reading as follows:

"With the power invested in it by the Crowned Lion on the Throne of the World, this court hereby grants the petition of the twenty-four 'Men of Austere Life' to have these nine foreigners remitted on appeal to the tribunal of the *aytau* of *aytaus* in the city of Peking, so that, with the mercy of the court, the sentence handed down against them may be moderated. Given on this seventh day of the fourth moon in the twenty-third year of the reign of the Son of Heaven."

Affixed to this document were the signatures of the *chaem* and eight *conchalins*[2] of the criminal bench, who are like appellate court justices.

The two counsellors for the poor who had undertaken to plead our cause immediately delivered the document to us, and as we took it from their hands, we expressed the wish that God would repay them for what they were doing for us, out of love for him.

"And may he guide you in the understanding of his works," they replied, "so that therein you may with patience gather the fruit of your travail, like all those who fear his name."

87
A Letter of Recommendation

After we had gone through all the misfortune I described above, they shipped us out in the company of thirty or forty other prisoners convicted of serious crimes who were also being sent to the proper appellate courts having jurisdiction over the crimes for which they had been sentenced, where the punishment they deserved would be carried out.

And the day before our departure, when we had already been placed aboard the *lanteia*, bound in threesomes with very long chains that hooked into our leg irons, these two defenders of the poor arrived. And once they had tended, first and foremost, to the people they saw suffering from the greatest privation, by distributing food and clothing to each according to his needs, they asked us if there was anything we lacked for the journey.

We told them that God only knew how sorely we were lacking in everything, but that if we had not said anything till then about all the misery we had endured, it was only because the charity we wanted of them was the favor of a letter to the *tanigores* of that holy brotherhood, asking them to take a special interest in us since, as they knew, we were so alone and friendless that no one in the entire country even knew our names.

"Do not say that," they both protested. "It is a grave sin to talk that way, though God will forgive you for your ignorance. You should know that the more you are oppressed in this world, because you are poor, the higher you will stand in the eyes of God, provided you accept with patience the suffering against which the proud flesh is wont to rebel; for just as the bird cannot fly without wings, so the soul cannot earn merit without deeds. As for the letter you requested, we will gladly give it to you, knowing how necessary it will be to you, in order to be sure of the favor of good people, when you need it."

Then they gave us a sack of rice, four silver *taels,* and a blanket with which to cover ourselves, and they recommended us highly to the *chifu,* who was the bailiff responsible for us. And they bade us farewell with many kindly words and returned to their rounds at the prison hospital I mentioned before, which had over three hundred patients at the time.

At daybreak the following morning, they sent us the letter we had asked for, sealed in green lacquer with their signet impressions on it, that read as follows:

"Servants of the Lord on high, that resplendent mirror of uncreated light, in comparison with whose merits ours are as none, we, the lowliest slaves of this holy House of *Tauhinarel,* founded in the interest of the fifth prison district of Nanking, with the sincerest expression of respect due to your humble persons, hereby inform you that the nine bearers of this letter are foreigners from very distant lands, whose goods and bodies were so unmercifully ravaged by the sudden fury of the sea that out of their original number of ninety-five, according to what they told us, only these poor survivors were washed ashore on the sands of the islets of *Tauta,* along the coast of the bay of *Sumbor* and *Fanjus;* and suffering from cuts and lesions, as we had occasion to see for ourselves, they set out on foot, begging in one town after another from people who, out of love for their fellow man, were willing to share what they had with them—as is only to be expected from the goodhearted and faithful—until they were arrested by the *Chumbim* of *Taypor,* without reason or justice, and sent to this fifth prison district of *Fanjau,* where they were condemned to the lash, a penalty that was promptly executed by the ministers of the Arm of Wrath, as set forth in the proceedings of his case. And since they had also been sentenced, with inordinate cruelty, to having both their thumbs cut off, they begged us, weeping as though they would never stop, that for the sake of the true Lord we serve, they might see in us the favor of his smile. In view of their utter helplessness, we then hastened to their aid by entering a plea for mercy on their behalf, to which the court of the Crowned Lion replied that no consideration could be given to a plea for mercy that reflected on the reputation of the court; wherefore, we, in our zeal for the honor of God, appealed immediately to the bench of the twenty-four 'Men of Austere Life,' who, with saintly fervor, at the sound of the bell, gathered in the holy House of the Shelter of the Poor, where they, desirous of helping these men, pronounced a curse against all the members of the high court and all the ministers of the criminal bench, to prevent their inclement anger from prevailing over the blood of these unfortunate men, in view of the fact that God's mercy is of as high a degree as we can see by the effects it has on us. Whereupon, they revoked the first sentence, amending it with a second opinion, and transferred the case to the jurisdiction of your city, as you can see from the record of the proceedings.

"Therefore, gentlemen and humble brethren, we all entreat you, in the name of God, to look out for them in all things and to see to it that justice is done, for otherwise it will be a great sin and will bring shame and disgrace upon us; and we also request that you help them with your alms and provide them with clothing to cover their bodies, so that they may not perish from neglect.

"For all the saintly deeds you perform on their behalf, you will please the Lord above, to whom the poor of the earth continually cry out, their voices reaching the highest heaven of all the heavens, which we believe as an article of faith. And may the divine Lord, for whose sake we do this, sustain us in this faith until death, and make us worthy of gazing upon his countenance in the House of the Sun, where he sits surrounded by his own.

"Written by the bench of zeal for the honor of God on this ninth day of the seventh moon, in the fifteenth year [1] of the throne and scepter of the Crowned Lion on the Throne of the World."

88
The City of Nanking

A day after this letter had been given to us we departed early at dawn, chained to each other in the manner I have described; and we proceeded on our way, though we could not keep to our daily schedule because of the swift currents and heavy flow of water carried by the river at that time of year. Shortly before sundown we dropped anchor at a little village called *Minhacutem,* which was the native village of the selfsame *chifu*—or bailiff, in whose custody we were traveling—who lived there with his wife and children; and he remained there for three days, making some preparations for the voyage.

After he had put his wife and family aboard, with their household goods and all, we proceeded on our course, in the company of many other ships using that river as a thoroughfare to get to different parts of the *anchacilados* and domains of the empire. And even though we were chained to the oarbanks of the *lanteias,* from where we rowed, our eyes could not fail to take in many magnificent sights we passed in the cities, towns, and villages located along this great river, and though we really were not able to get a close look at anything, I will make a few brief comments about the little we did see, beginning first with the city of Nanking, which was our point of departure.

This city is situated at latitude thirty-nine degrees and a third below the north and is sprawled out along the river called the *Batampina,* which means "fish flower" in our language. The headwaters of this river, according to what they told us at the time and what I later saw for myself, are in Tartary, in a lake called *Fãostir,* nine leagues from the city of *Lançame,* where Tamerlane,[1] king of the Tartars, resides most of the year.

Branching out from this lake, which is twenty-eight leagues long, twelve wide, and tremendously deep, are five of the most torrential rivers that have been discovered to date.

The first river is this one called the *Batampina,* which flows across the middle of the Chinese empire for a distance of 360 leagues and finds its way out to the sea through the Gulf of Nanking at latitude thirty-six degrees.

The second, called the *Lechune,* descends with tremendous force from the *Pancrùm* Mountains, dividing the land of the Cochin from the domains of the *Catebenão,* which border in the interior with the kingdom of Champa at latitude sixteen degrees.

The third river, called the *Tauquiday,* meaning "mother of the waters," cuts across to the west-northwest through the kingdom of *Nacatás,* which is the land from which the Chinese came in ancient times as I will explain later. This river enters the sea through the empire of the *Sornau,* commonly known as Siam, at the bar harbor of Cuy,[2] about 130 leagues below Patani.

The fourth river, called the *Batobasoy,* descends through the province of *Sansim,*[3] and is the same river that overflowed its banks in the year 1556,[4] about which more will be said later. It finds its outlet to the sea at the bar of *Cosmim*[5] in the kingdom of Pegu.

And the fifth river, called the *Leysacotay,* cuts eastward across the interior, in the opinion of all the Chinese, as far as the *anchacilado* of *Xinxipou,* which borders with the land of the Muscovites; and they say that it empties into a sea that is unnavigable owing to the climate prevailing at latitude seventy degrees.

But getting back to my main purpose, this city of Nanking, which, as I said before, is situated along the *Batampina* River at a fairly high elevation, dominates the surrounding countryside where the prevailing climate is somewhat cold but very wholesome. It is encircled on all sides by eight leagues of city walls measuring three leagues wide and one long on each side. The houses consist generally of two- or three-story buildings; however, the homes of the mandarins are all single-story buildings surrounded by walls and ditches, spanned by bridges of excellent stonemasonry leading into the gates, all of which are covered by very costly and richly decorated archways, with all sorts of ornamental devices on the turned-up eaves of the tile roofs, so that a complete view of the building creates a total effect of great majesty.

The homes of the *chaens, anchacis, aytaus, tutões,* and *chumbis,* men who were governors of provinces and kingdoms, have very tall towers, six or seven stories high, topped with gilded spires, where they store their weapons, household goods, treasures, silk furnishings, and other valuables, as well as endless quantities of very fine porcelain pieces, which are like precious jewels to them. This type of porcelain is not exported from the kingdom, not only because they value it more highly than we do, but also because there is a law, carrying the death penalty, that prohibits the sale of this porcelain to any foreigner, with the exception of the Persians of the Shah Tahmasp,[6] called the Sophy,[7] who are licensed to purchase a few pieces at exorbitant prices.

The Chinese we spoke to claimed that this city has a population of 800,000, and that there are 24,000 mandarin homes, 62 huge public squares, 130 slaughterhouses with eighty butchering blocks in each, and 8,000 city streets, 600 of which, that is, the most elegant ones, all have heavy brass railings fashioned by lathe, running along both sides of the street. They also claimed that there are 2,300 religious pagodas in the city, a thousand of them being used as monasteries for the people who have taken vows, and that they are very beautiful buildings with belfries containing sixty and seventy huge bells of bronze and wrought iron that make a horrible racket when they ring.

This city also has thirty very large fortified prisons, each of which holds two and three thousand inmates. Attached to each of these prisons is a building, something like our Houses of Mercy, where they arrange for all the poor people to receive legal defense counsel in all the civil and criminal courts, and where a great deal of charitable work is done.

All the elegant streets have archways over their entrances, with gates that close at night, and most of them have fountains of pure drinking water, which are themselves very decorative and finely wrought.

Every new and full moon they have great market days which are attended by huge crowds of people from all over, and where one can find enormous quantities of every sort of food imaginable, in the way of produce as well as meat.

There is so much fish in this river, and in such great abundance, especially the mullet and flatfish, that I think it is impossible to describe. They are all sold live, hanging from reeds that are strung through the snouts; and in addition to this fresh fish, there is an infinite supply of dried and salted fish that comes from the sea.

The Chinese also told us that there were ten thousand silk looms in the city, since Nanking is the main manufacturing center that supplies the entire kingdom.

The city itself is surrounded by a very sturdy wall of excellent stonemasonry, containing 130 gates that are reached by bridges spanning the ditches. A gatekeeper and two halberdiers are stationed at each of these gates to keep track of everything that comes in and goes out. It has twelve stone fortresses which are built somewhat like ours, with ramparts and very tall towers, but they have no artillery of any kind.

They also told us that this city provided the king with a daily income of two thousand silver *taels,* which are equivalent to three *cruzados,* as I have said many times before.

As for the royal palaces, I would rather not say anything since we only saw them from the outside and all we know about them is what the Chinese told us, and that in itself was so impressive that I am afraid to mention it; therefore I will pass over them for the time being because I still have to describe what we saw in the palaces of the city of Peking; and even though I have not yet come to it, I must confess that I am already beginning to worry about how I will be able to describe even the little that we did see of it, not that it would seem strange to anyone who has already seen the other wonders of the kingdom of China, but because I fear that those people who try to measure the many things that are to be found in the countries they have never seen, against the little they see in their native lands, will doubt, or perhaps refuse completely to believe, those things that do not conform to their ideas and limited experience.

89
The Pagoda of *Pocasser*

Continuing our journey up the river, the first two days we did not see any cities or towns that were particularly outstanding, nor any kind of building worth mentioning, just many little villages and hamlets of about two to three hundred inhabitants that were located all along the water's edge and which, judging from all the signs and the simplicity of the construction, looked like they were settled by fishermen and poor people who labored for a living.

And everywhere else, for as far inland as the eye could see, there were huge pine forests, woods, groves, orange orchards, and fields of wheat, rice, millet, sorghum, barley, rye, vegetables, flax, and cotton, and fenced-in gardens surrounding some elegant homes that must have been country estates of mandarins and noblemen of the kingdom.

All along the river there was such a large quantity of livestock of every kind and description that I can truly say it was equal to that of Ethiopia and the lands of Prester John. Higher up in the mountains many of their heathen temples could be seen, adorned with numerous gilded spires, looking so proud and magnificent on the exterior, that even from afar it was a pleasure to see, for the total visual effect was one of great wealth and splendor.

On the fourth day of our voyage we reached a good-sized city called *Pocasser,* twice as large as Canton and well protected by very sturdy stone walls, with towers and ramparts almost like ours, and a pier on the riverfront running along the entire face of the wall for more than twice the distance of a falcon shot, completely enclosed by a double row of iron railing with very stout gates providing access for people and for the discharge of cargo from the junks and other ships that were constantly loading all sorts of merchandise destined for different parts of the kingdom—mainly copper, sugar, and alum, of which they have enormous supplies. And in the middle of a large courtyard, almost at the end of the entire city, there is a very strong castle that has three ramparts and five towers, in one of which, the tallest, the Chinese told us the present king's father had kept imprisoned for nine years a Tartar king who had died there of poison, which his own vassals had arranged for him to be given so as to avoid payment of the ransom demanded by the Chinese king.

In this city the *chifu* allowed three out of the nine of us to go ashore to beg for alms, in the company of four *upos,*[1] or police guards, armed with halberds. They led us as we were, in our chains, through six or seven streets, where we collected more than twenty *cruzados'* worth of alms, both in clothing and cash, to say nothing of a good supply of food consisting of meat, rice, flour, and fruit, half of which we shared with the four *upos,* since that was the custom there.

Here they took us to a pagoda that was crowded with people at the time, for it happened to be the day of its invocation. They told us that this pagoda had formerly been a royal palace, and that it was said that the grandfather of the reigning king had been born there. And since his mother had died in childbirth, they had her buried in the same room where she had given birth to him; and to commemorate her death, these same buildings had been dedicated as a temple to the invocation of *Tauhinarel,* one of the main cults of the kingdom of China, which I will have more to say about when I come to the complicated subject of the thirty-two religions that are practiced there.

The entire compound with all its workshops, gardens, orchards, and everything else within its gates, stands high above the ground, supported by 360 columns, each of which is hewn out of a solid piece of rock almost as thick as a good-sized wine keg, and about twenty-seven handspans tall. These 360 columns have names for the 360 days of the year, and every day a feast is celebrated in the name of the respective idol, which is placed on that particular column in an ornate litter with a silver lantern in front of it. Each name day is observed with generous almsgiving and bloody sacrifices, accompanied by a great deal of music, dancing, and other kinds of ceremonies. Below, on the ground level, at the base of these columns, are eight very handsomely laid-out streets, lined on each side with brass grilles and gates at the entrances to provide access for the pilgrims who come from out of town, as well as for the many other people who continually flock to these festivals, as though it were a jubilee celebration.

On the upper level, the building housing the queen's tomb was designed in the form of a circular chapel, completely covered from top to bottom with silver, of far greater cost for its workmanship than for its intrinsic value, judging from the diversity of the ornamentation that was to be seen on it. In the center there was a round dais rising fifteen steps from the floor, designed in proper proportion to the building itself, completely enclosed by six rows of silver railings joined together with knots of gold. On the topmost step there was a silver lion standing on a large sphere, supporting a very fine quality gold casket on its head, nearly three handspans square, said to contain the queen's bones, which are worshipped as a precious relic by these blind, ignorant people. Overhead, in perfect proportion to the rest, braced into the ceiling and encircling the dais below, were four silver beams extending around the entire length and breadth of the building, from which hung forty-three silver and seven gold lamps, the silver ones in honor of each year of the life of the queen, who they said was forty-three years old when she died, and the seven gold ones in honor of the seven children they said she had borne.

Extending outward from the arch of this chapel, right at the entrance to the transept, were an enormous number of very large, richly adorned silver lamps hanging from eight beams that ran across the entire building. The Chinese told us that the wives of the *chaens, aytaus, tutões,* and *anchacis,* the most honorable women in the kingdom, who were present at the death of the queen, had ordered them hung there to commemorate that honor; and they said that there were 250 lamps altogether.

Outside the gates to the entire shrine, which was about the size of the Church of São Domingos in Lisbon, there was an enormous number of perfectly proportioned statues of giants, each about fifteen handspans tall, forming six large circles that stretched for row after row all the way around the entire shrine. They were all made of cast bronze and were holding halberds and maces, made of the same metal, and a few of them had small hatchets slung over their shoulders; and the entire complex presented such a splendid and magnificent spectacle, that one could never get tired of looking at it. Among these many statues which, according to what the Chinese told us, numbered twelve hundred, there were twenty-four huge serpents, made of the same type of bronze, and astride each of them was a woman with a sword in her hand and a silver crown on her head. These twenty-four women, they said, had been given the title of queen to honor their descendants, because they had all sacrificed their lives on the death of their queen in order to be able to serve her with their souls in the next life, just as they had served her with their bodies in this life. It is something that the Chinese who are descended from these women regard as a very high honor, and they bear it as an emblem on their family coats of arms. Beyond these rows of giants was yet another running all around them, this one consisting of gilded triumphal arches to which were attached, on silver chains, a large number of wind bells that tinkled incessantly in the breeze, making so much noise that it was impossible to hear one's own voice above them.

Beyond these arches, in the same proportion, surrounding all these works of art, are two rows of brass railings installed in quarter sections on brass columns in the form of a shield, with some lions rampant at the top, mounted on spheres, which, as I have said several times before, is the coat of arms of the kings of China. In the corners of this courtyard there are four monsters, also cast in the same type of bronze, fashioned in such a strange and disproportionately large size, with features so diabolically ugly, that it is next to impossible for the human mind to imagine; and it would have been better for me not to mention them because I realize, and I admit it freely, that I have neither the knowledge nor the vocabulary required to describe them fully. But since it is not right that they should be kept hidden without giving some account of their existence, I shall do my best to describe them, insofar as my limited understanding permits.

One of these monsters, which stands on the right-hand side just as one enters the courtyard, is the one the Chinese call the Ravenous Serpent of the Lower Depths of the House of Smoke, and—according to what is written in their chronicles—he is Lucifer. He is depicted in the figure of an incongruous serpent, with seven of the most hideous, frightful-looking snakes coming out of his chest, speckled all over in green and black, with many porcupine-like spines longer than a handspan completely covering their bodies, and each of them was holding the figure of a woman horizontally between its jaws, with her hair streaming down, looking as though she had fainted. Protruding halfway out of the monster's disproportionately large mouth was a lizard over thirty handspans long and as broad as a wine cask; and its nose, nostrils, and lips were dripping with so much blood that all the rest of this huge serpent's body was covered with it, from there on down. And he was grasping a huge elephant between his forelegs which he seemed to be squeezing so hard that his guts and lungs were bulging out of his mouth. And it all looked so real and natural that one could not help shaking with fear at the sight of a creature perhaps never before imagined by man.

Around its tail, which must have measured more than twenty armspans, it was entwined in another incredible monster, the second one out of the four I said were standing in the four corners of the quadrangle. This one, called *Turcamparó* by the Chinese, was fashioned in the shape of a man over a hundred handspans tall; and they said that he was the son of that serpent. This one was not only hideous, he had both hands stuck in his mouth, stretching it out to the size of a doorway, showing a row of teeth within its depths, and a black tongue sticking out for more than two armspans, a sight that was also most frightful and enough to make one's hair stand on end.

As for the other two monsters, one was in the form of a woman named *Nadelgau,* standing seventeen armspans high and six around. And right in the middle of her waist, scaled to the size of her body, was a face, measuring more than two armspans, emitting huge clouds of smoke from its nostrils and an endless number of real—not artificial—sparks from its mouth. And this they accounted for by explaining that they keep a fire going continuously there on top, inside the head, to show the people that she was the queen of the fiery sphere, for they say that she is the one who will set the earth on fire when the world comes to an end.

The fourth monster was a figure of a man in a squatting position, with enormously puffed up cheeks, blowing so hard he looked like a ship's foresail swollen with wind; and he too was of such an extraordinary size, and had such a hideous and frightful aspect that one could hardly bear to look at him. The Chinese call him *Uzanguenabó,* and they said that he was the one who caused the storms to blow at sea and the buildings to collapse on shore; and this one received many offerings from the people to keep him from doing them harm, and they all signed up as members of his confraternity with annual dues of one *mace*—which is equal to fifty *reals*—so that he would not flood their junks or harm their mariners. And there are many other different kinds of superstitions which they in their blindness believe in with such deep sincerity that they would die a thousand deaths for each one of them.

90
The Great Albuquerque Defamed

On the following day, after our departure from *Pocasser,* we reached another city called *Xinligau,* which was also very large and stately, with row on row of fine houses, completely surrounded by brick walls and a moat. Standing at both ends of the city were two well-fortified castles made of rough stone and smoothly trimmed, with towers and ramparts almost like ours; and at the gates there were drawbridges suspended from heavy iron chains; and in the middle of each of these castles there was a tower six stories high, covered with many interesting designs, painted in all different colors. The Chinese told us that in both of these towers there were fifteen thousand silver piculs in tax money collected from that *anchaci,* which had been stored there by the reigning king's grandfather in memory of a son born there by the name of *Leuquinau,* meaning "the joy of all," whom they regard as a saint because he died a monk. And he is buried there in a temple dedicated to the invocation of *Quiay Varatel,* god of all the fish in the sea, about whom these blind people tell so many ridiculous things with regard to the religious system he invented and the precepts he laid down, things that are appalling to hear and about which I will have more to say in due time.

It is here and in another city five leagues further on that most of the silk in the kingdom is loomed because of something in the local waters which they say makes the colors in the dye come out brighter than they do anywhere else. From these silk looms, which they said numbered thirteen thousand altogether, the king of China received an annual revenue of 300,000 *taels.*

Proceeding on our way up the river the next day, shortly before vespers we came to a very broad prairie where large herds of cattle as well as some old nags and mares were being tended by many men on horseback who sold them to the meat merchants to be butchered and retailed like any other meat.

After passing this prairie, which must have stretched on for ten or twelve leagues, we reached a small town called *Junquileu,*[1] surrounded by brick walls with huge spikes on top, and totally devoid of battlements, ramparts, or towers like the others I have mentioned.

On the outskirts of this town, along the riverbank, we saw some dilapidated old buildings, set on heavy wooden piles rising out of the water, that looked like warehouses. Near the entrance, in a small courtyard, there was a stone monument, enclosed all around by iron railings painted green and red, covered by a spired roof made of fine-quality black and white porcelain tiles, supported by four highly polished stone columns, beautifully finished; and on top of the monument there were five cannonballs of the camel gauge, and two others of cast iron that appeared to be of the half-sphere type.[2] On the front of the monument there was an inscription in Chinese characters, engraved in gold, that read as follows:

"Here lies Tuan Hassan Mudeliar,[3] uncle of the king of Malacca, whom death carried off before God had avenged him on Captain Albuquerque,[4] lion of the robbers of the sea."[5]

It took us all by surprise, and we asked them what was the meaning of that inscription. One of the Chinese there who seemed to be more honorable than the rest spoke up.

"Forty years ago," he said, "the man who lies buried there came to China as an ambassador, sent by a king of Malacca it was said, to ask the Son of Heaven to help him in his struggle against some people from a nameless country, who had come by sea from the ends of the earth and taken Malacca from him, as well as committing some other frightful atrocities, which are recorded in a book that was printed on the subject. For nearly three years he hung around the court, petitioning continuously for aid; and just when the *chaens* of the governing councils had decided to grant it, one night, in the middle of dinner, it was his misfortune to be taken sick with a chill, and he lasted for only a matter of nine days. Apparently, out of disappointment over the failure of his mission, he had that epitaph engraved for his tombstone, so that all men, until the end of time, would know who he was and what his purpose was in coming here."[6]

We departed soon afterwards and proceeded on our way up the river, which is narrower at this point than it is at the city of Nanking from where we originally started out. But there are many more villages and farms here than in all the other places, for it is impossible to throw a stone without hitting some kind of building, either a pagoda, or a farmhouse, or a workingman's home.

And when we had gone about two leagues further, we reached a large terraced area completely surrounded by extra heavy iron gratings, in the middle of which there were two monstrous bronze statues, one of a man and the other of a woman, braced upright and leaning against some thick cast-iron columns seven armspans tall and as wide across as a barrel. Both these monsters stood about seventy-four handspans high, and they had both hands in their mouths, with their cheeks puffed out, as though they were blowing hard, and with their eyes glaring so bloodthirstily that any-one looking at them was filled with horror. The male statue was called *Quiay Xinga-talor,* and the female, *Apancapatur.* When we asked the Chinese what those statues represented, they said that the male was the god who was always huffing and puffing with all his might to keep the hellfires burning, so as to torment the souls of those who had not given him alms in this life; and that the female was the gatekeeper of hell, and that she allowed all those who had given her alms in this life to escape down an icy cold river called *Ochileuday,* where she concealed them and protected them from all the devils.

One of the men in our group could not keep from laughing at such utter non-sense and the devilish blindness of these people. This so outraged three of the bonzes— as they call their priests—who were standing nearby, that they got it into the head of the *chifu* who had us in custody that if he did not punish us hard enough to placate those gods for having made fun of them, that without any doubt, his soul would be mercilessly tormented in hell by the two of them, with no hope of escape. The thought of it put such a fright into that dog of a *chifu* that, without any more ado, he had all nine of us bound hand and foot, and with a lash fashioned out of folded cords they gave each one of us more than a hundred strokes which left us all dripping with blood, and thenceforth we never again made fun of anything we saw.

At the time we arrived there, a group of twelve bonzes were offering incense to these two diabolical monsters in a pair of silver censers, filling the air with the mingled scent of eaglewood and benzoin as they chanted these words in loud, discordant voices, "Help us, just as we serve Thee!"

To which another large group of priests responded with a loud cry, "So it shall be, I promise thee, like a good Lord!"

And they marched this way in procession around the entire courtyard, shouting discordantly for well over an hour, and clanging continuously on many bronze and cast-iron bells that were hanging from beams outside the courtyard, while some others were beating the drums and shaking sistra, altogether making such a horrendous racket that I swear it was positively frightening.

91
Inez de Leiria

From this courtyard we continued on our way for eleven more days, sailing up the river, which at this point is so crowded with cities, towns, villages, hamlets, fortresses, and castles that in many places the distance between them is less than the range of a musket shot. And it was the same all the way inland for as far as the eye could see where the countryside was dotted with large numbers of magnificent villas and temples to their gods, topped by many gilded spires, presenting altogether a panorama of such breathtaking splendor and majesty, that it left us gasping with amazement.

In this manner we arrived at a city called *Sampitay*,[1] where we remained for five days because the *chifu*'s wife was not feeling well. Here, with his permission, we went ashore as we were, still in our chains, and we all went up and down the streets begging for alms, which the local inhabitants gave us most generously. Amazed to see people like us, they gathered in groups to ask us who we were, from what kingdom we came, or what was the name of our country. We repeated the same story we had told many times before, that we were natives of the kingdom of Siam, that we had been shipwrecked in a storm at sea while bound from Ning-po to the Gulf of Nanking, and that we had once been wealthy merchants with a great deal of property to our names, though they would not suspect it from the way we looked.

There was a group of women nearby, and one of them, after hearing our conversation, spoke up.

"That is not at all surprising," she remarked. "We have seen the same thing happen often enough. Most of the men who seek their livelihood at sea find their graves at sea. And that is why, my friends, the best and the surest thing for a man to do is to value the earth more highly, and to labor on the earth, since it pleased God to create us out of earth."

And so saying she gave us two *maces* with the charity one shows to the poor, and advised us strongly not to think of making long voyages where it had pleased God to make life so short. But thereupon she unbuttoned the sleeve of a purple satin coat she was wearing, and baring her arm, she showed us a well-defined cross on her skin that looked like the brand of a Moorish slave.

"Perchance," she inquired, "do any of you recognize this sign? The people of the true faith call it a cross. Have you ever heard of it?"

The minute we saw it we dropped to our knees, all of us assuming the proper attitude of devotion, some with tears in our eyes, and told her we had.

At this she uttered a cry and raised her arms heavenward.

"Our Father who art in heaven," she prayed out loud in Portuguese, "hallowed be thy name..."

Then she lapsed back into Chinese, giving us to understand that that was about the extent of her Portuguese, and begged us to tell her if we were Christians. We all answered yes, and all together we kissed the cross on her arm and finished reciting the Lord's Prayer where she had left off so that she would know that we were telling the truth.

When she heard this and understood from it that we were Christians, she said good-bye to the people there with the tears streaming down her cheeks, and turned back to us.

"Come with me, Christians from the end of the world," she said. "Come with this true sister of yours in the faith of Christ, who may even be related to one of you through the father who begot me in this land of exile."

As she started to lead us in the direction of her house, the *upos,* or the policeman guarding us, stopped her, refusing to let us go and insisting that we get on with our begging in the rest of the city as the *chifu* had ordered us to do, otherwise they would take us back to the ship. They were objecting on grounds of their own self-interest, for they would be losing their share which, as I said before, was half of everything we collected. And when they made as if to take us back to the ship, she stopped them.

"I understand you perfectly," she said, "and I can appreciate the fact that you do not want to lose what is coming to you. And it is only fair, considering that you have no other source of income."

Then, reaching into her purse, she gave them two silver *taels,* which made them happy; and with the *chifu*'s permission, she took us to her house, where she kept us for the entire five days of our stopover, constantly looking after us and treating us with great charity.

While we were here she showed us a little chapel containing a wooden crucifix finished in gold leaf, some silver candlesticks, and a lamp, and told us that her name was Inez de Leiria, and that her father, whose name was Tomé Pires,[2] had been sent from Portugal as ambassador to the king of China; and that owing to an uprising in Canton, for which one of our captains was to blame,[3] the Chinese took her father for a spy and not the ambassador he claimed to be, and threw him in jail along with the twelve men in his party. And after sentencing them to repeated floggings and torture, from which five of the men promptly succumbed, the others were separated and banished singly to different parts of the kingdom where they all died eaten up by lice, with the exception of one man named Vasco Calvo[4] who was still alive and who came from a town in our country called Alcochete,[5] as she had often heard her father say, weeping bitterly every time he spoke about it; and that it had fallen to her father to be banished to this part of the country, where he had married her mother, who had some means of her own, converting her to Christianity. And that during the twenty-seven years of their marriage both of them had always led a very Catholic life, converting many heathens to the faith of Christ, more than three hundred of whom were still living in that city, meeting every Sunday there in her house to practice their religion.

When we asked her what they would say or how they prayed, she replied that all they did was kneel down before that crucifix of hers, raise their hands, lift their eyes to heaven, and recite in unison, "Lord Jesus Christ, even as it is true that thou art the true Son of God, conceived in the womb of the holy Virgin Mary by the Holy Spirit for the salvation of all sinners, so it is true that thou wilt forgive us our trespasses in order that we may be worthy of gazing upon thy divine countenance in the glory of thy kingdom where thou art seated at the right hand of the Almighty. Our Father who art in heaven, hallowed be thy name. In the name of the Father, and the Son, and the Holy Spirit. Amen."

Then they would all kiss the crucifix, embrace each other, and return to their homes. And this was the kind of life they led, living with each other in friendship and harmony, with never the slightest trace of hatred or animosity among them; and that her father had written down some other prayers for her, but that the Chinese had stolen them afterwards, which was why they only knew the one prayer she had recited for us. We replied that what she had recited was very good but that we would leave some other very good ones with her before we departed.

"Do so," she said, "by the duty you owe to such a good God as yours, who has done so much for you and me and everyone."

Then she had the table laid with food and fed us most abundantly. She did the same thing on all five of the days we were at her house, where we stayed with the *chifu*'s permission which was obtained by means of a gift she had sent his wife, with an earnest request that she get her husband to treat us well because we were very special people in the eyes of God, which she promised to do, while at the same time thanking her profusely for the gift she had sent her.

In the five days we were at her house, we gave the Christians there seven lessons in doctrine, which raised their spirits a great deal; and Cristóvão Borralho prepared a notebook for them in Chinese with the Lord's Prayer, the Ave Maria, the Credo, the Salve Regina, the Commandments, and many other fine prayers that he left for them. And after that we bade farewell to the Christians and to Inez de Leiria, who, judging by what we saw of her in those few days we spent at her house, seemed to be a true Christian.

These Christians gave us a charitable gift of fifty *taels,* which stood us in very good stead afterwards in many needy situations we found ourselves in, as I will explain later on; and Inez de Leiria, on her own, also slipped us another fifty *taels* very quietly, without anyone seeing, and begged us to commend her to the Lord in our prayers since we could see how sorely she needed it.

92
The Legend of *Nancá*

  After leaving the city of *Sampitay* we continued on up the *Batampina* River until we reached a place called *Lequimpau,* which was a town of about ten or twelve thousand inhabitants, with what looked like fine housing from the outside, encircled by a wall and barbican, with a moat running all around. Nearby, located outside the wall, there was a rather long structure with thirty furnaces on either side, in which they were smelting and refining huge quantities of silver that was brought there by the wagonload from a mountain range five leagues away called *Tuxenguim.* And the Chinese here told us that upwards of a thousand men worked around the clock in those mines, digging for silver that provided the king of China with an annual revenue of five thousand piculs. They also told us some other things which we found very interesting but which I am not including here out of fear of being tiresome.

  From here we departed close to sundown, and at vesper time of the following day we dropped anchor between two small cities facing each other, a little over a quarter of a league apart, which is how wide the river was, one called *Pacão,* and the other *Nacau;* and both of them, although small from the outside, were very stately and surrounded by well-constructed walls of stout, wide stone slabs. They had many pagodas there, covered in gold leaf, with many ingeniously designed spires and weather vanes on them of very elaborate and costly construction, which was quite a beautiful and delightful thing to see.

  With regard to these two cities, I will relate what they told us there and what I heard a few times afterwards, so that something will be known about the origin and the founding of the Chinese empire, since the writers of antiquity to this day have not provided any information on the subject.

  In chapter 13 of the first of the eighty chronicles devoted to the kings of China, which I heard read aloud many times, it says that in the year 639 after the Great Deluge there was a land called *Guantipocau* in those days, which it seems, judging from the parallel in which it lies, must be located at sixty-two degrees north, in the latitude of the coasts of Germany,[1] in our own continent of Europe. Living in this land at that time was a prince of small power and estate by the name of *Turbão*[2] who they say, as a young bachelor, had fathered three children by a woman named *Nancá,* with whom he was madly in love, much to the displeasure of his mother, the dowager queen.

  Having been urged several times by the leading citizens of the kingdom, or domain—which is all it was at the time—to get married, he always brushed it aside with some excuse which they found unacceptable; and instead, in response to the pressure exerted on them by his mother, they became more insistent in their demands and pressed him so hard that, in order to get out of marrying against his will, he conceived a plan for legitimizing his oldest son by *Nancá* and making him his heir to the throne, by entering a monastery called *Gizom,*[3] which it seems was a Roman idol and sect that is found to this day in the Chinese empire, on the island of Japan, and in Cochinchina, Cambodia, and Siam, countries in which I saw many temples of this sect. And when he drew up his testament, declaring this to be his last will, the queen mother, who at that time was a widow of fifty, contested it and let it be known that as long as her son had chosen to devote the rest of his life to the religion he had professed, leaving the kingdom without a legitimate heir, then she would take it upon herself to deal with the crisis. And thereupon, she remarried, choosing a priest of hers as a husband, a twenty-six-year-old man named *Silau,* and had him sworn in as king, much to the dismay of many of the people.

Turbão was immediately informed of what his mother had done, and knowing full well that she had taken this step in order to deprive his son of his inheritance and vitiate the terms of his will, he left the monastery with the intention of regaining the kingdom he had renounced and devoted all his time and energies exclusively to that end. Fearing that if he were successful they might both end up losing their lives, his mother and this *Silau* she had married met secretly with some of their followers— thirty cavalrymen and eighty foot soldiers, so they tell—who one night broke into the house where *Turbão* was staying, killing him and all his people.

However, *Nancá* and her three sons managed to escape along with some other members of her household by embarking on an oar-propelled *laulé,*[4] and fleeing down the river until they reached a place seventy leagues from there, where she and her few followers disembarked. And there, along with some other people who joined her later, she fortified herself in a floodplain located in the middle of the river, which she named *Pilaunera,* meaning "harvest of the poor" in our language, intending to spend the rest of her life there, cultivating the soil and supporting herself by the labor of her people, for, according to what it says in the same chapter, the country from there on down was still uninhabited.

After she had been living in this miserable and impoverished state for five years, the tyrant *Silau,* who, because he was not well liked by the people, began to fear that when the three boys grew up they might remove him from the throne he had unjustly usurped from them—or at the very least might cause disturbances that would eventually lead to riot and rebellion should they lay claim to the throne—decided, they say, to search for them by sending out a fleet of thirty oared *jangás*[5] said to be carrying sixteen hundred men on board. Having been reliably informed that this force was coming against her, *Nancá* consulted with her council to decide what to do about it, and it was agreed that under no circumstances should she remain there to face them, in view of the fact that her sons were mere children, that she was a woman, and that her followers were too few, weak, unarmed, and sorely lacking in everything necessary to defend themselves against so many well-armed enemies. She had a count taken of her followers and discovered that altogether they numbered barely thirteen hundred and that only five hundred of them were men and the rest women and little children, and that on the entire river the only ships she had available for all those people were three small *laulés* and a *janga* with a total capacity of under a hundred.

Nancá was well aware of the fact that these ships were not enough for all her people, and she began looking about for other ways of meeting so great an emergency; and, as the history relates, once again she called her council together and informed them publicly about her fears, asking them all to advise her, which at the time they refrained from doing, protesting in all sincerity that they did not think themselves capable of making up their minds so quickly but that, in keeping with their ancient customs and rituals, they advised her to cast lots, as they were accustomed to doing in similar emergencies, and that to whomever it would fall to be the one to speak, that person should tell them what was in his heart, as God would inspire him to do; and that they should set aside three days for this, during which time they should all join together, fasting, weeping, crying out loud, and praying with one voice for support and assistance to the merciful Lord on high from whose hand the help they sought was sure to be forthcoming.

Once *Nancá* and all her people had decided to follow this advice, which was considered the best of all at the time, she issued a public proclamation to the effect that no one, on penalty of death, was to eat more than once in all those three days, so that through abstinence of the flesh they would be spiritually closer to God.

93
The Child Prophet

At the end of these three days of penitence, they cast the lots five times in a row, and all five times they fell upon a seven-year-old boy called *Silau,* which was also the name of the dreaded tyrant, a startling coincidence that spread gloom and confusion among them when it was ascertained that no one else in the entire compound went by that name.

After they had finished making their sacrifices with the playing of music and the burning of incense, which were all the ceremonies customarily performed by way of giving thanks to God, they commanded the child to raise his arms to heaven and to tell them what he thought was the best way of meeting the grave crisis confronting them. And the story goes that with his eyes fixed on *Nancá,* the child said, "O frail and wretched woman, now that human understanding has failed thee in this sad hour of anguish and affliction and thou art more bowed down by the weight of thy helplessness and art delivering thyself with humble sighs into the hand of the almighty Lord, free, free, free, or at least, try thy utmost to free thy heart from the mists of earth, turning thine eyes to heaven with a pure and steadfast gaze, where thou wilt see, in the justice of the One who created thee, what wonders can be wrought by the prayers of the innocent and the sorely afflicted; for at the moment that thou didst reveal thy frailty and impotence to him with humble sighs, the victory over the tyrant *Silau* was immediately granted to thee from on high, along with a great promise for the future which the Lord of all mankind commands me, his lowliest creature, to transmit to thee. And he commands thee to embark on the enemy's ships with thy children and all thy family, and to run along the shoreline, within sound of the waters, keeping painful vigilance through the night though thy arm grow weary at the oars, for he will show thee, before thou comest to a resting place on the river, the site where thou art to lay the foundation of a house that will endure for many generations to come and that will achieve such great renown that within its walls his mercy will be praised throughout all time by foreign nations in a clamor of voices and bloodshed that will be as pleasing to him as the cries of the just and faithful children of tender age."

And the history book says that no sooner had he finished speaking these very words than the boy fell lifeless to the ground, an astounding thing—that is, of course, if it actually did happen—that left a very deep impresson on *Nancá* and all her people.

This same history book, which I heard read many times, also relates that five days after this happened, they saw the fleet of thirty *jangás* coming down the river in the morning, in perfect formation, with not a soul on board. And the same history book—every word of which the Chinese believe to be absolutely true—explains it this way.

When this armada was heading towards them in a body, with orders to ruthlessly carry out the tyrant *Silau*'s cruel and desperate measures against poor *Nancá,* her three sons, and the other people with her, they stopped one night at a place called *Catebasoy;* and while they were anchored there, a black cloud formed above them, emitting flashes of lightning and pelting them with thick, heavy raindrops that were so extremely hot that when these drops began to fall on the people, who were still awake at the time, they threw themselves into the river, where in less than an hour all of them perished, for they say that those drops burned in such a way that wherever one of them fell, it penetrated the flesh, accompanied by excruciating pain, clear down to the marrow of the bone, and that no clothing or covering of any kind that they could put on could protect them against it.

It was then that *Nancá,* recognizing the fact that she was in the presence of a very deep mystery, accepted it with many tears as an act of mercy from the hand of the Lord, and she and all her people offered up many prayers of thanks for it. She embarked on the thirty *jangás* of the armada with her three sons and all of her followers and went sailing down the river; and keeping within sound of the swift current, which was running in her favor, the history states that at the end of forty-seven days they reached the spot where the city of Peking now stands, and she disembarked with all her people, intending to make their home there. And they say that because she was afraid of *Silau,* whom she had always feared, she built a fortress there as best as she could, with stockades and walls of dry masonry rubble, about which more will be said later on.

94
The Founding of Peking

Having disembarked with all her people, the history book says that only five days after her arrival *Nancá* had them swear fealty to her oldest son as their lawful prince, by way of reassuring herself about a few things that had been troubling her all along, and of alleviating the suffering she had endured till then.

As for her son, in the afternoon of the same day that that small group of people who were with him had sworn to obey him, he staked out that site where the fortress was to be built. When they opened the first ditch, which he had ordered them to dig with all speed, he emerged from his tent, accompanied by his mother—who was directing everything—his brothers, and some of the leading members of their community. Dressed in his finest clothes for his first public appearance, he came forward in their company with a stone that he had had cut for the occasion and that was ceremoniously being carried in the lead. When he reached the spot where the foundation had been prepared, he took the stone into his own hands, and beaming with pleasure, he got down on his knees, raised his arms heavenward, and addressed all those present.

"Brothers and dear friends," he exclaimed, "on this cornerstone, on which the foundation of a new house will rest, I have inscribed my name, for henceforth that is how it will be known. Therefore, I ask you all as my friends, and I command you all, as your king, never to refer to it by any other name, so that all who come after us will remember, from now until the end of time, that on the third day of the eighth moon in the year 639—after the Lord of all creation had made those then living see how deeply he abhorred the sins of mankind by flooding the earth with rain from the heaven above in accordance with his divine judgement—young Peking built this house, to which he gave his own name, a house within which—according to the prophecy we received from the child who died—the voices of foreign peoples will be heard throughout all time exalting the ways in which the Lord is to be feared and gratified with the sacrificial offerings that are just and pleasing to him."

And the same words that were spoken by him can still be seen today engraved on a silver escutcheon that hangs over the archway of one of the city gates, which is the main gate, now called *Pommicotay,* where, by way of honoring and perpetuating the memory of this prophecy, a guard of forty halberdiers and their captain are stationed around the clock, whereas only four men stand guard at each of the other gates to keep track of everything that passes in and out through them each day.

And because it was on the third day of the month of August—according to what the history books say—that the young king laid the cornerstone for the foundation of the city, ever since then the kings of China have always observed the custom, as they still do even now, of appearing in public on that day. And they do it with so much pomp and majesty, in such a strange and grandiose manner, that I must say in all truth, to describe what the least part of it is like, let alone all, is much too difficult, and for that reason, I did not want to get into something that I know for certain that I will not be able to deal with adequately.

And because of the words spoken by the first king when he laid the cornerstone, which the Chinese believe to be a true prophecy, his descendants later made a law that carried severe penalties with it, forbidding all foreigners to enter the kingdom, with the exception of ambassadors and captives who, when they are apprehended, must be exiled from place to place, just as was done to the nine of us.

And that was the way, as I have briefly explained, that the city of Peking was founded, and the Chinese empire populated by this prince called Peking, *Nancá's* oldest son. His two younger brothers, named *Pacão* and *Nacau,* later founded two other cities to which they too gave their own names. As for their mother, who was called *Nancá,* as I said before, one also reads that she founded the city of Nanking, the second-largest city of this monarchy, which took its name from her and still retains it to this day.

One reads that this Chinese empire continued in a direct line of succession from one king to the other from that time until a certain era, which, reckoned by our calendar, would seem to fall out in the year of our Lord 1113. And it was then that this city of Peking was ravaged and laid waste twenty-six times by enemy forces. But since by that time the population was already large and the kings very rich, they say that the reigning monarch, who was called *Xixipão,* spent twenty-three years building a wall around it, the way it stands today; and that another king, a grandson of his, by the name of *Jumbileytay,* built the second wall eighty-two years later. Both walls have a circumference of sixty leagues, or thirty each, that is to say—ten leagues long and five wide; and both walls, one reads, have 1,060 round bastions and 240 well-fortified towers that are wide and tall, topped by spires that are painted in all different colors, which make them look very bright and attractive. And all of them have gilded lions at the top, resting on spheres or round pommels, which represent the device or coat of arms [1] of the king of China, by means of which he wants it understood that he is the "Crowned Lion on the Throne of the World."

Beyond the outer wall there is a huge moat over ten fathoms deep and forty wide, in which at all times there are a large number of oared craft, covered with awnings, like houses, on which everything imaginable is sold, from foodstuffs to any kind of merchandise that one can name.

Also, according to what the Chinese told us, this city has 360 gates all around, at each of which, as I said a little while ago, four armed *upos,* holding halberds in their hands, are always stationed, whose responsibility it is to check on the traffic going in and out. They also have certain buildings there that are like a civic center, that the city has staffed for that purpose with their *anchacis* and magistrates, where lost children are also brought and kept until their parents can come and claim them.

About the rest of the wonders of this great city I will have more to say in due time, because what I have related thus far was only meant to provide a brief summary of the origin and founding of this empire, and of the founder of this city of Peking [2]—a metropolis that truly stands far above all other cities in the world, for its grandeur, good government, bounty, wealth, and everything else that one can possibly think of or say—and also, to explain a little about the founding and the beginnings of the second city of this great empire, which is Nanking, as I have said before, as well as about the other two cities, *Pacão* and *Nacau,* mentioned above, where both their founders' bodies lie enshrined in rich and noble temples, within tombs of gold-trimmed green and white alabaster, supported by silver lions that are surrounded by row on row of lamps and perfume censers, filling the air with many different kinds of fragrance.

95
The Great Wall of China

As long as I have dealt with the origin and the founding of the Chinese empire and the walls of the great city of Peking, I thought it would also be fitting to add, as briefly as possible, a few words about something else no less remarkable than each of the others.

One reads in the fifth volume of the *Guide to All Notable Places* in the empire, or monarchy, or however one chooses to call it—for really, any word signifying greatness is appropriate when referring to it—that in the year A.D. 528—which seems to be the right date, based on the book of eras they use—the ruling king, named *Crisnagol Dacotay,* went to war against the Tartar because of a dispute they had over the state of *Xenxinapau,* which borders in the interior with the kingdom of Laos, routing his forces and achieving a resounding victory in the field. However, immediately afterwards the Tartar began to gather a still larger and more powerful army than before, by entering into an alliance and league with some other kings who were friendly to him, and eight years later he invaded China again, capturing, it is affirmed, thirty-two important towns, including the large city of *Ponquilor*. And, out of fear that he would not be able to defend himself against him, the Chinese king signed a peace treaty with him, under the terms of which he agreed to relinquish his rights to the disputed territory and, in addition, to hand over the sum of two thousand silver piculs to pay for the foreign mercenaries in the Tartar's army. That settled the matter, and everything was peaceful and quiet for the next fifty-two years, as it says in the same history book.

However, since he was afraid that he might not be able to resist the combined force of another confederation similar to the last, the reigning Chinese king[1] decided to build a wall, sealing off the entire frontier between the two empires. He convoked a general assembly of the people and informed them of what he had decided, and they all thought it was an essential and highly desirable thing to do. To help meet the cost of such an important project, they voted him the sum of ten thousand silver piculs, which in our currency is equal to fifteen million gold *cruzados*, calculated at the rate of fifteen hundred *cruzados* per picul. And in addition, it is said that they voted to maintain, for as long as it took, a work force of 250,000, consisting of 30,000 trained engineers and the rest, unskilled laborers.

After assembling everything necessary for this extraordinary project, they got to work. And the history relates that within a period of twenty-seven years, the borders of these two empires were completely sealed off from one end to the other. This would mean, going by what it says in the same chronicle, that the wall extended for a distance of seventy *jaus*,[2] which is the equivalent of 315 leagues by our reckoning, calculating at four and a half leagues per *jau*. They say that 750,000 men worked continuously on this project, to which the common people, as I said before, contributed a one-third share of the cost, the priesthood and the Hainan islands another third, and the king, together with the princes, the lords, and the *chaens* and *anchacis* in high governing positions, contributed the remaining third.

This wall, which I saw a few times and which I measured, is on the average six armspans tall and forty handspans wide in the masonry work, but from four armspans down, there slopes a dirt-and-rubble fill, like a terreplein, braced on the outside face with a bituminous substance like mortar, nearly twice as wide as the wall itself, making it all so strong that not even a thousand basilisks could knock it down. And instead of towers or bastions, it has some two-story lookouts, erected on heavy timber piles of a black wood they call *caubesy*, meaning "iron wood," each one as thick as a wine barrel and very tall, as a result of which, these lookouts, it seems, turn out to be much stronger than if they had been made of stone and lime.

This wall, or *Chanfacau*,[3] as they call it, runs along like this uniformly until it meets the rough terrain of the mountains that appear along the way, which, in order that they may also serve as part of the wall, are all smoothed down and sloped with pickaxes, making these sections much stronger than the very wall itself. This means that in all this distance of land, the only wall there, is that which occupies the space between the mountains; and in all the rest, the mountains themselves serve as part of the wall.

And in the entire length of this wall, along all these 315 leagues, there are only five entrances, formed by the rivers of Tartary which descend with tremendous force, cutting across the interior for a distance of more than five hundred leagues before emptying into the seas of China and Cochinchina. And one of these rivers, since it is more powerful than the others, finds its outlet in the kingdom of *Sornau,* commonly known as Siam, at the bar harbor of Cuy. And both the Chinese king and the Tartar have troops stationed at all five entrances, and at each one the Chinese has a garrison of seven thousand men posted around the clock, consisting of six thousand infantry and one thousand cavalry men, who receive very high wages. And most of them are foreigners, such as Moghuls, *Pancrus,* Chams, Khorasanis,[4] *Gizares*[5] from Persia, and others recruited from many other nations and kingdoms located in the heart of the interior, because the truth is that the Chinese do not really make very good soldiers,[6] for aside from their lack of experience in warfare, they are fainthearted, a little short of firearms, and totally lacking in heavy artillery.[7]

Altogether there are 320 command posts along the entire wall with a five-hundred-man company stationed at each, making a total of 160,000 men, not counting the administrators, magistrates, and *upos* guarding the *anchacis* and *chaens,* and many other people who are necessary for running the wheels of government and for sustaining this huge population which altogether, the Chinese told us, came to 200,000 men who were constantly on duty and whose subsistence was the only expense borne by the king; for since all or almost all of them are conscripts, condemned to forced labor, they do not have to give them wages, just their food, as I will explain later when I discuss the prison located in the city of Peking, where these conscripts are held, which also happens to be another outstanding building of remarkable architectural grandeur and proportions. Within its walls there is a constant labor pool of over 300,000 prisoners, all, or most of them, ranging in age from eighteen to forty-five, who are kept there in readiness, waiting to be called out to work on this great wall. Among them there are many highly respected members of the nobility and wealthy upper class who had committed serious crimes but who had had the sentences they deserved commuted to serving what amounts to a life term at this forced-labor prison, where they remain, waiting to be called out to work on the wall. While they are there, they have recourse to appeal, as provided by the statutes of war enacted for that purpose and approved by the *chaens* who enjoy the same unlimited privileges and powers of life and death as does the king himself in these and all other matters. And every single one of these twelve high-ranking *chaens* in government service has the right to dispense funds, even as much as a million *cruzados* in gold, from the public treasury if he chooses to, with no one to say him nay.

96
The Submerged City

And now to get back to my story from which I strayed quite some time ago. After we departed from the twin cities of *Pacão* and *Nacau,* we proceeded on our way up the river, chained in the manner I described, until we reached another city called *Mindó,* not much larger than the last two, where half a league inland there was a very large saltwater lake with a huge number of solar evaporating ponds around it. The Chinese told us that the level of this lake rises and falls just like the ocean tides despite the fact that it is located more than two hundred leagues inland, and that it yielded the king of China an annual revenue of 100,000 *taels,* just for his one-third share of the salt. Apart from this, the city also provided him with another 100,000 *taels* in revenue from its silk looms, camphor, sugar, porcelain, vermillion, and mercury, all of which they told us were produced here in enormous quantities.

About two leagues beyond the city there were twelve rather long buildings that looked like warehouses where large numbers of people were employed in the smelting and refining of copper plates, and they were making such an infernal racket with their hammers that, if there is anything on earth resembling hell, it had to be this.

Curious about the cause of all this uncommon noise, we tried to find out from where it was coming and saw that in each of these buildings there were forty furnaces blasting away, counting twenty on either side, with forty huge anvils, on each of which eight men were hammering away with rhythmic strokes at such a rapid pace that there was barely time for our eyes to discern what their hands were doing. In each of these buildings they had 320 men working round the clock, which meant that in all twelve buildings there was a total work force of 3,840, not counting the many other people assigned to various other jobs.

When we asked how much copper was worked there annually, they said from 110,000 to 120,000 piculs, two-thirds of which went to the king, since the mines belonged to the crown, and that the mountain from which it was extracted was called *Coretumbagá,* which means "river of copper," so named because ever since it was discovered, which was more than two hundred years ago, the copper has never been exhausted; to the contrary, they kept on discovering more and more.

Close by the river's edge, about a league beyond these warehouses, in the middle of a rather large landscaped area enclosed by three iron grillwork fences, we saw a group of thirty buildings standing in five rows, six in each row, which were also very long and well constructed, with bronze and cast-iron bells hanging from tall towers, and a great deal of hand-carved workmanship, gilded columns, and hewn stone façades of very ingenious design. Here at this terraced area we went ashore with the permission of the *chifu,* who took us there because of a vow he had made to visit this temple, which was called *Bigay Potim,* meaning "the god of 110,000 gods," *corchó fungané ginaco ginaca,* as they say, signifying "bigger and stronger than all the others."

For one of the perversities these wretched people blindly adhere to is the belief that each thing has its own particular god who created it and who preserves for it its natural being, but that all of them are the offspring of this *Bigay Potim,* issuing from under his armpits, and that they receive their being from him, as from a father, by means of a filial union which they call *Bijaporentesay.*

In the kingdom of Pegu, which I have visited several times, I saw another pagoda similar to this one, which the natives call *Ginocoginana,* "god of all greatness." It had been built by the Chinese in ancient times when they ruled over India, which was from A.D. 1013 to 1072, as would appear from their chronological account of events. From this chronology one can see that the Chinese rule lasted only fifty-nine years because the successor of the king who conquered India, called *Oxivagão,* renounced it voluntarily when he realized how high a price he was paying in the blood of his people and how little he was getting in return.[1]

In the thirty buildings mentioned above there was a huge quantity of gilded wooden idols and as many more made of tin, copper, brass, cast iron, and porcelain—such a huge quantity that I would not dare hazard a guess at the number.

From here, we could not have gone more than six or seven leagues further when we saw a large city that appeared to extend for more than a league around with its walls and buildings completely demolished.

When we asked the Chinese why everything was in ruins, they told us that this city had formerly been called *Cohilouzá,* meaning "wildflower," and that it had been very prosperous in its day; and that about 142 years ago a foreigner had come there in the company of some merchants, from the Siamese port of Tenasserim; and that, apparently, from what was written about him in a book entitled *Toxefalém,* he was a holy man, in spite of the fact that the bonzes called him a sorcerer at that time because of the wondrous deeds he performed, for in less than a month he had raised up five persons from the dead and had wrought many other marvels that amazed everyone. And on several occasions, when the priests had engaged him in theological disputations, he confounded them and put them all to shame, so that in order to avoid getting into any more arguments with him, they incited all the people against him by getting them to believe that if they failed to kill him, God would punish them by sending down fire from heaven. As a result, inflamed by their words, the mob converged on the house of a poor weaver named Joane, where the foreigner lodged, killing the weaver, two of his sons-in-law, and a son, for trying to defend him. Then the holy man appeared before them in tears, and rebuked them for their mob action, arising out of their evil way of life. One of the things, among others, that he said when he spoke to them at the time was that the God in whose faith they would find salvation was called Jesus Christ, and that he had come down to earth from heaven to become a man of flesh and blood; and that it had been necessary for him to die for the sake of mankind; and that with the price of his blood, which he shed upon the Cross for all sinners, God in his justice was so thoroughly satisfied that he gave him the power of heaven and earth and promised him that all who professed his Law with good faith and good works would not be denied their due reward; and that all the gods that the bonzes worshipped and served with ritual blood sacrifices were false, and idols in which the devil hid to deceive them.

Upon hearing these words, the priests became so enraged that they began to shout, bringing down curses on any and all who refused to help gather firewood with which to burn him at the stake. This was soon done, with great haste; and as the fire began to spread with tremendous fury, he made the sign of the cross over it and uttered a few words which they could not remember but which were also recorded, and the fire went out immediately. Amazed by such a wondrous thing, all the people began to shout, "This man's God must be extremely powerful and most worthy of being worshipped throughout all the world!"

When he heard this and saw that the people were beginning to draw back because of what they had seen, one of the bonzes who had been the main instigators of the mob, threw a stone at the holy man, shouting as he did so, "Whoever fails to do as I am doing, may the Serpent of the Night swallow him in his fiery jaws!"

At these words, all the other bonzes followed suit, so that right there they succeeded in stoning him to death. And after they had thrown his body into the river, the current checked its flow to such an extent that, during the five days that the holy corpse remained in the river, it never followed its course downstream. And after witnessing that wondrous deed, many people became followers of that man's religion, and there were still a large number of them living around there.

Just as the Chinese were telling us this we rounded a bend in the river and saw a small terraced area completely surrounded by trees, in the middle of which there was an extremely large and well-fashioned stone cross, the sight of which affected us so, that I can honestly say, in all truth, that there are no words to describe the feelings that the Lord our God instilled in us there. We begged the *chifu* on our knees to let us go ashore to see for ourselves what those men had been talking about, but that heathen dog put us off with the excuse that we still had a long way to go to the next town where we were to spend the night, and his refusal left us feeling quite disconsolate.

But since the Lord our God, in His mercy, would grant us this blessing almost miraculously, He ordained that when he had already gone more than a league further, by dint of straining against the oars with the greatest difficulty, at that very moment, his pregnant wife, who was on board with him, began to get such severe labor pains that he was forced to turn back and put into the place we had left behind, which was a village of thirty or forty hearths called *Xifangau,* next to where the cross was located. Disembarking there, he took a house for his wife, where she died in childbirth nine days later.

In the meantime, we all went down to the place where the cross stood and there, prostrated on the ground, with the tears running down our cheeks, we paid it due reverence, to the open amazement of the townspeople who all came running up to us. They too got down on their knees, and raising their arms heavenward, they also kissed the cross over and over, as they chanted these words, "Cristo Jesu, Jesu Cristo, Maria, micau vidau late impone moudel," which in our language means, "Christ Jesus, Jesus Christ, Mary, ever a virgin, conceived him, a virgin bore him, and a virgin remained."

To which we replied, weeping, that indeed it was so. When they asked us if we were Christians, we said yes, which they were delighted to hear; and they took us to their homes and gave us shelter and treated us with loving-kindness, for these people were all Christians who descended from the weaver in whose house the holy man had lived.

Then we asked them if the story told us by the Chinese was true, and they related how the whole thing had come about and showed us a book that had been printed on the subject, dealing with some very wondrous things that had been wrought there by the Lord through that holy man whose name it said was Mateus Escandel, and that he had been a hermit on Mount Sinai. And it said that he was a Hungarian, from a town called Buda.

And in the same book it says that nine days after that holy man had been laid to rest, in the same town where he still lay buried, an earthquake struck the city of *Cohilouzá,* where he had been slain, with such a sharp jolt that all the common people fled in terror to the open fields, settling in tents, for none of them dared to go back to their homes. At this time the bonzes came running up in an effort to calm the crowds of people that were milling about, because they were all shouting at the same time, "The blood of the holy foreigner will demand vengeance for his death at the hands of our bonzes, for he was telling the truth!"

They reprimanded the people for what they were saying, telling them not to talk that way because it was a grave sin, and that they should not be afraid, for they promised that they would all ask *Quiay Tiguarém,* the god of night, to command the earth not to do that again, otherwise they would withhold their alms from him.

With that all the priests formed a procession and marched off to the temple of this idol, the most important one in their religion, but they went all by themselves because the people were too afraid of returning to the city to accompany them. And they say that the night after this earthquake, shortly before eleven o'clock, while all these ministers of the devil were in the midst of offering their sacrifices, with the burning of fragrant incense and other ceremonies they usually perform, the Lord our God, in his divine justice, ordained a righteous punishment for them by permitting the earth to tremble again, but this time with such tremendous force that temples, houses, walls, and every other kind of building in the city collapsed, bringing death to all the bonzes, without a single one of them escaping alive; and according to what the book says, there were more than four thousand of them. Then the earth opened up and water gushed out from beneath the surface, submerging the entire city and leaving in its wake a large lagoon more than one hundred fathoms deep. They also told us many other things that were utterly amazing.

And from that time on the city was called *Fiunganorsé,* meaning "punishment from heaven," though it had previously been known as *Cohilouzá,* which, as I have already said, means "wildflower."

97
Business and Trade Practices in China

After departing from the ruined city of *Fiunganorsé* we reached a large, very prosperous city called *Junquinilau,* where all kinds of things were available in abundant supply, its streets filled with many very distinguished-looking people going about on horseback and on foot, and the harbor teeming with an enormous number of vessels, from oared craft to huge sailing junks.

We stopped in this city for five days because our *chifu* wanted to arrange for the funeral of his wife there, for the sake of whose soul he distributed charity to all of us there in the form of both food and clothing, releasing us from the punishment of the oar bench and giving us liberty to go ashore whenever we felt like, without having to wear the iron collars and shackles, which was a tremendous relief for us.

From here, as we continued our journey upstream, all along the river, on both sides, we saw many fine cities and villages and other good-sized towns surrounded by strong, massive walls with rock-built castles along the shore, as well as many towers and sumptuous shrines belonging to their heathen sects, all topped by belfries and spires covered with gold leaf. In the fields there was such an enormous quantity of cattle that in some parts the herds covered a distance of six or seven leagues. And there were so many vessels on the river that in some places where they were holding fairs it was impossible for the eye to take them all in, to say nothing of many other smaller conglomerations of as many as 300, 500, 600, and 1,000 sails we met up with all along the way on both sides, where as wide a variety of things as one can name were being offered for sale.

Quite a few of the Chinese told us that in the Chinese empire there were just as many people living on the rivers as in the cities and towns, and that if it were not for the highly organized system they have of providing for the working people, and of regulating the businesses and trades in which they are forced to make a living, the competition would be so fierce that they would probably eat each other up alive, for every line of work and trade that men live by is divided into three or four different fields of specialization.

For instance, in the poultry line, let us say ducks, some men are just allowed to operate the egg hatcheries and the raising of ducklings for sale; others specialize in raising the ducklings to maturity for killing and selling them cured; others deal in feathers only, and the entrails and giblets; others only in eggs. And a man engaged in any single one of these operations is not allowed to mix into any other on pain of thirty strokes of the lash, a penalty for which there is no recourse either to appeal, protection, influence, or anything else.

In the pork business, some make their living as wholesalers, selling the pigs alive on the hoof; others only handle them for slaughter and selling them at retail; others for cutting them up to be sold as cured meat; others specialize in the sale of suckling pigs; others in chitterlings, lard, feet, blood, and edible organs.

In the fish business, the one who sells fresh fish is not allowed to sell salted fish, and the one who sells salted fish is not allowed to sell dried fish, and so on, with all other lines of fresh food, whether it be meat, game, fish, as well as fruits and vege-tables, all of them are subject to the same rules and regulations. And no one is allowed to switch from one kind of dealing to another without obtaining a license from the city council,[1] and even then he has to show just and lawful cause or face the penalty of thirty strokes.

There are also other people who make their living by selling live fish swimming around in large tanks or pools of water, loading them onto many oared barges, where they are kept in watertight compartments and carried alive to many far-off places.

Also, all along the shores of this great *Batampina* River on which we made our way from Nanking to Peking, which is a distance of 180 leagues, there are so many sugar mills and presses for making wine and oil out of so many different kinds of fruits and vegetables that there are entire streets all along both sides of the river two and three leagues long that are lined with these food processing plants, which is certainly enough to stagger the imagination.

In other parts there are many warehouses stocked with an infinite supply of pro-visions and just as many other rather long buildings, like storehouses, where they slice, salt, cure, and smoke every kind of game and meat that is found in the land. And they are piled high with stocks of ham, pork, bacon, ducks, geese, cranes, bustards, ostrich, venison, beef, buffalo, tapir, yak, horse, tiger, dog, fox, and the meat of every other kind of animal on earth, which left us all gasping with amazement, as one would natu-rally expect, at such an unusual, astounding, and almost incredibly marvelous thing, and many a time we would say that all the people in the world could not possibly consume that much food in one lifetime.

We also saw on this river a large number of ships they call *panouras*,[2] which are similar to the foist, their decks covered from stem to stern with woven reed cages like chicken coops, each measuring two spans tall, stacked three or four on top of each other and crammed full of ducks that men were carrying to be sold. These men travel up the river under sail and oar, or however they wish, selling these ducks for a living. When it is time to feed them, they bring the ships in close to shore, picking a marshy spot with some pools of water, and they lay planks down to the ground, and open the doors of these cages. At the sound of four beats of the drum, all these birds, numbering as many as six, seven thousand or more, leave the ship with a squawking and head all in a rush, straight for the puddles in the field. When the owner decides that they have had time enough to eat, he beats the drum again, and the moment they hear it they let out the same loud squawking and go back on board the ship they came from, with each one resuming its place in the same coop, and without a single one being lost in the process, after which the ship continues on its way.

When it is time for them to lay their eggs, the owner puts into shore again near some dry field with a good cover of grass, opens the cages carrying them, beats the drum again, and the minute they hear it they all go ashore to lay their eggs. After an hour has passed, or whatever length of time he thinks it takes them, more or less, to finish laying, he beats the drum again, and then they all rush to get back aboard the ship without, as I say, a single straggler being left behind in the field. Once they have found their places on board, the owner and two or three others who work with him go ashore carrying baskets, and when they reach the grass that has been whitened by the freshly laid eggs, they gather them in their baskets and return to the ship. And not a day goes by without their collecting from ten to twelve basketloads, after which they proceed on their way, selling these wares for a living.

And whenever their supply of ducks runs low and needs to be replenished, they buy them from other people who also make their living by raising and selling them wholesale to these retailers, who are not allowed to raise them as the others do because, as I said before, no one is permitted to deal in anything other than what he has been licensed for by the city council. The people who earn their living by raising the ducks have ponds near their houses where they keep as many as ten or twelve thousand ducklings, some smaller, some larger than others. And in their hatcheries, which are very long buildings that look like warehouses, they have twenty, thirty ovens packed with dung in which they bury 200, 300, and 500 eggs at a time, keeping the dung warm by covering the mouths of the ovens and letting them stay there until they think they are about ready to hatch. Then in each one of these ovens they install a half-plucked capon wounded in the breast, and cover the openings again. Within two days the capon has finished hatching them all, and then they put them in certain places underground that have been prepared for them with their bran mush inside. Then they are allowed to roam free for ten or twelve days until they find their way by themselves to the ponds where they are raised until they grow large enough to be sold to those retailers I mentioned, who in turn transport them for sale in various places and who are not allowed, as I said before, to raise them, as are the people from whom they were purchased, under pain of being sentenced to thirty strokes of the lash for doing so; for a dealer who specializes in one end of the line is not allowed to step over into another man's specialty.[3]

These regulations are so strictly observed that, whether it be on the street, the public squares, or any place else where food is marketed, if a man licensed for duck eggs is found with chicken eggs, presumably for sale, they punish him right there on the spot where he has been caught with the wrong merchandise, by administering thirty lashes on the buttocks, without giving him a chance to explain. And if he wants to keep them, he must show, in order to escape the penalty, that they are slightly cracked on top, to make it look like he was saving them for his own dinner. And what applies to one also applies to the other, not one whit more, not one whit less.

Also, those who sell live fish have to keep them in large tubs of water, with reeds strung through their mouths, so the buyer can hold them up if he wants to see how big they are, without squeezing them or dirtying them or otherwise damaging them. And if a fish should die, they have to slice it up and salt it immediately, to be sold at the price fixed for salted fish, which is somewhat less.

That way no one breaks the rules and regulations imposed on him by the *conchalis* of the government—who are like our market inspectors—under pain of being promptly and severely punished for it, because the king is so highly revered in this country, and his administration of justice so deeply feared, that not a single person, no matter how important he may be, dares to open his mouth or raise his eyes in the presence of any representative of the law, though he may be only a simple *upo* who wields the whip and whose function is similar to that of the executioner or bailiff in our country.

98
The Floating Cities of China

We also saw as we were traveling along this great river enormous herds of swine and draft animals, both wild and tame, that were being watched over by men on horseback, and in another place, numerous herds of domesticated deer, being tended by men on foot who were leading them to pasture. All these deer were lame in the right front leg, a defect that is inflicted on them when they are young and the risk is minimal, in order to prevent them from fleeing.

We also saw many animal pens in which they were raising a large number of dogs[1] to sell to the meat suppliers, for all sorts of flesh is eaten in this country, and one can tell the kind of meat according to the butcher shops and prices.

We also saw many barges full of suckling pigs, and others loaded with turtles, frogs, otters, snakes, eels, snails, and lizards, because everything, as I say, is bought for food. And since these types of food are cheaper, they allow the merchant who sells them to handle many different varieties, for they take everything into consideration; accordingly, certain concessions are made, more in some things than in others, so that there will be no lack of dealers in every line.

And while I am on the subject of what they sell, I may as well include something else we saw that came as no small surprise to us, for it amazed us to see how greed can lead men to seize upon the vilest, filthiest things in order to make a profit. I am referring to the fact that we saw many other people who make a living by buying and selling human excrement, which they do not regard as such a bad kind of merchandise, for there are many very wealthy and highly respected merchants who deal in it. And this excrement is used to renew the soil of fallow fields that are being replanted, because they think it is superior to the usual type of fertilizer.[2] And the dealers who buy this stuff go through the streets making noise on a wooden clapper of sorts, like our Lazarists begging for alms, by way of letting people know what they want to buy, for they are well aware of how dirty the word in itself is and that it would be in bad taste to go crying it out in the streets. And the demand for this merchandise is so great that at times it is possible to see as many as two, three hundred sails coming into port on the tide to pick up this cargo, the way the barges in our country come in to load salt, and even so, they very often have to resort to a system of allocations at fixed prices, depending on the available supply of the commodity. And because this fertilizer is so effective, they harvest three crops a year in China.

We also saw many vessels loaded with dried orange peel, which is used in the low-priced taverns for boiling with dog meat in order to eliminate its characteristic bad odor, improve its soggy texture, and make the flesh firmer.

We also saw going up this river, as I said before, many *vancões, lanteias,* and barges, loaded with as many different kinds of food as can be produced on land or in the sea, and all of it in such abundance that I am really at a loss for words, let alone numbers, that would give some idea of the quantity involved, for in speaking of the quantity of things they have there, one should not imagine for a moment that it is the same as we are used to seeing in the countries around us here, but rather two, three hundred shiploads of each one of these things alone, especially on the days when they hold their *chandeus*[3] and celebrate the religious festivals of their pagodas, at which time everything that enters is duty free owing to the large number of people attending. And all or nearly all of the buildings belonging to these pagodas are situated at the edge of the river, which gives them easier access to things and contributes to their splendor and wealth.

When the vessels gather for these festivities, they constitute a very large and stately city in themselves, stretching out along the shoreline for more than a league and nearly a third of that across, comprising over twenty thousand vessels, to say nothing of the *balões, guedés,*[4] and *manchuas,* which are very small boats, too numerous to count, that they use for carrying on business.

There are sixty captains in this city, as ordained by the *aitao* of *Bitampina*[5] who, as I said before, is the supreme head and president of the council of the thirty-two admirals of the thirty-two kingdoms of this monarchy; and thirty of these captains are responsible for the administrative affairs of this floating city and are charged with putting it in order and hearing all legal disputes. The other thirty captains are responsible for the protection of the out-of-town merchants, seeing to it that they are free to navigate in safety without fear of being attacked by thieves. And all these officials in turn are responsible to a *chaem* who wields the power of life and death in all matters civil and criminal, without recourse to appeal or review.

For two weeks, from the time of the new moon to the full moon, which is as long as these fairs last, the orderly administration, disposition, and stately beauty of this city, which is comprised of ships anchored in the river, is far more impressive than anything ever built on shore. For in this city, two thousand very long, straight lanes can be seen, lined on both sides by ships, and most of them dressed with silk awnings, with many banners, flags, streamers, and gaily painted afterdecks on which anything one could desire is sold. On other ships, there are skilled workmen representing all the different crafts and trades that exist in the world. And in the middle of these lanes are the people who come to trade, gliding back and forth in little *manchuas* ever so peacefully, without making any noise or causing the slightest disturbance. And if by chance they should catch a thief stealing something, he receives the punishment he deserves right then and there.

At nightfall all these lanes are cordoned off with ropes crossing from one to the other side so that no one can get through once the bell has been rung. And each of these lanes is illuminated by ten or twelve lanterns hanging from the mastheads, enabling them to see anyone passing at night, who he is, where he is heading, and what he is looking for, so that a complete report can be given to the *chaem* in the morning. And all these lights, when seen together at night, are one of the most beautiful things imaginable.

In each of these lanes there is a sentry bell, and whenever they ring the one on the *chaem*'s boat, all the others respond with such a loud clamor of tones that it astounded us, for it was something perhaps never imagined before, and was done in such a harmonious and well-organized fashion.

In each of these lanes, even the poorest of them, there are prayer houses installed on big barges, similar to the galley, which are spotlessly clean and beautifully arranged, with deck coverings adorned in gold leaf that serve as the chapel for the idol, and priests in attendance to perform the sacrifices offered by the common people who constantly provide them with enough alms and offerings to feast on handsomely.

Every honorable man or leading merchant in these stately lanes takes a turn at patrolling the area on different nights, along with certain members of his block squad, in addition to the thirty military captains who cruise around outside in extremely well armed *balões* to make sure that no thief escapes anywhere, and as they make their rounds they continuously call out loud to make their presence known.

Among some of the most noteworthy things we saw here was a lane of over a hundred ships loaded with all kinds of gilded wooden idols which were being sold as offerings for the pagodas, in addition to a complete assortment of wooden feet, legs, arms, and heads that sick people were buying to offer up in their devotional prayers.

There are also other ships, covered with silk awnings, on which they present many comedy skits and all different kinds of entertainment which are very popular with the common people who flock there to be amused.

There are others on which they sell bills of exchange, for transferring sums of money from earth to heaven, from which these priests of Satan promise them much profit and interest, while at the same time assuring them that without these bills of exchange there is no way they can possibly be saved, since God is a mortal enemy of those who do not give alms to the pagodas. And they fill their heads with so many lies and preach so much nonsense to them about these matters that very often the poor things go without food in order to give them money.

There are other ships piled high with human skulls which they buy to use as a graveside offering when someone dies; for they say that just as the deceased goes to the grave accompanied by those skulls, so will his soul enter heaven, accompanied by the alms of those to whom the skulls had belonged; for when the gatekeeper of paradise sees him there attended by so many servants, he will honor him as though he had been lord and master of all those people here in this life; and that if he is poor and comes unaccompanied, they will not let him in. And the more skulls a man takes with him, the more blessed he holds himself to be.

There are also other vessels displaying many cages full of live birds, tended by men who play music as they exhort the crowd to come and release these little creatures of God from captivity, and many people hasten to rescue them with their money, each one selecting the captive birds he wishes to redeem; and as they set them free, everybody cries out, "Pichau pitanel catao vacaxi," meaning, "Go and tell God up there how well we serve him down here."

In like manner, on other ships, there are men who display large pots of water with numerous little fish swimming in them, which they catch in the rivers with extremely fine meshed nets, and they also carry on in the same way, exhorting the people to do God a service by freeing the innocent captives who never did anything wrong. These people also give money to select the ones they want, and as they throw them back into the river they say, "On your way little fish, and inform everyone there of the good deed I have done for thee, for the sake of God!"

And the number of ships carrying these things for sale are not to be estimated at less than a hundred to two hundred or more, besides many others carrying other things in much greater quantity.

99
More about the Wonders of China

We also saw groups of men and women on board some barges playing different kinds of musical instruments for anyone who wanted to hear them. And they become quite wealthy just by doing that.

There are also other men who bring in ships loaded with animal horns, which the priests sell as cornucopias for banqueting in heaven. They say these horns were taken from animals sacrificed to the idols at devotional prayers and offered up in fulfillment of vows made by people because of misfortunes undergone or illnesses suffered. And they say that just as the flesh of these animals has been distributed to the poor on earth, out of love of God, in the same way the soul of the deceased person for whom one of these horns is offered also dines in the next world on the soul of the animal it had belonged to originally, and invites other souls among his friends to join him, the way people invite each other here on earth.

We also saw many ships, covered with symbols of mourning, that were carrying coffins, torches, candles, and women who can be hired to weep at a funeral, all for burying people, who die in as honorable a fashion as each one wishes to, depending on the number of attendants or mourners hired to accompany him to his grave.

There are others called *pitaleus* [1] who, on very large barges, carry all sorts of wild animal acts that they put on with music and dancing, which is a very interesting and frightening spectacle, for they include snakes, cobras, giant lizards, tigers, beasts of prey, and many other different kinds of animals, which are also exhibited for money.

There are others carrying huge stacks of books containing descriptions of historical events relating to everything one would want to know, not only about the creation of the world—about which they tell infinite lies—but also about the countries, kingdoms, islands, and provinces of the world, and their respective laws and customs, mainly of the kings of China, how many of them there were, what they accomplished, who founded which countries and cities, and the events that took place in each period. These people also draw up petitions, write letters, give legal advice, and perform other services of this nature, which enables them also to make a very good living.

Likewise, there are others who show up at these fairs in very swift boats, with armed men on board, who advertise their prowess by loudly proclaiming that anyone who wants to receive satisfaction for an insult or injury to his name should come and talk it over with them and he will soon have his honor restored.

There are also other ships carrying many elderly women who act as midwives and give concoctions for inducing labor, and for having or not having babies.

There are other ships with many wet nurses on board who can be hired to take care of abandoned children and others for as long as one wants.

We also saw other very nicely furnished ships on which there are honorable men of great authority, together with their wives of grave and dignified bearing, who act as marriage brokers, console bereaved women who have lost a husband or children, and provide assistance for other personal matters of this nature.

There are also other ships with a large number of nurses on board, many of whom are not unattractive, who specialize in giving enemas.

There are also other ships carrying many young men and women who hire themselves out for wages to anyone who needs them, after an exchange of references and other guarantees.

There are also other men, of more dignified bearing, called *mongilotos*,[2] who buy claims for damages in civil or criminal cases, as well as deeds and old land titles and the rights to unpaid debts and interest wrongfully withheld, settling on whatever terms agreed upon with the interested parties.

There are others to be found on other ships who treat buboes[3] by means of sweat baths, and take care of incurable sores and fistulas as well.

Finally, so as not to spend any more time trying to describe every little thing that is to be found in this city, for there would be no end to this story, I will sum it all up briefly by saying that there is nothing in the world that one can possibly ask for or desire that is not to be had there on those ships during this period, in even much greater quantity than I have described. And as for the other cities, towns, and villages situated throughout the land, there is no need to say anything about them here because one can get a pretty good idea of what they are like from what has been said of this river, since they all resemble each other.

One of the reasons, or rather the principal one, why this Chinese monarchy, comprised of thirty-two kingdoms, is so rich and magnificent and teeming with traffic and commerce, is because the land is completely covered by a network of superb rivers and estuaries, many of them natural, and many of them man-made waterways dug in ancient times by the various kings, lords, and peoples to provide for easy communication by making all parts of the country accessible to navigation. The narrowest of these waterways have very tall, long, wide bridges running across them, of very sturdy stonemasonry construction, similar to ours, and some are made of a single, solid block of stone running eighty, ninety, or a hundred spans across from one side to the other, and fifteen to twenty spans wide, which is certainly an extremely remarkable feat of engineering, for it is hard to understand how such a huge block of stone could be extracted from the quarry in a solid piece like that, or how they managed to transport it from there to where it was standing.

All the roads and avenues leading into the cities, towns, villages, hamlets, and fortresses are very broad and paved in extremely well hewn stone, with richly decorated columns and archways at either end displaying inscriptions in gold letters commemorating, with words of high praise, those people responsible for having them built; and they have costly stone benches on either side so poor people and weary travelers can stop to rest; and they have many public fountains and springs with good drinking water. And in barren and sparsely populated areas along the way there are unmarried women who take in, free of charge, poor people who have no money. This abuse and abomination, which they regard as an act of charity, is supported by funds from entailed estates, bequeathed by deceased persons for the salvation of their souls, in the form of lands, rents, and other revenues, to be used for these evil practices which they hold to be blessings. Likewise, there have been other deceased persons who have left rents for the construction and maintenance of buildings in uninhabited areas and wastelands, where they keep bright torches burning at night to guide the traveler along the way, as well as casks of water for them to drink, and wayside shelters for them to rest. And to make sure that these services are well maintained, they look for people who, given high salaries, pledge themselves to the constant upkeep of these things, just the way the founder ordered it for the good of his soul.

In view of all these marvelous things that are to be found in a few of the cities of the Chinese empire, one can well imagine how magnificent it must be when considered as a whole. But to clarify this point even more, I shall not fail to say—that is, if my personal testimony is worthy of belief—that in the twenty-one years that my misfortunes lasted, during which time, due to various accidents and mishaps that befell me, I traveled over much of Asia, as anyone can see from reading this *Peregrination*[4] of mine, in some countries I saw enormous supplies of many different kinds of food that we do not have in Europe, but I can solemnly declare, in all truth, that not even all of them put together, let alone taken separately, can compare with what China alone has to offer of these things.

And the same can be said of all the other things with which nature has endowed her, not only in the way of a pleasant and healthy climate, but also in political organization, wealth, splendor, magnificence, and grandeur in all things relating to her. And to top it all off, there is also such a strict observance of justice there, and such an excellent and even-handed government, that she is indeed to be envied by every nation in the world; for without these attributes, no matter how many other lofty and magnificent qualities a nation may have, they lose their luster and fade into obscurity.

And at times, whenever my thoughts turn to the many things of this nature that I saw in the region of China, on the one hand, I am overcome with amazement when I think of how lavishly our Lord shared the material blessings of this earth with these people; and on the other hand, it fills me with great pain and sadness to see how ungrateful they are for all these blessings, since they offend him continually with their many different and deeply sinful practices, not only with their repugnant, diabolical idolatries, but also with the depravity of the unspeakable sin,[5] for it is not only allowed among them publicly, but according to the doctrine of their priests, it is regarded as a great virtue.

And may I be forgiven for not going into any further details here on this matter, because Christian thinking does not condone it, nor would it be right to waste time and words on such bestial and abominable things.

100
Arrival in Peking

After departing from this utterly amazing and extraordinary city, we proceeded on our course up the river for the rest of the way until Sunday, October 9, in the year 1541,[1] which was when we arrived at the great city of Peking, where, as I said before, we were being sent on appeal. Tied together as we were by threes, they threw us into a prison called *Gofanjauserca*, where they welcomed each of us with thirty strokes of the lash that left us incapacitated for several days. As soon as the *chifu*, the bailiff who had us in custody, presented the records of the proceedings in our case— just as he had received them in Nanking with their twelve wax seals unbroken—to the *pilanga*[2] of the *aytao*, which is their appellate division, the twelve *conchalis* of the criminal bench, to whom our case was assigned for review, promptly sent one of their number to the prison where we were, along with two clerks and six or seven officers they call *upos*.

The moment he arrived he frightened the wits out of us by declaring in a threatening manner, "I, by the power and authority vested in me by the *aytao* of *Batampina*, supreme head and presiding officer of the House of the Thirty-two having jurisdiction over foreigners, within whose heart are locked the secrets of the Crowned Lion on the Throne of the World, do hereby admonish and command you in his name to tell me what manner of people you are, the name of the country in which you were born, and whether or not you have a king who, to serve God and carry out the obligations of his office, is well inclined to the poor and extends equal justice to them, thereby giving them no cause to cry out in despair, with upraised arms and tears in their eyes, to the Lord of celestial beauty, next to whom, all the pure in heart who reign with him, are like hempen sandals for his holy feet!"

We answered that we were foreigners, natives of the kingdom of Siam, who had been shipwrecked in a bad storm at sea while bound for the port of Ning-po with our cargo; that we had survived, naked and barefooted, without a scrap of clothing on our bodies and had gone on that way, begging from door to door, until we reached the town of *Taypor*, where the visiting *chumbim* had arrested us without cause and sent us to the city of Nanking, where solely on his word we had been sentenced to be flogged and to having our thumbs cut off, without being given an opportunity to defend ourselves; which was why, turning to the twenty-four Men of Austere Life, with our gaze fixed heavenward and tears in our eyes, we had asked them, for the love of God, to take pity on us, for we were poor and friendless, with no one to protect us; to which they had immediately responded, with holy fervor, by arranging for us to be sent here on appeal; therefore, we were asking him too, for the sake of God, to consider the fact that we were alone and friendless, and that a grave injustice had been done us because we did not know anybody in that country who could protect us or say a single word on our behalf.

After a moment's pause, he replied, "There is no need for you to say anything more. The fact that you are poor is reason enough for the case to be handled in an entirely different manner from the way it has been up to now. But I, by virtue of the powers vested in me, will give you five days, in accordance with the articles of the Third Book, which should give your attorneys time to enter a plea on your behalf. And I would advise you to send a petition to the *tanigores* of the holy office, requesting them, in their zeal for the honor of God, to take all your problems under their charge."

Then, as an act of charity, he gave us each one *tael*.

"A word of caution," he said. "Guard your possessions well from the inmates of this prison, for you must know that they make it their business to steal what others have, rather than share what they have with the needy."

From here, he went on to another big building crowded with prisoners where he held hearings for more than three hours, at the end of which he ordered the execution of twenty-seven men who had been sentenced to death some time before, all of whom died under the lash. It was a dreadful sight that nearly drove us out of our minds with fear.

At first light the next morning they put us in a chain with neck irons and handcuffs, which caused us much suffering. After seven days of this great torment, while we were lying in a corner, huddled on top of each other, lamenting our misfortune with bitter tears and gradually becoming more terrified at the thought of the cruel death awaiting us if they should chance to find out about what we had done in *Calempluy,* it was God's will that the four *tanigores* of the House of Mercy attached to this prison—which in their language is called *Cofilem Guaxi*—should happen to come by. The moment they appeared all the prisoners prostrated themselves and chanted these words: "Blessed be this day on which God visits us through the hands of his servants!"

To which they responded with grave and modest mien, "May his divine, powerful hand, which created the beauty of the night, keep you in its grasp as it does those who always weep for the misfortunes of the people!"

When they reached our side they asked us with courteous words what manner of men we were, or why we were lamenting our imprisonment more than the others there. We replied with tears in our eyes that we were poor foreigners who were so forsaken by all men that there was not a single person in the entire country who knew our names; as for the rest of what we could tell them about our poverty, for the purpose of asking them, for the love of God, to keep us in mind, they would find it all in the letter addressed to them by the brotherhood of the House of *Quiay Hinarel,* which we had brought from the city of Nanking.

Then Cristóvão Borralho handed them the letter, which they accepted with another ceremony of great courtesy.

"Praised be the Lord of all Creation," they replied, "for deigning to make use of sinners on this earth and permitting them thereby to reap the reward that he has in store for them on the last day of days when they will be more than compensated for their labors out of the riches of his holy treasures which, as we hold to be true, will be as plentiful as the raindrops falling from the clouds upon all the earth below!"

One of the four put the letter into the bosom of his robe and told us that once it had been presented for consideration to the Aid to the Needy Committee, they would reply to us and provide us with everything necessary, and with that they took their leave of us.

For three days they did not visit the prison, but on the morning of the fourth, they returned and asked us many questions which they read from a scroll they were carrying. We answered them all, fitting our replies to each question, and they were quite satisfied with the way we responded.

Then they sent for the clerk assigned to our case and informed themselves in great detail about it, after which they asked him to advise them how to proceed in the matter of our defense. After they had taken note of all the things that were helpful to us, they asked him to leave the file with them because they wanted to go over it together with the attorneys in their office, promising to return it the following day so that he could deliver it to the *chaem,* as had been decided.

IOI
A Favorable Ruling

So as not to linger over all the details of our case, which dragged on for six and a half months, while all that time we languished in jail suffering untold hardships, I will briefly relate all else that happened until a decision was finally handed down.

When the case came up before the twelve *conchalys* of the criminal bench—who are, to put it in terms that are familiar to us, the supreme court magistrates and justices empowered to review and rule on all matters under appeal—the two attorneys for the House of Mercy who were pleading our cause did everything in their power to obtain a reversal of the unjust sentence that had been handed down against us. In their efforts to have the indictment set aside, they submitted a petition on our behalf to the *chaem*—who was the chief justice of the high court—showing cause why the penalty involving bloodshed could under no circumstances be applied to us in view of the fact that no reliable witnesses had been produced who could testify that they had actually seen us steal anything, nor had we been found with any weapons on our persons as prohibited by the articles of book 1; but instead, we had been apprehended naked and barefooted like poor lost souls, which we were indeed, in every sense of the word; from which it would appear that our impoverished and forlorn state was more deserving of compassionate respect than of the severity with which the first officers of the Arm of Wrath had imposed the penalty of the lash upon us; and that as far as our guilt or innocence was concerned, the only real judge of that was God, in whose name they urged him once, twice, nay, many times, to bear in mind that he was but a mortal man, and that as such his lifespan was brief, and that when the time came for him to give up the carnal life he had received from God, he would have to render an account of everything that had been said to him and requested of him, for he had sworn a solemn oath to exercise his best judgement at all times, and to perform his duties with the utmost integrity, unswayed by worldly considerations that tend to upset the faithful balance of the scales of justice which have been delicately adjusted by God in the righteousness of his divine justice.

This plea was submitted to the district attorney who was prosecuting the case against us, who in turn presented a brief in which he said that he would prove by means of eyewitness testimony from both native and foreign witnesses that we were public thieves, robbers of other people's property, and not the bona fide merchants we claimed to be; for if our intentions in coming to the coast of China had been honorable, knowing that the royal duties had to be paid at the customs houses, we would have entered the port havens where they had been established for that purpose by order of the *aytao* of the administration; but since we had been drifting about like pirates from one island to another, God, who abhors stealing and all forms of wickedness, had ordained the shipwreck which resulted in our being arrested by the ministers of his justice, in order that we might reap the evil harvest we had sown, namely, the death penalty, which we deserved for our wicked deeds and which was mandatory under the criminal code section of book 2; and furthermore, even if the law itself might provide some grounds for leniency, though he could find none applicable to us, which would absolve us from the death penalty, still, due to the fact that we were foreigners and lawless people who had no true knowledge of God, for whose sake, out of love or fear, we would refrain from engaging in many evil and perverse activities, then that alone would be reason enough for us to be sentenced at the very least to having our hands and noses cut off and to being banished forever to the remote areas of *Ponxileytay*, where people of our occupation were usually sent, as he would show by the many precedents that had been set in such cases for which sentences had already been handed down and executed; wherefore, he urged the court to accept the arguments in the brief he was submitting to them, for which he hoped to present evidence within the time limit assigned him by the court.

In rebuttal to these arguments, the attorneys for the Society for Aid to the Poor, who were in charge of our defense, presented, within the time limit they had been given, many other arguments in our favor and requested the court repeatedly to reject the prosecutor's summary, in view of the fact that the allegations contained therein were highly defamatory and outside the bounds of legal propriety.

The *chaem* ruled that he would accept the prosecutor's arguments provided he could prove his charges within six days of the date of the issuance of the ruling, by means of unimpeachable and God-fearing witnesses, and with the understanding that any request for a postponement would be denied in view of the fact that the defendants involved were indigents, who are often forced by necessity to steal in order to satisfy their bare needs rather than out of a desire to commit a sin.

At the end of the six days, having failed to produce a single shred of evidence against us or a single person who could identify us, he appeared before the court asking for six more days, which were denied him on the grounds that the defendants were indigents whose defense was being handled at great expense by the House of God; and therefore, in order to avoid prolonged argumentation, designed solely as a dilatory tactic, the court ordered him to present his final summary immediately, in view of the fact that he had been denied, for valid reasons, the postponement he had requested. He was also instructed to allow the legal aid attorneys to examine it so that within the five-day period assigned to them they should present the proper arguments in our defense.

The prosecutor summed up his case against us in four paragraphs that were of such a defamatory nature, and phrased in such discourteous language, that the *chaem* was outraged by them. Reacting angrily to the improper and undignified terms contained therein, he had them all stricken from the record and issued a statement to this effect:

"Before pronouncing sentence in this case, I hereby charge the prosecuting attorney with contempt of court and fine him the sum of twenty silver *taels* for the relief of these needy foreigners, since he failed to prove any of the charges he has made against them; and for this first offense, he is to be suspended from the duties of his office until such time as the *tutão* shall provide. And let him be advised that henceforth he is not to express himself with such impropriety and such a lack of decorum, on pain of being punished the next time in accordance with the statutes enacted by the *chaens* and approved by the House of the Son of Heaven, Crowned Lion on the Throne of the World. Upon the satisfactory execution of this order within the next three days, he is to return to this court and present the rest of the arguments that both parties wish to make known."

The following morning at daybreak, the four *tanigores* of the brotherhood who were visiting the prison that week sent for us at the infirmary where they were distributing food to the sick, and informed us about the favorable ruling the court had issued, which augured well for us. At this, we all prostrated ourselves at their feet and weeping freely, we told them that we hoped that God would repay them for all the trouble they had gone to on our behalf, by granting them the reward they were seeking.

"And may he keep all of you in the knowledge of his Law," one of them replied, "for therein lies the reward of all good men."

Then he left instructions for us to be given two blankets with which to cover ourselves at night because we had been suffering a great deal from the cold.

"Do not hesitate to ask us for anything you need," he said, "for it is not the way of the Lord our God to be sparing with his alms."

At that moment the court clerk assigned to our case arrived and informed us of the *chaem*'s ruling of the day before; whereupon he gave us the twenty silver *taels* that the prosecutor had been fined, and made us all sign a form at the bottom of the page. We thanked him effusively and asked him to help himself to as much of the money as he felt like. However, he refused, with these words: "I would not exchange for such a trivial thing the merit I can earn with God on your account."

102
Of Judges and Influence

For twelve days nothing more was said about our case, but at the end of that time, on a morning when the four members of the brotherhood came by on their sick rounds, we begged them, with the greatest urgency, since they knew full well that we had neither money nor friends to help us, to please say a few words on our behalf to the *chaem*, who by this time had all the final documents lying on his desk, ready for his decision. They drew back in indignation at this request.

"If you were natives talking that way, instead of foreigners," they answered, "that alone would be enough for us to disavow the obligation the brotherhood has towards you and never to take another step in your affairs. However, we will overlook your shortcomings this time because of your ingenuousness and your ignorance, but you can believe us when we say that anyone who does what you suggested is not worthy of God's favor."

A little startled by their reply, and somewhat abashed by the manner in which it was spoken, we begged their pardon, pleading our ignorance as our excuse, before both God and them. Whereupon, turning to the other members of the group, one of them said, "Perhaps we do these men a greater wrong by reprimanding them than they do us by suggesting such a thing. For all we know, it may be the custom in their country. Since they are barbarians, who are lacking in the perfect knowledge of our true faith, it is quite possible that their ministers of justice are so devoid of conscience that the parties to a dispute may be forced to rely more on their connections than on a just determination of their cases."

Impressed by what we had heard, we said to them, "Dear brothers, since you are so virtuous in all that your calling demands of you, please tell us why you were so outraged when we asked you to do something that not only seemed quite proper to us, but extremely necessary, in view of our helplessness, of which you are well aware."

To this, one of them, who appeared to have greater authority than the others, replied, "It is only right that you should remind us about this matter which is of such great concern to you, in order to make us complete the necessary steps in less time, the sooner to obtain your release. But it is not right that you should ask us to speak to the judge, in order to influence him to do, for our sake, what a man in his position should not do, for then we would be responsible for his sinning against God and being condemned to hell, thereby making of us more properly servants of the devil than ministers of the poor and needy. And if, as you say, we should intercede for you because justice is on your side, that will be seen in the course of the proceedings and not because of what some outsider may suggest; for the controversies and differences of opinion that give rise to litigation are never well resolved by fruitless charges and countercharges, nor with written briefs and rebuttals that are out of order, which are presented more to obscure and delay justice, to the detriment of the rightful party, than to clarify it and bring it to execution, for those are all tricks of the trade invented by devious persons whom the poor unfortunate litigants call lawyers. But they can be verified with incontrovertible evidence and God-fearing testimony on which the judge bases his decision, if he is doing what he should do, relying on them alone to make the proper judgement. And if in your country, my brothers, this system is not followed, you must all be living in fear of divine punishment, for never a night goes by when God above finds it necessary to close his eyes in order to sleep, as do the kings here below, who are just as subject to all the imperfections of earth as any one of us, for they are men like us. Therefore, my friends, the best advice I can give you, if you want to make use of influence to help you out of your difficulties, is to turn your gaze humbly to the heavens above, because from there alone will come the sentence that will bring you freedom and forgiveness for the faults that are attributed to you. And we, for our part, will help you like good friends, if God sees fit to hear our prayers."

Then they handed us our usual supply of rations and went on to visit other needy people lying sick in the prison hospital, which was always filled to overflowing with them.

103
Sentenced to Hard Labor

We had been waiting for nine days, our hearts filled with fear, for our sentence to be read, when on a Saturday morning two *chumbins* of the law—who are, as I have said before, the bailiffs responsible for enforcing court orders—came to the prison to get us. They were accompanied by twenty guards—who, as I have also said before, are called *upos*—outfitted with halberds, spears, mail helmets, and other things of that sort which made them look so ominous that we were filled with fear and agony. They wrapped a very long iron chain around all nine of us and marched us off to the *caladigão*,[1] which was the courthouse where those condemned to death were executed.

On the way we were in such a state that I swear, in all truth, I cannot even begin to describe clearly what we were going through at the time, for at that hour none of us were in any condition to know where we were going, and all we could do was resign ourselves to the will of God our Lord and to implore him with many tears, by the pains of his sacred Passion, to accept, in satisfaction of our sins, whatever penalty that court would decree. And in some places along the way, suddenly overcome by terror at the thought of the cruel form of death that awaited us, we would all fall to our knees with our arms around each other and beg him for mercy, creating a scene that utterly amazed the Chinese.

Dragging our feet painfully every step of the way, under a shower of abuse hurled at us by a mob of screaming youngsters, we finally arrived at the outer courtyard of the *caladigão*, where the twenty-four executioners, whom they call the officers of the Arm of Wrath, were waiting, along with many other people who had come there as petitioners of the court. We remained there for a long time until a bell was rung and some other doors were opened under a large stone archway elaborately carved in bas-relief and richly painted, on top of which there was a monstrous silver lion, its paws resting on a huge round map, also made of silver, that represented the coat of arms of the Chinese kings, which is usually found on the façades of all the high court buildings where the *chaens* of the judiciary—who are something like our viceroys—sit in session.

As I was saying, once these doors were opened, the crowd surged forward into a large building resembling a church, its walls and ceilings covered from top to bottom with different kinds of paintings depicting strange forms of punishment being administered to all sorts of people by executioners who were shown in the most horrible and frightful attitudes. Each of these paintings had a caption on the bottom that read, "This is the kind of death that is mandatory for the commission of such and such a crime." So that by looking at the different kinds of horrendous paintings, one could tell what kind of capital punishment was mandated for each type of crime, and how extremely rigorous the courts were in carrying out the laws that ordained such executions.[2]

In the front part of this building, running across like a transept, there was another building, much more splendid and richer than the first, all covered in gold leaf, on which our eyes could have lingered with great pleasure had we been capable at the time of taking pleasure in anything.

In the middle of this structure there was a dais, seven steps high, set off by three rows of balustrades made of iron, brass, and ebony, inlaid with mother-of-pearl. The dais was overhung by a canopy of white damask, with green and gold fringes and wide lace borders to match. Underneath the canopy, surrounded by all the trappings of pomp and majesty, was the *chaem*, seated on an ornamental silver throne, with a small table in front of him and three young boys round about it, resting on their knees, who were gorgeously attired, with gold chains on their necks. The function of the boy in the middle was to hand the *chaem* the writing brush he used for signing documents, while the other two on either side were there to collect the documents from the petitioners and place them on the table for him to dispatch.

On the right-hand side, but on a higher step, almost on the same level with the *chaem*, was a little boy who appeared to be about ten or twelve years old, dressed in white satin embroidered with gold roses, wearing a rich string of pearls that went three times around his neck. His hair was very long, like a woman's, braided with a gold and crimson ribbon edged with pearls of great value. On his feet he wore a pair of gold and green sandals, decorated on top with baroque seed pearls, and in his hand he held as the insignia that symbolized his office a small stem of roses made of silk and gold thread, with a scattering of very valuable pearls. And he looked so genteel and handsome that no woman, no matter how fair, could surpass him. This boy's elbow was resting on the *chaem*'s throne, apparently to help him support the insignia he was holding, which was the symbol of Mercy.

In the same manner, on the left-hand side, there was another boy, also very handsome and splendidly attired in crimson satin garments embroidered with gold roses. His right sleeve was rolled up, exposing an arm stained with a vermillion dye that looked like blood, and his right hand was holding an ornamental sword, its naked blade also stained with the same vermillion dye, and on his head he wore a crown resembling a mitre, decorated all over with tiny knives, like the lancets that surgeons use for bleeding their patients. And even though he looked rich and handsome in every respect, nevertheless, his aspect was quite fearsome because of the insignia he carried. This one represented Justice. For they say that the judge who stands in lieu of the king, who in turn is God's representative on earth, must possess these two qualities—Justice and Mercy—and that if he does not show both these qualities, it is because he is a lawless tyrant and a usurper of the insignia he bears in his hand.

The *chaem* was dressed in very long purple satin robes trimmed in green and gold fringes, with a scapular at the neck, such as a friar wears, that had a large gold disk in the middle on which could be seen a sculptured hand holding an evenly balanced scale of justice, with a legend running around it that read, "It is the nature of the Lord on high, in his justice, to weigh, to count, and to measure. Therefore, take heed what thou doest, for if thou shouldst sin, thou shalt pay forever without end." On his head he wore something like a round cap, with little bars of gold, dotted with green and purple enamel, and at the top it had a small gold lion, its paws resting on a sphere that was also made of gold. The crowned lion, as I have already said several times before, signifies the king, whereas the sphere stands for the world, and together both these emblems signify that the king is the Crowned Lion on the Throne of the World. In his hand he held a sparkling white ivory staff, only three spans long, that resembled a scepter.

Standing on the first three steps of the dais were eight ushers holding silver maces, and kneeling on the floor below them were sixty sturdy Moghuls in two rows, holding damascened halberds in their hands. In front of them, standing at attention like squadron lieutenants or corporals, were two fantastic giants, fine looking and richly clad, with their broadswords slung bandolier style across their chests, and huge halberds in their hands. The Chinese themselves call these men *gigauhós*[3] in their language.

Down on the floor on both sides of the dais were two very long tables, with twelve men sitting at each of them, four of whom were like judges or magistrates, two were clerks, four others were attorneys, and two others were *conchalys,* who are like supreme court justices or chancellors. One of these tables of twelve attended to criminal matters while the other dealt with civil matters. All of the officials at both these tables were dressed in very long white satin robes with wide sleeves, designed that way to symbolize the generosity and purity of Justice.

The tables were covered with purple damask cloths that were very beautifully decorated with gold fringes and lace borders. Only the *chaem*'s table, because it was made of silver, was not covered, and all it had on it was a small brocade cushion on top of which was a little round desk set consisting of an inkstand and blotting powder.

Outside, in the other large audience hall, were the twenty-four executioners who, as I said before, are called officers of the Arm of Wrath, all standing in order in a single row.

And everywhere else a huge crowd of petitioners was standing, except for the women, who were sitting on benches. Just outside the doors of this building, six guards—whom they call *upos*—were stationed, holding copper maces.

All these things, when seen as a whole, in this highly organized fashion, represented a great being of impressive majesty, and the awesome aspect of their ministers inspired tremendous fear and terror in anyone who cast his eyes on them.

After four rapid strokes of a bell, one of the two *conchalys* rose to his feet, paid his respects to the *chaem,* and spoke in a loud voice for all to hear, "Silence in the court! Listen with humble attention to all that is said, under pain of incurring the punishment ordained by the *chaens* of the government for anyone disturbing the peace of this hallowed hall of justice!"

Then he sat down and the other stood up. And after performing the same ritual courtesies, he ascended the dais where the *chaem* was sitting, took the records from the hands of a court official, and began to read them aloud, one by one, with such long drawn out ceremoniousness that it took him over an hour.

When at length he came to the proclamation of our sentence, they made us all kneel down with our heads bowed to the floor and both hands raised as though in prayer, to show that we were listening with humility. It went as follows:

"I, *Pitau Dicalor,* in my capacity as *chaem,* newly appointed to this sacred court of justice having jurisdiction over foreigners, by the will of the Son of Heaven, Crowned Lion on the Throne of the World, to whom all scepters and crowns of all the kings who govern the earth are subject and placed beneath his feet, by the grace and will of the highest of the heavens, hereby make known to all those present the decision I have reached in the appeal of the nine foreigners whose case was transferred to my jurisdiction from the city of Nanking, at the request of the twenty-four Men of Austere Life, appearing as the aggrieved parties. I hereby declare, by the solemn oath I have sworn to discharge my duties faithfully on behalf of the *aytao* of the *Batampina* District, presiding over the thirty-two governors who rule over the length and breadth of the land, that on the ninth day of the seventh moon in the fifteenth year of the reign of the Son of Heaven,[4] an indictment against them was placed before me, drawn up by the *chumbim* of *Taypor,* in which they were charged as thieves and robbers of other people's property, an occupation in which they had been engaged for a long time, gravely offending and showing no fear of the Lord on high who hath created all things, as they went about bathing themselves in the blood of the victims who rightly offered them resistance; for which crimes they were condemned to the double penalty of the lash and loss of their fingers. The penalty of the lash was immediately executed, but before the finger-cutting portion of the sentence could be carried out, the attorneys for the poor entered a plea on their behalf, alleging that the sentence was unjust in view of the fact that there was no proof whatsoever of the charges made against them. Wherefore, they requested on their behalf that witnesses who fear God and the righteous punishment of his divine justice should be questioned anew, and that the defendants should not be convicted on the basis of hearsay evidence alone. The justices, meeting in full session, denied the plea on the grounds that it was not permissible to impugn the reputation of the court. Whereupon, the attorneys representing them appealed this ruling to the twenty-four Men of Austere Life, demonstrating just cause for their complaint in the petition they presented, and steps were immediately taken to provide for them in their defenselessness, in view of the fact that they were indigents, who came from foreign shores, so distant and alien to us that we never were able to ascertain exactly in what country they were born. In response to their pitiful cries for help, answer was made by the Tribunal of the Twelve that they were referring the case to this jurisdiction. In the regular course of the proceedings it became apparent that the *continão*[5] prosecuting the case, in the arguments he presented to this court, was unable to prove any of the charges against them; he only said that they deserved the death penalty by reason of the suspicion people had of them. But since holy justice, which is impartial and agreeable to the Lord, does not accept arguments of opposing parties without clear proof of what is said, it appeared to me that it would be unjust to accept the brief of the prosecutor, on the grounds that he had not proven what he alleged in it. And when he persisted in pressing his charges against these foreigners without showing just cause or sufficient grounds therefore, I declared him in contempt of court and fined him twenty silver *taels,* which were to be given to the defendants to provide for their needs. I had his arguments stricken from the record, since they were inspired by misplaced zeal and prejudice, with complete disregard for justice, and highly displeasing to God, whose mercy always inclines to the weakest creatures of the earth when they cry out to him, as is manifest in the merciful effects of his majesty. Wherefore, I instructed the *tanigores* of the holy brotherhood to present their final arguments, which they did, within the time limit I assigned to them. Being satisfied by both parties to the suit, in accordance with the procedure of this court, I ordered the hearings closed and the records delivered to me for adjudication and the passing of a just sentence. Therefore, all things duly considered, without deviating for any human considerations in any way from a righteous judgement in strict conformity with the laws sanctioned by the twelve *chaens* of the judiciary, as contained in volume 5 of the *Will and Pleasure of the Son of Heaven* who, in this case, owing to his magnanimity and majesty, is more inclined to heed the clamor of the poor than the bellowing of the pompous of the earth, I order that these nine foreigners be absolved of all the charges preferred against them by the *continão* who prosecuted them, with no punishment whatsoever for any felony, and I condemn them only to one year of banishment to the construction project at *Quansy*,[6] where they will work for their support. When they have finished serving eight months of their one-year sentence, I order the *chumbim,* the *conchalás,* the *monteos,*[7] and all the other officials concerned to whom this sentence of mine shall be presented, to immediately issue them a safe-conduct pass so that they may depart freely for their country or any place else they please."

We were still on our knees with arms upraised facing the *chaem,* when this sentence was finally pronounced; then, after performing many other ritual ceremonies that the officials taught us, we said out loud for all to hear, "Confirmed within us is the sentence of thy clear judgement, even as the purity of thy heart is agreeable to the Son of Heaven."

This said, one of the twelve *conchalys* at the table rose, made his obeisance to the *chaem,* and directed a question to the crowded auditorium in a very loud voice, repeating it five times: "Is there perchance any person present in this courtroom, in this city, or in this kingdom who has any objection to this sentence, or any qualms about releasing these nine prisoners?"

When there was no reply each of the five times the question was asked, the two boys representing Justice and Mercy touched each other lightly with the insignia they held in their hands and chanted in unison, "Let them be released and set free, in compliance with the sentence that has been justly pronounced."

Thereupon one of the guards they call *upos* struck a bell three times, which was a signal for the two law enforcement *chumbins* who had brought us there as prisoners to free us, first from the long chain linking us together, and then from the handcuffs, leg irons, and collars, thereby releasing us from all restraint. And for this we offered up deep prayers of thanks to our Lord Jesus Christ, for we had thought all along that we would have to suffer at the hands of the law because of some evil presumptions that had been made about us.

From here, now free of our chains, they led us back to the prison where an entry was made in the prison register, which both *chumbins* signed, and all of us along with them, not only to relieve the warden of his responsibility for us, but also as a means of acknowledging our obligation to carry out the terms of our banishment within a period of two months, or face the penalty of being made captives of the king, in accordance with his ordinances.

We wanted to go into the street at once to beg for alms, but the *chifu,* who was the warden of the prison, told us to wait until the next day when he would recommend us to the *tanigores* of the brotherhood and ask them to provide us with some charitable assistance.

104
The Kindly Captain of *Quansy*

Early the next morning the four *tanigores* of the brotherhood came to visit the prison hospital as was their custom, and they congratulated us for the favorable verdict, with which they were obviously quite pleased. We in turn expressed our appreciation to them with many words of gratitude, mixed with a few tears, which impressed them favorably. They told us not to fret about having to complete the full term of our banishment because the king was reducing one-third of our sentence by granting us a four-month pardon, which meant that we would only have to serve eight months out of our one-year term, and that he was doing so as an act of charity, for love of God, because we were poor, for if we had been rich and powerful, he would not have shown us any charity or favored us in the least; and that they would immediately see to it that the pardon was duly recorded on the reverse side of the sentence. They also said that they would speak to an honorable man in town who had just been appointed as captain and *monteo* of *Quansy,* the same place to which we had been banished, and ask him to favor us and arrange for us to be paid for the time we spent there, for he was a very kindly man and a friend to the poor, which was why they thought it would be a good idea for us to go along with them to pay a call on him, for it was possible that he might decide to take us in charge at once and arrange for us to be lodged somewhere, as he was doing for many others that were going with him, especially since we did not know anyone in that country. For this we all expressed our deep thanks, with the hope that God would repay him for the kind favor they were doing us for love of him.

After which we all set out together for the house of the *monteo,* who came out to the front courtyard to receive them, leading his wife by the hand as a sign of greater honor or ceremony, and throwing himself at their feet the moment he came near, exclaiming as he did so, "My lords and holy brethren, I now indeed regard my appointment as a good thing and shall accept it without complaint, since, because of these men, it was the reason that God saw fit to send his servants to my house, an honor I certainly never dreamed of, for I regard myself as unworthy of so great a favor."

After an exchange of courtesies involving all the ceremonious etiquette they observe, one of the *tanigores* replied, "May the Lord our God, out of the bottomless well of his mercy, repay you with the blessings of this life for all the charity you give to the poor, for love of him. Believe us, dear brother, when we say that the main rod and staff on which the soul leans to keep it from falling every time it stumbles is the charity we show to our neighbor, as long as, out of vainglory, it is not accompanied by worldly chaff that defiles the good zeal to which his holy Law obliges us; and in order that you may be deserving of coming into his presence and beholding the celestial smile of his sweet countenance, we have brought here to you these nine poor men, who are indeed so poor that it is hardly likely that there are any others in the entire land as poor as they—so that when you get to the city to which you have just been assigned as captain and *monteo* of the law, you may do for them whatever you think should be done, for the sake of so almighty a Lord as the One in whose name we request this favor."

To which he and his wife responded in such a well-spoken and remarkable manner that we were all amazed to see the way in which they attributed what happened to them to the principal cause of all blessings, as though they had received the light of faith, or some knowledge of our holy Christian religion.

Then they all withdrew into one of the buildings on the grounds, where they remained engrossed in conversation for nearly half an hour while we waited outside. When they were getting ready to leave, they had us come inside, and the *tanigores* spoke to him about us again, recommending us once more to his care. He asked us to sign a book that he had in front of him.

"I am doing this," he said, "so that, since I am not so good as to give you what is mine out of love of God, I may not be so bad as, out of forgetfulness, to deprive you of the sweat of your labor for which the king is obligated to you. From this day forward you will receive your keep, even though you have not yet begun to serve your sentence, because I want this to be counted as charity on my part. And for the time being you will stay in my house, where I will provide you with everything you need. As for the rest, I do not want to promise you anything, because I am afraid that any promises I make may fill me with excessive pride, and leave me prey to the devil, as so often happens, because of our weakness. However, for the present it is enough for you to know that I have taken you under my care, out of love of God and the holy brethren who have spoken to me on your behalf."

With this the four *tanigores* took their leave, and as they did so they gave us four *taels,* intended for all of us.

"Do not forget to thank God for the successful outcome of your case," they said to us, "for if you fail to acknowledge the great mercy he has shown you, you will be guilty of a grave sin."

And that was how we came to stay in the house of this *monteo,* who kept us very good company all the time we were there. At the end of the two months we had free to spend there, we departed for *Quansy* to begin serving our sentence, in the company of this *monteo,* who also, from then on, always treated us very well and did many favors for us right up to the time the Tartars invaded the city, bringing with them much destruction, death, and distress, about which I shall have more to say further along.[1]

105
The Splendors of Peking

Before I say anything about what happened to us from then until after the time we embarked with this Chinese who took us in charge and gave us high hopes of obtaining our freedom, I thought it would be fitting at this point to say a few words about the city of Peking—which can indeed be called the capital of the monarchy of the world—and about some of the things that I observed there, not only about its wealth, government, and grandeur, but also about the workings of its great system of justice, the admirable way they have of providing for the general welfare, the manner in which their war veterans are compensated for their services as set forth by law, and other matters of that nature. Though before I begin, I must confess that I have neither the ability nor the knowledge required to explain anything about the geographical region of the city or the latitude in which it lies, something I believe the learned and curious would probably like to know.

But since my intention in writing this book—as I have said before—was none other than to leave it to my children as a primer of sorts, for them to learn their ABCs by reading about the hardships I endured, I thought it mattered little if I wrote it in my own crude style, which is the only way I could do it, for it is my understanding that the best way to treat matters of this sort is the way that Nature taught me, without looking for circumlocutions or words borrowed from others with which to enhance my weak, unpolished wit, for I was afraid that if I did so I would get caught in the act and people would apply to me the proverbial saying, "When did Pedro learn to speak Galician?"

But since I feel obliged to discuss these things in order to keep the promise I have made above, I will begin by saying that this city which we call Paking, but which natives call by its original name of Peking, is situated at latitude forty-one degrees north.[1] And according to what the Chinese told us—and as I read later on in a little book called *Aquesendó* that I brought back to Portugal which describes its wonders— it is surrounded by walls measuring thirty leagues in circuit, ten in height, and five in width, though some people say they are fifty leagues in circuit, seventeen in height, and eight in width. Since there is such a wide difference of opinion among the people who deal with these matters, with some saying thirty and others fifty, I want to explain the reason for this disagreement, according to what I saw with my own eyes.[2]

Considering the way it stands today with its many fine buildings, the city probably measures the thirty leagues in circuit that some say it does and is completely surrounded by two rows of very sturdy walls constructed with an infinite number of towers and bulwarks, in the same fashion as ours. But outside these walls, which are those of the city proper, there is another wall of much greater height and width enclosing an area that the Chinese say had been completely populated in ancient times but is so no longer, for today there are only a large number of small towns and villages separated from each other, with many very elegant homes all around, including sixteen hundred which are much finer than any of the others. These are the homes of the local administrators[3] of the sixteen hundred cities and important towns of the thirty-two kingdoms[4] comprising this monarchy, who meet in Peking every three years, when they convoke the general assembly of the estates[5] to propose measures for the common welfare, as will be explained later.

Outside of this larger wall, which, as I say, runs outside the city proper, there is an area three leagues wide and seven long, used as a cemetery, where twenty-four thousand mandarins lie entombed in some sort of small chapels completely covered with gold leaf, all of which have atria, closed off by iron and brass balustrades fashioned by lathe, that are entered by passing under some very elaborate and costly archways. Located right next to these chapels, there are very large dwellings with beautiful gardens, densely wooded areas, and all kinds of ingeniously designed pools, waterspouts, and fountains. The inner sides of these city walls are lined with very fine porcelain tiles, and they are decorated along the top with many ornamental lions bearing golden banners, and at the corners of these sections there are very tall spires painted in different colors. In addition, there are five hundred very large buildings that are known as the "Homes of the Son of Heaven," where they shelter all the war veterans who have been wounded in the service of the king, and many others besides who had to retire from the army due to illness or old age. Each one of them receives a monthly stipend for his support, and according to what the Chinese told us, they have as many as 100,000 of these veterans, for they claimed that there were two hundred men living in each one of these buildings.

We also saw a very long street lined with one-story buildings that were used as residence halls for the twenty-four thousand oarsmen who row the king's *panouras*.[6]

We saw a similar street more than a good league long, with housing facilities for the domestic staff of fourteen thousand who work in the kitchens of the royal palace. And still another one like it where there were countless numbers of prostitutes who, because they are also attached to the palace, are exempted from the tribute usually paid by those women of the town. And many of them have run away from their husbands in order to pursue this unhappy profession. And if, for that reason, their husbands do them some harm, they are punished severely, because these women are protected by the royal *tutão*, who is the chief steward or administrator of the king's household.

All the *mainatos*[7] who do the laundry for the whole city also live within this wall, and according to what we were told, there are well over 100,000 of them, for there are large rivers and streams here with very deep reservoirs and ponds, all enclosed with walls of sturdy stonemasonry and prime-quality, well-hewn slabs.

In addition, according to what it says in this book called *Aquesendó*, there are within the confines of this great wall thirteen hundred stately residence halls and annexes of costly construction provided for men and women who have taken vows in the four main religious sects out of the thirty-two that exist in this Chinese empire.[8] They say that some of these halls provide living quarters, under a single roof, for well over a thousand people, not counting the people who serve them by attending to their needs from the outside.

Also, we saw many other compounds containing huge, splendid buildings, surrounded by high walls enclosing gardens and dense forests where all kinds of wild game that one can desire, whether big or small, is there for the hunting. These magnificent buildings are like public inns or amusement centers where endless crowds of people come streaming in continuously, not only to dine, but also to enjoy the shows, farces, games, bull fights, wrestling matches, and sumptuous banquets that the *tutões, chaens, conchacys, aytaos, bracalões,*[9] *chumbins, monteos, lauteás,*[10] and many other lords, captains, merchants, and rich noblemen put on there for their friends and relatives, complete with a dazzling array of many footmen carrying silver maces, and costly tableware, the complete service made of gold. Sleeping chambers are available, furnished with silver bedsteads covered with brocade canopies, and full service is provided by extremely lovely young maidens, attired in very expensive finery. But even so, all this does not amount to much when compared with the pomp and splendor we saw in some of these establishments. And the Chinese assured us that there are banquets given in the *charachina* style that last for ten days and cost more than twenty thousand *taels* because of the lavishness, pomp, and circumstance that go with them in the form of huge staffs of servants and attendants, musical entertainment, and amusements such as fishing, hunting, hawking, games, farces, theatrical performances, and competitions both on foot and horseback. These establishments, which cost more than a million gold *cruzados* to build, are maintained by companies of very wealthy merchants who invest the money they earn from business and trade in these enterprises, from which it is said they profit much more than by risking it at sea.

By this time it is all so well regulated and so well organized that when a person wishes to indulge himself at great expense, he goes off to see the *xipatom*,[11] who is the manager in charge of the place, and explains to him what he has in mind. The *xipatom* then shows him a book, completely divided into chapters, on the prescribed method and manner of the banquets available, with a list of the dishes and how and in what way they are served, from which he can choose what he likes. This book is called *Pinatoreu,* and I have seen and heard it read aloud several times.

The first part of this book, from chapters 1 to 3, contains a description of the feasts that should be offered up to God, along with the price of each. From there on, in descending order, it deals next with the king of China, who they say rules on earth by the special grace of heaven, as supreme head over all the other kings in the world. From the king of China on down, speaking now of ordinary human beings, it deals with the types of banquets given for the *tutōes,* who are the ten highest dignitaries in command of all of the foty administrative *chaens,* who are viceroys. They call the *tutōes* "splendid rays of the sun," and explain it by saying that even as the king of China descends from the sun, and the sun gives off rays of light, in the same manner the *tutōes* representing the king can be called "splendid rays" emitted by him.

But putting aside for the moment these barbaric heathen practices, I want to mention just one thing in particular here while I am dealing with the subject, and that has to do with the dishes they say should be served at the banquet tendered to God, some of which I have seen them prepare to the letter, though, for lack of faith, their good works will avail them little.

106
Chinese Banqueting Houses

The opening chapters of this banquet book, as I have said before, deal with the kind of feast that should be tendered to God on earth, and while we are on the subject, it reads as follows:

"Any banquet, no matter what the cost, has to be paid for with a certain amount of money, depending more or less on the generosity of the host; therefore, once he has paid for it, he has nothing more to show in return for all that he has spent but the fawning of the flatterers and the grumbling of the gossipmongers.

"Wherefore, my brother," it says in the introduction, "I would advise thee rather to spend thy money on banqueting God through his poor, and providing anonymously for the children of the good, so that they may not perish for want of that of which thou hast more than enough; for if thou wouldst reflect on the vile substance of which thy father engendered thee, and the still viler substance out of which thy mother conceived thee, thou wilt see how much less worth thou art than any other kind of brute animal who, without benefit of reason, is driven blindly to follow the instincts of the enemy flesh.

"And as long as thou, as a human being, art willing to invite thy friends who may not be thy friends on the morrow, why not, like a good, devout man, invite God's poor, whose cries of need move him to pity like a compassionate father, for with it goes a promise of infinite satisfaction in the House of the Sun, where we believe, as an article of faith, that those who serve him will possess him, with boundless joy."

And after these introductory remarks and many others worthy of note which, as required by the rules of the house, a priest reads to the host, the *xipatom*—who is, as I have said before, the one in charge of the staff running this huge labyrinth of a place—goes over all the chapters of the book with him, starting with the most elaborate kind of banquet available and continuing on down to the least expensive, and suggest that he begin by deciding on the quality of the man or lord he wishes to invite, the number of guests, and the number of days he wishes the banquet to last because, for guests such as kings and *tutões,* special dishes must be served by a certain number of servants in a special style, in special rooms, on special dinnerware, with special entertainment, with a certain number of attendants and spare horses, with a scheduled number of days for big- and small-game hunting, all of which, complete to the last detail, will cost him a certain amount of money. Then too, if the client decides that he wants a less expensive banquet, he turns to another chapter containing a description of parties that are given for the *chaens, aytaos, ponchacys,*[1] *bracalões, anchacys, conchalás, lauteás,* or military officers, or wealthy merchants, because every other class of people from there on down the social scale can sit right down at the table and eat as much as they like in any manner they like, and then go on their way; for there are always fifty or sixty of these banqueting houses constantly crowded with all sorts of men and women who are waited on by attendants of a lesser quality. Here too, as I say, there are many remarkable things to be seen, not only in the banqueting halls with their furnishings and decorations, but also in their kitchens, pantries, slaughterhouses, infirmaries, dormitories, stables, salons, courtyards, separate bedroom suites and cottages, all luxuriously appointed with comfortable beds, and tables set with many dishes, and the chairs in place, with nothing more for one to do than to sit right down and eat.

There are other buildings in the compound reserved for concerts where full orchestras perform with harps and rebecs in harmony with flageolets, flutes, cornets, sackbuts, and many other different kinds of musical instruments that are not in use among us. And there is such an abundance of everything that if the banquet is for women only, as is often the case, the service is provided in the same manner by women and by very beautiful young maidens, very richly attired, who, because they are so attractive, often find good husbands from among the many noblemen frequenting the place.

So that—to finish with the brief observations I wanted to make about these banqueting houses—of all the money spent on these banquets, 4 percent is set aside, 2 percent being contributed by the *xipatom,* and 2 percent by the banquet host, to pay for the upkeep of the table of the poor which is made available, for the love of God, to any and all who wish to come in and partake of the food. They also offer them a roof over their heads and a spotlessly clean, comfortable bed for a limited period of three days, making an exception to this rule only for pregnant women or others too sick to walk, who are allowed to stay longer, for they are extremely considerate of everybody, according to one's needs.

We also saw within the area encompassed by the outer walls—which run beyond the city proper for a distance of three more leagues in width and seven in length as I said before—thirty-two residence halls that were quite large and separated from each other by a little over a falcon-shot's range. These buildings are used as colleges for the thirty-two different religious sects existing in the thirty-two kingdoms of this empire. In each one of these colleges, judging by the large number of people we saw there, they must have over ten thousand students. And the *Aquesendó* itself—the book which deals with the subject—estimates the total enrollment to be about 400,000. Apart from these buildings there is another, standing separately, that is much larger and more imposing than the others, probably measuring nearly a league all around, to which all those who wish to prepare themselves for graduation,[2] both in theology and in the laws of the kingdom, come to study. Here, a *chaem* of the judicial branch of the government, to whom the heads of all the other colleges are subordinate, sits in residence. They call him the *xiley xitapou,* which is a title of supreme dignity, meaning "lord of all the nobility."

Since his position is more lofty than that of all the others, this particular *chaem* has the privilege of traveling in state, escorted by a retinue as magnificent as that of any *tutão,* for he has an honor guard of three hundred Moghuls, twenty-four mace bearers, thirty-six women mounted on white horses harnessed with silver trappings and silk saddlecloths, accompanying themselves on soft musical instruments as they sing, making sweet harmony in their fashion. Also included are twenty spare saddleless horses covered in cloths of brocade and silver, with collars of the same round the neck and silver bells on the bridle, each of them led by six halberdiers and four grooms, all in very well ordered formation. At the head of this magnificent cortège go more than four hundred *upos,* trailing a huge quantity of long iron chains behind them, making altogether such a frightful racket that it is enough to make one tremble with fear. Behind them go twelve horsemen called *peretandas,*[3] holding red satin umbrellas like canopies, fixed on very long poles, as well as another dozen horsemen carrying white damask banners trimmed with very wide gold fringes and laces. Behind all this comes the *chaem,* seated in a triumphal carriage, followed by sixty *conchalás, chumbins* and *monteos* of the courts, who are like the crown magistrates, chancellors, and chief justices in our court system, all of them marching on foot, with gold-plated swords hanging from the shoulder. Walking at the head of the whole noisy procession go the lesser officials, such as the court scribes, receivers, bailiffs, and interrogators, shouting to the crowds to go home so that the streets would be cleared[4] of every living soul; and trailing along at the very end of the whole cortège come the procurators and solicitors, also on foot. Beside the *chaem* or *tutão*—for either one of these titles can apply to him—keeping even with him on horseback, ride two richly attired little boys, one to his right and one to his left, carrying their respective insignias of Justice and Mercy as I described them before with the one on the right dressed in white symbolizing Mercy, and the one on the left dressed in red symbolizing Justice. And the horses these children ride are also covered with saddlecloths to match the clothes they are wearing, with gold trappings and harnesses, and a silver mesh cloth on top completely covering their haunches. Behind each of these boys come six youths ranging up to fifteen years of age, carrying silver maces. So that there is not a single person who, beholding all this, can repress a shudder of fear, though at the same time he cannot help but be overwhelmed by the grandeur and majesty for which it stands.

So as not to linger any longer on what we saw inside this large wall, I will leave out many other things of interest, not only about rich, stately buildings, but also about temples to their gods, bridges supported by heavy stone pillars, highways[5] completely paved with fine-quality stone slabs which are all very wide across and smoothly surfaced and of considerable length, with well-built iron railings running along both sides, for one can get a fairly good idea of what the things that I am omitting are like from what I have already said about the other things, since they are all similar. And now, I will describe as briefly as possible some of the buildings I saw inside the city, mainly four of them, which I observed with greater curiosity because they seemed to be more grandiose than the others—as well as a few other things worthy of mention.

107
Sightseeing in Peking

This city of Peking, about which I promised to say a few more words, is so extraordinary, and everything about it is so remarkable, that I almost regret having made such a promise, because I really do not know where to begin to carry it out.

One should not imagine for a moment that it is anything like Rome, Constantinople, Venice, Paris, London, Seville, Lisbon, or any of the great cities of Europe, no matter how famous or populous. Nor should one imagine that it is like any of the cities outside of Europe, such as Cairo in Egypt, Tauris[1] in Persia, Amadabad[2] in Cambay, Bisnaga[3] in Narsinga,[4] Gour[5] in Bengal, Ava[6] in *Chaleu*,[7] *Timplão* in *Calaminhan*,[8] Martaban[9] and Bagou in Pegu,[10] *Guimpel* and *Tinlau* in *Siammon*,[11] Ayuthia[12] in the *Sornau*,[13] Pasuruan[14] and Demak[15] on the island of Java, *Pangor* in the Ryukyus, *Uzangué* in Greater Cochin, *Lançame* in Tartary, or Miyako[16] in Japan—all capitals of great kingdoms; for I dare say that all of them put together cannot compare with the least thing, let alone the sum total of all the grandiose and sumptuous things that make up this great city of Peking, such as magnificent buildings, infinite wealth, excessive and overwhelming abundance of all the necessities of life, people, trade and countless ships, orderly government, justice, tranquil court life, the great state in which the *tutões, chaens, anchacys, aytaos, puchancys,* and *bracalões* live, for all of them are extremely high paid governors of very large kingdoms and provinces. They reside in this city permanently, as do others in their name when, owing to special circumstances, they are sent throughout the kingdom on important business.

But putting this aside for the moment, to be dealt with at the proper time, this city—based on what is written about it, not only in the aforementioned book *Aquesendó,* but in all the chronicles of the emperors of China—measures thirty leagues in circuit, excluding the buildings located within the area of the outer wall which I have discussed briefly, and all too briefly in comparison with the many things I left unsaid. As I mentioned before, it is completely surrounded by two very strong, well-constructed walls, with 360 gates, at each of which there is a stone fortress with very tall twin towers, moat, and drawbridge. Stationed at each of these gates, along with four gatekeepers armed with halberds, there is a clerk who has to account for all that passes in and out. These gates, by disposition of the *tutão,* are divided among the 360 days of the year in such a way that, on each day in turn, they celebrate, with great solemnity, the feast day of the idol for whom each one of these gates is named, and on this subject too I have already dwelt at some length.

Within the walls of this great city, according to what the Chinese told us, there are also thirty-eight hundred pagodas to their gods, where an enormous number of wild beasts and birds are continuously sacrificed. The explanation they give for this practice is that these animals are more acceptable to God than the domestic varieties people raise at home. The priests use many arguments in order to persuade the people to uphold this superstition as an article of faith. The pagodas to which I am referring consist of compounds of many sumptuous buildings, especially the ones belonging to the religions practiced by the *menigrepos, conquiais,*[17] and *talagrepos,* who are the priests of the four sects of *Xaca,*[18] Amida,[19] *Gizom,*[20] and *Canom,*[21] which take precedence by reason of seniority over the other thirty-two sects of this diabolical labyrinth, in which the devil sometimes reveals himself to them in various forms, the better to make them believe in all these deceptions and falsehoods.

The ordinary streets of this city are all very long and wide, lined with very elegant two- to three-story houses, and they are completely closed off by brass and iron railings running along both sides, with entrances to the passageways leading back from them. At the end of each of these streets there are archways spanning richly decorated gates that are closed at night, and alarm bells at the tops of these archways. Each one of these stately streets has its own captain and patrol units assigned to different watches, and every ten days they have to report to the city hall about everything that goes on there, so that the *ponchacys* and *chaens* of the administration can take any action that may be necessary, in conformity with the law.

According to what it says in this book devoted solely to the wonders of this great city, which I have quoted so many times, there are also 120 canals three fathoms deep and twelve wide, running across the entire length and breadth of the city. These waterways were built in ancient times by the kings and the people, and they are spanned by a large number of bridges supported by very sturdy stone arches, with pillars at both ends that have chains running all the way across, and stone benches with backs where people can rest. They claim that there are eighteen hundred of these bridges over these 120 waterways, each one finer and handsomer than the other, both in its workmanship as well as all else visible to the eye.

This book also states that there are 120 magnificent public squares, in each of which a fair is held every month, which means, as one can figure out, that there are four fairs taking place daily throughout the year. In the two months that we were free to roam around here, we saw about ten or twelve of them, where there were endless numbers of people, both on foot and horseback, who were selling, out of boxes they carried, like peddlers, everything one can think of, to say nothing of the regular market stalls owned by the rich merchants, neatly set up in their own lanes, with enormous quantities of bolts of silk, brocade, woven goods, garments of linen and cotton, sable and ermine skins, musk, eaglewood, fine porcelain, gold and silver tableware, pearls, also of the seed variety, gold dust, and bullion, the sight of which left the nine of us gasping in amazement.

But then, if one wanted to go into detail about all the other supplies of iron, steel, lead, copper, tin, brass, coral, carnelian, crystal, flintstone, quicksilver, vermillion, ivory, clove, nutmeg, mace, ginger, cinnamon, pepper, tamarind, cardamon, borax, indigo, honey, beeswax, sandalwood, sugar, conserves, provisions of fruit, flour, rice, meat, game, fish, and fresh produce—there is such a great abundance of all this that I believe there are no words to do it justice.

These Chinese also assured us that there are 160 ordinary slaughterhouses in this city, each of them equipped with a hundred chopping blocks for every kind of meat found on earth because these people eat all of them—veal, mutton, goat, pork, horse-meat, water buffalo, yak, tiger, lion, dog, mule, donkey, zebra, tapir, otter, badger, or to make it brief, every kind of animal that one can name. A fixed price is immediately set on every item sold on each of these chopping blocks. Apart from the butcher's own scales which he uses to weigh his meat, there are also others belonging to the city, located at each door, where the meat is weighed again to see if the customers get the correct weight, so that the people are not cheated. Besides these slaughterhouses, which are the common ones, there is not a single street that does not have five or six meat markets where all kinds of top-quality meat is sold. And in addition, there are also many public taverns where food is available, cooked to perfection and served with the utmost cleanliness.

There are also shops full of hams, fresh pork, cured meat, poultry, smoked pork, and beef, and all of it available in such large quantities that the less said the better, but I am only mentioning it to show how generous the Lord our God was to these blind people when he distributed the blessings he created on earth. And for this, may his name be praised forevermore!

108
Prison of the Outcasts

Putting aside now any attempt to dwell in detail on the enormous number of splendid, grandiose, and sumptuous buildings we saw in this city, I will limit myself to describing just a few that struck me as being more noteworthy than the rest, and from these few one may well imagine what the many others are like which I chose not to include to avoid being tedious.

I would not even mention these few if I did not think it were possible that some day—the Lord willing—the Portuguese nation might find itself so strong and imbued with such proud spirit as to make use of this information for the greater glory of God, and that by means of these human resources, aided by his divine favor, they might be able to make these barbarians see the truth of our Catholic faith, about which, for their sins, they have so little understanding that they make fun of everything we tell them about it, and carry their barbaric and irrational way of thinking so far as to say that there is no greater blessing for the soul than to gaze upon the countenance of the Son of Heaven, who is their king. This leads me to believe that if the Lord our God, out of his infinite kindness and mercy, should permit their king to become a Christian, then it would be an easy matter to convert all the rest of his people; otherwise, it would be very difficult to convert any of them. That is because they stand in great awe of his system of justice, for which they all have so much fear and veneration, as well as such an enormous respect for those who administer it, that it is hard to believe.

But getting back to what I was saying, the first of these buildings that I saw which I said were among the most noteworthy and memorable was a prison called *Xinanguibaleu,* meaning "prison of the outcasts." It is located in a walled-off area of perhaps nearly two leagues square, equal in length and breadth, and is surrounded by a very high wall devoid of battlements, protected only by sharp spikes on top, which are all covered with thick, heavy lead plates. On the outside there is a very deep moat running all around, spanned by drawbridges which are raised at night by means of brass chains suspended from very thick columns of cast iron. It has a very sturdy stone arch that ends in twin towers, and strung out along the very top of the arch are six huge sentry bells. When these bells are struck, all the others in the compound respond, and according to what the Chinese told us, there are more than a hundred of them and they make a terribly frightful noise.

By order of the king the prison population is maintained at a constant level of 300,000 men ranging in age from seventeen to fifty—a startling piece of information which naturally as a great surprise to us. When we asked the Chinese why they had built such a huge prison and why so many men were kept there, they told us that not long after the Chinese king called *Crisnagol Dacotay* had finished sealing off the frontier between China and Tartary with a wall that extended for three hundred leagues,[1] as mentioned above, he gave orders, with the approval of the peoples who were summoned to a national assembly of the estates convoked for that purpose, that all those who had been condemned to the penalty of exile by the courts of justice should be sent to serve a sentence of forced labor on the wall, in exchange for which they would only receive their food and keep, without any obligation on the part of the king to compensate them for their labor, since they were serving that sentence as a penalty for their crimes, and that after they had served for six consecutive years, they would be free to go on their way, without being forced by law to serve the rest of their original sentence, because the king chose to pardon them as compensation for what in all good conscience he would have had to pay them for their labor; but if before the end of the six years they should in any way distinguish themselves by some outstanding deed or show themselves superior to others, or be wounded three times in their border forays, or succeed in killing one of the enemy, then they will receive an immediate pardon for the rest of the time they would have served, with the *chaem* issuing them a certificate to that effect, describing the circumstances that had won them their freedom, wherein all could see that he had satisfied the law, in conformity with the statutes of war.

It was obligatory to maintain an army of 210,000 men on constant duty at this wall, who were assigned to it by order of the king. These forces were depleted by one-third each year for various reasons, such as death in the ranks, disabling injuries, and the departure of men who had either completed their terms or been pardoned for distinguishing themselves in action. When the *chaem,* who is supreme commander of all these forces, requested of the *pitaucamay,* which is the highest court of the land, that they call up this large number of men, they were not able to assemble them as quickly as necessary, since they were scattered all over the empire—which is so huge, as I pointed out before—and a great deal of time was lost before they were assembled. As a result, another king, *Goxiley Aparau* by name, who succeeded this *Crisnagol Dacotay,* ordered the construction of this large enclosed compound within the city of Peking, so that as soon as the prisoners had been banished to the wall, they could immediately be brought to this *Xinanguibaleu* prison where they would all be kept together, ready to report for duty without any delay whenever replacements were needed for the wall, as it is done today.

As soon as these condemned men are delivered to this prison by the law, in exchange for which the officers escorting them receive a certified statement, they are immediately released from their shackles and allowed to move around freely with no more than a small, very thin wooden tablet[2] measuring just under four fingers wide and a handspan long on which is recorded the prisoner's name, his native town, the crime for which he was convicted, and the date his sentence began. Thus, each one wears this reliquary around his neck, in witness of his virtues, making a public record of his crime and the day his sentence began, because they are all released in order of seniority depending upon the time they entered.

These prisoners consider themselves fortunate when they are taken out to work on the wall because they cannot, under any circumstances whatsoever, be released from the *Xinanguibaleu* prison, nor is any time served there taken into account, nor do they have other hope of freedom except for the hour when their turn comes to be taken out to the wall; however, once they are on the wall, they immediately have a definite possibility of being freed in accordance with the statute I mentioned above.

Now that I have explained the reason for building such a huge prison here, I thought it would be appropriate, before I drop the subject altogether, to say something about a local fair we saw there, one of two annual fairs held within its gates, that the natives call *Guxinem Aparau* of the *Xinanguibaleu,* meaning "the bountiful fair of the prison of the outcasts." These fairs take place during the months of July and January and are accompanied by remarkable religious festivals dedicated to the invocation of their deities, and involve the celebration, in their fashion, of plenary indulgences in which they promise them great wealth in the next world.

Admission to these fairs is free of charge, without any sort of excise tax, which accounts for the huge attendance of the well over three million which they claim. And since, as I pointed out before, the 300,000 men in the labor pool of this prison all walk around as freely as those who come from the outside, they have devised a method to prevent them from leaving with the others. When the free citizens enter, they place a stamp on the inner part of their right arm, made out of a concoction of oils and a bituminous mixture of lac, rhubarb, and alum, which, once it dries, is impossible to remove without the application of a very hot vinegar and salt solution. In order to stamp the arms of such a huge crowd of people, they have large numbers of *chanipatões*[3] posted on either side of the gates who, with some lead signets dipped in this bituminous mixture, press the mark on the arm of each person arriving before letting him in. This is done to the men only, not the women, because women are never exiled to the wall. On their way out of the gates they all come with their sleeves rolled up displaying the mark for the benefit of these same *chanipatões*—the gatekeepers and officers in charge of the whole operation—who check them and let them pass. And if for some reason someone should be unlucky enough to have the mark fade from his arm, he may as well suffer in patience and remain behind with the other prisoners because he does not have a chance of getting out if he cannot show them the mark that was stamped on his arm when he came in. This operation is handled so smoothly and efficiently by all these *chanipatões* that, within the space of an hour, 100,000 men come and go without anybody encountering any difficulty. And that is how they see to it that all 300,000 exiled prisoners always remain inside, without a single one of them being able to slip out along with the others.

This prison or labor supply depot contains within its walls three settlements like large towns, all consisting of one-story buildings lined up along very long streets without any intersections. The entrances to these streets are closed off by very strong gates with their sentry bells on top, at each of which a *chumbim* and twenty guards are stationed. Not far from these settlements, about a falcon-shot's distance, are the living quarters of the *chaem,* who is the superior officer in charge of this entire prison complex. His residence consists of a large collection of regal buildings with spacious courtyards and gardens with many water fountains and very cleverly designed rooms and salons in which a king would feel quite comfortable, no matter how big a following he had with him.

Running across from two of the settlements, which are the main ones, and leading right up to the *chaem*'s residence are two streets, each one more than a falcon shot long, all decorated with stone archways covered on top like those of the hospital of Lisbon, only much nicer, where they sell at all times everything one could ask for, from food to expensive luxury items. There one can find gold and silversmiths and shops belonging to very substantial merchants[4] who cannot take advantage of their wealth to avoid serving their sentences when it is their turn to be called. It is here, between these two arched streets, in a very wide open area, that they hold the two annual fairs I have been talking about that attract this huge crowd of people.

Also, within these prison gates, there are many forests with very tall trees and many streams and freshwater fountains which serve all these prisoners for their personal needs and laundry, as well as many small chapels and hospitals, and a dozen very wealthy and sumptuously appointed monasteries. So that all that a very fine wealthy city should contain is to be found in great abundance within these walls, and in many respects they are even better off because most of the prisoners have their wives and children with them and they are provided with a house by the king, according to the size of each family.

109
Treasure House of the Dead

The second thing of interest we saw—among the few I have chosen to describe—is another walled area almost as big as the first, called *Muxiparão,* meaning "treasure of the dead." It is surrounded by strong walls with their moats and many watchtowers of hewn stone, all of them topped by multicolored steeples. Instead of the usual parapets, the wall was ringed all around the top by iron rails, supporting a large number of idols of different shapes, some human, some in the form of serpents, horses, oxen, elephants, fish, cobras, and many other monstrous figures of strange-looking animals and beasts never seen anywhere else before, all made of bronze and cast iron, though some were made of tin and copper; yet the total effect of the structure, when seen altogether, was much more striking and agreeable than one would expect because of the way in which it was laid out.

Crossing a bridge that spanned the width of the moat, we came out on a large courtyard, leading to the main entrance, that was completely enclosed by very heavy brass rails, its floor all laid with black and white flagstones arranged in a checkerboard pattern which were so smooth and shiny that one's reflection was mirrored in them. In the middle of this courtyard there was a column of jasper thirty-six handspans high that looked as if it was made of one piece, at the top of which there was a silver idol in the shape of a woman who, with both hands, was strangling a serpent that was beautifully painted in green and black. A little further up, near the entrance to the door, which was located between two very high towers built upon twenty-four very heavy stone pillars, there were two statues of men, each with an iron mace in his hands, standing there as though they were guarding the entrance. In stature they measured 140 handspans tall, and their faces were so ugly, so much so, that the sight of them was almost enough to make one shudder with fear. The Chinese call them *Xixipitau Xalicão,* which means "fire-fanners of the House of Smoke." In front of this doorway there were twelve halberdiers and two clerks seated at a table making notes about every sort of person that entered and collecting a fee of two cash,[1] which is the equivalent of three *reals* in our money.

After passing through this doorway, we came out on a very wide street completely covered on both sides with richly decorated arches that were beautiful not only for their workmanship but for everything else about them, to which, in every curve of the arches, countless numbers of little brass bells were attached, swaying in the wind on little brass chains and making such an infernal racket with their constant tinkling that it was impossible to be heard above the noise no matter how loud one shouted.

This street was probably a little less than half a league long, and within these arches, on either side, there were two rows of one-story buildings as big as churches, built in proportion to the arches, with their steeples covered in gold leaf and many other painted designs. There were three thousand of these buildings, as the Chinese assured us, and they were all filled from top to bottom with human skulls, a thing so utterly amazing that from what one could judge, not even a fleet of a thousand of the largest *naos* afloat would suffice to carry them. Behind these buildings was a mountain of human bones[2] which rose high above the rooftops and was as long, from one end to the other, as the entire half league of the street, and extremely wide across.

When we asked the Chinese if they had any idea of how many bones there were, they said yes, that the *talagrepos* kept careful records of all the contents of the three thousand buildings and that they derived an annual income of two thousand *taels* or more from every one of those buildings, out of property willed to them by the deceased for the expiation of their sins, and that altogether it amounted to five million *cruzados* in gold, four-fifths of which went to the king and the rest to the *talagrepos* for the upkeep of that graveyard. Also, that the four-fifths share that fell to the king, as their patron, was spent on the support of the 300,000 exiles imprisoned in the *Xinanguibaleu.*

Still shaking our heads in amazement at what we had seen, we continued on up the street, and when we had gone nearly halfway, we came out on a large courtyard surrounded by a double row of brass railings, in the middle of which there was a large bronze snake all coiled up that had been pieced together, which measured more than thirty armspans all around, a thing so utterly amazing that there are no words to do it justice. Some of us guessed that it weighed more than one thousand quintals, presuming it was hollow inside, and despite its enormous size, it was, in every respect, so well proportioned, that not the slightest defect could be found in it. This applied as well to its workmanship, for it had all the beauty and perfection that one could desire in a work of art. This monstrous snake, which the Chinese called the "Ravenous Serpent of the House of Smoke," had a wrought-iron cannonball about fifty-two handspans in size set right in the middle of his head, which looked as though it had been thrown at him.

About twenty paces ahead there was a male figure made of bronze too, like a giant, which also looked rather odd because of its abnormal size and the thickness of its limbs. This giant was grasping a wrought-iron cannonball in both hands and was glaring at the serpent with a ferocious expression on his face, as though he were getting ready to hurl it at him. Encircling this statue were a large number of little gold-leafed idols kneeling before him with their arms stretched out towards him, as though in adoration, and on four iron beams running all around there were 162 silver candelabra, with as many as six, seven, and ten branches apiece.

The entire edifice was dedicated to this particular idol called *Muchiparom,* who the Chinese said was the keeper of all that treasure of bones, and that once upon a time he had caught the serpent we had seen in the act of stealing the bones and had thrown the cannonball that he was holding at him, causing the serpent to flee in terror to the Lower Depths of the House of Smoke where God had thrust him for his evil deeds, and that three thousand years ago he had thrown a ball at the serpent and was due to throw still another one at him three thousand years later, a process that would eventually finish him off after it had been repeated five times at intervals of three thousand years, and that once the serpent was dead, all those bones would return to their original bodies and dwell forever in the House of the Moon.

Apart from all this beastly nonsense they told us many other things in a similar vein which these miserably blind people believe so fervently that there is no way of convincing them otherwise because that is what they are taught by their priests, who assure them that all they have to do for the salvation of their souls is to have their bones brought there. As a result, not a day goes by without two thousand skeletons of these poor misguided creatures arriving there. Those who cannot bring the bones because the distance is too great bring one or two teeth along with a charitable donation which they say makes up for the rest. This explains why there are so many teeth stored in all those buildings, in such huge quantities that it seems to me that a great number of *naos* would not be able to carry them.

110
The Shrine of the Queen of Heaven

We also saw, in a large open area outside the walls of this city, another compound consisting of very rich and sumptuous buildings called *Nacapirau,* which means "the queen of heaven." However, when they say this, they do not mean the One who is really Queen of Heaven, who is our Lady the Virgin Mary, but these blind people believe that just as here on earth secular kings get married, so too in heaven the Lord our God is married, and that the children he begot with this *Nacapirau*, his wife, are the stars that we see at night in the sky, and that whenever a star falls and disintegrates in the air, they say that it is one of their children who has died and that the other sister stars, grieving over his death, shed so many tears that their excessive flow waters the earth below and is the means by which God has ordained our sustenance, as a charitable offering for the soul of the deceased.

But putting aside this piece of nonsense and countless others like it which these poor wretches practice in the thirty-two religious sects they have among them, I will confine my observations exclusively to the buildings we saw within this compound, which contain 140 monasteries for both men and women followers of this cursed religion, in each of which they told us there were four hundred people, which altogether comes to fifty-six thousand, not counting the large number of dervishes who serve them from the outside and who are not bound by the same vows as those inside. These, as a sign of their priesthood, go dressed in purple robes with their green *altirnas*[1] drawn up under the arm, somewhat like the stoles worn by our priests, with their heads, beards, and eyebrows shaved, and prayer beads around the neck. But they do not beg for alms[2] because they have enough money to support themselves.

The king of the Tartars stayed in this shrine of *Nacapirau* in the year 1544 when he laid siege to the city of Peking, which is something that will be dealt with later on.[3] At that time, in a diabolically bloody sacrificial rite, he had thirty thousand people beheaded, including fifteen thousand women, most of them young and beautiful, daughters of the noblest families in this kingdom who had taken their final vows in the various sects of *Quiay Frigau,* "god of the motes of the sun," *Quiay Nivandel,* "god of battles," *Compovitau,* and four others named *Quiay Mitru, Quiay Colompom, Quiay Muhelé,* and *Muhé Lacasá,* which are the five main sects of the thirty-two that exist in this kingdom, as we will see later on when we come to them.

But getting back to what I was saying, we saw some things within the walls of this large compound I have been talking about that I thought were worth remembering. One of them is another enclosure right in the middle of this one, nearly a league around, its walls set on very sturdy stone arches, and instead of parapets on top, it was enclosed all around with brass grillwork and with iron beams every six armspans, resting on bronze columns connected to each other, with an infinite number of bells hanging from chains constantly swaying in the breeze and keeping up such a frightful noise with their incessant movement that no one could stand it.

Here, within this second enclosure, flanking a large gate through which we passed, were a pair of very hideous figures representing what they call the "gate-keepers of hell," one named *Bacharom* and the other *Quagifau,* both of them with iron maces in their hands, and so extremely ugly that it gave one the shivers to look at them.

Passing through this gate beneath a heavy chain that ran all the way across it, connected at each end to the chests of these two devils, we came out on a very beautiful street that was as wide as it was long and completely covered on either side with arches all decorated with different kinds of paintings. On top of them, running along the entire length of the street, were two rows of idols in which there must have been more than five thousand statues. We could not very well tell what they were made of, but they were all covered in gold leaf and their heads were crowned with mitres of different sizes and shapes.

At the end of this avenue there was a large square courtyard, paved in checkerboard style with exceptionally fine black and white stone slabs, that was completely enclosed by four rows of bronze statues of giants, each one standing fifteen handspans high, with halberds in their hands and their unruly hair and beards all gilded, a marvelous sight indeed which was not only pleasing to the eye, but which also presented a very regal and magnificent spectacle. At the end of this courtyard was *Quiay Hujão,* the "god of rain," leaning on a staff more than seventy handspans long, standing so high that his head reached above the battlements of the tower, which must have been more than twelve handspans tall. This figure was also made of bronze, and twenty-six little jets of water, which the people below believed to be very holy, were spouting from his mouth, cheeks, forehead, and chest. The water came from the top of the tower against which he was leaning by means of pipes so well hidden that no one could find them.

After passing beneath his wide-spread legs, which formed a passageway for the people, we found ourselves in a large building, like a church, that was very long and had three naves supported by very thick, tall pillars of jasper. Along the walls, on both sides, were an enormous number of burnished idols large and small in different shapes and sizes, which, arranged on shelves in very good order, took up every bit of space along the entire length and width of the walls, and to the naked eye seemed to be all made of gold.

At the far end of the building, on a round dais fifteen steps high, there was an altar built in perfect proportion to the dais, on which stood the statue of *Nacapirau,* in the form of an extremely beautiful woman, with her hair streaming loosely over her shoulders and both arms raised heavenward. She herself shone there in dazzling splendor, fashioned as she was of such an extremely fine quality of highly polished gold that it was impossible to look directly at her for long, because the rays she cast were as blinding as those of a mirror. Arranged around this dais, on the first four steps, were twelve silver statues of Chinese kings with crowns on their heads and ceremonial maces on their shoulders. A little further down one could see three rows of gilded idols, kneeling before them with arms upraised. Encircling them from above, suspended from the beams running across the building, were a large number of silver candelabra of six and seven branches each.

Leaving this building we walked along another street, also covered with arches like the one through which we had passed before, and then two more streets after that, also lined with many sumptuous buildings, until we came out on a wide terrace where there were eighty-two huge bronze bells hanging on heavy chains from iron beams supported at both ends by cast-iron columns. Once we were also out of this area, we reached a very sturdy iron gate connected to four very tall towers, where a *chifu* and a company of thirty halberdiers were stationed, along with two clerks who were recording in some books the names of everyone leaving, as they also did with us, and to whom we gave thirty *reals* when we left.

III
The Shrine of the 113 Kings

To conclude with this subject—for if I were to dwell on it in all its details there would be no end to it—among the large number of magnificent, sumptuous buildings we saw here, there was one that, to my mind, stood out more prominently than the rest. It was a walled structure nearly a league in circumference that was situated in the middle of the *Batampina* River, on a small flat island, like a floodplain, completely surrounded by extremely beautiful stone walls rising on the outside more than thirty-eight spans above the surface of the water, but level with the ground on the inside. On top it was enclosed all around by a double row of brass railings, the outer ones measuring only six spans tall, or low enough to lean over them, while the inner ones, which measured nine spans, were decorated with silver lions atop round spheres representing, as I have pointed out several times before, the coat of arms of the kings of China.

Within these railings, arranged in orderly fashion, there are 113 chapels shaped like round bastions, each one containing an elaborate alabaster tomb, cleverly supported on the heads of twin silver serpents which looked like cobras because their bodies were coiled many times around, though they had women's faces with three horns on their foreheads, the meaning of which escaped us. There were thirteen silver candelabra of seven branches each burning in each one of these chapels, which meant that altogether there was a total of 1,439 candelabra in these 113 chapels.

In the middle of a large square, surrounded on all sides by three separate railings and a double row of idols, there was a very tall tower with five steeples painted in different ways with their silver lions at the very top. This tower, the Chinese told us, contained the skeletons of the 113 kings, which had been transferred there from the other chapels below. They say that these skeletons, which they worship as priceless relics, meet at every new moon to dine with each other, and that that is the reason why, on those days of the month, the common people are in the habit of bringing offerings for these banquets, of huge quantities of every variety of fowl, rice, beef, pork, sugar, honey, and every other kind of food one can name, and because of the contributions they make to these banquets, all of which the priests keep for themselves, they think they have been redeemed, as though by plenary indulgence, from all the foulness of their sins.

It was here too that we saw an elaborately decorated hall, covered from top to bottom with plates of silver, where these 113 kings of China were kept in hollow statues, also made of silver. They say that each king's skeleton was kept separately within each one of those statues because that enabled them all to communicate at night, and according to what their priests told them, they engaged in pastimes in each other's company, which no one was worthy of seeing, except for certain bonzes, they call *cabisondos*,[1] who are priestly dignitaries of higher rank than the others, like cardinals.

In addition to these tales of blindness and ignorance, they told us many others that these wretched people believe as firmly as if they were very plain and obvious truths.

Within the entire area encompassed by this large wall, in seventeen different places we counted 340 bronze and cast-iron bells, twenty at each location, that are rung all together on certain days of the months, namely, on the days they say these kings get together to hold their feasts.

Next to this tower, in a very richly appointed chapel poised in midair over thirty-seven solidly constructed pillars of hewn stone, was the statue of the goddess Amida,[2] her body of silver and her hair of gold, resting on a gold-plated dais, fourteen steps from the floor. The face was beautiful, and hanging from under both of her upraised arms, like a string of beads, was an enormous number of tiny little idols, no bigger than half a finger, while on her secret parts she had two very large pearl oyster shells, decorated in gold.

When we asked the Chinese to explain the meaning of all those things, they answered that after God had sent down water from the rivers of heaven, flooding the world and drowning all mankind, he saw that the earth was left uninhabited, with no one to sing his praises, so in order to replenish the earth with humankind to take the place of the people who had drowned, he sent down from the Heaven of the Moon the goddess Amida, first lady-in-waiting to his wife *Nacapirau*. The moment she set foot on a piece of land that was dry by then, which was called *Calempluy*[3] (the very same island or floodplain in the Gulf of Nanking, described before as the place where Antonio de Faria went ashore), she had turned to solid gold, and there, standing upright with her face turned heavenward, she had sweated an enormous number of children from her armpits, boys from the right side and girls from the left, for she had no other place in her body for bringing forth children, unlike earthly women who have sinned and been punished for it by God who has subjected them, by way of nature, to the wretchedness of filthy, stinking corruption in order to show how odious was the sin committed against him. After she had given birth or expelled these children from her armpits—and they claim there were 33,333 of them—with twice as many females as males (because, they say, that was the way of the world and always would be), she had been left so weak, having no one to attend to her needs, that she had collapsed from sheer exhaustion and fallen to the ground dead, without ever having risen again to this day, and that that is reason why the moon, remembering her passing with deep sorrow, covered itself with mourning, which are those patches of earthly shadow we usually see on it. But when she wakes up, an event that will occur after the passage of as many years as the number of children she bore—which is, as I have said, 33,333—then the moon will remove its mask of mourning and from that moment on, night will be as bright as day.

They told us so many of these ridiculous things and many more like them, that it is enough to make one gasp with amazement, but even more to make one weep to see with what clear and manifest lies these peoples, who are otherwise so rational, have been so deceived by the devil that they cannot find the path to our holy truth, which the Son of God came to reveal to the world. However, only he knows the secret of this.

After leaving the courtyard where we had seen all these things, we went to another temple reserved for nuns, very rich and sumptuous, in which they told us that the king's mother resided, whose name was *Nhay Camisama*,[4] but they would not let us enter this one because we were foreigners.

From here we went along a street completely covered by arches until we came to a wharf called *Hichariò Topileu*, where an enormous number of ships were tied up, laden with pilgrims from various kingdoms who continuously come to visit this temple for the purpose of obtaining plenary indulgence which the king of China and the *chaens* of the government have granted them, as well as other privileges in the form of many tax exemptions throughout the land, besides free and very abundant meals.

As for the many other temples we saw in this city during the two months we were at liberty to roam around there, I will not touch upon them, for it would be an endless task to try to describe all of them in detail. Instead, I will deal with some other things we saw that were particularly noteworthy. First of all, I will devote a few words—and will try to be as brief as I can—to the palaces and the state in which the king of China lives, and to the way in which he governs the republic, as well as to the ministers of justice, the treasury, and the court, in order to make known the way in which this heathen rules his people, and the means by which he provides for the general welfare.

112
Social Welfare in China

The king of China resides in this city of Peking most of the time, in keeping with the oath he swears on the day of his coronation when they place in his hands the scepter of government, about which I shall have a few words to say further on.

In certain sections of this city, on separate streets, there are houses which they call *laginampur,* meaning "education of the poor." There, by order of the city council, all idle fatherless youngsters are taught doctrine, as well as reading, writing, and all the mechanical trades, until they are ready to earn a living for themselves. And the number of these houses in the city is not so few that they do not exceed two hundred or perhaps five hundred.

There are an equal number of other houses where, also by order of the city, many poor women make a living as wet nurses, breastfeeding and taking care of all foundlings of whom neither father nor mother are known for certain. However, before these infants are accepted into these houses, a thorough investigation is carried out by the courts, and if the father or mother of the abandoned child is discovered, they are severely punished and banished to certain areas that are considered to be the most arid and unwholesome. When these deserted infants are old enough, they are transferred to the above-mentioned schools to be educated. And if any of them are handicapped by nature for learning a trade, they find some other means of earning a living for them too, each according to his needs. In the case of blind children, every miller in town who is the owner of a hand-operated flour mill employs three of them, two for the manual operation of the mill, and one for sifting flour. In that way the government ensures that not only the blind are provided for, but other needy people as well who are public charges, for no craftsman can ply his trade without first obtaining a license from the city council, and the moment he applies for such a license he must agree to employ one or more of these indigents who are fitted for his trade, so that the means from which he seeks to make his living will also improve the lot of the poor. For this, they say, is a good deed in keeping with God's commandment to love thy neighbor, and one much cherished by him, in return for which he overlooks the punishment due us for our sins. The miller must provide each of these three blind persons in his employ with food, clothing, shoes, and wages of six testons a year, so that when he dies he may have something to leave for the good of his soul and not perish, because of being poor, in the Lower Depths of the House of Smoke, in accordance with the fourth precept of the goddess Amida, who was the first to pass on to these blind people the superstitions and errors to which they adhere, and who apparently dates back to the year 636 after the Great Deluge.

This religious sect,[1] as well as all the other barbaric sects of China—which, from what I have learned from them, number thirty-two altogether, as I have mentioned several times before—reached Siam from the kingdom of Pegu and were spread from there by priests and *cabizondos* throughout all the mainland countries of Cambodia, Champa, Laos, the *Gueos,* the *Pafuás,* the empire of *Uzangué,* Cochinchina,[2] and over to the archipelago of the islands of Hainan, the Ryukyus, and Japan, as far as the borders of Miyako and Bandou,[3] infecting with the poison of their herpes as great a part of the world as did the cursed sect of Mohammed.

They also have another way of helping the handicapped to keep them from starving to death, which provides that the crippled who are unable to walk be given to the rope makers, who employ them for twisting esparto cordage and the rush fibers used for basket weaving, and other jobs for which they can use their hands.

As for those who cannot work with their hands because of some handicap, they are given baskets which they carry on their backs, hiring themselves out for money, to carry from the marketplaces meat, fish, produce, and other things for people who have no one to do it for them and cannot do it for themselves.

As for those who are crippled in both hands and feet and are thus totally incapacitated for making their own living, they place them in some very large buildings, like monasteries, where there are also large numbers of women mourners to pray for the dead, and out of the offerings that come in from all the funerals, they get half, and the priests the other half.

As for the deaf and dumb, they place them in another building, like a hospital, and set aside for their support a fund gathered from the fines of all the loud-mouthed and shameless women who dishonor themselves in public.

For the prostitutes who come down with incurable diseases in old age, there are also other houses of the same kind, where they are treated and provided for most generously at the expense of the other public women plying the same trade, each of whom contributes a certain amount of money every month, for each one of them may also come down with the same disease some day and then the others who are healthy will pay for her what she, who is still in good health, is now paying for the ones who are sick. And there are men stationed throughout the city for the purpose of collecting these taxes, who are paid well for doing this.

There are also other buildings, like monasteries, in which the city looks after large numbers of orphaned girls, finding them husbands with dowries gathered from property forfeited by women who have been accused of adultery[4] by their husbands. They justify this practice by explaining that, as long as there are women who choose to risk all they have by leading unchaste lives, then let their property be used for the benefit of the orphaned girl who is virtuous, so that in this manner some may be punished and others helped.

SOCIAL WELFARE IN CHINA

Also, in certain sections of the city they provide shelter for penniless men addicted to a free and easy life, who are also supported by the city at the expense of the lawyers who persist in bringing unjust claims before the court to which their clients have no right, as well as at the cost of judges who, swayed either by influence or bribes, do not uphold the lawful processes of justice. Thus, in every respect, these people govern themselves in a very orderly manner.[5]

113
Provisions against Famine

Also, it is only right to let people know about the highly organized and marvelously efficient manner in which this heathen Chinese king provides food for his kingdom so that the poor do not suffer for want of it. And to that end I will relate what their chronicles have to say on the subject, for though they are written in Chinese characters, I have heard them read a few times, and what they say may well serve as an example of both charity and good government to all Christian kingdoms and republics.

These chronicles tell the story of the great-grandfather of the present ruler of China, a king by the name of *Chausirão Panagor,*[1] who had lost his eyesight as the result of a serious illness, and who was dearly beloved by the people for his noble soul and gentle nature. Since he was desirous of performing a pious deed that would be exceptionally pleasing to God, this king summoned his estates general, where he issued orders that, for the relief of all the poor people, there should be granaries of wheat and rice established—as there still are today—throughout all the cities and townships of the realm, so that, if the earth should grow sterile and not bear fruit, as sometimes occurred, the people would have enough food to go around that year, and the poor would not perish for lack of it, and to implement it, he was prepared to contribute one-tenth of the crown revenues. After he had had them write into law the general procedure that was to be followed by all the cities which were the seats of government of the *anchacilado* districts, the chronicle states that when they brought it to him to sign with the gold signet he carried on his arm, which was the way he ordinarily did it because of his blindness, the moment he signed it, God granted him perfect vision, which he enjoyed continuously for the remaining fourteen years of his life. From this example—if indeed it happened so—it would seem that our Lord wanted to show how much it pleases him when charity is done for the poor, out of love for him, even among the infidels, who have no knowledge of him.

From that time on there have always been a large number of granaries located throughout the entire monarchy, and from what they say, there are fourteen thousand of these storehouses. The governing bodies responsible for always keeping the food supply replenished act as follows: As soon as it becomes apparent that the harvests are certain and safe, the wheat from the previous season is distributed among the entire population of the region, according to each one's means, in the form of a loan to be paid back in two months. At the end of the period fixed by law, these men return promptly to deliver the same quantity of new wheat as they had received of the old, plus 6 percent, to allow for losses, thereby ensuring that the supply of food stored in the granaries will always be maintained at a constant level. If they should happen to have a year of bad harvests, the wheat is still distributed among the general population, free of interest, at no profit to anyone. As for the food that is distributed to the poor who are unable to repay the loan, that portion comes out of the land taxes paid to the crown, in the form of a charitable contribution from the king, as stipulated in the original plan, which is duly recorded in all the local councils, so that the *anchacys* of the treasury may take account of it.

As for the rest of the royal revenues, which adds up to a huge amount of silver piculs, it is divided into three parts, one-third being set aside for the upkeep of the royal household and the administrative expenses of the kingdom, one-third for defense of the provinces and military supplies for the arsenals and armadas, and the remaining third is put into the treasury here in this city of Peking, which not even the king can touch under ordinary circumstances, because it is reserved for the military defense of the kingdom and for the wars that frequently take place with the Tartars, the king of the Cochinese, and other kings whose lands border on his. This portion of the treasury is called *chidampur,* meaning "wall of the kingdom," for they say that as long as these funds are available in the treasury, to be resorted to in case of need, the king will not levy any tribute or extra taxes on the poor, nor will the general population be oppressed, as they are in other countries where they fail to take such precautions.

Thus, in this as well as in all other matters, this kingdom is so well governed, with such a high degree of excellence and with such prompt execution in all its affairs, that when he became aware of it, back in the days when he traveled in China, the blessed Father Master Francisco Xavier[2]—the brightest star in his day of all the Orient and so well known throughout the world for his virtue and saintliness that there is no need to say any more about him—was so amazed by these things as well as many other excellent things he saw in this land, that he used to say that, if God one day should bring him back to Portugal, he would ask the king, our lord, as a favor to him, to examine the war and treasury decrees and statutes by which these people were governed, because he never had any doubt that they were far better than those of the Romans at the height of their glory as well as those of all the other nations about which the ancients have written.

114
Farewell to Peking

I fear that if I were to give a detailed description of everything that we saw in this city the reader might doubt what I say because of the rare splendor of all those things; moreover, since I do not wish to provide an opportunity for the gossipmongers and backbiters—who base their opinions on their limited experience and the little that their narrow, evil minds are capable of understanding—to pass judgement on the truthfulness of what I saw with my own eyes, I will refrain from describing many things that would perhaps afford great pleasure to those people who are high-minded, who possess a broad, profound intelligence, and who do not measure things in other countries solely by the meanness and misery they see in front of their eyes, for I know that these people, not only because of their loftiness of spirit, but also because of their natural curiosity and intellectual capacity, would really enjoy knowing all about them.

But on the other hand, I cannot blame anyone either who doubts or finds it difficult to believe what I say when I myself, who saw it all with my own eyes, often become confused when I recall the splendors of this city of Peking, the admirable pomp with which this heathen king is attended, the magnificence displayed by the *chaens* of the judiciary and the *anchacys* of the administration, the awe and respect that their ministers inspire in everyone, the sumptuousness of the buildings and temples raised to their idols, and everything else that is there. For in this city of *Minapau* alone, which is located within the palace grounds, there are 100,000 eunuchs,[1] 30,000 women, and 12,000 guardsmen who receive high salaries and pensions from the king; also, there are twelve *tutões,* the highest-ranking dignitaries in the land who, as I have said before, are ordinarily referred to as the "splendid rays of the sun," because they say that just as the king descends from the sun, in the same manner these twelve who represent him in all things, are called "splendid rays of the sun." Beneath them in importance come the forty *chaens,* who are something like viceroys, in addition to many other dignitaries of lesser rank somewhat like our appellate judges, governors, comptrollers of the treasury, admirals, and captains-major, who go by the titles of *anchacys, aytaos, ponchacys, lauteás,* and *chumbins.*[2] And even though there are more than five-hundred of them altogether in this city, which is the royal court, none of them has a retinue[3] of less than two-hundred men, composed mainly—which is even more impressive—of foreign mercenaries who come from all over, their ranks filled primarily by Moghuls, Persians, Khorasanis, Mons, *Calaminhãs,* Tartars, and Cochinese, as well as some Burmese from *Chaleu* and Toungoo. This is due to the fact that they do not have much respect for the natives, who are fainthearted and worthless as soldiers, though they are quite skillful and clever in all things relating to industry and agriculture, and they are very talented architects and expert inventors of highly sophisticated things, and their women are very fair and chaste and more inclined to all kinds of labor than the men are.

The land is naturally fertile and produces such rich and abundant crops of every kind of food that, in all truth, I cannot find the words to describe it, for it seems to me that the mind is not capable of understanding, let alone finding names for all the many different things that God chose to lavish on these infidels who are enemies of His and who are so ungrateful for all the favors they receive from Him that they actually believe that it is solely due to the merits of their king that the land produces all this abundance, and not to divine Providence and the love of the almighty Lord.

This blindness and incredulity on their part is responsible for the utter senselessness and the enormous jumble of superstitions they believe in, which entail sacrifices with human blood,[4] which they offer with all different kinds of incense, together with large bribes they give their priests in order to be assured by them of great blessings in this life and of infinite treasures of gold in the next. In exchange, the priests give them written documents like bills of exchange, called *cuchimiocós*[5] by the common people, so that up there in heaven, when they die, they will give them a hundred for one, as though they had bank correspondents there, waiting to honor them. In this respect these poor wretches are so blind that they frequently do without food and other necessities of life in order to have enough money to give to these priests of Satan, in exchange for what they regard as a safe and sound investment.

Also, in a different sect, there are other priests called *naustolins,* who, contrarywise, preach to their listeners and swear vehemently that there is nothing more than living and dying like any beast and that therefore we should enjoy our worldly possessions while we are still alive, for it is sheer ignorance to think otherwise.

There are others belonging to another sect called *Trimechau,* who believe that a man will lie dead under the ground for the same number of years as he lived on earth, and that afterwards, in response to the prayers of their priests, his soul will rise to enter into the body of a seven-day-old infant, in which he will live until he has grown strong enough to go in search of his former body which he left behind in the grave, in order to take it back to the Heaven of the Moon, where they say he will sleep for many, many years, until one day he will be converted into a star, and that there he will remain fixed forever.

Others, in another sect called *Gizom,*[6] believe that only the lowly beasts of the field will go to their eternal rest in heaven because of the penance they have done with the hardships they have endured in this life, and not man, who has always lived by the whims of the flesh, stealing, murdering, and committing many other sins, because of which he cannot under any circumstances achieve salvation, unless at the hour of death he leaves everything he owns to the pagoda and the priests so that they will pray for him.

So that fundamentally, all these diabolical sects of theirs are based on tyranny and are designed for the benefit of the bonzes, who are the ones who preach these things to the people, reaffirming them over and over. As a result, their poor, unfortunate listeners, in the belief that it is all true, give them everything they have, because they think that that way they are safe and free of the fears with which they threaten them if they fail to do so.

In discussing this subject I only wanted to mention these three sects and not to say anything about all the other abuses practiced by the thirty-two sects of this great Chinese empire, not only because it would be an endless process to describe them all, as I have said several times before, but also because one can get a good idea from these examples of what the others are like, since they are all similar.

Leaving the remedy for such great evil and blindness to the mercy and to the divine Providence of the only One to whom it pertains, I will limit myself from here on to describe the other hardships we endured during our exile in the city of *Quansy* until the time we were captured by the Tartars, which happened in the year 1544.

115
A Point of Honor

On a Saturday, January 13, in the year 1544,[1] after having spent two and a half months in the city of Peking, we were taken to the city of *Quansy* to begin our sentence in exile. As soon as we got there the *chaem* had us brought before him, and after asking us a few questions, he decided to assign us to his personal guards, a company of eighty halberdiers he was allowed by the king. We regarded this as no small favor on the part of our Lord, not only because the work was easy, but also because the food and pay were better and we had greater freedom of movement.

After we had been here for nearly a month, when all was going well and we were quite pleased with the treatment we were getting, which was better than we expected, the devil himself, who could not bear to see the nine of us living together in harmony and sharing our meager possessions with each other in brotherly fashion, decided to sow the seeds of discontent between two of our men, which proved to be disastrous for all of us. It arose out of a certain vanity, typical of our Portuguese nation, which I cannot really explain except by saying that they are by nature very sensitive people when it comes to questions of honor.

It all began when two of the nine men in our group got into an argument about which one of the noble families had better accommodations at the court of the king, our lord—the Madureiras or the Fonsecas.[2] One word led to another, and before we knew it they were resorting to the vulgar language of fishwives and asking each other, "Who do you think you are?" and "Well, who do you think *you* are?" when both of them had little more than nothing to their names.

By this time they had worked themselves up into such a rage that one of them gave the other a hard slap in the face and in reply received a wide slash with a knife across the face, which left him with half of his cheek hanging down. The wounded man then grabbed a poleaxe and chopped off the other's arm. After that a fight really began when all nine of us became embroiled in this unfortunate argument. The situation got so out of control that seven of us were badly wounded by the time the *chaem* himself came running up with all the *anchacys* of the law. After taking us in hand, they immediately gave each of us thirty strokes of the lash, which left us bloodier than we had been from our wounds, and they threw us into an underground dungeon where they kept us for forty-six days, adding to our misery by keeping us with fetters on our feet, manacles on our hands, and collars round our necks.

Our case was then placed in the hands of the prosecutor, who drew up an indictment against us. One of the charges he made against us, supported by evidence obtained from sixteen eyewitnesses, was that we were a people who had neither fear nor any knowledge of God, who only paid lip service to him, as any beast could do if it had the gift of language, for if men of the same nationality, the same flesh and blood, the same king and country, the same language and religion, could wound and kill each other so mercilessly, for no cause or reason, the only possible explanation for it was that we were slaves in the service of the Ravenous Serpent of the House of Smoke, a fact which we had amply demonstrated, for the serpent always acted that way; therefore, in accordance with the statutes of the third book of the "Golden Clasps of the Will of the Son of Heaven,"[3] known as *Nileterau,* he recommended that we should be isolated from all human contact, like a virulent, contagious plague, and banished to the mountains of *Chabaqué,*[4] or *Sumbor,* or *Lamau,* where the likes of us were usually sent, so that there we should hear the wild beasts howling at night, for they were of as vile a breed and nature as we.

From here one morning they took us to the *Pitau Calidão* of the ministry of justice, the tribunal where the *anchacy* sat in awesome pomp and splendor, surrounded by many other ministers and officials known as *chumbins, upos, lauteás,* and *sipatões,*[5] to say nothing of a large crowd of many other people who came from all over as auditors and petitioners, and there again, they gave each of us thirty strokes of the lash. After pronouncing sentence on us, they transferred us to another prison where our situation was somewhat better than in the previous one, but where we spent our days cursing the Fonsecas and the Madureiras, and still more the devil who had contrived the whole thing.

We languished in this prison for nearly two months, and though we recovered completely from our wounds and lashes, we suffered unbearably from hunger and thirst. At the end of this time, thanks be to the Lord, the *chaem* took pity on us, for on a certain day of the year usually set aside by them for acts of charity on behalf of their dead,[6] he reviewed our sentence and decided that, in view of the fact that we were foreigners, from a country and nation so remote that there was no one there who had ever heard of us or any book or document that mentioned our name, nor could anyone be found who understood our language, plus the fact that we were accustomed to suffering from misery and vile poverty, which in itself is often the cause for dissension among decent, peace-loving men, let alone people who had never been taught patience in the face of adversity, it was apparent from all that, that our quarrel had been the result of our misery and poverty, rather than of the evil nature to which the prosecutor had attributed it; moreover, in view of the fact that there was a shortage of conscript labor for the routine tasks that had to be taken care of in the service of the republic and the administration of justice, he had decided, as an act of charity, in the name of the king, that the lashes we had received should be accepted as sufficient penalty for our crime, and that we should remain there forever as captives until such time as the *tutão* should see fit to ordain otherwise; furthermore, if anyone should be found guilty of creating a disturbance in the bazaars, or of drawing blood from any person, he would be flogged to death that same day.

This sentence was immediately read to us, and though we wept uncontrollably when we heard it, overwhelmed by the realization that we had sunk so low, still we regarded it as an improvement over the previous one.

After this, they released us from prison, bound three by three, and took us to an iron foundry where we remained for five months, suffering from dire necessity and hardship, without clothing or bedding, crawling with lice, and starving to death until, at the end of that time, we all fell sick with a lethargic disease,[7] and since it was contagious, they threw us out in the street to beg for a living until such time as we would be cured, and they ordered our shackles removed.

After four more months of dragging ourselves about from door to door, sick as we were, begging for alms which we rarely got because of a famine in the countryside, we were forced to come to an understanding among ourselves. We made an agreement to get along with each other and pledged under solemn oath to observe it, swearing that thenceforth we would all live together in perfect harmony like the Christians we were, and that every month we would take turns acting as a leader who would be obeyed by all the others in keeping with the oath we had sworn, as though he were our true superior and prelate, without any one of us being allowed to have a will of his own or to do anything unless he were acting under his orders, and we were to be guided by the written rules we had drawn up.

Once we had made this agreement, it was the Lord's will that from then on, we lived together in peace and harmony, in spite of the fact that we were lacking in all the necessities of life and suffering from terrible hardship.

116
A Chance Encounter with Vasco Calvo

A few days after we had begun living together in peace and harmony, in keeping with the agreement I mentioned above, Cristóvão Borralho, our leader that month, realizing that we had to seek out all possible means of remedying our situation, divided us up in twosomes by the week, some to go begging for alms in the city, some to get water and prepare the food, and others to gather firewood in the forest to sell and to use for ourselves.

One day, when it was my turn to go into the woods with my partner, a fellow by the name of Gaspar de Meireles, we got up bright and early and left the house to do our chores. Since this Gaspar de Meireles was a musician who played the viola[1] and sang reasonably well, talents which are highly appreciated by these people because they spend most of their time on banquets and pleasures of the flesh, they were very fond of him there and often called upon him to entertain them at their affairs from which he would always return with alms that helped to tide us over a good part of the time.

Well, as I was saying, when he and I were heading for the woods as we had been told to do, we happened to run into a crowd of people on a street near the edge of town who, with a great show of joy and merrymaking and many symbols of funeral pomp, were carrying a corpse to be buried. In their midst was a large group of musicians who were singing and accompanying themselves on their instruments. The leader or music master of the group, who knew Gaspar de Meireles, laid hold of him to make him play and thrust a viola into his hands.

"Please sing as loud as you can," he said, "so that this dead man we are carrying will hear you. Believe me, he is very sad, for he was extremely fond of his wife and children and he misses them very much."

Gaspar de Meireles tried to free himself with some excuse, but the bandleader not only refused to accept it, he became quite angry.

"If you do not agree to give this dead man the benefit of the gift that God gave you for singing and playing," he protested, "then I will no longer say that you are the holy man we all thought you were till now, but rather that the excellent quality of your voice comes from the inhabitants of the House of Smoke whose natural attribute in the beginning was also to sing sweetly, though now they weep and wail in the Lake of the Night like famished dogs, gnashing their teeth and foaming with rage against mankind, as they wallow in the wickedness of their deeds which are discernible in the offenses they commit against the One who lives in the highest of the heavens."

After this, ten or twelve of them laid hold of Gaspar de Meireles and practically forced him to play, and they took him along with them to the place where the deceased was to be cremated,[2] as is the custom in their heathen sects.

Finding myself alone once my companion had been forcibly carried off, I went into the forest to gather my load of firewood, as I had been told to do. Sometime in the afternoon, when I was returning with it on my back, an old man crossed my path. He was wearing black damask clothes with a white lambskin lining, and he was alone. The moment he saw me, he made for a little lane that opened there in the woods and stood there waiting for me at the foot of the path. But when he saw that I was passing him by without looking his way, he cleared his throat, making a noise loud enough to attract my attention. When I heard it, I looked up and saw him beckoning to me with his hand to come near. This struck me as rather odd, so I said to him in Chinese, "Potau quinay?" meaning, "Are you calling me?"

Without a word in reply he beckoned again, giving me to understand from his gestures that he meant yes. Thinking this might be some kind of a trap laid for me by thieves who were out to steal my wood, as sometimes happens in the forest, I put my bundle down, which left me in a better position to defend myself. Then I took hold of a stick I used to lean on and started towards him with a rapid stride. When he saw me following him, he hurried off down the lane, which convinced me that the man was undoubtedly a thief. Turning back to where I had left my bundle, I slung it on my back as fast as I could, determined to make a run for the highway that the people took to get to the city. However, guessing my intentions, the man cleared his throat again, this time even more loudly than before, and when I looked back, I saw him get down on his knees, holding out a silver cross for me to see before raising both his arms to heaven. I was so taken aback by what I saw that I stood there staring at him in amazement, unable to figure out what it was all about, while all this time he kept on beckoning to me with pious gestures to come closer.

Regaining a little better control of myself, I made up my mind to find out who he was or what he wanted of me. I walked towards him with my stick in my hand and followed him into the lane where, by this time, he was waiting for me. When I got close to him, without thinking up to that time that he was anything other than Chinese, he threw himself at my feet. Sobbing uncontrollably and shedding many tears, he began to speak, saying, "Blessed and praised be the most sweet name of our Lord Jesus Christ for having permitted me, after so many years, in such a remote exile, to set eyes upon a fellow Christian who professes the faith of my God upon the Cross!"

This was the last thing I expected to hear and so far from what had been running through my mind that I jumped back, completely startled.

"I appeal to you in the name of our Lord Jesus Christ," I shouted at him, "tell me who you are!"

"My dear brother," he replied, the tears streaming down his face, "I am a poor Portuguese Christian by the name of Vasco Calvo,[3] and a brother of the Diogo Calvo who was captain of the *nao* owned by Dom Nuno Manuel,[4] a native of the town of

Alcochete. It is now twenty-seven years since they arrested me here along with Tomé Pires,[5] whom Lopo Soares[6] sent as ambassador to the Chinese king—a mission that later ended disastrously because of the misconduct of a Portuguese captain."[7]

By this time I had fully recovered my wits, and I lifted him from the ground where he lay crying like a baby. Shedding as many tears as he did, I urged him to sit down beside me, which he reluctantly agreed to because he would have liked us to go to his house immediately. Then he resumed his tale of woe, telling me about all the hardships he had suffered throughout his life and everything else that had happened to him from the time he had left Portugal up to then. He also told me about the death of the ambassador Tomé Pires and all the other men whom Fernão Peres de Andrade had left with him in Canton to visit the king of China, a story that does not agree much with what our chroniclers write.[8]

After we had spent the rest of the day exchanging tales of our misfortune, we returned to the city. He showed me the house where he lived and begged me to go bring my other companions immediately. I went to call them straightway and found them all waiting for me in the humble little house in which we lived. When I told them about my encounter and everything else that had happened to me, they were all as astounded as one would expect them to be, and they all accompanied me at once to Vasco Calvo's house, where we found him waiting for us in a great state of excitement, with the table set for dining. And once again, at this encounter, many a tear was shed all around to celebrate the arrival of my companions.

He took us to another part of the house to meet his wife and children, two boys and two girls. She also greeted us warmly and treated us as lovingly as if she had been the mother or sister of each one of us.

After the better part of the evening had passed we sat down to the table, where he himself brought each of us water to wash our hands, and throughout the entire meal there was not a single dry eye among us. When dinner was over, his wife very courteously got up from the table, and since she was in the habit every night of offering up a Christian prayer of thanks to God, which she did in secret, either out of fear of her heathen neighbors or her respected kinsmen who lived nearby, she took out a key that she kept hidden in her sleeve and with it she unlocked a little door to a small private chapel that contained a beautifully decorated altar with a silver cross and two candlesticks and a lamp, also made of silver. Then she and all four children kneeled down, raised their arms, and recited the following words in clearly enunciated Portuguese.

"O true God, we sinners kneel down before thy Cross like good Christians, to confess to the most holy Trinity, the Father, the Son, and the Holy Ghost, three persons and one God. And thus we promise to live and die in thy most holy Catholic faith like good, true Christians, confessing and accepting as thy holy truth everything that is held and believed by the Holy Mother Church of Rome; and with all our souls, which were redeemed by thy precious blood, we pledge thee homage and swear to serve thee with all our lives, and to deliver them up to thee at the hour of death, as to our God and Lord, to whom we confess they belong, by creation and by redemption."

After this they said the Pater Noster, the Ave Maria, the Credo, and the Salve Regina, which they recited and pronounced so well that the tears came rushing to our eyes, for it made us weep to see those innocent little children, living in such a far-off land with no knowledge of God, confessing to his faith with such holy words.

But since it was already past three in the morning by the time they finished, we went back to our lodging, as amazed by what we had seen as one would expect, in view of the circumstances.

117
The Tartar Invasion

We had been in captivity here for eight and a half months, suffering all the while from extreme hardship and deprivation for lack of any means of support, except for the few paltry alms we collected in the city, when shortly after midnight on a Wednesday, July 13, in the year 1544,[1] there arose such a tumult in the streets, with the pealing of bells and shouts and screams coming from all over the city, that it sounded as if the whole world were coming to an end. We all dashed over to Vasco Calvo's house to find out what was going on, and he told us, choking back the tears, that it had been definitely confirmed that the Tartar king was about to invade the city of Peking[2] with the largest army in the world ever assembled by any king since the days of Adam and Eve, and that it was reported that twenty-seven kings had joined forces with him, swelling his ranks, it was said, by 1,800,000 men, including 600,000 cavalrymen who had set out from the cities of *Lançame, Famstir,* and *Mecuy,* traveling overland with a train of eighty-thousand yak laden with all their food and supplies; also, that the 1,200,000 foot soldiers had come down the *Batampina* River in a fleet of sixteen-thousand ships composed of *laulés* and *jangás,* and that the king of China, not daring to offer any resistance to such a huge force, had fled unattended to Nanking, and that at that very moment, in the pine forest of *Manicatarão,* only a league and a half away, a *nauticor*[3] of the Tartar king was encamped with an army of seventy-thousand cavalrymen, with not a single foot soldier among them, ready to strike, and that in all likelihood he would be there within two hours. This news left us so beside ourselves that all we could do was stammer back and forth at each other without being capable of saying anything that made any sense. Finally, when we asked him what we should do or what steps we should take to save ourselves, he answered impatiently, "My dear brothers, I would say that right now the surest means of our salvation would be to find ourselves somewhere between Lavra and Coruche,[4] back home, beside a clump of bushes, where I used to go often, but since that cannot be, let us commend ourselves to the Lord our God to avail us, for I assure you that less than an hour ago I was ready to give a thousand silver *taels* to anyone who could lead me to safety with my wife and children, but it was too late because all the gates had already been shut and heavily guarded, and the walls were covered with an infinite number of troops that the *chaem* had placed along them, to say nothing of other captains posted in reserve in certain areas, to patrol and rush in with their support wherever necessary."

Following which, we nine companions spent what remained of that sad night in the throes of deep spiritual agony and affliction, without being able to decide upon what to do or which way to turn, just weeping and moaning out of fear and anxiety at the thought of what lay ahead for us.[5]

At the crack of dawn, just before sunrise, the enemy appeared in full view, and a frightening and bellicose spectacle they were, divided into seven huge battalions, flying numerous field banners quartered in green and white, which are the colors of the standard of this king of Tartary; and to the throbbing of many drums, beaten in their fashion, they came bearing down upon a pagoda called *Petilau Namejão,* located just a short distance from the walls, that had many large buildings attached to it. They were preceded by numerous runners on swift horses who, weaving back and forth with their lances in readiness, were patrolling all seven battalions as well as the rest of the baggage in the vanguard.

When they reached the pagoda, precisely in the order I have described, they halted for nearly half an hour, after which, to the sound of their war instruments, which blasted continuously, they fell into position in a huge half-moon circle that surrounded the entire city. And when they were within slightly more than a musket-shot's distance from the walls, they rushed at them with such frightful screams that it seemed as if heaven and earth had come together as one. Raising more than two-thousand ladders they were carrying for that purpose, they stormed the walls all around in as many different places as they could, climbing up the ladders boldly without the slightest trace of fear, and even though they encountered some resistance initially from inside the wall, it was not enough to deter the enemy who—after they had smashed the four main gates of the city by means of battering rams fashioned of wooden beams with iron fittings—promptly killed the *chuem* along with a large number of mandarins and noblemen who had rushed in with him to defend the gates.

After that, without any further sign of resistance, the unfortunate city was entered in eight different places by these barbarians, who put all of its inhabitants to the sword, sparing nothing that breathed; with the result, as was affirmed later on, that the death toll came to well over sixty thousand, including in that number many women, very beautiful young maidens, and daughters of wealthy families. After slaughtering all these people and setting fire to the city with all its beautiful private dwellings and sumptuous temples and leveling everything else they found there, without leaving anything standing, they remained there for seven more days. At the end of that time they turned back to the city of Peking, where their king was then staying and from where he had ordered them to this attack, taking with them a huge quantity of gold and silver, but no other booty, because they had no way of transporting it; however, before they left they set fire to it all so that the Chinese would not derive any benefit from it.

Two days later they came to a castle called *Nixiamcó* where the *nauticor* of *Lançame*—the general in command of these barbarous people—set up his camp and dug in all around with the intention of assaulting it on the following day because it was said that when he had passed through there on his way to *Quansy* the Chinese had slain a hundred of his men in an ambush they had laid for him there, which rankled deeply in his breast.

118
Jorge Mendes Takes a Chance

After the army was encamped and fortified and all was quiet, which was sometime around the hour for the Ave Maria prayers, the general set out on a tour of inspection, making the rounds six or seven times in the company of only five horsemen. Once he had posted the sentries and taken every precaution necessary, he retired to his *dopo*[1]—the area where his tent was located—and secretly sent for the seventy captains in command of all the troops. There he informed them of his decision, which they fully endorsed. Laying their plans for attacking the castle the next day, they agreed that it should be stormed by scaling the walls and that the assault should be carried out with five-hundred ladders which were prepared that night.

No sooner had the first rays of morning broken through when, to the sound of their martial instruments—which they call *paliguindoens*[2]—the main body of their forces, divided into fourteen battalions, began to converge on the castle, marching at a none too hurried pace. When they came within an arrow-shot's distance, with the din of many war instruments and shouts filling the air, the soldiers made a rush for the walls to set up their ladders, and as those on the outside scrambled up trying to get in, they clashed with those on the inside trying to keep them out, and the battle that ensued was fought so fiercely that in less than two hours three thousand of the Tartar's men lay dead. At that point, the men who had been fighting retreated in a disorderly fashion, after which he withdrew to his camp, where he remained quietly all that day, devoting his time exclusively to overseeing the burying of the dead and the care of the wounded—and there were many of them too, most of whom died later from the wounds inflicted by the Chinese, whose arrows are dipped in a poison so virulent that no remedy was of any avail to them.

In view of the unfortunate outcome of the assault, for which they feared their king would blame them—especially since there was already some grumbling about it in the camp—the captains told the *nauticor* that, if he was planning to make a second assault, he had better place the matter before a general meeting of the council, in conformity with the orders he was carrying, because they did not dare to take such a heavy responsibility upon themselves.

This was agreeable to him, and accordingly, he sent at once for most of the noblemen and had them assemble in the field where the tents were pitched, and there, seated on a horse, he addressed them in a loud voice, explaining his reason for bringing them together. They argued about it for quite some time, advancing so many different opinions that they were unable to come to any decision on anything. But since the hour was late and there were many wounded in the camp who needed attention, it was agreed that they should all meet again the following day in the same place in order to resolve their differences, and on that note they all returned to their quarters.

One of those present at this meeting was the man who had been assigned to guard us, and since he was a rich and highly respected man, he returned in the company of three of the most important members of the council whom he had invited to supper. When they had finished eating they began to talk about the unhappy outcome of the previous day's fighting and about how badly Mitaquer—which was the name of the *nauticor*—was taking it, for he was extremely upset about it.

One of the men taking part in the conversation, who was nearest to the place where we were being held, happened to look our way, and he noticed that we understood what they were saying. He asked us who we were, what the name of our country was, and how we happened to have been captured by the Chinese, questions which we answered as truthfully as we dared. He became somewhat intrigued, and in the course of our conversation he asked us if we fought battles in our country and if our king was inclined to warfare. To this question, one of our men, named Jorge Mendes, replied that we did, and that we had all been reared as soldiers and trained for warfare from early childhood. The Tartar was so delighted with this answer that he turned to his two companions and said, "Come here and listen to what these prisoners have to say, for I warrant you that they seem to be men of reason."

The other two joined him at once and stood there listening to a few things we had to say about our unfortunate arrest. They kept on plying us with questions which we answered as best as we could until one of them, apparently more curious than the others, said to Jorge Mendes, who was doing the talking for us, "Considering all that you men claim to have seen of the world, if any one of you happens to know or has ever heard of some stratagem that Mitaquer, the *nauticor* of *Lançame,* could use to take this castle, I can assure you, instead of you being his captives, he will be yours."

Without thinking twice, and without fully realizing what he was saying or what he was getting into, Jorge Mendes replied, "If Lord Mitaquer, the *nauticor* of *Lançame,* would give us a signed statement in the name of the king, guaranteeing to get us safely by sea to the island of Hainan, from where we would be free to depart for our own country, then maybe I will make it possible for him to take this castle with very little effort."

One of the Tartars standing there, an elderly man with a grave air of authority about him who was said to be very close to Mitaquer, broke in excitedly, "Consider carefully what you are saying, for if you can do that, rest assured, you will immediately be granted anything you ask for and far more than you would even dream of asking for."

As for the rest of us, when we saw what Jorge Mendes was getting himself into by committing himself so rashly, and that the Tartars were seriously considering his promise, we all remonstrated with him, telling him not to get involved in something that would only make matters more difficult for us and place our lives in danger.

"Frankly, men," he retorted somewhat peevishly, "as far as my own life is concerned, it is worth so little to me now that if any of these barbarians wanted me to stake it in a game of *primeira,*[3] believe me, I would venture it immediately with any two queens in my hand on the first call. You know perfectly well that these people are not the sort who will free us for ransom like the Moors of Africa, and since that is the kind of situation we are in now, what difference does it make whether we die today or tomorrow? And remember what you saw them do in *Quansy.* That should give you some idea of what they are capable of doing to you."

The Tartars were a little surprised to see us arguing with each other and raising our voices, since that is something that is not done among them. They reprimanded us in a kindly way, pointing out that it was more proper of women to raise their voices sharply, since they are incapable of keeping their mouths shut or holding their tongues, than it was of men who gird swords and shoot arrows in the furious storm of war; but that if Jorge Mendes could put his words into effect, Mitaquer would grant him every-thing he might ask for. And with that they took their leave of each other and went off to their respective tents, since it was already close to eleven o'clock at night and the first watch had just ended and the captains of the guard were making their rounds of the camp to the sound of their instruments, as is their custom at such times.

119
A Portuguese Hero among the Tartars

One of the three Tartars—the one I said was a close friend of the field general Mitaquer—immediately reported the conversation with Jorge Mendes to him. He made it seem much more important than it actually was and told him that he ought to send for him and listen to what he had to say because he might like his sug-gestions well enough to make use of them and that, in case he did not, little would be lost thereby. Mitaquer approved of his advice and promptly sent word to the *tileymay,* the captain who had us in custody, instructing him to bring us there, which he lost no time doing.

When we got to Mitaquer's tent, with our chains and all, we found him sitting in council with all seventy of his field captains, though it must have been nearly two in the morning by then. He welcomed us in a pleasant manner though the expression on his face was grave and severe. Then after having us come closer to him, he had them remove part of the chains that still bound us by threes and asked us if we wanted to eat, to which we answered yes, because it was three days since we had been given anything. This was something he had not expected of the *tileymay,* and he directed a few words of reproof to him. Then he immediately had them bring us two large plat-ters of boiled rice and thin slices of raw salted duck which we hungrily fell upon in such a manner that it seems that everyone there enjoyed watching us eat for they said to Mitaquer, "Sir, even if you had not sent for them for any other reason than to ap-pease their hunger, so that they should not die of want, which is probably what would have happened, what you did was no small matter, for you gained thereby nine slaves who may very well serve you in *Lançame* or whom, perhaps, you could also sell for more than a thousand *taels.*"

They joked about this remark among themselves for quite a while. Then he had them bring us more rice as well as some beans cooked with eggplant, urging us to eat because it gave him great pleasure to watch us doing so, and we proceeded to provide him with that pleasure most willingly.

After we had eaten he discussed with Jorge Mendes, in accordance with the in-formation they had given him, how they would go about taking the castle, and he made him many promises of high honors, wealth, and influence with the king, or free-dom for all nine of us, plus many other advantages that left us more than well satis-ified, for he assured him that if, by means of his help, God granted him that victory which would enable him to avenge himself on his enemies as he desired and as called for by the blood of his slain men, then he would make of him, in everything he requested, a personage similar to himself or, at least, to any of his own children. This left Jorge Mendes somewhat embarrassed because he had never expected things to go that far. As for that matter, he replied, he had only told that man that perhaps he would tell them how to take the castle if he saw it with his own eyes, but that early in the morning he would go all around it and look it over carefully, and then he would tell him how it could be done, an answer which satisfied Mitaquer and the others very much, and for which they praised him highly.

Then they put us up in another tent next to his, where they maintained a close watch over us for the rest of the night, and God alone knows how terrified we were because we knew all too well that if things did not turn out the way they wanted them to, we would all be drawn and quartered, for they have no qualms about killing twenty or thirty people over something worth little or nothing, with no respect for either God or man.

The next morning, shortly after nine o'clock, Jorge Mendes and two more of us, whom they allowed to go with him, were taken to see the castle by a company of thirty cavalrymen. After he had surveyed the castle and its site and seen from which side and how it could be captured, they took him back to where Mitaquer, flushed with excitement, was waiting for him. He gave him a report on what he had seen and showed him how he could capture the castle without any effort and at very little risk, which made Mitaquer so happy he could hardly contain himself for joy.

Then he had all nine of us freed from the remaining irons and chains that bound us at our feet and necks, and he swore by the rice he ate that as soon as he arrived in Peking he would present us to the king and that he would fulfill every one of the promises he had made to us without fail; moreover, he would immediately give us a *firmaun* [1] to that effect, signed in letters of gold, so that we might rest easy about his keeping his word.

After ordering food for us he made us sit next to him and honored us in many other ways, in keeping with their customs, which we enjoyed to a certain extent though we were quite fearful of the disasters that fortune might bring if, in the end, because of our sins, the whole affair should not turn out as well as he expected.

Immediately afterwards, on that same day, a decision was reached in consultation with all the captains on the strategy to be followed in attacking the castle, as outlined by Jorge Mendes, who was acting as field marshal in complete command over everything. A huge quantity of branches was cut for filling in the moat, and over three-hundred ladders were built that were very sturdy and wide enough for three men to climb them side by side. In addition, enormous numbers of baskets and spades were gathered in and around the houses of the abandoned villages, and most of the men were kept busy all that day collecting these things which were needed for the following day when the assault was scheduled to take place. And all the while Jorge Mendes rode horseback beside Mitaquer, highly favored by him which, as all of us soon observed, instilled in him a new spirit of pride and vanity in sharp contrast to the way he had been acting a few days before. We were so amazed at the change we saw in him that it was not long before some of us men, motivated by that ill nature of ours that begrudges such changes, began to grumble about him, sniffing, turning up their noses, and saying, as if in jest, "What do you think of that dog? Because of him, either we get drawn and quartered tomorrow, or if things turn out well, as he imagines they will, he will acquire such great prestige with these barbarians that we will have to consider ourselves honored to wait upon him for the rest of our lives."

The next day, at two hours before dawn, to the beat of the *palosguindões,*[2] as they call their drums, and many other martial instruments they use, the whole camp fell into battle position, divided into twelve battalions drawn up in five very long lines with another row in the vanguard running around the entire field in a half-moon formation. At the spearheads went the sappers carrying all the paraphernalia of tree branches, ladders, baskets, and spades needed to drain the moat and fill it to ground level. With everyone marching in this order it was already daylight when they reached the castle, which by this time had increased its troop strength and was flying many silk standards and long streamers in the *charachina* style.

As soon as they arrived, those inside and outside opened fire with a salvo of many arrows and missiles consisting of spears, stones, pans of powdered lime, and some fire pots, which lasted for about half an hour. After this opening round the Tartars immediately drained the moat in six or seven places and, working with great haste, filled it with fagots and dirt, and then the ladders were swung all together against the wall, which was now quite low because of the fill.

Jorge Mendes was the first to climb up along with two of our men who, like *amucks,* were determined either to distinguish themselves in battle or die in the attempt. As the Lord willed, it turned out well for them, not only because they were the first to enter, but also because they raised the first standard, leaving Mitaquer and all the others near him so utterly amazed that they said to each other, "If the king of these people had laid siege to Peking as we did, the Chinese king would have lost his honor in less time than we made him lose it!"

Then all the Tartars at the foot of the ladders clambered up after these three Portuguese, which they also did with a great show of bravery, not only because they were led by their captain, but also because they are by nature endowed with almost as much courage as the Japanese, and in a very short time more than five-thousand men from our side went swarming over the wall. As they rushed forward, they swept the Chinese back, and the battle that ensued was so fierce and so ruthless that in little more than half an hour the whole business was done with and the castle taken, with the death of two-thousand Chinese and Moghul defenders who had been inside, and only 120 on the Tartar's side. After this the gates were immediately swung open with a great deal of celebrating and the joyful sounds of many musical instruments as a sign of victory.

Then Mitaquer, accompanied by all the captains and noblemen, made his entry, and they were even more astonished to see the large number of corpses strewn over the courtyard of the castle. Disregarding his own men who had also died there, he issued orders to have the Chinese flags burned and the castle bedecked with his, along with another ceremonious burst of music and merrymaking in their fashion. He also dispensed rewards to the wounded and conferred knighthood on some of his followers with the insignia of a golden armlet.

Once this was over, which must have been at about one o'clock in the afternoon, he dined with some friends and intimates inside the castle as a sign of even greater triumph.

To Jorge Mendes and the other two Portuguese he also presented gold arm bracelets and arranged to have them seated next to him. After he had finished eating, he and all the others that were with him went outside the gates, and he issued orders to have the entire wall torn down. After the wall had been razed they set fire to it while performing many ceremonies, by way of a victory celebration, accompanied by many shouts and sounds of music. Then he sprinkled blood all over it and had the heads of all the corpses laying in the courtyard cut off, after which he ordered his own dead buried and the wounded looked after.

When this was over he withdrew to his tent with a great display of pomp, consisting of spare horses, mace bearers, and guardsmen, with Jorge Mendes constantly at his side, while the eight of us and all the other captains and noblemen followed on foot. When he reached his tent, which was also decorated with festive symbols, he saw to it that Jorge Mendes received a thousand *taels* as a reward, whereas each of the rest of us received only a hundred, which made some of the men who thought they were his betters feel sad and discontented because it showed that they were less respected than Jorge Mendes, due to whose efforts the battle began and ended so successfully, and thanks to whom we were all set free and given our liberty with honor.

120
On to Peking with the Tartars

At daybreak the following morning, since there was nothing more to be done here, Mitaquer decided to continue on his way to the city of Peking, where the king was then staying, as I have said before. At eight o'clock, with the entire camp lined up in its customary marching order, he was on his way. He kept up a brisk pace to the rhythm of the drums, stopping to rest shortly before noon at a cool spot near the bank of a river where there were many orchards, the trees heavy with fruit. In some of them there were gracious houses which must have been used as country homes, but by then all was completely deserted with not a sign of people, personal goods, cattle, or anything else on which these barbarians could lay their hands.

When the heat of the day had subsided, which must have been shortly before three, he rose and continued on his way. Half an hour after dark he stopped for the night at a fair-sized town near the edge of the river called *Lautimey*, which we also found deserted, for the entire countryside had fled in fear of this cruel barbarian who would spare nothing or no one.

At daybreak of the following day, this army, as cruel and barbaric as its captain, set fire to the town and to many other very pleasant little villages along the river, which was the same fate that befell a field called *Bumxay*, a very flat, fully cultivated plain that extended for more than six leagues around, less than half of which had been harvested at the time, setting fire to it and consuming the uncut wheat, or the major portion of the crop, so thoroughly that everything in it was reduced to ashes.

Once this was finished—a deed quite worthy of the one responsible for it—the entire camp departed from there. It was composed of about sixty-five thousand cavalrymen, since the rest had been slain in the capture of *Quansy* as well as the castle of *Nixiancó*.[1] Continuing on his way, he came to a mountain range called *Pommitay*, where he encamped for the night.

The next morning he departed, quickening his pace a bit, for he still had seven leagues to go in order to reach Peking by daylight. At three o'clock in the afternoon, when he arrived at the bank of a river called *Palemxitau,* he was met by a Tartar captain with an escort of about a hundred cavalrymen who had already been there for two days, waiting for him. He was carrying a letter from the king, which he delivered to Mitaquer, who esteemed it highly and who accepted it from the bearer with a great deal of ceremonious courtesy.

From this riverbank to the king's camp, which was probably about two leagues, he marched, breaking the ranks he had previously maintained, not only to avoid the many crowds of people waiting for him along the roads, but also because of all those that the lords had in their retinue, who were there in such great numbers that they were spread out all over the fields, leaving no space for anything to get through.

Arriving in this order, or rather disorder, at the castle of *Lautir*—the first stronghold of nine outposts that the camp had—which was manned by a huge force, we found Prince *Guijay Parão* already there. He was the son of the king of Persia, who had been sent there by the king to escort Mitaquer the rest of the way.

The moment Mitaquer reached him at the entrance to the castle where he was waiting for him, he dismounted from his horse, withdrew the sword he wore at his side, and offered it to him on his knees, after first kissing the ground five times, which is the ceremonious etiquette observed among them. The prince welcomed him warmly and, beaming happily, congratulated him for the honor and fame he had won with the capture of *Quansy.* After this, he stepped back two or three paces, as part of another ceremony, and raising his voice, addressed him now in a more impersonal manner, in his official capacity as representative of the king.

"The one to whom I pay constant homage by kissing his stately kimono," he said, "the mighty one who rules in grandeur over all the scepters of the earth and the islands of the sea commands me, his slave, to say unto thee, may thy honorable coming into his presence be as pleasing as the sweet summer morn when bathing in the cold waters most gratifies our flesh; and to bid thee hasten without delay to hear his voice and to return by my side, mounted on this fine steed, richly caparisoned with jewels from his treasury, so that thou mayest be equal in honor to the greatest men of his court, and all who gaze upon thee, mounted in such splendid fashion, may know that thou art one of the valiant who has earned such a reward in the trial of battle."

Prostrated on the ground, with arms upraised, Mitaquer replied, "May my head be trampled on a hundred thousand times by the heel of his foot, emblazoning thereon a device that may be passed on to all my descendants and remain as a badge of honor for my eldest son."

And so saying, Mitaquer mounted the horse the prince had given him with all the splendid trappings of gold, which they said belonged to the king himself. Then he took his place on the right hand of the prince, and they began to ride with an elaborate display of pomp and majesty, accompanied by many riderless horses and an escort of macebearers, in the same style as ours, as well as a guard of six hundred halberdiers, most of them mounted, and fifteen carts loaded with silver drums which, together with many other kinds of barbaric and discordant instruments, produced such a din that it was impossible to hear one another. And all the rest of the way, which was nearly a league and a half, there were so many people on horseback that there was absolutely no way of getting through them.

Upon his arrival in this triumphant state at the first ramparts of the encampment, Mitaquer had one of his men show us to the *dopo* where his quarters were located. There we were comfortably lodged and very generously supplied with everything necessary. And he told us that on the following day, when he would have more time, he would present us to the king.

121
Summoned in Audience

It was on a Wednesday morning, fourteen days after we arrived in this camp, that Mitaquer, our general, summoned us to his tent. There we found him in the company of several noblemen, in front of whom he said to us, "Be ready, all of you, at this time tomorrow, so that I may fulfill the promise I made to you to let you gaze upon the countenance of the one who is our lord, a favor accorded you out of regard for me and which is being granted you along with your liberty, which I obtained for you today at the foot of his throne as a very high honor, one which I assure you, in all truth, that I prized as much, for love of you, as the capture of *Nixiancó*, the particulars of which you may relate to him there if you should be fortunate enough to be called upon to do so. And bear in mind that I will appreciate it very much if, back there, in that land at the end of the world from which you say you come, you will remember that I kept my word to you and that I was so scrupulous about it that perhaps I forfeited an opportunity to ask the king for something else that would have been of greater benefit to me, in order to show him that I would derive more pleasure from this one favor alone, which he immediately granted to me, showing me such high honors as he did so, that I confess that in this respect it is I who am much more indebted to you than you are to me."

Thereupon all nine of us prostrated ourselves on the ground and responded with all the courtesy befitting such good news, "My lord, so great are the favors that thou hast bestowed on us that we believe that endeavoring to thank thee with mere words, as is the custom among men of the world these days, would be an act of ingratitude rather than true and proper acknowledgment, which is why we think it best to maintain silence, locked deep in the souls that God implanted in us. And as long as we cannot use our tongues for this purpose, since they cannot form words capable of expressing so great an obligation as we have all incurred towards thee, we will use them to pray constantly with many tears and sighs, to the Lord who created heaven and earth—who, out of his infinite goodness and mercy, chose to take it upon himself to redeem for the poor that which their own feeble strength cannot attain—that he may give thee and thy children after thee, such a deep understanding of his truth that thou mayest deserve to share in his promises after a life of many long years on this earth."

Among the men in Mitaquer's company at the time was one already advanced in years by the name of *Bonquinadau,* who was one of the most important lords in the kingdom. He was the captain in charge of the foreign mercenaries there as well as the camp guard's yak train, and was the most highly respected among all those present.

Upon hearing what we said, he turned his gaze heavenward and exclaimed, "Oh, if one could only ask God to explain this mystery that is beyond our poor human understanding! Why was it his will that people so averse to the knowledge of our true faith should reply so spontaneously with a sweet flow of words to charm the ears? I assure you that I am persuaded—and I would stake my head on it—that these people know more about God and heaven in their sleep than we all do awake. From the way they talk it may be inferred that they have among them priests who know much more about what lies above the stars than our bonzes of the House of *Lechune*[1] do."

"What Your Magnificence says is quite right," the others replied, "and so much so, that all of us should accept it almost as an article of faith. Therefore, we think it would be best to detain them here and use them as teachers so that we can learn from them what they know about the world."

"I can assure you all that the king would never do such a thing under any circumstances," Mitaquer interjected, "not for all the wealth in China, for if he were to do so it would mean breaking his word and thereby losing his reputation as a great man, so there is no use talking about things that can never be, nor is it right that they should be."

"As for you," he said, turning to us, "you may go now, but make sure that you are ready at this time tomorrow when I send for you."

At this we all departed, in as happy a mood as one would expect us to be.

The following day, at the appointed hour, he sent nine well-groomed horses to our tent, which we mounted and rode back to his. He himself climbed into a *piambre*,[2] similar to the litters we use, borne by two horses with fine trappings, and set out completely surrounded by his sixty halberdiers, with six handsomely attired pages on white ponies while the nine of us followed closely behind them on our horses, and all the rest of the people on foot. He also had his orchestra of state with him which played from time to time, but there was no more ostentation or display than that. And in this manner he set off on his way to where the king was lodged in that large and sumptuous temple of *Nacapirau,* whom the Chinese call the "queen of heaven," as I mentioned previously in chapter 110.

When he reached the outer fortifications of the king's *dopo,* which was called *Xuxiapom,* he descended from the *piambre* along with all the others, in order to speak to the *nautarão.*[3] Performing some heathen ceremonies, he asked for permission to enter, which was granted to him. Climbing into his *piambre* again, Mitaquer continued on past the gates in the same ostentatious manner as before, with us following him on foot, until he reached a very long, low veranda, on which a large group of noblemen were sitting. There he descended from his *piambre* again and told us to wait for him there because he was going in to find out if the king was ready to be spoken to, and we all stayed there for nearly an hour.

In the meantime, some of the noblemen sitting on the veranda noticed that we were foreigners, people of a kind that they had never seen there before, and they called to us to come inside. They very cordially invited us to sit next to them, and we stayed with them for quite a while watching some acrobats tumble and sing, which they enjoyed very much and we very little, not only because we could not understand them, but also because we thought they were very dull and clumsy.

Nearly an hour later Mitaquer came out with four very handsome little boys wearing long hooded robes with green and white trimming and gold bangles on their feet. The moment they appeared everyone stood up, withdrew the swords they wore at their sides, laid them on the ground, and performed an unusual form of ritual courtesy that we found very impressive, as they recited these words three times: "Faly hincane midó patinau dacorem!" which means, "May the lord of our heads live for a hundred thousand years!"

In the meantime, as we lay prostrate, with our faces touching the ground, one of the boys spoke up in a clear and well-pitched tone of voice.

"Rejoice, ye men from the end of the world," he said, "for the hour you have longed for has come when you will be granted the freedom that Mitaquer, here present at my side, promised you at the castle of *Nixiancó*. Lift you heads from the ground, raise your arms to heaven, and give many thanks to the Lord Who made the stars shine in the quiet night of our repose, for He alone ordained, without any kind of worldly merit, that you should encounter in your exile someone who, in His name, would set you free."

To which all of us, the way we were, prostrate on the ground, replied as the interpreter taught us to, "May it be our good fortune to have his feet trample our heads!"

To which the boys responded in turn, "May the Lord grant you that rich reward!"

122
The Tartar King

From here, these four boys and Mitaquer, who was guiding us, passed through a corridor built on top of twenty-six bronze columns by which we reached a large hall constructed of wood, like a warehouse, that was crowded with noblemen, among them some foreigners—Moghuls, Persians, *Berdios, Calaminhās,*[1] and Burmese from the *Sornau,*[2] king of Siam. Passing straight on through this building where there was no delay for reasons of etiquette, we reached another called *Tigihipau,* which was also filled with another large crowd of people; however, these were all armed and standing in five lines that extended for the entire length of the building, and all of them were wearing gold-plated swords slung over their shoulders. Here they detained Mitaquer a while as they asked him some questions in a highly ceremonious manner and administered an oath to him on the maces the four boys were carrying, which he swore on his knees, kissing the floor three times. After this, they let him pass through another door up ahead, and we came out on a large square courtyard like the cloister of a convent, in which stood four rows of bronze statues in human form that looked like savages, with maces and crowns also made of bronze, but completely covered in gold. These idols or giants or whatever they were, stood twenty-seven handspans tall and six across at the chest. Their features were quite ugly and forbidding and their hair was coarse and unruly like a kaffir's.

When we asked the Tartars what those figures represented, they told us that they were the 360 gods[3] who created the days of the year in order that the people should pray to them daily to nurture the fruit that the earth produces on those days of the year; which gods the Tartar king had brought there from a great temple called

Angicamoy, which he captured in the city of *Xipatom,*[4] in the sanctuary of the tombs of the kings of China, for the purpose of displaying them in triumph when he returned to his country, so that it would be known throughout the world that, in spite of the king of China, he had captured his gods.

In the middle of the courtyard I am talking about, between an orange grove surrounded by a trellised fence of ivy, rosemary, and rosebushes, as well as many other kinds of shrubs and flowers that do not grow in Europe, there was a fantastic tent erected on twelve camphorwood balusters, each of which was inserted into four rods of silver twisted like a friar's waist cord, thicker than a man's arm. Inside this tent there was a flat dais, like an altar, covered on all sides with an extremely fine quality of gold leaf, with a canopylike hood above it that was studded with many silver stars, the sun, the moon, and a few clouds, some white and others the color of rainclouds, all fashioned of enamel so skillfully and looking so natural that one's eyes could almost be deceived into thinking they had water in them; and everything else, both in proportion and the execution of the painting, was very perfect. In the center of the dais there was a large silver statue lying on a bed of silver that was called *Abicau Nilancor,* meaning "god of the health of kings," which had also been taken from the temple of *Angicamoy* that I have mentioned before. Around this statue, in two rows, there were thirty-four idols the size of five- or six-year-old children, all on their knees, with both arms upraised to it, as though worshipping it. Right near the entrance to the tent there were four boys, perfect little gentlemen in their rich attire, who, in twosomes, were spreading incense all around it. At the sound of a bell that was struck at certain intervals, they would throw themselves face down on the ground, covering each other with incense and chanting aloud, "Hixapu alitau xucabim tamy tamy ora pani maguo," which means, "May our cry ascend unto thee like a sweet fragrance, so that thou mayest hear us."

Guarding this tent a short distance away and encircling it all around were sixty halberdiers arrayed in dressed green leather with rich and well-wrought helmets on their heads, all of which together presented quite a beautiful spectacle of great majesty.

Once beyond this courtyard we entered another section of the compound comprised of four beautiful and richly appointed buildings, in which there were many noblemen, both native and foreign. Continuing on from here, close on the heels of Mitaquer and the four boys, we came to the door of a large one-story audience hall, built like a church, where six macebearers were stationed. After engaging in some other kind of ceremony with Mitaquer, they showed us all inside, without allowing anyone else to enter.

The Tartar king was in this building, accompanied by many princes, lords, and captains, both native and foreign, among them the kings of *Pafuá, Mecuy,* and Kamp'engp'et,[5] Rajah *Benão,* the *Anchesacotay,* and some other kings, making fourteen altogether, who, dressed in rich and festive costumes, were all sitting about two or three paces from the foot of the dais, and alongside it, a little further back, were thirty-two very beautiful women, playing different instruments and making music that was delightful to hear.

The king himself was seated above on top of the *piambre,*[6] as they call the dais, surrounded by twelve children on their knees with their small gold maces, like scepters, resting on their shoulders. A little further back there was a very beautiful girl, very richly attired, who kept fanning him from time to time. She was the sister of

Mitaquer, our general, and a favorite of the king, and it was through her that he had achieved such a high position and such great renown throughout the armed forces.

The king must have been about forty years old, lean and tall, a handsome man of stern and serious aspect, with a short beard, a Turkish-style moustache, and slightly slanted eyes. He was dressed in a purple kimono, somewhat like a surplice, embroidered with pearls; and on his feet he wore a pair of green sandals, worked with gold thread and garnished likewise with pearls; and on his head, a helmet of purple satin, its border all studded with rubies and diamonds.

We stopped ten or twelve paces in front of him and made our kowtows, kissing the ground three times, along with some other ritual courtesy the interpreters had showed us. The king then ordered the music to stop.

"Ask these people from the end of the world," he directed Mitaquer, "if they have a king, what their country is called, and how far it is from there to where I am now in the land of Chinese."

Acting as spokesman for us, one of our party replied that our country was called Portugal and that we had a king who was very great, rich, and powerful, and that it would take nearly three years to journey from there to the city of Peking, an answer which left him gasping with amazement, as though he could not conceive of the world as being so large. Hitting his thigh smartly three times with a small rod he was holding, he turned his eyes upward to heaven, as though giving thanks to God, and said aloud for all to hear, "Julicavão julicavão minaydotorcu pismão himacor davulquitaroo xinapoco nifando hoperau vuxido vultanitirau companoo foragrem hupuchiday purpuponi hincau," which means, "O Creator, Creator of all things, who among us, humble creatures that we are, crawling like ants on the face of the earth, can comprehend the marvels wrought by thee in thy grandeur?

"Fuxiquidane, fuxiquidane!"—"Come closer, come closer!" he said, beckoning to us to come up to the bottom step of the dais where the fourteen kings were sitting, and asking us again, as though he could not believe his ears, "Pucau, pucau?"—meaning, "How far? How far?"

We replied as we did before, that it would take almost three years, to which he responded by asking why we did not come by land instead of exposing ourselves to the perils of the sea? Our answer was that the earth was too large and that there were kings of different nations who would not permit it.

"What is it that you are looking for in those other lands? Why do you expose yourself to such great hardships?"

After we had explained why, in the best and most felicitous terms that occurred to us at the moment, he remained silent for a while, then shook his head three or four times.

"The fact that these people journey so far from home to conquer territory," he remarked to an old man sitting nearby, "indicates clearly that there must be very little justice and a great deal of greed among them."

"It would certainly seem so," the old man, called Rajah *Benão,* replied, "for when men, by dint of industry and ingenuity, fly over all the waters in order to acquire possessions that God did not give them, it means either that there is such great poverty among them that it makes them completely forget their homeland, or that the vanity and blindness engendered in them by their greed are so great as to cause them to deny God and their fathers."

Some of the men there, as we inferred, found this remark amusing and exchanged a few witty and courtly pleasantries about it, which the king enjoyed very much.

Then the women began to play their instruments once more, and after a little while the king withdrew to another apartment, accompanied only by the women who were playing and the girl who was fanning him, without allowing any of the men to join him. Then one of the twelve boys who had been carrying the scepters approached Mitaquer with a message from his sister to the effect that the king had asked him not to leave, which he considered a very great honor since it had been delivered in front of all the kings and lords who were present in the hall. With that he stayed on there and sent us back to our tent, assuring us that he would take care to remind the Son of Heaven about us.

123
The Tartars Lift the Siege

Since our arrival at this camp forty-three days before, there were a few battles and skirmishes between the besiegers and the besieged, as well as two assaults with scaling ladders which the defenders inside the walls resisted bravely, determined not to give ground. When he saw that this campaign, on which he had spent so much of his resources, had turned out to be quite the opposite of what he had expected, the Tartar king put the matter before a general council, attended by all of the twenty-seven kings who had accompanied him, as well as many princes and lords and most of the captains. There it was agreed that he had no alternative but to lift the siege and depart before winter set in completely, and that any further delay would mean total disaster in view of the fact that winter was already upon them, the fields were already beginning to flood, both rivers were rising rapidly and running with such great force and pressure that they had already washed out most of the trenches and earthworks throughout the camp, and many of the men had already died of disease, which was spreading so widely that not a day passed without four to five thousand men dying, and the shortage of food was becoming so acute that the captains did not have enough to supply the daily rations, nor were the horses, which they were allotted for that purpose, sufficient to take care of even half of the rabble.

The king held all these reasons to be sound and decided to follow their advice, much against his will, because he understood that it was necessary to do so. He immediately had all the foot soldiers embark with all the munitions in the camp, and the campgrounds put to the torch, and he departed overland with only 300,000 cavalrymen and a train of twenty thousand yak.

A casualty count, made in accordance with the captains' rolls, showed that 450,000 men had died, most of them from sickness, and that 300,000 horses and 60,000 yak had been eaten in the two and a half months of famine they endured. This meant that out of the 1,800,000 men with whom he had started out from his kingdom to lay siege to the city of Peking, which had lasted for six and a half months, he was leaving with an army reduced by 750,000, with 450,000 having died of the pestilence, hunger, and war and 300,000 having passed over to the ranks of the Chinese, attracted by higher pay and the many other advantages they received in the form of honors and cash bonuses, which were showered on them continuously. And there is nothing surprising about this, for experience has taught us that this alone has much more power than anything else on earth to compel a man to do something.

Having departed from the city of Peking on a Monday, October 17,[1] with only 300,000 cavalrymen, as I said before, out of the 600,000 he had originally brought with him, that same day, close to nightfall, the Tartar king encamped beside a river called *Quaytragum,* and on the following day, an hour before sunrise, to the beat of many fifes and drums as well as many other kinds of martial instruments they ordinarily use, the camp fell into the order assigned to them, sending lookouts and scouts ahead and organizing the captains of the vanguard and *teuguauxés,* which is a different kind of armed unit they usually place in the rear behind the baggage train and the service troops, a tactic which affords greater protection to an army on the march than we normally have. Marching in this order he arrived close to vesper time at a city called *Guijampé,* which he found completely deserted. After he had rested for an hour and a half, which was the length of time he usually allowed, he broke camp and resumed the march at full speed and encamped for the night at the foot of a mountain range called *Liampeu,* from which he also departed at the start of the dawn watch.

He marched in this order for seventeen days, covering eight leagues per day, and at the end of that time he reached a fair city by the name of *Guauxitim,* with a population of ten to twelve thousand, where he was advised to replenish his store of provisions because by then he was running low. With that end in view, the city was attacked on all sides with scaling ladders, and since the resistance encountered from within was weak, in very little time it was entered and put to the sack, with such cruel havoc visited on the miserable inhabitants of the city that all of us nine companions went about in a state of shock. After everything had been consumed and razed to the ground, both by fire and sword, and the camp had been plentifully supplied with many good stocks of provisions, he departed, setting forth at an hour before daybreak.

The following day, passing within sight of the city of *Caixiló,* he refused to attack it since it was big and strong, not only because it was learned that there were fifty thousand men inside, including ten thousand Moghuls, Cochinese, and Chams, people who are more resolute and experienced in warfare than the Chinese. Passing on from here, he arrived at the walls of *Singrachirau,* which are the ones that I said before divide these two empires of China and Tartary. Since he did not encounter any resistance there, he went on to make camp on the other side in *Panquinor,* which was the first city within his territory, located three leagues from this *Singrachirau* wall, and on the following day he reached *Xipator,* where he demobilized his army.

Staying here only seven days, during which he took care of the business of satisfying obligations, paying wages, and executing justice upon some of the prisoners they had brought along, he embarked, unencumbered but none too happy, and went on his way to *Lançame,* taking only 120 oar-propelled *laulés* with him, capable of carrying ten to twelve thousand men, on which, six days later, he arrived in the city of *Lançame,* where, without wanting any reception or celebration to be arranged in his honor, he disembarked at two hours after dark.

12. (*Above left*) The sultan of Cambay.
From a series of sixteenth-century Flemish
tapestries depicting the victory of Dom
João de Castro over the Turks besieging
the fortress of Diu in 1546. One of the few
principled but impecunious viceroys of
Portuguese India (1545–48), he amazed
his contemporaries by celebrating the victory in Goa with an extravagant Roman-
style triumph (see figures 13 and 14).
Kunsthistorisches Museum, Vienna

13. (*Below left*) Dom João de Castro entering Goa in triumph. From a series of
sixteenth-century Flemish tapestries.
Kunsthistorisches Museum, Vienna

14. (*Above*) Triumphant procession of
Dom João de Castro with elephants drawing siege catapults, and with mummers
and dancers. From a series of sixteenth-
century Flemish tapestries. Kunsthistorisches Museum, Vienna

15. (*Top*) Land animals of the East. From J.-T. de Bry, *Historiarum Orientalis Indiae,* vol. 3 (Frankfurt, 1598). Courtesy of the Edward E. Ayer Collection, The Newberry Library, Chicago

16. (*Bottom*) Sea animals of the East. From J.-T. de Bry, *Historiarum Orientalis Indiae,* vol. 3 (Frankfurt, 1598). Courtesy of the Edward E. Ayer Collection, The Newberry Library, Chicago

124
At the Tartar Court

The king waited in the city of *Lançame* for all his troops, both the infantry and the cavalry, to catch up with him, which delayed him for twenty-six days.
As soon as he had them all gathered together he departed for another much larger and
more magnificent city called *Tuymicão,* where he was greeted in person by some
princes from neighboring states, as well as by the ambassadors of other kings and
lords from more remote areas, the most important of whom were six very great and
powerful rulers, namely the Shah Tahmasp,[1] king of the Persians; the *Siammon,*[2] emperor of the *Gueos,* whose lands border in the interior on the Burmese kingdom of
Toungoo; the *Calaminha,*[3] "lord of the indomitable force of the elephants of the
earth," as will be explained when I discuss him and his dominions further on; the
Sornau[4] of Ayuthia, known as the king of Siam, whose domain extends for seven hundred leagues from Tenasserim to Champa, bordering, along the coast, on the lands of
the Malays, *Berdios,* and Pathans,[5] and in the interior on P'itsanulok,[6] Kamp'engp'et,[7]
Chiang Mai, Laos, and the lands of the *Gueos.* Thus he has a total of seventeen kingdoms in his domain alone where he goes by the supreme title among all these heathens
of "lord of the white elephant." Yet another was the king of the Moghuls, whose kingdom and sovereignty lies in the interior between the Khorasan,[8] which is next to Persia, and the kingdom of Delhi and Chitor;[9] and an emperor called the *Carão* whose
domain, from what we learned here, borders within the mountains of *Goncalidau* at
above sixty degrees, on a people whom the natives here call Muscovy,[10] some of whom
we saw in this city. They are tall, red-headed men[11] who go dressed in breeches, cassocks, and hats, after the fashion of the Flemish and Germans whom we see here in
Portugal. The most honorable among them were wearing long, fur-lined robes, some
with fine marten skins, and were carrying long, broad swords. We detected some
Latin words in the language they spoke, and when they sneezed they would say
"Dominus, Dominus, Dominus," three times. But everything else about them, from
what we observed, looked more like idolatry and paganism than true religion, and
above all, they were much inclined to the unspeakable sin.[12]

The ambassador of the *Carão* prince was given a much better reception than all
the others. He brought with him a retinue of 120 bodyguards armed with arrows and
panouras[13] inlaid with gold and silver, all of them attired in dressed leather dyed purple and green; twelve mounted macebearers with silver staffs; twelve spare horses all
decked out in crimson trappings, trimmed all over with laces interwoven with gold
and silver threads; and twelve gigantic men of the most unaccustomed stature dressed
in huge tiger-skin garments, the way savages are usually depicted, each with a large
greyhound of his own, all of them restrained with silver chains and muzzles made of
silver, with many little bells also made of silver attached to them, like horses' head-
stalls. These muzzles, which they wore to keep them from biting, were locked into
some brass rings with their gilded guards like those of a bridle bit. And there were
twelve little boys mounted on white horses, riding in stiff-legged style on green velvet
saddles covered with silk netting, all of them dressed alike in short robes of purple

satin lined with marten skins, with matching breeches and hats, and very heavy gold chains strung across their chests like baldrics. They were all of equal size, and in my entire life I have never seen such handsome features and fine, well-proportioned bodies as theirs, for not one of them showed the slightest defect of nature with which one could find fault. And those were all the people he had with him in the mounted portion of his retinue.

He himself rode in a carriage with three wheels on each side that was completely trimmed with silver, and in it was a silver chair on which he was seated. Around the *pirange,*[14] as this carriage was called, were forty footmen, handsomely attired in leather doublets and checkered green and purple cloth hose with red silk lace and buckled shoes very much like the old-fashioned Portuguese style. They were carrying swords more than three fingers wide, with silver pommels, grips, and chapes, and hunting horns hanging crisscross from their shoulders on chains that were also made of silver, and on their heads they wore some sort of helmets like shepherd hoods, with many feathers on them, lavishly decorated with silver trimming. All in all, the pomp and splendor displayed by this ambassador, whose name was *Leixigau,* was of such grandeur and majesty that one could immediately tell that he represented a very rich and powerful prince.

In the apartments where he stayed, which we went to see one day in the company of Mitaquer, who paid him a visit on behalf of the king, among the things we saw—which we noted particularly because they were the most unusual and rarest of all in that country—were five apartments decorated with wall hangings of very richly wrought Arras tapestries, like the ones we use, from which it appears that the ones they use are manfacturered in the same place as the ones that come to Portugal. In each of these five apartments there was a brocade canopy hanging over a table with a silver bowl and pitcher on it of very costly workmanship, a crimson chair of state decorated with gold and purple fringes, and a matching foot cushion to go with it. In certain parts the floor was covered with large carpets, and there was a silver brazier containing an incense burner, also made of silver, that gave off an extremely pleasant fragrance.

Standing at the door of each one of these five apartments were two halberdiers who made no attempt to bar the entrance to any noble person wishing to see it. In another very large room that, somewhat like a veranda, ran across the entire street front and was also furnished like the other apartments, there was a table on a tall raised platform, set like ours with damask tablecloths and another matching cloth on top of it, both fringed in gold, as well as a napkin on a silver salver with a gold spoon and fork and two small saltcellars likewise of gold. About ten or twelve paces from this table there were two sideboards fully laden with very fine silver plate with a great quantity of pieces of every size and shape, fashioned by lathe. In the four corners of this apartment there were four large earthenware jars, each with a capacity of nearly a quart,[15] with their little warming pans attached by chains adorned in sections with pieces of gilded material of some sort as thick as a man's arm, and two enormous candlesticks with their fresh candles unlit because it was still daylight.

At the door of this gallery there were twelve halberdiers standing smartly at attention, dressed in a very shaggy homespun, with matching hoods on their heads and short silver-plated swords in their belts, who answered in such a rude and arrogant manner when spoken to that everyone was afraid of them.

This ambassador, in addition to the official visit he came to pay, as did the others, also came to treat of a marriage between the *Carão* emperor and one of the Tartar's sisters named *Meica Vidau,* meaning "splendid sapphire," a woman who was already thirty years of age but very attractive and very charitable to the poor, whom she helped for the love of God. We saw her frequently in the city at important festivals that these people are accustomed to observing on set days of the year, which they celebrate with many pastimes and a great deal of merrymaking, albeit in the heathen style, in keeping with all their customs.

But putting all this aside for the moment, which I only brought up in order to give an account of the ambassadors that we saw at this court, especially this last one who I thought was more noteworthy than all the others, I will return to the subject I was dealing with, not only with regard to our freedom, but also the route we took to the islands of the China Sea where this king or emperor of Tartary arranged for us to be sent, so that men in this part of Europe may be informed about a few things they may never have heard of before.

125
Jorge Mendes Stays Behind

In the days following his return to *Taymicão,* some of which were taken up by a number of extraordinary festivities on account of the wedding of his sister, Princess *Meyca*[1] *Vidau,* to the *Carão* emperor I mentioned above, the Tartar king, influenced by the opinions and advice of his captains, decided to renew the siege of Peking he had abandoned, for he was taking his recent failure almost as a personal affront. For that purpose, he immediately convoked a general assembly from all over the kingdom and, with the help of enormous bribes, formed a number of alliances and confederations with many neighboring kings and princes. Aware of the fact that this might hurt our chance of obtaining the freedom promised us, we poor unfortunate souls appealed to Mitaquer once more, since he had been charged with the responsibility of seeing to it, and reminded him of a few things that were of vital concern to us, as well as of the obligation he had to keep his word with us.

"You are absolutely right in what you are saying," he replied, "and I even more so by refusing to deny what in all fairness you are asking of me. Therefore, it would be advisable to remind the king about this matter, for otherwise your freedom may be lost through sheer neglect. Moreover, I think that the sooner you leave here the better off you will be, for we are headed for difficult times because of what the king is now planning to undertake again, thanks to the advice of certain people who have greater need of counselling on how to govern themselves than the earth has need of water to make the fruit sprout from its seed. But tomorrow, God willing, I shall remind him about you, about your poverty, and the fatherless young children you have mentioned several times, and perhaps that will move him to act compassionately on your behalf, as he usually does in cases like yours, out of the nobility and greatness of his heart." And with that he dismissed us.

The following morning he went to the *pontiveu*—the audience hall where the king usually receives petitioners—and when he reminded him about us, the king told him that as soon as he dispatched one of his ambassadors to the king of Cochinchina, he would send us along with him, since that was what he had decided to do.

Mitaquer returned with this answer to his house where we were already waiting for him and told us what the king had said and that he had sensed in him a desire to make us a charitable gift for the journey. Overjoyed by this good news we went back to our lodgings where we waited from one hour to the next for this promise to be fulfilled, until finally, after ten days, acting on the king's orders, Mitaquer took us to the palace. As we approached him with the elaborate and stately ceremonies they observe in addressing him, which were the same as those used when he was in Peking, as I related before, he looked at us with a kindly expression on his face and told Mitaquer to ask us if we wanted to enlist in his service, for he would be very happy to have us, and that he would bestow higher honors and favors on us than on any of the other foreign mercenaries who served him in war.

Speaking on our behalf, Mitaquer told the king what he had heard us say several times before—that we were married and had left our wives with many small children behind, and that we were so poor that all we had to our names was what we earned with the sweat of our brows, which was barely enough to support them. He listened with obvious compassion, which raised our hopes of receiving favorable treatment from him.

"I am happy to hear that they have as much to return to as they say," he said to Mitaquer, "for then it will give me greater pleasure to fulfill the promise you made to them in my name."

Then Mitaquer, and the rest of us too, raised our hands as a sign of gratitude, and kissed the ground three times.

"Hipausinafapó lagão companoo ducure viday hurpane marcutó valem," we said, meaning, "May your feet rest upon a thousand generations so that you may be the lord of all who inhabit the earth."

This brought a smile to his lips and he turned to one of the princes in his entourage and said, "These people speak as though they had been raised among us."

Then he looked straight at Jorge Mendes who was at the head of our group, next to Mitaquer, and said to him, "What about you? Do you want to go or stay?"

To which Jorge answered, like someone who had long since made up his mind, "Since I am not married, nor do I have any children to mourn my absence, I would rather serve Your Highness, if that is your pleasure, than be *chaem* of Peking for a thousand years."

The king smiled and turning to some lords who were closer to him began talking about some other matters related to their pastimes, without saying another word to us.

Thereupon, quite contented, we returned to our house, where we remained for three more days, making ready to leave. At the end of that time, at the request of Mitaquer, and through the intermediary of his sister who, as I said before, was the king's favorite, he saw to it that we were given two thousand *taels* for all eight of us, and he handed us over to the ambassador he was sending to the city of *Uzangué* in Cochinchina, who was traveling in the company of the ambassador of the Cochinese king, and five days later we embarked on his ship. Jorge Mendes gave us one thousand *cruzados,* for by then he was receiving an income of six thousand. He stayed with us all that day and finally bade us farewell, shedding many tears and between them lamenting now and then the exile in which he would be living.

126
Departure from Tartary

We departed from the city of *Tuymicão* on 9 May 1544,[1] and that same day, just before dark, we went to spend the night at a seminary called *Guatipamor*, located within a pagoda by the name of *Naypatim*, where both ambassadors were warmly received by the *tuyxivau*,[2] who was the rector of the school. At daybreak the next morning they proceeded on their way down the river, each in his own boat, besides two others loaded with their baggage.

Two hours after vespers we reached a small city called *Puxanguim*, which was well fortified, with towers and ramparts constructed the same way as ours and wide moats spanned by three very sturdy bridges of hewn stone. They had a large quantity of wooden artillery there, like ship pumps, except that the mechanism that struck the powder chambers was set in tracks lined with iron plates, and fired the same type of cannonballs as the falcon and the half-sphere.

When we asked the ambassadors who had invented that kind of projectile, they said some people called *Alimanis,* who came there from a country by the name of *Muscó* after crossing a large, deep saltwater lake[3] in nine rowing vessels, in the company of a widowed noblewoman from a place called *Guaytor,* who was said to have been banished by a king of Denmark; and that after she had found refuge there with her three sons, the great-grandfather of the present Tartar king had made them great lords and married them off to kinswomen of his, from whom the principal families of the empire were now descended.

The following morning we departed from this city and spent the night at another much nobler one by the name of *Linxau*. Continuing our journey down this river for five more days, on a Saturday morning we reached a large temple called *Singuafatur,* surrounded by a wall that must have measured more than a league around, within which there were 164 long, wide buildings like warehouses that were filled from floor to ceiling with human skulls.[4] There were so many of them, in such large quantities, that I am really afraid to mention it, not only because it is something that is hard to believe, but also because of the blindness of these wretched people and the error of their ways. Outside of each of these buildings were the bones belonging to the skulls inside, all stacked up so high that they towered more than three armspans over the rooftops in such a way that the structure itself remained buried under this mountain of bones and only the doorway in front was visible from the street.

On higher ground to the south, completely enclosed by nine rows of iron railings, there was a terraced area that could be reached by climbing along four passageways. Within this terrace, standing upright and leaning against a very strong, tall, stone turret, was a cast-iron monster that was the most hideous, frightful thing imaginable. Judging by the eye one would say that it probably measured over thirty armspans tall and six broad, but in spite of its outlandish size, all of its members were well proportioned, except for the head, which was a little too small for such a huge body. Also, in both hands this monster was holding a cannonball cast in the same metal, measuring thirty-six handspans around.

We asked the Tartar ambassador to tell us what this strange monstrosity signified.

"If you only knew in what great awe this powerful god is held, and how important it is for you to have him for a friend," he replied, "then you would willingly give all you have to him, rather than to your own children, and consider the money well invested. You should know that this great saint you see here before you is the treasurer in whose safekeeping all the bones of all the people ever born have been placed; and that on the last day of days, when all men are to be born anew, he will give back to each body the bones it left behind on earth, for he can recognize everybody and he knows exactly which one of those skeletons came from which body. As for anyone who was foolish enough not to honor him in this life, or not to give him alms, he will match him up with the most rotten skeleton he finds on the ground, making a permanent invalid of him, or he will give him one or two bones less, leaving him crippled, mutilated, or one-eyed. Therefore, heed my advice, make friends with him now, offer him something, and you will see how much benefit you will derive from it."

We also asked him what was the significance of the cannonball the monster was holding and he told us that it was meant to be thrown at the head of the Ravenous Serpent who lives in the Concave Depths of the House of Smoke, in case he should try to rob those bones.[5] After that we asked him what the monster was called and he told us that his name was *Pachinarau dubeculem pinanfaqué*, and that he had been born seventy-four thousand years before from the mating of a tortoise named *Mijanga* with a sea horse 130 armspans long named *Tibremvucão*, who had been king of the *Gigaos* of *Fanjus*.[6] And in addition to these monstrous lies and absurdities, he told us many others they believe in, with which the devil carries them all straight to hell, or as they call it, "the Concave Depths of the House of Smoke."

This ambassador also assured us that the alms alone that this monster received from his devotees brought in an annual income of well over 200,000 *taels*, to say nothing of the income derived from the properties of the chapel tombs for the nobles, which, by itself, accounted for a much larger share of income than the alms, and that he ordinarily had twelve thousand priests whom he fed and clothed, whose duty it was to pray for the dead to whom the bones belonged. These priests never left the compound without the permission of their *chisangués*[7] whom they obeyed, but outside the walls there were six hundred servants who procured everything necessary for them, and only once a year they were allowed to break their vows of chastity within the walls, but outside they could do so anytime and with whomever they felt like without committing a sin. They also had their retreats where they kept many women designated for that purpose who, with the permission of their *libangús,* or prioresses, do not deny themselves to the priests of this bestial, diabolical sect.

127
A Heathen Pope

From this pagoda we continued on our way, and the following day we reached a very stately city at the edge of the river, called *Quanginau*, where both ambassadors remained for three days, buying a few things they were short of by then and taking part in the festivities then going on to celebrate the arrival of the *talapicor*[1] of *Lechune*,[2] someone like a pope to them, who was passing through on his way to visit the king to console him for the unfortunate turn of events in China.

Among the honors and privileges this *talapicor* conferred on the local inhabitants in compensation for the large sums of money expended on the reception they had given him was that of declaring them all to be priests with the right to perform sacrificial ceremonies wherever they happened to be, and to receive a stipend for it like any other priest ordained by examination. And he also gave them the power to issue documents like bills of exchange,[3] to be used in heaven to repay those who had benefitted them here on earth. As for the ambassador from Cochinchina, since he was a foreigner, he conferred on him the right to legitimize, through new family relationships, anyone in his country who could pay for it, as well as the right to confer patents of nobility on the courtiers, just as the king did. The poor ambassador considered himself so highly honored that it went to his head, and he stepped completely out of character—for he was stingy by nature—and gave all the money he had with him to the priests, and still not content with that, he borrowed the two thousand *taels* we got from the king, which he later repaid with 15 percent interest.

When they were all set to leave, these ambassadors went to visit the *talapicor* at a pagoda where he was staying, for in view of the fact that he was an exalted personage and enjoyed the reputation of a saint, he could not be expected to stay with any man, other than the king alone. However, he told them to put off their departure because he was to preach at a convent dedicated to *Pontimaqueu* that day, and since it was an invitation that flattered them highly, they set out at once for the pagoda where the sermon was to be delivered. So many people had already crowded into it that it became necessary to move the *agrém*,[4] as they call the pulpit, to a huge courtyard, which in less than an hour was encircled by stands covered with silk awnings, reserved for the wives and daughters of the nobility who were sitting there in all their costly finery, while in another section, the *vanguenarau*,[5] or the prioress, sat with the more than three hundred *menigrepas*[6] of the pagoda.

The *talapicor* then climbed up to the *agrém*, and after making all the many gestures and outward signs of sanctity, looking heavenward from time to time with upraised hands, launched into his sermon with this introduction: "Faxitinau hinagor datirem, voremidané datur natigão filau impacur, coilousaa patigão," etc., which means, "Just as by nature water washes all things clean, and the sun gives warmth to all creatures, so it is in the divine nature of God to do good to all. From this it follows that it is the duty of each and every one of us to imitate the ways of the Lord who created and sustaineth us, by doing unto those who are lacking in wordly goods, what we would have them do unto us, for by so doing we please him far more than in anything else; for as the good father rejoices when he sees his children shown favor, so our Lord, who is the true Father of us all, rejoices to see us sharing with each other in love and charity. From which it follows as the night the day, that the miserly man who closes his hand to those who are forced by necessity to beg for what they lack and need and turns his face aside without helping them, will find that God in his righteous judgement will turn his face aside from him and condemn him to the dark pool of the night where he will be forever croaking like a frog and tormented by his ravenous greed. Therefore, I admonish you and command you all, since you have ears, to hear me and do what the Law of God obliges you to do, which is to give of that whereof you have too much to the poor who lack what they need to sustain themselves, so that the Lord will not fail you when you breathe your last. And let your charity be so widely seen and distributed that even the little birds in flight will be uplifted by this generosity of yours which the Lord lays upon you as a commandment, so that the poor, for lack of what you have to spare, will not be forced to steal, a sin of which you will be just as guilty as if you had killed a child in the cradle. And furthermore, I charge you all to remember what is inscribed in the books of our true Law, about the good that you must do unto the priests who pray for you, so that they will not perish for lack of what you fail to give them, a sin which will be as great in the eyes of God, as if you were to kill a white calf feeding at its mother's teat, with whose death die a thousand souls that are entombed within it, as in a golden castle, waiting for the promised day when they will be turned into white pearls dancing in heaven like specks of dust in the sun's rays."

And so with these absurd notions and many others equally as absurd, he worked himself up to such a fever pitch of excitement and uttered so much nonsense that we eight Portuguese were amazed to see the devotion of those people and how eagerly they responded with arms upraised, repeating from time to time the word "Taximida!" meaning, "Thus we believe!"

One of the men in our group, a fellow by the name of Vicente Morosa,[7] began to join in with the audience, and every time he heard them say "Taximida!" he would exclaim, rhyming the Portuguese words with theirs, "Tal seja tua vida!"[8] And he would do this with such funny gestures, with such a sober look on his face, and with not the slightest trace of a smile, that not a single person present in the audience could keep from laughing, yet his own expression never changed, for he remained always very sure of himself, weeping crocodile tears of devotion and keeping his eyes fixed on the *talapicor,* who could not help laughing either when he looked at him, so that at the end of the sermon both the preacher and the audience broke out laughing with such obvious enjoyment that even the *vanganarau* was unable to restore the discipline she had maintained before over all the *menigrepas,* for everyone was convinced that the Portuguese fellow had been acting in earnest, taking part in the services with complete devotion. But to tell the truth, if they had known that he was actually making fun of them or even showing contempt for them, perhaps he would have been severely punished for it.

After this, the *talapicor* returned to the pagoda where he was staying, accompanied by the ambassadors and all the honorable people there, and on the way he kept on talking about the Portuguese fellow and praising him for his devotion.

"Even these bestial people," he exclaimed, "who have no knowledge of our true faith, cannot help feeling that I was talking about something holy."[9]

To which they all replied that there was no doubt about it.

128
En Route to Cochinchina

Early the next day we left *Quanginau* and proceeded on our way downstream for four days, passing many good-sized towns and villages along the way. At the end of those four days we reached a city called *Lechune,* which is the seat of the false religion of these heathens, as Rome is among us.[1] They have a very sumptuous temple there with many impressive buildings attached to it where twenty-seven kings or emperors of the Tartar monarchy lie buried in elaborate chapel tombs built at tremendous cost, as could be seen from both the richly carved ornamentation and the silver that covered them, in which they had large numbers of idols of different shapes and sizes that were also made of silver.

To the north, a short distance away from this temple, there was a wall remarkable both for its size and strength, within which 280 monasteries had been raised to their various idols, in equal numbers for men and women, and in them, they assured us, there were forty-two thousand priests and *menigrepos,*[2] to say nothing of the large numbers of people who provided them with services from the outside. Standing among these 280 buildings were an infinite number of bronze columns, each of them topped by an idol made of the same bronze covered in gold, though some of these idols were made of silver. These are the statues of those whom they regard as saints in their sects[3] and about whom they tell monstrous lies. They make these statues, at a greater or lesser cost, with more or less gold, depending on how virtuous a life each one led, to the end that the living who see them honored that way will be inspired and encouraged to emulate them so that they will do as much for them when they die.

In one of these monasteries I am talking about, dedicated to the worship of *Quiay Frigau,* "god of the motes of the sun," the widowed sister of the king lived in a richly furnished apartment. She had been married to Rajah *Benão,*[4] prince of *Pafuá,* and on his death she had entered the monastery with six thousand women she had brought with her, where, as the highest honor of all, she had assumed the title of "lowly broom of the House of God." The ambassadors went to visit this woman and kissed her feet reverently, as though she were a saint. She welcomed them affably, and in a very discreet manner she questioned them in great detail about some things that they in turn explained to her.

Then glancing our way, for we had remained a little further back, and perceiving that we were foreigners, such as had never been seen there before, she asked them what nationality we were. They told her we came from a country at the end of the world that no one had ever heard of, to which she reacted with open astonishment. Then she ordered us to come closer to her and asked us all sorts of questions which we answered as was proper, to her obvious enjoyment and that of all the other women in her company too. Amazed by the answers she received from one of our men, the queen remarked, "They speak like they have been raised among people who have seen more of the world then we have."

After detaining us a little while longer with a few questions she dismissed us in a kindly manner and saw to it that we received a hundred *taels* as an act of charity.

Having bade her farewell, the ambassadors proceeded on their course down the river, and at the end of five days we arrived at a large city called *Rendacalem* situated at the furthermost point of the kingdom of Tartary. From there on the seigniory of *Xinaleygrau* begins, through which we traveled for four more days until we reached a village called *Voulem*, where both ambassadors were welcomed by the feudal lord, who provided them with everything they needed for their voyage, including river pilots to guide them through those waters.

From here they proceeded on their course for seven more days without seeing anything worth mentioning in all that time, and at the end of those seven days we reached the mouth of an estuary called *Quantanqur*, which the pilots entered not only in order to shorten the distance we had to cover but also to avoid the possibility of encountering a well-known pirate who had plundered the greater part of that country. Running along this estuary in an easterly direction, then east-northeast, and at times east-southeast, depending upon the falls over which the water escaped, we came out on the lake of *Singapamor*,[5] called *Cunebeté*[6] by the local people, which, according to the information they gave us, measured thirty-six leagues in circuit. There we saw such an enormous variety of birds[7] of all different species, that I would not dare attempt to describe it.

In this lake of *Singapamor*, which is carved into the heart of the country by some admirable work of nature, four deep, wide rivers have their source;[8] one by the name of *Ventrau*,[9] which flows straight west across all the land of the *Sornau* of Siam and empties into the sea at the bar of *Chiamtabuu*[10] at twenty-six degrees latitude. Another, called *Jangumá*,[11] after flowing south and southeast across a great part of the land, such as the kingdom of Chiang Mai, the Laotians, the *Guéos*, and part of the *Dambambuu*, finds its outlet to the sea at the bar of Martaban,[12] in the kingdom of Pegu,[13] and the distance between them, going by the degrees of their latitudes, is over seven hundred leagues. The third river, called *Pumfileu*,[14] cuts across all of Kamp'engp'et and Suk'ot'ai[15] in the same way and, after turning above the second river, flows across the whole empire of *Monginoco*, as well as a small section of *Meleytay*[16] and *Sovady*,[17] emptying into the sea at the bar of *Cosmim*,[18] near Arakan.[19] As for the fourth river, which is similar to these three, the ambassadors were unable to tell us anything, but it is presumed, in the opinion of most people, to be the Ganges of Chittagong[20] in the kingdom of Bengal. So that these four rivers are believed to be the greatest of those known so far in all that has been discovered in those parts of the Orient; and from this lake onward the land is less populated than all the other areas through which we passed.

Proceeding on our way from here for seven more days, we reached a town by the name of *Caleypute*, where the inhabitants would not allow us to go ashore, and when the ambassadors tried to insist on disembarking, they were met by such a withering barrage of stones and missiles of *saligues*[21] and charred stakes that, when we finally saw ourselves free of them, we realized that God had shown us great mercy.

After departing from there, much bothered and bruised and, worst of all, sorely lacking in needed supplies, on the advice of the pilots we navigated along another river much wider than the estuary we had just left, for a period of nine days. At the end of that time, as God willed, we reached a pleasant village called *Tarem*, whose lord was a subject of the Cochinese and welcomed their ambassador in an extremely friendly manner and provided him with a very abundant supply of everything necessary.

We took off from here the next day near sundown and proceeded on our way down the river for another seven days until we reached a fine city called *Xolor,* where they manufacture all the damascened porcelain that goes to China. The ambassadors stayed here for five days, using the time to have the four boats careened, for by then they were very sluggish and full of worms. After seeing to it that everything necessary would be taken care of, the ambassadors went off to look at some mines in the area belonging to the Cochinese king, which produced large quantities of silver that was transported from here in carts to a smeltery that employed over a thousand men, to say nothing of those who worked in the mines, whose numbers were much greater. When the ambassadors inquired there how much silver those mines produced annually, they were told it amounted to six thousand piculs, which equals eight thousand quintals in our money.

129
Death on the Suicide Pyre

From the city of *Xolor* we proceeded on our way down this great river for five more days, and during all that time we passed in constant view of many very fine villages that were located along the shore, for here in this latitude the land is much better, more populous, rich, and productive, the rivers heavily trafficked with a multitude of rowing vessels, the fields cultivated with wheat, rice, vegetables of every sort, and great expanses of sugarcane which grows here all over in great abundance. The nobles go dressed in silk and ride about on richly caparisoned horses, and the women are very fair complexioned and beautiful.

After an extremely difficult and perilous passage down these two estuaries and the *Ventinau*[1] River I mentioned above, owing to the many pirates infesting those waters, we reached the city of *Manaquileu,* situated at the foot of the *Comhay*[2] mountains that separate the Chinese and Cochinese kingdoms, where the ambassadors were welcomed by the local captain. From here, they departed early the next morning and stopped for the night at a city called *Tinamquaxy,* where they both went to visit an aunt of the king, who was the feudal lady of the town. She welcomed them warmly and gave them the news that her nephew the king was already back from the war of the *Tinocouhós,*[3] highly pleased with the successful outcome of the campaign. She informed them of some other particulars that they were very happy to hear, especially when she told them that the king, after dismissing all the men he had brought with him, had left unattended for *Fanaugrem,* where he had been staying for almost a month now, occupied with fishing and hunting, and planning to spend the winter months in *Huzamgué,*[4] which is the capital of the Cochinese empire.

After discussing between them the news they had just heard, they decided to send all four boats on to *Huzamgué,* while the two of them, with just a small party of their men, would travel overland to *Tanaugrem,*[5] where they had been informed the king was staying. They lost no time putting this plan into effect, with the approval of the Princess too, who provided the necessary horses for them and their party, as well as a train of eight yak to carry their baggage. Three days later they departed, and after covering a distance of eighty-six leagues that took them thirteen days under the most arduous conditions, owing to the rugged terrain and the huge mountains they had to cross, they finally reached a large resthouse called *Taraudachit* at the edge of a river, where they spent that night, departing at the crack of dawn for a village called *Lindau Panó*, where they were welcomed by the local captain, a relative of the Cochinese ambassador, who had arrived there only five days before from *Fanaugrem*, where the king was staying, still fifteen leagues away.

After giving this ambassador, his relative, some of the news about the court and the events of the war, he also informed him that a son-in-law of his had died and that, as a result, his daughter, who was the wife of the deceased, had immediately thrown herself upon the funeral pyre,[6] which was a great consolation for all her kinsmen, for by that noble deed she had given proof of who she was and had always been. And the ambassador himself, father of the dead woman, was also much pleased about it and expressed his satisfaction openly.

"O daughter of mine," he exclaimed, "now that I know that thou art a saint and that thou art serving thy husband in heaven, I promise thee and swear to thee that because of thy noble deed, whereby thou hast given proof of the royal blood from which thou art descended, I shall, in memory of thy goodness, build thee a house of so honorable a name that thou wilt be desirous of coming down from where thou art to take pleasure therein, like those souls who we believe have done the same in days of yore."

After pronouncing these words he fell face down on the ground and remained that way until the following day when he was visited by all the local priests who consoled him at great length and assured him that his daughter was a saint and that, as such, he was entitled to erect a silver statue[7] to her, since he had the permission of all of them to do so. He regarded this as a very high honor for which he thanked them profusely and distributed money to them as well as to all the poor in the region.

We remained in this town for nine days in observance of the funeral rites for the deceased woman, departing immediately thereafter, and the following day we reached an abbey called *Litiparu*, meaning "succor of the poor," where both ambassadors stayed for three days waiting to hear from the king, whom they had already informed of their arrival. The king sent word for them to come on to a town called *Agimpur*, which was three leagues away from there and only one from *Fanaugrem*, where he would send for both of them when the time was suitable.

130
The Tartar Ambassador at the Court of Cochin

Having been informed by his ambassador of the presence of another from the court of Tartary, early the next day the king sent an honor guard to escort him from *Agimpur*, the village where he was staying. It was headed by a brother-in-law of his, a very rich and valiant prince by the name of *Passilau Vacão*, who was a brother of the queen, his wife. He arrived in a silver-covered coach with three wheels on each side, drawn by four white horses, all of them adorned with gold trappings. The *fiambra*,[1] as they call this type of coach, had sixty footmen disposed in two ranks all around it. They were dressed in green leather and were all wearing swords in gold-plated scabbards that hung from their shoulders, and together with them were twelve macebearers.

In the same order, marching at the outer edge of these ranks, were many other men with halberds adorned in silver, and kimonos and trousers made of green and brown silk, with their swords hanging from baldrics closely resembling ours. They were all stouthearted men whose stern and haughty looks, combined with their swaggering gestures, which were entirely in keeping with their natural arrogance, could not help but inspire fear in others. About thirty paces ahead of these guards there went eighty elephants in very good order, with silver-trimmed seats and castles on their backs, their *panouras*,[2] or battle swords, in their tusks[3] and good-sized bells around their necks. In front of these elephants, which were said to belong to the king's guard, rode another large group of men on horseback with fine dress and trappings. And in the vanguard of this display there were twelve carts carrying silver timbals, with their silken saddlecloths.[4]

When the prince, surrounded by all this pomp and majesty, reached the Tartar ambassador, who was already waiting for him, there was an exchange of all the compliments and courtesies that are customary among them, which lasted for a quarter of an hour. Following this, the prince gave the ambassador the *fiambra* in which he had arrived and mounted a horse, placing himself on his right and the king's ambassador on his left. Marching in the same order in which he had come, heralding their approach with many different kinds of musical instruments, they arrived at the outer courtyard of the king's apartments, where the *broquem*,[5] captain of the palace guard, was standing, waiting for him in the company of many noblemen as well as a corps of mounted guards drawn up in two rows that extended for the entire length of the courtyard. After another exchange of ceremonious greetings, they walked up to the main entrance of the palace, where they found an old man more than eighty years of age by the name of *Vuemmiserau,* said to be the king's uncle, who was waiting for them in the company of many lords and noblemen. In another ceremony, both ambassadors kissed the sword at his side, which he acknowledged as a supreme honor, after they had both prostrated themselves on the ground before him, by placing his hands on their heads. Allowing the Tartar to walk nearly side by side with him, he led him down a very long hall until they reached a door at the far end. He knocked three times, and a voice answered from within asking him what he wanted.

"In keeping with an ancient custom of true friendship," he replied in measured tones, "an ambassador from the great *Xinarau* of Tartary has arrived to seek an audience with the *Prechau Guimião*,[6] whom we all hold to be lord of our heads."

With this reply the doors were opened wide, and they entered with this prince leading the Tartar ambassador by the hand while the *broquem* and the king's ambassador followed a short distance behind, and after them the other members of the party walking in orderly formation, three by three. After passing through this hall, which was empty except for some guards kneeling with their halberds in their hands, we entered another much larger and more elegant hall called *Naguantiley,* where we saw sixty-four bronze and nineteen silver statues, all with iron chains around their necks.

Amazed by the sight, we asked what it meant, and one of the *orepos*[7] there, a priest, explained that the statues we were so surprised to see were the eighty-three gods of the *Timocouhós* which the king had taken, after beating them in battle, from the great temple where they were kept, for the greatest honor, and the one that the king prized most, was to triumph over the gods[8] of his enemies, whom he held captive, in spite of their efforts.

When we asked why they had those chains on them he said it was so that when he entered the city of *Huzangué,* where he was preparing to go, he would have them dragged by the chains that bound them, in a triumphal march arranged to celebrate the victory he had achieved over them.

Passing through this hall of the idols, we entered another where we saw a large number of very beautiful women seated along the walls, some working on embroidery, and others playing musical instruments and singing, which was indeed a delight to behold. And in another hall farther on, where six women macebearers stood guarding the door, there was the king, accompanied by some elderly men, though few in number, while the rest of the people present in the hall consisted of young women playing their instruments as they accompanied a chorus of little girls. The king was sitting on a raised platform like an altar, eight steps high, beneath a canopy supported on balusters, and both canopy and balusters were completely covered with gold leaf.

Kneeling beside him were six little boys with scepters in their hands, and a little farther back was an elderly woman with a heavy string of beads on her neck who was fanning him from time to time. The king must have been about thirty-five years of age, a handsome man with big eyes, a fair, well-trimmed beard, a stern face, and severe mien, who gave one the impression of being a great prince, one of grandeur not only in state but in everything else he represented.

As the ambassadors entered this hall they both prostrated themselves on the floor three times, and after the third time, his own ambassador remained face down in the middle of the hall while the Tartar went forward until he reached the dais where the king was sitting. Climbing the first step, he addressed him in a voice that all could hear.

"*O Otinão cor Valirate prechau com panó* of the forces of the earth!" he exclaimed. "May the sweet breath of the almighty God who created all things cause the state of thy grandeur to prosper, so that for a thousand years to come the sandals on thy feet will be like strands of hair on the heads of all the monarchs of the earth, making thee like to the flesh and blood of the great prince of the Silver Mountains by whose command I have come to visit thee in his name, as thou canst see from this *mutra*[9] to which his royal seal is affixed."

Looking at him, his face beaming with pleasure, the king replied, "As is his desire and mine, may the sun with the gentle warmth of its bright rays smile upon this true love until the ocean has ceased to roar, so that the Lord may be praised forever in its lasting peace."

To which all the lords present in the hall responded with one voice, "May the One who created the day and night so grant it!"

Then the women resumed their playing, and the king said nothing more until he was about to withdraw.

"I shall read the letter of my brother, the *Xinarau,*" he said to him, "and I shall reply according to thy desire, so that thou mayest depart happily from before me."

Without a word in reply the ambassador again prostrated himself at the foot of the dais, touching his head three times to the step on which he was sitting. Then the *broquem* took him by the hand and led him to his house, where he stayed for the entire thirteen days he spent there, up until the king's departure for *Huzangué.*

131
The Cochinese King Returns in Triumph

Thirteen days had passed since we arrived in *Fanaugrem,* and by then the king was already on his way to *Huzangué.* During that time the Tartar ambassador had only seen him twice, and on one of those occasions he had spoken to him about us, in accordance with one of the articles of the instructions he was carrying. To which they say he replied, his face wreathed in smiles, "So it will be done. And thou, for thy part, do not forget to remind me when thou seest that the winds call for it, so that they do not miss the monsoon they need to carry them to their destination."

This made the ambassador very happy, and when he came to tell us about it, in exchange for such good news he asked us to write down some of our God's prayers for him in a book he was carrying, since he wanted very much to become a slave of His because of the many wonderful things he had heard us say about Him. We were extremely pleased by this news, and we all thanked him effusively, for this was the only thing that we really wanted and that we desired far more than the many personal advantages the Tartar king had offered us a few times to remain in his service.

Departing from this village of *Fanaugrem* one Saturday morning, the king made his way by stages of only six leagues a day because of the large number of people in his party. On the first day he dined in a small town called *Benau,* where he stayed until very late in the afternoon, going on from there to spend the night at an abbey called *Pomgatur.* Early the following day he departed for *Mecuy,* and from there, reducing his party to only three thousand cavalrymen, he continued his journey for nine more days, passing through what appeared to be, judging from the exterior, many very noble towns, in all of which he refused to allow them to make any receptions or parties for him, with the explanation that public festivities of that nature provided an excuse for tyrannical officials to rob the poor, which was a great disservice to God. Traveling in this manner, he reached the city of *Lingator,* located on the banks of a freshwater river that was very wide and deep and heavily trafficked by oared craft, where, feeling indisposed, he stayed for five days to rest up from the strain of the journey. From here he departed in the predawn hours with only thirty men on horseback, refusing to allow any more than that to accompany him. That way, avoiding contact with people, he began to relax by spending a good deal of the time on hunting with his hawks, a sport of which they said he had always been fond. And with pastimes of this sort, as well as with hunts for boar and other wild game which the people organized for him, he covered the greater part of the journey, sleeping most nights, for love of the rugged life, in the thickest part of the woods in tents he carried for that purpose.

When he reached the *Baguetor,* one of the three rivers I referred to before that have their source in the lake of *Famstir*[1] in the kingdom of Tartary, he crossed it in oar-propelled *laulés* and *jangás* which they had ready for him there. He proceeded in them down the river until he came to a large town called *Natibasoy* where, close to nightfall, he disembarked, without any fuss or fanfare, and from here he completed the journey overland.

Thirteen days later he reached *Huzamgué,* where he was given a grand reception in which he carried before him in triumph all the spoils he had won in the war, the main part, and the part of which he boasted the most, being twelve wagons laden with the idols I mentioned above. They were all different, as is typical of those they have in their pagodas, and consisted of sixty-four gigantic bronze and nineteen silver statues of the same size and shape, for as I have already pointed out a few times, what these people prize most is to parade in triumph with these idols, boasting abroad that despite all their enemies' efforts they had captured their gods.

Surrounding these twelve wagons were a large number of priests, bound by threes with iron chains, and they were all weeping. A short distance behind these priests came forty carts, each drawn by a pair of yak and piled high with an endless assortment of weapons and many banners dragging in the dust. Behind them came another twenty carts similar to these, laden with huge iron-bound chests said to contain the treasure of the *Timocouhos.* In the same manner they displayed all the other things by which they usually set great store in their victory processions, such as two hundred elephants armed with castles and war *panouras,* which are the swords that are fastened to their tusks when they go into battle, and a large number of horses laden with sacks full of skulls and bones of the enemy dead. So that when he made this triumphal entry into the city, he showed the people everything he had won by the lance from his enemies in the battle he had waged with them.

After nearly a month in this city, during which we saw many noteworthy games and festivals and many other kinds of amusements that the nobles and the commoners were constantly arranging with splendid banquets every day, the Tartar ambassador who had brought us there reminded the king about our departure, to which he readily agreed. He immediately gave orders for them to provide us with passage to the China coast, where we thought we would find ships of ours on which we could get to Malacca and from there to India. His orders were promptly carried out and we made all the necessary preparations for our departure.

132
The Discovery of Japan

Flushed with excitement and joy, as one can imagine, at finding ourselves free at last after all the hardship and misfortune we had endured, we departed from this city of *Huzamgué* on the twelfth of January.[1] We made our way along a large sweet-water river more than a league wide, turning the prow in different directions owing to the bends in the river; and throughout the seven days that we ran along it we passed in constant view of many very magnificent cities both large and small which, judging by the outward splendor, gave one the impression that the people must be very rich because of the sumptuous buildings we saw there, both the private homes and the temples with their gilded spires, as well as the multitude of oared craft that were to be seen there, with all kinds of merchandise and food stuffs in great abundance.

When we reached a magnificent city called *Quangeparuu,*[2] with a population of about fifteen to twenty thousand, the *naudelum*—the man who was transporting us in obedience to the king's orders—stopped there for twelve days to trade with the local merchants in exchange for silver and pearls, turning over a profit, as he confessed, of fourteen times his cost, though if he had been carrying salt, he would not have been satisfied with less than thirty times as much. In this city they assured us that, just from the silver mines alone, the king received an annual income of twenty-five hundred piculs, which equals four thousand quintals, and that apart from this he receives a great deal of additional revenue from many other sources. The only defenses this city has to protect itself are just a weak brick wall eight times thicker than the span of my fingers, and a moat five armspans wide and seven handspans deep. The inhabitants are poor fighters and have no weapons, nor do they possess any artillery or anything else capable of warding off an attack by any company of five hundred good soldiers.

From here we departed on a Tuesday morning and proceeded on our course for thirteen more days, arriving at the port of *Sanchão*[3] in the kingdom of China—which is the island where the blessed Father Master Francisco died afterwards—about which more will be said later on.[4] Upon discovering when we got there that all the ships from Malacca had departed nine days before, we proceeded to another port seven leagues further on called *Lampacau*,[5] where we found two junks from the Malay coast, one from Patani and the other from Lakhon.

And since we Portuguese are by nature very fond of having our own way, there arose such sharp differences of opinion[6] among the eight of us about something that we would have been better off settling in peace and harmony, that we were almost on the point of killing each other. Since it is too shameful to tell how it happened, all I will say is that the *necodá,* the skipper of the *lorcha* who had brought us there all the way from *Huzangué,* was so shocked by our barbaric behavior that he departed in a rage, refusing to take back any kind of letter or message from any one of us, protesting that he would rather the king chopped his head off for doing so than offend God by taking anything belonging to us any place he might go. And so, at odds with each other, nursing our differences, we remained on this little island for nine more days, during which both junks departed, each of them also refusing to take us with them. As a result we were forced to stay there, hidden in the bushes, exposed to many hazards and great danger, from which I doubt we would ever have been able to escape if the Lord our God had not remembered us; for after we had been here for seventeen days, suffering from great misery and starvation, a pirate by the name of *Samipocheca* happened to anchor there, fleeing from the armada of the *aytao* of *Chincheo*[7] who had destroyed his fleet, capturing twenty-six out of his twenty-eight sails. He had managed to escape with just the two ships he had with him, and since most of the men on board were critically wounded, he was forced to remain there for twenty days for them to recover. As for the eight of us, compelled by necessity, we were forced to make a pact with him in order to get him to take us with him wherever he might go until God would provide us with a better and safer vessel to get back to Malacca.

At the end of these twenty days, during which the wounded recovered, without having reconciled our differences in all that time, we embarked with this pirate, still at odds with each other, three on his junk and five on the other one commanded by a nephew of his. Leaving here for a port called Lailó, seven leagues above *Chincheo* and eighty from this island, we proceeded on our course under fair winds along the coast of *Lamau*[8] for a period of nine days. One morning, when we were almost northwest-southeast with the Salt River[9] five leagues below the *Chabaqué,*[10] we were attacked by a robber with a fleet of seven very tall junks. He engaged us in a furious battle that lasted from six to ten o'clock in the morning with a heavy barrage of projectiles, both spears and fire balls, finally setting three ships aflame, two of the robber's and one of ours—the junk that the five Portuguese were on. But we were unable to go to their aid because by that time most of our people were wounded. Late in the afternoon, when the winds freshened a bit, with the help of God we were able to make a run for it and escaped from his clutches.

We proceeded on our voyage in the battered condition we were in, and three days later we were struck by a storm that blew over the land with such fierce gusts of wind that that same night we were driven out of sight of the shore. And since by then we were unable to approach it again, we were forced to make with full sail for the island of the Ryukyus where this pirate was well known to both the king and the other people there. With this in view we sailed ahead through the islands of this archipelago, but since at this time we were without a pilot, ours having been killed in the recent battle, and the northeast winds were blowing head on, and the currents were running strong against us, we went tacking with great effort from one board to the other for twenty-three days until finally, at the end of that time, our Lord brought us within sight of land. Coming in closer to see if it showed any sign of an inlet or harbor with good anchorage, we noticed a huge fire burning over to the south, almost at a level with the horizon. This led us to believe that it was probably inhabited and that there might be people there who would sell us water, which we were running short of.

As we were anchoring opposite the island in seventy fathoms of water, two small canoes with six men on board came rowing out from shore. They came alongside, and after an exchange of greetings and courtesies in their fashion, they asked us whence the junk had come. Our answer was that we had come from China, bringing merchandise to trade with them, if they would give us leave to do so. One of them replied that as long as we paid the duties that were customarily charged in Japan, which was the name of that big land mass outlined ahead of us, the *nautoquim*,[11] lord of that island of Tanegashima,[12] would readily grant us permission. He followed this up by telling us everything else that we needed to know and showed us the port where we were supposed to anchor.

Filled with excitement we immediately hauled in our moorings and, with the ship's longboat at the bow, moved in to drop anchor in a little bay to the south where a large town called *Miaygimá*[13] was located, from which many prows came rowing alongside with supplies of fresh food and water which we bought from them.

133
The Inquisitive Prince of Tanegashima

Hardly two hours had elapsed since we anchored in this bay of *Miaygimá* when the *nautoquim,* prince of the island of Tanegashima, accompanied by many merchants and noblemen, came out to our junk, laden with a large number of chests full of silver which they brought with them to trade. After the usual courtesies on both sides had been exchanged and he had been given assurance that it was safe to approach, he immediately drew up alongside. The moment he saw us three Portuguese on board he wanted to know what kind of people we were, for he could tell from looking at our faces and beards that we were not Chinese.

The pirate captain told him that we were from a country called Malacca, to which we had come many years ago from another by the name of Portugal, whose king, as he had heard us say several times, lived far away, at the end of the huge expanse of the world. Unable to hide his amazement, the *nautaquim*,[1] turning to the men in his party, exclaimed, "May heaven strike me dead if those men are not the *Chenchicogis*[2] of whom it is written in our scrolls that by flying over the waters they have conquered the inhabitants of the coastal regions where God created all the wealth of the world! If so, it will be our good fortune if they have come to our country in the name of friendship."

Then he called to his side a Ryukyu woman who had been acting as interpreter in his conversation with the Chinese master of the junk.

"Ask the *necodá*," he said to her, "where he found these men and why he brought them here to our land of Japan."

The captain replied that he could vouch for the fact that we were perfectly respectable merchants, and that he had found us shipwrecked in *Lampacau* where, out of charity, he had taken us on board, as was his custom whenever he came across anyone in similar circumstances, so that God in turn might protect him from the sudden disasters that ride the waves and strike the mariner down at sea.

Apparently, the pirate's answer was so convincing that the *nautaquim* immediately boarded the junk, selecting only a small group to follow him, for there were too many in his party for all of them to join him. After he had looked the junk over from stem to stern, examining every nook and cranny, he sat down on a chair near the quarterdeck and interrogated us about certain things in particular he wanted to know, to which we replied, telling him only what we thought he wanted to hear, and he was extremely pleased. He talked to us for a long time, and from the questions he asked we could tell that he was a curious person who was eager to learn about new things. He said good-by to us and the Chinese *necodá*, taking little notice of anyone else there, and saying as he left, "Come see me at my house tomorrow and bring me a wonderful present of information about the great wide world you have traveled, the countries you have seen and their names, for I can assure you that you have nothing else here I would purchase with greater pleasure."

And so saying he returned to shore.

At daybreak the next morning he sent a large prow out to the junk loaded with fresh food for us, including grapes, pears, melons and all the different vegetables they grow in Japan, at the sight of which we offered many praises and thanks to our Lord. In return for the fresh food the *necodá* of the junk sent him some expensive art objects and bric-a-brac from China. He also sent word with the messenger that, as soon as the junk was safely anchored and made secure against the weather, he would visit him ashore and bring him samples of the merchandise he had for sale. Early the next morning he went ashore, taking all three of us with him along with ten or twelve of the most decent and respectable-looking Chinese in the ship's company whom he wanted there in order to make a good impression at this first interview, which is when these people usually show themselves off in a most pretentious manner.

When we arrived at the *nautaquim*'s house he welcomed us all very cordially, and the *necodá* gave him a fine present, after which he showed him samples of everything he had for sale. He was satisfied with what he saw and immediately sent for the principal local merchants with whom prices were discussed. Once prices were agreed upon it was decided to have the goods brought ashore the next day to a building he had set aside for the use of the *necodá,* where he and his people could stay until they were ready to return to China.

After these matters were settled, the *nautaquim* resumed his conversations with us. He asked us about many things, in great detail, and in our answers we were less concerned with the real truth than we were with trying to please him. But this was the case only in certain instances when it was necessary to help ourselves out with a few little falsehoods so as not to undo the high regard he had for this country of ours. The first was his telling us that the Chinese and the Ryukyu had told him that Portugal possessed more territory and wealth than the entire empire of China, which we granted him. The second was that they had also assured him that our king had subjugated most of the world by means of maritime conquests, which we also said was true. The third was that our king was so rich in gold and silver that he had more than two thousand storehouses filled from floor to ceiling. To this we replied that, as to the number of storehouses, we could not be sure, because the country and the kingdom in themselves were so vast and contained so many treasures and peoples that it was impossible for anyone to be able to tell him the exact number with any degree of certainty.

He detained us for more than two hours with these questions and others like them and concluded by saying to his followers, "One thing is certain, that we know of no king on earth today who can consider himself fortunate unless he is a vassal of a monarch as great as the emperor of these people.

After dismissing the *necodá* and his entire company, he asked us to consent to spending the night ashore with him because he could not get his fill of asking us many things about the world, which he was very fond of doing, and that in the morning he would arrange to house us where we would be close to him, since it was the best part of town.

We readily agreed and he had us put up with a very wealthy merchant who wined and dined us most generously, not only that night but on all the twelve other nights we stayed with him.

134
How Firearms Came to Japan

In keeping with the *nautaquim*'s instructions, early the next day, the Chinese *necodá* unloaded his cargo and transferred it to a suitable warehouse assigned to him for that purpose, and within three hours it was all gone. It sold so fast, not only because there was very little to begin with, but also because there was a great scarcity of that kind of merchandise in the country. The pirate made so much money on these transactions that in the end he was more than compensated for the loss of the twenty-six ships confiscated by the Chinese authorities, for they readily accepted the merchandise at the prices he quoted. As a result, from what he confided to us, on just that small supply of goods, which had cost him twenty-five hundred *taels,* he made a profit of over thirty thousand.

As for us three Portuguese, since we did not have any business to attend to, we passed the time away hunting, fishing, and visiting the very rich and majestic temples to their gods, where we were most cordially received by the bonzes, or priests, for the Japanese are by nature a very friendly and sociable people. It was during this time, when we had nothing to do, that one of the three men in our group, a fellow by the name of Diogo Zeimoto,[1] who was very fond of shooting, would occasionally go off by himself with his musket, which he knew how to handle quite expertly. One day he came upon a swamp inhabited by an enormous number of birds of all different varieties, and while he was there he shot down about twenty-six wild ducks.

The Japanese had never seen firearms like that before and they promptly reported it to the *nautaquim,* who at the time happened to be watching the running of some horses that had just been shipped to him from the outside. Astounded by the news, he immediately sent for Zeimoto, who came straight from the swamp where he had been hunting. As he watched him coming towards him with the musket slung over his shoulder and his two Chinese helpers loaded down with game, he could hardly contain his excitement. From the way he carried on, it was apparent that he was simply delighted by it all, for they had never before seen target shooting with firearms in Japan, and since none of them knew the secret of the gunpowder and could not understand how it worked, they attributed it to some sort of witchcraft.

As for Zeimoto, when he saw them all staring at him in amazement, and the *nautoquim* especially looking so pleased, he fired three shots in the air, bringing down two doves and a seahawk right at their feet. But there is no point going into all the details because the whole incident was truly incredible. Suffice it to say that the *nautaquim* made Zeimoto climb up behind him on his horse and rode off with him, accompanied by many people, including four footmen carrying iron-tipped staffs who shouted to the crowds, which by then were increasing in great numbers.

"Hear ye! Hear ye! It is the will and command of the *nautoquim,* prince of this island of Tanegashima and lord of our heads," they proclaimed, "that you and all the inhabitants of the land bounded by the two seas, honor and revere this *chenchicogim* from the end of the world, for as of this day he has made him his kinsman, alike to the *facharões*[2] who sit beside him. Whosoever does not willingly obey this command shall lose his head!"

And the people responded with a tumultuous cry: "So shall it be forevermore!"

When Zeimoto arrived at the outer courtyard of the palace in the midst of all this ostentatious display, the *nautaquim* dismounted and took him by the hand, leaving the two of us a good distance behind. Keeping him by his side all the while, he led him into one of the buildings where he seated him at his own table, and then crowned it with the highest honor of all by inviting him to spend the night there. Thereafter he always showed great favor to him, and to us too, to some extent, out of consideration for him.

Before long Diogo Zeimoto realized that he could not find a better way to repay the *nautaquim,* if only in part, for all the honors he had received, and that nothing would please him more than having the musket,[3] so he offered it to him on a day when he had returned from the hunt with an especially large quantity of pigeons and doves.

He accepted it as though it were a priceless gift and assured him that it meant more to him than all the wealth of China. In return, he gave him a thousand silver *taels* and begged him to teach him how to make the powder, for without it, the musket was just a useless scrap of metal, which Zeimoto promised to do, and he kept his word. From then on, the *nautaquim*'s chief pleasure and pastime was in exercising with this musket. When his people saw that there was nothing that gave him greater joy, they decided to have some new ones made on the model of that musket, and they lost no time going about it.

As a result, the insatiable curiosity and demand for this musket increased from that moment on to such a remarkable degree that, when we left the island some five and a half months later, there were already more than six hundred of them around. And afterwards, the last time I was in Japan, when the viceroy Dom Afonso de Noronha[4] sent me there with a gift for the king of Bungo[5] in the year 1556,[6] the Japanese assured me that in the city of *Fucheo,*[7] which is the capital of the kingdom of Bungo, there were more than thirty thousand. When I expressed surprise, for it seemed incredible to me that they could have increased their production at such a rapid rate, some merchants told me—and they were noble, respectable men, who assured me in no uncertain terms—that in all the islands of Japan there were more than 300,000 muskets, and that they alone, in six voyages to the Ryukyus, had transported 25,000 to be sold there.

So that all because of the single musket that the well-intentioned Zeimoto presented to the *nautoquim* as a token of friendship, to repay him in part for all the honors and favors bestowed on him, as I mentioned before, the land became so flooded with them that today there is not a village or hamlet, no matter how small, where they do not produce a hundred or more, and in the important cities and towns they speak of them in nothing less than the thousands. From this alone it is easy to understand what kind of people they are and how naturally they take to military exercise, which they enjoy more than any other nation that is known to date.

135
The King of Bungo

After we had spent twenty-three restful and contented days on this island of Tanegashima, passing the time away hunting and fishing, of which the Japanese are generally quite fond, a *nao* from the kingdom of Bungo arrived in this port with a large number of merchants aboard. As soon as they landed they went to pay their respects to the *nautoquim,* bearing gifts for him, as is the custom there. Among them was an elderly gentleman, well attended by his personal staff and addressed with great deference by all the others, who kneeled down before the *nautoquim* and presented a letter to him as well as a fine broadsword trimmed with gold and a jewel case full of fans, which the *nautoquim* accepted with great ceremony.

After spending a great deal of time questioning him in some detail about certain matters, the *nautoquim* read the letter to himself, and as its substance sank in, his expression became a bit more somber. Then, after dismissing the bearer of the letter and giving instructions to have him housed in a manner befitting his station, he summoned us to approach and motioned to the interpreter who was a little farther away.

"My dear friends," he had him say to us, "please listen to the contents of this letter which I have just received from the king of Bungo, who is my uncle and liege lord,[1] and then I will tell you what I would like you to do."

He handed the letter to a treasurer of his and ordered him to read it aloud. It went like this:

"To *Hyascarão Goxo*,[2] *nautoquim* of Tanegashima, who sits beside me as an equal, like each of my loved ones, and who is as dear to me as the right eye in my face:

"I, *Oregemdó*,[3] your father in the true love of my heart as much as he from whom you took your name and being; king of Bungo and Hakata,[4] lord of the great House of *Fiancima*,[5] Tosa,[6] and *Bandou*,[7] supreme head of the lesser kings of the islands of Goto[8] and Shimonoseki,[9] wish to inform you, my son, in words spoken by me and addressed to you personally, that a few days ago I learned from some travelers returning from your port that you had in your city some three *chenchicogins* from the end of the world, men whose ways are very compatible with our own, who dress in silken garments and gird on swords, not like merchants engaged in trade, but like men who love honor, in the name of which they seek to cover themselves with glory. I was told that they have given you a great deal of information about everything going on in the outside world, and that they have declared to you, on their word of honor, that there exists another country, much larger than ours, inhabited by black and brown-skinned people, things which we find incredible.

"Therefore, I ask you, as a son who is as dear to me as my own, to do me the favor of letting me see with my own eyes one of the three men they say you have there. This can be done by sending him back here with *Fingeandono*,[10] whom I have sent to visit my daughter. As you know, I am in need of some distraction of this sort, owing to my prolonged illness and indisposition, beset with much pain, deep melancholy, and great tedium. But if they should show some reluctance to do so, you must give them your word and mine as well that I will send him right back, safe and sound, without fail. And like a good son who wishes to please his father, give me the joy of fulfilling this desire of mine by letting me see him. *Fingeandono* will tell you anything else I have neglected to say in this letter, and through him I beg you to share freely with me all the good news about you and my daughter who is, as you well know, the eyebrow of my right eye, and so dear to me that the very sight of her makes my face light up with joy.

"Dated on the seventh *mamoco*[11] of the new moon, from the House of *Fucheo*."

As soon as the reading of the letter was finished, the *nautoquim* spoke up.

"The king of Bungo," he explained to us, "is both lord and uncle to me, for he is my mother's brother, and he is, above all, a good father to me, and I call him that because he is my wife's father.[12] For all these reasons he loves me like a son; and because of the deep obligation I am under to him on this account, I assure you that I am so anxious to do his bidding that I would have given up right now a great part of my land for God to have made me one of you so that I might not only go to see him but give him this pleasure as well, which I am sure, from what I know of his temperament, would mean more to him than all the wealth of China. And now that I have explained to you how he feels, I pray that you will bend your will to his and that one of you two will consent to go to Bungo to visit this king, who is both father and liege lord to me.

As for the other one on whom I have conferred the name and being of kinsman, I will not allow him to leave my side until he has finished teaching me how to shoot as well as he does."

We two, Cristóvão Borralho [13] and I, answered that we kissed the hands of His Highness for the favor he did us by asking us to serve him, and that since such was his pleasure, he had but to command which one of us he wanted to send and that one would immediately prepare to go. He remained absorbed in thought for a moment deliberating on his choice, and then, pointing to me, he replied, "This one, because he is of a more cheerful and less solemn disposition than the other. He will be more agreeable to the Japanese and will relieve the patient of his melancholy. A doleful gravity like that of the other fellow among the sick only serves to make them feel sad and dsependent and adds to the depression of someone already suffering from it."

While he was joking about it with his courtiers and making some witty, urbane remarks, to which by nature they are very much inclined, *Fingeindono* arrived. He handed me over to him at once with very strict instructions regarding the safety of my person. This reassured me completely and relieved me of certain fears that had been preying on my mind, owing to my lack of prior contact with these people. He also ordered them to give me two hundred *taels* for the journey, which I used to prepare myself as fast as I could. And we departed, *Fingēdono* and I, in an oar-propelled vessel they call a *funce*. [14]

It took us only one night to cross over from this island of Tanegashima, and at dawn we found ourselves opposite land in a bay called Yamagawa, [15] from where we went on to a fine city called Kagoshima. [16] Sailing along our course that way with a fair wind behind us, on the following day we arrived at a stately town called Tano-ura; [17] and from here we went on the next day to another one called *Minato* [18] where we spent the night, and from there on to Hyuga. [19] And in this manner, resting on shore every day where we picked up fresh food, we arrived at a fortress belonging to the king of Bungo called Usuki, [20] located seven leagues from the city, where *Fingeandono* remained for two days because the commanding officer of the fort, who was his brother-in-law, was very sick.

Here he left the boat behind, and we traveled overland to the city, arriving at noon. But since it was not the proper time of day for an audience with the king, he went straight to his own house, where he received a warm welcome from his wife and children, who treated me very hospitably. After he had dined and rested up from the fatigue of the journey, he changed into his court robes, and accompanied by some of his relatives, he went to the palace, taking me along on horseback. When the king was informed of his arrival, he sent one of his young sons out to the palace courtyard to meet him. The boy, who was magnificently attired, appeared to be about nine or ten years old. He came forward in the company of a large group of noblemen, with six macebearers preceding him. Taking *Fingeindono* by the hand, he said to him, with a bright smile on his handsome face, "May your coming into this house of the king my lord be of such great honor and contentment to you that your sons, because they are your sons, will deserve the right to dine at table with me on all the festivals of the year."

To which he replied, as he lay prostrate on the ground, "May those who dwell in heaven—from whom you, my lord, have learned to be so good—answer for me, or else give me a tongue dipped in sunbeams so as to gratify you with music joyful to your ears for this great honor you have so magnanimously done me; for if I should speak without such a heaven-sent gift, I would be as guilty as all the ungrateful wretches confined for their sins to the lowest lake of the dark depths of the House of Smoke."

With this he moved forward to kiss the sword that hung at the boy's waist, but the latter would not allow it. Instead, he took him by the hand, and with the other noblemen behind them, led him into the room where the king was waiting. Despite the fact that he was lying on a sick bed, the king greeted him with another unusual ceremony, which I prefer not to describe for the sake of brevity. After reading the letter he had brought him from the *nautoquim* and inquiring after his daughter, the king told him to summon me, for during all that time I had remained a short distance behind. He immediately called me and presented me to the king who bid me welcome with these words: "May your arrival in the land over which I rule be as pleasant in my eyes as the rain from heaven in the middle of our rice fields!"

I was quite embarrassed by the novelty of his greeting and eloquence and for the moment I could not think of a single thing to say in reply.

Then, turning to the courtiers around him, he said, "I can sense that this foreigner is perturbed, perhaps because he is not accustomed to having so many people around him. Maybe it would be better to put this interview off for another day to give him an opportunity to become used to the palace, and then he will not feel so ill at ease at finding himself in a situation like this."

I replied to this through my interpreter, an excellent one I had with me, that it was true, as His Highness had said, that I felt perturbed, but not because there were so many people around me, for I had been surrounded by many more on other occasions; but the very thought of finding myself at his feet was of itself enough to leave me speechless for a hundred thousand years, if I should live that long, because the people around me were men like me, whereas His Highness had been made by God so superior by far to all other men, that He had immediately chosen him to be king and the others servants, and had made me a tiny little ant, so small in comparison to his greatness, that because of my diminutive size, he could neither take any notice of me, nor could I know how to reply to his questions.[21]

They were all so impressed by this crude, awkward reply of mine that they clapped their hands in amazement.

"Look, Your Highness, how appropriately this man speaks," they said to him. "He does not seem to be a merchant[22] who deals in the vulgar business of buying and selling. He must be a bonze who preaches and ministers sacrifice to the people, or a man who was bred to be a corsair of the sea."

"You are quite right," the king replied, "that is exactly the impression I have of him, but now that he has gotten up enough courage to loosen his tongue, let us get on with our questions. And all of you be quiet, because I want to be the only one to ask him questions. I swear to you that I enjoy talking to him so much, that perhaps in a little while I will have a bite of something to eat, for I no longer feel any pain in my body."

The queen and his daughters who were close beside him were so happy when they heard this that they knelt down, raised their hands heavenward and offered a prayer of thanks to God for the great blessing he had granted them.

136
A Shooting Accident

The king then commanded me to move closer to the bed where he lay quite ill, suffering from the gout.

"I hope it does not make you feel uncomfortable to be so close to me," he said, "for I enjoy seeing you and talking with you. Tell me, do you know of some remedy from that land at the end of the world that is good for this disease that has left me so crippled, or something for my lack of appetite, because it is almost two months now that I have not been able to eat a thing?"

I told him that I was not a doctor nor had I ever studied medicine, but that on board the junk on which I had come from China they had a certain kind of wood[1] out of which they made a brew that cured ailments far more serious than the one he was complaining about, and that if he were to take it he would be restored to health without fail, which he was very happy to hear.

Anxious to begin treatment with it at once, he had some brought from Tanegashima where the junk was anchored. He took it and within thirty days he was cured, and this after two years of being confined to his bed without being able to stir or lift his arms.

The first twenty days of my stay in this city of *Fucheo* were very much to my liking. I spent part of the time answering all sorts of questions put to me by the king, the queen, the prince, and the gentlemen of the court, questions that showed that these people knew absolutely nothing about the rest of the world outside of Japan. I shan't take the time here to repeat any of their questions or the answers I gave, because they all dealt with matters of no great importance and I can see no purpose it would serve other than to fill up space with things that would inspire more boredom than pleasure. The rest of the time was spent observing their festivals, their houses of worship, their military exercises, the ships in their fleet, and the fishing and hunting sports they are so fond of, especially the hawking and falconry after our fashion. Once in a while I would go hunting with my musket and shoot down a good supply of pigeons, doves, and quail which are very abundant throughout the land.

This kind of firearm was no less strange for the people here than it was for the people on Tanegashima, and now, seeing it for the first time, they made such ado about it that I cannot begin to describe it. The king's second son, of whom he was very fond, a youth about sixteen or seventeen years of age named *Arichandono*,[2] asked me several times to teach him how to shoot, but I always managed to put him off by telling him that it took a long time to learn. However, he would not be put off with my excuses, and he complained about me to his father, who asked me to please him by letting the boy try a couple of shots just to satisfy his curiosity. I replied that I would let him shoot two, four, a hundred, or as many times as His Highness commanded, but since the boy happened to be dining with his father at the moment, the lesson was put off until after the siesta hour. But as it turned out, that afternoon the boy had to accompany the queen, his mother, on an important religious pilgrimage to a pagoda where she was holding special prayer services for the health of the king, so the lesson could not take place that day.

On the following day, which was a Saturday, eve of the feast day of our Lady of the Snows,[3] he came by my house during the siesta hour, accompanied by just two young noblemen, and there he found me sleeping on a mat. He made no attempt to wake me, for he had seen my musket hanging on the wall and he wanted to get in a couple of extra shots, thinking, as he admitted later, that they would not be included in the number I had promised him. He ordered one of the young noblemen to light the fuse as quietly as possible while he removed the musket from its place and tried to load it as he had seen me do several times. But since he did not know how much powder to put in, he loaded the gun barrel more than two handspans deep, inserted the ball, held it up to his face, and aimed at an orange tree in front of the house. No sooner did he ignite the charge, bad luck would have it that the musket blew up in three pieces, hitting him and inflicting two wounds, one of which almost severed the thumb of his right hand and knocked him to the ground unconscious. Leaving him for dead, the two youths who were with him sped off toward the palace, shouting along the streets as they ran, "The foreigner's musket has killed the king's son!"

Their shouts roused the whole town, and people came running from all over the city. Brandishing their weapons and screaming, they converged in a solid mass on my house, where by then, poor unlucky me, God only knows what a state I was in, for I was awakened by all this milling and shouting around me to see the boy lying on the floor next to me all covered with blood, without stirring either hand or foot. I clasped my arms around him, but by this time I was so completely out of my mind that I had not the slightest idea of where I was or what I was doing.

In the meantime the king arrived, slumped forward in a litter borne on the shoulders of four men, looking more dead than alive with all the color drained out of his face. The queen arrived on foot, holding on to two women who supported her every step of the way, as did both her daughters, also on foot, without their wigs, hemmed in by a crowd of ladies and noblemen, all of them in a state of shock. When they all entered the house and saw the boy lying on the floor looking as though he were dead, clasped in my arms, and the two of us covered with blood, they all jumped to the conclusion that I had killed him. Two of the men there made a rush for me, brandishing naked swords in their hands, ready to kill me.

"Wait, wait, wait!" the king shouted out loud. "Let's interrogate him first! I suspect that there is more to this than meets the eye. This man may have been bribed by relatives of the traitors I had executed the other day."

Next they sent for the two young noblemen who had been there with his son and questioned them repeatedly, but all they would say was that my musket had killed the boy by some sort of magic it had inside the gun barrel.

"Sire!" all the bystanders protested loudly. "Why listen to any more of this? Show him no mercy! Let him be put to death at once!"

With this they sent for the *jurubaca*[4] in great haste. He was the interpreter through whom I usually communicated with them, but by this time he had also fled in fear for his life. They brought him back a prisoner, and there in the presence of the king and all the officials of justice they harangued him and threatened him with all sorts of dire consequences if he did not speak the truth, to which he replied, weeping and trembling, that he would. Then they sent for three scribes and five executioners with their double-grip swords drawn. By then I had my hands tied behind my back and was forced to kneel down before them. Then the bonze *Asquerão Teixe,* who was the chief justice there, took up his stance, with his sleeves rolled back, holding aloft a curved dagger that had been dipped in the boy's blood.

"I conjure you," he said to me, "son of the devil that you are, and as guilty of this heinous crime as those traitors who dwell in the House of Smoke in the Concave Depths of the bowels of the earth—tell me, here and now, and speak up loud so all can hear you—why did you want your enchanted musket to kill this innocent child who was as dear to us as the hair on our heads?"

I was absolutely incapable of uttering a single word in reply because I was so paralyzed with fear that even if they had killed me on the spot I do not think I would have felt a thing. However, glaring at me with a fierce and angry expression on his face, he addressed me again.

"If you do not answer my questions," he said, "you may consider yourself condemned to death by blood, fire, water, and whirling winds, whereby you may be torn to bits in the air, like the feathers of a dead bird, scattering in all directions." And he followed this up with a good, hard kick intended to rouse me from my stupor.

"Speak up!" he shouted at me again. "Confess who bribed you! How much did they pay you? What are their names? Where do they live?"

By this time I had recovered my wits somewhat and replied that God alone knew the truth and that I took him for my judge in this matter.

Still not satisfied with all that he had done, he threatened me again in a long speech, filled with all sorts of frightful horrors, which took him more than three hours to deliver. But by that time it was the will of God that the boy should regain consciousness. When he saw his mother and father beside him, all bathed in tears, he begged them to stop crying and not to accuse anyone of his death because he alone was to blame, and that what had happened was no fault of mine. Therefore, he entreated them earnestly, by the very blood that covered him, to set me free at once because if they failed to do so, he would die again. And the king immediately commanded them to remove the bonds that the executioners had put upon me.

In the meantime, four bonzes who were supposed to cure him had arrived. When they saw the condition he was in, with his thumb hanging loose, they made so much ado over it that I can find no words to describe it. Seeing how they were carrying on over him, the boy began to shout, "Get those devils out of here and bring me someone who will not stand there telling me what is wrong with me, since it was God's will that I should be in this condition!"

And so they dismissed these four and brought in some others who did not dare to treat the boy's wounds, making the father feel even sadder and more disconsolate when they told him so. Then he sought the advice of the people around him who suggested he send for a bonze named *Teixe Andono,* who was very famous among them but who happened to be in Hakata at the time, some seventy leagues away.

"I do not know how you can give my father such advice," the boy protested, weak as he was, "when I am in this condition which is plain for all to see. By this time my wounds should have been treated to stop the bleeding, but instead you want me to wait for a decrepit old man who is a hundred and forty leagues away coming and going, when it will take him more than a month to get here? Try to be nice to this foreigner! Reassure him in some way so that he will get over the fright you have put into him, then clear everybody out of the house and let him treat me as best as he can, because I would rather die at the hands of a man who has suffered as much on my account as this poor fellow than at the hands of the bonze from Hakata who is ninety-two years old and blind as a bat!"

137
The Prince's Recovery

The poor, unhappy king, by now thoroughly amazed to see his son acting that way, turned to me and, speaking very gently, said, "Please see if you can help me, for I can see that my son is in danger of losing his life. If you do so, I promise that I will treat you like a son too, and I will give you anything you ask of me, if you heal him for me."

I told His Highness that he should get rid of all those people because the noise they were making was driving me frantic with fear, and then I would see how serious the wounds were, and if I thought I could heal him, I would gladly do so. The king ordered them out immediately. Then I went over to the boy, examined him, and saw that he had only two wounds, one just above the forehead, which, though it was a wide cut, was not dangerous, and the other on his hand, where only the thumb was half severed. And the Lord instilled enough courage in me to tell the king that His Highness had no cause to be worried because I trusted in God that I would be able to heal his son in less than a month.

As I set about making my preparations to attend to his wounds, the bonzes chided the king severely for allowing me to do so. They told him that his son would die without fail that very night, so that he would do better to have my head chopped off than to give me the opportunity of killing his son a second time, for if that should happen, and there was every indication that it would, then the boy's death would be a great scandal and the king would be held in very low esteem by all his people.

The king told them that he knew only too well how right they were in what they were saying, but then would they please tell him what he should do. Their answer to this was that he should wait for the arrival of the bonze *Teixe Andono* and not to take anyone else's advice, for inasmuch as he was the saintliest of all the priests, they were sure that he would restore the boy to good health with just the touch of his hand as they had seen him do to others many times before. Just when the king had decided to take the unholy advice of these advocates of the devil, the boy began to complain that his wounds were hurting a great deal and that in any case they should do something for him any way they wished right away because he could not stand the pain.

This made the king turn again for advice to those who had stayed with him. He asked them all to consider on the one hand, the opposition of the bonzes, and on the other, the great danger in which his son found himself as well as the great pain he was suffering, and to advise him what to do in this dilemma since he could not make up his mind. They all told him that it would be much better to have the boy treated immediately rather than wait as long as the bonzes said. The king approved of this counsel as better and more sensible and as such, accepted it at once and thanked them for it. Getting back to me where he had left off, he again spoke very gently and promised to make me very rich if I would make his son well. With tears in my eyes I replied that His Highness would see for himself how carefully I looked after his son.

And so, commending myself to God and screwing up my courage, as they say, for I could see that I had no other alternative and that if I failed to do what they wanted they would chop off my head, I prepared everything I needed for the treatment. I began at once with the wound on the hand since it appeared to be more serious than the other, and I put seven stitches in it though, of course, if it had been done by a surgeon, perhaps fewer would have sufficed; and in the head wound, since it was smaller, I only put five. Then I covered the wounds with egg plasters and bound them up very carefully the way I had seen it done several times in India. After five days I removed the stitches and continued dressing the wounds, and within twenty days, the Lord willing, they were completely healed, without any other ill effect than a slight weakness of the thumb. As a result, from then on I was highly honored and treated with great cordiality by the king and all the courtiers, as well as by the queen and her daughters, who gave me gifts of many articles of silk clothing. Also, the noblemen gave me swords and fans, and the king gave me six hundred *taels,* so that, all in all, for healing the prince's wounds I got more than fifteen hundred *cruzados,* which I took with me from there.

Just about that time I was advised by letters I received from the two Portuguese who had stayed behind in Tanegashima that the Chinese pirate who had brought us there was preparing to leave for China. I so informed the king and asked him for permission to return, which he granted me without any difficulty, together with words of deep gratitude for curing his son.[1] He then gave orders to have an oar-propelled *funce* prepared for me and had it fully equipped with everything necessary, with twenty servants from his own household and a nobleman as captain of the vessel. I departed from this city of *Fucheo* on a Saturday morning, and the following Friday at sundown we reached Tanegashima, where I found my two companions, who welcomed me with great joy.

We waited here for two more weeks while the junk was finally made ready and we departed for Ning-po, a seaport in the kingdom of China, which I described before at great length, where the Portuguese used to trade in those days. We sailed along our course, and with God's will, made port safely, receiving a warm welcome from the local people, who were amazed to see that we had voyaged that way, relying on the bad faith of the Chinese, and they asked us where we were coming from and where we had embarked with them. We responded truthfully, telling them how it had come about, and we gave them an account of our entire voyage, informing them about the new land of Japan we had discovered, the great quantity of silver to be found there, and the huge profits that had been made on goods from China, which made them so happy they could hardly contain themselves for joy.

They immediately organized a religious procession to give thanks to our Lord for such a great blessing. It started at the main church, Our Lady of the Immaculate Conception, and ended at another, the church of Santiago, at the other end of town, where there was a special mass and sermon. Once this extremely pious and saintly act of devotion was over, greed soon gained control, filling the hearts of most of the men in town to such a degree that they became a community divided against themselves— since each one wanted to be the first to make the voyage—and they gathered into bands that went about at gunpoint trying to buy up all the merchandise in town. As a result, the Chinese merchants, watching the spread of this sudden and inordinate greed, raised their prices, and in only eight days, a picul of silk, which at that time was worth 40 *taels,* rose to 160, and even at that price it was grabbed up by force, and in a very nasty manner.

Driven by their hunger for profits, in only two weeks they readied nine junks that were in the harbor at the time, all of them so ill prepared and poorly equipped to sail that some of them were carrying as pilots only the ships' owners, who knew absolutely nothing about the art of navigation. And that was how they departed, all together, on a Sunday morning, against the wind, against the monsoon, against the tide, and against all reason, without a moment's thought for the perils of the sea, but so blind and obstinate in their determination to leave that none of these drawbacks were considered. And I too went along on one of them.

In this manner, that first day they picked their way blindly between the islands and the mainland, and at midnight, in a dense fog, with heavy rain and wind that descended upon them, they all foundered upon the shoals of *Gotom,*[2] at latitude thirty-eight degrees; with the result that only two of the nine junks, by a great miracle, escaped, while the other seven were all lost, with not a single survivor from any of them. The losses were estimated at more than 300,000 *cruzados* in merchandise, to say nothing of the much greater loss of six hundred people who died on them, including 140 Portuguese, all rich, honorable men.

We proceeded on our course in the two junks that escaped miraculously, sailing together in consort until we got as far ahead as the Ryukyu Islands,[3] and there, with the conjunction of the moon, we were struck by such a fierce contrary wind from the northeast that we never saw each other again. And there, sometime near afternoon the wind shifted to west-northwest, and the seas became so heavy with swells and waves so high that it was a most frightful thing to see. When our captain, a very courageous nobleman by the name of Gaspar de Melo,[4] saw that the junk was already leaking at the stern, with nine handspans of water filling the hold of the lower deck, he decided, after consultation with the ship's officers, to cut away both masts because they were splitting the junk. The dismasting was done as carefully and cautiously as possible, but in spite of all the precautions taken, it could not be accomplished safely enough to avoid catching beneath the weight of the big pole fourteen people, five of them Portuguese. All of them were crushed, each one bursting into a thousand bits—a most pitiful thing to see—which brought our spirits so low that we were left in a state of shock.

With all that, the storm grew gradually worse, and suffering great hardship, we abandoned ourselves to the fury of the sea until nearly sundown when the junk finally split wide open. Then, when the captain and all the rest of the people saw the sad state to which our sins had reduced us, we sought refuge in an image of our Lady, to whom we prayed, with many tears and loud cries, asking her to intercede for us with her blessed Son to pardon us for our sins, for by then none of us expected to come out of this alive. We spent most of the night this way, and with the junk half waterlogged we drifted on till the end of the midwatch, when we ran aground on a reef. At the first impact the junk was smashed to bits, and sixty-two people lost their lives, some drowned and others crushed under the keel, a tragedy as painful and heartrending as anyone of sound judgement can imagine.

THE PRINCE'S RECOVERY

138
Shipwreck off the Ryukyu Islands

There were only twenty-four of us, besides some women, who survived this miserable shipwreck. When day broke we could tell from the landmarks of *Fire* Island[1] and the *Taydacão* Mountains that we were off the main island of the Ryukyus. Wounded as we were from all the cuts and abrasions we had sustained on the oyster beds and rocks of the reef, we all gathered together, and commending ourselves tearfully to the Lord, we began to walk breast deep in the water, even swimming in some places. We kept on going this way for five consecutive days, suffering from extreme hardship as one can imagine, without finding a thing to eat in all that time except for some rockweed. At the end of these five days it was the will of the Lord that we should reach shore.

As we were walking through the forest, divine Providence presented us with sustenance of some herbs we call *azedas*[2] in our country, on which we lived for the three days we were there, until we were seen by a boy who was herding cattle. The moment he spied us he raced up the mountainside to bring word of our presence to a village a quarter of a league away. Once the townspeople were informed they immediately spread the alarm throughout the entire countryside by beating their drums and blasting away on their conch horns, and within three or four hours a crowd of over two hundred had gathered, including fourteen on horseback. As soon as they caught sight of us they split up into two groups and headed straight for us.

Mindful of the sad and wretched state to which we had been reduced by misfortune, our captain got down on his knees and spoke to us at great length. He began to lift our spirits by reminding us that everything that happens is the result of the divine will, so that, as Christians, we should understand that it served God's purpose to make this the last hour of our lives, and since that was so, we should all resign ourselves to His will and accept from His hand, with great forbearance, the unfortunate death that awaited us by asking Him earnestly, from the bottom of our hearts, to forgive us for all our past sins, because he had faith in His mercy that if all of us prayed, weeping and sobbing, as His holy Law obliged us to do, He would not remember our sins at that hour. Then raising his arms and his voice to heaven, the tears streaming down his cheeks, he repeated three times, "Lord God, have mercy on us!"

At these words there came from all of us such a loud outburst of devout, Christian lamentation that I can say in all truth that what we least regretted at that moment was that which one naturally fears most.

While we were all locked in this painful trance, six horsemen rode up to us, and at the sight of us there on our knees, naked and unarmed, with two dead women in our midst, they took such pity on us that four of them promptly headed back to the people following them on foot and kept them in check where they were, without permitting anyone to do us any harm. Then they returned, bringing with them six of the men on foot who appeared to be ministers of justice, or at least, the kind of justice that we thought God had in store for us at the time.

At the command of the men on horseback, these six tied us all up in groups of three. Showing signs of compassion, they told us not to be afraid because the king of the Ryukyus was a God-fearing man, well inclined by nature to the poor, to whom he was always very charitable, and they gave us their word, swearing by their faith, that he would do us no harm. These words of consolation, however pious they appeared to be on the surface, did not satisfy us in the least, for by then we had lost all hope of life so that even if we had been told this by someone we trusted completely, we still would have found it hard to believe, much less a group of cruel, tyrannical heathens who had neither religion nor any knowledge of God.

As soon as they finished tying us up, the people on foot formed a ring around us, with the horsemen preceding them, galloping from side to side, as though patrolling the area. As we started to walk, three of the women with us who were still alive, or rather, more dead than alive, were so terrified that they were unable to move from the spot, and they kept fainting out of both fear and exhaustion, so that it became necessary for those who were walking to carry them in their arms, taking turns at intervals. And before we reached our destination, two of them died and had to be left behind there in the woods, their bodies naked and exposed to the danger of being eaten by the forest beasts, the otters and the jackals we had seen lurking about in great numbers.

Close to sundown we reached a good-sized village of over five hundred households called *Sipautor,* where we were immediately placed in one of the temples of their worship, a pagoda that was surrounded by a very high wall, and put under guard of over a hundred men, who could be heard shouting and beating the drums throughout the night, during which each one of us got as much rest as the time and circumstances permitted.

139
Arrested for Piracy

After daybreak the following morning the honorable women of the town came to visit us. As an act of charity they brought us a large quantity of boiled fish and rice, with some of the locally grown fruit for us to eat. From the words they spoke and the tears they shed we could tell that they were deeply moved by our sad and miserable plight. Also, when they saw how short of clothing we all were, for at that time we had very little on us, or no more than we were wearing when we came out of our mothers' wombs, six of them, who were chosen by the rest, went off begging through all the streets of the town, shouting as they went, "O people, good people who profess the word of the Lord, whose nature—if one may say so—is to be prodigal with us in bestowing his blessings, come forth from behind your walls and behold the flesh of our flesh stricken by the wrath of the arm of the almighty Lord and help them with your alms so that his great mercy will not forsake you as it has forsaken them!"

The response to their call for alms was so generous that in less than an hour we were all abundantly provided with everything we needed.

It was past three in the afternoon when a courier on horseback came riding into town in great haste and delivered a letter to the *xivalém*,[1] who was their local military commander. As soon as he read it, he immediately ordered two drums to be beaten by way of summoning the townspeople, who responded to the call by assembling in a large temple of their worship. There, framed in a window, he addressed them, informing them of the orders he had received from the *broquem*,[2] governor of the kingdom, to the effect that they were to take us to the city of *Pongor*, seven leagues from there. The majority of the people protested, voicing their objections to this order six or seven times, and a heated argument ensued, as a result of which nothing was agreed on that day except to send the courier back to the *broquem* with an explanation of what was happening. Consequently, they were forced to keep us confined there until eight o'clock the following day when two *peretandas*[3]—who are like magistrates— arrived, accompanied by a crowd of people from the city, including twenty men on horseback. After taking us into custody with detailed documents drawn up by notaries public, they departed immediately. Late in the afternoon of the same day we reached a town called *Gundexilau*, where they put us into an underground dungeon, in which we spent the night, suffering unbearable hardship, in a pool of water swarming with leeches that left us all quite bloody.

Early the next morning they took us to the city, but since we did not get there until four in the afternoon, it was too late by then for the *broquem* to see us. Nor did he see us at all until three days later, when he ordered us to be brought before him, tied up as we were, along the four main streets of the city which were lined with huge crowds of people who, as far as we could tell from appearances, were deeply moved by our misery and misfortune, especially the women.

That was the way we arrived at the courthouse where the guard of the ministers of justice was stationed. There they kept us waiting for a long time because it was still too early to conduct proceedings. But at the appointed hour a bell was struck three times and another door up ahead was opened, through which they led us into a large hall where the *broquem* was seated on a silk-draped dais beneath a brocade canopy, with six macebearers on their knees forming a circle around him. And below, all along the walls of the entire structure, were a large number of armed men with halberds of gold and silver inlay, while the rest of the hall was filled with many other people of different nations that we had never seen before in that part of the world.

When the court was called to order we prostrated ourselves in front of the *broquem*'s dais, with our chains and all, and addressed him, weeping freely.

"Sir," we began, "we beseech thee, for the sake of the God who created heaven and earth, beneath whose power we all live, be moved to pity by our sad plight, for since the waves of the sea have already placed us in such a state of great misfortune, let thy kind inclination place us in a better state before the king, so that he will be moved to take pity on us, for we are poor foreigners, bereft of the favor and aid of the world, which God so permitted for our sins."

At these words, he looked at the people around him and shook his head a few times.

"What do you think of these people?" he asked. "They speak of God as though some word of his truth has reached them. There must be some great world out there in creation of which we have not yet heard. And since they are aware of the source of all blessings, it is only reasonable that we should proceed with them in accordance with their tearful plea."

Then he turned to us as we all lay prostrate on the floor, and with his hands upraised, as though in adoration of God, he said to us, "I have such great compassion for your misery, and I am so deeply pained by your poverty, that I assure you in all truth—and may the truth avail me before the king—that I would much rather be any one of you, having within me what I see in you, than have this office which, for my sins, I now hold, for I very much fear that I may give you offense, which I most certainly would not wish to do. However, since it cannot be avoided, for I must, of necessity, discharge my duty, I beg you, as I would my own friends, do not be alarmed by the questions I must put to you for the good of justice. And as for whatever else may be required for your release, if God gives me life, you shall have it. And you may rely on this promise of mine, for I know what a royal disposition the king, my lord, has toward poor people such as you."

We then thanked him for his promises with a flood of tears, for by this time we were in such a state that we were totally incapable of uttering a word in reply.

140
Under Sentence of Death

Next, the *broquem* sent for four scribes and the two court *peretandas,* who are something like magistrates, as I said before, as well as ten or twelve other ministers of justice. Then rising to his feet, with a look of wrath on his face and a naked sword in his hand, he began to interrogate us in an impersonal tone, raising his voice slightly for all to hear.

"I, *Pinachilau,*" he said, *"broquem* of this city of *Pongor,* by the power vested in me by the one whom we all hold to be the hair of our heads,[1] the king of the Ryukyu nation and all this land between the two seas, where the fresh and salt waters divide his treasure mines, do hereby admonish and command you with all the rigor and force behind my words to tell me, with pure and innocent hearts, what people or of what nation you are, where your country is and how is it called?"

To which we replied truthfully, that we were Portuguese residents of Malacca.

"Then who brought you to this land of ours?" he demanded, "or where were you going when you were shipwrecked?"

We answered that since we were merchants who made our living by trade, we had embarked from the port of Ning-po in the kingdom of China, bound for Tanegashima where we had already been several times before, and that when we had sailed as far as *Fire* Island we were struck by such a terrible storm that we were unable to hold the ship steady and as a result were forced to run before the wind for three days and nights until we were driven aground on the reefs of *Taidacão,*[2] where sixty-eight of the ninety-two people on board immediately drowned; and as for the twenty-four of us that he saw there before him, God had saved us by a miracle but had left us with nothing more to show for it but the wounds on our bodies, as he could see.

"How did you come by such a huge fortune in silks and other costly goods that the sea washed up on our shores, all of which came from your junk?" he demanded.

"From what I have been told it is worth more than 100,000 *taels,* and it is hard to believe that men can justly acquire so much wealth without having to resort to stealing, which is such a grave offense against God that it is an occupation worthier of those who serve the Serpent of the House of Smoke than of those who dwell in the House of the Sun, where the just and pure of heart bathe in the fragrant waters of the almighty Lord."

To which we replied that we most assuredly were merchants and not thieves as he had called us so many times because the God in whom we believed forbade us in his holy Law either to kill or to steal.

"If these people are telling the truth," he said, addressing the audience, "we can say that they are like us and that their God is far better than all the others; from which it appears that what they say must be so."

Then turning back to us he proceeded with his interrogation which lasted for nearly an hour, maintaining throughout a stern countenance and wrathful gestures like an incorruptible public official in the performance of his duty, and at the very end he asked us, "Well, why did your people slaughter ours so mercilessly when they conquered Malacca years ago, out of greed for her wealth, as proof of which, even today there are still some widows[3] alive in this land of ours?"

To this we replied that it must have been as an act of war, but certainly not one motivated by greed, for we were not in the habit of stealing from people any place in the world.

"Then what is this they say about you?" he retorted. "Do you deny that he who conquers does not steal? that he who uses force does not kill? that he who seizes power does not scandalize? that he who covets does not steal? that he who oppresses does not tyrannize? Well, all these things are said about you and affirmed as holy truth, from which it would appear that if God forsook you and permitted the waves of the sea to engulf you, it was not for lack of reason but rather the effect of his righteous justice."

Then, rising from the chair on which he had already sat down, he ordered the *peretandas* to take us back to the prison, from where we would be heard, depending on the compassion the king might feel inclined to show towards us. This saddened us and left us feeling disconsolate and completely bereft of hope for our lives.

Immediately on the following day the king was advised by letters from the *broquem* of both our imprisonment and of what he had learned about us during the audience. He also drew his attention to a few things in our favor, which persuaded the king to change his mind about having us put to death at once as they said he had decided to do because of the meddling of some Chinese mischief makers.

We remained in this prison for nearly two months, enduring great hardship, without anyone speaking to us in all that time about how our case was proceeding. However, since the king wanted some more information about us than the letters of the *broquem* contained, he secretly sent a man by the name of Raudivá to spy on us in prison. Posing as a foreign merchant, he was sent to find out, in greater detail, the truth about our coming to that place, for depending on the information given him by this spy, he would decide on what, in his view, would be the proper course of justice to follow.

Even though this was arranged with the greatest possible secrecy, someone still managed to get word to us the day before the arrival of this man, for which we armed ourselves with the saddest and the most wretched outward appearances that in the midst of all the misery we were going through at the time we were still able to feign, for, after God, it was always this make-believe that helped us more in this situation than all the other means we sought.

This man appeared one morning, well accompanied, and entered the *vileu*[4]— the dungeon where they kept us—and after he had looked us over one by one, he called the *jurubaça*[5] he had brought with him who, as I said before, was his interpreter.

"Ask these men," he said to him, "why God in the divine wisdom of his justice withdrew the protection of his mighty arm from them and permitted their lives to be judged by the opinions of men whose unremorseful conscience does not allow them to set before their eyes the terror of that dreadful vision that usually confronts the soul in the last hour of life? For this reason it is to be believed that sin after sin was the cause of what I see in them."

In reply we told him that he was absolutely right, for it was clear that the sins men committed were the principal cause of their suffering, but not even that would prevent God, who is a father and merciful lord, from having pity on those who called on Him constantly with tears and sighs, and in whose benevolence we had placed our hopes that He would inspire in the king's heart a desire to inform himself of the truth about us and treat us with justice because we were poor foreigners, without any influence, which was the principal means that counted most with men in this life.

"That is all very well," he replied, "if your hearts are in accord with your words and if such is the case, do not feel sorry for yourselves, for it goes without saying that He who painted what our eyes behold in the beauty of the night and all else we see by day in the sustenance of the smallest creature on earth,[6] will not deny you His help in obtaining your freedom since you pray to Him so often with such deep lamentation. Therefore, I beg you, do not be ashamed to confess truthfully to what I am about to ask you, which is, who are you people, from what nation, in what part of the world do you live, what is the name of the land or suzerainty of your king, if you have one, why did you come to where you are now, and where were you going with such an enormous amount of costly merchandise as has been cast up on the beaches of *Taydacão,* which so amazed all these people that they undoubtedly believe that you are masters of the China trade, the largest in all creation."

In answer to those questions and many others that he asked us at the time we replied according to the dictates of the moment, and he appeared to be so satisfied that he offered to speak to the king about our release, without ever revealing to us the truth about why he had been sent there; instead, he kept on pretending that he was a foreigner and a merchant like any one of us. When he left, he recommended us highly to the jailer and asked him to see to it that we were always provided with everything we needed, promising to reimburse him in a most satisfactory manner. We thanked him with quite a few tears that also moved him to compassion for us and he left us a gold bracelet worth thirty *cruzados* in weight and six sacks of rice and, on top of it, begged our pardon for giving us so little.

This man went directly to the king and gave him a report on what had taken place with us, assuring him that we definitely were not the kind of people the Chinese had told him we were, and that on that he would stake his life a thousand times, which they say relieved the king somewhat of all the evil suspicions he had been made to harbor about us.

Just when the king had made up his mind to order our release, basing his decision on what this man had told him as well as on what the *broquem* had written him, there arrived in port a fleet of four junks belonging to a Chinese pirate who enjoyed the protection of the king in exchange for a 50 percent share of the booty he brought from China, thereby winning for himself a considerable amount of influence with the king and all the grandees in the land. This pirate, for our sins, was the greatest enemy the Portuguese had in those days because of a battle our men had engaged him in the year before, in the port of *Lamau,* that was commanded by a Captain Lançarote Pereira,[7] a native of Ponte de Lima, in which they had set fire to three of his junks and killed two hundred of his men.

When he found out about our imprisonment and the king's decision to release us, this dog so embroiled matters and told the king so many lies about us, that he almost made him believe that very soon he would undoubtedly lose his kingdom because of us, for he told him that it was our custom to spy out a country in the guise of merchants and to return later to conquer it like thieves, killing and destroying everything in our path. This information had such a strong influence on the king that it led him to reverse his decision completely, and in view of what he had just been told about us, he changed the sentence and ordered us all to be drawn and quartered and exhibited publicly in the main streets for all to know that we had deserved that punishment.

141
The Compassionate Women of the Ryukyus

After pronouncing this cruel sentence against us, the king sent a *peretanda* to deliver it at once to the *broquem* of the city where we were being held prisoner, giving him four days within which to carry it out. The *peretanda* departed with it immediately and when he reached the city, it was the will of our Lord that he should go to stay at the home of a widowed sister of his, a highly respected woman who had been very generous to us with her alms. He told her in great secret what he had come there for, and that he was to bring back documents certifying that the king's sentence had been carried out.

This noble woman confided in one of her nieces, a daughter of the *broquem,* the governor of the city, who had taken into her home a Portuguese woman, the wife of our pilot, also imprisoned with us along with two of their sons. She could not wait to console her and in doing so, she revealed to her what she had found out. They say that the moment she heard this news, the poor Portuguese woman suddenly fell to the floor as though she had been struck dead. She lay there speechless for a long time, and when she finally regained consciousness, she dug her finger nails into her face, tearing at her flesh so mercilessly that both her cheeks were covered with blood. This was regarded as such an extraordinary thing among these people that news of it spread rapidly throughout the city, where it had such an astounding effect on all the women that most of them dropped what they were doing and ran out of their houses with their sons and daughters by the hand, without stopping to think that their husbands might take them to task for it and without fear of the malicious tongues of the idle gossipmongers who, prompted by their ill nature and evil inclinations, always have something bad to say about many things that because of the sincerity and good intentions with which they are done, would often be accepted by our Lord as having been done in his service.

In this manner they all converged on the house of the *broquem*'s daughter, where they found the Portuguese woman better prepared to die than to answer all the questions they put to her. Inspired by the first and foremost Cause, which is the Lord our God, Author of all blessings, who, out of his infinite kindness and mercy, when suffering and misfortunes are greatest, offers the most unfailing remedy to those most afflicted and despairing of all earthly remedies—these women, even though they were heathens, were so filled with compassion,[1] so deeply touched by the tears and the uncommon grief of the Portuguese woman that they all decided among themselves to write a letter to the king's mother on our behalf. And in the letter, which they wrote there at once, they told her the whole truth about us and what they had heard people saying, and how unjust the sentence was that had been handed down against us. They also told her what the Portuguese woman had done and the great pain and anguish with which she, with blood dripping down her face, loudly bemoaned the death of her husband and sons, adding that they were sure that God had taken it upon himself to punish the injustice of this crime. The text of the letter read as follows:

"To our sainted pearl, set in the largest oyster in the profoundest depths of the sea, heavenly star, shining as bright as fire, skein of golden hair interwined in a garland of roses, to thee, whose feet, as a sign of thy grandeur, rest upon the top of our heads like a ruby set in a priceless jewel: We, the lowliest of creatures, crawling like ants among the forgotten crumbs of thy larder, the daughters and relatives of the wife of the *broquem*, as well as all the rest of thy captive slaves whose signatures appear below, do hereby register a complaint to thee about something we witnessed today with our own eyes. It was a poor foreign woman lying in a pool of blood, her face stripped bare of flesh, her breasts torn with such astounding cruelty that it would frighten the wild beasts of the jungle and instill terror in the hearts of everyone; moreover, she was screaming so loudly that we can all affirm to thee as holy truth that if God should lend an ear to her—as we believe he will, for she is a poor woman, despised by the world— then dire punishment by fire and famine will be visited upon us all.

"Since we live in fear of the day when it shall come to pass, we raise our voices and beg thee, like famished children crying for their mothers, to consider the soul of the king thy husband, for whose sake we ask thee to grant us this favor as an act of charity and to take on the nature of the saints, putting aside completely all worldly considerations, for the more thou art moved to act for the sake of God, the closer thou shalt find the king thy husband, singing, to the sound of the harp played by the little children who never sinned, the hymn in praise of this pious act of charity which we beg of thee for the sake of God and the soul of thy husband; which is, that thou makest every effort to persuade thy son, the king, to let himself be moved by God, by thee, and by our tears and cries, to have pity on these foreigners, and to grant them a pardon, freeing them of all blame, for as thou knowest, the accusation against them was not made by any saint who came down from heaven but by men of bad character and evil ways, to whom it is not fitting to lend an ear.

"Conchanilau, a lovely, kindhearted maiden, and above all, more honorable than any of the women of this city, for having been raised in thy service by her aunt, will inform thee truly in the name of God and the king thy husband, for whose sake we beg this favor of thee, and she will tell thee about all the other particulars concerning this affair, describing the continual tears and sighs of all those poor people, as well as the deep fear and sadness that has fallen over the entire city whose inhabitants, with fasting and almsgiving, all implore thee to present their plea to thy most dearly beloved son, the king. May the good Lord bless him with such great prosperity that from the forgotten goods of his storehouse all those who dwell in the land and the islands of the sea shall have great abundance."

This letter was signed by more than a hundred of the most prominent women in town and delivered by a young girl who was the daughter of the mandarin Comanilau, governor of the island of *Banchá,*[2] which lies to the south of the Ryukyus. She departed on her errand the same day that the sentence arrived, leaving at about two hours after dark, as was deemed necessary, in the company of two of her brothers and ten or twelve other relatives, all of them members of the noblest and most important families in town.

142
The Dowager Queen of the Ryukyus

When she got to the town of *Bintor* where the king and his mother, the dowager queen, were then in residence, six leagues from the city of *Pongor,* this young girl went straight to the home of an aunt of hers who was chief lady-in-waiting to the queen, with whom she had a very close relationship. She told her why she had come and made her see how important it was to her honor and her good standing in the eyes of the other women who had chosen her for this mission that she return with this pardon which they were all asking of His Highness.

After making her comfortable and attending to her with all the love and affection that come from the heart, the aunt told her that, since she claimed that her honor depended on it, she would do everything possible to see to it that she did not go back unhappy and disappointed with the results of her mission, especially in view of the fact that their cause was in itself as just as she said it was, to say nothing of the fact that the petition was being presented as a request for charity and was signed by so many women, all of whom were among the most prominent members of society.

They say that, after giving due thanks to her aunt, the girl asked her, as an extra favor, to act as fast as possible because there were only two days left in which to prevent this senseless injustice from being perpetrated against us and also, that she could not wait any longer than that.

"I am very well aware of the need to act fast," the aunt replied, "because of the haste shown by the king, who was so anxious to punish those poor unfortunate people, solely on the basis of what the Chinese had told him. But when the queen wakes up, which should be in about an hour from now, she will find me at her feet, and that in itself will be so surprising to her that it will compel her to ask me why I am there, since I have not done anything like that for over six years, owing to my poor health."

Then, after leaving her niece comfortably settled in her apartment, she opened the door to a passageway for which she alone had the key and withdrew to the chamber where the queen was sleeping. And they say that two hours[1] had already gone by when the queen woke up and, seeing her there at her feet, exclaimed, "What is the meaning of this, *Nhay*[2] Meicamur [for that was the name of her chief lady-in-waiting]? What possessed you to remain here tonight? There must be something very strange going on."

"Indeed there is, madam," she replied, "and I think Your Highness will be just as amazed to hear about it as I was to see my niece arrive now from the city, at this hour, with feelings of such deep personal outrage that she cannot find the words to express it."

"If she is in such a state, then call her in right now," the queen replied.

She had her come in immediately, and when she found herself in the presence of the queen who was still lying in bed, the girl prostrated herself before her and, with all due reverence, explained to her in tears why she had come. And she handed her the letter she was carrying, which the queen commanded her to read aloud. The girl kissed her hand in gratitude and read the letter in a manner befitting her purpose, and they say the queen was so deeply touched that, even before the girl had finished reading it through, she interrupted her with tears in her eyes, saying repeatedly, "No more, no more! I have heard enough for now. And since that is the way matters stand, may neither God, nor the soul of the king, my husband, in whose name all these women are asking me for this charitable deed, allow those poor men to lose their lives so unjustly, because the sentence executed against them by the sea is punishment enough for what they have been accused of by the Chinese. Leave it to me, for I am taking it upon myself to see to it that your petition is granted. Go lie down and rest a little until morning, then all three of us shall go to see the king my son, before he rises, and you shall read the letter the way you read it to me, so that he may the more readily be moved to pity and grant us this perfectly reasonable request."

Promptly at daybreak the queen rose, and taking with her only her chief lady-in-waiting and the girl and no one else, she went through a passageway to the chamber where her son was still lying in bed. After explaining what it was she wanted of him, she ordered the girl to read the letter to him and to tell him in her own words everything that had happened in this regard. The girl complied fully with these instructions but not, as we later learned, without her and her aunt shedding many tears.

"Indeed, madam," they say the king replied, addressing his mother, "all night long I dreamed I saw myself a prisoner standing before a very irate judge who said to me, placing his hand on his face three times, as though he were threatening me, 'I promise thee that if blood of these foreigners comes before me or raises an outcry in my ears, thou and all of thine will be called to account for it.' Therefore, I hold it as beyond all doubt that this came through the will of God, for whose sake, as a charitable offering in praise of his name, I grant them all their lives and their liberty so that they may be free to go wherever they choose, and I will provide them at once with a ship and whatever else they need at the expense of my treasury."

The queen, his mother, thanked him for this and commanded the chief lady-in-waiting and her niece to kiss his feet for having granted them this favor, which they both did, and with that the queen retired to her apartments.

The king immediately sent for the *chumbim*[3] who had taken part in handing down the sentence and informed him of everything that had taken place, not only what he had dreamt, but also what his mother had requested and been granted, for which they all kissed his hand and praised him highly. Then, after issuing orders to have the sentence revoked and a pardon issued, he wrote a letter to the *broquem* of the city which went like this:

"To the *broquem* of my city of *Pongor:* I, lord of the seven generations and the hairs of thy head, send thee the smile of my mouth that thy honor may be increased. As a result of the information concerning the evil way of life of these foreigners, given to me under solemn oath by the Chinese, who swore by their faith in all their gods that they were, without any doubt, pirates of the sea and robbers on the land of the goods of others, their arms forever stained with the blood of those who righteously defended their property, as was common knowledge throughout the world which, driven by greed, they had circled a thousand times, sparing neither island, nor mainland, nor port, nor river, from devastation by fire and committing deeds so ugly and criminal that I dare not mention them out of respect for God; for all these reasons it seemed to me that there were sufficient grounds for punishing them, and in accordance with the laws of my kingdom, I placed the matter before the *chumbins* of the government, all of whom swore to me by their souls that the foreigners deserved to die, not once, but a thousand times, if such were possible; wherefore, guided by their opinion, I instructed the *nhay peretanda* to notify you, in my name, that within four days you were to carry out the punishment in accordance with the sentence I pronounced.

"And now, because all the noble women of *Pongor*, whom I regard as my relatives, have asked me, for the sake of the soul of the king my father, as a charitable gift to them, to spare the lives of the foreigners, setting forth reasons for it in their letter which moved me so that I could not deny them; therefore, I deemed it best to grant their wish because I feared that if I refused, their cries of protest would have penetrated the highest regions of heaven where reigns that Lord in whose nature it is to be moved to compassion by the tears of virtuous, well-intentioned women who are zealous in the observance of his Law. Once I was free of the blind passion provoked by the flesh, I did not wish my wrath to prevail over the blood of these poor men.

"Therefore, as soon as this lovely young maiden of noble lineage, who is a relative of mine, delivers this letter to thee over my signature—a letter in which I confess I take much pleasure out of regard for the one who requested it of me—I command thee to go to the prison where thou didst incarcerate the foreigners and set them free without any further delay. Also, thou art to provide them with a ship at my expense, as well as all the other charity thou mayest deem fit in obedience to the Commandments of the Lord, without letting miserliness close thy hand. As for their seeing me in audience before they depart, I deem it unnecessary, not only because of the hardship it might work on them but also because it does not behoove me in my office as king to speak to people who, knowing much about God, show little respect for his Commandments, by making a habit of stealing from others.[4]

"Dated at *Bintor,* on the third *chaveca*[5] of the first *mamoco*[6] of the moon, in the presence of the eyebrow of my right eye, my mother, and queen of my entire kingdom."

This was followed by the seal of the king, which read as follows: *"Hirapitau Xinancor Ambulec,* stout defender of all justice."

As soon as she had the king's letter in her hand, the girl delayed only long enough to take leave of her aunt and traveled so fast that in a very short time she reached the city where she delivered the letter to the *broquem*. No sooner had he read it than he gathered all the *peretandas* and *chumbins* of the court and went off to the prison where at that time we were already being held under very close guard.

When we saw him come in we raised our voices and cried out loud three or four times, "Lord God, have mercy on us!"—which had such a startling effect on him and everyone else in the building that some of them wept tears of compassion for us. Then the *broquem* consoled us with words that were truly remarkable for their charity and had the shackles removed from our hands and feet at once. He then led us out to a courtyard that was a little further on where he informed us about everything that had transpired in regard to our case, about which, up to that time, we had heard nothing because of the heavy security that had been placed around us.

After making public the letter that the king had sent to him, he said, "I beseech you, as a favor to me, now that God has shown you such great mercy, to learn to show your gratitude to him by constantly singing his praises and offering many prayers of thanks to him, for if he finds you truly grateful, he will grant you from on high, whence all things come, a happy and never-ending rest, which is more precious than living another four days down here below on this wretched earth where no rest is to be found, only hardship, pain, enormous suffering, and above all, poverty, which is the crowning evil of all, and usually the one through which our souls are completely consumed in the Concave Depths of the House of Smoke."

143
A Brief Description of the Ryukyu Islands

The *broquem* then had two hampers full of ready-made clothing brought in and gave each one of us what he thought we needed most, after which he took us to his house, where his wife and all the other Ryukyu ladies came flocking in to see us. Besides the pleasure they showed at our being released, they also offered us many kind words of consolation, which is something that is characteristic of them, for the women of this country are by nature very well inclined. And still not content with that, they also divided us up amongst themselves and offered us the hospitality of their homes, where we stayed until it was time for us to depart, which was forty-six days later. During that time we were always very well provided by them with everything necessary, in such abundance that there was not a single one of us who did not leave with at least a hundred *cruzados* or more. As for the Portuguese woman, in cash and goods, she came away with more than a thousand, with which her husband recovered his losses in less than a year.

At the end of these forty-six very restful days, with the arrival of the monsoon, the *broquem,* in keeping with the king's instructions, arranged for us to take passage on board a Chinese junk bound for the port of Ning-po in the kingdom of China, but not without demanding a good-sized bond from the captain of the junk to guarantee the safety of our persons against foul play once we were under way. And that is how we departed from the city of *Pongor,* capital of this Ryukyu island about which I have decided to give some brief information here as I have been doing all along with the other lands I have discussed before, so that if the Lord our God should one day see fit to inspire the Portuguese nation to undertake the conquest of this island—first and foremost for the greater glory and propagation of its holy Catholic faith and secondly for the great profit it can derive therefrom—they may know where to set foot, how much they can gain from its discovery, and how easy it will be for them to conquer it.[1]

This Ryukyu island[2] is situated at twenty-nine degrees latitude. It is two hundred leagues in circumference, sixty in length, and thirty in width. The land in itself is more or less on the order of Japan, a little mountainous in some parts, but it becomes more level in the interior, where many of its lush, fertile fields are irrigated by freshwater streams which produce an endless number of fresh crops, especially wheat and rice. There are mountain ranges where they mine a great quantity of copper[3] which, because it is so plentiful, is so cheap among these people that they load junks full of it to sell in every port of China, *Lamau*,[4] *Sumbor*,[5] *Chabaqué*,[6] Tosa,[7] Miyako,[8] and Japan, with all the other islands to the south, *Sesirau*, Goto,[9] *Fucanxi*, and *Pollem*. In addition, all this land of the Ryukyus has great quantities of iron, steel, lead, tin, alum, saltpeter, sulphur, honey, beeswax, sugar, and large amounts of ginger which is of a much better quality and far superior to the ginger produced in India. They also have large forests of angely wood,[10] *jatemar*,[11] *poytão*,[12] *pisu*, pine, chestnut, cork oak, oak, and cedar, from which thousands of ships can be made.

To the west, there are five very large islands which have many silver mines, pearls, amber, incense, silk, rosewood, brazilwood, wild eaglewood, and large quantities of pitch,[13] though the silk is somewhat inferior to that of China. The inhabitants of all these islands are like the Chinese, and they dress in clothes made of linen, cotton, and silk, along with some damasks that they import from Nanking. They are overly fond of food, given to the pleasures of the flesh, and have little inclination for bearing arms, which are in short supply, from which it appears that it will be very easy to conquer them. So much so that in the year 1556 there arrived in Malacca a Portuguese in the service of the grand master of Santiago[14] by the name of Pero Gomes de Almeida,[15] bringing a magnificent gift and letters from the *nautoquim*, prince of the island of Tanegashima, for King John III, may his soul rest in peace, which in essence amounted to an appeal for five hundred men to help him and his men conquer this Ryukyu island, in return for which he offered to pay an annual tribute of five thousand quintals of copper and one thousand of brass. Nothing ever came of this embassy because the message was sent to Portugal on board the galleon on which Manuel de Sousa de Sepulveda[16] was shipwrecked.

More to the north-northwest of this land of the Ryukyus, there lies a large chain of small islands from which they obtain very large quantities of silver. These islands, as it appears (and as I always suspected from what I saw in the Moluccas in the reports presented by the Castilian General Ruy López de Villalobos[17] to Dom Jorge de Castro,[18] then captain of our Ternate fortress), must be the islands of which these people have some intelligence, the ones they called the Silver Islands,[19] though I do not know with how much justification because, according to what we have seen and read in the works of Ptolemy as well as the others who have written on geography, not one of them ever went beyond the kingdom of Siam and the island of Sumatra, with the exception of our own cosmographers who, from the time of Afonso de Albuquerque on, have gone a little further and have already described the Celebes, Papua, Mindanao, Champa, China, and Japan, though they have not yet mentioned the

Ryukyus[20] nor the rest of the archipelagos in the vast expanse of this sea that still remain to be discovered.

From the brief report I have given here about the Ryukyu Islands, one can understand—and I think so from what I have seen—that with a mere two thousand men, one could conquer and occupy this island along with all the others in these archipelagos, from which we would derive far more profit than we do from India, and at much less cost to us in manpower and everything else, for from trade alone, as the merchants to whom we spoke assured us, the three customs houses on this Ryukyu island brought in a million and a half in gold, to say nothing of the combined revenue of the whole kingdom, and the mining of silver, copper, brass, iron, steel, lead, and tin, which yielded even far more than the customs houses.

As for the rest of the excellent things I could say in particular about this island, I will pass over them now because it seems to me that this alone will be enough to stimulate and arouse the spirits of the Portuguese to an undertaking of so much service to our Lord and so much honor and profit for them.

I44
Mission to Martaban

We made port safely in Ning-po, where we received a warm welcome and very hospitable treatment from the Portuguese who were there at the time. From here I embarked for Malacca on a *nao* belonging to a Portuguese by the name of Tristão de Gá[1] with the intention of returning from there once more to try my fortune which had been contrary to me so many times, as can be seen from what I have related thus far.

This *nao* arrived safely in Malacca where I still found Pero de Faria[2] in command of the fortress. Since he wanted to be of help to me before his term of office expired, he offered me the voyage to Martaban,[3] which in those days was very lucrative, on board a junk belonging to a Moor by the name of *Necodá* Mahmud, who had a wife and children living in Malacca. The purpose of my voyage was to arrange a peace treaty with the *chaubainhá*,[4] king of Martaban, as well as a commercial agreement whereby his junks would bring food to the fortress, which was in very short supply at the time as a result of the Java wars.

Another reason for my going, no less important than the first, was to look for a certain Lançarote Guerreiro,[5] a well-known mutineer who was then cruising along the coasts of Tenassarim with a hundred men in a fleet of four foists, to get him to come to the aid of the fortress because it was known for certain that the king of Achin[6] was mounting an attack against it. And since Pero de Faria was in no position to withstand a siege, for he was very short of men and everything necessary, he decided to try to avail himself of these hundred men, not only because they were nearer and could reach him faster, but also because, like all those engaged in that occupation, they were well supplied with munitions that were needed for the expected siege. And the third reason for sending me, also a very important one, was to warn the Bengal *naos* to come back all together in consort and to be on the alert for trouble on the way which might otherwise catch them unawares and lead to some disaster.

I willingly agreed to undertake this voyage and departed from the fortress of Malacca on a Wednesday, 9 January 1545.[7] I sailed on my course under favorable winds as far as *Pulo Pracelar*,[8] where the pilot hove to because of the reefs that run across the entire channel from the mainland to the island of Sumatra. After passing beyond them, though not without difficulty, we proceeded on our course up to the islands of Pulo Sambilang,[9] where I transferred to a well-equipped *manchua* I had with me. In keeping with Pero de Faria's instructions I continued navigating in her for more than twelve days during which I spied out the entire Malay coast for a distance of 130 leagues, as far as Junkseylon, penetrating all the rivers of *Barruhás*,[10] Selangor,[11] *Panaagim*,[12] Kedah, Perlis, *Pendão*,[13] and *Sambilão Sião*,[14] without being able to pick up any precise information about the enemy anywhere.

After nine more days of proceeding on our original course, which was our twenty-third day at sea, we anchored off a little island they called *Pisanduré*,[15] where the *necodá*, the Moorish captain of the junk, found it necessary to replace a cable and take on water and firewood. He went ashore for that purpose and set to work as quickly as possible, distributing among the crew the required tasks, on which a good part of that day was spent. While this was being done, a son of the Moorish captain asked me to go with him to kill a deer, for there were many of them on that island. I told him I would be glad to, and picking up a musket, I went ashore with him. We entered the thickest part of the woods, and we must have gone a little over a hundred paces when we discovered in a clearing a large herd of wild boar, rooting beside a pool of water.

Excited by all this wild game before our eyes, we crept up as close as we could get to the nearest one and fired both our muskets right into the middle of the whole herd, bringing down two of them. Shouting with glee, we went running into the clearing where they had been rooting and discovered nine half-buried corpses there, as well as another ten or twelve that were partially devoured, a horrible sight indeed that left us quite startled and confused, and we edged back a little because of the over-powering stench of the dead bodies.

"I think we had better go back to the beach and tell my father, who is there now working on the cable," said Çapetu, as the young Moor who was with me was called, "so that he can send out around the island right away to see if they can find any *lan-charas* of robbers hiding behind that point, for I fear that we may meet up with some disaster here, such as has already befallen some ships at various times, with a heavy toll of lives, because of the carelessness of their captains."

This seemed like a good idea to me, and I immediately went back to the beach with him where he told his father about what we had seen. And since the *necodá* was a sensible man who had been burned by disasters of this sort before, he quickly dispatched a patrol to go around the entire island, ordered the women and little children back on board the ship just as they were with their laundry half done, and set off for the pit from which we had just come, taking with him forty men armed with muskets and lances. Reaching the spot where the corpses lay, he looked them over, holding his nose because of the horrible stench which was quite unbearable, and out of pity for them, he ordered the sailors to dig a common grave for them. As they were moving the bodies to bury them, they found some daggers decorated with gold on a few of them and some arm bangles on others.

Realizing what all this meant, the *necodá* told me to immediately dispatch the rowing vessel he had with a message to the captain of Malacca, for he assured me that there was absolutely no doubt that the dead were Achinese who had been beaten in battle at Tenasserim, where their armadas were still at war with the Siamese king, because the gold armlets he had found belonged to Achinese officers who were usually buried wearing them, and that he would be willing to bet his life on it. And for further proof of this he decided to have more bodies dug up, which was promptly done. After digging up thirty-seven more that were there, they found sixteen gold armlets on them and twelve richly ornamented daggers, as well as many rings, which must have brought the spoils to even more than a thousand *cruzados* that the *necodá* came away with, to say nothing of what was concealed. But this was not done without paying a price, for nearly all our men fell sick from the horrible stench of the bodies.

I quickly dispatched our ship's rowing *balão* to Malacca with a letter to Pero de Faria, giving him a full report of all the events of the voyage, the course followed, as well as the ports, rivers, and bays I had entered, without being able to pick up any news or word of the Achinese enemy anywhere, except for a vague suspicion that they were in Tenasserim, where, from the corpses we had found here, it could be surmised that they had been routed; and that if I should hear anything more definite about it I would immediately send word to him, from wherever I happened to be.

145
The Pathetic Little King

Once the *balão* had been dispatched to Malacca with letters for Pero de Faria and the junk supplied with everything necessary, we set sail for Tenasserim where, as I said before, I had been instructed to go, in order to arrange for Lançarote Guerreiro and the other Portuguese in his company to come to the aid of Malacca, then under threat of attack by the Achinese.

Proceeding on our course, we came to a small island called *Pulo Hinhor,*[1] not much more than a league around, from where a prow came heading towards us with six dark-complexioned men on board, all wearing red caps,[2] but shabbily dressed. They drew up alongside the junk which was still under sail at the time, made a peaceful salute, to which we responded in kind, after which they inquired if there were any Portuguese on board. They were told there were. However, they did not have much faith in what the Moors told them and begged to be allowed to see one or two of them because it was a matter of the utmost importance that they should. The *necodá* then asked me to come up on deck, for at the time I was lying down below in my cabin, feeling indisposed, but I did so in order to please him. When I appeared above on deck, I called out to the people in the prow, who, the moment they saw me and recognized me for a Portuguese, let out a shout, clapped their hands for joy, and clambered aboard the junk.

"Sir, before I ask your leave to speak," said one of them, who appeared to be of greater authority, "please read this letter so that you may have confidence in what I am about to say and will know that I am the one to whom it refers."

Then he handed me a letter, wrapped in a filthy rag, which I opened and saw that it read as follows:

"Fellow Portuguese and true Christians: This honorable man, the bearer of this letter, is the king of this island, who has just become a Christian and taken the name of Dom Lançarote. All of the undersigned, as well as many others like us who sail along this coast, have been receiving valuable intelligence from him, warning us of the treacherous attacks that the Achinese and the Turks were preparing against us, and thanks to this good man, we were kept informed of everything going on. Also, because of him, our Lord has just granted us a resounding victory over them in which we captured a galley, four galliots, as well as five foists, killing more than a thousand Moors who were on board. In view of the above, we ask Your Graces, for the sake of the wounds of our Lord Jesus Christ and the agony of his sacred Passion, not to allow any evil or injury to be done to him, but rather like good Portuguese, to favor him in every way you can so that it may serve as an example to others who hear about it, to do the same as he did. We kiss Your Graces' hands a thousand times. Dated this third day of November, 1544."

The letter was signed by more than fifty Portuguese, among them the four captains I was looking for, namely, Lançarote Guerreiro, Antonio Gomes, Pero Ferreira, and Cosme Bernardes.[3]

Impressed by the contents of this letter, I offered to help the poor little king personally, even though my possibilities at the time were so limited that I could not afford to give him more than a scanty meal and a red cap that, although it was old, was still in better condition than the one he was wearing. Then, among some of the things he told me about himself and his wretched life, he said to me, raising his hands to heaven and shedding many tears, "Our Lord Jesus Christ and his Holy Mother Mary, whose slave I am, know how desperately I need the help and protection of some Christians, for since I am also a Christian, in the last four months a Moorish slave of mine has reduced me to the state in which you now see me, leaving me with no other recourse but to look up to heaven and weep, with great pain and small comfort, over my misfortune. I swear to you, by the truth of this new, holy religion I now profess, that it is only because I am a Christian and a friend of the Portuguese[4] that I have been persecuted this way. And as long as you cannot be of help to me, since you are just one person, I beg you, sir, take me along with you, lest I lose this soul God has given me, and I promise to serve you as a slave for as long as I live." And as he spoke these words he cried all the while, shedding so many tears that it was really a pitiful sight to behold.

The *necodá*, who was a very kind and generous person by nature, felt very sorry for him and gave him some rice and some cloth with which to cover himself, for he was so impoverished that not even the clothes he was wearing were enough to cover him completely. Then after he had obtained some information from him about a few things that were important for him to know, he also asked him about his enemy, where he was, and how powerful he was. He replied that he was a little over a quarter of a league from there, in a straw hut, and that he had only thirty fishermen with him, most, or practically all, of them unarmed. Then the *necodá* looked at me, and when he saw how sad I was because there was nothing I could do by myself to help this poor Christian, he made what he considered a gesture of friendship.

"Sir, if you were now captain of this junk, instead of me," he asked, "what would you do to help this poor fellow's tears as well as yours?"

I said not a word in reply for I was as sad and depressed as Christian brotherhood obliged me to be.

The shame and anguish of my predicament was not lost on the *necodá*'s son, who as I said before, was a spirited lad, raised among Portuguese. He asked his father to let him have twenty sailors from the junk, which was all he needed to restore that poor little king to his throne and run that robber off the island, to which he replied that he would gladly do so if I were to ask it of him. When I heard that, I threw myself at his feet to embrace them, which is the humblest form of courtesy observed among them, and told him with tears in my eyes that if he would do that for me, I would be his captive slave for as long as I lived and that I would repay such great friendship to him and to all his children, as he would see, for I swore it on my word of honor. And he readily granted my request.

He had the junk anchored close to the island while he and all his men made ready to go ashore in three rowing vessels with a falcon, five culverins, and sixty well-armed men, Javanese and Luzons, thirty of whom were carrying muskets and the rest lances and arrows, and a large quantity of fire pots and other firearms suitable for our purpose.

146
A Throne of Straw

It must have been about two in the afternoon when all of us disembarked and started marching towards the enemy stockade. The *necodá*'s son was in the lead with forty men, twenty of them armed with muskets, and the rest with lances and arrows. The *necodá* himself followed with thirty men in the rear, carrying a flag with the cross which Pero de Faria had given him before he left Malacca, so that by means of it he would be recognized as a vassal of His Majesty, our king, in case he should encounter any of our ships at sea.

Maintaining this order, with the poor little king as our guide, we marched further inland until we came to the field where the rebel had taken up a position in the open with his men, who were making a terrible racket, shouting and putting on a show of bravado, trying to make it look as if they were not the least bit afraid of us. There might have been fifty of them altogether at the most, but it was plain to see that they were weak and unarmed, and poorly equipped with the most essential weapons needed for their defense, for all they had between them were some sticks, about ten or twelve lances, and one musket.

As soon as our men spied them, they discharged the falcon and the culverins and, firing twenty muskets, made a rush for them, but by this time they were fleeing in total disorder, with nearly all of them wounded. Hot in pursuit, our men caught up with them at the top of a hill, and in less time than it takes to recite two Credos, they were all slain, with the exception of three, whose lives were spared because they said they were Christians. Reaching a village which consisted of twenty grass huts, all they found there were just sixty-four women and little children, all of them crying and shouting in one voice, "Christian, Christian, Jesus, Jesus, Holy Mary," with a few of them repeating the words, "Our Father who art in heaven, hallowed be thy name," without reciting the rest of the prayer.

Since it seemed to me that they were really Christians, as they said, I asked the *necodá* to make his son withdraw and not to allow a single one of them to be killed, because they were Christians, a request with which he promptly complied. Nevertheless their miserable huts were sacked, though altogether the booty collected was barely worth five *cruzados,* for these people are all so impoverished that they have not a single *real* to call their own, and they exist on nothing but a little fish which they catch on a line and eat roasted over live coals without salt. Yet in spite of everything, they are so vain and conceited, and have such an inflated opinion of themselves, that there is not a single one of them who does not call himself king of some little piece of land or other on which he has a hut and nothing more; besides, neither men nor women own any clothes with which to cover themselves.

Once the rebellious Moor and his followers were slain and the poor little Christian king reunited with his wife and children—who had been held captive by the enemy along with sixty-three other Christian souls—and a church set up there for catechizing the newly converted, we returned to the junk and set sail immediately, proceeding on our way to Tenasserim, where I was hoping to find Lançarote Guerreiro and his companions in order to discuss with them the matter I have mentioned above.

But since the Portuguese—in the letter the little king had shown me—had referred to a victory that God had granted them over the Turks and the Achinese of this coast, I have decided to relate here how it happened, not only because I think it would please the reader, but also to make it clear that, when the need arises, there is nothing that good soldiers cannot accomplish, and therefore, it is very important to indulge them and treat them favorably.

In almost eight months of cruising off this coast in a fleet of four well-rigged foists, these hundred men of ours had captured twenty-three *naos* laden with very rich plunder, in addition to many other smaller vessels, earning so fearful a reputation for the Portuguese that the people who used to sail along that coast abandoned their regular trading voyages and beached their ships. As a result, there was a sharp decline in the customs revenues of the ports of Tenasserim, Junkseylon, Mergui,[1] *Vagaru,*[2] and Tavoy,[3] so that the people in those places were forced to report it to the emperor of the *Sornau,* the king of Siam, who is the supreme lord of all this territory, and to ask him to take steps to remedy this evil about which everyone was complaining. The king, who was then residing in the city of Ayuthia, responded immediately by sending for one of his captains, a Turk by the name of Heredim Mohammed, who was stationed on the Laos frontier. This captain had originally come from Suez with Suleiman Pasha, viceroy of Cairo, in the armada that the Grand Turk had sent against India in the year 1538. His galley having strayed from the main body of the fleet, he landed on the coast of Tenasserim, where he accepted a commission from the *Sornau,* king of Siam, as commander-in-chief of the armed forces stationed on the border of the kingdom of Laos, at a salary of twelve thousand *cruzados* a year. And since the king thought this man was invincible, because he was a Turk, and had more confidence in him than in any of his own people, he recalled him from his border station, along with three hundred Janissaries serving under him. Favoring him with a huge sum of money, he appointed him general of this seacoast, with full and absolute powers of royalty over all the *oyás*[4]—who are like dukes—to avenge the people for the depredations of our men. And in addition, he promised to make him duke of *Banchá*,[5] which is a very large state, if he would bring back the heads of the four Portuguese captains.

This proud Turk, now more arrogant and vain than ever with the recent honors and promise he had received from the king, departed in all haste for Tenasserim, where he outfitted an armada of ten sails to do battle with ours, and so confident was he of victory that, in reply to some letters the *Sornau* had sent him from the city of Ayuthia, he wrote one that read as follows:

"Nine days after I lifted my head from the feet of Your Highness, at whose pleasure I departed to perform this minor service, I arrived in Tenasserim, where I promptly obtained the ships that were lacking here. I had only wanted to take two, for I have not the slightest doubt that those two vessels alone were all I needed to crush these ants' nests. However, to be in all things obedient to the written instructions bearing the royal *mutra*[6] that were handed to me by the *combracalão*,[7] governor of the empire, I am outfitting the large galley, the four small ones, and five foists, with which I mean to depart at once, for I fear that those dogs may get word of my coming and that God, for my sins, may be so great a friend to them that he will give them time to escape, a possibility that would cause me such great pain that I fear that just the thought of it would destroy my life or make me turn in desperation to a life like theirs. However, I am placing my trust in the Prophet Mohammed, whose faith I have professed since childhood, not to be so great an enemy as to allow my sins to count for so much."

As I was saying, when this Heredim Mohammed arrived in Tenasserim, he quickly fitted out an armada of five foists, four galliots, and a royal galley, and signed on a company of eight hundred Moorish fighters—not counting the hands at the oars—consisting of three hundred Janissaries, and the rest Turks, Greeks, Malabaris, Achinese, and Moghuls, all handpicked men experienced in warfare, which made a victory seem certain. With this armada he departed from the port of Tenasserim in search of our men, who were then on the island of *Pulo Hinhor,* where this Christian convert reigned as king and who, at the time that this armada was being readied, happened to be there in the city selling some dried fish. Suspecting that it was preparing to go against our men, he disposed of his merchandise and hurried back to this island of his, where he found our men very much at ease, completely unaware of what was going on, with all four of their foists on the beach. When he informed them of what was happening, they were all as alarmed as one would expect them to be under the circumstances, and they set to work immediately, devoting that night and the following day to making the ships seaworthy and getting them launched and loaded with provisions, water, artillery, and munitions. They remained on the alert with their hands on the oars, intending, as they told me later, to head for Bengal or Arakan,[8] because they did not dare to do battle with such a formidable armada.

There were mixed opinions among them, and while our men were trying to make up their minds, all ten ships appeared in view, followed by five large Gujerati *naos* whose owners had paid Heredim Mohammed thirty thousand *cruzados* to protect them against our men.

The sight of these fifteen ships threw our men into a state of confusion, and since, in the meantime, a strong contrary wind had sprung up and they no longer dared to head for the open sea, they decided instead to bring the ships into a sheltered cove on the southern end of the island that was surrounded by a rocky reef, for by then they had no alternative but to wait and see what fortune would bring.

The five Gujerati *naos* proceeded out to sea, but the ten oar-manned vessels headed straight for the island, arriving close to the hour for Ave Maria prayers. Acting on information that our men were there, the Turk immediately dispatched a reconnaissance party to spy out the port while he moved in under oar, anchoring in the mouth of the bay to cut off any chance of his prey escaping, for it was his intention, at daylight, to capture our men and to present them, bound hand and foot, as he had said, to the *Sornau* of Siam, who had promised him the state of *Banchá* for this feat, as mentioned above.

The *manchua* that had been sent to spy out the port returned to the armada about two hours after dark and reported to Heredim that our men had already slipped away. They say that this news had such a startling effect on him that he began hitting himself and tearing at his beard.

"Well did I fear all along," he said in tears, "that my sins would cause God in this undertaking to prove more Christian than Moslem, and that Mohammed would be just like each one of those dogs I was after!"

And with these words he fell to the floor as though he had been struck dead, and he remained there, incapable of speech, for more than a whole hour. However, when he finally came to he behaved in a manner befitting a captain. He immediately sent the four galliots in search of our men to an island called *Taubasoy,*[9] located further out to sea about seven leagues from *Pulo Hinhor,* in the belief that they must be hiding there since it offered much better shelter than they had here. Next, he divided the five foists up by sending them in three different directions, two of them to another island called Sambilang, two to still another island nearer to the mainland, because they all offered good refuge, and the other foist, which was swifter, he sent after the four galliots, so as to bring him before daybreak word of what they had found, promising five thousand *cruzados* as a reward for good news.

Meanwhile, our men were on the alert, and when they saw that the Turk had stripped himself of the major part of his force and that the only ship he had left was the galley he was on, they decided to strike. Slipping out of the cove, oars in hand, they approached her silently. Since it was already past midnight, the enemy, feeling secure and far from imagining that there was danger about, had failed to post a good lookout. Our four foists fell upon the galley simultaneously with tremendous force and courage, throwing sixty men aboard who, before the enemies had wits enough about them to reach for their arms—which was about the time it would take to recite two or three Credos—had put over eighty Turks to the sword. The rest jumped over the side, leaving the galley with not a live man on board nor a person whose life could be spared, including that dog of a Heredim Mohammed, who also perished there. And the Lord our God showed such great favor to our men in this great exploit, that he gave them this honorable victory at hardly any cost, for our only casualties were one slave dead and nine Portuguese wounded, whereas on the galley they assured me that very close to three hundred Moors had died either by the sword or by drowning, most of them Janissaries, wearing gold armlets, which is a sign of nobility among the Turks.

It must have been about two hours past midnight when this was over, and our men rested for the remainder of the night, feeling quite contented and keeping a sharp lookout. At daylight, our Lord in his mercy willed that two of the foists should return from the island to which they had been sent, and since they were unaware of what had happened in the meantime, they too were a little careless about their watch. As soon as they rounded the tip of the bay where the galley was anchored, all four of our ships attacked them, and in no time at all they were captured at very little cost to us. And in the belief that all this success had come to them as a special blessing from the hand of God, they fired a devout salvo to him, during which they all offered up many prayers of thanks and sang his praises over and over, imploring him with many tears not to abandon them, for with his favor they were prepared to sacrifice themselves in future exploits for the glory of his holy name, by laying down their lives for his holy Catholic faith.

After which, making haste to fortify the two foists and the galley they had captured, they grappled them to the riverbank on the south and installed five heavy pieces of artillery on board to defend the entrance to the bay. When it was close to vesper time, the other two foists that had been sent to the mainland returned, as negligent in their watch as the others, and even though they gave us a bit of trouble when we grappled them, they were both overcome, but it cost us the lives of two Portuguese, one of them Lopo Sardinha,[10] the factor of Ceylon. After fortifying themselves once more with these two additional foists, our men decided to wait there for the four galliots that had been sent to the island further out to sea. However, on the following day, our Lord sent such a violent north wind against them that two of them were cast upon the coast, with all hands lost. As for the other two, they came along in the afternoon, more than three leagues apart from each other, with their oarbanks destroyed. One of them reached the harbor at the hour of the Ave Maria prayers and met the same fate as the others without a single Moorish life being spared.

The next day, at an hour before dawn, when the wind was completely calm, our men sighted the other galliot limping in the distance, for she had jettisoned all her rowing equipment, and they calculated that she would not be able to make port until late in the afternoon when the winds blew out of the west. They decided to go out after her, and when they reached her they fired two broadsides into her, killing most of the men on board. Then they threw the grappling irons out and captured her without any difficulty since nearly all her men were either dead or wounded, after which they towed her into the bay where they had left the others.

So that out of the ten ships in the armada, our men captured the galley, two galliots, and four foists. As for the other three ships, two galliots were lost on the coast of *Tobasoy* Island, as I have said before, and nothing more was ever heard about the remaining foist, though it was presumed either to have gone down at sea or been cast upon the coast of one of the other islands.

And this glorious victory which the Lord granted to our men, took place in the month of September, in the year 1544, on the eve and day of the archangel Saint Michael.[11] It was an exploit that made the name of the Portuguese so famous and so feared all over this coast that for more than three years people could speak of nothing else; so that when the *chaubainhá*, king of Martaban, heard about it, he immediately sought them out, promising them a great share of wealth if they would help him fight against the king of Burma, who was then making preparations in the city of Pegu to lay siege to his city with an army of 700,000 men.

147
Arrival in Martaban

Having departed, as I said before, from this island of *Pulo Hinhor*, we proceeded on our course, bound for the port of Tenasserim to tend to the business I have already mentioned several times. Shortly after nightfall, as a precaution against the many reefs at the bow, the pilot ran out to sea, intending to head back to shore at daybreak with the westerly monsoon winds which were then blowing from India. After we had been navigating on this course for five days, tacking from side to side with great difficulty, it was the will of the Lord that one morning we should chance to see a small vessel. Believing it to be a fishing boat, we headed towards her, hoping to get a bearing from them and to find out how many leagues it was from there to Tenasserim. We hailed her as we passed but got no answer, which made it necessary for us to lower the ship's boat, though we took the precaution of sending some armed men along to oblige her to come alongside.

Our boat quickly reached the craft we had sighted and brought it back under tow without any difficulty. As it came alongside I was quite puzzled by what I saw, for it turned out to be a longboat with five Portuguese on board, two of them dead and the other three still breathing. There was also a chest with three sacks of coins—*tangas larins*[1]—and a bundle with many silver goblets, jugs, and two huge platters, all of which I immediately stowed away in a safe place, and the three Portuguese I brought on board the junk and made as comfortable as I could.

For the first two days that I had them there they were unable to speak, but after I had force-fed them with egg yolks and chicken broth, they recovered consciousness, and the Lord willing, within six or seven days they regained sufficient strength to be able to explain what had happened.

One of these Portuguese was a man by the name of Cristóvão Dória,[2] who later received an appointment in Portugal as captain of São Tomé,[3] and the other two were Luis Taborda[4] and Simão de Brito,[5] all three of them honorable, wealthy merchants. They told me that they had left India on a *nao* belonging to Jorge Manhoz[6]—a family man, residing in Goa—and were bound for the port of Chittagong in the kingdom of Bengal when, for lack of the proper precautions, they were shipwrecked on the reefs of Arakan. Out of the eighty-six people on board the *nao* only seventeen managed to get away on the ship's longboat. They followed the coast for five days, intending to put into the *Cosmim* River in the kingdom of Pegu and, from there, embark for India on His Majesty's lacquer *nao* or any other available merchantman in the harbor. But as they were proceeding on this course, they were struck by an easterly wind blowing from shore with such great force that, after a day and a night, they lost sight of land. They drifted helplessly like that with neither sail nor oars nor anyone knowledgeable enough to give them a bearing, enduring this hardship for sixteen days, with their water supply giving out completely, which was the cause of their deaths, and out of the seventeen who escaped on the ship's longboat, only three had survived the way I found them.

From here we proceeded on our course for four more days when it pleased God that one morning we found ourselves among five Portuguese *naos* that were bound from Bengal to Malacca. I showed them all the instructions Pero de Faria had given me and urged them to sail together in consort on account of the Achinese armada cruising along the coast, so as to avoid disaster that might arise out of heedlessness on their part. I asked them for a document to that effect which they all gave me, and they also provided me with everything I needed in great abundance.

Once this had been taken care of, we proceeded on our course from there, arriving nine days later at the bar of Martaban, on a Friday of Lazarus, the twenty-sixth of March, in the year 1545, after having passed by Tenasserim, Tavoy, Mergui, *Juncay, Pulo Camude,* and *Vagaru,* without finding any trace of the hundred Portuguese I was looking for in any of those ports, for by this time they had cast their lot in with the *chaubainhá,* king of Martaban, who, according to what I heard, had sent for them to help him defend himself against the king of Burma, who had laid siege to his city with 700,000 men in his camp, as mentioned above. However, by the time I got there, they were no longer in his service, as we shall soon see, but I did not know the reason why.

148
The Siege of Martaban

It must have been about two hours after dark when we reached the mouth of the river where we dropped anchor, intending to wait until morning before going on to anchor in the city. After all was quiet on board, we heard the sound of heavy artillery being fired at intervals, which disconcerted us somewhat and left us in a quandary about what to do. At daybreak the *necodá* called a general meeting, as was his custom in a situation like this, and told them that since everyone was exposed to the same danger they should all have a voice in the matter. Speaking to everyone in general, he called their attention to what he had heard during the night, on account of which he was afraid to go and anchor in the city. There were many different views and opinions on the subject, but finally it was decided that we should go and see for ourselves if there was any cause for apprehension.[1]

To that end we sailed up the river with the wind and the tide in our favor, rounding a point called *Mounay,*[2] from where we saw the city completely surrounded by hordes of people nearly everywhere we looked, and almost as many oar-propelled vessels in the river. Even though we suspected what this meant, because of the rumors we had been hearing all along, it did not stop us from sailing into port, where we very cautiously dropped anchor. As a matter of ceremony we fired our customary salvo of peace, in response to which, a well-armed longboat came towards us from shore with six Portuguese on board whom we were extremely happy to see. After climbing aboard our ship, where they were warmly welcomed by all, they told us everything we needed to know for our personal safety and advised us not to move from the spot under any circumstances, since we told them we had decided to slip out that night and head for Bengal, for if we did so, all would be lost and we would be captured by the armada the king of Burma[3] had stationed there, an armada that consisted of seventeen hundred vessels, including one hundred galleys, all well manned with foreign mercenaries. Instead, they suggested I go ashore with them immediately to see João Cayeyro,[4] who was in command of the Portuguese troops there, to tell him why I had come, and to do as he advised if I did not want to make the wrong move, because he was a very considerate person and a good friend to Pero de Faria, about whom they had often heard him speak with nothing but high praise for the nobility of his character and deportment. They also said that there I would find Lançarote Guerreiro and the other captains for whom I was carrying letters and that, in any event, they would discuss what would be the best thing to do in the service of God and the king, our lord.

This seemed like good advice to me and I immediately went ashore to see João Cayeyro. He welcomed me cordially as did all the others with him in his stockade, who altogether numbered seven hundred Portuguese, all of them very rich men of good family background. I showed João Cayeyro the letters and the instructions I had received from Pero de Faria and discussed with him the business that had brought me there. He made an urgent appeal to the four captains I had been trying to find, who answered that they were always ready to serve the king, our lord, whenever the need arose; however, they pointed out that the letter of Pero de Faria, captain of Malacca, was based entirely on his fear of the Achinese and the armada of 130 ships under the command of *Bijayá Sora*,[5] king of Pedir and admiral of the Achinese, which he was expecting to arrive in Tenasserim, but since that fleet had already been there and been beaten by the local inhabitants, with the loss of seventy *lancharas* and five thousand men, they saw no need to go, for according to what they had seen, the enemy forces were so completely destroyed, that it seemed to them that not even in ten years would he be able to recover what he had lost. In addition, many other reasons were given, as a result of which it was decided that there was no need for them to return to Malacca. I asked João Cayeyro to provide me with a written statement describing everything that had transpired in this case, for with it, they would believe me in Malacca, and as soon as it was delivereed to me I intended to return at once since there was nothing more for me to do here.

I remained there that way in the company of João Cayeyro with the intention of leaving on the junk when the time was right,[6] and I was with him throughout all the hardships of this siege until it was lifted forty-six days later by the Burmese king, about whom I will say a few words because I think that the reader with any curiosity will be interested to know how the tide of war turned out for the *chaubainhá*, king of Martaban.

At the end of the six months and thirteen days that this siege lasted, during which the city had been assaulted five times with over three thousand scaling ladders, the inhabitants had always risen valiantly to its defense, proving themselves to be men of great courage; but since, little by little, time and the ravages of war had sapped their strength, and no help came to them from any quarter, and the enemy outnumbered them many times over, the *chaubainhá* was faced with such a great shortage of everything that it was said that he had only 5,000 men left in the entire city, because the other 130,000 men of his original army had since perished by famine and the sword. Consequently, after counsel had been taken on what should be done to remedy their situation, it was decided that the king should appeal to the enemy's self-interest, a plan that he immediately put into effect, sending word to him that in exchange for lifting the siege he would give him thirty thousand *biças*[7] of silver, which was a million in gold, and in addition, he would become his tributary and pay him sixty thousand *cruzados* a year. To this the Burmese king replied that he would not agree to any terms unless he would first surrender himself to him personally.

The *chaubainhá* made another attempt, this time proposing that he be allowed to leave the city with his treasure, his wife, and his children, on board two *naos,* to seek asylum with the *Sornau,* king of Siam, and in exchange he would abandon the city and everything in it to him. This was also refused. The third time he proposed to him that he withdraw with his camp as far as *Tagalá,*[8] which was six leagues from there, enabling him and his people to depart freely, and that he would deliver up to him the city and the kingdom with all the treasure of the former king, or give him, instead, three million in gold, which was also refused.

Despairing now of ever reaching a peaceful agreement with his cruel enemy, the *chaubainhá* tried to think of some other way to escape from his clutches, and as a last resort, he turned to the Portuguese, thinking that with their help he would be able to get out of the dangerous situation confronting him. He proposed to João Cayeyro that he should embark at night on the four foists he had there, in order to save him with his wife and children, and in exchange he would give him half his treasure. To arrange this matter with the utmost secrecy, he sent a man by the name of Paulo de Seixas,[9] a native of the town of Óbidos,[10] who had remained in the city with him. He appeared one night in João Cayeyro's tent, wearing the costume of Pegu to avoid detection, and gave him a letter from the *chaubainhá* which read as follows:

"To the brave and loyal captain of the Portuguese, by the grace of the great monarch at the end of the world, mighty lion of the frightful roar, crowned with majesty in the House of the Sun:

"I, the unhappy *chaubainhá* that once was prince but is no more, of this unfortunate, captive city, do hereby make known to you with words spoken by me in all good faith, that I offer myself, now and forever, as vassal and subject of the great Portuguese king, whom I acknowledge as sovereign lord over my sons and me, with due homage and the payment of such rich tribute as it is his will to impose.

"Wherefore, I request of you on his part, that as soon as Paulo de Seixas presents this letter of mine to you, without a moment's delay, you bring the *naos* up to the ramparts of the *varela*[11] wharf, where you will find me standing in wait for you and where, without any further ado, I will deliver myself into your trust, with all the treasure I have with me in gold and precious stones, half of which I freely offer to be used in the service of the king of Portugal, with the proviso that he grant me permission to use the remaining half to recruit, from within his kingdom or the fortresses of India, two thousand Portuguese soldiers, to whom I promise to pay high wages, if they will help me regain possession of all that which, to my great misfortune, I am now forced to abandon.

"As for you and the others in your company who help me to escape, I give you my solemn word that I will share my treasure among them all so liberally that they will be well satisfied. And since I must be brief, for the time is short, Paulo de Seixas, who brings you this letter, will bear witness to you of all that he has seen as well as the rest that has passed between us."

No sooner had he read this letter than João Cayeyro, with the utmost secrecy, called a meeting of the most honorable and most reputable men in his company. After he had shown them the letter, he explained to them how important and advantageous it would be to the service of God and His Majesty to accept the *chaubainhá*'s proposition. Once Paulo de Seixas had taken another oath, he asked him for his opinion on the matter and if it was true that the *chaubainhá*'s treasure was as great as it was generally believed to be. To this he replied that, on the oath he had taken, he did not know for certain how large it was, but that five times he had seen with his own eyes a big building, about the size of an average church, filled from floor to ceiling with ingots and bars of gold, which he thought was enough to fill the holds of two good-sized *naos*. He had also seen twenty-six locked chests, bound with ropes, which the *chaubainhá* had told him contained the treasure of *Bresagucão*,[12] former king of Pegu, and as for the amount of gold involved, he told him it came to 130,000 *biças*, which, at five hundred *cruzados* per *biça*, brought the total to sixty-five million in gold. As for the silver bullion which he had also seen stored in the *bralla*[13] of *Quiay Adocá*, god of thunder, he did not know the exact amount, but that from what he had seen with his own eyes, there was such an enormous quantity of it that four good-sized *naos* would not be able to carry it all. In addition, he had also shown him the gold statue of *Quiay Frigau* that had been captured in Rangoon, all covered with precious stones of such great splendor and value that in his opinion there was nothing in the whole world to compare with it.

The declaration made by this man, there in public, under solemn oath, so amazed all his listeners that most of them did not think such a thing was possible. They asked him to wait outside while they discussed what action should be taken; but, for our sins, nothing ever came of it because there was such a wide divergence of opinions on the subject that even Babylon in its heyday had never produced a greater confusion of tongues. According to what was said, this was due mainly to envy on the part of six or seven of those present there, trying to put on airs of nobility, who actually believed that if God permitted the whole affair to turn out as well as expected, then João Cayeyro alone—whom they disliked—would as a result become so famous and so highly honored that it would be a small matter indeed, as they said later, for the king to make him a marquis or, at the very least, governor of India.

So that after pointing out some of the obstacles that would be encountered, which served as a shield for their cowardice and evil disposition, to say nothing of their fear of losing their goods and having their heads cut off by the Burmese king, these ministers of the devil concluded by totally rejecting this undertaking. On the contrary, they threatened to reveal it if João Cayeyro insisted on going forward with the *chaubainhá*'s proposition, as he had thought of doing, though at the time he had no alternative but to hide his thoughts because he was afraid that if he forced the issue they would denounce him to the Burmese king as they were threatening to do, with neither fear of God nor shame in the eyes of men.

149
Martaban Capitulates

When João Cayeyro realized that all his efforts were to no avail and that there was nothing he could do to bring it about, much as he desired, he wrote a letter to the *chaubainhá,* excusing himself in a very lame manner for not acceding to his request. He gave it to Paulo de Seixas, sending him on his way with the answer, and he left immediately. It must have been about three in the morning when he departed, and when he reached the city he found the *chaubainhá* waiting for him where he had said in his letter he would be, and handed him the answer he was carrying. When the *chaubainá* read it and realized that he could not be rescued by our men, as he had thought all along he would be, they say that he was so overwhelmed by pain and sorrow that he fell to the ground as though he had been struck dead. He lay there for a while, and after he regained consciousness he began hitting himself in the face again and again, bewailing his sad fate.

"Ah, you Portuguese, Portuguese!" he cried, sighing deeply and shedding many tears. "How shamefully you have repaid me—poor unfortunate wretch that I am—for all the many favors I have done for you time and time again, believing that in so doing I was accumulating a treasure in your friendship, so that you would stand by me loyally at a time like this when I find myself in such great need. And all I wanted or aspired to was to save my children's lives as well as to enrich your king and to have you with me in my land, where you all would have occupied the highest places. And would that it had been the will of the One who reigns amidst the beauty of his stars that you should have earned the merit in his eyes of doing me this good deed—which my sins prevented—for through me, you would have increased his faith and I would have found salvation in the promise of his truth!"

Then he bade farewell to Paulo de Seixas, along with a young girl who had borne him two children, and in appreciation for his having remained with him through all the hardship of the seige, he took two bracelets off his arms and gave them to him.

"I beg you," he said to him, "not to remember how little I give you now, but rather how much I have always loved you. And do not forget to tell the Portuguese how much pain they have caused me and how deeply I lament their ingratitude, of which I most assuredly shall render an account on the Day of Judgement when I accuse them of this crime before God."

This Paulo de Seixas came back the following night with his two small children and their mother, a beautiful, very genteel girl whom he later married in Coromandel,[1] where he sold the two bracelets the *chaubainhá* had given him for thirty-six thousand *cruzados* to Miguel Ferreira,[2] Simão de Brito, and Pero de Bruges, a lapidary, from whom Trimila Rajah, the governor of Narsinga,[3] bought them afterwards for eighty thousand.

Five days after this Paulo de Seixas left the city and came to the camp, where he told us all the things I have said here, the *chaubainhá,* fully aware by then that his situation was utterly hopeless, sought advice from his counsellors on all the evils and misfortunes that were besetting them day by day in rapid succession. At their meeting it was decided to kill every living creature incapable of fighting, to make a sacrifice of all their blood to *Quiay Nivandel,* war god of the *Vitau* battlefield, to throw all the treasure into the sea to prevent their enemies from making use of it, and after that, to set fire to the whole city, and for those who could bear arms, to run amuck and die on the battlefield fighting with the Burmese.

The *chaubainhá* gave his approval, for he thought that this advice was the best of all, and this was the only course of action he meant to follow. Fully committed to it, he immediately issued orders to have the buildings torn down and huge piles of firewood gathered in preparation for carrying out the plan that had been decided upon.

However, that very night, two of the three most important captains he had in the city, in fear of what was to take place the next day, passed over to the Burmese camp, taking four thousand men with them. The flight and disloyalty of these men had such a demoralizing effect on the remaining population that there was no longer anyone who would respond to the sound of the bells, nor would they man the bulwarks, as they had done before. Instead, they all agreed that if the *chaubainhá* did not reach some sort of understanding with the Burmese, they would open the gates, for they thought it was a lesser evil to die fighting than to let time take its toll, consuming them little by little like sick cattle. In order to quell the rebellion that was beginning to arise, the *chaubainhá* told them that he would do as they wished. And when, for that purpose, he ordered another count of the people who were fit for combat, it showed that there were only two thousand men and all of them in such a bad state and so broken in spirit that they would not even be able to resist an army of weak women.

He had now reached the lowest depths of despair, and the only person with whom he could discuss his misfortune was his wife, for by this time there was no one else to whom he could turn for advice or whom he could trust to speak the truth to him, and he decided, as a last desperate measure, to surrender himself into the hands of his enemy, to do with him as he saw fit.

On the following day, at six in the morning, a white flag of truce appeared on the wall. The enemy camp immediately responded with another, and the *Xemimbrum,*[4] their field marshal, sent a man on horseback to the ramparts where the flag was flying, and from its heights they informed him that the *chaubainhá* wanted to send a letter to the king and that they should send him a safe conduct for that purpose. The *Xemimbrum* immediately sent it to him with two high-ranking Burmese officers who came on horseback, bringing a safe-conduct pass that was written on a thin sheet of gold foil, bearing the seal of the king. While these two Burmese remained as hostages within the city, the *chaubainhá* sent him a letter with one of his people who was a sort of priest, an old man already in his eightieth year, who was highly regarded among them as a saint. And the letter read as follows:

"The love of our children is so powerful in this house of our weakness that there is not one of us who are fathers who, for their sake, would not willingly descend a thousand times into the darkest depths of the House of the Serpent, let alone place his life for them in the hand of the One who shows such great mercy to all. For which reason, I have resolved this night, on my own counsel and that of my wife and children, so as to avoid opinions contrary to what I believe to be the greatest good of all, to place myself in the hands of Your Highness, to do with me and with them as you see fit. As for the defense I can plead before you in my own vindication, it is my desire, my lord, that it not be counted in my favor, so that you may earn greater merit before God for the mercy you show me.

"Your Highness may order immediate possession to be taken of my person, my wife, and my little children, as well as of my city, my treasure, and the entire kingdom, all of which I regard from this moment on as having been handed over to you as king and my true and natural sovereign lord. And I beseech you on my knees and prostrate on the ground, to allow them and me to take vows of poverty and to live out our days in a religious retreat, where I promise to lament forever with profound repentance the guilt of my past crime. As for the worldly honors and estates with which Your Highness, as lord of the greater part of the land and isles of the sea can enrich me, I shall renounce them at your feet and again swear perpetual homage to you and take a solemn oath to the greatest God of all gods who moves the clouds in the sky with a gentle touch of his mighty hand, that, as long as I live, I will never leave the religious order in which you, my lord, may command me to profess. And may it be a place where God grant I shall lack everything, so that I shall be totally bereft of earthly promises and my penitence will be more pleasing to the One who pardons all.

"This saintly *grepo*,[5] chief *talapoy*[6] of the Golden House of the Holy *Quiay*,[7] by reason of his authority and austere life, has the power to act for me. He will relate, at your feet, everything else that I might have told you in this letter that is appropriate to my surrender, so that I, trusting in his word, will be relieved of the fears and doubts that ceaselessly beset my soul."

After he had seen the letter, the Burmese king replied immediately with one of his own, promising him many things and swearing repeatedly that the past would be completely forgotten, and that he would provide him with an estate of such lands and income that he would be quite contented—promises never kept, as I will explain further.

That day passed with everyone excited at the prospect of witnessing the surrender. Then early the next morning, the king's *dopo*,[8] or his camp fortifications, presented an unusual sight, for eighty-six luxurious field tents had been set up there, each one surrounded by thirty elephants drawn up in two rows as though ready for battle, their castles bedecked with streamers, and *panouras* in their trunks, making a total of 2,580 elephants. Surrounding the entire *dopo* on all four sides were twelve thousand Burmese cavalrymen on richly caparisoned horses, also drawn up in their regular battle formation, all of them arrayed in full battle dress and armed with cuirasses, breastplates, and skirts of mail, as well as lances, swords, and gilded shields.

Surrounding these cavalrymen were another four rows of more than twenty thousand foot soldiers, also Burmese, while the rest of the countless numbers of troops in the camp were lined up in company order under their respective captains, displaying a huge number of richly decorated flags and banners, and all this to the accompaniment of a wide variety of martial instruments, which together created such a deafening racket, to say nothing of its terrifying effect, that it was impossible to be either heard or understood with all that noise. And at the outer edges of this entire army, another large number of horsemen were running back and forth with their lances in their hands, hooting and shouting, trying to get the people in order.

Wishing to celebrate the surrender of the *chaubainhá* with a grandiose display of majesty, the Burmese king ordered all the foreign captains, with their men fully armed and dressed in their holiday best, to line up on two sides, leaving a path through which the *chaubainhá* could come, which they did at once, forming a passageway that ran from the city gate up to his tent, which must have been a distance of two-thirds of a league. There were thirty-six thousand foreign mercenaries in this formation who came from forty-two different nations, including Portuguese, Greeks, Venetians, Turks, Janissaries, Jews, Armenians, Tartars, Moghuls, Abyssinians, Rajputs, *Nobins*, Khorasanis, Persians, *Tuparás, Gizares*,[9] *Tanocos* of Arabia Felix, Malabaris, Javanese, Achinese, Mons,[10] Siamese, Luzons from the isle of Borneo, *Chacomás*, Arakanese, *Predins*, Papuans,[11] Celebes, Mindanaons, Peguans, Burmese, *Chalões, Jaquesalões, Savadis*,[12] *Tangus*,[13] *Calaminhãs*,[14] *Chaleus*,[15] Andamans, Bengalese, Gujeratis, Indragiris, Menangkabowans, and many, many more whose nationalities I never did learn.

All of the foreigners were lined up in accordance with the instructions issued by the *Xemimbrum*, the field marshal who placed the Portuguese at the head of all these troops, right next to the city gate through which the *chaubainhá* would have to pass. After them came the Armenians, then the Janissaries and the Turks, and all the rest in whatever positions he saw fit, organizing the foreign mercenaries, as I said before, in lines that stretched right up to the king's *dopo,* where the Burmese honor guards were stationed.

150
The Surrender Ceremony

It was nearly one in the afternoon when a bombard was fired, and at this signal the gates of the city were immediately thrown open. The first to appear were the guards that the king had placed in the city the day before, a special unit composed of four thousand Siamese and Burmese troops, all arquebusiers, halberdiers, and pikemen, as well as three hundred armed war elephants led by a Burmese captain named Mompocasser, who was the king's uncle and a *bainhá*[1] of the city of *Meleitay*[2] in the kingdom of *Chaleu.*[3] Ten or twelve paces behind this elephant guard came many lords who had been sent by the king to receive him, including among them the following:

The *chirca*[4] of *Malacou,* with another man next to him whose name I did not learn, both of them seated on elephants adorned with gold-plated harnesses and castles, and collars of precious stones at their necks. Right behind these two, in the same order, came the *bainhá Quendou,* who was lord of *Cosmim,*[5] an important city in the kingdom of Pegu, and the *Mongibray Dacosem.* After these two came the *Bainhá Brajá;* the *Chaumalacur;* the *Nhay Vagaru;*[6] the *Xemim Ansedá;*[7] the *xemim* of *Catão;* the *Xemim Guarem,* son of the *Moncamicau,* king of *Jangumá;*[8] the *bainhá* of *Lá; Rajah Savady;* the *Bainhá Chaque,* governor of the kingdom; the *Dambambuu,*[9] lord of Mergui; *Rajah Savady,*[10] brother of the king of *Berdio;* the *Bainhá Basoy;* the *Cou-talanhameydó;* the *monteo* of *Negrais;*[11] and the *chircá* of *Coulam.*

After these princes, and many others whose names I did not hear, keeping a distance of eight or ten paces behind them, came the *rolim* of *Mounay,*[12] the *talapoy* with the highest priestly rank in the kingdom, who was revered as a saint by the king. He alone was at the side of the *chaubainhá,* for he was acting as patron and interme-diary between him and the king; and right behind him, borne on three litters, came the *Nhay Canató,* daughter of the former king of Pegu[13]—whose kingdom had been taken from him by this Burmese—and wife of the *chaubainhá,* with her four little children, two boys and two girls, between the ages of four and seven. Around these litters came thirty or forty very lovely young maidens of the nobility, walking with their heads bowed, weeping and completely exhausted, all leaning on other women for support. All of them were surrounded by a circle of *talagrepos*—who, among them, are like our Capuchin friars—all elderly men walking barefoot, their heads un-covered, praying on their beads, trying to lift the spirits of these ladies and reviving them with water whenever they swooned, which happened many times. It was indeed such a pitiful sight that there was not a man present at the scene who was not overwhelmed with pain and sorrow.

Immediately behind this forlorn group came another guard corps of foot soldiers, and bringing up the rear were close to five hundred Burmese on horseback. The *chaubainhá* himself was seated on a small female elephant as a symbol of poverty and disdain for the world, in keeping with the precepts of the holy order he was intending to join soon, with no other sign of pomp or splendor about him. He was dressed in mourning in a very long black velvet robe, with his head, beard, and eyebrows freshly shaven. Around his neck there was a frayed rope of coir, with which to surrender himself to the king, and the expression on his face was so sad that no one there could hold back the tears when they saw him. He was sixty-two years old, tall and handsome, his eyes were sad and tired, his features grave and severe, and he had the look of a generous prince about him.

When he reached the courtyard inside the city gates, the entire population of women and children and a few old men who were waiting for him there, on seeing what he looked like before he passed through, all let out such a loud scream, six or seven times, that it sounded as if the world was coming to an end. This was followed by the sounds of loud wailing and lamentations, of people slapping themselves in the face and hitting their heads with stones so unmercifully that most of them were soon bathed in their own blood. As a result, the horror and pity of what was seen and heard there had such a mournful affect on everyone, that even the Burmese of the guard who were their enemies, and stouthearted by nature, were crying like babies.

At this point the *Nhay Canató,* wife of the *chaubainhá,* fainted twice, along with all the other ladies around her, so that it became necessary to help him down from the elephant he was riding, for him to console her and give her courage to go on, but when he saw her lying on the ground looking as though she were dead, with their four children in her arms, he kneeled down on the ground and lifted his eyes to heaven.

"O almighty power of the divine omnipotent God!" he cried, the tears flowing freely. "Who can fathom the righteousness of thy divine justice, that thou shouldst, without regard for the innocence of these poor creatures who have never sinned, allow Thy wrath to go beyond the limits of our understanding? Nevertheless, Lord, my Lord, remember who thou art and not who I am!"

And so saying, he collapsed face down on the ground beside his wife, which brought forth once more from that huge crowd of people, who were there in countless numbers, another outburst of weeping that was so horrible that I cannot find the words to describe the magnitude of it.

However, when he came to, the *chaubainhá* asked for water, which he used to sprinkle on his wife, bringing her back to consciousness, and then, cradling her in his arms, he remained with her that way for quite a while, speaking words of comfort to her, not in the manner of a heathen, which after all, he was, but like a good Catholic man endowed with deep understanding. After nearly half an hour had gone by this way, they mounted him on the elephant again, and the sad procession continued on its way, in the same order as before.

As soon as the king passed through the city gates and started down the path formed by the foreign mercenaries, despite his state of mind, he raised his eyes and saw the seven hundred Portuguese soldiers who were stationed right next to the entrance, all dressed in their holiday best, with short leather cuirasses, the caps on their heads adorned with plumes, all of them with their arquebuses on their shoulders, and João Cayeyro in their midst, dressed in crimson satin, with a gilded broadsword in his hands, clearing the way. The *chaubainhá* recognized him the moment he set eyes on him, and turning his face away, dropped forward on the elephant's neck, refusing to go a step further.

"O brothers and friends of mine," he protested to those around him with tears in his eyes, "I assure you, in all truth, that I find it less painful and offensive to sacrifice myself in the manner that God in his justice has ordained, than to have to bear the sight of people as ungrateful and as evil as these Portuguese! Either let them kill me here or else remove those people from there, for otherwise, I will not go any further!"

And with that he turned around to avoid looking at us and to let everyone see how offended he felt at us, and, all things considered, perhaps he had good reason for feeling that way, because of what I related above. When the captain of the guard saw that the *chaubainhá* had stopped in his tracks and heard his reason for refusing to go any further, though without being able to determine the reason why he was complaining about the Portuguese, he turned around very sharply on the elephant he was riding and came at João Cayeyro.

"Clear out of here!" he shouted. "People as evil as you should not be allowed to tread the earth that may bear fruit! May God forgive whoever got it into the king's head that you could serve some useful purpose. Shave your beards off so that people will not be fooled by you, and you will serve us as women for our money!"

With growing anger, the Burmese guards began to threaten us, and much to our disgrace and shame, they drove us out of there, heaping words of abuse on us. And I must say, in all truth, that in my whole life I never felt more aggrieved about anything than I did at that moment, for the honor of my countrymen.

This done, the *chaubainhá* proceeded on his way until they reached the tent of the king, who was waiting for the *chaubainhá* with all the trappings of royal pomp and splendor in the company of many lords, including fifteen *bainhás*, who are like dukes, as well as six or seven others with still higher and more exalted titles of nobility.

The moment he reached him, the *chaubainhá* threw himself down at his feet, and he lay there, prostrate on the ground, as though in a state of shock, unable to utter a word. At this point the *rolim* of *Mounay*, who had been by his side all the while, spoke on his behalf, in his capacity as priest.

"Sire," he said, "this is indeed a sight to move thy heart to pity, despite the nature of the crime. And bear in mind that the service that is most pleasing to God and to which he is most inclined to show mercy is the one that thou art now called upon to perform, for, by showing clemency in this instance, thou wilt be imitating him, as everyone wishes thee to do with all their hearts, though the desire remains unspoken. And thou mayest believe for certain that God will be so grateful to thee for this, that when he gazes upon thee in the hour of thy death, he will reach out his mighty hand upon thy head and absolve thee of all blame."

After this he said many other things which moved the king to pardon him freely. And he made him a promise to do so. At this, the *rolim* of *Mounay* and all the other lords present showed great pleasure and praised him highly for it, thinking that he would do as he had promised there in the presence of all.

Since it was close to nightfall by then, he dismissed them, and the poor *chaubainhá* was handed over to a Burmese captain called the *Xemim Coumidau,* while his wife and children, together with all the other women, were placed in the care of the *Xemim Ansedá* because he had his wife there with him and was an honorable old man whom the Burmese king trusted implicitly.

151
The Sack of Martaban

It was almost nightfall when the surrender ceremony ended, and since the king was afraid that the troops might enter the city and make off with the plunder for themselves, he had Burmese captains posted at all twenty-four of the gates to stand guard over them and, on pain of severe penalties, not to allow anyone to pass into the city until he should provide otherwise, in keeping with the promise he had made to the foreign mercenaries to give them a clear field. But these precautions were taken, not so much for the reasons he gave, but because he wanted first and foremost to safeguard the *chaubainhá*'s treasure.[1] That is why he let two days go by without doing anything about the captives in his power, for it was the time he needed to secure all the treasure, which was said to be so great that a thousand men had all they could do to gather it up.

One morning, after these two days had passed, the king climbed to the top of a hill called *Beidao,* located about two falcon shots away. From there he gave the order for the captains guarding the gates to withdraw, and then the unfortunate city of Martaban was delivered up to the field soldiers. At the sound of a bombard, which was the final signal, they made such a mad dash for the city that it was said that on entering the gates more than three hundred people were trampled to death. Since there was such an infinite number of people, from many different nations, most of them without king, or law, or fear, or knowledge of God, they were so blinded by their lust for plunder that they thought nothing of killing a hundred men for a single *cruzado.* And things got so out of hand that it became necessary for the king to intercede personally, six or seven times, in order to quell the disorder and tumult going on in the city.

The king, with another ceremony, complete with official proclamations and the blasting of trumpets, ordered the rich and noble palaces of the *chaubainhá* and thirty or forty others belonging to his most important captains to be torn down, along with all the *varelas,* pagodas, and *bralas*[2] in the entire city. The loss of these sumptuous temples with their buildings and magnificent artworks was said by many to have amounted to well over ten million in gold. Still not content with this, the king ordered the torch put to whatever else had been left standing, in over a hundred different places, and since it was a windy day, the flames spread so quickly that the destruction wrought by the fire on that first night alone was so complete that even the city walls in some places, with their towers, bulwarks, and guard stations, burned down to their very foundations.

A rough estimate and list of the losses suffered during this disastrous campaign of vengeance having been made, it was said that 160,000 people perished either by the sword or famine, to say nothing of nearly the same number that were taken captive, and that 140,000 buildings were burned, as well as sixteen hundred in which they say that sixty thousand statues of idols—most of them covered in gold—were destroyed, and that three thousand elephants were eaten during the siege. Other losses included six thousand pieces of both bronze and iron artillery, 100,000 quintals of pepper, and about the same quantity of spices, sandalwood, benzoin, lacquer, putchock,[3] storax,[4] eaglewood, camphor, silk, and many other kinds of expensive dry goods, and most of all, an infinite amount of clothing that had come there from all over India in more than a hundred *naos* from Cambay, Achin, Melinde, Ceylon, the Straits of Mecca, the Ryukyus, and China. As for the silver, gold, and precious stones, the losses could never be determined with any certainty, for such things are generally covered up or denied. But just what this Burmese king alone made off with in hard cash from the *chaubainhá*'s treasure was said to run well over a hundred million in gold, half of which—as was explained above—was lost by the king, our lord, because of our sins, and perhaps because of the cowardice or envy of some men of ill will.

Early the following day, after the city had been sacked, destroyed, burned, and razed to the ground, on the same hill where the king had stood, twenty-one gallows appeared in view, twenty of them alike and one a little smaller than the others, that had been erected on stone pillars enclosed by a rosewood fence and covered by a canopy with gilded spires at the top. The entire area was guarded by a hundred Burmese cavalrymen and surrounded on all sides by a barrier of very wide ditches where many black, bloodstained banners were flying. Since it looked like something unusual was afoot, for which nobody had any explanation at the time, six of us Portuguese decided to go and see for ourselves what it was all about. After walking around a while looking at all those death machines, we heard the loud murmur of voices coming from all the people in the camp, which disturbed us somewhat. Without being able to fathom what was going on, we saw coming from the direction of the king's headquarters a large number of men on horseback who were clearing a wide path in the crowd with their lances, shouting at the same time that, on pain of death, no one was to appear with arms or to express what he felt in his heart. At a considerable distance behind these guards came the *Xemimbrum,* the field marshal, with a hundred armed war elephants and a large number of foot soldiers, followed by fifteen hundred cavalrymen in four columns, six abreast, under the command of the *Talanhagibray,* viceroy of Toungoo[5]. Behind them came the *Chauseró Siammom* with three thousand Siamese troops armed with muskets and lances, moving all together in a crowd, in the midst of which walked a large group of women—140 of them, according to what was said there—all tied together four by four and accompanied by *talagrepos* of austere life—who are like Capuchin friars—who were trying to give them the courage to face the terrible ordeal of death which they were about to undergo.

Behind them, surrounded by twelve footmen bearing silver maces, came *Nhay Canató,* daughter of the king of Pegu[6]—whose kingdom had been taken from him by this Burmese tyrant—and wife of the *chaubainhá,* with her four little children, borne in the arms of some men on horseback. All of the 140 women in the death procession were the wives and daughters of the leading military captains who had remained in the city with the *chaubainhá,* and it was against these women that the Burmese tyrant, by way of revenge, chose to give vent to the deep-seated feelings of resentment and hatred he had always harbored against women.

All, or most, of the condemned women ranged in age from seventeen to twenty-five, and they were all extremely fair and beautiful, with their hair like skeins of gold.[7]

They were so weak and so beside themselves that they kept falling to the ground in a faint with each new proclamation they heard, and every time this happened, other women who were supporting them would come to their aid with sweets, to which the poor girls paid very little heed, for by then they were so far gone that their only reaction to what the *talagrepos* were telling them was to raise their arms heavenward now and then, though not very often.

Immediately behind this princess came sixty *grepos* in double file, reading from their prayerbooks, with their heads bowed and the tears streaming down their cheeks, who chanted some sort of litany from time to time that went like this: "O Thou who alone hast the being of who Thou art, justify our works in Thee so that they may find acceptance in Thy court of justice," to which others responded in tears, "May it please Thee, O Lord, to grant our prayer so that we may not, by our deeds, lose the rich rewards of Thy promises!"

These *grepos* were followed by a procession of over three hundred children, all naked from the waist down, with white wax candles in their hands and nooses of coconut fiber cord around their necks, who were chanting another litany with deep emotion: "O merciful Lord, hear the sound of our cry and grant pardon to these thy captives, so that they may rejoice in the blessings of thy rich treasures ...," and so on, in this manner, they went on chanting many other prayers like this on behalf of the doomed women.

Behind this procession came another guard of foot soldiers, also Burmese, armed with lances and arrows, and a few with arquebuses. At the very end came another hundred elephants of the guard, similar to the ones in the vanguard. So that altogether, those engaged in the execution of this sentence, as well as those in the guards and the ones taking part in the pomp and ceremony attending it, came to ten thousand men on foot and horse, and two hundred elephants, to say nothing of the common people, both native and foreign, who were there in countless numbers.

152
The Burmese Tyrant's Revenge

Keeping to this order, these forlorn people walked on through the middle of the camp to the ground where all of them were to be put to death, reaching it with enormous difficulty, for since they were women, feeble in strength and courage, and most of them very delicate young maidens, they fainted at every step of the way. When they finally got to where the twenty-one gallows stood, the six mounted macebearers raised their voices once again and proclaimed out loud, "Hear ye! Hear ye! Let the peoples of the world bear witness to the criminal justice decreed by the living god, lord of truth, and sovereign king over our heads, whose will and pleasure it is that all of these 140 women should be put to death and delivered up to the element of the air for having advised their husbands and fathers to rise up against us in this city where altogether they killed twelve thousand Burmese of the kingdom of Toungoo!"

At the stroke of a bell the entire mob of guards and ministers of justice let out a bloodcurdling scream that was frightful to hear and enough to make one tremble with fear.

Just as the cruel executioners were about to carry out their stern justice, the wretched condemned women embraced each other, shedding many tears. Then they all turned their gaze on the *Nhay Canató,* who by that time, looking more dead than alive, was leaning on the breast of an old woman, and most of them made their final *zumbaias* to her, while one of them, as though speaking in the name of the weaker ones who could not do so, said to her, "Madam, crown of roses for our heads, now that we are embarking with thee as thy slaves on these vessels of death, console us with the sight of thy presence, so that we may depart with less suffering from this painful flesh and enter into the presence of the righteous Judge of the mighty hand, before whom we protest we shall tearfully demand justice for thee, with eternal vengeance for this senseless crime."

Deathly pale, the *Nhay Canató* looked at them and replied in a voice so weak she could hardly be heard, "Hiche hocão finarato quiay vanzilau maforem hotapir," which means, "Do not leave me, sisters of mine, stay and help me carry these children." Thereupon, she leaned her head again on the woman's breast without saying another word.

Then the ministers of the Arm of Wrath,[1] as they call the executioners there, set about doing their work on the poor women, stringing them up on the twenty gallows, seven on each, tied by the feet with their heads down, which kept making loud, cracking noises, as if to show how grievous was the death they were dying, and there, in less than an hour, they all suffocated in their own blood.

Then the mounted guards made the people move back again, for there was such a huge mob that no one could get through, and the four women supporting the *Nhay Canató* brought her up to the gallows where she was to be hanged, along with her four little children. As the *rolim* of *Mounay,* whom they all regarded as a saint, was saying a few words of comfort to her, she asked for a little water, which was immediately brought to her, and after taking some in her mouth she shared it with the four children whom she had gathered in her arms by then. Kissing them over and over she exclaimed through her tears, "O my darlings, my dearest children, newly born in the deepest recesses of my soul! Would that I were so blessed that I could ransom your lives by receiving a thousand deaths in exchange! I swear to you, by this hour of fear and sadness, in which I gaze upon you with all eyes on me, that I would as gladly accept such a death at the hands of this cowardly enemy, as to gaze upon the presence of the almighty Lord in the peace of his heavenly abode."

And fixing her eyes on the executioner who by then had already tied up two of the children, she said to him, "I beg you, my friend, not to be so heartless as to make me witness the death of my children, for you would be guilty of a grave sin. Let me die first and I will be eternally grateful to you for this charitable deed that I ask of you in the name of God!"

Then she took the children in her arms once more and kissing them over and over as if bidding them farewell, fell lifelessly into the arms of the woman attending her. At that moment the executioner hurried forward and strung her up on the gallows as he had done with the other women, and then he did the same thing with the four little children, hanging two of them on each side of her, leaving the unfortunate mother swinging in the middle. At this heartbreaking and utterly cruel spectacle, such a tumultuous sound of cries and shouts arose among all the people that the earth trembled beneath our feet, and a riot broke out in the camp, which got so out of control that the king found it necessary to fortify the area around his tent with six thousand Burmese cavalrymen and thirty thousand foot soldiers. Even then he was afraid that what he had always dreaded might happen, and would have happened if the coming of nightfall had not prevented it, because there was absolutely no way of quieting that mob; for out of the 700,000 men present in the camp, 600,000 were Peguans, and the queen whose death they had witnessed was the daughter of their king, but they had been so thoroughly subjugated by the iron fist of the Burmese tyrant that they did not dare lift their eyes.

And so, with such a base and ignominious kind of death, *Muhé* [2] *Canató,* daughter of the king of Pegu, emperor of nine kingdoms, and wife of the *chaubainhá,* king of Martaban, a princess with an income of three million in gold, met her end. And her luckless husband was thrown into the sea [3] that same night with a stone weight around his neck, along with fifty or sixty of his vassals, some of whom were noblemen with incomes of between thirty and forty thousand *cruzados,* all fathers, husbands, and brothers of the 140 innocent women who suffered such a cruel, degrading death, among them three of the princess's ladies-in-waiting who had received from the Burmese king, while he was still a count, a proposal of marriage which neither they nor their fathers would even consider in those days, but such are the changes usually wrought by time and fortune.

153
Betrayed by a Portuguese Nobleman

After carrying out this stern justice, the Burmese tyrant remained in the area for nine more days, on each of which he inflicted further punishment on the inhabitants of the city. At the end of that time he departed for Pegu, leaving behind the *Bainhá Chaque,* [1] his chief steward, to attend to some matters that were necessary for the pacification of the kingdom and the rebuilding of what the fire had consumed. He left him a sufficient garrison for that purpose and took the rest of the army with him, including João Cayeyro and the seven hundred Portuguese mercenaries, with the exception of just three or four who were of no account. Besides these, there also remained one other by the name of Gonçalo Falcão, [2] a well-born gentleman of good blood whom the heathens called *Crisna Pacau,* meaning "flower of flowers," an honorary title among them, which the king of Burma had bestowed on him as a reward for his services. At the time that I left Malacca, Pero de Faria had given me a letter for him, asking him to help me, should the need arise, to carry out my mission, not only as a service to His Majesty, but also as a personal favor to him. When I reached Martaban and found him living there, I gave him the letter and also informed him of the nature of my mission, which was to confirm the peace treaty previously made by the *chaubainhá,* through the intermediary of his ambassadors, with Malacca, during Pero de Faria's first term of office [3] as captain of the fortress, with all of which he was well acquainted. I also told him that for that purpose I was the bearer of a letter of deep friendship for the *chaubainhá,* as well as a gift of luxury items from China.

Apparently, in the belief that he could curry even greater favor with the king of Burma—to whose side he had crossed over during the siege, deserting the *chaubainhá,* whom he had previously been serving—this Gonçalo Falcão, barely three days after the departure of the king, went to see this military governor of his and told him that I had come there on an embassy to the *chaubainhá* from the captain of Malacca, and that I had been instructed to offer him a substantial number of troops against the king of Burma, then in control of the land, in order to build fortifications in Martaban and throw the Burmese out of his kingdom. He told him many other things like that, as a result of which the governor promptly placed me under arrest. After putting me under heavy guard, he went down to the junk on which I had arrived from Malacca and seized the vessel and all the cargo in her hold, which was probably worth over 100,000 *cruzados.* Then he arrested the *necodá,* the captain-owner of the junk, together with all of the 164 persons he found on board, among them a group of forty wealthy merchants comprised of Malays, Menangkabowans, Moors, and heathen natives of Malacca, who were then all summarily sentenced to having their property confiscated and being made captives of the king like myself, for consenting to and covering up the treason that the captain of Malacca had secretly been plotting with the *chaubainhá* against the king of Burma.

He had them all thrown into a dungeon where they were flogged repeatedly, so that in the month or so that they were in prison, 119 of the 164 people there died of neglect, fever,[4] hunger, and thirst, and the forty-five who survived were put aboard a sampan with neither sails nor oars and left to drift down the river. Abandoned in this manner to the whim of fortune, they landed at an uninhabited island called *Pulo Camude,* twenty leagues from the bar of Martaban, where they gathered some food such as shellfish and berries from the woods, rigged up a sail out of the clothes they were wearing, and with a pair of oars they either found there or fashioned for themselves, proceeded along the coast as far as Junkseylon. After making another stop, which took them two months, they finally reached the Perlis River in the kingdom of Kedah, where most of them fell sick from some abscesses in the throat, similar to the ones that come with the plague, so that only two of them reached Malacca alive. There they reported to Pero de Faria[5] on the events of this unhappy voyage and told him about how poor unlucky me had already been sentenced to death—which was true at the time, but fortunately, the good Lord miraculously delivered me from such a fate; for after the *necodá* and the merchants had been exiled in the manner I described, they transferred me to a more tightly guarded prison where they kept me in irons for thirty-six days under the most harsh and cruel conditions. Meanwhile, this dog continued to press charges against me, defaming me and alleging all sorts of unheard of crimes, for the sole purpose of killing me and robbing me as he had done to all the others on the junk. Three times he interrogated me in public court, but I never answered any of his questions directly, which so infuriated him and all the others present that they accused me of arrogance and contempt of court. As a result, right there in public they flogged me repeatedly and treated me to fiery drops of molten lac, which nearly killed me on the spot and left me hovering between life and death for more than twenty days, an ordeal from which nobody ever expected me to recover.

But since I happened to say a few times that all these false charges were being brought against me so that they could rob me of my merchandise, but that it would not be long before Captain João Cayeyro, who was in Pegu, would report it to the king, those few chance words, spoken in desperation, without really knowing what I was saying, were—thanks be to God—what saved my life. For just when this dog was on the point of executing the sentence handed down against me, some of his friends intervened and advised him not to, pointing out to him that if he were to kill me, all the Portuguese in Pegu would complain to the king about him and accuse him of having condemned me to death in order to rob me of the 100,000 *cruzados* that the captain of Malacca had sent with me; moreover, the king was bound to ask him to account for all that money, and that even if he were to hand over the entire amount that he had taken from me, the king would not be satisfied and would think that it had been much more; with the result that he might be so discredited in the eyes of the king that he might never again be able to get back in his good graces, and his children would be completely ruined, debased, and deeply dishonored. Dreading such a possibility, that dog of a governor *Bainhá Chaque* decided not to go forward with what he had so willfully conceived. He revised the death sentence that had been handed down, commuting it to confiscation of property and imprisonment as a captive of the king.

As soon as my wounds from the floggings and fire drops had healed, they took me to Pegu in chains, where I was handed over as a captive to the king's treasurer, a Burmese by the name of *Diosoray,* who had been holding eight other Portuguese captive for the past six months, owing to misfortunes arising out of sins like mine, for they had been on board a *nao* belonging to Dom Henrique d'Eça of Cannanore[6] that had been driven ashore in bad weather.

Now as long as I have gone this far in describing the events of my voyage to Martaban and the benefits I derived from it in the service of the king, our lord—such as having my property stolen and being made a captive after having gone through so much hardship—I have decided before I go any further, to describe all else that happened to me in the course of the two and a half years I spent as a captive in these kingdoms, as well as the countries through which I wandered, owing to difficulties and misfortunes beyond my control, since I thought it was necessary before continuing my tale.

Having departed from the city of Martaban, as was mentioned above, this Burmese king marched by stages with his army until he reached Pegu where, before mustering out his captains, he took a census of the troops he had and found that there were 86,000 less than the original 700,000 men with whom he had laid siege to the *chaubainhá.* But since, by this time, rumors had reached him that the king of Ava, in league with the *Savadis* and the *Chaleus,* were allowing the *Siammon*[7] (whose country borders in the interior to the west and west-northwest with the territory of the *Calaminhan,*[8] "emperor of the indomitable force of the elephants of the earth," as I shall explain later on when I speak of him) to cross their borders to take the fortresses of the Toungoo kingdom away from this Burmese king, he, like a good captain and a highly experienced one, very astute in matters pertaining to warfare, immediately gave orders, before doing anything else, that his four main fortresses, for which he feared the most, should be well garrisoned and fully stocked with all the necessary supplies. Having made the decision to march on the city of Prome,[9] he retained the army that was with him and set about once more making great preparations for war throughout the entire kingdom. Within five months he had raised an army of as many as 900,000 men, with whom he departed from the city of Bagou,[10] which is commonly called Pegu, embarking on twelve thousand oared vessels, two thousand of which were *serós,*[11] *laulés,* cutters, and foists.

Departing on 9 March 1545, this fleet traveled up the *Ansedá* River,[12] stopping at

Danaplu[13] long enough to replenish their dwindling provisions, and from here, proceeding on his course along a great freshwater river more than a league wide that was called *Pichau Malacou,* on the thirteenth of April[14] he anchored within view of the city of Prome. There he learned from spies seized during the night that the king had died and been succeeded by his son, a boy of thirteen whom his father, on his deathbed, had given in marriage to his sister-in-law—that is, his wife's sister, the boy's aunt and daughter of the king of Ava[15]—who, as soon as she had learned that the Burmese king was marching on her city of Prome, had immediately sent to ask her father for aid. He was said to be sending his son, the queen's brother, with an armada carrying sixty thousand Mons, *Tarés,* and *Chalens,* all elite troops, very determined in battle. When this news reached him the Burmese king decided to act fast and to take the city before help arrived. Disembarking in a field called *Meigavotau,* two leagues below the city, he remained there for five days making all the necessary preparations.

After giving orders for what was to be done, he set off from there one day in the predawn hours and, marching to the sound of an infinite number of war drums and fifes, reached the city at eleven o'clock that morning without having encountered any opposition whatsoever up to then. He began at once to set up his camp the way they usually do, and before nightfall it was enclosed all around with very strong trenches and bulwarks, and six artillery emplacements.

154
The Burmese Attack Prome

Five days after the arrival of the Burmese king, the besieged queen, who was governing the city in her husband's name, sent one of her most highly revered priests—a *talagrepo* over a hundred years old—to pay a call on him and to deliver a handsome gift of gold serving pieces encrusted with precious stones, as well as a letter that went like this:

"Great, powerful lord, more highly favored in the House of Fortune than all the other kings who inhabit the earth, impregnable fortress of great power, flood tide of the salty seas where all the lesser rivers of the earth, alike unto this poor, unfortunate woman, bring their currents to rest, mighty shield, emblazoned with crests that bespeak grandeur, possessor of great states, upon whose throne thy feet are firmly placed, unchallenged, in great majesty.

"I, the *Nhay Nivolau,* a poor woman, governess and servant of this orphaned child, prostrate myself before thee with all the respect due thee as my lord, and implore thee with tears in my eyes not to draw thy sword against me, for I am but a weak woman, incapable of defending myself, nor can I do aught but bewail before God the wrong that is done me, for it is the very essence of his divine nature to succor with mercy and punish with justice, so that no matter how mighty the states of the world may be, he tramples them beneath his feet with such awesome power, that even those who dwell in the Lower Depths of the House of Smoke tremble in fear before this Lord, for whose sake I entreat thee, I implore thee, not to take away from me what is mine, for as you know it is so insignificant that thou wilt be none the greater for having it nor smaller for not having it; whereas, sire, if thou, on the contrary, show pity towards me, thou wilt achieve such greatness and renown that even the innocent little babes will leave off suckling at their mothers' breasts to sing thy praises with lips so pure and sweet, and all the people in the land, both native and foreign, will remember thee for the charity thou showest me, which I shall have written on the sepulchers of the dead so that both they and the living will give thee thanks, on my account, for this charitable deed which I beseech thee with all my heart and soul to grant me.

"To *Avemlachim,* the saintly bearer of this letter, written in my hand, I have given full power and authority to make, in the name of this fatherless child and my own, any kind of equitable agreement with thee and to concede to thee whatever tribute and homage thou mayest deem proper, on the condition that thou permit us to remain in possession of our houses so that, under the security of thy word, we may raise our children and harvest the produce of our fields for the sustenance of the wretched inhabitants of this poor, captive village, all of whom, and I with them, will serve thee with humble respect in whatever way it shall be thy will to employ us."

This letter and embassy was received with great authority by the Burmese king, who paid honor to the bearer, not only because of his age but also because he was revered among them as a saint. Right at the outset he granted him some of the things he asked for, such as a truce during the period of negotiations, and freedom for the besieged to communicate with the people in the countryside, and other things like that of minor importance. However, once he had seen the conditions proposed by the poor queen and noted the humble tone of her letter, which he attributed entirely to fear and weakness on her part, he no longer bothered to reply directly to the points raised by the messenger; but instead, he secretly issued orders to carry out raids throughout the land against the weak unarmed population who, feeling secure in their poverty, had not left their huts in the woods, and among whom these cruel, inhuman enemies spread such destruction, without encountering any resistence or opposition, that it was said that in only five days' time they killed fourteen thousand people, all or most of them women and children and old men unfit to bear arms.

Disenchanted by the false promises of the tyrant, and extremely unhappy about the lack of respect that had been shown him, the *rolim* who had delivered the letter asked for permission to return to the city, which was not refused him by the Burmese, who replied to the queen's letter orally by telling him that she should surrender to him first with all her people, treasure, and kingdom, and he would indemnify her with something else with which she would be happy; also, that he wanted an answer the same day, for that was all the time he would give her, and depending on her answer, he would decide on what he had to do.

The *rolim* took leave of him immediately and returned to the city, where he informed the queen of everything that had taken place. And he made her see the evil intentions of the tyrant, and how untrustworthy he was, reminding her of what he had done in Martaban to the *chaubainhá* when he surrendered to him, trusting in his word, only to be killed later along with his wife and children and all the nobles in the kingdom. As a result the queen decided then and there, in consultation with the members of her council, to defend the city until help arrived from her father, which should not take any more than two weeks; moreover, she made them all swear to this by taking new oaths of allegiance from them.

Having made this decision, without any further delay, she saw to all things that were important to the defense of the city, conducting herself with great courage and fervor and inspiring her people with great prudence and a manlike spirit. Sharing liberally with them from her treasury, she also promised them all that she would repay them in the future for their services with honors and rewards, thereby lifting their morale considerably.

When the Burmese king saw that the *rolim* failed to return within the time period stipulated, early the following day he proceeded to strengthen his fortifications with double the amount of artillery so as to be able to batter the city on all sides, and he ordered large numbers of ladders built for scaling the walls, after which he issued a proclamation to the effect that everyone was to be ready for action within three days, on pain of death.

On 3 May 1545, the day appointed for the assault, at an hour before dawn, the king sallied forth from his headquarters on the river where he was anchored with two thousand *serós* manned by elite forces. He gave a signal to the captains on shore, who by then were ready for action, and they charged the walls all together in a single body with such a horrible clamor of screams and shouts that it seemed as if heaven and earth had come together as one.

Then the enemies engaged, and the ensuing battle was so cruel and furious that in no time at all the air was filled with fire and the ground covered with blood, broken only by the occasional gleam of the iron lances and swords flashing through the fiery curtain, which altogether created such a frightful spectacle that we Portuguese went about gasping in horror.

The battle raged on without pause for more than five hours, but at the end of that time, when he saw that the people inside the walls were defending themselves bravely, while at several points along the lines his men were beginning to weaken, the Burmese tyrant jumped ashore with some ten or twelve thousand of the best troops in the armada and quickly threw them into battle, thereby reinforcing the companies still fighting, and the battle began anew with such force and fury on both sides that it seemed as if it had just started.

This second engagement lasted until nearly nightfall, but even that was not enough to make the king call a halt to the fighting, despite the advice of his people who urged him to withdraw. Instead, he swore that he would sleep inside the walls or else cut off the heads of any of his captains whom he saw unwounded. His obstinacy was responsible for serious losses in the ranks, for by letting the battle rage on until the moon set—which was sometime about two in the morning—when he finally gave the order to withdraw, the number of casualties, as revealed by the following day's muster, turned out to be twenty-four thousand dead and more than thirty thousand wounded, many of whom died later of neglect. This caused a serious pestilence to spread through the camp, not only because of the corruption of the air but also because of the blood flowing in the river, which had practically contaminated the water. This alone accounted afterwards for the deaths of more than eighty thousand men— according to what was said—including among them five hundred Portuguese whose only burial then was in the bellies of the vultures and crows that tore them apart bit by bit as they lay scattered in the fields and along the shores.

155
The Fall of Prome

When he saw how dearly he had paid for this initial assault, the Burmese king decided not to expose his men in the same way again. But he ordered the construction of a huge earthwork of fill and rubble, for which he had over ten thousand palm trees cut down, creating a mountain so high that it towered nearly two armspans over the walls of the city. On top of it he had eighty heavy pieces of artillery installed, with which he battered the entire city for nine days in a row, leveling most or practically all of it and bringing the death toll within the city to fourteen thousand. This broke the back of the poor queen's resistance, for by then she had only five thousand men still fit for battle, while the rest of the population consisted of women, children, and others unfit to bear arms.

After a session with her council which she called to decide what to do in this dire situation, it was agreed, upon advice of the leading citizens of the land, that they should anoint themselves with the oil from the lamps of the shrine of *Quiay Nivandel,* god of the *Vitau* battlefield, and offering themselves in sacrifice, they should storm the mountain and either conquer or all die as *amucks,*[1] in defense of their king, for he was only a child, and they had done homage to him and sworn to be good and loyal subjects. The queen and all the others agreed that this was the best and wisest course of action in view of the circumstances, and to reinforce their resolve, they all took a solemn oath to carry it out.

Once this was done, they immediately set to work mapping out the way in which they were to proceed with this undertaking, and they chose one of the queen's uncles as their captain, a man by the name of *Manica Votau,* who quickly gathered the five thousand men fit for combat. That same night, at the end of the midwatch, he sallied out of the two gates facing the mountain and fell upon it with such determination that in little more than an hour the camp was scattered into over a hundred parts, the mountain with all eighty pieces of artillery on it captured, the king wounded, the stockades burned, the ramparts leveled, the *Xemim Brum,* their field marshal, together with over fifteen thousand men—including six hundred Turks—slain, forty elephants captured and many more killed, and eight hundred Burmese taken prisoner, from which it would appear that these five thousand *amucks* accomplished a feat that would have taken 100,000 other men to do, no matter how brave, and even then only with great difficulty. When they finally withdrew at an hour before dawn, out of the original five thousand only seven hundred were found dead.

The Burmese king was so outraged by this turn of events, putting the blame on some of his captains for the careless watch they had kept and for their negligence in guarding the mountain, that on that very same day he ordered the beheading of over two thousand Peguans, who were the ones on duty during that watch. After this, things were quiet for a period of twelve days, during which there was no activity in the camp outside the walls.

About this time, one of the four main captains in the city, a man by the name of *Xemim Meleitay,*[2] who feared, as did most everyone by then, that there was no escape from this enemy who had besieged them, entered into secret correspondence with him, in which he proposed to deliver the city to him by allowing him to enter it through the gate he was guarding, on condition that he leave him freely in possession of his estate, that he not touch the house of any member of his family, and that he name him *xemim* of *Ansedá* in the kingdom of Pegu, with all the revenue the *bainhá* of *Malacou* had received there, which was thirty thousand *cruzados*.

The Burmese king accepted the proposal with all these conditions and pledged his word by sending him an expensive ring he had on his finger. And on the appointed day, which fell on the eve of Saint Bartholomew,[3] in the year 1545, at three o'clock in the morning, this treacherous plan was carried out with the ferocious and horrendous cruelty that the Burmese tyrant customarily employed in all matters of this nature.

Since it seems to me that it would take forever to describe everything that happened, suffice it to say that the gate was opened, the city entered, all her people put to the sword without sparing a soul, the king and queen taken prisoner, the treasury captured, all the buildings and temples razed, and many other different kinds of atrocities committed that are so utterly beyond the imagination or conception of men that I can truly say that I myself, whenever I look back on the way these events unfolded, which I saw with my own eyes, I nearly go out of my mind. For since his pride had been hurt, and he was still smarting from the humiliation of his recent defeat, the tyrant inflicted all sorts of cruel punishment on these unfortunate people in revenge for the reverses of fortune he had suffered from the beginning of the siege. But the truth of the matter is that it was because he was a coward who came of a base bloodline and extraction,[4] the sort that is more likely to show a streak of cruelty and a desire for revenge than someone who is courageous and generous by nature, and most of all, because he was basically dishonest and incapable of keeping his word, and because he was by nature a pederast and extremely hostile to women, despite the fact that those he had in that kingdom and in all the others he ruled were fairer and more beautiful by far than many another.

Following the cruel and bloody destruction of this unfortunate city, the tyrant, by way of a triumphal procession, marched in with great pomp and splendor, coming through an opening in the wall he had arranged to have knocked down for that purpose. When he reached the palace of the poor little king, he had himself crowned king of Prome, keeping the boy on his knees throughout the entire ceremony, with hands upraised, as though he were worshipping God, and every now and then they would make him put his head down to the ground and kiss his feet, which the tyrant pretended not to notice.

When this was over, he went to stand at a window overlooking a courtyard where they brought the bodies of more than two thousand children that had been lying in the streets, and right there in front of him he had them cut into very small pieces, rolled in rice chaff and grass, and fed to the elephants.

After this was done, in another sort of ceremony, accompanied by the sound of many musical instruments and loud cries, they led in more than a hundred horses laden with the quartered bodies of men and women, which, after being cut up, he also burned.

After this, they brought him the queen, the wife of the little king who, as mentioned previously, was only thirteen years old while she was thirty-six, a very fair, handsome woman, aunt to her husband, sister to his mother, and daughter of the king of Ava, the country from which the rubies, sapphires, and emeralds[5] come to Pegu.

Three years before, this Burmese had sent to ask her father for her hand in marriage, according to what was said there at the time, and he had refused, telling the ambassador that his daughter had much higher aspirations than that of becoming the wife of the *xemim* of Toungoo,[6] which was the seat of the family from which this cruel and cowardly tyrant descended. And now, not only to show contempt for her and her father, but also to avenge himself for the past insult he had received, he had her stripped naked right there in public and brutally flogged, after which she was taken all over the city and, to the accompaniment of the shouts and jeers of the vulgar and indecent crowds, again subjected to torture, from which she soon expired. After her death he had her bound embracing her husband, the little king, who was still alive, and, with a stone tied at each of their necks, had them both thrown into the river,[7] which was a most frightful form of cruelty from which the onlooker recoiled in horror. And in this manner he went on to perpetrate many other atrocities, the like of which had never been seen or dreamed of before.

And to crown it all, on the following day, which was Saint Bartholomew's Day, he had all the noblemen who had been taken alive—and there must have been nearly three hundred of them—impaled on *caloetes*,[8] and in that manner, impaled like suckling pigs, they too were thrown into the river. So that the means used here by this tyrant to punish these unfortunate people were so unheard of, that we Portuguese all went about gasping in horror.

156
The Fall of *Meleitay*

For fourteen days after these things happened, the tyrant devoted himself to fortifying the city, working with great care and haste. By that time he received confirmed reports from the spies he had sent abroad for that purpose that an armada of four hundred oar-propelled sailing ships had departed from the city of Ava and was coming down the *Queitor* River with thirty thousand of the *Siammon's* men, not counting the sailors and deckhands. It was commanded by a son of the king of Ava and brother to the poor queen, who on being advised of the fall of Prome and the death of his sister and brother-in-law, had encamped in the fortress of *Meleitay,* which was eighteen leagues up the river from Prome. The tyrant was so shaken by this news that he thought it necessary for him to go at once in person against these people before they received the additional help of an army of eighty thousand Mons, which he had heard was getting ready to join them under the command of the king of Ava.[1]

Having made this decision, the Burmese tyrant set out in search of these people at *Meleitay*[2] with an army of 300,000 men, sending 200,000 by land along the shore of the river under the command of his brother-in-law, the *Chaumigrem,*[3] while he proceeded up the river in a fleet of two thousand *serós,* taking 100,000 with him; and altogether, those by land and by water comprised an army of handpicked men.

When they came in sight of *Meleitay,* the Avans set fire to their ships, not only to avoid the possibility of their fleet being captured in the river, which would have been too great an affront to their pride, but also to show the enemy that they had come there determined to fight and that nothing, not even their fear of the huge army confronting them, would deter them from their purpose. Filled with savage pride, they had made up their minds, down to the last man, to avenge the outrage perpetrated against their king, and without a thought for what the flesh, by nature, fears most, they took to the field, divided into four battalions of ten thousand each. Three of these battalions were comprised of the thirty thousand Mons,[4] while the fourth, which was a little larger, consisted of the sailors and deckhands from the four hundred ships they had burned. These they placed in the front line of battle, the strategy being to use them to tire the enemy whom they attacked at once, engaging them in fierce combat which lasted half an hour and in which most of the seamen were slain. Immediately after this, the thirty thousand Mons, keeping in tight formation, rushed at the enemy with tremendous force and fury, and since by then they were exhausted from their recent encounter with the seamen, many of them were slain and many others wounded. At any rate, so as not to dwell on details that might seem doubtful, suffice it to say that the battle that raged between them was so extraordinarily cruel that of the thirty thousand Mons, only eight hundred escaped alive. Wounded and routed as they were, they withdrew to *Meleitay,* leaving 115,000 dead on the battlefield out of the 200,000 in the king of Burma's army, and the rest nearly all wounded.

Meanwhile, the Burmese tyrant, who had been coming up the river with his two thousand *serós,* arrived on the scene where the battle had taken place. He was as if thunderstruck and nearly out of his mind to see the devastation the Mons had inflicted on his men. Disembarking, he immediately laid siege to the fortress, determined, as he said, to take alive all of the eight hundred men inside.

This siege continued for seven days, during which those on the outside launched five assaults, and each time the eight hundred men inside defended themselves valiantly. However, realizing that their last hour had come and that they were not able to hold the fortress for their king as they had hoped to all along, owing to the reinforcements the Burmese had brought with him in the fleet, and wishing to follow the example of the others, they decided, like the brave men that they were, to go out and die on the battlefield as their comrades had done and avenge their deaths with that of their enemies, for by remaining inside, most of their efforts were going to waste and the Burmese artillery was destroying them little by little.

Having made up their minds, they sallied forth one night when it happened to be very dark, with dense fog and heavy rain, and fell upon the first two enemy positions nearest the landward gate from which they had issued, wiping them clear of the people there. Unswerving in their purpose, they pushed forward like men who were now fully committed and blind with desperation or desirous of laying down their lives for honor and glory. They did so much damage that the tyrant was forced to jump into the river and swim for his life, leaving the field in almost complete disorder and divided into more than a hundred parts, with a death toll of twelve thousand that included fifteen hundred Burmese, two thousand foreign mercenaries from various nations, and all the rest Peguans.[5] This battle lasted for a little more than a quarter of an hour and ended only after the death of the eight hundred Mons, who fought to the last man, for not a single one of them would surrender.

Once the Burmese tyrant saw that the battle was over and that all was now completely quiet, he returned to the field. He gathered his scattered forces together again and entered the fortress of *Meleitay,* where he immediately ordered the beheading of the *xemim*,[6] blaming him for the disaster he had suffered and justifying it by saying that anyone who would betray his own king could not be very loyal to him. And that was the reward he received from the tyrant for handing over to him the city of Prome—and a well-deserved reward it was for someone who had delivered his king and his own country into the hands of the enemy. After that they gave their complete attention to the care of the wounded who were there in great number, too.

157
New Military Alliances

That whole night went by with much fear and careful vigil. At daybreak the next morning, the first thing that was done, before all else, was to clear the field of the dead with which it was completely covered. A count made of the huge number of dead on both sides that this expedition to *Meleitay* had cost showed that on the Burmese side the death toll was 128,000, while on the side of the prince, son of the king of Ava, it was 42,000 including the 30,000 Mons who had come to his aid.

This done, and after the Burmese tyrant had fortified the city of Prome and the fortress of *Meleitay* and built two new fortresses along the riverbank in places of strategic importance for the security of the kingdom, he departed up the *Queitor* River with seventy thousand men on board a thousand swift oar-propelled *serós,* intent on personally spying out the kingdom of Ava, letting himself be seen in the city, and seeing for himself how strong its defenses were and the strength he would need to capture it.

At the end of this twenty-eight-day journey, during which he passed many noble towns of the king of *Chaleu* and *Jacuçalão* that were located along the shores of the river, without having anything to do with any of them, he reached the city of Ava on the thirteenth of October in that same year of 1545. During the thirteen days he remained in her port, the only damage he did was to burn two or three thousand commercial vessels he found in the harbor, and set fire to some nearby towns. But the price he paid was by no means cheap, for these assaults cost him the lives of eight thousand of his men, including sixty-two Portuguese, owing to the fact that, by the time we arrived, all precautions had already been taken, and the city, besides being strong, not only by reason of its location but also because of its fortifications, was garrisoned by twenty thousand Mons who, it was said, had arrived only five days before from the mountains of *Pondaleu* where the king of Ava, with the permission of the *Siammon,* emperor of this monarchy, was organizing a new army of eighty thousand men for the purpose of recapturing Prome. For when the king of Ava had been reliably informed of the dishonor and death of his daughter and son-in-law, as described above, knowing full well that by himself he was not powerful enough to avenge the evils and outrages committed against him by this tyrant and to protect himself against those he feared might be committed by him in the future, such as taking his kingdom from him as he had already threatened to do more than once, he went in person, with his wife and children, to throw himself at the feet of the *Siammon.* After telling him about his trials and tribulations and what he had in mind, they made an agreement, whereby he became tributary to him, for the sum of 600,000 *biças* a year, which is equivalent to 300,000 *cruzados* in our money, and a *ganta*[1] of rubies, which is a measure of capacity similar to the *canada*,[2] as a present for his wife. They say that he immediately paid ten years of this promised tribute in advance, to say nothing of other bribes he distributed in the way of precious gems, plate, and tableware that must have been worth more than two million in gold.

In exchange, the *Siammon* obligated himself to take him under his protection and to personally enter the field for him as often as the need arose, and to restore the kingdom of Prome to him within a year's time, for which purpose he then gave him 130,000 men, 30,000 of whom were the reinforcements that the Burmese had slain in *Meleitay,* 20,000 that were here in this city, and 80,000 that were due to arrive under the generalship of the king of Ava himself.

As a result, when the tyrant found out about all these things, he was afraid that this time he would be running a far greater risk of being defeated than he had ever faced before, and he immediately returned to Prome to fortify the city with much greater urgency than before.

However, before he departed from his anchorage in the river, about a league from the city of Ava, the Burmese sent his treasurer, a man by the name of *Diosoray*— in whose custody, as I have already said, we eight Portuguese captives had been placed—as ambassador to the *Calaminhan,*[3] a powerful prince who resides deep in the interior of these backlands (about whom I shall have a few words to say when I speak of him further on), to propose an alliance and a new friendship treaty whereby he would become his brother-in-arms.[4] In exchange, he offered him a certain amount of gold and precious stones as well as the income from some lands bordering on his kingdom, with the proviso that he engage the *Siammon* in a war the following summer that would prevent him from coming to the aid of the king of Ava, thus making it easier for him to capture the city without fear of the promised aid.

This ambassador departed from here, embarking on a *laulé* and twelve *serós* carrying three hundred men to serve him as attendants and guards, apart from an almost equal number of oarsmen. He took with him, as a gift for the *Calaminhan,* many expensive objects of gold and precious stones, including an elephant harness that they claimed was worth close to 600,000 *cruzados,* so that altogether the gift was said to be worth more than a million in gold.

Among some of the favors the Burmese king bestowed on this ambassador of his for this journey was one granting him ownership of all eight of us; so that from then on we were captives of this treasurer, who provided us most generously with clothing and everything else we needed and who was very happy to take us with him. And throughout the entire journey, he always took much more account of us than he did of any of the others that he had in his company.

158
Journey to the Land of the *Calaminhan*

It seemed fitting to me at this point for the proper telling of my tale to leave the Burmese tyrant aside for a while (to whom I will return in due course), in order to say something about the journey we made from here to the city of *Timplão*,[1] capital of the empire of the *Calaminhan*, meaning "lord of the world," for in their language *cala* means "lord," and *minhan* means "world." He is also known as the "absolute lord of the indomitable force of the elephants of the earth," and indeed, he fits that title more than anyone else[2] in the entire universe, as will become apparent from what follows.

Departing from Ava in October of the year 1545, this ambassador made his way up the *Queitor* River[3] with the bow facing west-southwest, and in some parts, due east, because of the bends in the river. Steering in different directions, we proceeded on our way for seven days until we came to an estuary called *Guampanó*, through which our pilot, a man by the name of *Robão*, made his way, in order to steer clear of the *Siammon*'s territory, as the king had instructed him to do, and we reached a large town called *Guatelday*, where the ambassador stopped for three days to take on some provisions he needed for his journey.

Departing from here, we proceeded up this estuary for eleven more days without finding or seeing anything worthy of note. All we saw were small straw-hut villages inhabited by extremely poor people. In the fields there were huge herds of cattle that apparently did not belong to anyone, because we were slaughtering from twenty to thirty head a day in full view of the local people without anyone trying to stop us or uttering a word of protest; on the contrary, in some places they even brought them to us free of charge, as though they enjoyed killing them.

After leaving this estuary of *Guampanó*, we entered a very large river called *Angegumá* that was more than three leagues wide and in some places 120 fathoms deep, with countercurrents so strong that they frequently drove us back over a good part of the distance we had already covered. After following the shores up this river for seven more days, we arrived at a small, strongly walled city called *Gumbim*, in the kingdom of *Jangomá*,[4] which was surrounded on the inland side for a distance of five or six leagues by forests of benzoin and fields of lac, products that are carried to market in the city of Martaban and transshipped from there on many *naos* to different parts of India, the Straits of Mecca, El Quseir, and Jiddah. There is also a large supply of musk in this city, which is much better than the Chinese kind, which they also ship to Martaban and Pegu where we Portuguese buy it and carry it for resale to *Narsinga*,[5] Orissa,[6] and Masulipatam.[7]

The women in these parts are generally very fair and beautiful; they go dressed in clothes of silk and cotton and wear gold and silver bangles on their feet and thick chain-link collars around their necks. There is a great abundance in the land of wheat, rice, and meat, and especially honey, sugar, and beeswax, of which they have an enormous supply. This city and its environs, which extend for ten leagues around, provide the king of *Jangomá* with an income of sixty thousand gold *alcás*,[8] or the equivalent of 720,000 *cruzados* in our money.

From here we coasted along the southern shore of the river for seven more days until we reached a large city called *Catammás*—meaning "golden shrimp"[9] in our language—that lay within the domains of the *raudivá* of *Tinlau*,[10] second son of the *Calaminhan*, who is someone like the duke of Orleans in France. The *naugator*[11] of this city gave the ambassador a fine welcome, provided his entourage with many refreshments, and informed him that the *Calaminhan* was in the city of *Timplão*.

From here we departed on a Sunday morning, and the following day, at vesper time, we came to a fortress called *Campalagor* that was situated on a rocky point protruding from the river like a small island. It was surrounded by a wall of fine-hewn stone with three ramparts and two towers seven stories high where, the ambassador was told, the *Calaminhan* kept a huge store of treasure, one out of twenty-four that were distributed throughout the kingdom, mainly in the form of silver of about six thousand *candins'*[12] weight, which is twenty-four thousand quintals by our standard of measures, all of it buried in underground wells.

From here we proceeded on our course for thirteen more days, passing along both sides of the river many very noble places, most of them probably rich cities, judging from the splendor of their outward appearance, and all the rest was forests of great trees, with many vegetable farms, flower gardens, and orchards, to say nothing of large wheat fields where we saw huge herds of cattle, deer, tapir, and yak, all shepherded by men on horseback. The river was teeming with oared craft, from which they were selling everything that the earth produces, in great abundance, which the Lord saw fit to lavish on the people of these parts of the world, for reasons He alone knows.

And because the ambassador got sick here of an inflammation of the chest, he was advised not to continue his journey until he recovered, and that is why he agreed, after consulting some of his men, to seek treatment in a large hospital located twelve leagues up the river, in a pagoda called *Tinagogo*[13]—meaning "god of a thousand gods"—for which he immediately set out, arriving there on a Saturday afternoon close to nightfall.

159
The Pagoda of *Tinagogo*

Early the next morning the ambassador disembarked and was taken to a hospital for noblemen called *Chipanocão* that had forty-two spotless, well-furnished cottages attached to it, one of which was assigned to him by order of the *puitaleu*, who was like their hospital administrator, where he received more than enough of everything he needed, both in the way of medical care and other kinds of attention. Besides this, the incense, the perfumes, the cleanliness and elegant service, the tableware, the bedclothes, the food, the entertainment and pastimes they provided were so unique and so perfect that he even had musical concerts performed for him twice daily by very attractive women who played and sang beautifully, and at certain hours of the day they staged elaborate comedy shows for him. And since I do not dare to dwell in full on the subject, I will keep silent about many things, about which others, who are more capable than I of describing them, would make much ado.

Twenty-eight days after we arrived here, during which time the ambassador recovered completely, we departed for a city called *Meidur*, located twelve leagues up the *Angegumá* River. However, so that I may not be accused of failing to keep the promise I made before to say something about this pagoda of *Tinagogo*, I will now let the ambassador go on his way, and I will return to the pagoda and say a few words about some of the many things we saw there, in order to show the Christians—and I am including myself among them—who are as careless about their lives as I am, how little we do to save our souls, in comparison with all that these blind wretches do to lose theirs.

During the twenty-eight days that the ambassador spent in the hospital, we nine Portuguese and all the others who were traveling with him were forced into idleness, and since we had nothing to do to while away the time, we spent it on different kinds of pastimes, each of us on the one that was most to his liking, for there was something there to please everyone. Thus, some occupied themselves hunting for game, which is plentiful in this land, especially deer and wild boar, while others hunted for tigers, yak, wildcats, zebra, lions, buffalo, wild cattle, and many other different kinds of animals never seen or mentioned here in Europe, so that the hardiest among us were always in the woods; others were in the fields hunting for quail, duck, and geese, others went after the high-flying birds with falcons and hawks, and still others went fishing for trout, *bogas, bordalos,* sole, *asevia,* mullet, and many other different varieties of fish that are found in all the rivers of this empire. And we, in the same way, spent our time now on one thing, then on another, though most of the time we just looked, listened, and asked questions about the laws, pagodas, and sacrificial rites we observed there, which were extremely fearsome and terrifying, only five or six of which I will describe, as I have already done in other instances, because I believe that should be enough to give one an idea of what the others are like that I will not describe.

One of them took place at the time of the new moon in December, which fell on the ninth day of the month. It is the day on which these heathens are accustomed to celebrate a festival called *Massunterivó* by the people of this land, *Forió* by the Japanese, *Manejó* by the Chinese, *Champas* by the Ryukyus, *Ampalitor* by the Cochinese, and *Sansaporau*[1] by the Siamese, Burmese, *Pafuas,* and the *Çacotais;*[2] so that even though, because of the diversity of their languages, the names in themselves are different, they all mean one and the same thing in our language, which is "remembrance of all the dead." This festival we saw them celebrate here on this day, with so many different things never before imagined that I cannot decide with which one of them to begin, because the very thought of them, coupled with the blindness of these wretched people, in such disparagement of the honor of God, is enough to make a man fall speechless.

At this time of year, enormous crowds of people stream into this place from every nation in those parts, to attend a fair that is held during this festival season, which lasts for fifteen days from the new moon to the full moon. At this fair they sell everything that nature has created on land and sea, in such highly abundant quantities that for every kind of thing sold there are ten, twelve, fifteen, twenty streets lined with houses, huts, and tents stretching as far as the eye can see, all occupied by very rich merchants, not to mention all the rest of the countless numbers of common people there, camping along a big river for more than two leagues in a flat wooded area forested with various kinds of trees, among which there are groves of walnut, chestnut, and pine, as well as coconut and date palms, from which everyone can take as much as they want since all this belongs to the pagoda.

The temple dedicated to this idol is an extremely sumptuous building that is located in the middle of this field, on top of a round hill more than half a league in circumference, all chamfered by pickaxe to a height of fifteen armspans. From there on up, a wall of pure-white hewn stone rises three armspans high, with ramparts, turrets, and guard towers in the same style as ours. Inside this wall there is a terreplein up to the level of the battlements more than a stone's throw in width, which, like the wall, runs all around the hill and looks like a veranda; and all along it there are 160 hostels. Each one of them comprises more than three hundred spotlessly clean, well-furnished, single-story dwellings where they shelter the pilgrims, *fancatões,* and dervishes who come with their whole clan, like gypsies, with their leaders, each clan numbering from two to three thousand people, some more, some less, depending on how near or far they are from their lands and kingdoms, and one can tell from which countries they come by the emblems on the banners they carry.

From here on up the entire area is enclosed by a dense forest of cedar and cypress, with many fountains of pure drinking water. On the highest point of the hill, which probably measures about a quarter of a league around, there are twenty-four cloisters of very rich and sumptuous temples, twelve of them for men and twelve for women, each of which, according to what they told us there, houses five hundred people. In the middle of these twenty-four cloisters, within a garden enclosed by three orders of brass grating, with arches every ten armspans carved out of rich inlaid wood, with gold-leafed finials and many silver bells that tinkled incessantly in the wind, was the chapel of the idol *Tinagogo,* "god of a thousand gods," set upon a round litter. The entire chapel from top to bottom was lined with silver panels, with many candelabra, also made of silver. His monstrous figure, which was either made of gold, or wood, or gilded copper—we could not tell for sure—was standing erect with both arms raised heavenward and a rich crown upon his head. Surrounding him were many other small idols on their knees, gazing at him in awe. Below him were twelve gigantic male figures made of bronze, extremely ugly, that stood thirty-seven handspans high. These, they said, were the gods of the twelve months of the year.

Outside this building there were two rows of 140 giants surrounding it. They were made of cast iron and were holding halberds in their hands, as though they were guarding the building. Between them were many bronze bells hanging from very thick iron bars that went from shoulder to shoulder of these giants. When seen as a whole, this building displayed such great splendor that, the moment a person set eyes on it, he was struck by the great opulence and sumptuousness of its construction.

And now, setting aside the rest of the information that I could give about the other dependencies of this rich temple, for it seems to me that what I have said is enough to give one an idea of what it was like, I will now say something briefly about the sacrifices we saw there at a festival they call *Xipatilau,* meaning "refreshing place of the good."

160
The Festival of *Xipatilau*

The fair that took place during this festival of theirs was attended by such huge crowds of people and diverse groups of pilgrims as I said before; and since it lasted for fifteen days with many different kinds of sacrifices and ceremonies, not a day went by without all sorts of things going on that were very unusual, very costly, very worthy of being seen, and even more worthy of being noted, one of which occurred on the fifth day of the moon, which is the day they published their jubilees.

It was a procession that must have extended for over three leagues, as our men estimated roughly, and taking part in it, as everyone claimed, were forty thousand priests representing the twenty-four religious sects of this empire, many of whom were dignitaries with different titles such as *grepos, talagrepos, rolins, neepois,*[1] *bicos,*[2] *sacureus,* and *chanfarauhos,* all of whom could be distinguished by the vestments they wore and the devices and insignia they carried, and they were revered by the people according to their rank.

However, none of these dignitaries walked in the procession as did the common priests, for on that particular day they were not permitted to let their feet touch the ground without committing a great sin, and instead, they rode on litters borne on the shoulders of their subordinate priests who were dressed in green satin with their *altirnas* of purple damask drawn up under their arms like stoles. In the middle of this procession went all their sacrificial devices mounted on richly adorned litters, bearing the idols to which each one was devoted, with their votaries dressed in yellow robes, holding candles in their hands. Behind every fifteen litters, a triumphal carriage rolled by, making a total of 226 carriages in all.

Each one of these carriages was four decks high, and some even five, with an equal number of wheels on each side, and each of them was carrying at least two hundred people among priests and guards. Mounted at the very top was a silver idol with a golden mitre on its head, all of them bedecked with pearl necklaces and splendid collars of precious stones. Immediately behind them came many censers[3] giving off most delightful fragrances, and children on their knees with silver maces resting on their shoulders, and some others holding thuribles in their hands who now and then, at the sound of certain instruments, would swing them three times and recite the following words in a sad voice charged with emotion: "Pautixorou numilem forandaché vaticur apolem," which means, "Assuage, O Lord, the pain of the dead so that they may praise thee in peaceful slumber!"

And to these words all the people responded in a thunderous voice, "Thus may it be for as long as thy sun shines upon us!"

Pulling at each of these carriages by six very long silk-covered ropes were more than five thousand people who, as a reward for their efforts, were granted plenary remission of their sins without restitution of any kind. And the method they used whereby the greatest number of people might receive absolution for pulling these ropes was to have each man close his fist over the rope, one after the other, and so on down to the end until the entire length of rope was covered with closed fists and nothing was left to be seen. Now in order to enable the many others who had been left out to earn the same jubilee and indulgence, they were allowed to help the ones who had their hands on the ropes by putting their hands on their shoulders. Others were allowed to do the same to them, so that all along the length of these ropes there were men helping in rows six and seven deep, bringing the total at each rope to more than five hundred persons.

All along the outer edges of this procession there were many men on horseback who were running back and forth with iron-tipped clubs in their hands, crying aloud to the huge crowds of people to make way and not disturb the priests at their prayers.+ At times they would hit them so hard that three or four of them would be sent sprawling and many others badly battered, all of which took place without anyone registering the slightest protest, or so much as blinking an eye.

In this order the amazing procession filed by, passing along more than a hundred streets that had been specially set aside for that purpose and adorned with palm fronds, woven branches of myrtle, and many silken flags and banners. In many places along the way there were many theatrical interludes where tables were set with food that was distributed for the love of God, to any and all who wished to partake of it. In other places clothes were given out, feuds reconciled, and debts forgiven, and many other pious deeds were performed, so much in keeping with Christian ethics that had they been done with faith and baptism in the name of Christ our Lord, without the intrusion of worldly matters, it seems to me that they would have been acceptable to him, but the best was wanting in them, for their sins, and for ours.

As this enormous welter of litters and carriages went by in a horrifying clamor of music, shouts, and all sorts of other things, from certain wooden huts that had been expressly constructed for the purpose along the way, six, seven, eight, or ten men would come forth, enveloped in the odor of many perfumes, wrapped in silken loincloths and adorned with golden bangles on their arms. As they came out of the huts, the crowd would fall back to make room for them, and after making several *zumbaias* to the idol mounted on top of the carriage, these men would throw themselves face down in the path of the vehicle, which passed over them, cutting them in two; whereupon, the crowds would shout loudly, "Pachiló a furão!" meaning, "May my soul go with yours!"

Then one of the priests would descend immediately from the carriage and, with ten or twelve others to help him, would go over to those blessed or cursed men who were lying there dead and gather up the pieces, the heads, and entrails, or whatever else was left of those unfortunate bodies, into some very large trays and show them to the people from the roof of the carriage where the idol was mounted and speak to them in a voice filled with sorrow, saying "Pray to God all you sinners to make you as worthy of sainthood as this man who has just expired in sweet-smelling sacrifice."

Then all the people prostrated themselves face down on the ground and responded with a frightful roar, "Let us hope that the god of a thousand gods will grant it so!"

And in like manner, many others followed the example of these unfortunate people, sacrificing themselves in numbers well over six hundred, according to what we were told there by some honorable merchants whose credibility was above reproach.

Apart from these, there were others too called *xixaporaus,* who also sacrificed themselves in front of these carriages by cutting off pieces of their own flesh so mercilessly that it seemed like something beyond the bounds of human nature. They would take the pieces of their flesh which they cut off with well-sharpened knives and place them in some sort of bow as if they were arrows and shoot them heavenward, saying as they did so that they were sending them to God as a present for the soul of their father, or son, or wife, or some other person in whose name they were doing it. Whereupon, so many people would rush forward to pick up these pieces wherever they fell that at times they trampled each other to death in the attempt to get at them, for they regarded them as extremely holy relics. In the meantime, these poor wretches would go staggering about, dripping with blood, without noses, or ears, or the semblance of men, until they finally fell to the ground dead. Thereupon the *grepos* would quickly descend from the carriages, run to their side, cut off their heads, and display them to the people, who in turn would kneel down with arms upraised and cry out loud, "O Lord, reach out to us in time for us to do the same thing in thy service!"

Then came others who were also inspired by the devil, though in a different way, who went among the crowd asking for alms with the words, *Minta dremá xixapurha param,* meaning, "Give me alms for the love of God, otherwise I shall kill myself!" If the alms were not produced quickly enough, they would slit their own throats there on the spot with some large knives they carried in their hands, or they would disembowel themselves and drop to the ground dead. The *grepos* would also come running up to them and cut off their heads [5] just as they had done with the others and display them to the people, who showed the same reverence for them too, shouting aloud and prostrating themselves face down on the ground.

Then there were others, extremely ugly and frightful looking, called *nucaramões,* who went about dressed in tiger skins, holding copper pots under their arms filled with a certain concoction of putrid urine mixed with human feces that was so noxious and so evil smelling that no one could bear to be within a whiff of it. They would go among the people begging for alms, saying as they did so, "Quick, give me some alms or I will eat the devil's food and spray you with it so that you will be as accursed as the devil himself!" At which everybody hastened to give them alms, for if they delayed but a moment in granting his wish, he would put the pot to his mouth, take a long draught of that malodorous concoction and spray it over those he wanted to harm. In the meantime, all the others who had seen them get sprayed would consider them accursed and mistreat them so badly that the poor wretches did not know what to do, for if anyone failed to dishonor them, he would in turn be considered just as unworthy of the respect of his fellowmen as they were. Thus, everybody would beat them and push them about and point to each one as having been excommunicated for causing that saintly man to eat the devil's filth, thereby becoming eternally foul in the eyes of God, so that he could neither go to paradise nor be seen by the eyes of men.

Thus, there are amongst these people, who otherwise are not lacking in good judgement and wit, many other kinds of blind spots and brutish customs [6] that are so far beyond all reason and human understanding, that they serve as a great motive for us to offer thanks continually for the infinite mercy and goodness He has shown us, by giving us the light of true faith wherewith to save our souls.

161
The Frightful Penitents of *Tinagogo*

When nine of these fifteen days had gone by, the huge crowds gathered here began to scream, pretending that the Ravenous Serpent of the Lower Depths of the House of Smoke—who is Lucifer,[1] as I said before—was coming to steal the ashes of those who had recently sacrificed their lives in order to prevent their souls from going to heaven; and the noise coming from all those people was so horrifying, so dreadful, and so frightful, that words cannot express it. Moreover, it was accompanied by the din of countless numbers of bells, gongs, drums, conch horns, and sistra, which altogether created such an incredible racket that the earth trembled beneath our feet—and all that commotion for the sake of frightening the devil.

This tumult lasted from one o'clock in the afternoon until the following morning near daybreak. During the night they consumed an enormous quantity of candles to light their lanterns which covered the ground for as far as the eye could see, making it look as if everything was on fire at the time. The reason for this, they said, was that *Tinagogo,* the "god of a thousand gods," had gone in search of the Ravenous Serpent, to slay it with a sword that had come down to him from heaven.

At the end of this incredibly noisy night, in the clear light of morning, the hillside surrounding the temple could be seen covered with white flags, at the sight of which the people prostrated themselves on the ground to give thanks to God. It was an extremely happy occasion for them, and they celebrated it by exchanging gifts with each other to show their gratitude for the wonderful news symbolized by the white flags, which was the official sign from the priests that the Ravenous Serpent had already been slain. Filled with joy, this huge crowd surged up the hill, heading for the temple, pouring through the twenty-four gates in its haste to congratulate the idol for the victory he had achieved the night before with the beheading of the serpent. For three days and nights the people kept on coming in such huge numbers that only with great difficulty could one get through any of the streets.

As for us Portuguese, since the nine of us who were there had nothing to do, we were determined not to miss seeing any part of this humbug, and we asked the ambassador for permission to go. He refused for the time being, but told us that we should go with him on the following day, for he had made a vow during his recent illness to pay a visit to the temple. His answer did not displease us, for it meant that it would be easier for us to get in and see more of what we felt like seeing.

Two days later the crowds had begun to thin out, and we went up to the temple of *Tinagogo* in his company, but even then we had some difficulty reaching the top of the hill where it stood. There were six very long streets there that were completely lined with scales hanging from bronze beams on which countless numbers of people were being weighed in fulfillment of vows they had made because of various illnesses and misfortunes, and for the remission of all the sins they had committed against God from the time they had learned to sin until that hour; and depending upon the promise made, or the degree of guilt, or the financial possibilities of each of them, that is how they were weighed.

The offering each one made was in conformity with the sin he had committed, so that the ones who believed they were guilty of the sin of gluttony and who had failed to observe any abstinence at all during that year, were weighed against an equal quantity of honey, sugar, eggs, and butter, since those are things agreeable to the priests from whom they were to receive absolution. The ones who thought they were guilty of sensuality balanced their weight against cotton, down, *panha*,[2] clothing, wine, and fragrances because they said those were the things that were used in the commission of that sin. Those who were lukewarm or lax in their devotion to God and who had been stingy with their charity, balanced the scales with copper, tin, and silver coins or pieces of gold.[3] Those guilty of sloth were weighed with firewood, rice, charcoal, pigs, and fruit. He who was guilty of envy, from which the only fruit one derives is grief over the good that God has chosen to bestow on another, paid for it by confessing it openly in public and being slapped in the face twelve times in praise of the twelve moons of the year. The sin of pride was paid for in dried fish, brooms, and ox dung, which are the lowliest things of all; while he who has sinned by saying very hurtful things about his neighbor without asking his forgiveness for it, offers a cow on the scale, or a pig, sheep, or deer; so that in this manner there were countless numbers of people being weighed on all the scales along these six streets, the benefits of which were reaped by the priests, who received such large quantities of these offerings that there were huge piles of each item.

As for the poorer people who had nothing to give or offer for the remission of their sins, they gave the hair of their heads, which was sheared off there on the spot by more than a hundred priests who were all seated there in good order for that purpose on three-legged stools with scissors in their hands. And there were huge piles of this hair too, out of which another group of more than a thousand *grepos*, all lined up in good order, were making ropes, braids, rings, and bracelets, which all the people were buying to take home, much the same way as among us it is the custom of the pilgrims returning from Santiago[4] to bring back those trinkets of jet.

Now in order that what I am discussing here may not seem like so much humbug, I must say, in all truth, that this ambassador of ours was astonished by the incredible things he saw here, for when the *grepos* explained the meaning of each one of them to him and how much income they derived from all these alms as well as from the other offerings received for various reasons in the course of these fifteen days, they assured him that these things alone that were made from the hair contributed by the poor, brought in more than 100,000 *pardaus*[5] of gold, which is equal to 90,000 *cruzados* in our money. And from this one can judge how much more all the rest could come to.

After spending a little while on these streets of the scales, the ambassador passed on along all the stations where the sacrifices, offerings, interludes, dances, farces, musical concerts, and wrestling matches were going on, until we reached the shrine of the god *Tinagogo*, though not without a great deal of difficulty and disrespect from the crowds, for there were so many people milling about that it was next to impossible to squeeze through them despite all our efforts. The building itself consisted of a single nave, but it was very long, wide, spacious, very beautifully and richly adorned, illuminated by an infinite number of wax-burning lanterns and silver candelabra of ten branches each, and filled with the fragrance of benzoin and eaglewood.

When we got there we saw the idol of *Tinagogo* standing in the middle of the nave on an ornate dais like an altar, surrounded by many silver candelabra and candle-

sticks, and by purple-robed children who were spreading incense around it with thuribles, to the sound of many different kinds of musical instruments[6] somewhat like
ours, that a large group of priests were playing in fairly good harmony. Also, to the
accompaniment of this music there were some very lovely, richly clad women dancing
around this idol, to whom the people would give the alms they brought as offerings
and from whose hands the priests would receive them and place them at the foot of
the dais of the idol in a highly ceremonious manner that entailed throwing themselves
face down on the ground from time to time.

The statue of this monster was made of silver in the shape of a gigantic man
which stood twenty-seven handspans tall. It had the hair of a kaffir, enormous nostrils,
thick lips, and an expression of deep sadness on its ugly face. One hand held a halberd
that resembled a cooper's adze, but with a much longer handle, which was the weapon
used the night before, as the priests told the people, to slay the Ravenous Serpent of
the Lower Depths of the House of Smoke for trying to steal the ashes of the men who
had sacrificed their lives. The Ravenous Serpent itself was lying in the middle of the
nave, in front of the idol's dais, in the shape of the most frightful-looking snake imaginable, and yet it looked so natural that it gave one the shivers just to see it stretched out
full length there on the floor with its head cut off. Its neck was as thick as a wine cask
and measured eight armspans in length, and even though we were looking at it and
knew full well that it was artificial, still it was enough to make one shiver and shake
since it looked, as I said, so natural in every respect that one would have taken it for a
real living creature. And all the people would go up and jab it with iron implements
resembling halberd tips, hurling many scornful and insulting words at it, and calling it
ugly names such as *turbacão, maxirané, való, hapacou, tangamur, cohilousa,* meaning
"arrogant one," "cursed thing," "storehouse of hell," "deep lake of damnation," "en-
vier of the blessings of God," "famished dragon in the deep of night," and many other
curses and insults that seemed so strange and yet so appropriate, considering the effect
the serpent had on everyone, that it left us gasping in amazement. Then they would
pass on ahead and throw their offerings of gold, silver, rings, bolts of silk, coins, and
fine cotton cloth into some basins placed at the foot of the dais, which contained large
quantities of everything.

From here we went with the ambassador to see the rock caves of the penitents
that were located in the woods below, about a cannon-shot's distance away. There
were 142 of these caves, and despite the fact that they did not appear to be man-made,
they had been carved out by hand in some cliffs of living rock, one after the other, in a
long row. There were men living in some of them who were revered as saints, practicing a strange form of penitence by leading lives of excessively harsh austerity. There
were about twelve of them right near the entrance to the first group of caves, dressed
in black vestments similar to those worn by the Japanese bonzes. They followed the
religion of an idol who had once been a man by the name of *Situmpor Micay,* who left
as a precept to his followers that as long as they were clad in rotting flesh and bones
they should spend their days in harsh renunciation, for, as he taught them, it was only
by punishing the flesh that they could become worthy of heaven, far more than by any
other means, and that the more pitilessly they mortified their own flesh, the more generously would God give them all the good things they could desire in the next world.

The ones we saw here told us that they ordinarily ate nothing but boiled greens
with roasted beans and some wild fruit that was handed to them through an opening

in the cave by other priests somewhat like cloistered monks whose responsibility it was to look after them in accordance with the precepts each one followed.

Further up, in some other caves of the same type, we saw others of another diabolical sect called *Angemacur,* who were living in some underground caves carved out from the solid part of the same rock in conformity with the precepts of these poor souls who eat nothing but flies, ants, scorpions, and spiders, with the juice of some herbs that are called wood sorrel in our country. They spend all their time in meditation, gazing heavenward night and day with both fists clenched as a sign that they desired nothing from the world, letting themselves die like brutes. These men are generally revered among them as the saintliest of all, and because they consider them so holy, after they die they burn them on fragrant and costly funeral pyres. These rites are carried out with a great deal of pomp and majesty and with offerings of expensive things, which are used to build sumptuous temples to them so that the living who see them will be inspired to emulate them in order to achieve the vainglory accorded them by the world merely as a reward and compensation for the extremely excessive penitence they practice.

We also saw others belonging to another diabolical sect founded by someone called *Gileu Mitray* who observe different forms of penitence, and who bear a close resemblance, for the diversity of their precepts, to the Abyssinians of Ethiopia in the kingdom of Prester John. Some of them, in order to make their fasting more meritorious because of the harshness with which they practice it, eat nothing but rotten, slimy mucous, grasshoppers, and chicken droppings. Others eat slices of coagulated blood from men who have been bled for a cure, along with bitter fruit and herbs of the forest, and as a result they generally last very few days and become so disfigured in the color and aspect of their faces that they are frightful to see.

We also saw other followers of a sect called *Godomem,*[7] who end their days by going up and down the mountains night and day, yelling continuously and hitting themselves with their hand on the mouth as they shout without respite, "Godomem, Godomem," until they drop dead for want of breath.

We also saw others belonging to another sect called *Taxilacões,* who die in the beastliest way of all by letting themselves down into very narrow, tightly covered caves made that way to suit their purpose, inside of which they burn thistles and branches of green spurgeflax and allow themselves to be asphyxiated by the smoke. So that all these people who practice these different forms of terribly harsh penitence become martyrs of the devil,[8] who rewards them with everlasting hell, and it is indeed an extremely pitiful and painful thing to see how much these poor wretches do to lose their souls and how little most of us Christians do to save ours.

162
Encounter with a Portuguese Woman

After we had seen all these things that so amazed us all, we departed from this pagoda of *Tinagogo* and continued our journey for thirteen more days until we came to two very large cities situated on opposite banks of the river just a little more than a stone's throw apart, one of which was called *Manavedé* and the other *Singilapau*. In the middle of the river, which narrowed down at this point, there was a round islet created by nature out of living rock that was thirty-six armspans high and more than a crossbow shot wide, and in the center of this little island they had built a stone castle with nine bulwarks and five towers. All around the outer ramparts of the wall it was enclosed by two rows of very heavy iron railings. Running across the river, from the four bulwarks facing the two cities, there were two iron chains connected to both of them, which had the effect of closing the river and cutting off all access.

At these two cities the ambassador went ashore at the one called *Singilapau*, where he was given a fine reception by the *Xemim Dum*, commanding officer of the city, who provided a lavish supply of refreshments for the ambassador's entire party.

The next morning he departed from here, accompanied by twenty oar-manned *laulés* with a thousand men on board, arriving close to vesper time at the *tavangrás*[1] of the kingdom, which were two very strong castles that blocked all traffic by means of five very heavy brass chains stretching from one to the other across the entire width of the river, so that nothing could pass through.

It was here that a man in a light *seró* came rowing up and told the ambassador to anchor at the divan[2] of *Campalagrau*—the castle on the southern bank of the river—in order to show them the letter he was carrying from his king to the *Calaminhan* so that they could see if it was written in the way he was accustomed to being addressed. The ambassador did so immediately and, after disembarking, entered a large hall where three men were sitting at a table, accompanied by another large group of noblemen, who welcomed him warmly and asked him what had brought him there, as if they did not know. He replied that he was the ambassador of the king of Burma, lord of Toungoo, and that he had been sent on a mission of vital importance to the holy *Calaminhan*, regarding matters of state.

After replying to a few ceremonious questions put to him by the three main people at the table, merely as a matter of formality, he showed them the letter which they changed slightly in order to make it conform to their own style and usage. He also showed them the gift he was carrying, which left them all gasping in amazement, especially when they saw the gold chair and the elephant's jewels that many dealers in precious stones had appraised at 500,000 to 600,000 *cruzados*, to say nothing of all the many other very costly objects he was carrying, as I mentioned previously.

After he had been dismissed from the reception desk of the first *tavangrá*, we went on to the other one, located a league up the river from there, where we found some other men of much higher rank who went through the same ceremony, examined the letter and the gift, and attached some red silk cords and three wax seals to all the pieces. This was the final stamp of approval required for the embassy to be received by the *Calaminhan*.

On this same day a message arrived from the city inland, from the *queytor*,[3] the governor of the kingdom, who sent greetings to the ambassador along with a gift of fresh food, both meat and fruit, and other things after their fashion. And on all the next nine days he was here, the ambassador was always kept very generously supplied with everything, both for his own personal use as well as for that of all the members of his party. In addition to this, he was treated to all kinds of pastimes in the form of fishing, hunting, banquets, concerts, and farces presented by very beautiful and richly attired women.

During these same nine days we Portuguese, with the permission of the ambassador, visited some of the local sights that had been highly recommended by the natives, such as the ancient buildings, rich and sumptuous temples, private estates, castles, and houses located all along the river, constructed in a strange fortresslike fashion at tremendous expense. One of them was a hospice for pilgrims known as *Manicafarão*, which actually means "prison of the gods" in our language. It was an enclosed area measuring more than a league around, with twelve streets of vaulted arches, on each of which there were 240 houses, counting 120 on each side, so that altogether there was a total of 2,880 housing units which at that time were nearly all filled to capacity with travelers from different parts who come here on pilgrimage all year round. They say that this pilgrimage is more highly prized than any other because the god imprisoned here was captured from foreigners and is not free to return to his native land.

These pilgrims, who number, according to what the natives say, more than 100,000 persons[4] throughout they year, are provided with food and lodging for the time they are here, out of the income and offerings the temple receives. These pilgrims are looked after by four thousand priests attached to the *Manicafarão* itself who, along with many others, reside here within this enclosure in 120 convents where there is also an equal number for women, serving in the same capacity.

The temple at this hospice was a very large building constructed with three naves like our churches, in the middle of which there was a round chapel enclosed by three rows of very thick brass gratings with great knockers on the doors, also made of brass. Inside this chapel there were eighty statues of idols in the shape of men and women, with an equal number of smaller idols lying on the floor. Only the eighty large ones were in an upright position, all of them bound with iron chains and heavy iron collars around their necks, and some with handcuffs, and the little ones lying on the floor, as though they were the children of the larger ones, were tied around the waist, six by six, with other lighter chains.

Outside the gratings, in two other rows, three across to each row, were 244 bronze giants, each twenty-five handspans tall, with their halberds and maces on their shoulders, looking as though they were standing guard over the others in chains; and above, hanging from iron beams running clear across the entire width of the nave, were many lights burning in ten-branched candelabra, similar to the ones in India, and they, as well as the walls of the building and everything else to be seen there, were covered with varnish, as a sign of sadness for the captivity of the gods.

The nine of us were amazed by what I have just described as well as by many other things I will not describe, and since we could not understand the significance of the imprisoned gods, we asked the priests to explain the meaning of what we were looking at. One of them, who appeared to have more of an air of authority about him than the others, replied, "Since you, as foreigners, are interested in learning about something that I believe you have never heard of or that has never been mentioned in your books, I will tell you what it means and how it actually came to pass, according to what is written in our chronicles. From the present date, it is now 7,320 moons—which is 610 years by the calendars of the other nations[5]—since a holy *Calaminhan* named *Xixivarom Meleutay* ruled on the throne of the twenty-seven kingdoms that make up this empire. During his reign differences arose between him and the *Siammon,* emperor of the mountains of the earth, and as a result, sixty-two monarchs on the two sides placed their forces in the field, and from one hour before dawn until past two-thirds of the day, they waged a fierce, cruel battle, in which sixteen *laquesás*[6] of men on both sides lost their lives—and there are 100,000 in each *laquesá*. Then, since the victory had fallen to our *Calaminhan,* with just the 230,000 of his remaining troops he laid waste to all the lands of his enemies in a march that lasted four months. During that campaign of destruction, he inflicted such ravages on the population that, if what our history books say is true, as many people affirm, we find, according to what it says, that fifty *laquesás* of people died.[7]

"This battle took place on the ninth day of the first moon in the year 7,320 of the era to which I am referring, on the famous field of *Vitau* where *Quiay Nivandel* appeared before them, seated on a wooden throne. From that time forward he acquired greater renown than all the other gods of the Mons and the Siamese and came to be worshipped by them as the god of battles, so much so, that in all the nations that inhabit the earth, when swearing that something incredible is true, all one has to say is "by the holy *Quiay Nivandel,* god of the *Vitau* battlefield," to be given credence. And in a large city called *Sorocatão,*[8] where 500,000 people were killed, all the gods you see here in chains were captured despite the kings who believed in them and the priests who administered the sweet fragrance of their sacrifices to them. As a result of this glorious victory, all these peoples became subject to us with the obligation of paying honorable tribute to the crown of those who now wield the scepter of *Calaminhan* justice, though it has cost a great deal in blood and suffering in the course of the sixty-four uprisings that have occurred intermittently over the years among all these peoples who cannot bear to see their gods in captivity. This is in truth a great dishonor for them, because of which they have vowed not to celebrate any joyous festivals until they have been freed, and to this day, they still have not lit any fires in their *bralas* and prayer houses, nor will they be lit as long as their gods remain here in captivity."

After some of the more curious among us had thought the matter over well, it is affirmed, according to what this *grepo* told us, and which he swore there on his word of honor was true, more than three million died over the years fighting for the liberation of these idols we saw here in chains, to say nothing of those killed in the previous battles, from which it is plain to see how deeply the devil holds these wretched people in his thrall and how many different preposterous and outrageous ways he has of leading them to hell in such large numbers.

From here we departed for another temple called *Urpanesendó* which I refuse to discuss so as not to have to deal with indecent and abominable subjects. Leaving aside the excessive abundance of riches as well as of everything else we saw in this temple, all I will say about it is the purpose it serves. It is a place where all the virgin daughters of the princes and lords of the kingdom and all the other members of the nobility go to fulfill a vow they are forced to make when they are little children, to sacrifice their honors, for otherwise no honorable man will marry them, not for all the money in the world, since it is regarded as a great dishonor among them to do so. This obscene, sensuous sacrifice[9] involves so great an expense that there are many of them on which they spend ten thousand *cruzados* or more, besides the offerings made to this *Urpanesendó* idol to whom they sacrifice their honor. This idol is kept in a round chapel all covered with gold. It is made entirely of silver and is fashioned in a sitting position on a dais, like an altar, encircled above by many candelabra, also made of silver, of six or seven branches each. Around this dais are other gilded idols in the shape of extremely lovely women who, kneeling on the ground with upraised arms, are worshipping it. The priests told us that these were the sainted souls of some young girls who had ended their lives there, which was an extremely great honor for all their relatives and one they prize more highly than any other the kings can bestow on them.

This cursed idol receives an annual income, according to what they told us there, of 300,000 *cruzados,* not counting the cash offerings and expensive items received for their abominable sacrifices, which are estimated at a much higher amount. In this diabolical temple there are over five thousand women leading religious lives in the many convents we saw, but what I noticed is that they are all old, with not a single young woman among them, and most of them are very rich. They all leave their estates to this pagoda when they die, which is why it has such a large income.

From here we went back to the *tavangrá* where we had left the ambassador and then walked over to see the caravans of the yogis who had come here on pilgrimage in the manner I have described before. There were forty-six of them camped along the river with one hundred, two hundred, three hundred, and five hundred persons to each caravan, though a few had many more. In one of them we came across a Portuguese woman, which surprised us much more than all the other things we had seen there. When we asked her what she was doing in such a strange place, she told us, with tears streaming down her cheeks, who she was and how she had come there and married a yogi who traveled with those caravans, and that she had been married to him for twenty-three years, though at the present time she was widowed. Since she did not dare to live among Christians, she would go on living in those unfortunate circumstances until God carried her to a land where she might end her days, doing penance for her past way of life; but that in spite of the way we saw her living there, dressed in those diabolical clothes, she had never stopped being a true Christian.

We were all so amazed by a case as strange as this and quite sad as well to see the poor woman living in such an unfortunate state, and we told her what, at the time, in our judgement, we thought was right. At the end of our conversation she agreed to go within ten days to the city of *Timplão* in order to accompany us to Pegu, and from there to take ship for Coromandel where she could end her days in the village of the apostle Saint Thomas.[10]

Having made this agreement to which she swore under oath, we took leave of her, fully believing that she would certainly keep her promise so as not to lose such a good opportunity to change the error of her ways and return to a state in which she might be saved, since it was ordained by our Lord that she should meet up with us in that distant land so far from what she could ever imagine or hope for. However, she failed us completely, for we never saw her again nor did we ever hear anything more about her, from which it seems that either some great obstacle must have kept her from returning, or else her sins had led her so far astray that, because of them, she did not deserve to take advantage of the favor that our Lord in his infinite mercy had placed within her grasp.

163
At the Palace of the *Calaminhan*

When the ambassador had been here for nine days, which according to the custom of the country was the ritual waiting period observed in honor of his embassy, one of the governors of the city, a man by the name of *Quampanogrem,* came to fetch him. He was accompanied by eighty *serós* and *laulés* that were very well equipped and splendidly manned, with music coming from so many different kinds of barbarous, discordant instruments that it nearly made the flesh quiver, for they consisted mainly of bells, gongs, drums, timbals, sistra, cornets, and conch horns which, especially since they were mingled with the shouts of the crew, made it seem like some sort of incantation, or better yet, music from hell, if there is such a thing down there.

In the midst of this discordant racket, we departed for the city, which was a little over a league from there, arriving close to noon. As we neared the first wharf, which was called *Campalarraja,* we could see a huge crowd of splendidly attired people waiting there, both on foot and on horseback, as well as many handsomely arrayed war elephants with their silver ornamented saddles and canopies and their battle *panouras* in their tusks, giving them a fearsome aspect.

Once the ambassador had landed, *Quampanogrem,* the mandarin escorting him there, led him by the hand and, on his knees, presented him to another mandarin, a man by the name of *Patedacão,* who was waiting for him on the pier in great pomp and splendor. He was one of the most important men in the government of the kingdom who, according to what they said, possessed many landed estates and vassals. After receiving the ambassador with another courteous ceremony, he offered him an elephant he had beside him, adorned with a saddle and trappings of gold, but the ambassador refused to accept it despite the mandarin's insistence. Then he sent for another that was almost identical and gave it to him, and for us, the nine Portuguese, along with another fifty or sixty Burmese, they brought up horses which we all mounted.

In this manner, we took off from here in a deafening clamor of music and shouts, along with sixteen carts full of silver timbals, and just as many loaded with drums and bells. Off we went, riding through a large number of very long streets, only nine of which were enclosed with brass railings, their entrances adorned with richly wrought archways topped by many gilded spires and very large bronze bells which, like clocks, sounded the hours every quarter of the day, which is the way the people ordinarily govern their lives.

After a great deal of difficulty, owing to the enormous crowds filling the streets, we arrived at the outer courtyard of the *Calaminhan's* palace, which measured nearly a culverin shot in length with its width in proper proportion. There we came upon a spectacle that was most pleasing to the eyes, for it was filled at the time—according to some of those who saw it—with more than six thousand cavalrymen whose horses were all adorned with silken cloths and silver trappings, the men all armed with copper and brass breastplates and silver helmets, and banners in their hands, and bucklers and shields on the horns of their saddles. Their commander was the *queitor* of justice, who is the highest official above all the ministers of civil and criminal law, which is a separate jurisdiction by itself with the power of life and death, from which there is no appeal or recourse.

When the ambassador reached him—for by this time he had already come forward to meet him—having dismounted with the two mandarins escorting him, they all prostrated themselves three times on the ground, just as they were, which is another unusual ceremony of courtesy practiced among them. To this the *queitor* responded only by touching him on the head with his hand and presenting him with a sword he wore at his waist, which the ambassador accepted, kissing it three times. Then the *queitor* placed him at his side, and leaving the two mandarins a short distance behind, set off with him down the middle of a lane of elephants lining the entire length of the courtyard, probably numbering over fifteen hundred, all harnessed with richly adorned castles and saddles ingeniously fashioned in different designs, with many silken saddlecloths and banners, and many halberdiers all around them, a sight that of itself displayed great pomp and majesty, which led us all to believe that this prince was one of the most important and most powerful in those parts, both in wealth and position.

After reaching a large gate between two very tall towers where two hundred men were stationed—all of whom fell to their knees the moment they saw the *queitor*—we passed through it and came out on another very long courtyard where the king's second company of guards was stationed. This company consisted of a thousand men armed with gilded swords and shields, their helmets plated with gold and silver and adorned with many plumes of different colors. After passing through the middle of all these people, we reached a large patio that served as the reception area for the palace compound, where a mandarin was waiting. He was an uncle of the king, an elderly man of more than seventy years by the name of *Monvagaru,* and he was there in the company of a large group of noblemen, along with many captains and lords of the kingdom. Around him there were twelve richly clad little boys, with heavy gold chains strung across their chests and silver maces resting on their shoulders. When the ambassador reached his side, the mandarin touched him lightly on the head with a fan he was holding and said to him, "May your coming into the palace of the lord of the world be as gratifying to him as the rain that falls on our rice fields, for if it should prove to be so, he will grant you what your king desires."

From here we climbed up a large staircase leading into a very long hall filled with lords and captains and many other noblemen who, on seeing *Monvagaru,* all rose to their feet, as though acknowledging his superiority over them. Passing through this hall we came out into another building where there were four beautifully decorated altars, all with silver idols, on one of which we saw a gigantic statue of a woman thirty handspans tall, with her arms outstretched, gazing heavenward. It was also made of silver and had very long gilded hair that fell loosely about her shoulders. There was also a dais here encircled by thirty giants of cast bronze with gilded maces at their sides and features as ugly as the devil himself.

After passing through this building we entered another that was very long, like a corridor, its walls covered from top to bottom with many rosewood shelves inlaid with ivory that were all filled with many human skulls, each one with an inscription on the brow in letters of gold, declaring the name of the one to whom it belonged. Running along the entire length of this building there were twelve gilded iron beams from which many richly wrought silver lamps were hanging, many of them that looked like thuribles, in which numerous little cones of sweet-smelling incense were burning, as well as censers containing amber and calambac. In a round altar enclosed by three rows of silver railings there were thirteen statues of kings, also made of silver, with gold mitres on their heads, and on top of each one there was a human skull. Below there were many silver candlesticks with white wax tapers, which the little boys were charged with keeping trimmed as they sang in harmony with other voices of *grepos,* chanting a sort of litany responsively with each other.

We were told by the *grepos* that those thirteen skulls crowning the statues had belonged in life to the thirteen *Calaminhans*[1] who, in ancient times, had won that empire from some foreign invaders called *Roparões* who, by force of arms, had usurped it from the original inhabitants from whom they all descended; and that the rest of the skulls we had seen there on those *sagiraves,*[2] which were the shelves, had also belonged to military captains who had died honorably in the restoration of the empire, performing heroic deeds on the battlefield; and inasmuch as death had deprived them of the rewards they had earned for their bravery, it was only reasonable that the world should not deprive them of their right to be remembered; and that the honors accorded them would instill envy in the breasts of other good, brave men and inspire them to similar deeds, and at the same time, would make the weak and the craven ashamed of their cowardice.

Leaving this hall we crossed over a long bridge resembling a thoroughfare that was completely covered above with costly and ornately fashioned arches and enclosed on the sides by brass railings with silver-pointed tips and coats of arms inscribed in gold which had as their crests, up above in the curvature of the arches, silver globes of the world more than six handspans in circumference that were finely wrought at great expense, in a magnificent display of royal pomp and majesty. We passed down this long thoroughfare, and when we got to the end of it we reached a large building, the doors of which were closed at the time. A ceremonious knocking four times brought no response from within, until a bell was rapidly rung another four times, when a woman over fifty years of age came to the door, accompanied by six richly clad little girls with their silver *altirnas* drawn up under the arm like stoles, and with gold-plated swords at their sides.

This old woman asked *Monvagaru* what he wanted or why he had rung the bell, to which he replied in respectful tones that he was bringing there an ambassador from the king of Burma, the lord of Toungoo, who had some important affairs of state to discuss at the feet of the *Calaminhan.* The old woman, owing to her high position of authority, did not appear to be impressed with this reply, which amazed us all because the one talking to her was the principal lord of the kingdom, and the uncle, according to what they said, of the *Calaminhan* himself, but one of the six little girls replied on behalf of the old woman.

"Let that ambassador wait, as well as Your Highness and all the others in his party," she said to him, "until we find out if it is the proper time for us to be able to kiss the foot of the throne of the lord of the world and reveal to his ears the arrival of that foreigner, and according to the favor the Lord our God may see fit to show us in this matter, so will his heart rejoice, and ours with him."

They went back inside and the door was closed again, and it remained closed, as part of the ceremony, for as long as it would take to recite three or four Credos. At the end of that time the six little girls opened it again, though this time we did not see the old woman who had first come with them, but we saw a little boy that could have been nine or ten years old who was splendidly attired, with a gold *hurfangá*[3] on his head—which is something like a mitre, only it is closed all around, without any opening—and a gold mace, like a scepter, resting on his shoulder. And without paying the least attention to *Monvagaru* or the other lords present there, he took just the ambassador by the hand and said to him, "At the feet of the *binaigá* of the holy *Calaminhan*, scepter of the kings who govern the earth, news of your arrival has come, so pleasing to his ears that with a smile on his lips he bids us send for you so that in his presence you may be heard concerning what is requested of him by your king, whom he welcomes once more into the ranks of his brothers with the love of a father for the son of his loins, so that he may remain powerful over his enemies."

Ushering the ambassador through the doors with just *Monvagaru* and the three lords in his party, he left all the others standing outside. Whereupon, the ambassador, finding himself alone and deprived of the company of his own people, glanced back three times, his face showing displeasure. Observing this, *Monvagaru,* who was in charge of everything there, motioned to the *queitor,* who was following close behind him, to allow the foreigners only to enter. They reopened the doors for that purpose, and as the Burmese started in, and we Portuguese with them, so many other people tried to push their way in with us that all the doorkeepers—and there were more than twenty of them—had quite a hard time closing the doors, distributing many blows with the staffs they had in their hands and injuring some very highly respectable men in the process, but there was nothing that could stem the tide of people rushing to get in, screaming and shouting in a way that was positively frightful.

Once we got beyond these doors we passed through the middle of a large garden landscaped with so many strange and different kinds of things so pleasing to the eye, that there are no words to do it justice, because it was interspersed with many walks enclosed by silver railings, and there were many trees of rare fragrances which they told us were by nature so adapted to the moons of the year that they bear flowers and fruit in all seasons. Apart from this, there were so many different varieties of roses, and many other blossoms and wildflowers, that I think it best to say nothing, for it is impossible to tell what really goes on there.

In the middle of this garden there were many very lovely, well-dressed young ladies amusing themselves in many different ways, taking part in beautifully arranged ballets and dances, as well as in the playing of a wide variety of soft musical instruments very much like our own, which they played so well together, with such sweet harmony, that there was no one who would not have enjoyed listening to them. Others were seated about, embroidering, sketching or plaiting ropes of gold, others playing games, and still others picking fruit to eat; and all of this was taking place in such a charming and orderly fashion, in a peaceful atmosphere of virtuous, dignified, and strict discipline, that all nine of us could hardly believe our eyes.

After leaving this garden, where *Monvagaru* urged the ambassador to linger a while, so that he would have something to tell his king in Pegu, we entered a very large reception hall they called *Cutamuilau,* where many lords and captains were seated, as well as some princes of great wealth and estates, who welcomed the ambassador with certain kinds of ceremonial etiquette, but without any one of them leaving his place. Once past this hall, we reached a door guarded by six men bearing silver maces, and after passing through it we found ourselves in another building, constructed in an extremely elaborate fashion, where the *Calaminhan* sat enthroned in a theater of great majesty, enclosed by three rows of silver balustrades, in the company of twelve very beautifully and splendidly attired women, who were sitting on the steps of the dais inside the enclosure, playing their delicate instruments to the accompaniment of which only two of them sang in turn. At the very top, where the king himself was sitting, there were twelve little girls about nine or ten years of age kneeling around him with small golden maces in their hands like scepters, and another one standing, who was fanning him. Below, along the entire length of the hall, were many old men with gold mitres on their heads, dressed in kimonos and *raudivás*[4] of satin and damask with broad trimmings of gold thread and with silver maces at their shoulders. There might have been sixty or seventy of them, and they were all standing along the walls. In the rest of the breadth of the hall were many fair and very beautiful young ladies sitting on luxurious rugs and carpets, and there must have been over two hundred of them, according to the estimate of our men.

As for this hall, both in its marvelous construction and the excellent order and harmony of everything in it, I can truly say that it represented a majesty so rich, so honorable, and so extraordinary that it filled us all with amazement, so much so, that we heard the ambassador himself say several times when talking about it, "If God takes me safely back to Pegu, I will not say anything about this to the king, not only because I do not want to make him feel sad, but also because I do not want to be taken for a man who tells incredible tales."

164
News of the Redeemer

As I was saying, after the ambassador entered this hall escorted by the four princes, he prostrated himself on the floor five times, without daring to lift his eyes to the *Calaminhan* because of the great reverence in which he is held, until *Monvagaru* commanded him to go forward. When he reached the first balustrade, keeping his head down all the while, he addressed the *Calaminhan*, raising his voice for all to hear: "The clouds that nourish the fruit that sustains us have made known the great majesty of thy power throughout the entire monarchy of the world, because of which my king, coveting thy friendship like a rich pearl, sends me, in his name, to deliver himself unto thee as a true brother with honorable obedience by reason of thou being older and he younger; and as such he sends this letter because it is the greatest jewel in his treasury, in which his eyes take more delight through honor and pleasure than in being lord of the kings of Ava with all the precious stones in the mountains of *Faleu, Jatir,* and *Pontau.*"[1]

"I accept this new friendship," the *Calaminhan* replied, with a grave and stern countenance, "and I take it upon myself to satisfy thy king in every way, as I would a son newly born of my own flesh and blood."

Then the women took up their instruments and resumed their playing, and six of them danced with six little boys for about as long as it takes to recite three or four Credos. After them, six tiny little girls danced with six of the oldest men in the hall, which we all thought was very nice. When this was over, they presented a play performed by twelve very beautiful, well-dressed women in which a king's daughter appeared, protruding from the mouth of a fish, which proceeded to swallow her right there in full view of everybody. At the sight of this, the twelve women, shedding many tears, fled in great haste to a hermitage located at the foot of a mountain, whence they returned with a hermit who offered up fervent prayers, in their fashion, to the god of the sea, *Quiay Patureu,* to have that fish cast up on shore so that a proper burial could be given the damsel, in accordance with her noble station in life. To which *Quiay Patureu* himself replied that the twelve maidens should convert their weeping into soft, sweet music to charm his ears and he would command the sea to cast up the fish, and then he would deliver it lifeless into his hands.

Next, six little boys appeared with gold crowns on their heads and wings also made of gold, just the way angels are depicted among us, except that they were naked, with not a stitch of clothes on them. They kneeled down in front of the twelve women and handed them three harps, three violas, and some other musical instruments, including two flageolets, and told them that *Quiay Patureu* had sent them those *caulanges*[2] from the Heaven of the Moon with which to lull the fish of the sea to sleep, thereby making their sweet music the means of fulfilling their desire.

The twelve women took the instruments from the hands of the six little boys with a ceremony of elaborate courtesy and began to play, accompanying themselves in song with such mournful harmony, shedding so many tears that some of the men who were there began to weep too. After they had been playing for nearly half a quarter of an hour they saw the fish that had swallowed the king's daughter rise up from the depths of the sea, and as though stunned, little by little it staggered ashore and fell lifeless at the feet of the twelve woman musicians. It was such a remarkable performance that no one thought it was staged, but real; moreover, it was executed with such great perfection, in a dazzling setting of magnificent splendor and beauty.

Next, one of the twelve women drew a jeweled dagger from her waist, and after slitting one side of the fish she helped out the king's daughter, who, to the accompaniment of the same music, went straight up to the *Calaminhan* and kissed his hand, and he in turn accorded her the signal honor of letting her sit next to him. This girl, it was said, was his niece, a daughter of one of his brothers, and all of the other twelve who had taken part in the play were daughters of princes and grandees whose fathers and brothers were all present there. Three or four more plays were also presented in the same manner and flawlessly executed by very noble young women with such dazzling beauty, pageantry, opulence, and with such perfection in every detail, that one could never grow weary of watching them.

Later in the afternoon the *Calaminhan* retired to another hall within the palace accompanied by the women only, and everyone else followed *Monvagaru,* as he held the ambassador by the arm, escorting him up to the last hall of the palace. There he bade him farewell after handing him over to the *queytor,* who took him to his house, where he stayed throughout the thirty-two days he was there until his departure. And during all that time he was wined and dined by the principal courtiers in a manner that was rare for its perfection and splendor. As for us, as members of his party, we were also very generously provided with everything necessary, and during our entire stay there were always many pastimes like fishing, hunting trips, and many other different kinds of sport.

Throughout the city and its environs we saw some notable buildings and temple compounds with extremely sumptuous pagodas and their dependencies of elaborate construction, one of which stood out from all the others for its majesty and grandeur. It was called *Quiay Pimpocau*, "god of the sick," and within its confines there were a large number of priests clad in dark gray habits and *altirnas* of purple damask drawn up under their arms, as I have mentioned several times before, like a stole. Since they are wiser and more learned than all the other priests in the twenty-four sects of this empire, they are allowed to wear a distinctive emblem of yellow cords around their waists. And as the highest mark of honor, the common people call them *sigiputões*,[3] which means "perfect men."

The ambassador visited this temple five times, not only to see the marvelous things they had there, but also to listen to the doctrines they preached, and he kept a record of everything he saw, heard, and experienced. He took back with him a volume full of humbug which he gave to the king of Burma, who later on, in Pegu, commanded that it be preached from the pulpits of all the *bralas* in his kingdom, as they still do today. I brought back to Portugal the translation of that book which a Florentine gentleman borrowed, and when I tried to get it back again he pretended that he had lost it, and he took it with him to Florence and presented it to the duke of Tuscany[4] who, I have been told, had it published under the title of "Strange Beliefs of the Heathens at the Other End of the World."

It was here one day in this pagoda that the ambassador, in a conversation he had with one of the *grepos* with whom he had struck up a friendship—for they are all by nature very kind and well inclined to foreigners, with whom they converse and communicate freely—asked him how many years ago the world had been created or whether there was a beginning to the things that God put so clearly before our eyes, like day, night, sun, moon, and stars, and all the other creatures who were not known to have a natural mother or father from whom they descended. The *grepo*, more confident of his knowledge than the others who were there, answered that, as for the world and the other things to which he referred that were not known by nature to have either mother or father, they actually did have mother and father, though not palpable and visible ones like other things had; and that the only creation the world by itself had ever had was the one that proceeded from the will of its Creator, which, at a certain time determined by his divine intelligence, he had manifested to the dwellers of heaven who already existed before, and that according to what was written about it, this occurred eighty-two thousand moons ago. He went on to say that when the earth emerged from the lake of the waters, God created a beautiful garden upon it in which he placed the first man, whom he named Adá, together with his wife Bazagom; and in order to keep them under a yoke of obedience, he commanded them not to touch the fruit of a certain tree called *hisaforão*, for that one alone he reserved for himself; and that if they should eat of it, they and all their descendants would feel the rigor of his divine punishment for ever after. When the great Lupantó, the Ravenous Serpent of the Concave Depths of the House of Smoke, heard of the commandment to which God had subjected them whereby they would earn merit in heaven, he went off to see the woman and bid her eat of that fruit and to make her husband do the same, assuring her that once they had tasted it, they would both become far more excellent in knowledge than God had created them, and freed of that heavy nature out of which

God had composed them, their bodies would rise to heaven in a single moment. Whereupon Bazagom, hearing what Lupantó had said to her, was so desirous of achieving the excellence he held before her eyes, that she ate of the fruit and made her husband do the same, and because they tasted of that unhappy morsel, both of them immediately became subject to the penalties of death, sorrow, and poverty. Upon seeing the disobedience of these first two beings he had created in the world, God made them feel the rigor of his justice by driving them out of the garden in which he had placed them and confirmed the penalties with which he had threatened them. Wherefore Adá, finding himself faced with the taste of death, fearing that the scourge of divine justice would proceed further against him, wept continuously for many years, which is why God sent word to him, with the promise that if he persevered in his repentance as much as he could, he would forgive him for having erred.

It was the first time the ambassador had ever heard anything like this and he was quite surprised.

"I am certain that the king, my lord, has never heard anything like what you have just told me," he said to the *grepo*, "nor have the priests in our *bralas* ever told us anything like that, for the only reward they hold out to us for our deeds is health and wealth in this life, and after death they say that the only reward that awaits us is to end our lives like the beasts in the wilderness, with the exception of the cows which, after death, are rewarded for the milk they give us by being transformed into sea cows, from whose eyeballs come the pearls that are found in the sea."

"Nor will anyone else in this land, except a *grepo* as learned as I am," he said, with an almost overweening pride, "tell you what I have just chosen to discuss with you, out of friendship."

Then, glancing with a vain air of presumption at the nine of us standing behind the ambassador, he addressed us, smiling like the devil's deputy that he was and assuming that we would be as impressed with him as he was with himself, "Since you, as foreigners, have no knowledge of the truth I have spoken, I would be very happy to have you come and listen to me more often so that you will learn about how God created all things and how much we are all beholden to him for the gift of this Creation."

Then one of the men in our group, a fellow by the name of Gaspar de Meireles,[5] who wanted to show that he was more interested in the subject than the rest of us, began by giving him due thanks in the name of us all, after which he begged permission to ask him a few questions about some other things he would be very happy to learn from him. The *grepo* became very expansive and said that he would be delighted to answer his questions, for it was a trait of the wise and curious man to ask questions in order to learn and of the ignorant to listen without knowing how to respond. Then Gaspar de Meireles asked him if, after God had created all those things he had been talking about, he had performed any deeds of justice or mercy on earth, and he said yes, for as was plain to see, man had never stopped committing sins that deserved to be punished, nor had God ever lacked the will to pardon him for them, and as the sins of man multiplied, owing to the corruptibility of nature, God had flooded the entire earth by commmanding the clouds in heaven to rain upon it and drown every living thing on it, except one just man and his family, whom God had commanded to take refuge in a large wooden house, and it was from him that afterward all the other people who inhabit the earth had descended.

Then again our man asked him if after this punishment God had sent any other and he replied that, in general, nothing similar to this had ever occurred again, but that in particular, he continuously punished everybody, not only entire kingdoms and peoples with wars and famine, but also individuals, with sickness, hardship, and other afflictions, and especially with poverty, which was the worst of all evils.

Continuing with his questions, our man asked him if there was any hope that God would one day be appeased, so that men too, might hope to gain entrance to heaven, and he said he did not know, but that it was evident and it was to be believed as an article of faith, that just as God was infinite good, so he would be inclined to the good that men did on earth, out of love and respect for him.

He also asked him if he had ever heard or read that after all those things he mentioned had taken place, some man had come into the world who, by dying on the cross, had satisfied God for all men, or if there was any word of this among them.

"No one can satisfy God completely," he replied, "except God himself, even though there have already been saintly and virtuous men in the world who have satisfied God for themselves and for some of their friends, like the gods of our *varelas,* as our *grepos* have assured us in this regard; but as for there being one man who could satisfy God for all, up to now we have never heard of it, nor is it possible for the earth by itself to produce so precious a ruby in so base a quarry. Still, in times past something to that effect was preached in this land by a man called John who happened to come to this city, about whom it is written that he was a holy man and had been a disciple of another called Tomé Modeliar,[6] a servant of God who was killed by the inhabitants of *Dumclé* because he preached publicly that God had made himself a man and had died for all men. It was something that deeply divided the people of this land, for many believed it to be true, while others, as with prohibited goods, condemned him for what he was saying, at the instigation of the *grepos* of the sect of *Quiay Frigau,* 'god of the motes of the sun.' As a result, he was exiled from this city to *Savady,* a kingdom of the Burmese, and from there, for the same reason, to the city of Rangoon, where he was killed for preaching about this publicly, that is, that God had made himself a man and suffered death on the cross[7] for men."

To this Gaspar de Meireles replied—as did all the rest of us with him—that everything that that man had preached here was without a doubt the absolute truth. Upon hearing this, the *grepo,* along with all the others in his company, was so overcome, that falling to his knees, with hands raised and his eyes turned heavenward, he cried out tearfully, "O God and Lord! Thou whose beauty and loving kindness are manifested in the star-studded heavens, I beseech thee with all my heart to permit that in our days the hour may come when the people of the world will give thanks to thee for so great a favor!"

After all these things had taken place, and many others of this nature that could be related had I but the aptitude and wit required to set them down here, the ambassador took his leave of this *grepo* with many courteous words which they use unstintingly among themselves, for that is how they are ordinarily accustomed to treating each other.

165
A Brief Description of the *Calaminhan*'s Empire

A month after our arrival in the city of *Timplão* where the court was then in residence, the ambassador petitioned for a reply to his embassy and was granted an audience with the *Calaminhan,* who welcomed him graciously. After a brief discussion concerning his mission, he handed him over to *Monvagaru* who, as I have already said, was the highest-ranking official in the government of the kingdom and the one in charge of military affairs, who ordinarily handled such matters. He gave him the *Calaminhan*'s reply along with a costly gift in return for the one the king of Burma had sent him, and wrote him a letter that went like this:

"Limb of flawless ruby, newly joined by God to my body by means of the alliance and friendship treaty I hereby grant thee, making thee part of my flesh and blood like one of my own brothers; I, the *Prechau Guimião,*[1] lord of the twenty-seven crowns of the Mountains of the Earth, inherited by lawful succession from the lord who rested his feet on my head but twenty-two months ago, for it is that long since he parted from me, never more to see me, by reason of the sanctified state in which his soul now rests, basking in the gentle warmth of the sun's rays; I read thy letter on the fifth *chaveca*[2] of the eighth moon of the present year, whereunto I have given the credit of a true brother and as such I accept the terms thou proposest to me, with the obligation to permit thee to pass freely through both the borders of *Savady,* so that, without fear of the Siamese, thou mayest be king of Ava, as requested in thy letter. As for the other points raised separately by thy ambassador, I shall reply to them through one of my own, whom I shall send from here at once, to the end that he may, in my name, reach a decision that will give thee the pleasure thou seemest to take in making war upon thy enemies."

Immediately after receiving this letter the ambassador departed from the court, on the third of November in the year 1546, accompanied by a group of noblemen who, by order of the *Calaminhan,* went with him as far as a town called *Bidor,* where he was given an elaborate farewell banquet and some personal gifts.

However, before I say anything about the journey we took from here to Pegu, where the king of Burma was then in residence, it seemed both fitting and necessary to provide some information about some things we saw in this country, which I shall do as briefly as possible, as I have done with all the other things I have been discussing thus far; for if I were to dwell in detail on everything that I saw and experienced not only in this empire, but in all the other kingdoms as well in which I found myself on this sad and arduous journey of mine, another much larger volume than this would be required, to say nothing of a knowledge, ability, and wit far superior to mine, which I know all too well is very inferior and inadequate, as I have already pointed out and confessed many times before. But rather than let such noteworthy things remain in obscurity, I shall do my best to describe them in my own awkward way.

The kingdom of Pegu has 140 leagues of coastline which lies at sixteen degrees latitude south. It reaches eastward through the heart of the interior for a distance of 130 leagues. In the upper reaches, it is surrounded by a stretch of land called *Pan-*

guassirau, which is where the Burmese live, an area 80 leagues wide by 200 long. At one time their monarchy was all one kingdom, but that is no longer true, for it is divided into thirteen states, ruled by rebellious lords who declared their independence, according to what their chronicles relate, after first poisoning their king[3] at a banquet they gave in his honor in the city of *Chaleu.* Of these thirteen states, eleven are now ruled by other nations whose lands encompass the Burmese territory, forming a circle above them for an even greater distance, in which two great emperors reside, one called the *Siammon,* and the other this *Calaminhan,* who is the only one I intend to discuss here.

They say that this prince's empire and overlordship covers an area of more than three hundred leagues, both in length and width, and though formerly it consisted of twenty-seven kingdoms, the inhabitants spoke the same language then as they do today. Here in this empire we saw many very prosperous and populous cities, filled with all kinds of food in the way of meat, freshwater fish, grains, legumes, rice, vegetables, wines, and fruit, and all of it in such huge quantities, that there are not words enough to do it justice. Their capital is this city of *Timplão* where the *Calaminhan* emperor resides with his whole court most of the time. It is situated lengthwise all along a large river called *Pituy,* which is frequented by an infinite number of oared craft. It is completely surrounded by two terrepleins of very strong masonry with their wide moats outside, and at all the gates it has castles with very high towers. Some merchants we asked informed us that there were 400,000 hearths in the city, where most of the houses are two and three stories high; and that some of them were quite expensive and luxurious, especially the ones belonging to the merchants and the nobility, to say nothing of the mansions owned by the lords which stand apart from the others within very large walls, with terraces for their pastimes; and that within the gates, which are decorated with Chinese-style arches, there are gardens, orchards with many trees, and water fountains, much suited to the joys and pleasures of life to which these people are very much inclined.

They further assured us that within and without the walls, for a league around this city, there were twenty-six hundred houses of worship, and some of them, which we visited, were very sumptuous temples, of extremely fine construction and richly adorned, though most of them are small structures, like hermitages. These people are followers of twenty-four different religious sects, among which there is so great a variety and confusion of diabolical errors and precepts, principally in the blood sacrifices they employ, that it is frightful to hear them, let alone see them, as we did a few times on the solemn festival days of their *terivós.*[4] But the largest and most popular sect by far is that of an idol I have mentioned many times before by the name of *Quiay Frigau,* "god of the motes of the sun," because this is the one the *Calaminhan* and all the most important lords in the kingdom believe in and worship. The priests of this sect, the *grepos, menigrepos,* and *talagrepos,* are also more highly revered than any of the others and are regarded as saints by the people. The chief dignitaries of this sect are given the lofty title of *cabizondos,*[5] and presumably they have nothing to do with women, but they have other diabolical ways of satisfying their base, sensual appetites, which is more to be deplored than discussed here, and that is why I regard it as both a duty and necessity to pass over them in silence, because they are totally unworthy of Christian tongues and ears.

Also, at the ordinary city fairs, which they call *chandeuhós,*[6] we saw all the things that the earth brings forth, and in addition to that, a great deal of iron, steel, lead, tin, copper, brass, saltpeter, sulphur, mercury, cinnabar, honey, beeswax, sugar, lac, benzoin, silk, all sorts of dry goods, pepper, ginger, cinnamon, linen, cotton, alum, borax, indigo, cornelian, crystal, camphor, musk, ivory, cassia fistula,[7] rhubarb, *trevite,*[8] scammony,[9] verdigris, woad,[10] incense, putchock,[11] cochineal, storax,[12] saffron, cutch,[13] myrrh, extremely fine porcelain, gold, silver, rubies, diamonds, emeralds, sapphires, and everything else one can name, and in such huge quantities that it is impossible to describe, for it has to be seen to be believed.

The women are generally very fair and beautiful, but what makes them more attractive is the fact that they are good-natured, chaste, charitable, and affectionate. The minor priests of all twenty-four sects, and there are large numbers of them in this empire, go dressed in yellow robes, like the *rolins* of Pegu, with their *altirnas* drawn up under the arm like a stole. They have neither silver nor gold coins because all trade is carried on by means of measures of weight, such as *cates,*[14] *taels,*[15] *mazes,*[16] and *conderins.*[17] The court of this *Calaminhan* is very rich and the courtiers very elegant. It is attended by many princes and lords of great wealth and state. The emperor himself is very much feared, extremely so, and at the same time very much revered, and he maintains a large number of foreign military captains at his court, at very high salaries.

The ambassador was told that in this city where the court resides there are always sixty thousand or more men in the cavalry and ten thousand elephants. The nobility's style of living is very clean and honorable, with silver and sometimes gold dinner services, while the commoners use porcelain and brass. They dress in satins, damasks, and Persian calicoes, and in the wintertime, sable-lined clothes. In their system of justice there is neither plaintiff nor defendant, nor do they draw up formal indictments; instead, the captains of the street patrols decide verbally any legal questions raised by the common folk. And if by chance any disputes should arise between persons of higher quality, they are settled by monks who are especially authorized to do so in certain temples, and their decisions may be appealed to the *queitor,*[18] who is the chief justice, whose decision is final, without any further recourse, no matter how serious and important the matter may be.

There are seven hundred political subdivisions within the twenty-seven kingdoms of this monarchy, or twenty-six per kingdom, and each one has its captain who resides in the city or town that is the capital of the district, all of whom have equal power, nor does anyone in his district have more power than any other in his. Every month each of these captains is obliged to take a general census of the troops levied by the *vagaru*[19] in each captaincy, which consist of two thousand foot soldiers, five hundred cavalrymen, and eighty war elephants. One of these elephants is given the name of the city or town that is the capital of the district, so that altogether the number of troops and elephants in these seven hundred district captaincies comes to 1,750,000 men, of whom 350,000 are mounted on horseback and 56,000 on elephants. And because there are so many of them in this land, in such huge numbers, this emperor has come to be styled the "lord of the indomitable force of the elephants of the earth."

The revenue from the royal duties, which are referred to there as the "price of the scepter," plus the income derived from all the mines, amount to twenty million in gold, not counting all the services rendered to him by the princes, captains, and lords, which are entered into a separate account and which also add up to a sizable figure, divided among them according to the merits of each. Pearls, amber, and salt are very expensive in this country because they are products of the sea, which is very far from this city, but of everything else there is very great abundance. The climate here is very healthy, with good air and water. When they sneeze they make the sign of the cross as we do and say, "Quiay dó sam rorpy,"[20] meaning, "The God of truth is three and one," from which it appears, as was said before, that these people had some knowledge of our evangelical faith, which is the only true one.

166
Strange Races and Places

The next day, after departing from this town of *Bidor,* we proceeded on our course down this great river of *Pituy,* and that same day we stopped for the night at an abbey belonging to the sect of *Quiay Jarem,* "god of married people." It was situated in a clearing at the edge of the river within a large wooded area amidst many splendid buildings, where the ambassador was treated very hospitably by the *cabizondo* and the *talagrepos* who lived there. From here, continuing our journey for seven more days, we arrived at a city called *Pavel,* where we stayed for three days provisioning the boats with the necessary supplies. The ambassador purchased many luxury items and trinkets from China which they sold very cheaply here, including a large quantity of musk, fine porcelain, silk fabric and yarn, ermine pelts, and many other kinds of furs which they wear during the winter, since it gets very cold here. These goods are brought in by elephant and yak caravans from very distant places across the hinterland, according to the information we got from some merchants here who told us that they were from a province called *Friucaranjá* beyond which lived some people called *Calogens* and *Fungaos* with whom they are constantly at war, a dark-skinned people who are excellent bowmen and whose feet are round at the bottom like an ox's but with toes and nails and all the rest like other men, except for their hands, which are very hairy. The men are by nature of a cruel and evil disposition, and down below at the bottom of the spine, they have a lump of flesh the size of two fists. They also told us that these people lived high up in some wild mountain ranges where, in some parts, there are underground caves so deep that in some of them, on winter nights, the sound of howling and other frightful noises could be heard coming from them.

Apart from these people there were others called *Colouhos, Timpates,* and *Bugem,* and still others from an even more distant land called *Oqueus* and *Magores,* who lived on wild animals which they hunted and ate raw, as well as on all different kinds of unclean animals such as lizards, insects, and snakes that are found there. When they go hunting for these wild animals they ride mounted on other animals about the size of horses, which have three horns or antlers in the middle of their foreheads, short thick legs, and a row of spines in the middle of the back with which they struck when provoked. The rest of the body is covered with scales the color of a green lizard, and at the neck, instead of a mane, they have more spines very much longer and thicker than the ones on the back, and where the shoulders meet, they have short wings, like the fins of a fish, with which, we were told, they take flying hops of twenty-five to thirty paces. They said that these animals were called *banazas,*[1] and that the people of that country would make frequent incursions mounted on them over the borders of other nations, with whom they were constantly at war, some of which paid them tribute in the form of salt, which they valued more highly than anything else because there was none to be had except at places very far from there.

We also spoke with some other people called *Bumioens* who came from a very high mountainous region where there were alum quarries, lac, and woad for dyes. We saw a caravan of more than two thousand oxen from this nation, laden with pack saddles very much like ours. These men were all tall and they had beards and eyes like the Chinese.

We saw men from another nation with bright red hair and some with freckles who had very thick beards and their ears and noses pierced and plugged with gold ornaments like clasps. These people were called *Ginafôgaos,* and they were natives of the province of *Surobasoy,* which borders on the lake of Chiang Mai in the mountains of Laos. Some of them wear hairy animal skins and others wear dressed hides, and they go about barefooted and always bareheaded. Some merchants told us that these people, generally speaking, were very wealthy and that among themselves the only thing they used was silver; however, they had great quantities of it.

We also spoke with others called *Tuparoens,* dark-complexioned, good-natured people, extremely gluttonous, and overly fond of the delights of the flesh and the palate. We were treated far better by these people than by any of the others we met, for most of the time was spent in banqueting us. At one of these banquets, which all nine of us attended with the ambassador, one of our men, a fellow by the name of Francisco Temudo,[2] outdrank them and came close to offending them for doing so. Since it was a great blow to their pride, they prolonged the banquet in an effort to restore their honor. However, the Portuguese did so well in a drinking contest with twenty of them who were still sitting at the table, that they were soon under it, while he remained in complete control of himself. After they came to, their captain, a man by the name of *Sapitou,* in whose house the banquet had been given, sent for all his men—and there must have been over three hundred of them—and much against his will, they placed the Portuguese on top of an elephant and led him through the whole city, followed by a huge crowd, to the accompaniment of trumpets, drums, and other musical instruments, while behind him came the captain and the ambassador, with us Portuguese and the rest of the Burmese on foot, with boughs in our hands, and two men on horseback who kept shouting to the crowds as they rode by, "O ye people, sing joyful praises to the rays that issue from the center of the sun, which is the god that brings forth our rice, for the time has come when you behold in your land a man so holy who, by drinking more than anyone ever born in the world, has brought down the twenty principal heads of our troop. May his fame be spread far and wide forever!"

The mob that accompanied him broke into such a loud roar that it was really frightful. And when, in this manner, they reached the house where we were staying with the ambassador, they dismounted him from the elephant in a highly ceremonious and honorable manner, and on bended knees they handed him over to the ambassador, admonishing him to treat him thenceforth as a saint, or the son of some great king, for he could not be otherwise, since God had endowed him with such a precious gift. Then they asked for contributions from everyone and collected right there more than two hundred *taels* in silver bars which they presented to him, for such is the custom of this nation. During the remainder of our stay they visited him constantly with many presents and bolts of silk, as though they were offerings that one would give to a saint on the day of his invocation.

We also spoke here with some other white men called *Pavileus,* expert bowmen and fine horsemen who dressed in silk kimonos like the Japanese and ate with sticks like the Chinese. They told us that their country was called *Binagorem* and that it was about two hundred leagues up the river from there. They carried a great deal of gold to trade with, of the same quality found in Menangkabau on the island of Sumatra, as well as eaglewood, lac, musk, tin, copper, silk, and wax, which they exchanged for pepper, ginger, salt, and rice wines. The wives of those we saw there are very fair, and they dress better than all the other women in those parts, and they are generally very kindhearted and gracious.

When we asked them what was their religion and what God they worshipped, they told us that their God was the sun, the heaven, and the stars because from them they received, by holy communication, the blessings they possessed on earth, and that the soul of man was the breath which ceased with the death of the body, rising into the atmosphere to mix with the clouds until it condensed into water and returned to earth to die, just as the body had done before.

They told us many other ridiculous things like this, which is enough to fill one with amazement to see how confused and blind these poor wretches are, and enough to make those whom God chose to deliver from such things give thanks to him continually for such favor.

And thus, from the great diversity of unknown nations we saw here, one may very well conclude that in this monarchy of the world there are still many undiscovered lands about which we know nothing.

167
Funeral Rites for the Holy *Rolim*

We continued on our way from this city of *Pavel,* and the day after our departure we reached a village called *Lunçor* that was surrounded for a distance of more than three leagues by trees from which they obtain the benzoin that is shipped to the kingdoms of Pegu and Siam.

From here we sailed down this great river for nine more days, passing in view of many different kinds of very noble cities and towns located along the shore, until we reached another river called *Ventrau,*[1] by which we made our way as far as *Penauchim,* the first town in the kingdom of *Jangumá,*[2] where the ambassador registered the vessels and all the men on board, in compliance with the local custom. Departing from here, we went on to spend the night at the *Rauditens,* which were two fortresses belonging to the prince of *Pancanor.*

Five days later we came to a large city called *Magadaleu,* from where they get the lac that is shipped to Martaban. At the time we were there the local prince gave the ambassador a review of a general levy of troops he was sending against the king of

Laos, with whom he was at war for having repudiated a daughter of his after three years of marriage in order to marry a concubine who had previously borne him a son he had legitimized and named heir to the kingdom, thereby depriving a grandson of his by this daughter of his right to the throne.

From here we proceeded on our way along an estuary called *Madur,* and five days later we arrived at a village called *Mouchel,* which was the first town in the kingdom of Pegu where, one night, we were attacked by a very famous pirate called *Chalagonim,*[3] who was on the prowl with a fleet of thirty well-equipped and well-manned *serós.* He fought with us until nearly daylight, giving us such a hard time that it was only by the great mercy of God that we escaped from the battle with the loss of five of our twelve vessels and the death of 180 of our men, including two Portuguese. The ambassador received a cut on the arm and two arrow wounds from which he nearly died, and we and all the others were badly wounded. Also, they made off with the gift the *Calaminhan* had sent, which was worth over 100,000 *cruzados,* as well as a great deal of other valuable merchandise that was on board those five vessels. And three days later, that was the way we reached the city of Martaban, routed and robbed, with the greater and better part of the company slain.

Here, the ambassador immediately sent a letter off to the king of Burma, advising him of all that had happened to him during both the voyage and this disaster. The king promptly responded by dispatching, at top speed, an armada of 120 *serós* with a large company of elite troops on board, among them a hundred Portuguese, which went in search of this pirate who, by the time it got there, had already beached the thirty *serós* with which he had attacked us, and he and all his men had withdrawn to a fortress that was full of the many prizes he had taken from many of the communities in the surrounding area.

Our men immediately laid siege to the fortress, and in their first assault they entered it at a cost in lives of a few Burmese and only one Portuguese, but many received arrow wounds from which they recovered in a few days without danger to life or limb for any of them. Once inside the fortress they put everyone there to the sword, sparing only the pirate and 120 of his men whom they brought back alive to the city of Pegu, where the king of Burma had them all thrown to the elephants which, in no time at all, crushed them to bits and pieces. The Portuguese did quite well for themselves in this foray against the pirate, for they all returned very rich, and there were five or six of them who they say received from twenty-five to thirty-five thousand *cruzados* each as their share of the booty, and the ones who came off worst got two and three thousand each.

After recovering here in Martaban from the wounds he had received in the battle, the ambassador departed for the city of Pegu, where at that time, as mentioned above, the king of Burma was residing with all his court. As soon as the king heard that he was arriving and that he was carrying a letter from the *Calaminhan* accepting his friendship treaty, he sent a reception party to meet him, headed by the *Chaumigrem,*[4] his foster brother and brother-in-law, who was accompanied by all the grandees, with an escort of four battalions of foreign mercenaries, including among them a thousand Portuguese under the command of one Antonio Ferreira,[5] a native of Braganza and a man of great courage, who was receiving a salary of twelve thousand *cruzados* from this king, to say nothing of personal gifts amounting to nearly as much.

Now that his desire for this alliance had been granted him by God, the Burmese king, by way of thanking him for so great a favor, arranged for elaborate celebrations among all the people and ordered sweet-smelling sacrifices to take place in the *bralas* of their heathen sects, during which they slaughtered more than a thousand deer, pigs, and cows, which were given away as alms to the poor, to say nothing of other charitable deeds, such as the distribution of clothing to five thousand needy people, the freeing of over a thousand prisoners, and the forgiving of large debts.

After these celebrations had been going on for seven days, in the full fervor of the festivities, and at tremendous cost to all the people, the king, and the nobility, a confirmed report reached the city of the death of *Aixquendó,*[6] *rolim* of *Mounay,*[7] the highest dignitary in their priesthood. As a result, everything came to a sudden stop, and expressions of deep sorrow were seen among all the people. The king went into retirement, the bazaars closed down, the windows and doors of all the buildings were shut tight, and there was not a living creature to be seen in the entire city. The *bralas* of their idols were filled with mourners who wept continuously, inflicting various kinds of extreme penitence on themselves from which some of them died.

That same night the king departed for *Mounay,* twenty leagues away, since it was necessary for him to be present at the funeral, in keeping with the ancient custom of the kings of Pegu. He arrived there the following afternoon at vesper time and saw to it that the necessary arrangements for the funeral proceeded so rapidly that on the same day all the preparations were completed and everything was in order.

When it was almost sundown the body of the deceased was taken from the house in which he had died and placed on a catafalque that had been erected in the center of a large plaza, draped all about with white velvet and covered above with three canopies of brocade. In the middle of it there was a platform twelve steps high, with a bier in a style similar to ours, decorated all over with many objects made of gold and precious stones, and all around it a large number of silver candlesticks and incense burners, owing to the decomposition of the body which was already beginning to smell bad.

It remained that way all through the night, during which there was so much going on, what with the cries and screams of all the people that were so frightful that there are no words to describe it, and it was said that just the number of *bicos, grepos, menigrepos, talagrepos, guimões,*[8] and *rolins* alone—who are the members of their orders and dignitaries of their priesthood—that were assembled there came to well over thirty thousand, not counting those who were arriving every hour. With the appearance of some mourning symbols that were very appropriate for those funeral rites, on the stroke of two hours past midnight, there issued forth from a temple called *Quiay Figrau,* "god of the motes of the sun," a procession in which there were probably more than five hundred naked children, with iron chains and ropes of coir around their waists and necks, small bundles of firewood on their heads, and knives in their hands. As they went, they were singing responsively in two choirs with such deep sadness and emotion that they brought many a tear to the eyes of the listeners as one of the choirs chanted in the manner of a sequence, "Thou who art about to enter into the joys of heaven, leave us not behind as captives in this earthly exile."

To which the other choir responded, "So that we may rejoice with thee in the blessings of the Lord."

And they continued chanting this in the manner of a litany, repeating many other verses in the same manner and the same tone. After they had all knelt down in front of the catafalque on which the body of the deceased lay, a *grepo* more than a hundred years old prostrated himself on the ground and, with arms upraised, addressed the corpse on behalf of these children, to which another, who was beside the bier, replied, as though speaking for the deceased, "God, who by his holy will saw fit to create me out of dust, ordained that on this day I should return to dust, wherefore I charge you, my dear children, to live in fear of this hour when the hand of the Lord weighs us in the scales of his justice."

To which, with a loud and mournful cry, they all responded, "May it please the Lord on high who reigns in the kingdom of the sun to look away from our deeds, so that we may be delivered from the pain of death."

Once these children had left, another group of eight boys about ten to twelve years of age appeared, dressed in long white satin robes, with gold bangles on their feet and many rich jewels and strings of pearls around their necks. After making many *zumbaias* to the deceased, which they performed in a highly ceremonious manner, they brandished the naked swords they held all around the bier, as if they were driving the devil away, saying as they did so, "Be gone, thou cursed one, to the Concave Depths of the House of Smoke where thou shalt endlessly suffer the torments of dying, as a punishment without end decreed by the rigorous justice of the Lord on high!"

With these words they departed, as though satisfied that they were leaving the body free of the evil spirits they had driven away. Next came six of their highest ranking *talagrepos,* each one more than eighty years of age, clad in purple damask, their *altirnas* thrown over their shoulders and drawn up under their arms like stoles, with silver incense burners in their hands, while before them, adding dignity to the ritual, walked twelve porters carrying silver maces. After spreading incense around the bier four times with a great deal of ceremony, these six priests all prostrated themselves face down on the ground and wept with deep emotion, while one of them spoke up, as though he were addressing the deceased.

"If the clouds in the sky were capable of explaining the reason for our sorrow to the beasts in the field, they would leave their pastures to help us mourn thy absence and the deep void left by thy death; or they would entreat thee, my lord, to take us with thee on that tabernacle of death where we can all see thee without being seen by thee, for we are unworthy of so great a blessing. But in order to console these people, give them some earthly sign, before the grave hides thy body from us, of the quiet joy and contentment of thy rest, so that they may all be roused from the heavy torpor into which they have sunk, weighed down by the suffering of the flesh, and may they inspire us poor wretches to imitate thee and follow in thy footsteps, so that when we breathe our last, we may see thee in a state of happiness in the House of the Sun."

To which all the people responded with a frightful roar of *Miday talambá!*— meaning, "Grant us this wish, O Lord!"

As the twelve macebearers began once more to clear a path through the crowd, encountering great difficulty in doing so because the people absolutely refused to make way, there came forth from a building to the right of the catafalque twenty-four splendidly attired little boys, with many jewels and gold chains around their necks, all of them carrying many native-style musical instruments. Forming two rows, they knelt down before the bier and played all these instruments, to the sound of which just two of the boys sang, with five of them responding from time to time. This caused the people to shed so many tears and provoked such deep feeling in them that some very honorable and highly respectable gentlemen struck themselves on their faces and at times hit their heads on the steps of the bier.

During the course of this ceremony as well as ten or twelve others that followed, six young noble *grepos* sacrificed themselves by taking deep draughts from a golden bowl that was on a nearby table containing a yellow liquid so venomous that they died immediately after drinking it, for which they were revered as saints, thereby earning the envy of all. And from where they had fallen they were immediately taken in procession to be cremated on a huge funeral pyre made of sandalwood, benzoin, and eaglewood, where their bodies were all reduced to ashes.

When morning came, the most elaborate ornaments on the catafalque were removed, though the canopies, the velvet coverings, the banners and flags, and other ornaments of great value were left as they were. Then, in an extremely ritualistic fashion, while the screams and wailing rose even higher, accompanied by the frightful din of many musical instruments, they set fire to the catafalque with all that had been left on it, sprinkling the body with many costly perfumes as it was rapidly consumed by the flames. As it burned, the king and all the grandees present offered up to it many objects made of gold, and precious rings of rubies and sapphires, as well as some priceless strings of pearls, and all of these costly items, so ill employed, were consumed by the fire along with the flesh and bones of the hapless corpse.

The cost of this elaborate funeral, according to what was said there, was well over 100,000 *cruzados,* to say nothing of the vestments that the king and the grandees gave to the thirty thousands priests, for which infinite amounts of cloth were used, all to the advantage of the Portuguese who sold theirs, which they had brought from Bengal, for whatever price they demanded and for which they received prompt payment in gold ingots and silver bars.

168
Election of the New *Rolim*

The next day between seven and eight in the morning, when the ashes of the deceased had cooled, the king himself, together with all the grandees of the kingdom, came to the place where the body had been cremated. He was accompanied by a sumptuous procession of all the *grepos* in his priesthood, including a group of 130 carrying silver incense burners in their hands and fourteen others with gold trays on their heads, who were wearing long robes of yellow satin, with their green velvet *altirnas* tucked under their arms. All the rest, probably numbering between six and seven thousand, were dressed in the same yellow color, though their robes were made of fine taffetas and *chautares,*[1] for which they must have gone to great expense considering the large number of people involved.

When they reached the place where the *rolim* had been cremated, some heathen ceremonies were performed with words and actions in their fashion to fit the occasion and the feelings demonstrated by all, and after that, a *talagrepo* climbed up to an *agrém,*[2] which was the pulpit. He was Burmese by nationality and an uncle to the king, his father's brother, who, because he was regarded by the majority of the people as the wisest among them, had been chosen to deliver the sermon of the hour. After a few introductory remarks eulogizing the life and deeds of the deceased, embellished with words and arguments to suit his purpose, he got so carried away that he turned to the king, his eyes brimming with tears, and raising his voice slightly in order to be better heard, said to him, "If the kings who govern or, to be more exact, who tyrannize the earth these days, would give some thought to how little time they have to prepare for this hour, and to how severe the punishment is that awaits them at the hand of the almighty Lord for all the crimes and outrages they have committed in their tyrannical lives, perhaps they would consider themselves more fortunate to be grazing in the fields like cattle instead of using their power so despotically and unreasonably, being cruel to the gentle sheep and lenient with the evildoers, whom they have honored with titles of nobility. For those whom fortune has placed in so perilous a state are indeed to be pitied, but that is precisely what we see happening these days to our kings who continuously lead dissolute lives without restraining their passions or feeling a moment of shame or fear.

"For know this, ye blind of the world, that if God made men to be kings, it was for them to be humane to men, to hear men, to satisfy men, and to punish men, but not out of sheer tyranny to kill men. However, you, wretched kings, by the way you carry out the duties of your office, you are denying the very nature with which God has endowed you, changing it as often as you change your clothes, acting like leeches toward some, depriving them bit by bit of life and property, never letting go until you have sucked up every last drop of blood from their veins. Whereas for others, you act as fierce as lions, proclaiming abroad with a terrible roar intended to mask your greed, that all those guilty of scandalous or wicked behavior shall forfeit life and property, which is your real goal, while for those who are your favorites, those whom you or the world in general, or I know not who, have ennobled with grand titles, you are so lenient in punishing their arrogant deeds and so prodigal in bestowing favors on them at the expense of the poor whom you have despoiled, stripping them of all but skin and bones, that the little people have good cause for accusing you of all these things before God, in whose presence you poor kings will find yourselves with no excuse to offer, nor words with which to defend yourselves, and with nothing but fear and turmoil to confound you!"

And he went on this way, saying so many things in favor of the little people, crying out so many times, and shedding so many tears on their behalf that the king listened as though astounded and quite beside himself. It made such a deep impression on him that he immediately sent for the *brazagarão,* the governor of Pegu, and commanded him to go at once and dismiss all the procurators of the kingdom whom he had called together in the city of *Cosmim*[3] to ask them to raise a huge sum of money to finance another military campaign he was planning against the kingdom of *Savady*. Also, he sword publicly on the ashes of the deceased that as long as he reigned he would not levy extra tribute on any of the common people, nor would he force them into his service as he had been doing all along, and that henceforth he would be at pains to lend an ear to the little people and to punish the grandees, each according to his merits. In the same manner he promised many other things that were very just and highly commendable, all of which, coming from a heathen, put us to great shame.

When the sermon was over, the ashes of the dead man, which had been gathered up in the meantime, were divided as a holy relic among the fourteen gold trays, one of which the king carried at the head, while the highest-ranking *grepos* carried the others. And from there, keeping the same formation in which they had come, the procession resumed its march, bearing the ashes to a sumptuous temple nearly a sphere-shot's distance away by the name of *Quiay Docó,* "god of the afflicted of the earth," where they were placed in a tomb that was level with the ground, without ostentation or any display of vanity, in obedience to the wishes of this *Aixequendó* who, as I have said, was their supreme *rolim,* highest in rank over all the *grepos,* just as the pope is among us Christians. The tomb was immediately enclosed by three rows of railings, two of silver and one of brass. Hanging from three beams that ran across the entire width of the building were seventy-two silver chandeliers, twenty-four on each beam, all very costly and valuable, of ten or twelve branches each, and all of them suspended from very heavy silver chains. The tomb within the railings was surrounded by thirty-six perfuming vessels, like incense burners, from which rose the delightful fragrances of eaglewood, daisy benzoin, and other preparations mixed with amber.

By the time these funeral rites were over it was already close to vespers, owing to the many ceremonies that had taken place, and the only thing else they did that day was to release a great quantity, in almost countless numbers, of little birds⁺ that they brought there in more than three hundred cages and coops. They explained this by saying that there were souls in those birds of people who had passed on from this life, and that they were waiting for the day when they would be released so that they could freely go and accompany the soul of this dead man. They also did the same thing with another enormous number of little fish which, out of devotion, they had brought there in wooden troughs full of water and, with another ceremony, set free by throwing them into the river, to go and serve the soul of the dead man. Also, a huge quantity of all the game in the forest was brought here, and this was far more interesting to see than anything else I have described thus far; however, the meat was distributed as alms to the countless numbers of poor.

Since it was already close to nightfall when these and many other ceremonies that formed part of the obsequies had ended, the king retired to his *dopo,* or his head-quarters, where he was spending the night in tents, out of grief for the deceased, as were the grandees too, along with all the other people who were gathered there.

At daybreak the following morning, the king issued a proclamation that every person, regardless of station, was to leave the island at once, on pain of death, and that those who were priests should retire to their prayers, on pain of being deprived of their dignity for failing to do so, all of which everyone hastened to obey.

With the island deserted, and the priests in retirement, ninety of them who had been appointed to elect the dead man's successor all gathered in the temple of *Guangiparau* to perform their duty. Since they were unable to do so within the first two days, which was the time limit they had been given to make their choice, owing to a wide diversity of opinions and the casting of votes among many candidates, it was decided, on the advice of the king, that out of the ninety electors, nine definitors⁵ should be chosen who would pick the successor by themselves alone.

Once they had been chosen, these nine definitors all got together and sat in session for five more days. During all those days and the nights that followed the bonzes said many prayers, and there were offerings, and alms, and clothing for the many poor, and tables laden with food for any and all, and processions in their manner.

The nine concluded the session with a unanimous vote, electing a man by the name of *Manica Mouchão,* who at this time was serving as *cabizondo* in the city of Rangoon, in a pagoda called *Quiay Figrau,* "god of the motes of the sun," which I have mentioned many times before. He was sixty-eight years of age and was re-garded by the people as a prudent man, of exemplary conduct, very learned in the laws and customs of their heathen sects, and above all, very charitable to the poor, a choice with which the king and all the grandees were highly satisfied. Without any further delay, the king immediately dispatched the *Chaumigrem,* his brother-in-law, on whom—in order to lend greater dignity to his mission—he then conferred the title of *coutalanhá,*[6] meaning "brother of the king," to go and fetch the newly elected *rolim.* He departed at once with a hundred oared *laulés* carrying on board the flower of Burmese society, along with the nine definitors, and they brought him back from his place of residence with all due authority and veneration.

Nine days after his departure, when he had reached a town called *Tagalá,*[7] five leagues from this island of *Mounay,* the king went to meet him in person, accompanied by all the grandees of his court, to say nothing of the countless other people, in a fleet of more than two thousand rowing vessels. Arriving with all this pomp and splendor at the place where the new *rolim* was staying, he prostrated himself before him, and kissing the ground three times, he said to him, "Thou, O holy pearl of purple splendor that glows in the center of the sun, blow gently upon my head with breath that is pleasing to the Lord of uncreated power, so that I may not fear on earth the heavy yoke of my enemies!"

To this the *rolim* replied, extending a hand for him to rise, "Faxy hinapó varite pamor dapou campanó, dacorem fapixãopau," meaning, "Labor, my son, to make thy works pleasing to God, and I shall pray for thee constantly."

Raising him from the ground where he still lay, he seated him next to him and placed his hand upon his head three times, a gesture that the king regarded as a very high honor indeed; and after saying a few words to him which we could not hear because we were a little too far away, he breathed upon his head another three times as the king knelt before him, while all the other people lay prostrate on the ground. After which, departing from here in a deafening noise of shouts and bells and sonorous instruments, he embarked on the king's *laulé,* seated on a splendid throne of gold and precious stones, with the king at his feet, as a signal honor accorded him by the *rolim.* A little further back, forming a circle around him, were twelve little boys clad in yellow satin robes and brocade *altirnas,* with golden maces, like scepters, in their hands. Along both sides of the vessel, in place of oarsmen, went all the lords of the kingdom, with their gilded oars beside them, and at the bow and stern were two choirs of young lads dressed in crimson, accompanying themselves with many different kinds of musical instruments as they sang with excellent voices, many praises to the Lord, among them one hymn that our men noted particularly, which went like this:

"O ye children pure of heart, sing praises to the divine, admirable Lord, for I am unworthy because I have sinned, and if you do not have leave to do so, then let the tears fall at his feet and he will be gladdened thereby!"

And so in like manner they sang many other songs as they accompanied themselves on their instruments, making such sweet music that if they had been Christians, they might well have been able to move their listeners to deep devotion.

Surrounded by all this pomp and splendor, the *rolim* arrived in the city of Martaban, and since it was then very late at night, he did not go ashore at once as originally planned but waited until the following morning to do so; and because it was strictly forbidden for him to let his feet touch the ground, owing to the great dignity of his person, the king carried him ashore on his shoulder, and thus he was passed along from one to the other in the arms of the princes and lords of the kingdom. He was carried that way to the pagoda of *Quiay Ponvedé,* since it was the greatest and most sumptuous temple in the entire city, in the middle of which there was a theater that had been very richly decorated and draped with yellow satin, which symbolized the priestly ornaments.

Here, as part of another ceremony, the *rolim* lay down in a golden coffin and pretended that he was dying. At the sound of a bell that was struck three times, which signalled that he was dead, all the *rolins* prostrated themselves face down on the ground for nearly half an hour, and during all that time the people kept their hands in front of their eyes, as a sign of mourning, shouting out loud, "Resurrect, O Lord, unto new life, this holy servant of thine, so that we may have someone to pray for us!"

Then they lifted him from the coffin wrapped in a yellow satin shroud and placed him in a tomb decorated with the same cloth. After circling the building three times, chanting many mournful dirges and shedding many tears, they left him in a grave that had already been dug for that purpose, covered above with a velvet cloth and surrounded all about with human skulls; and weeping freely, they recited some prayers for him in their fashion, by which the king appeared to be deeply moved.

Then, once the people had been silenced, a large bell was struck three times. And suddenly, in response to this signal, all the bells in the city began to ring, resounding with such a horribly frightful noise that the whole earth trembled beneath our feet. When that was over, two *talagrepos,* highly reputed as learned men in their sciences, climbed up to two *agréns,* which are the pulpits, as I have said several times before, that had been set up and decorated with silk cloth and luxurious carpets. Addressing the audience about the ceremony that was taking place, they explained to them the significance of each thing and related to them, step by step, the life and death of the previous *rolim* and the election of the new one, and his qualification for the exalted pontificate to which he had been summoned by God, as well as many other things, all of which the people were very pleased to hear. And by way of conclusion, after three strokes of the same bell that had been struck before, they immediately set fire to both of the *agréns,* with their ornaments and all, as part of another ceremony which I would rather not describe, because I think it is unnecessary to waste time on these superfluous heathen rituals, about which I have already said enough.

After things had quieted down and the silence was unbroken for as long as it would take to recite five or six Credos, there came from another temple, located nearly a crossbow-shot's distance away, a very elaborate procession of children. They were all dressed in white taffeta as a symbol of their purity and innocence and were adorned with many pieces of gold jewelry around their necks and ankles. They were holding candles of white wax in their hands, and on their heads they wore silvery wreaths of colored silk yarn and gold and silver thread interwoven with a great many pearls, rubies, and sapphires.

In the middle of this procession, covered by a gold cloth, there was a rich litter, borne on the shoulders of twelve of these children, and surrounded all about by many silver maces and incense burners with sweet-smelling perfumes. These children were all playing many different kinds of musical instruments and singing praises to God, imploring him to resurrect the dead man to new life. As soon as they reached the place where the *rolim* lay, the children set the litter down, and when they removed the cloth covering it, a little child stepped out who appeared to be no more than three or four years old at the most; and even though he was naked, none of his flesh was exposed because his body was completely covered with gold and precious stones in a costume made to look the way angels are depicted among us, with golden wings and a scepter in his hand, and a splendid crown on his head. The moment he descended from the litter, all the people prostrated themselves on the ground, reciting these words in voices loud enough to make the flesh quiver, "Angel of God, sent from heaven for our salvation, upon thy return, pray for us!"

Then the king approached the child and taking him reverently in his arms in a strange kind of ceremony as if to show that he was unworthy of touching him because he was an angel sent by God from heaven, he set him down at the edge of the grave. Once the velvet covering had been removed and the people were all kneeling down, gazing heavenward with arms upraised, six priests spread incense on him five times, after which the child, as though speaking to the dead man, said in a loud voice, "To thee, sinner that thou art, conceived in sin in the vile wretchedness and sordidness of the flesh, God has sent an insignificant creature like me to tell thee that thou shouldst rise up and return to a new life agreeable to him, one in which thou wilt always fear the punishment of his mighty arm, so that when thou hast breathed thy last, thy conscience will not be heavy like that of all the children of the world. Rise up at once from thy grave, for thou hast already been confirmed as the greatest of the greatest in the *bralas* of the earth. Rise up and follow me, follow me, follow me."

At that moment the king lifted the child in his arms once more, and the *rolim,* rising from the grave, looking as though he were dazzled by the vision he beheld, knelt down before the child who was still in the king's arms, and said, "I accept this new blessing from the hand of the Lord, in accordance with the message he sends me through thee, and I shall be bound until death to live as an example of humility and the least of all his creatures, so that the lowliest toad on earth be not lost in the troubled waters of the world."

The child was put down and then, with his own hand, he finished pulling the *rolim* from the grave, from which he had not as yet completely risen. At this time a bell was struck five times, in response to which all the people prostrated themselves on the ground and recited these words out loud, "Blessed art Thou, O Lord, for the great mercy thou hast shown us."

Then all the bells in the city began to peal with a thunderous noise that made it impossible to hear or be heard; and added to this, they fired an infinite number of salvos, both on land and on the river, where the two thousand ships were anchored, increasing the racket greatly and making it even more difficult to bear.

169
The New *Rolim* Ascends the Holy Throne

From here the new *rolim* was carried off in a splendid litter, richly adorned with gold and precious stones, and borne on the shoulders of the eight most prominent lords in the kingdom. He was preceded on foot by the king, walking with a rich ornamental sword at his side, who accompanied him in this manner all the way to his very own palace, which had in the meantime been splendidly decorated with pontifical ornaments, and there the *rolim* remained for three days while, on the island of *Mounay,* the necessary preparations were being made for his reception there.

During the time that he remained in the city of Martaban, the people, the princes, and the aristocracy arranged for a very ingenious and costly series of games, in two of which the king himself took part with a great deal of pomp and splendor, but about which I think I will remain silent because I confess, I do not really know how it was all done.

On the day appointed for the *rolim* to enter the island of *Mounay*—which, as I have already said, is to them what Rome is to us, and the seat of their diabolical pontificate—the fleet of *serós, laugoas,*[1] and *laulés,* and all the other kinds of vessels that were in the river—which numbered well over two thousand—were lined up in two rows that ran from the city all the way up to the island, for a distance of probably a league and a half. Lined up this way, they formed the most beautiful thoroughfare imaginable, for all these vessels were covered with boughs heavily laden with fruit and decorated with many roses, daisies, and all sorts of wildflowers as well as many silken awnings, banners, and bunting. And there was a joyous spirit of competitiveness in the air, for it seems that each one was trying to outdo the other in order to obtain plenary indulgence and absolution for all the robberies they had committed without any kind of restitution, and for other abominable practices in which they indulge throughout their depraved lives—which I prefer to pass over in silence since it is a subject unfit for pious ears—in keeping with the customs of their diabolical sects and the evil intentions of their founders, for they are just as dissolute and depraved as all the other infidels and heretics.

To escort the *rolim,* only thirty light, oared *laulés* had been reserved, which were manned entirely by lords and other members of the nobility. He was on board a magnificently decorated *seró,* seated on a silver dais beneath a gold cloth canopy, with the king at his feet, since he was unworthy of being assigned any other place, and on their knees all around him were thirty little boys, dressed in crimson satin, with silver maces at their shoulders. Standing upright were twelve others, dressed in white damask, with sweet-smelling incense burners in their hands, and all the rest of the company on board consisted of about two hundred *talagrepos,* honorable dignitaries, similar to our archbishops, six or seven of whom were the sons of kings. And since this vessel was too crowded with people to be rowed, it was towed by fifteen *laulés,* their oars manned by the highest-ranking priests in the nine sects of this kingdom.

Maintaining this order, he departed from this city of Martaban two hours before dawn, passing down the middle of the lane formed by the vessels on which there were an infinite number of ingeniously fashioned festival lights of many different kinds nestled among the boughs that covered them.

As he got under way, a signal was fired from three pieces of artillery, and the clanging and clamor that arose from all the bells that responded, the thunderous noise of the artillery they let loose, and the many different kinds of barbarous instruments they played, together with the screaming and yelling of the people, created such an unbelievable racket that it seemed as if earth and sea were coming together as one.

When he reached the landing where he was to disembark, he was received by a procession of *rolins* from the wilderness, known as *menigrepos,* who are like the Capuchins among us and are highly respected by all these heathens because they are believed to practice greater austerity than any of the others in their way of life and in the doctrines they profess. There must have been about six or seven thousand of them there, and they were all barefooted and dressed in black straw matting as a sign of contempt for the world, with skulls and bones on their heads, and heavy ropes of coir around their necks, their foreheads smeared with mud, with a sign that read, "Mud, mud, cast not thy eyes upon thy lowliness, but fix them on the reward that God has promised those who scorn themselves to serve him."

When they reached the *rolim,* who welcomed them graciously, they all prostrated themselves before him with their heads touching the ground, and after they had remained that way for a little while, one of them, who appeared to be their leader, looked straight at the *rolim,* and said, "May it please the One, from whose hand thou hast just accepted the charge of being the head of all on earth, to make thee so good and so saintly that all thy deeds may be as agreeable to him as the simplicity of the innocent babes of tender age whose cries are stilled at their mothers' breasts!"

To which all the others responded with a tumultuous cry, "May the great Lord of the mighty hand permit it to be so!"

Then, departing from here accompanied by this procession, which the king, to do him greater honor, was leading, along with some of the most prominent lords whom he summoned for that purpose, he went directly to the place where the deceased *rolim* was buried. When he got to the tomb he threw himself face down on it, and after shedding many tears, in a sad voice charged with emotion, he said, as though he were talking to the deceased, "May it please the One who reigns on high in the beauty of his stars to reward me for my labors by making me worthy of being thy slave, so that there in the House of the Sun where thou art now enjoying thyself, I may serve thee as a broom beneath thy feet, for that will make of me a diamond of such high grade that the whole world with all its riches will not be able to equal it in price."

To which the *grepos* responded, "Massirão fatipay," meaning, "O Lord, grant it thus!"

Thereupon he picked up the dead man's prayer beads which were lying on the tomb and put them around his neck as one would a precious relic and, as an offering, gave him six silver lamps, two censers, and six or seven bolts of purple damask.

From here he retired to his palace, accompanied all the while by the king, princes, and lords of the kingdom and the entire throng of priests who were assembled there, and he bade a general farewell to all of them, and tossed grains of rice upon their heads from a window, the way holy water is sprinkled among us, which the people received from him on their knees, with hands upraised.

When this ceremony ended—after what must have been nearly three hours—a bell was struck three times as a signal for the *rolim* to go inside and for the people to return to the ships, and that day there was plenty to do clearing all those people off the island. Sometime in the afternoon the king also bade the *rolim* farewell and went to spend the night in the city. Early the next morning he departed for the city of Pegu, eighteen leagues away, arriving the following day two hours after nightfall without any fanfare or fuss, as a sign of mourning for the death of the former *rolim,* to whom, they said, he had been very devoted.[2]

170
Escape from Burmese Captivity

Twenty days after his return to the city of Pegu, the Burmese king decided to send his brother-in-law, whom he had honored, as mentioned earlier, with the official title of "brother," to attack the city of *Savady,* which lay 130 leagues from there to the northeast. This decision was based on the letter his ambassador had brought from the *Calaminhan,* informing him that he would be sending his own ambassador to make the final arrangements for their joint alliance against the *Siammon,* which could no longer be done that summer because of the many details that had yet to be worked out; and also because it was not the proper season for making war on the kingdom of Ava, much as he desired.

Gathering an army of 150,000 men for that purpose, including 30,000 foreign mercenaries from various nations, and five thousand elephants—two thousand for combat and the rest for baggage and supplies—the *Chaumigrem* departed from the city of Pegu on the fifth day of March, in a fleet of thirteen-hundred oar-manned vessels, and on the fourteenth he arrived within sight of *Savady.* Anchored alongside a field called *Guampalaor,* he remained there for six days waiting for the five thousand elephants that were coming by land, and as soon as they arrived he set off for the city. After laying siege to it he launched three attacks with scaling ladders, but each time he was forced to withdraw with heavy losses in his ranks, not only because of the stiff resistance he encountered from those inside but also because the site on which the wall was built was all slate, making it difficult to set up the ladders.

Consulting with his captains about what to do next, they advised him to batter the city from two different positions and to concentrate their fire on what appeared to be, as far as they could tell from the outside, the two weakest sections of the wall, for once these two sections had been breached, it would be easier and less dangerous for him to enter the city. They lost no time putting it into effect, and for that purpose the engineers began to raise two bulwarklike earthworks on the outside of the wall, reinforcing them with wooden beams and fascines, building them both up in five days to such great height that they towered more than two arm's lengths above the walls. And on each of them they placed twenty pieces of artillery consisting of heavy-caliber spheres and camels, with which they began to batter the walls, knocking them down in two places. Apart from these guns, they had also set up more than three hundred falcons, which kept up a steady barrage for the sole purpose of killing people walking about on the streets and, in that way, inflicted a great deal of damage on them.

Outraged by this attack and the heavy losses they had sustained, those on the inside decided like truly brave men to sell their lives dearly to the enemy; and one morning, in the predawn hours, they sallied forth through the open sections of the wall that had been knocked down by the artillery and fell upon those in the field so fearlessly that in less than an hour the Burmese army came close to being totally routed. Since it was almost broad daylight by then, the *Savadis* withdrew to the city, leaving eight thousand enemy dead behind. And in no time at all they repaired the two fallen sections of the wall by shoring them up from behind with earthworks which they reinforced with logs, rubble, and fagots, making them so strong that none of the artillery that was fired later was able to penetrate them.

With the campaign going so badly for him up to then, the *Chaumigrem* decided to make war on the neighboring towns that were nearest to the city. He sent *Diossaray,*[1] the treasurer in chief—in whose custody we eight Portuguese were being held captive—appointing him colonel in command of five thousand men, with instructions to attack a village called *Valeutay* that had often supplied the city with food. This expedition was so disastrous for him that, before he had even reached the town, some two thousand *Savadis* fell upon him, and in less than half an hour every single one of the five thousand lay dead. During the battle, which was fought at night, it was the will of our Lord that all eight of us Portuguese who were there should make our escape,[2] since we deemed it the better part of wisdom to save our lives than to end up dead on the battlefield like the others.

From here, without the slightest idea of where we were going, we set out over a rugged mountain, crossing it after three and a half days with a great deal of difficulty, only to come out on some swamplands with not a sign of a road or any living thing other than the large numbers of tigers, snakes, and many other kinds of wild animals that filled us with terror. But since the Lord our God is the only true path for those who have lost their way, we called on him constantly, shedding many tears, and at the end of this time, the Lord in his mercy saw fit towards evening to permit us to see a fire burning over to the east. We headed straight for it and at dawn came out upon a large lake around which there were some villages inhabited, to all outward appearances, by poor people. Not daring to show ourselves, we hid that day in a swampy field overgrown with arrowhead, where we suffered great hardship because of the many leeches that were there which sucked a great deal of blood out of us.

When night fell we continued on our way until just before daylight when we found ourselves near a large river along which we walked for five more days until we came to another much larger lake, at the edge of which stood a small temple, like a hermitage, inhabited by a very old hermit who took us in and let us stay with him for two days. While we were here we asked him questions about many things that suited our purpose, and he answered them all truthfully. Also, he told us that the area we were in was still part of the territory of the king of *Savady,* and that the lake was called *Oregantor,* which means "yawning night," and the hermitage, *Quiay Vogarem,* "god of succor." When we asked him what that superstition signified, he assured us, placing his hand on a wire horse that stood on the altar as an idol, that according to what he had read many times in a book dealing with the founding of that kingdom, 237 years before, there had been a large city on that lake, called *Ocumchaleu,* that had been captured in battle by another king called *Avá.* Because of that great exploit, he was advised by his priests, who ruled him completely, that he would have to show his gratitude for that great honor to *Quiay Guator,* the god of war, for granting him that victory, by sacrificing all the young male children that had been captured there, for otherwise, he could rest assured that, when they grew to manhood, they would recapture the kingdom. In fear of the danger threatening him, the king had ordered them all to be brought together on a certain day, which fell on what was for them a very solemn one. There were eighty-five thousand of them, and they were all put to the sword in an extremely cruel and bloody manner, preparatory to their all being burned in sacrifice the following day. He also said, and he assured us at great length that it was so, that on that same night the earth shook, and that so many flashes of fire and lightning struck the city that within half an hour the entire city and everything in it was completely submerged,[3] and that in the punishment meted out by the righteous justice of God, the king and all his people died, with not a single one escaping alive. The dead included thirty thousand priests who from that time on could be heard, on every new and full moon, howling in the lake, making such terrifying sounds that the people trembled with fear. As a result, from that time forward, the land had become depopulated all around there, and all that remained was just eighty-five hermitages which had been built in memory of the eighty-five thousand children that the king had had slain for no reason other than the advice of his priests.

171
Back in Goa

As I was saying, we spent two days in this hermitage where we were hospitably treated by the hermit who lived there, and on the third day, bright and early, we took leave of him and departed, thoroughly shaken and frightened by what he had told us.

We continued on our way along the river all that day and night, and shortly before daybreak we found ourselves near a large field of sugarcane where we helped ourselves to a few stalks since we had nothing else with which to sustain ourselves. On we went, still following the river by which we had set the course of our journey, for it seemed to us that even though it might take longer, it was bound to lead to the sea, where we hoped that somehow the Lord would show us the way to salvation. The next day we reached a town called *Pommiseray,* where we hid in some thick bushes to avoid being seen by the people who frequented the highway.

Two hours after dark we resumed our journey, intending, as I said before, to keep on going blindly that way, following the river downstream to wherever fortune would lead us, or until God should see fit to put an end, with our death, to all the many hardships we endured night and day, living in the grip of fear and tormented by visions of death worse than death itself, which was our constant companion. After seventeen days of journeying in this sad and painful manner, it was the will of the Lord that, on a very dark and rainy night, we should see a fire burning about a culverin-shot's distance ahead of us. Somewhat fearful that it might be a village, we stayed where we were for quite a while without stirring, worried and undecided, until we noticed that the fire was moving. From this we concluded that it was a vessel moving on the water, and within little more than half an hour we could distinguish a boat coming towards us with nine people on board. When they got up close to where we were, they pulled her up even with the bank at the edge of the river, disembarked in a cove formed by a curve in the land like a bay, and once ashore they promptly built a fire over which they proceeded to cook their supper. When it was ready they fell to it in a festive mood and high spirits that lasted for quite a while. When they had had their fill of eating and drinking, it was the will of God that all nine of them, including three women, should fall into such deep slumber that they did not know what was going on around them.

Seeing that the moment was right for us to take advantage of the favor God showed us, all eight of us very quietly made our way to the boat which lay half stuck in the mud, tied to a branch. Putting our shoulders to it, we got it afloat, embarked in a flash, and went rowing down the river, without making the slightest sound or disturbance of any kind. With the wind and the current in our favor, by dawn we were more than ten leagues from there near a pagoda called *Quiay Hinarel*, "god of the rice fields," in which we found one lone man and thirty-seven women, most of them elderly and pious votaries of that temple, who very charitably offered us their hospitality even though, as it appeared, they did so more out of fear of us than out of a genuine desire to help us. When we asked them about a few things in particular that served our purpose, they were unable to answer a single one of our questions. All they would say was that they were women, detached by vows from worldly matters, and that the only life they knew was to be shut up there, praying constantly to *Quiay Ponvedé*, who moved the clouds in the sky to send down water on the fields they cultivated so that there would be no shortage of rice. We spent all that day repairing the boat, and we also provisioned it from the larder of these pious women with rice, sugar, beans, onions, and some cured meat, of which they had a plentiful supply.

An hour after dark we departed from here and proceeded on our way under sail and oar for seven whole days without any of us venturing ashore for fear of some disaster that might easily have befallen us in any one of the towns we saw along the river. But since no one can escape the fate that is determined for him on high, as we were going along this way, deeply troubled and frightened by thoughts of what might happen to us, falling prey to many terrors both real and imagined every hour of the day, early one morning, shortly before daybreak, as our sad luck would have it, just as we were passing the mouth of an estuary, we were attacked by thirteen pirate prows. They fell upon us with such great force, showering us with so many different kinds of missiles, that in less time than it takes to recite two Credos they had killed three of our companions.

The five of us who escaped quickly jumped into the sea, all covered with blood from the wounds we had received, which afterwards left two of us hovering between life and death. Reaching the shore, we hid in the woods where we remained all that day, lamenting with bitter tears this latest misfortune which had come on top of so many others we had endured.

Despite our wounds, we departed from this place with greater expectations of death than of life and resumed our journey by land with great difficulty, so troubled and undecided about what to do that many a time, overcome by fear, we would break down and cry on each other's shoulders with deep despair, for we had lost all hope of saving our lives by any human means. In the midst of this sad state of affairs, with two of our five companions on the verge of death, it was the will of the Lord—for wherever human means fail he is always to be found—that a boat should chance to pass by the very spot where we were at the edge of the water. On board was a Christian woman by the name of Violante, who was married to the heathen owner of that boat, which was on a trading voyage, bound for *Cosmim* with a cargo of cotton. The moment she spied us she let out a shriek.

"Jesus!" she cried. "Are those Christians I see before me?"

Giving orders to quickly haul in the sail, she came rowing up to where we were and jumped ashore, and her husband with her—for even though he was a heathen, he was a very charitable man—and they both embraced us, shedding many tears as they helped us into the boat. She immediately set about tending to our wounds and did the best she could at the time to provide us with clothes to cover ourselves, in addition to doing many other things for us like a good Christian.

Departing from here, with out past fears behind us, it was God's will that, five days later, we should reach the city of *Cosmim,* which is a seaport in the kingdom of Pegu, and there in the home of this Christian woman we received the best of care and recovered completely from our wounds. And since there is naught but perfection in God's favors, he ordained that at the time we arrived there should be here in port a *nao,* owned by Luis de Montarroyo,[1] that was bound for Bengal. After bidding our hostess farewell and giving her due thanks for all that we had received from her, we embarked with this Luis de Montarroyo, who also treated us very well and provided us most generously with everything we needed.

When we arrived at the port of Chittagong in the kingdom of Bengal, where at that time there were many Portuguese, I immediately embarked on a foist belonging to a certain Fernão Caldeira[2] that was bound for Goa, where, as God willed, I arrived safely. There I found Pero de Faria,[3] the former captain of Malacca, who had sent me to Martaban on the embassy to the *chaubainhá,* as related above, and I gave him a lengthy account of everything that had happened to me. He appeared to be deeply touched by my story and, moved by his conscience and nobility, gave me something to make up for what he thought he owed me for all that I had lost on his account.

With what he gave me I embarked, during the same monsoon, heading south to try my fortune once more in parts of China and Japan where I had so often lost my shirt, to see if this time I could better myself with another shirt less threadbare than the one I had on.

172
The Ambassadress from Java

After embarking here in Goa on a junk belonging to Pero de Faria that was bound for Sunda[1] on a trading voyage, I arrived in Malacca on the day of the demise of Ruy Vaz Pereira Marramaque,[2] who was captain of the fortress at the time. Departing from here for Sunda, in seventeen days I arrived in the port of Bantam,[3] which is where the Portuguese usually traded. But since the country was then suffering from a severe shortage of the pepper we were looking for, we were forced to spend the winter there that year, with the intention of going on to China by the following year.

When we had been in this port for nearly two months, peacefully going about our trading in the local market, a woman by the name of *Nhay Pombaya* arrived there, on an embassy from the king of Demak,[4] emperor of all the islands of Java, Kangean,[5] Bali,[6] Madura,[7] and all the other islands in this archipelago. She was a widow, nearly sixty years old, whom he had sent to deliver a message on his behalf to the *Tagaril,* king of Sunda—who was also his vassal, as were all the other kings in this monarchy—to the effect that within a period of a month and a half he was to meet with him in person in the city of Japara,[8] where he was then preparing to go to war against the kingdom of Pasuruan.[9]

When this woman disembarked in the port, the king went to meet her in person at the *calaluz*[10] in which she had arrived and led her with great pomp to his palace, where he lodged her with the queen, his wife, while he moved to another apartment far from there, since that was the highest honor he could pay her.

Now in order to understand why a woman,[11] rather than a man, was sent to deliver this message, one must know that it was always a very ancient custom among the rulers of these kingdoms, ever since they began, for matters of great importance requiring peace and harmony to be handled through women. This is true not only of private messages that the lords send their vassals as in this particular instance, but also of public and general affairs that some kings handle with each other through their embassies. The reason they give for this is that the female sex, owing to its gentle nature, has been endowed by God with more affability and authority, as well as other qualities that make them worthy of greater respect than men, who are blunt and therefore less likely to meet with favor by the parties to whom they are sent.

However, they say that the woman who is chosen by these kings for the kind of mission I am talking about must have certain qualities that they deem necessary in order for her to accomplish her mission satisfactorily. They say that she must not be single because an unmarried woman who leaves her home will lose the very essence of her being, for it is said that though a woman is loved by everyone for her beauty, at the same time it may also be more of a cause for dissension where peacemaking is required, than for bringing matters to a successful conclusion where peace and harmony are sought. Furthermore, they say that she must be a legitimately married woman, or at least, the widow of her legitimate husband; and if she had children by her husband, she must have documentary proof that she nursed at her breast all the children she bore him, for they say that the woman who has given birth and has not nursed her children if able to do so, is more properly a mother of pleasure, alike to any depraved and unchaste woman, than the true mother of her own child.

This custom is so strictly observed among the nobility of this country that if any woman gives birth and for some lawful reason cannot nurse her child at her breast, it is necessary for her, for the sake of her honor, to have a document drawn up to that effect, as though it were a question of something far more serious and important. And if a young girl should happen to become widowed, to add lustre to her virtue she must enter a nunnery to show that she had not married so much for the pleasures to be derived therefrom, as for the purpose of having children, in conformity with the purity and chastity with which God, in the earthly paradise, joined together the first two married people. Also, in order for their marriage to be wholly pure and in keeping with God's law, they say that after the woman feels that she is pregnant, she must not have any further intercourse with her husband, for then the cohabitation will no longer be pure and chaste but sensual and unclean. Also, they have other conditions of this sort which I will not discuss because I think it would be a waste of time to dwell on such insignificant matters.

The *Nhay Pombaya* who brought the message to the king of Sunda left the city of Bantam immediately after the conclusion of her mission. Not long afterwards the king completed his preparations and departed with an armada of thirty *calaluzes* and ten *jurupangos*[12] fully equipped with food and munitions. These forty sails carried seven thousand fighting men, in addition to the oarsmen, and that number included forty Portuguese out of the forty-six of us who happened to be there at the time, for in return, he offered us many commercial advantages and announced publicly that he would be pleased to have us, which is why we found it difficult to refuse.

173
The Javanese Lay Siege to Pasuruan

On the fifth of January in the year 1546, the king of Sunda departed from the port of Bantam, and on the nineteenth he arrived at the city of Japara where the king of Demak,[1] emperor of the island of Java, was then mobilizing an army of 800,000 men. On being informed of the arrival of the king of Sunda, who was both his vassal and his brother-in-law, he sent a reception party out to his ship, headed by the king of Panarukan,[2] the admiral of the fleet, who departed with 160 oared *calaluzes* and *lancharas* carrying Luzons from the island of Borneo. In the midst of all this company he escorted him to the waiting king, from whom he got a fine reception, with far greater honors than all the others.

Fourteen days after our arrival in the city of Japara, the king of Demak set out for the kingdom of Pasuruan with a fleet of twenty-seven hundred vessels, a thousand of which were ocean-going junks and the rest all oared craft, and on the eleventh of February he reached the river of *Hicanduré,* which is at the entrance to the bar. When the king of Panarukan, the admiral of the fleet, discovered that the large vessels could not anchor near the city which was two leagues from there, owing to the shoals and sandbanks in some parts of the river, he ordered the men on the big ships to disembark, and the oared craft went on to anchor in the city roadstead, with instructions to burn any vessels that might be up in the harbor, which they ultimately did, and with them went the emperor, the *pangueyrão*[3] in person, accompanied by all the grandees of the kingdom, who took part in this armada. His brother-in-law, the king of Sunda, who was field marshal, set out overland with the greater part of the army, and after they had all reached the site facing the city walls that had been selected for their camp, the first thing they did was to fortify it and set up the artillery emplacements from which to batter the most strategic areas, a task on which they spent the better part of the day.

After a night of great joy and merrymaking, during which a careful lookout was kept, at the break of day each captain applied himself to what he was duty-bound to do, without anyone stopping to rest until the engineers's orders had been carried out. As a result, on the second day the entire city was surrounded by huge ramparts, their earthworks reinforced with stout beams, on top of which they placed many pieces of heavy artillery, including a few bronze eagles[4] and lions[5] which Turks and Achinese had cast for them in a foundry directed by a renegade master gunsmith, a native of the Algarve, who was known at the time by his infidel name of *Coje Geinal,* though I will refrain from mentioning his Christian name to protect the honor of his family, for he was of no mean extraction.

Realizing that they had been negligent in allowing the enemy to work undisturbed on the fortification of their camp for two whole days without anyone trying to stay their hand, the people inside the city, outraged by it all, asked their king for permission to test the enemy that night, since it was obvious that they would be too tired to fight or put up any kind of resistance to this first assault.

The reigning king of Pasuruan at that time was a young man endowed with qualities that greatly endeared him to his people, for judging by what was said about him, he was extremely generous, with not a trace of the tyrant about him, well inclined to the common people, a great friend of the poor and the widowed, to whom he was so generous that they had only to inform him of their needs and he would immediately see to it that they received far more than they had asked him for. Apart from all these excellent qualities, he had a few others that were so attuned to the will of the people, that there was not a man among them who would not willingly risk his life for him, a thousand times over, if necessary. In addition to this, he had there with him all the flower of his kingdom, all young and very select soldiers, as well as many foreign mercenaries to whom he had also been very generous and granted many favors and honors accompanied by kind words, which are the means of winning the hearts of both the humble and the great and of making fierce lions out of meek lambs, for to do otherwise affects the morale and sometimes causes fierce lions to turn into meek and timid lambs.

Before granting them permission to attack, the king laid the matter before the oldest and wisest among them, and after a thorough discussion of the possible repercussions of such an undertaking, they concluded unanimously that, even if fortune should be completely adverse to them in this sally they were planning against their enemy, they still would regard it as less of a misfortune and less of an outrage than to see their king surrounded by people so base and despicable that, contrary to all reason and justice, they wanted to force them to renounce the faith in which their fathers had raised them and to accept another to which they themselves had only recently converted, on the advice and instigation of some *farazes*,[6] who placed their hope for salvation on nothing more than washing their behinds, refusing to eat pork, and marrying seven wives; from which it was clear, as any intelligent person could see, that God was so much their enemy that he would not help them in any of their undertakings, for it was a great offense to him that under the guise of religion, for such absurd reasons, they wanted to force their king to become a Moslem and a vassal of theirs. And so on, in the same manner they presented many other arguments that the king and everyone else present found so convincing that they all responded, as though in one voice, saying, "It is as fitting and proper for a good and loyal vassal to die for his king as it is for a virtuous woman to remain chaste for the husband that God has given her; therefore, it is not in our interest to delay such an important undertaking any longer, rather, it behooves us all in general and each one of us in particular, to show, by means of this sally, the love we feel for our good king and the love we are confident he feels for the families of those who fight best in his defense, for that is all the inheritance we desire to leave to our children."

Whereupon it was resolved that they should sally forth against their enemies that very same night.

174
The *Amucks* Sally Forth

Since everyone in the city was excited by the prospect of this sally, the men did not wait to be called, but at two hours past midnight, long before the time appointed by the king, they all assembled in the *passeyvão*[1] of the royal palace, a huge courtyard where the natives usually held their fairs and the important festivals they celebrate on the solemn days of invocation to their pagodas. Delighted to see such enthusiasm and high spirit among them, the king selected, out of the seventy thousand then present in the city, only twelve thousand to take part in this sally. He divided them under four banners, each unit consisting of three thousand men, under the overall command of an uncle of his, his mother's brother, named *Quiay Panaricão,* who from past experience had shown that he was just the man for this undertaking and who would also be in command of the first unit. The captain of the second unit was another important mandarin by the name of *Quiay Ansedá;*[2] of the third, a foreigner, a Cham called *Necodá Sòlor,*[3] who was a native of the island of Borneo; and of the fourth, another named *Pambacalhujo*—all of them fine officers and extremely brave, seasoned warriors.

When everyone was ready the king made them another speech in which he reminded them once more of the confidence he had in them regarding this undertaking, and he assured them that his heart went with each one of them and that inside were the hearts of all four of the captains, and together with theirs, those of all his brothers and loyal vassals who were accompanying them. After which, the better to encourage them and assure them of his love, he took up a golden goblet and offered all of them a sip from his own hand, and for those he could not reach, he begged their pardon a thousand times. These words, and the manner in which their king had shown his love for them, inspired them so, that without any further delay most of them began to anoint themselves with *minhamundy,*[4] which is a certain preparation of fragrant oil used by these people in cases like this, as final proof of their determination to die, and those who anoint themselves this way are called *amucks* by the common people.

When the hour appointed for the sally arrived, four of the twelve city gates were thrown open, and through each of them marched one of the four captains with his company, preceded by a scouting party composed of six *ourobalões*[5] chosen from among the bravest of the *ambarrajas*[6] in the king's entourage, on whom he conferred new titles of high honor, along with many other great favors and distinctions, which is the sort of thing that usually instills courage in the weak and spurs the brave to greater feats of derring-do.

Following closely behind the six spies they had sent ahead, the four captains joined forces in a safe area from which they were to launch their attack. Falling all at once upon the main enemy ranks, impelled by the strength of the determination that filled their hearts, they fought so courageously that, in less than an hour, which is as long as the force of the battle lasted, the twelve thousand Pasuruans left more than thirty thousand enemy dead on the field, to say nothing of the even larger number of wounded, many of whom died later. Morever, three kings were captured, as well as eight *pates,*[7] who are like dukes, while the king of Sunda, under whose banner we forty Portuguese were fighting, escaped with three spear cuts, though fourteen of our men lost their lives defending him, and the rest were badly wounded. Furthermore the camp was thrown into such utter confusion that it was almost destroyed, and the *pangueyrão* of *pates,*[8] emperor of Demak, was pierced by a spear and fell into the river where he nearly drowned, with no one to help him. From which one can see how effective a sudden attack like this can be when an army is caught off guard, for even before these people realized what was happening, and before the captains could call their men to action, they had twice been completely routed.

With the coming of morning, when the full extent of the damage could be clearly seen, the Pasuruans withdrew quite safely to their city with the loss of only nine hundred of their men and two or three thousand wounded. However, the successful outcome of this battle later filled the besieged with such great pride and self-confidence that eventually it was responsible for some disasters that befell them afterwards.

175
The Pasuruans Attack Again

The king of Demak was deeply distressed and appalled by the day's disaster, not only because of the losses in his ranks and the defeat he had received from those inside, but also because it meant that the siege was off to a bad start, and a few times he made some sarcastic remarks to our king of Sunda, while at other times he openly rebuked him since, as field marshal, he was responsible for the careless watch that had been mounted, and thus he blamed him alone for the widespread disorder that had occurred throughout the ranks.

After providing for the care of the wounded and the burying of the dead, he called to council all the kings, *sanguys de pates,*[1] and captains of both land and sea, and informed them that he had made a solemn vow and sworn to it on a *moçafo*[2] of Mohammed—which is the holy book of their faith—that he would not lift the siege until the city had been leveled, even if it cost him his entire state, and therefore he was also swearing to them that, if any one of them, for any reason, should oppose him, even though he did not agree with what he was saying, he would have him killed. This announcement aroused such deep fear in everyone present there that not a single one of them dared to contradict him; on the contrary, they praised him in every respect for his determination.

Following this, he gave orders to have the camp refortified in great haste with ditches and trenches and many bulwarks of dry rock reinforced inside with their terrepleins, and he had many pieces of bronze artillery installed, all of which left the camp far stronger than the city itself. As a result, at night, those inside would frequently taunt those on the outside who were standing guard, telling them that from the way they had fortified their camp, anyone could see how cowardly they were, for instead of coming to besiege their enemies like brave men, they had walled themselves in like weak women, and that it would be better for them to go home and spin on their distaffs, which would be more profitable for them, since they were not much good for anything else. They kept on taunting them this way, deeply offending those on the outside with insults of this sort and many others like them.

The siege lasted for nearly three consecutive months, during which time five artillery attacks were mounted as well as three assaults with more than a thousand scaling ladders, but each time those inside the city defended themselves with great spirit, like very courageous men, fortifying themselves from within by shoring up the fallen sections of the wall with timber torn from their houses, so that despite the powerful force he had with him, which numbered, as I have said before, 800,000 men—though somewhat diminished now by his recent losses—the *pangueyrão* was never able to enter the city.

As a result, when the chief engineer of the camp, a renegade of Mallorcan nationality, saw that the campaign was not progressing as much to the king's liking as he had led him to believe it would, he decided to try something else. He built a new, huge mountain of earth filled with rubble and fagots, reinforced with six rows of beams, which he gradually brought so close to the city that within nine days it towered nearly an armspan above the walls. Then he placed forty pieces of heavy artillery on this mountain, as well as an even greater number of falcons and culverins, with which he began to batter the entire city from above, inflicting a great deal of damage on those inside.

Realizing that this new contrivance spelled certain disaster for him, the king agreed to allow ten thousand volunteers to attack the mountain, honoring them with the title "tigers of the world." They were prepared to set out immediately, and the king, in order to raise their spirits still higher, decided to go with them as their captain, even though the full weight of the operation would be borne by the four *panaricões*[3] who had led the first sally.

One morning, shortly before sunrise, they threw themselves head on against the main force where all the artillery was concentrated, rushing upon it so fearlessly that, in less time than it takes to recite two or three Credos, most of them had reached the top where they promptly fell upon the enemy who must have numbered over thirty thousand, routing them completely in less than a quarter of an hour. The *pangueyrão* of *pates,* seeing his forces routed, came running to their aid in person with heavy reinforcements. As he was trying to climb the mountain with twenty thousand *amucks* preceding him, the Pasuruans, who had occupied it, defended it so courageously that it is hard to find words to describe it.

This bloody battle lasted until nearly vesper time, when the Pasuruan king, who by then had already lost most of his men, withdrew inside the walls against which the mountain was leaning, but first he issued orders to set fire to it in six or seven places. When the flames reached the many powder barrels they had there, in no time at all the fire spread with such intensity that at a distance of over a crossbow shot the heat was unbearable. So that this alone was enough to keep these enemies apart at the time, for it formed a barrier that prevented them from getting at each other, and was the reason why the city escaped this time from the danger threatening it.

But the price the Pasuruans paid for it was by no means cheap, for out of the ten thousand sworn volunteers, six thousand lost their lives on top of the mountain. As for the *pangueyrão*'s men, it was said that over forty thousand died, including three thousand foreign mercenaries from various countries, most of them Achinese, Turks, Malabaris, as well as twelve *pates*, five kings, and an equally large number of captains and gentlemen of very noble lineage.

176
A Portuguese Renegade

That sad night went by with much weeping, wailing, and lamentation on both sides, for each of them had much to mourn and it was impossible to get any rest at all that night, for everyone, both inside and out, spent most of it tending to the wounded and tossing the dead into the river. At daybreak the following morning, the *pangueyrão* of *pates*, seeing how badly the campaign had gone for him up to then— and in spite of that, refusing to call a halt to it as some of his men advised him to— once again issued orders to have all the men prepare for an assault against the city, for it seemed to him that by this time the besieged no longer had the strength to defend it, since the greater part of their walls had already been knocked down, their munitions all spent, many of their people dead, and according to what was said, their king badly wounded.

In order to ascertain if it was true, he set up ambushes in certain places where he had learned that people from the neighboring towns would be passing through with poultry and eggs and other things they were delivering to the city for the sick. That same night, those he had sent out for that purpose returned to camp shortly before dawn, bringing nine prisoners with them, one of them a Portuguese. After breaking eight of them on the rack, they started to prepare the Portuguese, who happened to be the last, for the same treatment. Believing that he would be set free if he confessed who he was, at the first turn of the rack he cried out that he was Portuguese, though up to that time he knew nothing about us nor we about him.

Upon hearing this, our king of Sunda had the torture suspended and immediately sent for us to find out if that man was telling the truth, and six of us—those who were least wounded—went at once to his tent, reaching it with a great deal of difficulty. When we saw him it seemed to us at first sight that he was Portuguese, and we all prostrated ourselves at the feet of the king and begged him to turn the man over to us, explaining the reasons why he should grant us that favor, since he was Portuguese, like us. He readily agreed and again, we all prostrated ourselves on the ground and kissed his feet. From there we brought this man with us to where our comrades were lying wounded and asked him if indeed he was Portuguese, because the poor fellow was in such a sad state that even by his speech we could not rightly tell, but after he had completely pulled himself together he began to speak, shedding many tears.

"Gentlemen and brothers," he said, "I am a Christian—though from the way I am dressed it may not seem so to you—and Portuguese, on both my mother's and father's side. I am a native of Penamacor,[1] and my name is Nuno Rodrigues Taborda. I came from Portugal with the marshal's[2] armada in the year 1513, on board the *nao São João*,[3] which was under the command of Ruy Dias Pereira,[4] and since I was and had always proven myself to be an honorable man, Afonso de Albuquerque[5]—may God keep him in His glory—favored me with the command of a brigantine, one of only four we had in India at the time. I was with him when he took Goa and Malacca, and I helped him to pacify Calicut and Hormuz. I was present at all the heroic exploits that took place in his time, as well as in the days of Lopo Soares[6] and Diogo Lopes de Sequeira[7] and the other governors of India down to the time of Dom Henrique de Meneses,[8] who succeeded to that office on the death of the viceroy Dom Vasco da Gama.[9] At the beginning of his governorship he dispatched an armada of twelve sails with three hundred men on board, under the command of Francisco de Sá,[10] with orders to build a fortress in Sunda, for at that time they were afraid of the Castilians who had begun sailing to the Moluccas via the new ocean route discovered by Magellan.[11] I came as a captain with that armada on board a brigantine called the *São Jorge,* with twenty-six brave men under me.

"We departed from the bar harbor of Bintang[12] when Pero de Mascarenhas[13] destroyed it, and after we had sailed about as far as the island of Lingga,[14] we were caught in a storm so fierce that we were unable to withstand it and were forced to seek shelter in Java, where six of our seven oar-manned vessels were lost, one of which was mine, for my sins. And here in this very land where we now find ourselves, I was cast ashore twenty-three years ago, escaping with only three companions out of all those on board the brigantine, though I am the only one still alive. And would to God our Lord I had died before, for though these heathens tried many times to convince me to follow their faith, for a long time I refused. But since the flesh is weak, and my hunger was great, and my poverty even greater, and all hope of freedom lost, the passage of time and my sins made me give in to their pleas, as a result of which the father of the present king always favored me. Then, yesterday, because they sent someone to the village where I lived, asking me to come and cure two of the most important noblemen in the land, it was God's will that I should be captured by these dogs, making of me worse than a dog; and for this, may the Lord be blessed forevermore."

We were all as amazed by this man's tale as one would expect us to be. Then, consoling him as best as we could, with the words we thought necessary, considering the circumstances, we asked him whether he wanted to go with us to Sunda, because from there he could get to Malacca where the Lord would be pleased to let him live out the rest of his life as a Christian, and in his service; to which he answered yes, for he had never wanted anything else but that. Then we provided him with some other clothes more appropriate for a Christian than the ones he was wearing, and he remained with us all the while, for as long as the siege lasted.

177
A Young Assassin

And now to return to the subject from which we strayed. Having learned from the enemies taken captive by his men that the city's defenses were weak, that a large number of people had already died, that their ammunition was completely exhausted, and that their king was badly wounded, the *pangueyrão* of *pates,* king of Demak, was more determined than ever to attack the city, only this time he resolved to scale the walls by day and throw in many more troops than he had used in the first assault. To that end, enormous preparations were made, and heralds bearing silver maces were dispatched on horseback to all corners of the camp, preceded by a blare of trumpets.

"Hear ye! Hear ye!" they proclaimed in loud voices. "The *pangueyrão* of *pates,* lord of the islands bounded by the seas, by the power of the Creator of all things, desiring to make known to all those present the secrets that lie deep in his heart, sends us to inform you that you have nine days in which to make ready, with the courage of a tiger and twofold strength, for the attack he is planning to launch against the city; and he magnanimously promises to bestow great favors, in both money and honorable titles, on the first five men who raise the standard on the enemy's walls or please him by distinguishing themselves in battle. And whosoever fails to live up to his expectations in the line of duty, shall die, regardless of rank or station!"

This proclamation, coupled as it was with a threat, fell like a thunderbolt over the entire camp, spreading such deep fear that the captains immediately set to work making all the preparations necessary for the assault, driving themselves relentlessly night and day, without a moment's rest, while the air was filled with a deafening clamor of voices, shouts, and sounds of music that was simply appalling.

Then, one morning, after seven of the nine days had passed, when the *pangueyrão* was sitting in council with his chief advisors discussing their combat strategy, how, when, and where and what time it should start, as well as other important decisions that had to be made, they say that a heated argument broke out, owing to a wide difference of opinion among the members of the council, because of which the *pangueyrão* wanted to have their votes in writing.

In the meantime, he asked his page, a young boy who was sitting nearby, to give him some betel,[1] which are some sort of leaves, similar to the plantain, that they chew constantly, because it sweetens the breath and purges the humors of the stomach, but it seems that he did not hear him. This young lad must have been about twelve or thirteen years old, which should be kept in mind in view of what I am about to say. As he continued arguing with the council, the *pangueyrão*'s mouth grew dry with rage, and he again asked for the betel which the boy carried with him in a gold box, but he did not hear him the second time either because he was so completely absorbed in following all the different arguments.

And when the king asked for it a third time, one of the lords who was near the boy tugged at his sleeve and motioned to him to give the betel to the king, which he promptly did, kneeling down before him with the box in his hand while the king selected two or three leaves as was his custom. As he did so, he touched him lightly on the head, without any show of emotion, breaking off the discussion just long enough to say, "What is the matter with you? Are you deaf?" and then continued with what he was saying. Now the Javanese are the most headstrong people on earth, and they are above all extremely treacherous and distrustful, and in their view the worst insult of all, and the greatest dishonor that could befall anyone, is a touch on the head.[2] Interpreting the king's gesture as a flagrant mark of contempt that besmirched his honor, the boy sat there sobbing for a while, without anyone attaching any importance to what the king had done or so much as giving it a thought. Finally, having made up his mind to avenge himself on the king for having dishonored him, he drew out a tiny dagger, like a toy, that he wore at his waist and stabbed the king in the left side of the chest. As though struck by a mortal blow, the king fell before he could say anything more than "*Quita mate!*" meaning, "My God, he killed me!"

This astounding deed, committed in the presence of all the lords, caused such an uproar that I cannot find the words to describe it. Once they had recovered from the initial shock, they tried everything possible to save the king, but to no avail, for the blade had pierced the heart, and he died two hours later. The boy was quickly seized and put to the torture because they suspected complicity, but he confessed to nothing, nor would he say any more than that he had done it because he felt like it inasmuch as the king had treated him disdainfully by hitting him on the head the way one would a mongrel cur that barked in the streets at night, when he was the son of *Pate Pandor,* lord of Surabaya. All the same, the youth was impaled alive on a fairly thick *caloete,*[3] which was thrust all the way through his anus to the nape of his neck. The same fate also befell his father, his three brothers, and sixty-two of his other relatives, which resulted in the entire family being wiped out.

This extremely harsh and cruel form of justice was the cause of the violent uprisings that occurred throughout Java and the islands of Bali, Timor, and Madura, which are rather large states, each governed separately by a viceroy who wields supreme power, in accordance with the age-old ways of their heathen customs.

Once they had finished with these executions, they then dealt with the problem of what to do with the king's body, about which they argued at great length, with some saying that if they were to bury him there it would be like leaving him behind as a captive of the Pasaruans, while others were opposed to taking him home to Demak for burial in his own tomb on the grounds that the body would of necessity decompose before it arrived, and that if they were to bury him in such an advanced state of decomposition his soul would not be allowed to enter paradise, according to the law of Mohammed in which he had just died.

After consulting among themselves in an effort to determine the best way to solve this problem, they finally decided to follow the advice of one of our fellow Portuguese, which turned out to be a very profitable thing for him, because he received prompt payment from the lords of over ten thousand *cruzados,* as a token of appreciation for his service to the late king. And all he advised them to do was to place the corpse in a box full of camphor and lime and then bury it deep in the hold of a large junk that had been filled with earth. It was a simple enough idea, but fortunately for the Portuguese, they thought it was rather extraordinary. And so the king's body was transported this way to Demak, without giving off any foul odor or showing any sign of decay.

178
Anarchy in Demak

As soon as the king's body had been taken to the junk and buried there, the field marshal, our king of Sunda, immediately had all the artillery and munitions loaded on board and the king's personal belongings safely stored, as well as all the treasure that was in the tents. But even though this was done with all expedient haste and secrecy, it was still not enough to prevent their enemies from becoming aware of what they were doing. Whereupon the king himself, in person, sallied forth with only three thousand of the volunteers who had all anointed themselves with *minhamundy* and taken a solemn oath to run amuck. They fell upon their enemies who at that time were busy dismantling the camp, dealing with them in such a way that in the space of half an hour, which was as long as the full fury of the battle lasted, twelve thousand men were cut down in the field, two kings and five *pates* were captured, along with three hundred Turks, Abyssinians, and Achinese, as well as their *caciz moulana*, the highest dignitary in the Moslem sect, on whose advice the *pangueirão* had come there. In addition, four hundred vessels that were beached at the time, with the wounded aboard, were set afire, so that the entire camp was nearly devastated. Withdrawing safely once again, with his ranks depleted by only four hundred men, he let them embark that same day, which was on the ninth of March.

After they had embarked with all possible haste, they departed immediately for the city of Demak, taking with them the body of the *pangueyrão,* where, upon arrival, it was received by all the people with loud cries and many tears that were generally shed for him. Early the following day a count of all the soldiers was made in order to determine how many had died, and it showed that 130,000 men were missing. As for the Pasaruans, it was said that they had lost only twenty-five thousand. But the price paid for these things is never so small—no matter how cheaply Fortune may sell them—that the battlefields are not left stained with the blood of the victors, let alone that of the vanquished, for whom they are always far most costly.

That same day they immediately set about the business of selecting a new *pangueyrão* who is, as I have said several times before, the imperial dignitary above all the *pates* and kings in that great archipelago which the Chinese, Tartar, Japanese, and Ryukyu writers refer to as *Rate na quem dau,* meaning "the outer edge of the world,"[1] as one can see from looking at a map, provided the degrees of latitude are drawn accurately.

Now since there was no lawful heir to the crown, they decided that one should be chosen by election; for which purpose, by the consent of all, they immediately chose sixteen men as a governing council over all the people, which in turn was to choose the *pangueyrão*. These men retired to a building where, once they had restored order in the city, they remained in session for seven days without, in all that time, being able to decide on who the successor should be. Since there were eight contenders to the throne, and they were the most important lords in the kingdom, there were many differences of opinion among the electors, for inasmuch as most or nearly all of them were relatives or related to relatives of the eight contenders, each one of them was trying to elect as *pangueyrão* the one that best suited his own interests.

When the population at large and the soldiers in the fleet saw how long it was taking, they thought that it would be a never-ending process and that there would be no justice in power to punish them. As a result, they began to behave in a shameless manner, robbing the merchant ships in port, both native and foreign, so flagrantly and boldly that it was said that in just four days they seized a hundred junks, killing over five thousand men on board. Whereupon the king of Panarukan and prince of Blambangan,[2] who was the admiral of the sea of that empire, hastily appeared on the scene, and of the delinquents who were caught in the act, he had eighty strung up along the beach one morning to inspire terror in the beholder.

When the *Quiay Ansedá*,[3] *pate* of Cheribon,[4] who was governor of the city and a very powerful man locally, saw what the king of Panarukan had done, he interpreted it as a sign of contempt for him, with total disregard for his official status. He was so highly offended by it and so suspicious that he gathered a force of between six and seven thousand men and descended upon the quarters of the king of Panarukan, where he attempted to arrest him for it. But the Panarukan resisted, with the aid of the men he had with him at the time, and, according to what they said, tried to reason with him in a polite manner and to justify his actions. However, the *Quiay Ansedá* not only rejected his explanations but, forcing his way into the house, killed thirty or forty of his guards. The noise they made attracted such an enormous crowd that it was frightful to see, and since the two were powerful noblemen, with the best family connections, one the admiral of the fleet and the other the governor of the city, the devil stirred up so much discord between them both that, if night had not come between them, putting an end to the fight, I have no doubt that nearly everyone there would have been killed.

However, this unfortunate incident did not end there, for the moment the men in the fleet—who at that time still numbered probably over 600,000—learned that their admiral, the king of Panarukan, had been offended by the *Quiay Ansedá*, governor of the city, they decided to avenge him for so deep an outrage. That same night they all went ashore—with the Panarukan powerless to stop them, much as he tried—and descending upon the quarters of the *Quiay Ansedá*, killed him along with more than ten thousand of his men. And not content with that, they attacked the city in ten or twelve different places and began killing and sacking everything they found, carrying on in such a way that in just the three days that the sack lasted, nothing was left of it that anyone could lay eyes on. Moreover, the cries and screams that accompanied it were so frightful that it seemed, in the judgement of men, as if the world was coming to an end.

To make it brief, the incident terminated with a fire that laid waste the entire city, destroying everything in it down to its very foundations. It was said that more than 100,000 buildings were burned down there, that 300,000 people were put to the sword and an almost equal number captured and sold as slaves in different places. It was also said that an infinite quantity of extremely valuable merchandise was carried off, of which the gold and silver items alone were said to have been worth more than forty million in gold so that altogether the spoils were estimated at a hundred million in gold, and the dead and captured at 500,000.

And this was what came of the bad counsel of a young king, reared among the young, and ruled by his own will, with no one there to gainsay him.

179
Struggle over a Life Raft

After three days of this utterly appalling and brutal uprising, calm descended on the city once more. However, in fear of reprisals from the new *pangueyrão*, who was bound to punish them for their part in this serious crime as soon as he was elected, the leaders of the riot decided to flee from the danger threatening them and sailed away, making good their escape in the same fleet in which they had come, with the king of Panarukan, their admiral, powerless to stop them; on the contrary, twice he and a handful of his supporters nearly lost their lives in the attempt. Thus, in a period of only two days, all of the two thousand sails that had been anchored in the harbor were gone, leaving behind nothing but a few *jurupangos* belonging to some merchants, and a landscape of smoldering ruins.

As a consequence, the few lords still remaining got together and decided they should move to the city of Japara five leagues from there, on the coast of the inland sea, and lost no time going about it. Once they were there, after quelling the unrest among the common people who were still milling about in countless numbers, they finished electing the *pangueyrão*—a word that actually means "emperor"—by promptly choosing a certain *Pate Sidayo,* prince of Surabaya, who had not been among the original group of eight contenders. This was a choice that seemed necessary for the general welfare and for keeping peace in the land, and one which completely satisfied all the people. The Panarukan was immediately sent to fetch him from the village of *Pisamannes,* twelve leagues from there, where he was residing at the time. He arrived nine days later, escorted by a fleet of fifteen hundred *calaluzes* and *jurupangos* with over 200,000 men on board, and was welcomed there by all the people with very joyous demonstrations and was immediately crowned, with all the customary ceremonies, as *pangueyrão* of all of Java, Bali, and Madura, which together comprise a very great monarchy, in population, power, and wealth. He left for Demak immediately afterwards with the intention of rebuilding it and restoring it to its former condition.

The first task he undertook was to punish those that could be found who were guilty of sacking the city, but by then, out of the huge multitude responsible for it, they could only find five thousand, since all the others had already scattered in different directions. During the four days that the executions lasted, all these unfortunate people were put to death in only two ways—some they impaled alive on *caloetes,* and others they burned on board the same ships on which they were captured, so that during these four days, not one went by without huge numbers of them dying, while all of us Portuguese who were there at the time went about as though in a state of shock.

Since there was still unrest all over the country, without any sign of normal activity, we requested permission from the king of Sunda to return to the port of Bantam, where our junk was anchored, for by then the monsoon for China had arrived and it was time for us to get underway. He granted it most readily and exempted us from paying duty on our merchandise. He also gave each of us a hundred *cruzados,* as well as three hundred *cruzados* for the heirs of each of the fourteen Portuguese who had died in battle, which at the time we thought was a very noble gesture, befitting a generous, kindhearted prince, and we were all quite pleased.

We left immediately afterwards for the port of Bantam, where we remained for twelve days completing our preparations for the voyage, and departed for China in consort with four other ships that were also going there. We took with us João Rodrigues,[1] the Portuguese heathen I mentioned previously, whom we had found in Pasaruan, where he was living as a Brahman under the name of *Guaxitau Facalem,* meaning "holy counsel," in a pagoda called *Quiay Nacorel.* This João Rodrigues, after we reached China, took ship for Malacca, where he was once more reconciled to our holy Catholic faith and where, to do penitence, he was asked to serve a year in the hospital for incurable diseases, which he did. At the end of that time he passed away, with the signs of a good and true Christian, from which it appears that we can believe that our Lord probably had mercy on his soul, for at the end of so many years of living as an infidel, he spared him so that he could come and die in His service, and for this may he be praised forevermore.

All of the five ships that had sailed in consort from Sunda reached the port of *Chincheo,* where the Portuguese used to trade in those days, and there we remained for three and a half months, under the most difficult conditions, at great risk to our lives, due to widespread unrest and uprisings all over the country, with armed fleets cruising up and down the coast because of the many robberies the Japanese pirates[2] had committed there. Under those circumstances things were not peaceful enough for carrying on trade, nor did the merchants dare to set foot out of their houses. As a result, we were forced by necessity to move on to the port of *Chabaqué,*[3] where we found 120 junks, anchored in the harbor, which set upon us. After a brief fight they captured three of our five ships, with the loss of four hundred Christian lives, eighty-two of them Portuguese.

Our remaining two ships that miraculously escaped from them headed out to sea, but we were unable to make it back to shore because of the east winds that blew all that month, and much against our will we were forced to head for the coast of Java. After twenty-six days of following this course, navigating under the most difficult conditions, we sighted an island called Pulo Condore[4] at a latitude, from where we were, of eight and a third degrees, northwest-southeast with the bar harbor of the kingdom of Cambodia. When we had almost reached it, a storm came out of the south with winds so fierce that we came close to total disaster. While we were running with the wind under bare poles, we came in sight of the island of Lingga, where the storm shifted to west-southwest, with such fierce gusts, mountainous waves, and crossed seas, that it was impossible for us to make use of any kind of sail. Afraid of the reefs and shoals looming ahead of us, we lay by with the ship athwart the seas until, after quite some time, the keelson cracked open at the stern, flooding the lower deck with nine spans of water. At this point, with death staring us in the face, we were forced to cut away both the masts and throw all the cargo overboard, thereby easing the junk somewhat.

We kept on riding this way at the mercy of the sea for the rest of the day and part of the night until God our Lord, in the rigor of his divine justice, without our knowing how or seeing anything before us, ordained that we should be driven onto a rocky reef where the junk broke into four pieces, with the loss of sixty-two lives. And since this unfortunate turn of events deprived us completely of our wits and strength, there was not one among us who had enough presence of mind to look for some means of salvation as did the Chinese sailors in our crew, who were so clever that before daybreak forty of them were comfortably ensconced aboard a raft they had made out of whatever pieces of wood and planks they could find at hand and lashed together with the ropes of the sails.

And since, as the saying goes, this was a case of "each man for himself," each one, both the Chinese sailors as well as our slaves, tried to do what was best for himself alone, without regard for anything else. Things went so far that when Martim Esteves, the captain and owner of the junk, asked his own boys who were on the raft to take him on board with them, they answered that under no circumstances could they do so. When word of this reached the ears of one of the men in our company named Ruy de Moura, he could not bear the ungrateful and discourteous treatment we were getting from all of them by that time, and rising to his feet on the very spot where he had been lying badly wounded, he made us all a short speech in which he told us that we should be mindful of how dishonorable and abhorrent a thing cowardice was, and that we should realize how necessary it was for our own salvation to make every effort to capture the raft. He said many other things to that effect, which did much to lift our spirits, imbuing us with a single purpose and renewed strength. Whereupon, all twenty-eight of us Portuguese flung ourselves in a single body upon the forty Chinese who were already on the raft, we with our swords and they with their little hatchets, fighting all in a heap with such fury that in the time it would take to recite three or four Credos, all forty of the Chinese and sixteen of the Portuguese were dead, while the other twelve who escaped sustained serious wounds, from which four of them died the following day. It was certainly something never dreamed of or imagined, which clearly demonstrates the wretchedness of human life, for less than twelve hours before we had all been embracing and treating each other with so much love that we would have died for each other, but our sins had brought us to such an extreme of necessity that we killed each other so mercilessly over four pieces of wood lashed together with two ropes, as if we had been mortal enemies or something even worse. But then too, it seems that we can be excused in part by the dire necessity which drove us to such utter madness.

180
Ransomed from Slavery

After we had become masters of this sorry raft at a cost to us, as well as the Chinese, of so much blood, thirty-eight people climbed aboard, twelve Portuguese and the rest our slaves and a few young children of the Portuguese, most of us so badly wounded that nearly all died later. Since the raft was too small for so many, we floated in the water up to our necks, but in spite of that we managed to get clear of that fatal reef on Christmas Day, which fell on a Saturday,[1] in the year 1547. And with just a scrap of blanket for a sail, we went drifting along at the mercy of the sea, without a compass or anything else to guide us but our hope in the Lord our God, on whom we called continuously, mingling our frequent sighs and cries with a great many tears.

For four days we navigated this way, without anything to eat in all that time, until the morning of the fifth day, when we were forced by necessity to eat one of the kaffirs who died. This sustained us for five more days of our voyage, making a total of nine, but on the remaining four days that this suffering lasted we ate nothing but algae we found on the surface of the water, for we were determined to let ourselves die rather than eat any of the four Portuguese who had died. As we were drifting along this way, the Lord in his mercy ordained that on the Day of the Epiphany² we should discover land, the sight of which, and the excitement accompanying it, proved to be fatal for four of the fifteen of us who were still alive, for just the sheer joy of it was enough to cause their sudden death, and two of these were Portuguese. This means that out of the thirty-eight of us who embarked on the raft, only eleven escaped— seven Portuguese and four of our slaves.

When we finally reached land we went ashore on a beach shaped like a bay, where we gave infinite thanks to the Lord for delivering us from the perils of the sea, trusting in him to deliver us likewise from those facing us on the land, after which we gathered some shellfish we found among the rocks. Observing that the land was unin- habited and thickly populated with elephants and tigers, we climbed some trees that grew wild there, seeking safety for the time being from the huge numbers of them as well as other animals we had seen there. When we thought it would be less dangerous to walk, we gathered together again and plunged into the dense jungle, going hither and thither, weeping and crying, searching in vain for some means of salvation.

However, divine mercy, which never forsakes the poor and wretched of the earth, ordained at the time that we should see a barge coming towards us on a fresh- water river winding through the jungle on its way to the sea, carrying a load of timber and firewood, with nine black Javanese and Papuans aboard. The moment they saw us, as they later confessed, they thought we were devils and they all jumped over- board, abandoning the vessel to its fate, but once they realized that we were victims of a shipwreck, they regained their composure and recovered completely from their ini- tial fright. After that they approached us and asked us many personal questions which, by nature, they are much inclined to do. We answered in complete accord with the truth and begged them, for the love of God, to take us with them to any town they chose and there to sell us as their slaves to people who would take us to Malacca, because we were merchants and could be ransomed there for a great deal of money or for as much merchandise as they wanted.

Now, inasmuch as the Javanese are an extremely greedy people, and since we had appealed to their own self-interest, in addition to which they could see how miserable and desperate we were, their attitude softened somewhat and they responded in a kindlier and more favorable manner, thereby raising our hopes that they would do as we had asked them to. However, this feeling lasted until they got back to the boat they had abandoned, but once they were aboard, they shoved off. Making as if they in- tended to depart without taking us along, they told us that in order for them to be sure that we were telling them the truth, we would, first of all, have to hand all our weapons over to them, for otherwise they would not take us on board, even if they saw us being eaten by the lions. As a result, forced by dire necessity and the desper- ateness of our situation, we had no other recourse but to give in to all their demands.

Bringing the barge in a little closer to us, they instructed us to swim out to it one by one because they did not have a *manchua* in which to pick us up, and this we also determined to do. Then two slaves and one Portuguese jumped into the water and started swimming towards a rope they had thrown out from the stern of the barge, but before they could get their hands on it, they were devoured by three huge lizards, without any trace left of the three of them but the blood staining the entire river crimson. When this happened, the eight of us waiting at the edge of the river were so paralyzed with fear that for a long time not one of us could recover his wits. But instead of being moved to pity, those dogs clapped their hands, laughing loudly and shouting, "Blessed are those three who ended their days without pain!" Then when they saw that the rest of us were stuck knee deep in the mud and too weak to pull ourselves out, five of them jumped ashore, tied us under the armpits and dragged us to the barge, which by this time they had brought close into shore, handling us roughly and shouting many curses and insults at us as they helped us aboard.

Setting sail, they took us to a village twelve leagues from there called Cheribon, where they sold all eight of us, six Portuguese, a Chinese boy, and a kaffir, for thirteen *pardaus*³—which is thirty-nine hundred *réis*⁺ in our money—to a heathen merchant from the island of Celebes, who kept us for twenty-six days. He treated us very well insofar as both food and clothing were concerned and then sold us to the king of *Calapa*⁵ for eighteen thousand *réis*. This king was so magnanimous to us that he sent us freely to the port of Sunda where there were three Portuguese *naos* under the command of a certain Jeronimo Gomes Sarmento, who gave us a hearty welcome and provided us generously with everything necessary until his departure for China.

181
Portuguese Mercenaries in Siam

After a stay of nearly a month in the port of Sunda, where the Portuguese saw to our needs, the monsoon for China arrived and the three *naos* departed for *Chincheo* with just two Portuguese remaining behind, who left with their merchandise in a Patani junk, bound for Siam. I was forced to go with them too because they were willing to pay my way back and had promised to lend me some money there with which to tempt Fortune once more, to see if by importuning her I could improve my lot. Departing from here, within twenty-six days we arrived at the city of Ayuthia, which is the capital of the *Sornau* empire—commonly known as Siam in those parts—where we were welcomed by the Portuguese we found there, who offered us their hospitality.

I remained in the city of Ayuthia for a little over a month, waiting for the China monsoon to take ship for Japan along with six or seven other Portuguese who were bound for those parts, where I was planning to invest the hundred *cruzados* lent me by the two men who had brought me from Sunda. While I was there, a confirmed report reached the king of Siam,¹ who was then residing in Ayuthia with his entire court, to the effect that the king of Chiang Mai, allied with the *Timocouhos,* the Laotians, and the *Gueos* (which are four nations in the northeast, dominating most of the hinterlands above Kamp'eng'et and P'itsanulok, ruled by very rich and powerful kings who are absolute lords in their domains, owing allegiance to none), had laid siege to the city of *Quitirvão*[2] and slain the *Oyá*[3] Kamp'eng'et, general of the armies of the frontier, along with more than thirty thousand of his men.

This news had such an alarming effect on the king that, without waiting for anything, that very day he crossed over to the other side of the river, refusing to seek quarters in anyone's house, preferring instead to pitch his tents in the field as an example to all the others. From there he issued proclamations throughout the entire city that every man who could not be excused from military service on the grounds of old age or infirmity must report for duty within twelve days, which was the maximum time he would allow, under pain of being burned alive at the stake, to the perpetual shame of all his descendants, and confiscation of all his property in the name of the crown. In addition to these penalties he imposed many others that were very severe and so appalling and terrifying to hear that all the people trembled with fear.

As for the foreigners, regardless of their nationality, who were residing in his country, they were not exempted from these penalties either, but he gave them three days in which to comply or leave his kingdom. As a result, everyone was going about as though in a state of shock, without knowing which way to turn for advice or decide what they should do. With regard to the Portuguese, who had always been shown the highest respect in this country, he sent the *combracalão*,[4] the governor of the kingdom, to ask them to voluntarily join his campaign, in view of the reputation they had, for he was most desirous of having them serve as his personal guards[5] since, from what he knew about them, they were better suited for it than all the others. Considering the nature of this message, which was accompanied by many liberal promises and expectations of high wages, favors, honors, and above all, permission to build churches[6] in his kingdom, we felt so deeply obligated to him that, out of the 130 of us Portuguese who were there at the time, 120 agreed to go with him.

When the twelve-day period was over, the king departed in a fleet of three thousand *serós, laulés,* and *jangás,* with an army of 400,000 men, including 70,000 foreign mercenaries from different nations. On the ninth day of his voyage he arrived at a border town called *Suropisem,* twelve leagues from the city of *Quitirvão,* which the enemies had besieged, and he remained there for seven more days, waiting for four thousand elephants that were coming overland. During this time he received word that the city was in difficult straits, not only along the bank of the river which the enemies had occupied with a fleet of two thousand ships, but also on the land side where there were a great many soldiers whose numbers were not known for certain but were estimated, from what could be seen, at 300,000 men, of which 40,000 were said to be mounted on horse, but that they did not have any elephants. After receiving this report, the king made haste and ordered a general muster of all his troops, the result of which showed that he had 500,000 men, for many had joined him along the way after his departure, as well as four thousand elephants and two hundred wagons of field artillery.

With this army he quickly departed from the town of *Suropisem* and continued on his way to *Quitirvão* in marches of only four leagues per day, arriving on the third day at a valley called *Siputay,* a league and a half from where the enemies were encamped. Once this huge multitude of soldiers and elephants had been placed in order by their field marshals, two Turks and a Portuguese by the name of Domingos de

Seixas,[7] he proceeded on his way to *Quitirvão*, arriving before sunrise. Since by that time the enemies were already prepared, having learned from their spies of the power and determination of the king of Siam, they were waiting for him in the field, with full confidence in the forty thousand cavalrymen they had.

As soon as he came in sight, they advanced in tight formation, divided into twelve battalions of fifteen thousand each, all fine-looking troops, marching in perfect order. Then their vanguard, comprised of the forty thousand cavalrymen, rushed forward to meet the king of Siam's vanguard, comprised of seventy thousand foot soldiers, and routed them in less than a quarter of an hour, killing three princes[8] who were among them. Seeing the defeat suffered by his men, the king of Siam, like a prudent man, realized that he would have to change his tactics, and he reorganized his troops into a single body composed of the seventy thousand foreign mercenaries and four thousand elephants and charged the enemy camp with such tremendous force that at the first encounter he succeeded in breaking it up, routing them completely and slaying an infinite number of men, for given the fact that their main strength was in their cavalry, as soon as the elephants charged into them, with the support of the many foreign arquebusiers and the two hundred wagons of artillery, they crushed them completely in less than half an hour, and once the cavalry had been routed, the rest immediately began to fall back.

Following up on his victory,[9] the king of Siam pursued them up to the riverbank where the enemy formed a new squadron out of all the more than 100,000 men who had managed to escape, counting both the sound and the wounded, who, protected by their fleet, stood their ground in a single body, which the king was afraid to attack because of the advantage they had with their fleet of two thousand ships, which also had large companies on board. However, as soon as night fell, the enemy marched quickly along the river, with the armada covering their flank for greater protection, which the king of Siam did not regret in the least, because most of his men were badly wounded and in need of care, to which he gave his immediate attention, spending the better part of the day and the following night looking after them.

182
The King of Siam Poisoned by the Queen

After he had won this glorious victory, the king of Siam attended with great haste to the fortification of the city and to everything else that was necessary for its security. To determine his losses in battle he ordered a review of his troops and found that he had lost only fifty thousand men, most of them the riffraff who, constrained by the severity of the proclamations, had come against their will and without defensive weapons. As for his enemies, it was learned the following day that 130,000 of them had died. As soon as the wounded recovered, he stationed as many troops along the border as he thought necessary for its defense and decided to make war on the kingdom of *Guibem*, fifteen leagues to the north, as his counsellors had advised him to do, because its queen[1] had allowed the king of Chiang Mai to cross her territory and had consented to the past wrongs as well as to the death of the *Oyá Kamp'engp'et*[2] and the thirty thousand men who had died with him.

In complete accord with their advice, the king departed from this city with an army of 400,000 men and headed for a town within the queen's territory called *Fumbacor,* which was easily captured and destroyed, and where the entire population was put to the sword, barring none. From here he continued by daily marches to a city called *Guitor,* the capital of this kingdom of *Guibem,* where the queen was then residing, and laid siege to the city. The queen, a widow, who was acting as regent for her nine-year-old son, was in no position to resist the powerful king of Siam and agreed to pay him an annual tribute of five thousand silver *turmas,*[3] which is the equivalent of sixty thousand *cruzados* in our money. She immediately paid for five years in advance, and in addition, she let him take her son, the boy king, back to Siam with him as his vassal. With that he lifted the siege and continued on his way to the northeast, heading for the city of *Taysirão,* where he received word that the king of Chiang Mai had already dissolved the alliance he had recently made.

After six days of marching through enemy territory, plundering every village and town in his path and refusing to spare the life of a single male, he arrived at Lake *Singuapamor,*[4] which most people call Lake Chiang Mai, where he remained for twenty-six days. During that time he captured twelve very noble and wealthy towns that were well fortified with walls, moats, and ramparts similar to ours, except that the materials used were different, for in those parts they are not accustomed to using stone and lime as we do, just bricks and mud, nor did they have any artillery to speak of, except for some culverins and bronze musketry.

Since winter had set in by then, bringing with it some showers, and the men were beginning to fall sick, the king withdrew to the city of *Quitirvão,* where he remained for twenty-three more days, during which he finished fortifying the city by constructing walls and very deep, wide moats. When everything had been taken care of and the city had been made strong enough to defend itself, he departed for Siam with the same three thousand vessels on which he had come, and within nine days he reached Ayuthia, the most important city in his entire kingdom, where he resided most of the year with the whole court. There he was given an extravagant reception accompanied by all kinds of splendid pageantry that cost the people a great deal of money and lasted for fourteen days, in accordance with the statutes of their heathen sects.

During the five months he had been away, the queen, his wife,[5] had committed adultery with one of the purveyors to the royal household, a man by the name of *Uquumchenirá,*[6] and by the time the king returned she was already four months pregnant. Since she was afraid of what would happen to her—as well she might be—she decided that the only way to save herself from the danger threatening her was to poison the king,[7] her husband, and without any more ado she put some in a porcelain bowl with his milk. He lived for only five days after that, and during that time he made some provisions in his will relating to the affairs of the kingdom and fulfilled his obligations to the foreigners who had served with him in the Chiang Mai war, from which he had returned barely twenty days before. With regard to us Portuguese who had gone to war with him, in this last will and testament of his he placed them before all the others, inserting a clause that read as follows:

"As for the 120 Portuguese who served as my personal guards and always protected me loyally, they shall be given half a year of the tribute collected from the queen of *Guibem,* and an exemption from the payment of duty in my customs houses for a period of three years, during which no charges of any kind shall be levelled against their goods; and their priests shall be allowed to go through all cities and towns of my kingdom preaching the religion they profess of the God who became a man for the salvation of mankind, as they have assured me several times."

It contained many other things in the same vein which are quite worthy of being repeated here but which I will not mention at this time because I expect to do so later on at great length. He also asked all the grandees who were present there to give him the consolation of crowning his oldest son[8] king while he was still alive, and they hastened to do so.

After the *oyás,* the *conchalys,* and the *monteos,* who are the highest dignitaries in the land, had all sworn allegiance to the prince, they led him to a window, and there, in full view of the crowds of people in the courtyard below, they placed a rich golden crown on his head resembling a mitre, and a naked sword in his right hand and balances in his left, in keeping with an ancient custom observed in their coronation ceremonies. Then the *Oyá* P'itsanulok, the highest dignitary in the land, kneeled down before him and, choking back the tears, pronounced these words in a loud voice so that all could hear: "Holy child of tender age, in whose high and fortunate star it was written that thou shouldst now be chosen by heaven to rule this *Sornau* empire which God has commanded me, thy vassal, to deliver to thee. I hereby do so, upon thy oath that thou shalt always rule it in obedience to his divine will, dispensing equal justice to all the peoples, without showing favoritism to any person, whether highborn or low, so that none may say of thee that thou hast not fulfilled the oath that thou hast sworn on this solemn occasion; for if thou shouldst, out of human considerations, deny justice to those who, in the eyes of the Lord of justice, deserve it, thou shalt be severely punished for it in the Concave Depths of the House of Smoke, that fiery and frightfully fetid lake where the wicked and the damned weep continuously, with the gloom of dark night in their hearts. If thou dost accept the obligations incumbent upon thee in this high office, signify by saying *xamxaimpom"*—which is like saying amen among us.

The boy repeated *"xamxaimpom"* through his tears, and as he did so, there arose from the crowd the most horrible sounds of weeping and crying, which lasted for a long time. Signalling to the people to be quiet, the *oyá* continued with the ceremony, saying, "And this sword, which has been placed unsheathed in thy hand, like a scepter, gives thee the power on earth to subdue those who rebel against thee; and with it too goes the obligation to protect with thy good faith the weak and humble, against those who, swelled by worldly power, would crush them beneath the weight of their pride—a thing so loathsome in the eyes of the Lord as is a blasphemous word directed against an innocent child who has never sinned. And if thou wouldst comply in every respect with the wishes of the burnished beauty of the stars in heaven, which is the manifestation in all its glory of the perfection, goodness, and justice of the all powerful God of creation, signify by saying *xamxaimpom."*

To which he responded twice, speaking through his tears, *"Maxinau, maxinau,"* meaning, "I promise to do so, I promise to do so."

Continuing his discourse in much the same manner, the *Oyá* P'itsanulok touched on other matters, interrupting his speech seven times while the boy responded with *"xamxaimpom,"* until finally the coronation ceremony was concluded. But still, at the end, they brought in a *talagrepo* by the name of *Quiay Pomvedé,* the highest dignitary in their priesthood, said to be over a hundred years old, who prostrated himself at the boy's feet and swore a solemn oath to him on a gold *charana*[9] filled with rice. After this they led him back inside, for the time would not permit any further delay, not only because the king, his father, was in the final throes of death, but also because the wailing and lamentations of the people had grown so intense that everywhere, as far as the eye could see, there were masses of people sobbing and weeping.

183
The Good King of Siam

That day and the following night went by like this, and the next morning at eight o'clock, the poor king finally expired in the presence of most of the lords of his kingdom. All the people were so deeply affected by his death that they cried and carried on in a way that seemed utterly beyond all reason and their normal customs. And since he had been a good king—benevolent in his almsgiving, splendid and open-handed in granting favors, generous in rewarding services done for him, compassionate and gentle with everyone, and above all, thoroughly incorruptible in dispensing justice and punishing wrongdoers—his people demonstrated it so amply with their tears and lamentations, that if everything they said about him was true, one would think that he was the best heathen king that ever lived in that land or, in his time, in any other part of the world. I would not go so far as to affirm what his people were saying about him through their tears because I did not see it and will therefore refrain from mentioning what they said, but neither would I doubt that it was so because of certain things that happened in my time, only three or four of which I shall relate here, out of the many I saw him do during the years between 1540 and 1545 when I was trading in this kingdom.

The first happened in the year 1540 when Pedro de Faria was captain of the fortress of Malacca. He had received a letter written by His Majesty, King John III of glorious memory, commanding him and strongly recommending that he do everything possible to ransom a certain Domingos de Seixas who had been held captive in Siam for twenty-three years, since it was a matter of the utmost necessity in God's service and his, inasmuch as he had been informed that this man, more than anyone else, could give him accurate information concerning the kingdom of Siam about which they had told him so many marvelous things; and that after obtaining his release, he was to send him immediately to the viceroy Dom Garcia[1] in India, to whom he had already written about him, so that he should send him back to Portugal in the *naos* scheduled to depart that year.

Acting in response to the king's urgent request, Pero de Faria sent an ambassador to Siam, a wealthy nobleman named Francisco de Castro,[2] to negotiate the ransom of this Domingos de Seixas as well as sixteen other Portuguese who were also being held captive there. This Francisco de Castro arrived in the city of Ayuthia at the time I was there and was given a fine reception by the king of Siam, to whom he delivered the letter he was carrying for him. After reading it and asking him a few questions about some of the latest and most interesting news, he replied to his embassy immediately—something he did not ordinarily do with any other ambassador—as follows:

"Regarding this Domingos de Seixas for whose freedom the captain of Malacca is asking, pointing out that the king of Portugal would be extremely pleased if I deliver him up to him, I am equally pleased to grant his request, and you may consider it done. This applies as well to the other sixteen Portuguese who are with him."

Francisco de Castro thanked him, prostrating himself three times, touching his head to the floor, which is the way they customarily kowtow to him since he is the foremost monarch of them all. As soon as the season arrived when Francisco de Castro was able to depart for Malacca, he sent to fetch Domingos de Seixas from the city of *Guntaleu* where he was stationed as general of the army of that frontier, in command of thirty thousand foot soldiers and five thousand horsemen, at an annual salary of eighteen thousand *cruzados*. He also ordered the sixteen Portuguese who were in his company to return with him and handed them all over to Francisco de Castro, who once again thanked him for the favor shown him. Later, when Domingos de Seixas and his companions were taking their leave of him, he gave them a bonus of one thousand silver *turmas,* which is twelve thousand *cruzados* in our money, and on top of it he begged his pardon for giving him so little.

Another time, in the year 1545, when Simão de Melo[3] was serving as captain of the same fortress of Malacca, a certain Luis de Montarroyo[4] was returning from China, bound for Patani, when he happened by chance to get caught in a turbulent crosswind that blew his *nao* against the coast, in the port of *Chatir,* five leagues below *Lugor*[5] where the local *shahbandar*[6] confiscated all the cargo that had been washed ashore and arrested him along with all the other survivors, a group of twenty-four Portuguese, fifty slaves, and little children, counting altogether seventy-four Christian souls. The cargo salvaged from the *nao* was worth fifteen thousand *cruzados,* and the reason the *shahbandar* gave for confiscating it was that everything belonged to him in accordance with an ancient custom of the kingdom. A number of Portuguese then living in that city learned about it from a letter Luis de Montarroyo had written them recounting his misfortune. After sending some much-needed clothing to him in prison, they got together and decided to buy an *odiá*[7]—which is a gift—of some expensive items worth a thousand *cruzados* to present to the king on the Day of the White Elephant, only ten days away, for on that solemn day the king customarily distributed a great deal of charity to all petitioners and granted many favors to his people.

When this solemn holiday arrived—on a day that is known as *Oniday Pileu,* meaning "joy of good people"—all the Portuguese, numbering about sixty or seventy altogether, posted themselves at a particular spot on one of the nine streets the king was to pass through with a great deal of pomp and majesty. As soon as he came near, they all prostrated themselves on the ground in Siamese fashion, and one of them who had been chosen as spokesman told him the whole story of what had happened to Luis de Montarroyo and his companions, and asked him for the release of the shipwrecked victims as an act of charity, without saying anything about the cargo confiscated by the *shahbandar* because he did not dare to go that far, nor did he think it would be appropriate to do so.

Knowing exactly what it was our people wanted, and observing the tears being shed by some of them, the king ordered the white elephant he was riding brought to a halt and studied them carefully, observing the expensive objects some of them held in their hands, which he realized were intended for him.

"As for the gifts you bring me," he said to them, "you may consider them accepted and I thank you for them. However, on this day I am not permitted to receive gifts, only to bestow them. Therefore, I pray you, for love of your God, whose humble servant I am and always will be, to distribute those gifts to the neediest among you, for it is far better to receive the divine reward that awaits you for giving charity in his name, than to receive whatever I—who am but an insignificant creature in his eyes—can give you for them. As for the prisoners, I am happy to grant your request for their liberty as an act of charity, so that they may freely depart for Malacca; and further, I command that all the goods which they say have been taken from them be restored to them, for the things which are done for the sake of God ought to be accomplished with far greater liberality than that which is sought by the poor, especially when tearfully requested in his name."

At these words, all the Portuguese prostrated themselves on the ground before him.

On the following day he had a *firmaun*[8] drawn up for them, instructing the *shahbandar* to bring the prisoners with all their confiscated goods to the city within a period of ten days, an order that was promptly and faithfully carried out. And the king made them a gift of the merchandise salvaged from the *nao*, which was worth more than fifteen thousand *cruzados*, as I said before, though all the rest of the cargo went down in the storm with the *nao*.

Two or three months later, in this same year of 1545, it became urgent for this king of Siam to defend his borders in the area of P'itsanulok against an invading army led by the king of the *Tuparahós* who was destroying and plundering some of the weaker towns around there, preparatory to laying siege to the fortress of *Xivau* and *Lantor*, on which the entire security of the nation depended. Having decided to lead his army personally in this action, he dispatched twenty colonels throughout the kingdom with orders to recruit a certain number of soldiers and to present themselves with them, within twenty days, in the city of Ayuthia, from where he intended to set out. The recruiting officers were under the strictest orders, which carried heavy penalties for disobeying, not to exempt anyone capable of fighting, aside from the sick, the poor, and men over the age of sixty, and each colonel was assigned an area from which to draw his recruits.

One of these colonels, a dauntless nobleman by the name of *Quiay Raudivá*[9] who had been of service to the king many times before, was assigned to the district of *Banchá*,[10] where most of the men are very rich, both in cash and goods, and generally given to the pleasures and delights of the flesh, always spending most of their time in banquets and gambling and many of the other agreeable things in life. When *Quiay Raudivá* tried to force them to go to this war, as he had been instructed to do, they took it very ill, for in their view, it was too heavy a burden to bear and one that conflicted with the refinement and luxury of the lives they led. As a result, the richest men in the district got together and decided to free themselves of the necessity of serving in this campaign by offering the colonel a huge bribe, to which they all contributed.

And since money, everywhere, is powerful enough to crush all resistance, Colonel *Raudivá* was impressed enough by the large sum these men gave him to allow them all to remain at home while, as a result, he was forced to recruit in their stead all the sick, crippled, poor, and aged—as many as he could find in the area—with complete disregard of the king's orders. On his return to Ayuthia he presented them for inspection to the king, as did all the other colonels with their troops.

From where he stood, framed in a window, the king could see these men, some of them so old and tattered and many of them sick, without a single decent-looking recruit in the lot, and he sent for four of them whom he saw filing by, all of them very old and patently ill. When he asked them about their age, what ailed them, and why they were so shabbily dressed, all four of them in one voice revealed the entire affair that had taken place in *Banchá*. This threw the king into a rage, and he immediately summoned the *Quiay Raudivá* to appear before him. After reviling him in public for it, he had him bound hand and foot, and having given the order to melt five *turmas* of silver, he had them poured down his throat, in his presence, which resulted in his immediate death. When he saw him lying there dead, he said to them, "If five *turmas* of silver were enough to kill thee, how couldst thou imagine that the five thousand that thou tookest as a bribe for exempting the cowards of *Banchá* would not kill thee? May God forgive thee for thy greed and me for not punishing thee sufficiently for it!"

And without a moment's delay he sent a party to the dead man's house, whence they returned with the five thousand *turmas* he had taken as a bribe—which comes to sixty thousand *cruzados* in our money—and he had them distributed in his presence to all those aged, sick, and poor people conscripted by *Raudivá*—who must have numbered over three thousand—and he sent them home, recommending that they pray to God to give them life. As for the exempted men who had paid the five thousand *turma* bribe, he had them dressed as women and banished to an island called Pulo Catão," and as punishment for their cowardice, he confiscated their estates, which he set aside to be distributed as a reward to those who fought best in that war.

And one day, noticing that a Portuguese soldier—one out of the 160 accompanying him at the time—had lagged a little behind the others during an assault that resulted in their capturing the main stronghold that had been taken by the enemy in the city of *Lantor,* he ordered him back to Siam because he was unlike the other Portuguese who stayed with him. Furthermore, he ordered him not to set foot out of the house for as long as he remained there, nor to call himself Portuguese, under pain of having his beard shaved off, like the exempted gentlemen of *Banchá,* because he was just as cowardly as they were. As for all the rest, who, as I said before, numbered 160, because of the honorable feat he had seen them perform, he ordered their pay tripled, exempted them from paying customs duties on their merchandise, and gave them permission to build churches in any part of his kingdom where the name of the Portuguese God could be worshipped, for it was obvious that He was much better than all the others.

And from these things and many more like them that I could relate about him, it is plain to see how magnificent and well inclined by nature this prince was, even though he was a heathen.

184
The Queen and Her Lover Usurp the Throne

Immense was the pain and sorrow shown by all the grandees of the kingdom for their good king who was lying dead before them, and infinite were the tears they shed for him. However, after one thing and another came to an end, all the priests in the city—who were said to number twenty thousand—got together with the leading citizens of the kingdom to discuss arrangements for the burial of the corpse and the ceremonies to be performed at the funeral rites. It was decided that he should be cremated immediately before the poison that had caused his death gave rise to an unpleasant odor, for if that should happen, there was absolutely no way for his soul to be saved, according to what was written in their books. Therefore, they hastened without delay to have a great funeral pyre built of sandalwood, eaglewood, calambac, and benzoin, and set it afire with another strange ceremony in which the body was consumed by the flames to the accompaniment of a pitiful lamentation of all the people. Then his ashes were placed in a silver coffer and put aboard a richly appointed *laulé* called the *cabizonda*,[1] which was towed forty *serós*, manned by *talagrepos*, who are the highest-ranking dignitaries in their heathen priesthood. In addition, they were accompanied by a great multitude of other vessels carrying an infinite number of people. Behind them all went a hundred big barges laden with different figures of idols in the shape of snakes, lizards, lions, tigers, toads, serpents, bats, ducks, goats, dogs, elephants, vultures, cats, hawks, crows, and many other animals, all of which were copied so closely from nature that one would think they were alive. As a sign of mourning the figures of all these idols were covered by pieces of silk cloth in colors to match each one of them, and there were so many of them, in such enormous numbers, that it was said—according to the estimate of those who witnessed it—that over five thousand bolts of silk had been used for the mourning cloths covering this huge throng of devils.

On another very large vessel went the king of all these idols—whom they call the "Ravenous Serpent of the Lower Depths of the House of Smoke"—in the shape of an extremely monstrous-looking snake wider than a wine barrel, wound in nine coils which, if stretched out full length, looked like they would probably be over a hundred handspans long, and holding its neck up high. Shooting from the eyes, mouth, and breast of this snake were huge jets of artificial fire, giving it so fearful and ugly an appearance that the sight of it was enough to make the flesh quiver. On a highly gilded and richly decorated platform that appeared to be almost three armspans high, there was a very beautiful child about four or five years of age, all covered with strings of pearls, chains, and bracelets of precious stones, with a pair of wings and tresses of gold thread, exactly the way angels are depicted here among us, and a richly ornamented sword in his hand, giving the onlooker to understand by means of this symbolism that he was an angel from heaven, sent by God to prevent that multitude of devils from harming the soul of the king before it reached the glorious abode prepared for him as a reward for the good works he had done in this world.

Keeping to this formation all the boats landed at a pagoda called *Quiay Pontar* where, after burying the silver coffer containing the king's ashes, they removed the child from the platform and set fire to the whole multitude of idols, just as they were, with the barges and all, to the accompaniment of such a horrendous din of shouts, screams, jeers, artillery and musket fire, mingled with the sounds of bells, gongs, cornets, conch horns, as well as many other different kinds of dissonant instruments that made the flesh creep.

This ceremony probably lasted for only an hour, for since the idols were made of straw and the barges had been purposely loaded with large quantities of tar and resin, in a very short time such an enormous and frightful fire broke out that it almost seemed like a portrait of hell, and the boats and everything on them were completely consumed.

Once this was over, as well as the many other clever pageants they enacted, all very natural looking and prepared at great cost—which I will pass over since they strike me as superfluous and unnecessary—this huge multitude of people went back to the city and retired one by one to their homes where they remained behind tightly shuttered doors and windows for ten days, during which not a living soul was to be seen stirring in the plazas and streets, except the poor who issued forth at night, crying and begging for alms.

At the end of this ten-day period of seclusion, they awoke at dawn to see the *varelas,* pagodas, and *bralas*²—which are their temples of worship—all gaily decked out in symbols of joy, with many silken awnings, standards, and banners, and richly arrayed tables giving off many delightful aromas. Then men on horseback, clad in white damask, appeared on all the streets, who, to the sound of melodious instruments cried aloud in voices choked with tears, "Hear ye! Hear ye, all ye disconsolate dwellers in this Siamese kingdom, hear the word of the Lord that is brought to you and praise his holy name with pure and humble hearts for the righteousness of his divine judgement! Come forth joyfully from your seclusion and sing praises to the Lord for his kindness in giving you a new king who is God-fearing and a friend to the poor!"

This proclamation was followed by the sound of many musical instruments played sweetly and harmoniously by men on horseback dressed in white satin, in response to which all the listeners prostrated themselves face down on the ground with arms upraised, as though giving thanks to God, crying aloud through their tears, "We call on the angels in heaven to praise the Lord continuously on our behalf!"

Thereupon, they all poured out of their houses, dancing and making merry all the way to the temple of *Quiay Fanarel,* "god of the joyous," with sweet-smelling offerings, and the poorest among them with hens, fruits, and rice for the priests to eat.³

That same day the new king allowed himself to be seen, passing through the entire city with great pomp and majesty, giving rise to great rejoicing among all the people.

However, since the king was but a child of nine, the twenty-four *bracalões* of the government ordained that the queen, his mother, should be his tutor and governess and president of the Council of Governors. Things went on like this for a period of four and a half months, during which all was quiet, with no sign of unrest or anything to disturb the calm, until the queen gave birth to a son,⁺ fathered by her purveyor.

Resentful of the evil things that were being said about her, she made up her mind to satisfy her longing to marry the father of this young son, for she was madly in love with him. To that end she decided to kill the little king, her legitimate son, so that his inheritance would pass to the bastard son.

She began by inventing all sorts of evil things never before dreamed of or imagined, which I will not mention here because they inspire me with fear, and ended by pretending that the deep love she had for the little king, her son, kept her in constant fear for his life. One day, while sitting in session with all the members of her council, she told them that, since she had only that one precious pearl embedded in her heart, she did not want it plucked from her breast by some disaster, and that therefore, she thought it would be advisable, not only to calm her fears, but also because of the evils that negligence at times is wont to cause in similar situations, if there were a special guard to watch over the palace and the person of the king.

The matter was immediately taken up by the council, and since the request in itself did not appear to be unreasonable, it was granted her. Delighted to see that her plan was proceeding so smoothly, the queen promptly sought out the people best suited for her nefarious scheme, the ones she could trust the most. She selected a corps composed of two thousand foot soldiers and five hundred horsemen—apart from the ordinary household guards—made up of six hundred Cochinese and Ryukyu Islanders. For their captain she chose a man by the name of *Tileubacus,* who was a cousin of the father of her child, so that, with his help, she would be more in control of what she was after and better able to achieve her ends.

Trusting in this large force which was already on her side, she began to avenge herself on some of the the grandees of the kingdom, because she knew she could not command from them the respect she desired. The first ones she laid hands on were two of the deputies of the government called *Pinamonteo* and *Comprimvão,* whom she accused of corresponding with the king of Chiang Mai and of plotting to give him access to the kingdom through their lands, and in the guise of justice she had them both executed and confiscated their estates, one of which she gave to her lover and the other to a brother-in-law of his who, it was said, was a former blacksmith.

Since these executions had been carried out with excessive haste, and without a shred of evidence, she was rebuked by most of the lords of the kingdom who reminded her of the merits of the dead men, their fine qualities, and the nobility and antiquity of their royal blood which descended in direct line from the kings of Siam. However, she paid them no heed, and instead, the next day, pretending that she was ill, she resigned the presidency of the council she held in favor of her lover, *Ucunchenirat,*[5] thereby making him more powerful than all the others and enabling him to freely distribute the possessions of the kingdom among those who would support him, leaving the way open for him to usurp the throne and make himself absolute lord of the *Sornau* empire, which yielded an income of twelve million in gold, to say nothing of its other resources, which amounted to nearly as much.

She went to such great pains to make her lover king and to marry him and make the son they had between them successor to the crown of the *Sornau* empire that, within the eight months that fortune smiled on her, carried away by the hopes she had of eventually fulfilling her desire, she murdered all the lords of the kingdom, confiscating their estates, their goods, and their treasures in her own favor and distributing them to others she newly created as lords, in order to have them on her side. And since the little king, her son, was the main obstacle in her path, not even he could escape this unbridled passion of hers because she killed him too,[6] by poisoning him.

Once he was out of the way she married *Ucunchenirat,* her former purveyor, and had him proclaimed king[7] in this city on November 11, in the year 1545, and on January 2 of the following year, they were both killed[8] by the *Oyá* P'itsanulok and the king of Cambodia at a certain banquet given by these princes in a temple called *Quiay Figrau,* "god of the motes of the sun," whose invocation was celebrated on that day.

With the death of these two, as well as of all their supporters who were slain along with them, all became peaceful and quiet, without detriment to the people of the kingdom, though it was left without any of the nobility it once had, for by then they had all perished in the manner and in the course of events I have described above.

185
The Burmese Invade Siam

In the meantime, following the death of the evil queen and her lover, inasmuch as the empire had been left without an heir to the throne or any successor who could claim the crown by direct descent, these two lords, namely, the *Oyá* P'itsanulok[1] and the king of Cambodia[2]—who was merely a duke at the time—along with four or five others of the remaining loyalists, decided that the one to be king was a monk named *Pretiem.*[3] He was chosen because he was a bastard brother of the late king, husband of the evil queen, who had been leading a religious life for thirty years[4] as a *talagrepo* in a pagoda called *Quiay Mitreu.* Having agreed on this choice, early the following day the *Oyá* P'itsanulok went to fetch him and returned to the city with him on the seventh of January, and on the ninth he was proclaimed king[5] in another rather magnificent ceremony of honor and state, which there is no need to describe here, for it would be a bit tedious, since I have dwelt a few times before on things of that nature. Also, leaving aside all else that occurred in this Siamese kingdom, I will confine myself to relating what all these events led to in the end, for the benefit of the curious who, I believe, will not fail to enjoy it.

On being informed of the sad state of affairs in the *Sornau* empire and of how all the grandees had died as a result of the events described above, and that the new king was a monk with no knowledge of warfare or experience with arms, pusillanimous by nature, and above all, a great tyrant, disliked by the people, the king of Burma, who at that time was reigning tyrannically in Pegu, called his council together in the city of *Anapleu,* where he was then residing, to consider undertaking an enterprise of such great importance. They all told him that under no circumstances should he allow this opportunity to escape him, since that kingdom was one of the best in the world, both for its riches and abundance of everything; moreover, the time and circumstances were all in his favor and gave promise of a victory so cheap that, to all appearances, its conquest[6] could not possibly cost him more than a year's revenue, no matter how much of his treasure he was willing to spend. They also pointed out that its conquest would make him monarch of the emperors of the world, for with it went the honor of that exalted title of "lord of the white elephant,"[7] as a result of which, all of the seventeen kings of Kamp'engp'et who professed the same religion there would perforce obey him, and with access through their lands and with their help, within ten or twelve days he would be able to reach China where, as everybody knew, that priceless pearl, unequaled in the entire world, was located, that great city of Peking, over which the Grand Tartar, the *Siammon,* and the *Calaminhan* had taken the field so many times with huge armies.

After listening to all these arguments and many others that the members of his council presented to him at this meeting, all of which were designed to appeal to his self-interest, which is a force that no one can resist, the king of Burma decided to follow their advice and to undertake this campaign. With this end in view he departed for Martaban, where in the space of two and a half months he gathered an army of 800,000 men, including 100,000 foreign mercenaries, among them 1,000 Portuguese, commanded by Diogo Soares de Albergaria,[8] nicknamed "the Galician," who had left Portugal for India in the year 1538, in the same fleet as the viceroy Dom Garcia de Noronha,[9] on board the *nao Junco,* commanded by João de Sepulveda of Évora, who was on his way to take up his appointment as captain of Sofala. At that time, which was in the year 1548, this Diogo Soares was already receiving an income of 200,000 *cruzados* from the Burmese king, who had also given him the title of "the king's brother," and the governorship of Pegu.

The king departed from the city of Martaban on Low Sunday, 7 April 1548,[10] with this army of 800,000 men, only forty thousand of whom were mounted on horseback and all the rest on foot, including among them sixty thousand arquebusiers. He also took with him five thousand tusked elephants, which are the ones they use for combat in those parts, and a nearly equal number of pack elephants for the baggage, and one thousand pieces of artillery carried alternately by four thousand yokes of buffalo and yak, in addition to an equal number of oxen for carrying the provisions. He marched in this manner until he crossed over into the territory of the king of Siam where, after five more days of marching, he reached a fortress called *Tapurau* that had close to two thousand inhabitants, under the command of a Moghul named *Khoja Tarão,* who was both brave and very astute in warfare.

After laying siege to it, the Burmese king mounted three daylight assaults in which he attempted to scale it on all sides with many ladders he had brought along for that purpose, and when he failed to enter it that time because of the stiff resistance encountered from those within, he fell back towards the river where, upon the advice of Diogo Soares, his field marshal, by whom he was always guided, he battered it with forty heavy artillery pieces, most of them capable of firing cast-iron cannonballs. After knocking down a section of the wall twelve armspans wide, he sent in ten thousand foreign mercenaries comprised of many Turks, Abyssinians, Moors, and Malabaris, and the rest Achinese, Javanese, and Malaysians. A fierce battle ensued between them, and in the space of about half an hour all six thousand Siamese inside the walls were slain, for not a single one of them was willing to surrender. As for the Burmese, he lost nearly three thousand of his men, over which he appeared to be deeply distressed, and to avenge himself for these losses, he had all the women put to the sword, which seemed like an extremely cruel thing to do.

From here, he set out for the city of Suk'ot'ai nine leagues away, bent on avenging himself more freely there, and arrived within sight of the city on a Saturday afternoon, close to sundown. He pitched camp along the bank of the *Leibrau* River—one of the three that have their source in Lake Chiang Mai" as I mentioned before—intending to strike out from there for the city of Ayuthia, which is the capital of the *Sornau* empire, where he learned that the new king was then making preparations to meet him on the battlefield. When this news reached him, the Burmese king was advised not to stop anywhere for any reason, on the one hand, so as not to lose time, and on the other, so as not to deplete his forces, for by then the entire country was up in arms and the strongholds they were hoping to capture had been so heavily fortified that he might possibly be delayed by fighting there and pay so high a price for it that, by the time he reached Ayuthia, most of his army would be decimated and his supplies completely exhausted.

The king approved of this advice, and early the next day he departed and made his way through thick jungle growth where the sixty thousand sappers who also formed part of his army had quite a difficult time clearing the roads for him. When he reached a town called *Tilau,* which is on the coast of Junkseylon, toward the southwest near the kingdom of Kedah, 140 leagues from Malacca, he took the city of *Juropisão,* which was handed over to him by its commander, to the latter's advantage. From here, this time taking guides along who were familiar with the country, nine days later he came within sight of the city of Ayuthia and pitched his camp nearby, which he fortified all around with very strong stockades and trenches.

186
The Siege of Ayuthia

Five days had passed since the king of Burma reached this city, and on each of those days there was much work to be done both in preparing the stockades and trenches and in providing everything else required for the siege, and during all that time there was never a sign of any kind of activity going on inside the walls. Observing this and the apparent lack of concern shown by the Siamese for the huge army massed outside their walls, and not knowing to what to attribute it, Diogo Soares, the field marshal, decided to proceed with what he had come there to do. To that end he divided most of the foreign mercenaries, who might have numbered eighty thousand, into two separate squadrons, in each of which there were eight battalions of five thousand men each, and he marched with them to the sound of their instruments, up to the two southernmost points of the city, since he thought it would be easier to penetrate there than elsewhere.

At an hour before dawn—which was on the nineteenth of June in the same year of 1548—this entire force rushed at the walls, raising more than a thousand ladders, and as they scaled them they encountered such stiff resistance from those within that in less than an hour more than ten thousand men lay dead on one side and the other. Observing how badly the assault was progressing, the king, who at the time was spurring on his men, ordered them to withdraw and renewed the assault with the full force of his five thousand war elephants, divided into twenty companies of 250 each, led by twenty thousand carefully picked Mons and *Chaleus* who receive double pay.

Unleashing this brute force all at once along the entire length of the wall, which probably measured more than three crossbow shots, he attacked it with such a frightful onslaught that there are no words adequate enough to describe it, for since they all carried castles from which they were firing muskets and bronze lizards,[1] as well as a large quantity of oversized muskets ten to twelve handspans long, the combined power of all these firearms inflicted so much damage on the defenders that, in less time than it takes to recite three Credos, most of them had been shot down. Wrapping their trunks around the shields that served as merlons behind which those inside protected themselves, the elephants crushed them all so completely that not a single one of them was left intact, as a result of which the wall was so thoroughly shorn of the defense it had afforded its people that none of them dared to climb up there again, thereby making its entry easier for those on the outside who, upon seeing this favorable turn of events, were anxious to grasp the opportunity that lay before them and once again raised the ladders they had previously abandoned and climbed up without any opposition whatsoever, shouting at the top of their voices as they planted a huge number of flags and standards on the wall as a sign of victory.

Wanting to show that they had a greater part in this than all the rest, the Turks asked the king, as a boon, to let them lead the way, to which he readily agreed, on the advice of Diogo Soares who, desirous of seeing them diminished, always gave them the most dangerous positions. Pleased and quite proud of the fact that the king had granted them this favor in preference to any of the many other foreign nationals in the camp, the Turks were determined to acquit themselves honorably in the performance of the favor they had requested of the king. Organizing a squadron of twelve hundred, which included a few Abyssinians and Janissaries, they climbed the ladders, shouting mightily all the way up the wall which, at the time, as I have said, was already in the hands of the king of Burma and had many people on top. The Turks, because they were either more rash or more unfortunate, ran along the length of the wall and climbed down one of the bulwarks into the inner courtyard, intending to open a gate there to let the king in, so that it could truly be said that they alone had delivered to him the most important city in the kingdom of Siam and had earned the reward that went with it, for the king had previously promised to give anyone who delivered the city to him one thousand *biças* in gold, which is worth 500,000 *cruzados* in our money.

Once they were all down in the courtyard, the Turks prepared to break open the gates with two ironclad battering rams they had taken with them for that purpose. While they were going about it, never doubting for a moment that they alone would be the ones to win the one thousand gold *biças* the king had promised to whoever opened the gates to him, three thousand Javanese *amucks* fell upon them so resolutely that, in little time than it takes to recite three or four Credos, not a single Turk was left standing on his feet. And not content with that, whipped to a frenzy and thirsting for more blood after killing the Turks, they immediately climbed the wall and threw themselves so fearlessly upon the Burmese troops who were at the top that none of them dared to face them, with the result that the ones who fared best at the time were the ones who threw themselves down.

This was not reason enough at that moment for the king of Burma to want to call off the assault, but instead, anxious to try again, in the belief that the elephants by themselves were sufficient to open the way for him, he came bearing down on the wall again. As soon as he got word of this, the *Oyá* P'itsanulok, captain-general of the city, came running to the scene in great haste, accompanied by his fifteen thousand men, most of them Luzons, Borneans, and Chams, with some Menangkabowans among them, and issued an order to throw open the gates through which the Burmese was trying to break in. He thereupon sent him a message, telling him that he had heard that His Highness had promised to give one thousand gold *biças* to whoever would open the gates[2] for him, which he had just done, and that he was free to enter anytime he wished, provided he kept his word, like the magnanimous king that he was, by sending him the one thousand *biças,* because he was waiting there to receive them.

Choosing to ignore the message of the *Oyá* P'itsanulok, though its mockery was not lost on him, the king of Burma urged his men on with great fury, and as a result the battle flared up on both sides in a manner frightful to see, raging violently at full force for more than three hours, during which time both gates were smashed and the city entered twice. Observing this, and believing that all was nearly lost, the new king of Siam came rushing in with all the men at his command, throwing into the battle probably close to thirty thousand of the finest troops in the entire city, and with these reinforcements the fighting flared up for another half hour with even greater fury than before. I would not even dare to describe it, for I must confess I am not so bold as to think I can tell how it all happened, because the ground was covered with rivers of blood, the air was filled with live fire, the shouting and confusion were so great that it seemed as if the earth were coming asunder, the dissonance and discordance of their barbarous instruments, of the jeers, bells, drums, sistra, the noise of the artillery and the musketry, the trumpeting of the five thousand elephants, filled us with so much fear it nearly drove us out of our minds, and the courtyard inside the city, which was then in Burmese hands, completely covered with dead bodies and rivers of blood on all sides, made such a horrendous spectacle that the sight of it alone affected us so, that we went about as though in a state of shock.

However, when Diogo Soares saw that the courtyard had been lost again, and a great number of the elephants wounded, and the rest so terrified of the artillery that it was impossible to get them back to the walls, and that the best men among those who had taken part in this assault with him were already all dead, and the sun was almost down by then, he went up to the king and asked him for permission to withdraw outside the wall, which he grudgingly granted because he saw that he was badly wounded, as were the other Portuguese in his company, but he did so with the determination to resume the very next day where he was leaving off for the time being.

187
The Final Burmese Assault

It was not until after he had returned to his tent that the king discovered that in the course of the day's fighting he had sustained an arrow wound which had gone unnoticed in the heat of battle, so that his plans to resume the assault on the following day had to be postponed because he was forced to remain in bed for twelve days. However, seventeen days later, when he had fully recovered, he immediately resumed where he had left off, for he was just as determined as ever not to lift the siege until he was lord and master of the city, even though he was risking his life and his entire estate in the attempt.

The second assault was carried out in practically the same manner as the first, and again he was forced to withdraw with heavy casualties, but this only made him more furious and more obstinate, and never once did he flinch at the thought of the many soldiers who had already died. And so he launched five more attacks, attempting again to scale the wall by daylight with a huge number of ladders as well as many ingenious military devices invented daily for him by a Greek engineer, but each time he withdrew with heavy casualties, and he went about without hiding his anger and, at times, insinuating that he had repented of ever having undertaken this campaign. At this time he ordered a general census of the troops and discovered that he had lost 140,000 men in the four and a half months of the siege, most of them of disease. Finally, after considering the situation he was in, he decided to launch another attack—which was now the eighth in the siege—in an entirely different manner. He made this decision after listening to the opinions of his counsellors who advised him to assault the city at night, pointing out to him a number of reasons why at that time the attack would be less dangerous for him and the walls easier to scale.

Having made this decision, he immediately commanded that all the preparations necessary for carrying it out be made in great haste. Within seventeen days they constructed twenty-five platforms out of stout wooden beams, each of them set on twenty-six iron wheels with more than a hundred winches operated from below, which made for easier movement of the heavy structures. Each platform was ten hand-spans wide, thirteen long, and five high and was reinforced with many extra beams overlaid with lead plates. All of them were loaded with firewood, and each one had six very long chains on the front, for protection against the fire. These platforms were pulled by the sappers to the accompaniment of many drums and bells which were so frightful and discordant that it made the flesh creep.

On a dark, rainy, gloomy Friday at midnight, the Burmese king ordered three rounds of fire to be discharged by all the artillery in the camp which, as I think I have said before, consisted of 160 heavy guns, most of them firing cast-iron cannonballs, in addition to many other smaller-caliber guns such as falcons, culverins, dogs,' and large muskets numbering well over fifteen hundred. The simultaneous discharge of all this artillery three times, one after the other, made the earth quake so horrendously and fearsomely that I think I can say in all truth that only in hell can there be anything resembling it, but not on earth, for no matter how much the human mind tries to imagine what it was like, it still is nothing compared to what actually happened, for during this time they were not only firing the light and heavy artillery I mentioned above, but along with it they were also discharging all the other firearms of every kind and description they had from both inside and outside the walls. This meant that there were nearly 100,000 of them all together because the Burmese, as I already said, had sixty thousand musketeers, and in the city there were more than thirty thousand, not counting seven or eight thousand falcons, culverins, and iron rock throwers. Well, the sight, I dare say, of all these guns firing continuously for more than three hours on end, on a dark, stormy night filled with lightning and thunder, was something bordering on the incredible that had never before been seen, heard of, read about, or imag-

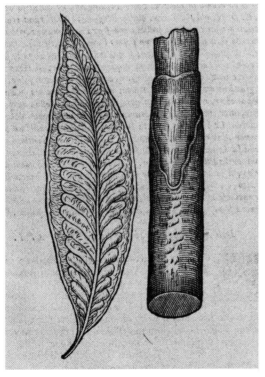

17. Merchants of Bantam. From William
Lodewijcksz, *Prima pars descriptionis itineris
navalis in Indiam Orientalem* (Amsterdam,
1598). Courtesy of the James Ford Bell
Library, University of Minnesota

18. Illustration of a cinnamon plant from Garcia de Orta, *Due libri dell'historia dei semplici,
aromati, et altre cose, che vengono portate
dall'Indie Orientali, pertinenti alla medicina*
(Venice, 1576). Courtesy of the James Ford
Bell Library, University of Minnesota

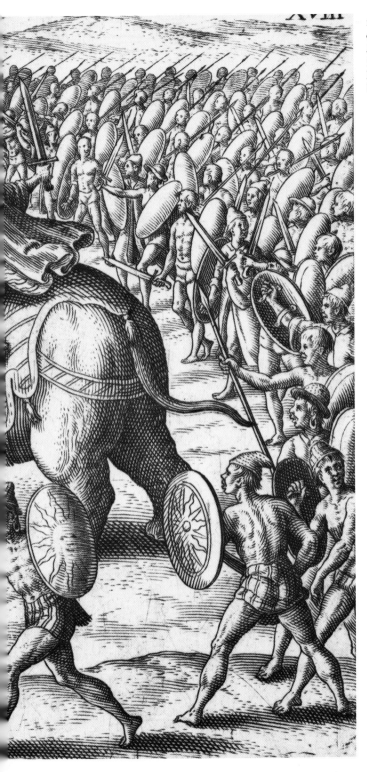

19. Single combat between the Kings of Pegu and Ava. From J.-T. de Bry, *Historiarum Orientalis Indiae,* vol. 7 (Frankfurt, 1598). Courtesy of the Edward E. Ayer Collection, The Newberry Library, Chicago

N.º 10

20. (*Above left*) Market scene, Bantam. From Willem Lodewijcksz, *Prima pars descriptionis itineris navalis in Indiam Orientalem* (Amsterdam, 1598). Courtesy of the James Ford Bell Library, University of Minnesota

21. (*Below left*) Market scene, Banda. From Jacob Corneliszoon Van Neck, *Journal ou comptoir, contenant le vray discours et narration historique, du voiage faict par les huict navires d'Amsterdam . . . l'an 1598* (Amsterdam, 1601). Courtesy of the James Ford Bell Library, University of Minnesota

22. (*Above*) Chinese merchants. From J.-T. de Bry, *Historiarum Orientalis Indiae,* vol. 3 (Frankfurt, 1598). Courtesy of the Edward E. Ayer Collection, The Newberry Library, Chicago

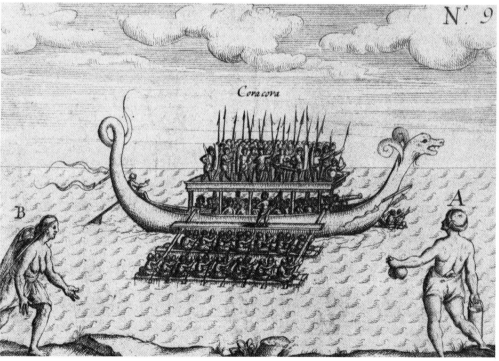

23. East Indian war ships (top) and a Bandanese war ship (bottom). Note the javelins. From Jacob Corneliszoon Van Neck, *Journal ou comptoir, contenant le vray discours et narration historique, du voiage faict par les huict navires d'Amsterdam . . . l'an 1598* (Amsterdam, 1601). Courtesy of the James Ford Bell Library, University of Minnesota

La nef ou prau Royale de Borneo.

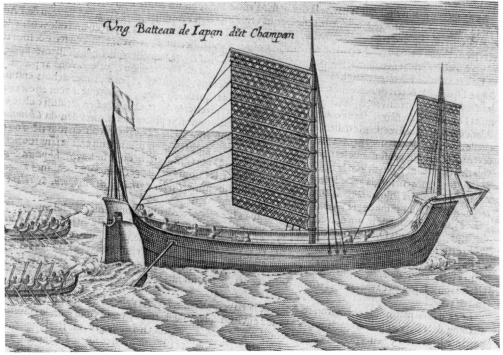

Vng Batteau de Iapan dist Champan

24. Royal ship or prahu of Borneo (top) and a Japanese sampan (bottom). From Olivier van Noort, *Description du pénible voyage faict entour de l'univers ou globe terrestre* (Amsterdam, 1602). Courtesy of the James Ford Bell Library, University of Minnesota

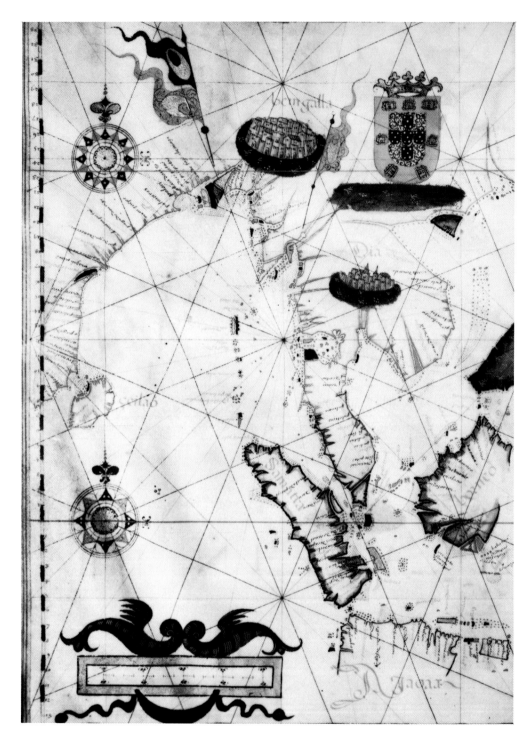

25. Chart of East Asia attributed to
Sebastião Lopez, from a Portuguese
manuscript atlas, ca. 1565. Courtesy of
the Edward E. Ayer Collection, The
Newberry Library, Chicago

26. Torture in China.
From J.-T. de Bry, *Histo-
riarum Orientalis Indiae,*
vol. 12 (Frankfurt, 1598).
Courtesy of the Edward
E. Ayer Collection, The
Newberry Library,
Chicago

27. A Chinese junk. From
J.-T. de Bry, *Historiarum
Orientalis Indiae,* vol. 2
(Frankfurt, 1598). Cour-
tesy of the Edward E.
Ayer Collection, The
Newberry Library, Chicago

28. *Namban* screen showing the arrival of a Portuguese *nao* in Japan. Attributed to Kano Naizen. Early seventeenth century. The black-robed figures are Jesuits; those in lighter robes Franciscans. The Japanese called the Portuguese *namban*—literally, "southern barbarians"—and developed a distinctive genre of painting, lacquerware, and ceramics called *namban* art to depict the first European visitors to Japan. Courtesy of the Kobe City Museum

29. *Namban* portrait of St. Francis Xavier. First half of seventeenth century. Courtesy of the Kobe City Museum

30. St. Francis Xavier. From
João de Lucena, *Historia da vida
do Padre Francisco Xavier*
(Lisbon, 1600). Courtesy of the
James Ford Bell Library, Uni-
versity of Minnesota

THE
VOYAGES
AND
ADVENTURES,
OF
Fernand Mendez Pinto,

A *Portugal* : During his

TRAVELS

for the space of one and twenty years in

The Kingdoms of Ethiopia, China, Tartaria, Cauchin-china, Calaminham, Siam, Pegu, Japan, and a great part of the East-Indiaes.

With a *Relation* and *Description* of most of the Places thereof; their Religion, Laws, Riches, Customs, and Government in time of Peace and War.

Where he five times suffered Shipwrack, was sixteen times sold, and thirteen times made a Slave.

Written Originally by himself in the Portugal Tongue, and Dedicated to the

Majesty of Philip King of Spain.

Done into English by *H. C.* Gent.

LONDON,
Printed by *J. Macock*, for *Henry Cripps*, and *Lodowick Lloyd*, and are to be sold at their shop in *Popes head Alley* neer *Lumbar-street*. 1653.

31. Title page from the first English edition, translated by H. Cogan (London, 1653; facsimile edition, London, 1969).

ined; so much so, that everybody was running about half-crazed with fear, with some throwing themselves flat on the ground, others jumping into trenches, others hiding behind the walls, others in water holes, others in cisterns, and still others diving into the river for fear of the multitude of cannonballs which were so dense that at times they collided with each other, bursting in midair.

At the height of this utterly fierce, horrendous storm that was raging at the time, they set fire to the twenty-five platforms which had been rolled up to the walls in the meantime, and the force of the fire, fanned by the howling winds, touched off the many barrels of tar lying nearby, once more creating such a horrible inferno—and that is the only word that fits, because there is nothing on earth with which it can rightly be compared—that even those on the outside trembled with fear, let alone those who were forced to sustain the full brunt of it; and with that, cruel and bloody fighting broke out everywhere.

The soldiers on the outside tried to force their way up the ladders, but those on the inside, who were no less prepared to meet them, kept them from doing so with such a tremendous show of force that nearly everyone, both inside and out, on several occasions, was on the point of total destruction. Since the soldiers on both sides were frequently reinforced, and the Burmese king was so utterly obstinate that he kept dashing about in person in the midst of his troops, spurring them on with many words and glowing promises of many rewards, fanning the flames of battle to such a degree, that not daring to describe the least part of what happened there, I leave it to the reader to imagine what it was like.

It was more than four hours past midnight when the castles had all burned down to the ground, leaving behind a heap of live coals of such intense heat that even at a stone throw's distance no one could stand it. It was then, at the request of the captains of the foreign troops, that the Burmese king ordered his men to retreat, since most of them were wounded, and there was much to do attending to them all of the following day and part of the night.

188
Rebellion in Pegu

When he saw that neither the artillery barrages launched against the city, nor the attempts to scale the wall with such huge numbers of troops, nor the ingenious platforms used for throwing so many fire missiles—in which he had placed such great confidence—had been effective in achieving the ends on which he had set his heart, the Burmese king, still refusing to desist from this campaign he had undertaken, called a general meeting of all the captains, *bainhás,* princes, and lords in his army and, once he had laid before them his intent and desire, asked them all to give him their opinions on the subject.

After a thorough and heated discussion of the matter, they all finally came to the conclusion that under no circumstances should he abandon the siege, inasmuch as no more honorable and profitable enterprise than this could present itself to him at that time, and since they had already invested so much of their resources in it, the assaults should be continued without pause until the enemy had been completely exhausted, because it was apparent, from what they had learned, that they no longer had strength enough to withstand even the slightest show of force.

Delighted with the consensus of opinion which was exactly what he had been hoping for, the king expressed his deep thanks and again distributed many gifts of cash to them and swore on the spot that if the city were captured he would make them all lords of the kingdom and reward them with very honorable titles along with large revenues and estates.

Once this was resolved, they immediately began to plan their strategy, and on the advice of Diogo Soares and the engineer, it was decided that they should begin construction of a mound of earth, reinforced with fagots, rising higher than the city walls, which would enable them to train all their artillery power against the main strongholds of the city where the sole defenses of the enemy were concentrated, and they quickly set about making the necessary preparations. The sixty thousand sappers in the camp were put to work on this project, and within twelve days they built the mound in a manner that suited the king's purpose.

Just when they had finished placing forty pieces of heavy artillery on it in a trench protected by twelve bastions, the way the Turks do, and were getting ready to batter the city on the following day, a courier arrived, bringing the king letters from the *chauseró*, lord of *Mouchão*, with the news that the *Xemindó*[1] had revolted against him in the kingdom of Pegu, killing 15,000 Burmese and capturing his main strongholds. This news had such a startling effect on the king that, without a moment's delay, he lifted the siege and withdrew to the edge of a river called *Pacarou*, where he stayed just that night and the following morning, long enough to collect the artillery and munitions. After giving orders to set fire to the ramparts and campgrounds, he departed for the city of Martaban on a Tuesday, the fifth of October, in the year 1548.

Covering ground rapidly in daily forced marches, within seventeen days he reached Martaban where he was more fully informed by his captain, the *chalagonim*,[2] about everything that had taken place in the kingdom and the manner in which the *Xemindó* had made himself king and seized the treasury, slaughtering the fifteen thousand Burmese, and also, that he had encamped with fifty thousand men in the cities of Rangoon, Syriam,[3] and Dalla,[4] and as far as Danobyu,[5] for the purpose of preventing him and his men from entering the kingdom.

This report was very disturbing to the Burmese king, and as he cast about in his mind for the method to employ in remedying the misfortune facing him, he tarried there in Martaban a few more days waiting for the rest of the army to catch up with him, intending, as soon as they arrived, to go after this enemy and settle the matter with him on the battlefield. But in just the twelve days that he waited there, 120,000 of the 400,000 men he had with him deserted, for since they were all Peguans and they were all anxious to be free of the yoke of the Burmese, and the *Xemindó*, the new king, was also a Peguan like them and a man of splendid disposition who constantly showered favors on them in addition to their regular pay, and moreover, one who was kind and gentle to his people, and so considerate and openhanded with everyone that never did a petition come before him that was not immediately granted, he had so completely won over the hearts of everyone that there was not a man among them who would not pass over to his side.

The Burmese king, who feared that the number of desertions would increase with each passing day, was advised by his staff not to delay another day since it was obvious that the longer he waited the more depleted his ranks would become because most or practically all of his soldiers were Peguans who were not likely to be very loyal to him.

The king approved of this advice, and he immediately set out for Pegu, where he received word that the *Xemindó* was awaiting him, since he had been informed that the king was coming and had also made ready to face him. As soon as they came in sight of each other they both set up their camps in a very large field called *Machão,* two leagues from the city of Pegu, the *Xemindó* with 600,000 men and the Burmese with 350,000.

Early the following day the two armies deployed their forces according to the strategy that suited them best and engaged each other on a Thursday, the twenty-sixth of November, in the same year of 1548, at six o'clock in the morning. From the moment they clashed, both sides fought so fearlessly that in little more than three hours the *Xemindó*'s army was routed, with the loss of 300,000 of his soldiers, while he himself fled on horseback with six of his men to a fortress called *Batelor,* where it took him only an hour to get hold of a small boat in which he fled that night up the *Ansedá* River.[6]

However, we will let him go on his way now, to return to him in due course, while we turn our attention to the Burmese who was quite contented with the victory he had won. The next morning he marched off to the city of Pegu, two leagues from there, as I said before, which surrendered to him on the condition that the lives and property of its inhabitants would be spared, and there he immediately tended to the wounded.

As for the men who had died on the battlefield fighting for the Burmese king, their number came to sixty thousand, including among them 280 Portuguese, while all the rest of them who survived were badly wounded.

189
The Marvelous Kingdom of Siam

Since I have dealt thus far with the outcome of the king of Burma's expedition to the kingdom of Siam and the uprising in the kingdom of Pegu, I think it would not be amiss at this point to deal, if only briefly, with the geographical location, extent, abundance, wealth, and fertility that I observed in this kingdom of Siam and empire of *Sornau,* and how much more profitable it would have been had we conquered it instead of all the possessions we have in India, and at far less than they have cost us up till now.

This kingdom, as one can see from the map, has nearly seven hundred leagues of coastline and reaches into the interior for 160 leagues. Most of the country consists of lowlands where there are many cultivated fields and freshwater streams which account for the high fertility of the region and the abundance of meat and agricultural products that are found there. The highlands are densely forested with angely-wood from which thousands of all kinds of ships can be built. There are many mines there, of silver, iron, steel, lead, tin, saltpeter, and sulphur. They also have a great deal of silk, eaglewood, benzoin, lacquer, indigo, cotton cloth, rubies, sapphires, ivory, and gold—all available in huge quantities. The coastal jungles produce great quantities of brazilwood and rosewood, which are shipped in more than a hundred junks every year to China, Hainan, the Ryukyus, Cambodia and Champa. They also have large supplies of wax, honey, and sugar. Ordinarily, the royal duties bring an annual revenue to the treasury of twelve million in gold, to say nothing of the feudal dues contributed by the lords, which also add up to a very large amount.

Within the jurisdiction of the king's realms, there are twenty-six hundred communities known as *produm*,[1] which are like cities and towns among us, not including the little villages of which they take no account. The majority of these communities have no fortifications of any kind, except for some wooden palisades, which means that they could easily be taken by anyone that attacked them with a minimal show of force. The inhabitants of these towns, besides being by nature a very weak breed, do not ordinarily possess defensive weapons. The coasts of this kingdom are bathed by both the northern and southern seas, by the Indian Ocean at Junkseylon and Tenasserim, and by the China Sea at *Mompolocota*,[2] *Cuy*,[3] *Lugor*,[4] *Chintabu*, and *Berdio*. The capital of the whole empire is this city of Ayuthia,[5] which I have been discussing thus far, and it is the only one which is surrounded by walls which are made of mud, brick, and adobe. Some people claim that there are 400,000 hearths within its walls and that 100,000 of them belong to foreigners from many different parts of the world. Inasmuch as this country is very rich and carries on an enormous amount of trade with all the provinces and islands of Java, Bali, Madura, Kangean, Borneo, and Solor, not a year goes by without more than a thousand junks setting sail from here, to say nothing of other smaller craft with which the rivers and ports are always crowded.

The king is by no means a tyrant, for it is not in his nature. The income derived from customs throughout the kingdom is set aside for certain pagodas as charity. Consequently, the duties paid here are very low, for since the pagodas are not allowed to accumulate any wealth, the merchants are only asked to pay what they wish, by way of charity, of their own free will. They worship in twelve different heathen sects, as do the Peguans. The king goes by the exalted title of *Prechau Saleu*,[6] which in our language means "the holy limb of God," and he appears in public only twice a year, surrounded on both occasions with a splendid show of majesty, not only of wealth, but of power and grandeur as well. Yet despite all this, he acknowledges the superiority of the emperor of China, to whom he pays tribute in order to have the right to send his junks to the port of *Comhay*,[7] where they carry on trade.

The kingdom also has great quantities of pepper, ginger, cinnamon, camphor, alum, cassia fistula, tamarind, and cardamom, so that I think that what I heard many times before from people in those parts is quite true, which is that this is one of the finest kingdoms in the world[8] and one that is easier to conquer and hold than any other province, no matter how small. Moreover, I can say in all truth that of things that I saw in this city of Ayuthia alone, there is so much more I could say than I have told of the entire kingdom. However, I prefer not to do so, so as to spare my readers the pain I feel when I think about how much we have lost there, for our sins, and how much we could have won.

190
The Burmese Tyrant Assassinated

Now to get back to what I was saying. After winning that tremendous victory against the *Xemindó* as described above, which left him in peaceful control of the entire kingdom, the first thing the Burmese king did was to punish the people responsible for the recent uprising. This involved the beheading of a considerable number of noblemen, captains, and lords and the confiscation of all their property in the name of the crown, an operation that allegedly netted him upwards of ten million in gold and silver alone, to say nothing of all the precious stones and elaborate serving pieces, which is why, as was generally said at the time, that many paid for the sins of just one.

After two and a half months of carrying on these reprisals, striking daily against various people here and there with mounting cruelty and injustice, the king was reliably informed that the city of Martaban was in revolt, that two thousand Burmese had been slain, and that the *chalagonim*, its commander, had declared himself in favor of the *Xemindó*.[1]

However, since many readers may be curious about the events leading up to this rebellion, I think it would be best, before I go any further, to say a few words about this *Xemindó*. He was a native Peguan priest of noble ancestry and, as some affirmed, a close relative of the former king who had been killed twelve years before by this Burmese, as mentioned above. This *Xemindó*, who had previously been known by his proper name of *Xoripamsay*, was forty-five years of age and a man of high principles whom everyone regarded as a saint. He was extremely learned in the canons and precepts of their heathen religion, and in addition to this, he was endowed with many fine qualities that endeared him so to the people who heard him preach that the moment he climbed up to the pulpit they would all prostrate themselves on the ground and at every word he uttered, they would exclaim, "Pitarul axinão davocó quiay ampaleu!" meaning, "Most assuredly it is God who speaks through thee!"

Knowing how much faith the people had in him, he was driven by the force of circumstance and his own inborn courage to try his fortune and see where it would take him. Thus, when the Burmese king marched against the kingdom of Siam and laid siege to the city of Ayuthia as described above, the *Xemindó*, who was preaching at the time to a huge crowd of people gathered in the *varela* of the *Comquiay* of Pegu (which is like a Holy See, higher than all the other temples), spoke to them at great length of the downfall of their kingdom, reminding them about the murder of their lawful king, the enormous outrages, the cruel executions, and many other evils perpetrated against the Peguan nation by the Burmese that were so offensive to God and disrespectful of him, that they had even destroyed and laid waste the beautiful houses of worship that had been built as temples in his praise out of the money donated by good people, while those that had received the best treatment from them were being desecrated, for some were being used as stables and others as garbage dumps and disposal sites for their fifth. And he went on preaching in this vein, telling them so many other things as bad as these, heaving so many sighs, and shedding so many tears which all together made such a deep impression on the people that everyone there, acting as a single body, swore him in, then and there, as their lawful king and named him the *Xemindó*, which is the highest title of all, though he had been known before as *Xoripamsay*.

Once he was king, the first thing he did, with the full support of the people who were swept up in the fervor of the moment, was to storm the Burmese king's palace, which was guarded by five thousand Burmese troops, putting them all to the sword, sparing none. Next, he did the same thing to all the others who were stationed in key positions throughout the kingdom, after which he seized the king's treasure, which was by no means small. Thus, as many Burmese as there were in the kingdom were all slain, and there were fifteen thousand of them, not counting their women. Also, the strongholds that supported them were captured and destroyed, so that within barely twenty-three days the *Xemindó* was in control of the entire kingdom. Then he mustered an army of 500,000 to meet the Burmese king in the battlefield when he returned to quell this uprising, which turned out the way I described above, and since I think that is enough to explain the events I have been discussing, I will return to where I left off.

As I was saying, having been informed of the rebellion and the slaying of his two thousand Burmese troops in the city of Martaban, the Burmese king[2] immediately issued orders to have all the lords of the kingdom hasten to his aid, each with as many men as he was obliged to levy, giving them only fifteen days in which to comply, since the urgency of the situation would not brook any further delay. On the very next day he departed with a small train from the city of Pegu, as an example for his people to do the same, and went to stay at a village called *Moucham*, intending to wait there for the entire fifteen-day period he had allowed them.

About six or seven days after he got there he was informed that the *xemim de Satão*,[3] commanding officer of a city by that name five leagues from there, had secretly sent a large amount of gold to the *Xemindó* and sworn fealty to him in the name of the city. The Burmese king was somewhat troubled by this news, and bethinking himself about how to prevent this rebellion from spreading any further, he sent for the *xemim de Satão*, who was then in the city he commanded, with the intention of having him beheaded. The latter however, took to his bed, feigning illness, and sent word that he would come as soon as he was well enough to leave his bed. As is the case with a guilty man, he suspected why he was being sent for and confided what he had done to ten or twelve of his brothers and relatives who were there with him and who all agreed that the only way to save themselves was to kill the king, and without further delay they went about laying their plans. Operating with the utmost secrecy and haste, they called all their followers together without letting them know why. They also won some other people over to their side on the strength of many promises, so that all together they comprised a company of six hundred strong.

Having learned that the king was staying at a pagoda, they descended upon it in a sudden rush and were so highly favored by fortune that they found him engaged in performing the necessities of nature, where they immediately killed him,[4] with no risk to themselves, and began retreating in a body to an outer courtyard. Here they were met by the soldiers, their treachery having been discovered in the meantime by the guards on duty, who engaged them in a fierce battle that lasted for nearly half an hour and left eight hundred men dead on both sides of the fray, most of them Burmese.

Retreating with about four hundred of his followers, the *xemim de Satão* went marching off to a large town called *Poutel,* where all the people in the surrounding area immediately joined forces with him upon learning about the death of the Burmese king, whom they all hated with a passion. Together they made up a good-sized company of five thousand men who went in search of the three thousand Burmese the king had brought with him but who by this time, crazed with fear, had scattered in many different directions, so that they were all easily killed that same day, barring none. Among them, eighty out of the three hundred Portuguese that Diogo Soares had there with him were also killed, though he, along with the others who escaped alive, agreed to surrender, since they had no other choice, and their lives were spared on condition that they swear to serve the *xemim de Satão* loyally from then on, as they would their own king.

Nine days after this uprising, finding himself so highly favored by fortune, with the support of so many people who had come running to his side from all over the neighboring villages and towns, raising the number of his supporters, it was said, to probably more than 300,000, the rebel had himself declared king, promising to distribute favors to all who would follow him and accompany him until he had won over the entire kingdom and thrown the Burmese out. This done, he withdrew to a fortress called *Tagalá,* intending to fortify himself there, out of fear of the forces that the slain king had been expecting to catch up with him, which, according to the latest reports, had already departed from the city of Pegu.

Among the Burmese soldiers slain by the *xemim de Satão* there was one who by chance had managed to excape, badly wounded though he was, by throwing himself into the river. After swimming over to the other side, he walked all that night and the next without stopping, out of fear of the Peguans. On the third day he reached a field called *Coutasarem,* a little over a league from the city, where he found the king's brother-in-law, the *Chaumigrem,* already encamped with an army of 180,000 men— only thirty thousand of whom were Burmese and the rest Peguan—waiting for the heat of the day to break before departing, which would have been in about two hours, and he informed him of the king's death and everything else that had happened in the meantime. Though he was thoroughly shaken by the news, the *Chaumigrem* disguised his feelings at the time with so much courage and prudence that no one could tell from looking at him that he was the least bit perturbed. Instead, he arrayed himself in a splendid robe of red satin embroidered in gold, with a collar of precious stones around his neck, and sent for all the captains and lords in the army and spoke to them cheerfully as follows.

"The courier you have just seen arriving so breathlessly," he said, "has brought me a letter from the king, my lord and yours, which you see here in my hand. Though he chides me a little for my negligence in tarrying so long, I trust in God that very soon I will be able to account to him for it and that His Highness will be grateful to all of us for the service we have rendered him in this respect. He also informs me that he has received a confirmed report to the effect that the *Xemindó* has been reorganizing his army with the intention of marching on *Cosmim* and Dalla and capturing the entire countryside from Danobyu to Henzada all along the river of Rangoon and *Meydó.*[5] That is why he commands me to act quickly and to take immediate steps to provide these very important towns with sufficient strength to resist the enemy and to see to it that nothing is lost through negligence on my part, for he will not accept any kind of excuse from me.

"Therefore, I think it best and absolutely necessary if we are to serve him well, that you, my Lord *Xemim Brum,* with all your soldiers, depart immediately for Dalla without a moment's delay, your brother-in-law, the *Bainhá Quem,* for Rangoon, with his fifteen thousand men, Captain *Gibray* and the *Mompocasser* with thirty thousand for Henzada and Danobyu, the *Ciguamcão* for the area from *Xará* to *Malacou* with twenty thousand men, and that the *Quiay Brazagarão,* with his brothers, brothers-in-law, and other relatives, go as general of the frontier, so that he can personally lead his fifty thousand men to the areas in the greatest need. As proof of the orders and instructions I have given you on his behalf, a document should be drawn up and signed by all of us because I do not want my head to be the only one to roll on account of inadvertence or negligence on your part."

These captains all obeyed him immediately, and without any further delay they all departed for their assigned destinations. And thanks to this very clever trick[6] which he carried off so well, he got rid of all of the 150,000 Peguans in little more than three hours, for he feared that once they learned about the king's death they would turn upon the thirty thousand Burmese he had there with him, and he knew all too well that they would not spare the life of a single one of them.

When night fell he returned to the city which was a little over a league from there and hastily gathered up all the treasure of the slain king which, it was said, came to more than thirty million in gold, to say nothing of the priceless gems, as well as all the women and children of the Burmese and all the arms and munitions he could carry. He had everything else that remained in the storehouses set afire, and had the lighter pieces of artillery destroyed by exploding them, and since the same could not be done with the heavier pieces, he had them all rendered useless by jamming them. Then he killed the entire brute force of the seven thousand elephants that were in the country, sparing only two thousand of them on which he loaded all his baggage, munitions, and treasure. Everything else was consumed by fire to such a degree that nothing but ashes was left of either the gilded palaces or the riverside warehouses and docks where there were two thousand oared ships careened on shore.

This done, he departed in great haste at an hour before dawn and continued on his way to Toungoo, his native land, 160 leagues into the interior, which he had left fourteen years before to conquer this kingdom of Pegu, and since fear usually gives wings to one's feet, it caused them to march so fast that they reached their destination within fifteen days.

Two days after the events I have just described, the 150,000 Peguans found out about the death of the Burmese king. Since they were mortal enemies of this nation, they organized an army of 120,000 and returned at top speed to look for the thirty thousand Burmese, but by the time they reached the city they were three days gone. Following in hot pursuit they reached a town called *Guinacoutel,* forty leagues ahead, where they discovered that the Burmese had passed through only five days before. Realizing that it would be impossible for them to fulfill their desire, which was to cut them to pieces, they turned back to whence they had come.

Gathering in council to decide what to do with themselves, they agreed, in view of the fact that their country was now rid of the Burmese and that they had no legitimate king, that they should throw their support to the *xemim de Satão.* This they did at once, and he received them with a great deal of joy and elation and promised them all sorts of favors, honors, and opportunities for advancement in the kingdom as soon as peace was restored, after which, he departed for the city of Pegu where he was received in triumph by the inhabitants as king and crowned in the *varela* of *Comquiay,* which is like a Holy See, higher than all the others.

191
The Abominable Crime of Diogo Soares

After he had been king for three months and nine days, reigning in peace in this city and kingdom of Pegu, with nothing to fear and without opposition from any quarter, this tyrant *xemim de Satão* began distributing and granting undeserved favors to anyone he felt like, at the expense of the crown. This gave rise to tremendous scandals which provoked wide rifts and quarrels among many of the lords who, because of the prevailing situation and the tyrant's lack of justice, betook themselves to various other lands and foreign kingdoms. Others threw their support to the *Xemindó,* who by this time was beginning to acquire a small measure of fame, for after he had fled from the past battle with the other six horsemen, as I mentioned before, he went to the kingdom of Henzada, where he gathered a considerable following, due to the effectiveness of his sermons and his personal prestige. With the help and support of these lords who had joined forces with him, he brought together an army of sixty thousand and marched with them to *Meidó,* where the local population welcomed him with open arms.

As for all else that he did in this country in the four months he remained there, I will put that aside for the moment to return to it in due time, and go on to tell of a strange incident that occurred in this city during those few days, so that people may know what came of the prosperity of the great Diogo Soares, onetime governor of this kingdom of Pegu, and the reward that the world usually reserves in the end for all those who serve and trust in it, no matter how kindly it smiles on them in the beginning. This is the way it happened.

Back in the days of the former Burmese king, when Diogo Soares was at the height of his power and glory, honored with the title of "the king's brother," and the highest position in the government, ranking far above all the princes and lords in the kingdom, there was a rich and well-known merchant in this city by the name of *Mambogoá,* who undertook to arrange a marriage between a daughter of his and the young son of another honorable merchant called *Manica Mandarin,* who was also very rich. After the fathers of the bride and groom had agreed on the marriage portion they would both provide for their children which, it was said, amounted to 300,000 *cruzados,* the day appointed for the marriage vows arrived. It was an elaborate affair, to which a large number of the local nobility had been invited, and it was celebrated with a great deal of merrymaking and a magnificent display of pomp and splendor, surrounded by all the trappings of wealth and honor.

That same day, close to sundown, Diogo Soares happened to be returning from the king's palace, accompanied as always by a large group of people both on foot and horseback. As he passed the residence of *Mambogoá,* the father of the bride, he heard the joyful sounds of music and merrymaking coming from the house. He inquired what the occasion was and was told that *Mambogoá* was marrying off his daughter. He then brought the elephant he was riding to a halt and sent someone in to congratulate him and to express the wish that God would grant the bride and groom a long and happy life together, with other fine words to that effect, and he also placed himself at their disposition in any way that he could be of service to them. This was so flattering to the old man, the father of the bride, who considered himself so highly honored by it that he did not know what to do to show his gratitude, in view of the fact that the dignity and exalted position of the person bestowing the honor on him was almost as great as that of the king himself. Anxious to reciprocate in part for something that he could not repay in full, he led his daughter, accompanied by many noblewomen, out to the street door where Diogo Soares was waiting. After prostrating himself before him in an obeisance of very deep respect, he thanked him, in their fashion, for the great honor and favor he had shown him. Then obeying her father's instructions, the young girl removed a very valuable ring from her finger and offered it to him as she knelt on the ground. But Diogo Soares, who was by nature an extremely lustful and sensuous man, instead of behaving with the decorum due her in the name of friendship and nobility, reached out, took the ring and then grabbed hold of her roughly, saying, "God forbid that anyone but me should possess so fair a maid as you!"

Shocked to see his daughter handled so roughly and insulted in such a shameless manner, the poor old father raised his hands, and, on his knees, cried out, with tears in his eyes.

"I beg you, my lord," he pleaded with him, "out of respect for the great God you adore, who was conceived in the womb of the Virgin, without the blemish of sin, as I confess and believe, according to what I have heard and been told about him—do not take my daughter away from me, for I shall die of a broken heart. If you want the dowry I have given her, together with everything else that I have in the house, and me as your slave besides, it is yours for the taking, as long as you let my daughter be the wife of her husband, for I no longer have any other loved ones in this world but her, nor do I want any other, as long as I live!" And with these words he grasped his daughter.

Seeing the poor man all bathed in tears holding on to his daughter, Diogo Soares said not a word to him in reply, but shouted to his captain of the guards, who was a Turk, "Kill him! Kill that dog!"

As the Turk rushed at him with upraised sword, the poor old man fled, leaving his daughter all disheveled, in the clutches of Diogo Soares. And because the tearful young groom also took hold of her, they killed him instantly, along with his father and six or seven other members of his family. By this time, the screams coming from the women inside the house were such that it was terrifying, and the earth below and the air above trembled, or better still, clamored aloud to God at this utterly senseless and outrageous insult, committed without the slightest fear of his divine punishment.

And may I be forgiven for not telling in full all the details of this ugly incident, but I must do so for the honor of the Portuguese name. Suffice it to say that the young girl strangled herself with a sash she was wearing before the lustful Galician could possess her. And afterwards he was heard to say more than once that he had regretted not having possessed her more than he repented of having kidnapped her.

For four whole years following this incident, the girl's father was never seen to set foot out of the house, but to show his grief he dressed in a piece of tattered matting and begged for food from his own slaves, with his face touching the ground. He carried on this way all the while, crying constantly, biding his time and waiting for the right moment to demand justice, which he did in the following manner.

When he saw that there was by then another king, other governors, and another kind of justice in the land—which are changes constantly wrought by time on all things, in all places—he left his house, dressed in the same sorry clothes he always wore, with a thick cord tied round his neck and a long white beard that by this time reached almost down to his waist, and went directly to a temple called *Quiay Fintareu*, "god of affliction," that was located in the middle of a large plaza. Removing the idol from its place on the altar, he walked out into the street with the idol in his arms, and there, after making his kowtows to it with all the customary ceremonies, in the heathen fashion, he shouted three times at the top of his voice to make sure that he would be heard by the crowd in the plaza.

"Hear ye! Hear, all ye good people who with pure and tranquil hearts profess the faith of this god of affliction you see here in my arms!" he cried through his tears. "Come forth like flashes of lightning on a rainy night and raise a hue and cry so loud that it will pierce the heavens, so that the merciful ear of the almighty Lord will be inclined to hear our lamentations and know thereby the right we have to ask that justice be done to this accursed foreigner—would he had never been born!—who has usurped our birthright and dishonored our generations. And whosoever does not join with me before this god I hold in my arms, in weeping and lamenting such an abominable crime, may the Ravenous Serpent of the Lower Depths of the House of Smoke consume his days and tear his flesh to pieces in the middle of the night!"

At these words a tremor of fear ran through the crowd and made such a deep impression on them that in less than a quarter of an hour more than fifty thousand people had joined him, all of them filled with frenzy, clamoring for vengeance and carrying on in a way that seemed as if they had gone mad. With the crowds growing bigger and bigger, they surged forward, heading straight for the king's palace, their voices reverberating so loudly through the streets that it made the flesh creep with fear. When they reached the courtyard of the royal palace they clamored loudly six or seven times, "Come out, O King! Come out from where thou art and hear the voice of thy God speaking through the mouths of these poor people who are here to demand justice of thee!"

In response to their shouts and cries, the king appeared at a window. Amazed by the unusual sight he asked them what they wanted.

"Justice!" they cried in one voice, with shouts so loud that seemed to be rending the heavens apart. "Justice upon a cursed infidel who, to rob us of our goods, has murdered our fathers, sons, brothers, and kinsmen!"

When he asked who it was, they replied, "A cursed thief, as treacherous in his deeds as the cursed serpent that struck down the first man created by God in the meadow of delight!"

Upon hearing these words the king covered his ears as though recoiling in horror. "Is it possible that anything like that exists out there?" he asked them.

"There is only one like that who resembles the serpent more than all others born on earth, due to his evil nature and wicked inclinations," they all replied, "and that is why we ask of thee, in the name of the god of affliction, that his veins be as empty of blood as hell is full of his wicked deeds!"

Turning to those who were at his side, the king asked, "What do you think I should do in such a strange and extraordinary situation?"

"My lord," they all replied, "if thou hast any doubts about what this god of affliction asks of thee, then he too will have doubts about sustaining thee in the dignity of thy high office."

So the king turned back to the tumultuous crowd below in the courtyard and told them to go to the plaza of the bazaar where he would have their man delivered to them, to do with him what they had asked of him. With that, he immediately sent the *chircá*,[1] their highest-ranking justice officer, to arrest Diogo Soares in his name and hand him over in chains to the people to punish him as they saw fit, for he very much feared that, if he failed to do so, God would punish him.

192
Stoned by the Mob

The *chircá* of police went directly to Diogo Soares's house and told him that the king had sent for him. When he saw him he was so terror-stricken and so beside himself that he was unable to speak for some time, as though he had completely lost his wits. However, once the initial shock had passed and he regained control of himself, he begged to be excused from going with him for the time being because he had a terrible headache, and that he would give him forty gold *biças* for his trouble.

"What you offer is very little to convince me to take upon myself a headache as big as the one you say you have," he replied. "But since you leave me no choice I must speak bluntly. Believe me, whether you like it or not, you are going with me."

When Diogo Soares saw that there was no way he could get out of going with him, he wanted to take six or seven of his attendants with him, but the *chircá* would not allow that either.

"I am only doing as the king commands me," he said, "and it is his wish that you alone come and not seven others, for those days are over when you used to go about so well accompanied, the way I have often seen you. And they were over the day the Burmese tyrant died, for it was he who filled you with such great arrogance, as is apparent from your ugly deeds, of which you stand accused today before God."

Taking him by the hand he led him away, keeping him close beside him all the while, surrounded by a company of more than three hundred guards, while we all looked on in amazement. With them escorting him in this manner street after street, they reached the *passeyvão* of the bazaar, which is the main city square where all their goods are marketed, and there it happened that they came face to face with his son, Baltasar Soares, who was on his way back from a merchant's house where his father had sent him that morning to collect some money they owed him. Upon seeing his father being led away like that, he quickly dismounted from his horse and threw himself at his feet.

"What is the meaning of this, sir?" he asked, in tears. "Why are they leading you away in this manner?"

"Let my sins answer for me," he replied. "They will tell you more than I can, for I assure you, my son, that in my present state, it all seems like a dream to me."

Then they embraced and remained that way for a long time, crying on each other's shoulders until the *chircá* ordered Baltasar Soares to get out of the way. However, he did not do so, for he could not bear to tear himself away from his father. But the guards removed him by force, and in doing so they pushed him so hard that they smashed his head, and on top of that they beat him so badly that his father's head began to swim and he fell to the ground in a faint. When he asked for some water, it was refused, upon which he exclaimed, once he had regained consciousness, raising his arms heavenward and shedding many tears, *"Si iniquitates observaveris Domine, Domine quis sustinebit*?[1] But trusting, my eternal God, in the infinite price of thy precious blood which thou didst shed upon the Cross for me, I shall be able to take heart and declare most boldly, *Misericordias Domini in aeternum cantabo!"*[2]

Then with a heavy heart, when he came in sight of a pagoda where the king had ordered him to be brought and saw so many people gathered there, he was utterly dismayed. After standing there motionless for a little while, he turned to a Portuguese who had been allowed to accompany him—in order to give him moral support and strengthen him in his faith—and exclaimed, "Jesus! Have all these people accused me before the king?"

To which the *chircá* replied, "This is no time to think about that, for you are a clever man and you know what the people are like when they get out of control. They always follow the course of evil, to which they are naturally inclined."

"I see it all clearly, and I understand all too well," Diogo Soares replied in tears, "that this disorder arises from my sins."

"Then you know," the *chircá* retorted, "that these are the wages of sin that the world reserves for people like you who lived all their lives without any fear of divine justice. May God grant you grace in the little time left to you to repent of what you have done and perhaps that will be worth more to you than all the gold you leave behind you now as an inheritance for the one who, perhaps, is the cause of your death."

At this point Diogo Soares dropped to his knees, and looking heavenward he prayed, with the tears coursing down his cheeks, "Lord Jesus Christ, by all the pains of thy sacred Passion, I beseech thee my God, for thy name's sake, to accept the accusations of these 100,000 hungry dogs in fulfillment of thy divine punishment, so that all that thou hast suffered for the salvation of my soul, unworthy as I am, shall not have been in vain."

As he mounted the stairs leading up to the terrace, he kissed the ground at every step he climbed and uttered the name of Jesus three times, as the Portuguese who was with him assured me, and the moment he reached the top, *Mambogoá,* who was holding the idol in his arms, began to incite the mob, shouting at the top of his voice, "Whosoever shall not, for the honor of the god of affliction whom I hold here in my arms, throw stones at this accursed serpent, may the brains of his children be consumed in the middle of the night, with a great outcry, so that the righteous justice of the Lord on high may be visited upon them as punishment for such a great sin!"

After these words such a heavy shower of stones rained upon the condemned Diogo Soares that, in less time than it takes to recite the Credo, he lay buried under an infinite number of rocks and stones which had been thrown so wildly that many of the people who had thrown them were injured themselves.

About an hour later they removed poor Diogo Soares from under the stones, with another tumultuous uproar of shouts and screams. They tore him to many pieces, which the young boys dragged along the streets, with the head and entrails, collecting alms from all the people, as though it were a very pious and holy deed.

Then the king gave the order to sack his house, unleashing those hungry dogs who were so frenzied with greed that they did not even spare the tiles on the roof. Since they did not find as much as he was presumed to have, they tortured all his slaves and servants in such an exceedingly cruel manner that thirty-eight of them were left dead, including seven Portuguese who suffered innocently for something about which they knew nothing.

Among all this plunder they found only six hundred gold *biças,* which is equivalent to 300,000 *cruzados,* and nothing else, except for some rich ornaments and furniture, but no precious stones, as a result of which it was said that Diogo Soares had buried it all by then, though no trace could ever be found of it, in spite of all the searches that were carried out. However, according to what I learned later, from what was said by men who had seen it in his possession several times when he was at the height of his prosperity, it is affirmed that, at the prices current there in that country, the collection was worth more than three million in gold.

And thus ended the life[3] of the great Diogo Soares, whom fortune had raised to such great heights in the kingdom of Pegu that he attained the title of "brother of the king," which is regarded there as the highest and most exalted style of all, with an income of 200,000 *cruzados,* and had become commander-in-chief of an army of 800,000 men and supreme governor over all the others in the fourteen kingdoms ruled by the king of Burma in those days. But such is the nature of worldly possessions, especially those that are ill-gotten, for they always lead to misfortune.

193
The *Xemindó* Proclaimed King of Pegu

And now to return to the *Xemindó,* about whom nothing has been said for quite some time.

As time went by, the reign of the greedy, despotic *xemim de Satão* became increasingly marked by acts of cruelty and tyranny which he inflicted on all sectors of the population, and each passing day saw fresh murders and robberies perpetrated against any and all he suspected of having money or anything else he could lay his hands on. Things got so bad that it was said that, in just the seven months that he remained in peaceful possession of the Peguan kingdom, he had killed six thousand people among the monied and merchant classes, to say nothing of the members of the ancient nobility who possessed the wealth of the crown in the form of entailed estates.

Consequently, he was already so much disliked by all the people that most of his followers deserted him and joined forces with the *Xemindó,* who by this time had won over to his side the cities of Rangoon, *Meidó,* and *Coulão,* up to the borders of *Xará,* from where he set out with an army of 200,000 men and five thousand elephants to lay siege to this tyrant. When he came in view of the city of Pegu where the tyrant was then residing with his entire court, he surrounded it on all sides with very strong ramparts and earthworks and assaulted it several times but was unable to enter it as easily as he had thought he would, because of the stiff resistance he encountered from those inside.

As a result, being a prudent man, he made a twenty-day truce with the tyrant on certain conditions, one of which was that if, within this twenty-day period, he would give him the sum of one thousand gold *biças*—which is equal to 500,000 *cruzados*—he would renounce his claim and all his rights to the kingdom; and all this, as I say, was done in a cunning manner, for he felt that he could get him to surrender this way at less risk to himself.

When the truce went into effect and all was quiet on both sides, those inside the city entered into a mystical form of communication with those on the outside. Every morning, during this period of calm, at about two hours before dawn, the sound of sweet music, played by many instruments in their fashion, would be heard coming from the *Xemindô*'s camp. Attracted by the music, all the people in the city would come running to the top of the walls to see what was going on. Then those on the outside would stop playing, and one of their priests, who was revered by all as a saintly man, would be heard proclaiming in a very sad and mournful voice, "Hear ye! O hear all ye good people whom Nature has endowed with ears to listen! Harken to the voice of this saintly captain *Xemindô,* a mirror of clarity, through whom God wills that you be restored to the peace and freedom you once knew. In the name of *Quiay Nivandel,* god of the *Vitau* battlefield, he charges and commands each one of you, just as you are, not to raise a hand against him nor against this holy assembly, for he is a zealous guardian of the people of Pegu and blood brother to the poorest of the poor among you. And whosoever goes against this army of the servants of God or allows any harm to befall them shall be damned for it and made ugly and black like the children of the night, who howl in vicious rage, foaming poisonously at the mouth, swallowed up in the fiery jaws of the Dragon of Discord, who was perpetually cursed by the true God of Gods! As for the blessed ones who obey this proclamation in the spirit of holy brotherhood, they shall be granted perpetual peace and prosperity in this life, and after death, their souls shall be as pure and pleasing to God as those of the saints that passed on, dancing over the sunbeams to their eternal rest in the almighty Lord."

Following this proclamation the music resumed, but this time it was so frightfully loud that it struck fear into the hearts of the listeners and made such a deep impression on them that in just the seven nights that it went on, more than sixty thousand people passed over to the *Xemindô*'s camp, all of them drawn to him by a deep conviction that what they heard was true, as though it had been spoken by an angel sent from heaven.

But when the besieged tyrant king saw that these proclamations were so damaging to him that they might destroy him completely, he broke the truce on the twelfth day. He sought the advice of his council on how to proceed in this matter, and they told him that under no circumstances should he allow the siege to continue, for, judging by the way the people were already rebelling against him, in less than ten days they would probably all desert him, and that therefore, in their opinion, the wisest course of action would be to engage the *Xemindô* on the battlefield before he became even more powerful.

Having decided to follow their advice, he immediately went about making his preparations, and two days later, in the predawn hours, he sallied forth from the city, passing through five gates with an army of eighty thousand men still loyal to him. Screaming and yelling, they rushed with great fury at the enemy who, by no means unprepared, came forward to meet them bravely. An extremely cruel battle ensued, fought by all with such eagerness that, in little more than an hour and a half, which was as long as the full force of the fighting lasted, more than forty thousand men lay dead on both sides. At the end of that time, the new king, the *xemim de Satão,* was brought down from the elephant he was riding by an arquebus shot fired by a Portuguese named Gonzalo Neto, a native of Setúbal.

As a result, all the rest of his army surrendered, and the city was handed over on condition that all life and property would be spared. The *Xemindó* immediately entered the city and was crowned king of Pegu[1] that same day in the great *varela,* on a Saturday, the twenty-third of February, in the year 1551.

And for his part in the battle, Gonzalo Neto was rewarded with twenty *biças* in gold, which is equal to ten thousand *cruzados,* whereas the rest of the eighty Portuguese received five thousand *cruzados.* In addition, he showered them with honors and allowed them many privileges in the land, exempting them from paying customs duties on their goods for a period of three years, and he adhered to it later on with the utmost integrity.

194
The Burmese Recapture Pegu

After he had been crowned king and had entered into peaceful possession of the entire kingdom of Pegu, the *Xemindó* began to entertain ideas that were different from those held by the *xemim de Satão* when he had found himself in the same position, for first and uppermost in the mind of this *Xemindó* was the preservation of the republic, with peace and justice for all. He bent all his efforts to that end, ruling with such great integrity and tranquility that none of the grandees dared to look askance at the members of the lower classes, not even the humblest among them. As for everything else related to the government of the kingdom, he maintained such high standards of truth and virtue that the foreigners who were there at the time were absolutely amazed to see what was going on, for all things considered, the peace, tranquility, and conformity at all levels of the population was indeed cause for amazement.

This happy state of affairs in the kingdom continued for a period of three and a half years until such time as the *Chaumigrem,* brother-in-law of the Burmese king who had been slain by the *xemim de Satão* as mentioned previously—having been informed that as a result of the uprisings and wars that had taken place in Pegu after his coming to power, the principal lords of the kingdom had been slain and that the present ruler, the *Xemindó,* was sorely lacking in everything necessary for its defense—decided to embark once more on the same campaign as before, which had been lost owing to the death of his king.

For that purpose he gathered a huge army of foreign mercenaries from many different nations who were hired at a salary of one *tical*[1] of gold per month, which is the equivalent of five *cruzados* in our money. On the ninth of March in the year 1552, he set out from Toungoo, his native land, with an army of 300,000 men that included only 50,000 Burmese, and all the rest were Mons, *Chaleus, Calaminhas, Savadis, Pamcrùs,* and Avans, so that the majority of all these people were from these six nations who inhabit, off to the east and east-northeast, for more than five hundred leagues, the interior of these kingdoms, as can be seen from a map, provided the scale is correctly drawn.

Once it had been confirmed that this force was marching against him, the new king of Pegu, the *Xemindó,* prepared to go out to meet it with the intention of engaging it in battle, and with that end in view he set up a huge camp of 900,000 men in this city where he was then residing. However, they were all Peguans, who were weakhearted by nature and more unsuited for warfare than all the other people I have mentioned thus far.

On a Tuesday at noon, on the fourth day of April, when he received word that the enemy was encamped along the *Meleitay* River twelve leagues from there, he made such great haste that overnight all the soldiers were in battle position, for since their captains had been preparing and training them for quite some time, very little was required to mobilize them.

On the following day at nine o'clock, this force set out, and marching at a not-too-hurried pace, to the beat of an infinite number of martial instruments, pitched camp that night two leagues away, along the banks of the *Pontareu* River, which was as far as he wanted to go. On the following afternoon, at an hour before sunset, the Burmese *Chaumigrem* appeared in full view with an army so huge that it spread out for nearly a league and a half, comprised of 70,000 cavalrymen, 230,000 infantrymen, and 6,000 war elephants, to say nothing of an almost equal number for the baggage and provisions. Since by then it was close to nightfall, he pitched his camp along the mountain so as to be in a more secure position.

That night went by with great vigilance and the deafening noise of shouts and screams on both sides. At dawn of the following day, which was a Saturday, in the seventh day of the month of April, in the year 1552, at five o'clock in the morning, these two armies approached each other along the river with entirely different objectives—that of the Burmese, to ford the river and take up a position at an elevation on the opposite bank, and that of the *Xemindó* to prevent him from doing so—and their cross-purposes resulted in a few skirmishes that took their toll on both sides, though not more than five hundred died. This struggle took up the better part of that entire day. Nevertheless, the *Chaumigrem* gained the ground he sought, and there he remained for the rest of the night with a heavy guard posted and his camp brightly lit by many fires.

The following morning at daybreak, the *Xemindó,* king of the Peguans, offered battle to the opposing side and was not refused. Rushing at each other with the fury that cruel hatred engenders, the two front lines containing the principal leaders of both armies fought so mercilessly that in little more than half an hour the entire battlefield was strewn with corpses, at which point the Peguans began to show signs of weakening. Then the *Xemindó,* observing that his men were badly wounded and, as a result, losing a great deal of ground, reinforced their ranks by bringing up a corps of three thousand elephants, which fell upon the seventy thousand cavalrymen so fearlessly that the Burmese were forced to relinquish all the ground they had gained. But then the *Chaumigrem,* like someone with greater experience in warfare, perceiving which way he could win, pretended that he was retreating, as though he were beaten, a ruse which the *Xemindó* did not see through. Instead, eager for victory, he spurred his men on and pursued him for a distance of nearly half of a quarter of a league. However, the Burmese suddenly veered about with all his men and fell upon him with tremendous force and such bloodcurdling screams that not only made the men tremble, but the earth and all the other elements as well. With that, the battle flared up again and raged so fiercely that in a very short time the air was filled with fire and the ground was flooded with blood. When the Peguan captains and lords saw their king so deep in the thick of the battle and, by then, showing signs of defeat, they broke ranks in order to go to his rescue. Then the *Panousaray,* brother of the Burmese, did the same, rushing in with forty thousand men and two thousand elephants, and at this encounter, the bloody battle raged on so fiercely that, in truth, there are no words to describe it. Therefore, all I will say is that with just half an hour of daylight left, the Peguan camp of 900,000 men was completely routed with a toll in lives, according to what was said there, of 400,000 and all the rest, or most of them, badly wounded. As for the *Xemindó,* heeding the advice of his men, he disappeared from among them.

Finding himself in control of the field, the *Chaumigrem* had himself crowned king of Pegu in the short period of daylight still left, with the same royal insignia of rapier, crown, and scepter that had once belonged to the Burmese king who was assassinated by the *xemim de Satão.* And since it was almost dark by then, all they did was attend to the wounded and post lookouts for the night.

195
Permission to Sack Pegu Denied

At first light the next day, all the victorious soldiers, both the wounded and the nonwounded, were busy despoiling the corpses of their valuables, which made many of them quite rich, since they came away with great quantities of jewelry in gold and precious stones, for it is a common practice among these heathens, as I think I have said before, to carry all their possessions with them when they go off to war. Once the soldiers had been satisfied in this respect, the new monarch of this wretched kingdom left the scene of his victory and set out for the city of Pegu, a little over three leagues from there. Since he did not want to enter the city that same day— for several reasons that will soon be explained—he pitched his camp within view of the city, a little over half a league away in a field called *Sunday Patir,* and there, once he had encamped, he saw to the posting of guards at the twenty-four city gates, stationing a Burmese captain with five hundred cavalry at each one of them.

He remained there for five days, hesitating to enter the city out of fear of the sack the foreign mercenaries were demanding, in keeping with an agreement he had made with them in Toungoo. Since it is ordinarily the custom of hired soldiers who live by their wages to show little regard for anything but their own interests, when it became apparent to the six foreign nations that the king was delaying his entry into the city, which they could ill abide, three of them began to mutiny, at the instigation of a Portuguese from Braganza, who was always in their company, an arrogant fellow, though a fine, brave captain, by the name of Cristóvão Sarmento.[1] This mutiny grew so out of hand that for his own protection the Burmese king was forced to withdraw to the safety of a large pagoda compound where he fortified himself with all his Burmese troops and remained on the alert until nine o'clock the following morning when a truce brought some respite to the rioting, during which the king revealed his intentions, speaking to them from on top of the wall, in a loud voice for all to hear.

"My most valiant captains and friends! Despite the fact that you have violated the oath of obedience you swore to me in Toungoo, I have summoned you to meet me here at this sacred burial ground so that, under solemn oath, I may declare my intentions to you, and here, on my knees, with my hands raised up to heaven, I call upon *Quiay Nivandel,* god of the *Vitau* battlefield, to be my witness, beseeching him to be the judge in this matter. And may he strike me dumb if I do not tell you the truth. I remember very well the promise I made to you in Toungoo in regard to the sack of this troubled city, a promise I made not only because I thought of your strength as the means of my vengeance, but also to satisfy your greed, to which I know that by nature you are very much inclined. Because of that promise, which I pledged you on my honor, I confess that I am duty-bound to keep my word. However, when I consider all the difficulties it presents, and that I shall have to give a strict account of it before that stern and righteous Judge who sits on high, I confess that I am very much afraid of assuming such a heavy burden. Therefore, for the same reason, I would rather be at fault in the eyes of men than incur the hatred of God, for it is unjust to make the innocent pay for the guilty who, I am satisfied, have already paid with their lives, thanks to all of you, in the recent battle. That is why I beg you, as I would my own flesh and blood sons, to respect my good intentions. Do not kindle the fire that will cause my soul to burn, for you can see how just what I am asking of you is, and how unjust it will be for you to refuse me. Nevertheless, in order to compensate you for any losses you have suffered, I will make up for it in part by giving you whatever you think is reasonable, from my own property, person, kingdom, and estate."

In view of the king's explanation and the promises he made, the leaders of the three rebellious nations all gave in and agreed to do as he wished. Nevertheless, they asked him to be mindful of the soldier's expectations, for it was necessary for him to respect their wishes. The king told them that they were right and that in all respects he would abide by whatever they thought best. So as to avoid any further disagreements, they resolved to submit the matter to a court of arbitration which was to be made up of three judges chosen by the rebels and three others chosen by the king, making a total of six. However, one of the conditions laid down was that three out of the six were to be priests and the other three foreigners, so that, in this way, their decision would be above suspicion.

Once they had all agreed on this, they selected as the religious members of the court three *menigrepos* from a pagoda called *Quiay Hifarom,* the "god of poverty." As for the other three who were to be chosen from among the foreigners, it was decided that the king and the rebels should draw lots to determine which of them would choose one or two of the judges on his side. And it was God's will that it fell to the king to choose the two, so that he—by divine permission—chose two Portuguese, both of them from among the 180 then residing in the city, one of whom was Gonzalo Pacheco, a very conscientious nobleman who was acting as agent in charge of all lacquer shipments for His Majesty, and the other, an honorable merchant by the name of Nuno Fernandes Teixeira, who was highly respected by this king who knew him from the days of the former king. Then the rebel leaders chose another foreigner, whose identity I did not learn.

Once the judges had been selected in this manner, they were immediately called to begin their deliberations because the king was afraid to leave before the matter was settled, so that he could thus send them all peacefully on their way before entering the city himself, for he feared that if they should ever gain entry to the city they would not keep their word. That was why, that very same day at midnight, the king sent a Burmese messenger on horseback to the foreign quarter of the city where the Portuguese resided, all of whom at that time were just as apprehensive as the Peguans were of the sack and loss of life that threatened them all. When he reached the city, the Burmese went about enquiring in a loud voice—since that is the custom when they are on a mission for the king—where he could find the captain of the Portuguese, and the people led him to his house without knowing what it was all about. When he was face to face with him, the Burmese delivered his message.

"It is as natural for the almighty Lord who created the firmament of all the heavens above," he said, "to create good men to undo the wrong done by evil men, as it is natural for the archenemy dragon to stir the spirit of reckless rebellion in their hearts so as to disturb the peace that keeps us in the way of the Lord. One of your countrymen, an evil man, has sent a spark flying from his devilish heart into the furnace of accursed discord, spreading the flames of rebellion in the camp of the king, my lord, among three foreign nations, the *Chalões, Meleitais,* and *Savadis.* It grew out of the malice and greed of both the instigator and the rebels, and the evil they caused became so uncontrollable that it resulted in the near destruction of the entire camp and the death of three thousand Burmese. And the royal personage was placed in such a dangerous and difficult position that he was forced to withdraw to a fortress where he stayed for three days. Even now, he is still there, for he does not dare to trust any of the foreign mercenaries. To control this unrest, it pleased God, who is the Father of holy peace, to fill the king's heart with the patience to suffer this evil like a prudent man, in order to pacify these three tumultuous and rebellious nations who inhabit the desolate regions of the mountains of Mons—may they be accursed by God among all the nations!

"In the interest of peace and tranquillity, an agreement was reached between the king and the rebel leaders and sworn to on both sides, that in exchange for delivering the city from the sack he had promised the soldiers, the king would pay from his personal funds a certain sum of money to be determined by a panel of six judges chosen for that purpose, four of whom have already been selected. Only two more are needed to complete the panel—you and another Portuguese the king has chosen to act on his behalf, whose name is in this letter which will confirm what I am saying."

And with that he placed in his hand a letter from the Burmese king, which Gonzalo Pacheco received on bended knee and then placed on top of his head in a ceremonious display of such great courtesy that the Burmese was deeply impressed.

"The king, my lord, knew quite well what he was doing," he said, "when he chose you to sit in judgement on his honor and estate."

Gonzalo Pacheco then read the letter aloud before all the Portuguese present there, who heard it standing with their hats in their hands, the contents of which went like this:

"To my dear friend, Captain Gonzalo Pacheco, alike to a pink-hued pearl in my eyes, as virtuous in the tranquil life you lead as the saintliest *menigrepo* in the forest: I, the former *Chaumigrem,* now king of the fourteen states of the land which, upon the death of my lord, the saintly king, God has delivered unto me, do send you the smile of my mouth, thereby making you as dear to me as those I seat at my table on festive occasions. I have decided, based on what I have heard about you, that you should be a judge in this case, to which I summon you and my good friend, Nuno Fernandes Teixeira, a man of pure gold of the highest quality; whereby it behooves you both to join me here immediately in order to settle this matter that I have entrusted to you, above all others. As for your personal safety, about which I know you must be concerned in view of the recent revolt, by means of this letter I give you my word, sworn to on my honor as king anointed by God, that I shall grant safe conduct to you both, as well as to all the others of your nation who believe in the God of your faith."

When he had finished reading the letter, to the amazement of those of us who heard it, we all agreed that it had come from heaven, by the divine will of God, to ensure the safety and tranquillity of our lives, about which, up until that moment, we had entertained grave doubts. Gonzalo Pacheco and Nuno Fernandes, along with ten other Portuguese who were selected for that purpose, immediately arranged to buy a gift of many rich objects of art to present to the king, and that same night, at an hour before dawn, they departed in the company of the Burmese who had brought the letter, because time and the king's urgency would brook no delay.

196
The *Chaumigrem*'s Triumphant Entry into Pegu

Gonzalo Pacheco, Nuno Fernandes, and the other Portuguese in their party reached the campgrounds an hour after sunrise, where the king had arranged for them to be met by the *Gibraidão Sedá,* lord of *Meidó,* one of the most important and most highly trusted of the Burmese captains he had there with him, who arrived with an escort of over a hundred horsemen and six macebearers and took them to the pagoda where the king was staying. He welcomed them all most cordially, particularly Gonzalo Pacheco and Nuno Fernandes, who were singled out for special honors.

After chatting with them on some topics of particular interest to him, he went on to review the important case for which he had summoned them. He instructed them to lean more in favor of the captains than himself for, as he assured them, that would give him the greatest pleasure, and he said other things to that effect. From there he had the same Burmese take them to a tent where the other four judges were already waiting for them along with the treasurer-in-chief and two scribes.

After commanding the noisy crowd outside to be silent, they fell to deliberating the matter for which they had assembled, in the course of which various opinions were expressed. This took up most of the day, but finally, all six of the judges reached the conclusion that although, on the one hand, the king was duty-bound to keep his word to allow the foreign mercenaries to sack the places captured in battle because of the promise he had made to them in Toungoo, on the other hand, honoring that promise would cause untold hardship and suffering to innocent people, thereby offending God. In view of which, they decided that the king, because of his promise, should pay them all one thousand *biças* from his treasury, to the satisfaction of the captains of each nation, and that as soon as they received the money they should cross over to the other side of the river and return freely to their lands. But first, they had to be given everything that was due them before the rebellion, as well as sufficient food to last them for twenty days.

When this decision was announced, it was accepted by both sides with great satisfaction, and the king issued orders for it to be carried out immediately. Moreover, as further proof of his generosity, after disbursing this huge sum of money, he distributed many other extra bonuses to all the captains and line officers, which added to the general feeling of satisfaction. In that way, these three rebellious foreign nations were discharged, for the king would not ever again trust them or make use of their services. Furthermore, he also issued orders that they should not all depart at once, but that they should be divided into units of a thousand men each, so that they might travel through the countryside without spreading fear and without sufficient strength to plunder the towns through which they passed, and that was the way they departed the following day.

As for Gonzalo Pacheco and Nuno Fernandes Teixeira, for acting as his two judges in this dispute, the king awarded them ten *biças* in gold, which more than compensated them for the gratuities and the gift they had brought him. Moreover, he granted permission, in his own handwriting, for all the Portuguese to depart freely for India as often as they liked without having to pay any customs duties on their goods, which they appreciated more than any amount of money they might have received, because for the last three years all the former kings had detained us against our will, subjecting us to many annoyances and acts of tyranny, occasionally at great risk to our lives, as in the case of the events I have just described.

Late that same afternoon, many proclamations were read by mounted criers, informing everyone that the next day the king would be entering the city in peace—as an act of great mercy, accorded them out of the nobility of his heart, at tremendous personal expense—along with threats of the cruellest form of death for those who were opposed. At nine o'clock the following morning he departed from the pagoda where he had been staying, and at ten he reached the city, passing through a gate called *Sabambainhá,* where he was welcomed by a delegation, in the form of a procession, of five thousand priests from all of the twelve different sects in the kingdom. One of them, called *cabisondo,*[1] made him a speech, which began this way:

"Blessed and praised be the Lord on high, who must needs be acknowledged by all as the true Lord and whose holy deeds, wrought by his divine hands, are manifested in the light of day and the painted sky of night, and in all the other wondrous works he has so mercifully performed for us, he who in his omnipotence has been pleased to designate thee king over all others who govern on earth! Since we hold thee to be the chosen one of God, we beseech thee, my lord, henceforth to dwell no more on the sins and errors of the past, but to console these unhappy subjects of thine, out of the nobility of thy heart, with a promise to that effect."

And all of the five thousand priests, who were also kneeling on the ground, with their arms upraised, implored him to do the same, raising their voices in a frightful tumult, as they intoned this plea: "Our lord and king, grant peace and pardon to all the peoples of this Peguan kingdom of thine, so that they will not live in fear of their sins, which they publicly confess before thee."

The king replied that he would do so gladly, and he swore to it by the head of the holy *Quiay Nivandel,* god of the *Vitau* battlefield. And with that promise, all the people prostrated themselves face down on the ground and recited this prayer: "May God grant thee prosperity, for days without number, in victory over thy enemies, so that thou mayest place thy feet on their heads."

As the band struck up and the joyful sounds of music were heard, played in their fashion by numerous instruments, albeit extremely barbarous and discordant in tone, this *grepo* placed upon his head a rich crown,[2] like a mitre, fashioned of gold and precious stones. Wearing this crown, he made his entry into the city with an enormous show of pomp, displaying triumphantly before him all the spoils of battle, the elephants and carts, the statue of the vanquished *Xemindó,* bound with a heavy iron chain, and forty banners trailing in the dust, while he himself rode on top of a powerful elephant in trappings of gold, accompanied by forty macebearers and all the lords and captains on foot, with their swords richly decorated in gold resting on their shoulders, and a guard of six thousand caparisoned horses and three thousand war elephants with their castles ingeniously decorated in different styles, to say nothing of countless numbers of others who followed on foot and horseback.

197
The *Xemindó* Captured and Condemned

After this Burmese king had been in the city of Pegu for twenty-six peaceful days, he turned his attention first of all to gaining control of the principal strongholds in the kingdom, which at this time were still holding out for the *Xemindó,* without knowing of his defeat. Dispatching a few captains for that purpose, he wrote many endearing letters to the people, addressing them here and there as "my beloved children," pardoning them for bygones and promising on his solemn oath that he would thenceforth provide for the general welfare in peace and tranquillity and always do them justice in all things without ever imposing any tribute or any other burden on them, but that, on the contrary, in all things he would treat them as well as he would his own Burmese troops who were serving him in the war. In addition, he said many other things best suited to the circumstances and to his own personal interests, which were supported by the inhabitants of the city, describing at great length the generous treatment and favors everyone had received from the king. All of this, combined with what rumor had already spread to all corners, was so effective that the forces all surrendered and swore obedience to him. The same thing happened in all the other towns, cities, states, and provinces of the kingdom. In my opinion, this newly reconquered territory over which the Burmese had just regained control is the finest, the most bountiful, and the richest in gold, silver, and precious stones that one can find in a great part of the world.

Once these matters had been so favorably resolved for the Burmese, he then quickly dispatched large numbers of men on horseback in all directions to look for the *Xemindó* who, as it was said, had been wounded when he escaped from the recent battle. He was unlucky enough to be recognized in a town called *Fancleu,* just one league from the city of *Potem,* which borders with the kingdom of Arakan. He was brought back to the Burmese king with a great deal of excitement by a man of base condition[1] who was rewarded for his efforts by being made a lord with an income of thirty thousand *cruzados* a year. He had him brought before him immediately just as he was, in the chains that bound him, with an iron collar around his neck and his wrists in handcuffs.

"Welcome, king of Pegu!" he greeted him scornfully. "Well mayest thou kiss this ground, for I assure thee, I have already set my feet on it, and from this thou canst see how good a friend I am to thee for according thee so high an honor which thou didst never dream thou wouldst have."

The *Xemindó* said not a word in reply. Once again the king taunted the poor *Xemindó,* who lay prostrate on the ground before him.

"How now?" he said to him. "Art thou so overcome at seeing me or at seeing thyself so highly honored? How is it that thou makest no reply to what I ask thee?"

To this the *Xemindó,* either because he was so offended, or because he could no longer control himself, replied, "If the clouds in heaven, the sun, and the moon, and all the other creatures incapable of speech, created by God for the benefit of man as a beautiful painting on the firmament hiding from us the rich treasure of his power, had been granted the power by nature to declare, in the terrible sound of their frightful thunder, to those who see me now before thee in this manner the deep affliction I feel in my soul, they would answer for me and explain the reasons I have for remaining silent here in this place to which my sins have brought me. And since, as both accuser and willing executioner, thou canst not be the judge of what I say, I see no need to reply, as I would before that gentle Lord above who, no matter how deep my guilt, would be moved to pity by a single tear I shed."

With that he collapsed face down on the ground, calling out twice for a little water which the Burmese king, to hurt him more, had brought to him by one of the daughters of the *Xemindó* himself, whom he was holding captive, a girl, it was said, dearly beloved by her father, who in the days of his decline had already arranged for her to be married to the prince of *Nautir,* son of the king of Ava. Seeing her father lying that way with his face down on the ground, they say the girl threw herself at his feet, and after she had kissed him on the cheek three times, she cradled him in her arms.

"O my dear father, my lord, my king," she cried, her face bathed in tears. "I beg thee, by the deep love I have always borne thee, and thou for me, take me with thee in thy arms this way, so that in this bitter pass thou mayest have someone to console thee with a cup of water, since the world, because of my sins, has denied thee the respect it owes thee."

Her father made several attempts to reply, but they say the effort was too much for him, so overcome was he by his deep love for her which choked off all speech. Again he fell face down on the ground where he had been sitting at the time, and where he remained unconscious for a long while. Some of the lords who were present were so moved to compassion that they could not hold back the tears that rose to their eyes. Observing this and the fact that these lords were Peguans who were former vassals of the *Xemindó,* the Burmese king, doubting their loyalty to him, ordered their heads cut off on the spot.

"As long as you feel such deep compassion for that *Xemindó* king of yours," he exclaimed in anger, "you can precede him to the grave and prepare his resting place for him, and there he will repay you for the love you bear him!"

Unable to control his rage, he also ordered the girl killed right there on top of her father, because he saw her embracing him, manifesting cruelty of a sort worse than brutal and worse than savage, that seeks to thwart the feelings of nature. And also, because he could no longer bear the sight of the *Xemindó,* he had him taken from there to a narrow prison cell where he spent that night under heavy guard.

198
The Execution of the *Xemindó*

The following morning at daybreak urgent proclamations were delivered throughout the city commanding all the people to be present at the execution of the unfortunate *Xemindó,* former king of Pegu. The reason the Burmese did this was so that once they saw him dead they would give up all hope of ever having him for their king again, a desire generally shared by all and foretold for the future. Since he was their native countryman, and the Burmese a foreigner, they very much feared that this Burmese might eventually turn out to be like the previous one, slain by the *xemim de Satão,* who throughout his entire reign had been most inimical to this Peguan nation, treating them with such extraordinary cruelty that there was never a day that he did not have five hundred or more people killed and beheaded and, at times, as many as four or five thousand, for the most insignificant offenses which would have been dismissed without penalty in a true court of justice.

Shortly before ten o'clock or thereabouts, the poor *Xemindó* was taken from his dungeon and led out in the following manner: Heading the procession, to clear the streets through which he was to pass, came forty horsemen brandishing their lances, followed by an equal number with naked swords in their hands, shouting out loud for the people who were there in countless numbers to make way. Directly behind them came a company of armed men who, according to the estimate of some bystanders, probably numbered more than fifteen hundred, all carrying arquebuses with lighted wicks. These *tixe lacauhos,* as they were called—meaning "those who prepare the way for the wrath of the king"—were followed by 160 armed elephants with their castles covered by silken awnings which, lumbering by five abreast, made a total of thirty-two rows. Behind them, keeping in the same order of five abreast, came fifteen horsemen, carrying bloodstained black banners and shouting aloud as though delivering a proclamation.

"Hear ye! Hear all ye wretched people held in the thrall of hunger and constantly beset by the afflictions of fortune!" they cried. "Harken to the powerful roar of the arm of wrath executed upon those who have offended their king, so that the fear of the penalty it carries with it will remain fixed in their memory!"

Behind them in the same manner came another group of fifteen, dressed in a certain kind of scarlet clothing that made them look quite ugly and frightful. At the sound of five rapid strokes coming simultaneously from three bells, they would recite the following words, chanting them aloud in such sad tones that they made the listeners cry: "This righteous sentence has been decreed by the living god, lord of truth, for whose holy body the hairs on our heads are the feet. It is his command that the *Xeri Xemindó* die for having usurped the states of the great Burmese king, lord of Toungoo!"

To this proclamation the huge crowd of people marching in front of them responded with such a loud roar of voices that it made one shake with fear as they bellowed the words, "Faxio turque panau acontamidó!"—which means, "Let him die, let there be no pity for one who has committed such a crime!"

Following on their heels came a company of five hundred Burmese on horseback. Behind them all came another company on foot carrying naked swords and shields, some of them wearing corselets and skirts of mail. In their midst came the condemned man mounted bareback on a sorry-looking nag, with the executioner behind him on the horse's rump, supporting him under the arms. The wretched victim was so poorly dressed that the flesh all over his body was exposed, and as a sign of the utmost contempt for his person, he was wearing a crown of straw on his head that looked like a urinal cover, decorated all around on the outside with mussel shells strung on blue threads. Around his neck, on top of the iron collar that held him captive, hung a great number of strings of onions. But even though he was dressed in this manner and his face was deathly pale, there still was a look in his eyes, which he raised from time to time, that showed that here was a king, in every sense of the word, with so dignified an expression of tenderness on his face that it made everyone cry. Around this company of guards surrounding him there was another made up of more than a thousand horse, interspersed with many armed elephants.

In this manner he passed along the twelve main thoroughfares of the city lined with infinite numbers of people until he finally reached a street called *Sabambainhá,* which was the one through which he had sallied forth—as I mentioned above—only twenty-eight days before, when he went to meet this Burmese on the battlefield. At that time the *Xemindó's* exit from the city had been accompanied by such magnificent pomp and splendor that, judging from what all the eyewitnesses had to say—and I was one of them—it must have been one of the most remarkable of its kind ever seen anywhere before, though I deliberately avoided any mention of it, either out of fear that I would not be able to do it justice or that, if I recounted it, it might raise some doubts about the truth of what I am saying.

However, since I saw both these events with my own eyes, and even though I concealed the grandeur of the first, I chose to describe the wretchedness of the second, so as to make people realize, from the tremendous changes that took place in so short a time, how little importance can be attached to earthly prosperity and to all the good things that false and fickle Fortune has to offer.

Continuing on his way along *Sabambainhá* Street, the poor condemned man reached a certain spot where our Captain Gonzalo Pacheco was standing with more than a hundred Portuguese in his company, among them an individual of low birth and of even much lower intelligence who, it seems from what he said, had been robbed two years before during the reign of the condemned man, and when he had lodged a complaint with him against the parties guilty of the theft, he had not been given the hearing he desired. This man now, still resentful about it, thought he could avenge himself by letting loose some words that were both foolish and unnecessary, for as soon as the condemned man reached the spot where Gonzalo Pacheco was standing with all the other Portuguese he shouted out loud for all to hear, "You thieving *Xemindó!* Do you remember when I went to you to complain about the men who stole my goods and I never got any justice out of you? Well, now you will get what's coming to you for your deeds, for this very day I shall dine on a piece of your flesh and invite my two dogs to join me!"

Upon hearing this madman's words, the poor condemned man raised his eyes to heaven, and after a brief moment of thoughtful silence he turned to him with a stern expression on his face and said, "I beg you, my friend, by the kindness of the God you believe in, to pardon me for what you say I did to you. Bear in mind that it is not a Christian thing to do, to remind me of what I did in the past at such a difficult moment as this, especially when it cannot restore to you the losses you claim to have suffered and can only cause me deep pain and distress."

When Gonzalo Pacheco heard what this man said, he shouted to him to shut his mouth, which he promptly did, and the *Xemindó,* with a grave expression on his face, gave him to understand that he was grateful for it. After this he appeared to be much calmer, and apparently out of a desire to thank him for it with words as well, since he could not then do so with anything else, he said to him, "All that I could wish for now, if it would please God, is one hour of life in which to confess to the excellence of the faith in which you men believe, for according to what I have heard on more than one occasion, yours is the only true God, and all the others false."

Upon hearing these words, the executioner dealt him such a severe blow that the blood spurted from his nose and the poor condemned man quickly cupped his hands over his face.

"Let me not waste this blood, my brother," he said to him as he lay face down, "so that you will have enough in which to cook my flesh."

Continuing on his way in the same order as before, he reached the execution grounds, but by this time he was so moribund that he was barely conscious of what was going on around him. After he had climbed the steps of a huge scaffold that had been erected there, the *chircá* of justice read the sentence to him in a very loud voice from the top of a pulpitlike structure. It consisted of very few words that went like this:

"The living god who reigns over our heads, lord of the crown of the kings of Ava, commands that the false *Xemindó* die for having instigated the peoples of the land to rebel, and for being a mortal enemy of the Burmese nation."

At this point, bringing his arms down sharply, the executioner cut off his head in one swift stroke. After holding it aloft for the huge crowds of people to see, he cut his body up into eight parts, separating the viscera and other organs from it, which were placed elsewhere. After covering everything with a yellow cloth, which is the color of mourning among them, they left him that way until close to sundown when they cremated him in the manner I shall presently describe.

199
Funeral Rites for the *Xemindó*

The eight quarters of the dismembered body of the *Xemindó* were left on display until three o'clock in the afternoon, in full view of the huge crowds of people that had assembled there, not only on account of the threat of punishment that hung over them but also because their priests had granted them *aixiparão,* which is a form of plenary indulgence, without the need to make restitution of any kind for robberies committed.

By then, the tumult and the shouting of the people having died, in compliance with the proclamations of men on horseback threatening them with heavy penalties, a bell was heard to toll five times, each time with fifteen strokes. At this signal, a dozen hooded men dressed in bloodstained black robes, all with their silver maces on their shoulders, issued forth from a wooden building that was five or six paces from the scaffold. Behind them came another twelve priests called *talagrepos* who, as I have said several times, are the highest dignitaries in their heathen faith and revered by the people as holy men. After them came the *Xemim Pocasser,*[1] the uncle of the king of Burma, a man who, judging by his face, was more than a hundred years old. He too was covered with symbols of mourning and was surrounded by twelve richly attired little children with gold-plated swords on their shoulders. With great ceremoniousness he prostrated himself three times on the ground by way of deep reverence and began to speak, his voice choked with tears, as though he were addressing the deceased.

"O thou holy flesh, more precious than all the kings of Ava!" he exclaimed. "O thou pure white pearl, of as many degrees of perfection as the motes one sees in the rays of the sun, thou who hast been most highly honored by God with the scepter of command over the mighty armies of kings! I, the lowliest ant in thy larder, feasting on the forgotten crumbs of thy munificence, a creature so lowly compared to thee and one so minute that I can hardly be discerned—I beseech thee, o master of my head, by the cool meadows where thy soul now dwells in delight, lend me thy suffering ears and harken to what I have to say to thee in public, so that thou mayest receive due satisfaction for the wrong that has been done thee on earth.

"Thy brother, the *Oretanau Chaumigrem,* prince of *Savady* and Toungoo, commands me, thy slave, to ask thee, before thou departest from this life, to forgive him for the past, if ever he caused thee pain, and at this very moment, he asks thee to take possession of the entire kingdom and all that is in it, without any reservations. And he protests through me, his vassal, that he renounces everything in thy favor so that any charges thou mayest present against him in heaven will not be heard before God. Furthermore, as a punishment for all the displeasure he has caused thee, he will assume the burden of remaining here in this earthly exile as captain and guardian of this thy kingdom of Pegu, swearing allegiance to thee and promising under oath that here on earth he will always obey all the commands that thou sendest him from heaven, on condition that, out of charity, for his own sustenance, thou grant him the revenue thereof, for he is well aware of the fact that he cannot otherwise possess it legally, nor would the *menigrepos* consent to it, nor would he receive absolution at the hour of death for so great a sin."

One of the priests there, who appeared to have greater authority than all the others, responded to this, as though he were speaking in the name of the deceased:

"My son," he said, "now that thou hast confessed to thy past errors, for which thou hast asked me to pardon thee before this public gathering, I can say that I forgive thee with all my heart, and it gives me great pleasure to hand this kingdom over to thee as pastor of my flock as long as thou dost not violate the oath thou hast sworn to me, which would be as grave a sin as if thou wert now to lay a hand on me without permission from heaven."

Then all the people responded joyfully with a deafening roar of approval, "Miday cutarão, dapanó dapanó!"—meaning, "My Lord, my Lord, grant that it be so!"

Following this, the same priest climbed up to the *agrém,* or the pulpit, and addressed the crowd:

"Make me a gift of a portion of your tears for my soul to imbibe, in exchange for the good news I bring you at this moment. For it is now, by the will of God that our king, the *Chaumigrem,* remains on earth, without having to make restitution of any kind to anyone, for which you should all rejoice, like good, loyal vassals."

At this, the entire throng of people gathered there demonstrated their joy by clapping their hands in gratitude and responding with a deafening clamor, "Exirau opatu!"—"Praised be the Lord!"

Having completed this part of the ceremony, the priests then gathered up all the pieces of the dismembered body of the deceased king, and while the fervor of the crowd was still at its height, they reverently carried them down to the courtyard below where a funeral pyre had been prepared of sandalwood, eaglewood, and benzoin—apparently at great cost—and placed his remains on it, including the viscera and all the other organs that had been removed from his body. Then three priests set fire to it while they engaged in a strange ceremony in which they offered up many sacrifices to him, consisting mainly of slaughtered sheep.

The body burned all that night and well into the following morning, and his ashes were placed in a silver coffer which was carried in a solemn procession of over ten thousand priests to a temple called *Quiay Lacasá,* "god of a thousand gods," where he was laid to rest in a gilded recess, like a chapel, all richly adorned.

And that was the end of this great, powerful *Xemindó,* king of Pegu, as venerated in the two and a half years[2] of his reign as I believe no other monarch ever was. But that is the way of the world.

200
The Second Voyage to Japan

The death of the good king of Siam and the adultery of his wife, the evil queen, which I described above at great length, were both the root and the beginning of all the dissensions and cruel wars that took place in the two kingdoms of Pegu and Siam, which lasted for three and a half years at such great cost in life and property as can be seen from what I have related thus far, paving the way in the end for the *Chaumigrem*, king of Burma, to become absolute lord of the kingdom of Pegu. However, I will not deal with him any longer. Instead, I will go on from here to describe the events that took place elsewhere, up until the time that this same *Chaumigrem* invaded the kingdom of Siam again [1] with the largest army that had ever been gathered in India by any other king—consisting of 1,700,000 men and sixteen thousand elephants, nine thousand for baggage and seven thousand for battle. This undertaking, as I was later told, cost us the lives of 280 Portuguese, among them two Dominican friars who were preaching there at the time.

But now, I want to get back to the main purpose of my story from which I strayed quite some time ago. After the disturbances described above had all been quelled, Gonzalo Pacheco departed from this city of Pegu along with all the rest of us Portuguese who were there, whom this new Burmese king had freed in the manner described above, issuing orders to have their goods freely restored to them, and granting them many other favors in the way of both honors and privileges. All 160 of us Portuguese embarked on five *naos* that were then in the part of *Cosmim*, one of the most important cities in that kingdom. On those ships we spread out, like the wanderers we are in India, in all different directions, wherever each of us thought it would profit him most.

I, along with twenty-six of my companions, went to Malacca, where, after we arrived, I remained for only a month and reembarked for Japan with one Jorge Alvares,[2] a native of Freixo de Espada à Cinta,[3] who was going there on a trading voyage, on board a *nao* owned by Simão de Melo, the captain of the fortress. After sailing on our course for twenty-six days under a strong, favorable monsoon, we sighted an island called Tanegashima,[4] nine leagues below the southernmost point of the land of Japan. We set a heading for it, and on the following day we dropped anchor in the middle of the bay that serves as the harbor for the city of *Guanxiró*. There, the prince of the island, *Nautaquim*,[5] out of curiosity and a desire to see something new that he had never seen there before, immediately came alongside. Amazed by the magnificence of the *nao* and her rigging, since it was the first one ever to arrive there, he showed how delighted he was that we had come and urged us several times to remain there and trade with him. However, Jorge Alvares and the merchants refused, because it was not a safe harbor for the *nao* in the event of a storm.

We departed the following day, bound for the kingdom of Bungo,[6] a hundred leagues to the north. It pleased our Lord that on the fifth day of our voyage we dropped anchor in the harbor of the city of *Fucheo*[7] where we were well received by the king and the local inhabitants who showed us much favor and generosity, especially with regard to the customs duties they charged on our merchandise. And there would have been yet much more if, for our sins, he had not been killed[8] in the short time we were there by one of his vassals—a man by the name of *Fucarandono*, himself a powerful prince and lord of many vassals, large revenues, and great estate. It was a disastrous affair that happened like this:

At the time we arrived there was a young man living in the king of Bungo's court by the name of *Axirandono*, who was the nephew of the king of Arima. Because of some grievances he had against his uncle, the king, he had come to this court more than a year before and had already made up his mind never to return to his native city.

But it was his good fortune that the king, his uncle, happened to die in the meantime, and since there was no one in the kingdom to succeed him, he had named him his heir. This *Fucarandono* whom I have just mentioned, realizing that it would be most advantageous for him to marry the prince to a daughter of his, asked the king, as a favor, to act as his intermediary in arranging the marriage, to which the king readily agreed. With that in view, the king invited the prince one day to join him on an outing to a forest two leagues from there where there were good hunting and other amusements of which they say the king was very fond. He took him along with him, and there he broached the subject of the marriage to him, letting him know that it would make him very happy if he did not refuse. The prince accepted gladly and the king was extremely pleased. On the following day he called *Fucarandono* to the city and told him what he had done with regard to the marriage of his daughter to the king of Arima, which made it necessary for him to call on him at once to thank him and to treat him from then on as a favorite son in order to win him over to his side, for both he and his daughter had much to gain thereby. He also gave him his word as a king that he himself had often wished that he could have him for a son-in-law.

Fucarandono threw himself at the king's feet, kissed them, and thanked him in a manner befitting the obligation he had incurred towards him for his part in the great honor and favor he had received from God. From there, happy and excited, he went straight home to inform his wife, children, and relatives, who were all delighted by the news and congratulated each other by exchanging gifts, as is customary among them in betrothals as honorable as this. The bride's mother, who derived the greatest pleasure of all from this, happily went to fetch her daughter from a chamber where she was engaged in needlework with a group of young noblewomen in her service. She took her by the hand and led her back to the room where her father was waiting with the entire family gathering of brothers, sisters, uncles, aunts, and other relatives. Everyone congratulated her for such an honorable match and addressed her as "Your Highness," as though she were already queen of the kingdom of Arima. In this manner that happy day went by in celebrations, banquets, and visits from ladies during which many expensive gifts were received.

But since the good or bad in affairs of this nature depends not so much on the way they begin but rather on the way they end, the joyful and auspicious beginnings of this betrothal were followed later by events of such profound evil and misfortune that they eventually came to be almost equal to those I described earlier in Siam. I say this because I can affirm it in all truth, having witnessed both these events with my own eyes, and my presence on both occasions placed me in great jeopardy.

That entire day was spent receiving callers from among the nobility of the kingdom, and in the midst of this general feeling of contentment, the only unhappy person was the bride herself, who was madly in love with a certain young gentleman, the son of a nobleman called *Groge Arum*, which is like baron among us, but far different in his person, estate, and worth from *Fucarandono*, the father of the bride. Therefore, compelled by her love for him, as soon as night fell she sent him a message by the go-between she always used in these affairs of hers, telling him by all means to come at once and take her away from her father's house before she did something foolish to herself.

The young man, who was no less in love with her, came to meet her at their usual trysting place, where she pleaded with him so urgently that he was forced to carry her off from her father's house at once and place her in a convent where an aunt of his was the abbess and where she stayed for nine days without anyone knowing what had become of her.

Early the next day, when the girl's governess did not find her in the same room where she had left her the night before, she went to the mother's room, thinking that since it was a holiday she would be there getting all dressed up in her finery or something to that effect. But when she did not find her there either, she went back to the girl's bedroom. Only then did she notice that a window facing on a garden was open and there was a rope made of knotted strips of a sheet hanging from the railing, and one of the girl's sandals down below on the ground. Suspecting what had happened, she became panic-stricken and, without a moment's delay, ran to inform the girl's mother, who all this time had been lying in bed. Startled by the news, she rose quickly and began a thorough search of all the women's quarters where she thought she might be, but when she could not find her, they say she was so terrified that she suddenly collapsed and fell to the floor, suffering a stroke from which she later died.

Hearing all the screams and commotion among the women, *Fucarandono,* who up until then still had no idea of what had happened, quickly ran to see what was going on. When he learned that his daughter had run away from home, he immediately sent word to some of his relatives who, amazed by this sad, unexpected news, came running to his side. A family council was held, and it was decided that they should act with the geatest possible severity. They began at once with the women, and out of the one hundred female members of the household not a single one was spared, for all of them were beheaded, though the highest ranking among them, who were accused of complicity in the girl's escape, were drawn and quartered.

They began speculating among themselves about where the girl could be, and they all thought it best at this point not to take any further action without first letting the king know what had happened. They did so at once and urged him to authorize a search of certain houses they indicated to him. The king refused, not only on the grounds that the owners would be highly offended, but also out of fear of the disorders that might follow upon such intrusions.

Vexed by the king's refusal to do what he had asked of him, *Fucarandono* went back home with his kinsmen, and there they decided to take matters into their own hands and do whatever they thought necessary for their honor, for it was only the weak and helpless who demanded that justice do for them what they were incapable of doing for themselves.

Since the Japanese are much more zealous about their honor than any other nation in the world, *Fucarandono* decided to go all the way in carrying out his intentions, without stopping to think of the consequences. With that in mind, he sent for all his kinsmen who resided at the court. That night, when they had all gathered together with him, he informed them of his decision, which they all thought was proper and gave their approval. Without any further ado they descended upon the houses of those suspected of harboring the girl, but by this time they too were fully prepared, having sent for their followers in fear of such an eventuality. As a result, the rioting and misfortune that ensued was such that in just the few remaining hours of the night, over twelve thousand people were killed on both sides of the fray.

On the heels of this uprising, the king himself finally came running in person with his guard to see if he could restore order, but by then the fighting had become so intense and their reaction to him was such that, after defying his authority several times, they turned all their fury against him and they killed so many of his men that he was finally forced to withdraw to his castle with the very few that remained. But by then even that was of no avail because they followed him all the way and finally killed him and all the others there who, it was said, numbered over fifteen thousand persons, including twenty-six Portuguese out of the forty that were with him.

And still not content with this enormous outrage and all the evil they had committed, these ministers of Satan also broke into the queen's apartments where she was lying sick in bed at the time, killing her and three of her daughters along with more than five hundred other women. Driven on by their fury and madness, they set fire to the city in six or seven places which, aided by the winds that were blowing hard at the time, spread so rapidly that in less than two hours most of it was completely destroyed. The seventeen of us Portuguese who escaped managed to get back on board the *nao* with a great deal of difficulty, miraculously saving our lives by weighing anchor and running out to sea.

When morning came, all the rebels who, at this time, still must have numbered more than ten thousand, after sacking the entire city, divided up into two battalions and withdrew to a steep hill called *Canafama,* where they dug in, with the intention of choosing a new king to govern them because by then, *Fucarandono,* as a result of a lance wound in the throat, had died, along with all the rest of his kinsmen who had started this infernal uprising.

201
The Prince Avenges His Father's Death

That same day, everything that had happened was reported to the prince, the king's son, who was then staying at his fortress of Usuki,[1] seven leagues from the city of *Fucheo*. He was quite shocked by the news, and after lamenting the death of his father, he wanted to leave for the city at once, accompanied by just a few close friends who were then with him. However, his tutor, *Fingeindono,*[2] would not hear of it and pointed to the many reasons that existed for not doing so until they could find out what the situation was like in the city at the time, for most likely, whoever had decided to kill his father would not hesitate to kill him too, since he still had the power to do so, whereas he had no way of defending himself at that moment. Instead, he urged him not to lose any time gathering as large a force as possible, which would enable him to subdue and punish his enemies.

The prince approved of his advice, and after attending to the most urgent matters at hand, he issued orders to blow his conch horn, in the Japanese *chara*[3] manner, along with all the others they had there, which roused the entire countryside and created so much excitement among the people that words are inadequate to describe it. In order for this to be better understood, some explanation is required.

According to a law or ancient custom in this kingdom of Japan, every inhabitant, no matter where he resides, from the noblest to the humblest, is required to keep a conch shell in his house, which he is forbidden to blow, at the risk of heavy penalties, except in one out of four emergencies caused by fights, fire, robbers, or treason. And just from the manner in which the horn is blown they can tell to which situation it applies, for it is one blast for fights, two for fire, three for robbers, and four blasts in the event of treason.

The moment the first horn is sounded, everyone within hearing range is obliged to blow his own horn, on pain of death, in exactly the same manner, so as to avoid the possibility of confusing the message it carries. Since the signal for treason is not heard as often as the other three, which they are accustomed to hearing frequently, when, perchance, it does sound, the people become so alarmed that, without a moment's delay, they all drop what they are doing and come running to the place where the first horn was blown. In this manner the news spreads so rapidly that, within an hour, more than twenty villages in the area respond to the call.

To return to what I was saying—as soon as the prince had taken care of things in this manner, demonstrating great courage and the qualities of a good captain, he withdrew to a monastery in the middle of the forest where he remained shut up for three days to mourn once more the death of his father, mother, and sisters, shedding many tears and grieving deeply for them. At the end of that time, since a large number of people had already gathered there, he came out of his retreat in order to make the necessary arrangements for the security of his kingdom and the punishment of the guilty, whose estates he immediately had confiscated and their houses destroyed, to the accompaniment of the most frightful proclamations that sent shivers down one's spine, just to hear them.

Seven days after this unfortunate event had taken place, the prince was advised—in view of the fact that many people had already gathered and that there was a shortage of food in the area—to proceed with his plans before the ten thousand people involved in the rebellion scattered in all different directions. He departed for the fort of Usuki, heading for the city with a huge camp of well-armed, fine-looking soldiers, whose numbers were estimated at 130,000—with seventeen thousand of them mounted, and the rest on foot—and all of them capable of distinguishing themselves in battle.

Upon his arrival in the city he was welcomed by all the people, though with signs of deep sadness and grief over the death of his father. He chose not to go directly to the royal palace, but instead, on his way, just as he was, he stopped at the pagoda where his father was buried, and there he celebrated his funeral rites which were conducted with solemn pomp and pageantry in their manner, at great cost, and lasted for two nights in a row, lit up by an infinite number of lanterns. When it was all over he was shown the clothing his father had been wearing when he was slain, still soaked with blood. He swore an oath over it not to forgive any of the guilty parties, even if they were to be ordained bonzes a thousand times over, and to burn down all the temples where they were found if they were meant to be used as sanctuaries.

On the fourth day following his entry into the city he was acclaimed king with a minimum of pomp and ceremony in deference to his grief, and immediately afterwards he set off from there with 160,000 men for the place where the guilty ones had withdrawn. He laid siege to them, surrounding the mountain on all sides so that they could not escape. For nine days he kept them in his grip, and when they saw that they did not have enough food or any hope of receiving aid, they decided that it would be better to die fighting in the field like brave men than to remain surrounded like cowards.

Since all of them were of the same opinion, they descended from their mountaintop in four columns, on a dark and rainy night, and fell upon the king's camp which by then had been forewarned and was ready to receive them. The battle that ensued was fought with such hatred and fury on both sides that it lasted until two o'clock in the afternoon. Finally, it was confirmed that thirty-seven thousand had died on the field, including all ten thousand of the rebels, for not a single one of them chose to save himself though some could have done so, resulting in a loss of life that appeared to affect the king very deeply.

Withdrawing immediately to the city, the first thing he attended to was the care of the wounded, which took a long time because—according to what was said—there were over thirty thousand more of them, many of whom died still later.

202
Two Japanese Passengers Taken Aboard

With the end of this revolt which had taken such a heavy toll on all sides and brought about the complete devastation of the land, the flight of all the merchants, and the determination of the king to abandon the city, the few of us Portuguese still there (for as soon as the weather permitted, we had returned to anchor in the port), out of concern for our safety and the dearth of buyers for our merchandise, set sail for another port called Yamagawa,[1] ninety leagues from there, on the Bay of Kagoshima.[2]

We remained there for two and a half months without being able to sell a thing because there was such a glut of Chinese merchandise in the entire area that people were losing more than twice their investment, for there was nary a port, or bay, or inlet on all this island of Japan that did not have thirty or forty junks anchored in it, and in some parts over a hundred, as was the case in *Minató*,[3] *Tano-ura*,[4] *Hyuga*,[5] *Hakata*,[6] *Angune, Ubra,* and Kagoshima. This meant that in that year more than two thousand ships had sailed from China to Japan, flooding the market with goods that sold so cheaply that a picul of silk, which at that time was being bought for a hundred *taels* in China, was selling in Japan for twenty-five, twenty-eight, and at most thirty, and even then as a special favor. Moreover, every other kind of merchandise suffered a corresponding drop in price, as a result of which we found ourselves faced with total ruin, without being able to decide what to do with ourselves.

But since the Lord our God, with his mysterious judgements, quietly ordains all things in ways that surpass our understanding, it was his will, for reasons he alone knows, that with the coming of the new moon in December, which fell on the fifth day of the month, a dreadful storm should arise, bringing with it such high winds and heavy rains that every single one of these ships was dashed against the coast. This storm was responsible for the destruction of 1,972 junks, twenty-six of them belonging to Portuguese, five hundred of whom perished, to say nothing of more than a thousand Christian souls and the loss of an 800,000-*cruzado* investment in Chinese merchandise. As for the Chinese, it was said that in addition to their 1,936 ships, they lost more than ten million in gold and 160,000 lives. Out of this enormous number of miserable shipwrecks, only ten or twelve vessels were saved—one of which I happened to be on—and even those escaped miraculously and were able afterwards to sell their merchandise at any price they asked.

With our goods sold and everything in readiness for our departure, we decided to set sail on the morning of Epiphany,[7] and even though, on the one hand, we were very happy because we had made so much profit here that we were all leaving rich, still, on the other hand, it made us feel quite sad to think that it had happened at the cost of so many lives and so much property, both of our own people as well as of the foreigners.

Just as we had cast off the lines and hoisted the foresail and were preparing to get under way, the halyards of the mainsail suddenly snapped and the spar came crashing down, breaking into four pieces on the *nao's* gunwales. As a result we were forced to drop anchor again and to send the longboat ashore to look for a sail yard and carpenters to rig it for us, along with a gift as a bribe for the port captain, to get him to attend to our needs as quickly as possible. He took such good care of us that on that very same day the *nao* was restored to its former condition, and even better.

As we were casting off again and preparing to sail, the anchor cable broke at the end of the buoy rope to which it was lashed, and since we had only one other anchor left on board the *nao,* we were forced to work as hard as possible to raise it because we could not afford to leave it behind. For this job we sent ashore for divers who, for the price of ten *cruzados* went down twenty-six fathoms to where the anchor lay and attached a hawser to it, which enabled us to hoist it up with the capstan, though it was no easy task and kept us all busy most of the night. With the first light of dawn we got ready to sail, and as the *nao* was getting under way, with the foresail rigged and the mainsail unfurled, the wind suddenly died down; thereupon the strong undercurrent drove us alongside a cliff where we found ourselves on the brink of disaster despite all our struggling and straining. As a result, we resorted to the best and most effective remedy, which was to cry out urgently to the Virgin Mary, with whose favor we escaped from that danger.

In the midst of this fear and hardship under which we were all laboring, we saw two men on horseback riding down the cliff in a great hurry, waving at us with a cloth and shouting excitedly for us to take them on board. Since the situation was most unusual, we were anxious to find out what was going on, and a well-armed *manchua* was immediately sent ashore. In view of the fact that one of my slaves had fled during the night, along with three others, I thought they might have some word of him and I asked Jorge Alvares, the captain, to let me go on the *manchua,* and he sent me with two other companions of mine. When we reached the beach where the two riders were waiting, one of them, who seemed to have a more honorable bearing than the other, spoke up.

"Sir," he said to me, "since there is no time to lose, for I am in fear of many people who are coming after me, I beg you, by the goodness of your God, to take me on board with you, without asking any questions."

I was so taken aback by his words that I did not know what to do, but since I had already seen that man twice before in the town of Yamagawa, in the company of some merchants, I decided to take him along. After I had gotten him and his companion into the *manchua,* fourteen horsemen who were pursuing him appeared in sight.

"Hand over that traitor if you value your life!" they said to me when they reached the beach, shouting all the way. Immediately behind them came another nine, so that altogether there were twenty-three horsemen gathered there, with not a man on foot.

Afraid of what might happen, I moved out to sea for a good crossbow-shot distance, and from there I asked them what they wanted.

"If you take that Japanese man along with you," they replied, paying his companion no heed, "a thousand other heads like yours will roll."

To these words I chose not to reply. When I came alongside the *nao* I got them both on board, though it was not easy, where the captain and the other Portuguese there provided both of them with everything they needed for such a long voyage.

And if I have dwelt at such great length here on the minor details of the hardships we encountered, it was because of the events that followed, which I mean to discuss presently, so that the ways in which our Lord chooses to be praised may become apparent, as will be seen when we come to the case of this Japanese man, whose name was Anjiro.[8]

203
With Francis Xavier in Malacca

We departed from the Yamagawa River and the Bay of Kagoshima on 16 January 1547. After fourteen days of a fair monsoon, the Lord willing, we reached *Chincheo,*[1] one of the rich, well-known ports of the kingdom of China. However, at the time we arrived, a famous pirate by the name of *Chepocheca*[2] was blocking the mouth of the river with a fleet of four hundred large sailing ships and sixty oared *vancões*[3] with sixty thousand men on board, only twenty thousand of whom were seamen and the rest fighting men, a huge company indeed, which he maintained with food and pay by means of the plunder he took at sea.

Since we were afraid of entering the river at the time because it was blocked on all sides by this pirate, we ran on ahead to *Lamau,*[4] where we took on enough provisions to last us all the way to Malacca. There we found Father Master Francis Xavier, universal rector of the Society of Jesus in India, who had arrived a few days before from the Moluccas, where he had acquired a reputation of a saint, for people were all talking about the miracles they had seen him perform there, or rather, which the Lord our God had performed through him. When he heard about our passenger, he immediately came looking for Jorge Alvares and me at the home of a certain Cosme Rodrigues,[5] a married man living in Malacca, with whom we were both staying.

He spent a good part of the day with us, asking questions out of a curiosity prompted solely by a lively zeal for the honor of God. After he had obtained the information he was seeking from us, we told him, without realizing that he had already heard about it, that we had two Japanese back on the *nao* and that one of them seemed to be a person of some consequence who was very intelligent and well informed about all the religious doctrines and sects of Japan, about which His Reverence would be pleased to hear. He could hardly contain his excitement and in order to please him, we went down to the *nao* to get the Japanese and brought him to the hospital where he was residing. He took charge of him and from there took him to India, where he was then preparing to go, and after he arrived in Goa he converted him and gave him the Christian name of Paul of the Holy Faith. Within a short time he knew how to read and write and had learned all of the Christian doctrine, in keeping with the plans of this blessed father, who had decided, come the April monsoon, to go and preach to the barbarians of the Japanese island the word of "Christ, son of the living God, crucified by sinners," as he used to say, and to take this man along with him as his interpreter, as indeed he did later on. He also took his companion, who together with him had also been converted, to whom the father had given the Christian name of John. Afterwards they were both very faithful to him in all things befitting the service of God, because of which, Paul of the Holy Faith was eventually banished to China where he was killed by some robbers, as I shall explain presently, when I come to the subject of his exile.[6]

When this holy father left Malacca for India to make arrangements with the governor for his voyage to Japan, Simão de Melo, who was then captain of the fortress of Malacca, as I mentioned earlier, wrote a letter about him, describing all that he had done for the propagation of our holy faith in those parts of the Moluccas, and the marvels that the Lord our God had performed through him. Among some of the things he reported to Governor Dom João de Castro[7] was an eyewitness account of what this holy father had said in a moment of prophetic inspiration while preaching at the See of Malacca about what the common people there call "the miracle of the Achinese." But in order to explain what this was about, I shall have to go back to the beginning.

It so happened that on a Wednesday, 9 October 1547,[8] at two hours past midnight, a huge armada of the king of Achin sailed into the harbor where our *naos* were anchored. It was a fleet made up of seventy *lancharas*, foists, and oared galliots carrying five thousand gangplank men, or what we would call fighting men, not counting the rowing hands. Under cover of the night, which was extremely dark, they sent a landing party ashore to attack the city by scaling the walls of the stockade with a number of ladders they were carrying for that purpose, but since they found it very well guarded, with God's help, their efforts ended in failure.

The rest of the enemy troops on board the armada simultaneously attacked the island of the *naos* and set fire to six or seven ships that were in port, one of them a huge *nao* belonging to His Majesty which had arrived from Banda[9] five days before, laden with nutmeg and mace, which was a total loss. By that time the noise and confusion among the people was so great that it was impossible to understand one another or to get together to take counsel, for inasmuch as the enemy had appeared out of nowhere and caught us unawares, and the night was very dark and rainy, and alarm bells and shouts were coming from all sides, all these things combined created so much havoc and confusion in our ranks that nobody knew what to do.

This state of affairs lasted for quite some time, until the return of the three *balões* that Simão de Melo had sent to find out what was going on, at which time they confirmed the fact that it was the Achinese. By then it was beginning to dawn, and a large number of oared sailing vessels, flying many silk flags and standards, could be seen from the fortress. When the captain ordered some of the heavy artillery fired to scare them off, they did not alter their formation, but in single file, just as they were, they began to withdraw to the tip of the island of Upi,[10] a little more than a third of a league away, where they remained with oars at the ready until close to vesper time, shouting and carrying on all the while as though they were celebrating a great victory.

Unfortunately, it happened that at that time one of our prows, with seven natives on board, was out fishing in the vicinity of those waters with their women and children. As soon as the enemy sighted it, they sent their well-armed *balões* in pursuit, captured it, and in no time at all brought it in. They had the noses and ears of all seven men on board cut off, adding insult to injury by hamstringing some of them at the ankles and releasing them that way with a letter for the captain, written in the blood of the very same unfortunate bearers of the letter, which went like this:

"I, *Biyayá Sòra*,[11] son of *Seribiyayá, Pracamá de Rajá,* who, for his honor, has stored away in golden jewel boxes the favor of the great Sultan Alaradim,[12] in the form of a candleholder sweetened with incense tablets from the holy House of Mecca, king of Achin and the land from sea to sea, hereby make known to thee so that thou in turn mayest inform thy king that in this sea of his where I have come to rest, terrifying his fortress with my might, I intend to keep on fishing here in spite of him, come what may, for as long as I please. And to prove that I mean what I say, I am taking over this land and its inhabitants with all the other elements on up to the lunar heaven. Furthermore, I hereby certify, with words that come from my own mouth, that thy king has been vanquished and stripped of all honor, and that his standards lie trampled in the dust, never again to be raised with the permission of one who has conquered him, signifying that he has laid his head beneath the feet of my king, as all-conquering lord, whose slave he shall be from this day forward. And to make thee confess to the truth of what I say, I challenge thee, from here where I stand, to come forth if, on his behalf, thou wouldst contradict me."

This letter came signed by the captains of the armada, as though it were something they had all agreed on in council. As soon as they reached the city, the seven unfortunate men who had had their noses and ears cut off were immediately taken to the fortress to see the captain, just as they were, all bloody and deformed. They gave him the letter they were carrying, which was read in public then and there, in front of everyone, while the captain and some of his intimates exchanged some witty, urbane remarks about it. In the meantime, Father Master Francis arrived, having just finished saying mass at the Church of Our Lady of the Mount, as was his custom. The captain rose to his feet and came forward to receive him two or three paces from where he had been sitting.

"What advice would Your Reverence give me on this challenge?" he asked with a smile, as though he attached no importance to the letter. "I think I shall have to refer it to a higher jurisdiction, like an ordinary judge remitting a criminal case to a higher court."

"Since Your Grace asks me, it is my opinion," the father replied, "that this is not a matter to be treated so lightly. We should make an effort, if possible, to equip some sort of fleet that is at least capable of barking at their heels, so that the Moors will not think we are so completely unprepared that we cannot cause them some discomfort, if they should come back here again."

"That would be fine," the captain said to him, "if it were in any way possible. But Your Reverence is well aware of the situation we are in here, with nothing but the rotting hulks of four foists which are beyond repair, and even if they were not, it would take much longer to make them seaworthy than to build new ones."

"If it is just a matter of repairing the foists," the father replied, "I wish, for the honor of God and the king, our lord, to take care of that myself and to go, if necessary, in the company of these servants of Christ and brothers of mine to fight against those enemies of the Cross."

At these words, those who were present—and there were a number of very noble gentlemen there—all responded in one voice, "If Your Reverence will do that, what more is there to say? For any Christian who refuses to take part in such a holy undertaking is a dirty Jew!"

Suddenly all the people were caught up in a holy spirit that nearly led to a riot with everyone so anxious and determined to fight for God that it was generally regarded as the work of a supernatural force. Then the captain, who had been sitting by the fortress gate, rose to his feet, quite pleased to see the spirit and holy fervor displayed by all the people, and taking the father by the hand, he led him down to the beach to show him the fleet that was careened there. He found seven foists and a small cutter. There, he immediately sent for the factor, Duarte Barreto,[13] and told him to deliver, with the utmost speed, everything necessary for repairing the ships. He answered that there was not even a single nail in the factory, nor tar, nor tow, nor a scrap of sailcloth, nor anything else that was needed for him to comply with His Grace's instructions. This news left the captain quite crestfallen and all the people even more so.

"Come now, brothers, gentlemen!" the father said, raising his eyes and inviting with his kindly expression all the bystanders to fix their gaze on him. "Do not be disheartened, for I assure you that the Lord our God is with us, and in his name I urge each one of you not to refuse to go along on this holy expedition because it is his will that we do so. As for the difficulties raised by the factor regarding the lack of supplies for repairing the fleet, that is not reason enough to deter us from our holy purpose."

After which he gazed directly at a group of seven men standing around him who were captains and owners of their *naos,* all of them rich and honorable men. Addressing each one of them by his name, he went up to them one by one and embraced them many times.

"Brother," he said to each, his face wreathed in smiles, "the honor of our Lord Jesus Christ requires that you, as his servant, take personal charge of repairing that foist over there (pointing to a different one for each of them), with the greatest possible speed, which is also required if we are to serve him properly. As for the reward for your labors, I promise you that you will be repaid a hundred times over."

He cajoled all seven of them this way, urging each one to accept the responsibility of repairing the foist assigned to him, which they all agreed to do with such holy fervor and zeal that it was said by all present there that it was due rather to the work of God than of men. Each of these seven men immediately took charge of the foist that the father had assigned to him, and that very hour, without any further delay, they all set to work. So great was the holy fervor and rivalry in them that they competed with each other to see which one would do it better and faster. As a result, a task that had seemed impossible to complete in a month—even with an abundant supply of material—was finished in a period of only five days because there were over a hundred men working on each foist.

During the time that this fleet was being made ready, the captain of the fortress, Simão de Melo, appointed his brother-in-law, Dom Francisco de Eça,[14] as admiral of this expedition, and Father Master Francis definitely made up his mind to accompany them. When the Brothers of Mercy heard about his decision, they got together with all the married men living in the fortress, and taking Dom Francisco de Eça himself with them, they all went to see him. They urged him, in the name of God, not to forsake them at a time when the fortress was being left so defenseless, because if he insisted on going, then they would all go with him too.

The father was somewhat troubled by their request, as one could tell from looking at him, for he was so noble and generous a soul that he would have liked to do both, which, of course, was impossible.

After a discussion in which many different opinions were expressed on both sides, the admiral of the fleet, Dom Francisco de Eça himself, seeing the need for it, finally turned to the father and asked him again to do what the people wanted, in view of the earnestness of their request, and the father conceded.

After he had decided to remain on shore, he consoled them all with a brief spiritual talk in which he discussed the many reasons one and the other had for risking their lives for so worthy a God who, in order to redeem them, had placed himself on a cross—which we all believed and confessed to as an article of faith—allowing himself to be scorned, disdained, flogged, crowned with thorns, and finally crucified on a rough piece of wood in order to crucify us in his sweet love and ennoble our souls with his priceless blood, thereby absolving our unworthiness before the Eternal Father. And so on in this manner he said many other things with his usual fervor and devotion, making such a deep impression on all the people that the captains and the soldiers who were going on the fleet vowed then and there that all together, united in Christian conformity, they would die for the faith of our Lord Jesus Christ.

204
Repairing the Fleet

Within eight days, during which the people continued in the grip of this holy fervor, our armada was readied and fully outfitted with everything necessary and all set to leave on the following day. It consisted of seven foists, a small cutter for carrying messages, and a company of 180 brave soldiers under the respective commands of Dom Francisco de Eça, his brother Dom Jorge de Eça,[1] Diogo Pereira,[2] Afonso Gentil,[3] Belchior de Sequeira,[4] João Soares,[5] and Gomes Barreto,[6] with the cutter under the command of the surrogate judge for orphans, André Toscano,[7] a married man living in Malacca.

The following day, with everyone on board and ready to depart, the admiral Dom Francisco de Eça hoisted the sail amidst general rejoicing and cheers on all sides, but just as he did so, his foist capsized, without anything on it being saved at the time but the men, and even that with great difficulty. All the people were so dazed and dejected, and the men in the fleet so dispirited, that everyone seemed to be in a state of shock.

As a result of this unfortunate accident, tongues started wagging, and some people began to make remarks that were completely unjustified, attributing this expedition to the work of the devil, in dire offense to God. They blamed the whole idea on the captain and Father Master Francis, even going so far as to accuse them of intending to hand over to the Achinese that fragile little fleet of only seven foists and 180 men who never had a chance of surviving in combat against the enemy's sixty ships and five thousand men. These disproportionate numbers lent such plausibility to their arguments that all of the common people were inclined to agree with them, and there was no way the captain or the constabulary could make them keep quiet, hard as they tried.

Outraged by these diabolical disorders, Captain Simão de Melo and Admiral of the Fleet Dom Francisco de Eça quickly sent someone to fetch the father from the Church of Our Lady of the Mount where he was then saying mass. Hurrying to get there, the messenger arrived when he was in the middle of the *Domine non sum dignus* with the Host in his hands. Undecided about what to do, he waited until the end of Communion before he approached him. And just as he opened his mouth to give him the message, the father motioned to him to be silent or not to disturb him and went right on with the mass without losing his composure.

After he left the altar he spoke to the messenger to whom, up to that moment, he had not said a word: "Go brother, and tell the captain that I will be there shortly and for His Grace not to worry about anything because the Lord is with us in our moments of greatest despair."

Entering the sacristy he removed his vestments, after which, he went and kneeled before the altar and prayed to the image upon it.

"O Jesus Christ, love of my soul," he was heard to say with a deep sigh, "consider who thou art and look upon the ornament of thy precious wounds wherein thou wilt see how deep is the obligation thy divine majesty hath chosen to assume for us, then, O my God and my Lord, what is there at this moment that I, miserable creature that I am, can ask of thee that thou, for thy name's sake, wilt not grant as a remedy for our present affliction?"

After these few words, spoken with many tears, he went down to the fortress, where he found the captain and everyone else looking unhappy and hard at work bailing out the foist in an effort to salvage the artillery and some other arms still aboard. The moment he saw the father, the captain came forward six or seven steps to meet him.

"Did you ever hear anything like this, Your Reverence?" he complained in a tone of near outrage at the insults being flung about by the disorderly crowd. "Listen to what these people are saying and make my excuses to them, for there is nothing I can do to shut their mouths."

"Bless my soul, why does Your Grace fret over such a small matter?" the father asked gently, with a thoughtful but cheerful expression on his face. "Don't be that way, let us have firm faith in the Lord and in his omnipotence because he will provide for our needs."

Then he embraced all the captains and soldiers and lifted their spirits by citing holy examples from the sacred Scriptures, praising them highly for the good intentions and the determination they had shown from the beginning. This done, he and the captain went off to the gate of the fortress some fifteen or twenty paces away, where they sat and talked about the capsizing of the foist, lamenting the loss of what was considered the best ship in the entire fleet, so much so that the admiral had chosen to embark on it. Following this discussion, Simão de Melo wanted to come to some decision, based on a consensus of opinion among those present, about what to do next, for he thought that would shut the mouths of the ones who were blaming him for heeding the father's advice to send such a small fleet against such a large one.

Each one's vote was recorded by Baltasar Ribeiro, clerk of the customs house and trading post, in the presence of all the justice and treasury officials, and it showed that the consensus felt that what they had tried to do was extremely rash. The reason they all gave for taking that stand was the disaster itself, which they claimed was a manifestation of the divine will, and that it proved that God was trying to avert an even greater one which most certainly would have occurred had they proceeded with the plans of the captain and the father. However, when it was their turn to voice their opinions, the admiral and the other captains and soldiers in the fleet said that even though they were facing death they would not go back on their promise to God, a promise which they repeated and swore to again, because it made little difference whether there were six foists or seven in view of the fact that the same number of soldiers would be going on the remaining six.

With this they rejected out of hand the vote that the clerk was taking which, it was said, did not displease the captain because of the honor he hoped the expedition would bring, not only to the fortress in general, but to his brothers-in-law in particular, Dom Francisco de Eça, who would be serving as admiral of the fleet, and his brother Dom Jorge, as the next in command.

Seeing that the captains and the soldiers were fully determined to carry out their noble intentions, Father Master Francis praised them highly for it. Among other things he said while he was talking to them was that they should all place their complete trust in God our Lord, for there was no doubt that in place of the lost foist he would very shortly send them two others, and of that they could all be very certain because it was going to happen that very same day without fail. All those who were present believed him because of what they had heard about him, but there were also a few who made some double-edged comments, born of their lack of faith, to the effect that the father was inventing something to lift their spirits and dispel the general feeling of gloom left by the unfortunate incident.

With that, Simão de Melo withdrew into the fortress, taking with him the admiral and the other captains of the fleet, whom he invited to join him for dinner; and the father also withdrew, heading for the hospital to tend to the poor, as was his custom.

Later that afternoon, with everyone watching for what he had predicted, though with different feelings, depending on the faith that each one had, at about an hour before sundown or thereabouts, an alarm was sounded from the top of the mount of our Lady, that off to the north two lateen-rigged vessels had been sighted. The news sent such a tremendous wave of excitement among the people that it was indeed amazing. Captain Simão de Melo immediately dispatched an armed *balão* to find out who they were. It returned with the message that they were two foists with sixty Portuguese on board, one of which was commanded by Diogo Soares,[8] the Galician, and the other by his son, Baltasar Soares, and that they were both on their way from Patani, with the intention of passing on straight for Pegu, which was their destination. The father, who by that time was at Our Lady, was immediately informed. He was very happy as he came out of the hermitage to see what was going on, and on the way he ran into the captain, who was hurrying to find him to thank him for his fine prophecy.

"Go pray to our Lady, Your Grace," he said to him, "and then have the *balão* made ready for me because I want to go speak with Diogo Soares before he bypasses Malacca, which is what they say he intends to do!"

The captain had the *balão* made ready at once and ordered the harbormaster to accompany him. He departed immediately, reaching the foists about an hour after dark, where he was received by Diogo Soares with a great deal of fuss and fanfare. He informed him about what was going on and begged him, for the sake of God our Lord and his wounds, to choose, for his own honor, to accompany Dom Francisco de Eça on this pilgrimage, because from there he would be able to go on more freely wherever he wished.

Diogo Soares replied that he had not intended to put in at Malacca so as to avoid paying customs on the little merchandise he was carrying, for that was all he had on which to support himself and his soldiers, but that since His Reverence was asking him to do so in such an urgent manner, with words so holy that there was much to fear from disobeying them, considering, as he said, that it was out of pure zeal for the Law of God on whose behalf he was making this request, he would be very happy to comply. However, as long as he was stopping there, he would have to enter the port to pick up the munitions he needed to do battle, so His Reverence would have to bring him a document, signed by the captain and the customs officers, granting him exemption from the payment of duty on his cargo; otherwise, if His Reverence did not arrange for an exemption, he would not enter the port. For all of this the father expressed his gratitude, promising to do everything he wanted and much more, if necessary, and with that he took leave of him since it was already close to midnight.

However, before going any further, I think I should point out the following, in order to satisfy the curious reader and lay to rest any doubts he may have on the subject: this Diogo Soares, the Galician, that we are dealing with here now is the same one I have mentioned earlier, who was put to death in Pegu by order of the *xemim de Satão*.[9] However, the events I am describing now took place long before his death, and if I mentioned it earlier, I was forced to do so in order to maintain the proper order of events in my story.

205
Diogo Soares Saves the Day

When he got to the fortress where Simão de Melo was waiting for him, Father Master Francis told him about the agreement he had made with Diogo Soares and that it would be necessary for His Grace to send him the document he was asking for, which the captain had drawn up at once, without delay. They all thought it would be better, for the greater satisfaction and reassurance of Diogo Soares, if the admiral Dom Francisco delivered it to him, and he set out immediately.

At daybreak, Diogo Soares anchored in the port with a demonstration of great joy. When he disembarked he found the captain waiting for him on shore where he was warmly welcomed not only by the captain but by all the people as well. From there, they went to the main church, which is now the See, where they heard mass said by Father Master Francis, who had played the major part in this expedition all along. Then, after the mass, they all went and sat at the gates of the fortress, where for a long time they talked about the best strategy to be employed for the expedition and the things they would need for the forthcoming battle with the enemy, all of which was provided for with the greatest possible diligence.

After four more days had gone by, during which they finished outfitting the fleet completely, the admiral Dom Francisco de Eça embarked on the foist of his brother Dom Jorge, since his own was still hopelessly waterlogged, so that altogether the ships in our fleet came to eight foists and a small cutter, which would be carrying a total of 230 men, all handpicked soldiers.

This armada departed from the port of Malacca on a Friday, the twenty-fifth of October, in the year 1547.[1] Sailing all together on their course, within four days they reached Pulo Sambilang,[2] sixty leagues from where they had departed. Since the orders that Dom Francisco was carrying did not extend beyond that point, he did not dare to go any farther. He remained there for several days, without encountering a single person or vessel along the entire coast that could tell him where the enemies were to be found. All they had to go by was a suspicion that by this time they were probably in Achin, where it was presumed they had been heading.

The matter was placed in council, during which many opinions differing widely from each other were expressed. Finally, in the end, the admiral decided to adhere to the orders he was carrying which forbade him to go beyond that point. Then just as he was setting his course back to Malacca, the Lord ordained that, with the conjunction of the moon, winds coming out of the northwest should suddenly arise, striking him at the prow, with the result that they were tied up for twenty-three days without being able to make the least bit of headway. Moreover, since the fleet had been carrying provisions for only a month, and they had already been out to sea for thirty-six days, and by this time they no longer had anything to eat, they were forced to look for something in Junkseylon or Tenasserim, which were ports very far from there, towards the coast of the kingdom of Pegu.

With this in view, they set out from where they were and started on their way with everyone thoroughly disgusted by this turn of events. But it pleased our Lord, who is the author of all blessings, for the weather to bring them to the coast of Kedah, and as they were entering the Perlis River[3] for the purpose of taking on water there and proceeding on their course, they saw a fishing prow passing along the shore at night. The admiral sent someone after it to find out where the watering station was. Once the prow had been brought alongside he gave the men on board a friendly reception, which made them happy. When they were interrogated one by one about a few necessary details, they all replied that the land was completely deserted, and that the king had fled to Patani on account of a huge armada that had been anchored there for a month and a half with five thousand Achinese who were building a fortress and lying in wait for the Portuguese *naos* bound from Bengal to Malacca, with the intention, as they claimed, of not sparing the life of a single Christian. They also disclosed many other things that suited our purpose, which made the admiral so happy that he donned his holiday clothes and had the entire fleet bedecked with flags.

Called in council, the captains discussed the matter, and it was their unanimous opinion that the three armed *balões* should immediately be sent up the river to the town where the enemies were located, twelve leagues from there, to try to find out if all this was true and, once they knew, to return at once to the armada so that they could decide on their strategy for the battle, and that in the meantime they should all make ready for what lay ahead of them, and that they should not forget what Father Master Francis had recommended to them, which was that inwardly, to always carry Christ crucified in their souls, and outwardly, to show pleasure and joy with great courage, so that from these outward signs the weak who were at the oars would take heart.

The admiral attended to everything necessary with all possible speed and gave orders for all the artillery of the armada to be fired and the foists bedecked, and that there be merrymaking aboard and no rationing of food, all of which was fully carried out.

When the three *balões* had been fitted out with everything necessary, and the oarsmen carefully chosen and well bribed, the admiral sent Diogo Soares in the first one in command of the others, his son, Baltasar Soares, in the second one, and João Álvares de Magalhães in the third, and each of these captains had with him two soldiers of the same caliber. The *balões* departed up the river, and when they had gone about five or six leagues, as luck would have it they ran head on into four enemy *balões*, and before either side had time to get into battle formation, our men captured three of them, while the other escaped by dint of hard rowing. Since the three *balões* captured by our men were far better than the ones they had, they transferred over to them, set fire to the ones they abandoned, and immediately returned to our fleet, flushed with excitement over this good beginning, and the admiral welcomed them with great joy and merrymaking.

Of the enemies that had been on board the *balões* captured by our men, the only ones to escape with their lives were six Achinese, whom our men brought back with them. When they were interrogated about matters of importance to us, none of them would talk, except to say with dogged obstinacy, "Mate, mate, quita fadulé," meaning, "Kill us, kill us, for all we care!" so that it was necessary for us to apply torture. They began to flog them and to drip boiling oil on them so mercilessly that two of them died immediately, and two others, tied hand and foot, were thrown into the river. As they were about to do the same to the remaining two who were still alive, they cried out to the admiral, begging him not to kill them, for they swore to tell the whole truth.

The admiral ordered the punishment stopped, and they said that for the past forty-two days they had been in control of that land where they killed two thousand people and captured almost as many others, to say nothing of the spoils in pepper and spices and other kinds of merchandise, a large part of which had already been sent to the king of Achin; and since one of the provisions in the orders carried by their admiral contained an express command from the king that they stay there in that river and lie in wait for the *naos* coming from Bengal and other parts on their way to Malacca, and to capture them all without sparing the life of a single Portuguese or any other Christian, he had remained there so long; and that he had decided to wait one more month, until the monsoon was fully spent; and that when they had heard the sound of our artillery they thought that the *naos* had already arrived, so the entire fleet was making ready, at top speed, to go in search of them, and there was no doubt whatsoever that they would be there on the following day. Armed with this information, the admiral Dom Francisco immediately prepared himself, as was fitting, to receive the guests he was expecting, always keeping a few *balões* on the lookout that kept coming and going without pause.

The following day, which was a Sunday, at nine o'clock, our *balões* came back in great haste, shouting out loud, "Get ready, get ready, get ready, in the name of Jesus!

Here come the enemies!" stirring the entire fleet into frenzied activity with their cries of warning. The admiral, armed with a laminated breastplate of crimson satin studded in gold and a broadsword in his hands, climbed into a well-equipped *manchua* and ran among all the ships, spurring on all the captains and soldiers. With his face bathed in smiles, displaying tremendous courage, he addressed them as brothers and gentlemen and reminded them of who they were and of what had been recommended to them by Father Master Francis, who was praying to our Lord constantly for them and whose tears and prayers were bound to be heard and to be well received before God, for he was such a saintly person, as everyone knew; so that it was necessary for all of them to strive with all their might to carry themselves with honor, since this fleet and her soldiers were called "The Name of Jesus," which was the name that the blessed father had given them when they departed; and so on, with other words to that effect, which were called for by the time and circumstances. All of this was received with great joy, with all of them protesting loudly that without fail they would lay down their lives for Christ like the true Christians they were. As the admiral got back to his foist, and almost before he was well aboard it, the enemy fleet was sighted. Raising a frightful hue and cry and making a horrendous racket with various martial instruments, they came down the river disposed in the following order.

206
Victory in the Perlis River

At the head of the enemy armada came three Turkish galliots accompanied by the *lanchara* carrying the Biyayá Sòra,[1] admiral of the fleet, who called himself king of Pedir. Behind these four came nine rows, six abreast, making a total altogether of fifty-eight sailing ships in the armada, whereas the rest consisted of *lancharas* and foists capable of firing camelets[2] over the prow, and some half-spheres, with their falcons on the gangway, in addition to many culverins and other light artillery pieces with which they were well equipped. Since the current was in their favor, and the ships were well manned, and they were rowing with might and main to the sound of many martial instruments, all this, combined with the cries of the crew and frequent bursts of arquebus fire, had such a terrifying and incredibly frightful effect, that it made the flesh quiver with fear.

As soon as the enemy vanguard, keeping this formation, rounded the tip of a bend on the southern shore behind which our men were waiting, also ready by then to receive them, the forward line comprising the three Turkish galliots and the *lanchara* carrying *Biyayá Sòra* rushed at our forward wing where the admiral was stationed with two foists, his in the middle, flanked by Diogo Soares and Gomes Brito,[3] a nobleman of the duke of Braganza's household.

The enemies fired their artillery a little too soon, but as the Lord willed, it did us no harm, and with that, the battle broke out between both vanguards in which both the admirals were stationed. Fighting each other with great courage and with as little pity as one would expect from the hatred with which they fought, God willed that a camel shot, fired from the foists of João Soares, should hit the mark so well that the *lanchara* carrying the *Biyayá* was promptly sent to the bottom, with the death of more than a hundred Moors. In their anxiety to hasten to the aid of those floundering in the water and especially to keep their admiral from drowning, all three of the galliots got so entangled with each other that the second row of ships, with the full force of the current, collided with them, and the next row after them, and all the rest, one after the other, on top of them, becoming so ensnarled with each other that way that they formed a jumbled heap that took up the entire width of the river, upon which all our artillery directed three broadsides, so well aimed, that not a single shot was wasted, sending nine *lancharas* to the bottom and destroying nearly all the others, since most of our cannon consisted of stone shot.

Seeing how well things were going for them and how God had ordained everything in their favor, our men were filled with such great spirit and courage that, calling on the name of Jesus, they fell upon them so fearlessly that four of our foists grappled six of theirs. Then they showered them with a great quantity of powder pots and stones—to say nothing of the large number of muskets that kept on firing continuously without pause. The fervor of this honorable battle reached such a high pitch that in only half an hour nearly two thousand of these enemies died.

At this point, their oarsmen became so panic-stricken that they all threw themselves into the river. However, with the current and force of the water, which was very strong, nearly all of them drowned in a very short time. Seeing this, the others who were still alive fought on bravely for quite some time though things were getting steadily worse for them. After a while, when they finally realized that all was lost and that our men were picking them all off with their muskets, which they were no longer able to do, nor were they able to make use of their artillerty, and above all, that most of them had been burned by the numerous powder pots, they were either forced or perhaps thought it a better means of escape to surrender themselves to the waters of the river, rather than to those who were mistreating them as badly as our men were. But soon after throwing themselves in the river they all drowned, for by then they were already badly wounded, burned, battle weary, and so exhausted that they could hardly move their arms. Thus, our men were fully avenged for not a single one of them escaped alive.

Offering up deep prayers of thanks and many praises to our Lord for the fortunate outcome of such a glorious victory as this, they took possession of the entire fleet of forty-six sailing ships—not counting the nine that were sunk at the start of the battle—with the exception of three that escaped, on which the *Biyayá Sòra* was saved, although, according to what was said, with a wound from an arquebus shot which left him hovering between life and death.

In this armada three hundred pieces of artillery were found, most of them falcons and culverins, including sixty-two bearing the coat of arms of the king, our lord, which they had captured from us in former days. Also found were eight hundred muskets, as well as an enormous quantity of javelins, lances, swords, Turkish bows and many arrows, krisses, and assegais[4] decorated in gold, to which some of our men helped themselves liberally.

The admiral then had a count made of his forces which showed that 26 of our men had died, only 5 of whom were Portuguese, and the rest slaves and sailors who had been rowing the foists, as well as 150 wounded, 70 of them Portuguese, 3 of whom died later and 5 who were permanently disabled.

The fame of this utterly glorious and honorable victory spread rapidly through-out the land. When it reached the king of Perlis,[4] who had been hiding in the jungle where he had fled for fear of these enemies, he gathered five hundred of his followers as best he could and fell upon the stockade they had captured from him where all their prizes of war were kept, guarded by their sick who must have numbered as many as two hundred. After killing them all, without sparing a single one, he won back the spoils, including two thousand of his people who had been held captive, but they were all women and children and other poor people.

This done, the king came at once to visit Dom Francisco and congratulated him on the victory, raising his hands to heaven over and over for it and promising under solemn oath, in their fashion, from then on to be a vassal of the king, our lord, with an annual tribute of two catties of gold, which equals five hundred *cruzados*, excusing himself for promising so little on the grounds that his limited resources did not permit him to pay more. An agreement was drawn up to that effect which the king signed, along with some of his followers.

Dom Francisco then made ready to return to Malacca, but when he saw that he did not have enough hands to sail so many ships, he set fire to them and returned with only twenty-five, including fourteen foists and the three galliots on which the sixty Turks had come, all of whom perished in the battle. Following this, they also captured a prow with fifteen Achinese on board who confessed under torture that, counting those who had drowned, over four thousand men had died in the battle, most of them fine soldiers in the service of the king of Achin, and that five hundred of them were *orabalões*[6] wearing golden armlets, which is a sign of nobility, and that among the dead were sixty Turks and twenty Greeks and Janissaries who had arrived only a few days before on two *naos* bound from Jidda[7] to Pasay.[8]

207
Francis Xavier's Revelation

I think it is time now to leave our armada behind and deal briefly at this point with the events that took place in Malacca after the armada departed, so that one may see the ways in which it pleases our Lord to lend credence to those who serve him on earth, much to the amazement of those who are worldly, indifferent, and half-hearted in the faith and trust that should be placed in this Lord who chose to die to give us life.

Ordinarily, this saintly Father Master Francis would preach twice a week—on Fridays at the House of Mercy, and on Sundays at the main church, which is now the See. For two consecutive months, beginning with the time our men left Malacca until they returned, he would always end his sermons by recommending that they say an "Our Father" and a "Hail Mary" to our Lord Jesus Christ, that he see fit to grant victory to our brothers who had gone on the armada to fight against those enemies of our holy faith, so that by means of this victory, his holy name would be made known throughout the land. The people continued to recite the "Our Father" for about fifteen or twenty days, during which they naturally thought it might have some effect. But as time went by and nothing more was heard of the armada, they came to the conclusion that, without a doubt, the armada had been captured by the Achinese. What gave them even more reason to think so was a false rumor that the Moors had circulated throughout the land to the effect that a *lanchara* arriving from Selangor[1] had made contact with another, bound for Bintang,[2] which had informed them that on a certain day, near the bar of Perak,[3] the enemies had met our men, defeated them, captured the entire fleet, and without sparing the life of a single man, had carried the foists off to Achin. Thus, in this manner, a scheme was devised by these ministers of Satan, based on so many lies that the captain never could, hard as he tried, put a stop to this false rumor. As a result, either out of remorse for what he had done or out of annoyance with what was being said publicly, he no longer dared to leave his house as often as he used to. However, the gossipmongers, who are always eager to add fuel to the fire, observing this change in his habits, also took this to mean that what was being said was the absolute truth. This rumor spread so far and wide that the king of Jantana,[4] son of the former king of Malacca, who was then residing in Indragiri,[5] one of his ports on the island of Sumatra, on being informed of what was being said among us, immediately appeared in the Muar River[6] with a fleet of three hundred sails, six leagues from our fortress, from where he dispatched some oared *balões* all along the coast to confirm this rumor, with the intention—as soon as he received word that what he so ardently desired was true—of invading Malacca, which from the way things looked at the time, he could very easily have done, without spilling much blood. But the better to disguise his intentions, he sent to pay a call on the captain and wrote him a letter that went like this:

"My brave Lord Captain, while I was in Indragiri with this fleet during the waxing of the moon, ready to send it against the king of Patani for various reasons that moved me to punish him, about which thou hast probably heard by now, I was reliably informed of the cruel deaths the Achinese had inflicted on thy men, which grieved me as deeply as if they had all been my sons. Since I have always wanted to demonstrate the deep love I feel for my brother, the king of Portugal, as soon as I heard this sad news, I put aside the vengeance I was seeking against my enemies and entered this river so that, from here, like a good friend, I might succor thee with my forces, my men, and my fleet. Wherefore, I beg thee, and on behalf of thy king, my brother, I request thee to grant me permission to show him favor and assist him, by anchoring in thy port before the enemies do so, in spite of thee, as I have been informed they are desirous of doing.

"*Sapetu de Raja*, my *ourobalão*, will tell thee verbally of the great love with which I desire to please, in every respect, the king of Portugal, my brother. It is as his true friend that I remain here awaiting thy reply, on receipt of which I will immediately put into effect all that I desire to do for him."

After reading this letter, the captain, pretending that he did not perceive his evil intentions, replied to his offer of help with the appropriate words of thanks, while completely concealing his deficiencies and letting him know that, for the present, he was not in need of any kind of assistance because he was very well supplied with everything. And so, with these feigned compliments on both sides, this enemy remained here within arm's reach of us for twenty-three days, giving us enough to worry about on each one of those days, until his *balões* returned from the kingdom of Kedah,[7] where he had sent them to bring back news. They brought him confirmation of the victory that God granted us, which distressed him so, that out of sheer disgust he had the first man who brought him the news killed. Without waiting there any longer he immediately set sail for Bintang, on the pretense that he was ill with a fever, after which there were many processions held in Malacca to give thanks to the Lord our God for having rid us of this enemy.

To return to Father Master Francis. As I was saying, he kept on asking at the conclusion of all his sermons that an "Our Father" and a "Hail Mary" be said for the victory of our men who had departed from Malacca. His listeners did so for as long as they thought it might be helpful, which was for fifteen or twenty days. But by the end of that time, which they thought was long enough for the matter to be resolved, since they no longer believed it possible that our men could still be alive—not only because of the false rumors that the Moors had spread, but also because of the length of time that had elapsed since their departure without any word from them in all that time—they decided, owing to their lack of faith, that the father was making that recommendation more as a matter of form than because he thought it was still necessary. As a result, all, or practically all of them, upon hearing him say it, would nudge each other, grinning and twisting his words, saying things like, "On my faith, Father, it would have been far better to say that 'Our Father' for their souls than for that victory you are talking about, for which you and the captain will have to give a strict accounting to God, since you are both responsible for their deaths." Others would make fun of him in a different manner by saying, "There are so few of these and the anointed that it is as if there were none at all." Still others would say, "If you should encounter them at some future hour, you would do well to make the sign of the cross." And others would make fun of the father in the same way, saying things of which they were later quite ashamed, and some of the most discreet among them were deeply pained.

One Sunday, on the sixth of December in the same year,[8] while this blessed father was saying mass that day as was his custom, just as he was coming to the end of his sermon, he turned toward the crucifix hanging above the chapel arch, and with the tears coursing down his cheeks he spoke to it, with words of deep devotion that left his listeners gasping with amazement. Drawing figures in the air with his hands, he showed how the battle with our men was taking place, and he implored Him with all his heart to remember His people, for even though they were sinners, and great sinners, still, they professed His holy name like the faithful followers they were, vowing constantly to live and die in His holy Catholic faith. And at many points he would clench his fists, carried away by deep emotion, and his face all aglow, he would say, "O Jesus Christ, love of my soul, by the suffering of thy sacred Passion, do not forsake us!"

In this manner he said many things which I cannot quite recall, at the end of which he leaned his head on the pulpit as though resting from the exertion. He remained still for about as long as it takes to recite two or three Credos and then, raising it again, with a bright, cheerful expression on his face, he said to all those present, "Recite an 'Our Father' and a 'Hail Mary' for the victory that the Lord our God has just granted our men against the enemies of his holy faith," at which the entire church was filled with the murmur of prayers and weeping.

Six days later, close to sundown of the following Friday, a very well-armed *balão* that had belonged to the enemy arrived, carrying a soldier by the name of Manuel Godinho, who asked the captain to reward him for bringing news of this victory. There in public, he described everything that had happened on the previous Sunday at ten o'clock in the morning, which, counting the number of days involved, showed that it had taken place on the very same day and hour that the father announced it from the pulpit. As a result, everybody realized, without any doubt—and they confessed it publicly—that the Lord our God had revealed it to him in spirit,[9] as had already been seen on previous occasions with other things he had done and said, which were discussed there at the time in front of everybody. One of the things mentioned was that after his departure from the Moluccas,[10] while saying mass one day in Amboina, sixty leagues from there, just when he had finished reciting the Credo and had not yet launched into the preamble, he said to those present in the church, "Say an 'Our Father' and a 'Hail Mary' for the soul of our brother, So-and-So de Araujo, who has just departed this life."

Fifteen days later when the *naos* arrived to load clove, among various items of news they brought, one was that a Gonzalo de Araujo[11] (for I believe that was his name) had died, and that it had been on the very same day and hour that the father had announced it when he was in Amboina.

Our Lord wrought many other marvels through this blessed father, some of which I saw and others I heard, of which I make no mention at this point because I hope to deal with some of them presently.

208
Francis Xavier in Japan

After this glorious battle was over in which the Lord our God chose to give credence to this blessed servant of his, first with what he did for the armada and then with what he said about it afterwards—much to the embarrassment and repentance of the slanderers through whom the infernal enemy tried so hard to discredit him—he left this city of Malacca for India the following December in the same year of 1547, to make arrangements for his voyage to Japan. He took with him Anjiro, who, after becoming a Christian, was called Paul of the Holy Faith, as I said before. Once there, he was unable to carry out his plans, much as he desired, because of the obligations of his office as universal rector of the Colleges of India of the Society of Jesus, and of the death of the viceroy Dom João de Castro,[1] who passed away in Goa the following June of the year 1548. However, Garcia de Sá,[2] who succeeded him in the government, sent him off in April of the following year of 1549, with orders for Dom Pedro da Silva,[3] who was then captain of Malacca, to provide him with passage for wherever God chose to lead him.

With these orders the father reached Malacca on the last day of May in the same year of 1549, and delayed there for a few days on account of the poor arrangements that had been made for his passage. But finally, after enduring many hardships there in Malacca, he embarked on Saint John's Day of the same year, at sundown, on a small junk that belonged to a Chinese who was known as the *Necodá Ladrão,*[4] and on the following morning it weighed anchor and departed. On that voyage he also suffered a great deal of hardship on which I will not dwell here because I do not think it is necessary to discuss these matters in great detail. I will only touch briefly on what I consider most important for my purpose, within the limits of my feeble wit.

On Assumption Day, the fifteenth of August, the father arrived at the Japanese port of Kagoshima,[5] the native town of this Paul of the Holy Faith, where he was well received by all the people and much more so by the king, who made a greater fuss over him than anyone else, showering him with many high honors and letting it be seen that he was very pleased by the noble purpose that had brought him to this kingdom. For the entire length of time that the father was there, which was nearly a year, the king always showed him many favors, which the bonzes, who are their priests, deeply resented, and many a time they complained to him about his having given permission for a religion, so contrary to theirs, to be preached so freely in their land.[6] To which the king, by then thoroughly annoyed with them, replied, "If his religion is so contrary to yours, then refute it with contrary arguments from yours, provided that I am the judge in this case, for I shall not allow this foreigner, who trusted in my word, to be offended by your anger"—a reply which all the bonzes found highly outrageous.

But since the intention of this blessed father had always been to spread the holy name of Christ among the nobility because he thought it would be easier to convert the common people that way, he decided to leave shortly afterwards for the kingdom of Hirado,[7] a hundred leagues further to the north, which he did, when he felt the time was right. He left behind, in the company of eight hundred souls he converted there with his teaching, Paul of the Holy Faith, who continued to indoctrinate them for five more months that he remained there with them, but at the end of that time, because he had been offended by the bonzes, he embarked for China, where he was killed by some pirates[8] who were ravaging the kingdom of Ning-po. As for the eight hundred Christians that were there, even though they had been left without the father or any other brother to instruct them, our Lord ordained that they should all so persevere in the faith, with the help of the doctrine the father had left them in writing, that during the seven years that they were there alone without being visited by a priest, none of them wavered from his holy purpose.

A little more than twenty days after his arrival in the kingdom of Hirado, the father thought it would be a good idea to sound out all the heathens there in order to determine which part of the country would be best suited to his purpose. He had with him at the time Father Cosme de Torres,[9] a Castilian who had come as a soldier to the Moluccas, via Panama, in a fleet sent there in the year 1544 by the viceroy of New Spain. Through the encouragement and guidance of Father Master Francis he later joined the society in Goa and accompanied him afterwards, as did another lay brother, also a Castilian, a native of the city of Cordova, whose name was João Fernandes,[10] a very humble and virtuous man.

Father Master Francis now left this Father Cosme de Torres behind in the kingdom and city of Hirado and set out in the company of the other father, João Fernandes, for the city of Miyako,[11] which is the easternmost point of all of the island of Japan, because he had been informed that their *kubo-sama,*[12] who is the supreme head of their priesthood, resided there permanently along with three other dignitaries who call themselves kings, each of whom in turn attends to the administration of justice, military affairs, and the general welfare of the republic.

On the way there he endured tremendous hardships, not only because of the rough mountain terrain but also because of the time of year at which he traveled, for the winter season had set in by then and at a latitude of forty degrees where the cold, rain, and winds are so harsh that no one can stand them. Moreover, he was sorely lacking in what he needed not only for this, but for keeping alive, and in some places along the way, where foreigners were not allowed to pass without paying a certain toll, since he did not have the means to pay it, he passed as a footman in the service of some nobleman who happened by, which made it necessary for him, in order to pass safely, to keep up with the pace set by the horseman he was accompanying.

When he finally reached this famous city of Miyako, the capital of the entire monarchy of the Japanese nation, he was not allowed to see the *kubo-sama* as he had wished, because they asked him to pay 100,000 cash[13] for the privilege, a sum equal to six hundred *cruzados,* and there were times when he showed how deeply he regretted not having the money to achieve the goal on which he had so set his heart. So that, in all this land, he garnered no fruit, in part due to the wars and dissensions then going on between some of the people (which is quite common among them), as well as to many other difficulties[14] too numerous to relate, from which it is plain to see that the enemy of the Cross was deeply aggrieved by what this servant of God was trying to do in this land.

When he saw what little fruit he was harvesting there, so as not to spend his time in vain the father passed on from this city of Miyako to the city of Sakai,[15] eighteen leagues away, and from there he reembarked for the kingdom of Hirado where he had left Father Cosme de Torres, and remained there for a few more days. However, he did not spend them in resting from his past hardships, but in dedicating himself anew to other greater ones. At the end of that time he went on to the kingdom of Yamaguchi,[16] where he converted more than three thousand souls in the little more than a year he spent in that city, which was up until 5 September 1551, when he heard that a Portuguese *nao* had arrived in the kingdom of Bungo.[17] He immediately sent a Christian by the name of Matthew,[18] who traveled overland a distance of sixty leagues to deliver a letter to the captain and merchants on board, which went like this:

"May the love and grace of Jesus Christ, our true God and Lord, dwell by his mercy constantly in your hearts, amen. By means of some letters that have come from Bungo, the merchants of this city received word of the safe arrival of your lordships, but since I did not think this report was as true as I, with all my heart, desire, I decided to make certain of it by sending this Christian to you. Therefore, I beg you to inform me where you come from, what port you sailed from, and when you intend to return to China, for I would like, if God our Lord would be served thereby, to do everything possible to return to India this year. Also, please write me about yourselves, your names, that of the *nao* and of her captain, as well as everything else you know for certain about the state of peace and tranquillity in Malacca. At the same time I urge you to make ready for the voyage by stealing a few moments from your trading activities to examine your consciences, for that is the one item of merchandise from which you are sure to derive greater profit than you would from the silk of China, no matter how many times you double your investment, for I intend, if it please God our Lord, to be there with you as soon as I receive word from you. May Christ Jesus, for his name's sake, watch over us all and keep us in this life, by his grace, in his holy service, amen.

"Written in the city of Yamaguchi, 1 September 1551. Your lordships' brother in Christ, Francis."

The messenger arrived with this letter at the port where we were anchored and received an extremely cordial reception from everyone, as was his due. Six or seven letters were immediately written in reply by both the captain and the merchants, in which they gave him a great deal of news about India and Malacca and informed him that the *nao* was due to depart within a month for China, where there were three *naos* loading cargo which were scheduled to depart for Goa in January, and that on one of them he would find his friend Diogo Pereira,[19] with whom His Reverence would feel at ease.

Then the Christian who had brought them the letter was dismissed with this reply, and he departed quite content, not only because of all the things they gave him, but also because of the gracious hospitality with which they treated him during the time he spent there.

After five days on the way he reached the city of Yamaguchi where the father welcomed him, elated by his confirmation of the *nao's* arrival and the letters he had brought him. Three days later he departed for the city of *Fucheo*,[20] which is the capital of the kingdom of Bungo, where this *nao* I have mentioned, which belonged to Duarte da Gama,[21] was then anchored in the port with thirty of us Portuguese on board, trading our merchandise.

One Saturday, three Japanese Christians who were traveling in his company came to see us. Through them, Captain Duarte da Gama learned that the father had remained behind two leagues from there, in a town called *Pimlaxau*, suffering from a headache and swollen feet, brought on by the exertion of walking sixty leagues all the way up to there, and that owing to his indisposition, they thought he needed a few days to recover in order to be able to come the rest of the way, or a horse on which to ride, if he would accept one.

209
An Invitation from the King of Bungo

Having learned that the father was in the town of *Pinlaxau*,[1] feeling indisposed, as the three Japanese had told him, Duarte da Gama, the captain of the *nao*, immediately sent word to the Portuguese who were then installed in the city selling their merchandise, a league away from the port where the *nao* was anchored. They came at once, filled with excitement, and after discussing what to do about it, they decided that they should go and bring him back from the town where he had fallen ill, a decision that they immediately put into effect.

When we had gone little more than a quarter of a league, we met him coming on the way, in the company of two Christians who had converted to the faith less than a month before, important noblemen from the kingdom of Yamaguchi whom the king had deprived of their revenues of two thousand *taels* (which equals three thousand *cruzados*), because they became Christians. Since we were all dressed in our holiday clothes and riding on good horses, we felt quite embarrassed to see him coming the way he was, on foot, with a pack on his back containing all the things he needed for saying mass, which these two Christians took turns helping him carry—a sight indeed, that made us feel quite sad and ashamed. But since he refused to accept a horse, we were forced to accompany him on foot, in spite of his objections, which the two Christians found very edifying.

When we arrived at the *Finge*[2] River where the *nao* was anchored, he was welcomed with every possible demonstration of joy that could be shown him, and in his honor four rounds of all the artillery were fired, including sixty-three shots that came from culverins, falcons, and camels, all, or most of them, firing iron and stone cannonballs which, owing to the hollows in the mountains, resounded frightfully.

When he heard that horrendous noise, the king, who was in the city at the time, startled by the unaccustomed sound, thought we were fighting with a fleet of pirates, whose presence had already caused some alarm in the city, and he immediately sent a nobleman to find out what was going on. When he arrived, he gave Duarte da Gama a message from the king and offered to provide whatever help he could under the circumstances. Duarte da Gama replied with the courtesy demanded by the message and the offer of help and explained that we were celebrating the arrival of the father, because he was a holy man and one for whom the king of Portugal had a great deal of respect.

"I am uncertain about what I am to tell the king," the nobleman replied, as amazed by what he had heard as he was by everything else he had seen, "for our bonzes have been assuring him that this man is not a saint as you all say, but that he associates with demons, with whom they have seen him in conversation on several occasions, and that by means of witchcraft he has worked some marvels that have frightened the ignorant, and that he was poor, so poor that even the lice that covered him were loath to eat his flesh. As a result, I fear that now they will lose their credibility with the king to the point where he will never again see them or listen to them, for it is obvious that any man for whom you do so much and honor so highly by welcoming him in this manner must indeed be what you say he is and not what they tried to persuade the king he is."

The Portuguese reaffirmed what they had said and assured him anew of what he had already perceived himself, and they told him the whole truth, which he found utterly amazing.

He departed at once, and when he reached the city he informed the king of what was going on and told him that the sound of the artillery he had heard had been fired in celebration of the arrival of the father, which had made us all as happy as if we had gotten the *nao* loaded with silver, from which it was plain to see that everything the bonzes had said about him was a lie. He also assured His Highness that he was a man of such grave countenance that anyone who saw him would be inspired with deep respect for him.

"They are right in what they are doing," the king replied, "and you, even more so, in what you presume of him."

Then he immediately sent a young nobleman who was closely related to him to pay a visit to the father and to deliver a letter to him that went like this:

"Father Bonze of the *Chem ahicogim:*[3] May thy coming to my land be as agreeable to thy God as the praises of all his saints are satisfying to him. Through *Quamsio Nafama,* whom I sent down to your *nao,* I was informed of thy coming from Yamaguchi to *Finge,* which made me as happy as all my people will tell you. Therefore, I entreat thee earnestly, since God did not make me worthy of being able to command thee, in order to satisfy the love I feel for thee in my soul, to knock before the break of day on the door of the house where I await thee, or to command me to importune thee, without sparing stern words of anger, by begging thy God, on my knees, prostrated on the ground before thy God who I confess to be the God of all gods and the best of the best, who dwells in the heavens above, to manifest through the lamentations of thy doctrine, to all the pride-swollen men of the times, how agreeable to him is thy holy life of poverty, so that in their blindness the children of our flesh may not be deceived by the false promises of the world.

"Please send me tidings of thy health, so that I may sleep contentedly in the repose of the night until the cocks' crowing awakens me to announce thy arrival."

The young man who brought this letter arrived in an oared *funé*[4] as big as a good-sized galliot, accompanied by thirty young noblemen and his tutor, a very old man by the name of *Pomindono,* the bastard brother of the king of *Minâto,* who bade farewell to the father and all of us other Portuguese who were with him at the time. When he reembarked on the *funé* in which he had come, the *nao* fired a salvo of fifteen rounds of artillery in his honor, which made the youth feel quite pleased and proud.

"The God of these people must be very great indeed, and his secrets deeply hidden from us," he said, turning to his tutor who was at his side, "since he permits a man as poor as the bonzes assure the king that this man was, to be obeyed by the *naos* of the rich, and that they should demonstrate with the booming of their cannon that the Lord is satisfied with merchandise so lowly and so despised in the opinion of those who inhabit the earth, that it seems like a grave sin for the mind to even dwell on it."

"It may well be," the old man replied, "that this man's poverty is so agreeable to the God he serves that, by adhering to it, out of respect for his God, he comes out richer for it than all the rich men in the world, despite what our bonzes so boldly declare to the contrary, to whoever will listen to them."

As soon as the young man reached the city he went directly to the king, and still feeling a glow of pleasure for the high honor that had been paid him, out of respect for the father, he said to him, "It would not do for Your Highness to speak to this man the way the bonzes spoke to you about him, for I assure you it would be a great sin, nor should Your Highness think of him as poor, for the captain and all the merchants told me that if he were to ask for the *nao,* just as it was, they would give it to him immediately, without fail."

"I am confused by what thou sayest," the king replied, "and even more so by what the bonzes have told me, but I promise thee that from now on I shall treat them the way they deserve."

The following morning at daybreak, Captain Duarte da Gama met with all the merchants and the other Portuguese on board the *nao* to discuss the manner in which this first audience of the father with the king should be conducted. They all agreed that for the honor of God he should go surrounded by as much pomp as possible, since it would make the bonzes look like liars in what they had said about him, for it was obvious that the way they saw him treated was the way they would regard him. For that reason, among people who had no knowledge of God, it was most essential that it be done the way they suggested, and even though the father was not completely in favor of this decision, nevertheless, because of the reasons that were expressed, he was forced to bow to the opinions of the others.

Once this was settled, we all got ready as best as each one could at the time and departed for the city on board the *nao*'s longboat and two *manchuas* covered with awnings and silken banners, with trumpets and flutes playing alternately from time to time. The local people were so amazed by this unusual sight that by the time we reached the pier it was impossible to get ashore. At this point, the *Quamsy-andono,* the captain of the *Canafama,*[5] arrived by order of the king, with a sedan chair for the father, which he refused to accept, out of consideration for us. From here, he proceeded directly to the palace on foot, accompanied by a crowd of noblemen and all thirty of the Portuguese with about an equal number of our slave boys, all very well dressed, with gold chains around the neck.

The father was wearing a cassock of black unwatered camlet with a surplice over it and a green velvet stole with a brocade border. Our captain was walking with a staff in his hand like a majordomo, and five of the most honorable and richest men of the highest reputation were carrying certain objects in their hands, as though they were servants of his. One was carrying a book in a white satin pouch; another, a Bengal cane with a gold knob; another, a retable of our Lady in a purple damask wrapper; another, a parasol with a short handle; and so on, in this order and with this ostentation, we passed through the nine principal streets of the city which were so thronged with people that even the rooftops, everywhere, were full.

210
At the Court of Bungo

Keeping to the order I described, we reached the outer courtyard of the king's palace where the *Fingeindono,*[1] the captain of the palace guard, was stationed with a company of six hundred archers, lancers, and others armed with ornamented swords, which was regarded as a magnificent state for a great king.

Passing through the midst of all these people, we entered a very long veranda where the five men who were carrying the objects I mentioned above kneeled down and offered them to the father. The gentlemen present there were so amazed that they turned to each other, saying things like, "Hang our bonzes, and may they never show their faces again because this man is not what they told the king, but something sent by God to confound the envious!"

Once past this veranda we came out on a large hall crowded with noblemen dressed in *altirnas*[2] of multicolored satins and damasks with their gold-plated swords. Among them was a little boy six or seven years of age, that an old man was holding by the hand, who went up to the father and said to him, "May thy happy coming into the house of the king, my lord, be as gratifying to thee and to him as the water that God sends from heaven when the cultivation of our rice fields calls for it! Enter without fear and with that rejoice, for I assure thee in all truth, that all good men wish thee well and the wicked grow gloomy as a rain-filled night of deep darkness!"

The father responded after his fashion, with similar words, while the boy remained silent. After listening to all that he had to say, he replied, "Great indeed must be thy fortune which brought thee from the end of the world to be defamed with the name of a pauper in foreign lands, and much greater beyond compare the goodness of God, who is gratified by this confused opinion of the world, from which our bonzes are so far removed that they swear publicly that neither women nor the poor can be saved in any way."[3]

"The Lord who reigns in the heavens above will permit the cloud that covers their eyes to be removed," the father replied, "and then they will know the error of their ways, and when God gives them this light, then he will give them grace to disavow the false opinion they hold."

As the boy went on conversing with the father this way on lofty matters of great substance—which quite amazed us all because of his tender age, to judge by his appearance—we entered another hall where there were many young men, sons of the nobility of the kingdom, who all rose to their feet when they saw the father. After making their *gromenares*[4] to him, by touching their heads to the floor three times—which among them is a sign of such deep courtesy that it is only done by a son to his father or a vassal to his king or overlord—two of them, as though speaking for the others, said to him, "May thy welcome, holy Father Bonze, be as gratifying to the king our lord as the smile of the beloved infant for the mother who fondles him in her arms, for we swear to you, by the hair of our heads, that even the very walls that thou seest with thine eyes, command us to celebrate thy coming, for the glory of the God about whom, in Yamaguchi, thou didst preach all the marvelous things we have heard here."

Then they all made as if they wished to accompany him, but the child who was leading him by the hand signalled to them to sit down again. From here we entered a very long veranda that ran along some orange trees, and passing through it we came to another hall as large as the first two. The *Facharandono*[5] was there, the king's brother, who later became king of Yamaguchi, before whom the father made a deep bow. At this, he too responded with the same courtesies, saying, "I assure thee, Father Bonze, that today is a day of great rejoicing in this palace, a day on which the king my lord considers himself richer than if he possessed the thirty-two treasure houses of the silver of China. May thy coming here be as gratifying to him and as honorable to thee as thou couldst possibly desire."

The boy who was leading him then handed him over to him and remained a short distance behind in what was a different manner of courtesy which appealed to us.

From here we entered another hall in which there were many noblemen of the kingdom who also honored him highly, and he stood here a while conversing with them until, from the recesses of another hall, word came for him to enter. He went in immediately, along with most of those lords accompanying him and found himself in a very splendid hall where, the moment he saw him, the king, who had already risen to his feet, came forward to meet the father five or six steps from where he had been sitting. The father tried to bow low at his feet, but he would not allow it, and instead, he lifted him by the arms and performed the *gromenare* to him three times, which, as I said before, is a courtesy paid by a son to a father, or a vassal to an overlord, while all the lords present there looked on in astonishment and we, even more so. He took him by the hand while his brother, who had brought him this far, remained a short distance behind. Then he sat down on the dais, placing the father on an equal footing with him, and his brother a little further down, with the Portuguese facing them right next to the lords of the kingdom who were present there.

During the conversation that ensued, with both sides exchanging compliments, the king behaved in a very friendly fashion to the father, who in turn responded, in his manner, with such pleasant words, that the king looked at his brother and the rest of the lords present in the hall and said out loud for all to hear, "If one could only ask God where all this is leading, or why he made us so blind and this man so bold, for on the one hand, we now see with our own eyes what everyone in general says about him and what he says, which he proves with words that cannot be gainsaid and which conform so well to all natural reason that anyone who reflects carefully upon this marvel will be confounded and will not deny it, but rather, if he possesses good judgement, will confess it to be true. On the other hand, we see our bonzes so confused in matters of our faith, and so deluded in what they preach, that today they say one thing and tomorrow another, so that all their doctrine, for men of clear judgement, results in confusion and, in part, raises doubt about our salvation."

Embarrassed by what the king had said, a bonze who was present there replied, "This is not a matter that Your Highness can resolve so hastily, since he has not studied in *Fiancima*.[6] And if he has any doubts, he should ask questions, or let him ask me, and I will clarify matters for him, and then he will see how much truth there is in what we preach and that what they give us for doing so is indeed well employed."

"Since thou knowest the answers," the king replied, "speak up, and I shall be silent."

The *Faxiandono* then propounded his arguments to the king, the first of which was that, as far as the saintliness of the bonzes was concerned, there was no doubt about it because they lived all their lives in a religious order pleasing to God, and they spent most of the night praying for those who left their possessions to them, and they maintained perpetual chastity, did not eat fresh fish, healed the sick, instructed the sons of men in good customs, settled differences between kings so that the people might live in peace, gave *cuchimiacòs*[7] as letters of exchange in heaven so that all the dead could be rich there and enjoy most of their possessions. Also, in the night they sustained with their alms the souls who came crying to them for counsel in the afflictions and hardships they suffered because of their poverty; and they had received degrees from the colleges of Bandou,[8] confirmed by the *kubo-samas* and *groxos*[9] of Miyako; and above all, they were good friends of the sun, the stars, and the saints in heaven and thus were always able to speak with them at night and often hold them in their arms. And on he went in this manner, saying many other senseless things, occasionally raising his voice to the king with such uncontrolled anger that four times he called him *foxidehusa*, meaning, "blind, eyeless sinner."

The king was so upset by what this bonze said to him and by the deranged manner in which he said it that he motioned to his brother, glancing at him two or three times, to silence him, which the *Facharandono*—for that is what the king's brother is called—promptly did. Making the bonze rise from where he was sitting, the king said to him, "From what we have heard of the arguments thou hast chosen to present as proof of thy saintliness, we do not wish to deny it to thee, but at the same time, I must confess that the arrogance of thy unbridled language has scandalized us so, that I dare say—and I may swear to it without risk—that hell has greater sway over thee than thou hast over the heavens where God abides."

"There will come a time," the bonze replied, "when I shall not want to be served by men, nor will they, nor thou, nor all the kings who now reign on earth be worthy of touching me."

Smiling at the vanity of the bonze, the king looked at the father as if to say, "What do you think of that?"

"Your Highness," he replied, trying to placate him, "let the matter rest for another day, when the bonze will be calmer."

"Thou are quite right in what thou sayest," the king answered, "and I am quite wrong in listening to him."

Commanding him to rise, he said to him, "If thou must speak of God, do not justify thyself with God, for thou wouldst be committing a grave sin; but, instead, with patience, for his sake, purge thyself of the anger thou hast within thee, and we will listen to thee."

As though offended, the bonze turned to those present and said: "Hiacatá passiram figiancor passinau!" meaning, "A king who speaks that way—may the fire of heaven consume him!"—and rising abruptly, without the slightest show of courtesy, he stalked out the door, muttering to himself, with all the lords ridiculing him and exchanging witty remarks in their fashion, thereby softening the king's anger and putting him in such good humor that he burst out laughing with pleasure six or seven times.

After this, since by then it was time for dinner, they brought it to him and he invited the father to dine with him, which, three times, he very courteously refused to do, excusing himself by saying that he had no need of food.

"I understand that thou probably art not hungry, since thou sayest thou hast no need of food," the king replied, "but I also understand that by now thou shouldst know—if thou art Japanese like us—that this offer among kings is the surest sign of love that can be shown, and since I hold thee in such esteem, I regard it as a high honor to invite thee."

At this, the father, making an attempt to kiss the sword the king wore at his side by way of thanking him, as is the custom among them, said to him, "May the Lord our God, on whose behalf thou dost this for me, communicate to thee from heaven above, so much of his grace that thereby thou mayest deserve to profess his Law, like a true servant of his, so that at the end of thy days thou mayest earn the merit of possessing him!"

"I consent to what, for my sake, thou art asking of him," the king said, "provided thou and I both remain here together to talk about these things that are now happening to us."

With his face bathed in smiles, he offered him the dish of rice that he had before him, again begging him to eat, and the father did so at once; because of which, all of us, the captain as well as the rest of us Portuguese there, got down on our knees for the great honor that he was bestowing on the father publicly, in spite of the bonzes and the way they had slandered him.

211
Francis Xavier and the Japanese Bonzes

Forty-six days had gone by since this blessed father arrived in the city of *Fucheo,* the capital—as I said before—of the kingdom of Bungo on this Japanese island. In all those days he devoted himself so completely to the conversion of souls, with no time to spare for anything else, that rarely could any of the Portuguese spend a single hour with him, except at night in spiritual conversation and mornings at confession. Some of his more intimate friends complained to him about it, telling him that it almost seemed as if he were avoiding them, and one day he answered them this way, "I beg you, brothers of mine in Christ the Lord, don't ever wait for me at mealtimes, nor think of me as being alive when it comes to inviting me for dinner, for I assure you in all truth that it would only cause me pain. You should know that the banquet I most enjoy and which gives me the greatest pleasure is to see a soul surrender to the One who redeemed it and to confess out loud what *Saquay Girão,* an important bonze of *Canafama,* confessed today. After conceding what he had always denied before, he kneeled down with arms upraised, in the middle of the square thronged with people, and in front of everyone spoke these words, with tears in his eyes, 'To thee, eternal Jesus Christ, Son of God, I surrender my soul and I confess with my mouth what I feel deep in my heart. Wherefore, I beseech all who hear me to tell the people with whom they speak, to forgive me for all the times I preached to them as truth what I now see and understand is falsehood and lies.' And brothers, you may be sure that the holy confession of this new servant of God and brother of ours made such a deep impression on all the people that today, if I allowed it, more than five hundred persons would become baptized. But it is better to handle this matter with great prudence and not let it come about so easily, on account of the bonzes who advise them that as long as they are going to lose their souls by becoming Christians, they should ask me for a large sum of money in exchange. That is because they think that if I do not give them the money, I may, since I am poor and do not have anything to give them, lose the faith they tell them they have in what I say. But the Lord in his mercy will provide for this obstacle which the crafty enemy of the Cross seeks to place in the way."

Throughout all this time the king engaged him in such intimate conversation and gave so much of himself to him that all the while he was here not a single bonze was ever able to obtain an audience with him; and instead, ashamed of all the many depravities they had taught him in the guise of virtue, he gave up many vices he had by first sending away a young boy he was very fond of, with whom he maintained a vile sensual relationship.[1] Also, where previously he had been extremely miserly with the poor, owing to the precepts taught him by the diabolical bonzes, later on, moved by what this servant of God preached to him, he came to be so generous with them that one could almost call him extravagant. He also commanded that from then on, on pain of extremely severe penalties, no woman could kill the child[2] to which she had given birth, which previously was a very common practice among most of them, on account of the same teachings and persuasion of the bonzes.

He also forbade three or four other things of a similar nature, often telling his people in public that in the father's face he could see himself as clearly as in a mirror and that he was becoming ashamed and mortified at what he had practiced up to then on the advice of the bonzes. That is why we always thought, judging from these changes we saw in him, that there would have been very little to do to convert him to the faith if this blessed one had spent more time with him. But since the king's mind was set on something far different from this facility which in our minds is often perplexing, to this day he still has not converted,[3] though God alone understands the secret of this which we cannot fathom.

In the meanwhile, the time for our embarkation had arrived, and when the *nao* was ready to depart, Captain Duarte da Gama and the rest of us Portuguese went with the father one morning to bid farewell to the king and to thank him for having treated us so well in his land. After welcoming us with a bright, cheerful expression on his face, he said to us, "I confess that my heart grieves that I cannot be each one of you, for I envy you the company you take with you, leaving me as forlorn as the soul within me that weeps, for I very much fear that I shall never see him again in this land."

After thanking him for the love he had shown him, the father replied that, if God gave him life, he would return to see His Highness very soon, for which the king thanked him kindly.

In the middle of this conversation, as well as others that he had had with him, the father reminded him again about several things he had touched on before that were important for his salvation. He urged him to remember how brief were the days of man and how constant a companion death was to us all, and he assured him that, without any doubt, anyone who did not die a Christian would be condemned forever, and that if he were a true Christian and persevered to the end in His Grace, Jesus Christ himself, the Son of God, would have just cause to accept him for his own son and to justify him before the Eternal Father with the infinite price of his precious blood. And in this manner he went on discussing the matter of his salvation, saying things that were so amazing to hear that twice the king's eyes filled with tears, which greatly astonished us all and about which his people who were there with him made much ado.

By this time, the bonzes, like the ministers of the devil they were, were going about distorting what they had learned from him, because in the past conversations the father had had with them, he had confounded and shamed them all with arguments they could not refute. For this reason the people were beginning to lose respect for them. This they resented deeply, and many a time they called this servant of God *inocosēm*,[4] "foul-smelling dog," "poorest of all the poor," "lice-infested one," saying that he ate bedbugs and the flesh of human corpses he dug up at night, and that the words he used to embarrass them were inspired more by pure witchcraft and the devil's guile than by any virtue or knowledge he possessed, and that the king, because he had favored him and showered him with honors, would burn by fire and lose his kingdom, as had already been foretold by all four *fatoquis*[5]—meaning the gods of their faith—*Xaca*,[6] Amida,[7] *Gizom*,[8] and *Canom*.[9]

In this manner they pronounced many other curses against the king and the people for allowing the father to remain in the land—curses so frightful to hear that we Portuguese all went about in a state of fear. But what helped us was that we always had the king on our side, who, next to God, was the reason why the bonzes did not dare to go forward with a wily scheme they had devised, which was to stage an uprising in which they would kill the father and all of us with him.

When they realized that they could not achieve their ends this way, they thought that they would be able to do so by means of a formal debate in which the father would be totally discredited. For that purpose they decided to call upon one of their great bonzes, the head of a temple called Miyajima,[10] twelve leagues from there, who represented the epitome of all their learning. With this in mind they went to see him and urged him to help them, for the honor of their gods. Since he thought it would bring him great honor and credit to vanquish someone who had vanquished many others, he came hurrying to their aid at once, accompanied by six or seven others like himself, whose help he sought.

He arrived in the city at the time that the father, as I said, was in the king's palace with our captain and the rest of us Portuguese, taking our leave of him, prior to our departure on the following day. Anxious not to let slip out of his hands what he thought was an easy prey, and confident of his learning, since he had earned the degree of *tundo*[11] from the University of *Fiancima*[12]—where it was said that he had spent thirty years as the foremost professor in a school regarded among them as the most outstanding, like the faculty of sacred theology among us—when he arrived at the palace at the time I indicated, he sent one of the bonzes in his party to inform the king that the *Fucarandono,* as he was called, was there. At this, the king's face darkened and he looked sad, for he thought that, with his great learning, he might embarass the father, thereby causing him to lose the esteem he had won from the others. The father understood this and begged the king, as a great favor, to let him come in, to which the king finally agreed, with a heavy heart.

Once the bonze had entered and paid his due respect, the king asked him what he wanted. He replied that he had come to see the father of the *Chenchico*[13] to bid him farewell before he departed. This was said with such an air of self-importance, arrogance, and overweening pride that one could immediately tell that he was a true advocate of the one who had sent him. He approached the father, who invited him to sit next to him, and after an exchange of compliments, with which they are ordinarily quite liberal, he asked the father if he knew him. He answered no, because he had never seen him before. The bonze made merry of this, laughing derisively.

"There is very little to be accomplished here," he said to the six members of his party, "since, after buying and selling with me ninety or a hundred times, he says he does not know me, which means that we cannot expect him to answer our other questions very much to the point."

Turning back to the father, he asked him: "Do you still have some of that merchandise you sold me in *Frenojama?*"[14]

"I do not answer anything I do not understand," the father replied, "so explain yourself more fully and then I shall answer to the point. Since I have never been a merchant, nor do I know where *Frenojama* is, nor have I ever spoken with you, how could I have sold you any merchandise?"

"You must have forgotten," retorted the bonze, "which makes me think that you probably have a bad memory."

"Since I have forgotten," the father replied, "you tell me about it, since you have a better memory, but remember that you are in the presence of the king."

The bonze, very sure of himself, proudly said: "It is now fifteen hundred years since you sold me a hundred piculs of silk, on which I made a great deal of money."

Looking at the king, the father very serenely and gently asked him for leave to reply, and the king told him he would be delighted to hear his reply. Then, after paying him due respect, he turned to the bonze and asked him how old he was.

"Fifty-two," he replied.

"Well then," retorted the father, "if you are only fifty-two years old, how could you have possibly been a merchant and bought merchandise from me fifteen hundred years ago? Also, since Japan has been populated for only six hundred years, as you all publicly proclaim, how can it be that fifteen hundred years ago you were a merchant in *Frenojama,* which at that time, as it would appear, must have been uninhabited land?"

"I shall tell you," the bonze said, "and you will see how much more we know of things past than you do of things present. I would have you know, since you do not, that the world never had a beginning, nor can the men born in it ever have an end, except for these bodies in which we go about, which end with the last breath we draw, in order to permit nature to pass us on to newer and better ones, as is plain to see when we are reborn of our mothers, either as males or females, depending on the conjunction of the moon at the time they bring us forth; and after we have been born here into the world, we undergo in succession a variety of these changes to which death holds us subject, due to the weak nature of which we are composed. He who has a good memory will always remember what he did and what happened to him in the other phases of his previous life."

The father responded to this false argumentation by destroying it three times with words and reasons so clear and obvious, and by means of comparisons so appropriate and natural, that the bonze was left at a loss for words. I am not giving them here merely because I want to be brief, but mainly because they are not within the grasp of my poor wits. However, in spite of all of them the bonze would not budge from his false opinion, so as not to lose the reputation and high regard which he thought everyone had for him. As he persisted in his line of argumentation—in order to demonstrate, for the benefit of the king and his other listeners how learned he was in matters of their laws—maintaining on behalf of the bonzes what the father was contradicting, he asked him, making much ado about it, why he forbade the Japanese to indulge in their depraved sensual practices.

To this second question the father also responded with such clear and vivid arguments—which are also beyond my ken—that the king was quite pleased and the bonze bewildered, yet so stubborn and unyielding in his stupidity that he still refused to accept any reason they gave him, no matter how clear it was, until all the lords present there told him, "If you want to fight, then go to the kingdom of Yamaguchi[15] which is now at war, and there you will find some heads to split because we—God be praised—are all at peace here. However, if you come to debate, maintain, or refute, let it be in a quiet and gentle manner, as you see this foreign bonze do, who responds only when you give him leave to do so. If you follow his example, His Highness will listen to you, otherwise he will have his dinner now, for it is almost time."

In response to this, which was spoken by one of the lords there, the bonze used such ill-mannered language that the king, in outrage, ordered him to rise and had him shown to the door, swearing to him that if he had not been a bonze, he would have had his head cut off.

212
Theological Disputations

The harsh manner in which the king had treated the *Fucarandono* led to an uprising of all the bonzes against him and all the lords in the kingdom, for they felt that he had done so in contempt of their doctrines. As a result, they closed all the temples in the city, refusing to perform any sacrifices for the people or accept any of their offerings. In view of the situation, it was necessary for the king to handle matters with great prudence, in order to quell the riots and disorders among the populace which were already beginning to get out of hand, with a shameless and total lack of respect.

Out of fear that what we had always dreaded might happen to us, we Portuguese embarked the next day—a bit more hastily than we should have—and we also insisted that the father do the same, since there was no longer anything for him to do there, but at the time he refused. Discussing the father's refusal among themselves, all those on board the *nao* agreed that Captain Duarte da Gama himself should immediately go ashore to look for him in person, before some disaster befell him, and he did so at once.

When he arrived at a humble abode where the father had sought shelter with eight Christians, Duarte da Gama gave him the message he was carrying from all the Portuguese and tried to make him see that it was in his own best interest, for many reasons, to embark at once, before some disaster befell him, which clearly, from all indications, was bound to happen if he did not do so.

"O my dear brother," he replied, "would that I were fortunate enough to deserve to have God our Lord visit upon me the disaster which you fear! But I know all too well that I am not worthy of so great a favor. As for my embarking as hastily as those gentlemen ask me and Your Lordship also advises me to do, it does not behoove me to do so at this time because it would be much too scandalous a thing in the eyes of these new converts to the faith. It would only serve as a bad example and provide them with both motive and cause to feel free to resort to that which the devil, through his advocates, places within their reach. And now that Your Lordship understands what my true purpose is, he is free to depart with all the other gentlemen, to whom he is deeply obligated, on account of their cargo, just as I am, perhaps even more, to so merciful a God who died, nailed to a cross, in order to save me."

Disappointed and shedding a few tears, the captain returned to the *nao*, so deeply troubled by the virtuous words he had heard from this blessed one that, after telling the Portuguese what had happened he said to them that, as for the obligation he was under to them, because of their freight, to take them back to the port of Canton from whence he had come, he was handing over and releasing the *nao* to them, then and there, with all its cargo, to do with it all as they saw fit, for he vowed to return to shore and under no circumstances to abandon the father. All the merchants were deeply impressed by the captain's holy resolve, and they granted him all the time he thought necessary to achieve it. Filled with holy zeal, they all resolved to join the captain, and the *nao* was returned to where it had been berthed before. This greatly consoled and pleased the father, lifted the spirits of the Christians, and embarrassed and annoyed the bonzes, for they realized that the life of poverty followed by the father, for which they vilified him so much, was dictated rather by a desire to serve God than by necessity, as they said. Even though they very well knew that the king was already convinced of the truth of this, and that the father was prepared to withstand all the opposition and difficulties they placed in the way of what he said and preached, nevertheless, they again concluded among themselves that the *Fucarandono* should continue his disputations with the father.

They promptly informed the king of their decision, who agreed under certain conditions that were quite contrary to those they proposed, the first of which was that they were not to shout out loud or speak discourteously; the second, that they were to yield to whatever their listeners deemed reasonable; the third, that they would abide by whatever decision was reached at the end of the disputations by a majority of votes; the fourth, that neither they, nor others representing them, were to stand in the way of those who might want to become Christians; the fifth, that regardless of the subject under discussion, when they wanted to prove or disprove a point, they would have to submit the matter to a panel of judges; the sixth, that they were to accede to whatever could be proven by means of natural reasons to which human judgement is subject— to which they all objected, protesting that it was dishonorable for them to submit to the decision of arbitration judges who were not bonzes like them themselves. Nevertheless, the king insisted that they abide by his rules which he thought were reasonable, and they gave in, very much against their will, because there was nothing else they could do.

Early the next day the *Fucarandono* arrived from Miyajima accompanied by more than three thousand bonzes who had gathered for this disputation. However, the king would only allow four of them to enter, explaining that he was doing so in order to avoid a commotion as well as for their own honor, for it would not do to have three thousand appear against only one.

He immediately sent a message to the father, whom he had already apprised of this some time before. He came accompanied by the captain and all the Portuguese with even greater pomp than when he had first met with the king, for the richest and most honorable among them waited on him as servants with the deepest respect, kneeling before him at every opportunity and holding their hats in their hands all the while, which were adorned with pearls and many gold chains.

The sight of all this wealth, honor, and splendor was highly offensive to the *Fucarandono* and the other bonzes, and they could not hide the fact that they were deeply pained and amazed by the spectacle before them. However, the king and the lords present in the palace were obviously delighted by it all, and by way of taunting the bonzes they were saying things to each other like, "Would that my sons were as poor as he is. . . . Let them say whatever they like for the truth is apparent to all. . . . The envy of those who claimed the contrary bears witness to the lie . . ."

The king, picking up his ears at what the lords were saying, smiled and said to them, speaking in our favor, "The bonzes had sworn to me that the moment I laid eyes on the father I would vomit out of nausea. At the time I believed it, because it was told to me by persons of authority, but from now on I shall hold their truths to be as trust-worthy as this one."

These words and other pleasantries which the king exchanged with the lords out loud, in front of everyone, spoken, so it seemed, in a scornful and derisive manner, made the *Fucarandono*—as well as the other bonzes who were with him—feel so embarrassed that they did not dare raise their eyes, and they were all so deeply hurt and filled with envy that the *Fucarandono,* turning to one of the four nearest him, said meekly, "By what my eyes have just seen and heard, it appears that we shall leave here today with the same honor as we left with the other day, and perhaps with more than a fair share of abuse."

When the father reached the palace where the king was waiting, making his entrance in the manner I described, accompanied by many lords and nobles, the king made him sit next to him with greater honors than all the others and almost equal to those he showed his brother. After exchanging a few words with him he called for silence in the hall and told the *Fucarandono* to speak up on behalf of the bonzes and explain why they thought that the new law the foreign father had come to preach to the inhabitants of their city should not be allowed in Japan.

The bonze, a bit more restrained by then, speaking in a gentler tone and keeping his pride in check—or perhaps disguising his lowly ancestry and the base bloodline from which they said he was descended—replied that it was because it was an extremely antagonistic law, directly opposed to all of theirs, which brought public dishonor on the servants of God who had taken religious vows and had led exemplary lives in his service by introducing new precepts forbidding everything that the *kubo-samas* of old had taught them, and affirming publicly in all the gatherings at which he was present that only by following what he preached and taught could men be saved and not by any other means; and that their saintly *Fatoquins,*[1] *Xaca,* Amida, *Gizom,* and *Canom,* were condemned to eternal punishment in the Concave Depths of the House of Smoke, delivered up by divine justice to the Ravenous Serpent of the House of Darkness; wherefore, it seemed that, out of holy zeal, they were all obliged to avoid this evil from which so many others proceeded.

The king then told the father to reply to this complaint, one which was heard in general, not only from this man but from others as well.

Turning his eyes heavenward with arms upraised, the father replied that His Highness should ask the *Tundo* to point out specifically the reasons he and the other bonzes had to complain about what he said, and then he would answer each one of them, point by point, and that whatever decision His Highness, together with all the others present there, reached on the matter, they would abide by it without either the bonze or him arguing any further about it. The king approved of this and commanded that it be done so.

Then, after silence had been imposed on the listeners once more, the bonze asked him, why did he speak ill of their gods. To this the father replied that it was because they were unworthy of that venerable name which was given to them by the ignorant, for by all the laws of reason and truth, it could only be applied to the almighty Lord who had created heaven and earth, whose omnipotence and incomprehensible marvels our minds were incapable of probing, let alone understanding, and that from the little that our eyes could perceive of him, one would judge him to be the true God, and not *Xaca,* or Amida, or *Gizom,* or *Canom,* who were merely very rich men, as was written in their scriptures. To this reply they all said, "What he says seems right."

When the bonze attempted to refute this argument, the king told him to go on to something else because that point had already been decided in the opinion of the listeners, which did not please him at all. Proceeding with his questions, he asked the father why he objected to the bonzes issuing letters of exchange for heaven, since they provided the souls of the dead with riches in heaven, without which they were poor and bereft of any means of livelihood.

To which he replied that the wealth of those who went to heaven did not consist of the *cochumiacos* that the bonzes gave them here, which were a form of tyranny, but of the deeds which they performed in this life with faith, and that it was by means of this faith, together with charity, that one earned the right to go to heaven, and that was the faith he was preaching to them, which was called the Christian religion, and that the giver of this holy faith and Christian Law was Jesus Christ, the Son of God, who had become a man in this world and suffered death on the Cross in order to redeem all sinners who, when baptized, would keep his Commandments and persevere in his holy faith until the end of their lives; and that this pure, holy, perfect faith was not so selfish as to make exceptions among individuals, as they preached, for it did not exclude women[2] from gaining salvation only because nature had made them the weaker sex, nor could they remedy their situation by the amount of money they were able to pay, as they had given him to understand; from which it was clear that their laws were based more on the self-interest of those who preached them than on the truth of the God who had created heaven and earth and worked by himself for the salvation, not only of men, but women as well, as they had heard him say several times before.

To this the king replied, "He is quite right in what he says." And all the others who were with him said the same thing, which made the *Fucarandono* and the other four feel quite ashamed and embarrassed, but still persisting in their errors as obstinately as before. But even though I have at times been heard to say that the Japanese people are more capable of reasoning than all the other heathens in those parts, still, their bonzes, because they are by nature very proud and conceited about knowing more than the others, consider it a matter of honor not to retract anything they have once said, nor yield a point in any argument touching upon their credibility, even though they might be risking their lives a thousand times because of it.

213
The Disputations Continue

The disputations[1] of our sainted father with the bonze *Fucarandono* did not end here, for he was joined by six others whom he trusted, and they came to see him many times, propounding many questions and always arguing many things anew against the truth that the father preached to them. These disputations went on for five more days and were always attended by the king in person, not only because he enjoyed listening to them, out of curiosity, but also because he had given the father his word to protect him the first time they had met in the city of *Fucheo*.

During this time, all the bonzes, in an attempt to embarrass or discredit him, asked him questions about things that the human mind has never imagined, slipping them in between others that were so simple and easy that anyone could have answered them with little effort. At times they also dealt with very profound, weighty questions over which there were many altercations on both sides. Of these, as best my meager wit will allow, I shall mention only three or four that I thought were of greater substance than the others, which I do not consider important enough to discuss.

To this end, our sainted father often asked us to help him with our prayers, for he assured us that he had great need of them, not only because of the weakness of his wit, but also because he realized that the devil was speaking through these advocates of his, disputing the law of God.

After the bonzes had propounded a few arguments to him, they tried to prove, by means of some diabolical philosophy, that God was extremely hostile to all the poor, for since, as they said, He denied them the good that he gave the rich, it meant that he did not love them. The father refuted this false proposition with reasons so clear, so obvious, and so true that the bonzes, even though they had replied twice, still, since the truth cannot be denied, were forced, despite their natural pride and presumption, to concede to what the father had said.

This one vanquished, another took to the field. He went up to the father and told him that there was no need for him to come from the end of the world, to put into the heads of the people that only in the religion he preached, and in no other, could a human being be saved, for since there were two paradises, one on earth and the other in heaven, only one of which necessarily was to be enjoyed according to God's precepts, one for work and the other for rest, it was clear that man's paradise was the one on earth, since all born men, each in his own way, gloried in earthly rest—the kings, by the power and command they exercised throughout the earthly monarchy; the grandees who come after them, such as princes, captains, the rich and powerful, in the injustice with which they treated those beneath them; and the common people, in the joys and pleasures of life; so that each and every one of them was his own judge, handing down sentences against himself; and the beasts and the oxen, because in this life they spent their days in suffering and hardship, had the right, and justly so, to possess the heaven that man, by his own inclination and as a consequence of his sins, chose to reject; and so on in this manner he propounded many other arguments as stupid and senseless as these, which the father also refuted very easily.

Furthermore, they told him that they did not deny that God, as all-powerful, had created everything in the world for the benefit of man, but, being subject to sin, the things that later proceeded from them were so imperfect by nature that they were bitter, hard, wild, and of absolutely no substance in themselves, which made it necessary, if they were to return to their original state of perfection, for Amida to be born from all of them, she who they believed had been born eight hundred times, in order to bestow a state of perfection on eight hundred different kinds of things in the world; for it if were not so, as indeed it was, and of this their scriptures assured them, there would no longer have been people, nor world, nor anything, nor any trace of those who had been born in it; so that it was only right that men should offer as many praises to Amida for this work of preservation, as well as to God for the benefit of creation.

The father destroyed this argument and false philosophy with few words, since the subject matter in itself was clearly of very little substance; but the arguments the father presented were such that the king and all the other listeners deemed quite satisfactory. Since the partnership of all seven of these bonzes had been arranged by the Infernal Enemy, the father of all discord, at that very moment, a dispute broke out among them that became so heated, with such great differences of opinion between them, that three or four times they nearly came to blows in front of the king, who lost his patience and told them that matters relating to God were not to be disputed with blows, but with favor and fervor, founded on meekness, for in the meek and humble spirit God took shelter to sleep his peaceful slumber. After which, he rose and left the hall accompanied by some of the lords who went with him to watch some games at the queen's apartments, and the bonzes each went his own way, and the father with the captain and the other Portuguese went off to the Christians' house where they slept that night.

The following afternoon, the king in person, pretending that he was passing down the street by chance, sent to ask the father if he wanted to come and see his garden, for he had just received word that the game was already waiting for him, and that he should arm himself well, for perhaps even today he would bring down a couple of buzzards out of the seven that wanted to pluck his eyes out yesterday.

The father understood the metaphor and went right out into the street where the king was waiting for him on foot, in the company of only three or four of his intimates. Taking him by the hand, with the Portuguese a short distance behind, he led him, with an elaborate show of honor, through all the streets, up to the palace, where the bonzes were already waiting with a large number of noblemen.

Once he was seated and the hall was silenced, the bonzes again raised other questions on the subject of the day before, holding up a long scroll full of rebuttals which the king refused to look at, saying, "That which has already been judged once, cannot be judged twice as you would have it. Therefore, go on to speak of something else because this father is already embarked for sailing and the captain is not so indebted to you, either out of kinship or friendship, that on your account, he should care to lose his voyage. Therefore, make the best of him these two days that he will still be here, if you please, or else go back to Miyajima whence you came."

To which he replied that he would do as His Highness commanded, but that as long as they were there he should give them leave to talk with the father about good things that they wanted to find out from him, which were not controversial, because they had pledged themselves to that purpose.

The king gladly granted them permission and urged them to proceed.

Then they went up to the father, and after begging his pardon for the past, asked him many curious and pleasant questions which the king enjoyed hearing. Among them one was that if to God, in his infinite wisdom, everything, both past and future, is present, how is it that he did not see, when he created the angels, that Lucifer himself, along with the others, would offend him by causing trouble, thereby making it necessary for him, by reason of his divine justice, to condemn them to eternal punishment. And if he did not see it—as one would expect him to—why was he not, in his infinite mercy, moved to intercept an evil from which, afterward, so many followed, in offense to him. Also, if he did not forsee it, which would excuse him, then what he was telling the people about him in this respect was false.

The father, after pausing a moment, as though he were giving some thought to the question the bonzes had posed, answered at great length, explaining the truth of the matter, which they at times contradicted with such astute arguments that the father turned around to Duarte de Gama who was a short distance behind him and said, "Mark well what Your Lordship hears and you will see that what they say does not proceed from them, but from the devil himself who teaches them. However, I trust that God our Lord will reply for me."

After some altercations on the subject, which caused some delay because the bonzes refused to accept the reasons they were given, the king decided to step in as mediator.

"According to what I have been able to make out from what has been said on the subject thus far," he said, "it is my understanding that the father is right in what he says but that you lack the faith to acknowledge the truth; for if you had it, then you would not contradict him; and since you do not have it, then avail yourselves of reason, like men, and do not bark like dogs all day long with such obstinacy and rage that you are slavering at the mouth like mad curs that run around biting people."

At this, all the lords present burst out laughing, showing their approval of what the king had said. The seven bonzes complained bitterly about this and asked the king how His Highness could consent to them all acting like kings in his presence. At this point the father came between them, and at his intercession, peace was restored.

The bonzes continued with their questions for more than four hours, dwelling on profound matters like men who—which cannot be denied—are endowed by nature with better understanding than the other heathens in those parts, from which it seems that the effort it takes to convert these people to the faith will be more fruitful and therefore better employed than on the Singalese[2] of Comorin and Ceylon; but even so, I do not mean to say that it is ill employed on them; by no means, it is very good.

Since he was more learned than the others, the *Fucarandono*, still anxious to come out ahead by posing questions that would embarrass the father, renewed his arguments by asking him why he gave indecent names to the Creator of all things as well as to the saints in heaven who served in his praise, defaming him as a liar, when, as everyone believed, he was the God of all truth.

In order to understand what made him say such a thing, it should be pointed out that in the Japanese language the word for "lie" is *diusa*.[3] Since the father, when he preached, would say that the faith he came to propagate was the true Law of *Deus*,[4] a name which, owing to the crudeness of their language they were unable to pronounce as clearly as we do, they would say *Dius* instead of *Deus*. That is what prompted these servants of the devil to tell their people that the father was a demon in the flesh who had come to defame God by calling him a liar. But the listeners were completely satisfied with the father's explanation, and they all said in one voice: "Sitá, sitá,"[5] meaning "Enough, enough, enough," as if to say, "We understand what you are saying."

Also, at the same time it should be pointed out that the reason why the bonze said he was giving indecent names to the saints was because every time he finished saying mass the father was in the habit of reciting a litany in unison, praying to our Lord for the augmentation of the Catholic faith, and as part of the litany, as is the custom, he would always say, "Sancte Petre ora pro nobis, Sancte Paule ora pro nobis," and so on, for the rest of the saints. Now because the word *santi*[6] is an obscene and disgraceful word in the Japanese language, that is how it came about that he accused the father of calling the saints bad names. But then he gave them the true explanation of how that had happened, which the king enjoyed immensely, and from then on, the father had the word *sancte* stricken and replaced it with "Beate Petre, beate Paule," and so on for the other saints, because all the bonzes had been making poisonous remarks about this to the king all along.

Still continuing with their arguments, not out of any zeal for converting, nor asking for the sake of learning, but only to vilify the Law of God and to vex this servant of his, they said to him that if God, who is infinite wisdom, saw that the work he was doing in creating man was to lead to man's committing so many offenses against him, why did He not desist, which obviously would have been better, for it would have avoided what happened afterwards. The father also gave them satisfactory explanations for this that were quite clear, yet adequate enough to confound them, just as he had done in every other instance. As for the way they replied to this and to all the other questions I have touched on, I can say no more here because I am too dim-witted to do so, as I have confessed many times before, and also because I realize that it does not behoove me to meddle in matters of this nature. Suffice to say that the answers were always such that all the bystanders were highly satisfied with them.

Nevertheless, that did not stop the bonzes from dwelling two to three hours on the rebuttals they made to some of them. But finally, after very grudgingly conceding this last point, they still went on to say that since God had decided, after Adam had been overthrown by the serpent, to send his son into the world to redeem the descendants of this same Adam, why did he not hasten to act, given the necessity for doing so. For if by chance his answer to this was that his reason for not doing so was to teach men the gravity of sin, that still was not reason enough to clear him of guilt for his negligence in delaying so long.

To this the father replied the way he usually did. However, on this point they raised many different objections and were so obdurate in conceding to the reasons they were given that the king, annoyed by their persistence in denying everything the father said, rose to his feet, saying, "Anyone who would argue about a religion so well founded on all reason as this one is, ought not to be so far beyond reason as you are."

Then taking the father by the hand, accompanied by all the grandees who were with him, he led him to the house of the Christians where he was staying, which provoked the bonzes enormously and made them feel deeply ashamed; and they said out loud, publicly, that fire from heaven should strike the king for allowing himself to be so easily deceived by a nameless, vagabond sorcerer.

214
The Miracle of the Sloop

The next morning our sainted father, along with all the rest of us Portuguese, went to say good-bye to the king. He treated him at this farewell meeting with the same honor and attention as he had always done. After this, we finally embarked and departed from the city of *Fucheo*.

We sailed on our course, keeping within sight of land as far as an island called *Meleitor* that belonged to the king of *Minacó*. From here we began our crossing and proceeded on our way with a following wind for a period of seven days. At the end of that time, with the conjunction of the new moon, the wind suddenly shifted to the south, threatening us with showers and signs of winter. It grew steadily stronger, forcing us to put about with the prow facing north-northeast, through unknown seas never before navigated by any nation, without knowing where we were going, delivered up totally to the whims of fortune and the weather, in a wild and raging storm beyond all human imagination, which lasted for five days. In all that time, since we never saw the sun by which the pilot could get a bearing, just by dead reckoning, without any idea of degrees or minutes of the latitude we were in, he set a course, more or less, for the area around the islands of the Papuas,[1] Celebes, and Mindanao, six hundred leagues from there.

On the second day of this storm, along about afternoon, the seas began to swell, with the waves rising so high that the thrust of the *nao* could not cut through them. As a result it was decided, on the advice of the officers, that the ship's castles, both fore and aft, should be razed to the floor of the deck, so as to make the *nao* lighter and better able to respond to the helm. Once this was done, with all possible speed because everyone without exception took part in it, our next task was to secure the sloop which, by dint of hard labor, was made fast alongside and immediately tied with a splice of two new coconut-fiber ropes. By the time this task was completed, darkness had closed in and the night was pitch black, making it impossible for the men on the sloop to climb back on board the *nao*. As a result, they were all forced to spend the night there. Altogether there were fifteen men on it, five of them Portuguese, and the rest, sailors and slaves.

In the midst of all these hardships and misfortunes, this blessed father was always at our side, night and day, either working physically like each one of us, or encouraging and consoling everyone in such a way that, after God, he alone was the captain who spurred us on and gave us the strength that kept us from succumbing completely to the hardship and from surrendering totally to the whims of fortune, as some were at times tempted to do, had it not been for him.

When it was almost midnight, the fifteen men on board the sloop let out a loud cry of "Lord God, have mercy on us!" and when everyone on board the *nao* came running to find out what was going on, they saw the sloop on the horizon of the sea, lashing about, because both the towlines with which it was fastened had snapped.

Heartsick at this disaster, the captain, without a moment's thought or consideration for what he was doing, ordered the *nao* to tack to leeward in the wake of the sloop, thinking that he would be able to save it. But since the *nao* was hard to maneuver and responded slowly to the helm, for there was little canvas to help her, she was caught between two waves where a huge mountain swept over the poop, spilling such a heavy load of water onto the deck that she nearly sank, at which the people, with a loud cry that pierced the air, called out urgently for our Lady to come to their aid. Hearing this, the father—who at the time was on his knees, leaning over a chest in the captain's cabin—came running in great haste. When he saw the precarious situation of the *nao* and all of us piled along the gunwales on top of each other, with most of the men battered by the cages on the deck, raising his arms to heaven, he prayed out loud,

"O Jesus Christ, love of my soul, help us, Lord, by the five wounds thou didst suffer for our sake, on the tree of the true Cross!"

Then, in that brief instant, the *nao* rose up again on the ocean wave, and they lost no time, working at top speed to trim the bonnet that was fastened as a forecourse to the bottom of the foremast, and as God willed, the ship righted itself and was promptly trimmed at the stern. But the sloop disappeared completely from view in the wake of the *nao*, leaving everybody in tears, praying for the souls of those who were on board.

In this manner we ran the rest of the night, under great duress, and at daybreak, for as far as the eye could see from the top of the crow's nest, there was nothing visible except the breaking waves on the storm-tossed sea. At a little more than half an hour past daylight, the father, who had been resting in the captain's cabin at the time, appeared on the poop deck where the master and the pilot, along with six or seven other Portuguese, had gathered. After greeting them all with a relaxed and cheerful "good morning," he asked them if the sloop had been sighted, and the answer he got was no. Then when he asked the master to send a sailor aloft to see if it could be sighted from the crow's nest, one of the men there told him that it would appear when another was lost.

Pained by these words, the father exclaimed, "O Brother Pero Velho² [for that was his name], what little faith you have! And why? Do you perchance think that there is anything impossible for the Lord our God? Well, I trust in him and his Mother, the most holy Virgin Mary, to whom, on his behalf, I have promised three masses in her blessed Church of the Mount in Malacca, for she will not allow those souls on the sloop to be lost."

Pero Velho was somewhat abashed by this and did not say another word. Then, in order to better satisfy the father's request, the ship's master, in person, along with another sailor, climbed up to the crow's nest, and after searching the seas from up there for nearly half an hour, they told him that there was nothing on the entire ocean for as far as the eye could see.

"Then you may as well come down," the father replied, "since there is no longer anything to be done."

Then he called me over to the poop deck where he was at the time, looking quite sad as everyone thought, and asked me if I would have a little drinking water heated for him because his stomach was very upset, a request which, for my sins, I could not satisfy, since there was no stove on the *nao*, for it had been thrown overboard the day before when the deck had been jettisoned at the beginning of the storm. Then he complained to me that his head was reeling and that he was subject to occasional dizzy spells.

"Little wonder that Your Reverence feels that way," I said to him, "since you have not slept for three nights and it is very likely that you haven't tasted a bite of food either, as one of Duarte da Gama's slaves told me."

"I assure you," he answered, "that I feel sorry for him when I see how disconsolate he is, for all last night, after the sloop was lost, he wept continuously for his nephew, Afonso Calvo, who is on it, along with our other companions."

Then, because I saw the father yawning frequently, I said to him, "Your Reverence, go lie down for a while in my cabin, and perhaps you will get some rest."

He agreed to this, saying that it should be for the love of God, and he asked me to have my Chinese boy close the door behind him, and to stay there, so that when he called he should open it for him, which would probably be between six or seven in the morning, more or less, and he retired to the cabin where he remained all that day until nearly sunset. In the meantime, when I happened to call the Chinese boy who was outside the door to bring me a dipper of water, I asked him if the father was still sleeping.

"He never slept a wink," he replied, "but he is on his knees, crying face down on the bunk."

I then told him to go back and wait outside the door, and be ready to attend him the moment he called.

In this manner the father remained given over to his prayers until nearly sundown, and then he came out of the cabin and went up to the poop deck where all the Portuguese were sitting on the boards because of the frequent lurching and reeling of the *nao*. After greeting them all he asked the pilot if the sloop had appeared. He replied that it was only to be expected that it would be lost in such heavy seas, and that assuming that God miraculously wanted to save it, by this time it was more than fifty leagues behind us.

"It would naturally seem so," the father said, "but it would make me very happy, Pilot, since there is nothing to be lost thereby, if, for the love of God, you would climb up to the crow's nest or send one of the sailors up there to scan the seas, so that we can say that we have left nothing undone."

The pilot repled that he would gladly do so. He climbed up, and the ship's master with him, more to satisfy the father's earnest entreaty than because they thought they might be able to see something, which only seemed reasonable. They stayed there for a long time, and finally, they assured him that they had seen nothing on the entire surface of the sea which, as everyone thought, made the father feel quite sad.

Resting his head on the poop deck bitts, he remained that way for a while, with the same air of sadness, heaving as though he would cry. Finally, opening his mouth and taking a deep breath, as though shaking off his sadness, he raised his hands to heaven and prayed, with tears in his eyes, "Jesus Christ, my true God and Lord, I entreat thee, by the pain of thy most sacred death and Passion, have mercy on us, and save the souls of the faithful who are on that sloop!"

With that, he again rested his head on the bitts against which he had been leaning and remained that way, as though he were sleeping, for about as long as it takes to recite two or three Credos, when a boy, sitting in the rigging, began to shout, "It's a miracle, it's a miracle, here's our sloop!"

At the sound of his voice everyone, just as they were, rushed over to port side where the boy was shouting and saw the sloop coming at more or less a musket-shot's distance from the *nao*. Struck with amazement by such a strange and unusual thing, they were all crying on each other's shoulders like children, so that it was impossible to be heard above all the wailing that was going on all over the *nao*.

Then they all ran to throw themselves at the father's feet. However, he would not consent to it and withdrew to the captain's cabin, locking himself inside so that no one should speak to him.

Our companions on the sloop were immediately brought on board with as much pleasure and excitement as one can imagine; and for that reason too, I shall give no further details of their reception, for they are more to be thought about than written about.

The short time left before darkness closed in completely—which could have been a little over half an hour—was spent this way, and when it had passed, the father sent a boy to call the pilot and told him to praise the Lord our God who had wrought such deeds, and to have the *nao* made ready because the storm would not last long.

As the father's command was being carried out, with all possible speed and devotion, the Lord willed that suddenly, before the main mast was raised and the sails rigged, the storm subsided completely and the wind shifted to the north; upon which, under a following wind, we proceeded on our voyage, with great joy and contentment on the part of all.

And this miracle I related took place on the seventeenth of December 1551.[3]

215
The Death of Francis Xavier

Proceeding on our way from here, from the vicinity where the Lord our God in his mercy, responding to the prayers of this blessed father, saw fit to grant us so miraculous a favor as this, and in thirteen days of our voyage it was his will that we should reach the kingdom of China.

We anchored in the port of *Sanchão*,[1] where we used to trade in those days, but since it was already late in the season by the time we arrived, we found only one *nao* there, and even that one was getting ready to sail for Malacca on the following day. The father embarked on it because it was necessary for the *nao* on which Duarte da Gama had come from Japan to lay up for the winter in Siam, since it was split at the stempost, owing to the severe stress it had undergone in the storm I have described above, and it had to be repaired there and fitted out with many things it needed.

On that part of the voyage that the father made from China to Malacca in the company of Diogo Pereira, who was a very good friend of his, he told him about how the affairs of Christianity stood in Japan and how important it was for him to do everything possible to see if he could gain admission to China, not only to propagate and make known the law of Christ our Lord to those heathens, but also to settle a matter once and for all with the bonzes of the kingdom of Yamaguchi who, finding themselves hard pressed in the conversations and disputation he had had with them about the faith, had in the end told him that since the laws they preached had come to them from China and had served them well for six hundred years, they would under no circumstances reject them, until they learned that he had convinced the Chinese with the same arguments he had used to make them confess that this law was good and true, and that what he was preaching deserved to be heard.

That is why this servant of God departed for India, driven by a desire that grew out of deep zeal for his honor and his faith, not to leave any stone unturned, not only in order to settle this matter once and for all with the Japanese, but also to make the truth known to others; for his intention was to apprise the viceroy of all these things and to ask him to help him in every possible way to carry out his plans.[2]

The father discussed this matter with the best-informed people on board the *nao* and asked for their opinions, since they were men who had a great deal of knowledge and experience in matters concerning this monarchy of China. They told him that there was absolutely no way the father could gain admission to China for that purpose, unless the viceroy of India would send an ambassador there in the name of the king, our lord, to make it official, along with an expensive gift and a new offer of friendship, worded in the style to which they are accustomed. Since a great deal of money would be needed for such an important undertaking as this, as well as a gift of many costly objects, it was doubtful that the viceroy would be willing to do this. The father was saddened by what they told him, for he believed it to be true, and also because he was mindful of the obstacles that hard times and troubles in the State of India might place in his path.

They talked often about this matter on that voyage, and Diogo Pereira offered to take it upon himself, as a service to God and out of friendship for the father, to get him into China at his own cost and to cover all the necessary expenses, both for the gift as well as everything else that was involved, an offer that the father accepted, promising him that he would be compensated for it by the king, our lord.

With this in view, immediately after their arrival in Malacca the father embarked for India, and Diogo Pereira remained in Malacca with the *nao,* preparing to go on to Sunda from there to load pepper. He sent in the company of the father a certain Francisco de Caminha, his steward, with thirty thousand *cruzados* in musk and silk to be used to buy everything that was necessary. When he reached Goa, the father communicated his plans to the viceroy Dom Afonso de Noronha,[3] who praised him highly for his noble and saintly intentions and offered to help in every way possible.

Quite pleased with the viceroy's favorable reply, he made all the necessary preparations as quickly as possible and returned to Malacca with the official orders the viceroy had given him for Diogo Pereira to go on this holy expedition as ambassador to the king of China, orders that were entrusted to Dom Alvaro de Ataide,[4] who was then captain of the fortress.

However, the captain refused to obey those orders because at the time the father arrived he had had a serious quarrel with Diogo Pereira over the latter's refusal to lend him the ten thousand *cruzados* he had asked him for. Even though the father tried as hard as possible, in his own virtuous way, to patch up this quarrel and discord, he was never able to do so. Since it was based on hatred and greed, and the devil was the one who was fanning the fire, in the twenty-six days during which some attempts at reconciliation were made, the captain would never give in to what the father was asking of him. Neither would he grant permission for Diogo Pereira to take him to China, in accordance with instructions from India, when so much money had already been spent, twisting the viceroy's instructions around by saying derisively that the Diogo Pereira to whom His Lordship was referring was a nobleman who remained in Portugal,[5] and not the one the father was presenting to him, who only yesterday had been a servant of Dom Gonzalo Coutinho[6] and did not have the qualifications required to go as ambassador to such a great monarch as the king of China.

As a result, when they saw that the situation was steadily deteriorating, with the captain refusing to account for his behavior or take anything they said into consideration, a group of honorable men, motivated by their zeal for the honor of God, all got together one morning and went to ask him not to take upon himself something that would be so detrimental to the honor of God, for he would be held strictly accountable for it in the next life. They also warned him to take heed of the fact that all the people were rising up in protest against him for preventing such a holy man as the father from going to preach the law of Christ to those heathens, through whom it seemed our Lord wanted to open a door to his Gospel, for the salvation of so many souls.

To which they say he replied that he was too old for them to be giving him advice, that if the father wanted to go to all that trouble for God, then let him go to Brazil or Monomotapa,[7] lands where there were also heathens, like in China, because he had sworn that as long as he was captain, Diogo Pereira would not go to China, neither as a merchant nor as an ambassador, and let God take that into account, for he was ready to give it to Him whenever He asked for it, because the voyage that Diogo Pereira wanted to make in the father's shadow in order to bring back 100,000 *cruzados* from China rightfully belonged to him, because of the services rendered by his father, the count admiral,[8] rather than to a servant of Dom Gonzalo Coutinho, whom the father wrongfully wanted to support in such a wretched matter, and with that he dismissed them.

When the revenue officer, the factor, and the customs officials saw how unreasonably he had answered these men, they all went one morning to present him with a petition in the name of the king stating that there was a regulation in their customs house, laid down by the past governors, that expressly commanded that under no circumstances whatsoever should any *nao* be prevented from sailing abroad as long as it obligated itself to return there to pay the duties; and that Diogo Pereira had given them a written statement that they had brought with them, in which he obligated himself to give the king, just in the duties from that *nao,* thirty thousand *cruzados* for the needs of the fortress, half of which he would pay immediately, and for the other half, depositary guarantors for when he returned; therefore, they requested His Lordship not to hinder his voyage, for were he to do so without cause, as in this instance, they protested in the name of the king that His Highness would have the thirty thousand *cruzados* out of the captain's estate.

To which he replied that if Diogo Pereira was obligating himself to give the king thirty thousand *cruzados* in customs duties from his *nao,* as they claimed, then he was also obligating himself, on account of the petition they had brought him, to give them all thirty thousand blows with the shaft of that halberd, and as he made a dash for a wall rack on which it hung, they very hastily withdrew.

In that way, twenty-six days went by after our arrival, during which there was nothing that could soften the captain's obstinacy; on the contrary, he used some very harsh terms in speaking of the father that were quite uncalled for and most inappropriate for a man of his authority and virtue.

Finding himself so vexed and insulted with ugly names, this servant of God bore it all very patiently, without anyone ever hearing him say anything except, "Blessed be Jesus Christ!" spoken as he gazed heavenward, with such vehemence, as though it were coming from the depths of his soul, and at times not without many tears. Thus it was being said publicly in Malacca that if the father desired—as was presumed of him—to suffer martyrdom for God, he had indeed been a martyr as a result of this persecution.

In all truth I can say that whenever I look back on what I saw with my own eyes of the great honors that the king of Bungo, a heathen, lavished on this father only because they had told him that he was teaching the law of God, as described above, and about what I saw later on in Malacca, I am struck with amazement, as I believe any Christian would be who had seen one and the other.

In spite of it all, the father embarked for China on this same *nao,* but it was quite different from the way it would have been had he gone with Diogo Pereira. However, he remained behind in Malacca, and the *nao* was taken over completely by the captain and his henchmen with his handpicked skipper, and the father went under arduous circumstances, without any authority, dependent on the charity of the quartermaster, and without any baggage other than the cassock he wore on his back. But since it had always been his intention to suffer among the infidels so as to make them confess to the truth of what he preached, for his part he did not want to do anything to jeopardize it by raising objections or placing obstacles in his path, and so he chose to embark that way, exposing himself to whatever time would bring.

At two hours past midnight, when the *nao* was ready to depart, the quartermaster sent a boy, a nephew of his, to Our Lady of the Mount where he was then staying, to tell him that His Reverence should embark at once on the *manchua* he was sending him because the *nao* was about to sail.

As soon as he received the message the father came out, holding the boy by the hand, along with two others, devotees of his, who accompanied him to where the *nao* was anchored, right next to the fortress. One of these two—the João Soares[9] who later lived in Portugal in the town of Covilhã[10]—watched him embark with deep sadness and melancholy, and as he was bidding him farewell, said to him, "Your Reverence, now that you are going so far away, you ought to speak to Dom Alvaro, if only to silence the tongues of his henchmen who claim that he says Your Reverence resented this as though it were a physical blow."

"Would to God, dear father," he replied, as he was about to step into the *manchua,* "that I were the sort who resented it for the honor of God, as would be right, but no imperfection was to blame for this. As for my speaking to Dom Alvaro as you advise, it is too late for that, for he and I shall never meet again in this life. But we shall see each other in the valley of Jehoshaphat, on that day of tremendous majesty, when Jesus Christ, the son of God and our Lord, sits in judgement on the living and the dead, before whom he and I shall be judged, and a reckoning will be taken from him of the reason he had for preventing me from going to preach to infidels the word of Christ, Son of God, nailed to the Cross by sinners. I assure you that very soon, at the onset of his punishment for this sin, he will face some difficulties with respect to his honor, his property, and his life. As for his soul, may Jesus Christ, God our Lord, have mercy on it!"

Then, fixing his gaze on the main door of the church in front of him, he kneeled down with arms upraised, as though he were praying for him, and with a sudden rush of tears that impeded his speech, exclaimed, "O Jesus Christ, love of my soul, by the pains of thy most holy death and Passion, I beseech thee my God, to look upon that which thou dost continuously present before the Eternal Father on our behalf, when thou showest him thy precious wounds, and that which thou didst earn for us. Grant it thus for the salvation of the soul of Dom Alvaro, so that he may walk in the path of thy mercy and be pardoned by thee!"

Bending down with his face to the ground, he remained that way for a while without making another sound. After he had risen to his feet, he took off his boots and beat them against a stone, as though he were shaking the dust from them. Then he climbed aboard the *manchua* and bade farewell to the two who had accompanied him, shedding so many tears that the Father Vicar João Soares, who was also crying, said to him, "Come now, what is this? Is this separation forever? Why does Your Reverence leave us so disconsolate? Well, I trust in God our Lord that very soon I shall see you back in this land again with greater leisure."

"May it please his divine mercy," he replied, and with that he embarked.

That morning at dawn the *nao* sailed out of the port of Malacca, and after a voyage of twenty-three days it dropped anchor in the port of *Sanchāo,* an island twenty-six leagues from the city of Canton, where at that time trade was carried on with the local people.

A few days after the *nao* had anchored here, while the merchants were attending to their affairs, and all was peaceful, and trade was brisk, this servant of God made an agreement with one of the honorable Chinese merchants of the port who was called *Chepocheca,*[11] to take him to the city when he went back. And even though some of the Portuguese objected to it, for they did not want to see him go that way all by himself, with nothing to lend authority to whatever he might say, still, after a thorough discussion of one thing and another, an agreement was reached with this merchant as follows: that the father was to give him two hundred *taels*—which is worth three hundred *cruzados* in our money—to take him from where the *nao* was anchored all the way to the city with his eyes blindfolded, so that in case—since he was a foreigner— the police got hold of him, as was bound to happen, and tried to make him confess under torture who had brought him there, he would not be able to tell them nor recognize the one who had brought him there, for fear that if he were discoverd they would have his head chopped off. The father agreed to all these conditions without fear of anything and without letting himself be frightened by the fears the others generally expressed to him, since they understood how anxious he was to receive martyrdom for God our Lord.

Nevertheless, since God himself, whose secrets no one can penetrate, did not see fit to let him enter China, and he alone knows the reason why he prevented him from doing so, in a way that naturally seemed just—as are all the things of God, by having this heathen *Chepocheca* confess that although he was quite satisfied with what they were paying him for the journey, nevertheless, his heart told him that he should not do such a thing because it was bound to cost him and all his children their lives.

After this the father allowed himself to remain on board the *nao* without putting this holy deed into effect, much as he desired. And since by then he had already taken ill with the fevers and dysentery, on top of the melancholia and disappointment from which he was suffering, the sickness gained such mastery over him, becoming increasingly worse each day, that he finally took to his bed, with severe loss of appetite, from which he suffered, under the worst conditions, for more than fourteen days. At the end of that time, realizing that his illness was a mortal one, he asked to be taken ashore, where he was then carried and placed in a makeshift hut they fashioned for him there, covered with reeds and branches. There he remained for seventeen days, and —according to what three men who were there with him told me—ill provided with the barest of necessities, not only because some people thought they were pleasing someone who they believed would not be unhappy about it, but also because—in my opinion—our Lord, by permitting this servant of His to be left destitute at that moment on earth, wanted to show that his passing was in conformity with that of others whom we know, as an article of faith, are now reigning with him in heaven.

At the end of these seventeen days, during which, from all outward appearances, he suffered deep physical discomfort and distress, when he became aware, both in spirit and from the weakness of the flesh, that his hour was already drawing near, he bade farewell to everyone, shedding many tears. He asked them to pray God for his soul, for, as he assured them, he was already on the way and was in great need of their prayers. With that he asked a boy who was taking care of him to close his door because the noise of the people disturbed him.

He remained this way for two more days, unable to hold anything down by that time. At the end of these two days he took a cruxifix in his hands, without lifting his eyes from it and without another sound being heard from him other than the words, "Jesus Christ of my soul!" which he uttered from time to time like a sigh.

Finally, when he was no longer able to pronounce a single word, the ones who were with him—according to what they all related—saw him publicly shed some tears that flowed somewhat more forcefully, with his eyes ever fixed on the crucifix, until he surrendered his soul completely to God, which happened on a Saturday, the second of December, in the year 1552,[12] at midnight—a death that was deeply regretted and mourned by all those present there.

216
The Miracle of Incorruptibility

They immediately attended to the burial of this blessed corpse, making all the necessary arrangements as best they could at the time, insofar as local conditions would allow. On Sunday afternoon, at two hours past vespers, they carried him to the place where the grave had been dug, which was perhaps a little more than a stone's throw above the beach, and there he was buried with deep feeling on the part of all, especially the most virtuous and God-fearing among them. However, there were some in whom this feeling could not be discerned outwardly, and whether they felt it inwardly or not, God only knows, and let him be the judge who knows the truth of things and the reasons for them. But what came to light publicly was that two weeks later, a man—whose name I will not mention for the sake of his honor—sent off a letter to Dom Alvaro on a *vancão* that left China for Malacca, in which he told him quite bluntly, "Master Francis has died out here, but in his death he worked no miracle. He lies buried on the beach here in *Sanchão* along with the others who died on the *nao,* and we will take him with us when we leave if the body is in fit condition, so that the scandalmongers of Malacca will not say that we are not good Christians like them."

Three months and five days later,[1] when the *nao* was ready to sail, the Portuguese went ashore and had the grave opened in which the saintly corpse had been buried, with the intention of taking his bones back to Malacca if they were in fit condition. They found the body completely intact, with no sign of decomposition or defect of any kind, so much so, that not even the shroud and the cassock he wore were found to have any spots or blemishes, for both were as clean and white as if they had just been washed, with an extremely sweet smell about them. This had such an astounding effect on everyone that some, who were perturbed by what they saw with their own eyes, smote themselves repeatedly for the things they had said before, and with tears streaming down their cheeks they publicly exclaimed, "Oh, wretched are the ones who tried to please the devil, acting as his advocates by causing thee vexation in Malacca, when thou wert as pure a servant of God as we see here now and publicly confess of thee! And wretched are we, who often denied thee our alms, knowing thou wert lacking in the barest of necessities to sustain thy saintly life! Hang the world and all its lies! Hang Malacca and all the promises it holds out, for in the end, thou alone, O blessed one, didst travel the right path in serving God as truly as all of us now confess of thee, in spite of ourselves, and much to our chagrin!"

They carried on in this manner, shedding many tears and scratching their faces as they lamented their past error, for which our Lord, because of the prayers of this servant of his would surely have mercy on them.

The saintly corpse was placed in a coffin that was made then and there to fit his measurements, and it was carried to the same *nao*[2] on which he had come, traveling all the way to Malacca in the pilot's cabin. At ten o'clock on the day after it arrived, the supervisor of the House of Mercy, the entire brotherhood, the vicar, and all the priests of the main church, accompanied by all the local population—with the exception of the captain and his henchmen—went down to the *nao* to get him. From there, they carried him to the chapel of Our Lady of the Mount, which was where he had always made his home in Malacca and from where, nine months and twenty-two days before,[3] he had embarked for China.

He was buried in this chapel with deep pain and grief on the part of all, and there he remained for nine more months, which was from the seventeenth of March until the eleventh day of the following December in the year 1553. On that day his body was disinterred and placed in another coffin that Diogo Pereira had ordered for him, lined with damask and covered on top with a brocade cloth. From here, from the chapel of Our Lady of the Mount, he was carried in procession, accompanied by many noblemen, until they placed him on a sloop that was already waiting, beautifully adorned with luxurious carpeting and a silk awning, on which he was taken to a *nao* belonging to a certain Lopo de Loronha[4] who was about to depart for India, and transferred aboard. With him went two brothers of the Society of Jesus, one called Pero de Alcáçova[5] and the other João de Távora[6]—who later on was at the College of Évora—both of whom accompanied him to India. On the way, which is a distance of five hundred leagues, some obvious miracles[7] were observed, according to the testimony later given to the viceroy Dom Afonso de Noronha in Goa, by all those on board the *nao,* which I see no point in discussing here since they are well known to everybody and it would only be a waste of time writing about what I know that others have already written.

217
The Final Resting Place of Francis Xavier

The *nao* carrying this holy corpse reached Cochin on the thirteenth of February in the year 1554. By that time the northwesterly monsoon was blowing along the coast, and the *nao,* along with all the others that had sailed in consort[1] with her from Malacca, owing to the foul wind, could make no more headway than one or two leagues a day, tacking from one board to the other with great difficulty. As a result, the pilots decided that the captain should send a message to the College of Saint Paul in Goa, asking the fathers to arrange for an oared vessel on which to carry the holy corpse because the *nao* could not reach Goa before March 25 or thereafter, which was the time when Holy Week fell that year. Since the holy Church was commemorating the Passion of the Son of God that week, it would then be impossible for him to be received with the pomp and pageantry on which they had all set their hearts.

Lopo de Loronha himself, the captain of the *nao,* chose to be the one to carry this message and departed immediately. When he got to the College of Saint Paul in Goa he delivered the message to Father Master Belchior,[2] universal rector of the Society of Jesus in India, and returned to the *nao* immediately afterwards. The father rector consulted with the other fathers of the college, and among them all it was agreed that the father rector himself should immediately go in person to inform the viceroy and to ask him for a well-equipped cutter. This was done and the viceroy immediately gave him one that was under the command of a certain Simão Galego, who was very sick in bed at the time, but a man who was a devoted follower of the deceased holy man offered to go in his stead, which made the viceroy very happy.

Father Master Belchior, along with three brothers[3] and four orphaned children of the college, embarked on the cutter and left Goa on a Monday morning. The following Wednesday he found the *nao* close to the bar harbor of Bhatkal,[4] along with seven others that were also becalmed, all within sight of each other, without being able to make any headway. Recognizing the cutter, because of the way it was festooned with branches and gaily bedecked, the *nao* saluted them in the same manner. As soon as the cutter came alongside the *nao,* Father Belchior climbed aboard with all the members of his party, leading the orphaned children before him with garlands on their heads and branches in their hands, singing *Gloria in excelsis Deo,* and so forth, as well as many other hymns in praise of God. After everyone had climbed aboard and been warmly welcomed by the captain and the rest of the ship's company, the brother who had the deceased holy man in his charge took the father rector by the hand and, holding a lighted candle aloft, led the way below to the cabin where he lay and showed him to the father and all the others who had come with him. The moment they saw him they all fell to their knees and with many tears in their eyes they kissed his feet. After they had gazed at him for a long time, they transferred him to the cutter, chanting the psalm *Benedictus Dominus Deus Israel,* as the bystanders joined in, shedding no less tears than the fathers did. Once unmoored from alongside the ship, where everyone remained showing signs of the devotion they felt for him, the *nao,* along with the seven others that were around when the cutter cast off, fired a deafening salvo of artillery which frightened the heathens and brought them running all along the shore to see what was going on.

Having departed from the bar of Ancola[5] here, five leagues below Bhatkal, bound for Goa, the cutter arrived on Thursday, at eleven o'clock at night, at our Lady of Rebandar, half a league from Goa, where the body was taken ashore, carried to the church, and placed next to the main altar, surrounded by many burning torches and tapers. Father Master Belchior, who was now in charge of it, immediately sent someone to inform the viceroy, as he had asked him to do. He also sent word to the fathers of his college for them all to come and wait for him on the pier at daybreak, for he would be there by eight o'clock. After the father rector had taken care of everything he thought necessary at the time and had rested a while, in the wee hours of dawn he said mass, which was attended by all the people who lived in the area, both native and Portuguese.

By this time, as day was breaking, six vessels arrived from the city with forty or fifty men on board who, during the lifetime of the deceased, had been very devoted followers of his, all of them carrying freshly lit candles in their hands, with their slaves carrying tapers. Upon entering the church they all prostrated themselves before the tomb or coffin where he lay and paid him reverence, shedding many tears, and at sunrise they set out for the city.

On the way they saw Diogo Pereira, who was there on a sloop with many people on board carrying lighted torches and tapers, all of whom prostrated themselves face down on the deck as the cutter passed by them. Close behind them, in the same order, were ten or twelve other vessels, so that by the time it reached the pier it must have been accompanied by twenty rowing vessels carrying about 150 Portuguese from China and Malacca, all very rich and respectable people. They were also carrying lighted torches and tapers while their servants, who probably numbered over three hundred, were carrying candles as big as torches, creating altogether a magnificent Christian spectacle that inspired deep devotion in all those who beheld it.

218
A Letter from the King of Bungo

When the cutter carrying this holy corpse arrived at the city pier where it was to dock, the viceroy was already there, waiting in full state with footmen bearing silver maces, accompanied by all the nobility of India, in addition to such an enormous crowd of people from among the general population that four constables had all they could do to clear the way. Also there were the canons of the cathedral chapter, the supervisors and brothers of the House of Mercy, all in their vestments, with white tapers in their hands, and a coffin with a brand-new cloth of brocade decorated with gold embroidery and fringes, which was not used because it seemed better to have him carried in the one in which he had come from Malacca.

The fathers and brothers of the Society of Jesus—who were there in great numbers—boarded the cutter, which by this time had been made fast to the landing.

When they lifted the coffin that was on top of the deckhouse, a very devout crucifix appeared, which a large group of orphaned children from the college had kept covered. One of them began to chant the psalm *Benedictus Dominus Deus Israel,* to which all the others responded together with a lamentation of very fine voices in perfect harmony that was so amazingly pious that it made everyone's hair stand on end just to hear them. Also, the tears and sobs were so widespread throughout that crowded Christian assembly that the mere sight of it was enough to make every sinner undergo a truly genuine conversion. [1]

The entire crowd set out from the pier in a very orderly procession, and the holy corpse followed behind them in the coffin in which it had come from Malacca, with a large brocade cloth on top and silver thuribles scenting it from both sides with the most delightful aromas, and the coffin belonging to the House of Mercy preceding it to the right. So that all in all, this funeral was conducted that day with such great cost and splendor, for the honor of God and this servant of his, that the native heathens and Moors stuck their fingers in their mouths [2] to show how deeply amazed they were, as is their custom.

They passed through the city gate, proceeding in this manner along the main street, which at the time was very splendidly decorated from top to bottom with many carpets and silken hangings, and the windows were well fitted out and crowded with the wives and daughters of all the noblemen, with many ingenious devices at the doorways below giving off perfumes and sweet-smelling aromas. And not only this street, but all the others through which it passed, as far as the College of Saint Paul to which it was taken, were like this. Even though it was a Friday of Lazarus, the college was festively bedecked with brocade frontals on all the altars, and lamps, candlesticks, silver crosses, and everything else in sight were arranged in like manner.

After they reached the church this way, it was placed next to the high altar on the Gospel side, where a solemn mass was said with a brocade pontifical and celebrated with a beautiful chorus and many musical instruments befitting the solemnity of such an important festivity. But because the hour was very late and everyone was very anxious to view the holy corpse, they dispensed with the sermon.

Once mass was over, the saintly body was exhibited to all the people who paid reverence to him with many tears. But since, as I said, there were so many people there and each one was trying to get a closer view of it, the crush and press of the crowd were such that the grilles of the chapel, despite the fact that they were very sturdy, were broken into many pieces. Seeing that the tumult was steadily increasing and that they were unable to control it, the fathers covered the coffin again and told them that they would be able to view it more comfortably in the afternoon, and with that they all departed. Nevertheless, it was shown several times afterwards, and on some of those occasions, because of the enormous crowds that came, there was a great deal of shouting and disorder on the part of both women and children who were in danger of being suffocated. [3]

Later that same afternoon there arrived in the city of Goa a Portuguese by the name of Antonio Ferreira, a married man residing in Malacca, who brought a gift of luxury items for the viceroy that had been sent to him from Japan by the king of Bungo, along with a letter that read like this: "Illustrious and splendid Majesty, lord viceroy of the lands of India, frightful lion of the ocean waves by force of great ships and heavy bombards—I, *Yacatá-andono,* [4] king of Bungo, Hakata, Yamaguchi, and the land bounded by the two seas, lord of the lesser kings of the islands of Tosa, Shimonoseki, and Miyajima, hereby make known to you that some days past, while I was listening to the Father Francis *Chenchicogim* speak of the new religion of the Creator of all things that he was preaching to the people of Yamaguchi, I made a secret promise to him deep in my heart that when he returned to this kingdom of mine I would receive from his hand the name and the water of holy baptism, even though the news of such an enormous change of heart would cause discord between me and my vassals. He also promised me that if God gave him life he would return very soon. Because his delay in returning is so much longer than I had hoped for, I decided to send this man to find out from him and Your Excellency, what keeps him from coming. Wherefore, my lord, I am asking you, in any event, to beg him, on your behalf and mine, since the kings of the earth cannot command him, to come immediately with the next monsoon, because his coming to this kingdom of mine will be of great sevice to God and will lead to a new friendship with the great king of Portugal, enabling this land of mine and his to be bound in love as one. Moreover, his vassals will be exempted from customs duties in all the rivers and ports where they may anchor, just as they are in your port of Cochin.

"Your Excellency may command me how best to serve your king in friendship, for I will do so as quickly as the sun turns the night to day. Antonio Ferreira will give you some arms which I used to conquer the kings of Hyuga and Shimonoseki, and clad in them as I was on the day on which I gave them battle, I give obedience, through you as my older brother, to that invincible king from the end of the world, lord of the treasures of great Portugal."

The viceroy Dom Afonso showed this letter to the Father Rector Master Belchior and asked him why he did not leave immediately for Japan to do something of such great service to God and take with him the entire College of Saint Paul of Goa. The father gave him many thanks for the favor shown him and told him that as long as His Lordship was both advising and commanding him to do so, he would go at once and make ready to depart during that very monsoon.

The viceroy praised and thanked him for it very much, for he realized that it was a matter of great service to our Lord.

219
Anarchy in Malacca

Fourteen days later, on the sixteenth of April, in the year 1554, Father Rector Master Belchior departed for Malacca on board a *nao* that was carrying Dom Antonio de Noronha,[1] son of Dom Garcia de Noronha,[2] former viceroy of India, to take possession of the captaincy of that fortress because the viceroy had ordered the arrest of its captain, Dom Alvaro de Ataide, for disobeying his orders and for other complaints he had against him which I do not care to dwell on here since they have nothing to do with my purpose.

On the fifth of June the new captain, Dom Antonio, arrived in Malacca. He was warmly welcomed there and conducted in a procession singing *Te Deum Laudamos* to the church, where mass was said and a sermon preached. After he left the church, which was sometime around eleven o'clock, the licentiate Gaspar Jorge, chief magistrate of India, who had been assigned to this case, had them ring a bell, at the sound of which all the people gathered together. He showed them the orders he was carrying from the viceroy, after which he pulled out some notes he had brought with him. Referring to these notes, he asked Dom Alvaro many questions which were duly recorded by two notaries and signed by both of them as well as by the magistrate and the captain, all of which took quite some time.

When the interrogation was over, Dom Alvaro was deposed from the captaincy and placed under arrest, and all of his property was confiscated. The same thing was done to all his supporters who had taken his side when he arrested Gamboa, the revenue officer, and tore up the viceroy's orders, as well as other excesses that were committed in this case. All this was carried out with such great severity, to such an extreme, that most of the men fled to the Moors, leaving the fortress so deserted and in such an abandoned state that it stood in danger of falling, if the new captain, Dom Antonio, had not handled the matter with great prudence, by issuing a general pardon to all. Even so, they returned very reluctantly, for since Malacca was deprived of its former status as a city, because of these abuses and others committed by Dom Alvaro, and her city council and government stripped of its powers amidst ugly, shameful public proclamations, all the inhabitants became so alarmed and panic-stricken by these unprecedented measures that they abandoned their homes and property, as I said, and passed over to the Moors.

So that from all these indignities and many others committed against Dom Alvaro it was clear to see how true the prophecy made by Father Master Francis turned out to be when he told the vicar João Soares that Dom Alvaro would soon find himself beset with vexations and difficulties involving his honor, his property, and his life. As for his death, it is a well-known fact that he died in Portugal trying to free himself on bond of several charges filed against him by the crown prosecutors, and that the cause of his death was a huge abscess that formed on his neck, spreading infection throughout his entire body with such an unbearable smell that no one dared to go near him. But from here on I will have nothing more to say about him. Suffice it to say that his death came very fast[3] and was the result of God's judgements, which He alone understands.

These disturbances and excesses in the name of justice, which had the entire city in turmoil, made it impossible for Father Master Belchior and the others in his party[4] to continue their voyage to Japan that year as he had planned, and as a result they were forced to spend the winter here in Malacca until April of the following year 1555, which delayed them ten months.

During this time, the magistrate Gaspar Jorge went right on rigorously administering punishment day after day, against this one and that one, giving cause for much outrage in the entire land. And not content with that, relying on the wide powers the viceroy had granted him, he tried to interfere in the jurisdiction of the captain, Dom Antonio, encroaching so much on his powers that he was left as captain in name only and overseer of the fortress, which, though he resented it bitterly, still, in the beginning he tolerated it with a great deal of patience.

However, after all these excesses and high-handedness on the part of the magistrate had been going on for more than four months, during which there was a great deal of dissatisfaction throughout the land, which I will not dwell on here for there would be no end to it, one day, when Dom Antonio saw that the time had come to put into effect a plan it seems he had decided on beforehand, he arrested him on a Friday, inside the fortress, where he was put in a room by certain people who had been prepared for that purpose, and there, according to what was said, he was stripped bare and tied hand and foot with a rope. After he had been soundly whipped and tortured with the drippings from some hot oil wicks, from which he nearly died, they put iron shackles on his legs, manacles on his hands, a collar around his neck, and plucked out his beard without leaving a trace of hair on his face. They did some other things like that to him, according to what was said publicly at the time, so that the poor licentiate Gaspar Jorge, who bore the titles of chief magistrate of India, custodian-in-chief of orphans' and deceased persons' property, and revenue officer of Malacca and parts south, in the name of the king, our Lord, was treated that way by Dom Antonio, if what was said was true.

When the monsoon came he was sent to India in irons like that, along with an ugly deposition that had been drawn up against him, which the learned justices of the appellate court of Goa later declared invalid and ordered a new one to be drawn up in Malacca.

As for Dom Antonio, because of what he had done, the viceroy Dom Pedro de Mascarenhas, [5] who, by this time, was governing the State of India, ordered him brought back prisoner to stand trial along with Gaspar Jorge and to answer for what he had done. Dom Antonio immediately came to India where, while he was engaged in trying to clear himself of the charges, the court ordered him to reply within three days to an ugly complaint filed against him by Gaspar Jorge. Since Dom Antonio was naturally opposed to these judicial proceedings filled with charges and countercharges with which it was said the judges wanted to annoy him, it seems (according to what the scandalmongers said at the time, for I neither saw it nor do I know it for a fact) that he did not want to spend all three days they had given him to reply to the complaint, but within twenty-four hours he met up with Gaspar Jorge and laid him out in a spot from which he never again rose—and according to what was also said—with a good mouthful of a delicacy they gave him at a banquet, which put an end to this entire affair. Dom Antonio was exonerated and allowed to serve out his captaincy, whither he set out from there a month later. However, after he arrived in Malacca and was once more in possession of his office, he lasted in it only two and a half months, at the end of which he died of dysentery. [6]

And that is how Malacca finally was rid of all the discord and difficulties that beset her at that time.

220
En Route to Japan

Once the monsoon had arrived and Father Master Belchior was able to continue his voyage, we departed from Malacca on the first of April in the year 1555 aboard a caravel belonging to the king, our lord, which Dom Antonio, the captain of the fortress, provided for the father in keeping with the viceroy's instructions.

On the third day of our voyage we reached an island called Pulo Pisang[1] just outside the mouth of the Strait of Singapore, where the pilot, owing to his lack of experience in those waters, ran aground under full sail on a rocky shoal, which spelled total disaster for us. As a result, it was necessary for Father Master Belchior, on the advice of all, to go in a *manchua* to ask for the aid of a longboat and sailors from a certain Luis de Almeida,[2] whose ship had passed us two hours before and was anchored two leagues away on account of contrary winds.

On that trip, for the entire distance, the father, as well as two brothers and I who were with him, were exposed to considerable hardship and danger, for the entire country was in a state of war. Since it belonged to the king of Jantana, the grandson of the former king of Malacca, our greatest foe, his *balões* and *lancharas,* which were cruising about in armada formation, kept on harassing us all the way, with the intention of ramming us, but the Lord did not permit that to happen.

When we finally reached the ship, worn out and trembling with fear, her captain provided us with a longboat and crew in which we headed back to the caravel with all possible speed to rescue her from the precarious situation in which we had left her. When we got there the following day—as the Lord willed—we found her floating free but taking on a great deal of water at the stempost, which was later pumped out in Patani, where we arrived seven days later.

I disembarked along with two others and went to see the king and deliver a letter to him from the captain of Malacca. He welcomed us most hospitably, and on reading the captain's letter he understood that our reason for coming there was to buy provisions and other things that we had not brought with us from Malacca, and to proceed on our voyage to China, and from there to Japan, in order for the father and the others in his party to preach the Christian faith to the heathens of Japan. At which the king, after a moment of thoughtful silence, smiled to his people and said to them, "Wouldn't it be better for these people, as long as they are exposing themselves to such great hardship, to go to China to get rich rather than to foreign kingdoms to preach nonsense?"

Then he called to the *shahbandar*[3] who was in front of him and said, "Do everything for these men that they require, for the sake of the captain of Malacca, who recommends them to me very highly, and remember that I give an order only once."

After we had taken our leave of the king, delighted with the favorable reception he had given us, we immediately set about buying everything necessary, both in the way of provisions as well as all the other things we were lacking, and within eight days we had laid in a very abundant store of everything.

Departing from this port of Patani we ran for two days under favorable southeasterly winds along the coast of *Lugor*[4] and Siam. As we were crossing over from the bar of Cuy, in order to set our course for *Pulo Cambim*[5] and from there for the islands of Canton,[6] intending to wait there for the conjunction of the new moon, we were struck by a storm with winds from the west-southwest (which are the ones that ordinarily prevail along that coast most of the year) that were so fierce that we were faced with total disaster. As a result, we were forced to turn back again to the coast of Malaysia. When we got to an island called Pulo Tioman,[7] there too we were exposed to many dangers from both the storms and the treacherous natives on shore. Five days after we got there, without any water or provisions since we had thrown everything overboard, the Lord willed that one morning we should meet up with three Portuguese *naos* bound from Sunda,[8] and with their arrival all our worries were over.

Father Master Belchior immediately spoke with their captains about what he should do, and they all agreed that he should send back the caravel on which he had come from Malacca since it was not seaworthy enough for a voyage as long as it was from there to Japan. This was done, and the father embarked with a certain Francisco Toscano,[9] a rich and honorable man who paid his expenses on the entire voyage and during much of the time that he spent in China, as well as those of all the other members of his party.

We sailed from this island of Pulo Tioman on a Friday, the seventh of June in the year 1555, and after passing the mainland of the kingdom of Champa,[10] we sailed along the coast with a following breeze, and in twelve more days we dropped anchor at an island called Pulo Champeiló[11] in the gulf of Cochinchina, where we took on water from a very fresh stream that descended from the top of the mountain through a huge agglomeration of boulders, beside which, on a very tall slab, a very beautiful cross was sculptured, with the four letters of the inscription, and below, about four fingers from the foot, was the date, 1518, and about six letters that read in short, Duarte Coelho.[12] From this stream southward, about two crossbow shots away, hanging from some trees that ran all along the beach, were the bodies of sixty-two men and many others besides, lying on the ground partially devoured already, which was something that seemed to have happened six or seven days before. On another tree was a large banner with some Chinese characters on it that read, "Let any ship or junk stopping here take on its water and depart immediately, weather permitting or not, on pain of suffering the penalty paid by these wretches who fell within the reach of the Wrathful Arm of the Law, by the authority of the Son of Heaven."

No one was able to provide a satisfactory explanation for this strange thing, but it was surmised that a Chinese armada had landed there and, coming upon those poor men, had robbed them, as is ordinarily their custom, and under the guise of justice, had done to them what we saw.

221
Arrival in China

We departed from this island of Pulo Champeiló, setting a course for the islands of Canton, and after five days of sailing, as it pleased our Lord, we arrived in *Sanchão,* the island on which, as I said before, Father Master Francis had been buried.

The following morning everyone in the fleet went ashore, and we all walked in procession to the burial place of the sainted father, which by this time was completely overgrown with weeds and brush, with nothing to be seen but the tips of the crosses encircling it. However, it was immediately cleared and smoothed by everyone with deep devotion and then fenced with strong wooden stakes and still another fence that was built outside of that one. Then the ground all around it was carefully swept and leveled, and the whole area was enclosed with a very nice embankment and a very tall, beautiful cross was erected at the entrance.

After this had been done in a way that seemed fitting at the time, Father Master

Belchior said a festival mass to music, at which the orphan children and some men with a talent for singing officiated, with an excellent chorus and with brocade ornaments and silver lamps and candlesticks. Also, there was a brief sermon, appropriate to the solemn occasion that was being celebrated, which dealt with the life and labors of the holy departed man, the great zeal he had always shown for the honor of God, the propagation of His holy faith, the salvation of souls, and the holy purpose that had brought him to the kingdom of China, where our Lord had seen fit to call him to his glory. This sermon was heard by all with deep devotion and not without some tears.

On the following morning we departed from this island of *Sanchão,* and at sundown we reached another island six leagues further north called *Lampacau,* [1] where in those days the Portuguese traded with the Chinese and where they continued to trade up until the year 1557 when the mandarins of Canton, at the request of the local merchants, gave us the port of Macao, [2] where it is carried on today. There, on what was formerly an uninhabited island, our people have built a noble town with houses worth three or four thousand *cruzados* and a cathedral with a vicar and ecclesiastical beneficiaries. They also have their own captain-major, crown magistrate, and officers of the law, and they live there so confident and secure in the thought that it is ours, as if it were situated in the safest part of Portugal. But let us hope that our Lord in His infinite goodness and mercy will permit their security to be of more certain and of longer duration than it was in Ning-po, [3] another Portuguese town I mentioned earlier at great length, located two leagues to the north of Macao, which, because of the misconduct of a Portuguese, was totally destroyed and laid waste in a very short time. I was present at that unfortunate event in which there was an incalculable loss of life and property, for that town had three thousand inhabitants, twelve hundred of whom were Portuguese and the rest, Christians from various nations. According to what was said by people who were in a position to know, the commerce carried on by the Portuguese was worth more than three million in gold, the bulk of it consisting of silver from Japan, a country that had been discovered two years before, and no matter what kind of merchandise you brought there, you doubled your money three and four times over.

This town had a captain who lived on shore, apart from the individual captains of the *naos* on the China run who would come and go. There was also a crown magistrate, judges, councilmen, a custodian-in-chief of orphans' and deceased persons' property, market inspectors, a council clerk, night patrols, tax collectors, all other offices of government, four notaries public, and six for court duty, and each of these offices sold for three thousand *cruzados* and others went for a much higher price yet. There were three hundred men married to Portuguese and half-caste women; there were two hospitals and a House of Mercy maintained at a cost of more than thirty thousand *cruzados* a year, and the city council had revenues of six thousand, so that it was generally said that it was the noblest, wealthiest, and most affluent community in all of India and, for its size, in all of Asia. And when the clerks would transmit certain writs to Malacca, or the notaries would draw up certain documents, they would say, "In this very noble and ever loyal city of Ning-po, on behalf of the king, our lord."

As long as we are on the subject, I do not want to go ahead without explaining how and why such a rich and notable city as this was lost. It happened in the following manner. There was an honorable man there of good family background by the name of Lançarote Pereira, [4] a native of the town of Ponte de Lima, [5] who, they said, had given about a thousand *cruzados'* worth of poor-quality merchandise on credit to some unreliable Chinese men who made off with the goods without ever giving him anything in return for it or ever being heard from again. In an effort to make up for this loss on those who were not to blame for it, he gathered together for that purpose some fifteen or twenty Portuguese idlers of evil conscience and perhaps worse judgement, and fell one night on a village about two leagues from there called *Xipatom*,[6] where he robbed ten or twelve of the farmers living there and carried off all their women and children, killing thirteen people, without any possible reason or justification for doing so.

The news of this outrageous deed spread rapidly the next day throughout the entire countryside, and the inhabitants went to the *chumbim*[7] of justice to lodge a complaint. An investigation having been conducted into what had happened, a report was prepared in the form of a petition by popular demand, which they call a *macalixau,* and sent to the *chaem*[8] of the government, who is the viceroy of that kingdom. He immediately dispatched an *aitao,*[9] who is like an admiral among us, with an armada of three hundred junks and eighty oared *vancões*[10] with a company of sixty thousand men, which they got ready in seventeen days. This armada fell upon this unfortunate enclave of the Portuguese one morning, and what happened there was such that I daresay in all truth that I cannot summon up either the ability or the wit or words adequate enough to describe it fully. However, I leave it to the imagination of any intelligent person. I will just say, as an eyewitness, that in the less than five hours that this incredibly frightful punishment from the hand of God and the power of his divine justice lasted, nothing one could put a name to was left intact, for everything was burned down and razed to the ground, with a loss in life of twelve thousand Christians, including eight hundred Portuguese who were all burned alive on board thirty-five *naos* and forty-two junks; and it was said that in silver, pepper, sandalwood, clove, mace, nutmeg, and many other kinds of merchandise, more than two and a half million in gold was lost.

The cause of all this evil and misfortune was the lack of scruples and poor judgement of a greedy Portuguese. As a consequence of this evil, still another of no small significance followed, which was that we became so discredited in the land that no one wanted to see us, for they said that we were devils in the flesh, engendered as a curse by the wrath of God for the punishment of sinners. And this happened in the year 1542 when Martim Afonso de Sousa[11] was the governor of the State of India and Ruy Vaz Pereira Marramaque[12] was captain of Malacca.

Two years later, when the Portuguese wanted to settle in another port called *Chincheo,*[13] in this same kingdom of China, a hundred leagues below the port of Ning-po, in order to have a depot for their trade and goods, the local merchants, because of the great profit they derived from it, managed to get the mandarins to consent to it by bribing them handsomely to look the other way. Trade was carried on here quietly between us and the local people for a period of nearly two and a half years, more or less, until there arrived from Malacca, by order of Simão de Melo,[14] captain of the fortress, another man of practically the same stuff as Lançarote Pereira, whose name was Aires Botelho de Sousa. He was carrying orders from Captain Simão de Melo, who had appointed him to be captain-major of the port of *Chincheo* and custodian of deceased persons' property. He arrived, according to what was said, so anxious to get rich that he earned the reputation for helping himself to everything he could lay his hands on, with a total disregard for any and all.

During this time a foreigner happened to arrive, an Armenian national who everyone regarded as a very good Christian. This man had about ten or twelve thousand *cruzados* of his own, and since he was a foreigner and a Christian like us, he disembarked from a Moorish-owned junk on which he had come and transferred to a *nao* owned by a Portuguese named Luis de Montarroyo.[15] After he had been living here peacefully among us for about six or seven months, favored and sheltered by all because he was, as I said, a very good man and a good Christian, he happened to fall ill of the fevers and die. On making his last will and testament, he declared that he was a married man with a wife and children in a town in Armenia called *Gaborem,* and that of the twelve thousand *cruzados* he owned he was leaving two thousand to the House of Mercy of Malacca, with the stipulation that a certain number of masses be said for the salvation of his soul. As for the rest, he asked the supervisor and the brothers of the House of Mercy to hold it in trust until they could have it transferred to his children to whom he had instructed them to give it; and in the event that his children were dead, he named the House of Mercy as his residuary legatee.

No sooner was this Christian buried than Aires Botelho de Sousa, the custodian of deceased persons' property, took possession of all his goods, without benefit of inventory or any other formality, claiming that it was necessary to send a demand to the heirs who lived in Armenia more than two thousand leagues away, to see if there were any liens outstanding so the matter could be settled by their courts.

About this same time, two Chinese merchants arrived in town, carrying three thousand *cruzados*' worth of silk, bolts of damascus, porcelain and musk, which were owed to the deceased Armenian. The custodian also took possession of these items, and along with them, advancing the claim that all the rest of the merchandise the Chinese had with them also belonged to the deceased Armenian, they say that he took about eight thousand *cruzados* from them and told them that they should go to Goa to demand justice from the chief custodian because he had to do what he was doing in order to comply with the obligations of his office. At any rate, so as not to dwell on all the details of this case, suffice it to say that the two merchants went home empty-handed. As soon as they got back they both went immediately, with their wives and children, to throw themselves at the feet of the *chaem* and reported to him, in the form of a petition, everything that had transpired in this case, and in addition, they told him that we were people who had no fear of God's justice.

Desirous of giving immediate satisfaction to these merchants as well as to others who had also complained to him about us on previous occasions, the *chaem* issued a proclamation forbidding anyone to communicate with us from that day forward, on penalty of death. Since that was the reason for our being cut off completely from our source of supply, the shortage of food among us reached such drastic proportions that what had been selling before for a *vintem*[16] could not even be obtained later for a *cruzado*. This made it necessary to go in search of it in some of the surrounding villages, where serious disorders occurred. This in turn caused the entire countryside to rise up against us with such great hatred and fury that within sixteen days a fleet of 120 huge junks appeared on the scene which, for our sins, treated us in such a way that, out of the thirteen *naos* in port, not a single one of them escaped being burned, and out of the five hundred Portuguese on shore, only thirty escaped, with nothing on them that was worth as much as a single *real*.

Thus, from these two sad incidents that I have described, I have come to the conclusion that it appears that the present state of our affairs in China and the peace and confidence we enjoy in our relations with her based as they are on a firm and secure treaty of friendship, will endure only as long as our sins do not give her some reason, similar to those in the past, to make her rise up against us, which may our Lord in his infinite mercy forbid.

And now to return to my story from which I have strayed. As I was saying, when we arrived at the port of *Lampacau,* we anchored there with all three of the *naos* in which we had come, and a short time later another five *naos* dropped anchor in the same port. But since the local merchandise was not selling at that time as well as it usually did before, none of the *naos* went on to Japan during that monsoon, and as a result, we were forced to winter here in this port another year, with the intention of continuing our voyage the following May, which was ten months later, in keeping with our original plans. [17]

222
Earthquake in China

When Father Master Belchior realized that he would not be able to go to Japan that year, not only because the monsoon was over but also because of some other obstacles that had arisen, he immediately arranged for a shelter to be built on shore where he and the members of his party could stay. He also ordered the construction of a sort of church where divine services could be held and where the Sacraments necessary for the salvation of men could be administered on a regular basis, all of which was promptly carried out. [1]

During the time we spent here, neither Father Master Belchior nor the others in his company remained idle. On the contrary, they continuously gathered a harvest of souls, not only because of the frequent attendance at confession, but also with the freeing of two Portuguese [2] who had been held in prison in the city of Canton for five years, whose release cost more than twenty-five hundred *cruzados* which came from funds contributed by faithful Christians.

When we had been here for six and a half months, on the nineteenth of February 1556, a reliable news report reached this city of Canton to the effect that on the third day of the same month and year, the province of *Sansy* [3] had been completely destroyed, in the following manner:

On the first day of February the earth shook from eleven o'clock at night to one in the morning, and on the following day from midnight until two o'clock, and on the day after that from one to three, with the most dreadful claps of lightning and thunder, when the entire earth erupted into a boiling mass of water that seemed to rise up from the center of the earth, and suddenly, an area of sixty leagues around was submerged, with only one lone survivor from among the entire population, a seven-year-old child who, in amazement, was taken to the king of China.

When this news reached the city of Canton, it struck the greatest fear and terror into the hearts of all the inhabitants. But since our people thought it could not possibly be true, some fourteen out of sixty of us Portuguese who were there at the time decided to go and see for themselves and set out immediately. On their return they declared that the story was true indeed, and a public document was drawn up to that effect by fourteen eyewitnesses, all of them in agreement and all of them Portuguese. Francisco Toscano sent this document to Portugal, addressed to King John III, may he rest in glory, through the intermediary of a clergyman by the name of Diogo Reinel, who was one of the fourteen who saw it.

Over this catastrophe,[4] strange manners of penitence were observed in this city of Canton among all the people, and even though they were heathens, they put all of us who saw it to shame, in spite of our being Christians, for on the first day that the news reached them, at two o'clock in the afternoon, there were proclamations through all the main streets of the city that six men on horseback, covered in very long mourning robes, read in very sad, mournful tones, heralding the news as follows:

"Hear ye, hear ye, ye wretched people who continuously offend the Lord, hear the news of a most grievous and sorrowful event that we bring you now in voices choked with tears! Know ye, that because of all our sins, God has brandished the sword of his divine justice over the people of Cuy[5] and *Sansy,* bringing destruction down on the entire province of the *anchacilado*[6] by fire, water, and lightning, with not a single survivor except for one child who was taken to the Son of Heaven."

Then, at the sound of a bell that was struck three times, all the people prostrated themselves on the ground, responding with a most horrendous shout, "Xipató varocay!" meaning "God is just in all that he does!"

Then all the people immediately withdrew to their houses, and for five days the city was so deserted that not a living soul appeared in sight. All of us Portuguese who were there at the time went about in amazement, for not a single person with whom one could speak was to be seen on any of the streets.

When this five-day period was over, the *chaem,* together with the *anchacys* of the government and all the people (that is to say, the men only, for they do not think that women have the ability to be heard by God because of the disobedience of Eve when she committed the first sin) spread out through all the main streets of the city in an amazing procession, and with a clamor of voices that shook the heavens, their priests, who must have numbered over five thousand, shouted out loud, "O admirable and merciful Lord! Do not take account of our evil deeds, for then we shall remain mute before thee!" To which all the people responded with another frightful shout, "Xaputey danacó fanaragy paleu!" meaning, "We confess before thee, O Lord, the error of our ways!"

Shouting continuously in this manner they reached a sumptuous temple named for *Nacapirau,*[7] whom they regarded as the queen of heaven, as I have mentioned several times before. From here, on the following day, they went to another temple called *Uzangue Nabor,* "god of justice." And in this manner they continued for fourteen days, during which many charitable deeds were performed, many prisoners released, and many sacrifices offered up with sweet-smelling incense of eaglewood and benzoin, and some others of blood offerings, in the course of which they slaughtered many cows, deer, and pigs, which were given to the poor as charity.

Thus, throughout the remainder of the time we were here, which was probably about three months, they performed many other pious deeds at great expense, which if, with the benefit of the faith of Christ, they had done for love of him, I believe he would have found them very acceptable.

Also, it was generally affirmed by all that during the three days that this happened in *Sansy,* blood had rained down continuously on the city of Peking, where the king of China was then in residence, and that as a result, most of the city was deserted and he fled to Nanking, where it was also said that he had had many generous alms distributed and an infinite number of prisoners released, counting among them—as God willed—five Portuguese who had been imprisoned[8] in the city of *Pocasser*[9] for more than twenty years. Here in Canton, where they eventually arrived, they told us many amazing things, among which they assured us that the alms distributed by the king, because of this catastrophe, came to well over 600,000 *cruzados,* to say nothing of the many sumptuous temples he built to placate the wrath of God, which included one that was built in this city, called *Hifaticau,* "god of love," a very sumptuous and extremely majestic building.

223
The Farce of the Wooden Hands

Once the monsoon had arrived and we were able to continue our voyage, we departed from this island of *Lampacau* on the seventh of May in the year 1556 on board a *nao* whose captain and owner was Dom Francisco Mascarenhas,[1] nicknamed "Old Straw," who had resided there the past year as captain-major. We proceeded on our course for fourteen days when we sighted the first group of islands[2] at thirty-five degrees latitude which, by scale, lie west-northwest of Tanegashima. When the pilot realized that his navigation was in error, he turned about to the southwest, heading for the tip of the mountains of *Minató,* and hugging the coast of Tano-ura, we sailed within constant sight of land as far as the port of Hyuga.

Here in this latitude, since the compass needles swung to the northeast, and the currents were running to the north, the pilot lost his bearings completely, so that by the time he recognized his error—though something in the nature of a pilot would not let him admit it—we had already gone sixty leagues beyond the port we were bound for. Thus, it was with great difficulty, since the winds were against us, that we found it again two weeks later, and with quite a bit of vexation and at great risk to our lives and property, for that entire coast was in revolt against the king of Bungo, our friend, and against its inhabitants, because they were very receptive to the doctrine of the Lord which our priests were spreading there.

Once we had anchored by God's mercy in the bay of the city of *Fucheo,* capital of the kingdom of Bungo—which I have mentioned many times before—and presently the most flourishing center of Christianity in all of Japan, everyone agreed that I should go to the fortress of Usuki,[3] where we heard that the king was then staying, and even though I had some qualms about making the journey because the countryside was in revolt at this time, still I was forced to give in since everybody insisted on my going. I promptly made ready, as did the four other companions I took with me, and after I received a present that Dom Francisco, the captain of the *nao,* was sending to the king—which must have been worth about five hundred *cruzados*—I left the *nao.* Once I had disembarked at the city wharf, I went directly to the quarters of the *Quansio-andono,* admiral of the sea and captain of the *Canafama.* He received me in a most hospitable manner, which relieved me somewhat of my fears. After explaining the purpose of my visit to him, I asked him to supply me with horses and men to take me to where the king was staying, which he promptly did, generously providing me with far more than I had asked for.

I departed from this city, and the following day at nine o'clock I arrived at a town called *Fingau*, [4] which was about a quarter of a league from the fortress of Usuki. From there, I sent a message through one of the Japanese in my party, to the *Osquim-dono,* the captain of the fortress, informing him of my arrival and of the embassy [5] I was bringing from the viceroy of India for His Highness, regarding which I asked him to let me know when I could speak to him.

To this he immediately sent me a reply with one of his sons, welcoming me along with all my companions and informing me that he had already sent a message to the king on the island of *Xeque*, [6] where he had gone at dawn with a large party to kill a huge fish of unknown species that had come there from the middle of the ocean with a large school of small fish, and since it had already been encircled in an estuary, he thought that he would not be able to return before nightfall, but that as soon as he received a reply from His Highness he would immediately let me know, and that in the meantime I should rest in the more comfortable lodgings he had arranged for me, where I would be provided with everything necessary because that whole land belonged as much to the king of Portugal as did Malacca, Cochin, and Goa. One of his men, who had arrived by then for that purpose, put us up immediately in a pagoda called *Amidamxó,* where the bonzes in charge wined and dined us splendidly.

As soon as the king was informed of my arrival, he immediately dispatched three oared *funés* [7] from the island where he was trapping that huge fish, and with them he sent a highly trusted chamberlain of his by the name of *Oretandono,* who arrived sometime in the afternoon at the place where I was staying. He immediately sought me out, and after telling me in his own words the reason why the king had sent him, he drew a letter from him from his breast and kissed it with the customary ceremonies and rituals observed among them, before handing it to me. The letter read as follows:

"While engaged in a task that gives me great pleasure, I was informed of thy safe arrival at the place where thou art, together with the others in thy company, which made me so happy that I assure thee that if it had not been for the fact that I had sworn not to leave this spot until I had killed a huge fish I have trapped, I would have personally hastened to fetch thee. That is why I beg thee, like a good friend, since I cannot go for the reason I explained, to come at once in the boat I am sending for thee, for with thy coming, and my killing this fish, my happiness will be complete."

Upon seeing this letter, I, together with all my companions, immediately boarded the *fune* on which *Oretandono* had come, while the boys carrying the present got on the other two. Since they were all very swift and well manned, in little more than an hour we reached the island which was two and a half leagues from there. At the time we arrived the king, with more than two hundred men, all with their harpoons, were moving about in boats, chasing after a big whale that had happened to come there in the midst of an enormous school of fish. [8] The name "whale," and the fish itself, were then entirely unknown to them because they had never before seen one like it in that country.

Once it had been killed and brought ashore, the king was so delighted that he exempted all the fishermen there from a certain tribute they had always paid and bestowed new aristocratic names on them. As for some noblemen there, who were intimates of his, he increased their stipends. As for the *guesos,*[9] who are like gentlemen-in-waiting, he rewarded them with a thousand *taels* of silver. As for me, he welcomed me with his face bathed in smiles and asked me about many things in great detail, to which I replied, enlarging on the truth of many of the things he asked because I thought it necessary to do so for the sake of the reputation of the Portuguese nation and the esteem they had for us in that land up to that time, for in those days they were all convinced that the king of Portugal was the only one who could truly be called the monarch of the world, not only for the lands he possessed, but for his power and treasure as well, and that is why they attached so much importance to our friendship in that country.

When he had done with this he departed immediately from the island of *Xeque* for Usuki, reaching his house about an hour after dark, where he was greeted by all his people with a great deal of joy and merrymaking in their fashion. They congratulated him for such an honorable deed as that of catching the whale, giving him all the credit for what the others had done, for this harmful vice of adulation is so natural in the courts and palaces of princes that even among the barbarous heathens it was not out of place.

Dismissing all the people who had accompanied him, the king dined privately with his wife and children, refusing to allow any of the men to attend him at the time because the banquet was being given by the queen. Nevertheless, from there, he sent someone to his treasurer's house where we had already been installed, to fetch all five of us, begging us, as a favor, for his sake, to eat in his company, with our hands, just as we did in our country, because the queen would enjoy watching us. Then he had the table set with generous portions of very clean, well-prepared delicacies, served by very beautiful women, and we all very heartily threw ourselves upon what they placed in front of us. However, the charming, courtly remarks of the ladies, and the way they made fun of us when they saw us eating with our hands, provided the king and queen with far greater pleasure than any kind of farce that could have been presented for their amusement, for since all these people are accustomed to eating with two sticks, as I have mentioned several times before, they consider it a very dirty thing to eat with one's hands[10] as is our custom.

Then one of the king's daughters, a young girl between fourteen and fifteen years of age and very beautiful, asked her mother for permission to perform a little skit that six or seven of the girls wanted to present on the subject with which they were dealing, and the queen, with the consent of the king, agreed to it. They then disappeared into another room where they remained a little while. In the meantime, those who remained outside amused themselves at our expense by making many funny, witty remarks, which we all found quite embarrassing, at least four of the five of us, since it was all quite new to them and they did not understand the language, whereas I, in Tanegashima, had already seen another farce about the Portuguese similar to this one, and I had seen them several times in other places as well.

While we were in the midst of this indignity, though we were better able to tolerate their making fun of us when we saw how much pleasure the king and queen derived from it, the princess, looking very lovely, came out of the other room. She was dressed as a merchant, with a gold-plated sword at her side and everything else about her very appropriate to the role she was playing. Kneeling down in front of the king, her father, she said to him, "Powerful king and lord, though my boldness is deserving of severe punishment, because of the great inequality that God saw fit to place between Your Highness and my lowliness, the great need in which I find myself has made me put aside my fear of being punished. Since I am old by now and have many children by the four wives I married, and what I possess is so paltry, I have been desirous, as a father should be, of leaving them provided for, which is why I asked my friends to help me out by lending me money, which some of them did. After investing it in a certain kind of merchandise which, for my sins, I have not been able to sell in all of Japan, I decided to trade it for whatever I could get for it. While I was complaining about it to some of my friends in Miyako, which is where I come from, they assured me that only Your Highness could be of help to me in this matter. That is why I beg you, my lord, out of consideration for my gray hair, my advanced age, the many children I have, and the dire need in which I find myself, please help me in my distress, for by doing what I ask of you, you will be performing a very charitable service for me and a great favor for the *Chenchicos* who have just arrived on that great ship, since this merchandise of mine suits them more than anyone else, because of the great physical defect from which they suffer all the time."

While she was speaking the king and queen were laughing uncontrollably, knowing that the merchant who was so old, with so many gray hairs on his head, so many children and such great need, was their own daughter, the princess, who was very young and very beautiful. Nevertheless, restraining his laughter somewhat, the king replied very gravely that he should bring him a sample of the merchandise he had and that if it was something that might be of use to us, he would ask us to buy it from him. At this, she bowed deeply and then went back into the other room.

Up to that point we were so embarrassed by what we had seen that we could not decide what it was all about. The women who were in the room, and there must have been more than sixty of them—with no other man present there except for us five companions—began to squirm and nudge each other with their elbows, whispering among themselves and laughing softly.

As soon as they had quieted down, the merchant returned with the samples which six very lovely, richly clad young girls were carrying. They were dressed as merchants with gold swords and daggers at their sides and bore themselves in a solemn, dignified manner, for all of them were daughters of the principal noblemen of the kingdom, whom the princess had chosen to help her perform this farce for the king and queen. Each of these six girls had a green taffeta bundle slung over her shoulder, and all six of them were acting the part of the merchant's sons. They made their entrance with a dance which they performed very well, in their fashion, to the sound of music played by two harps and a rebec, and from time to time they would sing ballads in very sweet voices that were a delight to hear.

"O lofty and powerful lord of riches, for thy sake, be mindful of our poverty. We are wretched creatures in a foreign land, despised by the people because we are orphans and the object of scorn and disrespect. Wherefore, O lord, we implore thee, for thy sake, be mindful of our poverty."

And in this manner they sang two or three more stanzas which in their language were very well constructed, always repeating at the end of each one, "For thy sake, be mindful of our poverty!"

When the music and dancing were over, they all kneeled down before the king, and after the merchant had thanked him with another very well composed speech for offering to help him sell his merchandise, the six girls unwrapped the bundles they were carrying, spilling out on the floor an enormous number of wooden arms—like those that are offered here in Portugal to Saint Amaro—with the merchant saying in a very charming manner, with carefully chosen words, that inasmuch as nature, for our sins, had subjected us to a form of misery so dirty, that our hands of necessity would be smelling all the time of fish, or meat, or whatever else we ate with them, the merchandise he had there suited us perfectly, for while we were using one pair of hands, the other could be washed.

At this, the king and queen broke into rollicking laughter, and all five of us were so embarrassed that the king, sensing it, begged our pardon, explaining that since he wanted the princess, his daughter, to see how fond he was of the Portuguese, he had allowed her that little pastime, in which we alone, as brothers of his, had been participants.

To which we replied that we hoped that the Lord our God would repay His Highness for the honor and favor he had bestowed on us, which we confessed was quite overwhelming, and that we would make it known throughout the entire world for as long as we lived.

For which he and the queen and the princess, still dressed in the clothes of a merchant, thanked us profusely, in their fashion. And the princess said to us, "Well, if your God should wish to take me for his servant, I would invent still other farces for him, much better and more to his liking than this one, but I trust that he will not forget me."

At this, all five of us, kneeling and kissing the hem of her kimono, replied that we hoped that indeed God would, and that if she were to become a Christian we were bound to see her queen of Portugal one day, which brought peals of laughter from her and her mother, the queen. Then, taking our leave of the king, we returned to our lodgings.

In the morning he sent for us and inquired in great detail about the arrival of the priests, the viceroy's intentions, his letter, the *nao,* the cargo she was carrying, and many other particulars, which took up more than four hours. Then he dismissed me, saying that he would be leaving for the city within six days and that there I should give him the letter, and he would meet with the father and reply to everything.

224
Embassy to the King of Bungo

Six days later the king departed from the fortress of Usuki for the city of *Fucheo,* accompanied by a large train and many noblemen, including a guard of six hundred foot soldiers and two hundred horsemen in a display of great majesty. On his arrival in the city all the people welcomed him with great joy and merrymaking, farces, and very costly forms of entertainment in their fashion. Then he went to spend the night in some magnificent, sumptuous palaces that he had there.

The next morning he sent for me and told me to bring him the viceroy's letter, for that was his sole purpose in coming there, and that after he had seen it he would speak with Father Master Belchior concerning the other matters of importance.

I returned to my lodgings immediately to make all the necessary preparations, and at two o'clock in the afternoon the king sent the *Quansio Nafama*,[1] the captain of the city, along with four of the highest-ranking men in his court to fetch me. They led me to the palace, accompanied by many people. However, they as well as I and the forty Portuguese in my party all went on foot, since that is their custom. All the streets through which we passed were very clean, nicely decorated, and so crowded with people that the *nautarões,* who were the gatekeepers, carrying iron-tipped staffs, had plenty to do clearing the way for us. The gifts were carried by three Portuguese on horseback, and a short distance behind them came two other riders, handsomely attired in their cloaks and arms, as though for a joust.

When we crossed the outer courtyard of the palace, we found the king there, seated on a platform or dais that had been specially constructed for the occasion, accompanied by all the nobility of the kingdom, along with some ambassadors from foreign kingdoms, one from the king of the Ryukyus, another from the Cochinese and the island of Tosa, and another from the *kubo-sama,*[2] emperor of Miyako. All around, filling the entire area of the courtyard, there were over a thousand arquebusiers and four hundred men mounted on well-caparisoned horses, to say nothing of the commoners of the land who, as I say, were there in countless numbers. When I and the forty Portuguese in my party reached the dais where the king was sitting, we all performed the customary obeisances and courtesies that are called for on such formal occasions. Then I went up to him and handed him the letter I was carrying from the viceroy. He stood up to receive it from my hand and, sitting down again, handed it to a *Quansio Gritau* of his—who is like a secretary—and the latter read it aloud for all to hear.

After it was read, he asked me, in the presence of the three ambassadors and the princess in his entourage, a few things he wanted to know, out of curiosity, about that Europe of ours, one of which was how many armed men, of all types of arms, including cavalrymen arrayed like those we had brought, did the king of Portugal place in the field. Since I was afraid to tell him a lie, I confess that I was hesitant to reply. Observing this, one of my companions who was next to me, took the lead and answered, between 100,000 to 120,000, which amazed the king, and me even more. Then the king, who seemed to enjoy the grandiose replies he was getting from this Portuguese, kept on plying him with questions for more than half an hour, leaving him and all those present completely wonderstruck by such marvelous things.

"I assure you in all truth," he said to his followers, "that nothing would please me more now than to see the monarchy of that great land about which I have been hearing such marvelous things concerning both their treasures and the multitude of ships on the sea, for with that I would be quite content for the rest of my life."

Then bidding me and the others in my party farewell, he said to me, "Whenever you think it fitting, you can tell the father to come and see me, for he will find me here ready to listen to him and to all the others in his company."

225
Failure of the Evangelical Mission

As soon as I got back to the house where I was staying, I informed Father Master Belchior about the warm reception I had been given by the king and all the rest that had happened between us and how anxious he was to see him. That is why I thought it would be better, as long as the Portuguese were all there together, dressed in their finery, that he should go to see him at once, and he and all the other fathers agreed. Adorning himself with some outer garments necessary for his good name, he set out from the church, accompanied by the forty Portuguese, all very well dressed, with their collars and heavy gold chains across their chests, four orphan children, dressed in white taffeta cassocks and hats, with silk crosses on their breasts, and Brother João Fernandes,[1] to act as their interpreter.

When he reached the outer courtyard of the king's palace, some lords were already there, waiting for him, and in the most courteous manner, with a deep show of affection, they ushered him into a chamber where the king was already waiting for him. With a beaming countenance he took him by the hand and said to him, "Believe me, foreign Father, I can truly regard this day as mine alone because of the great pleasure it gives me to see you before my eyes, for it is as though I were seeing the holy Father Francis whom I loved as much as my own self."

Taking him further inside into another room that was luxuriously appointed, he seated him beside him. As for the four children, since it was something unusual, never before seen in that land, he also welcomed them very graciously. The father expressed his thanks for the many great honors he had bestowed on him, acting in the manner customary among them, which Brother João Fernandes had already taught him. Immediately after this he spoke about his main reason for coming there, namely, that the viceroy had sent him there to serve him and to show him the true path to his salvation. For this, from his facial expressions and the way he nodded his head, the king showed that he was grateful. The father continued talking, in the form of a holy discourse, like a sermon, which he had prepared in advance for that purpose, and in it he touched upon everything it behooved him to say.

"I cannot find the right words to tell thee, blessed Father," the king replied, "how much pleasure I derive from seeing thee in this house and from hearing everything thou hast said. But the times are such, as thou hast probably heard, that I cannot give thee an answer now. Therefore, I beg thee, since God has already brought thee here, to stay and rest a while from all the hardship thou hast endured in his service. As for what the viceroy writes me concerning what I wrote to him through Antonio Ferreira, even now I do not disavow it. However, the times at present are in such a state[2] that I very much fear that if my vassals see any change in me, they will follow the advice of the bonzes. Moreover, I know all too well—as thou hast probably learned by now from the fathers who are here[3]—that I am in a very precarious position in this land because of what happened in the recent uprisings, during which I was exposed to greater risks than any man ever was, so that one morning, for my own personal safety, I was forced to kill thirteen of the principal lords of the kingdom, along with sixteen thousand of their counsellors and fellow conspirators, to say nothing of an almost equal number whom I exiled or who fled. But if God should one day grant me what my soul asks of him, it will not be too difficult for me to follow the advice the viceroy gives me in his letter."

The father replied that he was very pleased with his good intentions, but that he should remember that men had no control over their lives, for they were all mortal, and that if he should happen to die before he could put them into effect, what would become of his soul. "God knows," he replied with a smile.

When the father saw that for the time being the king had nothing more to say other than kind words and polite remarks, and that he was unwilling to made a definite commitment about something of such great importance to him, he pretended not to notice and changed the subject, turning to other matters that, from what he had observed in him, were more to his liking. After spending a good part of the evening with the father this way, plying him with questions about things that were new to him—which he was very fond of doing—he dismissed him with honorable and well-chosen words, leaving him with the hope of his becoming a Christian[4] sometime in the not too distant future, for reasons which, at that time, we all understood.

On the following day, two hours after vespers, the father met with the king again, but apart from the great hospitality he showed him, as was always his custom, in the rest of their conversation he never once touched on that subject, but after he had left the city and returned to his fortress of Usuki, he sent word to him to stay on and begged him to come to see him without fail within a few days because he enjoyed very much talking about the grandeur of God and the perfection of his law.

After two and a half months had gone by, during which nothing more was forthcoming from the king regarding this matter, with the exception of a few vague promises at times accompanied with a few excuses which did not satisfy the father, he decided it would be better for him to return to India, not only to fulfill the obligations of his office, but for other reasons as well that moved him to do so. Added to this also was the fact that he had received a letter, via Hirado, which a certain Guilherme Pereira[5] had brought him from Malacca, informing him that a brother of his, by the name of João Nunes,[6] had arrived from Portugal, with an appointment as patriarch to Prester John.[7] This also made a deep impression on him because he thought that, if he joined him, he would gather a much greater harvest there in Ethiopia than here, where he already realized that he was wasting his time and efforts. However, these good intentions of his also came to naught because, in the meantime, the empire of Prester John was conquered by the king of Zeila,[8] with the help of the Grand Turk, and he withdrew with a few followers to the mountains of Tigremahom, where he died of poison some Moors gave him. And when his oldest son, named David, succeeded to the throne of what little was still left of the empire, he chose as his patriarch an Alexandrian, who had been his teacher and who was such a schismatic, and one who persisted so stubbornly in his errors, that he preached publicly that only he, in the dogma he followed, was the true Christian, and not the supreme pontiff. In this manner the five years of the governorships of Francisco Barreto[9] and Dom Constantino[10] went by without any of these things being carried out, and both the priest brothers died,[11] one in Goa and the other in Cochin, without anything further being achieved down to this day in regard to the salvation of the Abyssinians, nor do I believe that anything ever will be, unless God our Lord so ordains by a miracle, because of the evil neighbor we have in the Turk in the Straits of Mecca.

When I realized that the mission of the fathers in the city of *Fucheo* was going this way, and that Father Master Belchior was by this time almost completely embarked on the *nao,* I went to Usuki to see the king and asked him for the answer to the letter I had brought him from the viceroy. He gave it to me at once because it had already been prepared, and in return for the gifts, he sent some decorative arms, two golden swords, and a hundred Ryukyuan fans. The letter he had written went like this:

"Lord Viceroy of honorable majesty, I, *Yaretandono,* king of Bungo, seated on the throne of those who dispense justice by power of the scepter, hereby make known to you that in this my city of *Fucheo,* there came to me, at your command, Fernão Mendes Pinto, [12] bearing a letter from Your Royal Lordship, and a gift of arms and other objects that suited my purposes admirably and which I greatly prized because they came from the land at the end of the world known as *Chenchicogim,* where reigns, by the power of very great fleets and armies comprised of people from different nations, the crowned lion of great Portugal, to whom I offer myself from this day forward, as servant and vassal, with the loyalty of a friend as true and sweet as the song of the siren on the stormy sea. Wherefore, I beg you, as a favor, for as long as the sun does not fail to produce the effect for which God created it, nor the waters of the ocean cease to rise and fall over the shores of the earth, not to forget the homage I am paying, through the bearer, to your king and elder brother of mine, for whom I hope that this obedience of mine may be honorable, as I trust that it always will be, and that he will accept the arms that I am sending to you there as a symbol and token of my word of honor, as is the custom among us, the kings of Japan.

"From this my fortress of Usuki, on the ninth *mamoco* of the third month in the thirty-seventh year of my age."

With this letter and present I returned to the *nao* which was anchored two leagues from there in the port of *Xeque,* where I found Father Master Belchior and the rest of his party already embarked. From there we departed on the following day, which was the fourteenth of November in the year 1556.

226
Return to Portugal

Departing from the port of *Xeque* we sailed along our course with fair northerly winds, and on the fourth of December we arrived in *Lampacau,* where we found six Portuguese *naos* under the command of a merchant named Francisco Martins, an agent for Francisco Barreto, who was then governing the State of India, having succeeded Dom Pedro Mascarenhas [1] to the post. But by that time, since the monsoon for India was almost at an end, our captain, Dom Francisco Mascarenhas, [2] delayed here only long enough to take on provisions for the journey.

From the port of *Lampacau,* we departed on the first octave of Christmas, and on the seventeenth of February we arrived in Goa, where I immediately informed Francisco Barreto about the letter I had brought for him from the king of Japan, which he instructed me to deliver to him on the following day. I brought it to him, along with the arms, swords, and the other objects that comprised the gift I was carrying. After he had examined everything very carefully, he said to me, "I assure you, in all truth, that I prize these arms and objects you have just brought me as highly as I do the governship of India itself, for with them, and with this letter from the king of Japan, I hope to find such high favor with the king, our lord, that after God, they will be the means of delivering me from the castle of Lisbon, where most of us who govern this state eventually disembark, for our sins."

To compensate me for the trouble and expense I had gone to, he offered me many things which I at the time refused, but I proved to him, by means of documents and eyewitness accounts, how many times, in the service of the king, our lord, I had been captured and had had my property stolen, thinking that that was enough, and that in my own country, on that basis alone, I would not be denied what I thought was due me for my services.

He instructed me to draw up a document setting forth all these things, to which he added the rest of the certificates I presented to him. He also gave me a letter, addressed to His Highness, which made me feel, as a matter of course, that I would be more than amply compensated here for my services. Filled with confidence born of these hopes and the conviction that right was clearly on my side, I embarked for Portugal, so happy and proud of the papers I was carrying that I regarded them as the most precious possession I had, for I was persuaded that all I had to do was present them to receive satisfaction.

With God's will I arrived safely in the city of Lisbon on the twenty-second of September in the year 1558 at the time that the queen, our lady Dona Catarina [3]—may she rest in peace—was governing this kingdom. I gave her the letter I was carrying from the governor of India and an oral report of everything I thought would redound to my credit. She sent me to the official then in charge of these matters who, with fine words and finer hopes—which I fully believed at the time because of what he said to me—held on to those poor papers for four and a half years. At the end of that time, the only harvest I reaped was the hardship and grief I suffered in presenting my petition, which I dare say was far worse than all that I had suffered throughout the previous years.

When I saw how little either my past hardships or all my present petitioning profited me, I decided to retire with the miserable pittance I had brought back with me, acquired at the cost of so much hardship and misfortune, which was all that was left after what I had spent in the service of this kingdom, and to leave the matter to divine justice. I immediately acted upon this decision, regretting the fact that I had not done so sooner, for if I had, perhaps I would have saved a good share of my wealth.

And this was what came of my services of twenty-one years, during which I was captured thirteen times and sold into slavery sixteen times, [4] as a result of the unfortunate series of events that took place in the course of this long peregrination of mine which I have narrated above at great length.

But despite all this, though I did not get the satisfaction I sought in exchange for so many hardships and services, I realize that it was due more to the workings of divine Providence which ordained it so, for my sins, than to any negligence or fault on the part of whoever, by the will of heaven, had the responsibility for compensating me. For inasmuch as I have always observed in all the kings of this kingdom (who are the pure source from whence flow all compensations, though at times through channels affected more by favor than by reason) a saintly and grateful zeal and an extremely generous and grandiose desire, not only to reward those who serve them, but also to bestow many favors even on those who do not serve them, from which it is clear that if I and the others as neglected as I have not been compensated for our services, it was merely the fault of the channels and not the source, or rather, it was so ordained by divine justice, in which there can be no error, and which disposes all things as it sees fit and as is best for us.

Therefore, I give many thanks to the King of Heaven, who has seen fit in this manner to carry out his divine will on me, and I am not complaining about the kings of the earth, since I did not deserve any better, for having sinned so deeply.

Notes

Introduction

1. Henry Charles Lea, *A History of The Inquisition of Spain*, 4 vols. (New York: Macmillan Co., 1906–7), 3:238.

2. Letter of Gil Vicente to John III, dated 26 January 1531, in *Obras completas de Gil Vicente*, ed. Marques Braga (Lisbon: Sá da Costa, 1942–44), 6:251–55.

3. Jordão A. de Freitas, "A inquisição em Goa," *Archivo Historico Portuguez* 5 (1907): 216–27.

4. Letter from Cipriano Soares, S. J., to Diogo Mirón, S. J., in Rome, as cited by Georg Schurhammer, S. J., in "O descobrimento do Japão pelos Portugueses no ano de 1543," *Gesammelte Studien: Orientalia 2* (Rome: Bibliotheca Instituti Historici, 1963), 21:485–580.

5. A record of this interview was discovered in the Jesuit archives by Father Schurhammer, who claims that the information contained therein was never used by Maffei. See "Um documento inédito sobre Fernão Mendes Pinto," *Revista de História* (Lisbon) 13 (1924): 81–88.

6. Maurice Collis, *The Grand Peregrination* (London: Faber & Faber, 1949), 297.

7. Dorothy Osborne, *The Letters of Dorothy Osborne to William Temple*, 4th ed., ed. G. C. Moore Smith (Oxford: Clarendon Press, 1968), letter 59, dated 19 February 1653/54, 148.

8. William Alfred Rae Wood, "Fernão Mendes Pinto's Account of Events in Siam," *Journal of the Siam Society* 20, no. 1 (June 1926), 25–39.

9. Albert Kammerer, "Le Problématique Voyage en Abyssinie de Fernand Mendez Pinto (1537)," in *La Mer Rouge, l'Abyssinie et l'Arabie aux XVIème et XVIIème siècles et la cartographie des Portulans du monde oriental*, 21–30 (Cairo: Société Royal de Géographie d'Egypte, 1947).

10. Brother Fulgencio's letter was published in *Copia de algunas cartas que los padres y hermanos dela compañia de Iesus que andan en la India y otras partes orientales, escrivieron alos dela misma Compañia de Portugal* (Barcelona: Claude Bornat, 1562).

11. Georg Schurhammer, *Francis Xavier: His Life, His Times*, trans. M. Joseph Costelloe (Rome: Jesuit Historical Institute, 1982), 4:251.

12. Charles Ralph Boxer, *The Christian Century in Japan, 1549–1650*, 2d ed. (Berkeley: University of California Press, 1967), 27.

13. Edward W. Rosenheim, Jr., *Swift and the Satirist's Art* (Chicago: University of Chicago Press, 1963; Midway Reprints, 1982), 25.

14. As cited in Collis, *Grand Peregrination*, 202.

15. Ibid., 287.

16. Ibid., 292.

Chapter 1

1. *sold . . . seventeen times:* What appears to be a lapse of memory on the part of the author occurs in the final chapter of the book, in which he states that he was "captured thirteen times and sold into slavery sixteen times."

2. *"outer edge of the world":* The author is here referring to the Malay Archipelago, the largest of island groups in the world, comprising the islands of the East Indies, including Sumatra, Java, Lesser Sunda Islands, Moluccas, Timor, New Guinea, Borneo, Celebes, and the Philippines. The expression appears again in chapter 178.

3. *Gueos or Gueus:* A great deal has been written about the identity of this mysterious nation. The Portuguese historian João de Barros (1496–1570) describes the *Gueos* as ferocious cannibals who dwell in the mountains north of Siam and brand their bodies with hot irons. He also adds that they fight on horseback and descend periodically from their mountain strongholds to attack the Laotians who have reluctantly accepted the overlordship of the king of Siam in order to receive protection against the marauders; and were it not for the military might of the Siamese, the *Gueos* would long ago have destroyed the Laotians and conquered Siam. Barros also claims that he got his information from Domingos de Seixas, a Portuguese held captive for twenty-five years in Siam, where he served as an officer in the Siamese army and accompanied the king of Siam on one of his raids against the *Gueos*. See *Ásia de Joaõ de Barros* 6th ed., ed. Hernâni Cidade and Manuel Múrias (Lisbon: Divisão de Publicacões e Biblioteca, Agência Geral das Colónias, 1945), 3:78. Interestingly enough, Pinto refers to this Domingos de Seixas (chaps. 181 and 183) and the manner in which he was granted his freedom by the king of Siam. Duarte Barbosa, writing before Barros (1518?), describes a similar race of cannibals in the same region north of Siam, but does not name them. See *The Book of Duarte Barbosa,* ed. Mansel Longworth Dames (London: Hakluyt Society, 1918–21), 2:xxviii, 167 n. 1. The epic poet Camões seems to have relied on Barros for his description of the *Gueos* in *The Lusiads* (canto 10, stanza 126) when he wrote (Bacon's translation),

> Look! Those far heights to other clans belong,
> Where self-styled *Gueos* live grim lives and fell.
> Man's flesh they eat and with hot iron brand
> Their own, a cruel custom of the land.

The Dutch traveler, Jan Huyghen van Linschoten, who worked as secretary to the archbishop of Goa in 1583–89, appears to have based his description of the *Gueos* on either Barros or Camões when he wrote, "Others [nations] that dwell upon the hills called *Gueos,* which live like wild men, and eat man's flesh, and mark all their bodies with hot iron." See Linschoten, *The Voyage of John Huyghen van Linschoten to the East Indies,* ed. Arthur Coke Burnell and P. A. Tiele (London: Hakluyt Society, 1885), 1:122–23. As for modern scholarship on the subject, Dames, in the *Book of Duarte Barbosa,* xxviii, quotes Sir James George Scott, author of *Burma from the Earliest Times to the Present Day* (New York: Alfred A. Knopf, 1924), who identifies the *Gueos* with the Was and Lawas of Burma, as does Joaquim de Campos, who points out that the Siamese name *Ngiu* for the Shans indicates that the ancient name of the Was and Lawas passed to the Shans who occupied their land. See Joaquim de Campos, "Early Portuguese Accounts of Thailand," in "Relationships with Portugal, Holland, and the Vatican," *Selected Articles from the Siam Society Journal* (Bangkok: Siam Society, 1959), 7:220 (originally published in *Journal of the Thailand Research Society* 32 [1940]). For a description of these two primitive groups, see William Alfred Rae Wood, *A History of Siam from the Earliest Times to the Year A.D. 1781* (London: Unwin, 1926), 41. Donald F. Lach also has some interesting comments to make about earlier speculations on the identity of the *Gueos* in his *Southeast Asia in the Eyes of Europe: The Sixteenth Century* (Chicago and London: University of Chicago Press, Phoenix Books, 1968), 523–24.

4. *Montemor-o-Velho:* A town north of Lisbon, halfway between the university city of Coimbra and the seaport of Figueira da Foz. This has generally been accepted by Pinto's biographers as the designation of his birthplace; however, no proof has ever been adduced.

5. *Manuel I:* (1469–1521), known as Manuel the Fortunate. It was during his reign (1495–1521) that Vasco da Gama discovered the maritime route to India (1497–99) and Cabral discovered the coast of Brazil (1500). The wealth of the East began to pour into Portugal, making her the leading commercial nation of the West. Manuel kept a splendid court and was the envy of all Europe. However, it was during his reign that the seeds of decline were sown, for the sudden wealth had corrupting effects on officials—one of the themes of Pinto's book—and

started the process of turning interest away from the agricultural and industrial development of Portugal.

6. *Alfama:* One of the oldest districts of Lisbon, with narrow, winding streets, located on a hill overlooking the Tagus River. Today, where the Stone Wharf once stood, is a small pier known as the *Cais das Colunas* (pier of the columns). See illustration of the Alfama waterfront in the third-quarter of the sixteenth century in Julio de Castilho, *A ribeira de Lisboa* (Lisbon: Publicações Culturaes da Camara Municipal de Lisboa, 1942), vol. 3, n.p.

7. *Setúbal:* Formerly called in English Saint Ubes or Saint Yves. A seaport nineteen miles southeast of Lisbon, on the Bay of Setúbal, one of the finest harbors in Portugal. It was a royal residence from the time of John II, who reigned 1481–95.

8. *King John III:* (1502–57), known as John the Pious, son of Manuel I. It was during his reign (1521–57) that the Portuguese empire was at its apogee. The great Asiatic possessions were extended by further conquests, and systematic colonization of Brazil was begun. However, decadence had set in, with the corruption of officials abroad, the abandonment of agriculture and industry at home, and the debilitating effects of depopulation. Portugal's North African conquests were abandoned, but many slaves were brought into the country. The Inquisition was introduced by John, who favored the clerical party and the ideas of the Counter-Reformation. A rich literature on the discoveries flourished during his reign, but Portugal was falling into the stagnation that characterized the reign of his grandson Sebastian I (1557–78), who succeeded him.

9. *Sesimbra:* Town on the edge of the Atlantic Ocean, about six miles west of the port of Setúbal (see above, n. 7).

10. *cruzado:* An old Portuguese coin of silver or gold, nominally translated as "ducat" and roughly equivalent to "a piece of eight."

11. *Larache:* Al-Araish in Arabic. City and seaport on the North Atlantic coast of Morocco. The Phoenicians founded a trading post on the site, which was later captured by the Romans and called Lixus. Spain held the city twice, 1610–91 and 1911–56. From the sixteenth to the eighteenth century it was a favorite haunt of the Barbary Coast pirates.

12. *nao:* Literally "great ship," often translated as "carrack" in English. A large merchant vessel, also fitted for warfare, with three or four decks, but not very maneuverable. During the sixteenth and seventeenth centuries the Portuguese *naos* were the largest vessels in the world, averaging between eight hundred and twelve hundred tons, rivalled only in size by the great Manila galleons which sailed yearly between Mexico and the Philippines. For a more detailed description of the *nao,* see Charles Ralph Boxer, *The Great Ship from Amacon,* 2d ed. (Lisbon: Centro de Estudos Históricos Ultramarinos, 1963), 13–14.

13. *Vila do Conde:* City in Northern Portugal about eighteen miles from Porto, near the mouth of the Ave River.

14. *São Tomé:* Saint Thomas in English, an island in the Gulf of Guinea, on the equator, in west Africa. Together with Príncipe Island, it formed the Portuguese province of São Tomé e Príncipe, discovered by the Portuguese in 1471. After 1975 it became an independent republic.

15. *Melides:* Today a parish of the municipality of Grandola, southwest of Lisbon, in the district of Setúbal, on the right bank of the Melides River. In Pinto's day it was a parish of the Order of the Knights of Saint James, and until 1855 formed part of the municipality of Santiago de Cacém.

16. *Santiago de Cacém:* Municipality of the district of Setúbal, not far from Melides. See above, notes 7 and 15.

17. *grand master . . . Saint James:* The grand master of the Order of the Knights of Saint James was Dom Jorge, duke of Coimbra and illegitimate son of King John II. The Knights of Saint James was a powerful military religious order founded in Spain in 1170, but a separate Portuguese order was established in 1290. In 1862 it became known as "the Ancient, Very Noble and Enlightened Order of Saint James for Scientific, Literary, and Artistic Achievement."

Chapter 2

1. *no flagship:* It was unusual for the king not to commission an admiral for an India-bound fleet, but the fact that he did not do so that year is confirmed by a letter of John III dated 29 October 1536, in which he says that he had decided not to send a fleet admiral to India the following year. See Jeremiah D. M. Ford and Lucius Gaston Moffatt, eds., *Letters of John III, King of Portugal, 1521–1557* (Cambridge, Mass.: Harvard University Press, 1931), letter 258, 291.

2. *commanded . . . by the following captains:* The *Livro das Armadas* published by the Academia das Ciências of Lisbon (1979) agrees in all respects with Pinto's description of the fleet that sailed from Lisbon in March of 1537, though other contemporary accounts do not. This is not at all surprising if one considers that Luis de Albuquerque, in his introduction to the *Livro das Armadas,* lists twenty different sources, both published and unpublished (and the list is by no means complete), for the composition of the annual India fleets, while at the same time pointing out that there are striking differences between them, and that only rarely do they agree on the dates, number and names of the ships, commanders comprising the fleets, etc.

3. *Dom Pedro da Silva:* One of the six sons of Vasco da Gama. He served as captain of the fortress of Malacca (1548–52), where in 1551 he bravely defended the fortress-city against the besieging Moslem forces. He was also a close friend and admirer of Francis Xavier, to whom he lent money in 1552, which the saint used to repay Pinto for a sum of money borrowed from him the year before in Japan. The money Pinto lent him was used to build the first Christian church in Japan. See letter of Francis Xavier from Malacca, dated 16 July 1552, in Rebecca Catz, ed., *Cartas de Fernão Mendes Pinto e outros documentos* (Lisbon: Biblioteca Nacional, 1983), document 2, 19–20.

4. *Dom Fernando de Lima:* In 1538 the governor of Portuguese India, Nuno da Cunha, appointed him captain of the fortress of Hormuz, where he died of the fevers after three months in office, "deeply grieved by all, for the many virtues he possessed," according to Diogo do Couto (João de Barros and Couto, *Da Ásia de João de Barros e de Diogo de Couto* [Lisbon: Na Régia Officina Typográfica, 1778–88], década 5, bk. 2, chap. 6, 8). See note 5 below.

5. *Hormuz:* Island in the Persian Gulf on the Strait of Hormuz. In 1506 it was captured by Afonso de Albuquerque, who allowed it to remain an autonomous sultanate, tributary to Portugal and subject to the jurisdiction of the resident Portuguese captain. It remained under Portuguese sovereignty until the first quarter of the seventeenth century.

6. *Jorge de Lima:* Though he was appointed captain of the fortress of Chaul (see n. 7 below) in January of 1537, he did not take up his duties until the end of the following year.

7. *Chaul:* Ancient city and port on the west coast of India about thirty-nine miles southeast of Bombay. In 1521 the Portuguese received permission from the local ruler to build a fortress in Chaul, on condition that they import three hundred horses annually from Persia and Arabia. For a decade it was the only important naval base the Portuguese had on that part of the coast. It remained in their possession until about the middle of the eighteenth century.

8. *Lopo Vaz Vogado:* His name appears briefly in the Portuguese chronicles as captain of the *Flor de la Mar,* which sailed for India in March of 1537, and also in a letter of King John III, dated 10 January 1537, naming him as captain of the same ship. See Ford and Moffatt, *Letters of John III,* letter 265, 296.

9. *Pero Lopez de Sousa:* He went to India in 1539 as admiral of a fleet of six ships, but on the return voyage to Portugal, in command of the *nao Galega,* he died in a shipwreck near the island of Madagascar. He was the younger brother of Martim Afonso de Sousa, governor of India 1541–45. According to Gaspar Correia, his death was "a just punishment of God, because he was a great tyrant" (*Lendas da Índia,* ed. M. Lopes de Almeida [Porto: Lello & Irmão, 1975], vol. 4, chap. 37, 99–101).

10. *Martim de Freitas:* After reaching India and discharging the soldiers and munitions at the fortress of Diu (see n. 15 below), he anchored at the nearby port of Daman (see n. 11 below), where, according to Gaspar Correia, he went ashore with a group of men to sell some

merchandise to the local Moslems. A fight broke out because of the overbearing manner of some of the Portuguese, and Martim de Freitas lost his life defending his men. In addition, thirteen men were killed, twenty taken captive, and the rest, though wounded in the fray, managed to get back to their ship, which sailed immediately for Goa (vol. 3, chap. 103, 818). According to Barros, Martim de Freitas went ashore with a group of noblemen to visit some friends and lost his life in an ambush laid for them by the local Moslems (Barros and Couto, déc. 4, bk. 8, chap. 11). Diogo do Couto says that Martim de Freitas went ashore to sell some merchandise and was never heard from again (déc. 5, bk. 2, chap. 13). Fernão Lopes de Castanheda says simply that, after reaching India, Martim de Freitas was killed by the Moors in an unknown manner (*História do descobrimento e conquista da Índia,* ed. M. Lopes de Almeida [Porto: Lello & Irmão, 1979], vol. 2, bk. 8, chap. 171, 846). Francisco de Andrade, as usual, agrees with Correia (*Crónica de Dom João III* [Porto: Lello & Irmão, 1976], pt. 3, chap. 46, 221).

11. *Daman:* A port city of Portuguese India, located at the mouth of the Daman River, about a hundred miles north of Bombay. It was conquered by the Portuguese in 1536 and remained in their possession until 1961.

12. *Duarte Tristão:* Gaspar Correia mentions a homebound merchant ship that spent the winter of 1537 in Mozambique, but he says it was owned by a Jacomé Tristão (vol. 3, chap. 103, 817).

13. *Vicente Pegado:* Served as secretary to Vasco da Gama when the latter took up his duties as viceroy, on his third voyage to India, where he died in 1524. Due to political difficulties with da Gama's successors, he was shifted to a post in Africa in 1530, where he remained until 1538. That same year he was back in Goa where he joined the armada that Governor Nuno da Cunha (see n. 14 below) was preparing to send to the aid of the besieged fortress of Diu (see n. 15 below). However, when in the midst of these preparations Nuno da Cunha was recalled and replaced by the viceroy Garcia de Noronha (see chap. 8, n. 4 below), Vicente Pegado decided to return to Portugal.

14. *Nuno da Cunha:* (1487–1539), governor of Portuguese India from 1528 to 1538. During his ten years in office he founded the fortresses of Diu, Chaul, and Bassein, and inadvertently caused the death of the sultan of Cambay. He was much feared and respected but had many political ememies, and at their instigation John III ordered him home. There was a fleet waiting for him at the Azores to arrest him, but he died on the homebound ship on 5 March 1539, as it was rounding the Cape of Good Hope, and he was buried at sea. He was said to have uttered as his dying words, "*Ingrata patria ossa mea non possidebus.*" See José F. Ferreira Martins, *Crónica dos vice-reis e governadores da Índia* (Nova Goa: Imprensa Nacional, 1919), 1:286. See also chapters 4, 6, and 12, below in which he is mentioned.

15. *Diu:* Island and seaport town on the west coast of India, at the entrance to the Gulf of Cambay, 170 miles northwest of Bombay. It came into the possession of the Portuguese in 1535 as the result of an agreement with the local ruler, Sultan Bahadur of Cambay, who allowed them to build a fortress there, though he later regretted it. It withstood two devastating sieges in 1538 and 1546 laid against it by combined Moslem forces, and remained in Portuguese possession until December of 1961.

16. *Sultan Bahadur:* The historical accounts of the death of Sultan Bahadur differ in some respects, but they all agree more or less on the most important details: Once the sultan's war with the Moghul was over and he no longer needed the aid of the Portuguese, which had been less substantial than promised, he regretted the fact that he had allowed them to build a fortress in Diu and began to plot against them. Though he was aware of the plot, the governor sailed to Diu, at the invitation of the wily sultan, hoping to outwit him. Pretending that he was too sick to go ashore, the governor invited the sultan to visit him aboard his ship, intending to seize him. Bahadur came, but suspecting danger, fled to his boat. However, the governor, anxious not to lose his prey, issued vague instructions to his men to go after him, which they did, killing the sultan, much against the wishes of the governor. This gave rise to the siege of the autumn of 1538, which the Portuguese were expecting at the time that Pinto arrived in Diu. See Barros

(Barros and Couto, déc. 4, bk. 8, chap. 5), Correia (vol. 3, chap. 95, 781–82), Castanheda (vol. 2, bk. 8, chap. 165, 838–41), Andrade (pt. 3, chap. 41, 709–11). Also of interest is the Indian version of this incident quoted by the English historian F. C. Danvers in his *The Portuguese in India* (London, 1894; 2d ed., New York: Octagon Books, 1966), 1:419–20, which was taken from the "Akbar-Nama" of Shaikh Abu'-l-Fagl and published by Sir H. M. Elliot in his *The History of India as Told by Its Own Historians* (London, 1867–75). Also, it should be pointed out that *bahadur* (*bhadur, bahaudur,* or *badur*), is not a proper name, but a term, possibly of Mongolian origin, meaning "a hero or champion." It was assumed as a title by some of the Moslem rulers of India, who also conferred it upon their most honored subjects. See Henry Yule and Arthur Coke Burnell, eds., *Hobson-Jobson: A Glossary of Colloquial Anglo-Indian Words and Phrases, and of Kindred Terms* (1903), 2d ed. (Delhi: Munshiram Mancharlal, 1968), as well as Sebastião Rodolfo Dalgado's *Glossário Luso-Asiático,* 2 vols. (Coimbra: Imprensa da Universidade, 1919–21). Generally speaking, any reference by Portuguese writers to Sultan Bahadur of Cambay applies specifically to the Moslem sovereign who reigned from 1526 to 1536.

17. *Cambay:* Principal port of the former kingdom of Gujerat on the west coast of India, 240 miles north of Bombay, at the head of the Gulf of Cambay. It was one of the favorite residences of the Moslem kings of Gujerat, which is why they were often referred to as the kings of Cambay. Soon after their arrival in India, the Portuguese became aware of the importance of this port to the commerce of India and tried to take it, either by force or by coming to an understanding with the kings of Cambay.

18. *Goa:* Former colony and capital of Portuguese India, with one of the best ports on the coast of Hindustan. It was founded in 1510 by Afonso de Albuquerque from territory he seized from the sultanate of Bijapur. Old Goa, the original capital of the colony, was a very prosperous city in the late sixteenth century. In 1842, New Goa, or Pangim, was built to replace Old Goa as the capital. It remained in the possession of the Portuguese until 1961 when it was annexed by India. For a description of Portuguese Goa in the sixteenth century, see Boies Penrose's bilingual edition of *Goa—Rainha do Oriente/Goa—Queen of the East* (Lisbon: Comemorações do V Centenário da Morte do Infante D. Henrique, 1960).

19. *that same year of 1538:* Obviously an error. The year should be 1537 and not 1538 as it appears in the text. Apart from the fact that the outbound voyage to India normally took about six months, Pinto relates in chapter 7 that he sailed past Diu a year later when it was under siege, an event that took place during the late summer and autumn of 1538.

20. *Antonio da Silveira:* Famous in the history of Portuguese India for his heroic defense of the fortress of Diu during the siege of 1538. He arrived in India in 1526 and served as captain of the fortresses of Hormuz, Bassein, and finally Diu, where he withstood the siege mounted against Diu by the combined forces of Islam. He received a hero's welcome on his return to Portugal in 1539.

21. *Luis da Silveira:* (1481–1532), count of Sortelha and brother of Antonio da Silveira (see n. 20 above). He held many important posts at court during the reigns of Manuel I and John III.

22. *Cochin:* Former princely state in southwest India on the Arabian Sea. The first Portuguese fleet to enter the harbor of Cochin was that of Pedro Alvares Cabral in 1500. He was welcomed by the local ruler, who accepted an alliance with the Portuguese and consented to the establishment of a factory there. With the arrival of Albuquerque (1503), he gave them permission to build a fortress there—the first European fortress in India. After the conquest of Goa by Albuquerque (1510), Cochin ceased to be the center of Portuguese dominion in Asia, but it continued to be the first port of call for the ships coming from Europe. Its ruler was the most faithful ally of the Portuguese until the end of Portuguese dominion, which passed to the Dutch in 1663.

23. *Manuel de Macedo:* From the days of Albuquerque he served as captain of the royal ships in India. Also served as captain of the fortress of Bassein 1536–37.

24. *"cannon of Diu"*: The basilisk is a large cannon used in the sixteenth century, gener-

ally made of brass. The one that Pinto is referring to is described as "colossal" in the catalog of the Military Museum of Lisbon, where it may be seen today. It bears an inscription in Arabic that, according to the catalog, states that it was built in 1533 for Sultan Bahadur of Cambay. (See sec. R-18, "Artilharia Ultramarina" of the catalog of the Military Museum, Lisbon, 1979). According to João de Barros, Nuno da Cunha found it in the arsenal of the sultan after the latter's death in 1536, or two years prior to the first siege of Diu (1538). He also says that there were three basilisks of amazing size, one of which had belonged to the sultan of Babylon (Egypt), which Rumi-Khan (see n. 25 below) brought with him when he came to Diu, and since it was a most remarkable piece of artillery, Nuno da Cunha sent it to the king, in Portugal (Barros and Couto, déc. 4, bk. 8, chap. 8).

25. *Rumi-Khan:* Name given by the Portuguese to the Turkish general Mustafa who, after a falling out with the Grand Turk, went to offer his services to Sultan Bahadur of Cambay. He arrived in Cambay in 1527 with two ships and a large quantity of artillery, accompanied by the renegade Coje Çofar (Khodja Tzaffar?), his uncle's former slave, believed to be the son of an Albanian father and an Italian mother, who had risen to become the treasurer of Cairo and, later, captain of Cambay. Concerning the manner of their arrival in Cambay, see Barros, in Barros and Couto, déc. 3, bk. 1, chap. 3; déc. 4, bk. 1, chap. 8. However, one should not confuse this Rumi-Khan with the son of Coje Çofar who at a later date was honored with the same name. The latter succeeded his father to the captaincy of Cambay and fought against the Portuguese in the second siege of Diu (1546). The name Rumi-Khan is a compound of the honorific *khan,* meaning "lord or prince," and the term *rumi,* meaning "a Roman," applied by the Indians to the Turks of the Ottoman Empire. In older Oriental books it is used for a European, but *rum,* for the Roman Empire, continued to be applied to what had been part of the Roman Empire after it had fallen to the Turks. (See Yule and Burnell.)

26. *Dom Pedro de Castelbranco:* In 1533 King John III received word from his spies in Venice that the Turks were preparing a fleet in Suez at the request of Sultan Bahadur. Also, Governor Nuno da Cunha received the same news from Red Sea merchants who came to India. He sent a ship to Portugal with a message, which arrived after the departure of the annual fleet. As a result, another fleet was made ready, which departed from Lisbon in October of 1533 under the command of Dom Pedro de Castelbranco. According to Gaspar Correia, the fleet comprised three galleons and nine caravels (vol. 3, chap. 45, 541), though Francisco de Andrade says there were two galleons, one *nao,* and nine caravels (pt. 3, chap. 2, 583). As it turned out, there was no need for this emergency fleet because the sultan, after suffering a series of losses in his war with the Moghul, decided to make peace with the Portuguese and gave them permission to build a fortress in Diu, which was finished in February of 1535. It was only after the death of Bahadur in 1536 that the Turks sent an armada, at the request of the sultan's mother, which laid siege to the fortress of Diu in 1538. See notes 14–17, 20, 24, and 25 above.

Chapter 3

1. *foist:* A light single-masted vessel, propelled by sail and oar, used for both cargo and warfare.

2. *Straits of Mecca:* The Portuguese writers of the period often referred to the Red Sea as the Straits of Mecca.

3. *concern in India:* See chapter 2, notes 16 and 26 above.

4. *monsoon:* Winds that blow at a certain time of the year, especially in the Indian Ocean. Generally speaking, there are two monsoons in the Indian Ocean, one from the northeast which is called the "dry" or "summer" monsoon, and the other out of the southwest, which is called the "rainy" or "winter" monsoon, though it is well known that there is no winter in the tropics. The former prevails from October to March, and the latter, which is stronger, from April to September. The foist on which Pinto embarked departed in September, as he says, "at the wrong time of year" and "at the end of winter."

5. *Kuria-Muria:* A group of five rocky islets in the Arabian Sea off the southwest coast of Oman, southeast Arabia.

6. *Abd al-Kuri:* A rock and coral reef in the Arabian Sea off Cape Guardafui (Africa), west of the island of Socotra. (See n. 7 below.)

7. *Socotra:* Island in the Indian Ocean, south of Arabia and about 130 miles east of Cape Guardafui, near the entrance to the Red Sea. In 1507, Tristão da Cunha and Afonso de Albuquerque conquered the island of Socotra, where the Arabs already possessed a fortress, which the Portuguese rebuilt after it had been partially destroyed in the fighting. Since it proved too costly to occupy, it was abandoned three years later in 1510. However, the island was frequently visited by the Portuguese on their way to the Red Sea ports.

8. *Dom Francisco de Almeida:* First viceroy of Portuguese India (1505–9). He sailed from Lisbon on 25 March 1505 (and not in 1507 as Pinto states). On his way back to Portugal, he and the men who had gone ashore with him to take on water were killed by the natives of southwest Africa on 1 March 1510.

9. *Apostle Saint Thomas:* It is not known when the Socotrans were converted to Christianity, but it was mistakenly assumed by some of the sixteenth-century chroniclers, among them Gaspar Correia (Anno de 1507, vol. 1, chap. 3, 683–85) and Castanheda (vol. 1, bk. 2, 298), that they were converted by the apostle Saint Thomas on his way to India. Others, like João de Barros (in Barros and Couto, déc. 2, bk. 1, chap. 4, 18) and Manuel de Faria e Sousa (*Asia Portuguesa* [Porto: Livraria Civilização, 1945], vol. 1, pt. 2, chap. 1, 228), realized that they were a branch of the Abyssinian or Jacobite church. By the time the Portuguese arrived in Socotra, Christianity was in a vestigial state. Today, no traces of Christianity exist on the island, which has been Islamized, but many Ethiopian inscriptions have been found. For a thorough discussion of the history of Christianity in Socotra, see Henry Yule, ed. and trans., *The Book of Ser Marco Polo, the Venetian,* 3d ed. (London: John Murray, 1929), vol. 2, bk. 3, chap. 32, 408–10, n. 2.

10. *Coromandel:* Name applied to the southeast coast of India from Point Calimere north to the mouths of the Kistna River.

11. *mouth of the straits:* Refers to Bab el Mandeb, a strait twenty miles wide between southwest Arabia and the African coast, uniting the Red Sea and the Gulf of Aden (Indian Ocean). The Portuguese writers often referred to it as the "mouth or the gates of the strait," meaning the entrance to the Red Sea.

12. *Massawa:* Once the principal seaport of Ethiopia, on a small island, on the western coast of the Red Sea, at the northern extremity of Arkeeko Bay.

13. *First Watch:* The hours from 8:00 p.m. to midnight, so called because it is the first of the three night watches on board a ship.

14. *Grand Turk:* Suleiman I, or Suleiman the Magnificent (1494–1566), the most famous of the Ottoman sultans, who reigned from 1520 to 1566. Under him the Ottoman Empire reached the height of its power and prestige. He continued his predecessor's conquests in the Balkans and the Mediterranean and conquered the Arabian coastlands of the Red Sea, preventing the Portuguese from gaining a foothold there. He undertook several successful campaigns in Persia, and in Europe he inflicted a crushing defeat on Hungary in 1526, but was stopped at the gates of Vienna in 1529.

15. *Falcon:* A cannon of the sixteenth and seventeenth centuries, of small caliber, firing iron balls.

16. *stone thrower:* Or *roqueiro.* A short, thick, iron cannon of the sixteenth century, used for hurling stones at great elevation.

17. *Culverin:* Or *berço.* A short swivel cannon of the sixteenth and seventeenth centuries, of small caliber, firing iron or lead balls. It had various chambers which, loaded in advance, permitted greater rapidity in firing. The culverin and the falcon belonged to the so-called small artillery designed for use on ships as defense against boarding.

18. *powder pans:* A crude grenade or incendiary bomb, made of clay, containing powder and thrown by hand.

19. *Jidda:* Also Jedda or Djedah. Town and seaport on the east coast of the Red Sea, in the province of Hejaz, Saudi Arabia. It is the chief port for pilgrims going to Mecca.

20. *Aden:* Port of Yemen, on the Gulf of Yemen, 110 miles east of the Strait of Bab el Mandeb (See n. 11 above). It was an important trading center in Roman times and the chief port on the medieval trade route between the Red Sea and the Persian Gulf and India. In 1513 it was unsuccessfully attacked by the Portuguese under Afonso de Albuquerque. In 1538 it was captured by Turkish forces sent by Suleiman I to drive the Portuguese out of India. In 1548 it was held briefly by the Portuguese, who were invited to come in after an uprising against the Turks, which only resulted in their strengthening their fortifications, enabling them to hold Aden until the seventeenth century. (See n. 14 above and n. 21 below.)

21. *Pasha of Cairo:* Or "the Eunuch," as the Portuguese called him, governor of Cairo, commander of the armada that Suleiman I sent against the fortress of Diu in 1538. On the way to India, he stopped in Aden where, after receiving valuable presents and provisions from the king, he sent armed men ashore, on the pretext that they were ill, and while his "sick" men were taking over the city, the pasha cold-bloodedly murdered the king, who had come to visit him aboard his ship. Once Aden was taken, he proceeded to Diu, where he arrived in September of 1538. He was also known as Suleiman Pasha. (See chap. 2, n. 26 above.)

22. *Cerdagne:* An old division of Europe in the east Pyrenees, partly in France, partly in Spain. It belonged to the ancient kingdom of Mallorca, formed in 1276 out of the inheritance of Jaime I of Mallorca, which comprised the Balearic Islands, Roussillon, Cerdagne, and some feudal lands in the south of France. In 1343, Pedro IV of Aragon took the kingdom from Jaime II, annexing it, along with Catalonia, to Aragon. In 1462, Juan II passed Cerdagne, along with Roussillon, to Louis XI; Charles VIII returned them in 1493. In 1659, after the Treaty of the Pyrenees, Spain ceded to France the part situated to the north of the Pyrenees. It should be pointed out that there is some confusion here with regard to the renegade, who says first that he is a native of Jidda and then later, "a Mallorcan national, native of Cerdagne." Also, there is a chronological error here because the fleet of Suleiman Pasha departed a year later, in 1538. (See chap. 2, n. 19 above.)

23. *pastel:* A blue dyestuff prepared from the leaves of the woad plant, *Isatis tinctoria,* powdered and fermented, forming a paste (hence pastel); now generally superseded by indigo, in the preparation of which it is still used. It is sometimes called "dyer's or garden woad," and "dyer's weed."

Chapter 4

1. *Arkeeko:* Also written Arkiko, Harkiko, or Arqiqo. Port on the west coast of the Red Sea, about five miles south of Massawa and five hundred from Addis Ababa. It was the principal port of entry to Ethiopia.

2. *Prester John:* Legendary Christian priest and monarch of a vast wealthy empire in Asia or Africa. Like many legends, it was based on a historical fact—the existence of Christian communities throughout the East. The legend first appeared in the latter part of the twelfth century and persisted for several centuries, given credence by Marco Polo, among others, and by letters supposed to have been written by him and about him which were widely circulated in western Europe. At first the utopian realm of the Christian king was supposed to be in Asia, but later it was placed in Africa. The identification of Prester John with the king of Ethiopia came about at the end of the fifteenth century as a result of the voyages of the Portuguese who, in their age-old struggle with Islam, were anxious to make contact with a Christian kingdom in the East. It was partly confirmed by a letter of Pero da Covilhã (1487), who had been sent by King John II to look for Prester John and who believed he had found him in Ethiopia. Since

then, the monarch of Ethiopia (or the *negus* as he was called by his subjects) was referred to by the Portuguese chroniclers as the "Prester John of the Indies." Paradoxically, at the same time that the sixteenth-century chroniclers refer to the *negus* as the prester, they reject his identification with the legendary Christian priest and monarch. Cf. Castanheda (vol. 1, bk. 3, chap. 96, 724) and Barros (in Barros and Couto, déc. 3, bk. 4, chap. 1, 360).

3. *Shihr:* Also Shehr or, with the article, Es-Shihr. City and District on the coast of Arabia, about 330 miles east of Aden. It was an important city at the time because of an active trade with India, in spite of its poor port facilities. The Portuguese of the sixteenth century frequently traded there.

4. *Dom Manuel de Menezes:* Towards the end of 1535, Governor Nuno da Cunha sent Dom Manuel with seventy men in his company to investigate the complaints of the sultan of Shihr regarding the outrageous behavior of Portuguese traders in his port. According to Barros, the sultan's complaints were entirely justified, but Dom Manuel was arrested on his arrival, though he was later released after a new treaty of peace had been signed with the Portuguese. Regarding the Portuguese captives, it was a shrewd gesture on the part of the sultan, who, realizing that he had incurred the anger of the Portuguese by arresting Dom Manuel, and knowing that the Turks were preparing a fleet in Suez to send against them, decided to curry favor with the Grand Turk by making a gift to him of thirty-four of the Portuguese captives (and not sixty, as Pinto claims). See Barros, in Barros and Couto, déc. 4, bk. 8, chaps. 15–16. Gaspar Correia also relates the history of the capture and release of Dom Manuel de Menezes, but his version is quite different from that of Barros' (cf. Correia, vol. 3, chap. 108, 843).

5. *Suleiman Pasha:* A native of Greece, he was governor of Egypt in the service of Suleiman the Magnificent (see chap. 3, n. 14 above). When, after the death of Bahadur Shah of Cambay, Suleiman I decided to send a powerful fleet against the fortress of Diu, he appointed Suleiman Pasha as commander, in spite of the latter's seventy years of age. After his failure to take Diu, the pasha retreated to Constantinople via the Red Sea, leaving destruction in his wake. Called to court to explain his defeat, the aged eunuch, fearing for his head, preferred to put an end to his life by taking poison. Castanheda gives us an interesting portrait of Suleiman Pasha: "Even though he was a great lord and had reached the age of seventy, and was so fat that when he sat down he could not get up and needed two men to lift him, and had such a big double chin that it hung down to his chest, he was so hungry for glory and money that in order to obtain so great a glory as it would be to take India from the Portuguese and make himself lord of the many great treasures there, he asked the Turk for the command, offering to pay the salaries of the men in the fleet himself" (vol. 2, bk. 7, chap. 191, 874). See also chapter 2, note 26 and chapter 3, note 21 above.

6. *Mohammed:* The reference here is to the grand sherif of Mecca. Pinto writes *Mafamede*, a variant spelling for Mohammed.

7. *Óbidos:* Town in the district of Leiria, west central Portugal, about fifty miles north of Lisbon, famous for its medieval castle.

8. *Gileytor:* The name has not been identified; however, Viscount Lagoa believes that the fortress was "probably located in the Jebel Halibó of our modern maps, to the northwest of Massawa, at 15° 58' Lat. N and 38° 45' Long. E." See "A Peregrinação de Fernão Mendes Pinto (tentativa de reconstituição geográfica)," in *Anais da Junta de Investigações Coloniais do Ministério das Colónias* (Lisbon: Junta das Missões Geográficas e de Investigações Coloniais, 1947), vol. 2, bk. 1, 37.

9. *Tigremahom:* Probably a reference to the province of Tigre, in the north of Abyssinia, taken from the title of the governor, *Tegre Makuannen,* which means "the governor of Tigre." The Jesuit Manoel de Almeida, in his *História da Ethiopia a alta, ou Abassia,* says that it was also the name of a small district in the "kingdom" of Tigre. See *Some Records of Ethiopia, 1593–1646,* ed. C. F. Beckingham and G. W. B. Huntingford (London: Hakluyt Society, 1954), xcvi.

10. *Mother of Prester John:* Regarding the possible identity of the queen mother, see Albert Kammerer, "Problématique Voyage," pt. 1, 21–30.

11. *Bitonto:* Kammerer believes that *Bitonto* is a transcriber's error for Bisonto, which could only be Bisan or Bizan, the name of the town where a monastery of Saint Michael did indeed exist (ibid., 28).

12. *Barnagais: Bahar Nagaes* or *Bahr Nagas,* the title of the governor of northern Ethiopia, meaning literally "lord of the sea." In the fifteenth and sixteenth centuries he was the governor of Tigre and the lowlands stretching to the coast at Massawa. After 1580 his office was absorbed in that of the *Tegre Makuannen,* but when the Portuguese first arrived (1520), the two were still distinct, the domain of the *bahar nagaes* ending at the Marab and including the provinces of Sarawe, Hamasen, Akala Guzay, and Bur. See Francisco Alvares, *The Prester John of the Indies,* ed. C. F. Beckingham and G. W. B. Huntingford (London: Hakluyt Society, 1961), 54 n. 4.

13. *Lopo Chanoca:* The name of a Lopo Chanoca appears in the sixteenth-century chronicles as one of the ship captains who departed for India in 1505 with the armada of the viceroy Francisco de Almeida, but it is not known if he is the same man mentioned here or later on in chapter 17.

14. *Azebibe:* Zabid, city on the coast of the Red Sea, in the present-day Arab Republic of Yemen. Also written Azebybi or Zeibide by the Portuguese chroniclers.

15. *oquea: Waqet* in Ethiopic and Amharic, a unit of gold weight, of uncertain value, given the wide disagreement among the experts. In the sixteenth century Ethiopia had no coinage.

16. *Betenigus: Beit-el-negus* in Amharic, meaning literally "house of the king." It applies specifically to the round houses and not to the rectangular ones, according to Beckingham and Huntingford, eds., *Prester John of the Indies,* by Alvares, 98 n. 2.

17. *Jews:* Probably the Falasha, an ethnic group of Ethiopia, practicing a form of Judaism. They believe only in the Old Testament and have no knowledge of the Talmud or the postbiblical Judaic literature. In ancient times they probably ruled their own state.

18. *Sunday, October 4:* J. I. de Brito Rebello, in the introduction to his edition of the *Peregrinação de Fernão Mendes Pinto,* states that the first Sunday in the month of October 1537 fell on the seventh and not on the fourth ([Lisbon: Livraria Ferreira Editora, 1908], 1:xviii).

19. *Queen Helena:* There was indeed a Queen Helena who played an important part in the history of Abyssinia. It was she who procured the throne for the king Lebna Dengel (d. 1540) and sent an ambassador to Portugal in 1512. She died in 1525, during the mission of Dom Rodrigo de Lima, the first Portuguese ambassador to Abyssinia. See Kammerer, "Problématique Voyage," 28.

20. *King Solomon:* According to tradition, the kingdom of Ethiopia was founded in the tenth century B.C. by Menelik I, son of the queen of Sheba by King Solomon after her famous visit to Jerusalem (1 Kings 10). The kings of Ethiopia claim to be descended from him.

21. *Naique:* Or *naik.* From the Sanskrit *nayaka,* meaning a "leader, chief, general." The term is used in several applications among the Portuguese chroniclers as meaning a "native captain" or "headman" of some sort. For its other uses, see Yule and Burnell.

22. *Present:* According to Kammerer ("Problématique Voyage," 29 n. 2), the generosity of the Ethiopians as described by Pinto in this chapter is exaggerated, for in the year 1537 the kingdom was completely ruined by its wars with the Arabs.

Chapter 5

1. *6 November 1537:* According to Brito Rebello, Wednesday was the seventh and not the sixth (1:15).

2. *Abyssinian bishop:* The queen mother could not possibly have sent a bishop because there was only one bishop (called the *abuna*) in the Coptic Church, chosen by the patriarch of Alexandria, who never left the country. It is possible that Pinto is referring to a Jacobite priest of the lesser clergy. See Kammerer, "Problématique Voyage," 29, n. 3.

3. *Santiago de Galicia:* Better known as Santiago de Compostela, in La Coruña Province

of Galicia, northwest Spain. It was famous for a thousand years as one of the chief shrines of Christendom, next in importance to Jersualem and Rome.

4. *Gocão:* Lagoa attempts to identify it with the Guddcan of modern British charts, located near Mount Guddcan, at the western entrance to the Bay of Annesley ("Peregrinação," 38).

5. *Isle of the Reef:* Kammerer remarks that there are so many reefs in this part of the Red Sea that it is impossible to identify ("Problématique Voyage," 29 n. 4).

6. *gelva:* Arabic *djelba.* A small vessel similar to the caravel, propelled by both sail and oar, used mainly in the Red Sea.

7. *terrada:* Variously described by the chroniclers as a vessel of India and the Persian Gulf, propelled by sail and oar, used in warfare or for transporting provisions and water. The large ones carried artillery and were similar to galleys or small galleons. Barros uses the word to signify light shore boats used for carrying supplies to Hormuz from the mainland (in Barros and Couto, déc. 2, bk. 2, chap. 5).

8. *opposite coast:* The eastern shore, or the Arabian coast of the Red Sea.

9. *Janissaries:* An elite corps in the service of the Ottoman Empire, composed of war captives and Christian youths pressed into service, converted to Islam, and trained under the strictest discipline. It was originally organized by Sultan Murad I in the fourteenth century. The Janissaries gained great power in the Ottoman Empire and made and unmade sultans. By 1600, Moslems had begun to enter the corps, largely through bribery, and in the seventeenth century membership in the corps became largely hereditary, while the drafting of Christians gradually ceased. In 1826, Sultan Mahmud II rid himself of the by then unruly Janissaries by having them massacred in their barracks.

10. *Mocha:* Seaport on the Red Sea, South Yemen. It was noted for the export of the coffee to which it gave its name, but declined as a trading port in the late nineteenth century with the rise of Hodeida and Aden.

11. *Qasis:* More often spelled *caciz* by Pinto. From the Arabic *kashish,* meaning a "Christian priest." Strangely enough, the term is frequently employed by old Christian writers on Eastern subjects as if it were the special title of a Mohammedan theologian, when, in reality, it is the special and technical title of a Christian priest.

12. *moulana:* From the Arabic *mawlana;* also *mullah.* A Moslem religious leader or teacher, or any man of learned reputation. Used also as a title of respect. Both terms are used interchangeably, but *mullah* is more common.

Chapter 6

1. *mocadão:* From the Arabic *muqaddam* or *mukaddam,* meaning a "headman." The technical applications of the term are many. It can be applied to the headman of a village, to the local head of a caste, or to the headman of a gang of laborers, etc.

2. *guazil:* From the Arabic *wazir,* meaning a "minister," usually the prime minister of a king, or the governor of a city, especially among the Arabs and Persians. The term was known on the Iberian peninsula long before the Portuguese reached India, but it was used with the Arabic article and had acquired a different meaning: *alguazil,* "a constable." In English it became "vizier."

3. *Noby:* From the Arabic *nabi,* meaning "prophet," and by extension, "Mohammed."

4. *dato:* A prelate in Malacca, derived from the Malayan *datok,* from which the Timor term *dató* is also derived, meaning "a headman or foreman."

5. *Medina:* In Arabic, Medinat an-Nabi (city of the Prophet) or Madinat Rasul Allah (city of the Apostle of Allah), city of the Hejaz in west Saudi Arabia, about 110 miles inland from the Red Sea. In 622, after his flight (*hegira*) from the city of Mecca, Mohammed quickly gained control of Medina and used it as a base for converting and conquering Arabia. The chief

building is the large mosque that contains the tombs of Mohammed, his daughter Fatima, and the caliph of Omar. A pilgrimage to Mecca usually includes a side trip to Medina.

6. *khoja:* Or *khojah,* from the Persian *khwajah,* a respectful title applied to various classes, as in India especially to eunuchs; in Persia, to wealthy merchants; in Turkistan, to persons of sacred families. Pinto writes *Coja.*

7. *cabaya:* A surcoat or long tunic of muslin, one of the most common native garments of the better classes in India. From the Arabic *gaba* or *caba,* meaning a "vesture."

8. *réis* (*real,* sing.): Small Portuguese copper coin of low value which was abolished in the sixteenth century, but its multiples were retained and used as money of account. During the period 1555–1640, the value of the *cruzado* was theoretically fixed at four hundred *réis.* See Boxer, *Great Ship from Amacon,* 337.

9. *Tor:* Also spelled Tur, a town on the Sinai Peninsula, northeast Egypt, on the east coast of the Gulf of Suez.

10. *Mount Sinai:* Probably a mountain of the Gebel Musa group in south Sinai Peninsula, but not identified with certainty; supposed to be the same as the biblical Mount Horeb (Exod. 3:1).

11. *Babylonia:* According to Kammerer this means that the caravan Pinto was traveling in departed from Egypt (or Cairo), which was the normal route in those days ("Problématique Voyage," 30 n. 2).

12. *Qishm:* Also Queshm or Kishm, an island sixty-eight miles long at the southeast end of the Persian Gulf in the Strait of Hormuz. It is also the name of the chief town at the eastern tip of the island.

13. *Doctor Pero Fernandez:* In 1538, due to the many complaints he had received about Dom Pedro de Castelbranco, then captain of Hormuz, Governor Nuno da Cunha sent Doctor Pero Fernandez there to remove him from office. The doctor's position was that of *ouvidor-geral da Índia,* or special magistrate for India, appointed by the king. He installed Dom Fernando de Lima as captain of Hormuz, an office he held until his death three months later. See Correia, vol. 3, chap. 107, 841–42. See also chapter 2, note 4 above.

14. *pardau:* Name formerly applied to two types of coins in India, one of gold, worth 6 *tangas,* or about 360 *réis;* the other of silver, worth 5 *tangas,* or 300 *réis.* See Boxer, *Great Ship from Amacon,* 336.

Chapter 7

1. *Dom Luis, Infante of Portugal:* (1506–55) fourth son of King Manuel I. From what Damião de Góis writes, there was some substance to this rumor. It appears that plans had been made for a fleet of sixty ships to take him to India, but the king would not permit his brother, of whom he was very fond, to go abroad to fight the Moors. Nevertheless, in 1535, Dom Luis secretly left the court to join the army of Emperor Charles V in Tunis. See *Crónica do Felicíssimo Rei D. Manuel* (Coimbra: Universidade de Coimbra, 1949), vol. 1, chap. 101, 247–48.

2. *Patemarcá:* Or *Patemarcar,* as the Portuguese writers called him, probably a combination of *patel,* a Gujarati word used as a title of respect, and the proper name Marcar or Maracar (Marakkan?). He was a wealthy Moslem merchant and navigator of the Malabar coast of India and admiral of the fleet of the *samuri* or king of Calicut (see n. 3 below), in the early part of the sixteenth century. He belonged to the well-known family of the Maracares, shipowners and merchants of the Red Sea. He stood high in the favor of the *samuri,* who granted him a monopoly of the pepper trade. The early relations of *Patemarcar* with the Portuguese were friendly, and during the administration of Governor Diogo Lopes de Sequeira (1518–21) he formed a partnership with a Portuguese named Antonio de Brito; but when the governor ordered two of *Patemarcar*'s ships to be seized, "against all reason," in the words of Gaspar Correia, he declared war on the Portuguese. In this he was heavily financed and protected by the *samuri* and by a

syndicate of Moslem merchants. During the administration of Governor Nuno da Cunha (1528–38), the Portuguese were determined to destroy him. Defeated, he gave over the command of the fleet to his nephews and emigrated to Ceylon, where he died in 1539. The Moslem war against the Portuguese armadas ceased temporarily but broke out again in the seventeenth century under the leadership of the descendants of this *Patemarcar*. See Correia, vol. 2, chap. 2, 569; chap. 3, 680.

3. *samorim:* Or *samuri,* a Malayal word meaning "sea king or sea rajah." Title of the former Hindu kings of Calicut, port city on the Malabar coast of India and capital of a wealthy kingdom that went into decline with the rise of Goa. From the days of Vasco da Gama and Pedro Alvares Cabral, the Portuguese had demanded a monopoly of the spice trade, which they enforced by sinking the Arab fleets and expropriating their cargos. However, the *samuri* had centuries-old commercial ties with the Moslem traders of the Indian Ocean, which he was reluctant to break. In the ensuing struggle, the *samuri* tried to remain neutral, but he was caught between Moslem intrigue and Portuguese intransigence. During the administration of Afonso de Albuquerque (1509–15) there was some reconciliation, but it did not last long. Later, the *samuri* financed and supplied the Maracar corsairs (see n. 2 above) in his ports, who preyed on unescorted Portuguese ships. The succeeding *samuris,* jealous of their sovereignty, continued to harass the free trade of the Portuguese during the sixteenth and seventeenth centuries. The power of the *samuris* of Calicut ended in the eighteenth century when their kingdom came under British dominion.

4. *Simão Guedez de Sousa:* Served as captain of the fortress of Chaul from 1534 to 1538. During the first siege of Diu (1538) he frequently sent aid to the Portuguese besieged by the Turks. At the end of 1538 he was replaced as captain by Dom Jorge de Lima. See chapter 2, note 6 above.

5. *Royal and bastard galleys:* The royal galley had more than twenty-four oarbanks on each side, usually twenty-nine, and probably a greater number of rowers per bench than the bastard galley, which had twenty-four on each side.

6. *wall-breaker:* The Portuguese usually named their early artillery according to their characteristics or after wild beasts, real or imagined. As the name implies, the wall-breaker was intended to break through walls. This gun has been classified as a culverin or colubrine (meaning "snakelike"), one of the three types of Portuguese artillery; i.e., culverins, cannons, and stone throwers. The culverins were long guns of more than twenty-five calibers, capable of reaching distant targets. See General Henrique Pereira do Valle, "Nomenclatura das bocas de fogo portuguesas do século XVI," *Revista de Artilharia,* 2d ser., 58 (1962): 381–90.

7. *lion:* The most powerful of the Portuguese cannons of the sixteenth century, made of bronze, of approximately twenty-centimeter caliber, measuring 3.60 to 4 meters in length, firing iron balls of fifty-four pounds (ibid.).

8. *sphere:* This was later called a "third of a cannon." Made of bronze, of twelve-pound caliber, with a bore of twelve centimeters and a barrel length of 2.20 to 2.40 meters (ibid.).

Chapter 8

1. *Carapatão River:* Former name of the Vaghotan or Vaikunthan, which flows through Bombay. Its mouth is about sixty miles north of Chaul. See Lagoa, "Peregrinação," 38.

2. *Fernão de Morais:* One of the captains of India, whose name is mentioned by the chroniclers for various heroic deeds as early as 1525. In 1539 the viceroy Dom Garcia de Noronha sent him on a mission to Pegu (Burma), where he died the same year. See Correia, vol. 2, chap. 7, 947–48; vol. 3, chap. III, 851.

3. *Dabul:* Or Dabhol, city on the west coast of India, in the state of Gujerat, about twenty miles southeast of Baroda. Formerly an important pepper emporium, visited by merchants from all over the Indian Ocean. In 1509 it was reduced to ashes by the viceroy Dom Francisco de Almeida to avenge the death of his son, Dom Lourenço. The same year it was

conquered by Albuquerque and incorporated into the Portuguese State of India. It was also bombarded during the administration of the viceroy Dom João de Castro (1545–48), after which it declined in importance.

4. *Dom Garcia de Noronha:* Third viceroy and tenth governor of India. First served in India as an admiral under his uncle, Afonso de Albuquerque, but returned to Portugal on the latter's death in 1515. In 1538 he was appointed viceroy and arrived in Goa at the time that the fortress of Diu was under siege. He had been sent with orders to relieve the fortress, but instead, he limited himself to sending minor expeditions until the heroic resistance of Antonio da Silveira (see chap. 2, nn. 15 and 20 above) forced the enemy to withdraw. According to Gaspar Correia, he was only interested in enriching himself and was not above selling offices and pardoning crimes for money. He died on 3 April 1540, after only a year and seven months in office. See Correia, vol. 4, chap. 34, 94.

5. *paguel:* "Buggalow," in English; probably a corruption of the Mahrati word *bagla,* or *bagala,* a name given on the west coast of India to Arab vessels of the old form. It is also used in the Red Sea under the name *bakala* or *baghla,* for the larger native vessels. See Yule and Burnell; also, René de Kerchove, *International Maritime Dictionary* (Princeton, N.J.: D. van Nostrand Co., 1961).

6. *Adil-Khan:* Generally referred to by the Portuguese chroniclers as the *Idalcão* (as Pinto calls him) or the *Idalxá.* It is a title by which the Portuguese distinguished the kings of the Mohammedan dynasty of Bijapur, which rose at the end of the fifteenth century on the dissolution of the Bahmani kingdom of the Deccan. The title is composed of the Arabic word *adil* (just, or justice), and the Persian *khan* (lord, or prince). Ismail Adil Shah, the son of Yussuf Adil Shah, who succeeded his father in 1510, is the person most frequently referred to by the Portuguese writers as the *Idalcão.* With regard to the significance of the *cabaya* as a gift among the Moors, Barros writes that it is presented as a sign of love, or to do honor to someone (Barros and Couto, déc. 4, bk. 5, chap. 14, 293).

7. *Gonzalo Vaz Coutinho:* The chroniclers do not mention the expedition to Honowar described by Pinto. However, a Gonzalo Vaz Coutinho is mentioned as a captain of India, charged with various missions during the years 1530–38. Up to that time, Castanheda, Barros, and Correia agree. Only Correia goes on to mention a Gonzalo Vaz Coutinho who, in the year 1540, was imprisoned for ugly crimes, but who eventually escaped and turned corsair, operating along the Coromandel coast of India and Ceylon. In the year 1546, he spied against the Portuguese on behalf of the *Adil-Khan,* who endowed him with property beyond the reach of the Portuguese, where he lived as a "perfect Moor" with his wife and children. See Correia, vol. 4, chap. 56, 540.

8. *Honowar:* Variants: Onor, Hannur, Hinawr, Honnavara, etc. An ancient town and port on the west coast of India, in the state of Kanara, located just south of Goa, near the entrance of a saltwater river.

9. *Bardez:* The northern province of the former Goa territory of Portuguese India, situated on a peninsula opposite Panjim. It was conquered by Albuquerque and later retaken by the *Adil-Khan.* In 1544 it was ceded to the Portuguese and remained in their possession until 1961.

Chapter 9

1. *king of Narsinga:* For the Portuguese writers of the sixteenth and seventeenth centuries, Narsinga was synonymous with the kingdom of Bijayanagar or Vijayanagara, which they wrote variously as Bisnagá, Bisnaguer, or Bisnagua. It was the capital of a powerful Hindu state which flourished for two centuries until it was destroyed by the Moslems in 1563. At the time that the Portuguese arrived in India, its sovereign, who reigned from 1487 to 1508, was called Narasinha, and for nearly two centuries the Portuguese applied his name to that of the kingdom. At the time, Honowar was a vassal of the king.

2. *almadia:* *Al-ma'-diya* in Arabic. Properly, it means a "raft," but it is generally used by the writers on India for a canoe, or the like small native boat.

Chapter 10

1. *camel:* Like many of the early Portuguese guns, this one was named after an animal, and a gentle animal at that, which is an indication of a lower power of destruction. It is classified as a *pedreiro*, or "stone thrower." It was made of bronze and was capable of firing stone balls of sizes varying between eighteen and thirty-four pounds. (See Pereira do Valle, 385.)

Chapter 11

1. *sauguate:* Also, *saguate* or *saugate*, from the Hindi-Persian *saughat*, meaning a "gift," especially one that is given on festive occasions or as a symbol of homage.
2. *linha:* The triple cord, or sacred girdle, that the high-caste Hindus wear across the breast, from left to right, from the day of their investiture into the priesthood, as a symbol of their regeneration, or *dvija*, meaning "twice-born."

Chapter 12

1. *Pero de Faria:* It appears from the chronicles that he spent most of his life in India. In 1511 he was present at the conquest of Malacca with Afonso de Albuquerque. Later he served as captain of Goa (1526–28) and twice as captain of Malacca (1528–29 and 1539–43). In 1544 he accompanied the armada of Governor Martim Afonso de Sousa on an expedition to Cannanore. In that year, Diogo do Couto describes him as "a nobleman, 80 years of age, who was highly respected by all the Governors" (Barros and Couto, déc. 5, bk. 9, chap. 10, 367).
2. *nizam-ul-mulk:* Literally, "administrator of the state." It was the title of one of the chiefs at the court of the Bahmani king of the Deccan, who had originally been a Brahman and a slave. His son Ahmed set up a dynasty at Ahmednagar in 1490, which lasted for more than a century. The *nizam-ul-mulk* referred to here was *Buhran Nizam Shah*. He reigned from 1508 to 1555, in close contact with the Portuguese, who referred to the sultans of this dynasty variously as the *nizamaluco, inezamaluco, nizamoxá,* or *nizam xá,* the last being the correct title: *nizam shah.*
3. *Asad-Khan:* Title of a high-ranking dignitary of the *Adil*-Khan's states. The term is a compound of the Arabic *asad* (tiger), and the Turco-Persian *khan* (prince). The Portuguese chroniclers use it with reference to a dignitary of the *Adil-Khan*, who ordinarily resided in Ponda. The *Asad-Khan* referred to here was called *Sufolarim,* the *Adil-Khan's* captain from whom Albuquerque seized Goa. The Portuguese spelled the title variously as *açadacan, açadecão, açedecan, açedecão.*
4. *14 November 1538:* According to Brito Rebello, the Saturdays in the month of November of that year fell on the second, ninth, sixteenth, and twenty-third (1:31).
5. *The news . . . Holy Faith:* Gaspar Correia writes that the men in the armada were so angry at the viceroy for his dilatoriness that they "uttered blasphemies against him" (vol. 4, chap. 23, 67). Diogo do Couto agrees, but from his point of view, it was a prudent and well-calculated move on the part of the wily old viceroy, who knew that word of the huge fleet he was gathering would be enough to frighten the Turks into lifting the siege, as indeed it was (in Barros and Couto, déc. 5, bk. 5, chap. 5).
6. *Martim Afonso de Sousa:* (1500–1564) Nobleman of the court of King John III, one of the most illustrious warriors and navigators and the first to institute a methodical colonization of Brazil (1530–33), though he never again returned to Brazil. In 1534 he departed for India as admiral of the sea, and remained there until 1539, when he returned to Portugal, dissatisfied with the viceroy's action, or rather, lack of action. In 1542 he was back in Goa, this time as governor

of India. During his administration the city of Bhatkal was destroyed and the Portuguese took possession of the Moluccas; and as the result of an agreement, Salsette and Bardez were taken over by the Portuguese crown. In 1545 he returned to Lisbon to take up a position at the council of state. (See chap. 2, n. 9 above.)

7. *Vicente Pegado:* See chapter 2, note 13 above.

8. *Doctor Fernão Rodriguez de Castelbranco:* He departed for India with the armada of the viceroy Garcia de Noronha in 1538, with the appointment of comptroller-general of India (*Vedor da Fazenda Geral da India*). His business was to keep account, on behalf of the crown, of all valuable products acquired by the fleet. Next to the viceroy, the comptroller-general was a person of the greatest consequence. However, he returned to Portugal in 1541, having resigned his position, as a result of a disagreement with the viceroy's successor, Governor Estêvão da Gama.

9. *Nuno da Cunha:* With regard to the viceroy's high-handed treatment of Nuno da Cunha, Barros writes that he had a document in his possession from the king, which allowed him to use his former powers as governor, while in Cochin, to choose a crown ship to take him and his family back to Portugal, and to load pepper for his own account, none of which was honored by the viceroy. Instead, he was forced to book passage on a privately owned merchant ship, and "this lack of respect which was shown to the person of Nuno da Cunha, in the land that he governed for so long, when he asked for homeward passage, which had never been denied to any man of small or great estate, hurt him so deeply, that it is believed that this, in addition to his poor health, was the cause of his death" (Barros and Couto, déc. 4, bk. 10, chap. 21, 737). See also chapter 2, note 14 above.

10. *Thursday, the six of December:* Brito Rebello writes that Thursday was the fifth, and that Diogo do Couto says that the viceroy departed on November 20 (1:32). However, I have not found any mention of the date of the viceroy's departure in Diogo do Couto. Actually, it was Gaspar Correia who wrote that "on the 20th of November, he [the viceroy] departed for Diu with 90 ships" (vol. 4, chap. 25, 70).

11. *Dahanu:* Or *Danu.* A town on the west coast of India, at the entrance to the Gulf of Cambay, just south of Daman.

12. *Dom Alvaro de Noronha:* Son of the viceroy Dom Garcia de Noronha and grand-nephew of Afonso de Albuquerque. In 1539 his father appointed him admiral of the sea, a post left vacant when Martim Afonso de Sousa returned to Portugal (see n. 6 above). In 1540, when his father became ill, Dom Alvaro was sent to negotiate a peace treaty with the *samuri* of Calicut (see chap. 7, no. 3 above). Too sick to carry out his duties, the viceroy tried to name his son to take over the reins of government, but the captains of India preferred to have the comptroller-general take over his duties until the viceroy's death on 3 April 1540, when the letters of succession were opened and Estêvão da Gama became governor. Ten years later, Dom Alvaro was appointed captain of Hormuz (1550–53), where he resisted the siege laid against the fortress by the Turkish troops sent by Suleiman the Magnificent, whose forces had laid siege to Diu in 1538. On his way back to Portugal in 1554, he lost his life in a shipwreck off the coast of Africa.

13. *João de Sousa:* One of the captains of India who sailed in the armada commanded by Martim Afonso de Sousa. Barros gives his full name as João de Sousa Rates so as to distinguish him from other captains of the period, also named João de Sousa.

14. *Dom Cristóvão da Gama:* (1515–42) Fourth son of Vasco da Gama. He went to India for the first time in the armada of 1532 with his older brother, Dom Estêvão da Gama (see chap. 13, n. 1 below), who had been appointed captain of Malacca, fighting at his side against the Moslems of Ujantanah and Achin. In 1535 he was back in Lisbon. He returned to India for the second time in 1538 with the armada of the viceroy Dom Garcia de Noronha. He accompanied the viceroy's fleet to Diu, where, during the storm described by Pinto, he revealed himself to be not only a great humanitarian, but a master navigator as well. In 1541 he accompanied his brother Dom Estêvão da Gama (who succeeded the viceroy as governor of India in 1540) on his

expedition to the Red Sea. His brother then sent him to Abyssinia, in command of a force of four hundred men, to defend the *negus* of Abyssinia against the sheik of Zeila, and there, in September of 1542, he was captured, tortured, and slain. The actions of Dom Cristóvão and his brave companions are described by Miguel Castanhoso in his *História das cousas que o muy esforçado capitão Dom Christóvão da Gama fez nos reynos do Preste João, com quatrocentos Portugueses que levou consigo* (Lisbon, 1564). According to R. S. Whiteway, translator of Castanhoso's book, the expedition of Dom Cristóvão da Gama "was decisive in that Abyssinia has since remained Christian; it is seldom that results so momentous have been attained by means so disproportionate" (*The Portuguese Expedition to Abyssinia in 1541–1543* [London: Hakluyt Society, 1902], xviii). See also Charles Fernand Rey, *The Romance of the Portuguese in Abyssinia* (London: H. F. & G. Witherby, 1929), 127–69.

Chapter 13

1. *Dom Estêvão da Gama:* (?–1575) Second son of Vasco da Gama. He served as captain of Malacca (1534–39) and as governor of India (1540–42). As captain of Malacca he twice defeated the sultan of Ujantanah and drove off the invading Achinese (see n. 14 below), thereby avenging the death of his brother, Paulo da Gama, whom he succeeded as captain of Malacca. The most notable event of his term as governor of India was the expedition to the Red Sea, where he went in 1541 with the intention of destroying the fleet that the pasha of Egypt was preparing in Suez. However, the enemy's resistance prevented him from achieving his objective, and he returned to Massawa, from where he dispatched the expedition to Abyssinia, under the command of his brother, Christóvão da Gama (see chap. 12, n. 14 above). He returned to Portugal, where he was offered a term as viceroy of India, which he refused. He died, a bachelor, in September of 1575.

2. *term of office:* See letter of Pero de Faria to King John III, written from Malacca on 25 November 1539, in which he complains that he is unable to accomplish anything because Estêvão da Gama was still in office. This letter is of interest for other reasons. First, because it contradicts what Pinto writes in chapter 12 with regard to the composition of the fleet and the date of its arrival in Malacca, as well as other facts that contradict each other. Second, because it contains a series of impertinent remarks, which he dared to address to the king for not having appointed him governor of India. Of even greater interest is a footnote appended to this letter by Brito Rebello (who published it in his edition of the *Peregrinação* 4:139–51), in which he quotes another letter written to the king by Governor Nuno da Cunha on 10 December 1537, complaining about appointments of unqualified persons to high office, and especially that of Pero de Faria! He reminds the king that he had previously recommended that he retire Pero de Faria, with a pension, which he deserved because of long years of service in India, and adds that it would be more to the advantage of the king to have him in Portugal than in India (148–49). Both letters give us some insight into the character of Pero de Faria and how others viewed him.

3. *Battak:* What is known about the Battak today does not fit the description that Pinto gives of them in the following chapters. Although there are references to the Battak in the early writers (Marco Polo, Friar Odoric, Nicolo di Conti, Duarte Barbosa, Antonio Galvão, and João de Barros), little is known about them, prior to the eighteenth century. According to William Marsden (*History of Sumatra,* London, 1783), the country of the Battak was located in the northwestern part of the island of Sumatra, bounded on the north by Achin and to the south by Passumman and Aru, or Rou. Writing two hundred years after Pinto, he says that "the country is very populous but that the bulk of the people reside at a distance from the sea, in the central parts of the land, in extensive plains between two ridges of hills, on the borders of a great lake . . . their towns lie, as well as on the rivers that discharge themselves into the Straits of Malacca, as those which have their course towards the West coast" (292). Marsden affirms that the Battak were a primitive people who practiced a form of ritual cannibalism. He also adds that he doubts that the whole of the country was ever united under the jurisdiction of one monarch.

Other early writers refer to the cannibalism of the Battak, among them João de Barros, who describes them as the "wildest and most warlike people on earth" (in Barros and Couto, déc. 3, bk. 5, chap. 1, 509). In defense of Pinto, Maurice Collis (*Grand Peregrination,* 48) says that Marsden's statements hardly suffice to prove a case against Pinto, and that possibly, in the sixteenth century, the kingdom of the Battak extended to the coast, and that even if most of Battak was very primitive, it does not necessarily follow that the king and his court were at the same level. In support of Collis's arguments is the fact that the Battak possessed an alphabet, written documents, and some form of literature. See also Yule, *Marco Polo* 2 : 288 n. 3.

4. *Isle of Gold:* Many years before the Portuguese arrived in India, Sumatra was famous for its production of gold. When they arrived in India at the beginning of the sixteenth century, the Portuguese heard talk of an isle of gold, off the coast of Sumatra, that was difficult to reach because of the many reefs and shoals. In 1520, it was said that Diogo Pacheco, the first Portuguese to round the island of Sumatra, had discovered the Isle of Gold, but died in the attempt. Later it was said that a French ship, which foundered off the coast of Sumatra in 1528, had also discovered the Isle of Gold, but there were no survivors. In 1542, other expeditions were sent out, but the elusive (or illusive) Isle of Gold was never found. Marsden writes that "if these islands [of gold], so celebrated about this time, existed anywhere but in the region of fancy, they were probably those called the Ticos, to which it is possible that much gold might be brought from the neighboring country of Menangkabow" (328).

5. *Eaglewood:* Aloeswood, garrow and garroo-wood, aglawood, uggerwood, etc. The name of an aromatic wood from Cambodia and other regions of Southeast Asia. It is the "odorous wood" referred to by Camões. The best quality of this wood, once much valued in Europe as incense, is the result of disease in a tree of *N.O. Leguminosae,* the *Aloexylon agallochum, loureiro,* growing in Cambodia and south Cochinchina (Yule and Burnell, 335). See Garcia da Orta for a detailed description of types, origin of word, and provenance of aloeswood (*Colóquios dos simples e drogas da India* [Lisbon: Imprensa Nacional, 1891–95, 2 : 60–65 n. 1.])

6. *Calambac:* It is the Malayan name, *kalambaq,* adopted by the Portuguese, for the finest quality of eaglewood. Some writers make a distinction between eaglewood and calambac and indicate the differences between them.

7. *quintal:* The Portuguese hundredweight, which was widely used in the East. It was generally reckoned at about 130 pounds avoirdupois.

8. *Benzoin:* An aromatic resin, taken from the trees of the genus *Stirax,* which is indigenous to Sumatra, Siam, Java, Borneo, and the Malay Peninsula. Garcia da Orta, who was the first European to write with exactitude about the origin of this drug (colloquy 9), distinguishes between three varieties of benzoin, i.e., the almond, which was considered very good, the black variety, which was of a lesser quality, and the daisy (or *beijoim de boninas,* the type referred to by Pinto), which was worth ten times more. Benzoin is still used today in the manufacture of expectorants and antiseptic drugs. Also called gum benzoin, benjamin, gum benjamin, and *asa dulcis.*

9. *palm leaf:* Examples of this ancient form of writing are preserved today in many museums. In the summer of 1982 I saw an exposition in the British Library of Indian books. Among the books exhibited there were many fashioned of palm leaf, the letters incised with a metal stylus. In southern India, this traditional method of book production from palm leaves was preserved until the nineteenth century. See Jeremiah P. Losty, *The Art of the Book in India* (London: British Library, 1982).

10. *Angeesiry Timorraja:* This should probably be written as *Angé Siri Timor Raja.* The name of this presumed king of the Battak does not appear in any of the chronicles. However, Tomé Pires, in his *Suma Oriental* (written between 1512 and 1515) states, with reference to the kingdom of the Battak, that "the king of this country is called *Raja Tomjam,*" which is fairly close to Pinto's *Timor Raja,* or rajah of Timor. See Armando Cortesão, ed., *The "Suma Oriental" of Tomé Pires* (London: Hakluyt Society, 1944), 145.

11. *safe-conduct pass:* The Portuguese, in their effort to obtain a monopoly of the trade in

the Indian Ocean, would issue such passes, or *cartazes* as they called them, to ships of friendly nations, which protected them against harassment from Portuguese vessels.

12. *lanchara:* From the Malay *lancharan,* a coasting vessel equipped with a single mast, sail, and oars.

13. *jurupango:* From the Malay *jurubung,* a coasting vessel similar in size to a small caravel.

14. *Achinese:* People of the ancient kingdom of Achin (also written Acheen, Atchin, and Atjeh), situated at the extreme northwestern point of the island of Sumatra. During the sixteenth and seventeenth centuries it grew to be the most powerful Malay state in the archipelago, frequently sending its armadas against the Portuguese of Malacca. In 1524 they expelled the Portuguese from Sumatra and in the following century aided the Dutch in expelling them from Malacca. After the defeat of the Portuguese in Malacca (1641), the power of Achin declined.

15. *mamoco:* From the Persian *mah,* meaning "moon." A term used by the Mohammedans to describe the course of the moon. Pinto uses it in the sense of "day of the lunar month."

16. *bahar:* Also written *bar* or *baar,* meaning a "load" in Arabic, though the word is of Indian origin and was adopted and spread by the Arabs throughout the Far East. It is a unit of weight, used in large trading transactions, that varied widely from 141 to 330 kilograms, depending on the locality and the commodity.

17. *Pasay:* Also written Paser, Pasei, and, by the Portuguese, Pacém, Pacé, or Pacē. An ancient kingdom near the northwestern point of the island of Sumatra. At the time the Portuguese arrived in India, Pasay was considered one of the most important ports in the archipelago. In 1516 the Portuguese built a fortress there, from which they were expelled by the Achinese in 1524. Soon afterwards, Pasay lost its importance and did not figure as a leading port in later times. Today, the name of this ancient kingdom survives in the Pasay River, in latitude 5°9′ north.

18. *ourobalões:* From the Malay *hulubalang, hulu* meaning "head," and *balang,* "missile." Usually written by the Portuguese as *orabalão* or *urubalão* (in the plural, *orabalões, urubalões*). The word was used for a military leader, chosen warrior, or champion. Dalgado points out that the spelling used by Pinto was probably an allusion to the gold bracelets worn by these warriors, *ouro* meaning "gold."

19. *Quiay Hocombinor:* According to Dalgado, the word *quiay, quiai,* or *quiar,* comes from the Malay-Javanese *kiai,* meaning "venerable." It is a title of respect used in Indochina and China. It is also placed before the names of divinities, as Pinto does in this instance and many others. The title is commonly used by the Portuguese writers. According to Marsden, *Hocombinor* is a Malayan name, somewhat corrupt (304).

20. *salt:* Marsden writes that it was customary among the Battak, when accused of a crime, to protest one's innocence by swearing not to eat salt, among other things (310).

Chapter 14

1. *balões* (*balão,* sing.): A large dugout canoe used in India and Malaysia. Yule and Burnell give various Anglo-Indian spellings for the word; i.e., "ballong," "balaum," "baloon," "balloon."

2. *Upi:* Also, Upeh, Upé. A small island about two and a half miles west of the mouth of the Malacca River, which was also called Tranqueira. It was the most important of the three suburbs of Malacca. In reality, it included a large part of the actual town of Malacca, having as its boundaries the Malacca River, the sea, and the *tranqueira,* a Portuguese word meaning "palisade" or "rampart." See R. Cardon, "Portuguese Malacca," *Journal of the Malayan Branch of the Royal Asiatic Society* 12, no. 2 (1934): 7.

3. *bendara:* Tomé Pires (1512?), who has given us the first European description of the Malacca high officials, writes that "the *bendara* is a kind of chief justice in all civil and criminal

affairs. He also has charge of the King's revenue. He can order any person to be put to death, of whatever rank and condition . . . but first of all he informs the King." The Portuguese retained the office of *bendara* when they took over Malacca, but with some restrictions. See Cortesão, *Suma Oriental,* 264.

4. *finger in his mouth:* Maurice Collis describes this gesture as an Oriental mannerism of great antiquity, denoting stupefaction. He adds an interesting note to the effect that "among the figures carved on the pedestal for an alms-bowl, a Kushan work of the second century A.D., which was in the 1947 Exhibition of Indian Art at Burlington House, was a man with his finger in his mouth as he gazed at the miraculous birth of the Buddha" (*Grand Peregrination,* 42).

5. *Surotilau:* Unidentified. However, the Hollander, P. Roo de la Faille, seems to see in this toponym a Portuguese corruption of the Malay *Soera-ti-la-woe,* a phrase that describes the outline of the coast of Aaru. See "Mendez Pinto op Sumatra," in *Historische curiositeiten uit Malajve en Java* (Amsterdam: Tropical Museum Library, 1954), 7–12.

6. *Aaru:* Lagoa (Glossário toronímico da antiga historiografia ultramarina [Lisbon: Junta de Investigações Coloniais, 1950–54]) situates this ancient kingdom on the eastern coast of Sumatra at latitude 4°10' north and longitude 98°08' east, but the kingdom or state of Aaru has long since disappeared from our maps. The name, which appears on the ancient charts as Daru or De Aru, survives today in the Bay of Aru or Aroe, on the northeast coast of Sumatra. In 1524, the king of Aaru sent an armada to the aid of the fortress of Pasay, but by the time he arrived the Portuguese had already abandoned it. (See chap. 13, n. 16 above; and Barros, in Barros and Couto, déc. 3, bk. 8, chap. 4, 280.) Correia claims (vol. 2, chap. 17, 796) that the king of Aaru was defeated by the Achinese in 1524 and took refuge in Malacca, where he died in poverty, but that is not correct.

7. *Hicanduré:* Unidentified. However, Roo de la Faille (7) identifies the first part of this toponym as the word *ikan,* from the Wangsalan language, meaning a "searoad," which would indicate that there were still Hindus living in the area.

8. *Minhatoley:* Unidentified. Roo de la Faille (7) says that the name is probably a corruption of the Malay *mina-ng-k-a da-toe oleh-leh,* meaning the territory of the *Datoe,* the *Soekoe* head of the *Olèholèh,* or the present-day Achin Head, where one rounds the tip of Sumatra to the south.

9. *Pedir:* Ancient kingdom in the northwestern part of the island of Sumatra that included the present port of the same name, but now a place of no importance. According to Barros, it was the greatest and most celebrated state in those parts before Malacca was populated (Barros and Couto, déc. 3, bk. 5, chap. 1, 511). It was the first place on the island of Sumatra visited by the Portuguese in 1509, when Diogo Lopes de Sequeira erected a commemorative pillar there; and two years later it was visited by Albuquerque on his way to Malacca. Today the name survives in Pedir Point, or Kuala Pedir, at latitude 5°30' north.

10. *Guateamgim:* Unidentified. However, Marsden sees a similarity between Pinto's *Guateamgim* and *Atay Angin,* a name applied to the western coast of Sumatra, bordering on Menangkabow, "which extends from thirty-two minutes N. to 40 minutes south latitude" (36; see also 282, 304). It is interesting to note that Roo de la Faille, who has made a careful study of Pinto's Sumatran place-names, does not mention this one.

11. *lizards:* Alligators.

12. *caquesseitão:* Pinto is referring here to the huge bats of the genus *Pteropus edwardsi,* found only in the tropical regions of the East and in Australia. According to Marsden (94), they resemble the fox in color and size, hence the name "flying foxes," as they are popularly called in English. By day they live suspended from the branches of trees and derive their sustenance only from fruit, and not from "monkeys and other animals," as Pinto claims. Roo de la Faille says that they are called *kalang* or *kalong* in the Malay language; and that the word *caquesseitão* means literally "ancestors of the devil."

13. *hooded cobras:* Popular name of a venomous snake of the genus *Naja tripudians,* found

in India and adjacent countries, remarkable for its power of dilating the neck and sides of the head when irritated, so as to produce the semblance of a hood.

14. *other cobras:* Pythons.

15. *apes:* Orangutans.

Chapter 15

1. *Batorrendão:* Unidentified. Roo de la Faille (7) reads this as *Batoe Rendang* and says that it is a pun of sorts on *Batoe,* an island group on the equator, off the west central coast of Sumatra.

2. *shahbandar:* From the Persian *shah* (king) and *bandar* (seaport). Title of an officer at native ports all over the India seas, who was the chief authority with whom foreign traders and shipmasters had to transact. The *shahbandars* had multiple duties, for they functioned as harbormasters, customs officers, protectors of immigrants, and superintendents of trade. At the time the Portuguese held sway in Malacca, there were four *shahbandars* assigned to four different quarters of the city, inhabited by people of different races or religions. See Richard Winstedt, *The Malays* 6th ed. (London: Routledge & Kegan Paul, 1961), 76.

3. *Campalator:* Unidentified. Roo de la Faille (8) says that this name does not appear to be correct and that Pinto might have taken it from the Malay *kam-pong-ke-palar.*

4. *amborrajas:* From the Malay *hamba-raja,* meaning "servant of the king." Marsden points out that these were Malay and not Battak officers (304).

5. *bailéu:* From the Malay, meaning "audience hall" or "magistrate's tribunal." The word was given secondary meanings by the Portuguese writers, who used it variously in the sense of tribune, veranda, porch, lean-to, public banquet hall, or a raised fighting platform on a ship.

6. *skull of a cow:* Roo de la Faille (8) sees in the cow's head with gilded horns a symbolic reference to the ancient kingdom of Menangkabow, which was held in deep veneration by all the states of Sumatra.

7. *prayer:* Marsden, writing in 1783, says that it is very difficult to find traces of what can be called religion among the Battak. "They have some idea of a powerful Being, disposed to benevolence, and of another, the worker of ill to mankind, but they pay no worship to either. . . . Their only ceremonies that wear the appearance of religion are those used on taking an oath, in their prognostications, and at their funeral rites" (309).

8. *Turbão:* Unidentified. Roo de la Faille (8) sees a possible connection between *Turbão* and the Malay *Batoe-poer-wa-Boewana,* but does not explain why. My thanks to Ms. Vera Rubinstein of Holland for her help in translating Roo de la Faille's article from the Dutch.

Chapter 16

1. *Menangkabow:* Or Menangkabau. An ancient kingdom on the island of Sumatra, formerly the seat of a monarchy that had ruled over the entire island and whose sovereign was spoken of with deep respect in the far corners of the East. At the time that the Europeans arrived in Asia, Menangkabow was in decline and its borders reduced to the center of the island. Nevertheless, two hundred years later, Marsden was able to write that Menangkabow still "received a shadow of homage from the most powerful of the other kingdoms which had sprung up from its ruins" (35). Menangkabow was also famous for its gold mines. See chapter 15, note 6 above.

2. *Luzon:* Largest of the Philippine Islands, known to the Portuguese before the arrival of Magellan in 1521. The first European reference to the Philippine archipelago appears to have been made by Tomé Pires (1512–15), who writes, "The Luzons are about ten days' sail beyond Borneo. They are nearly all heathen; they have no king, but they are ruled by groups of elders. They are a robust people, little thought of in Malacca. They have two or three junks at the most.

They take the merchandise to Borneo and from there they come to Malaccca" (Cortesão, *Suma Oriental,* 133 n. 2).

3. *Indragiri:* Or Indiragiri, former kingdom on the island of Sumatra, extending to the east coast of Sumatra where the Indragiri River empties into the Strait of Berhala. Tomé Pires refers to Indragiri as a kingdom of great importance because of its trade with Malacca and because of its river or port, which was accessible to large ocean-going vessels (ibid., 282).

4. *Jambi:* Or Djambi. Former kingdom of south central Sumatra, extending nearly across the island from the Barisan Mountains to the South China Sea. Its capital, of the same name, a river port on the Hari River about sixty miles from its mouth, is today an important oil center and trading town.

5. *half-sphere:* An ancient cannon, firing iron balls weighing six pounds, with a diameter at the mouth of 9.5 centimeters and a barrel length of from 1.80 to 2.00 meters, according to General Pereira de Valle, 389.

6. *Lopo Vaz de Sampaio:* Governor of Portuguese India (1526–29), called the Usurper. Following the death of Viceroy Vasco da Gama on 2 December 1524, after only three and a half months in office, the first letter of succession was opened, naming Henrique de Meneses as governor of India. He died on 2 February 1526, after thirteen months in office. The second letter of succession named Pero de Mascarenhas, who was absent in Malacca and unable to reach India until the following monsoon. The third letter was opened, on condition that the person named would rule until the return of Mascarenhas. The third person was Lopo Vaz de Sampaio, who refused to hand over his office to Mascarenhas and continued to rule until 1529. On his return to Portugal he was chastised by the king, fled to Spain, but was later pardoned. He died in 1534.

7. *Rosado:* In 1527, three French *naos* sailed for India from the port of Dieppe. One reached São Lourenço (Madagascar), and according to Correia, this vessel eventually returned to France, laden with poor-quality merchandise. The second *nao,* commanded and piloted by a Portuguese named Estêvão Dias Brigas, arrived in Diu, where the entire company converted to Islam and died in the service of Sultan Bahadur, king of Cambay. The third *nao,* commanded by the Portuguese pilot Rosado, reached the Isle of Gold, off the coast of Sumatra, where it was wrecked on the reefs. The survivors headed for shore in a ship's boat, laden with gold, but were killed by some fishermen they ran into (vol. 3, chap. 2, 238–41). Barros mentions only two French *naos,* one that landed in Diu and the other in Madagascar (Barros and Couto, déc. 4, bk. 3, chap. 2, 261–62; bk. 5, chap. 6, 583). See also chapter 13, note 4 above.

8. *Gujeratis:* People of the ancient kingdom of Gujerat, which extended along the west coast of India at latitude 22°30' north and longitude 72° east and included, during the period alluded to by the Portuguese chroniclers, the regions of Kathiawar and Kutch. In 1297 Gujerat was annexed to the sultanate of Delhi; in 1401 its Mohammedan governor founded an independent kingdom which reached its height under Sultan Mahmud, who at the end of his reign constructed a fortress to stop the Portuguese maritime expansion and joined the naval coalition against them, which was destroyed in 1509 by Viceroy Francisco de Almeida, at the battle of Diu. His son, Muzaffar II, maintained cordial relations with Afonso de Albuquerque. His successor, Bahadur Shah, ceded the territories of Bassein, which included the fortress of Diu, to Governor Nuno da Cunha (1535). He died at the hands of the Portuguese in 1536. (See chapter 2, nn. 14–17 above.) In 1572 Gujerat was annexed by the Moghul emperor Akbar, whose assault on the Portuguese territories failed. In the eighteenth century it was overrun by the Marathas, who later ceded it to the British.

Chapter 17

1. *amucks:* From the Malay *amoq,* meaning "frenzied attack, or a man possessed by fury." Dalgado distinguishes between two types of Oriental *amucks,* those who, moved by vengeance, seek desperately to do as much harm as possible to their enemies, as in India; and those

who, dominated by fury, kill innocent people, as in the Malaysian archipelago. In English the word is used only in the phrase "to run amuck."

2. *Tenasserim:* A division of extreme south Burma which was formerly part of the kingdom of Pegu. It is a narrow strip of coast between Thailand on the east and the Andaman Sea on the west, extending southward for nearly six hundred miles, from the Gulf of Martaban to the Isthmus of Kra, and including many offshore islands. Tenasserim was long subject in turn to Siam and Burma, but remained in Burmese hands when the long wars of the Thai and Burmese ended late in the eighteenth century. As a result of the first Anglo-Burmese War (1824–26) it passed under British rule. Today it forms part of the Republic of Burma.

3. *Sornau:* A name often given to Siam in the early part of the sixteenth century. It is a corruption of the Persian *Shahr-i-nao,* meaning "new city," the name by which Ayuthia, the capital founded on the Menam about 1350, seems to have become known to the traders of the Persian Gulf. See also chapter 36, note 10 below.

4. *Pedir:* In 1524 the kingdom of Pedir was conquered by the Achinese, who had formerly been subject to it. See chapter 14, note 9 above.

5. *Pasay:* See chapter 13, note 17 above and note 6 below.

6. *captured your fortress at Pasay:* In 1524 the Portuguese abandoned their fortress at Pasay, fleeing in disorder from the Achinese enemy. According to João de Barros, it all began when in 1519 Gaspar da Costa was shipwrecked off the coast of Achin and the survivors taken captive to Raja Abraemo, king of Achin. The king of Pedir, a friend of the Portuguese, asked Abraemo to release the captives to him, which he refused to do. This led to war between Achin and Pedir, in which the latter was eventually defeated. This was followed by the capture of two other Portuguese vessels, as a result of which the king of Achin found himself so well equipped with Portuguese artillery and munitions that he was able to achieve a decisive victory over the king of Pedir, who fled to the Portuguese fortress at Pasay, by then reduced to starvation, with its food supply cut off. Its commander, André Henriques, got word to Rafael Perestrello in Bengal, who sent Domingos de Seixas to buy food in Tenasserim, where he was captured by the king of Siam, and mistakenly charged with piracy committed by other Portuguese freebooters in the area. (See chapter 1, n. 2 above.) Henriques also requested aid from the king of Aaru and, at the same time, wrote to the governor of India, asking to be relieved of his duties, owing to poor health. However, when Lopo de Azevedo arrived to replace him, he refused to hand over the command of the fortress to him and Azevedo departed for Malacca. Thereupon Henriques handed over the command to his brother-in-law, Aires Coelho, and set out for India. On the way he met up with two Portuguese ships and convinced them to return to Pasay with him. In spite of these reinforcements, the Portuguese decided to abandon the fortress. At sea, they met up with a fleet of thirty *lancharas* carrying food and men that was being sent to their aid by the king of Aaru, who was himself marching overland with his army. To add to their shame, when they reached Malacca, they found two ships preparing to come to their aid. As for their Sumatran allies, the king of Pasay found refuge in Malacca, where he died in poverty, and the kings of Pedir and Dayá lived out their lives in exile, in the kingdom of Aaru. See Barros, in Barros and Couto, déc. 3, bk. 8, chaps. 1–4, 239–81; Correia, vol. 2, chap. 13, 766–69; chap. 17, 790–96. Castanheda (vol. 2, bk. 6, chap. 16, 179–80; chaps. 50 and 51, 232–34) and Andrade (pt. 1, chap. 43, 106; chap. 50, 127–28; chap. 51, 129–32) give shorter versions of these events, which differ in some respects from those given by Barros and Correia.

7. *galley bound for the Moluccas:* In the year 1528, Simão de Sousa Galvão departed from Cochin, bound for the Moluccas to take up his duties as captain of the fortress. Caught in a storm, his galley was blown against the coast of Achin, where it was captured and the survivors taken to the king, who, much to their surprise, treated them as honored guests. Unbeknownst to them at the time, the good treatment they received was because the wily king had learned of the presence in Malacca of an ambassador from the king of Aaru who had gone there to request aid from the Portuguese in their war against Achin. To forestall such action, he sent some of the

Portuguese captives to Malacca with an offer of peace and friendship. As a result, Pero de Faria, then serving his first term as captain of Malacca, withdrew the help he had promised Aaru, and the ambassador departed in anger. To test the sincerity of the king of Achin, Pero de Faria sent some Portuguese envoys to Achin, who were well received, but who died mysteriously on the return voyage. Nothing more was heard of the projected peace treaty until the arrival of Garcia de Sá, who replaced Pero de Faria as captain of Malacca the following year. See Barros, in Barros and Couto, déc. 4, bk. 2, chap. 17, 227–33; bk. 6, chap. 18, 103–10; Couto, in Barros and Couto, déc. 4, bk. 4, chap. 7, 282–92; bk. 5, chap. 8, 378–85; Castanheda, vol. 2, bk. 7, chap. 83, 513–15; Correia, vol. 3, chap. 6, 267–71; and Andrade, pt. 2, chap. 37, 389–92; chap. 46, 418–20.

8. *Kedah:* Former kingdom, south Malay Peninsula, in the Strait of Malacca. Converted to Islam in the fifteenth century, tributary to Malacca prior to its conquest by the Portuguese (1511), it was conquered by the Achinese in the seventeenth century, leased to the British East India company in 1786, subject to Siam in 1821–1909, transferred to Great Britain in 1909, taken by the Japanese in 1941, and, finally, in 1948 became part of the Federation of Malaya. As for what happened to the three *naos* off Kedah, the chronicles are silent.

9. *the Malacca galleon:* Once he learned of the arrival of Garcia de Sá, who replaced Pero de Faria as captain of Malacca in 1529, the king of Achin sent another party of Portuguese captives to arrange for a treaty of peace, on the same conditions offered to Pero de Faria the year before. Convinced of the sincerity of the king, Garcia de Sá sent the two-hundred-ton galleon *São Jorge* to Achin, richly laden with goods and guns. Upon their arrival in the port of Achin, they were treacherously attacked, the galleon seized, and those who survived were taken to the king, who had them slain along with the other Portuguese who had been taken captive the year before and so lavishly entertained. See note 7 above. See also Barros, in Barros and Couto, déc. 4, bk. 6, chap. 18, 103–10; Couto, in Barros and Couto, déc. 4, bk. 5, chap. 9, 385–91; Castanheda, vol. 2, bk. 7, chap. 100, 545–47; Correia, vol. 3, chap. 12, 303–5; and Andrade, pt. 2, chap. 46, 418–20.

10. *Selangor:* Former kingdom, south Malay Peninsula, in the Strait of Malacca. Prior to the sixteenth century, Selangor was subject to the powers that in turn dominated the Malay Peninsula. After Malacca fell to the Portuguese in 1511, it was nominally ruled by the kings of Bintang (modern Riouw) and Ujantana (Johore), but in the late seventeenth century it was conquered by Bugis tribesmen from the Celebes, who for a time threatened to dominate Malaya from Selangor. In 1874 it accepted the protection of the British; in 1895 it became part of the Federated Malay States and of the Federation of Malaya in 1948. Its capital, Kuala Lampur, is also capital of the federation.

11. *Lopo Chanoca:* See chapter 4, note 13 above.

12. *none-too-secure position:* In reality, the Portuguese were never very secure in their fortress of Malacca. Throughout the 130 years of its existence, except for rare periods of peace, they had to defend themselves constantly against their Malaysian enemies. After the conquest of Malacca by Albuquerque in 1511, the deposed Moslem king, Mahmud Shah, fled to Bintang (Riouw), from where, together with his Javanese allies, he continued to harass the Portuguese, in a constant struggle to regain possession of his throne, a struggle that was continued by his son, the king of Ujantana (Johore), until his defeat in 1534, when he was forced to make peace with Estêvão da Gama, then captain of Malacca. But the Portuguese could never assuage the implacable hatred of the Achinese, who throughout the sixteenth century continued to send their armadas against Malacca. Later, in the seventeenth century, with the arrival of the Dutch, the fortress had to defend itself in 1601, 1606, 1613, 1615, 1620, and 1635, before it finally fell in 1641 to the combined forces of these two enemies. It is interesting to note that during Pero de Faria's two terms of office as captain of Malacca (1528–29 and 1539–44), the fortress enjoyed some of its rare periods of relative peace and stability. See Ian A. Macgregor, "Notes on the Portuguese in Malaya," *Journal of the Malayan Branch of the Royal Asiatic Society* 28, no. 2 (1955): 5–47; and Marsden, 322–64. With respect to the defeat of the king of Ujantana in 1534, see Castanheda,

vol. 2, bk. 8, chaps. 85–88, 708–9; Barros, in Barros and Couto, déc. 4, bk. 9, chap. 13, 534–41; Couto, in Barros and Couto, déc. 4, bk. 8, chap. 12, 283–92; and Andrade, pt. 3, chap. 6, 597–602.

Chapter 18

1. *passeivao:* From the Malay *paseban,* meaning a "veranda or terrace surrounding an audience hall," in Malaysia.

2. *kaffir:* The word is properly the Arabic *kafir,* (pl. *kofra*), meaning "an infidel, an unbeliever in Islam." As the Arabs applied this to pagan blacks, among others, the Portuguese adopted it in this restricted sense and passed it on to other European nations. The term is often applied contemptuously by Mohammedans to Christians, as in this instance.

3. *Al-Koran:* The word has two meanings: (a) the Koran, or sacred book of the Mohammedans; (b) the tower or minaret of the mosque from which the muezzin calls the faithful to prayer. Pinto uses it here in the second sense.

4. *assegai:* Also spelled "assagai" or "hassegai." Short lances or spears used for both throwing and stabbing. From the Arabic *az-zagaya,* a term adopted by the Arabs from the Berber *zaghaya,* and later by the Portuguese to designate various lances of their own.

5. *catty:* From the Malayo-Javanese *kati.* A variable unit of weight introduced from China into the Malayan archipelago. Though it varied greatly in different parts of the East, the usual English equivalent is given as one and one-third pounds.

6. *Apefingau:* Unidentified. Strangely enough, this toponym appears in chapter 19 as *Fingau.* See chapter 19, note 1 below.

7. *Siak:* Formerly a small kingdom on the eastern shore of the island of Sumatra that had been tributary to the sultan of Malacca. In 1613 it was subjugated by the Achinese.

Chapter 19

1. *Fingau:* Unidentified. This appears to be the same island that is called *Apefingau* in chapter 18 (see chap. 18, n. 6 above). Lagoa attempts to identify it as an island off the west coast of Sumatra, near Achin, between King Point and Point Baba Nipa, at the entrance to Surat Passage, though he concedes that identification is not viable (*Glossário*).

2. *Minhagaru Strait:* Lagoa identifies this strait with Swang Arus Kechil or the Surat Passage of modern maps, which separates the northwestern part of Sumatra from the island of Lampujang or Pulo Bras (*Glossário*).

3. *Junkseylon:* Former name of modern Phuket, Puket, or Bhuket. Island and province of Thailand, off the west coast of the Malay Peninsula, in the Andaman Sea. Contested by the Siamese and Burmese during their wars of the eighteenth century, the island was finally incorporated into the kingdom of Siam in the nineteenth century.

4. *Perlis River:* Empties into the Strait of Malacca at latitude 6°24′ north and longitude 100°08′ east. The state of Perlis, which formed part of the kingdom of Kedah until 1842, is the smallest of the Malay states, located between Thailand and northwest Kedah, with a short coastline on the Andaman Sea. It became part of the Federation of Malaya in 1948.

5. *odiá:* Or *adiá,* from the Arabic *hadyia,* meaning "a gift given to a superior or a teacher of the Koran." The word was introduced into Hindustani, from where João de Barros took it and into the Malay tongue, from where Pinto took it, spelling it *odiá.* Pinto also writes *Odiá* for the city of Ayuthia, the former capital of the kingdom of Siam.

6. *conto:* Portuguese term for a million, thus "two *contos* of gold" would be two million *cruzados* (ducats), although *cruzados* were usually silver coins.

7. *Patani:* Or Pattani. Former kingdom on the east coast of the Malay Peninsula, near the mouth of the Gulf of Siam. In the nineteenth century it was reduced to a province of Siam.

With Ayuthia, the former capital of Siam, it was one of the first ports opened to the Portuguese in the sixteenth century.

8. *gregoge:* Ancient form of torture in Malaysia. From the Melay *gergaji,* meaning "to saw."

Chapter 20

1. *Pulo Sambilang:* Or Nine Islands, a group of small islands of the Malay Archipelago, in the Strait of Malacca, near the mouth of the Perak River. (*Pulo* is a Malay term meaning "island" and is often used with names of islands in the Malay Archipelago.)

2. *Pegu:* Division of Lower Burma. Formerly an important and powerful kingdom. Founded by the Talaings (as they are called by the Burmese) or Mons (as they call themselves), circa 573, Pegu was the center of one of the three chief states of Burma from the fourteenth to the late fifteenth century. In the sixteenth century it was the capital of a united Burmese kingdom. After it was destroyed in 1564, and again in 1599, the Burmese moved their capital to Ava. In the eighteenth century the Talaings rebelled against the Burmese and set up their own capital in Pegu. It was destroyed by the Burmese in 1757, but was later rebuilt as the center of a Burmese province. In 1852 the city and the province came under British rule. In March 1942 Pegu was taken by the Japanese and retaken by the British in May 1944. Portuguese trade with the kingdom of Pegu was opened up in 1519 and flourished under the Talaing kings and their Burmese successors. Pinto devotes twenty-four chapters to the wars between the Talaings (whom he calls "Pegus") and the Burmese, and to the part played in those wars by his countrymen. See chapters 147–57, 170, 188, and 190–200 below.

3. *Tristão de Gá:* He had a long and distinguished career in Asia, beginning in 1505 with his departure for India in the armada of the viceroy Francisco de Almeida. In March 1508 he was taken captive by Malik Aiyaz, captain of Sultan Mahmud of Cambay (1458–1511) in the battle of Chaul, in which Dom Lourenço, the viceroy's son, was slain (see n. 4 below). In 1509, after the defeat of the combined forces of Malik Aiyaz and Emir Hussein (captain of the sultan of Egypt), followed by a peace treaty, the viceroy named him treasurer of Diu. In 1510, after the conquest of Goa, Afonso de Albuquerque named him treasurer of Goa, and in 1515 he accompanied Albuquerque on his expedition to the Red Sea; and again, in 1517, he joined a similar expedition under Governor Lopo Soares de Albergaria. In 1527 he was one of the judges chosen to decide who was the lawful governor of India. In 1533 he was sent by Governor Nuno da Cunha as ambassador to Sultan Bahadur to negotiate for the building of a fortress in Diu; and in that year, Gaspar Correia describes him as wise and prudent and says that "he was already an old man" (vol. 3, chap. 40, 495–96).

4. *Dom Lourenço:* The viceroy Francisco de Almeida's only son, who departed for India with his father in 1505. He distinguished himself in various exploits as admiral of the sea of India. At the beginning of January 1508 he departed from Cochin with a fleet of eight ships intended to convoy the annual cargo fleet returning to Portugal. Lying in wait off the coast of Chaul were the combined forces of Malik Aiyaz and Emir Hussein. A mistaken maneuver on the part of the pilot caused Dom Lourenço's ship to become entangled in some fishermen's nets, and he was fatally wounded. The Mohammedan forces threw themselves against his *nao,* permitting the cargo ships to go safely on their way. (See n. 3 above and n. 5 below, as well as chap. 3, n. 8 above.)

5. *Emir Hussein:* The Mirocem of the Portuguese chronicles; admiral of the fleet that the sultan of Egypt sent in 1508 to Sultan Mahmud of Cambay, in a combined effort to expel the Portuguese from India. (See nn. 3 and 4 above.)

6. *chronicles:* See Castanheda, vol. 1, bk. 2, chaps. 80–81; Barros, in Barros and Couto, dec. 2, bk. 2, chaps. 8–9; Correia, vol. 1, chap. 16, 762–71; Góis, vol. 2, chaps. 25–26.

7. *Rosado:* See chapter 16, note 7 above.

8. *Moghul wars:* The Moghul king who went to war against Sultan Bahadur of Cambay was Humayun (reigned 1530–56), son of Baber and father of Akbar. Defeated by Humayun in 1535, Bahadur turned to the Portuguese for help. Having decided that they would be less of a threat to his sovereignty than the Moghul, he signed a peace treaty with the Portuguese, giving them permission to build a fortress in Diu, which he later regretted. See chapter 2, note 16 above.

9. *Pulo Butum:* Lagoa identifies this island as Pulo Betong, which he situates at latitude 5°18′ north and longitude 100°11′ east, in the Strait of Malacca (*Glossário*). However, C. Eckford Luard, editor of the English version of the *Itinerário* of Fray Sebastian Manrique, identifies it as Pulo Butum, an island he places at 6°10′ north and 96°30′ east, off the Malay Peninsula (2:9 n. 20).

10. *nao Biscay:* The *Livro das Armadas* (15v) has an illustration of a *nao* called *Bastiana*, which arrived in India with the armada of 1512, commanded by Pero de Albuquerque. Gaspar Correia (vol. 2, chap. 35, 289) refers apparently to the same *nao* as the *Biscay Bastiana* (*Biscaynha Bastyayna*), but there is nothing in the chronicles to prove that it ever belonged to Magellan, who went to India in 1505 with the armada of the viceroy Francisco de Almeida.

11. *Sunda Straits:* Channel between the islands of Sumatra and Java, connecting the Java Sea with the Indian Ocean, sixteen miles wide at its narrowest part.

12. *Lampong River:* Probably the Bay of Lampong, at the southern end of the island of Sumatra, which opens into the Sunda Straits.

13. *Menangkabow:* See chapter 13, note 4 and chapter 16, note 1 above.

14. *Kampar:* The kingdom of Kampar no longer exists, though the name survives in the Kampar River on which it stood. Writing in the sixteenth century, Tomé Pires describes Kampar as a sterile land, of little profit, with no villages on the sea, bounded on one side by Siak, on the other by Campon, and inland by Menangkabow (Cortesão, *Suma Oriental*, 150–51). Writing in the eighteenth century, Marsden refers to Kampar as a once-famous kingdom now fallen into obscurity (290). After Albuquerque's conquest of Malacca, the king of Kampar was the first of the neighborhood rulers to offer his submission to the king of Portugal (Barros, in Barros and Couto, déc. 2, bk. 6, chap. 7, 101).

15. *Jambi River:* Or the Hari River, as it is known today, a river about 450 miles long in south central Sumatra. It rises in the Barisan Mountains, flows east to Berhala Strait, and is navigable for about one-third of the way.

16. *Broteo River:* Unidentified. Marsden (290) says that the principal rivers of Sumatra are the Indragiri, the Siak, and the Battoo Bara, and that the latter descends from the Battak region, emptying into the Strait of Malacca. Pinto's *Broteo* River may possibly be a corruption of Battoo Bara.

17. *queen of Sheba:* It is possible that such a legend existed in those parts at the time that Pinto was there and that, like many legends, it had a grain of truth. The kingdom of Menangkabow was celebrated in ancient times for its gold mines, throughout the Orient and the Middle East. When the queen made her famous visit to King Solomon in the tenth century B.C., the kingdom of Sheba was a region of great wealth, due in great part to its geographical situation on the trade route from India to Africa. See chapter 4, note 20 above.

18. *Prester John:* See chapter 4, note 2 above.

19. *Pulo Ticos:* The Ticos are three small islands on the west coast of Sumatra, about one and a half miles apart, the outermost lying in latitude 0°23′ south, longitude 99°50′ east. See chapter 13, note 4 above.

20. *Francisco de Almeida:* Not to be confused with the viceroy Francisco de Almeida mentioned at the beginning of the chapter. Homonyms are very common in Portuguese.

21. *Banda Islands:* A group of ten volcanic islands, about seventy square miles, East Indonesia, in the Banda Sea, in the south central Moluccas. The islands were discovered and claimed by the Portuguese in 1512. The Dutch ousted the Portuguese in 1599. For centuries these islands were important in the spice trade.

22. *Jailolo:* Or Halmahera, largest island of the Moluccas, in East Indonesia, lying on the equator between New Guinea and the Celebes. Known to the Portuguese and the Spaniards as early as 1525, Halmahera came under Dutch influence in 1660. Taken by the Japanese (1942) in World War II, it was frequently bombed by the Allies.

23. *Nicobar Islands:* A group of nineteen small islands at the entrance to the Bay of Bengal, northwest of Sumatra. They are separated from the Andaman Islands to the south by a channel ninety miles wide. In the middle of the eighteenth century the Danes tried unsuccessfully to colonize them. Occupied by the British in 1869, they were joined to the Andaman Islands to form an administrative division. Occupied by the Japanese in 1942–45.

24. *Martim Afonso de Sousa:* Governor of India, 1542–45. See chapter 12, note 6 above.

25. *Jerónimo de Figueiredo:* Gaspar Correia gives us some insight into the character of this Jerónimo de Figueiredo, whom he describes as a mischief maker. It appears that, in the year 1542, Figueiredo wrote a letter to the incoming governor, Martim Afonso de Sousa, addressed to him in Mozambique, maligning the outgoing governor, Estêvão da Gama, whose term of office ended when Martim Afonso de Sousa arrived in India, unannounced, and ahead of schedule, in order to catch Estêvão da Gama *in flagrante delicto,* though he never found proof of the irregularities he had been accused of by Figueiredo (vol. 4, chap. 39, 224). Correia also says that Figueiredo was the mischief maker who, in the following year, informed the governor that Diogo Cabral had cursed him. As a result, Cabral, described by Correia as a highly respected nobleman who had served his king well, was put in chains and removed from the command of the discovery expedition to which he had been appointed by the king, and the command given instead to Jerónimo de Figueiredo, in compensation for his scandalmongering (vol. 4, chap. 35, 306).

26. *El Quseir:* Or Al Qusair, El Qoseir, Al-Qasir, etc.; also, formerly, Kosseir. Seaport, east Egypt, on the Red Sea, east of Qena, which was an ancient caravan route to the Nile. It was one of the cities burned by Estêvão da Gama on his expedition to the Red Sea in 1541. (See Correia, vol. 4, chap. 27, 185–87; Couto, in Barros and Couto, déc. 5, bk. 7, chap. 8.) Father Jerónimo Lobo, writing in 1640(?) says that it was "the most famous town on this coast because it is the usual port used by pilgrims going to Mecca . . . when they wish to avoid the inhospitable overland route. . . . They embark here at Alcocer because the crossing at this place is very short." See Donald M. Lockhart, ed., *The "Itinerário" of Jerónimo Lobo* (Hakluyt Society Publications, 2d ser., vol. 162 (London, 1984), 92.

27. *Galle:* City and capital of southern province, extreme south Sri Lanka (Ceylon), on the Indian Ocean. Famous as a trade center for Chinese and Arabs by 100 B.C., Galle rose to prominence under Portuguese rule (1507–1640), when it became Sri Lanka's chief port. It was the capital of Sri Lanka under the Dutch (1640–56), whose original fort still stands. The city passed to the British in 1796. Its commercial importance continued until the opening of the Suez Canal in 1869 and the construction (1885) by the British of a modern harbor at Colombo. Since the 1960s congestion and other problems at the port of Colombo have diverted some shipping to Galle.

28. *Dom João de Castro:* Fourth viceroy of India, scientist and navigator, famous for his strength of character as well as for his military and administrative abilities. During his term in office (1545–48), the second siege of Diu was lifted (1546). (See chap. 2, n. 15 above, and note 29 below.) He was responsible for so many other notable exploits in India that the king wished to reward him by renewing his term of office for three more years, but he died on 6 July 1548. He is also remembered for the many scientific works he authored.

29. *Dom João de Mascarenhas:* (1500?–80), hero of the second siege of Diu (1546). He first went to India as an obscure military officer, but later, during the governorship of Martim Afonso de Sousa (1542–45), he was given command of a caravel. It was then that he began to be noticed, for he protested openly against the governor, accusing him of employing crown ships for common acts of piracy. In 1545, he received a royal appointment as captain of the fortress of Diu, where he was stationed when Dom João de Castro arrived in India. Shortly afterwards the

fortress was besieged by combined Moslem forces. The siege lasted a year, until November 1546, when Dom João de Castro arrived with fresh troops, forcing the enemy to withdraw. The viceroy rebuilt the fortress and delivered it to the brave captain, who returned to Portugal in 1548, where he learned, too late, that he had been named to succeed Dom João de Castro as viceroy of India.

Chapter 21

1. *Dom Estêvão da Gama:* Captain of Malacca, 1534–39. During his term of office he twice defeated the king of Ujantana (1534 and 1535) and repelled an attack by the Achinese in 1537. The second battle against Ujantana (modern Johore) was so decisive that, for the first time since the conquest of Malacca (1511), the deposed kings of this dynasty, who had never ceased to make war against Malacca, were forced to sign a treaty of peace. As a result of Dom Estêvão's energetic action, Pero de Faria, the incoming captain, was able to enjoy a period of relative peace during his administration (1539–44). See Correia, vol. 3, chaps. 50, 63, 86, 115. See also chapter 13, note 1 and chapter 17, note 12 above.

2. *Ambassador from the king of Aaru:* The chronicles only mention the presence of an ambassador from Aaru in the year 1528, and not in 1539. (See chap. 14, n. 6 and chap. 17, n. 12 above.) While it is true that the king of Aaru was very friendly with the Portuguese of Malacca, his friendship was due to the historic hatred of the Aarus for the former kings of Malacca deposed by the Portuguese. And in spite of the sympathetic portrait painted by Pinto of the king of Aaru as poor and powerless, the Aarus had a reputation for being extremely bellicose and were much feared by their neighbors, with whom they were constantly at war. See Cortesão, *Suma Oriental,* 147.

3. *nearby base:* According to Tomé Pires, it was possible to cross over to Malacca from Aaru in one day (ibid.).

4. *in office for another month and a half:* According to Diogo do Couto, when Dom Estêvão da Gama arrived in Malacca in 1534, his brother, Dom Paulo, who was outgoing captain, "immediately handed over the fortress to him, without the usual inconveniences and impediments laid upon the Captain and other officials today; because in those days any Captain, at any time that he arrived in India, if his appointment was prior to that of the one who was in the fortress, was able to remove him from office; but this was later revoked by the King with a special regulation to the effect that when a Captain was already in office, he could not be removed by another recently arrived from Portugal, even if his appointment was an earlier one, which he did to avoid many inconveniences" (vol. 4, bk. 8, chap. 9).

5. *whatever military assistance he deemed necessary:* In a letter (quoted in chap. 13, n. 2 above) written to King John III on 25 November 1539, Pero de Faria complains that he is unable to do anything because Dom Estêvão has not stepped down from office. Yet in the same letter he contradicts himself by enumerating all the things he has done in spite of Dom Estêvão. See Brito Rebello 4:143.

6. *Japan:* In the year 1539 the Portuguese had not yet begun to trade with Japan, which was discovered accidentally in the year 1542 or 1543 by a group of three Portuguese. Pinto himself claims to be one of the three who were the first Europeans to set foot in Japan. See Pinto's account of the discovery of Japan in chapters 132–37 below.

7. *returning with such bad news:* If the king of Aaru sent an ambassador to Malacca in 1539, then it was not the first time that one of his envoys had left Malacca unhappy with the results of his mission. The chronicles relate that in the year 1528 the king of Aaru did indeed send an ambassador to Malacca to ask for military assistance against the Achinese, when Pero de Faria was serving his first term as captain of the fortress. Concurrently, the wily king of Achin, having learned of the ambassador's mission, offered to sign a peace treaty with Malacca. Believing in the sincerity of the Achinese, Pero de Faria withdrew the promised military aid, and the Aaru ambassador departed in anger. Nothing ever came of the peace offer, but the king of

Achin had achieved his end, that of preventing the Portuguese from helping Aaru. See note 2 above and chapter 17, note 7 above.

8. *Arroba:* A weight equal to a quarter of a quintal, or thirty-two pounds avoirdupois; from the Arabic *ar-ruba,* meaning "a fourth." The arroba today is reckoned in Portugal as equivalent to fifteen kilograms.

9. *laminated breastplate:* Breast armor of the sixteenth century, made of narrow horizontal, overlapping plates, fastened together by sliding rivets, which was more common in the East than the solid breastplate. It is also called "anime." See illustration in George Cameron Stone, *A Glossary of the Construction, Decoration, and Use of Arms and Armor,* 2d ed. (New York: Jack Brussel, 1961), 10.

10. *5 October 1539:* According to Brito Rebello, the fifth day of October, in the year 1539, fell on a Sunday and not on a Tuesday (1:60).

11. *Puneticão River:* Unidentified. However, Roo de la Faille (8) suggests that it comes from the Malay *roe-pané-moes-tika-no-e-sa,* meaning "a small stone amulet, or bezoar," a name formerly applied by the Malays to an islet today called Pulo Kumpei, located in the Bay of Aru, in northeast Sumatra (see chap. 14, n. 6 above), because its shape resembles that of a bezoar stone. Marsden, on the other hand, sees a possible connection with the river Racan or Arracan, on whose banks the kingdom of Aaru was located (290–91).

Chapter 22

1. *good Moslem:* Pires writes that Muzaffar Shah, fifth king of Malacca, who converted to Islam, tried throughout his life to destroy the king of Aaru precisely because he did not consider him to be a good Moslem; and that from the time of Muzaffar until the reign of Mahmud Shah, eighth king of Malacca, deposed by the Portuguese, the kings of Malacca were always at war with Aaru. See Cortesão, *Suma Oriental,* 245.

2. *huge sums of money:* Modern historians attribute the increasing wealth and power of Achin at this time to the commerce that Achin maintained with the Indian states, which stopped sending their ships to Malacca out of fear of the constant warfare between the king of Bintang and his allies, and the Portuguese of Malacca. See J. Kennedy, *A History of Malacca* (London: Macmillan & Co., 1962), 34–35; and Richard O. Winstedt, "A History of Malaya," *Journal of the Malayan Branch of the Royal Asiatic Society* 13, no. 1 (1935), 74–79. With regard to the king of Bintang, see note 7 below.

3. *kings . . . poor as I am:* According to Tomé Pires, the king of Aaru was greatly feared by his neighbors with whom he was constantly at war; also, Pires writes that the kingdom maintained itself by piracy at sea, and not by trade, because it had nothing to exchange (Cortesão, *Suma Oriental,* 147).

4. *Antonio Garcia:* The Portuguese chronicles make no mention of an Antonio Garcia during Jorge de Albuquerque's time as captain of Malacca, but that does not mean that such traitors did not exist, for there was much hunger and hardship among the Portuguese soldiers in that time and place. The chroniclers do mention the case of a Portuguese by the name of Martim de Avelar who joined up with the king of Bintang at that time. See Castanheda, vol. 2, bk. 6, 101; Barros, in Barros and Couto, déc. 3, bk. 10, chap. 3, 474; and Correia, vol. 2, chap. 17, 798.

5. *Jorge de Albuquerque:* Admiral of the sea of India during the governorship of his cousin Afonso de Albuquerque, at whose side he fought during the conquest of Malacca (1511). He served as captain of Cochin (1512) and twice as captain of Malacca (1514–16 and 1521–25). He returned to Portugal in 1519 but came back to Malacca in 1521 when he was named captain for the second time. During his two terms in office as captain of Malacca he carried on fierce warfare with the sultan of Bintang, not infrequently coming off the worst for it. In 1525 he returned to Portugal and retired from the military. Barros describes him as a virtuous man who trusted in others too much, who lacked foresight, and who failed to take the necessary precautions in

warfare (Barros and Couto, déc. 3, bk. 5, 4). Correia confirms this opinion when he says that "the orders he issued were never carefully conceived, which is why the affairs of Malacca in the time of Jorge de Albuquerque were always in a bad state" (vol. 2, chap. 17, 797).

6. *king of Bintang:* After the conquest of Malacca (1511) Sultan Mahmud, eighth king of Malacca, expelled by the Portuguese, fled to Pahang on the Malay Peninsula. But he did not stay long out of fear that his relatives there would rob him of the treasure he had brought with him. He went instead to the island of Bintang (the largest island of the Riouw Archipelago, opposite Singapore), where he established his capital and from where he continued to make war on the Portuguese. Routed by the Portuguese in 1526 under the command of Pero Mascarenhas, who succeeded Jorge de Albuquerque as captain of Malacca, Mahmud Shah fled to Kampar, where he died in 1528. He was succeeded by his son 'Ala'u'd-din, who established his capital above the Johore River where he proclaimed himself king of Ujantana (Jantana or modern Johore). See Winstedt, "History of Malaya," 74. Correia writes (vol. 3, chap. 5, 91) that the king of Bintang "went to another place called Ujantana, from where he continued to make war against the Portuguese until he died," but he is confusing the son with the father.

7. *saligues:* Dalgado says the word comes from the Malay-Javanese *saligi,* meaning "wooden lance or pointed stick." Ramusio describes the preparation of some charred sticks, made from the heavy wood of the sago tree, which "will pierce any armor, and much better than iron would do" (cited in Yule, *Marco Polo* 2:305 n. 4). Castanheda refers to some "charred wooden assagais made from the areca palm, which are capable of piercing deeply" (vol. 2, bk. 6, chap. 98, 305). And Pedro Teixeira makes reference also to some "salikhes, which are charred sticks, so hard as to pierce like iron; and easily broken, whereupon they have the wound full of a thousand splinters that make it almost incurable" (*The Journey of Pedro Teixeira from India to Italy by Land, 1604–1605,* trans. and ed. William F. Sinclair [London: Hakluyt Society, 1902], 2d ser., 9:6).

8. *batéis* (sing. *batel*): The *botella, pattello,* or *patellee* (from Hindu *patela*) is described in Yule and Burnell as a large flat-bottomed boat in use on the Ganges, or a dhow in miniature.

9. *loya:* Pinto appears to be the only one of the sixteenth-century writers to use this word, which is not found in Dalgado. For a description of the manufacture of gold bracelets in Sumatra, see Marsden, 143–45.

Chapter 23

1. *Anchepisão Islets:* Lagoa makes a heroic attempt to identify these islets, but ends by saying that the author must have suffered a lapse of memory ("Peregrinação," 41).

2. *crossbow shot:* A measure frequently used by the sixteenth-century writers for a distance of approximately 400 yards, or 365 meters, according to C. F. Beckingham and G. W. B. Huntingford in Alvares, 54 n. 3.

3. *reimões:* (sing. *reimão*): Pinto makes a distinction between the tiger and the *reemow,* which is the word for "tiger" on the island of Sumatra. So says Marsden, who claims that the size and strength of this animal are prodigious and that he has known instances of entire villages being depopulated by these tigers. Marsden also mentions the tiger cat, another common species of Sumatra, called *cochin-reemow,* which is a wildcat, similar to, but smaller than, the tiger (93–94, 149–50).

4. *breath-snakes:* These so-called breath-snakes are mentioned by other early writers, among them, Tomé Pires, who heard of them in Malabar but who very judiciously adds that he has never met a man who has seen one. To this, Armando Cortesão appends a note: "They must be a product of the natives' imagination" (*Suma Oriental,* 72 n. 2).

5. *lizards:* Marsden writes that the alligators kill many of the inhabitants of the island of Sumatra, especially when they go to the river to bathe, which they frequently do, in spite of the danger (150).

Chapter 24

    1. *Palembang:* Capital of South Sumatra Province, Indonesia, on southeast Sumatra. It is a port on the Musi River, one of the largest cities on the island and an important trade and shipping center. In the eighteenth century it was the capital of the powerful Hindu-Sumatran kingdom of Sri Vijaya. In the sixteenth century it was an independent sultanate, under the economic and political influence of Malacca, though the Portuguese never occupied it. Later, it came under Dutch rule, passing intermittently under British rule.

    2. *pardau:* Popular name among the Portuguese of a gold coin from the native mints of western India, the name of which afterwards attached to a silver coin minted by the Portuguese, of constantly degenerating value. Also used for money of account. See chapter 6, note 14 above.

Chapter 25

    1. *mace:* From the Javanese and Malay *mas; maz* in Portuguese. (a) A gold weight used in Sumatra, being one-sixteenth of a Malay *tael,* or about forty grains; (b) the name of a small gold coin of Achin, weighing nine grains; and (c) term adopted in the language of the European traders in China to denominate the tenth part of the Chinese *tael* of silver.

    2. *Surabaya:* Variously spelled Surabaja or Soerabaja. Port city, capital of East Java Province, northeast Java, Indonesia, on the Kali Mas River just above its mouth at the western end of Madura Strait. It is one of the most important trade centers of the Far East. Also spelled *Surabaja, Soerabaja.*

    3. *jars:* Probably the so-called Martaban jars. This name was given to vessels of a peculiar pottery, of very large size, glazed, which were famous all over the East for many centuries and were exported from Martaban. Yule quotes the fourteenth-century traveler Ibn Batuta, who says he received a gift of "four Martabans, or huge jars filled with pepper, citrons, and mango, all prepared with salt, as for a sea voyage" (*Hobson-Jobson,* 559).

    4. *married to a native woman:* Early in the sixteenth century it was the policy of the Portuguese government to favor such marriages, enthusiastically encouraged by Afonso de Albuquerque, the idea being that the Portuguese would populate the conquered territories and that their descendants would constitute a loyal population of permanent residents. In the beginning the government paid a stipend to these married men, but the practice was soon abandoned, and they were paid only when called upon to defend the fortress. With regard to the number of married men in Malacca, see Ian A. Macgregor, 12 n. 37.

Chapter 26

    1. *Mandovi:* Chief customs house of the Portuguese State of India, located on the Mandovi River, which forms the northern boundary of the island of Old Goa. Mandovi is said to signify "customs house" in the regional languages of the Malabar Coast.

    2. *Dom Estêvão da Gama:* See chapter 17, note 12 and chapter 21, note 1 above.

    3. *Paneticão:* Spelled *Puneticão* in chapters 21, 22, and 32, and *Paneticão* in chapters 26 and 31.

    4. *Sabang:* Seaport of the island of Weh (or Pulo Way), about fourteen miles off the extreme northwestern tip of Sumatra. It is the first port of call from Indian and western ports on routes to Singapore and east Asia.

    5. *calaluz:* A swift oar-propelled sailing vessel, often mentioned by the Portuguese writers as used in the Indian archipelago.

    6. *Barros:* Also Baros or Baruez. Formerly an important seaport on the northwest coast of Sumatra.

    7. *Six thousand Aaru soldiers:* In chapter 22 the king of Aaru says there are only five thousand Aaru soldiers in his army.

Chapter 27

1. *Cutiale Marcá:* Probably Khutb-Ali Maracar (or Marakkan), nephew of *Patemarcá* and member of a family of wealthy Moslem merchants who had sworn to drive the Portuguese out of Asia. See chapter 7, note 2 above.

2. *Sultan Alaradim:* The king of Achin at this date had widened his conquests to the states on both the west and east coasts of the island of Sumatra, hence the self-styled "king of the land from sea to sea." Also, it is interesting to note that the name Radin, according to Marsden, is very common among the Malays, to which the Arabic particle "al" is here prefixed (345).

3. *Prophet Nobi:* Spelled *Noby* in chapters 6 and 59. See chapter 6, note 3 above.

Chapter 28

1. *set herself afire:* Pinto may be referring here to *suttee,* or the rite of widow burning, as practiced formerly by people of certain castes among the Hindus. But he says the queen was a Moslem, hence it is doubtful that her suicide would have received religious sanction, since the practice was forbidden by Islamic law.

2. *Minhasumbá:* Unidentified. However, Roo de la Faille says that it represents the Malay *Minjak Sembawa,* the name for an area near Aaru that was famous for its *oleum terra,* or whitish earth oil, which was formerly exported as a medicine or balsam, called *minjak tanah.*

3. *prow:* Generic name used in Indonesia and the Indian Ocean for undecked native boats or vessels, some of which have platforms or portable decking. It is used indiscriminately for dugout or plank-built craft with or without outriggers, whether rowed, paddled, or sailed. Also called *prahu, prau, parao,* and *perahu.*

Chapter 29

1. *Alvaro de Faria:* Son of Pero de Faria by an Asian wife. Pero de Faria named him captain of the sea of Malacca, or the commander of the naval squadron based in Malacca. It was probably the death of this son (1539 or 1540?) that Faria recounted in a letter to King John III, written from Malacca, on 22 November 1540. In another letter, of 8 September 1545, written from Goa, Faria complained that on account of his poverty his children would suffer disadvantages if he died, for they were Eurasians. See Corpo Cronologico, 1-68-86 and 1-76-102, cited in Macgregor, 20 n. 61. See also chapter 12, note 1 above.

2. *Hilir:* A village outside the walls of Malacca that extended from the stream of Ayer Laleh to Ujon Pasir. It corresponds to the southeast part of the town of Malacca, called Banda Hilir today.

Chapter 30

1. *Jantana:* Former kingdom at the southern extremity of the Malay Peninsula, opposite Singapore, which included all or part of the modern state of Johore. It was also called Ujantana or Ujungtanah. See above, chapter 21, note 1 and chapter 22, note 6.

Chapter 31

1. *Ramadan:* The ninth month of the Mohammedan year, rigidly observed as a thirty days' fast during the hours of daylight, by all Mohammedans.

2. *island of Kampar:* Unidentified. However, Pinto may be referring to one of the islands in the Straits of Kampar, off the east coast of Sumatra, at the southern end of the Strait of Malacca; probably one of the two called Great and Little Karimun islands, which are separated

by a deep-water channel that begins in front of the former kingdom of Kampar. See chapter 20, note 14 above.

3. *Lingga:* Chief island of the Lingga Archipelago, off the east coast of Sumatra, on the equator. Together with the Riouw Archipelago to the north, it forms the Riouw-Lingga Archipelago of Indonesia. See chapter 22, note 6 above.

4. *Dervish:* A Mohammedan monk or friar who has taken vows of poverty and austere life.

5. *Laué River:* Possibly the Laye River, which Marsden mentions as one of the principal rivers of the Rejang country of western Sumatra (38).

6. *Daya:* Former kingdom on the island of Sumatra, which Barros (Barros and Couto, déc. 3, bk. 3, chap. 3, 266) situates twenty leagues from Achin, to the west, on the tip of the island, in the present region of the Daya River. It appears on Marsden's map of 1783 as Dyah, just below Achin. See chapter 17, note 6 above.

Chapter 32

1. *joangá:* Large oared vessel of the Moluccas. The word does not appear in the Malayan dictionaries, but it was used by other writers of the period, among them Castanheda (vol. 6, bk. 11, 172), who describes it as a long vessel with 180 oars on each side.

2. *laque xemena:* Also written *lassamane* or *lasamane,* from the Malay-Javanese *laksamana.* It is not a name, but the title of one of the five principal dignitaries of the Malay States, commander of the armed forces both on land and sea. It is possible that the *laksamana* referred to here was the famous warrior Hang Nadim, who fought the Portuguese for forty years. He died in battle in the year 1550. See Marsden, 348 n., and Winstedt, "History of Malaya," 70.

3. *bailéu:* From the Malay *balai,* which means a "raised platform, either on a ship or in a building." In this chapter it refers to such a platform or scaffold on which soldiers fought on board ancient ships. For its other meanings, see chapter 15, note 5 above.

4. *Perak:* Today, a state of the Federation of Malaya, on the west coast of central Malay Peninsula, on the Strait of Malacca, bounded on the north by Thailand. Perak was once a vassal of the king of Malacca ousted by the Portuguese in 1511, whose heir later became the king of Jantana referred to in this chapter.

5. *Dom Leonis Pereira:* Captain of Malacca (1567–72), famous for his heroic defense of the undermanned fortress, which, according to Diogo do Couto, began on 20 January 1568, when a huge Achinese armada appeared before Malacca on the day that the Portuguese were celebrating the birthday of King Sebastian. After some diplomatic skirmishing, intended to facilitate the capture of Malacca, all of which failed, finally, on February 14 the Achinese stormed the fortress with scaling ladders. Unable to breach the walls, on February 25 the king of Achin departed as suddenly as he had appeared. A day later the king of Jantana, who had been advised by Dom Leonis of the presence of the Achinese, arrived in Malacca with a fleet of sixty ships, not so much out of a desire to aid the Portuguese, with whom they were then at peace, but to avenge himself on the king of Achin, for having taken Aaru from him. So confident had he been of taking Malacca that the king of Achin had brought with him his wives and three sons, the eldest of which, the king of Aaru, was slain on the first day of fighting. See Couto, in Barros and Couto, déc. 8, chap. 22, 133–63.

Chapter 33

1. *Pahang:* A state of the Federation of Malaya, on the east coast of the Malay Peninsula, on the South China Sea. It is the largest state on the peninsula. After the fall of Malacca (1511), Pahang formed part of the sultanate of Riouw (Bintang) and Johore (Jantana)—except in the seventeenth century, when it was captured by Achin—until its own rulers established themselves as independent sovereigns in the nineteenth century.

2. *Tomé Lobo:* A person by that name is mentioned by both Castanheda (vol. 2, bk. 57, chap. 52, 236) and Correia (vol. 2, chap. 13, 770–71) as the sole survivor of a foist attacked by the forces of the king of Bintang, who swam ashore and made his way back to Malacca, in 1523, through enemy territory. Perhaps it is the same.

3. *monteu of Banchá:* According to Dalgado, *monteu* means "a Chinese authority who performs military and judicial functions," and it probably comes from the Chinese root *man-sz',* meaning "counsellor." As for the toponym Banchá, Armando Cortesão identifies it with Bang-taphong or Bang Sabhan, a port in the kingdom of Siam, at latitude 11°12' north (*Suma Oriental,* 106 n.).

4. *morning watch:* Hours between 4:00 and 8:00 a.m.

5. *Pulo Tioman:* Island in the South China Sea off southeast Pahang, south Malay Peninsula.

6. *Achinese attacked . . . second time:* The Achinese attacked Malacca twice in the year 1537; the first time in the month of September, when they were driven off after one day of fighting. Shortly afterwards they returned with a larger force and were driven off after three days of fighting. See Barros, in Barros and Couto, déc. 4, bk. 2, chap. 14, 548; and Correia, vol. 3, chap. 115, 861.

7. *Talangame:* A port of the island of Ternate, one of the Moluccas. Being free of reefs, Talangame offered a better berth for ships than the Portuguese fortress of Ternate, which was located about a league away. Despite its relatively small size, Ternate was for centuries a major spice center and one of the most important islands of the Moluccas.

Chapter 34

1. *tuão:* From the Malay *tuan* or *tuwan,* meaning "lord or master."

Chapter 35

1. *Tanjampura:* Armando Cortesão identifies this with Tanjong Puting, a port on the south coast of Borneo, mentioned by other writers of the period, among them Barros (in Barros and Couto, déc. 4, bk. 6, chap. 19), Castanheda (vol. 8, bk. 21), and Orta (colloquy 43), as being rich in diamonds (*Suma Oriental,* 223 n. 1). *Tanjong* is the Malay word for "cape."

2. *Solor:* A small mountainous island of the Lesser Sunda Islands, of Indonesia, in the Savu Sea.

3. *Khoja Geinal:* Pinto uses the name Geinal (Zainal?) with the honorific *khoja* for three different individuals: in chapter 6, for a Turkish Janissary, and in chapter 173, for a Portuguese renegade. See chapter 6, note 6 above.

4. *Kelantan River:* A river about 150 miles long in Kelantan State, Malay Peninsula. It rises in the mountains on the southwest border, and flows north-northeast into the South China Sea.

5. *necodá:* Also *nacoda, nacoder,* etc., from the Persian *na-khuda,* meaning "a skipper, or master of a native vessel." The term, which was adopted by the Malays, denotes a person who is at the same time navigator and owner of a trading vessel, a condition of much respectability among them.

6. *tael:* A weight and money of account in the Far East, representing a varying weight of silver in different localities. Often called "the ounce of silver." The word was apparently taken from the Malay *tahil,* the name of a weight.

Chapter 36

1. *Antonio de Faria e Sousa:* Attempts have been made to identify this character with a historical figure, possibly a relative of Pero de Faria, captain of Malacca. No one by that name is

mentioned in the Portuguese chronicles; however, in one of his letters to King John III, Pero de Faria praises some of the fidalgos who accompanied him to Malacca for their service to the king, among them one by the name of Antonio de Faria. See letter of Pero de Faria to King John III, written from Malacca on 25 November 1539 (Arquivo da Torre do Tombo, Corpo Cronologico, Pᵉ 1° maço 66, n° 37) as cited in Brito Rebello 4:151.

2. *Lugor:* Also, Ligor, Ligore, Lakon, Lakhon, or the modern Nakhon Sri Thammarat (*nakhon* means "town" in Thai), at latitude 8°18′ north, on the east coast of the Malay Peninsula, on the Gulf of Siam.

3. *Japara:* Or Djapara. Town on the north coast of Central Java Province, in Indonesia, thirty-five miles north-northeast of Samarang. The province, which forms a projection or peninsula, is bounded on the south by Samarang and on the other three sides by the Java Sea.

4. *Demak:* Town just south of Japara, bounded on one side by Samarang and on the other by Tidunan, on the island of Java.

5. *Panaruca:* Or Panaroekan. Town and province on the northeast coast of the island of Java, in the Strait of Madura, seventeen miles east-northeast of Bezocki, on a bay of its name.

6. *Sidayo:* Or Sedayu. Seaport at the east end of the island of Java, in Indonesia, off the west coast of the Strait of Surabaya.

7. *Pasuruan:* Or Paseeroean, Passaroewang. Seaport and province on the east end of the island of Java, in the Strait of Madura. The town is located about thirty miles south-southeast of Surabaya.

8. *zumbaia:* From the Malay *sembahyang*. An act of deep courtesy or reverence, paid to a king or other person of exalted rank. The term is used today in modern Portuguese, but in a pejorative sense.

9. *Prechau Saleu:* The word *prechau* is used by Pinto and other writers, mainly in connection with Burma, Siam, and the countries of the Indochinese peninsula. C. Eckford Luard, in the *Travels of Fray Sebastien Manrique* (1:195 n. 10), says that *prechau* appears to be the Siamese word *phra-chao, phra* meaning "excellent" and *chao* meaning "lord." According to Donald F. Lach (*Southeast Asia*, 526 n. 156), *Prechau Saleu* represents *P'ra Chao Chang Phenak*, meaning "lord of the white elephant."

10. *Sornau:* Joaquim de Campos disagrees with the derivation of the word *Sornau* given by Yule in *Hobson-Jobson* (see chap. 17, n. 3 above). He believes that it comes from the word *suvarna*, meaning "land," or *suvarnabhumi*, meaning "land of gold," which was a geographical expression encompassing a great part of the Indochinese peninsula. See Campos, 224–25.

11. *Ayuthia:* Ayudhya, Ayutthaya, or Phra Nakon Si Ayutthaya. City and capital of Ayuthia Province, south central Thailand, forty miles north of Bangkok. It was the capital of a Thai kingdom founded circa 1350, located on the site of a Khmer settlement, on an island in the lower Chao Phraya River. Like Venice, it is intersected by many canals, and many of its inhabitants live in boats. Destroyed by the Burmese in 1559, it was rebuilt by the Siamese in the late sixteenth century, but was again devastated by the Burmese in 1767, after which the capital was moved to Thon Buri and then to Bangkok.

12. *poyho:* According to Dalgado, *poyho* comes from the Siamese *pù-phra*, meaning "viceroy." However, the word *phra* is also used in composition with various names throughout Burma and the Indochinese peninsula. See note 9 above.

Chapter 37

1. *Hainan:* The second largest island off the China coast (Taiwan is the largest), in the South China Sea. Administratively part of Kwangtung Province (China), it is separated from the mainland by Hainan Strait (about thirty miles wide). Under Chinese control since the first century A.D., Hainan was not fully incorporated into China until the thirteenth century. It became part of Kwangtung in the late fourteenth century.

2. *brazilwood:* Common name for several trees of the family Leguminosae, whose wood

yields a red dye. The East Indian redwood, or sapanwood (*Caesalpinia sappan*), was called "bresel wood" when it was first imported to Europe in the Middle Ages. Portuguese explorers used this name for a similar South American tree (*Caesalpinia brasiliensis*), from which the name Brazil, for its native country, purportedly derives.

3. *Heitor da Silveira:* Arrived in India in 1523, where he served as naval captain and as captain of the fortress of Cannanore. He led three expeditions to the Red Sea, where he did indeed capture many of the Arab merchant vessels en route to India. In 1531 he was killed in battle before Diu. He was highly respected by his compatriots.

Chapter 38

1. *Banchá:* Pires spells this toponym *Bamcha* and describes it as a port belonging to "the lords of the land of Siam." Armando Cortesão identifies it with the modern Bang-taphang or Bang-Sabhan at latitude 11°12′ north (*Suma Oriental,* 105–6 n. 2).

2. *pate:* An honorific title equivalent to "prince" or "duke" in Malaysia, according to Dalgado. From the Malay-Javanese *patih,* Sanskrit *pati,* meaning "lord." According to Armando Cortesão, Tomé Pires was the first European to define the term, describing the *pates* as "governors with capital powers, both civil and criminal over every person in their lands." The title is still used for some native Java dignitaries (ibid., 154 n. 3).

Chapter 39

1. *Champa:* Ancient coastal kingdom of Indochina, occupying the region in the southeast of the peninsula, closely corresponding to South Annam, which flourished from the third century A.D. to the end of the fifteenth century. Its inhabitants were the Chams, closely related to the Cambodians.

2. *Pulo Condore:* An island group in the South China Sea, lying off the southern coast of Cochinchina, South Vietnam, just southeast of the Mekong Delta.

3. *nautaquim:* Used frequently by Pinto as the Japanese word for "prince," and spelled elsewhere as *nautoquim.* There is no doubt that he took it from *Naotoki,* one of the various names of the feudal lord of the island of Tanegashima who ruled at the time the Portuguese first landed in Japan (1542 or 1543). See Yoshitomo Okamoto and J. Abranches Pinto, "Mendes Pinto e o descobrimento do Japão," *Boletim da Sociedade Luso-Japonesa* (1929): 78–84.

4. *Tosa:* Former name of the Japanese island of Shikoku, and name of a former province on south Shikoku Island, now Kochi Prefecture. Home of the influential Tosa clan.

5. *river of . . . Pulo Cambim:* Pinto is obviously referring here to the delta of the Mekong River, a region between the kingdoms of Cambodia and Champa, both of which were tributary to Siam at that time. However, the toponym *Pulo Cambim* has not been identified.

6. *last day of May:* According to Brito Rebello (1:109), the last day of May in the year 1540 fell on a Monday, not Sunday.

7. *Catimparu:* Identified as Cantho-Paru by José de Ramos, who writes that Pinto "definitely entered through the estuary of the Mekong called Bassac," and that "some miles higher there is still today the village of Cantho in Cochin-China." See "Cambodia and Diogo Velloso," *Boletim do Instituto Português de Hongkong* 4 (1955): 138 n. 6. *Webster's Geographical Dictionary* (1966 ed.) describes Can-Tho as a "town, Central Cochin China, S. Vietnam, on the right bank of the Mekong in its delta, 90 miles southwest of Saigon . . . a port of call for river and coastal steamers."

8. *Lake Pinator:* Lagoa ("Peregrinaçao" 3:51) points out that Manuel de Faria e Sousa (whose *Asia Portuguesa* was published 1666–75) also mentions this lake, which he locates 260 leagues from the mouth of the river. Based on Faria e Sousa's information, Lagoa situates the lake somewhere in Tibet and suggests a possible identification with one of the Tibetan lakes, either Charing Nor, Oring Nor, Toso Nor, or Kuku Nor. As we know today, the Mekong

does indeed rise in the highlands of east Tibet, but that was not known to Pinto or his contemporaries.

9. *Quitirvão:* Pinto mentions this kingdom again in chapters 181 and 182 as bordering with Siam.

10. *Xincaléu:* Lagoa ("Peregrinaçao" 3:286) speculates that this town, which is also mentioned by Faria e Sousa, may be located in Tibet and suggests a possible identification with the town of Shigatse, located west-southwest of Lhasa. However, there is also the possibility that Faria e Sousa plagiarized Pinto, whom he staunchly defended against his detractors.

11. *diamonds:* Regarding these diamonds, see Orta 2:198–99, 210–11, notes.

Chapter 40

1. *charachina:* From the Malay *chara,* meaning "mode or manner"; hence, in the manner of the Chinese.

2. *lorcha:* A modified sailing junk, the hull constructed in European fashion, but rigged in Chinese fashion.

3. *Santiago!:* An old Iberian war cry, invoking the help of Saint James.

4. *hoist . . . on the rack:* Torture, practiced by the Inquisition, that consisted of tying the victim with ropes to a pulley and raising and stretching the body on a rack till the bones cracked.

5. *Ning-po:* Former name of the city of Ning-Hsien, referred to by the Portuguese chroniclers in a corrupted form as Liampó, a city and treaty port, northeast Chekiang Province, east China, about ninety miles east-southeast of Hangchow on the south side of Hangchow Bay, and on a small stream about thirteen miles from its mouth. Visited by Portuguese traders as early as 1515.

6. *crossbar:* This consisted of placing a tourniquet around the head of the victim and twisting a bar or stick until the skull split and the gray matter burst out.

7. *manchua:* Portuguese corruption of the original Malayalam word *manji,* for a single-masted cargo boat used on the Malabar coast of India.

8. *teston:* *Testão* in Portuguese. Ancient coins minted for the first time in the reign of King Manuel I (1495–1521). There were gold testons valued at twelve hundred reals and silver testons valued at one hundred reals.

9. *fire rafts:* Crude wooden rafts, laden with combustibles, set adrift on the tide or current, in the direction of an enemy ship.

Chapter 41

1. *Corpus Christi Eve:* Fell on May twenty-sixth that year, according to Brito Rebello 1:115.

2. *Varela:* There is a Cape Varela (or Mui Nai) on the coast of Cochinchina, but not a river by that name. *Tinacoreu* has not been identified.

3. *hoyá:* Or *oyá,* from the Siamese *húa,* meaning "chief, or captain." It is also a title of nobility in Siam, equivalent to that of duke, according to Barros (Barros and Couto, déc. 3, bk. 2, chap. 5, 171).

4. *Gueos:* See chapter 1, note 3 above.

5. *yak:* Pinto uses the word *bada* here, a borrowing from the Malay *badak,* which in the sixteenth century had the indefinite meaning of a "wild animal" or a "domesticated animal that goes wild." In the seventeenth century the word *bada* (or *abada*) began to be applied to the rhinoceros. When speaking elsewhere of the *badas* that were used as beasts of burden, Pinto is undoubtedly referring to the yaks of Tartary, for which there was no word in Portuguese. Unfortunately, Pinto's seventeenth-century translators rendered the word as "rhinoceros," which added to his reputation as a liar. In this passage Pinto may be referring to the wild yak or a large

wild animal for which he could not find an exact Portuguese term. The best explanation for the meaning of this vague term, in my view, is given by Joaquim de Campos, 228. See also Yule's note on the yak of Tartary in his *Marco Polo* 1:277–79, as well as Charles W. Loch's article, "Rhinoceros Sindaicus: The Javan or Lesser One-Horned Rhinoceros and Its Geographical Distribution," *Journal of the Malayan Branch of the Royal Asiatic Society* 15, no. 2 (1937): 130–49.

6. *Lake Chiang Mai:* The name of an imaginary lake, which in the maps of the sixteenth century, followed by most of those in the seventeenth century, is made the source of most of the great rivers of Further India, including the Brahmaputra, the Irawaddy, the Salween, and the Menam. The actual name seems to have been taken from the state of Chiang Mai.

7. *jau:* From the Malay *jauh,* a measure of distance, which, at the rate of 3 leagues per *jau,* would make it equivalent to 9.6 miles. In chapter 95, Pinto uses this measurement again, but at the rate of 4.5 leagues per *jau,* making it equivalent to 14.4 miles. For further clarification, see Cortesão, *Suma Oriental,* 302–3 n.

8. *Passiloco:* Probably Phitsanulok, also spelled P'itsanulok, or Bisnulok. Today, a province of west central Thailand, and a town, its capital on the Nan River, seventy-five miles north of Nakhon Sawan and on the railroad north from Bangkok. In ancient times, a region of the Siamese empire that reached the border.

9. *Savady:* Probably the modern Sandoway or Sandoe, a town of Arakan in Lower Burma, near the coast of the Bay of Bengal, sixty-three miles west-southwest of Prome. The Burmese name is Thankwe (Sandwe).

10. *Toungoo:* Or Taunggyi, a town in Yawnghwe State, southern Shan States, Burma, ninety-five miles southeast of Mandalay, on the Sittang River. Also, capital of the Federated Shan States and chief town of the Southern Shan States. From the late fourteenth century it was the center of one of the three chief states of Burma; in the late sixteenth century, under the kings of Pagan, it preceded Pegu as the capital of a unified Burmese kingdom.

11. *Prome:* A city in Pegu, above the delta, on the left bank of the Irawaddy River, 150 miles north of Rangoon. It is one of the oldest towns in Burma and was once the capital of a flourishing kingdom.

12. *Calaminhan:* In chapters 158–65 Pinto describes his voyage to *Calaminhan,* long considered a figment of his imagination, but since identified as the kingdom of Luang Prabang. See José de Ramos, "Império do Calaminhão," *Mosaico* (Macau) 3, no. 13 (September 1951): 1–12; Campos, 230; and *Manrique* 1:299–300 n. 2.

Chapter 42

1. *Tinaçoreu:* Spelled *Tinacoreu* in chapter 41.

2. *Pulo Champeiló:* Appears as such on early maps, but on modern maps is marked as Cham Calao or Culao Cham, an island off the coast of Annam (northeast South Vietnam), just southeast of Cape Tourane (or Da Nang).

3. *Gulf of Cochinchina:* The Gulf of Tonkin or Tonking, at latitude 20° north and longitude 107° east.

Chapter 43

1. *Parsee:* A member of a religious community of India practicing a form of Zoroastrianism, whose ancestors migrated from Persia in the eighth century to avoid Moslem persecution.

2. *Saint Catherine:* Several writers of the period refer to the convent on Mount Sinai where Saint Catherine of Alexandria was buried and which was a great resort for pilgrims. However, there seems to be some disagreement about the location of Mount Sinai proper. *Webster's Geographical Dictionary* states that Mount Sinai has never been identified with cer-

tainty. Mansel Longworth Dames, in his version of the *Book of Duarte Barbosa* (1:45 n. 1) says that Jebel Tur (or Tor) is a name for the Mount Sinai group of mountains, which contains several peaks, the highest of which, Jebel Katharin, is dedicated to Saint Catherine, and that the peak of Mount Sinai proper lies just north of it. See chapter 6, note 10 above.

3. *Surat:* City, west Central India, in Gujarat State, 160 miles north of Bombay, on the Gulf of Cambay.

4. *Garcia de Sá:* Arrived in India in 1518 with appointment as captain of Malacca, in which post he served until 1521, and again in 1529–33 and briefly in 1545. However, on his return to Goa in 1533, he was placed under house arrest and ordered to return to Portugal to face charges before the king by his enemies at home. The order was ignored by Governor Nuno da Cunha, who defended him and who, in 1537, appointed him captain of Bassein, where he raised a fortress and played an important part in the defense of the besieged fortress of Diu. Though he was exonerated of the charges placed against him at home, he never returned to Portugal. On 7 June 1548 he succeeded the viceroy João de Castro as governor of India and died in office, on 6 July 1549, according to Correia (vol. 4, chap. 11, 679), one year and one month later. During his brief term as governor, Bardez and Salsette were annexed to Goa and many of the warring, neighboring potentates of India signed peace treaties with him. See chapter 17, notes 7 and 9 above.

5. *Bassein:* This is a corruption of three entirely different names, and is applied to various places remote from each other: (a) Wasai, an old port on the west coast of India, twenty-six miles north of Bombay; (b) a town and port on the river that forms the westernmost delta arm of the Irawaddy River in the province of Pegu (Burma); (c) Basim, or properly Wasim, an old town in Berar, west Central India, today part of Madhya Pradesh State. Pinto is referring to Wasai at the time that Garcia de Sá was serving as captain of the Portuguese fortress of Bassein, or Baçaim as they called it. See note 4 above.

6. *Dom Estêvão da Gama:* See chapter 13, note 1 and chapter 21, note 1 above.

7. *Christóvão Sardinha:* His name is not mentioned by the Portuguese chroniclers of the period; however, Castanheda (vol. 2, bk. 8, chap. 115, 756; chap. 119, 763; chap. 155, 819) and Correia (vol. 3, chap. 51, 567; chap. 63, 637; chap. 86, 729, 735; chap. 101, 800) mention a Diogo Sardinha who was admiral of the Moluccan seas, to whom he may have been related, since nepotism was not uncommon in those days.

Chapter 44

1. pearl fishers of *Quemoy:* An island off the southeast coast of China, in the Formosa Strait, east of Amoy. However, from Pinto's description it does not seem likely that the Portuguese pirates had sailed that far north at this point of the narrative. In general, Pinto's travels in and around the South China Sea are difficult to follow.

2. *lanteia:* A swift rowing vessel used in Chinese waters, described by Gaspar da Cruz as having six or seven oars on each side, propelled by two men standing at each oar, with one foot forward. See Charles Ralph Boxer, ed., *South China in the Sixteenth Century* (London: Hakluyt Society, 1953), 114, as well as note 1, to which Boxer adds that the word was later applied to the large lighterlike barges that brought down goods by the inland waterways from Canton to Macao.

3. *Chincheo:* Some confusion as to the application of this name has existed for centuries. However, Boxer states that it applies to Fukien Province of China and, more particularly, to the region of the Bay of Amoy where the Portuguese traders met Chinese smugglers from the cities of Chang-chou and Ch'uan-chow, both of which, as well as the entire province, were termed "Chincheo" by the Portuguese. See Boxer's appendix 1, "Chincheo," in *South China*, 313–26.

4. *Lamau:* Lagoa (*Glossário*) identifies this as the Lamock Islands at latitude 23°16' north and longitude 117°19' east off the east coast of China; but at the same time he points out

that the name Lamau, which appears on map 12 of the atlas of Vaz Dourado of 1568, extends to the island of Namoa, to the northwest and in the immediate vicinity of Lamock, in latitude 23°25' north and longitude 117°04' east.

5. *Comhay:* Lagoa (*Glossário*) identifies this as Kwang-hoi or Kwanghai, in latitude 21°58' north and longitude 112°43' east, on the coast of the Chinese province of Kwangtung, west-southwest of Macao.

6. *Sumbor:* Identified as Song-Men by Georges Le Gentil in *Les Portugais en Extrême-Orient* (Paris: Hermann, 1947), 102.

7. *tutão:* From the Chinese *tu-t'ang,* abbreviated from the title *hsun-fu-tu-t'ang,* meaning "viceroy," "governor," or "inspector-general." According to Boxer, this was a temporary provincial appointment conferred on a high official of the central government who was detached for the duration of some regional emergency. Mainly owing to the depredations of Japanese pirates and their Chinese collaborators, such appointments were made for the two Kuang provinces, with a general headquarters at Wu-chou, and for Fukien and Chekiang conjointly known as the *Minchê.* These "viceroys," as the Portuguese and Spaniards called them, were civil officials but often exercised supervisory control over the armed forces in their provinces. See Boxer, *South China,* 6.

8. *Cochinchina:* To the Portuguese, and to all Europeans until the middle of the nineteenth century, Cochinchina meant Annam, the southern Vietnamese kingdom with its capital at Hué. With the coming of French rule in the nineteenth century, the term Cochinchina came to be used for the Saigon region, that part of Vietnam which was the first French annexation on the Southeast Asia mainland. In the 1850s Saigon was indeed part of Annam, and hence part of Cochinchina in its original meaning; but in earlier periods Saigon and the Mekong Delta had not yet come under Vietnamese rule. See Alastair Lamb, *The Mandarin Road to Old Hué* (Hamden, Conn.: Archon Books, 1970) 12; and ibid., 29 n. 2, 64 no. 2.

9. *vancões:* Plural form of *vancão, bancão, wankan,* etc., from the Malay *vankan.* Gaspar da Cruz describes it as a swift Chinese rowing vessel, smaller than the junk, having three oars to each side, capable of loading a great deal of goods. Like the *lanteia* (see n. 2 above), the rowing is done by two men standing at each oar with one foot forward. See Boxer, *South China,* 113–14.

Chapter 45

1. *anchacilado:* A term, probably invented by Pinto, for the district of the *anchaci* (from the Chinese *an-ch'a-shih*), a provincial judge or chief justice in China. Also translated as "criminal judge," "judicial commissioner," etc. See Boxer, *South China,* 6 n. 2.

2. *prechau:* See chapter 36, note 9 above.

3. *lacasá:* Or "lack" in the Anglo-Indian colloquial, from the Sanskrit *laksha,* meaning "100,000." The English adopted the term to designate 100,000 rupees, or the equivalent of £10,000, in the exchange rate of those days. Yule and Burnell state that the word was adopted in the Malay and Javanese and other languages of the archipelago, but that in all of those languages, it is used in the sense of 10,000 instead of 100,000, with the exception of the Lampungs of Sumatra, who use it correctly.

4. *hoyha:* See chapter 41, note 3 above.

5. *chaens:* From the Chinese *ch'a-yuan,* an abbreviation of *tu-ch'a-yuan,* the censorate or court of censors in Peking. It is applied to the censors or imperial commissioners who toured the provinces of China in various capacities. See Boxer, *South China,* 6.

6. *piculs:* From the Malay-Javanese *pikul,* meaning "a man's load." A measure of weight used in China and the East generally, equal to 100 catties; i.e., about 133 1/3 pounds avoirdupois or 60 kilograms.

Chapter 46

1. *Pulo Catão:* Pulo Canton or Kulao Rai, an islet fifteen miles east of Cape Bantan, at latitude 15°23' north, off the coast of Annam.

2. *tucão:* From the malay *tukan,* meaning a "craftsman" or "skilled workman," in Malaysia.

3. *Pero Borges:* Gaspar Correia mentions a Pero Borges who, in 1511, was a clerk in the trading factory of the Moluccas (vol. 2, chap. 30, 265), and Castanheda mentions someone by that name who survived a shipwreck near the Red Sea (vol. 2, bk. 5, chap. 32, 58).

4. *João de Oliveira:* Mentioned previously in chapter 43 as the owner of a junk that was captured by the pirate *Quiay Taijão,* alias Cristóvão Sardinha. But this name does not appear in any of the sixteenth-century chronicles.

Chapter 47

1. *Antonio Borges:* Someone by that name is mentioned briefly by Castanheda (vol. 2, bk. 8, chap. 65, 675) as a fidalgo, or nobleman, who accompanied an ambassador of Governor Nuno da Cunha to Diu in 1533.

2. *chileu:* Dalgado believes that this word comes from the Tonkinese *kinh luoc,* which is pronounced "kileu."

3. *anchaci:* See chapter 45, note 1, above.

4. *chi-fu:* Or *chih-fu,* the title of the mandarin governing the largest of the provincial subdivisions in China; prefect. (See Boxer, *South China,* 298 n. 7.)

Chapter 48

1. *Church of Our Lady of the Mount:* Built in 1521, it was originally called "Our Lady of Grace." Later it was successively rebuilt and renamed "Our Lady of the Mother of God," "Our Lady of the Mount" or "the Hill," "Our Lady of the Annunciation," and finally, the "Church of Saint Paul." Its ruins can still be seen today on the hill of Malacca. For the history of this church, see R. Cardon, "The Old Church on the Malacca Hill," *Journal of the Malayan Branch of the Royal Asiatic Society* 20, no. 1 (1947), 188–234.

2. *Quangepaarù:* The 1614 *princeps* edition has six different spellings for this place-name.
   (a) *Quangepaarù:* chap. 48, 51r
   (b) *Quangiparù:* chap. 52, 56r
   (c) *Quoanjaparù:* chap. 56, 61r
   (d) *Quãogeparu:* chap. 61, 67r
   (e) *Quoangeparù:* chap. 70, 78r
   (f) *Quangeparuu:* chap. 132, 157r

Chapter 49

1. *nautarel:* Pinto uses this word in the sense of "highest-ranking customs officer," in Annam. Dalgado suggests a derivation from the Siamese *nai-dan,* which means the same.

2. *capisondo:* Or *cabisondo, cabizonda.* Pinto uses this word with three different meanings, all of them with reference to Indochina: (a) in this chapter as a "high-ranking customs official"; (b) in chapters 111, 112, 165, 166, 168, 196 as a "high-ranking Buddhist priest"; (c) in chapter 184 as a "flagship or lead vessel." According to Dalgado, in Tonkinese, *cai* means "chief," *binh,* "troop," and *xin,* "to pray." Thus *cabisondo* would mean "chief of the faithful or believers." But there is also *song,* which means "river." Substituting *song* for *xin, cabisondo* would mean "chief or authority of the river," and *cabizonda,* "flagship or lead ship which is carrying the *cabizondo.*"

Chapter 50

1. *September 8:* This fell on a Wednesday, in the year 1540, according to Brito Rebello 1:145.

Chapter 51

1. *Dom Paulo da Gama:* Vasco da Gama's third son, who accompanied his father to India in the year 1524 when the latter was appointed viceroy. On the death of his father the following year he returned to Portugal but came back to India in 1533 with an appointment as captain of Malacca. With the arrival of his brother Estêvão a year later he resigned his appointment in favor of his brother but remained in Malacca as admiral of the sea of Malacca. Eight days later he was killed in combat with the forces of the king of Jantana. See chapter 13, note 1 above.

2. *Quiay Necodá:* See chapter 13, note 19 and chapter 35, note 5 above.

3. *Luis de Paiva:* A Luis Alvares de Paiva is mentioned briefly by Castanheda (vol. 8, bk. 27, 608; bk. 106, 745) as one of the captains who arrived in India in 1528; and by Correia (vol. 3, chap. 9, 292) as one of the captains who took part in a foray against Cambay in 1529.

4. *Rui Lobo:* A Rui Lobo is mentioned briefly by Castanheda (vol. 6, bk. 97, 304; bk. 101, 312; bk. 126, 356) as one of the captains who distinguished himself in battle against the king of Bintang's forces, in the year 1525; and by Correia (vol. 2, chap. 3, 887; vol. 3, chap. 104, 828) as one of the captains who accompanied the fleet of admiral of the sea of India, Martim Afonso de Sousa, in the year 1537.

Chapter 52

1. *bichara:* Consultation, meeting, conference, etc., from the Sanskrit *vichara.*

2. *Quangiparú:* See chapter 48, note 2 above.

3. *angely-trees:* From the Tamil *anjili* or *anjali-maram.* A wood of great value on the west coast of India, for shipbuilding, house building, etc.

Chapter 54

1. *Feast of the Archangel Saint Michael:* Michaelmas Day, observed on the twenty-ninth of September.

2. *Habakkuk:* One of the minor Hebrew prophets mentioned in the stories of "Bel and the Dragon" that form the fourteenth chapter of *Daniel* in the Vulgate; according to which, Daniel remained unharmed in the lion's den, protected and fed by the prophet Habakkuk, who was brought to Babylon by an angel.

Chapter 55

1. *Lailó:* Liau-lô, the southeast corner of Quemoy Island in the Bay of Amoy.

Chapter 57

1. *Goto Islands:* In Japanese, "Goto-Retto," literally, "five-island group"; a chain of islands in the east China Sea, off western Kyushu, Japan.

2. *sucão:* Pinto uses this word as the title of a reigning prince or petty king of an island in the China Sea. Dalgado suggests a possible derivation from the Malay word *suku,* meaning "principality or petty state," and *hang,* an obsolete title.

Chapter 58

1. *dogs:* According to Pereira do Valle (390), this was the name for an iron artillery piece of three-pound caliber, frequently used on board ship and in the close defense of fortifications. For the half-sphere see chapter 16, note 5.

Chapter 59

1. *Lah . . . halah:* The Mohammedan profession of faith, which Pinto gives us in fairly correct Arabic: "La ilaha illa-llahu Muhammad rasul allahi" (There is no God but Allah. Mohammed is the apostle of Allah).

Chapter 60

1. *Foochow:* A seaport on the Min River, thirty-five miles from its mouth, and capital of Fukien Province in southeast China, halfway between Hong Kong and Shanghai. However, Pinto calls it *Fucheo,* a place-name he also uses for the city of Oita in Japan. See chapter 134, note 7.

Chapter 63

1. *chifanga:* Pinto uses this word for "prison," which, according to Dalgado, is *kien-lau* in Chinese. However, he suggests possible derivations from *chi-fan* (government bureau or department), *tse-fan* (customs duties), or *chah-fang* (guard house).

2. *our lady of Nazareth:* Probably a reference to a medieval shrine in the town of Nazaré, located about eighty-five miles north of Lisbon. It was begun as a small chapel in 1182 and was successively enlarged over the years. It is known that both Vasco da Gama and Saint Francis Xavier made a pilgrimage to the shrine before they departed for India.

Chapter 64

1. *odiá:* See chapter 19, note 5 above.

2. *particular point:* As Maurice Collis points out (*Grand Peregrination,* 105), this is one of the earliest mentions of Chinese objection to the diplomatic claim of brotherhood between a foreign sovereign and the emperor of China. As for the first point the mandarin objected to, regarding the legality of Portuguese trade with China, it is clear from the records that for thirty years or so preceding the establishment of Portuguese Macao (1557), trade with China was carried on in a more or less clandestine manner. For more on the subject, see Boxer, *South China,* xix-xxxvii, and other works mentioned by him.

3. *brala:* Also *varela,* or *varella.* According to Yule and Burnell, this is a term frequently applied by the early Portuguese writers to the pagodas of Indochina and China. It is probably derived from the Malay *barahla,* or *brahla,* meaning an "idol."

4. *tansu:* From the Chinese *tung-sz',* meaning "interpreter."

Chapter 65

1. *Tomé Pires:* The first European ambassador to enter China, in 1517, where he and the members of his embassy were said to have perished after a lengthy imprisonment. Pires had served previously in India and Malacca as the crown pharmacist or "feitor das drogas" where, before his departure for China, he wrote his *Suma Oriental* (sometime between the years 1512–15), the earliest description of Southeast Asia written by a Portuguese. The manuscript was lost until Armando Cortesão discovered it in Paris in 1937. Portions of an early copy had been

published by Ramusio in Venice, in 1550 (vol. 1 of the *Navigatione e Viaggi* under the title "Sommario di tutti li regni, città, e populi orientali . . ."), but without the author's name and with the suppression of the portions relating to Malacca and the Moluccas, since at that date the Spice Islands were "top secret" information. See Armando Cortesão, *Suma Oriental,* as well as Cortesão's smaller work on the subject, *Primeira embaixada européia à China* (Lisbon: Seara Nova, 1945). See also Barros, in Barros and Couto, déc. 3, bk. 2, chap. 8, 217; bk. 6, chap. 1, 4, 11, 13; bk. 8, chap. 5, 287.

2. *Fernão Peres de Andrade:* Arrived in India in September of 1515 with an appointment from King Manuel as captain-major of a fleet that was to go "to discover China" and to take an ambassador there. In February 1516 he left India and arrived in Canton in June 1517, after a difficult voyage of nineteen months. After a stay of fourteen months in China, during which he seems to have established peaceful and prosperous relations with the local officials at Canton, in September 1518 Andrade set sail for India, leaving behind the ambassador, Tomé Pires, who was to proceed to Peking. The following year he returned to Portugal with glowing accounts of prospects for future commercial relations with China. However, this was not to be, for in 1521–22 his brother, Simão de Andrade, commander of the next royal squadron that visited China, behaved in a high-handed manner that contributed to a break in relations and the arrest of the ambassador and his party. See Armando Cortesão's introduction to the *Suma Oriental.*

3. *Lopo Soares de Albergaria:* Succeeded Afonso de Albuquerque as governor of India in 1515 and devoted most of his three years in office to undoing many of the farsighted programs introduced by his predecessor. He is remembered for his disastrous expedition to the Red Sea in 1517, and for the construction of a fortress in Ceylon in 1518. Also, it was during his administration that the first royal squadron visited China.

Chapter 66

1. *Pulo Hinhor:* Pinto applies this unidentified toponym to three different islands, located at considerable distances from each other: in chapter 50, to an island in the Gulf of Tonkin; in chapters 66 and 67, to an island off the coast of China, near Ning-po; and in chapters 145–47, to an island in the Bay of Bengal, off the coast of Tenasserim. *Pulo* is the Malay word for "island."

2. *Hirado:* Island off the northwest coast of Kyushu, Japan. It was the first trading port opened to European vessels: to the Portuguese, circa 1550 to 1639, when they were driven out by Iyemitsu; to the Dutch, 1610 to 1641, when they were transferred to Deshima; to the English, who had a factory there from 1613 to 1624.

3. *Santarém:* City in west central Portugal, on the right bank of the Tagus River, about forty-five miles northeast of Lisbon.

4. *city of Ning-po:* See chapter 40, note 5 above. Pinto's description of a Portuguese enclave in Ning-po is believed to be highly exaggerated. While it is true that the Portuguese carried on a more or less clandestine trade along the coasts of Chekiang and Fukien for some thirty-five years before settling down in Macao (1557), no trace of such an enclave in Ning-po has ever been found. For more information on the subject, see William C. Milne, "Notes of a Seven Months' Residence in the City of Ningpo," *Chinese Repository* (Canton) 13, no. 7 (1844): 338–57; Donald W. Ferguson, "Letters from Portuguese Captives in Canton, Written in 1534 and 1536," *Indian Antiquary* (Bombay) 30 (October 1901): 439–41; Henri Cordier, "L'Arrivée des Portugais en Chine," *T'oung Pao,* 2d ser., 12 (1911): 483–543; L. da Cunha Gonçalves, "A famosa cidade de Liampó segundo Fernão Mendes Pinto e a verdade histórica," *O Instituto,* 4th ser., 75–76 (1928): 113–20; and Albert Kammerer, "La Découverte de la Chine par les Portugais au XVIème siècle et la cartographie des portulans," *T'oung Pao,* 2d ser., 39, supplement (1944): 71–82. Also of interest is Lagoa's article, "A Dupla Liampó das crónicas portuguesas," *Anais da Junta de Investigações Coloniais* (Lisbon, 1950), in which he claims that Pinto uses the toponym Liampó (or Ning-po) to refer indifferently to two different cities, one the river port of Ning-

po, and the other the seaport of Chin-Hai, at the mouth of the Yung River, the latter being the one visited by Pinto in this chapter.

Chapter 67

1. *Gates of Ning-po:* Z. Volpicelli identifies the Gates of Ning-po with the islands forming the Blackwell Channel. He also places the Portuguese settlement of Ning-po at Chin-Hai, twelve miles from the seaport of Ning-po, on Hangchow Bay. See his "Early Portuguese Commerce and Settlements in China," *Journal of the China Branch of the Royal Asiatic Society,* 2d ser. 27 (1892): 69. See chapter 66, note 4 above.

2. *death of the king of China:* The emperor Chia-Ching died in 1567 and not in 1541.

3. *Prechau Muão:* See chapter 36, note 9 above.

4. *Oeiras:* Town on the right bank of the Tagus River, about ten miles below Lisbon.

Chapter 68

1. *panoura:* The word appears to be of Malay origin, but Dalgado is unable to identify it. It is not used by any of the Portuguese chroniclers of the period, nor is it mentioned by Yule and Burnell. In this chapter it is used in the sense of a "ceremonial weapon or sword." Elsewhere, Pinto uses the same word for a ship.

2. *Tristão de Gá:* Not to be confused with the Tristão de Gá mentioned in chapter 20 (see chap. 20, n. 3 above).

3. *Farias:* One of the oldest and noblest families of Portugal, which traces its ancestry back to the founding of the nation in the twelfth century. Of course, we have no way of knowing if the pirate Antonio was a member of that family or if the author is speaking tongue in cheek. The tableau described by Pinto depicts the death of the most famous member of the Faria family, a Nuno Gonçalves de Faria, who was captured and slain by the Castilians while defending his country in the year 1373, an episode that has been romanticized in Portuguese poetry and prose, as a symbol of patriotism, down to modern times. The other Farias that appear in the book, Francisco, Pero, and Alvaro, are indeed historical figures.

4. *Spain:* In this instance, Spain means the Iberian peninsula.

Chapter 69

1. *péla:* A type of public entertainment in which the dancer practices certain movements of the head and arms while leaping in the air, like a ball.

Chapter 70

1. *Mateus de Brito:* A Mateus de Brito was taken prisoner by the Chinese, probably off Fukien, in the year 1548 or 1549, and later sent to Canton, where he was ransomed in 1556 by the Jesuit father Melchior Nunes Barreto. In a letter written from Macao on 23 November 1555, Father Melchior describes his efforts to ransom Mateus de Brito, along with several other Portuguese held by the Chinese. Pinto himself, who accompanied the father on one of his trips to Canton, mentions the ransoming of Mateus de Brito in a letter from Macao, dated 20 November 1555. Upon his release from prison, Mateus de Brito wrote a report on China ("Informação da China"), which was sent by the Jesuits, via Malacca, to Portugal. See Jack M. Braga, "Some Portuguese Captives in China," *Mosaico* (Macao) 1, no. 1 (September 1950), 112–16. See also Rebecca Catz, *Cartas,* document 9, 59–65 (Pinto's letter), and document 10, 65–73 (Melchior's letter).

2. *Lançarote Pereira:* In this chapter Pinto introduces a Lançarote Pereira who is a distinguished member of the Portuguese enclave of Ning-po (1541?). In chapters 140 and 221 he

places the blame for the destruction of that enclave (1548–49?) on a Lançarote Pereira, described as a native of the town of Ponte de Lima in Portugal. Castanheda, alone of all the Portuguese chroniclers, mentions a Lançarote Pereira (vol. 2, bk. 9, 902) who was one of the captains in the armada sent to the Red Sea (1539) by the viceroy Garcia de Noronha to destroy some Turkish ships said to be anchored there. Other modern sources consulted repeat Pinto's version of the destruction of the Portuguese enclave of Ning-po, owing to the high-handed conduct of Lançarote Pereira, or deny its existence as a year-round settlement.

3. *Prechau Muhão:* For *prechau,* see chapter 36, note 9 above. Also, *Muhão* is spelled *Muão* in chapter 67.

4. *Chiang Mai:* Or Chieng Mai. Province of northwest Thailand and name of capital city located on the upper course of the Ping River about eighty miles east of the Burma border. Formerly the capital of a united Lao kingdom, later subject to Burma.

5. *Similau:* The pirate killed by Antonio de Faria in chapter 40 was also named Similau.

6. *Calempluy:* An island never identified with any certainty, but vaguely placed in Korea by some investigators, among them Lagoa (*Glossário*) and A. J. H. Charignon and M. Médard (*A propos des voyages aventureux de Fernand Mendez Pinto,* [Peking: Imprimerie des Lazaristes, 1935], 138–45), and by E. H. Parker, who informs us that Korea was once called Kalo or Kara ("Pinto in Corea," *China Review* (Hongkong) 16, no. 3 (November–December 1887): 182)

Chapter 71

1. *panoura:* See chapter 68, note 1 above.

Chapter 72

1. *sea horse:* Pinto is obviously referring to the fabulous horselike marine animal, with the foreparts of a horse and the tail of a fish, like the steeds depicted in ancient art, drawing the chariots of Neptune and Proteus. Also, the name was formerly applied to the hippopotamus. Interestingly enough, the word was omitted from all the seventeenth-century translations (with the exception of the Spanish), and in a recent Portuguese edition of Pinto's book (Lisbon, 1983), it carried the following footnote: "Name also applied to the hippopotamus. I don't see why Mendes Pinto mentions them here since they do not exist in the Orient."

2. *Alimania:* Old name for Germany. Pinto's reference to a province called *Alimania* is not as incredible as it seems. Boxer writes that the Chinese characters representing the sound of the word (*A-lu-mang-ni-a*) are shown in the extreme northwest corner of Europe on a Chinese world map of 1300. Moreover, the idea that China, or at any rate, Tartary, bordered on Germany was widespread among the Portuguese in Asia at that time. See Boxer, *South China,* 71–72, 71 nn. 2, 3.

Chapter 73

1. *bada:* See chapter 41, note 5 above.

2. *caleu:* Dalgado is unable to identify this word, which he thinks might mean "wolf," but he spells it *calem* (*calens* in the plural), though in the 1614 *princeps* edition it is very clearly printed *caleus* (*caleu* in the singular) and not *calens.*

3. *Pocasser:* Armando Cortesão writes that Pinto's *Pocasser* seems to correspond to Chinkiang, a port city of Kiangsu Province, east China, on the south bank of the Yangtze, forty-three miles below Nanking at the junction of the Grand Canal with the river. However, he quotes the sinologist A. C. Moule, who has assured him that "in the sixteenth century Chinkiang was not called anything like *Pocasser.* The only loop-hole is that some towns occasionally had popular names which have not been recorded in the official histories." See Cortesão, *Suma Oriental,* lv, lvi n. 2.

4. *Nan-t'ou:* Or Lantau, Nantoo, Nantó, as it is called by other early Portuguese writers, is Nan-t'ou or Nam-t'au (Cantonese pronunciation), an important town in the San On (Hsien-an) District, where a military post was located. See Jack M. Braga, "The 'Tamão' of the Portuguese Pioneers," *T'ien Sha Monthly* (May 1939): 428–29, and T'ien-tse Chang, *Sino-Portuguese Trade from 1514 to 1644,* (Leyden: E. J. Brill, 1933), 41, 116.

5. *catties:* See chapter 18, note 5 above.

Chapter 75

1. *almud:* Or *almude,* from the Arabic *al-mudd.* A measure of dry or liquid capacity in Portugal, Brazil, and other countries, varying widely in dimensions, from about two to thirty-two quarts.

Chapter 77

1. *talagrepo:* Pinto uses this word frequently with reference to the Buddhist monks of China and Indochina, but the usually dependable Dalgado is unable to trace the etymology of the word and its compounds. For a discussion of the possible derivations, none of them certain, see *Manrique* 1 : 223 n. 5.

2. *menigrepo:* As the text implies, a Buddhist monk of a lesser category than the *tala-grepo* (see n. 1 above). In this instance, Dalgado suggests a possible derivation for the first part of the word, *meni-,* from the Siamese *mo'hinn,* meaning "great, powerful," or *mo'n,* "to disdain worldly matters." For his explanation of *grepo,* see chapter 78, note 3 below. Other possible derivations are discussed in *Manrique* 1 : 223 n. 5.

Chapter 78

1. *bonze:* A term long applied by Europeans in China to the Buddhist clergy, but originating with early visitors to Japan. It has been suggested by Yule, Dalgado, and others, that the Japanese term *bonzi,* or *bonzo,* corresponds to the Chinese *fan-seng,* "a religious person," or *fa-sze,* "teacher of the Law," pronounced "bo-zi" in Japanese. For a more recent explanation, see Tai Whan Kim, "O étimo do Português 'Bonzo,'" *Anais do XIV Colóquio de Estudos Luso-Brasileiros* (1980): 90–97.

2. *Amida:* The Japanese name for the Buddha Amitabha (infinite light) or Amitâyus (infinite life). Devotion to Amida or Amitabha, which first developed in China, gave rise in Japan to a special branch of Buddhism called Amidism. For further details, see Masaharu Anesaki, *History of Japanese Religion,* 3d ed. (Rutland, Vt., and Tokyo: Charles E. Tuttle Co., 1966), 148.

3. *grepo:* See compound forms (with *talagrepo* and *menigrepo*) in chapter 77, notes 1 and 2 above. Dalgado believes this is a general term for a Buddhist priest and suggests a possible derivation from the Siamese *khru* (Pali *garu,* from the Sanskrit *guru*), meaning a "religious preceptor," and from *pho,* meaning "father." See also *Manrique* 1 : 223 n. 5.

Chapter 80

1. *Ponte de Lima:* Small town in the province of Minho, in northern Portugal, located on the banks of the Lima River.

Chapter 81

1. *aytao:* From the Chinese *haitao, hai-tô,* or *hai-tao-fu-shih,* commander of the provincial coast-guard fleet, or "general of the sea of Kwangtung Province." Sometimes translated as

"commissioner of the sea route" and sometimes as "admiral." The Portuguese also used the forms *aytão, haytao,* etc.

Chapter 83

1. *nivator:* Though Pinto uses this word with reference to China, Dalgado says that the word is certainly not Chinese. He suggests a possible borrowing from the Concani *niphatar,* the name of a bird of Goa, which is not a pheasant but which Pinto may have seen or heard of in Goa.

Chapter 84

1. *chumbim:* Initially, Dalgado attributes the same meaning to this word as does Pinto, i.e., "a magistrate or judge in China," and gives *hing-ming* as the etymology of the word. But in the supplement to his *Glossário* he quotes the French sinologue, Paul Pelliot, who gives *tsong-ping* as the etymology. However, Armando Cortesão, in discussing the meanings of various Chinese words used by the old Portuguese writers, injects a word of caution when he writes, "The question as to what Chinese expressions are meant by these old Portuguese versions has been a matter of controversy and it is still not quite settled." See *Suma Oriental,* xxxiii n. 1.

2. *chaem:* See chapter 45, note 5 above.

Chapter 85

1. *gerozemo:* Dalgado believes that Pinto borrowed this word not from the Chinese, but from the Japanese *gero-sama,* which means "jailer."

2. *ferucua:* In this instance Dalgado writes that "if the word is really Chinese, it must come from *pwan-sze-kwan,* 'judge,' or from *kwan-fu,* 'magistrate,' with a transposition of terms."

3. *German:* See chapter 72, note 2 above. The Portuguese word for German is *alemão.*

4. *Batampina:* Armando Cortesão identifies this toponym with the Yangtze Kiang River (*Suma Oriental,* lv).

Chapter 86

1. *conchaci:* In this chapter Pinto uses the words *conchacis* and *conchalins* in the sense of "judge or magistrate," which Dalgado says may be derived from the Chinese *kwan-chah-sz'* or *-li.* However, with particular reference to these Chinese expressions, Cortesão writes that Dalgado's conclusions "must be taken with all reserve" (*Suma Oriental,* xxxiii n. 1).

2. *conchalins:* See note 1 above.

Chapter 87

1. *fifteenth year:* In chapter 86, Pinto dates the letter from the "defenders of the poor" on the seventh day of the fourth moon in the twenty-third year of the reign of the emperor. Here, in chapter 87, he dates the response to this letter on the ninth day of the seventh moon in the fifteenth year of the reign of the emperor—or eight years earlier. Whatever the reason for the discrepancy, whether intentional or accidental, it should be pointed out that the Ming emperor Chia-ching reigned from 1522 to 1566 and that, in any case, the dates of both these letters are inconsistent with the events described by Pinto, which presumably took place in the year 1542, when the shipwreck occurred (chap. 79) that cast him and his companions ashore on the coast of China.

Chapter 88

1. *Tamerlane:* Also known as Timur-Leng (Timur the Lame), Timour, Timur, and Tamburlaine. The reference is, of course, to the Mongol conqueror who held sway from the Euphrates to the Ganges in 1387 and who died in 1405, while planning an invasion of China. However, in Europe his name was applied, as a title, to his successors, which is what Pinto has done here.

2. *Cuy:* Menangkui, Menangkuwi, or Meng Kuwi, on the west coast of the Gulf of Siam.

3. *Sansim:* The province of Shensi, the characters for which are pronounced "shasi." In English it is written Shensi for the province in northwest China, simply in order to distinguish it from Shansi, the province in north China, separated by the Yellow River where it flows north-south. See Cortesão, *Suma Oriental,* 126 n. 1.

4. *river that overflowed its banks in the year 1556:* Pinto is referring to a natural disaster that occurred in China during the great earthquake of January 1556, about which he has more to say in chapter 222. The Dominican missionary, Gaspar da Cruz, devotes the last chapter of his *Tratado das cousas da China* (1569) to the series of natural disasters that occurred in China during the years 1555–56. For an English version, see Boxer's *South China,* 223–27.

5. *Cosmim:* Or *Cosmin.* According to Yule and Burnell, this name was given by many travelers in the sixteenth and seventeenth centuries to a port on the western side of the Irrawaddy Delta, which must have been near Bassein, if not identical with it. But the exact site seems lost.

6. *Shah Tahmasp:* (1514–76), shah of Persia (1524–76), who succeeded to the throne when a mere boy. Unfortunately for him, he was a contemporary of Suleiman the Magnificent, who repeatedly invaded Persia. Continual warfare during the reign of Tahmasp brought about internal decline.

7. *Sophy:* The name by which the king of Persia was long known in Europe, in the same way that the sultan of Turkey was known as the "Grand Turk," and the king of Delhi as the "Great Mogul." This title represented Sufi, Safavi, or Safi, the name of the dynasty that reigned over Persia for more than two centuries (1449–1722, nominally to 1736).

Chapter 89

1. *upo:* Dalgado believes this word is Chinese and that Pinto is using it correctly, but at the same time he cites other authorities who disagree with him.

Chapter 90

1. *Junquileu:* Armando Cortesão believes that Pinto's *Junquileu* may correspond to a small town—Wei-Ch'ueh-Lou in English—between Fanshui and Paoying, about fifty-six miles from Shaopo (*Suma Oriental,* lvii). Interestingly enough, this town, spelled *Janquileu,* is also mentioned in the *Commentaries of the Great Afonso Dalboquerque* (Afonso de Albuquerque, ed. and trans. Walter de Gray Birch [London: Hakluyt Society, 1875–84], vol. 3, chap. 30, 134), from which Pinto may have copied this portion of his narrative, though Cortesão thinks it was the other way around, giving as his reason the fact that the *Commentaries* were first published in 1557 (while Pinto was still in Asia) and that he did not begin to write his book until about 1569 or 1570. Cortesão is more inclined to believe that Pinto's companions, or even Pinto indirectly, had supplied the information used by the author of the *Commentaries.*

2. *description of the mausoleum:* Described in Albuquerque, *Commentaries* (vol. 3, chap. 30, 134), as a "sepulchre surrounded by steps of lateen."

3. *Tuan Hassan Mudeliar:* Or *Trannocem Mudeliar.* Name of the Malay Ambassador sent to China by the ex-king of Malacca, to ask the Chinese emperor, of whom he was nominally a

vassal, to help him regain his kingdom, from which he had been ousted by the Portuguese in 1511. Pinto's spelling of the name probably represents Tuan (from the Malay, meaning "lord or master;" see chap. 34, n. 1 above) Nassim Mudeliar, or possibly, as Cortesão suggests (*Suma Oriental*, lvi n. 1), Tuan Hassan Mudeliar. In Barros, it appears as Tuam Mahamed (Barros and Couto, déc. 3, bk. 6, chap. 1).

4. *Afonso de Albuquerque:* Governor of Portuguese India (1509–15), whose farsighted policies and military genius laid the foundation for the Portuguese overseas empire. He first went to India in 1503, and again in 1506, carrying secret instructions to supersede the viceroy Francisco de Almeida. Albuquerque had forts built at Goa, Calicut, Malacca, and Hormuz; reconstructed those at Cannanore and Cochin; began shipbuilding and other industries in Portuguese India; and established good relations with the rulers of Southeast Asia. He was a just and honest governor, widely respected and feared throughout the East. The main goals of his policy—control over the sources of spices and of the trade routes—were nearly attained during his brief tenure of office.

5. *inscription:* Cf. Albuquerque, *Commentaries* (vol. 3, chap. 30, 134), in which the inscription on the tombstone or mausoleum is almost the same.

6. *fate of the Malay ambassador:* Cf. version of the death of the Malay ambassador in *Commentaries* (ibid.), in which the author, son of Afonso de Albuquerque, attributes the ambassador's death to sheer grief over the failure of his mission and to the demise of his wife. Also, as pointed out by Brito Rebello (2:76 n. 1) and Cortesão (*Suma Oriental*, lvi n. 1), the voyage of the Malay ambassador to China had been made about thirty, not forty, years before, since Malacca was captured by Albuquerque in 1511. Barros writes (Barros and Couto, déc. 3, bk. 2, chap. 7, 195) that it was not unusual for an ambassador to die on the way to Peking, since the journey was long and arduous. Generally, he would be buried in a sumptuous tomb with an inscription giving his name and that of the person he was representing. Regarding Malacca's tributary relationship with China, see J. J. L. Duyvendak, "The True Dates of the Chinese Maritime Expeditions in the Early Fifteenth Century," *T'oung Pao*, 2d ser., 34 (1938): 341–99.

Chapter 91

1. *Sampitay:* Armando Cortesão (*Suma Oriental*, lv) deduces from Pinto's account that *Sampitay* corresponds to the present town of P'ei chou or Hsin-p'ei-chou, a place near the northern limit of Kiangsu Province at latitude 34°25′ north, longitude 118°6′ east; and on page lviii he makes a fairly strong argument in support of this identification.

2. *Tomé Pires:* See chapter 65, note 1 above.

3. *one of our captains was to blame:* The captain referred to here is Simão Peres de Andrade, who arrived in China two years after his brother, Diogo Peres de Andrade (see chap. 65, no. 2 above), had brought Tomé Pires's embassy to China and whose prudence and diplomacy made a good impression on the Chinese. In contrast to his brother, Simão Peres de Andrade was a man of violent character and little tact. Historians agree that his high-handed behavior was in great part responsible for the failure of the embassy.

4. *Vasco Calvo:* Pinto was mistaken in referring to Vasco Calvo as a member of the ill-fated embassy. Actually, he was a merchant who arrived in China on board a ship commanded by his brother Diogo Calvo, at the time that the Chinese had hardened their attitude toward the Portuguese. He was arrested while trading ashore but claimed to be a member of the embassy in the hope of obtaining diplomatic immunity. In 1524 he managed to get a letter out of China in which he describes the harsh imprisonment of the Portuguese and says that the ambassador Tomé Pires had died that same year. His letter, along with that of Cristóvão Vieira, another Portuguese prisoner, was published by Donald W. Ferguson in "Letters from Portuguese Captives," *Indian Antiquary* 30 (October–November 1901): 421–51, 467–91, and 31 (January–February 1902): 10–32, 53–65. In his introduction to the *Suma Oriental*, Armando Cortesão has shown that both these letters were written in 1524 and not 1534 and 1536 as Ferguson mistakenly

thought (xlv–xlviii). A fragment of the original of Vasco Calvo's letter (Ferguson had used a Paris copy) was published by E. A. Voretzsch in "Documento acerca da primeira embaixada à China," *Boletim da Sociedade Luso-Japonesa* 1 (1929): 50–69. Also, Barros made use of these letters in his *Décadas* (déc. 3, bk. 6, chap. 2, 24). See chapter 116 below, in which Pinto describes his meeting with Vasco Calvo.

5. *Alcochete:* Ancient town in the district of Setúbal, located on the left bank of the Tagus River, eight miles from Lisbon.

Chapter 92

1. *Germany:* See chapter 72, note 2 above.

2. *Turbão:* In chapters 15 and 16, *Turbão* appears as the name of a town in Sumatra. See chapter 15, note 8 above.

3. *Gizom:* From the Japanese *Jizoo,* one of the Bodhisattvas or titular gods of Japanese Buddhism, protector of children.

4. *laulé:* Dalgado is not sure of the provenance of this word but suggests the Malay words *lalai* or *laley,* both of which refer to various parts of a vessel; or the Burmese *hlay-loung,* meaning "canoe or dugout."

5. *jangá:* Pinto seems to be the only writer of the period to use this word for a vessel of the Far East. A similar word, *joangá,* is used elsewhere by Pinto (see chap. 32, n. 1) for a vessel of the Moluccas. However, Dalgado believes that the word *jangá* comes from the Malay *changgah,* meaning "a boat hook or grapple," and points out that many of the names of Malaysian vessels are derived from some particular circumstance or peculiarity.

Chapter 94

1. *coat of arms:* Pinto makes several references to the lion on a sphere as a coat of arms, and to the emperor as the "Crowned Lion on the Throne of the World." If there was anything resembling a heraldic or national symbol in Ming China, it most certainly was a representation of the dragon—especially the five-clawed dragon—and not the lion, which was a European symbol. See Justus Doolittle, *Social Life of the Chinese,* (New York: Harper & Brothers, 1865), 2:264–65.

2. *Peking:* I do not know where Pinto got his version of the founding of Peking, but there is no doubt that the history of the city, on the site of Peking, goes back to very old times, for it had been the capital of the kingdom of Yen prior to 222 B.C. when it was captured by the prince of the Ch'in (or T'sin) dynasty. According to Yule (*Marco Polo* 1: 375 n. 1), it was given the name of Yen-ling in the year 1013. As for the founding of the empire, it is interesting to compare Martin de Rada's version, taken from Chinese chronicles he claims to have seen, containing what he calls "scores of fables." Yet at the same time he adds, "If this history is true, they began to have kings shortly after the Flood." See the "Relation of Fr. Martin de Rada," in Boxer's *South China,* 278–82.

Chapter 95

1. *the reigning Chinese king:* The construction of the Great Wall of China is usually attributed to the emperor Shih Huang Ti of the Ch'in dynasty (221–210 B.C.), but that is not quite correct. As a matter of fact, the work was done in sections, parts of it built before his time, and a great many people had a hand in it. But he had the existing portions improved and added to, and it was he who made one great whole out of what was but a series of sections before the Chinese empire was unified. He was also responsible for the construction of the underground army of terra-cotta soldiers built to guard his tomb near Sian, in Shensi province. Discovered in 1974, it is undoubtedly the most spectacular archeological find of the twentieth century.

2. *jau:* See chapter 41, note 7 above. The wall extended for about fifteen hundred miles.

3. *Chanfacau:* Or *Chang-hai-koan,* which is actually the name of one of the fortified gates of the wall, on the east side. The wall itself is called *Wan-li-chang-ching.* For a description of the wall, see Robert Silverberg, *The Great Wall of China* (Philadelphia: Chilton Books, 1965) or Jonathan Fryer, *The Great Wall of China* (London: New English Library, 1975). Of particular interest, for its many illustrations, is William Edgar Geil's *The Great Wall of China* (New York: Sturgis & Walton Co., 1909).

4. *Khorasanis:* A people of Khorasan or Khurasan, today a region of northeast Iran, which at one time extended from Russia to Afghanistan.

5. *Gizares:* A people of Al-Jazira, a region of upper Mesopotamia, in the Tigris and Euphrates valley, northwest of Baghdad.

6. *not . . . good soldiers:* This opinion was shared by many Europeans for centuries. Boxer (*South China,* lxxvii n. 4) cites a letter written to King Philip II in January of 1574, in which the writer, a Fernando Riquel, goes so far as to say that China, despite its large population, could be subjected with less than sixty good Spanish soldiers.

7. *totally lacking in heavy artillery:* This assertion is not true. The Chinese did have artillery, but it was inferior to the best European artillery of the period.

Chapter 96

1. *Chinese conquest renounced:* Similar statements are to be found in Barros (Barros and Couto, déc. 3, bk. 2, chap. 7, 196) and other writers of the period, though without the fanciful names and dates given by Pinto. However, at that time the Portuguese never fully understood the nature of the Chinese tributary system, which began less than a century before they arrived in India and arose, not out of conquest, but respect. In the early part of the fifteenth century the Ming emperor Yung-lo sent out a number of maritime expeditions under the able command of an ambitious eunuch of the court named Cheng-ho. During the years 1405–33, the Chinese made seven voyages, touching at the harbors of the South Pacific, the Bay of Bengal, and the Indian Ocean, and sailing as far as the Persian Gulf, the Red Sea, and the east African coast. These enigmatic expeditions were designed, not to encourage trade or to make conquests in the sense that the Portuguese understood the word, but to satisfy the luxurious tastes and curiosity of the imperial court, while at the same time enhancing the emperor's prestige and ministering to the ambitions of the eunuchs. Many ambassadors came to China bringing tribute, engaging in trade, and at times requesting and receiving military assistance. The tribute bearers undoubtedly received more than they gave, and the system resulted in a heavy drain on Chinese treasure and manpower. Upon the death of Yung-lo, his successor put a sudden stop to the overseas expeditions and issued a decree—which was often disobeyed—forbidding his nationals from leaving the country. For a discussion of these Chinese voyages, see J. J. L. Duyvendak; G. B. Sansom, *The Western World and Japan* (New York: Alfred A. Knopf, 1951), 141–45; and Daniel J. Boorstin, *The Discoverers* (New York: Random House, 1983), 186–201.

Chapter 97

1. city council: This is obviously a European concept. There was nothing resembling a city council in Ming China.

2. *panoura:* See chapter 68, note 1 above.

3. *ducks:* Cf. Pinto's description of the raising and selling of ducks in China with that of Gaspar da Cruz in chapter 9 of his *Tratado da China.*

Chapter 98

1. *dogs:* The original has *gozo,* a common breed of dogs with short legs and a long body.

2. *fertilizer:* "Night soil" is still used today in China.

3. *chandeu:* From the Chinese *chin-hu* (there is no *d* in Chinese), meaning a "fair or bazaar."

4. *guedé:* From the Malay *gaeng,* meaning a "dugout or flatboat."

5. *Bitampina:* Spelled *Bitampina* in the *princeps* edition of 1614. Elsewhere it appears as *Batampina.*

Chapter 99

1. *pitaleu:* Pinto uses this word in the sense of "animal trainer or acrobat," for which, according to Dalgado, the Chinese word is *kin-tan-wang.*

2. *mongiloto:* From the Chinese *mun-wei-li-to,* meaning a procurator or attorney authorized and employed to act for and manage the affairs of others.

3. *bubo:* An inflammatory swelling of a lymph gland in the groin or armpit. In the sixteenth century the term was also applied to venereal diseases.

4. *Peregrination:* The book was originally published under the title, *The Peregrination of Fernão Mendes Pinto. . . .*

5. *unspeakable sin:* Sodomy.

Chapter 100

1. *9 October 1541:* This date conflicts with that given in chapter 79, where we are told that the shipwreck that cast the protagonist on the shores of China occurred on Monday, 5 August 1542.

2. *pilanga:* From the Chinese *ping-liu,* meaning, according to Dalgado, "military tribunal."

Chapter 103

1. *caladigão:* From the Chinese *ta-li-sz'-king,* meaning "high tribunal," according to Dalgado.

2. *executions:* According to the early accounts of Portuguese prisoners in China, capital punishment was inflicted in the form of beheading, once a year, at the autumn assizes, after the death sentence had been confirmed by the emperor. Once confirmed, it was actually carried out in small numbers and was often delayed for many years. However, most of the prisoners died of hunger, cold, or the lash, which was cruelly inflicted. See Boxer, *South China,* 18–23, 176–180. For the many other forms of punishment and torture, both official and unofficial, see Doolittle, which is profusely illustrated.

3. *gigauhós:* In chapter 73 above, Pinto refers to the *Gigauhós* as a monstrous race of people whom he meets on the voyage to *Calempluy.*

4. *reign of the Son of Heaven:* The fifteenth year of the reign of the emperor Chia-ching (1522–66) would place the action in the year 1537. This is the same emperor said to have died in chapter 67.

5. *continão:* Probably derived from the Chinese *kwa-ti-nien,* meaning "prosecutor," according to Dalgado.

6. *Quansy:* Possibly Kansu, a province of north central China, a great part of which is traversed by the west end of the Great Wall. Under the Ming emperors (1368–1644) it was part of Shensi Province, but was made a separate province in 1911. However, this toponym has

never been identified with any degree of certainty. See hypotheses offered by Lagoa in his "Peregrinação" 89–91.

7. *monteo:* Elsewhere Pinto used the term *monteo* with particular reference to a Siamese official. See chapter 33, note 3 above.

Chapter 104

1. *Tartar invasion:* See chapters 117–23 below.

Chapter 105

1. *latitude:* The latitude of 41° north is not too far from the mark. Modern atlases situate the city of Peking in latitude 39°54' north and longitude 116°28' east, but it was not until the seventeenth century that a method was devised for fixing longitude.

2. *with my own eyes:* It is doubtful that Pinto ever saw Peking with his own eyes. His description is not to be trusted any more than that of some of his compatriots who, like him, were in China, but based their accounts on hearsay. A full and detailed description of the city was given by the Jesuit Father Gabriel de Magalhães in his *Doze excellencias da China,* written in 1668 and published posthumously, in French, under the title *Nouvelle relation de la Chine* (Paris, 1688) and in English (London, 1688) as *A New History of China.*

3. *homes of the local administrators:* These were the "yamen" or "yamun," as they came to be called in English, which served both as office and official residence of the public functionaries or mandarins, but it is doubtful that they numbered sixteen hundred.

4. *thirty-two kingdoms:* There were fifteen provinces in Ming China, all under the direct control of the central government. However, whenever an emergency arose, a *tu-t'ang* (Pinto's *tutão*) was sent by Peking to govern the province for as long as the emergency lasted. The Portuguese called these high officials "viceroys," which may explain why Pinto refers to the provinces, thirty-two or otherwise, as "kingdoms." See Boxer, *South China,* 5–6.

5. *general assembly of the estates:* There never was anything in China resembling the estates general, which was a European institution.

6. *panoura:* See chapter 68, note 1 above.

7. *mainato:* From the Tamil-Malayal *mainatta,* meaning a "washerman." The *mainatos* were of a low caste in India who did the washing for the entire community, but the term was widely used by the Portuguese throughout Asia.

8. *religious sects . . . empire:* There were three main religious sects in China, namely, Confucianism, Buddhism, and Taoism, though there were many popular deities to whom sacrifices were performed in both private homes and temples. Confucianism, though essentially a moral code, was the official state religion down to the twentieth century. Though Pinto speaks of thirty-two sects, the renowned Jesuit scholar and missionary Matteo Ricci (1552–1610), who was the first to explain the differences between these three main religious sects to the West, writes that "under these three captions, one could number nearer to three hundred different and disparate sects." See *China in the Sixteenth Century: The Journals of Matthew Ricci, 1583–1610,* 2d ed., trans. Louis J. Gallagher (New York: Random House, 1953), 104.

9. *bracalões* (*bracalão,* sing.): Pinto uses this word with relation to Siam and China in the sense of a "high dignitary" or "minister or counsellor of state." From the Siamese *boromo,* "royal, preeminent," and *kromo,* "minister."

10. *lauteá:* A title of respect used for high Chinese officials in general, in the sense of "sir, lord." The term is derived from the Amoy vernacular *ló-tia,* or the Chaun-chou form *lau-tia,* meaning "venerable father."

11. *xipatom:* In chapters 105 and 106 this word is used in the sense of "manager of a banquet hall," which Dalgado says is derived from the Chinese *xi-fan-táu.* However, in chapter 115 it is used as the title of a courtroom official, and in chapters 122 and 221 it is used as a place-name.

Chapter 106

1. *ponchacys:* Also spelled *puchancys*. From the Chinese *pu-chêng-shih*. Originally a civil governor and comptroller, whose functions later became essentially those of a provincial treasurer.

2. *graduation:* The Chinese had a highly standarized national system of education comprising central and local schools of different levels, and an examination system connecting school education with civil service appointments. The five recognized Confucian classics formed the chief substance of the curriculum and were concerned primarily with the cultivation of good moral character, since the main purpose of higher education was the preparation of officials. They were chosen on the basis of an examination system known as *K'e Chu,* the foundation for which was laid in the T'ang dynasty (A.D. 618–907). See Howard S. Galt, *A History of Chinese Educational Institutions* (London: Arthur Probsthain, 1951), 1: 204, 236, 241, 363, 385. For a more detailed description of the examination system, which was followed down to the closing years of the Ch'ing dynasty (1905), see Doolittle, vol. 1, chaps. 15–17.

3. *peretanda:* From the Malay *pretanda,* meaning (according to Dalgado), "an early day magistrate, hangman, or a cruel person." This word would be more applicable to the lictors who cleared the way than to the men who carried the umbrellas of state before the officer, whose rank could be ascertained by the color and the number of flounces on the umbrellas. See Doolittle 1: 299.

4. *streets would be cleared:* Those who shouted to the crowds to go home were the lictors (see n. 3 above) who, according to Doolittle, were in the habit of "beating unceremoniously and unmercifully" anyone who did not hasten to comply (1: 300).

5. *highways:* Pinto may have been echoing Galeote Pereira, Gaspar da Cruz, and others before him who praised the roads and highways they saw in southern China, but as for those of Peking, Ricci writes, "Very few of the streets in Pekin are paved with brick or stone, and it is difficult to say which season of the year is more objectionable for walking" (310).

Chapter 107

1. *Tauris:* Ancient name of Tabriz, city in northwest Iran, second in size to Teheran. For centuries an important commercial city, of which early travelers have left glowing accounts. Became Persian under Shah Abbas I in 1618.

2. *Amadabad:* Or Ahmadabad, Ahmedabad. City and capital of Gujerat State (formed 1960), 290 miles north of Bombay. Founded in 1411 by Ahmad I of Gujarat on site of previous Hindu cities. At its height in the fifteenth century as capital of Gujerat kingdom. Declined 1512–72, but revived under the Moghul emperors 1572–1709.

3. *Bisnaga:* Bisnagar, Beejanugger, or Vijayanagar. These and other forms stand for the name of the ancient city and capital of the most important Hindu kingdom in India during the later Middle Ages. The city, located thirty-six miles northwest of Bellary, is now known as Humpy (or Hampi) and is entirely in ruins. Both the city and the kingdom were commonly called by the early Portuguese Narsinga, from Narasimha (1490?–1508), who was king at the time of their first arrival.

4. *Narsinga:* See chapter 9, note 1 above.

5. *Gour:* Gaur, Laknauti, or Lakhnaoti. Ancient city, medieval capital (1200?–1340, 1455–1563) of Bengal, about 163 miles north of Calcutta. It was the residence of a Hindu dynasty at the time of the early Mohammedan invasions (end of twelfth century), and was popularly known as Lakhnaoti. Gour was afterwards the residence of several Mussulman dynasties, famed for its size and splendor.

6. *Ava:* Today, a ruined city on the Irawaddy River, Upper Burma, six miles southwest of Mandalay. Founded in 1364, it was the capital of Burma for four hundred years, replaced by Amarapura in 1783, and again the capital 1823–37.

7. *Chaleu:* Mentioned in early maps, which place it between Ava and Prome on the Irawaddy River. It appears to have been a subordinate principality at one time, though here and in subsequent chapters Pinto speaks of the "kingdom of *Chaleu.*" See *Manrique* 1:238 n. 9.

8. *Timplão in Calaminhan:* See chapter 41, note 12 above.

9. *Martaban:* The city of Martaban, situated on the mouth of the Salween River, in southeast Lower Burma, is of great antiquity and was formerly an entrepôt of great importance, much disputed by Burma, Pegu, and Siam. At the time the Portuguese became acquainted with it, it was under the Talaing king of Pegu. In chapters 147–53 Pinto gives us a detailed description of the siege and sack of Martaban by the Burmese. It never recovered from the destruction of 1540, and in later times its place was taken by Moulmein on the southeast bank of the Salween estuary.

10. *Bagou in Pegu:* The Burmese name for Pegu is Bagó, which belongs to the Talaing language. The form Pegu appears to come through the Malays who called it Paigu. Pinto may have heard both names and is confusing the two. See chapter 20, note 2 above, and Yule and Burnell.

11. *Guimpel and Tinlau in Siammon:* I cannot identify *Guimpel,* which is mentioned only once. *Tinlau* appears in chapters 58 and 61 as the name of a river in China, and in chapter 158 as the name of a duchy or principality in *Calaminhan. Siammon* is mentioned frequently in subsequent chapters, apparently as the title of the emperor of the *Gueos.* See chapter 1, note 3 above.

12. *Ayuthia:* See chapter 36, note 11 above.

13. *Sornau:* See chapter 36, note 10 above.

14. *Pasuruan:* See chapter 36, note 7 above.

15. *Demak:* See chapter 36, note 4 above.

16. *Miyako:* Former name of the city of Kyoto. It was the capital of Japan until 1869, when the government was moved to Tokyo.

17. *conquiai:* Dalgado says that *conquiai* seems to be etymologically the same as *conquão* (which Pinto does not mention), but that it is employed with a religious significance. The meaning he gives for *conquão* is "administrative dignitary in China."

18. *Xaca:* Shakya, or Sakya, the clan or family name of the Buddha.

19. *Amida:* Or Amita (Japanese), Omito (Chinese), from the Sanskrit Amithaba. A fabulous personage who abides in the western heaven. He is worshipped by the northern or Mahayana Buddhists but is unknown to the southern or Hinayana Buddhists of Siam, Burma, and Sri Lanka (Ceylon). The western paradise promised to the worshippers of Amida-Buddha is inconsistent with the doctrine of nirvana, since it promised immortality instead of annihilation. See E. T. C. Werner, *A Dictionary of Chinese Mythology* (Shanghai: Kelly & Walsh, 1932), 6. See also chapter 78, note 2 above.

20. *Gizom:* See chapter 92, note 3 above, and chapter 114, note 6 below.

21. *Canom:* The Bodhisattva Kuan-yin (Chinese) of Kwannon (Japanese), often called, in Western books on China, the goddess of mercy.

Chapter 108

1. *Three hundred leagues:* In chapter 95 Pinto gives the length of the wall as 315 leagues. In his *Great Wall of China* (1909), Geil gives the length as "over 2,550 miles" (373). It would seem that over the years the size of the wall was not constant for long. In his *Great Wall of China* (1975), Fryer writes that approximately five hundred miles of the wall were constructed by Ch'in Shih Huang-ti between 221–210 B.C. The rest of the structure, approximately thirteen hundred miles in length, was made up of already existing state walls. Eventually it was to stretch on for nearly four thousand miles, but nobody has ever seen the entire length of the wall and no two authoritative maps agree as to its exact course (50, 373).

2. *wooden tablet:* Pinto's wooden tablet is reminiscent of the cangue, a wooden collar or yoke, used as a form of punishment throughout the Ming and Manchu dynasties. It is described

by the sixteenth century Portuguese prisoners in Boxer, *South China*, 21, 180, 183–184, 301. See also Doolittle 1:165, 335.

3. *chanipatões* (*chanipatão,* sing.): From the Chinese *chau-mo-ting,* meaning "stamp or seal."

4. *merchants:* Cf. Galeote Pereira's description of trade carried on in prison in Boxer's *South China*, 23, and that of Gaspar da Cruz, 181.

Chapter 109

1. *cash:* A Chinese coin of low value with a square hole in the middle. Originally minted of copper, and later of increasingly base metal.

2. *human bones:* Such a custom would have been repugnant to the Chinese, and certainly in conflict with their ancestor worship.

Chapter 110

1. *altirna:* Pinto uses this word for the upper or outer garment worn by the Buddhist priests of China, which Dalgado believes is derived from the Pali *uttariyam.*

2. *alms:* The Buddhist priests of China did indeed beg for alms.

3. *dealt with later on:* In chapter 121 below.

Chapter 111

1. *cabisondo:* See chapter 49, note 2 above.

2. *Amida:* See chapter 107, note 18 above.

3. *Calempluy:* See chaps. 75–77 above.

4. *Nhay Camisama: Nhay* comes from the Siamese *nai,* meaning "sir or madame." *Camisama* appears to be composed of the Japanese *kami,* which is the name for the Shinto gods, and the Japanese *sama,* meaning "sir or madame."

Chapter 112

1. *religious sect:* A confused reference to Buddhism and a pantheon of minor deities.

2. *Cochinchina:* See chapter 44, note 8.

3. *Bandou:* Kanto, former daimiate on the island of Honshu, in Japan, comprising eight provinces. See Schurhammer, *Francis Xavier* 4:95 n. 76.

4. *adultery:* Women accused of adultery by their husbands were condemned to death. See Doolittle 1:339.

5. *orderly manner:* Pinto's ideas on orderly government in China seem to have been borrowed from chapter 10 of Gaspar de Cruz's *Tratado da China.*

Chapter 113

1. *Chausirão Panagor:* The emperor in Pinto's time was Chia-ching (1522–66). His great-grandfather was Ch'êng-hua (1464–87). However, the author is more concerned with the morality than with the reality of this tale of the blind emperor.

2. *Francisco Xavier:* Xavier never set foot on the mainland of China, hard as he tried. His failure to do so is described by Pinto in chapter 215 as well as in the many biographies of the saint, the best of which was written by Georg Schurhammer, S. J. See his *Franz Xaver, Sein Leben and Seine Zeit,* vol. 4 (Freiburg: Herder, 1973) or the recent translation thereof by M. Joseph Costelloe, S. J., *Francis Xavier,* vol. 4, chaps. 6–7.

Chapter 114

1. *eunuchs:* There were indeed many eunuchs and women at the court who were often presented to the emperor as gifts, but certainly not in the numbers described by Pinto. Cf. chapter 16 of the *Tratado da China* of Gaspar da Cruz.

2. *anchacys . . . chumbins:* As does Gaspar da Cruz (ibid.), Pinto lists the titles of the principal office holders in China, but describes their functions in a very general way. See glossary 1.

3. *retinue:* When an official appeared in public processions in the course of performing his duties, he was accompanied by a procession appropriate to his rank. Everything about the procession was regulated by strict rule, from the number of sedan bearers to the number of soldiers. But it is doubtful that the soldiers numbered two hundred or that the soldiery was composed of foreign mercenaries. For a description of a high-ranking mandarin's procession, see Doolittle 1 : 298–302.

4. *human sacrifices:* Human sacrifices were performed in a very early period of Chinese history but were abolished during the Chou dynasty (1028–500 B.C.). See Wolfram Eberhard, *A History of China,* 4th ed. (Berkeley and Los Angeles: University of California Press, 1977), 27.

5. *cuchimiocó:* From the Japanese *kuchi* and *myokuan.* Called *lu-in* in Chinese. This is probably a reference to the "spirit-money" or "mock-money" usually burned at funerals or in worship, a practice that continued down to modern times. When burned in worship, it was believed that these slips of paper, designed to look like money, actually turned into money that could be used by the divinity or the deceased person for whom they were intended. For a description of this ceremony in the nineteenth century, see Doolittle. 1 : 16. Spelled *cuchimiacò* in chapter 210 and *cochumiaco* in chapter 212.

6. *naustolins, Trimechau, Gizom:* I have not been able to identify the words *naustolins* and *Trimechau. Gizom* has been identified elsewhere (chap. 92, n. 3 above) as *Jizoo* or *Jizô,* the Japanese name for a Buddhist god, known in China as *Ti-tsang.* His connection with Buddhism is obscure. See Christmas Humphrey, ed., *A Popular Dictionary of Buddhism,* 2d ed. (London: Curzon Press, 1976). However, Pinto seems to have been aware of the fact that there were three main religions in China, plus a plethora of spirits and divinities, though he presents a much distorted version of them, either out of ignorance or satiric design.

Chapter 115

1. *Saturday, 13 January 1544:* According to Brito Rebello (2 : 172), the first two Saturdays in the year 1544 fell on the fifth and the twelfth of the month, whereas in the previous year of 1543, January 13 fell on a Saturday.

2. *Madureiras and Fonsecas:* Two noble families that trace their lineage back to the beginnings of Portugal as a nation.

3. *Book of Golden Clasps:* Pinto is fond of referring metaphorically to important books. Compare his use of the "Book of Flowers" for the Koran (chap. 27 above), probably inspired by the flowery designs that often illuminated the chapter headings.

4. *Chabaqué:* Both Lagoa (*Glossário*) and Le Gentil (102) identify *Chabaqué* with Chuaun or Tchuaun. It is listed in modern gazetteers as Choan or Chao-chow, a city in east Kwantung Province, southeast China, on the Han River about twenty miles above Swatow. It was the scene of banishment of the great poet, philosopher, and opponent of Buddhism, Han Yu (A.D. 768–824), under the T'ang dynasty.

5. *sipatões:* Dalgado believes this word is derived from the Chinese *xi-pin,* meaning "secretary."

6. *on behalf of their dead:* Pinto is probably referring to *Tsing Ming,* the "festival of the tombs," which took place every year 106 days after the winter solstice, as specified in the impe-

rial calendar. It was a time when the Chinese visited the graves of their ancestors and presented offerings before them. See Doolittle 2:44.

7. *lethargic disease:* The original has "modorra," which means somnolence, but I cannot determine the pathology of the disease.

Chapter 116

1. *viola:* The original has "viola," which conjures up an image of a European instrument of the viol family. While it is true that the Chinese had similar instruments, they were smaller than their European counterparts and different in sound and other respects. Ricci tells us that all the Chinese stringed instruments had strings that were made of twisted cotton and that "the whole art of Chinese music seems to consist in producing a monotonous rhythmic beat, as they know nothing of the variations and harmony that can be produced by combining different musical notes" (22). See also Boxer's note on Chinese musical instruments in *South China,* 144 n. 2.

2. *cremated:* The Chinese did not cremate their dead. However, the bodies of Buddhist priests and lepers were cremated. See Doolittle 1:244−45, 2:257.

3. *Vasco Calvo:* See chapter 91, note 4 above.

4. *nao owned by Dom Nuno Manuel:* This was the *nao Madalena,* which set out from Lisbon on 7 April 1515. See facsimile edition of the *Livro das Armadas,* 17.

5. *Tomé Pires:* See chapter 65, note 1 above.

6. *Lopo Soares:* See chapter 65, note 3 above.

7. *Portuguese captain:* The Portuguese captain referred to here was Simão Peres de Andrade, brother of Fernão Peres de Andrade. See chapter 65, note 2 and chapter 91, note 3 above.

8. *chroniclers write:* Barros (in Barros and Couto, déc. 3, bk. 6, chaps. 1 and 2; and bk. 8, chap. 5) is the only chronicler who mentions the fate of Tomé Pires after 1517, the year he was left behind in Canton by Fernão Peres de Andrade. He appears to have read the letters written by Vasco Calvo and Cristóvão Vieira in 1524. See chapter 91, note 4 above.

Chapter 117

1. *Wednesday, 13 July 1544:* According to Brito Rebello (2:181), 13 July 1544 fell on a Sunday, not a Wednesday.

2. *Tartar king . . . invade . . . Peking:* Pinto may be referring to the great Tartar raid of 1550, under the leadership of Altan (Anda or Yen-ta) Khan (1507−83), who by the middle of the sixteenth century had carved out an empire for himself stretching from the China Sea to the borders of Tibet. The "Tartar king" did indeed invade China in the year 1544 as Pinto claims and, for that matter, almost every year thereafter for the next twenty years, ravaging the border provinces of Shensi and Shansi. However, it was only in the year 1550 that Altan Khan came close to threatening Peking. Moreover, the 1550 raid is mentioned by both Galeote Pereira and Gaspar da Cruz, whose accounts were undoubtedly read by Pinto. See Boxer, *South China,* 38 (for Galeote Pereira's report) and 85 (for Gaspar da Cruz's report). For Altan Khan's incursions across the border during the years 1541−50, see Father J. A. M. de Moyriac de Mailla, *Histoire générale de la Chine* (Paris: Clousier, 1779), 10:313−17. As for the name Tartar, it should be pointed out that it was originally applied by the Chinese to a petty tribe of the northeast corner of Mongolia. Later, they applied it to all the Mongols, and finally, it was applied by both Chinese and Westerners to the tribes inhabiting Central Asia, as well as to the Manchus. Cf. Geil, 161 n. 1.

3. *nauticor:* Pinto uses *nauticor* as a title for a Tartar general, but Dalgado says that he may have taken it from the Siamese *nai-to-roi-ek,* meaning "great captain."

4. *Lavra and Coruche:* Two Portuguese towns, the one, Lavra, located northwest of the

city of Porto, and the other, Coruche, just northeast of Lisbon. Metaphorically, it would be somewhat like saying, "somewhere between Lisbon and Porto."

5. *lay ahead for us:* Gaspar da Cruz writes that the Portuguese who were prisoners in China in 1550 were overjoyed by the news of the Tartar raid, hoping thereby to be set at liberty. See Boxer, *South China,* 85.

Chapter 118

1. *dopo:* According to Dalgado this word comes from the Burmese *tat* or *dat,* meaning "fortress."

2. *paliguindoens:* Pinto uses this word for the Tartar war drums. However, Dalgado claims that the word comes from the Malay *palu-kidong,* meaning "an instrument played with sticks."

3. *primeira:* An old Iberian card game in which each player is given four cards. The numbers on the cards have different point values. The best hand is a flush, with which the winner takes all.

Chapter 119

1. *firmaun:* From the Persian *farman,* "an order, patent, or passport," issued by high-ranking Mussulmen of the East. It is derived from the Persian *farmudan,* meaning "to order."

2. *palosguindões:* Spelled *paliguindoens* in chapter 118.

Chapter 120

1. *Nixiancó:* Spelled *Nixiamcó* in chapter 117 and *Nixiancó* in chapters 120 and 121.

Chapter 121

1. *House of Lechune:* The House of *Lechune* is Pinto's name for an ecclesiastical citadel or capital of Tibetan Buddhism, which Lagoa (*Glossário*) identifies with Lhasa. See chapters 127 and 128 below. Also, in chapter 88 above, *Lechune* is the name given by Pinto to a river that empties into the Gulf of Tonkin.

2. *piambre:* Pinto uses this word four times in chapter 121 in the sense of a "horse-drawn carriage or litter." In chapter 122, the same word is used to denote a "platform," or "dais." In chapter 124, he uses the word *pirange,* which he describes as a six-wheeled horse-drawn carriage. In chapter 130, he uses the word *fiambra* for a similar vehicle. Dalgado says that he has not been able to identify these three words, which are not used by any of Pinto's contemporaries. However, he points out that, phonetically, one can relate *pirange* or *pirangue* to *pelanki* or *planki,* the Malay and Javanese forms of the word "palanquin."

3. *nautarão:* Unidentified. However, Pinto uses the same word in chapter 224, with reference to Japan.

Chapter 122

1. *Calaminhãs:* See chapter 41, note 12 above.

2. *Sornau:* See chapter 17, note 3 above.

3. *360 gods:* See chapter 75 above, in which there is a reference to "360 chapels dedicated to the gods of the year," on the island of *Calempluy.*

4. *Xipatom:* See chapter 105, note 11 above.

5. *Kamp'engp'et:* Or Kam-phaeng Phet. Today, a province of west Thailand. Pinto spells it *Capimper.*

6. *piambre:* See chapter 121, note 2 above.

Chapter 123

1. *Monday, October 17:* Only in the years 1541 and 1547 did the seventeenth of October fall on a Monday. See Brito Rebello 2:206.

Chapter 124

1. *Shah Tahmasp:* See chapter 88, note 6 above.
2. *Siammon:* The *Siammon* is mentioned frequently by Pinto as the emperor of the *Gueos,* but the term has not been identified. For the *Gueos,* see chapter 1, note 3 above. See also chapter 107, note 11 above.
3. *Calaminhan:* See chapter 41, note 12 above.
4. *Sornau:* See chapter 17, note 3 above. For Ayuthia, see chapter 36, note 11 above.
5. *Pathans:* The Afghan dynasty that ruled western Bengal in the sixteenth century, destroyed with the defeat and death of Daud Khan Kararani, by the armies of the Moghul emperor Akbar in 1576.
6. *P'itsanulok:* See chapter 41, note 8 above.
7. *Kamp'engp'et:* See chapter 122, note 5 above.
8. *Khorasan:* See chapter 95, note 4 above.
9. *Chitor:* Name of the old fort and early capital of the Indian state of Mewar (Udaipur) in Rajputana. It was taken by Akbar in 1586.
10. *Muscovy:* Very little was known about Tartary in Pinto's day, but his notion about the geography of the region can be traced to Gaspar da Cruz (chap. 3), who writes, "Among the many and great kingdoms which adjoin China, running along it from above the lake whence originates the river Thanas on the European side, one is Russia, where Europe ends, which belongs to Scythia. . . . This Russia lies at the end of Almayne, and it either borders on China or is part thereof." See chapter 72, note 2 above.
11. *tall, red-headed men:* This too seems to have been borrowed from Gaspar da Cruz (ibid.), who writes that "the King of China has many mercenaries who guard the weak passes along the border of Tartary, and these are said to be big men, ruddy, and heavily bearded, wearing cut-hose and blunt swords."
12. *unspeakable sin:* As Boxer points out, "The prevalance of pederasty in Ming China was frequently mentioned in the accounts of European travellers and missionaries. A study of contemporary Chinese literature shows that the practice was neither condemned nor encouraged, but regarded with indifference" (*South China,* 17 n. 1).
13. *panouras:* See chapter 68, note 1 above.
14. *pirange:* See chapter 121, note 2 above.
15. *quart:* The Libson quart was the equivalent of more than six almuds.

Chapter 125

1. *Meyca:* Spelled *Meica* in chapter 124.

Chapter 126

1. *9 May 1544:* Note the inconsistency of Pinto's dates. In chapter 117 he tells us that the Tartar invasion occurred on 13 July 1544, and now, after several months of captivity, he departs from the Tartar capital of *Tuymicão* (spelled *Taymicão* in chapter 125) on 9 May 1544, or a little more than two months before his capture by the Tartars.
2. *tuyxivau:* Rector of a Buddhist temple in Indo-China, according to Dalgado. From the Burmese *thin'oke'ksa'yah.*
3. *saltwater lake:* In the geography of the Middle Ages this would be the Caspian Sea,

according to Le Gentil (128), who also points out that very little was known about Tartary in Pinto's day, and that his confused notions about the geography of the region can be traced to Gaspar da Cruz (chap. 13), who in turn seems to have based his account on that of the medieval Franciscan travelers. See also chapter 72, note 2 above.

4. *human skulls:* Compare with Pinto's description of the "treasure house of the dead" in chapter 109 above.

5. *rob those bones:* Compare with the idol *Muxiparom* (or Muchiparom) in chapter 109 above.

6. *Fanjus:* This is an example of Pinto's multiple use of place-names. In chapter 71 *Fanjus* is the name of a mountain range in north China. In chapter 85 we are told that Nanking is the "capital of the three kingdoms of Ning-po, *Fanjus,* and *Sumbor*" (Song-Men?). In chapter 87 the Portuguese prisoners were washed ashore on the "coast of the Bay of *Sumbor* and *Fanjus.*"

7. *chisangué:* Dalgado believes that this word is derived from the Sanskrit *crisanghi,* meaning "venerable chief of the monastery."

Chapter 127

1. *talapicor:* Pinto uses *talapicor* as the title of a popelike figure bearing a striking resemblance to the Dalai Lama, of whom he seems to have heard. Though the origin of the expression is obscure, it bears some resemblance to other words, i.e., *talapoi, talapoin, talapoimor,* etc., used by European writers of the sixteenth and seventeenth centuries to designate the Buddhist monks of Ceylon and the Indochinese countries. For the explanation offered by C. Eckford Luard, see chapter 77, note 1 above.

2. *Lechune:* See chapter 121, note 1 above.

3. *bills of exchange:* Compare these "bills of exchange" with the *cuchimiocós* described by Pinto in chapter 114. See also chapter 114, note 5 above.

4. *agrém:* Pinto uses this word for a Buddhist pulpit in Indochina. Dalgado says that it is probably derived from the Pali *agaram,* from the Sanskrit *agara,* meaning "house or room."

5. *vanguenarau:* Or *vaganarau.* In this chapter *vanguenarau* is used to designate a Buddhist prioress, whereas in chapter 126 the word *libangú* is used in the same sense. For *vanguenarau,* Dalgado suggests a derivation from the Pali *vagganariyo,* meaning "women of the congregation," but he cannot identify *libangú.*

6. *menigrepas:* This is the feminine plural form of the word *menigrepo,* which has appeared before in chapters 77, 78, 85, and 107. It is spelled *menigregas* in the first edition, but that is obviously a printer's error. See chapter 77, note 2 above.

7. *Vicente Morosa:* This Vicente Morosa has appeared in chapters 58 and 59, in which he took a prominent part in the battle against the pirate *Khoja* Hassim.

8. *"Tal seja tua vida!":* "May thy life be so!" or "Such be thy life!"

9. *something holy:* As pointed out by Georges Le Gentil (128–29) and Maurice Collis (*Grand Peregrination,* 140–41), Pinto seems to have had some notion of Tibetan Buddhism and the existence of the Dalai Lama, whom he compares to the pope. In this respect he was far ahead of his contemporaries. The sermon preached by the *talapicor,* by its insistence on charity, certainly has a Buddhist flavor.

Chapter 128

1. *as Rome is among us:* It is impossible to trace Pinto's footsteps at this juncture of the narrative, but he seems to have traveled westwards, toward the borders of Tibet, possibly Yunnan or Szechuan, where he met the popelike figure he calls the *talapicor* (Dalai Lama?). Four days later he reaches *Lechune* (Lhasa?), which he describes as a religious capital. Though his description is far from exact, he realized that it was a huge, monastic settlement. Collis (*Grand Peregrination,* 141) suggests that Pinto may have used Odoric and other odd references

in early books, together with the unpublished talk of his age, as the basis of his account. While it is true that Lhasa did not become the permanent headquarters of the Dalai Lama until the middle of the seventeenth century, other monastic citadels existed elsewhere at an earlier date. Friar Odoric, who claims to have been in Tibet about 1328, mentions its pope and his capital but gives no description. See *The Travels of Friar Odoric,* in Henry Yule, ed., *Cathay and the Way Thither* (Liechtenstein: Kraus Reprint, 1967), reprint of Hakluyt edition of 1913–16, 2:250.

2. *menigrepos:* Spelled *menigregos* in the first edition. See chapter 127, note 6 above.

3. *saints in their sects:* The statues of these saints would seem to suggest that Pinto had some vague notion of the Mahayana doctrine relating to Bodhisattvas, or those who have vowed to become Buddhas for the sake of the world's salvation, but who refrain from entry into perfect bliss as long as one soul is still left in pain and sorrow. See Samuel Couling, ed., *The Encyclopaedia Sinica* (Shanghai: Kelly & Walsh, 1917), 53.

4. *Rajah Benão:* In chapter 122 a Rajah *Benão* is present at the court of the Tartar king, and very much alive.

5. *Singapamor:* In chapter 182 Pinto speaks of a lake *Singuapamor* called Chiang-mai by the local people.

6. *Cunebeté:* In chapter 41 Pinto speaks of "a big lake the natives call *Cunebeté,* though others call it the Chiang Mai."

7. *birds:* In chapter 41 Pinto refers to a marshland formed by the *Tinacoreu* River, where there were so many birds that the entire kingdom of the *Chintaleuhos* had to be abandoned.

8. *source:* Cf. source of the rivers given in chapter 88. Though Pinto appears to be describing the same lake, the names and number of the rivers are different.

9. *Ventrau:* This appears to be the river called *Tauquiday* in chapter 88. Also, in chapter 129 it is spelled *Ventinau,* and *Ventrau* in chapter 167.

10. *Chiamtabuu:* Chanthaburi, Chantaburi, or Chantabun. Today, a province of Thailand, also a commercial town, its capital near the northeast coast of the Gulf of Siam, 140 miles southeast of Bangkok.

11. *Jangumá:* Lagoa (*Glossário*) identifies this with the Salween River, which fits the description given by Pinto.

12. *Martaban:* See chapter 107, note 9 above.

13. *Pegu:* See chapter 20, note 2 and chapter 107, note 10 above.

14. *Pumfileu:* This appears to be the river called *Batobasoy* in chapter 88.

15. *Suk'ot'ai* or *Sukhot'ai:* Village on the Yom river, west Thailand, thirty miles northwest of P'itsanulok. Called *Sacotay* by Pinto.

16. *Meleytay:* Meady. See chapter 150, note 2 below.

17. *Sovady:* Spelled *Savady* elsewhere. See chapter 41, note 9 above.

18. *Cosmim:* See chapter 88, note 5 above.

19. *Arakan:* Today, a division of Lower Burma, extending along the northeast coast of the Bay of Bengal. Once the seat of a powerful kingdom (after the fifteenth century), it came under Burmese rule at various times and was finally absorbed into Burma in 1783.

20. *Chittagong:* Today, a town, port, and district of East Bengal, Pakistan. Conquered by the nabob of Bengal in 1666.

21. *saligues:* See chapter 22, note 7 above.

Chapter 129

1. *Ventinau:* See chapter 128, note 9 above.

2. *Comhay:* The *Comhay* mountains have not been identified, but Lagoa has identified the port city of the same name, which is mentioned in chapters 44, 55, 81, 82, and 189. See chapter 44, note 5 above.

3. *Tinocouhós:* Spelled *Timocouhós* in chapters 130 and 131 and *Timocouhos* in chapter 181.

4. *Huzamgué:* Spelled variously as *Uzangué* in chapters 107, 112, and 125; as *Huzamgué* in

chapter 129; as *Huzangué* in chapter 130; and as both *Huzangué* and *Huzamgué* in chapters 131 and 132.

    5. *Tanaugrem:* Elsewhere in this chapter, and in chapter 131, it is spelled *Fanaugrem.*

    6. *funeral pyre:* Pinto may have read Friar Odoric, who writes, speaking of Champa (southern Indochina), "When a married man dies in this country his body is burned and his living wife along with it." (See Yule, *Cathay and the Way Thither* 2 : 166.) Though suttee, or the rite of widow burning, was not practiced by Buddhists, but by people of certain castes among the Hindus, the practice prevailed in various other regions beside India. (See Yule and Burnell, 878–79.)

    7. *silver statue:* Cf. the statues of the saints described in chapter 128.

Chapter 130

    1. *fiambra:* See chapter 121, note 2 above.

    2. *panouras:* See chapter 68, note 1 above.

    3. *in their tusks:* The battle sword was tied or attached to the elephant's tusks.

    4. *saddle cloths:* There seems to be something missing from this sentence, but that is exactly what the original says.

    5. *broquem:* A Japanese governor. From the Japanese *buraku,* meaning "province." It is used here in the sense of "captain of the palace guard," but in chapters 139–43 it is used as the title of the governor of the Ryukyu Islands.

    6. *Prechau Guimião:* Presumably the title and name of the king of Cochinchina. For *prechau,* see chapter 36, note 9 above.

    7. *orepo:* Presumably a Buddhist priest in Cochinchina, or a misspelling of the word *grepo.* See chapter 78, note 3 above.

    8. *triumph over the gods:* Cf. description of the captive gods of China in chapter 122 above.

    9. *mutra:* Seal, stamp, signature, in India. From the Sanskrit *mudra.*

Chapter 131

    1. *Famstir:* In chapter 88 a Lake *Faõstir* is given as the source of five rivers. In chapter 128 Lake *Singapamor,* in the same geographical area, is given as the source of four rivers. As for the *Baguetor* River, this is the first and only time it is mentioned in the work. In chapter 117, *Famstir* is the name of a city.

Chapter 132

    1. *twelfth of January:* Ordinarily, the absence of the year in any of the many partial dates given by Pinto would not be deserving of our attention, but in this instance it is of special significance because this is the year (?) that Pinto lays claim—and a much disputed claim it is— to being among the first group of Europeans to have set foot in Japan.

    2. *Quangeparuu:* Whether by design or by accident, Pinto fails to draw the reader's attention to the fact that he had reached the city of *Quangeparuu,* which Antonio de Faria and his band of Portuguese pirates had been planning to attack. See chapters 48, note 2 and 52, note 2 above.

    3. *Sanchão:* Or Saint John's Island as the English called it. This is a corruption of San-Shan, or more correctly Shang-Ch'uan, the Chinese name of an island about fifty miles to the southwest of Macao where, prior to the establishment of Macao (1557), the Portuguese engaged in smuggling with merchants from Canton. For a description of *Sanchão,* see Schurhammer's *Francis Xavier* 4 : 621 n. 1. For the many different spellings of *Sanchão,* see "The Name Sancian," in appendix 3, pp. 662–64 of the same volume. See also chapter 113, note 2 above.

4. *later on:* In chapter 215 below.

5. *Lampacau:* Lang-pa-kao or Lam-Puk. In the years 1555–57 the Portuguese transferred their trade from *Sanchão* to the more easterly island of Lang-pa-kao, near the modern Bullock Horn island. In a letter dated Macao, 20 November 1555, written by Pinto when he was a novice in the Society of Jesus, he says that *Lampacau* is six leagues from Macao. See Catz, *Cartas,* 61.

6. *differences of opinion:* Cf. argument among the same group of Portuguese in chapter 115 above.

7. *aytao of Chincheo:* The commander of the provincial coast-guard fleet. See chapter 44, note 3 and chapter 81, note 1 above.

8. *Lamau:* See chapter 44, note 4 above.

9. *Salt River:* A Salt River appears in the south of *Chincheo* on Diogo Homem's map of 1568. See Schurhammer, "Descobrimento do Japão" 21:564 n. 153. Translated from the German into Portuguese by Francisco Rodrigues, S.J., this work was also published in the *Anais da Academia Portuguesa da História,* 2d ser., 1 (1946): 9–172.

10. *Chabaqué:* See chapter 115, note 4 above.

11. *nautoquim:* See chapter 39, note 3 above.

12. *Tanegashima:* Largest of the Osumi Islands, a group just south of Kyushu Island, Japan, part of Kagoshima Prefecture, separated from the southern tip of Kyushu by the Osumi or Van Diemen Strait. It was here, in the year 1542 or 1543, that a group of three Portuguese arrived in Japan on board a Chinese junk. They were the first Europeans to set foot on Japanese soil. That much is known for certain. What is not known for certain is that Pinto was one of that historical group of three, as he claims to be. Unlike his account of China, what he has to say about Japan is fairly accurate, yet some historians refuse to accept his version of the discovery of Japan or to accord him the honor of being among the first group of Europeans to set foot in Japan. The question still hangs fire.

13. *Miaygimá:* Possibly intended for Miyajima, which Pinto mentions in his letter of 5 December 1554. However, in that letter he correctly situates the island of Miyajima (or Itsukushima) off the southwest coast of Honshu, which is far from Tanegashima. (See Catz, *Cartas,* 45.) Lagoa (*Glossário*) identifies it as the island of Make-Jima or Make-Shima, off the coast of Tanegashima, which Father Schurhammer says is impossible. See Schurhammer, "Descobrimento do Japão" 21:565 n. 157.

Chapter 133

1. *nautaquim:* Spelled variously as *nautoquim* or *nautaquim.*

2. *Chenchicogis:* Or more correctly *Chenchicogins,* as it appears in the plural in chapter 135. In chapter 134 it appears in the singular as *Chenchicogim.* It is composed of two Japanese words, *tenjiku,* meaning "India," and *jin,* meaning "individual" or "individuals," hence "man or men from India," since the Japanese does not distinguish between singular and plural. It was applied to the Portuguese who came to Japan via India.

Chapter 134

1. *Zeimoto:* the names of the three Portuguese discoverers of Japan appear in two other European accounts of the sixteenth century, one written by Antonio Galvão (1563), who was governor of the Moluccas from 1536 to 1539, and the other by Diogo do Couto (1597), who was the official chronicler of Portuguese India. Both writers give the names of the first Portuguese to arrive in Japan as Antonio da Mota, Francisco Zeimoto, and Antonio Peixoto. Japanese sources, first brought to light by Hans Haas in his *Geschichte des Christentums in Japan,* 2 vols. (Tokyo: Hobunsha, 1902–4), give a garbled version of two of the names as Mura Shukusha and Kirishita (or Krishta) Ta Mota. Pinto's name does not appear in either the Japanese or European sources. See Antonio Galvão, *Tratado dos descobrimentos,* 3d ed. (Porto:

Livraria Civilização, 1944), 273, or Hakluyt's bi-lingual edition of *Galvano's Discoveries of the World* (London, 1862), 229–30; and Diogo do Couto, in Barros and Couto, déc. 5, bk. 8, chap. 12, 262. Chapter 3 (vol. 1) of Haas's work, which deals with the Japanese sources, was translated into Portuguese from the original German by J. de Sousa Monteiro and published in the *Boletim da Segunda Classe* (Lisbon) 2 (1910): 84–110.

2. *facharões:* Pinto uses this word in the sense of "companion or colleague." Dalgado suggests a derivation from the Japanese *hoyu-tsure*. (Initial *f* for *h* is normal in the Portuguese transcription.)

3. *musket:* It is certain that the introduction of firearms into Japan coincided with the arrival of the Portuguese in Tanegashima, a fact not mentioned by either Galvão or Diogo do Couto. It is confirmed by the Japanese chronicle *Teppo-ki,* or "history of the introduction of firearms into Japan." It was first printed in 1649, but was written during the Kaicho period (1596–1614). The author was connected with the feudal lords of Tanegashima and was in a good position to ascertain the facts. He places the arrival of the first Portuguese in Tanegashima on the Japanese date corresponding to 23 September 1543. Also of interest is the fact that for many years all firearms of this type became known in Japan as *tanegashima,* a word that was applied to pistols and carbines down to the nineteenth century. See Haas, vol. 1, chap. 3.

4. *Dom Afonso de Noronha:* Served as viceroy of Portuguese India from 6 November 1550 to 16 September 1554.

5. *king of Bungo:* Pinto's "king" of Bungo at that time was the *daimyo* Otomo Yoshishige (1529–87). He succeeded his father, Otomo Yoshinori, as daimyo in the year 1550 when the latter was assassinated. He was a friend and protector of the Portuguese merchants and missionaries who frequented his ports. He converted in 1578 and was baptized with the name of Francisco, probably after Xavier. See Schurhammer's article, "Ein fürstlicher Gönner des hl. Franz Xaver, Otomo Yoschischige, König von Bungo," in *Gesammelte Studien,* ed. Laszlo Szilas (Rome and Lisbon: Bibliotheca Instituti Historici, 1963), 4:127. Bungo is the name of a former daimiate in the northeast corner of the island of Kyushu. In the sixteenth century, under Otomo, it controlled nearly all of the island of Kyushu. The name survives today in the Strait of Bungo, a channel twenty to twenty-five miles wide northeast of Kyushu, separating it from the island of Shikoku.

6. *in the year 1556:* Pinto was appointed ambassador to Japan in 1554 by the viceroy Afonso de Noronha (see n. 4 above) when he learned that Pinto was planning to accompany a party of Jesuit missionaries to Japan, headed by Father Melchior Nunes Barreto, vice-provincial of the Society in India and successor of Francis Xavier to that post. However, the missionaries did not reach Japan until 1556. Their hazardous voyage is described by Pinto in chapters 220–23 below, and in his letter of 20 November 1555. The same voyage is described by Father Melchior Nuno Barreto in his letter of 23 November 1555. See Catz, *Cartas,* document 9, 60–65 (Pinto's letter) and document 10, 66–72 (Melchior's letter). What the viceroy did not know when he appointed him ambassador was that Pinto had joined the Society of Jesus, a fact that was not disclosed at the time. For some reason, Pinto also thought it best to omit that information from his book, which purports to be an autobiography.

7. *Fucheo:* The seaport city of Funai, as it was formerly called, in the northeast corner of the island of Kyushu. Today it is known as Oita and is the capital of Oita Prefecture. In chapter 60 above, Pinto uses the place-name *Fucheo,* but there he is referring to the city of Foochow in China. See chapter 60, note 1 above.

Chapter 135

1. *my uncle and liege lord:* The "king" of Bungo in 1542 (or 1543) was Otomo Yoshinori, father of Otomo Yoshishige, who was "king" of Bungo when Pinto was there in 1556. (See chap. 134, n. 5 above.) Moreover, as James Murdoch points out, Tanegashima was never subject to the

House of Otomo of Bungo, and at that date, it acknowledged Shimadzu of Satsuma as its feudal superior. See James Murdoch and Isoh Yamagata, *A History of Japan during the Century of Early Foreign Intercourse (1542–1651)* (Kobe: Asiatic Society of Japan, 1903), 2:33–42.

2. *Hyascarão Goxo:* Haas believes that *Hyascarão* is a corruption of Hyôbunojô, a title then used by Naotoki. *Goxo* (or *gosho*) was the title of the regent who, in the name of the emperor, exercised civil control over all of Japan. The ruler of Tanegashima did not have the right to use this title. See Schurhammer, "Descobrimento do Japão" 21:569 nn. 165 and 166.

3. *Oregemdó:* At that time the "king" of Bungo was Otomo Yoshinori (see chapt. 134, n. 5, and n. 1 above). *Oregemdó* is probably a corruption of Yoshinori-dono. *Dono* or *tono* is the Japanese for "feudal lord or large landholder."(*Tono* changes to *dono* when it is added to the name of an individual or land.) The Japanese lords who had the right to use *dono* after their names and who had converted to Catholicism were given the title of *dom* by the Portuguese.

4. *Hakata:* Spelled *Facata* by Pinto, a normal transposition, since *f* and *h* are almost indistinguishable in Japanese pronunciation. It is the former name of Fukuoka, city, port, and capital of Fukuoka Prefecture in northern Kyushu. The name survives today in the Bay of Hakata, which forms the outer harbor of Fukuoka, as well as in the name of the well-known Hakata dolls that have been made there for centuries. The ancient port area of Hakata was in medieval times one of the chief ports of Japan. The Mongols under Kublai Khan were twice defeated at Hakata, in 1271 and 1281.

5. *Fiancima:* Possibly a corruption of Firoshima or Hiroshima.

6. *Tosa:* See chapter 39, note 4 above.

7. *Bandou:* Kantô, or Kwantô. See chapter 112, note 3 above.

8. *Goto:* See chapter 57, note 1.

9. *Shimonoseki:* Pinto writes *Xamanaxeque*. Formerly Akamagaseki, popularly called Bakan. A seaport city on the southwestern tip of Honshu, on Shimonoseki Strait, opposite Moji. It should be pointed out that in the year of the Portuguese discovery of Japan, neither Shimonoseki nor any of the other places mentioned in the king's letter were subject to Bungo. However, by the year 1556, when Pinto arrived at the court of Bungo as ambassador from the viceroy of India, there had been a great expansion of the Bungo domains, but even then they did not extend beyond the island of Kyushu.

10. *Fingeandono:* Possibly Hiji-dono, since, in chapter 209 below, Pinto writes *Finge* for Hiji, a port of the northwestern part of Bungo. However, Dalgado says it is a compound of the Japanese *kinji,* meaning "a court official," and *dono,* meaning "sir or lord."

11. *mamoco:* See chapter 13, note 15 above. This is a term in the lunar calendar of the Moslems and as such is out of place in a Japanese letter.

12. *my mother's brother . . . my wife's father:* According to Haas, neither Naotoki nor his wife were related to the diamyo of Bungo. Naotoki's mother was the daughter of Shimazu Tataoki and his wife was the daughter of Yakubo Yamato-no-Kami Takashige. See Schurhammer, "Descobrimento do Japão" 21:568 n. 163.

13. *Cristóvão Borralho:* Here, Pinto introduces the third member of his group of "discoverers." Some historians have tried to connect the name Kirishita that appears in the Japanese chronicle *Teppo-ki* with that of Christóvão. Kirishita is also the Japanese word for Christian.

14. *funce:* A small oared vessel, from the Japanese *funé,* meaning "boat," and *se,* meaning "river or canal."

15. *Yamagawa:* Spelled *Hiamangó* by Pinto. Seaport at the entrance to the Bay of Kagoshima, a deep inlet in South Kyushu.

16. *Kagoshima:* Spelled *Quãguixumá* by Pinto. Seaport city, capital of Kagoshima Prefecture, in southern Kyushu, on Satsuma Peninsula and Kagoshima Bay. It was here that Francis Xavier landed in 1549.

17. *Ta-no-ura:* Spelled *Tanorá* by Pinto. Town located north of the Bay of Ariake in the province of Hyuga.

18. *Minato:* Minato means "port," but what is meant here is Chino-no-minato (Sakita-no-ura), one of the ports of Ariake Bay on the southeastern coast of Osumi, today part of the city of Kushima. It is spelled *Minâto* in chapter 209 and *Minató* in chapters 202 and 223.

19. *Hyuga:* Pinto writes *Fiungá.* A province in eastern Kyushu.

20. *Usuki:* Pinto writes *Osquy.* Today, a town in Oita Prefecture, northeast Kyushu, about twelve miles southeast of Oita (see chap. 134, n. 7), with a good harbor on the Bungo Strait. After an uprising in 1556, Otomo Yoshishige, whose family had always lived in Funai, decided to move to Usuki, where he built himself a stronghold high on a rock, surrounded on three sides by the sea. See Luis Fróis, S.J., *História de Japan* (Lisbon: Biblioteca Nacional, 1976) 1:105.

21. *reply to his questions:* Pinto may be parodying the court language of Lisbon. Cf. with Gulliver's speech to the queen of Brobdingnag.

22. *merchant:* Regarding the attitude of the Japanese feudal nobility toward the merchant classes, see Boxer, *The Christian Century in Japan,* 2d ed. (Berkeley and Los Angeles: University of California Press 1967), 30.

Chapter 136

1. *certain kind of wood:* China wood or China root (*Smilax china*), a climbing, prickly plant grown in China and some parts of India. First used in India in 1535 for its supposed medicinal virtues. It was brought to Europe by Martim Afonso de Sousa (see chap. 12, n. 6 above) in 1539, where it acquired a favorable reputation after it was prescribed for the emperor Charles V, who suffered from gout. Its properties and uses are described by Garcia da Orta (1500?–1568) in the forty-seventh colloquy of his *Colóquios dos simples e drogas da Índia.* There is also an English translation by Sir Clements Markham, *The Colloquies on the Simples and Drugs of India* (London: Henry Sotheran and Co. 1913), 378–89, but it is not as well annotated as the Portuguese edition of 1891–95. It was also described by Orta's contemporaries, among them the Flemish anatomist Andreas Vesalius and the Portuguese physician Amato Lusitano, to say nothing of the many modern herbals that still list it. It is still used in China today in the treatment of various ailments, among them, rheumatoid arthritis. See *A Barefoot Doctor's Manual,* DHEW Publication NIH 75-695 (Washington, D.C.: National Institutes of Health, 1974), 598.

2. *Arichandono:* Probably intended for Hachiro-dono, one of the names of the younger brother of Otomo Yoshishige, son of Yoshinori. Hachiro later became daimyo of Yamaguchi, where he ruled from 1551 to 1557 under the name of Ouchi Yoshinaga. Since Otomo Yoshishige was sixteen years old in 1544, Hachiro must have been younger than the sixteen or seventeen years of age attributed to him by Pinto. See Schurhammer, "Descobrimento do Japão" 21:571 nn. 185 and 186.

3. *our Lady of the Snows:* The feast day of our Lady of the Snows falls on August fifth. Brito Rebello (2:252 n. 1) fixes the date as 4 August 1543, which he regards as a most significant date because the only years in which the eve of that feast day fell on a Saturday were (a) 1537, the year in which Pinto departed for India; (b) 1548, when Pinto was in Siam; and (c) 1543, which is the year most historians agree was the year of the European discovery of Japan.

4. *jurubaca:* The first edition has *iurubaca,* but it is intended for *jurubaça,* as it appears in chapter 140, and as most of Pinto's contemporaries wrote it. It is derived from the Malay-Javanese *juruba-hasa, juru* meaning "master, expert," and *bahasa,* from the Sanskrit *bhasa,* meaning "tongue," hence, "interpreter."

Chapter 137

1. *curing his son:* Schurhammer points out that this story of the shooting accident and the cure of the young prince *Arichandono* (see chap. 136, n. 2 above) is very similar to something

that did happen to Otomo Yoshishige's younger brother Hachiro (later known as Ouchi Yoshinaga) in the year 1545 or 1546. The implication, of course, is that Pinto heard the story when he was in Japan and appropriated it as his own. See Schurhammer, "Descobrimento do Japão" 21:533 n. 81.

2. *Gotom:* Lagoa identifies this with the shoals of the Seven Sisters that appear on the British Admiralty Chart at latitude 30°17' north and longitude 121°33' east (*Glossário*). In chapter 140 below Pinto refers to these shoals under the name of *Taidacão*.

3. *Ryukyu Islands:* Boxer writes that both the Chinese and the Portuguese had only vague and confused ideas at this period of the relative position of the modern Lu-chu (Ryukyu) Islands and of Formosa. See *Great Ship from Amacon*, 309 n. 5.

4. *Gaspar de Melo:* A person of that name is mentioned by Diogo do Couto (Barros and Couto, déc. 7, bk. 1, chap. 11, 97) as captain of Goa in the year 1555, but that does not mean necessarily that he is the same person to whom Pinto is referring.

Chapter 138

1. *Fire Island:* Cortesão says that *Fire* Island appears for the first time on Lopo Homem's map of 1554 and that it corresponds to Nakano-shima or Suwanose-shima, two islands with active volcanoes. The former is described in *Webster's Geographical Dictionary* (1966) as a volcanic island 3,215 feet high, Tokara Island, in north Ryukyu Islands, Japan. Suwanose-Shima is not listed. See Cortesão, *Suma Oriental*, 128–29 n. 2.

2. *azeda:* Wood sorrel.

Chapter 139

1. *xivalém:* From the Japanese *shihai-nin*, meaning "provincial governor."

2. *broquem:* See chapter 130, note 5 above.

3. *peretanda:* See chapter 106, note 3 above.

Chapter 140

1. *hair of our heads:* This curious expression may be explained by the fact that there is, or was, a taboo against touching the head and hair of the royal personage in Siam, where Pinto is known to have lived. Quaritch-Wales tells us that this taboo is founded in part on the supposition "that the hair must be the most sacred part of the body by reason of the superior position that it occupies, and it is evidently this belief that has given rise to the use of the word *pham*, 'hair,' for 'I' when speaking to superiors, meaning that only the most noble part of the speaker dares to address the superior person spoken to." Pinto freely applies this concept to other Asian potentates. See H. G. Quaritch-Wales, *Siamese State Ceremonies* (London: Bernard Quaritch, 1931), 33.

2. *Taidacão:* In chapter 138 above Pinto refers to the *Taydacão* Mountains. In this chapter he refers both to the reefs of *Taidacão* and to the beaches of *Taydacão*, none of which have been identified with any degree of certainty. See also chapter 137, note 2 above.

3. *widows:* It is doubtful that Pinto ever visited the Ryukyu or Lu-chu Islands, about which little was known at the time. However, it is certain that the Luchuans or Ryukyu, who were tributaries of China in the sixteenth century, made trading voyages to Malacca. The assumption here is that the Ryukyu traders were slain in Malacca when it was conquered by Albuquerque in 1511. Pires, writing in 1512–15, says that "they [the Ryukyu] take the merchandise that goes from Malacca to China, and go to Japan" and that "one, two, or three junks come to Malacca every year." See Cortesão, *Suma Oriental*, 130.

4. *vileu:* Dalgado suggests a possible derivation from the Chinese *kien-lau*, meaning "prison, dungeon," or from the Malay *bileq*, meaning "room, chamber."

5. *jurubaça:* See chapter 136, note 4 above.

6. *He who painted . . . earth:* Pinto uses this expression, which he and some of his contemporaries believed to be the essence of the heathen religion, quite frequently. He probably borrowed it, though in a more poetic manner, from Gaspar da Cruz, who writes, with particular reference to the Chinese, "They believe that everything depends from on high, both the creation of all things as the conservation and ordering of them, and not knowing who in particular is the author of these things, they attribute it to the same sky." See *Tratado de China,* chap. 27, or Boxer's *South China,* 213.

7. *Lançarote Pereira:* See chapter 70, note 2 above. A Lançarote Pereira was taken prisoner by the Chinese in 1549, off the coast of Fukien. See Schurhammer, *Francis Xavier* 4:310, 632. Also, Schurhammer, "Descobrimento do Japão" (21:564 n. 152) identifies *Lamau* with Amoy, a port in the province of Fukien. For a map and description of the Bay of Amoy, see Boxer's *South China,* xx, 245 n. 3.

Chapter 141

1. *compassion:* Boxer says that early travelers to the Ryukyus speak of the mild and gentle nature of the inhabitants, which seems to accord well with what Pinto writes in this episode (*Christian Century in Japan,* 12); and Pires, in one of the earliest written accounts (1512–15), says of them, "They are very truthful men. . . . They do not buy slaves, nor would they sell one of their own men for the whole world, and they would die over this" (Cortesão, *Suma Oriental,* 130).

2. *Banchá:* See chapter 38, note 1 above for identification. This toponym is used in chapters 38 and 183 with reference to Siam, but it appears to be out of place with reference to the Ryukyus.

Chapter 142

1. *two hours:* The original says that the queen woke up in the middle of the *quarto da lua,* which means "a quarter of the moon." As Brito Rebello points out (3:20), this is a mistake, and it should read *quarto d'alva,* which is a nautical expression meaning "morning watch." Since the morning watch takes place between the hours of 4:00 and 8:00 a.m., we can say that the queen woke up at 6:00 a.m., or that two hours had gone by.

2. *Nhay:* See chapter 111, note 4 above. *Nhay* appears again in this chapter for *nhay peretanda.*

3. *chumbim:* See chapter 84, note 1 above. This is the only instance when this word is used without reference to China.

4. *stealing from others:* Pinto seems to have developed this episode from a historic event about which he heard or read. On 5 December 1554, during his brief career as a member of the Society of Jesus, Pinto wrote a letter from Malacca to his brethren in Portugal in which he says, "Two hundred and fifty leagues from here [from China] and a hundred leagues before arriving in Japan, are the Ryukyus, where some Portuguese were shipwrecked. The king of the Ryukyus gave them a ship *and everything else they needed, but he refused to see them, saying that it would not please God for him to see with his own eyes, people who were in the habit of stealing from others. He said that because of the lands conquered by the Portuguese in India. I mention this, dear brothers, to show you the kindness of these people who have no knowledge of their Creator."* The portion in italics was deleted from the copies of this letter in the codexes of the three Jesuit colleges in Portugal, as well as from the many printed copies of the Jesuit letterbooks published in the sixteenth and seventeenth centuries, with the exception of the Italian version, *Diversi avisi particolari dall'Indie di Portogallo,* published in Venice in 1565. For the complete letter (in Portuguese), see Catz, *Cartas,* document 6, 39–45; and (in Spanish) Joseph Wicki, S.J., ed., *Documenta Indica III (1553–1557), Monumental Historica S.I.,* vol. 74, *Monumenta Missionum S.I.,* vol. 6, *Missiones Orien-*

tales (Rome: Instituti Historici, 1954), document 32, 140–55. Pinto may also have been aware of a report written by the Spaniard, Garcia de Escalante Alvarado, to the viceroy of Mexico in 1548. Escalante was a surviving member of the ill-fated Villalobos expedition to the Philippines, to which Pinto refers briefly in chapter 143. Escalante writes that, during his sojourn in Tidore, he was told by a Portuguese named Diogo de Freitas that some Portuguese bound for China "had been driven by storm to one of the Ryukyu islands where they were well received by the King. . . . After they had procured provisions they left the islands. Attracted by the kindly reception they had received and the wealth they had witnessed, other Portuguese merchants undertook the voyage . . . but this time they were not allowed to go ashore. They were ordered to hand over a list of the goods they carried, and the price of their purchase. . . . This they did and received full payment. Upon their being supplied with necessary provisions they received orders to leave." See Erik Wilhelm Dahlgren, "A Contribution to the History of the Discovery of Japan," *Transactions and Proceedings of the Japan Society* 11 (1913): 243–44.

5. *chaveca:* Not in Dalgado or Yule and Burnell. Moraes attempts to define it as "hour of the day" or "unit of time," but gives no etymology. See Antonio de Moraes Silva, *Diccionario da lingua portuguesa,* 7th ed. (Lisbon: Typographia de Joaquim Germano de Souza Neves, 1877–78), 1:373.

6. *mamoco:* See chapter 13, note 14 and chapter 135, note 11 above.

Chapter 143

1. *easy to conquer it:* In chapter 140 the king of the Ryukyus was told that it is the custom of the Portuguese "to spy out a country in the guise of merchants and return later to conquer it." Here, the author, in his assumed role of the *faux ingénu,* invites his countrymen to do what the prisoners said their religion forbids them to do. This is undoubtedly the highest point of irony in a work completely dominated by the rhetoric of satire.

2. *Ryukyu island:* By this is meant the Grand Lu-chu or the island of Okinawa, near the center of the Ryukyu Archipelago, and the only one of the islands of considerable size. The chain consists of about thirty-six islands located between latitude twenty-six to twenty-eight degrees north. Okinawa is about sixty miles long by ten miles wide. Modern gazetteers describe it as volcanic in origin, mountainous, and densely covered with vegetation. Semitropical products are grown, such as sugarcane, pineapples, and bananas, in addition to wheat and rice. Pinto's description, though not quite accurate, is no more inaccurate than those of his contemporaries, while Barros and Couto surprisingly have little or nothing to say about the Ryukyus.

3. *copper:* The *Imperial Gazetteer* (London: Blackie & Son, 1855) says that copper, tin, and sulphur abound in the Ryukyus. Yet Boxer writes that then, as now, they were poor in natural resources and they have never produced gold or copper (*Christian Century in Japan,* 12).

4. *Lamau:* Amoy. See chapter 140, note 7 above.

5. *Sumbor:* Song-men, according to Georges Le Gentil, 102.

6. *Chabaqué:* See chapter 115, note 4 above.

7. *Tosa:* See chapter 39, note 4 above.

8. *Miyako:* See chapter 107, note 16 above.

9. *Goto:* See chapter 57, note 1 above.

10. *angely wood:* See chapter 52, note 3 above.

11. *jatemar:* According to Dalgado this word may come from the Malay *játi-mérah,* meaning "red teakwood."

12. *poytão:* Dalgado is unsure of the provenance of this word, but suggests the Malay *po'ta,* meaning "incomparable, excellent."

13. *silver mines . . . pitch:* The products of manufactures named by Pinto were not native to these islands, which, as Boxer points out (*Christian Century in Japan,* 12), were poor in natural resources. But it is probable that some of these products, and others named by Pires, were

exchanged by the Ryukyu, who acted as middlemen on their trading voyages between Japan, Korea, China, Indonesia, and Siam. After the conquest of Malacca by the Portuguese, the Ryukyu voyages to Malacca ceased.

14. *grand master of Santiago:* Professor Francis Dutra of the University of California at Santa Barbara informs me that in 1556 King John III was grand master of the Order of Santiago (or Knights of Saint James), but that Dom Afonso de Lencastre, son of Dom Jorge who died 22 July 1550 (see chap. 1, n. 17 above), remained as commander or "comendador-mor" of the Order of Santiago.

15. *Pero Gomes de Almeida:* I have not been able to identify this Pero Gomes de Almeida, nor have I been able to verify Pinto's statement about Naotoki's request for military aid. However, as Le Gentil points out (163), Pinto seems to have anticipated the coming events by about fifty years, for in 1609 the Satsumas of Kyushu took possession of the northern part of the Ryukyu Archipelago, which they found easy to conquer, without the help of the Portuguese, and without becoming tributary to the king of Portugal. They extended their conquest progressively, and by the year 1879 the Ryukyus became an integral part of Japan.

16. *Manual de Sousa de Sepulveda:* Captain of the great galleon *São João* which was shipwrecked off the coast of Natal on 24 June 1552, or four years before the letters were supposed to have been written. The tragic fate of Manuel de Sepulveda and his wife and children was the subject of one of the most famous of the shipwreck narratives collected and reprinted by Bernardo Gomes de Brito in the *História trágico-marítima* (1735–36), of which numerous editions exist in several languages. See Charles Ralph Boxer, ed., *Further Selections from the "Tragic History of the Sea, 1559–1565"* (London: Hakluyt Society, 1968), 32 n. 2.

17. *Ruy Lopez de Villalobos:* Commander of the fleet sent out by the viceroy of Mexico on 1 November 1542 to take possession of the Philippine Islands, discovered by Magellan twenty years earlier. His fleet landed in Mindanao on 2 February 1543 but was met with hostility by the inhabitants. Villalobos sailed further south and remained for about a year on an island between Mindanao and the Celebes. Finally, after a losing battle with famine, illness, and hostility, Villalobos was forced to seek refuge in the Moluccas, then in the possession of the Portuguese, and in March 1544 he landed in Tidore. See Dahlgren, 240–41 and Galvano, *Discoveries of the World,* 238.

18. *Dom Jorge de Castro:* Captain of the fortress of Ternate (1539–44). It was he who complained to the viceroy of India about the Spaniards forcing their way into the Portuguese line of demarcation established by the Treaty of Tordesillas (1494; Dahlgren, 258).

19. *Silver Islands:* Imaginary islands sought by the Spaniards. In 1552 Francis Xavier wrote a letter to the Jesuit provincial in Portugal asking him to urge the Spanish monarch to desist in his efforts to discover these islands, for "besides the islands of Japan, no other island has been discovered on which silver is found." See Dahlgren, 258; Schurhammer, "Fernão Mendes Pinto und seine *Peregrinaçam,*" *Asia Major* 1st. ser., 3 (1926): 243, or *Gesammelte Studien: Orientalia 2* 21:84.

20. *Ryukyus:* Pinto was unaware of the *Suma Oriental* of Tomé Pires (written between 1512 and 1515), which had long lain forgotten until it was rediscovered by Armando Cortesão and published by the Hakluyt society in 1944. Pages 128–31 deal with the Ryukyus.

Chapter 144

1. *Tristão de Gá:* See chapter 20, note 3 and chapter 68, note 2 above.

2. *Pero de Faria:* Faria's last year in office was 1543. See chapter 12, note 1 above.

3. *Martaban:* See chapter 107, note 9 above.

4. *chaubainhá:* Saw binnya, meaning "lord of wisdom," was the title of the governor or viceroy of Martaban, who held his position under the king of Pegu, capital of the Talaings or Mons. See chapter 20, note 2 above.

5. *Lançarote Guerreiro:* Correia (vol. 4, chap. 41, 110) mentions a Lançarote Guerreiro

who, in the year 1540, detached his ship from a fleet that had been sent to the Red Sea by the governor of India and went off on his own, operating as a freebooter in many parts; and, Correia adds, "In six years he took many prizes and committed many robberies, but he was pardoned later by Governor Garcia de Sá [1548–49], who was from his home town, and afterwards, Governor Jorge Cabral [1549–50] favored him and gave him an honorable position in the Moluccas."

6. *king of Achin:* See chapter 17, note 12.

7. *9 January 1545:* This conflicts with the date that Pero de Faria left office. (See n. 2 above.) Moreover, it is known that he left Malacca for Goa in 1543, where he lived until his death in 1546.

8. *Pulo Pracelar:* Schurhammer identifies this as Pulo Parcelar ("Pinto und seine *Peregrinaçam*" 21:80). Lagoa (*Glossário*) calls it Pulo Parcela or Pracelar, an islet in the Strait of Malacca, mentioned in the British Admiralty charts and by Portuguese pilots of the period, though there is some disagreement as to its precise location.

9. *Pulo Sambilang:* See chapter 20, note 1 above.

10. *Barruhás:* Schurhammer identifies this as the Bruas River, ("Pinto und seine *Peregrinaçam*" 21:80). It appears in Pires as *Baruaz* (Cortasão, *Suma Oriental,* 107 n. 1).

11. *Selangor:* See chapter 17, note 10 above.

12. *Panaagim:* Schurhammer identifies this as Penang ("Pinto und seine *Peregrinaçam*," 21:80), an island off the west coast of the Malay Peninsula, at the northern end of the Strait of Malacca, also called Prince of Wales Island.

13. *Pendão:* Schurhammer identifies this as Pendang (ibid.), but I cannot confirm this. Not in Lagoa.

14. *Sambilão Sião:* Sambilang Siam (?), but I cannot explain the distinction between this and the Sambilang in note 9 above.

15. *Pisanduré:* Collis says that this may be what is now called Domel Island, on the Tenasserim coast, not far from Mergui. He points out (*Grand Peregrination,* 168) that, since Pinto's time, the British Admiralty has renamed most of the islands.

Chapter 145

1. *Pulo Hinhor:* See chapter 66, note 1 above.

2. *red caps:* In chapter 56 Pinto says that red caps were the usual headgear of the Portuguese when fighting at sea.

3. *Cosme Bernardes:* The names of Cosme Bernardes, Pero Ferreira, and Antonio Gomes are not mentioned by the chroniclers.

4. *friend of the Portuguese:* This is the same complaint voiced by the ambassador of the king of Aaru in chapter 21 above.

Chapter 146

1. *Mergui:* Seaport town, capital of the district of Mergui, South Tenasserim Division, in Lower Burma (then part of Siam). It includes the Mergui Archipelago, a group of about eight hundred islands in the Andaman Sea, which Collis describes as follows: "These islands are all similar in appearance . . . and must look today as they did in Pinto's time. They are thickly wooded, often surrounded by a white beach of coral and shells, some of them large and mountainous, with waterfalls and glades, full of game and occasionally inhabited" (*Grand Peregrination,* 167).

2. *Vagaru:* Wagayu, according to Schurhammer, "Pinto und seine *Peregrinaçam*" 21:80. Barros (Barros and Couto, déc. 1, bk. 9, chap. 1, 308) describes *Vagaru* as a town on the east coast of the Gulf of Martaban between the mouth of the Sittang River and the port of Martaban.

3. *Tavoy:* A town, capital of Tavoy District, Tenasserim Division, Lower Burma, on the left bank of the Tavoy River, about thirty miles from its mouth. Also, Tavoy Island, in the Andaman Sea, off the west coast of Lower Burma, south of Tavoy Point, the northernmost island of the Mergui Archipelago.

4. *oyás:* See chapter 41, note 3 above.

5. *Banchá:* See chapter 38, note 1 above.

6. *mutra:* See chapter 130, note 9 above.

7. *combracalão:* Cf. *bracalão* in chapter 105, note 9 above.

8. *Arakan:* See chapter 128, note 19 above.

9. *Taubasoy:* Also spelled *Tobasoy* later in this chapter. This island has not been identified. *Tobasoy* is used for a Cambodian river in chapters 40 and 41.

10. *Lopo Sardinha:* Not mentioned by any of the Portuguese chroniclers.

11. *eve and day of Saint Michael:* September 28 and 29.

Chapter 147

1. *tangas larins:* In the first edition there is a comma after *tangas,* but that is not correct. Though the *tanga* and the *larim* were separate units of currency, in this instance the *larim* is used as an adjective to describe a peculiar form of currency in the shape of a little rod of silver that was bent double unequally. The theoretical value of the ordinary silver *tanga* was fixed at sixty réis, but the *tanga larim* was worth from sixty to one hundred réis. See Boxer, *Great Ship from Amacon,* 338.

2. *Cristóvão Dória:* Castanheda (vol. 2, bk. 8, chap. 184, 864, 887) mentions this Cristóvão Dória as a ship captain who, in the year 1538, was sent by Governor Nuno da Cunha on a mission to Bengal, where he distinguished himself by capturing a Turkish vessel with a rich cargo. Also, Schurhammer ("Pinto und seine *Peregrinaçam*" 21:80–81) cites a letter written by Cristóvão Dória on 19 November 1545 to the then governor João de Castro, in which he says, "I was twice in Bengal and three times in Pegu with Francisco de Moura, Tristão de Gá, and Fernão de Morais." For the last named, see chapter 8, note 2 above. As for Tristão de Gá, Pinto says in chapter 144 above that he sailed from Ning-po to Malacca on a ship belonging to de Gá.

3. *São Tomé:* See chapter 1, note 14 above.

4. *Luis Taborda:* Not mentioned by the Portuguese chroniclers.

5. *Simão de Brito:* Not mentioned by the Portuguese chroniclers.

6. *Jorge Manhoz:* Not mentioned by the Portuguese chroniclers.

Chapter 148

1. *cause for apprehension:* Unbeknownst to Pinto, he had stepped into the middle of a war, the background of which is important to understand in order to follow the events he describes. Collis puts it succinctly (*Grand Peregrination,* 172–73) when he says that the history of Burma is a record of how the Burmese made themselves the ruling race in that region. In addition to numerous tribes there were four main ethnic groups in Burma: the Burmese, the Shans, the Talaings, and the Arakanese. The Burmese became the dominant race when they established the Pagan dynasty that ruled over a united Burma from 1044 to 1287. That dynasty fell after the Tartar invasion of 1287, when Kublai Khan was emperor of China. For three centuries after the withdrawal of the Tartars, the Burmese failed to reestablish their hegemony, and the country was divided into four independent states—the Shans in the north and east, the Arakanese in the west, the Talaings in the south, and the Burmese in the center. In 1535 the Burmese set out to reunite the country, and by 1539 they had overthrown Pegu, the capital of the Talaing kingdom. But Prome and Martaban, the two other principal Talaing cities, held out. When Pinto entered the mouth of the Salween River, the Burmese army was besieging

Martaban, and the Portuguese freebooters who had been hired by the *saw binnya* (Pinto's *chau-bainhá*) to defend him, had passed over to the Burmese camp. The most important historians of the period are Godfrey Eric Harvey, *The History of Burma* (New York: Longmans, Green & Co., 1925); Arthur P. Phayre, *History of Burma,* 2d ed. (London: Susil Gutpa, 1967); and James George Scott, *Burma from the Earliest Times to the Present Day.* However, there is some disagreement among them concerning dates. Phayre says that the siege of Martaban took place in 1540; Harvey, in 1541. Scott says that the dates (1544–45) given by the Portuguese writers, Pinto included, are more trustworthy than the dates given by the Burmese chronicles.

2. *Mounay:* According to Lagoa (*Glossário*), this would be Moulmein, on the east shore of the Gulf of Martaban, at the mouth of the Salween River, opposite Martaban.

3. *king of Burma:* Pinto's king of Burma was Mengtara, who was known as Tabin Shwehti (or Tabeng Shwehti), a title meaning "the topmost golden parasol." He became king of Burma in 1531, at the age of sixteen.

4. *João Cayeyro:* The modern spelling of his surname is Caeiro, but I have left it the way Pinto wrote it. His name appears in most of the European accounts of Burma, but strangely enough he is not mentioned by any of the Portuguese chroniclers of the period, perhaps because he was an adventurer and mercenary, operating beyond the pale of the Portuguese administration. Schurhammer ("Pinto und seine *Peregrinaçam*" 21:80) cites a letter written from Bassein on 24 December 1548 by Simão Botelho, the financial superintendent of Portuguese India, to King John III, informing him that he had taken possession of thirteen to fourteen thousand *pardaus* left by João Caeiro on his death.

5. *Bijayá Sora:* Obviously a title, or Pinto's version of the title, among the Malays, which I cannot identify. It is used again in chapters 203 and 206 with reference to the Achinese, but is spelled differently. See chapter 203, note 11 below.

6. *when the time was right:* Possibly a reference to the monsoon, or an opportune moment to escape.

7. *biças:* A weight used in south India and in Burma. The word is derived from the Tamil *visai,* meaning "division." In Madras it was equal to about three pounds, two ounces avoirdupois. In Burma, the "viss," as the English called it, was equal to about three pounds five ounces.

8. *Tagalá:* Pinto uses this unidentified toponym again in chapter 168, where he says it is a town located five leagues from Moulmein, and in chapter 190 as the name of a fortress.

9. *Paulo de Seixas:* One of the Portuguese mercenaries who, unlike João Caeiro, remained loyal to the *saw binnya.* Not mentioned by any of the Portuguese chroniclers.

10. *Óbidos:* See chapter 4, note 7 above.

11. *varela:* A term that the old Portuguese writers applied to the Buddhist pagodas and monasteries of Indochina and China. It is probably derived from the Malay *barhala* or the Javanese *brahala,* meaning "idol." An idol temple is *rumah-barhala* or *barahla,* "a house of idols," but *barahla* alone may have been used elliptically by the Malays or misunderstood by the Portuguese. Pinto also uses the term *brala* in the same sense, in this chapter and elsewhere.

12. *Bresagucão:* I cannot find anything vaguely resembling *Bresagucão,* the name or title that Pinto applies to the former king of Pegu. The last Peguan king of any stature was Binnya Ran, who ruled peacefully and prosperously for thirty-five years. In 1526 he was succeeded by his son, a frivolous youth of fifteen, called Takarwutbi, whose poor judgement, followed by his death in 1538 or 1539, led to the fall of Pegu. See Phayre, *History of Burma,* 83–95.

13. *bralla:* Or *brala.* See note 11 above.

Chapter 149

1. *Coromandel:* See chapter 3, note 10 above.

2. *Miguel Ferreira:* Mentioned by all the Portuguese chroniclers, who speak highly of him as a rich and able captain of India who could be counted on in great emergencies. He

served under all the governors of India from Albuquerque (1509–15) to Garcia de Noronha (1538–40). Couto (Barros and Couto, déc. 5, bk. 5, chap. 8, 477) says of him that in 1540 he was more than seventy years old, that he never married, and that he died in São Tomé.

3. *Narsinga:* See chapter 9, note 1 and chapter 107, note 3 above.

4. *Xemimbrum: Xemim* represents *smim,* the Talaing word for "lord," and is spelled variously by the English historians as *thamin* or *thamein.* Collis (*Grand Peregrination,* 177) identifies this personage as Smim Payu. In chapter 151 and 155 it is spelled *Xemin Brum.*

5. *grepo:* See chapter 78, note 3 above.

6. *talapoy:* A word frequently used by European writers to designate the Buddhist monks of the Indochinese countries. It is derived from the Pegu *tala,* meaning "lord," and *poi,* meaning "our," hence, "our own spiritual advisor." See *Manrique* 1:223–24 n. 5.

7. *quiay:* See chapter 13, note 19 above.

8. *dopo:* See chapter 118, note 1 above.

9. *Gizares:* See chapter 95, note 5 above.

10. *Mons:* One of the four principal ethnic groups of Burma. They are called Talaings by the Burmese, but they call themselves Mons, in their own language. See chapter 20, note 2 and chapter 148, note 1 above.

11. *Papuans:* The people of Papuas, the name by which the Portuguese designated New Guinea and the surrounding islands. See Hubert T. T. M. Jacobs, *A Treatise on the Moluccas* (Rome: Jesuit Historical Institute, 1971), 330 n. 2.

12. *Savadis:* The people of Sandoway, as it is called by the Arakanese, Hongsavadi by the Siamese, and Hanthawaddy by the Peguans (Schurhammer, "Pinto und seine *Peregrinaçam*" 21:83 n. 162). See chapter 41, note 9 above.

13. *Tangus:* The people of Toungoo. See chapter 41, note 10 above.

14. *Calaminhãs:* See chapter 41, note 12 above.

15. *Chaleus:* See chapter 107, note 7 above.

Chapter 150

1. *bainhá:* Title of a high government officer in Burma and Pegu. From the Burmese *ba-yin,* meaning "lord." Spelled variously by the English historians as "binnya" (Collis), "bayin," (Harvey and Phayre), "buyin," (Scott). See chapter 144, note 4 above.

2. *Meleitay:* Meady or Myédé, in the Thayetmyo District, Magwe Division, Upper Burma. The town is located on the Irrawaddy River, opposite Allanmyo, forty miles north of Prome. In chapter 128 it is spelled *Meleytay.* See chapter 128, note 16 above.

3. *Chaleu:* See chapter 107, not 7 above.

4. *chircá:* Pinto uses this term as a title (chaps. 191, 192, 198) in the sense of a "high court justice" in Pegu. However, as Dalgado points out, the Burmese *sit-kai,* from which it is probably derived, means "lieutenant."

5. *Cosmim:* See chapter 88, note 5 above.

6. *Nhay Vagaru:* In chapters 146 and 147, *Vagaru* is used as a place name, identified as Wagayu. (See chap. 146, n. 2 above.) In chapter 165, it is used as the title of a high-ranking military officer in the kingdom of *Calaminhan.* For this title Dalgado suggests a possible derivation from the Burmese *voni-gyi,* meaning "minister of state," or *bo-gyi,* meaning "general." Also in chapters 163–65, Pinto uses the title *monvagaru,* which Dalgado says may be derived from the Burmese *min-voni-gyi,* meaning "minister or governor." *Nhay* is the Siamese *nai,* for "sir or madame." (See chap. 111, n. 4 above.)

7. *Ansedá:* This would be Henzada, a district and town in Lower Burma, located on the Irrawaddy River, seventy-five miles north of Rangoon.

8. *Jangumá:* Also *Jangomá.* The town and state of Siamese Laos, called by the Burmese Zimmé, by the Siamese Xieng-mai, or Kiang-mai, or Chiang Mai. See chapter 70, note 4 above. It is spelled variously as *Jangomay, Zangomay, Jamahey,* or *Iamayhey,* in the English and Dutch

narratives if the seventeenth century. However, the Portuguese chroniclers write *Jangomá* as does Pinto, i.e., Barros (in Barros and Couto, déc. 3, bk. 2, chap. 5, 158; Couto (in Barros and Couto, déc. 5, bk. 6, chap. 1, 3); and Antonio Bocarro (*Década XIII da história da Índia,* ed. Rodrigo José de Lima Felner [Lisbon: Academia Real das Sciências de Lisboa, 1876], part 1, chap. 33, 136). Pinto also refers to a *Jangumá* River, for which see chapter 128, note 11 above.

9. *Dambambuu:* Used as a place-name in chapter 128.

10. *Rajah Savady:* Appears twice in the same sentence. For *Savady,* see chap. 41, note 9 and chapter 149, note 12 above.

11. *monteo of Negrais: Negrais* has been identified by Phayre (*History of Burma,* 11 n. 2) as Nagarît, the bluff of land so called by the Burmese, and known to Europeans as Cape Negrais, a corruption of the Burmese name. As for *monteo,* in chapters 103 to 106 Pinto uses this word for a Chinese official whose powers are both military and judicial. In chapters 33 and 182 he uses it with reference to Siam, and in chapter 150 he applies it to Burma. See chapter 33, note 3 above.

12. *rolim of Mounay:* According to Collis (*Grand Peregrination,* 196), *rolim* is a corruption of the Burmese word *yahan* or *rahan,* which is the highest monastic grade among the Buddhists. For *Mounay,* see chapter 148, note 2 above.

13. *daughter of the former king of Pegu:* She could not have been the daughter of the last king of Pegu, Takarwutbi, who was only twenty-six years old when Pegu fell to the Burmese. He was sixteen years old when he succeeded his father, Binnya Ran, in 1526. See Phayre, *History of Burma,* 85–95.

Chapter 151

1. *chaubainhá's treasure:* Pinto may have exaggerated the wealth of Martaban, but most historians agree that it was a town of the greatest importance, since it was an entrepôt on the trade route from China to the West. Though Martaban had been a great trade center for centuries, its wealth increased with the opening of trade with Europe by the Cape of Good Hope. See Collis, *Grand Peregrination,* 166, and Phayre, *History of Burma,* 96.

2. *varelas, pagodas, and bralas:* Pinto seems to be making a distinction between these three words, but basically they mean the same thing. See chapter 148, note 11. However, whatever he chooses to call them, it seems strange that Tabin Schwehti would have given the order to have them torn down. Both he and his brother-in-law, Bureng Naung, who succeeded him, represented themselves as upholders of religion and founded many costly religious buildings. Generally speaking, throughout their respective reigns they were very careful not to offend the priests. See Phayre, *History of Burma,* 99, and Scott, 76.

3. *putchock:* Or putchuk. The trade name for the root of the plant *Apletaxis auriculaia,* a native of Kashmir, exported to China and other eastern countries and used as a medicine and for making the Chinese joss sticks. Described by Garcia da Orta, who was the first to recognize that the drug known as "costo" or "costus" (the *Aucklandia costus* of Falconer) was identical to the putchock. See *Colóquios* 1:267 n. 1.

4. *storax:* Or styrax. A fragrant gum resin obtained from any of several trees or shrubs. In early modern use applied to the resin of the tree *Styrax officinalis;* in later commercial and pharmaceutical use, to the balsam of the tree *Liquidambar orientalis* (liquid storax). See Orta 2:112–13 n. 4.

5. *viceroy of Toungoo:* Possibly Thingathu, the father of Bureng Naung (Pinto's *Chaumigrem*), who ruled the hereditary kingdom of Toungoo in the absence of Tabin Shwehti and Bureng Naung. See Phayre, *History of Burma,* 100.

6. *daughter of the king of Pegu:* She may have been a daughter of Binnya Ran and sister to Takarwutbi, who was the last king of Pegu. See chapter 148, note 12 and chapter 150, note 13.

7. *hair like skeins of gold:* Collis writes (*Grand Peregrination,* 182 n. 1), "That Talaing women should have seemed so to Pinto is strange. Their natural complexions were probably

blanched with white powder and they may have been wearing yellowish turbans or head-scarves."

Chapter 152

1. *ministers of the Arm of Wrath:* The same expression is used with reference to China in chapters 87, 101, and 103.

2. *Muhé:* The first edition has *Muhé,* which may be a name or, as Brito Rebello seems to think, an error for *nhay* (3:66 n. 1).

3. *thrown into the sea:* Collis writes (*Grand Peregrination,* 183–84), "The Burmese chronicles, after recording the fall of the city, do not mention the execution of Saw Binnya and his wife, but such executions were normal in Burmese history and it is likely that this one took place." A similar statement was made by Harvey, 342 n. 2.

Chapter 153

1. *Bainhá Chaque:* Mentioned in chapter 150, where he is described as "governor of the kingdom."

2. *Gonçalo Falcão:* Schurhammer cites a letter written by a Gabriel de Ataide from São Tomé on 18 May 1546 to Don Álvaro de Castro in which he says that he has heard from Pegu, from Gonçalo Falcão, who has been there for fifteen or sixteen years. This is undoubtedly the Gonçalo Falcão to whom Pinto refers. See Schurhammer, "Pinto und seine *Peregrinaçam*" 21:80. Diogo do Couto mentions a Gonçalo Falcão who was ordered home in chains by Queen Catherine in 1558 but who was later absolved and appointed captain of the fortress of Sofala by King Sebastian, an appointment which his subsequent death prevented him from assuming. He was the last of a noble family that traced its ancestry back to the beginnings of Portugal, and may possibly be the same Gonçalo Falcão to whom Pinto refers. See Couto in Barros and Couto, *déc.* 7, bk. 10, chap. 1, 422–44.

3. *Pero de Faria's first term:* He served two terms as captain of Malacca, from 1528 to 1529 the first time, and 1539 to 1543 the second time.

4. *fever:* The original has "modorra." See chapter 115, note 7.

5. *Pero de Faria:* In 1543 Pero de Faria left Malacca for Goa, where he lived until his death in 1546. See Schurhammer, "Pinto und seine Peregrinaçam" 21:83.

6. *Dom Henrique d'Eça:* Appears to have had a long career in India, where he distinguished himself in action as early as 1518. He was appointed captain of Cannanore in 1542.

7. *Siammon:* According to Phayre (*History of Burma,* 266), Pinto's *Siammon* is a corruption of Shan Meng, as the chief of Unbaung was known. He was the leader of a federation formed by the northern Shan states to resist the designs of Tabin Shwehti upon Ava. According to Le Gentil (53), Pinto borrowed the word from Gaspar da Cruz, who uses *Siões Mãos* (Siamese Mons) as a synonym for Laos (chap. 3). *Siammon* is also used as a place-name in chapter 107. Also spelled *Siammom.*

8. *Calaminhan:* See chapter 41, note 12 above.

9. *Prome:* See chapter 41, note 11 above.

10. *Bagou:* See chapter 107, note 10 above.

11. *seró:* Pinto uses this term to designate a small Burmese vessel. Dalgado believes it is a borrowing from the Malay *seroh,* meaning "shrunken, reduced," or *seroq,* meaning "small."

12. *Ansedá River:* By this the Irrawaddy River is meant, since *Ansedá* (the modern town of Henzada) is located at the head of the Irrawaddy Delta, seventy-five miles north-northwest of Rangoon.

13. *Danaplu:* Danubyu (or Danobyu), a city in the Burmese district of Maubin, located on the left bank of the Irrawaddy River, about sixty miles from Rangoon.

14. *thirteenth of April* [1545]: Phayre (*History of Burma,* 99) says that Tabin Shwehti

marched on or reached Prome in 1541; Harvey (157) says that he marched on Prome in 1542, and Scott gives no date.

15. *daughter of the king of Ava:* According to Phayre (*History of Burma,* 98), Narabadi was succeeded by his brother Meng Khaung, as king of Prome, and his wife was the daughter of Tho Han Bwa, king of Ava. According to Scott (71), the queen of Prome was a sister of Sao Han Hpa (Phayre's Tho Han Bwa), the king of Ava. Harvey does not clarify the relationship.

Chapter 155

1. *amucks:* See chapter 17, note 1 above.

2. *Xemim Meleitay:* I have found no mention of such a personage in any of the histories consulted, but it seems that this type of treason was not uncommon. According to Phayre (*History of Burma,* 100), there were other instances of royal refugees in the countries of Indochina who offered, in exchange for such favors, to become tributaries of ruling kings. Also, as Harvey points out (157), "after a five months' siege, starvation set in at Prome and the besieged deserted in great numbers."

3. *eve of Saint Bartholomew:* August 23.

4. *base bloodline and extraction:* Pinto seems to be confusing Tabin Shwehti with Bureng Naung, his general and successor to the throne, who was said to be a commoner. Tabin Shwehti, or his father for him, claimed descent from the ancient kings of Burma, as set forth in the royal chronicles. See Phayre, *History of Burma,* 92–93, and Scott, 65.

5. *rubies, sapphires, emeralds:* The Pali or classical name of Ava was Ratanapura, meaning "city of gems." See Phayre, *History of Burma,* 63.

6. *xemim of Toungoo:* Smim or lord of Toungoo, which was the hereditary kingdom of Tabin Shwehti, and an insignificant one before he set out on his wars of conquest to re-unite Burma.

7. *thrown into the river:* According to Phayre (*History of Burma,* 99), "The king, the queen, and the chief officers were massacred with revolting cruelty." Scott (71) relies on the Burmese chronicle, *Maha Yazawin,* which says that the king and queen were taken off to Toungoo and so dismisses them. Harvey (342 n. 2) quotes a different source that shows that the king and queen of Prome were kept in captivity till 1553, when the husband was executed and the wife passed into the harem of Bayin (or Bureng) Naung, Pinto's *Chaumigrem,* who appears for the first time in chapter 156.

8. *caloetes:* Or *caluetes.* The punishment of impalement, in Dravidic India, from the Tamil-Malayalam *kaluvirri* (pronounced kaluvitti), *kalu* meaning "punishment stake," and *luvirri* "to impale." Pinto applies this word to areas outside of India.

Chapter 156

1. *under the command of the king of Ava:* Pinto presents a somewhat confused version of the fighting that took place during and after the siege of Prome. He may not have been aware of, or perhaps, for his own rhetorical purposes, chose to ignore, the fact that two armies came to the relief of Prome while the siege was in progress, and a third, after the fall of Prome, which attempted to recapture it. The first army was commanded by Thobanbwa (or Sao Han Hpa), the king of Ava and father of the queen of Prome. Simultaneously, a second army, sent by the king of Arakan (see chap. 128, n. 19 above) who was married to the sister of the king of Prome, marched across the mountains to operate on the flank of the invader. Both armies were defeated by Bureng Naung (see n. 3 below) north of Prome, while the siege was in progress. In the meantime, Thobanbwa, the king of Ava and father of the queen of Prome, having been murdered, the Shan chief of Unbaung (see chap. 153, n. 7 above) was invited to take his place. This new king of Ava, six months after the fall of Prome, marched with a Shan army in an attempt to recapture the city. The Shans were again defeated near Prome and were chased to the very gates

of Ava (see chap. 107, n. 6 above) by Bureng Naung. After which, he and Tabin Shwehti returned to Pegu, being convinced that the confederation of the northern Shan chiefs were still too strong to be successfully attacked. See Phayre, *History of Burma,* 98; Scott, 70–71; and Harvey, 155–57.

2. *Meleitay:* See chapter 150, note 2 above.

3. *Chaumigrem:* Pinto's name for Bureng Naung, the brilliant general of Tabin Shwehti and perhaps the greatest man of action in Burmese history. The title by which he was best known is Bureng Naung (spelled variously as Bayinnaung or Buyin Naung), meaning "the king's elder brother," which designated him as heir to the throne. Popular tradition makes him out to be of humble birth (see chap. 155, n. 4 above), the son of a toddy-palm climber. His mother was said to be the wet nurse of Tabin Shwehti, with whom he was raised from childhood and whose sister he married. Throughout the reign of Tabin Shwehti (1530–51), Bureng Naung was all-powerful in the direction of affairs. He succeeded Tabin Shwehti in 1551 and reigned until his death in 1581. See Phayre, *History of Burma,* 94; Scott, 66; and Harvey, 342 n. 1.

4. *Mons:* Though Prome was a Mon, or Talaing, city, the army sent by the king of Ava to the relief of Prome was comprised of Shans, a distinct ethnic group similar in language and customs to the Siamese and Laotians.

5. *Peguans:* These were Mons, or Talaings, who had capitulated to Tabin Shwehti in 1541(?) and in whose capital he had been consecrated king. They served in his armies. See chapter 149, note 10 above.

6. *Xemim Meleitay:* See chapter 155, note 2 above. Meady or Myédé was subject to Ava.

Chapter 157

1. *ganta:* From the Malay *gantang,* a weight or measure mentioned by some old voyagers by which pepper was sold in the Malay Archipelago. Crawfurd (in Yule and Burnell, 364a) defines it as a "dry measure, equal to about a gallon." Garcia da Orta mentions it as a weight of twenty-four ounces. Dalgado defines it as a variable measure of capacity in Malaysia, which, in general, was equal to a *canada.* See note 2 below.

2. *canada:* Boxer (*Great Ship from Amacon,* 342) defines the *canada* as a Portuguese liquid measure equivalent to three English pints.

3. *Calaminhan:* See chapter 41, note 12 above.

4. *brother-in-arms:* Of all the episodes in the book, the embassy to *Calaminhan* has been regarded by some critics as the most fantastic. Schurhammer for one ("Pinto und seine *Peregrinaçam*" 21:82) dismisses it as a figment of the author's imagination. Except for Pinto's confused geography, others, like Phayre, have no difficulty accepting the general facts of the story, which he finds quite probable. Phayre writes, "As the Northern Shan chiefs had entered into an alliance to resist the designs of Tabeng Shwehti upon Ava, the account by Pinto of a Burmese officer of high rank being sent . . . to secure the good-will or active support of the eastern Shan states and the king of Zimmè [Chiang-mai or Siamese Laos] . . . is credible and probable" (*History of Burma,* 266).

Chapter 158

1. *Timplão:* According to José de Ramos, *Timplão* or *Timplan* is a Burmese corruption of *Xieng Luang,* meaning "big city." The Siamese *Xieng* is *Thieng* in Burmese, since the initial letters *x* and *s* are pronounced like *t.* Therefore, *Timplão* of *Xieng Luang* is the city or capital of the former Shan or Laos state known today as Luang Prabang. See Ramos's article, "Império do Calaminhão."

2. *he fits that title more than anyone else:* Ramos also tells us (ibid.) that *Calaminhan* comes from the Siamese *kala,* meaning "lord," and *mouen* or *muong,* meaning "earth or world," hence, "lord of the earth or world," i.e., "king." He also tells us that in Lanchang (the early name for Luang Prabang) the king was known as *chao mouen* or *chao muong.* On the other hand, the kings of Lanchang had many titles, one of which was *chao muong chang* or "king of elephants," *chang* meaning "elephant." And since *lan* means "a million," Lanchang, the name of the country itself means "a million of elephants." Writing at an earlier date (1940), Joaquim de Campos states, "The Empire of Calaminham of which Pinto gives a glowing description is not an invention. Calaminham (Mon *Kala,* from *Trala,* and *muong*: *lord of the country*) refers certainly to the King of Lan Chang who was Photisarat at the time and who received two embassies from King Ṭaben Shweti of Burma, as recorded in the *Annals of Lanchang*" (230).

3. *Queitor River:* This would be the Irrawaddy River, on which the town of Ava is located.

4. *Jangomá:* Also *Jangumá.* See chapter 150, note 8 above.

5. *Narsinga:* See chapter 9, note 1 and chapter 107, note 3 above.

6. *Orissa:* The name of the ancient kingdom and modern state in east India, on the Bay of Bengal.

7. *Masulipatam:* Or Masulipatnam. A seaport city, northeast Andhra Pradesh, India, on the Bay of Bengal, 215 miles north-northeast of Madras. A popular name for the city is Bunder.

8. *alcá:* Pinto seems to be the only one of the early Portuguese writers to use this word, which Dalgado suggests may be related to the Malay *laku,* meaning "currency (coin)."

9. *"golden shrimp":* Ramos ("Império do Calaminhão") cannot identify the city of *Catammás* but points to the fact that *k'tam* (pronounced *k'dam*), means "crab," and *mas* (pronounced *meas*), means "gold" in the Cambodian language and perhaps in the Mon language as well. He mentions a city called Catamasai (as does Eckford Luard, in Manrique 1:299 n. 2), located to the south of Viengchan, but admits that it was not on the route traveled by Pinto.

10. *raudivá of Tinlau:* According to Ramos ("Império do Calaminhão") the second prince of Luang Prabang is still to this day called *ratsabout* or *rajavu. Tinlau* or *Tinleu,* he says, in the Burmese transcription would represent Xieng Lau or Xieng Leu, but gives no identification or location for them.

11. *Naugator:* Captain or chieftain of a city, in Indochina. Dalgado believes this word is a phonetic variant of *nauticor* (see chap. 117, n. 3), which is similar in meaning.

12. *candins:* (*candil* or *candim,* sing.): An Indo-Portuguese weight, corresponding roughly to about five hundred pounds, but varying much in different localities.

13. *Tinagogo:* Schurhammer believes that Pinto took the name *Tinagogo* from that of a city called Theng-gan-ngok, located between Tavoy and Mergui ("Pinto und seine Peregrinaçam" 21:82). However, Le Gentil says it is useless to try to identify Pinto's *Tinagogo* with a city located much too far from the region described by Pinto (56).

Chapter 159

1. *Sansaporau:* Fray Sebastian Manrique uses this word in his *Itinerario* (1629–43) to describe a similar festival in Arakan, for which both Collis (*Grand Peregrination,* 189 n. 2) and Eckford Luard (Manrique 1:246 n. 2) have accused him of plagiarizing Pinto. Manrique (1:234) says that the word means "feast in commemoration of the dead," but Eckford Luard says it appears to mean the "full moon" feast, from the Siamese *sasi,* meaning "moon," and *punna,* "full." José de Ramos ("Império do Calaminhão") gives a similar derivation. Pinto, however, employs it as the god's name.

2. *Çacotais:* Probably the people of Sukhothai or Sukotai, today a village on the Yom River, West Thailand, thirty miles northwest of P'itsanulok. Important formerly as the capital of a Thai-Khmer state of the same name that flourished 1256–1350.

Chapter 160

1. *neepois:* This word is not found in either Dalgado or Yule and Burnell. Eckford-Luard, in his edition of Manrique's *Itinerario,* suggests a possible derivation from the Talaing *naai-puiai,* meaning "our master," i.e., the head of a monastery. He also remarks that Pinto's minute classification of monks is unusual, for as a rule they are classed simply as *gama-bhikku* or village monks and *aranya-bhikku* or forest monks. See Manrique 1 : 224 n. 5.

2. *bicos:* Described simply by Dalgado as a Buddhist monk who begs for alms. From the Pali *bhikku* (see n. 1 above). In Siamese it is *pikkhu.*

3. *censers:* In Burmese Buddhism incense sticks are sometimes used, but censers are quite unknown. See Manrique 1 : 246 n. 2.

4. *prayers:* Eckford Luard writes (ibid.), "A feast of the dead and prayers for souls can have no place in a religion which denies the continuance of personality after death. In theory also no Burman Buddhist can pray, but in practice every one does. But they never pray for the dead."

5. *cut off their heads:* "That Buddhist monks would touch the remains of the immolated devotees is . . . not to be believed in for a moment" (ibid.).

6. *brutish customs:* The festival described here by Pinto is certainly reminiscent of the Hindu fesival of Juggernaut, our corruption of the Sanskrit word *Jagannatha,* meaning "lord of the world." It is the title under which Vishnu is worshipped at the shrine of Puri in Orissa, on the Bay of Bengal. This cult, unique in India, has no caste distinction. Although pilgrims have thrown themselves to death beneath the wheels of the Juggernaut car and committed other acts of self-immolation, contrary to popular belief these acts are not part of the religious ritual. A similar festival is described by Friar Odoric, who stated in his *Travels* (1330) that as many as five hundred pilgrims perished every year beneath the wheels of the car. The festival is also mentioned by Nicolo Conti (1420) and Gaspero Balbi (1581), as well as by Pinto's contemporary, Diogo do Couto. Other examples are quoted in Yule's and Burnell's *Hobson-Jobson,* under "Juggurnaut." For Friar Odoric's description, which Pinto may well have read, see Yule's *Cathay* 2 : 145. Later travelers, such as Sonnerat (*Voyages aux Indes,* 1782), say the suicides had decreased in number, and again, a hundred years later, they are spoken of as a rare exception. But, as Collis points out (*Grand Peregrination,* 189), "in the sixteenth century the car procession was reputed to be an occasion of nightmare, the most dreadful scene of religious frenzy in Asia."

A poem of the early nineteenth century (1809), quoted by Yule (*Hobson-Jobson,* 467), that dramatizes the phantasmagoria of the Juggernaut festival is given here for its interest.

> A thousand pilgrims strain
> Arm, shoulder, breast, and thigh, with might and main,
> To drag that sacred wain,
> And scarce can draw along the enormous load.
> Prone fall the frantic votaries on the road,
> And calling on the God
> Their self-devoted bodies there they lay
> To pave his chariot way.
> On Jaga-Naut they call,
> The ponderous car rolls on, and crushes all,
> Through flesh and bones it ploughs its dreadful path.
> Groans rise unheard; the dying cry,
> And death, and agony
> Are trodden under foot by yon mad throng,
> Who follow close and thrust the deadly wheels along.
> (*Curse of Kehama,* XIV, 5)

Collis also points out that Pinto "did not properly understand Hinduism nor appreciate the distinction between the two forms of Buddhism, the Mahayana and the Hinayana . . . and treats them as existing all three in one place. In point of fact, he was not entirely wrong. While it has been the practice of modern writers to demarcate the geographical boundaries of these three forms of Oriental religion, they are not in actual practice so insulated. Even in Burma, which has always prided itself on the purity of its Hinayana faith, there have always coexisted important elements of Hindu and Mahayanist worship, though the orthodox monks have not countenanced them."

Chapter 161

1. *Lucifer:* Eckford Luard writes (Manrique 1:246 n. 2) that "The serpent, Swallower of the House of Smoke, and the Devil, are incompatible with Buddhism or Burma, where the snake is worshipped as an incarnation of Buddha."

2. *panha:* Also *paina,* from the Malayalam *paññi.* A type of cotton from the plant *Bombax malabaricum,* not suitable for weaving. It is used only for stuffing.

3. *silver coins . . . gold:* Diogo do Couto (Barros and Couto, *déc.* 5, bk. 6, chap. 31) mentions a religious festival in Bengal where the devotees also brought offerings worth their weight in gold and silver.

4. *Santiago:* See chapter 5, note 3 above. Also, cf. Odoric's "people come to say their prayers to the idol from great distances, just as Christians go from far on pilgrimage to Santiago in Galicia, or to Saint Peter or Saint Paul in Rome." See Yule, *Cathay* 2:143 n. 3.

5. *pardaus:* See chapter 6, note 14 above.

6. *musical instruments:* Speaking of the Burmese monks, Eckford Luard writes (Manrique 1:246 n. 2), "Musical instruments they would not deign to touch, such being 'anathema Maranatha,' quite as much as to a seventeenth century Puritan."

7. *Godomem:* This represents Kodam' or Khdam', which is one of the most common names for Buddha in the Indochinese countries. It comes from the Pali *Gotamo,* or the Sanskrit *Gautama.* It is the priestly surname, according to Buddhist legend, of the Sakya tribe from which the Buddha is descended.

8. *martyrs of the Devil:* Collis writes (*Grand Peregrination,* 194) that "such kinds of hermits, yogis, recluses and anchorites . . . were to be found at that date, and continue till the present day, in India, Tibet, China, and also, to a less degree, in Burma and Siam, though never all of them in one place. The austerities mentioned by Pinto are facts and he might have added others of an even grimmer sort." Also, with particular reference to Luang Prabang at that date, Joaquim de Campos writes (230) that the religious practices described by Pinto "were the relics of Brahmanism and Buddhist Mahayanism with an admixture of animism which King Photisarat, a fervent Hinayanist, tried to stamp out."

Chapter 162

1. *tavangrá:* From the Burmese *ta-ghá-va,* meaning an "estate," a "farmhouse," or any kind of "abode at the edge of a river," in Indochina.

2. *divan:* In the Near East, a room used for councils of state or similar formal functions; a council of state.

3. *Queytor:* In chapters 156–158, *Queitor* appears as the name of a river (see chap. 158, n. 3). In chapters 162–65, it is used as the title of a governor or minister of justice. It is spelled *Queytor* in chapters 162 and 164.

4. *100,000 persons:* With reference to the number of pilgrims who flock to the festival of Orissa each year, Le Gentil cites (58) the *Imperial Gazetteer of India* (1886), 312, which says that

"more than 100,000 come each year and that the cortege of certain Rajahs who come from hundreds of miles away, number more than 3,000 persons."

5. *calendar of other nations:* As José de Ramos points out ("Império do Calaminhão"), the Laotians have a lunar calendar with each month divided alternately into twenty-nine and thirty days. The lunar year is adjusted to the solar by dividing it into twelve months and adding intercalary days or a supplementary month every three years. Therefore, 7,320 moons or lunar months make exactly 610 solar years.

6. *laquesá:* See chapter 45, note 3 above.

7. *fifty laquesás of people died:* There are a number of points in this paragraph for which José de Ramos ("Império do Calaminhão") offers the following explanation: Since Pinto was in Laos in 1545, the priest is referring to events that took place in the tenth century, or 610 years earlier. The first and second quarter of the tenth century is exactly when the first king of Laos, the legendary Kun Lo of the Thai race, established his supremacy over what was then called Muang Sua. However, the facts described seem to conform more with the reign of King Fa Ngum, who ascended the throne in 1353 and who, after many wars, enlarged the frontiers of the kingdom which constituted the empire of Lanchang or "Calaminhan." He may have had twenty-seven small tributary kings under his sway. As for the reference to him as the "holy *Calaminhan,*" in Siam as in Laos, the king was always regarded as absolute temporal and spiritual leader. Also, Pinto's *Xixavong* or *Xixavarom* is a common name of the Laotian kings. *Meleutay* seems to be related to Fa Ngum's title, "San Seu Thai," meaning 300,000.

8. *Sorocatão:* Though no clue to the whereabouts of this city has ever been traced, *Sorocatão* is undoubtedly a corruption of *s'ramana Gautama,* meaning "the ascetic Gautama." See Manrique 1:255 n. 8.

9. *sensuous sacrifice:* Pinto may be thinking of the *deva-dasi* ("slave girl of the gods"), the official name of the poor girls who are devoted to dancing and prostitution in the idol temples, particularly in southern India. See Yule and Burnell.

10. *village of the Apostle Saint Thomas:* Probably refers to Meliapur, a suburb of Madras, in southeast India, where Saint Thomas is supposed to have been killed by Brahmans in A.D. 68. Legend places the martyrdom and original burial place of the saint upon a hill known as Saint Thomas's Mount, which lies about eight miles southwest of Madras City. On it stands a Portuguese church erected in 1547 on the spot where a cross popularly connected with Saint Thomas was found. It is a place of pilgrimage for Indian Roman Catholics or the "Christians of Saint Thomas," said originally to have been converted by the apostle Saint Thomas. At the request of the king of Portugal, Saint Thomas of Meliapur was created into a suffragan bishopric of the metropolitan see of Goa on 9 January 1606. A curious note may be added to all this. The Roman martyrology calls the city Calamina. Schurhammer ("Pinto und seine *Peregrinaçam*" 21:83) says that Pinto may have taken the name of his *Calaminhan* from this, but it is located much too far from the region described by Pinto. For the best summary of the traditions and legends relating to the apostle Saint Thomas in India, see Yule's *Marco Polo* 2:356–59 n. 4. See also chapter 3, note 9 above.

Chapter 163

1. *thirteen Calaminhans:* See José de Ramos ("Império do Calaminhão"), who says that from the time of King Fa Ngum (1353–73), who was the first king of the empire of *Calaminhan,* to the time of King Photisarat, there were indeed "thirteen *Calaminhans.*"

2. *sagirave:* Or *sanguirave.* Dalgado thinks this word comes from the Malay *sagi-ravang.*

3. *hurfangá:* Dalgado seems to think that this word is related to the Burmese *tha-ra-hpu,* meaning "crown."

4. *raudivá:* This word is used as a proper name in chapter 140, as a title in chapter 158, and here as an article of clothing that Dalgado says is derived from the Malay *randi.*

Chapter 164

1. *Faleu, Jatir, and Pontau:* We find a similar reference in Manrique to the "mountains and ranges of Pondaleu, Jatir and Faleu," which Eckford Luard says (1:253 n. 7) "have not been traced." But Manrique may have copied Pinto.

2. *caulanges:* Dalgado suggests a possible derivation from the Malay *kalangar,* which means "a fainting away, or a gradually passing away."

3. *sigiputões:* In this instance Dalgado "presumes" that the word comes from the Pali *sijjipito,* meaning "well-educated, cultured, ready."

4. *duke of Tuscany:* There may be some truth to this. In the year 1569 the Grand Duke Cosimo de' Medici (1519–74) sent an embassy to Lisbon with instructions to obtain maps and other geographical information on China. While in Lisbon, the Florentine ambassador, Bernardo Neri, contacted Pinto for such information. See Pinto's letter of 15 March 1571 to Bernardo Neri in Catz, *Cartas,* 114–16.

5. *Gaspar de Meireles:* A Gaspar de Meireles is mentioned in chapter 116, but he died, presumably, in chapter 132, on the way to Japan.

6. *Modeliar:* From the Tamil *mudaliyar, muthaliyar,* an honorific used in the Tamil districts of Ceylon for a native headman.

7. *death on the cross:* The thinly veiled Christian theology expounded in this chapter appears to be an attempt on the part of the author to support the widely held belief that Saint Thomas had converted parts of inner Asia. The search for these Christians begins in chapter 48, in which Antonio de Faria learns that the natives of Hainan have never heard of Christ. In chapter 96 the Portuguese prisoners in China come across a group of Christians who claimed to have been converted by a hermit called Mateus Escandel. The whole story of Saint Thomas is probably apocryphal, but there is no doubt that in very early times there were Nestorian Christian communities in China and southern India.

Chapter 165

1. *Prechau Guimião:* See chapters 36, note 9 and chapter 130, note 6 above.

2. *chaveca:* See chapter 142, note 5 above.

3. *poisoning their king:* Manrique also alludes (1:238) to the Burmese chronicles, which tell of a king who was killed by his nobles at a banquet they had given him in the city of *Chaleu.*

4. *terivós:* According to Dalgado, this would mean a "solemn festival or pilgrimage" in which a large number of *theras,* or religious elders, take part. *Theriyo* in Pali, from the Sanskrit *sthaviraya,* is an adjective, with the sense of "related to the *theras.*" In chapter 159 it is used in a compound form as *massunterivó.*

5. *cabizondos:* See chapter 49, note 2 above.

6. *chandeuhós:* This appears to be a variant spelling of *chandeus.* See chapter 98, note 3 above.

7. *cassia fistula:* An ornamental tropical tree whose dried pods yield a mild laxative.

8. *trevite:* Apparently a medicinal drug of India, which I have been unable to identify.

9. *scammony:* A climbing plant of the morning glory family, native in Asia Minor, with tuberous roots containing a milky juice. The dried resin of the roots are used as a strong cathartic.

10. *woad:* See chapter 3, note 23 above.

11. *putchock:* See chapter 151, note 3 above.

12. *storax:* See chapter 151, note 4 above.

13. *cutch:* Also called catechu and caut. An astringent extract from the wood of several species of acacia.

14. *cates:* See chapter 18, note 5 above.

15. *taels:* See chapter 35, note 6 above.

16. *mazes:* See chapter 25, note 1 above.

17. *condorins:* Or "candareens," in English. From the Malay *kanduri*. The term was formerly applied to the hundredth of the Chinese ounce or weight, commonly called by the Malay name *tahil* or *tael.*

18. *queitor:* See chapter 162, note 3 above.

19. *vagaru:* See chapter 150, note 6 above.

20. *"Quiay dó sam rorpy":* Both Ramos and Campos believe that Pinto, without knowing it, is referring to the Buddhist Triad or the Trinity of Buddhist doctrine (the Three Precious Jewels): Buddha, Dharma (the Law), and Sangha (the Monastic Order), which is invoked in all the cremonies and Buddhist prayers. Eckford Luard quotes Wood, who writes, "*Quiay doo samrorpi* may be Siamese *Chao Du Sam Roi Pi,* which may conceivably mean 'Lord guard me for 300 years'" (Manrique 1:300 n. 2).

Chapter 166

1. *banazas:* Neither this word nor any of the places or names of the monstrous creatures mentioned by Pinto have ever been identified and probably never will, though the wily Pinto is careful to say that he heard about them from merchants he met. This is not unusual, as descriptions of fabulous creatures appear in many of the medieval travel accounts. Odoric, for one, describes the strange creatures he saw in the garden of Kublai Khan (Yule, *Cathay* 2:230). Similar descriptions appear in the recollections of the fourteenth-century traveler Marignolli, who also mentions those described by Saint Augustine (Yule, *Cathay* 3:254–55). However, unlike Pinto, the last two very sensibly conclude that no such creatures exist as a species, though there may be an individual monster here and there. We must agree with Le Gentil (44), who says that Pinto's "natural history" is certainly at the level of the credulity of his contemporaries.

2. *Fransisco Temudo:* His names does not appear in any of the Portuguese chronicles of the period. Pinto may have invented this amusing anecdote as a satiric allusion to the drinking talents of his countrymen.

Chapter 167

1. *Ventrau River:* See chapter 128, note 9 above.

2. *Jangumá:* See chapter 128, note 11 above.

3. *Chalagonim:* Here the name of a pirate; in chapters 188 and 190 it is the name of a Burmese captain. Another example of Pinto's multiple use of names.

4. *Chaumigrem:* See chapter 156, note 3 above.

5. *Antonio Ferreira:* Some of the Portuguese who, according to Pinto, took part in the Burmese wars of the sixteenth century are mentioned by both the Portuguese chroniclers and the modern English historians. Some are mentioned by one and not the other, as in the case of João Caeiro (chaps. 148, 149, 150, 153) and Paulo de Seixas (chaps. 148, 149) who, as mercenaries, were ignored by the Portuguese chroniclers though they are mentioned by the later English historians who probably got their information from Pinto. The Antonio Ferreira mentioned here does not appear in either the Portuguese chronicles or the English historians of Burma.

6. *Aixquendó:* Spelled *Aixequendó* in chapter 168.

7. *rolim of Mounay:* See chapter 150, note 12 above.

8. *guimões* (sing. *guimão*): Pinto uses this word only once, whereas the other names for various priestly ranks are used frequently throughout the Indochinese episodes. Dalgado says it must be derived from a confusion of combination of two Burmese words; i.e., *kyung,* meaning a "Buddhist temple or monastery," and *pungui* (or *p'hun-gyi,* meaning "great glory"), which is the name for a priest.

Chapter 168

1. *chautar:* Or "chudder," as the English called it, from the Hindi *chadar.* A sheet, or square piece of cloth of any kind; also, the ample sheet commonly worn as a mantle by women in northern India.

2. *agrém:* See chapter 127, note 4 above.

3. *Cosmim:* See chapter 88, note 5 above.

4. *birds:* The freeing of birds or other animals is a common Buddhist method for gaining merit. It is still done today in Thailand, much to the delight of foreign tourists. In his translation of Manrique's *Itinerario,* Eckford Luard remarks (1:141 n. 10) that in the nineteenth century Indians would come with bird cages in their hands, run alongside the carriage of an English gentleman occupying a high position in the land, and set the birds free in his honor. See chapter 98 above, where Pinto describes the same practice in China.

5. *definitor:* An officer of the chapter in certain monastic orders, charged with the "definition" or decision of points of discipline.

6. *coutalanhá:* Pinto's *Chaumigrem,* who succeeded Tabin Shwehti as king of Burma, went by many titles during his thirty-year reign, but the one by which he was best known is Bureng Naung (a variant of Baringyinaungsaw), meaning "the king's elder brother," a title akin to "heir apparent." When he was consecrated king in 1551, he took the style of Hanthawadi Sin-Byi-Shin (Scott, 74) or Tsheng-phyú-myá-sheng Meng-tará-gyi (Phayre, "On the History of the Burma Race," *Journal of the Asiatic Society of Bengal* 38, no. 1 [1869]: 71). However, of all his titles, none even faintly resembles *coutalanhá.* See chapter 156, note 3 above.

7. *Tagalá:* See chapter 148, note 8 above.

Chapter 169

1. *laugoa:* Or *lagão* (from the Burmese *hlo-gah*), described by Dalgado and Couto (in Barros and Couto, *déc.* 8, bk. 1, chap. 12, 78) as a ship similar to a galley.

2. *very devoted:* Pinto may be exaggerating the king's devotion to the *rolim,* but there is no doubt that both Tabin Shwehti and Bureng Naung were careful to present themselves as great upholders of religion and founded many costly religious buildings in their lifetimes.

Chapter 170

1. *Diossaray:* Spelled *Diosoray* in chapter 153 and 157.

2. *make our escape:* The historical events leading up to Pinto's escape from captivity can be summarized as follows: Chance enabled Tabin Shwehti to pursue his plan of subduing the whole territory formerly dependent on, or tributary to, the ancient monarchy of Burma, and also to take revenge for the assistance given to his enemies by Arakan and Ava (see chap. 156, n. 1 above). About this time the king of Arakan died, and his son U'ba-Ra-dzá succeeded him. The deceased king's brother, who was governor of Sandoway (see chap. 41, n. 9 above), a town of Arakan, was discontented. He fled to Pegu and offered, if placed on the throne of Arakan, to hold it as tributary. In November of 1546, after the rainy season, both a land force and a fleet were put in motion. The town of Sandoway was occupied, and the Arakanese retreated. It was while the fighting at Sandoway was in progress that Pinto made good his escape. He resumes his account of the Burmese wars in ch. 185 below. See Phayre, *History of Burma,* 100, and his article "History of the Burma Race," 67, as well as Harvey, 158. Also, it should be pointed out that Lagoa disagrees with the generally accepted identification of Pinto's *Savady* with Sandoway ("Peregrinação," 134).

3. *completely submerged:* Cf. Pinto's version of a submerged city in ch. 96 above. Toward the end of the book (chap. 222), Pinto gives a third account of a submerged city, which has been authenticated.

Chapter 171

1. *Luis de Montarroyo:* A Portuguese merchant and shipowner who appears later in Siam (chap. 183) and China (chap. 221). His name is not mentioned by any of the Portuguese chroniclers.

2. *Fernão Caldeira:* A Fernão Caldeira is mentioned by Castanheda, Correia, and Couto, but he was assassinated in 1516. He is not to be confused with this Fernão Caldeira, whom I cannot identify.

3. *Pero de Faria:* See chapter 153, note 5 above.

Chapter 172

1. *Sunda:* The western and most mountainous part of the island of Java. The Sunda country is considered to extend from the extreme western point of the island to Cheribon, i.e., embracing about one-third of the whole island of Java. Hinduism appears to have prevailed in the Sunda country and held its ground longer than in "Java," a name which the proper Javanese restrict to their own part of the island. From this country the sea between Sumatra and Java got from Europeans the name of the Straits of Sunda (which Pinto mentions in chapter 20).

2. *Ruy Vaz Pereira Marramaque:* Succeeded Pero de Faria as captain of Malacca in 1543. Since he died the following year, we can place the date of Pinto's arrival in Malacca in 1544. See Correia, vol. 4, chap. 62, 415–17.

3. *Bantam:* Town on Bantam Bay, on the north coast of west Java. Early in the sixteenth century it became the capital of a powerful Mohammedan sultanate. It produced much pepper, which caused it to be frequented by European traders. It was a Portuguese trading station after 1545, the site of a Dutch settlement in 1596, and of a British factory in 1603.

4. *Demak:* Town in the north of Java, just south of Japara, which was formerly the capital of a powerful state. It was here in the fifteenth century that a dynasty of Muslim princes was founded. Their turbulent proselytism made them for a time the moral rulers of central Java. Today, in the words of A. Cabaton, "Demak lingers, rather than survives." See his *Java, Sumatra, and the Other Islands of the Dutch East Indies* (London: T. Fisher Unwin, 1911), 68.

5. *Kangean:* An island group of Indonesia in the Java Sea, eighty miles east of Madura. Also, the name of the largest island of the group.

6. *Bali:* This well-known island of Indonesia lies off the eastern end of Java and between the Bali Sea and the Indian Ocean. Colonized direct from India in early times, its civilization remained Hindu. It had little contact with the Dutch before the nineteenth century, when the Balinese princes recognized Dutch supremacy but retained local autonomy.

7. *Madura:* Or Madoera. Island about one hundred miles long by twenty-four miles wide, off the northeast coast of Java. Dutch influence was established there at the end of the seventeenth century.

8. *Japara:* See chapter 36, note 3 above.

9. *Pasuruan:* See chapter 36, note 7 above.

10. *calaluz:* See chapter 26, note 5 above. Pires (Cortesão, 194) describes the Javanese *calaluz* as follows: "They are not fit to go out of the shelter of the land. They are carved in a thousand and one ways, with figures of serpents, and gilt . . . very much painted . . . in a very elegant way, and they are for kings to amuse themselves in, away from the common people. They are rowed with paddles."

11. *why a woman:* A woman ambassador in a Moslem country? Le Gentil, for one, thinks it is possible and points to other historical instances of Moslem women in high places (78–79). Lending support to his argument are the words of an authority like Cabaton who writes, "The moral and material situation of woman among the Malayo-Polynesians has always been a high one, the matriarchate, with all its consequences, having for a long period been the basis of Malay society, and among the Negri Sambilan of the Peninsula it is still practiced. That is why,

in spite of Islam, the Javanese woman goes about unveiled, shares the interests of her husband, has her place at festivals, and speaks freely at home" (110).

12. *jurupangos:* See chapter 13, note 13 above.

Chapter 173

1. *king of Demak:* There is no doubt that this personage is historical. However, the expedition he led against Pasaruan, as described by Pinto in the following chapters, has not been confirmed. Nor is there any mention of it in the native chronicles, which are missing for that period. The Dutch historian, P. A. Tiele, writing in 1880, doubts that Pinto was an eyewitness to the campaign against Pasaruan. Nevertheless, he concludes, "For all that, Pinto provides us with a document which cannot be disregarded, for little is known of Javanese history at this period" (as cited in Schurhammer's "Pinto and seine *Peregrinaçam*" 21:84–85). On the same page, Schurhammer also quotes a letter that gives us some insight into the character and motivations of the king of Demak. Written in Malacca on 7 December 1548 to the bishop of Goa, it reads as follows: "We were forced by the weather to land in Java [the writer was returning to Malacca from a voyage to the Celebes undertaken at the end of 1545], where the King of Java was. He sent for me and asked me many questions. . . . It seems to me that this King of Java has been very victorious in overcoming the heathens who do not wish to convert to Islam. When they agree to accept his religion, he gives them many presents and treats them very well. He takes many soldiers with him and strives only to convert these people to Mohammedanism. He wants no gold or silver. All he wants is for them to become Mohammedans. Then, the King of Java says, after he has converted the heathens to Mohammedanism, he will become a second Grand Turk."

2. *Panarukan:* See chapter 36, note 5 above.

3. *pangueyrão:* From the Malay *pangeran,* the title of a native chief in Malaysia, according to Dalgado, who says that at times it is synonymous with "nobleman." Marsden (182 n.) says that "*Pangeran* is properly a Javanese title, introduced on Sumatra, and prevailing only in the southern part." Sir Stamford Raffles, in his list of Javanese titles, writes, "The sovereign . . . is either called *Susuhúnan, Susunan,* or Sultan. . . . His family are called *Pang'érans,* his queen, *Ratú,* the heir apparent, *Pangeran Adipati,* and the prime minister *Raden Adipati*" (*The History of Java* [London: Block, Parbury, & Allen, 1817], 1:79).

4. *eagles:* General Pereira do Valle describes the eagle as a cannon, smaller than the lion, with a relative length of 18 to 20 calibers, from 16.0 to 18.0 centimeters in the diameter of the mouth, firing iron balls of 30 to 40 pounds, with a bore between 3 and 3.5 meters (388).

5. *lions:* See chapter 7, note 7 above.

6. *farazes:* Also *farash, ferah, frash,* etc., from the Arabic *farrash,* (*farsh,* literally "to spread a carpet"). The *farazes* were menial servants, whose proper business it was to spread carpets, pitch tents, etc., and, in a house, to do housemaid's work.

Chapter 174

1. *passeyvão:* See chapter 18, note 1 above, where it is spelled *passeivão.* Here and in chapter 192 it is spelled *passeyvão.*

2. *Quiay Ansedá: Ansedá* is apparently a place-name for Henzada (see chap. 150, n. 7). It appears for the first time in chapter 150, where it is used with the title *xemim,* or *smim,* meaning "lord" (see chap. 149, n. 4). In chapter 153 it is used for the name of a river (see chap. 153, n. 12). In chapter 155 it appears as the *xemim* of *Ansedá.* Again, in chapter 188 it is the name of a river. In chapter 190 it appears twice as the name of a city, and in chapter 191 it appears as the name of a kingdom. Here in chapter 174, it is used with *quiay,* or *kiai,* which is a Malay title of respect (see chap. 13, n. 19 above).

3. *Necodá Sòlor:* For the title *necodá,* see chapter 35, note 5 above. For the toponym *Solor,* see chapter 35, note 2 above.

4. *minhamundy:* Or *minhamundi,* from the Malay *minyaq-múndi.* It is the oil of the tree *Garcinia dulcis,* which bears a savory fruit similar to the apple. The *amucks* anoint themselves with the oil as a sign of their determination to die. See chapter 17, note 1 above.

5. *ourobalões:* See chapter 13, note 18 above.

6. *ambarraja:* See chapter 15, note 4 above. Spelled *amborraja* in chapters 15 and 31.

7. *pates:* See chapter 38, note 2 above.

8. *pangueyrão of pates:* Pinto seems to have combined the words *pangueyrão* (see chap. 173, n. 3 above) and pates (see chap. 38, n. 2 above) to form something akin to "king of princes" or "emperor."

Chapter 175

1. *sanguys de pates:* This represents the Malay title *Sangadipati,* meaning the "sovereign lord or prince." It is a compound of *adipati,* meaning "prince, king," and *sang,* which is an honorific, usually prefixed to the names or titles of princes and divinities. See other combinations with *adipati* in chapter 173, note 3 above.

2. *moçafo:* From the Arabic *mushaf,* meaning "book, volume." It was used frequently by the early Portuguese writers to designate the Koran.

3. *panaricões:* Or *panicarões,* from the Malay *panjirakan,* meaning literally "comrade captain." It is used in chapter 174 with the honorific *quiay.*

Chapter 176

1. *Penamacor:* Town in east central Portugal, in the province of Beira Baixa, about ten miles from the Spanish border.

2. *marshal's armada:* Dom Fernando Coutinho, marshal of Portugal during the reign of King Manuel I, sailed for India in 1509, and not in 1513, as appears in the text. See *Livro das Armadas,* 18.

3. *nao São João:* Sailed from Portugal in 1508, under the command of Jorge de Aguiar, and was shipwrecked on the outbound voyage (ibid., 17).

4. *Ruy Dias Pereira:* Sailed from Portugal in 1506, in the armada of Tristão da Cunha. The name of the ship he commanded is not recorded (ibid.).

5. *Afonso de Albuquerque:* See chapter 90, note 4 above. He captured Goa in 1510, Malacca in 1511, made peace with Calicut in 1512 and with Hormuz in 1515. See Barros, in Barros and Couto, déc. 2, bk. 7, chap. 6; Correia, vol. 2, chap. 40, 329.

6. *Lopo Soares [de Albergaria]:* Governor of India from 1515 to 1518. See chapter 65, note 3 above.

7. *Diogo Lopes de Sequeira:* Governor of India from 1518 to 1522.

8. *Dom Henrique de Meneses:* Governor of India from 1524 to 1526.

9. *Dom Vasco da Gama:* Went to India for the third time in 1524, as viceroy of Portuguese India. He died in office on 24 December 1524, after serving only three months and twenty-four days of his term. See Martins 1:279.

10. *Francisco de Sá:* In 1526, Governor Lopo de Sampaio sent him to Sunda, in command of a small fleet, to build a fortress in Sunda. By the time he arrived, a new sultan, unfriendly to the Portuguese, in a surprise attack drove him away. After his defeat in Sunda he returned to Portugal. See Correia, vol. 3, chap. 6, 92.

11. *Magellan:* After Magellan's historic voyage, the second expedition to the Moluccas left Spain on 24 July 1525. It was the last Spanish fleet to sail to the Moluccas by the Strait of Magellan. In 1529, by the Treaty of Zaragoza, Charles V sold to the king of Portugal his "rights" to the Moluccas. See Mairin Mitchell, *Elcano: The First Circumnavigator* (London: Herder Pub-

lications, 1958), 115, 127; and R. A. Skelton, ed. and trans., *Antonio Pigafetta, Magellan's Voyage* (London: Folio Society, 1975).

12. *Bintang:* See chapter 22, note 6 above.

13. *Pero de Mascarenhas:* It was undoubtedly due to the destruction of Bintang by Pero de Mascarenhas, captain of Malacca (1526–27), that Francisco de Sá, who took part in the battle, was so savagely attacked when he arrived in Sunda. See note 10 above and Correia, vol. 3, chap. 5, 82–90.

14. *Lingga:* See chapter 31, note 3 above.

Chapter 177

1. *betel:* For details on the preparation and chewing of betel leaves, see Orta's "Coloquio do betere," 2:389–96, 402 n. 1; or "The Last Colloquy" in Markham's translation, 473–79, which, unfortunately, does not contain Ficalho's scholarly note.

2. *a touch on the head:* Other allusions to this notion of the sanctity of the head are found in Duarte Barbosa (Dames, 192 n. 1), Couto (Barros and Couto, déc. 4, bk. 3, chap. 1, 168–69), and strangely enough, in the Chinese author of the *Ying Yai Sheng Lan* (1425–32), who writes, "When in a crowd if anyone strikes another's head [literally, 'offends against his head'] or starts a brawl, the other strikes him with the dagger he carries in his belt." See W. W. Rockhill, "Notes on the Relations and Trade of China . . . ," *T'oung Pao* 16 (1915): 240.

3. *caloete:* See chapter 155, note 8 above.

Chapter 178

1. *"the outer edge of the world":* See chapter 1, note 2 above.

2. *Blambangan:* Formerly an ancient kingdom in east Java. On modern maps Blambangan survives in the name of the easternmost peninsula of Java.

3. *Quiay Ansedá:* See chapter 174, note 2 above.

4. *Cheribon:* Former name of Tjirebon, once the capital of a sultanate that was abolished after 1815. Today, a city and seaport of northwest Java, on the coast of the Java Sea.

Chapter 179

1. *João Rodrigues:* The same person is called Nuno Rodrigues Taborda in chapter 176.

2. *Japanese pirates:* These were the Wako, who ravaged the coasts of China for many years. For a succinct account of their depredations, see Boxer, *Christian Century in Japan,* 248–58.

3. *Chabaqué:* See chapter 115, note 4 above.

4. *Pulo Condore:* See chapter 39, note 2 above.

Chapter 180

1. *Saturday:* According to Brito Rebello (3:190 n. 1), Christmas fell on a Sunday in the year 1547.

2. *Epiphany:* January 6, also called Twelfth Day.

3. *pardau:* See chapter 6, note 14 above.

4. *réis:* See chapter 6, note 8 above.

5. *Calapa:* The modern Batavia.

Chapter 181

    1. *king of Siam:* King P'rajai (reigned 1538–46).

    2. *Quitirvão:* See chapter 39, note 9 above.

    3. *oyá:* See chapter 41, note 3 above.

    4. *combracalão:* See chapter 146, note 7 above.

    5. *personal guards:* W. A. R. Wood, the English historian of Siam, writes that on his accession in 1538 King P'rajai engaged 120 Portuguese to form a bodyguard and to instruct the Siamese in musketry. See Wood's *History of Siam* (1959), 102.

    6. *build churches:* Writing in 1924, Wood states that the Portuguese served King P'rajai so well that they were rewarded with various commercial and residential privileges, and that the "ruins of the houses and the church given by King P'rajai to the Portuguese can still be seen at Ayuthia" (ibid., 102, 103 n. 1).

    7. *Domingos de Seixas:* See Barros, in Barros and Couto déc. 3, bk. 8, chap. 2, 254–58. See also chapter 1, note 3 above.

    8. *killing three princes:* These may have been the "three generals" who, according to Wood, were killed in an ambush attack when King P'rajai was retreating to Ayuthia (*History of Siam,* 106).

    9. *victory:* According to Wood (ibid., 103–7), the Chiang Mai wars of 1545 were due, not to a border dispute, as Pinto claims, but to a dispute over the succession to the throne. Since Chiang Mai was a vassal state of Siam, King P'rajai was called upon to intervene. He made two expeditions to Chiang Mai in the year 1545, the second of which is described by Pinto. Though Pinto claims victory for the king, he was defeated, pursued, and ambushed by his enemies during his retreat to Ayuthia. Though Wood states that Pinto's account is confused, he concedes that the Siamese chronicles dealing with this period are either silent or unreliable.

Chapter 182

    1. *Queen:* This "queen" is probably meant to be Maha T'ewi, the princess regent of Chiang Mai. She was responsible in great part for the defeat suffered by King P'rajai on his second expedition to Chiang Mai. See Wood, *History of Siam,* 107.

    2. *Oyá Kamp'engp'et:* The governor of Kamp'engp'et was indeed slain in the wars of Chiang Mai, but not under the circumstances described by Pinto (ibid., 104).

    3. *turmas:* Ancient Siamese silver coin, equivalent to twelve Portuguese cruzados in Pinto's time (Dalgado).

    4. *Lake Singuapamor:* See chapter 128, notes 5 and 6 above.

    5. *queen, his wife:* King P'rajai did not have a wife who ranked as queen. This woman held the title of T'ao Sri Suda Chan, a style reserved for one of four senior nonroyal consorts of a king (Wood, *History of Siam,* 108).

    6. *Uquumchenirá:* This was P'an Sri But T'ep, who held a petty official appointment. After he won the "queen's" favor he was transferred to a post in the palace with the title of K'un Jinarat.

    7. *poison the king:* As for Pinto's statement that the king was poisoned by his wife, Wood writes that "the subsequent actions of that infamous woman were such as to justify the accusation" (*History of Siam,* 106).

    8. *his oldest son:* King P'rajai had two sons by the Princess Sri Suda Chan, Prince Keo Fa (or Yot Fa), born about 1535, and Prince Sri Sin, born about 1541 (ibid.).

    9. *charana:* Deep dish or tray on a pedestal, used in India especially for betel. From the Malay *charana,* meaning "foot."

Chapter 183

1. *Dom Garcia:* Dom Garcia de Noronha, viceroy of India from 1538 to 1540. See chapter 8, note 4 above.
2. *Francisco de Castro:* Two different men by that name are mentioned by Barros, Couto, and Correia for various noteworthy deeds, none of which have anything to do with Siam.
3. *Simão de Melo:* Captain of Malacca 1545–48.
4. *Luis de Montarroyo:* See chapter 171, note 1 above.
5. *Lugor:* See chapter 36, note 2 above.
6. *shahbandar:* See chapter 15, note 2 above.
7. *odiá:* See chapter 19, note 5 above.
8. *firmaun:* See chapter 119, note 1 above.
9. *Raudivá:* Used in chapter 140 as a proper name, in connection with the Ryukyus, and in chapter 158, as a title of nobility in *Calaminhan.*
10. *Banchá:* See chapter 38, note 1 above.
11. *Pulo Catão:* See chapter 46, note 1 above.

Chapter 184

1. *cabizonda:* See chapter 49, note 2 above.
2. *varelas, pagodas, and bralas:* See chapter 151, note 2 above.
3. *for the priests to eat:* Pinto's description of a royal cremation contains some very un-Siamese details, notably the "Ravenous Serpent" (devil) and the bejewelled child with wings (angel), symbols he applies repeatedly to Asian religions. For a description of what a royal cremation was probably like in the sixteenth century, see Quaritch-Wales, 143–67.
4. *gave birth to a son:* Wood says she gave birth to a daughter (*History of Siam,* 109).
5. *Ucunchenirat:* The "queen" managed to obtain the appointment of K'un Jinarat as regent during the minority of King Keo Fa, with the title of K'un Worawongsa (ibid.). Also, note the variant spelling of *Ucunchenirat.*
6. *she killed him too:* Wood writes, "Before the end of the year 1548 the short reign and the short life of this unfortunate little king both came to a sudden end" (*History of Siam,* 110).
7. *proclaimed king:* According to Wood, K'un Worawongsa (the former K'un Jinarat), was publicly crowned king of Siam on 11 November 1548 (ibid.).
8. *both killed:* Wood gives a different date and a gorier version of the death of the guilty pair. He writes that early in January of 1549 the royal barge was ambushed in a creek, where "the trembling usurper and his guilty partner were dragged ashore and beheaded, together with their infant daughter. Their bodies were impaled and left as a meal for the vultures" (*History of Siam,* 111).

Chapter 185

1. *Oyá P'itsanulok:* This must be K'un P'iren, the ringleader of the conspiracy to oust the usurper. The new king bestowed upon K'un P'iren the hand of his eldest daughter in marriage and conferred upon him the high title of Somdet Maha T'ammaraja, with the position of governor of P'itsanulok (Wood, *History of Siam,* 112).
2. *king of Cambodia:* This was probably the governor of Sawank'alok. He was a Cambodian prince who had been adopted by King P'rajai (ibid., 111 n. 1).
3. *Pretiem:* Prince P'ra T'ien Raja, a younger half-brother of King P'rajai (ibid., 108).
4. *thirty years:* Wood states that Prince T'ien could not have been a Buddhist priest for over thirty years, for it is known that he was about forty-two years old at the time of his accession (1549), and that he had several grown-up children. However, he had taken the wise step of

retiring to a monastery when he saw the direction in which events were tending after his brother's death (ibid., 110).

5. *proclaimed king:* Prince T'ien was brought forth from his monastery and crowned as king of Siam in 1549, with the title of Maha Chakrap'at. He reigned for twenty years (ibid., 112).

6. *conquest:* Pinto seems to agree with the Siamese account in attributing the first Burmese invasion solely to the aggressive spirit of Tabin Shwehti, encouraged by the disorganized state of the government of Siam after the death of King P'rajai. However, the Burmese histories agree that it was provoked by the Siamese who, hearing that Tabin Shwehti was away in Arakan, had been unable to resist the temptation of raiding Tavoy and Tenasserim, the possession of which was an open sore between the two countries for many years. See Scott, 71.

7. *lord of the white elephant:* According to Maurice Collis, a white elephant was one of the nine gems of Hinayana Buddhism, and its possession by a king was held indispensable if he aspired to be lord of the world and world savior. That was one of the reasons why an invasion of Siam had such a fatal attraction for the Burmese, who were at war with Siam, off and on, for over three hundred years. See *The Burmese Scene* (London: John Crowther, 1953?), 25. With particular reference to the period of which Pinto is writing, W. A. R. Wood says that King Maha Chakrap'at (Pinto's *Pretiem*), who spent most of his reign (1549–69) in fighting against Burma, had no less than seven white elephants, more than had been owned by any of his predecessors, and that it was he who assumed the title of "lord of the white elephants." See Wood's *Land of Smiles* (Bangkok: Krungdebarnagar Press, 1935), 184. In his letter of 5 December 1554, Pinto describes the ritual bath of a white elephant he claims to have seen, and the reverence in which the animal is held. See Catz, *Cartas,* 43–44.

8. *Diogo Soares de Albergaria:* For the checkered career of Diogo Soares in India, see Correia 4:154, 226, 266, 275. According to Correia, he was a pirate and a ruthless murderer who fled Goa when Governor Estêvão da Gama issued a warrant for his arrest. He was pardoned by the incoming governor Martim Afonso de Sousa (1542–45), whom he served well. From the time he was driven by the weather to the shores of Burma, where he rose to power under Tabin Shwehti and where he died ignominiously, see Couto, in Barros and Couto, déc. 5, bk. 8, chap. 2, 180; déc. 6, bk. 1, chap. 1, 8–22; bk. 5, chaps. 1–2, 346–59; bk. 7, chap. 8, 118; déc. 7, bk. 2, chap. 5, pp. 136–47. It should be pointed out that Couto refers to him as Diogo Soares de Mello. It may be coincidence, but one of his partners in crime, in the year 1542, was a Cristóvão Mello, and in the year 1545, he sailed for Malacca with Simão de Mello. See Brito Rebello (3:244 n. 1) regarding same.

9. *same fleet as the viceroy Dom Garcia de Noronha:* According to the *Livro das Armadas* (22), one of the ships that sailed from Portugal with the viceroy (see chap. 8, n. 4 above) in 1538 was called the *Junco,* and it was commanded by João de Sepulveda, who took up his appointment as captain of the fortress of Sofala in 1540 (Correia, vol. 4, chap. 8, 143). This agrees with what Pinto has to say. However, Brito Rebello (3:214 n. 1), who gives the *Ementa da casa da India* as his source, says that João de Sepulveda was in command of the ship *São Lourenço.*

10. *7 April 1548:* Phayre says that Tabin Shwehti departed in November of 1548, when the country is dry after the rainy season. See his article, "History of the Burma Race," 67. Moreover, Brito Rebello says that Easter fell on April 1 that year, and Low Sunday on April 8 (3:214 n. 2).

11. *Lake Chiang Mai:* See chapter 41, note 6 above.

Chapter 186

1. *lizards:* General Pereira do Valle (390) cannot identify this firearm, but he believes that, generally, the artillery pieces named after small animals, in this case a lizard of the garden variety, were small cannon, designed primarily for use on board ship.

2. *open the gates:* The Siamese also had Portuguese mercenaries fighting on their side.

Harvey (159) says that Tabin Shwehti "tried to bribe them, but they treated the offer with derision, and one of the Siamese commanders, flinging open the town gate, dared Tabinshwehti to bring the money." See also Couto, in Barros and Couto, déc. 6, bk. 7, chap. 9, 128.

Chapter 187

1. *dog:* A small iron artillery piece of three-pound caliber (eight centimeters), frequently used on board ship and in the close defense of fortifications. See Pereira do Valle, 390.

Chapter 188

1. *Xemindó:* Harvey calls him the Smim Htaw, though this title is spelled variously by the historians of Burma as Thamindaw, Tha-Mein-Htau-Ra-Ma, or Thaminhtoa Rama. He was a son by an inferior wife of the former king of Pegu and had been a Buddhist monk. In the year 1549 he threw off his religious robes, roused the people to rebel, and took the title of Smim Htaw.

2. *Chalagonim:* See chapter 167, note 3 above.

3. *Syriam:* Town in the Hanthawaddy District of Lower Burma, on the Rangoon River, opposite Rangoon. Pinto spells it *Surião.*

4. *Dalla:* Formerly an important city in Lower Burma; today, a suburb of Rangoon. Pinto writes Dalá.

5. *Danobyu:* See chapter 153, note 13 above.

6. *Ansedá River:* See chapter 153, note 12.

Chapter 189

1. *produm:* From the Siamese phrae-don, meaning "city" or "town" (Dalgado).

2. *Mompolocota:* Spelled *Mompollacota* in chapter 46.

3. *Cuy:* See chapter 88, note 2 above.

4. *Lugor:* See chapter 36, note 2 above.

5. *Ayuthia:* For one of the earliest eyewitness descriptions of the city of Ayuthia in the sixteenth century, see Pinto's letter of 5 December 1554 in Catz, *Cartas,* 43–44.

6. *Prechau Saleu:* See chapter 36, note 9 above.

7. *Comhay:* See chapter 44, note 5 above.

8. *finest kingdoms in the world:* Cf. Campos, 211–37; Barros, in Barros and Couto, déc. 3, bk. 2, chap. 5, 152–73; and Couto, in Barros and Couto, déc. 6, bk. 7, chap. 9, 123–30.

Chapter 190

1. *in favor of the Xemindó:* After being driven from the vicinity of the capital, Smim Htaw, pursued by Bureng Naung, had set himself up with his supporters in Martaban. See Harvey, 161–62.

2. *the Burmese king:* Tabin Shwehti did not take part in this expedition. Since his return from the war in Siam he had become a confirmed alcoholic. The Burmese chronicles blame the king's drinking habits on his association with a young Portuguese. See ibid., 343 n. 2.

3. *xemim de Satão:* The governor of Sittang, a Talaing nobleman, who had been appointed guardian of the drunken king. He later assumed the title of Smim Sawhtut (Harvey), spelled variously as Thaminsaw-tut (Scott), and Tha-Mein-Tsaw-Dwut (Phayre, *History of Burma*).

4. *killed him:* The official version of the murder of Tabin Shwehti, as set forth in the Burmese chronicles, is that, in the absence of Bureng Naung, the governor of Sittang lured the king into a jungle by telling him that a white elephant had been sighted. There, his followers cut

off the king's head, slew his Burmese attendants, and raised their compatriot to the throne. See Harvey, 161.

5. *Meydó:* Spelled *Meidó* in chapters 191, 193, and 196.

6. *clever trick:* Bureng Naung was in a difficult position when Tabin Shwehti was murdered. As Harvey writes (162), "There he was, a king without a kingdom, grappling with one Talaing rebel in the west [*Xemindó*] while another sat on his throne in the east [*xemim de Satão*]. Moreover, his own brother, who had been acting as Viceroy, was driven out of Pegu."

Chapter 191

1. *chircá:* See chapter 150, note 4 above.

Chapter 192

1. *Si iniquitates . . . sustinebit?:* "If thou, o Lord, shouldst mark iniquities, o Lord, who can stand?" Psalm 129 (Douay Version; 130, King James Version), or the sixth of the Penitential Psalms, the *De Profundis,* used in the liturgy of the church as a prayer for the faithful departed.

2. *Misericordias . . . cantabo!:* "The mercies of the Lord I shall sing forever!"

3. *thus ended the life:* Cf. Couto's account (Barros and Couto, déc. 7, bk. 2, chap. 5, 144−47) of the death of Diogo Soares, which, in many respects, agrees with the one given here by Pinto. Harvey (163) says that he "was mortally wounded in a brawl with the townsfolk, and then, holding the hand of a friendly lord *smim,* 'for he needed a little hope, he confessed his sins and died.'"

Chapter 193

1. *king of Pegu:* Phayre writes that the Smim Sawhtut (*xemim de Satão*) reigned only three months but gives no dates. The Smim Htaw (*Xemindó*) was consecrated king and is recognized in the Talaing chronicle, under the title of Zaggali Meng, as the last representative of a native dynasty. See Phayre, *History of Burma,* 104−5.

Chapter 194

1. *tical:* Spelled *tincal* by Pinto. A term that has long been in use by foreign traders to Burma, for the quasi-standard weight of uncoined current silver. It is equivalent to the hundredth part of the *biça* or "viss." See chapter 148, note 7 above.

Chapter 195

1. *Cristóvão Sarmento:* None of the Portuguese named in this chapter are mentioned by any of the writers of the period.

Chapter 196

1. *cabisondo:* See chapter 49, note 2 above.

2. *a rich crown:* Bureng Naung was formally consecrated as king of kings in 1551 (or 1552) and reigned over a united Burma for thirty years.

Chapter 197

1. *a man of base condition:* Scott (73−74) gives Faria e Sousa (*Asia Portuguese,* 1666−75) as his source when he says that the Smim Htaw hid in the hills, poor and unknown, till he took

a village girl to wife and told her his secret. She guilelessly told her father, who handed him over when a reward was offered for his head. Harvey (164) gives a similar version of the capture of the Smim Htaw, but no source.

Chapter 199

1. *Xemim Pocasser: Xemim* represents the Burmese honorific *smim. Pocasser* appears in chapters 73, 89, 90, and 222 as the name of a city in China. See Chapters 73, note 3 above.

2. *two and a half years:* In Chapter 194 Pinto says that the Smim Htaw reigned for three and a half years. None of the historians consulted give any specific dates for his reign.

Chapter 200

1. *invaded the kingdom of Siam again:* The second Burmese invasion of Siam took place in 1563–64. See Harvey, 167.

2. *Jorge Alvares:* Portuguese merchant and sea captain on whose ship Pinto sailed to Japan in 1546. Alvares is remembered for having written, at the request of Francis Xavier, one of the earliest European reports on Japan, which he gave to the saint in December of 1547. For a summary of that interesting report, see Boxer, *Christian Century in Japan,* 32–36.

3. *Freixo de Espada à Cinta:* Town in the northeastern part of Portugal, in the district of Braganza.

4. *Tanegashima:* See chapter 132, note 12 above.

5. *Nautaquim:* See chapter 39, note 3 above.

6. *Bungo:* See chapter 134, note 5 above.

7. *Fucheo:* See chapter 134, note 7 above.

8. *if he had not been killed:* According to Japanese sources, the daimyo of Bungo, Otomo Yoshinori (or Yoshinaki) was murdered in 1550 by one of his vassals, Tsukumi Mimasaka, because he wanted to make a bastard son his successor, instead of his firstborn son, Yoshishige. For the details of this palace revolution, see Schurhammer, *Francis Xavier* 4:253 n. 60. See also chapter 134, note 5 above.

Chapter 201

1. *Usuki:* See chapter 135, note 20 above.

2. *Fingeindono:* In chapter 135 it is spelled variously as *Fingeandono, Fingeindono,* and *Fingēdono.* In chapters 201 and 210 it is spelled *Fingeindono.*

3. *chara:* See chapter 40, note 1 above.

Chapter 202

1. *Yamagawa:* See chapter 135, note 15 above.

2. *Bay of Kagoshima:* See chapter 135, note 16 above.

3. *Minató:* See chapter 135, note 18 above.

4. *Tano-ura:* See chapter 135, note 17 above.

5. *Hyuga:* See chapter 135, note 19 above.

6. *Hakata:* See chapter 135, note 4 above.

7. *Epiphany:* January 6.

8. *Anjiro:* The first Japanese convert to Christianity. Pinto picks up his story in chapter 203.

Chapter 203

1. *Chincheo:* See chapter 44, note 3 above.

2. *Chepocheca:* In chapter 215 the same name is applied to a Chinese described as an honorable merchant.

3. *vancões:* See chapter 44, note 9 above.

4. *Lamau:* See chapter 44, note 4 above.

5. *Cosme Rodrigues:* See letter of Luis Fróis, S.J., dated Malacca 1 December 1555, in which he describes this Cosme Rodrigues as both a very good friend of Fernão Mendes and captain of the caravel that set out from Malacca on 1 April 1555 on what was to be Pinto's last voyage to Japan. See Catz, *Cartas,* 77–78. See also Schurhammer, *Francis Xavier* 4:263 n. 118. Pinto describes this last voyage to Japan in chapters 220–25.

6. *exile:* In chapter 208.

7. *Dom João de Castro:* See chapter 20, note 28.

8. *Wednesday, 9 October 1547:* According to Brito Rebello, October 9 fell on a Sunday that year (4:19 n. 1).

9. *Banda:* See chapter 20, note 21 above.

10. *Upi:* See chapter 14, note 2 above.

11. *Biyayá Sòra:* See chapter 148, note 5 above, where it is spelled *Bijayá Sora.* Spelled *Bijayá Sòra* in chapter 206.

12. *Sultan Alaradim:* See chapter 27, note 2 above.

13. *Duarte Barreto:* Mentioned briefly by Correia (vol. 3, chap. 88, 743) as captain of a ship that reached Goa with the armada of 1536.

14. *Francisco de Eça:* His military career spanned many years in India. He served as a naval commander under Governor Nuno da Cunha (1529–38) until the time of the viceroy Dom Constantino de Braganza (1558–61). In 1560 he was appointed captain of Malacca. See Couto, in Barros and Couto, déc. 4, bk. 4, chap. 3, 21; déc. 6, bk. 5, chap. 1, 347; déc. 7, bk. 9, chap. 4, 336; bk. 9, chap. 11, 380; déc. 7, bk. 10, chap. 10, 520; déc. 10, bk. 2, chap. 4, 176–77.

Chapter 204

1. *Dom Jorge de Eça:* After seeing action in Malacca he was appointed admiral of the sea of the Moluccas, where he seems to have served until 1558. See Couto, in Barros and Couto, déc. 6, bk. 7, chap. 6, 108; bk. 10, chap. 8, 455; déc. 7, bk. 5, chap. 2, 360–67.

2. *Diogo Pereira:* Military captain and merchant who, in 1551, offered to defray the expenses of Francis Xavier on a missionary voyage to China, in the guise of an embassy. Their plans were later foiled by Alvaro de Ataide for reasons Pinto explains in chapter 215. In 1569 Diogo Pereira was rewarded by King Sebastian with the captaincy of Macao, which he held to the general satisfaction of all until 1587. See Cardon, "Old Church," 222 n. 30. Also, see chapter 6 of Schurhammer, *Francis Xavier* 4:585–91.

3. *Afonso Gentil:* See Couto, in Barros and Couto, déc. 6, bk. 5, chap. 1, 349.

4. *Belchior de Sequeira:* Ibid.

5. *João Soares:* Ibid.

6. *Gomes Barreto:* Ibid. He was later appointed admiral of the sea of Malacca and took part in defending her against the allied Malay forces that besieged Malacca in 1551. (See Schurhammer, *Francis Xavier* 4:321 n. 6, 372, 331–32.) In chapter 206, Pinto refers to him (spelling his name Brito) as a nobleman of the household of the duke of Braganza.

7. *André Toscano:* See Couto, in Barros and Couto, déc. 6, bk. 5, chap. 1, 349.

8. *Diogo Soares:* See chapter 185, note 8 and chapter 192, note 3 above.

9. *xemim de Satão:* See chapter 190, note 3 above.

Chapter 205

1. *Friday, 25 October 1547:* According to Brito Rebello (4:30 n. 1), the twenty-fifth of October fell on a Tuesday in the year 1547.
2. *Pulo Sambilang:* See chapter 20, note 1 above.
3. *Perlis River:* See chapter 19, note 4 above.

Chapter 206

1. *Biyayá Sòra:* See chapter 203, note 11 above.
2. *camelets:* A stone thrower of smaller caliber than the camel, as the name implies. See Pereira do Valle (385), who describes the camelet as a bronze cannon capable of firing stone balls of twelve pounds. For the camel, see chapter 10, note 1 above.
3. *Gomes Barreto:* See note 6 to chapter 204.
4. *assegais:* See chapter 18, note 4 above. The term is listed in most English dictionaries.
5. *Perlis:* See chapter 19, note 4 above.
6. *orabalões:* See chapter 13, note 18 above. Also, note variant spelling.
7. *Jidda:* See chapter 3, note 19 above.
8. *Pasay:* See chapter 13, note 17 above.

Chapter 207

1. *Selangor:* See chapter 17, note 10 above.
2. *Bintang:* See chapter 22, note 6 above.
3. *Perak:* See chapter 32, note 4 above.
4. *Jantana:* See chapter 30, note 1 above.
5. *Indragiri:* See chapter 16, note 3 above.
6. *Muar River:* A river about a hundred miles long in northwest Johore State, at the south end of the Malay Peninsula. Its head streams rise in Negri Sembilan and Pahang and flow south-southwest into the Strait of Malacca at Bandar Maharani.
7. *Kedah:* See chapter 17, note 8 above.
8. *Sunday, 6 December 1547:* According to Brito Rebello (4:41 n. 1), Sunday fell on the fourth and not the sixth of December in the year 1547. However, the same day, month, and year is also given in Couto (in Barros and Couto, déc. 6, bk. 5, chap. 2, 354).
9. *revealed it to him in spirit:* Cf. Couto's account of the "miracle of the Achinese" and Xavier's vision of the victory in the Perlis River (in Barros and Couto, déc. 6, bk. 5, chaps. 1–2, 348–60). See also Schurhammer, "Pinto und seine *Peregrinaçam*" 21:91.
10. *Moluccas:* Ternate is meant.
11. *Gonzalo de Araujo:* References to this "miracle" are found in various forms in all the biographies of the saint. See Léonard Joseph-Marie Cros, *Saint François de Xavier: Sa vie et ses lettres* (Toulouse: Edouard Privat, 1900), 1:380. Cros may have used Pinto as his source.

Chapter 208

1. *viceroy Dom João de Castro:* See chapter 20, note 28 above.
2. *Garcia de Sá:* See chapter 43, note 4 above. See also Schurhammer, *Francis Xavier* 4:406 n. 23, regarding the different dates given by the Portuguese chroniclers for his death.
3. *Dom Pedro da Silva:* See chapter 2, note 3 above.
4. *Necodá Ladrão:* His name was Avan and he was a Chinese merchant who lived in Malacca. The Portuguese had given him the nickname of *Ladrão,* meaning "thief or robber" in Portuguese. *Necodá* is the Malay word for "captain" or "owner" of a merchant vessel. For fur-

ther details on Xavier's stay in Malacca and his difficulties in finding a Portuguese ship to take him to Japan, see Schurhammer, *Francis Xavier* 4:9–10.

5. *Kagoshima:* See chapter 135, note 16 above. Kagoshima was the capital of Satsuma, the southernmost province of Japan and the native city of Anjiro. Today Satsuma is part of Kagoshima Prefecture. For a map of the province in the sixteenth century, see ibid., 61.

6. *preached so freely in their land:* For the details of Xavier's missionary efforts in Kagoshima, see ibid., 52–117.

7. *Hirado:* See chapter 66, note 2 above.

8. *killed by some pirates:* On the unfortunate end of Anjiro, see Schurhammer, *Francis Xavier* 4:129–30 nn. 22–23. Most of the Jesuit writers accept Pinto's version.

9. *Father Cosme de Torres:* A Spanish priest who sailed from Mexico to the Moluccas where, in 1546, he met Francis Xavier, under whose guidance he joined the Society of Jesus. He accompanied Francis to Japan in 1549, and when Francis returned to India in 1551, he left him behind as superior of the Jesuit mission, a charge he held until his death in Japan, in the year 1572. See Catz, *Cartas,* 95, and Fróis, *Historia de Japam* 1:18 n. 7.

10. *João Fernandes:* Or Juan Fernández de Oviedo, a Spaniard who entered the order in Lisbon in 1547. He sailed to India in 1548 and from there to Japan with Xavier in 1549, where he remained until his death in 1567. He was not only one of the first Jesuits in Japan, but also the first European who learned to speak Japanese. He acted as interpreter for Xavier and for the priests who came later. Catz, *Cartas,* 67 n. 9, and Fróis, *Historia de Japam* 1:21 n. 28.

11. *Miyako:* See chapter 107, note 16 above.

12. *kubo-sama:* Pinto is referring here to the Emperor Go-Nara-Tenno (1527–57). However, he is confusing the emperor (*dairi* or *o*) with the shogun (*kubo-sama* or *bakufu*) who, during the course of more than two hundred years, had appropriated all authority, though he allegedly ruled in the name of the emperor. His original title was *sei-i-tai-shogun* (supreme commander for the overthrow of the barbarians). Anjiro called the shogun *Gosho,* which is the name of the imperial palace, though it was later applied also to the shogun. Their prime ministers were called *kanryo.* The court nobility were called *kuge.* See Schurhammer, *Francis Xavier* 4:200–1 nn. 57, 59.

13. *cash:* See chapter 109, note 1 above.

14. *difficulties:* For details of the difficulties encountered by Xavier in the capital, see Schurhammer, *Francis Xavier* 4:199–200.

15. *Sakai:* In Xavier's time it was the port city for Miyako. Today, it lies in Osaka Prefecture in west central Honshu, six miles south of Osaka, on Osaka Bay. In the fifteenth and sixteenth centuries it developed important trade with the Chinese and the Portuguese. It declined after 1635, and in recent years, with the silting up of the harbor, it has lost its standing as a seaport.

16. *Yamaguchi:* Today, the capital of Yamaguchi Prefecture, at the southern tip of Honshu, northeast of Shimonoseki. From the fourteenth and sixteenth century it was ruled by the Ouchi family and was one of the leading cities of feudal Japan. Xavier was twice in Yamaguchi. The first time was at the end of October 1550, when he passed through there on his way to Miyako. After his disillusionment with the emperor and the ruined city of Miyako, he decided to settle in Yamaguchi. He went back to Hirado and picked up the gifts that had been destined for the emperor, returned to Yamaguchi, and presented them to the duke, who received him warmly and gave him an empty Buddhist monastery to be used as a residence. For a map and description of Yamaguchi in Xavier's time, see Schurhammer, *Francis Xavier* 4:148–53.

17. *Bungo:* See chapter 134, note 5 above.

18. *Matthew:* A young Japanese converted by Francis, who sailed with him to Goa in order to go on from there to Portugal and Rome. He died a few months after he arrived in India. See Schurhammer, *Francis Xavier* 4:231 n. 90.

19. *Diogo Pereira:* See chapter 204, note 2 above.

20. *Fucheo:* Today it is called Oita, but in Pinto's time it was known as Funai or Fuchu, meaning "provincial capital." See chapter 134, note 7 above.

21. *Duarte da Gama:* Captain and owner of the ship on which Xavier sailed from Bungo to China in 1551. He was formerly captain of Quilon (India) and an old acquaintance of Xavier. He is described by Schurhammer (*Francis Xavier* 4:244) as "a zealous Christian who had at heart the welfare of the missionaries and the progress of the Gospel." He seems to have made a number of trading voyages to Japan. In a letter written from Macao on 20 November 1555, Pinto says that Duarte da Gama had arrived from Japan the month before, bringing good news of the progress of Christianity there. See Catz, *Cartas,* 64.

Chapter 209

1. *Pinlaxau:* Spelled *Pimlaxau* in chapter 208. Unidentified.

2. *Finge:* Hiji, a port in the northwestern part of Bungo, three leagues from *Fucheo* (the modern Oita). See chapter 135, note 10 above.

3. *Chem ahicogim:* Appears to be a variant form or a misspelling of *Chemchicogim.* See chapter 133, note 2 above.

4. *fune:* See chapter 135, note 14 above.

5. *Canafama:* According to Schurhammer (*Francis Xavier* 4:244 n. 24), this is meant to be Okinohama, the name of the harbor of the capital of Bungo, located less than half a league from *Fucheo* (modern Oita), at the mouth of the Dojirigawa (or the Oitagawa) River. In chapter 200 above, Pinto uses *Canafama* as the name of a steep hill.

Chapter 210

1. *Fingeindono:* See chapter 201, note 2 above.

2. *altirnas:* See chapter 110, note 1 above.

3. *neither women nor the poor can be saved:* In a letter written from Cochin in January 1552, Xavier explains to his brethren in Europe that the poor in Japan have no remedy since they cannot pay the bonzes to pray for them to free them from hell. As for women, the bonzes preached that "every woman had more sins than all the men of the world because of her monthly purifications. Such a filthy being as a woman could consequently be saved only with great difficulty, and only if she gave more alms than her husband" (Schurhammer, *Francis Xavier* 4:443).

4. *gromenares:* A respectful form of salutation or obeisance. From the Japanese *go-me-nare* (Dalgado).

5. *Facharandono:* Otomo Hachiro, younger brother of Otomo Yoshishige (daimyo of Bungo). Hachiro (or Haruhide) succeeded Ouchi Yoshitaka as daimyo of Yamaguchi, taking the name of Ouchi Yoshinaga upon his accession. A few days after Xavier's departure from Yamaguchi in September 1551, Yoshitaka was overthrown and the city nearly destroyed. In 1556 there was another rebellion and the city was burned a second time. Yoshinaga committed harakiri. In chapter 136 above, Pinto refers to him as *Arichandono.* See chapter 136, note 2 and chapter 137, note 1 above.

6. *Fiancima:* See chapter 135, note 5 above.

7. *cuchimiacòs:* From the Japanese *ku-chi* and *myokuan,* which Dalgado translates roughly as a "passport to heaven." In a letter to his brethren in Europe after reaching Cochin from Japan in 1552, Xavier writes that the Japanese bonzes "preached that individuals who gave much money to the bonzes in this life would receive tenfold for this in the other life, and in the same coin, so that they might take care of their needs in that world. The bonzes consequently gave them a receipt for these, and when they died they had these receipts buried with them so that they would scare the devil away." See Schurhammer, *Francis Xavier* 4:443. For Pinto's use of this word in China, see chapter 114, note 5 above.

8. *colleges of Bandou:* Kwantô or Kantô. Site of the largest and most important university in Japan, the Ashikaga-gakko, in Shimotsuke, one of the eight provinces of Kantô (or Bandô as Xavier always wrote it). See chapter 112, note 3 above.

9. *groxo: Goro-ju* in Japanese. A member of the council of state in ancient Japan (Dalgado).

Chapter 211

1. *sensual relationship:* The letters written from Japan by Francis and the Jesuit missionaries who followed him contain frequent references to the practice of pederasty. With particular reference to the Tokugawa period (1600–1867), the historian Yoshi S. Kuno writes that "it is an undeniable fact that in certain provinces of Kyushu the practice of this unnatural vice was a prevailing custom." See his *Japanese Expansion of the Asiatic Continent* (Berkeley and Los Angeles: University of California Press, 1940) 2:369.

2. *kill the child:* According to Schurhammer, Yoshishige did not forbid infanticide until 1555, and he did so on the insistence of Brother Luis de Almeida, who established an orphanage for the unwanted children (*Francis Xavier*) 4:259 n. 93.

3. *he still has not converted:* Otomo Yoshishige converted in the year 1578, a fact that Pinto may not have known at the time, since it took about a year for the information to reach Portugal. It is presumed that Pinto finished his book in 1578.

4. *inocosém:* A corruption of the Japanese *inu* (dog) and *kusai* (smelly, stinking).

5. *fatoqui:* A corruption of the Japanese *hotoke(s)*, meaning "Buddhist gods."

6. *Xaca:* See chapter 107, note 18 above.

7. *Amida:* See chapter 107, note 19 above.

8. *Gizom:* See chapter 92, note 3 above.

9. *Canom:* See chapter 107, note 21 above.

10. *temple called Miyajima:* Or more properly Itsuku-shima. A Shinto shrine located on an island about twelve miles southwest of Hiroshima. It is known that Xavier stopped there at the end of 1550 on his way to Miyako. For a description of the temple and grounds, see Schurhammer, *Francis Xavier* 4:171–73.

11. *tundo:* Buddhist priest in Japan. (Dalgado thinks it should be written *hondo.*)

12. *Fiancima:* Perhaps intended for the monastic school of Hiei-zan near Kyoto. It was the main site of the Tendai sect and of Japanese Buddhism in general. It was burned down by Nobunaga in 1571. See Schurhammer, *Francis Xavier* 4:95 n. 74.

13. *Chenchico:* A corruption of the Japanese *Tenjiku* (India). See chapter 133, note 2 above.

14. *Frenojama:* Hienoyama, according to Schurhammer, *Francis Xavier* 4:244. It appears to be another name for the famous Buddhist university of Hiei-zan, northwest of Miyako, which was destroyed by Nobunaga in 1571. See also Fróis 1:81 n. 1.

15. *Yamaguchi . . . at war:* See chapter 210, note 5 above.

Chapter 212

1. *fatoquins:* Spelled *fatoquis* in chapter 211.

2. *exclude women:* See chapter 210, note 3 above.

Chapter 213

1. *disputations:* Regarding the time, place, and circumstances under which the disputations were held, see Schurhammer, *Francis Xavier* 4:227, 240, 267, 292–93, 444.

2. *Singalese:* Pinto is referring here to the natives of the southernmost tip of India and Ceylon, where Xavier labored for fifteen months (1542–44) and where he was credited with thousands of conversions, particularly among the pearl fishers of Cape Comorin, whose igno-

rance and simplicity he described repeatedly in his letters to Loyola and other correspondents in Europe. See Cros, 1:292, 295–96, 314, 374, 376, 408, 422–23.

3. *diusa:* A corruption of the Japanese *dai* (big, great) and *uso* (lie).

4. *Deus:* At the beginning of his apostolate in Japan, Xavier had been misled into thinking that *Dainichi* was the Japanese equivalent of God. When he learned that *Dainichi* was the name of the principal god of the Shingon sect and that there was no equivalent word in the Japanese language for God, he replaced it with the Latin word *Deus,* which is pronounced *diusu* in Japanese. See Schurhammer, *Francis Xavier* 4:239.

5. *sitá:* This should be *shita,* the perfective form of the verb "to do."

6. *santi:* The nearest word I can find to this is *santan,* which means "terrible, wretched, miserable." However, this does not quite convey the meaning given by Pinto.

Chapter 214

1. *Papuas:* See chapter 149, note 11 above.

2. *Pero Velho:* He sailed to India in 1524 as the captain of a caravel in the fleet of the viceroy Vasco da Gama. He fought against the Moors in Malabar as the captain of a ship under the viceroy's successor in 1525. He had already served his king for many years and had become rich through his trade with China when Xavier made his acquaintance in Bungo in 1551. See Schurhammer, *Francis Xavier* 4:265, 451 n. 61; Castanheda, vol. 2, bk. 6, 283, 330; bk. 9, 914, 920–23; Correia 2:816, 876, 912.

3. *17 December 1551:* Pinto ascribes the miracle of the sloop to 17 December 1551, but as Schurhammer points out (in *Francis Xavier* 4:307 n.), this date is impossible. Xavier left Japan on November 15 and arrived in Malacca on December 27. It took ten to twelve days to sail from Japan to China and about a month to sail from China to Malacca. For a slightly different version of the so-called miracle of the sloop, see *Francis Xavier* 4:301–5.

Chapter 215

1. *Sanchão:* See chapter 132, note 3 above.

2. *carry out his plans:* Schurhammer has shown that Xavier fully intended to return to Japan the following year and that it was not until after he reached *Sanchão* that he altered his plans and decided instead to go to China with an official embassy from the viceroy of India. The idea was put forward in the letters that reached Diogo Pereira from the Portuguese prisoners in China, who hoped to gain their freedom in that way. See his "Der Uhrsprung des Chinaplans der hl. Franz Xaver," *Archivum Historicum Societatus Iesu* 22 (1953): 38–56; or *Francis Xavier* 4:306–14.

3. *Viceroy Dom Afonso de Noronha:* See chapter 134, notes 4 and 6 above.

4. *Dom Alvaro de Ataide:* Son of the famous Admiral Vasco da Gama. He succeeded his brother Dom Pedro da Silva as captain of Malacca in October of 1552. However, Ataide's term as captain of Malacca had not yet begun when Xavier returned to Malacca in May of 1552, bringing with him the confirmation of Ataide's appointment as admiral of the sea of Malacca. Ironically, it was this appointment, which Xavier helped him to obtain, that gave Ataide the right to decide which ships could sail from Malacca. For further details on how Ataide frustrated Xavier's plans for the China mission, see Schurhammer, *Francis Xavier* 4:585–91.

5. *a nobleman . . . in Portugal:* According to Schurhammer (*Francis Xavier* 4:587 n. 11), the edict of the viceroy mentions a nobleman in Portugal named Diogo Pereira.

6. *Dom Gonzalo Coutinho:* Naval commander who saw action in India, the Red Sea, and Ormuz, where his brother (Garcia Coutinho) was serving as captain of the fortress in 1522 (Correia, vol. 2, chaps. 5–6, 694–95). He must have gone back to Portugal, for the *Livro das Armadas* (21) mentions him as coadmiral of the royal fleet that sailed from Lisbon in 1533. He arrived with an appointment as captain of Goa, which was to begin upon the expiration (in 1536) of the

term of João Pereira (Correia, vol. 3, chap. 45, 540). In 1538, Correia says (vol. 4, chap. 1, 11) he presented the keys of the fortress of Goa to the newly arrived viceroy Dom Garcia de Noronha. After that his name disappears from the chronicles.

7. *Monomotapa:* Ancient native empire of South Africa that was at the height of its powers when the Portuguese discovered it early in the sixteenth century. It covered an enormous territory from the Zambesi to the middle of the continent. Today the region is divided between Mozambique and Rhodesia (Zimbabwe). See Barbosa, *Book of Duarte Barbosa* 1 : 12 n. 1.

8. *the count admiral:* Vasco da Gama.

9. *João Soares:* Vicar of Malacca. Xavier, as papal nuncio, had instructed him to publicly announce Ataide's excommunication, but his request had not been carried out. The vicar could not bring himself to do it, for he would have incurred the wrath of Ataide, and his life for the next three years would have been unbearable. See Schurhammer, *Francis Xavier* 4 : 588, 606.

10. *Covilhã:* Commune, in the district of Castelo Branco, in east central Portugal.

11. *Chepocheca:* See chapter 203, note 2 above.

12. *Saturday, 2 December 1552:* Schurhammer writes that Xavier died before dawn on Saturday, 3 December 1552 (*Francis Xavier* 4 : 643).

Chapter 216

1. *three months and five days later:* The ship carrying Xavier's body back to Malacca left *Sanchão* on 17 February 1553, which means that it was disinterred two and a half months after his death on 3 December 1552. See Schurhammer, *Francis Xavier* 4 : 644.

2. *the same nao:* the *Santa Cruz,* which belonged to Diogo Pereira (ibid.).

3. *nine months and twenty-two days before:* Xavier had embarked for China on 22 July 1552. His body was brought from China to Malacca on 22 March 1553 (ibid.).

4. *Lopo de Loronha:* Schurhamer writes Lobo de Noronha (ibid., 645).

5. *Pero de Alcáçova:* In 1552 Alcáçova arrived in Japan, where he was sent by Xavier with the return gift of the viceroy for the king of Bungo. The following year, Cosme de Torres, the superior of the Jesuit mission in Japan, sent him back to India to explain the needs of the mission to the authorities. On his way to Malacca he stopped in *Sanchão,* where he learned of Xavier's death (ibid.).

6. *João de Távora:* This should be Manuel de Távora. In 1553 he was on his way to the Jesuit mission in the Moluccas with João de Beira, the superior of the mission there, who left him behind in Malacca to stand guard over Xavier's remains (ibid.).

7. *obvious miracles:* In December of 1553 the only ship in Malacca that was bound for India was a decrepit old vessel belonging to Lopo de Noronha. Many people did not believe it could survive a storm. Nevertheless, despite the many perils encountered at sea, the fact that it made port safely was attributed to the presence of Xavier's body on board (ibid.). In chapter 217 Pinto again refers to the shipowner as Lopo de Loronha.

Chapter 217

1. *sailed in consort:* Schurhammer says that it was the only ship that sailed from Malacca to India in December 1553. See chapter 216, note 7 above.

2. *Father Master Belchior:* or more correctly, Melchior Nunes Barreto (1520–71). He arrived in India on 5 September 1551 with a doctorate in theology. In accordance with Xavier's instructions, after the deaths of Gaspar Barzaeus and Manuel de Morais, Nunes Barreto became rector of the College of Saint Paul in Goa and vice-provincial of the Society of Jesus in India. He succeeded to the position on 18 October 1554. Pinto refers to him here and in his letters as Belchior.

3. *along with three brothers:* What Pinto fails to mention is that he also went along with

Melchior to pick up the body of Francis. See his letter of 5 December 1554 in which he writes, "Because of my past friendship with him [Xavier] I offered to go with the Father [Melchior] . . . and he took with him three Brothers and four children . . . and only me, with no other outsiders" (Catz, *Cartas,* 41).

4. *Bhatkal:* A city often named in the sixteenth-century narratives, situated in the former district of North Kanara, in the province of Bombay. Writing in 1512–15, Pires says that it used to be a great port, but that its importance diminished after the Portuguese captured Goa. See Cortesão, *Suma Oriental,* 62.

5. *Ancola:* Pires describes it as a town in a creek thirteen miles southeast of the Kali Nadi River, or between Bhatkal and Goa (ibid., 55 n. 1).

Chapter 218

1. *undergo a truly genuine conversion:* That is precisely what happened to Pinto, for it was about this time that he joined the Society of Jesus, from which he was separated two years later, apparently at his own request. See Catz, *Cartas,* documents 3–7, 21 (pp. 26–27, 31, 35, 39–41, 50–51, 121).

2. *fingers in their mouths:* See chapter 14, note 4 above.

3. *suffocated:* Cf. Catz, Cartas, 22–23, 30, 31, 41, 49.

4. *Yacatá-andono:* *Yakata* was a title given by the shogun to feudal lords or provincial governors which, at the same time, made them members of the shogun's family. *Andono* is a corruption of the honorific *dono.* See chapter 135, note 3 above.

Chapter 219

1. *Dom Antonio de Noronha:* Captain of Malacca, 1554–55.

2. *Dom Garcia de Noronha:* Viceroy of India, 1538–40. See chapter 8, note 4 above.

3. *death came very fast:* Most of the contemporary accounts agree that Ataide died of leprosy. However, this seems unlikely, given the signs and symptoms and the rapid course of the disease. See Schurhammer, *Francis Xavier* 4 : 605 n. 28.

4. *others in his party:* Belchior departed from Goa with Gaspar Vilela, Antonio Dias, Estêvão de Gois, Melchior Dias, Fernão Mendes Pinto, Luis Fróis, and five orphaned children. Fróis was left behind in Malacca in 1554 to take charge of the Jesuit mission there, but he was later sent to Japan (1562), where he spent the rest of his life with the exception of two years in Macao (1592–94). He is the author of a history of the early Jesuit missions to Japan, from which he omitted Pinto's name. Apparently, it was a Jesuit custom to omit from their published works the names of members who left the order. Fróis died in Nagasaki in 1597. See his *Historia de Japam* 1 : 93–94. Schurhammer translated this work into German under the title *Die Geschichte Japans* (Leipzig, 1926).

5. *Dom Pedro de Mascarenhas:* Viceroy of India, 1554–55.

6. *died of dysentery:* In Malacca, in 1555 (Couto, in Barros and Couto, déc. 7, bk. 3, chap. 1, 191).

Chapter 220

1. *Pulo Pisang:* A group of small islands in the Malay Archipelago, situated at latitude 1°27′ north and longitude 103°17′ east, at the entrance to the Strait of Singapore.

2. *Luis de Almeida:* Captain of the *Santa Cruz,* appointed by Alvaro de Ataide, who sailed with Xavier to *Sanchão* in 1552. In 1555, shortly before the royal ship on which Barreto and Pinto began their voyage to Japan, he sailed as captain of a galleon from Malacca to China. This Luis de Almeida is not to be confused with the New Christian of the same name who, in the

same year, sailed in the ship of Duarte da Gama from China to Japan, where he joined the Society of Jesus and where he labored until his death in 1583. See Schurhammer, *Francis Xavier* 4 : 602 n. 12.

3. *shahbandar:* See chapter 15, note 2 above.

4. *Lugor:* See chapter 36, note 2 above.

5. *Pulo Cambim:* Possibly Pulo Gambir, at latitude 13°38′ north and longitude 109°19′ east, off the coast of Annam.

6. *islands of Canton:* See chapter 46, note 1 above, where it appears as Pulo Catão.

7. *Pulo Tioman:* See chapter 33, note 5 above.

8. *Sunda:* West Java, not to be confused with the Sunda Islands.

9. *Francisco Toscano:* Shipowner who was a benefactor of the Society of Jesus. In 1554 he had sent his son to be educated at the Jesuit College of Saint Paul in Goa. See Fróis 1 : 97 n. 33.

10. *Champa:* See chapter 39, note 1 above.

11. *Pulo Champeiló:* See chapter 42, note 2 above.

12. *Duarte Coelho:* Distinguished navigator and explorer of the sixteenth century whose exploits took him to both Asia and Brazil. Schurhammer (*Francis Xavier* 4 : 45 n. 147) points out that Pinto contradicts himself when he writes here that Duarte Coelho carved the cross and the inscription in 1518, whereas in his letter of 20 November 1555 he writes that Duarte Coelho had carved the cross thirty-two years earlier, thereby placing the event in 1523. Barros states that on a discovery voyage to Cochinchina in 1523, where he was sent by King Manuel, Duarte Coelho erected a "padrão" or commemorative pillar to mark the discovery (Barros and Couto, déc. 3, bk. 8, chap. 5, 290–91). On the other hand, Fr. R. Cardon, in his article "The Old Church on the Malacca Hill" (188–89), writes that Duarte Coelho discovered Cochinchina eighteen years after the coming of the Portuguese to India (1498? 1500?). He also cites Fr. Jacinto de Deos, who says that "to commemorate the occasion he erected a cross bearing the date of this occurrence together with the name of the discoverer." Perhaps the confusion arises from the fact that Duarte Coelho made several voyages to China with stops at Pulo Champeiló.

Chapter 221

1. *Lampacau:* Lang-Pa-Kao. See chapter 132, note 5 above.

2. *Macao:* For the founding of Macao, see Jack M. Braga's interesting article, "The Western Pioneers and Their Discovery of Macao," *Boletim do Instituto Português de Hongkong* 2 (September 1949): 7–214; and Boxer's *South China,* xxxiii–xxxv.

3. *Ning-po:* See chapter 66, note 4 above.

4. *Lançarote Pereira:* See chapter 70, note 2 and chapter 140, note 7 above.

5. *Ponte de Lima:* See chapter 80, note 1 above.

6. *Xipatom:* See chapter 105, note 11 above.

7. *chumbim:* See chapter 84, note 1 above.

8. *chaem:* See chapter 45, note 5 above.

9. *aitao:* See chapter 81, note 1 above. Spelled variously as *aytao* or *aitao.*

10. *vancões:* See chapter 44, note 9 above.

11. *Martim Afonso de Sousa:* Governor of India, 1542–45. See chapter 12, note 6 above.

12. *Ruy Vaz Pereira Marramaque:* Captain of Malacca, 1543–44. See chapter 172, note 2 above.

13. *Chinceo:* See chapter 44, note 3 above.

14. *Simão de Melo:* Captain of Malacca, 1545–48.

15. *Luis de Montarroyo:* See chapter 171, note 1 above.

16. *vintem:* An old Portuguese copper coin of little value.

17. *original plans:* Cf. Pinto's letter of 20 November 1555 in Catz, *Cartas,* 59–65.

Chapter 222

1. *carried out:* Cf. Belchior's letter of 23 November 1555 in Catz, *Cartas,* 66–73.

2. *freeing of two Portuguese:* In Belchior's letter of 23 November 1555 he speaks of his efforts to free a Mateus de Brito and five other captives (ibid.); in Pinto's letter of 20 November 1555, he mentions Mateus de Brito and "one other man" (ibid., 61); and in Luis Fróis's letter of 7 January 1556, he just mentions the release of Mateus de Brito (ibid., 83).

3. *Sansy:* This may be a corruption of Shensi, which was the province most affected by the catastrophic earthquakes described by Pinto in this chapter. See Boxer's *South China,* 223 n.3.

4. *catastrophe:* Cf. Gaspar da Cruz's account of the series of earthquakes that struck China in the years 1555–56, ibid., 223–27.

5. *Cuy:* Identified elsewhere as a city in Siam. See chapter 88, note 2.

6. *anchacilado:* See chapter 45, note 1 above.

7. *Nacapirau:* See chapter 110 above.

8. *five Portuguese imprisoned:* It is known that a large number of Portuguese were captured by the Chinese in 1549. Over the years some died and some were exiled, others escaped or were ransomed by the Portuguese. However, Mateus de Brito, whose release Father Belchior was able to obtain, could not have been among the earlier group of captives, since he was known to have been present at the siege of Malacca in 1551. See Schurhammer, *Francis Xavier* 4:448 n. 41.

9. *Pocasser:* See chapter 73, note 3 above.

Chapter 223

1. *Dom Francisco Mascarenhas:* Couto gives his full name as Francisco Mascarenhas Palha (*Palha* means "straw"). In later years the viceroy Antonio de Noronha (1571–73) appointed him admiral of a large fleet on the coast of Malabar, where he distinguished himself in action (Barros and Couto, déc. 8, chap. 18, 104).

2. *first group of islands:* According to Schurhammer (*Francis Xavier* 4:302 n. 3), Pinto's ship came to the Koshiki Islands instead of to Tanegashima through a pilot's error. See chapter 132, note 12 above.

3. *Usuki:* See chapter 135, note 20 above.

4. *Fingau:* This unidentified toponym is used in chapter 19 with reference to Sumatra. See chapter 19, note 1 above.

5. *embassy:* In 1554, shortly before his departure for Japan, the viceroy Afonso de Noronha (1550–54) had appointed Pinto as his ambassador to the king of Bungo. See chapter 134, note 6 above.

6. *Xeque:* Possibly the island of Saiki, at the northeastern tip of Kyushu, at latitude 32°57' north and longitude 131°54' east.

7. *funé:* "Boat," in Japanese. See chapter 135, note 14 above.

8. *school of fish:* Izaak Walton alludes to this fishing episode in the following manner: "And let me tell you that angling is of high esteem and of much use in other nations. He that reads the *Voyages of Ferdinand Mendez Pinto* shall find that there he declares to have found a king and several priests a-fishing" (*The Compleat Angler* [Mt. Vernon, N.Y.: Peter Pauper Press, 1955], 32). This quotation did not appear in the first edition of 1653 but is in all subsequent editions.

9. *gueso:* A counsellor of state in Japan. From the Japanese *giso* (Dalgado).

10. *to eat with one's hands:* Cf. chapter 83 above, in which the Portuguese, eating with their hands, provide amusement for a Chinese family.

Chapter 224

1. *Quansio Nafama:* Spelled *Quamsio Nafama* in chapter 209.

2. *kubo-sama:* See chapter 208, note 12 above.

Chapter 225

1. *Brother João Fernandes:* See chapter 208, note 10 above.

2. *times . . . in such a state:* It should be borne in mind that the arrival of the Jesuits in Japan coincided with what was known in Japanese history as the *Shengoku-jidai* or the period of the "country at war." On the island of Kyushu where the missionaries first came, there were intermittent wars for supremacy among three principal clans. At the time that Barreto arrived in 1556, Otomo was engaged in a war with the Motonari clan, which had just overthrown his brother, the feudal lord or daimyo of Yamaguchi, causing the Christians to flee from there to Bungo, where Otomo protected them. Moreover, Otomo had to contend with his Zen bonzes and some of his own followers, including several members of his family, who were opposed to the Christians. See Boxer, *Christian Century in Japan,* 41. See also letter of Cosme de Torres of 7 November 1557 (document 15, 96–98) and letter of Melchior Nunes Barreto of 10 January 1558 (document 16, 100–108) in Catz, *Cartas.*

3. *fathers who are here:* The fathers and brothers present at the time were Cosme de Torres, João Fernandes, Luis de Almeida, Duarte da Silva, and Baltasar Gago.

4. *becoming a Christian:* Otomo eventually converted in the year 1578. See Fróis 3: 25–27.

5. *Guilherme Pereira:* Probably the brother of Diogo Pereira (see chapter 204, n. 2 above) and one of the richest men in the Far East at that time. It is known that he sailed to Japan in 1558 and 1559. See Boxer, *Great Ship from Amacon,* 24–25, and *Fidalgos in the Far East, 1550–1770* (The Hague: Martinus Nijhoff, 1948), 32–33. But he is not to be confused with the Guilherme Pereira who was one of the orphaned children who came to Japan in 1556 with Father Nunes Barreto and later became a priest in Japan. See Fróis 1: 93 n. 15.

6. *João Nunes [Barreto]:* Born in Porto around 1510. He entered the order in Coimbra in 1545, arrived in Goa in 1556, and died there in December of 1562, without ever taking up his appointment as Roman patriarch of Ethiopia. See Fróis 1: 92 n. 3. As for the reasons why the so-called patriarch never set foot in that country, see Whiteway, *Portuguese Expedition to Abyssinia,* lxxvi, xcv.

7. *Prester John:* Emperor of Ethiopia. See chapter 4, note 2 above.

8. *king of Zeila:* The Iman Ahmad, whom the Portuguese called the king of Zeila, was slain in battle in the year 1543 by Cristóvão da Gama's men (see chap. 12, no. 14 above). But, as the Portuguese learned after the failure of Bishop Oviedo's mission in 1557, regardless of the fortunes of war neither the Emperor Galawdewos nor his brother Minas, who succeeded him in 1559, had any intention of abandoning the customs of their ancestors to adopt the Latin ritual (Whiteway, *Portuguese Expedition to Abyssinia,* lxxvi, xcv).

9. *Francisco Barreto:* Governor of India, 1555–58.

10. *Dom Constantino [de Braganza]:* Viceroy of India, 1558–61.

11. *priest brothers died:* Melchior died in Cochin in 1571, and João died in Goa in 1562.

12. *Fernão Mendes Pinto:* This is the only time the author mentions his own name.

Chapter 226

1. *Dom Pedro Mascarenhas:* Viceroy of India, 1554–55.

2. *Dom Francisco Mascarenhas:* The same ship captain with whom the Jesuit missionaries sailed from China to Japan. See chapter 223, note 1 above.

3. *Dona Catarina:* Granddaughter of Isabel and Ferdinand of Spain and sister of the emperor Charles V. She married John III of Portugal in 1525. None of their nine children lived to succeed their father, who died in 1557. She served as regent for her three-year-old grandson Sebastian until 1562, when she handed over the reins of government to her brother-in-law, Cardinal Henrique. She died in 1578, the same year that Sebastian died in a quixotic campaign against the Moors of North Africa.

4. *sixteen times:* See chapter 1, note 1 above.

Glossary 1

Foreign and Uncommon Words

The following words were defined the first time they appeared in the text but are given here in alphabetical order for the convenience of the reader who wishes to consult them. They are derived in great part from the following works: Yule and Burnell, *Hobson-Jobson* (London, 1903), and its equivalent in Portuguese, Dalgado's *Glossário Luso-Asiático,* 2 vols. (Coimbra, 1919–21). These, as well as some other less important works that are mentioned, are listed in the Bibliography.

Also appended to this list are words of uncertain provenance that have not been identified. The numbers following the definitions refer to chapters.

agrém: Pinto uses this word for a Buddhist pulpit in Indochina. Dalgado says that it is probably derived from the Pali *agaram,* which is in turn derived from the Sanskrit *agara,* meaning "house" or "room." 127, 168, 199.

Al-Koran: The word has two meanings: (a) the Koran, or sacred book of the Mohammedans; (b) the tower or minaret of the mosque from which the muezzin calls the faithful to prayer. 18, 27, 31, 51.

altirna: Pinto uses this word for the upper or outer garment worn by the Buddhist priests of China, which Dalgado believes is derived from the Pali *Uttariyam.* 110, 160, 163–65, 167, 168, 210.

amborraja: From the Malay *hamba-raja,* meaning "servant of the king." According to Marsden the *amborrajas* were Malay and not Battak officers, as Pinto would have us believe. 15, 31, 174.

Amida: The Japanese name for the Buddha Amitabha (infinite light) or Amitâyus (infinite life). Devotion to Amida or Amitabha, which first developed in China, gave rise in Japan to a special branch of Buddhism called Amidism. Amida is a fabulous personage who abides in the western heaven. He is worshipped by the northern or Mahayana Buddhists but is unknown to the southern or Hinayana Buddhists of Siam, Burma, and Sri Lanka. The western paradise promised to the worshippers of Amida-Buddha is inconsistent with the doctrine of nirvana, since it promised immortality instead of annihilation. Amida is a male deity, though Pinto makes him female, probably because the word ends with an *a.* 78, 107, 111, 112, 211–13.

amuck: From the Malay *amoq,* meaning "frenzied attack, or a man possessed by fury." Dalgado distinguishes between two types of Oriental *amucks,* those who, moved by vengeance, seek desperately to do as much harm as possible to their enemies, as in India; and those who, dominated by fury, kill innocent people, as in the Malaysian archipelago. 17, 28, 59, 119, 155, 174, 175, 186.

anchaci: A provincial judge or chief justice in China. Also translated as "criminal judge" or "judicial commissioner." 47, 85, 88–90, 94, 95, 106, 107, 113–15, 222.

anchacilado: A term, probably invented by Pinto, for the district of the *anchaci* (see above). 45, 83, 88, 113, 222.

assegai: Also spelled "azagaia," "assagai," or "hassegai." A short lance or spear used for both throwing and stabbing. From the Arabic *az-zagaya,* a term adopted by the Arabs from the Berber *zaghaya,* and later by the Portuguese to designate various lances of their own. 18, 206.

aytao, aytau, aitao: From the Chinese *haitao, hai-tô, or hai-tao-fu-shih,* commander of the provincial coast-guard fleet, or "general of the sea of Kwangtung province." Sometimes translated as "commissioner of the sea route" and sometimes as "admiral." 81, 85, 86, 88, 89, 98, 100, 101, 103, 105–7, 114, 132, 221.

azeda: A Portuguese word meaning "wood sorrel." 138.

bada: From the Malay *badak,* meaning (in the 16th century) a "wild animal" or a "domesticated animal gone wild." Pinto uses the word to refer to the yak of Tartary. 73.

bailéu: From the Malay, meaning "audience hall" or "magistrate's tribunal." The word was given secondary meanings by the Portuguese writers, who used it variously in the sense of tribune, veranda, porch, lean-to, public banquet hall, or a raised fighting platform on a ship. 15,32.

bainhá: Title of a high government officer in Burma and Pegu. From the Burmese *ba-yin,* meaning "lord." Spelled variously by the English historians as *binnya, bayin, buyin,* etc. 150, 153, 155, 188, 190.

barnagais: Bahar nagaes or *Bahr nagas,* the title of the governor of northern Ethiopia, meaning literally "lord of the sea." In the fifteenth and sixteenth centuries he was the governor of Tigre and the lowlands stretching to the coast of Massawa. After 1580 his office was absorbed in that of the *Tegre makuannen,* but when the Portuguese first arrived (1520), the two were still distinct, the domain of the *bahar nagaes* ending at the Marab and including the provinces of Sarawe, Hamasen, Akala Guzay, and Bur. 4.

bendara: Tomé Pires (1512?), who has given us the first European description of the Malacca high officials, writes that "the *Bendara* is a kind of chief justice in all civil and criminal affairs. He also

has charge of the King's revenue. He can order any person to be put to death, of whatever rank and condition . . . but first of all he informs the King." The Portuguese retained the office of *bendara* when they took over Malacca, but with some restrictions. 14, 15, 28.

betenigus: Beit-el-Negus in Amharic, meaning literally "house of the king." It applies specifically to the round houses and not to the rectangular ones. 4.

bichara: Consultation, meeting, conference, etc., from the Sanskrit *vichara.* 52.

bico: A Buddhist monk who begs for alms. From the Pali *bkikku.* 160, 167.

bonze, bonzo: A term applied by Europeans in China to the Buddhist clergy, but originating with early visitors to Japan. 78, 90, 96, 111, 114, 121, 134–37, 161, 168, 201, 208–13, 215, 223, 225.

bracalão (bracalões, pl.): Pinto uses this word with relation to Siam and China in the sense of a "high dignitary" or "minister or counsellor of state." From the Siamese *boromo,* "royal, pre-eminent," and *kromo,* "minister." 105–7, 184.

brala: According to Yule and Burnell, this is a term frequently applied by the early Portuguese writers to the pagodas of Indochina and China. It is probably derived from the Malay *barahla* or *brahla,* meaning an "idol." (See *varela.*) 64, 148, 151, 162, 164, 167, 168, 184.

broquem: A Japanese governor, from the Japanese *buraku,* meaning "province." It is used in chapter 130 in the sense of "captain of the palace guard," but in chapters 139–43 it is used as the title of the governor of the Ryukyu Islands. 130, 139–43.

cabaya: A surcoat or long tunic of muslin, one of the most common native garments of the better classes in India. From the Arabic *qaba* or *caba,* meaning a "vesture." 6, 8, 53.

cabisondo, cabizonda, capisondo: Pinto uses this word with three different meanings, each of them with reference to China and Indochina: (a) in chapter 49 as a "high-ranking customs official"; (b) in chapters 111, 112, 165, 166, 168, 196 as a "high-ranking Buddhist priest"; (c) in chapter 184 as a "flagship or lead vessel." 49, 111, 112, 165, 166, 168, 184, 196.

caciz, qasis: From the Arabic *kashish,* meaning a "Christian priest." Strangely enough, the term is frequently employed by old Christian writers on Eastern subjects as if it were the special title of a Mohammedan theologian, when, in reality, it is the special and technical title of a Christian priest. 5, 6, 13, 27, 31, 50, 51, 59, 178.

Caladigão: From the Chinese *Ta-li-sx'-king,* meaning "high tribunal." 103.

caloete, caluete: The punishment of impalement, in Dravidic India, from the Tamil-Malayalam *kaluvirri* (pronounce *kaluvitti*), *kalu* meaning "punishment stake," and *luvirri* "to impale." However, Pinto applies this word to Malaysia. 155, 177, 179.

Canom: The Bodhisattva Kuan-yin (Chinese) or Kwannon (Japanese), often called in Western books on China the goddess of mercy. 107, 211, 212.

chaem (*chaens,* pl.): From the Chinese *ch'a-yuan,* an abbreviation of *tu-ch'a-yuan,* the censorate or court of censors in Peking. It is applied to the censors or imperial commissioners who toured the provinces of China in various capacities. 45, 52, 68, 84–86, 88–90, 95, 98, 100–103, 105–8, 111, 114, 115, 117, 125, 221, 222.

chandeu, chandeuhó: From the Chinese *chin-hu* (there is no *d* in Chinese), meaning "a fair or bazaar." 98, 165.

Chanfacau: Or *Chang-hai-koan,* which is actually the name of one of the fortified gates of the Great Wall, on the east side. 95.

chanipatão (*chanipatões,* pl.): From the Chinese *chau-mo-ting,* meaning "stamp" or "seal." 108.

charachina: From the Malay *chara,* meaning "mode or manner"; hence, in the

manner of the Chinese. Pinto also uses the term *chara-japão,* meaning in the manner of Japan. 40, 47, 48, 50, 62, 68, 69, 77, 105, 119, 201.

charana: Deep dish or tray on a pedestal, used in India especially for betel. From the Malay *charana,* meaning "foot." 182.

chaubainha: *Saw binnya,* meaning "lord of wisdom," was the title of the governor or viceroy of Martaban, who held his position under the king of Pegu, capital of the Talaings or Mons. 144, 146–54, 171.

chautar: Or "chudder" as the English called it, from the Hindi *chadar.* A sheet, or square piece of cloth of any kind; also, the ample sheet commonly worn as a mantle by the women of northern India. 168.

chaveca: Pinto seems to employ this term as a division of both the lunar day and month. 142, 165.

Chenchicogim, Chenchicogi, Chenchico (*Chenchicogins,* pl.): This term is composed of two Japanese words, *tenjiku,* meaning "India," and *jin,* meaning "individual or individuals," hence "man or men from India," since the Japanese does not distinguish between singular and plural. It was applied to the Portuguese who came to Japan via India. 133–35, 209, 211, 218, 223, 225.

chifanga: Pinto uses this word for "prison," which, according to Dalgado, is *kien-lau* in Chinese. However, he suggests possible derivations from *chi-fan,* "government bureau or department," *tse-fan,* "customs duties," or *chah-fang,* "guard house." 63, 65.

chifu: Or *chih-fu,* the title of the mandarin governing the largest of the provincial subdivisions in China; prefect. 47, 87–91, 96, 97, 100, 103, 110.

chileu: A commanding officer and governor of a province. Dalgado believes that this word comes from the Tonkinese *kinh luoc,* which is pronounced "kileu." 47.

chircá: Pinto uses this term as a title in the sense of a "high court justice" in

Pegu. However, as Dalgado points out, the Burmese *sit-kai,* from which it is probably derived, means "lieutenant." 150, 191, 192, 198.

chisangué: Dalgado believes that this word is derived from the Sanskrit *crisanghi,* meaning "venerable chief of the monastery." 126.

chumbim (*chumbins,* pl.): Initially, Dalgado attributes the same meaning to this word as does Pinto, i.e., "a magistrate or judge in China," and gives *hingming* as the etymology of the word. But in the supplement to his *Glossário* he quotes the French sinologue Paul Pelliot, who gives *tsong-ping* as the etymology. However, Armando Cortesão, in discussing the meanings of various Chinese words used by the old Portuguese writers, injects a word of caution when he writes, "The question as to what Chinese expressions are meant by these old Portuguese versions has been a matter of controversy and it is still not quite settled." 84–88, 100, 103, 105, 106, 108, 114, 115, 142, 221.

cochumiaco: See *cuchimiocó.*

Coje: See *Khoja.*

conchaci, conchacy: Criminal judge or magistrate, in China. 86, 105.

conchala: Appellate court judge, in China. 103, 106.

conchalim, conchaly: Inspector of weights and measures; chancellor, or appellate court judge, in China. High-ranking dignitary, in Siam. 86, 97, 100, 101, 103, 182.

conquiai: Administrative dignitary in China. 107.

continão: Probably derived from the Chinese *kwa-ti-nien,* meaning "prosecutor," according to Dalgado. 103.

cuchimiocó, cuchimiacó, cochumiaco: From the Japanese *kuchi* and *myokuan.* Pinto uses the word in the sense of "letter of exchange" or "passport to Heaven," which Francis Xavier described in the following manner: "The Japanese bonzes preached that individuals who gave money to the bonzes in this life

would receive tenfold for this in the other life, and in the same coin, so that they might take care of their needs in that world. The bonzes gave them a receipt which they had buried with them when they died so that they would scare the devil away" (Schurhammer, *Francis Xavier* 4 : 443). 114, 210, 212.

dato: A prelate in Malacca, derived from the Malayan term *datok* meaning "a headman or foreman." 6, 31.

diusa: A corruption of the Japanese *dai,* "big, great," and *uso,* "lie." 213.

dopo: According to Dalgado this word is derived from the Burmese *tat* or *dat,* meaning "fortress." 118, 120, 121, 149, 168.

facharão: Companion or colleague. Dalgado suggests a derivation from the Japanese *hoyu-tsure.* (Initial *f* for *h* is normal in the Portuguese transcription.) 134.

faraz: Also *farash, ferah, frash,* etc., from the Arabic *farrash* (*farsh,* literally "to spread a carpet"). The *farazes* were menial servants, whose proper business it was to spread carpets, pitch tents, etc., and, in a house, to do housemaid's work. 173.

fatoqui, fatoquin: A corruption of the Japanese *hotoke(s),* meaning "Buddhist gods." 211, 212.

ferucua: Dalgado writes that, "if the word is really Chinese, it must come from *pwan-swe-kwan,* 'judge,' or from *kwan-fu,* 'magistrate,' with a transposition of terms." 85.

fiambra: A six-wheeled carriage. 130.

firmaun: From the Persian *farman,* "an order, patent, or passport," issued by high-ranking Mussulmen of the East. 119, 183.

gerozemo: A judicial civil servant in China. Dalgado believes that Pinto borrowed this word, not from the Chinese, but from the Japanese *gero-sama,* which means "jailer." 85.

Gizom: From the Japanese *jizoo,* one of the Bodhisattvas or titular gods of Japanese Buddhism, protector of children. 92, 107, 114, 211, 212.

Godomen: This represents Kodam' or Khdam', which is one of the most common names for Buddha in the Indochinese countries. It comes from the Pali Gotamo, or the Sanskrit Gautama. It is the princely surname, according to Buddhist legend, of the Sakya tribe from which the Buddha is descended. 161.

goxo: The title of the shogun or cubo who, in the name of the emperor, exercised civil control over all of Japan. (See kubo-sama.) 135.

gregoge: Ancient form of torture in Malaysia. From the Malay *gergaji*, meaning "to saw." 19.

grepo: A general term for a Buddhist priest, possibly derived from the Siamese *khru* (Pali *garu*, from the Sanskrit *guru*) meaning "a religious preceptor." Cf. *menigrepo, talagrepo*, and *orepo*. 78, 149, 151, 160–65, 167–69, 196.

gromenare: A respectful form of salutation or obeisance, from the Japanese *go-me-nare*. 210.

groxo: A member of the council of state in ancient Japan. 210.

guazil: From the Arabic *wazir*, meaning a "minister," usually the prime minister of a king, or the governor of a city, especially among the Arabs and Persians. The term was known on the Iberian peninsula long before the Portuguese reached India, but it was used with the Arabic article and had acquired a different meaning. 6.

gueso: A counsellor of state in Japan. From the Japanese *giso*. 223.

guimão: A Buddhist priest of a certain category, in Indochina. 167.

hoyá: See *oyá*.

inocosém: A corruption of the Japanese *inu*, "dog," and *kusai*, "smelly, stinking." 211.

jurubaça: The word is derived from the Malay-Javanese *juruba-hasa, juru* meaning "master, expert," and *bahasa*, from the Sanskrit *bhasa*, meaning "tongue," hence, "interpreter." 136, 140.

kaffir: An infidel or unbeliever in Islam, in Arabic. As the Arabs applied this word to pagan blacks, among others, the Portuguese adopted it in this restricted sense and passed it on to other European nations. The term was often applied contemptuously by Mohammedans to Christians. 18, 40, 122, 161, 180.

khoja, khojah: From the Persian *khwajah*, a respectful title applied to various classes, as in India especially to eunuchs; in Persia, to wealthy merchants; in Turkistan, to persons of sacred families. 6, 19, 35, 37, 41, 42, 50, 52, 53, 57–63, 69, 173, 185.

Koran: See Al-Koran.

kubo-sama, cubo: Former governor or shogun of Japan. Originally, he was a military leader who seized temporal power, reserving the spiritual power and some royal honors for the "dairi," or mikado. 208, 210, 212, 224.

lauteá: A title of respect used for high Chinese officials in general, in the sense of "sir, lord." The term is derived from the Amoy vernacular *ló-tia*, or the Chuan-chou form *lau-tia*, meaning "venerable father." 105, 106, 114, 115.

libangú: A prioress, in charge of Buddhist priestesses, in Indochina. 126.

linha: The triple cord, or sacred girdle, that the high-caste Hindus wear across the breast, from left to right, from the day of their investiture into the priesthood, as a symbol of their regeneration, or *dvija*, meaning "twice-born." 11.

loya: Gold filigree bracelet, in Sumatra. 22.

mainato: A washerman, from the Tamil-Malayal *mainatta*. The *mainatos* were of a low caste in India who did the washing for the entire community, but the term was widely used by the Portuguese throughout Asia. 105.

mamoco: From the Persian *mah*, meaning "moon." A term used by the Mohammedans to describe the course of the moon. Pinto uses it in the sense of "day of the lunar month." 13, 135, 142, 225.

menigrepo: A Buddhist monk of uncertain category, in Burma. 77, 78, 85, 107, 127, 128, 165, 167, 169, 195, 199.

minhamundi: A fragrant oil, in Malaysia, with which the *amucks* anoint themselves as a sign of their determination to die. 174, 178.

mocadão: From the Arabic *muqaddam* or *mukaddam,* meaning a "headman." The term can be applied to the headman of a village, to the local head of a caste, or to the headman of a gang of laborers. 6.

moçafo: From the Arabic *mushaf,* meaning "book, volume." It was used frequently by the early Portuguese writers to designate the Koran. 175.

modeliar, mudeliar: Chief, native captain, honorific title, in India. 90, 164.

mongiloto: From the Chinese *mun-wei-li-to,* meaning a "procurator or attorney authorized and employed to act for and manage the affairs of others." 99.

monteu, monteo: An authority figure who carries out military and judicial duties in China, Siam, and Burma. 33, 103–6, 150, 182.

monvagaru: Governor of the kingdom, in Calaminhan. 163–65.

moulana: A mullah, from the Arabic *mawlana.* A Moslem religious leader or teacher, or any man of learned reputation. Used also as a title of respect. 5, 6, 31, 51, 178.

mutra: A seal, stamp, or signature, in India. From the Sanskrit *mudra.* 130, 146.

naique, naik: From the Sanskrit *nayaka,* meaning a "leader, chief, or general." The term is used in several applications among the Portuguese chroniclers as meaning a native captain or headman of some sort. 4.

naugator: Captain or chieftain of a city, in Indochina. 158.

nautaquim, nautoquim: Used frequently by Pinto as the Japanese word for "prince," and spelled elsewhere as *nautoquim.* There is no doubt that he took it from *naotoki,* one of the various names of the feudal lord of the island of Tanegashima who ruled at the time the Portuguese first landed in Japan (1542 or 1543). 39, 132–35, 143, 200.

nautarel: Pinto uses this word in the sense

of "highest-ranking customs officer," in Annam. 49.

nauticor: Title of a Tartar general. 117, 118.

necodá, nacoda, nacoder, etc.: From the Persian *na-khuda, meaning* "a skipper, or master of a native vessel." The term, which was adopted by the Malays, denotes a person who is at the same time navigator and owner of a trading vessel, a condition of much respectability among them. 35, 46, 51, 52, 132–34, 144–46, 148, 153, 174, 208.

neepoi: A Buddhist dignitary. 160.

nhay: "Sir or madame," from the Siamese *nai.* 111, 142, 150, 151, 152, 154, 172.

nivator: Name of a species of bird or pheasant. 83.

Nobi, Noby: From the Arabic *nabi,* meaning "prophet," and by extension, "Mohammed." 6, 27, 31, 59.

odiá, adiá: From the Arabic *hadyia,* meaning "a gift given to a superior or a teacher of the Koran." 19, 64, 183.

orepo: A buddhist monk of uncertain category. 130.

ourobalão, orabalão (ourobalões, pl.): Military leader, chosen warrior, or champion. From the Malay *hulubalang, hulu* meaning "head" and *balang* "missile." 13, 15, 31, 174, 206, 207.

oyá, hoyá, hoyha, oya: From the Siamese *húa,* meaning "chief" or "captain." It is also a title of nobility in Siam, equivalent to that of duke. 41, 45, 146, 181, 182, 184–86.

paliguindão, palesguindão (paliguindoens, palosguindões, pl.): Tartar war drum. 118, 119.

panaricão: From the Malay *panjirakan,* meaning literally "comrade captain." 174, 175.

pangueirão, pangueyrão: From the Malay *pangeran,* the title of a native chief in Malaysia, at times synonymous with "nobleman." 173–79.

panha, paina: From the Malayalam *pañni.* A type of cotton from the plant *bombax malabaricum,* not suitable for weaving. It is used only for stuffing. 161.

panoura: In chapter 68 the word is used in the sense of a ceremonial weapon or sword. Elsewhere, Pinto uses the same word for a ship. Dalgado is unable to identify it. 71, 75, 79, 97, 105 (ship); 68, 124, 130, 131, 149, 163.

passeivão, passeyvão: From the Malay *paseban,* meaning a "veranda or terrace surrounding an audience hall," in Malaysia. 18, 174, 192.

pate: An honorific title equivalent to prince or duke, in Malaysia. 38, 174–79.

pela: A type of public entertainment in which the dancer practices certain movements of the head and arms while leaping in the air, like a ball. 69.

peretanda: From the Malay *pretanda,* meaning "an early day magistrate, hangman, or a cruel person." 106, 139–42.

piambre: Pinto uses this word in two different senses: (a) a vehicle resembling a litter; and (b) a tribune or dais. 121.

pilanga: From the Chinese *ping-liu,* meaning, according to Dalgado, "military tribunal." 100.

pirange: A wheeled vehicle of sorts, in the Orient. 124.

pitaleu: Pinto uses this word in the sense of "animal trainer or acrobat." 99.

ponchacy: Also spelled *puchancy.* From the Chinese *pu-chêng-shih.* Originally a civil governor and comptroller, whose functions later became essentially those of a provincial treasurer. 106, 107, 114.

poyho: From the Siamese *pu-phra,* meaning "viceroy." 36.

prechau: Title of the king of Siam, from the Siamese *phra-chao, phra* meaning "excellent" and *chao* meaning "lord." 36, 45, 48, 67, 70, 130, 165, 189.

primeira: An old Iberian card game in which each player is given four cards. 118.

produm: From the Siamese *phrae-don,* meaning "city" or "town." 189.

qasis: See *caciz.*

queitor, queytor: Governor of the kingdom or supreme magistrate. (In chaps. 156-58 used as the name of a river.) 162–65.

quiai, quiay: Venerable, respectable form of address, in China and Indochina. 13, 43, 51, 56–59, 61, 62, 64, 66, 70, 90, 96, 100, 110, 128, 148, 149, 155, 162, 164–68, 170, 171, 174, 178, 179, 182–85, 190, 191, 193, 195, 196, 199.

raudivá: Silk cloth, in China or Siam. 163.

reimão (*reimões,* pl.): Pinto makes a distinction between the tiger and the *reemow,* which is the word for "tiger" on the island of Sumatra. 23.

rolim: The highest monastic grade among the Buddhists in Burma, from the Burmese word *yahan* or *rahan.* 150, 152, 154, 160, 165, 167–69.

sagirave, sanguirave: A shelf, with pigeon-holes, in Calaminhan. 163.

saligue: Wooden lance or pointed stick, from the Malay-Javanese word *saligi.* 22, 128.

samorim: From the Malayal word *samuri,* meaning "sea king," or "sea rajah," title of the former Hindu kings of Calicut. 7.

sanguys de pates: This represents the Malay title *sangadipati,* meaning "sovereign lord or prince." 175.

sauguate: From the Hindi-Persian *saughat,* meaning a "gift," especially one that is given on festive occasions or as a symbol of homage. 11, 13.

shabandar: A port superintendent, or chief customs officer. 15, 18, 38, 183, 220.

sigiputão: The highest-ranking Buddhist priest, in Calaminhan. 164.

sipitão: A civil servant, in China. 115.

talagrepo: A Buddhist monk, in Indochina. 77, 86, 107, 109, 150, 151, 154, 160, 165–69, 182, 184, 185, 199.

talapoi: A word frequently used by European writers to designate the Buddhist monks of the Indochinese countries. It is derived from the Pegu *tala,* meaning "lord," and *poi,* meaning "our," hence "our own spiritual advisor." 149, 150.

tansu: Interpreter, in China, from the Chinese *tung-sz'.* 64.

tavangra: From the Burmese *ta-ghá-va,* meaning an "estate, "a "farmhouse," or "any kind of abode at the edge of a river," in Indochina. 162.

terivó: A solemn festival or pilgrimage. 165.

tuão: From the Malay *tuan* or *tuwan*, meaning "lord, or master." 34.

tucão: From the Malay *tukan,* meaning a "craftsman or skilled workman," in Malaysia. 46.

tundo: Buddhist priest, in Japan. 211, 212.

tutão (*tutões,* pl.): From the Chinese *tu-t'ang,* abbreviated from the title *hsun-fu-tu-t'ang,* meaning "viceroy," "governor," or "inspector-general." This was a temporary provincial appointment conferred on a high official of the central government who was detached for the duration of some regional emergency. 44, 45, 52, 67, 88, 89, 101, 105–7, 114, 115.

tuyxivau: Rector of a Buddhist temple in Indochina, from the Burmese *thin'oke'ksa'yah.* 126.

upo: A bailiff, in China. 89, 91, 94, 95, 97, 100, 103, 106, 115.

vanguenarau: A Buddhist prioress, possibly from the Pali *vagganariyo,* meaning "women of the congregation." 127.

varela: Pagoda and monastery of the Buddhists, in Indochina. See *brala.* 148, 151, 164, 184, 190, 193.

vileu: Prison or dungeon, in China. 140.

xaca: Shakya, or Sakya, the clan or family name of the Buddha. 107, 211, 212.

xemim: Represents *smim,* the Talaing word for "lord," and is spelled variously by the English historians as *thamin* or *thamein.* 149, 150, 151, 155, 156, 162, 190, 191, 193, 194, 198, 199, 204.

xipatom: A caterer, in China. (Also used as a place name in chaps. 122, 221.) 105, 106.

xivalêm: From the Japanese *shihai-nin,* meaning "provincial governor." 139.

yacata: This was a title given by the shogun to feudal lords or provincial governors, which at the same time made them members of the shogun's family. 218.

zumbaia: From the Malay *sembahyang.* An act of deep courtesy or reverence, paid to a king or other person of exalted rank. The term is used today in modern Portuguese, but in a pejorative sense. 36, 48, 152, 160, 167.

Unidentified

aixiparão 199
banaza 166
binaigá 163
caleu 73
caquesseitão 14
caubesy 95
caulange 164
chanfarauho 160
chidampur 113
combracalão 146, 181
comquiay 190
conquiai 107
fancatão 159
gigauhó 73, 103

hurfangá 163
jatemar 143
laginampur 112
macalixau 221
naudelum 132
naustolim 114
nautarão 121, 224
nucaramão 160
pitaucamay 108
pocausilim 23
pontiveu 125
poytão 143
puchissucão 72
puitaleu 159

sacureu 160
santileu 4
sucão 57
talapicor 127
tanigores 81, 87, 100, 101, 103, 104
teuguauxé 123
tileymay 119
tiquaxy 4
trevite 165
vagaru 165
xixaporau 160

Glossary 2

Weights, Measures, and Units of Currency

The information that follows was compiled chiefly from Boxer's *The Great Ship from Amacon* (Lisbon, 1963), 335–42, as well as from Dalgado's *Glossário Luso-Asiático,* 2 vols. (Coimbra, 1919–21) and Yule and Burnell's *Hobson-Jobson* (London, 1903).

alcá: Pinto seems to be the only one of the early Portuguese writers to use this word, which Dalgado suggests may be related to the Malay *laku,* meaning "currency (coin)." "This city . . . provides the king of *Jangomá* with an income of sixty thousand gold *alcás,* or the equivalent of 720,000 *cruzados*" (chap. 158).

almud: A measure of dry or liquid capacity in Portugal, Brazil, and other countries, varying widely in dimensions from about two to thirty-two quarts. In general, equal to about twenty-five liters. "about as thick as a four-*almud* barrel" (chap. 75).

arroba: A weight equal to a quarter of a quintal, or thirty-two pounds avoirdupois; from the Arabic *ar-ruba,* meaning a "fourth." The *arroba* today is reckoned as equivalent to fifteen kilograms. "He arranged to send him . . . two *arrobas* of musket powder" (chap. 21).

bahar, bar, bare: An Indian weight that varied widely in different regions and according to the different commodities for which it was used. In the Far East, the Portuguese usually reckoned the *bahar* as equal to three *piculs* or four hundred pounds avoirdupois. "signed a peace treaty that called for the Achinese to make reparations of five *bahars* of gold, or the equivalent of 200,000 *cruzados*" (chap. 13). See also chapters 18, 27, 33, 39, 43, 51.

biça, viss: A weight used in South India and Burma. The word is derived from the

Tamil *visai,* meaning "division." In Madras it was equal to about three pounds, two ounces avoirdupois. In Burma, the "viss," as the English called it, was equal to about three pounds, five ounces. "he became tributary to him, for the sum of 600,000 *biças* a year, which is equivalent to 300,000 *cruzados* in our money" (chap. 157; in chap. 186 Pinto writes, "one thousand *biças* in gold, which is worth 500,000 *cruzados* in our money"). See also chapters 148, 192, 193, 196.

canada: A Portuguese measure for liquids containing four *quartilhos* (one-twelfth almud), or three English pints. "they made an agreement whereby he became tributary to him for . . . a *ganta* of rubies, which is a measure of capacity similar to the *canada,* as a present for his wife" (chap. 157).

candim, candil, (candins, pl.): An Indo-Portuguese weight, corresponding roughly to about five hundred pounds, but varying much in different localities. "the *Calaminhan* kept a huge store of treasure . . . mainly in the form of silver of about six thousand *candins'* weight, which is twenty four thousand quintals by our standard of measures" (chap. 158).

cash: A Chinese coin originally of copper, and later of increasingly base metal. Ten cash went to the *conderin,* one hundred to the *mace,* and one thousand to the (silver) *tael,* in money of account. The Portuguese equivalent was given as half to one *ceitil,* which was the sixth of a *real* or *réis.* "they asked him to pay 100,000 cash for the privilege, a sum equal to six hundred *cruzados*" (chap. 208). See also chapter 109.

catty, cáte: A variable unit of weight introduced from China into the Malay Archipelago. Though it varied greatly in different parts of the East, the usual English equivalent is given as one and one-third pounds, with one hundred catties going to the picul. "twenty thousand catties of these skins had been traded; and with sixty skins to the catty . . . the total number of skins traded amounted to 1,200,000" (chap. 73). See also chapters 18, 165, 206.

conderin, canderin, candareen: Chinese money of account, valued at one-tenth of a *mace,* or one-hundredth of the silver *tael,* which contained ten cash. The term *conderin* was formerly applied to the hundredth of the Chinese ounce or weight, commonly called by the Malay name *tahil* or *tael.* "They have neither silver nor gold coins because all trade is carried on by means of measures of weight, such as *catties, taels, maces,* and *conderins*" (chap. 165).

conto: In the sixteenth century, the Portuguese term for a million. Today, it means a thousand. "whose property he had confiscated, thus enriching his treasury by two *contos* of gold" (chap. 19).

cruzado: A Portuguese gold coin whose value was fixed at four hundred *réis* in 1517, but which was mainly used in the Orient as money of account. It is nominally translated as "ducat" and roughly equivalent to "a piece of eight." "which the poor merchants . . . valued at forty thousand *cruzados*" (chap. 1; used liberally throughout the book).

ganta: From the Malay *gantang,* a weight or measure mentioned by some old voyagers by which pepper was sold in the Malay Archipelago. Crawfurd de-

fines it as a "dry measure, equal to about a gallon." Garcia da Orta mentions it as a weight of twenty-four ounces. Dalgado defines it as a variable measure of capacity in Malaysia that, in general, was equal to a *canada.* "they made an agreement, whereby he became tributary to him for . . . a *ganta* of rubies, which is a measure of capacity similar to the *canada*" (chap. 157).

jau: From the Malay *jauh,* a measure of distance that, at the rate of 3 leagues per *jau,* would make it equivalent to 9.6 miles. In chapter 95 Pinto uses this measurement for the second time (the first time in chap. 41), but at the rate of 4.5 leagues per *jau,* making it equivalent to 14.4 miles. "the lake measures sixty *jaus* in circumference, with three leagues to a *jau*" (chap. 41). But in chapter 95 he writes; "This would mean . . . that the Wall extended for a distance of seventy *jaus,* which is the equivalent of 315 leagues . . . calculated at four and a half leagues per *jau.*"

lacasa, laquesá: Or "lack" in the Anglo-Indian colloquial, from the Sanskrit *laksha,* meaning "100,000." The English adopted the term to designate 100,000 rupees, or the equivalent of £10,000, in the exchange rate of those days. The word was adopted in the Malay and Javanese and other languages of the archipelago, but in all of those languages it is used in the sense of 10,000 instead of 100,000, with the exception of the Lampungs of Sumatra, who use it correctly. "a total of sixteen *lacasás* of men—a *lacasá* being equal to 100,000—perished by the sword in only four and a half years" (chap. 45). See also chapter 162.

mace, mas, maz: (a) Chinese money of account, equivalent to one-tenth of the silver *tael,* or to ten *conderins;* (b) a gold weight used in Sumatra, being one-sixteenth of a Malay *tael,* or about forty grains; (c) the name of a small gold coin of Achin, weighing nine grains. "they all agreed to sell me

. . . for a price of seven *maces* of gold, which is equal to fourteen hundred *réis* in our money, at the rate of half a *cruzado* per *mace*" (chap. 25). See also chapters 89, 91, 165.

oquea: *Waqet* in Ethiopic and Amharic, a unit of gold weight, of uncertain value, given the wide disagreement among the experts. In the sixteenth century Ethiopia had no coinage. "he sent them a charitable gift of three hundred gold *oqueas,* which are worth about twelve *cruzados* in our money" (chap. 4).

pardau: Name formerly applied to two types of coins in India, one of gold, worth six *tangas* or about 360 *réis*; the other of silver, worth five *tangas* or 300 *réis*. "they assured him that these things alone . . . brought in more than 100,000 *pardaus* of gold, which is equal to ninety thousand *cruzados* in our money" (chap. 161). See also chapters 6, 24, 180.

picul, pico: A measure of weight used in China and the East, generally equal to one hundred catties; i.e., about $133\frac{1}{3}$ pounds avoirdupois, or sixty kilograms. "When the ambassador inquired there how much silver those mines produced annually, they were told it amounted to six thousand piculs, which equals eight thousand quintals in our money" (chap. 128). See also chapters 45, 48, 90, 92, 95, 96, 113, 132, 137, 202, 211.

quart: The Lisbon quart was the equivalent of more than six almuds, the almud being equal to about twenty-five liters. "There were four large earthenware jars, each with a capacity of nearly a quart" (chap. 124).

quintal: The Portuguese hundredweight, which was widely used in the East. It was generally reckoned at about 130 pounds avoirdupois. "they were told it amounted to six thousand piculs, which equals eight thousand quintals in our money" (chap. 128). See also chapters 13, 21, 43, 58, 109, 132, 143, 151, 158.

real (*réis,* pl.): Small Portuguese copper coin of low value which was abolished in the sixteenth century, but its multiples were retained and used as money of account. During the period of 1555–1640, the value of the *cruzado* was theoretically fixed at four hundred *réis*. "they all agreed to sell me to the merchant for a price of seven *maces* of gold, which is equal to fourteen hundred *réis* in our money, at the rate of half a *cruzado* per *mace*" (chap. 25). See also chapters 6, 89, 109, 110, 146, 180, 221.

tael (*taéis,* pl.): A weight and money of account in the Far East, representing a varying weight of silver in different localities. Often called "the ounce of silver." "there was a report . . . that they had been carrying 200,000 *taels* in silver alone—which comes to 300,000 *cruzados* in our money" (chap. 35; used frequently up to chap. 223).

tanga larim: Though the *tanga* and the *larim* were separate units of currency, in chapter 147, the *larim* is used as an adjective to describe a peculiar form of currency in the shape of a little rod of silver that was bent double unequally. The theoretical value of the ordinary silver *tanga* was fixed at sixty *réis,* but the *tanga larim* was worth from sixty to one hundred *réis*. "There was also a chest with three sacks of coins—*tangas larins*—and a bundle with many silver goblets" (chap. 147).

teston: Ancient coins minted for the first time in the reign of King Manuel I (1495–1521). There were gold testons valued at twelve hundred *réis* and silver testons valued at one hundred *réis*. "When an inventory of the plunder was made, thirty-six thousand *taels* in Japanese silver were found; and in our money, calculated at the rate of six testons per *tael,* that comes to fifty-four thousand *cruzados*" (chap. 40). See also chapters 49, 112.

tical: A term that has long been in used by foreign traders to Burma, for the quasi-standard weight of (uncoined) current silver. This weight is by the

Burmese themselves called *kyat* and is the hundredth part of the viss (*biça*), being thus equivalent to about one and a half rupees in value. "For that purpose he gathered a huge army of foreign mercenaries . . . who were hired at a salary of one *tical* of gold per month, which is the equivalent of five *cruzados* in our money" (chap. 194).

turma: An ancient Siamese silver coin, equivalent to twelve Portuguese *cru-zados* in Pinto's time. "The queen . . . agreed to pay him an annual tribute of five thousand silver *turmas,* which is the equivalent of sixty thousand *cruzados* in our money" (chap. 182). See also chapter 183.

vintem: An old Portuguese copper coin of little value. "what had been selling before for a *vintem* could not even be obtained later for a *cruzado*" (chap. 221).

Glossary 3

Sixteenth-Century Ships and Other Vessels

The information given below was derived chiefly from the following works: Leitão and Lopes, *Dicionário da linguagem de marinha antiga e actual* (Lisbon, 1963); René de Kerchove, *International Maritime Dictionary* (Princeton, N.J.: D. Van Nostrand Co., 1961), and Esparteiro, *Dicionário ilustrado de marinha* (Lisbon, 1936). Other sources mentioned are in the Bibliography. The numbers following the definitions refer to chapters.

almadia: Properly it means a "raft," but it is generally used by the writers on India for a "canoe," or the like small native boat. 9, 14.

balão (*balões*, pl.): A large dugout canoe used in India and Malaysia. The various Anglo-Indian spellings are "ballong," "balaum," "baloon," and "balloon." 14, 15, 29, 50, 56, 63, 68, 98, 144, 145, 203–5, 207, 220.

batel (*batéis*, pl.): A large flat-bottomed boat in use on the Ganges, or a dhow in miniature. The various Anglo-Indian spellings are "botella," "pattello," and "patellee." 22.

calaluz: A swift oar-propelled sailing vessel, often mentioned by the Portuguese writers as used in the Indian archipelago. Pires (Cortesão, *Suma Oriental*) describes the *calaluz* as follows: "They are not fit to go out of the shelter of the land. They are carved in a thousand and one ways, with figures of serpents, and gilt . . . very much painted . . . in a very elegant way, and they are for kings to amuse themselves in, away from the common people. They are rowed with paddles." 26, 32, 38, 172, 173, 179.

caravel: Single-deck, lateen-rigged vessel of shallow draft, used by the Portuguese from the fifteenth to the seventeenth century. It had a castle at the stern and two or three masts. 1, 2, 7, 12, 14, 20, 220.

foist: A long, narrow vessel of shallow draft of the sixteenth century. It had three masts with a large square-rigged foresail, a forepeak at the prow, and a deck awning at the stern. It varied a great deal in its dimensions and the number of oars it carried. 3–8, 10, 12, 20, 29, 35, 36, 44, 47, 97, 144–47, 153, 171, 203–7.

funce: A small oared vessel, from the Japanese *funé*, meaning "boat," and *se*, meaning "river or canal." 135, 137.

funé: The Japanese word for "boat." 209, 223.

galliot: A vessel similar to the galley, but smaller. Generally, it did not have more than twenty oars on each side. It had two lateen-rigged masts and a deck awning at the stern. 5, 26, 32, 71, 145, 146, 203, 206, 209.

gelva: A small vessel similar to the caravel, propelled by both sail and oar, used mainly in the Red Sea. 5.

guedé: From the Malay *gaeng*, meaning a "dugout or flatboat." 98.

jangá: Unidentified. A similar word, *joangá*, is used elsewhere by Pinto for a vessel of the Moluccas. 92, 93, 117, 131, 181.

joangá: Large oared vessel of the Moluccas. Castanheda describes it as a long vessel with 180 oars on each side. 32.

jurupango: A coasting vessel similar in size to a small caravel. From the Malay *jurubung*. 13, 14, 19, 35, 172, 179.

lanchara: A coasting vessel equipped with a

single mast, sail, and oars. From the Malay *lancharan.* 13–15, 17, 21, 23, 25, 26, 32–35, 37, 38, 144, 148, 173, 203, 206, 207, 220.

lanteia: A swift rowing vessel used in Chinese waters. It had six or seven oars on each side and was propelled by two men standing at each, with one foot forward. The word was later applied to the large lighterlike barges that brought down goods by the inland waterways from Canton to Macao. 44, 47, 48, 50, 52, 54, 55, 57–59, 61–63, 67, 68, 74, 81, 82, 84, 87, 88, 98.

laugoa, lagao: From the Burmese hlo-gah, described by Dalgado and Couto as a ship similar to a galley. Chapter 169.

laulé: Dalgado is not sure of the provenance of this word but suggests the Malay words *lalai* or *laley,* both of which refer to various parts of a vessel. Another possibility is the Burmese *hlayloung,* meaning "canoe or dugout." 92, 117, 123, 131, 153, 157, 162, 163, 168, 169, 181, 184.

lorcha: A modified sailing junk, the hull constructed in European fashion, but rigged in Chinese fashion. 40, 42, 47, 58, 59, 62, 63, 65, 66, 74, 132.

manchua: The Portuguese corruption of the original Malayalam word *manji,* for a single-masted cargo boat used on the Malabar coast of India. 40, 46, 57, 68, 98, 144, 146, 180, 202, 205, 209, 215, 220.

nao: A large merchant vessel, also fitted for warfare, with three or four decks. During the sixteenth and seventeenth centuries the Portuguese *naos* were the largest vessels in the world, averaging between eight hundred and twelve hundred tons, rivalled only in size by the great Manila galleons which sailed yearly between Mexico and the Philippines. The word is often translated as "carrack." 1–4, 7, 8, 12, 13, 15–17, 20, 26, 37, 40, 43, 55, 57, 65, 68, 71, 82, 109, 116, 135, 144, 146–48, 151, 153, 158, 171, 176, 180, 181, 183, 185, 200, 202, 203, 205–9, 211, 212, 214–17, 219–21, 223, 225, 226.

paguel: Called "buggalow" in English, which is probably a corruption of the Mahrati word *bagla,* or *bagala,* a name given on the west coast of India to Arab vessels of the old form. It is also used in the Red Sea under the name *bakala* or *baghla,* for the larger native vessels. 8.

prow: Generic name used in Indonesia and the Indian Ocean for undecked native boats or vessels, some of which have platforms or portable decking. It is used indiscriminately for dugout or plank-built craft with or without outriggers, whether rowed, paddled, or sailed. Also called *prahu, prau, parao,* and *perahu.* 28, 41, 47, 55, 57, 58, 132, 133, 145, 171, 203, 205, 206.

seró: Pinto uses this word for a small Burmese vessel. Dalgado believes it is a borrowing from the Malay *seroh,* meaning "shrunken, reduced," or *seroq,* meaning "small." 153, 154, 156, 157, 162, 163, 167, 169, 181, 184.

terrada: Variously described by the chroniclers of a vessel of India and the Persian Gulf, propelled by sail and oar, used in warfare or for transporting provisions and water. The large ones carried artillery and were similar to galleys or small galleons. Barros uses the word to signify light shore boats used for carrying supplies to Hormuz from the mainland. 5.

vancão (*vancões,* pl.): Gaspar da Cruz describes it as a swift Chinese rowing vessel, smaller than the junk, having three oars to each side, capable of loading a great deal of goods. Like the *lanteia,* the rowing is done by two men standing at each oar with one foot forward. 44, 52, 68, 98, 203, 216, 221.

Gazetteer

The place-names that have not been identified or which are quite different from their modern versions are given in italics, here and throughout the *Travels*. The numbers used in the Gazetteer refer to chapters.

Hainan 37, 42, 44–46, 48–50, 52, 53, 55, 56, 95, 112, 118, 189
Hakata 135, 136, 202, 218
Henzada 190, 191
Hicanduré River 14, 173
Hiji see *Finge*
Hilir 29
Hiquegens 85
Hirado 66, 208, 225
Holy Land 4
Honowar 8, 12
Hormuz 2, 6, 7, 176
Huzamgué 129, 131, 132
Huzangué 130–32
Hyuga 135, 202, 218, 223
India, State of 12, 16, 26, 65, 215, 219, 221, 226
Indian Ocean 189
Indragiri 16, 19, 22, 31, 207
Jacuçalão 157
Jacur 13, 14
Jailolo (Halmahera) 20
Jambi 16, 19, 24
Jambi River 20
Jangomá 158
Jangumá 150, 167
Jangumá River 128
Jantana 30–32, 51, 207, 220
Japan 21, 26, 92, 107, 112, 132–34, 136, 137, 143, 171, 181, 200–203, 208, 211, 212, 215, 218–23, 225, 226
Japara 36, 172, 173, 179
Jatir 164
Java 20, 33, 36, 38, 39, 57, 107, 144, 172, 173, 176, 177, 179, 189
Jerusalem 4, 5, 20
Jidda 3, 20, 26, 37, 43, 158, 206
Juncay 147
Junkseylon 19, 144, 146, 153, 185, 189, 205
Junquileu 90
Junquinilau 97
Juropisão 185
Kagoshima 135, 202, 208
Kagoshima, Bay of 202, 203
Kampar 20, 31, 32
Kamp'engp'et 122, 124, 128, 181, 185

Kangean 172, 189
Kedah 17, 19, 144, 153, 185, 205, 207
Kelantan River 35
Khorasan 124
Kuria-Muria 3
Kwantô. See Bantou
Lá 150
Lailó (Liau-Lô) 55, 57, 58, 132
Lakhon. See *Lugor*
Lamau 44, 51, 52, 56, 62, 86, 115, 132, 140, 143, 203
Lampacau (Lang-pa-kao) 132, 133, 221, 223, 226
Lampong River 20
Lançame 88, 107, 117–19, 123, 124
Lantor 183
Laos 95, 112, 124, 146, 166, 167
Larache (Al-Araish) 1
Lasapará 38
Laué 35, 36, 39
Laué River 31
Lautimey River 120
Lavra 117
Lechune 121, 127, 128
Lechune River 88
Leibrau River 185
Lequimpau 92
Leysacotay River 88
Liampeu 123
Lindau 39
Lindau Panó 129
Lingator 131
Lingau 13, 14
Lingga 31, 176, 179
Linxau 126
Lisbon 1, 2, 66, 67, 89, 107, 108, 226
London 107
Lugor (Lakhon) 36, 38, 50, 132, 183, 189, 220
Lunçor 167
Luxitay 55
Luzon 16, 28, 57, 59
Macao 221
Macassar 1
Madeira 2, 20, 35
Madel 50, 52
Madel River 50

Madur 167
Madura Island 172, 177, 179, 189
Magadaleu 167
Malabar 26
Malacca 12–15, 17–28, 30–38, 43, 46, 48, 51, 55–57, 60, 64, 86, 90, 131–33, 140, 143–48, 153, 171, 172, 176, 179, 180, 183, 185, 200, 203–8, 214–21, 223, 225
Malacca Straits 21
Malacou 150, 155, 190
Malasia 36, 220
Malaya 20, 41, 46, 57, 58, 132, 144
Manaquileu 129
Manavedé 162
Mandavi 26
Manicatarão 117
Martaban 107, 128, 144, 146–48, 151–54, 158, 167–69, 171, 185, 188, 190
Massawa 3, 4
Masulipatam (Masulipatnam) 158
Meady. See *Meleitay*
Mecca 5, 6, 18, 27, 31, 59, 203
Mecca, Straits of. See Red Sea
Mecuy 117, 122, 131
Medina 6
Meidó 190, 191, 193, 196
Meidur 159
Meleitay (Meady or Myédé) 128, 150, 156, 157
Meleitay River 194
Meleitor 214
Meleytay. See *Meleitay*
Melides 1
Melinde 151
Menangkabow (Menangkabau) 16, 20, 31, 35, 39, 166
Mergui 146, 147, 150
Meydó. See *Meidó*
Miaygimá (Miyajima?) 132, 133
Micuy 61
Minacaleu 17
Minacó 214
Minapau 114

Bibliography

Albuquerque, Afonso de. *Comentários de Afonso de Albuquerque*. 5th ed. Edited by Brás de Albuquerque. 2 vols. Lisbon: Imprensa Nacional-Casa da Moeda, 1973.

———. *Commentaries of the Great Afonso Dalbuquerque*. Translated and edited by Walter de Gray Birch. 4 vols. Hakluyt Society Publications, 1st ser., vols. 53, 55, 62, 69. London, 1875–84.

Almeida, Manoel de. *Some Records of Ethiopia, 1593–1646*. Translated and edited by C. F. Beckingham and G. W. B. Huntingford. Hayluyt Society Publications, 2d ser., vol. 107. London, 1954.

Alvares, Francisco. *The Prester John of the Indies*. Revised and edited by C. F. Beckingham and G. W. B. Huntingford. Hakluyt Society Publications, 2d ser., vol. 114. London, 1961.

Andrade, Francisco de. *Crónica de Dom João III*. Introduction and revision by M. Lopes de Almeida. Porto: Lello & Irmão, 1976.

Anesaki, Masaharu. *History of Japanese Religion*. 3d ed. Rutland. Vt., and Tokyo: Charles E. Tuttle Co., 1966.

Ayres, Christovam. *Fernão Mendes Pinto e o Japão: Pontos controversos*. Lisbon: Academia Real das Sciencias, 1906.

Barbosa, Duarte. *The Book of Duarte Barbosa*. Edited by Mansel Longworth Dames. 2 vols. Hakluyt Society Publications, 2d ser., vol. 44, 49. London, 1918–21.

———. *Livro em que dá relação do que viu e ouviu no Oriente*. Edited by Augusto Reis Machado. Lisbon: Divisão de Publicações e Biblioteca, Agência Geral das Colónias, 1946.

A Barefoot Doctor's Manual. DHEW Publication NIH 75-695. Washington, D.C.: National Institutes of Health, 1974.

Barros, João de. *Ásia de João de Barros*. 6th ed. Edited by Hernâni Cidade and Manuel Múrias. 4 vols. Lisbon: Divisão de Publicações e Biblioteca, Agência Geral das Colónias, 1945.

Barros, João de, and Diogo do Couto, *Da Ásia de João de Barros e de Diogo de Couto*. 24 vols. Lisbon: Na Régia Officina Typográfica, 1778–88.

Bocarro, António. *Década XIII da história da Índia*. Edited by Rodrigo José de Lima Felner. Lisbon: Academia Real das Sciências de Lisboa, 1876.

Boorstin, Daniel J. *The Discoverers*. New York: Random House, 1983.

Boulnois, Luce. *The Silk Road*. Translated by Dennis Chamberlain. New York: E. F. Dutton & Co., 1966.

Boxer, Charles Ralph. *The Christian Century in Japan, 1549–1650*. 2d ed. Berkeley and Los Angeles: University of California Press, 1967.

———. *Fidalgos in the Far East, 1550–1770*. The Hague: Martinus Nijhoff, 1948.

———. *The Great Ship from Amacon: Annals of Macao and the Old Japan Trade, 1555–1640*. 2d ed. Lisbon: Centro de Estudos Históricos Ultramarinos, 1963.

———, ed. and trans. *Further Selections from the "Tragic History of the Sea, 1559–1565."* Hakluyt Society Publications, 2d ser., vol. 132. London, 1968.

———, ed. and trans. *South China in the Sixteenth Century*. Hakluyt Society Publications, 2d ser., vol. 106. London, 1953.

Braga, Jack. M. ("Some Portuguese Captives in China," "Alguns portugueses cativos na China.") *Mosaico* (Macao) 1, no. 2 (October 1950): 173–77.

———. "The 'Tamão' of the Portuguese Pioneers." *T'ien Sha Monthly* (May 1939): 428–29.

———. "The Western Pioneers and Their Discovery of Macao." *Boletim do Instituto Português de Hongkong* 2 (September 1949): 5–244.

Brito Rebello, J. I. de. *Peregrinação de Fernão Mendes Pinto,* by Fernão Mendes Pinto. 4 vols. Lisbon: Livraria Ferreira Editora, 1908–10.

Brodrick, James. *Saint Francis Xavier (1506–1552).* New York: Wicklow Press, 1952.

Cabaton, A. *Java, Sumatra, and the Other Islands of the Dutch East Indies.* Translated by Bernard Miall. London and Leipzig: T. Fisher Unwin, 1911.

Camões, Luis de. *The Lusiads.* Translated with an introduction and notes by Leonard Bacon. 3d ed. New York: Hispanic Society of America, 1980.

Campos, Joaquim de. "Early Portuguese Accounts of Thailand." *Journal of the Thailand Research Society* 32 (1940): 211–37. Reprinted in "Relationships with Portugal, Holland, and the Vatican." *Selected Articles from the Siam Society Journal* 7: 211–37. Bangkok: Siam Society, 1959.

Cardon, R. "The Old Church on the Malacca Hill." *Journal of the Malayan Branch of the Royal Asiatic Society* 20, no. 1 (1947): 188–234.

———. "Portuguese Malacca." *Journal of the Malayan Branch of the Royal Asiatic Society* 12, no. 2 (1934): 1–23.

Castanheda, Fernão Lopes de. *História de descobrimento e conquista da Índia pelos Portugueses.* Edited by M. Lopes de Almeida. 2 vols. Porto: Lello & Irmão, 1979.

Castilho, José Feliciano de. *Fernão Mendes Pinto: Excerptos seguidos de uma notícia sobre a sua vida e obras.* 2d ed. 2 vols. Paris and Rio de Janeiro: B. L. Garnier, 1865.

Castro, Joaquim Mendes de. "Relendo a Peregrinação." *Brotéria* 107 (August–September, 1979): 162–86.

Catz, Rebecca. *Cartas de Fernão Mendes Pinto e outros documentos.* Lisbon: Biblioteca National/ Editorial Presença, 1983.

———. *A sátira social de Fernão Mendes Pinto.* Lisbon: Prelo Editora, 1978.

Chang, T'ien-tse. *Sino-Portuguese Trade from 1514 to 1644: A Synthesis of Portuguese and Chinese Sources.* Leyden: E. J. Brill, 1933.

Charignon, A. J. H., and M. Médard. *A propos des voyages aventureux de Fernand Mendez Pinto.* Peking: Imprimerie des Lazaristes, 1935.

Cirillo, Teresa. "Francisco de Herrera Maldonado apologeta di Fernão Mendes Pinto." *Quaderni Portoghesi* (Pisa) 4 (Autumn, 1978): 183–97.

———. "Note sulla traduzione spagnola della *Peregrinação* di Fernão Mendes Pinto." *Annali dell'Istituto Universitario Orientale, Sezione Romanza* (Naples) 19, no. 2 (1977): 407–15.

Collis, Maurice. *The Burmese Scene.* London: John Crowther, 1953(?).

———. *The Grand Peregrination.* London: Faber & Faber, 1949.

Cooper, Michael. *They Came to Japan: An Anthology of European Reports on Japan, 1543–1640.* Berkeley and Los Angeles: University of California Press, 1965.

Cordier, Henri. "L'Arrivée des Portugais en Chine." *T'oung Pao,* 2d ser., 12 (1911): 483–543.

Correia, Gaspar. *Lendas da Índia.* Edited by M. Lopes de Almedia. 4 vols. Porto: Lello & Irmão, 1975.

Correia-Afonso, John. *Indo-Portuguese History: Sources and Problems.* Bombay: Oxford University Press, 1981.

———. *Jesuit Letters and Indian History (1542–1773).* 2d ed. Bombay: Oxford University Press, 1969.

Cortesão, Armando. "Fernão Mendes Pinto não era de origem judaica." *Seara Nova* (Lisbon) no. 842 (2 October 1943).

———. *Primeira embaixada européia à China.* Lisbon: Seara Nova, 1945.

———. *The "Suma Oriental" of Tomé Pires and the "Book of Francisco Rodrigues."* Hakluyt Society Publications, 2d ser., vols. 89, 90. London, 1944.

Couling, Samuel. *The Encyclopaedia Sinica.* Shanghai: Kelly & Walsh, 1917.

Couto, Diogo do. *O soldado prático*. Edited by M. Rodrigues Lapa. Lisbon: Livraria Sá da Costa, 1937.

Cronin, Vincent. *The Wise Man from the West: The True Story of the Man Who First Brought the Message of Christianity to Fabled Cathay*. New York: E. P. Dutton & Co., 1955.

Cros, Léonard Joseph-Marie. *Saint François de Xavier: Sa vie et ses lettres*. 2 vols. Toulouse: Edouard Privat, 1900.

Cruz, Gaspar da. *Tratado das cousas da China*. In *Peregrinação de Fernão Mendes Pinto e Itinerário de António Tenreiro, Tratado das cousas da China, Conquista do reino de Pegu*, 11–678. Introduction by Aníbal Pinto de Castro. Porto: Lello & Irmão, 1984.

Cruz, Maria Augusta Lima. "Década 8° da *Ásia de Diogo do Couto*: Informação sobre uma versão inédita." *Arquipélago* 6 (January 1984): 151–66.

Cusati, Maria Luisa. "O léxico marítimo na *Peregrinação* de Fernão Mendes Pinto." *Annali dell'Istituto Universitario Orientale, Sezione Romanza* (Naples) 20, no. 1 (1978): 141–61.

Dahlgren, Erik Wilhelm. "A Contribution to the History of the Discovery of Japan." *Transactions and Proceedings of the Japan Society* (London) 11 (1912–13): 239–60.

Dalgado, Sebastião Rodolfo. *Glossário Luso-Asiático*. 2 vols. Coimbra: Imprensa da Univesidade, 1919–21.

Danvers, Frederick Charles. *The Portuguese in India*. 2d ed. 2 vols. New York: Octagon Books, 1966.

Dias, José Sebastião da Silva. *Os descobrimentos e a problemática cultural do século XVI*. Lisbon: Editorial Presença, 1982.

———. *A política cultural da época de Dom João III*. Coimbra: Imprensa da Universidade, 1969.

Doolittle, Justus. *Social Life of the Chinese*. 2 vols. New York: Harper & Brothers, 1865.

Doria, Antónia Álvaro. "Um aventureiro português do século XVI: Fernão Mendes Pinto." Reprinted from *Revista Gil Vicente* (Guimarães, 1951): 5–16.

Duyvendak, J. J. L. "The True Dates of the Chinese Maritime Expeditions in the Early Fifteenth Century." *T'oung Pao*, 2d ser., 34 (1938): 341–412.

Eberhard, Wolfram. *A History of China*. 4th ed. Berkeley and Los Angeles: University of California Press, 1977.

Edkins, Joseph. *Religion in China: Containing a Brief Account of the Three Religions of the Chinese*. London: Trubner & Co., 1878.

Esparteiro, António Marques. *Dicionário ilustrado de marinha*. Lisbon: Livraria Clássica Editora, 1964(?).

Faille, P. Roo de la. "Mendez Pinto op Sumatra." In *Historische curiositeiten uit Malajve en Java*, 7–12. Amsterdam: Tropical Museum Library, 1954.

Ferguson, Donald W. "Letters from Portuguese Captives in Canton, Written in 1534 and 1536, with an Introduction on Portuguese Intercourse with China in the First Half of the Sixteenth Century." *Indian Antiquary* (Bombay) 30 (October–November, 1901): 421–51, 467–91; 31 (January–February, 1902): 10–32, 53–65.

Flores, Alexandre M., Reinaldo Varela Gomes, and R. H. Pereira de Sousa. *Fernão Mendes Pinto: Subsídios para a sua bio-bibliografia*. Almada, Portugal: Câmara Municipal de Almada, 1983.

Ford, Jeremiah D. H., and Lucius Gaston Moffatt, eds. *Letters of John III, King of Portugal, 1521–1557*. Cambridge, Mass.: Harvard University Press, 1931.

———. *Letters of the Court of John III, King of Portugal*. Cambridge, Mass.: Harvard University Press, 1933.

Freitas, Jordão A. de. "Fernão Mendes Pinto: Sua última viagem à China (1554–1555)." *Archivo Historico Portuguez* 3 (1905): 466–70.

———. "A inquisição em Goa: Subsidios para a sua historia." *Archivo Historico Portuguez* 5 (1907): 216–27.

———. "Literatura de viagens." In *Historia da literatura portugueza ilustrada*, edited by Albino Forjaz de Sampaio, 3: 53–64. Lisbon: Livraria Bertrand, 1929–32.

———. "Macau: Materiaes para a sua historia no seculo XVI." *Archivo Historico Portuguez* 8 (1910): 209–42.

———. *Subsidios para a bibliographia portugueza relativa ao estudo da lingua japoneza e para a biographia de Fernão Mendes Pinto, grammatica, vocabularios e diccionarios, com observações philologicas pelo Exmo. Sr. A. R. Gonçalves Vianna.* Coimbra: Imprensa da Universidade, 1905.

Fróis, Luis. *História de Japam.* Edited by Josef Wicki. 5 vols. Lisbon: Biblioteca Nacional, 1976–84.

Fryer, Jonathan. *The Great Wall of China.* London: New English Library, 1975.

Galt, Howard S. *A History of Chinese Educational Institutions.* Vol. 1. London: Arthur Probsthain, 1951.

Galvano, Antonio. *The Discoveries of the World, from Their First Original unto the Year of Our Lord 1555.* Edited by Vice-Admiral Bethune. Hakluyt Society Publications, 1st ser. London, 1862.

Galvão, António. *Tratado dos descobrimentos.* 3d ed. Edited by Viscount Lagoa, João António de Mascarenhas Júdice, and Elaine Sanceau. Porto: Livraria Civilização, 1944.

Geil, William Edgar. *The Great Wall of China.* New York: Sturgis & Walton Co., 1909.

Giese, Wilhelm. "Mots malasiens empruntés au Portugais." *Boletim de Filologia* (Lisbon) 18 (1959): 275–94.

Góis, Damião de. *Chrónica do felicíssimo rei Dom Manuel.* 4 vols. Coimbra: Universidade de Coimbra, 1949–55.

Gonçalves, L. da Cunha. "Camões não esteve em Macau." *O Instituto,* 4th ser., 75 (1928): 14–42, 161–77, 318–42.

———. "A famosa cidade de Liampó segundo Fernão Mendes Pinto e a verdade histórica." *O Instituto,* 4th ser., 75–76, (1928): 113–20.

Gray, John Henry. *China.* 2 vols. London: Macmillan & Co., 1878.

Haas, Hans. *Geschichte des Christentums in Japan.* 2 vols. Tokyo: Hobunsha, 1902–4.

Hall, Basil. *Voyage to Loo-Choo and Other Places in the Eastern Seas in the Year 1816.* Edinburgh: Archibald Constable & Co., 1826.

Hammer-Purgstall, Joseph von. *Historie de l'Empire Ottoman.* 12th ed. Translated by M. Dochez. 3 vols. Paris: Parent-Desbarres, 1840–42.

Handbook of Oriental History, by members of the Department of Oriental History, School of Oriental and African Studies, University of London, 1951.

Harrison, J. B. "Five Portuguese Historians." In *Historians of India, Pakistan, and Ceylon,* 155–69. London: Oxford University Press, 1961.

Harvey, Godfrey Eric. *The History of Burma.* London and New York: Longmans, Green, & Co., 1925.

Hoffman, Helmut. *The Religions of Tibet.* Translated by Edward Fitzgerald. London: George Allen & Unwin, 1961.

Huc, E. *Souvenirs of a Journey through Tartary, Tibet, and China, during the Years 1844, 1845, and 1846.* 2 vols. Peking: Lazarist Press, 1931.

Humphrey, Christmas, ed. *A Popular Dictionary of Buddhism.* 2d ed. London: Curzon Press, 1976.

The Imperial Gazetteer. 2 vols. Glasgow, Edinburgh, and London: Blackie & Son, 1855.

Jacobs, Hubert T. T. M., ed. *A Treatise on the Moluccas.* Rome: Jesuit Historical Institute, 1971.

Kammerer, Albert. "La Découverte de la Chine par les Portugais au XVIème siècle et la cartographie des portulans." *T'oung Pao,* 2d ser., 39, supplement (1944).

———. "Le Problématique voyage en Abyssinie de Fernand Mendez Pinto (1537)." In *La Mer Rouge, l'Abyssinie et l'Arabie aux XVIème et XVIIème siècles et la cartographie des portulans du monde oriental,* 21–30. Cairo: Société Royale de Géographie d'Égypte, 1947.

Kennedy, J. *A History of Malaya.* London: Macmillan & Co., 1962.

Kerchove, René de. *International Maritime Dictionary* (Princeton, N.J.: D. van Nostrand Co., 1961.

Kim, Tai Whan. "O étimo do português 'bonzo.'" *Anais do XIV Colóquio de Estudos Luso-Brasileiros* (Tokyo, 1980): 90–97.

Kuno, Yoshi S. *Japanese Expansion on the Asiatic Continent.* 3 vols. Berkeley and Los Angeles: University of California Press, 1940.

Lach, Donald F. *Asia in the Making of Europe.* Vol. 1, books 1 and 2. Chicago: University of Chicago Press, 1965.

———. *Southeast Asia in the Eyes of Europe: The Sixteenth Century.* Chicago and London: University of Chicago Press, Phoenix Books, 1968.

Lagoa, João António de Mascarenhas Júdice, Visconde de. "A Dupla Liampó das crónicas portugesas." *Anais da Junta de Investigações Coloniais* (Lisbon, 1950).

———. *Glossário toponímico da antiga historiografia ultramarina.* 4 vols. Lisbon: Junta de Investigações Coloniais, 1950–54.

———. "A Peregrinação de Fernão Mendes Pinto (tentativa de reconstituição geográfica)." In *Anais da Junta de Investigações Coloniais do Ministério das Colónias.* Vol. 2, bk. 1. Lisbon: Junta das Missões Geográficas e de Investigações Coloniais, 1947.

Lamb, Alistair. *The Mandarin Road to Old Hué: Narratives of Anglo-Vietnamese Diplomacy from the Seventeenth Century to the Eve of the French Conquest.* Hamden, Conn.: Archon Books, 1970.

Le Gentil, Georges. *Les Portugais en Extrême-Orient: Fernão Mendes Pinto, un précurseur de l'exotisme au XVIème siècle.* Paris: Hermann, 1947.

Leitão, Humberto, and José Vicente Lopes. *Dicionário da linguagem de marinha antiga e actual.* Lisbon: Centro de Estudos Históricos Ultramarinos, 1963.

Linschoten, John Huyghen van. *The Voyage of John Huyghen van Linschoten to the East Indies.* 2 vols. Edited by Arthur Coke Burnell and P. A. Tiele. Hakluyt Society Publications, 1st ser. London, 1885.

Livro das armadas. Facsimile edition. Lisbon: Academia das Ciências, 1979.

Ljungstedt, Anders. *An Historical Sketch of the Portuguese Settlement in China.* 2d ed. Boston, 1936.

Loch, Charles. W. "Rhinoceros Sindaicus: The Javan or Lesser One-Horned Rhinoceros and Its Geographical Distribution." *Journal of the Malayan Branch of the Royal Asiatic Society* 15, no. 2 (1937): 130–49.

Lockhart, Donald M., ed. *The "Itinerário" of Jerónimo Lobo.* Hakluyt Society Publications, 2d ser., vol. 162. London, 1984.

Losty, Jeremiah P. *The Art of the Book in India.* London: British Library, 1982.

Lusitano, Amato. *Centúrias de curas medicinais.* Translated and edited by Firmino Crespo. Lisbon: Universidade Nova [1980].

Macgregor, Ian A. "Notes on the Portuguese in Malaya." *Journal of the Malayan Branch of the Royal Asiatic Society* 28, no. 2 (1955): 5–47.

Magalhães, Gabriel de. *A New History of China Containing a Description of the Most Considerable Particulars of That Vast Empire.* Translated from the French by John Ogilby. London, 1688.

Mailla, Joseph-Anne-Marie de Moyriac de. *Histoire générale de la Chine; ou, Annales de cet empire, traduite du Tong-Kien-Kang-Mou.* Vol. 10. Paris: Clousier, 1779.

Manoel, Jerónimo da Camara. *Missões dos Jesuitas no Oriente nos séculos XVI e XVII.* Lisbon: Imprensa Nacional, 1894.

Manrique, Sebastião. *The Travels of Fray Sebastien Manrique 1629–1643.* Translated and edited by C. Eckford Luard and H. Hosten. 2 vols. Hakluyt Society Publications, 2d ser., vols. 59, 61. London, 1926–27.

Marchiori, Laura. "Fernão Mendes Pinto e la sua opera: Una vita romanzata del XVI secolo." *Quaderni Ibero-Americani* 41 (December 1972): 7–17.

Margarido, Alfredo. "Fernão Mendes Pinto: Um herói do quotidiano." *Colóquio/Letras* 74 (July 1983): 23–28.

Marsden, William. *The History of Sumatra*. London, 1783.

Martins, José F. Ferreira. *Crónica dos vice-reis e governadores da India*. Vol. 1. New Goa: Imprensa Nacional, 1919.

Maurício, Domingos. "A *Peregrinação* de Fernão Mendes Pinto e algumas opiniões peregrinas." *Brotéria* 74 (January–June 1962): 637–50.

Mendonça, A. P. Lopes de. *Damião de Goes e a Inquisição de Portugal*. Lisbon: Academia Real das Sciencias, 1859.

Milne, William C. "Notes of a Seven Months' Residence in the City of Ningpo, from December 7, 1842, to July 7, 1843." *Chinese Repository* (Canton) 13, no. 7 (1844): 338–57.

Mitchell, Mairin. *Elcano: The First Circumnavigator*. London: Herder Publications, 1958.

Moraes Silva, Antonio de. *Diccionario da lingua portuguesa*. 7th ed. 2 vols. Lisbon: Typographia de Joaquim Germano de Souza Neves, 1877–78.

Morais, Wenceslau de. *Relance da história do Japão*. Porto: Edição Maranus, 1924.

Murdoch, James, and Isoh Yamagata. *A History of Japan during the Century of Early Foreign Intercourse, 1542–1651*. 3 vols. Kobe: Asiatic Society of Japan, 1903–10.

Nachod, Oskar. "Ein Brief von Fernão Mendez Pinto." In *Festschrift den XIII Internationalen Orientalistenkongress*, 28–43. Hamburg: German-Japanese Society of Berlin, 1902.

Nykl, Aluísio Ricardo. "Algumas observações sobre as línguas citadas na *Peregrinação* de Fernão Mendes Pinto." *Petrus Nonius* 3 (1941): 180–85.

———. "Mais observações sobre as línguas citadas na *Peregrinação* de Fernão Mendes Pinto." *Petrus Nonius* 4 (1942): 57–58.

Okamoto, Yoshitomo, and J. Abranches Pinto. "Mendes Pinto e o descobrimento do Japão." *Boletim da Sociedade Luso-Japonesa* 1 (1929): 78–84.

Orta, Garcia da. *Colóquios dos simples e drogas da Índia*. Edited by the Conde de Ficalho. 2 vols. Lisbon: Imprensa Nacional, 1891–95. Translated by Clements Markham, under the title of *The Colloquies on the Simples and Drugs of India*. London: Henry Sotheran and Co., 1913.

Ortega, Noel W. *A Frequency Study of the Vocabulary in the "Peregrinaçam" of Fernão Mendes Pinto*. 2 vols. Unpublished doctoral dissertation, presented to Harvard University, 5 March 1974.

Osborne, Dorothy. *The Letters of Dorothy Osborne to William Temple*. 4th ed. Edited by G. C. Moore Smith. Oxford: Clarendon Press, 1968.

Paez, Simão Ferreira. *As famozas armadas portuguesas, 1496–1650*. Rio de Janeiro: Ministério da Marinha, 1937.

Parker, E. H. "Pinto in Corea." *China Review* (Hongkong) 16, no. 3 (November–December 1887): 182.

Pauthier, M. G. *Chine moderne; ou, description historique, géographique et littéraire de ce vaste empire, d'après des documents chinois*. Paris: Firmin Didot Frères, 1853.

Pelliot, Paul. "Un ouvrage sur les premiers temps de Macao." *T'oung Pao*, 2d ser., 31 (1934): 58–94.

Penrose, Boies. *Goa—Rainha do Oriente/Goa—Queen of the East*. Lisbon: Comemorações do V Centenário da Morte do Infante D. Henrique, 1960.

———. *Travel and Discovery in the Renaissance, 1420–1620*. Cambridge, Mass.: Harvard University Press, 1952.

Phayre, Arthur P. *History of Burma*. 2d ed. London and Santiago de Compostela: Susil Gupta, 1967.

———. "On the History of Pegu." *Journal of the Asiatic Society of Bengal* 43, no. 1 (1874): 6–21.

———. "On the History of the Burma Race." *Journal of the Asiatic Society of Bengal* 38, no. 1 (1869): 29–82.

Pinto, Fernam Mendez. *Peregrinaçam de Fernam Mendez Pinto, em que da conta.* . . . Lisbon: Pedro Crasbeeck, 1614. Facsimile edition. Tokyo: Tenri Central Library, 1973.

Playfair, G. M. H. *The Cities and Towns of China: A Geographical Dictionary.* 2d ed. Shanghai: Kelly & Walsh, 1910.

Quaritch-Wales, H. G. *Siamese State Ceremonies: Their History and Function.* London: Bernard Quaritch, 1931.

Raffles, Thomas Stamford. *The History of Java.* 2 vols. London: Block, Parbury, & Allen, 1817.

Ramos, José de. "Fernão Mendes Pinto's Early Times and His *Peregrinaçam.*" *Mosaico* (Macao) 3, no. 15–16 (November–December 1951): 193–200.

———. "Império do Calaminhão." *Mosaico* (Macao) 3, no. 13 (September 1951): 1–12.

Rau, Virginia. "Affari e mercanti in Portogallo dal XIV al XVI secolo." *Economia e Storia* (Milan) 14, no. 4 (October–December 1967): 447–56.

Ravenstein, E. G., ed. and trans. *A Journal of the First Voyage of Vasco da Gama, 1497–1499.* Hakluyt Society Publications, 1st ser., vol. 99. London, 1898.

Rego, António da Silva. *Documentação para a história das missões do Padroado Português do Oriente.* Vols. 5 (1551–54) 6 (1555–58). Lisbon: Agência Geral das Colónias, Divisão de Publicações e Biblioteca, 1951.

———. *História das missões do Padroado Português de Oriente: India (1500–1542).* Vol. 1. Lisbon: Agência Geral das Colónias, Divisão de Publicações e Biblioteca, 1949.

Reis, Eduardo. "Ensaio crítico sobre a digressão piedosa que fez Fernão Mendes Pinto." *Boletim Eclesiástico da Diocese de Macau* 36 (1938–39): 917–44.

Revah, I. S. *La Censure inquisitorial portugaise au XVIème siècle.* Lisbon: Instituto de Alta Cultura. 1960.

Rey, Charles Fernand. *The Romance of the Portuguese in Abyssinia.* London: H. F. & C. Witherby, 1929.

Ribeiro, Aquilino. "A máscara de pirata de Fernão Mendes Pinto." In *Portugueses das sete partidas: Viajantes, aventureiros, trocatintas,* 4th ed., 259–85. Lisbon: Livraria Bertrand, 1950.

Ricci, Matthew. *China in the Sixteenth Century: The Journals of Matthew Ricci, 1583–1610.* 2d ed. Translated by Louis J. Gallagher. New York: Random House, 1953.

Rockhill, W. W. "Notes on the Relations and Trade of China with the Eastern Archipelago and the Coast of the Indian Ocean during the Fourteenth Century." *T'oung Pao,* 2d ser., 16 (1915): 236–71.

Rodrigues, Graça Almeida. *Breve história da censura literária em Portugal.* Lisbon: Instituto de Cultura e Lingua Portuguesa, 1980.

Rogers, Francis M. "Fernão Mendes Pinto, S.J." Lecture delivered to the Modern Language Association, Chicago, 28 December 1965.

Rogers, Francis M., Louise G. Cohen, and Constance H. Rose, eds. *Fernan Mendez Pinto: Comedia famosa en dos partes,* by Antonio Enríquez Gómez. Cambridge, Mass.: Harvard University Press, 1974.

Rossi, Giuseppe Carlo. "Ancora su Fernão Mendes Pinto." *Anali dell'Istituto Universitario Orientale, Sezione Romanza* (Naples) 15, no. 2 (1973): 235–57.

Russell-Wood, A. J. R. *Fidalgos and Philanthropists: The Santa Casa da Misericordia of Bahia, 1550–1755.* Berkeley and Los Angeles: University of California Press, 1968.

Sá, Artur Basílio de, ed. *Documentação para a história das missões do padroado português do Oriente.* Vol. 2. Lisbon: Agência Geral do Ultramar, Divisão de Publicações e Biblioteca, 1955.

Sanceau, Elaine. *Good Hope: The Voyage of Vasco da Gama.* Lisbon: Academia Internacional da Cultura Portuguesa, 1967.

Sansom, G. B. *The Western World and Japan.* New York: Alfred A. Knopf, 1951.

Saraiva, António José. *Fernão Mendes Pinto ou a sátira picaresca da ideologia senhorial.* Lisbon: Jornal do Foro, 1958. (Reprinted in *História da Cultura em Portugal* 3 [1962]: 343–496.)

Saras, Phra. *My Country Thailand.* 6th ed. Bangkok: Chitrasan, 1960.

Schlagintweit, Emil. *Buddhism in Tibet.* New York: Augustus M. Kelley, 1969.

Schurhammer, Georg. "The Church of Saint Paul, Malacca." *Journal of the Malayan Branch of the Royal Asiatic Society* 12, no. 2 (1934): 40–43.

———. "O descobrimento do Japão pelos Portugueses no ano de 1543." Translated by Francisco Rodrigues. In *Gesammelte Studien: Orientalia 2,* edited by Laszlo Szilas, 21:485–580. Rome and Lisbon: Bibliotheca Instituti Historici, 1963. (Reprinted from *Anais da Academia Portuguesa da Historia,* 2d ser., 1 [1946]: 9–172.)

———. "Um documento inédito sobre Fernão Mendes Pinto." In *Gesammelte Studien: Orientalia 2,* edited by Laszlo Szilas, 21:105–9. Rome and Lisbon: Bibliotheca Instituti Historici, 1963. (Reprinted from *Revista de História* [Lisbon] 13 [1924]: 81–88.)

———. "Fernão Mendes Pinto und seine *Peregrinaçam.*" In *Gesammelte Studien: Oritentalia 2,* edited by Laszlo Szilas, 21:23–103. Rome and Lisbon: Bibliotheca Instituti Historici, 1963. (Reprinted from *Asia Major,* 1st ser., 3 [1926]: 71–103, 194–267.)

———. *Francis Xavier: His Life, His Times.* Translated by M. Joseph Costelloe. 4 vols. Rome: Jesuit Historical Institute, 1973–82.

———. "Ein fürstlicher Gönner des hl. Franz Xaver, Otomo Yoschischige, König von Bungo." In *Gesammelte Studien,* edited by Laszlo Szilas, 4:127. Rome and Lisbon: Bibliotheca Instituti Historici, 1963.

———. "Historical Research into the Life of Francis Xavier in the Sixteenth Century." *Revista de História* (Lisbon) 12 (1923): 192–223.

———. "Milagres e lendas de São Francisco Xavier à luz da crítica." *Anais da Academia Portuguesa de História,* 2d ser., 13 (1963): 37–55.

———. "Der Ursprung des Chinaplans des hl. Franz Xaver." *Archivum Historicum Societatus Iesu* 22 (1953): 38–56.

———. "Zwei ungedruckte Briefe des hl. Franz Xaver." *Archivum Historicum Societatus Iesu* 2 (1933): 44–45.

Schwartzberg, Joseph E., ed. *A Historical Atlas of South Asia.* Chicago and London: University of Chicago Press, 1978.

Scott, James George. *Burma from the Earliest Times to the Present Day.* New York: Alfred A. Knopf, 1924.

Silverberg, Robert. *The Great Wall of China.* Philadelphia: Chilton Books, 1965.

Skelton, R. A., ed. and trans. *Antonio Pigafetta, Magellan's Voyage.* London: Folio Society, 1975.

Soothill, William Edward, and Lewis Hodous. *A Dictionary of Chinese Buddhist Terms.* London: Kegan Paul, Trench, Trubner & Co., 1937.

Sousa, Francisco de. *Oriente conquistado a Jesus Cristo.* Introduction and revision by M. Lopes de Almeida. Porto: Lello & Irmão, 1978.

Sousa, Manuel de Faria e. *Asia Portuguesa.* Edited by M. Lopes d'Almeida. 6 vols. Porto: Livraria Civilização, 1945–47.

Stone, George Cameron. *A Glossary of the Construction, Decoration, and Use of Arms and Armor in All Countries and in All Times.* 2d ed. New York: Jack Brussel, 1961.

Tcuzzi, João Rodrigues. *História da igreja do Japão.* Edited by João do Amaral Abranches Pinto. 2 vols. Tokyo: Notícias de Macau, 1954–56.

Teixeira, Pedro. *The Journey of Pedro Teixeira from India to Italy by Land, 1604–1605.* Translated and edited by William F. Sinclair. Hakluyt Society Publications, 2d ser., vol. 9. London, 1902.

Vale, Maria Teresa. *Fernão Mendes Pinto: O Outro Lado do Mito.* Lisbon: Direcção-Geral da Comunicação Social, 1985.

Valle, Henrique Pereira do. "Nomenclatura das bocas do fogo portuguesas do século XVI." *Revista de Artilharia,* 2d ser., 58 (1962): 381–90.

Van Scoy, Herbert A. "Fact and Fiction in Mendez Pinto's *Peregrinaçam.*" *Hispania* 32 (1949): 158–67.

Volpicelli, Z. "Early Portuguese Commerce and Settlements in China." *Journal of the China Branch of the Royal Asiatic Society,* 2d ser., 27 (1892): 33–69.

Voretzsch, E. A. "Documento acerca da primeira embaixada à China." *Boletim da Sociedade Luso-Japonesa* 1 (1929): 50–69.

Waddell, L. Austine. *Tibetan Buddhism.* 2d ed. New York: Dover Publications, 1972.

Werner, E. T. C. *Chinese Weapons.* Extra volume of the Royal Asiatic Society North China Branch (Shanghai), 1932.

———. *A Dictionary of Chinese Mythology.* Shanghai: Kelly & Walsh, 1932.

Wheeler, Stephen. "Mendez Pinto." *Geographical Journal* (1893): 139–46.

Whiteway, R. S., ed. and trans. *The Portuguese Expedition to Abyssinia in 1541–1543, as Narrated by Castanhoso, with Some Contemporary Letters, the Short Account of Bermudez, and Certain Extracts from Correa.* Hakluyt Society Publications, 2d ser., vol. 10. London, 1902.

———. *The Rise of Portuguese Power in India, 1495–1550.* 2d ed. London: S. Gupta, 1967.

Wicki, Josef, ed. *Documenta Indica III (1553–1557). Monumenta Historica S.I.,* vol. 74. *Monumenta Missionum S.I.,* vol. 6, *Missiones Orientales.* Rome: Instituti Historici, 1954.

Winstedt, Richard Olaf. "A History of Malaya." *Journal of the Malayan Branch of the Royal Asiatic Society* 13, no. 1 (1935): 60–82.

———. *The Malays: A Cultural History.* 6th ed. London: Routledge & Kegan Paul, 1961.

Wood, William Alfred Rae. "Fernão Mendes Pinto's Account of Events in Siam." *Journal of the Siam Society* 20, no. 1 (June 1926): 25–39. (Reprinted in "Relationship with Portugal, Holland, and the Vatican," in *Selected Articles from the Siam Society Journal* 7 : 195–209, Bangkok: Siam Society, 1959.)

———. *A History of Siam from the Earliest Times to the Year A.D. 1781.* London: Unwin, 1926. 2d ed. Bangkok: Chalermnit Bookshop, 1959.

———. *Land of Smiles.* Bangkok: Krungdebarnagar Press, 1935.

Yule, Henry. *The Book of Ser Marco Polo, the Venetian,* 3d ed. Revised by Henri Cordier. 3 vols. London: John Murray, 1929.

———. *Cathay and the Way Thither.* Revised by Henri Cordier. Hakluyt Society Publications, 2d ser., vols. 33, 37, 38, 41. London, 1913–16. Reprint. Liechtenstein: Kraus Reprint, 1967.

Yule, Henry, and Arthur Coke Burnell. *Hobson-Jobson: A Glossary of Colloquial Anglo-Indian Words and Phrases, and of Kindred Terms,* 2d ed. Edited and revised by William Crooks. Delhi: Munshiram Mancharlal, 1968.

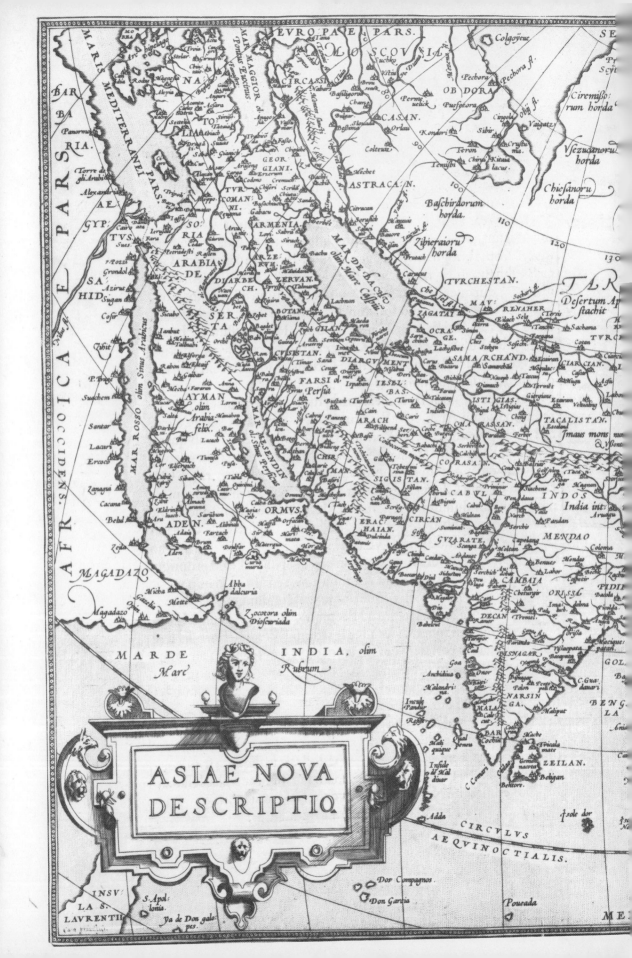

ASIAE NOVA
DESCRIPTIO.